▶ MANAGERIAL ACCOUNTING

Eighth Edition

Geraldine F. Dominiak
Texas Christian University

Joseph G. Louderback III
Clemson University

SOUTH-WESTERN College Publishing

An International Thomson Publishing Company

Accounting Team Director: Mary H. Draper
Sponsoring Editor: Elizabeth Bowers
Developmental Editor: Leslie Kauffman
Production Editor: Jason M. Fisher
Production House: Cover to Cover Publishing
Internal Design: Barbara Libby
Marketing Manager: Sharon Oblinger
Cover Design: Tin Box Studio/Sandy Weinstein

Cover Photographs:
Tony Stone/Andrew Sacks
Direct Stock/Marc LaFavor/Parallel Productions
Comstock
Superstock

ISBN: 0-538-85612-2
1 2 3 4 5 6 7 KT 2 1 0 9 8 7 6
Printed in the United States of America

Dominiak, Geraldine F.
    Managerial accounting / Geraldine F. Dominiak, Joseph G. Louderback. -- 8th ed.
        p.   cm.
    Includes index.
    ISBN 0-538-85612-2
    1. Managerial accounting.   I. Louderback, Joseph G. II. Title.
HF5657.4.D66 1997
658.15--dc20

96-19924
CIP

preface

In the tradition of the first seven editions, *Managerial Accounting*, eighth edition, continues its leading-edge coverage of management accounting topics within a decision-making framework. *Managerial Accounting* parallels the shift in today's business world, focusing not just "on the numbers," but on the functions of management: planning, decision making, controlling, and performance evaluation. This emphasis is apparent even in the "traditional" chapters on product costing (Chapters 13-15), a topic that accounting textbooks seldom discuss with the non-accountant in mind. Those chapters approach product costing from the standpoint of analyzing results under different costing systems, rather than concentrating on cost-accumulation procedures or the accounting problems related to those procedures.

Because the book emphasizes the uses of managerial accounting information, it is appropriate not only for accounting majors but also for other business majors (marketing, management, finance, etc.). It can also be used by majors in nonbusiness areas such as engineering, mathematics, and the physical sciences. The real-world examples and decision situations illustrated throughout the text and assignment material help students put information into a business perspective, rather than strictly an accounting focus.

The eighth edition of this book is, like the previous seven editions, intended for an introductory course in managerial accounting. Though we wrote the book with the undergraduate student in mind, it has seen successful use in graduate courses and in management development programs. The wide variety of assignment material allows instructors to use the book at various levels by selecting assignments consistent with students' backgrounds.

We assume that a student has had one or two terms of financial accounting or a working exposure to basic financial statements. We expect some understanding of the most basic principles on which financial statements are based. The journal-entry/T-account framework appears only in Chapter 15 and is not otherwise necessary to understanding the concepts. For those instructors wanting to cover the statement of cash flows and financial statement analysis, we have added two chapters (Chapters 17 and 18) on these topics. Assignment materials for these topics are included in the text, study guide, and test bank.

TEXT OBJECTIVES

Our objectives in this edition remain essentially the same as those for the first seven editions:

1. To present clearly and understandably the most important conceptual and practical aspects of managerial accounting.
2. To order the material in a way that allows the reader to build from elementary concepts to more complex topics and thus to integrate and expand early understanding.
3. To illustrate some of the interrelationships between managerial accounting and other courses in a normal business curriculum.
4. To show students, through discussion, illustration, and assignment material, the manifold applications of managerial accounting principles to decision making in economic entities of all types (including personal decisions).
5. To help students recognize that *people*, not entities, make decisions and are responsible for the results of those decisions.

We use various means to achieve these objectives. First, we use examples and illustrations liberally. Second, we proceed through the text (and its increasingly complex concepts) in a building-block fashion. We begin with the principles of cost behavior and cost-volume-profit analysis, which underlie virtually all of managerial accounting, and use this basis to approach the more complex problems encountered in decision making, comprehensive budgeting, responsibility accounting, and product costing. A reader will see the reliance on previously developed concepts by the use of references to earlier chapters.

The applicability of managerial accounting concepts to a wide variety of economic entities is most obvious in sections of the text that specifically refer to nonbusiness situations. But both the examples used in other parts of the text and the decision situations posed in assignment material also reflect our efforts to demonstrate the opportunities for using managerial accounting concepts in a nonbusiness context.

We regularly draw attention to qualitative and difficult-to-quantify aspects of a topic. As part of the qualitative considerations, we discuss behavioral problems and point out the implications of such problems. We raise these qualitative issues to emphasize that decisions are made by individuals with differing opinions, values, and moral standards. We expect students to recognize that accounting data provide relevant information but do not dictate courses of action.

Throughout the book we emphasize that decisions are based on estimates and that some factors important to a decision are difficult to quantify. Our intentions are to underscore (1) the presence of uncertainty and (2) the importance of recognizing all the available alternatives and all the factors relevant to each alternative. Both the text and many of the problems emphasize that a major problem in managing any enterprise is determining the right questions to ask and, concomitantly, what kinds of information to seek. In our opinion, students should learn that real-world problems do not present themselves in the form of schedules to be filled in and manipulated. Indeed, sometimes a manager's most difficult task is to discern, from the mass of economic activity taking place all around, exactly what the problem is that requires investigation and resolution.

NEW TO THIS EDITION

Based on user and reviewer feedback, we have added many new features to the eighth edition.

Learning Objectives. Each chapter now begins with a set of learning objectives. These learning objectives provide an overview of chapter concepts and serve as a framework for study and comprehension.

Better Integration of Real-World Examples. An important change in this edition is the increased number of references to actual companies, many from annual reports. The *vignettes* that begin each chapter are a new feature that uses real-world material to set the stage for the chapter material. *More examples* from the real world are included with more references to actual companies. Much of the real-world material appears in boxed *Insights*, which are new to this edition. *Assignment material* includes more items related to activities and policies of real companies. Real-company names are highlighted throughout the text for easy identification. A *company index* appears at the back of the text.

Chapter "Links." A strength of our text has always been its building-block approach—using the basic concepts and principles of managerial accounting as a basis for learning about more complex topics. New "link" margin icons now help students quickly identify references to related concepts. A left arrow represents a concept that was covered in an earlier chapter, while a right arrow indicates a concept that will be covered in more detail in a later chapter.

More Activity-Based Costing. In response to the widespread usage of activity-based costing (ABC) in today's business world, we have expanded the discussion of ABC in Chapter 3. ABC is also integrated into virtually every succeeding chapter, rather than isolated in a separate chapter.

More on Strategy. We discuss several managerial accounting principles and techniques in the context of corporate strategy. Most apparent are the use of a **General Mills** annual report in Chapter 1 and elsewhere, as well as more attention to strategic issues in Chapters 4, 5, 8, 9, and in some of the product costing material.

Additional Integration of JIT. The eighth edition includes increased coverage and integration of the terminology and techniques of the just-in-time (JIT) philosophy. These ideas are incorporated throughout the book, consistent with its overall plan, so that almost every chapter is affected. More complete integration of the new manufacturing environment is evident and nearly every chapter refers to the just-in-time (JIT) operating philosophy. As with ABC, this subject should be integrated and not treated as an add-on.

New Chapter Coverage.   Chapter 16 on quantitative methods replaces an appendix and now includes discussion of the theory of constraints. The statement of cash flows and analyzing financial statements are included as Chapters 17 and 18.

ADDITIONAL FEATURES

Ethics. Material on ethics has been expanded and includes a reprint of the IMA Standards for Professional Conduct. Most chapters have assignments dealing with ethical issues.

International Coverage. We have maintained, and in many cases expanded, attention to international matters, such as cultural differences as well as currency translation.

Guidelines for Preparing Memoranda. Virtually all chapters have assignments that require preparing memoranda with regard to the Accounting Education Change Commission. Appendix A gives guidelines for preparing memoranda.

ASSIGNMENT MATERIAL

One of the strongest features of this book is the assignment material, because of its integration with the text, its volume, and its variety with respect to degree of difficulty and economic entities. Users of previous editions have told us that these factors make it possible to teach this course, and the individual topics therein, at various levels of difficulty. Users cite the same factors in successful offerings of the course to students with widely diverse backgrounds. (Comments in the Solutions Manual aid in judicious choice of assignment items to accommodate different objectives.)

End-of-chapter material includes questions for discussion, exercises, problems, and cases. There are now short-answer review questions that can be solved by referring to a sentence or two in the chapter. Discussion questions are designed to increase students' understanding of concepts and use of critical-thinking skills; thus, many have no clearly correct answers. Exercises are usually short and cover basic applications of one or two key concepts. Problems tend to be longer than exercises and are more challenging, sometimes contain irrelevant information, and often ask the student to state reservations about whatever solutions are proposed. Both exercises and problems are generally arranged in order of increasing difficulty.

Cases normally contain less information than needed to develop a single solution; our intention is to emphasize this inconvenient characteristic of real-life situations. For most cases, the student must propose an analytical approach appropriate to the available, relevant information. Cases, and the later problems, require the student to determine what principles are relevant and how those principles apply in a given situation. That is, these assignments are designed to encourage the student to think, since a manager must do so.

ALTERNATIVE SEQUENCES

The text contains more material than is needed for a one-term course, and we expect most users to omit one or more chapters. Several users have found alternative sequencing to be practical. The text does offer considerable flexibility in the order of coverage.

Chapter 16, which discusses several quantitative methods of analysis, can be covered separately at nearly any time. Or, individual segments of that chapter can be assigned in conjunction with earlier chapters. The section on statistical decision theory has illustrations that use materials from Chapters 6, 8, and 12. The illustrations, while concentrating on applying the quantitative methods, draw on topics discussed in these earlier chapters. (The concept of expected value can be introduced as early as Chapter 5.) We have dropped the section on inventory control models. The linear programming section extends the material in Chapter 5 on alternative uses of limited resources. Similarly, the section on learning curves can supplement the discussion in Chapter 3 on cost prediction methods.

Instructors desiring an earlier and greater emphasis on product costing can move to Chapters 12 through 15 after Chapter 3. (Beginning product costing early requires incorporating Chapter 12 in the coverage of that topic rather than as part of the study of responsibility accounting, because some understanding of standard costs is assumed in Chapters 14 and 15.) Some users increase the time available to cover product costing by omitting Chapters 10 and 11. Alternatively, some users omit all product costing material, or omit all or parts of Chapters 14 and 15. Chapter 4 can be omitted without loss of continuity. Also, one or both chapters on capital budgeting (Chapters 8 and 9) can be omitted without serious loss of continuity.

Appendix B, which deals with the time value of money, is available for use with Chapters 8 and 9 on capital budgeting. It assumes no previous exposure to the principles of present and future value, but those who have had such exposure are likely to find this material useful for review.

SUPPLEMENTARY MATERIAL

Check Figures.   Key figures for solutions to selected assignment material are provided at the back of the text.

Study Guide.   (Prepared by Jay Holmen, University of Wisconsin-Eau Claire) The study guide is designed to help students obtain full value from the study of this text. This supplement, which offers key statements to use as guides in reading the chapters, includes not only objective questions but also a variety of short- and medium-length problems (solutions included) to test understanding. The final section of the study guide for each chapter identifies those concepts, practices, or approaches that cause the most difficulty or greatest misunderstanding for students.

Solutions Manual.   The solutions manual contains solutions for all assignment material and suggested times for completing assignments. It also provides notes to the instructor regarding class use of the material. These notes offer (1) alternative approaches for arriving at solutions, (2) suggestions for eliciting class discussion, and (3) suggestions for expanding individual assignments to cover new issues, pursuing existing issues in more depth, or highlighting relationships between managerial accounting concepts and concepts studied in other business disciplines. Also, the solutions manual contains suggested time allocations for alternative course lengths and chapter sequencing.

Solutions Transparencies.　Acetate transparencies for many solutions are available to adopters.

Test Bank.　(Prepared by Jay Holmen, University of Wisconsin-Eau Claire) The test bank, which contains true-false and multiple-choice questions and short problems, is available in both printed and microcomputer (MicroExam) versions. The eighth edition test bank has been expanded significantly to permit the preparation of several exams without repetition of material.

Spreadsheet Templates.　(Prepared by Marvin Bouillon, Iowa State University) Lotus 1-2-3®[1] templates for various end-of-chapter assignments are complimentary to adopters. Spreadsheet assignments are identified in the text with a margin icon.

PowerPoint Slides.　(Prepared by Marvin Bouillon, Iowa State University) PowerPoint®[2] teaching transparencies provide an electronic slide-show outline of each chapter, including key concepts, examples, and exhibits from the text.

Videos.　Three videos are available to adopters to assist in classroom presentations of new manufacturing environment techniques, such as continuous-flow manufacturing, activity-based costing, and JIT.

Cases in Cost Management: A Strategic Emphasis.　(Written by John K. Shank, Dartmouth College) This set of cases is offered for those instructors who want to augment their management accounting course with richer, longer "fun" problems. Each case includes specific numerical questions to challenge and help develop the students' calculation skills with management accounting techniques. Each case also includes broader discussion questions to sharpen the controversial aspects of the calculations and emphasize the managerial issues behind the numbers. Accompanying the book is an instructor's manual, which contains comprehensive teaching commentaries for each of the cases.

Readings and Issues in Cost Management.　(Edited by James Reeve, University of Tennessee) This text is designed to expose students to the concepts and information they need to become responsive and flexible managers. Articles in the text cover topics such as TQM, employee empowerment, reengineering, continuous improvement, and short-cycle management.

ACKNOWLEDGMENTS

We wish to thank the many instructors and students whose comments and suggestions have helped us significantly in the preparation of all eight editions of this book. In particular, we want to thank the reviewers of the eighth edition:

---

1 *Lotus 1-2-3 is a registered trademark of Lotus Development Corporation. Any reference to Lotus 1-2-3 refers to this footnote.*
2 *PowerPoint is a registered trademark of Microsoft Corporation. Any reference to PowerPoint refers to this footnote.*

Wagby M. Abdallah
Seton Hall University

Susan C. Borkowski
La Salle University

Wayne G. Bremser
Villanova University

James W. Damitio
Central Michigan University

Robert C. Elmore
Tennessee Technological University

Charles F. Grant
Skyline College

Carol A. Hilton
Ohio University

Leon B. Hoshower
Ohio University

Royal E. Knight
University of North Alabama

William V. Luckie
Mercer University

Keith A. Russell
Southeast Missouri State University

Neil Wilner
University of North Texas

Special thanks goes to James Emig, Villanova University, for verifying the accuracy of the solutions manual, test bank, and study guide.

We also express our appreciation to the American Institute of Certified Public Accountants and Institute of Management Accountants for their generous permission to use problems adapted from past CPA and CMA examinations, respectively.

Many people at South-Western have been extremely helpful. We particularly appreciate the work of our Developmental Editor, Leslie Kauffman. Others who made the work go more smoothly were Jason Fisher (Production Editor) and Mary Draper (Accounting Team Director).

Finally, we thank our respective institutions, and our colleagues at those institutions, without whom the development of this volume, in its current and prior editions, would have been a much less pleasant task.

Geraldine F. Dominiak
Joseph G. Louderback

brief contents

1	Introduction	1
Part One	**COST-VOLUME-PROFIT ANALYSIS**	
	AND DECISION MAKING	**29**
2	Profit Planning	30
3	Cost Analysis	77
4	Additional Aspects of Cost-Volume-Profit Analysis	130
5	Short-Term Decisions and Accounting Information	180
Part Two	**BUDGETING**	**241**
6	Operational Budgeting	242
7	Financial Budgeting	293
8	Capital Budgeting—Part I	347
9	Capital Budgeting—Part II	387
Part Three	**CONTROL AND PERFORMANCE EVALUATION**	**435**
10	Responsibility Accounting	436
11	Divisional Performance Measurement	492
12	Control and Evaluation of Cost Centers	548
Part Four	**PRODUCT COSTING**	**603**
13	Introduction to Product Costing	604
14	Standard Costing and Variable Costing	655
15	Process Costing and the Cost Accounting Cycle	707
Part Five	**SPECIAL TOPICS**	**757**
16	Quality and Quantitative Methods in Managerial Accounting	758
17	Statement of Cash Flows	795
18	Analyzing Financial Statements	836

APPENDIX A: Guidelines for Preparing Memoranda   877

APPENDIX B: Time Value of Money   882

COMPANY INDEX   896

INDEX   900

CHECK FIGURES   910

contents

1   **INTRODUCTION**   **1**

Management Functions and Accounting   3
   Planning   3
   Control   5
Managerial Accounting and Financial Accounting   6
   Illustration—Management and Accounting   8
Advanced Manufacturing   10
   Conventional Manufacturing: Its Background
    and Its Problems   11
   Just-In-Time (JIT) Manufacturing   11
Activities of Managerial Accountants   15
Ethics   18
International Aspects of Managerial Accounting   20
Deregulation   21

Part One   **COST-VOLUME-PROFIT ANALYSIS**
AND DECISION MAKING   **29**

2   **PROFIT PLANNING**   **30**

Cost Behavior   31
   Variable Costs   32
   Contribution Margin   32
   Fixed Costs   32
   Contribution Margin Income Statement   33
   Emphasis on Expectations   34
   Income Statement Formats—Financial Accounting
    and Contribution Margin Formats   35
   Unit Costs   35
Relevant Range   36
Cost-Volume-Profit Graph   37
Achieving Target Profits   39
   Break-Even Point and Target Dollar Profits   39

Contribution Margin Percentage   41
Target Return on Sales   42
Changing Plans   43
Target Selling Prices   43
Target Costing   44
Cost Structure and Managerial Attitudes   45
Margin of Safety   46
Indifference Point   47
Assumptions and Limitations of CVP Analysis   48
Appendix: Income Taxes and Profit Planning   53

3   COST ANALYSIS   77

Objectives of Analyzing Costs   78
Cost Management   78
Managing Activities—Cost Drivers and Cost Pools   80
Value-Adding and Non-Value-Adding Activities   81
Estimating Cost Behavior   82
Account Analysis   83
Engineering Approach   84
Interviews   84
High-Low (Two-Point) Method   85
Scatter-Diagram Method   86
Regression Method   87
Problems and Pitfalls in Cost Behavior Analysis   88
Historical Data   88
Correlation and Association   89
Spurious Correlation   90
Step-Variable Costs   91
Committed and Discretionary Fixed Costs   92
Avoidable and Unavoidable Costs   93
Direct and Indirect (Common) Costs   93
Manufacturing Costs   94
Activity-Based Costing   95
Appendix: Regression Analysis   102
Simple Regression   102
Correlation and the Standard Error   103
Selecting a Cost-Prediction Equation   105
Problems and Pitfalls   105
Multiple Regression   106

**4   ADDITIONAL ASPECTS OF
       COST-VOLUME-PROFIT ANALYSIS   130**

Analyzing Contribution Margin Variances   131
Sales Volume Variance   132
Sales Price Variance   133
Multiple Products   134
Weighted-Average Contribution Margin Percentage   136
Changes in Sales Mix   138
Weighted-Average Contribution Margin Per Unit   139
Fixed Costs and Multiple-Product Companies   141

Relevance of Activity-Based Costing	142
ABC and Ethics	143
Pricing Strategy	143
CVP Analysis in Not-For-Profit Entities	145
Benefit-Cost Analysis	146

5 SHORT-TERM DECISIONS AND ACCOUNTING INFORMATION **180**

The Criterion for Short-Term Decisions	182
Differential (Incremental) Revenues and Costs	182
Sunk Costs and Opportunity Costs	183
Basic Example	184
Developing Relevant Information	186
Allocated Costs	188
Activity-Based Allocations	189
Typical Short-Term Decisions	189
Dropping a Segment	189
Make-or-Buy Decisions	194
Joint Products	196
Special Orders	199
Factors in Limited Supply	203
Decision Making Under Environmental Constraints	205

Part Two BUDGETING **241**

6 OPERATIONAL BUDGETING **242**

Comprehensive Budgets	244
Budgets and Planning	245
Budgets and Control	246
Organization of Budgets	246
Developing the Comprehensive Budget	248
Sales Forecasting	249
Indicator Methods	249
Historical Analysis	250
Judgmental Methods	251
Which Method to Use	252
Expected Values and Forecasting	253
Interim Period Forecasts	254
Expense Budgets	254
Budgeting Variable and Mixed Costs	254
Budgeting Discretionary Costs	257
Budgeting and Human Behavior	257
Conflicts	258
Imposed Budgets	259
Stretch Goals	260
Budgets as "Checkup" Devices	261
Unwise Adherence to Budgets	262
Budgeting and Ethics	262
International Aspects of Budgeting	263

Illustration of a Comprehensive Budget
for a Retailer (Crane Company) 265
Budgeted Income Statement 266
Purchases Budget 267
Purchases Budget—Manufacturing Firm (Brandon Company) 268

7   FINANCIAL BUDGETING 293

Completion of Illustration—A Retailer (Crane Company) 294
Cash Budget 295
Pro Forma Balance Sheet 301
Concluding Comments 302
Minimum-Cash-Balance Policies 304
Cash Budget for a Manufacturer (Brandon Company) 306
Annual and Long-Term Budgets 307
Asset Requirements 308
Financing Requirements 308
Illustrations of Annual and Longer-Term Budgets 310
Annual Budgets (Strand Company) 310
Longer-Term Planning (Klep Company) 313
Budgeting in Not-For-Profit Entities 314
Zero-Based Budgeting 317
Program Budgeting 318

8   CAPITAL BUDGETING—PART I 347

Importance of Capital Budgeting Decisions 349
Types of Capital Budgeting Decisions 350
Capital Budgeting Fundamentals 350
Cost of Capital and Cutoff Rates 350
Methods of Analyzing Investment Decisions 352
Cash Flows and Book Income 353
Capital Budgeting Methods 353
Net Present Value (NPV) Method 355
Internal Rate of Return (IRR) Method 355
Generality of the Analysis 356
Taxes and Depreciation 357
Uneven Cash Flows 358
Salvage Values 358
Variations in Annual Flows 359
Decision Rules 360
Qualitative Considerations 361
Other Methods of Capital Budgeting 362
Payback 362
Advantages 363
Flaws of Payback 364
Book Rate of Return 364
Summary Evaluation of Methods 365
Investing Decisions and Financing Decisions 366
International Aspects of Capital Budgeting 367

9   CAPITAL BUDGETING—PART II   **387**

Complex Investments   388
    Changes in Working Capital   388
    Replacement Decisions   390
    Total-Project Approach   393
Mutually Exclusive Alternatives   394
    Unequal Lives   394
    Ranking Investment Opportunities   396
Sensitivity Analysis   398
More on Income Taxes   401
MACRS   402
Criticisms of DCF Methods   405
Social Consequences of Decision Making   406

Part Three   CONTROL AND PERFORMANCE EVALUATION   **435**

10   RESPONSIBILITY ACCOUNTING   **436**

Goal Congruence and Motivation   437
Responsibility Centers   438
    Cost Centers   439
    Revenue Centers   439
    Profit Centers and Investment Centers   440
Performance Evaluation Criteria   441
Organizational Structure   443
    Responsibility Reporting for Cost Centers   444
    Responsibility Reporting for Profit Centers   448
    Choosing an Organizational Structure   450
Cost Allocations on Responsibility Reports   452
    Reasons for Allocating Costs   452
    Reasons for Not Allocating Costs   454
Allocation Methods and Effects   454
    Allocating Actual Costs Based on Actual Use   456
    Allocating Budgeted Costs Using Dual Rates   457
    Allocating Through Transfer Prices   458
    What to Do About Allocations in Performance Reporting   460
Ethics and Allocations   460
Appendix: Other Allocation Methods   462
    Step-Down Method   462
    Reciprocal Method   464

11   DIVISIONAL PERFORMANCE MEASUREMENT   **492**

Decentralization   493
    Benefits of Decentralization   494
    Problems of Decentralization   495
Measures of Performance   496
    Income   496
    Return on Investment   497
    Residual Income   498
    Behavioral Problems   499

ROI Versus RI 501
ROI and RI 502
Problems in Measurement 504
    Income 504
    Investment 504
    Liabilities 506
    Fixed Assets 508
The Subject of Evaluation—Division or Manager 509
    Internal Ranking 510
    Historical Comparisons 510
    Industry Averages 510
    Budgets 511
Transfer Prices 511
    Pricing Policies 512
    Illustrations 513
Multinational Companies—Special Problems 516

12 CONTROL AND EVALUATION OF COST CENTERS 548
Cost Control 549
    Standards and Standard Costs 549
    Standard Costs and Budgets 550
Standard Variable Costs and Variances 550
    Labor Variances 551
    Variable Overhead Variances 555
    Materials Variances 557
    Standards in Multiproduct Companies 558
    Standard Costs and Activity-Based Costing 559
    Variances and Performance Evaluation 560
    Investigating Variances 561
    Setting Standards—Behavioral Problems 562
    Standard Costs, Product Life Cycle, and Strategy 564
    Reporting Variances 565
Control of Fixed Costs 565
    Budget Variance 567
    Fixed Costs on Performance Reports 567
    A Problem Area—Separating Fixed and Variable Costs 568
Standard Costs, Variances, and Continuous Improvement 569
    Kaizen Costing and Target Costs 569
    Nonfinancial Measures 570
Standard Costs for Nonmanufacturing Activities 573

Part Four PRODUCT COSTING 603

13 INTRODUCTION TO PRODUCT COSTING 604
Cost Flows 606
Manufacturing Processes 607
Absorption Costing and Variable Costing 608
Job-Order Costing 609
    Actual Costing 611
    Normal Costing 612

Misapplied Overhead 614
Overhead Variances 615
Income Statements, Actual and Normal Costing 617
Activity-Based Overhead Rates 619
Ethics in Product Costing 621
Product Costs and Value-Chain Analysis 622
Overhead Application, Behavior, and Strategy 622

14 STANDARD COSTING AND VARIABLE COSTING 655

Standard Absorption Costing 656
Calculating a Standard Fixed Cost 657
Variances 658
Income Statements 660
Review Problem 661
Multiple Products and Activity-Based Costing 662
Comparison of Standard and Normal Costing 664
Variable Costing 666
Comparing Variable and Absorption Costing Results 670
Absorption Costing, Production, and Income 671
Evaluation of Methods 672
External Reporting 672
Internal Reporting and Cost Strategy 672

15 PROCESS COSTING AND THE COST ACCOUNTING CYCLE 707

Process Costing 708
Equivalent Unit Production and Unit Cost 709
Ending Inventory and Transfers 710
Beginning Inventory 710
Materials and Conversion Costs 711
Multiple Processes 712
The Cost Accounting Cycle 714
Illustration of Actual Process Costing 715
Illustration of Job-Order Costing 717
Illustration of Standard Costing 721
Product Costing in an Advanced Manufacturing Environment 724
Final Comparative Comments 727
Appendix: Process Costing—The FIFO Method 732
Illustration of FIFO 733
Why Choose FIFO? 734

Part Five SPECIAL TOPICS 757

16 QUALITY AND QUANTITATIVE METHODS IN MANAGERIAL ACCOUNTING 758

Cost of Quality 759
Measuring Quality Costs 760
Statistical Decision Theory 763
A Caveat 766
Payoff Tables 766

Developing Probabilities	770
Linear Programming	770
Sensitivity Analysis	774
Shadow Prices	775
Theory of Constraints	777
Learning Curves	779

17 STATEMENT OF CASH FLOWS   **795**

Interest in Cash Flows	796
Cash Flow Statement	797
Defining Cash	797
Reporting Operating Cash Flows	798
Noncash Transactions	799
Cash Flow Statement Format	799
Illustration	801
Cash from Operations	802
Investing and Financing Activities	805
Cash Flow Statement	806
Operating Flows—Special Considerations	807
The Direct Method, Inflows and Outflows	807
Nonoperating Gains and Losses	811
Concluding Comments	812

18 ANALYZING FINANCIAL STATEMENTS   **836**

Expectations and Performance	837
Methods of Analysis	837
Areas of Analysis	838
Illustration	838
Liquidity	840
Working Capital and the Current Ratio	840
Quick Ratio (Acid-Test Ratio)	841
Working Capital Activity Ratios	841
Profitability	844
Return on Assets (ROA)	844
Return on Common Equity (ROE)	845
The Effects of Leverage	846
Earnings Per Share (EPS)	847
Price-Earnings Ratio (PE)	849
Dividend Yield and Payout Ratio	849
Economic Value Added (EVA)	850
Solvency	850
Debt Ratio	851
Times Interest Earned	851
Cash Flow to Total Debt	852
Ratios and Evaluation	853

APPENDIX A: GUIDELINES FOR PREPARING MEMORANDA   **877**

General Guidelines	878
Audience Analysis	878

Analysis Versus Restatement 878
Names and Abbreviations 878
Supporting Schedules 878
Use of Jargon 879
Environmental Constraints 879
Assignments 879
Reading the Assignment 879
Perspective of Writer and Reader 880
Headings 880
General Writing Guidelines 880

APPENDIX B: TIME VALUE OF MONEY **882**

Present Value of a Single Amount 883
Present Value of a Stream of Equal Receipts 884
Streams of Unequal Amounts 885
Computations for Periods Other Than Years 886
Uses and Significance of Present Values 887
Determining Interest Rates 887
Determining Required Receipts 889

COMPANY INDEX **896**

INDEX **900**

CHECK FIGURES **910**

Introduction

LEARNING OBJECTIVES

After reading this chapter, you should be able to

1 *Describe four managerial functions and their relationships to accounting.*

2 *Distinguish between financial accounting and managerial accounting.*

3 *Describe some of the problems that arise in conventional manufacturing and how advanced manufacturing techniques overcome them.*

4 *Describe the activities of managerial accountants.*

5 *Describe the code of ethics that managerial accountants follow.*

6 *Discuss some factors influencing the development of managerial accounting.*

The 1994 annual report of **Duke Power** described strategies to face increased competition. One strategy is continuous improvement. Employees work in teams, are much more customer-oriented, and are aware of the competition Duke faces. Pay depends not only on individual performance, but also on team, department, and business unit performance. **Panhandle Eastern**, a natural gas company, has established a program whereby employees will share in profits above a given level. Cost control had never before been important at Panhandle, or other regulated companies for that matter. In fact, the higher their costs, the higher the revenues they were allowed to earn by state regulators.*

Factory work has changed radically over the past few years. At the **Toyota** plant in Georgetown, Kentucky, workers have multiple duties, rather than one duty as characterized by traditional production *systems. Toyota workers can stop the production line when they find a defective unit, while at traditional plants, workers do not inspect work in progress. Instead, someone inspects at the end of the process. Many managers of U.S. companies have visited the Toyota plant and taken ideas back to their own companies for implementation.***

The Institute of Management Accountants (IMA), the leading professional organization of management accountants, has established a Continuous Improvement Center (CIC), which offers services to financial managers in four areas: Assessment Assistance, Benchmark Database, Performance Improvement and Best Practices, and Recognition Programs. The first three have to do broadly with assisting managers in developing opportunities for improvement and enabling managers to determine how well they are performing in relation to similar organizations and to the best organizations.

The common thread in these descriptions is that change has made it necessary for organizations to operate differently—deregulation for the utility companies, foreign and domestic competition for many others. The need to streamline and improve financial processes to be competitive in the global marketplace lies behind the IMA's CIC. The study and practice of managerial accounting itself faces a whole host of changes brought on by globalization, the adoption of advanced manufacturing techniques, and new discoveries in various areas affecting what managerial accountants do and how they do it.

* *Emily Nelson, "Gas Company's Gain-Sharing Plan Turns Employees into Cost-Cutting Vigilantes,"* The Wall Street Journal, *September 29, 1995, B1.*
** Greenville Piedmont *(SC), May 5, 1992, B1.*

Accountants develop and communicate much of the economic information used by managers of businesses and other economic organizations and by external parties, such as creditors, stockholders, and governmental agencies. Providing information to outsiders is **financial accounting**. **Managerial accounting** (or *management accounting* or sometimes *internal accounting*) has to do with providing information to help meet the needs of managers inside an organization. Managerial accounting defies attempts at comprehensive, concise definition; it changes constantly to adapt to technological changes, changes in managers' needs, and new approaches to other functional areas of business—marketing, production, finance, organizational behavior, and corporate strategy. Managerial accounting is an indispensable part of the system that provides information to managers—the people whose decisions and actions determine the success or failure of an organization.

Managerial accounting is relevant to many activities of managers. Managers develop strategies for achieving goals, evaluate the performance of workers and of other managers, and make a host of decisions. Managers decide what prices to charge for their products, whether to continue selling particular products, and whether to build a new factory. Many activities performed by managers have to do with acquiring and using economic resources (money, people, machinery, buildings), and managers need information to help them make those decisions. Managerial accountants generate much of the information managers use to plan operations and make decisions.

Managerial accounting obviously applies to businesses because it deals with economic information, and businesses seek profits and other economic goals. Managerial accounting also applies to organizations that do not seek profits— government units, universities, hospitals, churches—because those organizations, like businesses, use economic resources to meet their objectives. Hence, an understanding of the concepts of managerial accounting is important to managers in any organization. Therefore, in this book, we do not assume that you plan to major in accounting or to become an accountant; we assume only that you are interested in managing.

MANAGEMENT FUNCTIONS AND ACCOUNTING

Planning and control are two important management functions for which managers require information. The managerial accountant is the primary, though not the only, provider of information required for these functions. Useful information includes such historical data as prices of materials, wages paid to employees, rent on leased facilities or equipment, costs of fringe benefits, and various taxes. Managerial accountants prepare performance reports that assist managers in controlling their operations. They also provide information about the probable effects of proposed actions. Managerial accountants will estimate the profit that is likely to result from a successful advertising program. Managers also use information originating outside the firm. For example, statistics on the state of the economy are helpful in forecasting sales; patterns of population growth are relevant to decisions about locations for stores, warehouses, and manufacturing plants; statistics on the state of each industry in which a company operates are useful in forecasting both sales and related expenses.

PLANNING

Planning is setting goals and developing strategies and tactics to achieve them. Some planning is routine, recurring, and relates principally to periods of a year or less. Such planning includes the important process of **budgeting**, which is relating goals to the means for achieving them. For example, if a $1 million profit is a goal, budgets will determine what machinery, cash, labor force, and other resources will be needed to achieve that goal and how to acquire the necessary amount of each resource. Without careful planning, a company achieves its goals only by accident.

A company that budgets a profit for a year must also determine how to reach that target. For example, what products should it emphasize, and at what prices? Managerial accountants develop data that help managers identify the more profitable products. Often, managerial accountants determine the effects of alternatives, such as different prices and selling efforts. (What will profit be if we cut prices 5% and increase volume 15%? Would spending $250,000 on advertising, or offering a 10% sales commission, be wise if it led to a 20% increase in sales?)

Managerial accountants prepare budgeted financial statements, often called **pro forma statements**. Among the most important statements is the budget of cash receipts and disbursements. The finance department uses forecasts of cash requirements to determine whether borrowing will be necessary. The management of cash is extremely critical; more companies fail because they run out of cash as a result of inadequate planning than because they are unable to make a profit. Making profits and maintaining adequate cash are two very different things, and managers must understand that profitability does not guarantee generating enough cash to pay the bills.

Longer term planning, often called *strategic planning*, is also critical to organizations. In recent years managerial accountants have played important roles in formulating and implementing long-term strategies that relate to cost. Some of the changes in managerial accounting relate to increasing emphasis on strategic concerns such as value chains and supply chains. Today, companies often join forces with their suppliers and customers to benefit all parties. A **value chain** is "a linked set of value-creating activities all the way from basic raw material sources ... To the ultimate end-product ...."[1] In other words, the value chain is the entire set of processes that transform raw materials into finished products. Companies that operate in many segments of the value chain are called *vertically integrated*. The major oil companies are good examples, as they explore and drill, pump oil from fields, transport it, refine it, and sell it to customers. Companies try to gain advantages in the value chain by establishing cooperative relationships with suppliers and customers. **Compaq Computer**, the world's largest manufacturer of personal computers, had been awash in inventories of parts until it began to work with its suppliers to improve operations. Several suppliers agreed to build plants near Compaq's main plant in exchange for Compaq's giving them information on its production in advance. The suppliers were thus able to plan better, produce in a smoother cycle, and avoid costly rush orders for needed parts.[2]

Decision Making

Much of the information provided by managerial accountants is used in **decision making**, which is an important part of planning. Some decision making is carried on continually. Managers decide daily or weekly how many units of a product to buy or make, or how much advertising to place in specific newspapers or on specific radio stations. They also set prices for products or services.

Some decisions are made infrequently, such as whether to build a new factory, buy a new warehouse, introduce a new product line, or enter a foreign market. Accounting systems do not routinely generate data for such analyses, so managerial accountants do special analyses. They determine what data are needed, present the data in an understandable way, and explain the analyses to the managers making the decisions.

Managerial accountants assist managers in making decisions not only by providing information, but by using analytical techniques that help managers understand the implications of a decision. For example, managerial accountants can tell managers how many units of a new product they must sell to earn a desired profit or what cost savings are necessary to justify buying new machinery. We discuss many of these techniques in this book.

1 John K. Shank and Vijay Govindarajan, Strategic Cost Management, NY, The Free Press, 1994, 13.
2 Ronald Henkoff, "Delivering the Goods," Fortune, November 28, 1994, 76.

Decision Making and Behavior

Although managers use accounting data extensively in making decisions, such data do not *answer* the questions that managers face. *People* make decisions, and people bring to decision making their experience, values, and knowledge that usually cannot be incorporated into quantitative analyses. Managers might take actions because of some qualitative factor not captured in the accounting data. For example, managers of a company whose strategies include technological leadership might launch a new product that they expect to be unprofitable. Quantifying the benefits of such leadership is very difficult. A report of the quantitative analysis quite likely would include a comment about those benefits. That is, reports from managerial accountants recognize factors whose financial implications are not incorporated in the quantitative analyses.

CONTROL

Control is determining whether goals are being met, and if not, what can be done. What changes might we make to achieve our goals? Should we change our goals? Managerial accounting is used extensively in control because many goals are expressed in dollar terms—so much sales, so much cost—and because managerial accountants use analytical tools to help managers understand the reasons for not achieving goals. Implicit in control is **performance evaluation**—managers reviewing the accomplishments of their employees and weighing them against standards. Many such evaluations use managerial accounting information. For many managers, **control reports**, which often show actual and budgeted results, are the most common contact with managerial accounting information.

Low-level managers and managers of small enterprises control through close physical supervision, but the size of modern organizations precludes such close contact across several organizational levels. Even managers in relatively small companies usually cannot exercise constant oversight of the activities of their staffs. The principle of management by exception helps managers to control operations. Applying this principle, managers rely on reports to keep informed. Reports reduce the need for minute-by-minute, physical supervision and allow managers time to perform their other functions. Many such reports detail costs that managers are responsible for and usually relate those costs to budgeted costs. As a rule, when budgeted and actual results are very close, managers conclude that operations are going according to plan and need no special investigation. When budgeted and actual results differ significantly, managers usually investigate to determine what is going wrong and who might need help. Thus, accounting reports partially substitute for managers' personal supervision of activities.

Control reports do not tell managers what to do. That actual results differ greatly from planned results does not tell managers why the results differed. Control reports provide feedback to help managers determine where attention might be required. They do not tell managers how to correct any problems that might exist nor do they establish which people performed satisfactorily or unsatisfactorily. Substandard performance could result from conditions outside a manager's control.

Performance Evaluation

Evaluating performance and controlling are closely related. Managers are evaluated partly on the basis of how well they control their operations: whether they achieve budgeted sales, meet budgeted cost levels, or produce budgeted quantities of product. Higher-level managers who are not involved directly in day-to-day activities rely on the information reported by management accountants about the performance of lower-level managers.

Developing suitable measures of performance for a given manager is a behavioral problem. Many people think of accounting data as factual, neutral, or objective. On the contrary, accounting data and reports can motivate people to act in various ways—some desirable, some not. For example, evaluating the performance of sales managers on the basis of total sales dollars, a seemingly objective accounting figure, will motivate them to concentrate on obtaining the highest dollar sales without regard to the *profitability* of the products sold. The result might be very high sales but very low profits. Gross profit or other measures that reflect costs as well as revenues are better measures. Similarly, evaluating production managers by whether they meet budgeted costs might tempt them to ignore product quality, postpone preventive maintenance, or take other actions that harm the company in the long run. Selecting appropriate measures of performance is a constant concern of both managers and managerial accountants.

Effective performance evaluation requires that performance measures capture the essential aspects of the job. Failure to do so can be counterproductive to the company's best interests as the examples above show. Managerial accountants continue to research the ways in which the form and content of reports influence the actions of those who receive them. The reports developed by managerial accountants should continue to improve as a result of such research. In any case, the likelihood of misdirected managerial efforts is reduced when a manager is fully informed about the bases on which his or her performance will be evaluated.

MANAGERIAL ACCOUNTING AND FINANCIAL ACCOUNTING

Both managerial and financial accounting deal with economic events. Both require quantifying the results of economic activity, and both are concerned with revenues and expenses, assets, liabilities, and cash flows. Both, therefore, involve financial statements, and both suffer from the difficulties of capturing, in quantitative terms, the many aspects of an economic event. The major differences between financial and managerial accounting arise because they serve different audiences.

Financial accounting serves persons outside the firm, such as creditors, customers, government units, and investors. Hence, financial accounting reports are concerned mostly with the company as a whole. In contrast, managerial accounting reports usually deal with segments of a firm; managers receive information related to their own responsibilities rather than to the entire firm. The different audiences for accounting information use information for different purposes. Creditors and investors use information to decide whether or not to extend credit to the firm, and whether to buy, sell, or hold its stock. People inside the company use accounting information to make decisions such as which of several products to sell, whether to issue bonds or stock, which employees to reward for good performance, and what prices to charge.

The classification schemes used in managerial accounting reports usually differ from those in financial accounting reports. In financial accounting, costs are usually classified by the object of the expense (salaries, taxes, rent, repairs) or by the function of the expense (cost of goods sold, selling expenses, administrative expenses, financing expenses). In contrast, reports for managerial accounting purposes often follow other cost classification schemes. Some reports are based on the behavior of costs, separating costs that change when activity levels change from costs that do not change regardless of the level of activity. Other managerial accounting reports concentrate on the concepts of responsibility and controllability; costs are classified according to whether or not a particular manager is responsible for the cost and can control it. These classification schemes—behavior, responsibility, and controllability—underlie much of the material in this book and are critical to almost all aspects of planning and control.

Information in financial accounting reports might also differ in source and nature from that in managerial accounting reports. Financial accounting reports are developed from the basic accounting system, which captures data about completed transactions. Some managerial accounting reports incorporate information that is not found in the financial accounting system. Such information might relate to expected future transactions (such as budgeted sales and costs) or alternatives to past transactions (such as showing what income would have been if we had sold more units at a lower price). Some very important analyses in managerial accounting use hypothetical transactions. As later chapters describe, one of the costs associated with product quality is the cost of external failure, which is all of the costs of selling a unit that fails when used by the customer. Perhaps the most important cost is the lost sales from the ill will such failures cause, a cost that will never be recorded in the company's accounting system.

Managerial accounting reports are specifically designed for a particular user or a particular decision; financial accounting reports are general purpose. For this reason, a particular cost might appear on one internal report and not on another; the cost might be relevant for some internal decisions and not for others. We can illustrate this point with an example from everyday life. Suppose you own a car and pay $450 for insurance per year. That cost is part of the total cost of owning the car, but it is irrelevant if you are trying to determine how much it will cost to take a 200-mile trip. Because you pay the same $450 for insurance whether you take the trip or not, you can ignore it in determining the cost of the trip. The phrase "different costs for different purposes" describes the idea that relevance depends on the specific purpose.

Financial and managerial accounting information differ in that the former is primarily historical while the latter is concerned more with the future. Although many items in financial statements incorporate expectations (e.g., estimated useful life and residual value in the computation of depreciation, estimated warranty work to be done on items sold, and so on), financial accounting reports concentrate on the results of past decisions. Internal reports to managers often concentrate on what is likely to happen in the future.

Managerial accounting has no external restrictions such as the generally accepted accounting principles (GAAP) that govern financial accounting. For managerial purposes, relevance is the important concern, and managerial accountants respond to specific information requirements. For example, market price (replacement cost, fair market value, or some other measure) will be used in a managerial accounting report if it will help the manager make a better decision. Such alternatives are usually not allowed in financial accounting.

Advances in computer technology, especially in the ability to store and retrieve large amounts of information, have been accompanied by an unfortunate side effect called information overload. Some managers receive far more information than they can possibly use. One challenge in managerial accounting is to develop ways to determine what information is relevant for particular managers, summarize the information, and present it in a usable form. The general manager of a factory employing 500 people cannot effectively use weekly reports showing the actual costs in 823 categories. That manager could, however, use a report showing which costs differed significantly from their budgeted amounts. Communication between managers and managerial accountants is important so that managers receive the information they need and need the information they receive.

ILLUSTRATION—MANAGEMENT AND ACCOUNTING

Exhibit 1-1 diagrams some managerial processes and related accounting activities. Usually the topmost level of management sets overall objectives that are then formalized into strategies and plans. The accompanying Insight describes the objectives and strategies of **General Mills.**

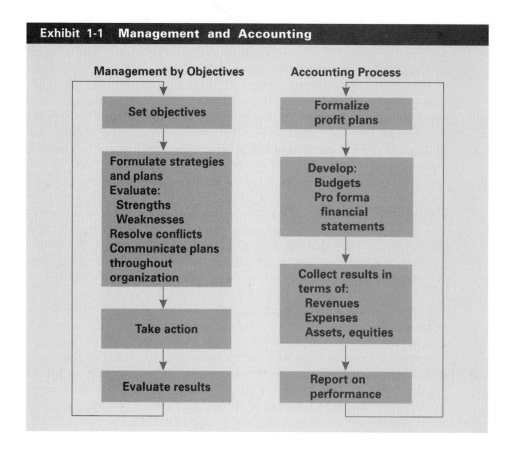

Exhibit 1-1   Management and Accounting

SIGHT

Recent annual reports of **General Mills, Inc.** have listed the following financial objectives, among others.

- *Averaging 12 percent earnings per share growth*
- *Improving after-tax return on sales (net income/sales) to a minimum of 7.0 percent*
- *Meeting or exceeding a 20 percent after-tax return on invested capital and 38 percent return on equity (net income/common stockholders' equity)*
- *Maintaining a solid balance sheet with a strong "A" bond rating*
- *Increasing dividends in line with long-term growth in earnings per share, with a target of paying out 50 percent of earnings*

The Consumer Foods segment has a goal of reducing manufacturing and distribution costs from 20 percent of sales to 17 percent by the year 2000.

General Mills experienced difficulties in 1994, especially in its Big G cereal line. The following paragraph from the 1994 annual report describes the problem and response.

"The first problem affecting Big G was escalating promotional activity by all competitors in the U.S. ready-to-eat cereal market. This activity resulted in reduced profits and little change in market share. It also generated increasing inefficiencies in using coupons and in-store promotions to deliver value to consumers. For instance, 98 percent of cereal coupons issued are thrown away and not redeemed, and roughly half of promotional expenditures do not reach consumers in the form of lower prices. Big G moved decisively to address the promotional escalation by eliminating $175 million annually in inefficient promotional spending and delivering increased value directly to consumers by lowering prices on its largest brands by $110 million. Combined with a focused series of product improvements, promising new products and marketing innovations, these actions are expected to restore Big G's profit growth in 1995. So far, all the signs are positive, as our cereal prices are coming down at retail and promotional activities by industry competitors are scheduled at substantially lower levels."

The 1994 annual report also described increases in productivity.

*"**General Mills** people found ways to improve productivity significantly, benefiting operations throughout the company. Betty Crocker Products, Gold Medal, Yoplait and Red Lobster were among those divisions whose increasing productivity contributed to margin and earnings growth in 1994. Additional productivity initiatives launched during the year will contribute to earnings growth in future years."*

Source: 1994 Annual Report of General Mills, Inc.

Companies describe various objectives, such as those related to product quality, pollution abatement, and employee satisfaction, and the costs of achieving them formally in plans. For example, a recent annual report of **Chase Manhattan Bank** stated that it wants to be the "employer of choice" and it has "reduced levels of management so more employees have personal responsibility for serving customers."

Managers set broad objectives and strategies, then make detailed plans to realize them. Should we move into other links of the value chain? (For example, should **General Mills** acquire agricultural businesses?) What new products can we introduce? What can existing products contribute to future profits and sales? What will foreign competitors do? Can some of our products be marketed more widely? Should we stress overseas operations or pay more attention to domestic business? Strategic and tactical questions like these and others are thrashed out, and planning is based on the company's strengths and weaknesses and the opportunities and threats that it faces. These plans are expressed in budgets and pro forma financial statements. The Insight mentions the Consumer Foods goal of cost reduction. The annual report further states that achieving the goal will come partly through increasing utilization of manufacturing capacity and using self-directed teams of workers who are responsible for all aspects of production. The latter strategy should reduce the layers of management and supervision.

Having established plans that are consistent with the broad objectives of the firm, managers implement these designs. They direct research programs on new products, advertising, and other sales efforts, add plant capacity to meet anticipated demand, and fill requirements for workers, managers, and other personnel. Many results of these actions show up within the framework of the accounting system. The results of sales efforts show up as revenues, while the firm's efforts show up as expenses and assets. The financing aspects of the various efforts are reflected in equities—long-term debt, common stock issuances, and increases in retained earnings.

In Exhibit 1-1, we have shown the boxes labeled "Take action" and "Evaluate results" as independent, but there is usually continual feedback. Note how **General Mills** responded to increased promotional spending by its competitors. Managers evaluate results quickly so that corrective action can be taken if necessary. Evaluations of results also can lead to reconsidering the original objectives or the plans formulated to meet them. Thus, the cycle shown rarely runs a complete course without any modifications. Plans and budgets are not static; managers change them continually. As described in the Insight, General Mills changed its promotional strategy in response to actions by its competitors.

ADVANCED MANUFACTURING

One of the driving forces behind many recent developments in managerial accounting is profound changes in manufacturing. These changes have carried over to service and merchandising organizations as well. At various points throughout this text we use such terms as advanced manufacturing environment, **advanced manufacturing**, world-class manufacturing, or just-in-time manufacturing to describe such developments. To help you better understand these references, we discuss those changes and some of their implications here.

CONVENTIONAL MANUFACTURING: ITS BACKGROUND AND ITS PROBLEMS

Following World War II, American companies were the unchallenged world leaders in manufacturing. They had strong advantages in product quality, capacity, and distribution facilities, and, exaggerating only a little, they could sell nearly anything they made. Production was the critical activity and the philosophy was to "get it out the door."

In this environment, many U.S. manufacturers adopted practices that reflected a "just-in-case" philosophy. As insurance against production delays caused by defects in components or the unavailability of materials, companies routinely purchased more than required to meet production needs. (They inspected all incoming shipments, though they often adopted sophisticated statistical techniques to cope with this growing task.) To avoid production shortfalls caused by manufacturing errors (or by delays because of defects in materials), companies produced more than required and also scheduled production much earlier than required to meet shipping dates. As a result, **lead time** or **cycle time**—the period that begins with the arrival of materials and ends with shipment of a finished unit—extended well beyond the time needed for the manufacturing process alone. A product that could be manufactured in a day or two might have a lead time of one, two, or even three months. This type of manufacturing is called "push," because parts and components push their way through the system whether they are needed or not.

Not surprisingly, these manufacturing practices generated significant costs. The high inventories of materials and finished units increased the risk of spoilage and obsolescence, as well as the costs of storage, insurance, financing, and handling. Inspecting raw materials, component parts, and finished units also was costly. Inevitably, prices rose to cover the increased costs. An unfortunate outcome of striving to meet output requirements on a timely basis was that waste, scrap, and the reworking of defective units came to be thought of as normal. This attitude did not encourage high quality and might even have discouraged quality-control efforts. Thus, practices that were wise if quality was suspect actually contributed to lowering quality.

Philosophies and practices that characterize the new manufacturing environment surfaced as overseas companies began to compete with U.S. manufacturers. In searching for a competitive edge, overseas manufacturers concentrated on the weaknesses of conventional manufacturing practices, particularly mediocre quality and high inventories. Terms used to describe a manufacturing environment that eliminates those weaknesses include just-in-time manufacturing, world-class manufacturing, and advanced manufacturing.

JUST-IN-TIME (JIT) MANUFACTURING

Just-in-time (JIT) manufacturing is a philosophy that focuses on timing, efficiency, and quality in meeting commitments. Companies that employ JIT strive for continual improvement and relentlessly search out and eliminate waste of materials, time, and space. One aspect of this philosophy is to increase customer satisfaction by reducing lead time. (How do you respond when told that you must wait two months for something you want to buy and use now? A commitment to reducing cycle time was thought important enough at **IBM** to be mentioned by the chair of its Board of Directors at an annual stockholders meeting.) Advocates of the JIT philosophy continually strive to promote a smooth and rapid flow of materials and components into finished products. Companies committed to JIT sometimes use the term "reengineering" to describe their efforts.

Inventory and Lead Time

The term "just in time" refers to one way of characterizing the goals of advanced manufacturing techniques. Under ideal conditions, purchased materials and components arrive just in time to be used, partly assembled units arrive at work stations just in time for the next step in production, and finished units emerge from production just in time to meet the shipping date requested by the customer. This is a "pull" environment, where the need for a finished unit pulls the parts and components along. Of course, ideal conditions are virtually impossible to achieve, but they serve as goals against which to measure progress, and progress has been dramatic in many cases. As examples, some factories receive deliveries of some items several times a day, and some have eliminated loading docks in favor of entrances allowing trucks to deliver materials directly to work stations. The delivery system reduces space requirements and eliminates the steps of putting materials in storage and then later taking them to work stations when needed. The trucks also carry away finished products so that they do not have to go into storage and then be taken out again for delivery to customers. (**Allen-Bradley** reports that its "factory within a factory" can take an order one day, produce the required units, and ship the order the following day, with only a small amount of material, and no finished or unfinished units, on hand at the end of the day.) Progress toward achieving just-in-time goals means shortened lead times, as well as reduced inventories and inventory costs.

As we mentioned earlier, companies today are forging links with suppliers and customers in efforts to benefit all concerned. The **Compaq** example is one instance of reducing cycle time through such links. **Toyota** provides its suppliers with its production schedule sufficiently far in advance so that the suppliers, whose factories are close to Toyota's, can have the right parts ready at the right time. **Ryder System**, the truck rental company, keeps the **Saturn** plant in Spring Hill, Tennessee, running smoothly by managing a supply chain of extreme complexity. Saturn has over 300 suppliers averaging 550 miles from Spring Hill. Saturn uses electronic data interchange (EDI), which means that its computers are linked to its suppliers' computers, to order all of its parts. It orders a new set of parts as soon as an automobile is finished, the ultimate in pull manufacturing.[3] **Merck**, the giant drug maker, saved $100 million in 1994 by reengineering its procurement processes. Employees had been spending most of their time in mechanical tasks such as processing requisitions and invoices. They now "spend 80 percent of their time establishing relationships that integrate suppliers into our supply process." Merck reduced its suppliers by 50 percent and has become a partner with them in increasing quality, reducing cost, and shortening cycle time.[4]

---

3 *Henkoff, op. cit., 78.*
4 *Merck 1994 annual report, 28.*

The JIT philosophy is concerned with all aspects of cycle time, not just inventory reduction. Managers continually scrutinize each step in the production process itself, trying to determine which cost-producing and time-consuming activities add value to the final product and which do not. For example, moving partially finished units from one work station to another is a non-value-adding activity. Hence, work stations in a JIT environment are often adjacent, rather than being spread throughout a factory, so that as much work as possible is done in a small cluster of machinery and workers, called a **manufacturing cell**. Coupling the use of cells with reduced needs for space to store inventories of various types, JIT operations use less space than conventional operations. Exhibit 1-2 illustrates production flows in a conventional operation and a JIT operation.

Multiskilled Workers

People are critical to any organization and especially so in JIT companies that give workers much more responsibility than do conventional manufacturers. Workers in a JIT company must master all of the skills required in cells. They must do much of their own maintenance and repair work. Some JIT companies, such as **Harley-Davidson**, give raises only to employees who learn new

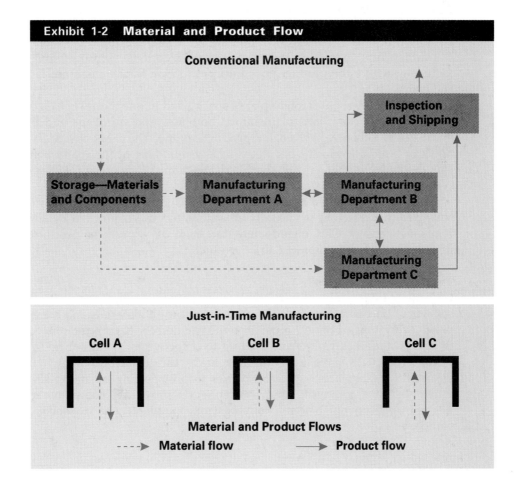

Exhibit 1-2   Material and Product Flow

Conventional Manufacturing

Just-in-Time Manufacturing

Cell A   Cell B   Cell C

Material and Product Flows

- - - → **Material flow**   ⟶ **Product flow**

skills. People work in teams and often earn bonuses based on the performance of their teams. **New Balance**, the maker of athletic shoes, recently changed from assembly line to team manufacturing. JIT workers are usually more productive than their conventional counterparts, in part because of higher morale that accompanies jobs with higher responsibility. As mentioned earlier, **General Mills** uses self-directed teams in its cereal manufacturing plants. The team approach extends beyond the manufacturing floor. Many companies are rewarding teams of managers for achieving goals in cost reduction, quality, and customer satisfaction.[5]

Flexible Manufacturing

In their efforts to reduce production time, JIT managers also have emphasized reducing setup time, the time required to change machine settings from making one product to making another. Conventional manufacturers often make long production runs of each product, which result in setup times measured in hours. The term **flexible manufacturing system** describes a JIT operation with a setup time of a few minutes that can respond very quickly to customer orders. For example, some modern plants for the manufacture of wearing apparel, which often has a high risk of obsolescence, can make and ship an order of ten pairs of walking shorts, in various sizes, colors, and patterns, within 24 hours of receiving the order. A manufacturer's ability to achieve flexible manufacturing depends partly on the available technology. But the goal of a flexible manufacturing system is to produce by units, rather than by batches. Jerry Jasinowski, president of the National Association of Manufacturers, has said that the ultimate goal is simultaneous manufacturing, where the product goes into production as the customer is placing the order.

For many years, automobile plants specialized in one model because of lack of flexibility. A new **Ford** plant builds both Aerostar minivans and Explorer sport-utility vehicles on the same production line. The plant cost $674 million and can build 50 vehicles per hour, in any mix. One of the many benefits of this flexibility is that jobs in the plant are more secure because they do not rely on only one vehicle.

Computer-integrated manufacturing (CIM) goes beyond flexible manufacturing so that a factory is virtually all automated and controlled by computer. Some versions of CIM include integration of all aspects of products, from design through development into production.

Total Quality Control

Of course, total quality control or total quality management is critical to the success of JIT operations. If little or no inventory of materials and components exist, everything received must be without defects or production could be delayed. Manufacturing errors leading to defective units cannot be tolerated. Several practices have evolved to achieve this condition, which is often referred to as *zero defects*. JIT companies stop inspecting incoming shipments when they are convinced that a supplier is providing components of the desired quality, and they stop buying from suppliers who do not meet that standard.

---

5 *Robin Couch Cardillo, "Business Talk,"* Financial Executive, *September/October 1994, 11.*

Similarly, JIT operations pinpoint problems early because workers inspect units throughout production instead of only at a few formal inspection points. Moreover, to reduce costs and increase quality, JIT manufacturers design quality and ease of manufacturability into products. Because of this lack of coordination in conventional manufacturing, product designers rarely talk with production people. Production engineers develop a manufacturing process to accommodate the design specifications, even though a minor design change might greatly simplify production. Design flaws often surface as manufacturing difficulties or in customer dissatisfaction. The conventional company is often described as a field of silos, with no connections among marketing, product, design, and customer service.

JIT companies stress cooperation and the blurring of lines of authority. **Nokia**, the $5 billion Finnish manufacturer of cellular telephones, built research and development laboratories next to each of its five major factories so that it could move quickly from the lab to the factory. It engineers "concurrently" with research and development, saving much valuable time and ensuring coordination of the two functions. Cellular phones have life cycles of 18 months, so quick response is critical.[6] **Culp, Inc.** is a $260 million manufacturer of decorative fabrics for the home furnishings industry, where design is important. The company has learned that over 80 percent of total costs are built into products at the design stage. The company's cost management and design people now work together. The company uses redesign as a strategic tool with new products that do not meet profit targets, rather than simply try to reduce their manufacturing costs.[7]

Evidence abounds of the importance companies now place on quality. **Eastman Kodak** used a full page of a recent annual report to discuss the awards the company had won for quality. An Eastman unit won a Baldridge Award, given for world-class quality, and 70 percent of its customers named Eastman their best supplier. **Intel**, the leading manufacturer of computer chips, bought a full page advertisement in *The Wall Street Journal* to congratulate three of its Preferred Quality Suppliers.

Quality is not limited to manufacturing. Service and merchandising companies can use JIT principles to improve their operations and increase profitability. **Red Lobster Restaurants**, a subsidiary of **General Mills**, has given teams of servers responsibility for portions of dining areas, which leads to faster service (shorter cycle time). Servers also take payments, eliminating the need for separate cashiers, which saves about $12 million annually, as well as time for customers. Red Lobster reports that its customers highly approve of the changes and believe that the value of a dinner is enhanced.

The table on p. 16 summarizes and contrasts JIT and conventional manufacturing.

ACTIVITIES OF MANAGERIAL ACCOUNTANTS

Managers of line functions are concerned with the primary operating activities of the organization—manufacturing (or buying) and selling a physical product or performing a service. A staff manager manages a department that serves

---

6 *"Grabbing Markets from the Giants"* Business Week, *November 28, 1994, 156.*
7 *John M. Brausch, "Target Costing for Profit Enhancement,"* Management Accounting, *November 1994, 45-49.*

JIT Manufacturing	Conventional Manufacturing
Manufacturing cells concentrating on one product	Departments working on all products
Multiskilled workers	Single-skilled workers
Small batches, smooth flows	Large batches, erratic flows
Total quality control	Some defects seen as inevitable
Short production cycle	Long production cycle
Zero or trivial inventories	Large inventories held as buffers
Daily delivery of materials/components	Large deliveries at irregular intervals
Relentless search to improve, eliminate all waste	Achieve acceptable performance
Integrate design and manufacturing	Design and manufacturing separate

other departments. For example, financial managers obtain the cash to keep operations running smoothly. The manager of the legal department advises other managers regarding the legal ramifications of actions.

Accounting is a staff function, with managerial accountants providing information to other managers. Information can relate to financial statements, tax problems, dealings with governmental authorities, and other matters. The managerial accountant, like other staff managers, often recommends courses of action to those using the information. But neither the managerial accountant, nor any other staff manager, can impose recommendations on line managers. Nevertheless, because of their expertise, staff managers can influence decisions. In fact, in some organizations "management accountants have votes on some line decisions, and, on certain decisions, their prior approval is sought."[8] Staff managers, like all managers, also manage their own departments.

Managerial accountants in businesses include people in the controller's office, as well as budget analysts, cost analysts, and financial analysts. A large company, or a division of a large company, might have several hundred people performing managerial accounting functions. In small businesses the controller and an assistant might carry out all of the other managerial accounting functions. Many managers look at managerial accountants as people who can identify and solve problems, help in implementing programs of continuous improvement and total quality management, and evaluate actions, products, and decisions.

The specific duties of managerial accountants include (1) assisting in the design of the organization's information system, (2) ensuring that the system performs adequately, (3) periodically reporting information to interested managers, and (4) undertaking special analyses.

The information system must meet the needs of all people who require information to perform their jobs. Managers responsible for sales of a particular product might need weekly sales reports for each territory. Their supervisor, who also supervises other sales managers, might need only a weekly report for a group (or line) of products. The chief sales executive might want only monthly, not weekly, reports of sales by product groups and sales territories. Managerial accountants must ensure that the system meets these varying needs.

8 Gerald H. Lander, James R. Holmes, Manuel A. Tipgos, and Marc J. Wallace, Jr., Profile of the Management Accountant, New York: National Association of Accountants, 1983, 10.

Computers usually record transactions in journals and ledgers. Accountants are responsible for supervising the gathering of data and for monitoring the system, making sure it functions as intended and is used appropriately. Regular, periodic reporting is the heart of managerial accountants' work in many organizations. One of the challenges here is ensuring that other managers receive relevant information and are not overwhelmed by irrelevant information. For some years, many people believed that managers should receive all of the information that could possibly be relevant. This view no longer prevails; managers' time is too valuable to spend sifting through material until they find what they need.

Special analyses are required when managers consider nonroutine actions. In some cases, such as the location of a new plant, relevant data might not be available in a form that enables managers to decide on the best course of action. Accountants must develop relevant information to serve such special purposes.

Managerial accountants have gained status in recent years as they now spend more time analyzing a company's operations and less with the problems of recording and computing costs of products. The Institute of Management Accountants (IMA), the principal organization of managerial accountants in the United States, has instituted a program to provide certification for managerial accountants. The Certified Management Accountant (CMA) examination was first given in 1972. About 15,500 people had successfully completed the examination by the end of 1994. A listing of the required subject areas in the CMA examination indicates the breadth of knowledge expected of the professional managerial accountant. The examination consists of the following four parts: Economics, Finance, and Management; Financial Accounting and Reporting; Management Reporting, Analysis, and Behavioral Issues; and Decision Analysis and Information Systems. The IMA also promulgated a code of ethics for management accountants, which is discussed further in the next section.

Additional evidence of the increasing importance and status of managerial accountants appeared in an article on **3M**, which is one of the most admired corporations in America according to a *Fortune* study. At 3M, divisional controllers are seen as "business advisors and financial consultants who are part of the operating/decision-making team."[9] This attitude was not prevalent 20 years ago. Controllers and other management accountants were then viewed as "bean counters" whose only purpose was to harass operating managers with trifling reports.

The role of the controller is expanding in many ways, in many companies. The controller at **Adolph Coors Company** is an important manager who participates in management meetings and is consulted on all major decisions. However, this was not always so. Many managers at Coors once thought of accountants as bean counters. A new controller came in with a plan to "transform 'accounting' reports into management reports, and place more emphasis on a forward financial perspective rather than on historical reporting of the company's financial results." Now, Coors' "accounting system produces management reports that present a combination of financial and

---

9 *Kathy Williams, "The Magic of 3M, Management Accounting Excellence,"* Management Accounting, *February 1986, 20.*

nonfinancial data important for performance evaluation, forecasting, and strategic planning."[10]

ETHICS

A decade ago, the Institute of Management Accountants published the Standards of Ethical Conduct for Management Accountants. The Institute also established an Ethics Committee and an Ethics Counseling Service. Management accountants are expected to abide by the Standards, which are reproduced in Exhibit 1-3 on pages 19 and 20.

Should you work as a controller or in some other managerial accounting position, you will be expected to comply with the Standards. Even if you are not subject to the code, there are two reasons why it is important that you know something about it. First, as a manager you have the right to expect ethical behavior from the managerial accountants with whom you work. Second, you should be aware that managerial accountants are prohibited from committing unethical acts on behalf of managers in the company by which they are employed.

Evidence indicates that pressure to violate the code is a serious problem. One study showed that a third to nearly half of management accountants felt pressured to achieve a specific income and that pressure was more common in companies that had formal codes of conduct.[11]

The Standards have four sections: competence, confidentiality, integrity, and objectivity. The competence provisions require management accountants to develop their knowledge and skills and to do their tasks in accordance with relevant laws, regulations, and standards. The confidentiality provisions forbid them to act on, or even appear to act on, confidential information they acquire in doing their work. This provision thus forbids "insider" actions such as selling the company's stock upon learning that it is likely to lose a major lawsuit. The integrity provisions cover avoidance of conflicts of interest, improprieties of accepting gifts or favors, and other matters generally associated with professional behavior. The objectivity provisions require management accountants to "communicate information fairly and objectively" and to "disclose fully all relevant information. . . ."

Management accountants ethically cannot ignore relevant data or use wildly optimistic projections to justify a course of action. Managers in charge of a product line that is not doing well, who fear for their jobs, might pressure management accountants to use exceedingly optimistic sales projections in an analysis. For management accountants to do so would compromise their professionalism. Moreover, management accountants could not ethically recommend buying office equipment from a company owned by a family member unless they disclosed the family member's interest to the persons making the decision.

The Standards require professional behavior, especially in avoiding conflicts of interest. They require management accountants to bring bad news to the attention of their supervisors, and to work competently. They also

---

10 Kenton B Walker, *"Coors, Brewing a Better Controllership,"* Management Accounting, *January 1988, 23.*
11 *Anne J. Rich, Carl S. Smith, and Paul H. Mihalek, "Are Corporate Codes of Conduct Effective?"* Management Accounting, *September 1990, 34.*

Exhibit 1-3 Standards of Ethical Conduct

Standards of Ethical Conduct for Management Accountants

Management accountants have an obligation to the organizations they serve, their profession, the public, and themselves to maintain the highest standards of ethical conduct. In recognition of this obligation, the Institute of Management Accountants, formerly the National Association of Accountants, has promulgated the following standards of ethical conduct for management accountants. Adherence to these standards is integral to achieving the *Objectives of Management Accounting.** Management accountants shall not commit acts contrary to these standards nor shall they condone the commission of such acts by others within their organizations.

COMPETENCE

Management accountants have a responsibility to:

♦ Maintain an appropriate level of professional competence by ongoing development of their knowledge and skills.
♦ Perform their professional duties in accordance with relevant laws, regulations, and technical standards.
♦ Prepare complete and clear reports and recommendations after appropriate analyses of relevant and reliable information.

CONFIDENTIALITY

Management accountants have a responsibility to:

♦ Refrain from disclosing confidential information acquired in the course of their work except when authorized, unless legally obligated to do so.

♦ Inform subordinates as appropriate regarding the confidentiality of information acquired in the course of their work and monitor their activities to assure the maintenance of that confidentiality.
♦ Refrain from using or appearing to use confidential information acquired in the course of their work for unethical of illegal advantage either personally or through third parties.

INTEGRITY

Management accountants have a responsibility to:

♦ Avoid actual or apparent conflicts of interest and advise all appropriate parties of any potential conflict.
♦ Refrain from engaging in any activity that would prejudice their ability to carry out their duties ethically.
♦ Refuse any gift, favor, or hospitality that would influence or would appear to influence their actions.
♦ Refrain from either actively or passively subverting the attainment of the organization's legitimate and ethical objectives.
♦ Recognize and communicate professional limitations or other constraints that would preclude responsible judgment or successful performance of an activity.
♦ Communicate unfavorable as well as favorable information and professional judgments or opinions.
♦ Refrain from engaging in or supporting any activity that would discredit the profession.

(continued)

OBJECTIVITY

Management accountants have a responsibility to:

◆ Communicate information fairly and objectively.
◆ Disclose fully all relevant information that could reasonably be expected to influence an intended user's understanding of the reports, comments, and recommendations presented.

RESOLUTION OF ETHICAL CONFLICT

In applying the standards of ethical conduct, management accountants may encounter problems in identifying unethical behavior or in resolving an ethical conflict. When faced with significant ethical issues, management accountants should follow the established policies of the organization bearing on the resolution of such conflict. If these policies do not resolve the ethical conflict, management accountants should consider the following course of action:

◆ Discuss such problems with the immediate superior except when it appears that the superior is involved, in which case the problem should be presented initially to the next higher managerial level. If satisfactory resolution cannot be achieved when the problem is initially presented, submit the issues to the next higher managerial level.
◆ If the immediate superior is the chief executive officer, or equivalent, the acceptable reviewing authority may be a group such as the audit committee, executive committee, board of directors, board of trustees, or owners. Contact with levels above the immediate superior should be initiated only with the superior's knowledge, assuming the superior is not involved.
◆ Clarify relevant concepts by confidential discussion with an objective advisor to obtain an understanding of possible courses of action.
◆ If the ethical conflict still exists after exhausting all levels of internal review, the management accountant may have no other recourse on significant matters than to resign from the organization and to submit an informative memorandum to an appropriate representative of the organization.

Except where legally prescribed, communication of such problems to authorities or individuals not employed or engaged by the organization is not considered appropriate.

* *Institute of Management Accountants, formerly National Association of Accountants,* Statements on Management Accounting: Objectives of Management Accounting, *Statement No. 1B, New York, N.Y., June 17, 1982.*

recognize that management accountants faced with a serious ethical conflict might have to resign and explain why to "an appropriate representative of the organization." Periodically, the Standards are reprinted in *Management Accounting,* the monthly magazine of the Institute, and the magazine's monthly column on ethics contains case studies and other materials that serve to remind management accountants of their ethical responsibilities.

INTERNATIONAL ASPECTS OF MANAGERIAL ACCOUNTING

In today's global economy, managers face new and more complex decisions. Should capital be raised in the U.S. or elsewhere? Where should the company manufacture the products it sells to customers in and outside of the U.S.? What products should the company make and in which countries? Should the company make some parts for its products in one country and complete the manufacturing process in others? Would it be profitable to change some products to accommodate differences among countries in tastes and culture? These decisions expand the information needs that managerial accountants must meet and influence the development of managerial accounting.

Perhaps the most pervasive problem facing multinational companies is the management of foreign currency. **The Toronto Blue Jays** illustrate the problem of changing currency values. The Blue Jays pay their players in U.S. dollars, but collect gate receipts in Canadian dollars. (They pay some expenses in Canadian dollars, but player salaries are the major expense.) Suppose the Canadian dollar is worth 0.90 U.S. dollars ($0.90). Then the U.S. dollar is worth $1.111 Canadian dollars ($1.00/$0.90). Paying each dollar of salary requires 1.111 Canadian dollars. If the value of the Canadian dollar drops to $0.80, is the team better off or worse off? It is worse off because each U.S. dollar in salary now requires 1.25 Canadian dollars ($1.00/$0.80). The team must take more of its Canadian dollars to the bank to exchange for U.S. dollars than it previously did. Of course, if the Canadian dollar rises to $0.95, the team is better off. The Blue Jays and other organizations with similar dealings can hedge against unfavorable foreign currency movements by purchasing futures contracts that allow them to buy U.S. dollars at future dates at specific prices. Such actions make certain what the companies will have to pay, but eliminate the possibility of their making money from a favorable move in the dollar.

The following excerpt from a **Coca-Cola** annual report indicates the importance of foreign currency management.

> "With approximately 79 percent of operating income in 1993 generated by operations outside the United States, foreign currency management is a key element of the Company's financial policies. The Company benefits from operating in a number of different currencies, because weakness in any particular currency is often offset by strengths in other currencies. The Company closely monitors its exposure to fluctuations in currencies and, where cost-justified, adopts strategies to reduce the impact of these fluctuations on the Company's financial performance. These strategies include engaging in various hedging activities to manage income and cash flows denominated in foreign currencies, and using foreign currency borrowings when appropriate to finance investments outside the United States."

At various points in this text we consider some of the special issues raised when analyzing the decisions confronting managers of international companies.

DEREGULATION

Deregulation is increasingly important to many companies and is among the factors that are influencing management accounting. In some regulated environments companies are guaranteed a stipulated rate of profit. Such companies do not need to control costs because they can pass them along to consumers. Many such companies now face competition and the market will set prices, not a regulatory agency. **Pacific Gas & Electric** now sells electricity for $0.073 per kilowatt hour. But it will soon have to compete against other power companies and its managers expect competition to reduce that price to $0.05 within the next few years. The company has already begun to reduce costs, but will have to scramble to stay ahead of its competition.[12] The regional Bell telephone companies have also begun to face competition from cellular companies and personal service communications enterprises. Such competition requires different information, especially measures of performance. Airlines were deregulated in the early 1980s, which required them to pay much more attention to costs and allowed carriers such as **Southwest Airlines** to grow profitably while offering very low fares.

SUMMARY

Managerial accounting and financial accounting both deal with economic events and reports about them. But the two areas of accounting differ in many ways, primarily because they serve different audiences. Managerial accounting serves internal managers in organizations. In businesses, top executives and managers in sales, production, finance, and accounting, use accounting data for planning and control, including decision making and performance evaluation. Managers of not-for-profit organizations perform many of these same functions and use much of the same accounting data as managers in businesses.

As you study managerial accounting, you will be introduced to some of the activities managers carry out in several areas of a business or other economic organizations. Changes in the manufacturing environment continue to prompt changes in managerial accounting as well as in related disciplines. Some managerial accounting concept or type of report relates to almost every area of managerial activity, and managerial accounting draws heavily on the concepts from related business disciplines. Management accountants are expected to carry out their activities in a manner consistent with their ethical responsibilities.

KEY TERMS

advanced manufacturing   (10)
budgeting   (3)
computer-integrated manufacturing
    (CIM)   (14)
control   (5)
control reports   (5)
cycle time   (11)
decision making   (4)
financial accounting   (2)
flexible manufacturing system   (14)

just-in-time (JIT) manufacturing
    (11)
lead time   (11)
managerial accounting   (2)
manufacturing cell   (13)
performance evaluation   (5)
planning   (3)
pro forma statements   (3)
value chain   (4)

---

12 *"PG&E: One Step Ahead of Future Shock,"* Business Week, *November 14, 1994, 68.*

ASSIGNMENT MATERIAL

QUESTIONS FOR DISCUSSION

1-1   *Everyday planning and control*   For each of the following activities, find an analogy to the planning and control process described in the chapter. Describe the process to be undertaken in these activities and compare with the process described in the chapter.

(a) Taking a course in college, including preparation and study, taking examinations, and evaluating test results.
(b) Taking a long automobile trip.
(c) Decorating your room or apartment.
(d) Coaching an athletic team.

1-2   *Ethics*   For each of the following situations, indicate which, if any, of the Standards of Ethical Conduct are violated.

(a) Al Nims, an assistant controller, informs his sister, a financial analyst, that the company he works for will report record earnings in the coming quarter. Al's sister has given him some profitable tips in the past and he wants to repay her.
(b) In order to please his superior, Bart Roberts, an ambitious management accountant, slants an analysis on building a new factory that makes the project appear profitable when it probably will not be. His superior will be promoted to controller if the plant is built and told Roberts he "sure hoped the analysis would be favorable."

1-3   *Who needs financial accounting?*   The chapter points out that differences between financial and managerial accounting relate to differences in the decisions made by managers and those made by parties external to the firm. If managerial accounting is supposed to serve the information needs of managers, why should managers know and understand financial accounting?

1-4   *Conventional versus world-class manufacturing*   Indicate whether each of the following costs should be higher or lower for a world-class (or JIT) manufacturer than for a conventional manufacturer. Briefly state why.

(a) Product warranty costs.
(b) Salaries of quality control inspectors.
(c) Amounts paid to vendors for parts and components.
(d) Wage *rates* for direct laborers.
(e) Total supervisory salaries.
(f) Warehousing costs, including rent or depreciation on space, salaries and wages of employees, utilities, etc.

PROBLEMS

 1-5   *Review of financial statement preparation*   Following is the balance sheet for Illustrative Company as of December 31, 19X4, and selected information relating to activities in 19X5.

Illustrative Company
Balance Sheet
as of December 31, 19X4

Assets

Current assets:		
Cash		$ 10,000
Accounts receivable		40,000
Inventory		70,000
Total current assets		$ 120,000
Property, plant, and equipment:		
Cost	$ 400,000	
Less: Accumulated depreciation	100,000	
Net		300,000
Total assets		$ 420,000

Equities

Current liabilities:		
Accounts payable		$ 10,000
Taxes payable		12,000
Total current liabilities		$ 22,000
Long-term debt:		
Bonds payable, 7%, due 19X8		100,000
Total liabilities		$ 122,000
Stockholders' equity:		
Common stock, no par value,		
10,000 shares issued and outstanding	$ 200,000	
Retained earnings	98,000	
Total stockholders' equity		298,000
Total equities		$ 420,000

During 19X5 the following events occurred.

(a) Sales on account were $350,000.
(b) Collections on receivables were $340,000.
(c) Credit purchases of inventory were $180,000.
(d) Cost of goods sold was $190,000.
(e) Payments to suppliers for inventory were $165,000.
(f) Cash paid for operating expenses was $80,000; interest on bonds was also paid.
(g) Plant and equipment were bought for $70,000 cash.
(h) Taxes payable at December 31, 19X4, were paid.
(i) Depreciation expense was $30,000.
(j) Income taxes are 40% of income before taxes. No payments were made on 19X5 taxes in 19X5.
(k) A dividend of $10,000 was declared and paid.

Required

1. Prepare an income statement for Illustrative Company for 19X5.
2. Prepare a balance sheet for Illustrative Company as of December 31, 19X5.

1-6   Review of the cash flow statement   Using the information from the previous assignment, prepare a cash flow statement for 19X5 for Illustrative Company.

1-7   Review of financial statement preparation   Following is the balance sheet for Example Company as of December 31, 19X4, and selected information relating to activities in 19X5.

Example Company
Balance Sheet
as of December 31, 19X4

Assets

Current assets:		
Cash		$ 20,000
Accounts receivable		80,000
Inventory		120,000
Prepaid expenses		8,000
Total current assets		$ 228,000
Property, plant, and equipment:		
Cost	$ 350,000	
Less: Accumulated depreciation	130,000	
Net		220,000
Total assets		$ 448,000

Equities

Current liabilities:		
Accounts payable		$ 40,000
Taxes payable		25,000
Accrued expenses		12,000
Total current liabilities		$ 77,000
Long-term liabilities:		
Bond payable, 6%, due 19X7		200,000
Total liabilities		$ 277,000
Stockholders' equity:		
Common stock, $10 par value,		
8,000 shares issued and outstanding	$ 80,000	
Retained earnings	91,000	
Total stockholders' equity		171,000
Total equities		$ 448,000

Other data relating to activities in 19X5 were as follows.

(a) Sales on account were $480,000.
(b) Collections on accounts receivable were $430,000.
(c) Credit purchases of goods for resale were $220,000.
(d) Cost of goods sold was $240,000.
(e) Payments of accounts payable were $210,000.
(f) Interest expense on bonds payable was paid in cash.

(g) Prepaid expenses at the beginning of the year expired and new prepayments in the amount of $6,000 were made in 19X5.

(h) Accrued taxes payable at the beginning of the year were paid.

(i) Accrued expenses payable are for wages and salaries. Total cash payments for wages and salaries during 19X5 were $95,000. At the end of 19X5, $7,000 was owed to employees.

(j) Other cash payments for expenses during 19X5 were $65,000, not including the $6,000 prepayments in (g).

(k) The company issued common stock to the public for $40,000 (4,000 shares).

(l) Plant and equipment were purchased for $30,000 cash.

(m) Depreciation expense was $40,000.

(n) The income tax rate is 40%. Income taxes for 19X5 were unpaid at year end.

(o) A dividend of $5,000 was declared and paid.

Required

1. Prepare an income statement for Example Company for 19X5.
2. Prepare a balance sheet for Example Company as of December 31, 19X5.

1-8   *Review of the cash flow statement*   Using the information from the previous assignment, prepare a cash flow statement for 19X5 for Example Company.

1-9   *Different costs for different purposes*   Suppose you are going to drive home this weekend, a round trip of 180 miles. Your car gets 30 miles per gallon of gas and you expect gas to cost $1.15 per gallon. Insurance and depreciation are $1,000 per year. You usually drive 10,000 miles per year. A friend asks you to take her along. She lives a block from your home.

Required

1. What are the costs of taking your friend along, as opposed to going by yourself?
2. Suppose now that you are not planning on going home. Your friend asks for a ride and you are willing to go. What are the costs of going, as opposed to not going?

1-10   *JIT*   You have been telling your fellow managers about the potential benefits of adopting the JIT philosophy, but some remain unconvinced. A couple of them seem not to hear what you have been saying. Manager A says, "Look, we just can't hit production right on the nose so that stuff arrives just when a guy finishes the last batch. We need some extra units so that our people aren't waiting around for the guys before them to finish." Manager B chimes in, "It all sounds great, but we're doing fine the way we work now. Some of our problems are caused by bad design of products, but we have to please our customers."

The quality control manager says, "We use the latest techniques to inspect both incoming shipments of parts and components and outgoing shipments of finished product. We are sure our quality is good on what goes out the door. And we catch plenty of stuff before we ship it, maybe 10 to 15 percent defectives that have to be reworked or scrapped. So we earn our keep around here." The production manager argues that the functional factory arrangement, with all machines of a given type in the same area, makes the company more efficient because the workers "... can really learn how to operate that one machine they're responsible for."

Required
Comment on each of the statements and indicate how JIT could help the company.

1-11   Ethics   You are the newly hired controller of TM Enterprises, a large manufacturer of industrial products. Yesterday morning the president of the company called you and other senior executives to her office where she stated that a competitor was about to file suit against TM for patent infringement. Regardless of the merits of the case, it will tie up company talent for a long while and will be quite costly to fight. The effects on the company's prospects cannot be measured, but it is possible that they will be severe.

This evening your father called from Florida, where he and your mother have lived in retirement for a few years. You chatted about the weather, the children, dad's golf game, and other such things. Then he told you that he had just bought shares of stock in TM Enterprises because he knew that any company you worked at would do well.

Required
What do you say to your father?

1-12   Ethics   You work as the data processing manager of Acme Products, a manufacturer of various consumer products. You recently asked for bids on new microcomputers and asked the controller's office to assist you in evaluating the costs and benefits of the suppliers' proposals. Eventually, you settled on systems offered by Micro Technologies, a relatively new company with a good reputation. The decision was based partly on a favorable analysis by Larry Bowman, an assistant controller.

A week or so after deciding on the Micro systems, you happen to see Bowman eating lunch with Paul Coleman, one of the Micro sales engineers. You later ask Bowman about it and he says that he and Paul were college classmates. He says that he didn't mention their friendship because it wasn't relevant; he did his analysis strictly on the facts.

Required
1. Has Bowman violated the IMA Standards of Ethical Conduct? If so, which standard?
2. Suppose instead of seeing Bowman and Coleman at lunch, you saw them at the airport. Bowman waved to you and said Coleman was paying for a weekend of sun and surf in the Bahamas. Has Bowman violated the Standards now? If so, which?

1-13   Conventional and JIT manufacturing   Jason Company manufactures five basic products that are similar and relatively standard. That is, they are not made-to-order. Product design and features are updated periodically in response to customer suggestions. Product designers come up with improvements and production is responsible for re-tooling and other activities required to implement the redesign.

Jason receives orders from customers, then fills the orders from stock or manufactures the required units. The company has a warehouse where it keeps finished units, raw materials, and components. The Quality Control Department inspects all incoming shipments of raw materials and components and rejects those with defects above a certain percentage. The percentage differs for different items. For instance, a relatively high percentage, say 10 percent, of defectives is considered acceptable for sophisticated, hard-to-manufacture components, while a low percentage, say 1 percent, is acceptable for mass-produced items like simple valves.

The company usually buys a two- or three-month supply of high-volume raw materials. Jason receives a 1 percent average discount on prices by buying in large quantities. Jason's purchasing manager is responsible, and rewarded, for obtaining raw materials and components at the lowest possible cost and so scours the country looking for the best deals. Jason therefore deals with a great many suppliers.

Production begins by withdrawing the necessary raw materials and components from the warehouse, inspecting them for possible deterioration during storage, and transporting them to the first station that will work on the batch of product. No job begins until all raw materials and components are available. Each station does one function, such as drilling, planing, welding, or various assembly operations.

Each station has an area to store raw materials and components for work that has not yet started. The raw materials wait there until the station is ready to begin the job. Significant setup time is required in changing over from one product to another at some stations. After the workers at the station have finished their part of the job, they send the semi-completed units along with the raw materials and components not yet installed to the next station. At that station the same process is repeated and so on until all work is completed. In some cases, a job will go to the same station more than once during production because it requires the same operation at different stages of production.

At the conclusion of the process, the finished units go to the Quality Control Department where they are tested and inspected. They then are sent to the warehouse to await shipment. The company usually makes 10 percent more units than needed for an order to allow for defects. Any spare good units are held in the warehouse until another order arrives. Defective units sometimes are reworked or sold as scrap. Reworked units are stored in the warehouse. If the work station that produced the defective part has been determined, the work station's manager is held responsible. (Bonuses for station managers are based largely on total good output.) In many cases, determining the source of the defect is not possible, so no one is held responsible.

The factory manager has said that "it gets pretty hectic at the end of each month when we're trying to finish up jobs and get the stuff out to the warehouse."

Cycle time varies among types of products, but spans from 10 days to 45 days depending on various factors.

Required

Prepare a memorandum describing how Jason differs from a JIT company and what changes in its operations you would recommend. Use the guidelines in Appendix A at the back of the book.

PART ONE

cost-volume-profit analysis and decision making

The first part of this book discusses the basic principles of decision making, the principles of cost-volume-profit analysis. These principles underlie the chapters in Part One and most of the material in the rest of the book. Much planning and decision making depends on classifying costs according to their behavior and on understanding what activities drive costs. An understanding of cost drivers and behavior is essential if a manager is to have the best information for making rational decisions.

The principles and techniques developed in this section are discussed and illustrated primarily in a business context. But nearly all are applicable to not-for-profit economic entities, such as hospitals, universities, charitable institutions, and government units.

Profit Planning

LEARNING OBJECTIVES

After reading this chapter, you should be able to

1 Describe and apply the concepts of fixed and variable costs.

2 Describe and apply the concept of contribution margin.

3 Prepare contribution margin format income statements.

4 Describe and discuss the significance of the relevant range.

5 Construct and interpret a cost-volume-profit graph.

6 Determine the sales volume or selling price needed to achieve a target profit.

7 Describe and illustrate target costing.

8 Describe and discuss the importance of cost structure.

9 Discuss the assumptions that underlie cost-volume-profit analysis.

The schedule below shows percentage increases in sales and income before taxes for two recent years for four large, successful companies.

	Percentage Increase in	
	Sales	Income before Taxes
Coca-Cola	16%	20%
Wal-Mart	25%	29%
Southwest Airlines	27%	50%
Motorola	31%	60%

Why did **Southwest** and **Motorola** show increases in income nearly double their increases in sales? Why were **Coca-Cola's** and **Wal-Mart's** income increases only slightly more than their sales increase? What factors besides sales determine a company's profit performance? One important reason for the differences in sales and profit increases of the listed companies is their cost structures. Some companies' costs remain relatively constant, so that even small increases in sales filter down to income. Other companies' costs rise and fall as sales rise and fall, so they experience much lower increases in profit from increases in sales. Other factors act on sales/profit relationships as well. The sales/profit street runs both ways, though. If Southwest's sales fall, its profit will fall more rapidly than that of Coca-Cola or Wal-Mart. The ability to raise prices to meet cost increases is also an important factor. Coca-Cola has more ability to raise prices than does Wal-Mart, which competes fiercely on its low prices. As you study this chapter, you will learn more about the relationships among sales volume, costs, and profits.

Companies must earn profits to stay in business. Managers want to increase profitability and therefore need to predict how their actions will affect profits. For example, what will happen to profits if increasing promotional efforts by $250,000 increases sales by 50,000 units? Managers also are concerned with questions such as the following: How many units must we sell to earn $50,000? What selling price should we set? Should we hire another salesperson? Would staying open another two hours each day be profitable?

Cost-volume-profit analysis helps managers plan for change and answer questions such as those posed above. **Cost-volume-profit (CVP) analysis** is a method for analyzing the relationships among costs, volume, and profits.[1] Managers use these relationships to plan, budget, and make decisions. The first step in CVP analysis is classifying costs according to behavior.

Classifying costs according to behavior is distinctive to managerial use of accounting information. In financial accounting reports prepared for external use, costs normally are grouped according to the functional areas of business: production (cost of goods sold), marketing (selling expenses), administration (general and administrative expenses), and financing (interest expense).[2] A functional classification does not provide the necessary information to predict what is likely to happen to costs and profits if circumstances change, and a manager must plan for change and take actions to make changes.

COST BEHAVIOR

A cost is classified as either fixed or variable, according to whether the *total* amount of the cost changes as activity changes. *Activity* is a general term denoting anything that the company does; examples of activity include units of product sold or produced, hours worked, invoices prepared, and parts

---

1 *Other terms you may encounter that mean essentially the same thing as CVP analysis are* break-even analysis *and* profit-volume analysis.
2 *In financial accounting the term* cost *denotes the expenditure for an asset and* expense *denotes expired costs—costs assigned to the income statement for a period of time. We shall generally use the more general term* cost.

inspected. *Volume* is, for many purposes, virtually synonymous with activity, and both terms are used throughout this book. In this chapter, we use sales as the measure of volume and classify costs as either fixed or variable with sales. Not all costs fall into these categories, and other measures of activity are often important. We consider other measures of activity in Chapter 3. For CVP analysis we care how a cost behaves, not whether it is cost of goods sold, salaries, or depreciation.

3▶

VARIABLE COSTS

Variable costs change, in total, in direct proportion to changes in volume. To illustrate this concept, consider TFL Company, a wholesaler of backpacks. The following schedule shows data for TFL.

TFL Company Data		
Selling price of backpacks	$10.00	
Cost of backpacks from manufacturer	$5.00	
Variable cost to pack and ship	0.50	
Sales commission at 5% of $10	0.50	per backpack at $10 price
Total unit variable cost	$6.00	
Total monthly fixed costs (rent, salaries, depreciation, etc.)	$20,000	

Notice that the $0.50 commission depends on the selling price, but that the per-unit amounts of the other variable costs do not. All three costs vary *in total* with the volume of sales. That is, the costs are incurred each time a backpack is sold, and the total of each increases or decreases in proportion to changes in sales.

CONTRIBUTION MARGIN

Contribution margin is the difference between selling price per unit and variable cost per unit. The term often is used to denote *total contribution margin*, the difference between total sales and total variable costs. In some cases, expressing contribution margin as a percentage is useful and convenient. The **contribution margin percentage** is per-unit contribution margin divided by selling price, or total contribution margin divided by total sales dollars. (Both calculations give the same result.) The percentage of variable costs to selling price, per unit or in total, is called the **variable cost percentage**.

We use the term *contribution* because what is left from a sale after variable costs are covered *contributes* to covering other costs and producing profit. In TFL's case, contribution margin per unit is $4 ($10 - $6) and contribution margin percentage is 40% ($4/$10).

FIXED COSTS

Fixed costs remain the same in total over a wide range of volume. The schedule shows that TFL has monthly fixed costs of $20,000. As well as the items listed, these costs include utilities, insurance, property taxes, advertising, and others that do not change in response to changes in sales volume. Note that we do not say that fixed costs never change. A company can hire more salaried personnel, increase or decrease advertising, turn up the air conditioning, and take other actions that change costs. But the costs do not change *automatically* as volume changes. For planning purposes, we think of them as fixed. Knowing total monthly fixed costs and unit variable costs, we can determine total costs as

$$Total\ costs = fixed\ costs + (variable\ cost\ per\ unit \times unit\ volume)$$
$$= \$20,000 + (\$6 \times units\ sold)$$

Knowing how to determine total costs, we can also determine profit as

Profit = (selling price × unit sales) - total variable costs - total fixed costs

CONTRIBUTION MARGIN INCOME STATEMENT

The following income statements for TFL show the effects of fixed costs and of changes in sales. Unlike financial accounting income statements, these statements group costs only as variable or fixed and show contribution margin as a subtotal.

TFL
Income Statements at Various Sales Levels

	5,000 Units	6,000 Units	7,000 Units
Sales ($10 per unit)	$50,000	$60,000	$70,000
Variable costs ($6 per unit)	30,000	36,000	42,000
Contribution margin ($4 per unit)	$20,000	$24,000	$28,000
Fixed costs	20,000	20,000	20,000
Income	$ 0	$ 4,000	$ 8,000

Notice that the $4,000 change in contribution margin as sales increase by 1,000 units is also the change in income. *As sales change, income changes by unit contribution margin multiplied by the change in sales.* We can also calculate income by multiplying per-unit contribution margin by unit sales and then subtracting total fixed costs.

Thus, to calculate TFL's income for sales of 6,000 backpacks, we can multiply the $4 contribution margin by 6,000. This gives total contribution margin of $24,000, and when we subtract fixed costs of $20,000, we find income of $4,000. We also could determine total contribution at that level of sales by multiplying sales of $60,000 (6,000 × $10) by the 40% contribution margin percentage, giving $24,000. Again, income is total contribution margin minus fixed costs.

An important use of CVP analysis is to help managers predict how income will change if volume changes. If TFL managers wonder what will happen to income if sales increase by 100 backpacks per month, CVP analysis can tell them that income will increase by $400, the 100-backpack increase multiplied by the $4 per-backpack contribution margin. The $400 change in income also can be determined by computing the increase in sales revenue (100 units ×

$10 = $1,000) and multiplying by the contribution margin percentage of 40%. Note that the increase in income is $400 no matter what the current level of sales.

EMPHASIS ON EXPECTATIONS

At this early stage we are dealing with a simplified case, looking at the costs in a single period (a month, a quarter, or perhaps a year) and predicting costs and income for the following period. The important point is that predictions are about the future. To expect either per-unit variable costs or total fixed costs to remain the same month after month, or year after year, is unreasonable. Total fixed costs, per-unit variable costs, and selling prices can change for many reasons.

Inflation is a major cause of changes in both fixed and variable costs—suppliers might raise their prices, lessors might raise rents, salaries might rise, and so on. Profit planning must take into account expected changes in costs. Based on expectations, CVP analysis does not assume that costs remain constant over time. Thus, if TFL managers expect the price they pay for backpacks to go up by $0.80 next month, they will use $5.80 (instead of $5.00) in planning for next month. Rapid inflation is a serious problem for managers in many countries and forces them to be creative. In Russia, for example, a manufacturer of shirts raised prices 15-20 times per month to cover rising costs. Having a good idea of how cost increases affect fixed and variable costs is necessary to make such adjustments.

Because of inflation, competition, or for other reasons, managers might change selling prices. For example, TFL might raise its price to $11 to counter an increase in the price it pays for backpacks. (Of course, an increase in the selling price will also increase TFL's per-unit commission, so it would use both the new price *and* the new variable cost in its plans.)

As mentioned earlier, managers can change some costs. TFL could hire another employee at a monthly salary, increasing fixed costs, or it could increase advertising (also increasing fixed costs). In a more complex company, many cost changes are the result of managerial actions. A large company could increase (or decrease) its office staff or change its level of spending on such items as travel and employee training. Thus, fixed costs might change during a period. But they are still fixed because they do not change with the level of activity. For planning purposes, then, managers predict fixed costs based on what they expect for the coming period, knowing they might change costs to meet changing conditions.

As a general rule, managers can change some fixed costs more easily than they can change per-unit variable costs, especially over short periods of time (more about this in Chapter 3). Some accountants, therefore, use the term **nonvariable costs** instead of *fixed costs*. The point, as we briefly introduced earlier, is that fixed costs are not fixed in the sense that they cannot be changed, but rather that, unlike variable costs, fixed costs do not change automatically when volume changes. In this book, we call such costs *fixed* because that term is more common. Regardless of terminology, the emphasis in planning is on expectations. If actual conditions (selling prices, prices from suppliers, etc.) do not coincide with expectations, or if managers later change decisions, differences will occur between actual and predicted costs and profit. Such differences between actuality and expectations are inherent in business but do not reduce the need to plan.

INCOME STATEMENT FORMATS—FINANCIAL ACCOUNTING AND CONTRIBUTION MARGIN FORMATS

The format used for income statements in this chapter and throughout most of this book differs from that used in financial accounting. As stated earlier, in financial accounting costs are usually classified by function or by object. The income statements in Exhibit 2-1 highlight the differences between the two approaches. Notice that the sales and income figures are the same under both approaches, but the costs are classified in different ways. The statements are for a month when TFL sells 6,000 backpacks.

The obvious differences between the statements are in terminology and the placement of costs. The principal difference is that a manager who receives a statement in the financial accounting format cannot perform CVP analysis, because that format tells little about cost behavior. The manager must determine how much of each cost is fixed and variable, which is not possible without additional analysis. One unfortunate result is the tendency of some managers to treat fixed costs as if they were variable and to use average total cost per unit for planning.

UNIT COSTS

You should see that, because total fixed costs remain the same at different levels of activity, the average fixed cost per unit changes whenever volume changes. Thus, the average fixed cost per unit when TFL sells 5,000 units is $4.00 ($20,000/5,000), while the average at 7,000 units is about $2.86 ($20,000/7,000). The average *total* cost per unit, then, depends on the level of activity, with the average total per-unit cost for TFL being $10.00 ($4.00 fixed plus $6

Exhibit 2-1 Comparison of Contribution Margin and Financial Accounting Income Statements

Financial Accounting Format (Functional)		Contribution Margin Format (Behavioral)	
Sales, 6,000 × $10	$60,000	Sales, 6,000 × $10	$60,000
Cost of sales, 6,000 × $5	30,000	Variable costs:	
Gross profit	$30,000	Cost of sales	$30,000
Operating expenses:		Packing and shipping	3,000
Packing and shipping	$ 3,000	Commissions	3,000
Commissions	3,000	Total variable costs	$36,000
Rent, salaries,		Contribution margin	$24,000
depreciation, etc.	20,000	Fixed costs	20,000
Total operating expenses	$26,000		
Income	$ 4,000	Income	$ 4,000

variable) at 5,000 units, and $8.86 ($2.86 fixed plus $6 variable) at 7,000 units. Notice that TFL earns zero profit at 5,000 units and that its average *total* cost of $10 at that volume equals its $10 selling price. TFL earns an $8,000 profit at 7,000 units because only its variable costs increase and its fixed costs remain constant.

Failing to recognize that average total per-unit cost changes as activity changes creates problems for managers who—unwisely—use averages to predict future costs. Managers should not use the average total per-unit cost for one level of activity to predict total costs at another level.

To illustrate this point, suppose TFL uses the $8.86 average total cost per unit (at 7,000 units) to predict total costs at a volume of 8,000 backpacks. The predicted cost is $70,880 ($8.86 × 8,000 backpacks). But TFL's income statements at volumes of 7,000 and 8,000 backpacks are

	7,000 Backpacks	8,000 Backpacks
Sales ($10 per unit)	$70,000	$80,000
Variable costs ($6 per unit)	42,000	48,000
Contribution margin ($4 per unit)	$28,000	$32,000
Fixed costs	20,000	20,000
Income	$ 8,000	$12,000
Average cost per unit	$8.86	$8.50
Profit per unit	$1.14	$1.50

Total costs at sales of 8,000 backpacks are $68,000 ($48,000 + $20,000), not $70,880. What appears to be additional profit per unit at the higher level of activity is simply the result of spreading the fixed costs over a larger number of units. The *behavior* of TFL's costs has not changed at all; variable costs remain at 60% of sales ($6 per unit) and fixed costs remain at $20,000. Using average total cost per unit to predict total costs works only if all costs are variable.

In the preceding example, notice that income as a percentage of sales (called **return on sales**, or **ROS**) differs at the two levels of volume. At sales of 7,000 units, income is about 11.4% of sales ($8,000/$70,000), while at sales of 8,000 units, income is 15% of sales ($12,000/$80,000). Perhaps the most common mistake managers make is to use the ROS percentage at one level of volume to predict income at another volume level. If a company has *any* fixed costs, its income as a percentage of sales increases as volume increases. Moreover, the percentage increase in income is greater than the percentage increase in sales. In the income statements just shown, a 14.3% increase in sales ($10,000/$70,000) produced a 50% increase in income (from $8,000 to $12,000).

RELEVANT RANGE

As stated earlier, per-unit variable costs and total fixed costs change over time. They might also change when activity changes by a large amount. That is, the per-unit variable cost and total fixed cost will behave as expected only over some range of activity.

For example, TFL might be able to handle up to about 10,000 backpacks with its current level of staff. But at some point around that level of sales, it will need additional help, increasing fixed costs. If TFL orders more than 10,000 backpacks per month it might get a discount on the purchase price, thus reducing per-unit variable costs.

The examples illustrate an important assumption underlying CVP analysis: that the company will operate within a **relevant range**, a range of volume over which it can reasonably expect selling price, per-unit variable cost, and total fixed costs to be constant. The width of the range varies among companies. Managers cannot expect these factors to remain constant when they operate outside the relevant range.

A company might have more than one relevant range, within each of which a particular price/cost combination prevails. For instance, a company could go from one shift to two shifts per day. Two-shift operation necessitates leaving the heat and lights on, hiring additional supervisors, and taking on other fixed costs. For planning purposes, managers forecast the approximate range of activity and use the selling price and costs they believe will hold within that range.

A special case of operating outside the relevant range occurs when a business shuts down for a short period. A company that closes for a week or a month should find its total costs for that period to be less than its normal total fixed costs. A company closing for a month would turn out the lights, turn down the heat, and probably not advertise. The company might also lay off some employees. Thus, to think of fixed costs as the costs that the company would incur at zero activity is not appropriate. Fixed costs are better thought of as the planned costs that will not change in total as volume changes within the relevant range.

TFL's volume, and relevant range, are expressed in units of product, or dollars of sales. Businesses that sell services, rather than goods, often charge their clients for the hours that they work. CPA firms, law firms, and consulting firms are examples. For these firms, chargeable hours (the number of hours worked that are chargeable to client business) is an appropriate and useful measure of activity. Still other companies use percentage of capacity as the measure of volume. Airlines use seat-miles or passenger-miles to measure volume. (A seat-mile is one seat flown one mile. A passenger-mile is a seat-mile occupied by a paying passenger.) Annual reports of airlines cite various statistics regarding seat-miles and passenger-miles. For example, **Delta Airlines** stated that its break-even point in 1993 was about 65 percent of available seat-miles. **American Airlines'** break-even point was 61.6 percent in a recent year.

Alternative measures are usually available and managers might use several of them, perhaps relying more on one than on others. According to the 1994 annual report, **The Coca-Cola Company** ". . . measures soft drink volume in two ways: gallon shipments of concentrates and syrups, and equivalent unit cases of finished product . . . Management believes unit case volume more accurately measures the underlying strength of the global business system because it measures trends at the retail level and is less impacted by inventory management practices at the wholesale level."

COST-VOLUME-PROFIT GRAPH

Exhibit 2-2 gives a graphical representation of the CVP picture for TFL. The revenue line shows total sales dollars at any volume, which is simply the

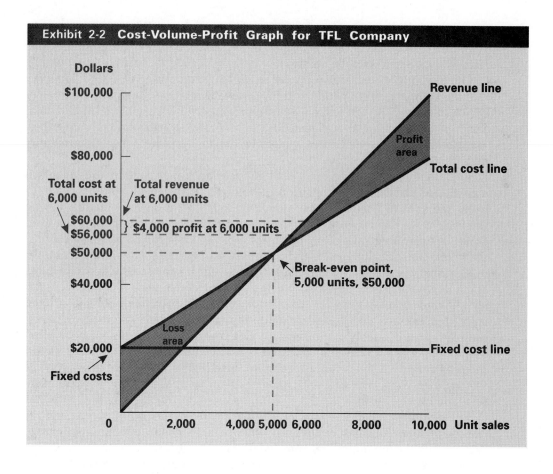

Exhibit 2-2   Cost-Volume-Profit Graph for TFL Company

selling price per unit multiplied by the level of unit volume. At any volume, the vertical distance between total costs and fixed costs is total variable costs at that volume.

Although the lines on the graph extend far to the right and back to the vertical axis on the left, doing so is not legitimate because of the relevant range. As suggested earlier, TFL's fixed costs should be less than $20,000 if the store is closed for the month (zero activity), and either per-unit variable or total fixed costs, or both, are likely to change if volume exceeds 10,000 backpacks per month. We extend the lines to zero volume and to 10,000 units to make it easier to read the graph.

At any volume, the vertical distance between the revenue line and the total cost line is the amount of profit or loss (shaded areas) at that volume. The graphical presentation directs attention to the **break-even point**—the point at which profits are zero because total revenues equal total costs. A company operating above the break-even point makes profits; below that point, it incurs losses. Managers of business firms do not want to break even—they want to earn profits. But they still want to know how low volume can be before losses appear. Knowing the break-even point is useful for many purposes. Managers of not-for-profit organizations frequently seek to break even, or show only a small profit or loss, on some of their activities.

The graph highlights an important lesson. As long as selling price exceeds variable cost (contribution margin is positive), selling more units will benefit the company, either by increasing profits or by decreasing losses. Thus, companies can often do better by staying open because their losses would be greater if they closed. Such is often the case with seasonal businesses. Businesses in summer resort areas expect losses during the winter, but might remain open. Many seasonal businesses continue to operate in the off-season because they recognize that the contribution margin from the additional, though lower, sales reduces their losses. Chapter 3 considers this point in more detail.

3▶

ACHIEVING TARGET PROFITS

BREAK-EVEN POINT AND TARGET DOLLAR PROFITS

The break-even point is of interest, but managers of profit-seeking organizations are concerned more with meeting a desired or **target profit**. Managers can express targets as absolute dollar amounts, ROS percentages, or in other ways. We can use the same general relationships to find both the break-even point and the volume required to earn a target profit. Profit equals total sales minus total variable costs minus total fixed costs. That is,

$$Profit = \begin{array}{c} total \\ sales \\ dollars \end{array} - \begin{array}{c} total \\ variable \\ costs \end{array} - \begin{array}{c} total \\ fixed \\ costs \end{array}$$

Understanding the relationships in this equation allows you to solve virtually any CVP problem. Using Q to denote the quantity of units sold, we can restate the formula as

$$Profit = \left(\begin{array}{c} per\text{-}unit \\ selling \\ price \end{array} \times Q \right) - \left(\begin{array}{c} per\text{-}unit \\ variable \\ cost \end{array} \times Q \right) - \begin{array}{c} total \\ fixed \\ costs \end{array}$$

Knowing that selling price minus variable cost per unit equals contribution margin per unit, we can combine those two components. We then add fixed costs to both sides, and get

$$Profit + \begin{array}{c} total \\ fixed \\ costs \end{array} = \left(\begin{array}{c} contribution \\ margin \\ per\ unit \end{array} \times Q \right)$$

Let us first use the above equation to find the break-even point (where profit is zero). At break even, the profit term drops out. Now we can solve for Q (the break-even sales in units) by dividing both sides by contribution margin per unit, producing

$$Q\ (\textit{break-even sales in units}) = \frac{total\ fixed\ costs}{contribution\ margin\ per\ unit}$$

TFL managers can interpret this formula as saying: "How many units must we sell to cover fixed costs of $20,000, if each unit contributes $4 to cover those fixed costs?" Applying the formula, TFL can determine that the break-even point is 5,000 backpacks.

$$\text{Break-even sales in units} = \frac{\$20,000}{\$10 - \$6} = \frac{\$20,000}{\$4} = 5,000 \text{ backpacks}$$

At the break-even point, total contribution margin equals total fixed costs. We can therefore find the volume required to achieve a target profit (zero is a target) by finding the sales required to earn total contribution margin equal to the sum of total fixed costs and the target profit.

Suppose TFL wishes to earn a profit of $2,000 per month. How many backpacks must it sell? We know that total contribution margin must equal fixed costs of $20,000 for TFL to break even. Hence, to achieve a profit of $2,000, total contribution margin must be $2,000 greater than fixed costs, or $22,000. To achieve total contribution margin of $22,000 when contribution margin per unit is $4 ($10 - $6), TFL must sell 5,500 units. Expressed in general terms, our basic equation is

$$\left(\begin{array}{c} \text{Sales, in units,} \\ \text{to achieve} \\ \text{target profit} \end{array} \times \begin{array}{c} \text{contribution} \\ \text{margin} \\ \text{per unit} \end{array} \right) - \begin{array}{c} \text{total} \\ \text{fixed} \\ \text{costs} \end{array} = \begin{array}{c} \text{target} \\ \text{profit} \end{array}$$

Restating this equation to solve for the needed level of sales yields

$$\text{Sales, in units, to achieve target profit} = \frac{\text{fixed costs} + \text{target profit}}{\text{contribution margin per unit}}$$

Applying this formula in TFL's case, we have

$$\text{Unit sales to achieve target profit} = \frac{\$20,000 + \$2,000}{\$10 - \$6} = \frac{\$22,000}{\$4} = 5,500 \text{ units}$$

Notice that the numerator of the formula is the total contribution margin required to earn the target profit, consisting of the $20,000 contribution margin required for break even plus the $2,000 required for the target profit. Target dollar sales is $55,000 (5,500 × $10).

An alternative approach also can be useful. We can construct an income statement filling in what we know and solving for what we do not know. First, we know profit and fixed costs, which enables us to determine total contribution margin.

Sales ($10 per unit)	?
Variable costs ($6 per unit)	?
Contribution margin ($4 per unit)	$22,000
Fixed costs	20,000
Profit	$ 2,000

We know that total contribution margin of $22,000 is unit contribution margin of $4 multiplied by volume, so we can divide total contribution margin by unit contribution margin to get the same 5,500 ($22,000/$4) unit result we obtained with the equation.

CONTRIBUTION MARGIN PERCENTAGE

Both the graph in Exhibit 2-2 and the target profit formula derived previously show sales in units. We could just as well use dollars and some managers find dollars more convenient than units. The following equation shows the contribution margin percentage alternative applied to TFL. We can rearrange the terms in the basic equation to yield

Profit = (sales dollars × contribution margin percentage) - fixed costs

So the volume required for a target profit is

$$\frac{\textit{Sales, in dollars, required}}{\textit{to earn target profit}} = \frac{\textit{total fixed costs + target profit}}{\textit{contribution margin percentage}}$$

TFL can interpret this version of the formula as saying: "How many dollars of sales must I have to cover fixed costs of $20,000 and earn a target profit, given that each sales dollar yields $0.40 of contribution margin (the 40% contribution margin percentage, [$4/$10])?"

For break even,

$$\textit{Break-even sales, in dollars} = \frac{\$20,000 + \$0}{40\%} = \$50,000$$

The units required to break even are still 5,000 ($50,000/$10 selling price per unit), and both this formula and the one using sales units give the same answer for the break-even point, 5,000 units or $50,000.

For a $2,000 profit, TFL needs sales of $55,000.

$$\textit{Sales dollars} = \frac{\$20,000 + \$2,000}{40\%} = \$55,000$$

Once again, the answer is the same regardless of approach. Target sales in units are 5,500 units, whether computed directly or as a result of the computation of target sales dollars ($55,000/$10), and target sales in dollars are $55,000 (5,500 × $10).

A single-product company can use either way of stating contribution margin (and of determining required sales); the choice depends on computational convenience. The contribution margin percentage approach is especially useful to companies that sell several products. For instance, managers of a department store that sells thousands of items cannot easily work with unit sales. (It makes little sense to speak of sales of 12,500,000 units when the units are as diverse as handkerchiefs, shoes, refrigerators, and television sets.) They prefer to work with sales dollars because their experience allows them to interpret numbers such as $4,000,000 of sales. Chapter 4 discusses multiproduct companies in more detail.

TARGET RETURN ON SALES

Managers might also state a profit target as an ROS (profit divided by sales). Managers with such a profit target are saying that their desired dollar profit varies with sales.

Suppose that TFL wishes to earn a 15% ROS. We already know that variable costs are 60% of sales ($6/$10). Therefore, it wants 75% of its sales to cover variable costs and profit, leaving 25% to cover fixed costs. We use a variation of the break-even formula based on contribution margin percentage to find target sales. Starting with the basic equation, then substituting the values we know,

$$Profit = sales - variable\ costs - fixed\ costs$$
$$15\% \times sales = sales - (60\% \times sales) - \$20,000$$

Gathering terms,

$$15\% \times sales = 40\% \times sales - \$20,000$$
$$25\% \times sales = \$20,000$$
$$Sales = \$20,000/25\% = \$80,000$$

Or,

$$\frac{Sales,\ in\ dollars,\ to}{achieve\ target\ ROS} = \frac{fixed\ costs}{contribution\ margin\ percentage - target\ ROS}$$

$$\frac{Sales,\ in\ dollars,\ to}{achieve\ target\ ROS} = \frac{\$20,000}{40\% - 15\%} = \frac{\$20,000}{25\%} = \$80,000$$

The logic of this later formula is that TFL needs 75% of sales for variable costs and profit (60% for variable costs, 15% for profit), so 25% is left to cover fixed costs. TFL's income statement shows that logic. We could have approached this problem by filling in the percentages in the income statement, with contribution margin at 40% and profit at 15%. We then see that fixed costs must be 25% of sales.

	Dollars	Percentages
Sales	$80,000	100%
Variable costs (60% of sales)	48,000	60%
Contribution margin	$32,000	40%
Fixed costs	20,000	25%
Income	$12,000	15%

To achieve sales of $80,000, TFL has to sell 8,000 backpacks ($80,000/$10). Warning: Don't forget that the percentages of fixed costs and of profit to sales are valid only at this volume.

We could also translate TFL's goal of a 15% ROS into a $1.50 profit per backpack ($10 × 15%). Subtracting the variable costs of $6 and the $1.50 profit from the $10 selling price leaves $2.50 to cover fixed costs. In a variation of the basic break-even formula (fixed costs/contribution margin), we could determine the sales volume needed for a target 15% ROS as 8,000 units ($20,000/$2.50). Note that this answer agrees with the one computed earlier.

CHANGING PLANS

The concepts of contribution margin and target profit are useful when managers are contemplating changes in plans in the hope of increasing profits. A typical example is an increase in advertising, with the expectation of increasing sales.

Suppose that TFL's marketing manager has proposed an advertising campaign that will cost $5,000 and is expected to increase sales by 2,000 units. Total contribution margin will increase by $8,000 (2,000 × $4), but fixed costs will be $5,000 higher, so that profit will be $3,000 higher than it would have been without the extra advertising. But suppose that some managers are concerned that sales might not rise by 2,000 units. They wonder how many additional units they must sell to make the additional advertising pay off. We can apply the target profit formula to determine the sales increase that is needed to cover the additional advertising.

Additional sales required = $5,000/$4 = 1,250 units

TFL needs 1,250 units just to cover the increase in fixed costs. Total profit will increase only if the advertising can increase sales by more than 1,250 units.

The preceding analysis does not require knowing what sales the company expected without the advertising campaign. That is, knowing if sales expected without the additional advertising were 0, 5,000, or 10,000 units does not matter. As long as the increase in volume is greater than 1,250 units, taking the proposed action increases profits over what they would have been.

TARGET SELLING PRICES

TFL's target is $5,000 per month and it expects to sell 6,000 backpacks per month. Remember that TFL's variable costs are $5.00 to purchase a backpack, $0.50 for packing and shipping, and a 5 percent sales commission. Thus, per-unit variable cost is $5.50 plus 5% of selling price. We still use the basic income statement equation,

Profit	=	*sales*	-	*variable costs*	-	*fixed costs*
$5,000	=	*S*	-	*[(6,000 × $5.50) + 5%S]*	-	*$20,000*
$5,000	=	*S*	-	*$33,000 - 5%S*	-	*$20,000*
$58,000	=	*95%S*				
$61,053	=	*S*				

Dividing the required sales of $61,053 by the expected volume of 6,000 backpacks yields a target price of $10.18 (rounded). Notice that we cannot use the contribution margin percentage approach because the percentage changes when we change the selling price. Notice that if TFL's variable costs did not depend on selling price (as the $5.50 does not), the calculation is simpler. In fact, a rearrangement of the basic equation gives

$$Price = \frac{total\ fixed\ costs\ +\ target\ profit}{unit\ volume} + unit\ variable\ cost$$

Notice that the first term on the right side is the required contribution margin per unit, the total required contribution margin divided by unit volume. Adding contribution margin to unit variable cost gives the selling price. For TFL,

$$Price \quad = \frac{\$20,000\ +\ \$5,000}{6,000} + (\$5.50 + 5\% \times price)$$
$$95\%\,Price = \quad \$4.17 + \$5.50$$
$$Price \quad = \quad \$10.18\ rounded$$

Whatever the basis used for setting a target profit, the manager must then ask: are we likely to sell 6,000 units at $10.18? CVP analysis cannot answer this question. The more competitive the market, the less control a company has over selling prices. Most companies have some discretion in pricing, but the amount of discretion changes as market conditions change. Personal computers used to be high-priced because people needed support and wanted to be able to call someone when they could not get the computer to work correctly. Now users are more sophisticated, so many buy from mail-order companies or from large retailers who offer little or no support, but charge very low prices.

TARGET COSTING

Some companies use a planning technique called **target costing** to help decide whether to enter a new market or bring out a new product. The essence of target costing is to determine how much the company can spend to manufacture and market a product, given a target profit. That is, the price and volume are estimated first, then the costs. Target costing is useful especially in deciding whether to enter an established market where selling prices are relatively stable. Proponents of target costing argue that its use increases the involvement of manufacturing, designing, and engineering people in planning because they have a cost to aim at, and will be encouraged to be creative in reaching the target cost. Recall from Chapter 1 that much of a product's cost is determined during the design stage, so close cooperation among the functional areas is important.

Analytically, the technique simply requires solving the basic CVP equation for total cost, variable cost, or fixed cost. For instance, if the managers agree on a target profit of $300,000 and that unit volume of 100,000 is achievable at a $20 price, the total allowable cost is

Revenue (100,000 × $20)	$2,000,000
Target profit	300,000
Total allowable cost	$1,700,000

If managers expect total fixed costs to be $1,200,000, total variable costs can be $500,000, or $5 per unit. The $5 then, along with the $1,200,000 fixed cost, becomes an objective for the managers responsible for designing and manufacturing the product. Note, however, that as with target pricing, the answer given by the analysis might not be achievable with existing manufacturing techniques. The managers responsible for manufacturing might be unsuccessful in reaching the target cost objective. In such cases, the top managers might decide against introducing the new product or entering the new market. Or they might decide to re-examine their profit target and estimates of price and volume. For example, reconsidering the profit target is more likely when the new product (or market) is one the managers believe is especially important for, say, the company's reputation as an innovator, or for pursuing a long-range strategy. The accompanying Insight describes several uses of the technique.

12▶ Chapter 12 will describe a related technique popularized by some Japanese manufacturers called *Kaizen*. Kaizen is a form of continuous improvement, which seeks to reduce costs by target amounts each period.

COST STRUCTURE AND MANAGERIAL ATTITUDES

Businesses can operate in different ways. A company can use a great deal of labor and little machinery or vice versa. Salespeople might be on salary, commission, or a combination of the two. When making choices, managers must consider the effects of their decisions on the *cost structure*—the relative proportions of fixed and variable costs. For example, a company might take on higher fixed costs to reduce variable costs and thereby increase contribution margin. (Automation does exactly that.) Such an action increases potential profitability, but also increases risk. The break-even point will probably rise, and, if volume drops, profits will fall more rapidly with the higher contribution margin.

To illustrate, consider Benson Company. Its managers decide to introduce a new product. They expect to sell 20,000 units at $10. They can make the product in either of two manufacturing processes. Process A uses a great deal of labor and has variable costs of $7 per unit and annual fixed costs of $40,000. Process B uses more machinery, with unit variable costs of $4 and annual fixed costs of $95,000. Given these estimates, Process B yields more profit, as shown in the following income statement.

	Process A	Process B
Sales (20,000 × $10)	$ 200,000	$ 200,000
Variable costs at $7 and $4	140,000	80,000
Contribution margin at $3 and $6	$ 60,000	$ 120,000
Fixed costs	40,000	95,000
Profit	$ 20,000	$ 25,000

If the managers are certain that the numbers are correct, they will choose Process B. But the numbers are estimates, so the managers should do some additional analysis before deciding which process to use. One item the managers should look at is the break-even point for each process.

SIGHT

A major world-wide maker of motion control components and systems, with $2.25 billion sales, uses target costing at the design stage to enable management to emphasize cost even before the product is ready. The company's managers believe that competition has increased the pressure to shorten development time, but they recognize that most cost is built in at the design/ development stage. Thus they look at costs over the life cycle of the product.

H. J. Heinz Pet Products unit took a similar approach with its 9-Lives cat food. Prices in the industry had fallen for several years. Heinz raised prices and lost so much volume that its profits dropped significantly. The unit then approached the problem from the consumers' point of view. The managers estimated the price that consumers were willing to pay for cat food, then worked on cost targets. It has reduced costs by closing old plants and automating new ones and forming partnerships with vendors to ensure stable supplies at favorable prices.

Some British companies use the term "drifting cost" to refer to costs of a product based on existing conditions (production methods, distribution channels, suppliers' prices, etc.) and then seek to reduce drifting cost to target cost. In a case history Morgan describes, a company identified two critical problems in reducing costs: a high percentage of defective units and a high number of tools used in a production operation. The company was able to reduce both defectives and the number of tools sufficiently to bring the drifting cost down to the target cost. Various techniques are used to reduce costs, including value engineering, procurement analysis, and design appraisal.

Sources: John P. Campi, "Total Cost Management at Parker-Hannifin," Management Accounting, January 1989, 51.
"How to Escape a Price War," Fortune, June 13, 1994, 84.
Malcolm J. Morgan, "Accounting for Strategy," Management Accounting (England), May 1993, 20-22.

$$\text{Process A: } \$40,000/\$3 = 13,333 \text{ units}$$
$$\text{Process B: } \$95,000/\$6 = 15,833 \text{ units}$$

Process B's higher break-even point is one indication that it is riskier, but that analysis ignores sales expectations. To incorporate those expectations in their assessment of the alternatives, managers often express risk by referring to the margin of safety.

MARGIN OF SAFETY

The decline in volume from the expected level of sales to the break-even point is called the **margin of safety (MOS)**. As the name suggests, the MOS is the difference between expected sales and the break-even point. The MOS can be expressed as a unit amount, dollar amount, or percentage. In our example, the MOS for Process A is 6,667 units (20,000 expected - 13,333 break even), or $66,670 (6,667 units at $10 each), or 33.3% (6,667/20,000). For Process B it is 4,167 units (20,000 - 15,833), $41,670 (4,167 units at $10), or 20.8% (4,167/20,000). Generally, the higher the MOS, the lower the risk. Our illustration shows the MOS for a single product, but the concept can be applied to a group of products or to an entire company.

INDIFFERENCE POINT

Another tool that managers use to help them choose between alternative cost structures is the indifference point. The **indifference point** is the level of volume at which total costs, and hence profits, are the same under both cost structures. If the company operated at that level of volume, which alternative was used would not matter because income would be the same either way.

We calculate the indifference point by setting up an equation where each side represents total cost under one of the alternatives. (Because selling price is the same under both of these alternatives, profits will be the same when total costs are the same.) At unit volumes below the indifference point, the alternative with the lower fixed cost gives higher profits; at volumes above the indifference point, the alternative with the higher fixed cost is more profitable. The indifference point for Benson's new product is 18,333 units, calculated as follows, with Q equal to unit volume.

$$
\begin{array}{lcl}
\textit{Total Cost for Process A} & = & \textit{Total Cost for Process B} \\
\textit{Fixed cost} + \textit{variable cost} & & \textit{Fixed cost} + \textit{variable cost} \\
\$40,000 \quad + \quad \$7Q & = & \$95,000 \quad + \quad \$4Q \\
\$3Q & = & \$55,000 \\
Q & = & 18,333 \ (\textit{rounded})
\end{array}
$$

At volumes below 18,333 units, Process A gives lower total costs (and higher profits); above 18,333 units, Process B gives higher profits.

The line $3Q = $55,000 gives a clue to the trade-off between the alternatives: Benson gains $3 per unit in reduced variable costs by increasing fixed costs $55,000. The indifference point shows that the company needs 18,333 units to make the trade-off desirable; that volume is only 1,667 units (or 8%) below the estimated volume of 20,000. If Benson's managers believe that a high likelihood exists that volume will be lower than their estimate of 20,000 units, they might decide to use Process A.

Exhibit 2-3 shows Benson's choices in a variation of the CVP graph shown earlier. As in the earlier graph, the axes represent volume and dollars. Each line represents profit at each level of volume for the associated alternative. Notice that the line for each process begins at a negative point equal to fixed costs for that process and crosses zero at the break-even point for that process. Where profit is the same under both alternatives, the two lines cross. This form of the graph is useful especially in examining alternatives because it reduces the number of lines needed to represent an alternative.

Benson's managers have no correct answer in their choice of cost structure. Analytical tools such as the indifference point, margin of safety, and CVP graph help them evaluate alternatives, but the decision depends on their attitudes about risk and return. If they want to avoid risk, they will choose

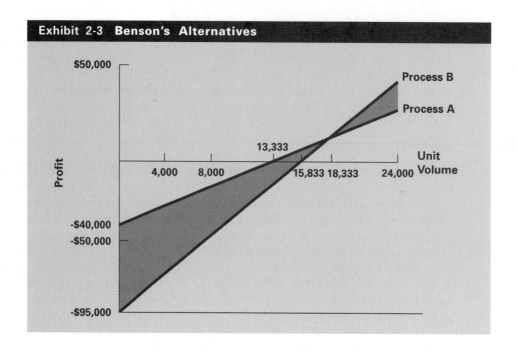

Exhibit 2-3 Benson's Alternatives

Process A, foregoing the potential for higher profits from Process B. If they are venturesome, they probably will be willing to take some risk for the potentially higher returns and choose Process B. The accompanying Insight describes the risk-reward characteristics of two prominent U.S. companies.

ASSUMPTIONS AND LIMITATIONS OF CVP ANALYSIS

We have already mentioned some of the conditions necessary for CVP analysis to give useful predictions. It must be possible to graph both revenues and total costs as straight, rather than curved, lines within the relevant range. This requirement means that selling price, per-unit variable cost, and total fixed costs must be constant throughout the relevant range. We introduce two other assumptions here, but we discuss them in detail in later chapters.

First, CVP analysis assumes either (1) that the company sells only one product or (2) that the sales of each product in a multiproduct company are a constant percentage of total sales. The term **sales mix** describes the percentage of each product's sales to total sales. If a change in sales mix occurs, the contribution margin percentage probably will change. Chapter 4 discusses multiproduct CVP analysis.

The second assumption is relevant only to manufacturing companies, not to merchandising and service companies. To apply CVP analysis to a manufacturing firm, production must equal sales. (That assumption was implicit in the analysis of Benson Company's alternative cost structure.) Because of certain requirements of financial accounting (and tax laws) for manufacturing companies, income reported for financial accounting (or tax) purposes usually does not agree with income predicted by CVP analysis. Chapter 14 explains how those requirements cause differences between reported income and income predictions using CVP analysis.

SIGHT

Managers can use CVP relationships to evaluate strategies and tactics. The following data are from the 1993 annual report of **Delta Airlines**, in millions, except for percentages.

	1993	1992
Operating revenues	$11,997	$10,837
Operating expenses	$12,572	$11,512
Operating loss	$(575)	$(675)
Available seat-miles (ASM)	132,282	123,102
Revenue passenger miles (RPM)	82,406	72,693
Load factor, RPM/ASM	62.30%	59.05%
Break-even load factor	65.53%	62.99%

An available seat-mile is a seat flown one mile. An airplane with 100 seats flying a 200-mile trip has 20,000 available seat-miles (100 × 200). A revenue passenger mile is one passenger flown one mile. If the 100-seat airplane carries 60 passengers it generates 12,000 RPMs (60 × 200). The load factor and break-even point are expressed as percentages of available seat-miles, so the airplane has a 60% load factor (12,000/20,000). Using a method discussed in Chapter 3 we estimate variable costs of $0.011 per RPM in 1993, and fixed costs of $11,665 million.

What are the keys to success for an airline? Its fixed costs are extremely high and variable costs extremely low. Moreover, its product, seat-miles, is perishable because once a plane is in the air **Delta** cannot sell another seat.

Companies with high fixed costs and perishable products (hotels, radio and TV stations) often lower prices to increase volume, but many times wind up pricing so low that they cannot be profitable without extraordinarily high volumes. The years shown above were extremely difficult for the airline industry; only one carrier was profitable in both years. Contrast these problems with those of a company such as **Wal-Mart**, some of whose results appear below, in millions of dollars.

Sales		$ 32,602
Cost of sales	$25,500	
Operating expenses	5,132	30,632
Operating income		$ 1,970

Wal-Mart has much higher variable costs than **Delta** (cost of sales is variable as are some operating expenses, though we cannot tell how much), so it will not have the feast or famine characteristic of high fixed cost companies. Wal-Mart must pay careful attention to prices, because slight changes can have major effects. But consider the effect of a $0.01 increase in seat-mile revenue for Delta, or $10 for a 1,000 mile trip. If Delta could have held its RPMs constant, and assuming that all of its variable costs vary per RPM, not per dollar, it would have earned $824 million, enough to turn a $575 loss into a $249 profit. Unfortunately, as one airline official pointed out, "a $10 price on a two-hour flight will grab anybody's passenger."

The companies in our illustrations, TFL and Benson Company, are relatively simple operations compared with most companies today. Analyzing a bigger, more diverse company in its entirety is more difficult. Yet CVP analysis is a tool that is used, in various forms, by managers of the largest and most complex organizations. Managers apply CVP analysis to segments of their companies, such as products or product lines and geographical areas.

SUMMARY

Cost-volume-profit analysis is critical to planning and requires classifying costs by behavior. A cost is either fixed or variable depending on whether the total amount of the cost changes as activity changes. Contribution margin, the difference between price and variable cost, is important in CVP analysis. Contribution margin can be expressed as a per-unit amount, a total, or a percentage of selling price. The critical points in the chapter are the recognition of the fixed/variable cost classification scheme, the analytical value of this classification, and the usefulness of contribution margin.

Managers use cost-volume-profit analysis to answer questions such as the following: What profits are earned at different levels of sales? What sales are needed to earn a particular profit? What are the effects of changes in selling prices? What price must we charge to earn a particular profit?

With varying degrees of ease, managers can change both costs and prices. Within limits, managers also can control the relative proportions of fixed and variable costs in their cost structure. The usefulness of CVP analysis as a planning tool depends, therefore, on managers' estimates about future conditions, not those prevailing in the past. A basic CVP graph presents a single set of conditions that managers expect. The indifference point, margin of safety, and a variation of the basic CVP graph help managers assess the risks and returns of alternative cost structures. Managers' attitudes toward risk-return relationships influence decisions about cost structure.

Managers in multiproduct and/or manufacturing companies can apply CVP analysis if they recognize that certain assumptions underlie that analysis.

KEY TERMS

break-even point (38)
contribution margin (32)
contribution margin
   percentage (32)
cost-volume-profit (CVP)
   analysis (31)
fixed costs (32)
indifference point (47)
margin of safety (MOS) (46)

nonvariable costs (34)
relevant range (37)
return on sales (ROS) (36)
sales mix (48)
target costing (44)
target profit (39)
variable costs (32)
variable cost percentage (32)

KEY FORMULAS

$$\text{Break-even sales, in units} = \frac{\text{total fixed costs}}{\text{contribution margin per unit}}$$

$$\text{Break-even sales, in dollars} = \frac{\text{total fixed costs}}{\text{contribution margin percentage}}$$

$$\text{Profit} = \text{sales} - \text{variable costs} - \text{fixed costs}$$

$$\text{Sales, in dollars, to achieve target profit} = \frac{\text{total fixed costs} + \text{target profit}}{\text{contribution margin percentage}}$$

$$\text{Sales, in units, to achieve target profit} = \frac{\text{fixed costs} + \text{target profit}}{\text{contribution margin per unit}}$$

$$\text{Sales, in dollars, to achieve target return on sales} = \frac{\text{fixed costs}}{\text{contribution margin percentage} - \text{target return on sales}}$$

$$\text{Total costs} = \text{fixed costs} + (\text{variable cost per unit} \times \text{unit volume})$$

REVIEW PROBLEM

Cost-volume-profit analysis assumes that important variables (selling price, variable cost per unit, total fixed costs) do not change within the relevant range. Nevertheless, as we saw in the section on price determination, a manager may want to know what value for one of these variables is consistent with a particular target profit. Moreover, because prices and costs can change quickly, a manager must be alert to the effects of such changes. The following problem tests your basic understanding of CVP analysis. Solve the problem, one part at a time, and check your answers with those provided. Consider each question independently of the others.

Glassman Company sells its one product at $20 per unit. Variable costs are $12 per unit and fixed costs are $100,000 per month.

Required
1. If Glassman can sell 15,000 units in a particular month, what will be its income?
2. What is the break-even point in units?
3. What is the break-even point in sales dollars?
4. What unit sales are required to earn $40,000 for the month?
5. What sales, in dollars, are required to earn $40,000 for the month?
6. Suppose Glassman reduces its selling price to $18 because competitors are charging that amount. What is its new break-even point (a) in units? (b) in dollars?
7. Suppose that fixed costs are expected to increase by $10,000 (to $110,000 per month). What is the new break-even point (a) in units? (b) in dollars? Price is $20.
8. Suppose that Glassman is currently selling 10,000 units per month. The marketing manager believes that sales would increase if advertising were increased by $5,000. How much would sales have to increase, in units, to give Glassman the same income or loss that it is currently earning?

(Although you know how many units are now being sold, you do not need this fact to solve the problem.)

9. Suppose Glassman is selling 20,000 units per month at $20. What is its margin of safety?

10. Glassman currently pays its salespeople salaries that total $40,000 per month, but no commissions. The vice president of sales is considering a plan whereby the salespeople would receive a 5 percent commission, but their salaries would fall to a total of $25,000 per month (a drop of $15,000). At what sales level is the company indifferent between the two compensation plans?

ANSWER TO REVIEW PROBLEM

1. Glassman will earn $20,000. An income statement is shown below.

Sales (15,000 × $20)	$ 300,000
Variable costs (15,000 × $12)	180,000
Contribution margin (15,000 × $8)	$ 120,000
Fixed costs	100,000
Income	$ 20,000

A shortcut is to multiply contribution margin per unit of $8 by 15,000 units (which gives $120,000 in contribution margin), then subtract fixed costs of $100,000 to get $20,000 income.

2. 12,500 units. The break-even point in units is the result of dividing fixed costs ($100,000) by the $8 contribution margin per unit.

3. $250,000. This amount can be determined either by multiplying the break-even point in units (from item 2) by the selling price per unit (12,500 × $20) or by applying the break-even formula using the contribution margin percentage ($100,000/40%). The contribution margin percentage is determined by dividing the selling price of $20 into the contribution margin of $8 (from item 2).

4. 17,500 units. The profit of $40,000 is added to the fixed costs of $100,000, and the target profit formula is then applied. Thus, the total to be obtained from sales is $40,000 plus $100,000 in fixed costs. If Glassman gets $8 per unit and desires total contribution margin of $140,000, it must sell 17,500 units ($140,000/$8).

5. $350,000. This amount can be determined either by multiplying the 17,500 units (from item 4) by the $20 selling price per unit or by applying the formula using the contribution margin percentage. To return the fixed costs of $100,000 plus a profit of $40,000, when the contribution margin percentage is 40%, requires sales of $350,000 ($140,000/40%).

6. (a) 16,667 units. If fixed costs of $100,000 must be covered when each unit carries a contribution margin of $6 ($18 selling price - variable cost of $12), a total of 16,667 units must be sold ($100,000/$6).

   (b) $300,000. This amount can be determined either by multiplying the number of units (16,667) computed in part (a) by the selling price of $18 or by using the formula with the contribution margin percentage. Thus, 16,667 × $18 is $300,000 (rounded) or $100,000/[($18 - $12)/$18] = $300,000.

7. (a) 13,750 units. With fixed costs of $110,000 and a contribution margin per unit of $8, the number of units to produce a contribution margin equal to the fixed costs is 13,750 ($110,000/$8). Another approach is to determine what additional sales volume (beyond that required to

break even with the current cost structure) provides sufficient contribution margin to cover the additional fixed costs. It will take the contribution margin from an additional 1,250 units ($10,000/$8 per unit) to cover the added fixed costs, and the break-even point is already 12,500 units, so the total number of units required to break even with the new cost structure is 13,750 (12,500 + 1,250).

   (b) $275,000. The most direct approach to this answer is to multiply the number of units (13,750) computed in part (a) by the selling price per unit ($20). Or, the answer could be determined by dividing the fixed costs ($110,000) by the contribution margin percentage (40%).

8. 625 units. Income will not be affected as long as the contribution margin from the additional units sold is sufficient to offset the expenditure for advertising. Hence, we need to determine only what additional sales will produce contribution margin sufficient to cover the cost of the advertising. Because contribution margin per unit is $8, the number of units needed to cover the $5,000 advertising campaign is $5,000/$8 or 625 units. (Note that the current level of sales is irrelevant to the decision of whether or not to undertake the advertising campaign. As long as the campaign will increase sales by 625 units, Glassman will be neither better nor worse off than it would have been without it.)

9. 7,500 units, or 37.5%. At sales of 20,000 units Glassman earns $60,000 (20,000 × $8 - $100,000) and the break-even point is 12,500 units (from item 2).

10. 15,000 units. Fixed costs fall to $85,000 under the proposal and variable costs increase to $13 ($12 + .05 × $20).

Total Costs Now		Total Costs Under Proposal
$100,000 + $12Q	=	$85,000 + $13Q
$1Q	=	$15,000
Q	=	15,000

Below 15,000 units the proposed method is more profitable for Glassman, while above 15,000 units the existing method gives higher profit. Note that this situation differs from one in which the company was changing the way it manufactures a product. The method of manufacture probably does not affect the sales of the product (quality remaining constant). But for Glassman motivational questions might arise. The salespeople might sell more units under one method than they would under the other. We cannot be certain which method would better motivate the salespeople.

This review problem has emphasized the possibility of changes in the structure of costs and selling prices. Managers must be alert for changes from outside (for example, a supplier raising prices) and should understand their effects on profits. Additionally, managers can analyze changes that they propose to see if they will increase profits. Item 8 of this problem gave an important practical example: an increase in a fixed cost was expected to lead to some increase in volume. If the marketing manager believes that the added cost will generate additional sales in excess of 625 units, the proposal for additional advertising would be wise.

APPENDIX: INCOME TAXES AND PROFIT PLANNING

Income taxes are a cost of doing business and should be considered, as should all costs, in the planning process. Income taxes are based on the amount of income before taxes. For our purposes, it is reasonable to assume that income taxes are a constant percentage of income before taxes. In most large corporations, this assumption is reasonable, but we hasten to point out that tax law is exceedingly complex, not all businesses are incorporated, and generalizations are risky.

Income taxes must be considered if managers seek an after-tax target profit. An after-tax target requires a revision of the basic target profit formula. The revision requires converting the after-tax target profit to a before-tax profit, which is accomplished by dividing the after-tax target profit by 1 minus the income tax rate. For example, suppose TFL wants to earn an after-tax profit of $6,300 and its tax rate is 30%. To earn $6,300 after taxes, TFL must earn $9,000 before taxes ($6,300/70%). Of the before-tax income of $9,000, $2,700 goes to the government ($9,000 × 30%), leaving $6,300 ($9,000 - $2,700). Accordingly, when the target is an after-tax profit, the basic formula for calculating the volume needed to achieve the target is as follows:

$$\text{\textit{Sales to achieve target after-tax profit}} = \frac{\text{\textit{fixed costs}} + \dfrac{\text{\textit{after-tax profit}}}{1 - \text{\textit{tax rate}}}}{\text{\textit{contribution margin percentage}}}$$

or

$$\text{\textit{contribution margin per unit}}$$

We already know that TFL's fixed costs are $20,000 and that its contribution margin percentage is 40%. Solving the above formula for sales dollars to achieve a $6,300 profit after taxes gives

$$\text{\textit{Sales}} = \frac{\$20,000 + \dfrac{\$6,300}{70\%}}{40\%}$$

$$= \frac{\$20,000 + \$9,000}{40\%} = \frac{\$29,000}{40\%}$$

$$= \$72,500$$

We could calculate the unit sales required either by dividing the $72,500 sales by the $10 selling price, or by dividing the $4 contribution margin per unit into the $29,000 (fixed costs plus required before-tax profit). Either way, the answer is 7,250 backpacks.

You needn't concern yourself with any formulas beyond those in the chapter if you recognize that the key step in both of the above calculations was converting an after-tax target ($6,300) to a before-tax target ($9,000). That conversion is the key whether the target is an absolute dollar amount of profit or a specific ROS.

To demonstrate, suppose TFL's target is an after-tax ROS of 14%. Once again, its after-tax target is 70% (1 minus the 30% income tax rate) of a before-tax target; so its before-tax ROS target is 20% (14%/70%). Using the formula on page 42, the sales target is $100,000, as shown below.

$$\text{\textit{Sales, in dollars, to achieve target ROS}} = \frac{\$20,000}{40\% - 20\%} = \$100,000$$

The income statement below, with both dollar amounts and percentages of sales, shows that sales of $100,000 will produce the after-tax ROS target of 14%.

Sales	$ 100,000	100%
Variable costs	60,000	
Contribution margin	$ 40,000	40%
Fixed costs	20,000	
Income before taxes	$ 20,000	20%
Income taxes, at 30%	6,000	
Net income	$ 14,000	14%

One final reminder. Planning for income taxes is important if the entity is subject to income taxes and if there is income to tax. Therefore, income taxes do not affect the determination of the break-even point, at which there is no income to tax.

ASSIGNMENT MATERIAL

QUESTIONS FOR DISCUSSION

2-1 Assumptions and misconceptions about CVP analysis A classmate is having trouble with CVP analysis and asks for your help. He has the following questions.

1. "How can CVP analysis work when you really don't know what's going to happen? You might change your selling price. Your suppliers might change their prices. Inflation can cause other costs to go up. You might not sell the number of units you need to sell in order to earn a target profit. All sorts of things can happen that will invalidate your calculations."
2. "When I took economics, I learned that the higher the price, the less you sell. So how can you draw a straight revenue line?"
3. "I don't see how you can say that some costs are fixed. I'll accept depreciation and a few others, but salaries can be raised or lowered easily, your insurance premiums can go up or down, you can spend more or less on advertising, travel, and all sorts of other elements that you would call fixed."
4. "Most companies cannot sell everything at their normal prices. A clothing store has to discount goods at the end of a season."

Required
Answer your classmate's questions.

2-2 Effects of events The newsletter of a national brokerage firm stated the following points about profitability of **Cooper Tire & Rubber**.

1. Industry-wide selling prices are rising, including Cooper's.
2. Raw material costs are rising.
3. The rise of the yen against the dollar should increase Cooper's export business.

Required
State the effect of each item, if any, on Cooper's CVP graph.

2-3   Will Sears' stockholders understand? The following statement appeared in the **Sears, Roebuck and Co.** report to stockholders for the first quarter of a recent year.

Traditional buying patterns in the merchandise business generally result in the lowest sales of the year in the first quarter, producing a relatively high ratio of fixed costs to sales and lower ratio of income to sales.

Required

Discuss this statement in relation to the concepts introduced in Chapter 2 and the traditional, late-January "white sales" at most department stores.

EXERCISES

2-4   Income statement and CVP analysis The following data are available for Quincy Company's one product.

Unit selling price	$8
Unit variable cost	$6
Total fixed costs	$80,000
Unit volume	60,000

Required

1. Prepare an income statement using the contribution margin format.
2. Determine the break-even point in (a) units and (b) sales dollars.
3. Determine the (a) unit volume and (b) dollar volume required to earn a 15% return on sales.
4. Determine the price that the company must charge to double the profit you determined in item 1, still selling 60,000 units.

2-5   Income statement and CVP analysis The following data relate to McFarland, Inc.

Sales	$800,000
Variable cost percentage	60%
Total fixed costs	$250,000

Required

1. Prepare an income statement using the contribution margin format.
2. Determine the break-even point in sales dollars.
3. Determine the dollar volume required to double the profit you determined in item 1.

2-6   Income statement and CVP analysis with taxes (related to Appendix) Use the data from 2-4 for this assignment. Also assume a 30% income tax rate.

Required

1. Prepare an income statement that incorporates income taxes.

2. Determine the (a) unit volume and (b) dollar volume required to double the after-tax profit you determined in item 1.
3. Determine the selling price that will double the before-tax profit at the original volume.

2-7 *Income statement and CVP analysis with taxes (related to Appendix)* Use the data from 2-5 for this assignment. Also assume a 40% income tax rate.

Required

1. Prepare an income statement that incorporates income taxes.
2. Determine the dollar volume required to double the after-tax profit you determined in item 1.

2-8 *Basic CVP analysis* Sea-Crest Company sells frozen fish dinners to super-markets for $30 per case. Variable cost is $12 per case and annual fixed costs are $600,000.

Required

1. Determine the break-even point in (a) units and (b) dollars.
2. Determine the volume required to earn a $120,000 profit in (a) units and (b) dollars.
3. Determine the volume required to earn a 15% return on sales in (a) units and (b) dollars.
4. If Sea-Crest can sell 30,000 cases, what price would it have to charge to earn a $100,000 profit?
5. Redo item 4 assuming that the variable cost of $12 consists of $9 related to the case and a 10% commission on sales ($3 per case at the $30 price).

2-9 *Basic CVP relationships, with income taxes (related to Appendix)* In one of its factories, M&J Company manufactures a water pump that it sells to auto parts dealers throughout the country. M&J sells the pump for $30. Variable costs are $18 and annual fixed costs are $2,000,000. The tax rate is 40%.

Required

1. Determine the volume required to earn a $300,000 after-tax profit in (a) units and (b) dollars.
2. If M&J can sell 180,000 pumps, what price would it have to charge to earn a $300,000 after-tax profit?
3. Redo item 2 assuming that the variable cost of $18 consists of $15 for manufacturing and a 10% commission on sales ($3 per pump at the $30 price).

 2-10 *Relationships among variables* Fill in the blanks for each of the following independent situations.

	(a) Selling Price per Unit	(b) Variable Cost Percentage	(c) Number of Units Sold	(d) Contribution Margin	(e) Fixed Costs	(f) Income (Loss)
Case						
1.	$40	60%	—	—	$60,000	18,000
2.	80	—	4,000	$80,000	—	$(10,000)
3.	25	—	15,000	—	25,000	50,000

2-11 *Relationships among variables* Fill in the blanks for each of the following independent situations.

	1	2	3
Selling price per unit	—	$5	—
Variable cost per unit	$6	$3	$6
Number of units sold	1,000	—	4,000
Total contribution margin	$2,000	$4,000	$16,000
Total fixed costs	—	$1,500	$ 8,000
Income	$1,200	—	—

2-12   CVP graph   The following graph portrays the operations of Richmond Company.

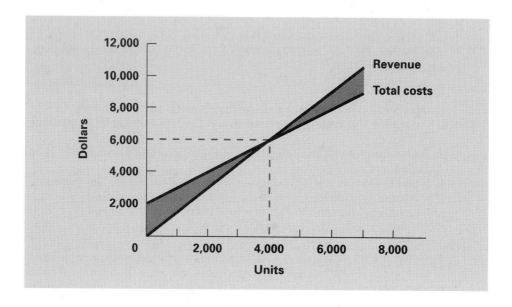

Required

Determine the following.

1. Sales dollars at the break-even point.
2. Fixed costs at 4,500 units sold.
3. Total variable costs at 4,000 units sold.
4. Variable cost per unit at 2,000 units sold.
5. Variable cost per unit at 5,000 units sold.
6. Selling price per unit.
7. Total contribution margin at 3,000 units sold.
8. Profit (loss) at sales of 3,000 units.
9. Profit (loss) at sales of 5,000 units.
10. Break-even sales, in units, if fixed costs were to increase by $500.

2-13   Graphs of cost behavior   The following graphs depict the behavior of costs in relation to volume.

Required

Answer the following questions using the letters from the graphs (A-D). One letter may be the answer to more than one question.

1. Which graph shows the behavior of total variable costs?
2. Which graph shows the behavior of total fixed costs?

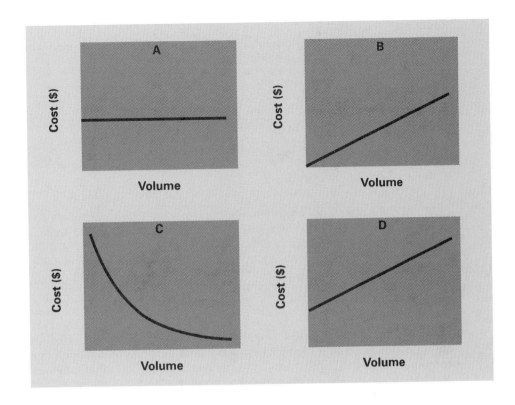

3. Which graph shows the behavior of variable costs per unit?
4. Which graph shows the behavior of fixed costs per unit?
5. Which graph shows the behavior of total costs?

2-14   CVP chart   The following chart portrays the operations of Weyand
Company.

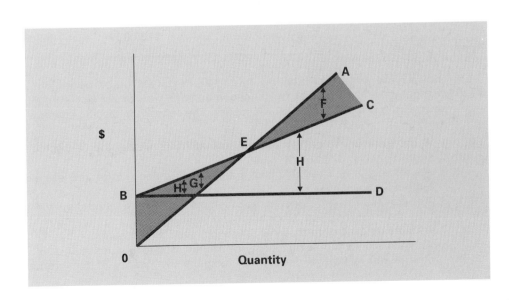

Required

Match the following descriptions with the appropriate letter(s) from the chart. You may have to indicate additions or subtractions.

1. Revenue line
2. Variable costs
3. Fixed costs
4. Profit area
5. Loss area
6. Total cost line
7. Break-even point
8. Total contribution margin

2-15 *Margin of safety* Trivia Inc. plans to market a new electronic game. The game would sell for $120, and Trivia expects sales to be 11,000 units. Per-unit variable manufacturing cost is $82. The only other variable cost is a 15% sales commission. The fixed costs associated with this game are $160,000.

Required

Compute the margin of safety at the expected sales volume.

2-16 *Alternative CVP graph (extension of 2-15)* The managers of Trivia Inc. have determined that the new game also could be brought out using a different combination of production and marketing strategies. The alternative strategies would reduce per-unit variable manufacturing cost to $71, but annual fixed costs would increase to $175,000 and the sales commission would be raised to 20%.

Required

In a CVP graph like Exhibit 2-3, plot the results of the two alternatives that Trivia is considering.

2-17 *CVP graph, analysis of changes* You have prepared a CVP graph for NMA Shoes. It reflects the following expectations.

Selling price	$50
Unit variable cost	$30
Total fixed costs	$400,000

NMA's managers are wondering what the effects will be on operations if some changes take place, either by management decision or by some outside force such as the prices charged by a supplier. The following specific changes are the most likely possibilities.

1. A decrease in the selling price resulting from greater-than-expected competition.
2. A decrease in unit variable cost arising from a decision to use less expensive leather in the shoes.
3. An increase in total fixed costs accompanied by a decrease in unit variable cost from introducing labor-saving machinery.
4. A decrease in the number of units expected to be sold.
5. An increase in the selling price combined with an increase in unit variable cost resulting from a decision to increase the quality of the product.

Required

Treat each change independently of the others. For each, state the effects on (a) the revenue line, (b) the total cost line, and (c) the break-even point. Some changes will have no effect on one or more of the items. In at least one case, the effect on the break-even point cannot be determined without additional information. Note that both the intercept and slope of the total cost line could be affected by a set of changes.

2-18   Converting an income statement Sandy Goode, president of SG Enterprises, has given you the following income statement for a recent month.

Sales		$ 250,000
Cost of goods sold		150,000
Gross profit		$ 100,000
Operating expenses:		
Salaries and commissions	$42,000	
Utilities	11,200	
Rent	13,300	
Other	23,000	89,500
Profit		$ 10,500

SG sells one product, an exercise glove, at $20 per pair. Cost of goods sold is variable. A 10% sales commission, included in salaries and commissions, is the only other variable cost. Goode tells you that the income statement is not helpful, for she cannot determine such things as the break-even point or the price that will achieve a target profit.

Required

1. Redo the income statement using the contribution margin format.
2. Determine the break-even point in (a) units and (b) dollars.
3. Determine the price that would give a $15,000 profit at 12,500 units. The cost of the product is a constant $12 per unit.

2-19   Target costing Managers of TNC Enterprises are thinking about a new product in the industrial electronics area. TNC has considerable technical expertise in the field but has never entered the segment of the market in which the new product would compete. Before writing specifications for performance, the managers want to determine what costs are allowable. They estimate sales of 200,000 units per year at a $100 selling price. They also want a profit of $6,000,000.

Required

1. Determine the total costs that TNC can incur and meet its profit objective.
2. Suppose that the designers, engineers, and manufacturing managers estimate that annual fixed costs will be about $9,000,000 per year. Find the maximum per-unit variable cost that TNC can incur and meet its profit objective.

2-20   Profit planning Tinney Company, a wholesaler of jeans, had the following income statement in 19X5.

Sales (40,000 pairs at $15)		$ 600,000
Cost of sales		300,000
Gross margin		$ 300,000
Selling expenses	$150,000	
Administrative expenses	90,000	240,000
Income		$ 60,000

Mr. Tinney informs you that the only variable costs are cost of sales and $2 per-unit selling costs. All administrative expenses are fixed. In planning for the coming year, 19X6, Mr. Tinney expects his selling price to remain constant, with unit volume increasing by 20%. He also forecasts the following changes in costs.

Variable costs:	
Cost of goods sold	up $0.50 per unit
Selling costs	up $0.10 per unit
Fixed costs:	
Selling costs	up $10,000
Administrative costs	up $15,000

Required

1. Prepare an income statement for 19X6 using the contribution margin format and assuming that all forecasts are met.
2. Determine the number of units that Tinney will have to sell in 19X6 to earn the same profit it did in 19X5.
3. If 19X6 volume is 48,000 units, what selling price will earn $60,000? All variable costs are constant per unit.

2-21   Basic income taxes (related to Appendix)   Hughes Company is introducing an electronic printer that will sell for $140. Unit variable manufacturing cost is $92, and Hughes pays a 10% sales commission. Fixed costs for the printer are $250,000 per year. The tax rate is 40%.

Required

1. Determine the profit after taxes that Hughes would earn selling 12,000 printers.
2. Determine the number of units that Hughes has to sell to earn an after-tax profit of $120,000.
3. Determine the price that Hughes has to charge to earn a $180,000 pretax profit selling 11,000 units.

PROBLEMS

2-22   Indifference point   Travelco sells one of its products, a piece of soft-sided luggage, for $60. Variable cost per unit is $34, and monthly fixed costs are $60,000. A combination of changes in the way Travelco produces and sells this product could reduce per-unit variable cost to $30 but increase monthly fixed costs to $84,000.

Required
1. Determine the monthly break-even points under the two available alternatives.
2. Determine the indifference point of the two alternatives.

2-23 Cost structure Ben Skove, the owner of SKE Company, is trying to decide which of two machines to rent. He needs a machine to sand the surfaces of a picnic table that SKE manufactures. The following data are related to the two alternatives.

	Hand-Fed Machine	Automatic Machine
Annual rental payments	$ 14,000	$ 36,000
Other annual fixed costs	100,000	110,000

Skove expects the variable cost per table to be $34 using the hand-fed machine and $27 using the automatic machine. He also expects annual volume of about 3,000 tables.

Required
1. Determine the total annual cost to manufacture 3,000 tables under each alternative.
2. Determine the annual volume of tables at which total manufacturing cost would be the same for each machine.

2-24 Changes in contribution margin Mr. Pahl, owner of Jeantown, a specialty clothing store, asks you for some advice. Last year, his business had the following income statement.

Sales (10,000 units at $20)	$ 200,000
Variable costs	100,000
Contribution margin	$ 100,000
Fixed costs	50,000
Income	$ 50,000

Mr. Pahl expects variable costs to increase to $11 per unit next year.

Required
1. Determine the volume Mr. Pahl needs to earn $50,000 in the coming year.
2. Mr. Pahl decides to increase his selling price so that he can earn $50,000 next year with the same unit volume he had last year. (a) What price will achieve that objective? (b) What dollar sales will he have?
3. Suppose that Mr. Pahl raises his price so that the contribution margin percentage is the same as it was last year. (a) What price will he set? (b) What dollar volume will give a $50,000 profit? (c) What is the unit volume?

2-25 Pricing and return on sales Rogers Construction builds steel structures for commercial and industrial customers. The buildings are various shapes and sizes, with the average price being $30 per square foot and the average variable cost $18 per square foot. Annual fixed costs are $5,000,000.

Required

Answer each of the following items independently.

1. Determine the volume that will give Rogers a 20% return on sales in (a) sales dollars and (b) square feet of construction.
2. If Rogers can sell 600,000 square feet of construction in the coming year, what selling price will give a $400,000 profit?
3. If Rogers can sell 600,000 square feet of construction in the coming year at $30, how high could variable cost per square foot rise and still allow Rogers to earn a $280,000 profit?
4. If variable cost increases to $22 per square foot and Rogers can sell 500,000 square feet, what price will give a $280,000 profit?

2-26   Per-unit data The controller of Walker Company provides the following per-unit analysis, based on a volume of 50,000 units.

Selling price		$ 20
Variable costs	$8	
Fixed costs	7	
Total costs		15
Profit		$ 5

Required

Answer each of the following questions independently of the others.

1. What total profit does Walker expect to earn?
2. What total profit should the company earn at 60,000 units?
3. What is its break-even point in units?
4. Walker's managers expect to increase volume to 55,000 units by spending an additional $40,000 on salaries for more salespeople. What total profit will Walker earn?
5. The managers expect to sell 60,000 units and want a $280,000 profit. What price per unit must it charge? Variable costs are constant per unit.
6. Redo item 5 assuming that the variable cost of $8 consists of a $6 purchase price and a 10% sales commission ($2 at the $20 price).

2-27   CVP analysis for a CPA firm Bret McConnell, a certified public accountant, has estimated the following fixed costs of operation for the coming year.

Office salaries	$ 42,000
Rent, utilities	21,000
Other	14,000
Total	$ 77,000

McConnell's operation has no variable costs. He charges clients $70 per hour for his time.

Required
1. How many hours must McConnell work to earn a profit of $50,000?
2. McConnell is thinking about hiring one or two senior accounting majors from a local university for $8 per hour to do some routine work for his clients. He expects each to work about 300 hours, but about 30 of those hours (training and temporary idle time) will not be chargeable to clients. McConnell wants each student to provide at least $3,000 profit. What hourly rate must he charge for their time to achieve his objective?

2-28   Pricing decision—nursery school   The Board of Directors of First Community Church is considering opening a nursery school. Members of the board agree that the school, which would be open to all children, should operate within $100 of the break-even point.

The school will be open for nine months each year with two classes, one in the morning and one in the afternoon. The treasurer prepares an analysis of the expected costs of operating the school, based on conversations with members of other churches that run similar programs.

Salaries—teacher and assistant	$28,000 for nine months
Utilities	$1,200 for nine months
Miscellaneous operating costs	$800 for nine months
Supplies, paper, paint	$2 per child per month
Snacks, cookies, juice	$4 per child per month

The best estimate of enrollment is 20 children in each of the two classes, which is all that the teacher and assistant can handle and still achieve the quality that the board thinks is essential.

Required
1. Determine the monthly fee per child that would have to be charged for the school to break even (round to nearest dollar) with its maximum enrollment.
2. If the monthly fee is $80, what is the break-even point in enrollment?

2-29   Sensitivity of variables   Cranston Jellies expects the following results in 19X5.

Planned sales in cases—19X5	40,000
Selling price	$20
Variable costs	$14
Total fixed costs	$200,000

Required
Answer the following questions, considering each independently.
1. Which of the following would reduce planned profit the most?
   (a) A 10% decrease in selling price.
   (b) A 10% increase per case in variable costs.
   (c) A 10% increase in fixed costs.
   (d) A 10% decrease in sales volume.
2. Which of the following would increase planned profit the most?
   (a) A 10% increase in selling price.

(b) A 10% decrease per case in variable costs.
(c) A 10% increase in sales volume.
(d) A 10% decrease in fixed costs.
3. If the selling price declined by 10%, how many cases would have to be sold to achieve the planned profit?
4. If the selling price increased by 20%, by how much could variable cost per case increase and the planned profit be achieved?

2-30 CVP analysis—changes in variables During two recent months, Thompson Company had the following income statements.

	March	April
Sales	$ 200,000	$ 222,000
Variable costs	130,000	154,200
Contribution margin	$ 70,000	$ 67,800
Fixed costs	40,000	40,000
Income	$ 30,000	$ 27,800

You learn that the price of the product Thompson sells generally changes each month, though its purchase cost is stable at $11 per unit. The only other variable cost is a 10% commission paid on all sales.

Required
Determine the selling price, unit volume, and variable cost per unit in each of the two months.

2-31 Changes in cost structure Newberry Company makes a product with variable production costs of $12 per unit. The production manager has been approached by a salesperson from a machinery maker. The salesperson offers a machine for rent for five years on a noncancelable lease at $36,000 per year. The production manager expects to save $0.80 per unit in variable manufacturing costs using the machine.

Required
1. Determine the annual unit production that would make renting the machine and continuing with current operations yield the same profit to the firm.
2. Suppose that the expected volume is 80,000 units per year. Determine the change in annual profit that would occur if the company were to rent the machine.
3. Would you be more likely or less likely to rent the machine if the lease were cancelable at your option rather than noncancelable for a five-year period? Explain your answer.

2-32 Cost structure Michael Cooper owns a beauty parlor. He has some space and wants to install a tanning bed. The following estimates are based on observations and discussions with knowledgeable people.

Annual volume, 2-hour sessions	800
Price per session	$6.00
Variable cost per session, mostly electricity	$0.80

Michael can lease a suitable bed from a manufacturer for $2,000 per year. He also can lease one for $1,200 per year plus $1.50 per two-hour session. The beds have instruments to verify use. There are no other fixed costs.

Required

1. Suppose that Michael leases the bed for $2,000. (a) Determine the expected profit from the bed. (b) What is break-even volume in number of sessions?
2. Redo item 1 assuming that Michael elects the $1,200 plus $1.50 per-session option.
3. Which lease arrangement would you prefer? Write a memorandum using the guidelines in Appendix A to support your position.

2-33   *CVP analysis on new business* Managers of Harter Enterprises, a medium-sized manufacturer of dress gloves, want to branch out from the company's traditional business into exercise gloves. Doing so requires leasing additional equipment for $550,000 per year. Other fixed costs associated with the new venture—including new personnel, advertising, and promotion—are estimated at $380,000 annually.

The variable cost of the new gloves is expected to be about $7 per pair and the selling price about $15 per pair. The managers are reluctant to try the new gloves unless they can be fairly confident of earning $150,000.

Required

1. Determine how many pairs of gloves Harter must sell to earn the target profit.
2. The marketing people believe that unit sales will be 120,000 units. What selling price will yield the target profit at that volume?
3. Suppose again that 120,000 units is the best estimate of volume and that Harter will stick with the $15 price. How much must Harter reduce the expected variable cost to meet the profit target?

2-34   *CVP analysis for a hospital* The administrator of the Caldwell Memorial Hospital is considering methods of providing X-ray treatments to patients. The hospital now refers about 200 patients per month to a nearby private clinic, and each treatment costs the patient $65. If the hospital provides the treatment, a machine will be rented for $2,200 per month and technicians will be hired for $3,600 per month. Variable costs are $10 per treatment.

Required

1. The administrator considers charging the same fee as the clinic. By how much will the hospital increase its income if it provides the service?
2. How much must the hospital charge to break even on the treatments?

2-35   *CVP in a service business* Microprog develops microcomputer programs to customer order, primarily for business applications. The company charges its customers $40 per hour for programming time. The managers are planning operations for the coming year and have developed the following estimates.

Total estimated chargeable hours	80,000
Total fixed costs, salaries, rent, etc.	$1,750,000

Microprog employs 15 full-time programmers at an average salary of $30,000. These salaries are included in the cost figure given above. Each programmer works about 2,000 chargeable hours per year. The company does not wish to hire additional programmers, but rather wants to use freelancers to meet demand. Freelancers charge an average of $25 per hour.

Required

1. If the company meets its goal of 80,000 chargeable hours, what profit will it earn?
2. How many chargeable hours must it obtain from freelancers, in addition to the hours its full-time programmers work, to earn a $300,000 profit?

2-36   Developing CVP information   The manager of Sans Flavour Food Store, a franchise operation, is confused by the income statements she has received from her accountant. She asks you to help her with them. She is especially concerned that her return on sales dropped much more than sales from April to May.

	April	May
Sales	$ 100,000	$ 80,000
Cost of sales	40,000	32,000
Gross profit	$ 60,000	$ 48,000
Operating expenses:		
Rent	$ 1,200	$ 1,200
Salaries, wages, commissions	34,500	30,500
Insurance	1,100	1,100
Supplies	2,000	1,600
Utilities	1,500	1,500
Miscellaneous expenses	6,000	6,000
Total operating expenses	$ 46,300	$ 41,900
Income	$ 13,700	$ 6,100
Return on sales	13.7%	7.6%

The manager informs you that the salaries, wages, and commissions account includes the salaries of several clerks and herself, as well as commissions. All salespeople earn commissions of 20% of sales. Supplies are primarily wrapping paper and tape and vary directly with sales. The manager had expected the $20,000 decline in sales, but expected income of $10,960, 13.7% of expected sales. She is now concerned that income will continue to be 7.6% of sales.

Required

Prepare income statements using the contribution margin format for April and May, and explain to the manager the advantages of this format.

2-37   Margin of safety   Nelson Wallets is considering two new wallets for introduction during the coming year. Because of a lack of production capacity, only one will be brought out. Data on the two wallets follow.

	Model 440	Model 1200
Expected sales	$ 200,000	$ 250,000
Expected contribution margin	$ 60,000 (30%)	$ 150,000 (60%)
Expected fixed costs for production, advertising, promotion, etc.	39,000	120,000
Expected annual profit	$ 21,000	$ 30,000

Required

1. Determine the margins of safety for each wallet, in dollars and as percentages of expected sales.
2. Suppose that the company is relatively conservative; its top managers do not like to take significant risks unless the potential profits are extremely high. Which wallet would you recommend be introduced? Why? Explain in a memorandum using the guidelines in Appendix A in the back of the book.

2-38   Changes in operations Bart Packard operates the 15th Street Parking Lot, leasing the lot from the owner at $12,000 per month plus 10% of sales. Packard is thinking about staying open until midnight. He now closes at 7 p.m. Keeping the lot open requires paying an additional $800 per week to attendants, with increases in utilities and insurance being another $100 per week. The lot pays a 5% city tax on its total revenue. The parking charge is $0.80 per hour.

Required

1. Suppose that Packard expects additional business amounting to 2,000 hours per week. Should he stay open until midnight?
2. How much additional business, stated in hours, does Packard need to break even on the additional hours of operation?

2-39   Converting income statement to contribution margin basis Clarkston Manufacturing Company has been profitable over the past few quarters and the top managers are taking steps to continue the increased profitability. Following is the most recent quarterly income statement. All amounts are in thousands.

Sales		$3,882.6
Cost of sales:		
Materials and parts	$ 763.3	
Labor	588.1	
Fringe benefits	69.0	
Repairs and maintenance	322.1	
Depreciation	189.2	
Supplies	56.1	
Power	118.6	
Miscellaneous	47.8	2,154.2
Gross margin		$1,728.4
Operating expenses:		
Sales salaries and commissions	$ 489.2	
Sales expenses	112.7	
Advertising	377.4	
Administrative expenses	541.3	1,520.6
Income before taxes		$ 207.8
Unit volume		415.3

The controller is concerned about the format of the income statement, which has been in use for several years. The controller, relatively new to the job, prefers income statements that use the contribution margin format. After talks with the relevant managers, she determines the following.

	Variable Amount per Unit	Quarterly Fixed Amount
Materials and parts	$1.838	$ 0
Labor	1.416	0
Fringe benefits	0.166	0
Repairs and maintenance	0.323	188.0
Depreciation	0.000	189.2
Supplies	0.135	0
Power	0.131	64.2
Miscellaneous	0.032	34.5
Sales salaries and commissions	0.789	161.5
Sales expenses	0.124	61.2
Advertising	0.000	377.4
Administrative expenses	0.022	532.2

Required

1. Prepare a new income statement using the contribution margin format.
2. What is the break-even point? What would happen to profit if unit volume increased 10%?
3. Comment on the differences between your statement and the one above. For example, what decisions are easier, or more difficult, to make with your statement?

2-40   Unit costs   Carl Murphy owns a chain of shoe stores. He recently opened a store in a shopping mall and was not pleased with the results for the first month.

Sales		$ 80,000
Cost of sales		40,000
Gross margin		$ 40,000
Salaries and wages	$ 23,000	
Utilities, insurance, rent	3,500	
Commissions at 15% of sales	12,000	38,500
Profit		$ 1,500

Noting that sales were 4,000 pairs at an average price of $20, Murphy calculates the per-pair cost at $19.625 ($78,500/4,000), leaving only a $0.375 profit per pair. He did expect sales to rise to 5,000 pairs at an average price of $20 over the next month or two, but he figured that profit would increase only to about $1,875 (5,000 × $0.375), which was still not adequate.

   Murphy asks for your advice, and, in response to your questions, says that even with the increase in sales additional salaried personnel will not be needed and that utilities, insurance, and rent will remain about the same. The cost of sales percentage will also remain at 50%.

Required

Prepare an income statement based on sales of 5,000 pairs of shoes. If profit is different from Mr. Murphy's estimate, explain the fallacy in his reasoning.

2-41   *CVP analysis and break-even pricing—municipal operation* Gardendale operates a municipal trash collection service. Analyses of costs indicate that monthly fixed cost is $15,000 and variable cost is about $0.80 per pickup per customer. The city collects trash in the business district 12 times a month and in the residential districts 4 times a month. The difference in frequency results from the much larger volume of trash in the business district. There are 250 businesses and 1,500 residences served by trash collection.

Required

1. The city manager is aware that other cities charge business customers $20 per month and residential customers $6 per month. What profit or loss would the operation generate at these prices?
2. The city manager would like to break even or show a small profit on trash collection. She believes it is fair to charge businesses three times as much as residences because the businesses get three times as much service. What monthly prices would make the operation break even?

2-42   *CVP analysis for a service business* Walker Associates is a market research firm. Companies contact Walker Associates for various types of studies regarding consumers' preferences, and Walker develops a plan for the study. If the company approves the plan, Walker does the job.

Walker's business involves interviewing people near supermarkets, drugstores, and department stores. Walker hires people part-time to do the interviews for $9 per hour and pays such expenses as mileage and meals. These expenses average $11 per day per person. Each person works about six hours per day. Fixed costs associated with Walker's operation consist largely of salaries to the permanent staff. These, along with rent and utilities, total $400,000 per year.

Walker wants to develop a pricing policy based on an hourly rate, that is, charging the client company an amount per hour that Walker's part-time employees spend interviewing.

Required

1. Walker's managers expect enough business to require about 10,000 six-hour days of interviewing. What hourly charge will give a $75,000 profit?
2. Suppose that Walker sets the charge at $17 per hour. How many six-hour days must it achieve to earn a $75,000 profit?
3. Walker is considering using full-time, salaried interviewers rather than part-time people. What are some of the implications of such a change?

2-43   *Alternative cost behavior—a movie company (continued in Chapters 3 and 4)* Blockbusters Incorporated, a leading producer of movies, is currently negotiating with Sky Kirkwalker, the biggest box-office attraction in the movie industry, to star in War Trek, a science fiction film. For a starring role, Sky normally receives a salary of $1,500,000 plus 5% of the receipts to the producer. (The producer normally receives 40% of the total paid admissions wherever the movie is shown.) However, Sky is quite optimistic about the prospects for Trek and has expressed some interest in a special contract that would give him only 25% of his normal salary but increase his portion of the receipts to the producer to 20%. Other than Sky's pay, costs of producing the picture are expected to be $2,500,000.

Required

Answer the following questions, calling the alternative compensation schemes N (for the normal contract) and S (for the special contract).

1. What are the break-even receipts to the producer under each of the compensation schemes?
2. If total paid admissions in theaters are expected to be $14,000,000, what will be the income to the producer under compensation schemes N and S?
3. At what level of receipts to the producer would Sky earn the same total income under compensation schemes N and S?

2-44   Conversion of income statement to contribution margin basis   The controller of Wassenich Company prepared the following budgeted income statement for 19X4. Materials and labor are both variable costs.

Wassenich Company
Budgeted Income Statement for 19X4

Sales (10,000 units)		$150,000
Cost of goods sold:		
Materials	$ 20,000	
Labor	10,000	
Other manufacturing costs:		
Variable	25,000	
Fixed	50,000	105,000
Gross profit		$ 45,000
Selling and administrative expenses:		
Variable	$ 19,000	
Fixed	35,000	54,000
Loss		$ (9,000)

Required
1. Prepare a new income statement using the contribution margin format.
2. What is the break-even point in units?
3. The president believes that spending an additional $15,000 on advertising will increase sales by 4,000 units. His son, the general manager, says that would be silly because the company is losing enough already. Is the son right?

2-45   Occupancy rate as measure of volume   Norman Motels is a chain operating in small cities throughout the Midwest. Its most relevant measure of volume is the occupancy rate, the percentage of available rooms rented to guests. Monthly revenue is $100,000 per percentage point of occupancy. (For example, at 40% occupancy, revenue is $4,000,000.) Contribution margin is 70%, and monthly fixed costs are $4,200,000.

Required
1. Find the monthly break-even point in (a) dollars and (b) occupancy rate.
2. Determine Norman's profit at a 75% occupancy rate.
3. Determine the occupancy rate Norman needs to earn $700,000 per month.
4. Determine whether Norman should increase advertising $100,000 per month if doing so increases the occupancy rate by two percentage points.

2-46   Assumptions of CVP analysis   Last year you were engaged as a consultant to Thompson Products Company and prepared some analyses of its CVP relationships. Among your findings was that the contribution margin percentage was 40% at the planned selling price of $20. The company expected to sell

10,000, which you estimated would yield a $46,000 income. You told Ms. Thompson, the owner, that profit would change at the rate of $0.40 per $1 change in sales.

Ms. Thompson has just called to tell you that the results did not come out as you had said they would. The company earned $63,200 on sales of $226,800. Variable costs per unit were incurred as expected, as were total fixed costs. Ms. Thompson was very pleased at the results. However, she asks you why profit did not increase by 40% of the added sales volume of $26,800, but rather by somewhat more.

Required

1. Prepare an income statement for the year, based on the actual results.
2. Determine (a) the number of units sold and (b) the selling price per unit.
3. Write a memorandum to Ms. Thompson explaining why the results were not as you had forecast. Use the guidelines in Appendix A at the back of the book.

2-47 *Cost structure* Wink Company manufactures replacement parts for automobiles and sells them to distributors in the northeastern United States. The president of the company wishes to begin selling in the Southeast but is uncertain how to expand most profitably. Two alternatives have been selected for final consideration. Under the first, Wink would use the services of independent sales representatives who would sell to distributors for a 15% commission. This plan would increase the clerical costs at the company's central office by $20,000 per year. Under the second alternative, Wink would hire its own salespeople to work on straight salary. Salaries for salespeople are estimated to be $100,000 per year; additionally, an office would be opened in the region and would cost $25,000 per year to operate.

The variable cost on parts is now 35%. The president is uncertain about demand in the Southeast and asks that you analyze profitability under both plans at various volumes. He selects $500,000, $700,000, $1,000,000, and $1,200,000 as the sales volumes to be used for comparison.

Required

Prepare a memorandum using the guidelines in Appendix A at the back of the book. Choose an alternative and defend your choice. Identify any qualitative factors that you believe are related to the alternatives.

CASES

2-48   *Opening a law office (CMA adapted)*   Don Masters and two of his colleagues are considering opening a law office in a large metropolitan area that would make inexpensive legal services available to those who could not otherwise afford these services. The intent is to provide easy access for their clients by having the office open 360 days per year, 16 hours each day from 7 a.m. to 11 p.m. The office would be staffed by a lawyer, paralegal, legal secretary, and clerk-receptionist for each of the two 8-hour shifts.

In order to determine the feasibility of the project, Masters hired a marketing consultant to assist with market projections. The results of this study show that if the firm spent $500,000 on advertising the first year, it could expect about 50 new clients each day. Masters and his associates believe the estimate to be reasonable and are prepared to spend the $500,000 on advertising. Other pertinent information about the operation of the office is given below.

The only charge to each new client would be $30 for the initial consultation. All cases that warranted further legal work would be accepted on a contingency basis with the firm earning 30% of any favorable settlements or judgments. Masters estimates that 20% of new client consultations will result in favorable settlements or judgments averaging $2,000. Masters expects no repeat clients during the first year of operations.

The hourly wages of the staff are projected to be $25 for the lawyer, $20 for the paralegal, $15 for the legal secretary, and $10 for the clerk-receptionist. Fringe benefit expense will be 40 percent of the wages paid.

Masters has located 6,000 square feet of suitable office space which rents for $28 per square foot annually. Associated expenses will be $22,000 for property insurance and $32,000 for utilities. The group will purchase malpractice insurance for $180,000 annually. The initial investment in office equipment will be $60,000, which will be depreciated over four years. The cost of office supplies has been estimated to be $4 per expected new client consultation.

Required

1. Determine the income the law office can expect if all goes according to plan.
2. Determine how many new clients must visit the law office for the venture to break even during its first year of operations.
3. Write a memorandum using the guidelines in Appendix A stating whether Masters and his associates should proceed.

2-49   *A concessionaire*   Ralph Newkirk is considering a bid for the hot dog and soft drink concession at the 14 football games for the season. There will be 7 college games and 7 professional games. Average attendance at college games is 30,000; at professional games attendance is 60,000. Ralph estimates that he sells one hot dog and one soft drink for each two persons attending a game.

Revenue and cost data are as follows.

	Hot Dogs	Soft Drinks
Selling price	$1.50	$1.00
Variable costs:		
Hot dog	0.32	
Roll	0.14	
Mustard, onion, etc.	0.02	
Soft drink and ice		0.22

In addition, salespeople earn a 20% commission on all sales. Fixed costs per game are $8,000 for rentals of heating, cooking, mixing, and cooling equipment.

The stadium management requested that bids be made in the form of royalties on sales. The highest percentage of sales bid will win the contract.

Required

1. What percentage of sales can Newkirk pay as royalty to the stadium and earn $180,000 for the season? (Round to nearest one-tenth of a percentage point.)
2. If Newkirk bids 12% of sales, what income can he expect? (Is your answer consistent with your answer in item 1?)
3. Assume that Newkirk gets the concession at a royalty of 12% of sales. He wants to know how much margin of safety he has in two ways. First, he is uncertain about total attendance and second, about the percentage of total attenders who buy a hot dog and drink. What is his break-even point for the season, expressed as (a) total attendance assuming one hot dog and drink per two attenders, and (b) the percentage of attenders who must buy a hot dog and drink if total attendance is as expected but the number of hot dogs and drinks each buys is uncertain?
4. What kinds of information does Newkirk need if he is also deciding to bid for the concession at baseball games at the same stadium?
5. After forecasting attendance for football games, Newkirk learns that the star quarterback of the local professional team will retire before the coming season. What effect does this information have on his planning?

2-50   Soccer camp   Since Jean Longhurst has been head soccer coach at Oldberne College, she has enjoyed considerable success. Longhurst has coached at summer camps for children and now is considering a summer camp for Oldberne. The college would provide room and board for the campers at a price and would also take 10% of revenue. Longhurst asks you for advice. You say that some of the important factors are setting a price, estimating enrollment, and estimating costs. After a few weeks, Longhurst returns with the following information, gathered from various sources.

Average enrollment	90 campers
Average price for one-week camp	$ 190
Costs:	
Food, charged by college	$ 50 per camper
Insurance and T-shirts	$ 12 per camper
Room rent charged by college	$ 15 per camper
Coaches' salaries	$ 450 per coach
Brochures, mailing, miscellaneous	$2,800 total

Longhurst also says that other camps have typically employed one coach for each 15 campers, excluding the director (Longhurst in this case). One problem is that you generally need to engage the coaches before you know the enrollment, although it is usually possible to find one or two at the last minute. It is, however, necessary to engage some of the coaches early so that you can use their names in brochures. Furthermore, while the enrollment and price given are averages, wide variations exist, with enrollments ranging from 40 to 120 and prices ranging from $160 to $230. As might be expected, the better-known camps have higher enrollments at higher prices, but they also pay better, as high as $800 per week for a well-known coach. Longhurst will keep the profits and suffer the losses, so she wants to be fairly confident before proceeding.

Required

1. If Longhurst hires enough coaches to meet the average enrollment and achieves all of the averages given above, what will be her profit?
2. What price will enable her to earn $4,000 enrolling 100 campers?
3. The college offers to take over the cost of brochures, mailing, and miscellaneous ($2,800 estimated) in exchange for a higher share of the revenue. If Longhurst achieves the results from item 1 (meets the averages), what percentage of revenue will she be able to pay the college and earn the same profit expected in item 1?
4. Write a memorandum to Longhurst explaining the advantages and disadvantages to her and to the college of the proposed arrangements. Use the guidelines in Appendix A at the back of the book.

Cost Analysis

LEARNING OBJECTIVES

After reading this chapter, you should be able to

1 *Understand the importance of cost management.*

2 *Describe the two ways of managing costs.*

3 *Distinguish between value-adding and non-value-adding activities and costs.*

4 *Describe and use the principles of cost drivers and cost pools.*

5 *Describe and use methods of analyzing cost behavior.*

6 *Understand the limitations of methods of cost behavior analysis.*

7 *Classify costs along several dimensions including whether managers can change them at short notice.*

8 *Describe and apply activity-based costing.*

- **United Airlines** *recently introduced ticketless air travel. Passengers no longer need to pick up tickets and show them at the airport.*
- *A few years ago,* **Levi Strauss** *announced that it was going to stop doing business with retailers whose purchases were less than $10,000 per year.*
- *A large manufacturer of golf equipment empowered production employees by turning over to them responsibility for product quality, reducing costs of quality control and of supervision.*
- *A large university empowered staff to order goods and supplies costing up to $500 without seeking authorization.*

- **Ernst & Young**, *the giant international firm of Certified Public Accountants, has reduced the floor space allotment per employee by 40 percent in the past few years.*
- *A recent annual report of* **Shawmut National Corporation**, *a large bank, describes how it has reduced layers of bureaucracy and sped up approval of loans.*

What do these actions have in common? They are all intended to manage costs better, reducing some costs and increasing others to provide better value to customers. Some of the actions reduce a special category of costs called non-value-adding costs, *which are costs that do not enhance the value of the company's products to its customers.* **United's** *saving passengers the trouble of picking up tickets, carrying them around, and producing them at an airport gate adds value. The university's allowing staff more leeway to run their operations means less paperwork and ultimately lower costs and better efficiency. Costs of approving small expenditures do not contribute to the education of students.*

Other cost-reduction efforts listed above aim at performing essential functions in less expensive ways, and without reducing the quality of the products and services the organizations provide to their customers.

Costs do not come with labels saying they are fixed or variable. Some costs do not vary with sales, but with some other activity. For example, some costs of a purchasing department vary with the number of vendors that the company uses and the number of parts and components the company buys. Some costs have both fixed and variable components. An example is maintenance, which typically includes a fixed component for regularly scheduled work and a component that varies with the use of the machinery.

Identifying and analyzing the activities that cause costs is also important in cost management, and we discuss a range of issues related to this topic. We also introduce some other categories of costs that are useful for various purposes and refine the concepts of Chapter 2.

OBJECTIVES OF ANALYZING COSTS

 From Chapter 2 you know that managers must understand the behavior of costs to plan and make decisions. To plan income for a future period, managers must be able to predict costs for that period, which requires estimates of fixed and variable costs. Managers also need good estimates of variable cost so they can compute contribution margin. Much important planning and decision-making activity requires knowledge of contribution margin.

COST MANAGEMENT

 Managers also must understand cost behavior to manage and control operations. Chapter 1 described some recent changes in the competitive environment, especially the emergence of companies that compete world-wide. That discussion showed that reducing costs and increasing quality have been critical to the success of many modern companies. Cost reduction is one key to increasing competitiveness and profitability. Of course, cost reduction is not necessarily desirable; reductions might sacrifice product quality, prompt delivery, technological superiority, or quick response to changing conditions, style, and fashion. The accompanying Insight describes some companies' attitudes about cost management, all taken from annual reports.

Managing costs has two basic aspects: One is managing the cost itself — for instance, buying materials, parts, and components at better prices. This aspect has traditionally been the principal focus of managerial accounting. The second, and usually more important, aspect is managing the *activity* that causes the costs — for instance, reducing the material content of a product without sacrificing quality. Managers now pay much more attention to this latter aspect.

Cost management is especially important for companies that cannot compete by differentiating their products or service. Some authorities believe that a company must select one of three basic strategies: (1) cost leadership (exemplified by such companies as **Southwest Airlines** and **Wal-Mart**), (2) differentiation of products or services (**Mercedes Benz, Calvin Klein**), or (3) focusing on a market niche (publishers of narrow-interest magazines such as *Runner's*

IN SIGHT

General Mills described three ways in which the company would grow. First was generating strong unit growth through innovation, next was increasing contributions from international operations, and third was improving productivity. General Mills seeks to improve productivity through investments in manufacturing operations and adopting high-performance work methods. The company has been successful; its most efficient lines have achieved manufacturing cost reductions of 33 percent compared to the least efficient lines.

One technique that **General Mills** found useful is benchmarking, which is finding the best practices and evaluating your operations against those practices. The company benchmarked the equipment changes of professional race-car pit crews and applied the lessons to cereal production. In one case the company applied the lessons of the race crew and reduced changeover time from eight hours to ten minutes.

Shawmut National Corporation, a large New England bank, lists cost control as "a strategic imperative" and goes on to say that "The winners in industries with excess capacity are those who most effectively control costs." Shawmut is reducing costs in various ways, including simplifying and delayering its bureaucracy. With fewer layers come quicker and more creative responses to customers, which is valuable even without the cost savings. One manifestation of lower costs and better responses is in lending, where the bank has speeded up credit approval. Shawmut has also consolidated branches based on analyses of the banking habits of segments of customers.

World). Companies that produce commodities, products that are virtually the same regardless of who makes them, must be cost leaders to survive. Such companies must have good estimates of the costs of all of their products and must be able to manage those costs and their underlying activities to thrive. But even companies that follow differentiation or niche strategies must also pay attention to costs.

MANAGING ACTIVITIES—COST DRIVERS AND COST POOLS

To manage costs effectively, managers associate costs with activities. Activities that cause costs are **cost drivers** and include sales, production, and various others such as the number of products the company makes and the number of customers it serves. A group of costs driven by the same activity is a **cost pool**. A cost pool might consist of all of the costs incurred by a department, such as the assembly department in a factory. A pool also could consist of only some of the costs of a department. For instance, the number of purchase orders drives some costs of the purchasing department, and the number of vendors drives others, while four or five other drivers might drive other costs. A pool could also consist of costs from more than one department. The number of employees drives some costs of both the payroll and personnel departments.

As later sections of this chapter show, identifying cost drivers and their associated cost pools is an important step in estimating the behavior of the cost. Identifying cost drivers also enables managers to focus their attention where it is likely to do the most good. Suppose setting up machines to run particular products drives a pool of $250,000 annual costs, and storing materials and components drives a pool of only $30,000 annual costs. Managers are likely to reduce costs more by concentrating on doing fewer machine setups, or doing them faster, than by trying to streamline storage procedures. Of course, *all* cost savings are helpful, but managers should concentrate their attention where the payoff will probably be the highest. Even if most of the costs of setups are fixed, large reductions in setups almost certainly will reduce the costs in the related pool.

After identifying a cost driver, managers estimate the fixed and variable components of each cost that is driven by that activity. They use methods that we explain in this chapter. But even if managers fail to estimate successfully how much of a cost is fixed and how much is variable, they can still manage costs better when they know what drives them. A manager who knows that increasing the number of parts in a product will increase particular costs can make some decisions even without knowing how much of each cost is fixed or variable.

For many years, labor time drove most other manufacturing costs. As manufacturing became more sophisticated, machines and computers took over many of the tasks that people had performed, and labor requirements declined. Now, more costs are driven by such activities as procurement, machine setup, and recordkeeping than was once the case. This newer environment therefore has more cost drivers.

Identifying cost drivers is an important part of managing costs as well as estimating cost behavior for planning purposes. As we illustrate later in this book, the increased attention to identifying cost drivers also has contributed to the development of activity-based costing, a relatively new approach to assigning costs to products.

VALUE-ADDING AND NON-VALUE-ADDING ACTIVITIES

As managers came to understand the changed environment and identified cost drivers, they also looked harder at why cost-driving activities occur and whether they add value to products. Such examination is part and parcel of advanced manufacturing environments because activities that do not add value are waste. Some activities, such as sewing together shoe soles and uppers, are clearly necessary to making products. These activities are **value-adding activities** and their costs are value-adding costs. Activities such as moving materials into and out of warehouses are **non-value-adding activities** because they do not make the product more valuable to the customer. The costs that non-value-adding activities drive are non-value-adding costs. Of course, classifying activities as value-adding or non-value-adding is not always easy and disagreements will arise about activities at the margin.

Managers strive to perform value-adding activities more efficiently and at lower costs consistent with quality and other objectives. A manager's goal with non-value-adding activities is simple: eliminate them. No company has eliminated all non-value-adding activities, but the goal is nonetheless valid. Trying to perform non-value-adding activities more efficiently is a poor tactic. Workers in many companies now inspect for defects as they make products instead of making a separate, final inspection that is a non-value-adding activity. From efforts to eliminate the non-value-adding activities of final inspection and reworking defective units came the emphasis on quality work—doing things right the first time.

Consider the different views taken by U.S. and Japanese auto makers. Most American auto makers try to keep cars on their assembly lines moving at all times. In contrast, Japanese companies try to have work being done on the cars at all times. Japanese companies want to be adding value to the cars at all times, rather than moving them more rapidly. In another example, **Hewlett-Packard**, the highly successful electronics company, simplified its accounting system in one plant. The company had been collecting considerable information about labor, but stopped after it went to a highly mechanized manufacturing process. As the company stopped collecting detailed information about labor, it was able to cut out some 100,000 journal entries per month and thereby experienced "... significant savings in staff time and costs ... "[1]

Non-value-adding activities and costs are themselves usually driven by other factors.[2] Think a moment about some non-value-adding activities and costs. From Chapter 1 we know that a functional factory arrangement, where machines of a given type are grouped together in departments, causes excessive movement of materials and semi-finished products. The *factory arrangement* is therefore driving the activity and cost of moving materials and product. Or consider supervision, an activity and cost that many would not even classify

1 R. Hunt, L. Garrett, and C. M. Merz, *"Direct Labor Not Always Relevant at H-P,"* Management Accounting, *February 1985, 58-62.*
2 *Michael R. Ostrenga and Frank R. Probst, "Process Value Analysis: The Missing Link in Cost Management,"* Journal of Cost Management, *Fall 1992, 4-14.*

as non-value-adding. Organizations employ supervisors for several reasons, perhaps the most common being that management does not trust workers to perform their jobs without supervision. For those organizations, management attitude, or policy, is driving a non-value-adding activity and cost. Many companies have greatly reduced or eliminated supervision and experienced increased productivity as workers become better motivated through their greater autonomy and responsibility. Teams of workers take full responsibility for their jobs in many companies today.

Nonmanufacturing companies also benefit from identifying non-value-adding activities. For example, many service companies discovered that the activity of following up on customers' complaints seldom added to customers' perception of value received. Such companies determined that improving the quality of service was less costly than following up complaints.

The accompanying Insight describes how **Southwest Airlines** eliminated non-value-adding activities and became one of the most productive companies in America.

ESTIMATING COST BEHAVIOR

Managers use several methods to estimate the fixed and variable components of costs. The methods range from simple to sophisticated. Each method has advantages and disadvantages, and managers in most companies will use more than one method.

A **mixed** (or **semivariable**) **cost** has both a fixed component and a variable component. For example, maintenance costs are likely to have a fixed component related to normal preventive maintenance carried out more or less routinely every month. There is also likely to be a variable component related to the amount of machine use. Exhibit 3-1 shows the behavior of a mixed cost; the pattern is like that of total costs when both fixed and variable costs are present.

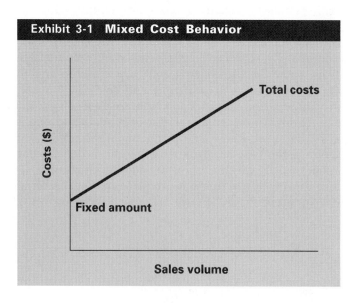

Exhibit 3-1   Mixed Cost Behavior

Southwest Airlines was the only major U.S. airline to be profitable in the early 1990s, which was a very difficult time for airlines. Much of the credit belongs to Herb Kelleher, its founder and president. The company is admired as a place to work, and its people are very loyal and very productive. Average salaries rival those of competitors and Southwest has excellent profit-sharing and pension plans.

Southwest calls itself the "nation's low fare, high Customer Satisfaction airline" and wants to continue to be the airline with the lowest cost structure. Southwest concentrates on short flights at low fares, eliminating meals and frills. Passengers cannot check baggage through if they are connecting with another airline. Southwest has pared non-value-adding activities to a bare minimum. It does not use the computerized reservation system that virtually all travel agents use. Travelers and travel agents alike must call the company to make a reservation. This policy alone saves $30 million annually. (It is interesting to note that other major airlines recently announced that they would stop compensating travel agents at the standard 10% of the fare and impose a $50 limit on the commission. This action not only reduced costs, but also changed the way consumers will purchase airline services. It should be obvious that the cost to a travel agent of booking a flight does not depend on the fare for the flight, although one cost driver is probably the number of legs on the flight.) But Southwest does not scrimp on service: it is the only airline to lead the industry in the categories of Ontime Performance, Baggage Handling, and Customer Satisfaction, and it led all three categories two years in a row.

Time that aircraft spend on the ground is non-value-adding. **Southwest** turns its planes around in 15-20 minutes, while other airlines take close to an hour. Such speed enables Southwest to operate its schedule with fewer aircraft and fewer flight crews. Southwest planes make about twice as many flights per day as those of other major carriers, spending about eleven hours per day in the air. By flying only one type of aircraft, the Boeing 737, Southwest saves millions of dollars because mechanics, pilots, and flight attendants need learn how to maintain and operate only one airplane.

Southwest has the lowest operating costs in the industry. For airlines, the most-watched measure of productivity/cost control is cost-per-seat-mile, the average cost of flying a seat, occupied or not, one mile. Southwest, at about seven cents per seat mile, was two to four cents below its major competitors. Southwest flies over 2,400 passengers per employee, compared with as few as 800 for other major carriers. Southwest employs only 81 people per airplane, while other airlines all employ over 100 people per airplane, some over 150.

Sources: Southwest Airlines Annual reports, 1993, 1994.

ACCOUNT ANALYSIS

A simple, yet sometimes effective, method of classifying the behavior of a cost is **account analysis**. Applying this method, the manager decides how to classify a cost by looking at its name and then checking this judgment by scanning the account for that cost for several periods. For instance, costs such as rent, depreciation, salaries, and advertising are generally fixed. If the amounts in the account for a cost vary only a little from month to month, it is likely that the cost is fixed. If the cost varies considerably from month to month, it is probably variable or mixed.

One weakness of account analysis is that it shows only what costs have been, not what they should be. Another is that considerable misclassification is possible. For example, stores in some malls pay rent as a percentage of sales, making rent a variable cost. But rent is fixed for most companies and someone looking at accounts would probably so classify it. Perhaps the most important weakness of this method is that it ignores the importance of identifying the cost-driving activity. Hence, account analysis is of limited usefulness.

ENGINEERING APPROACH

Another widely used method of ascertaining cost behavior is the **engineering approach**, which has been used most successfully to determine per-unit variable costs in manufacturing firms. Under this method, engineers study the material and labor requirements of products and related operations, then make per-unit estimates of the costs that should vary with production. The engineering approach has not been used as successfully when applied to non-manufacturing costs. The approach is most effective with standard products and processes that remain the same over time.

An important advantage of the engineering approach is that it indicates what costs *should be* rather than what they have been. This is important because simply knowing that, for instance, labor cost per unit of product has been $3.50 does not tell you that the labor is being used efficiently. It could well be that the company should be using a good deal less labor and that a cost of $2.80 is readily achievable if workers make changes in the way they do their jobs.

INTERVIEWS

A simple tool that has proven useful in determining what drives many costs is interviewing managers to determine what is likely to happen to particular costs, given specific actions. For instance, the purchasing manager probably could estimate what increase in workload might follow the introduction of a new product that requires parts not used in any other products. Using such parts would require evaluating new vendors, establishing testing procedures, doing paperwork, and so on. The new parts also could require additional personnel in purchasing, and perhaps in receiving and inspection.

Interviewing does not help determine how much of a particular cost is fixed or variable. However, it does help to identify cost drivers, which is an important part of applying the methods discussed in the remainder of this section. Interviewing might be useful in developing ballpark estimates of the effects of various decisions. For instance, a manufacturing manager might be able to tell a cost analyst how many additional people might be needed to speed up the introduction of a new product. The analyst could then assign dollar amounts to the additional needs.

To aid the presentation of the remaining methods, we will use the following data related to maintenance costs of RFC Manufacturing Co. In this situation, we assume RFC already has identified hours of machine use as the cost-driving activity, and that all of the observations are within the relevant range.

Machine Hours	Maintenance Cost
5,000	$14,800
10,800	28,200
12,200	27,300
7,300	19,100
10,000	25,400
8,100	24,900
18,000	40,800
13,400	31,800
5,400	18,100
14,100	31,900
15,100	36,100
17,300	35,900

HIGH-LOW (TWO-POINT) METHOD

A relatively unsophisticated, yet widely used, method of estimating the components of a mixed cost is the **high-low** (or **two-point**) **method**. This method uses two past levels of activity and the amounts of the cost incurred at those levels. The high and low points selected should be the highest and lowest levels of activity (as opposed to the highest and lowest costs) *within the relevant range*. To find the variable component of the cost, divide the difference in cost at the two levels by the difference in volumes of the cost-driving activity. The formula for finding the variable cost factor in a mixed cost is

$$\frac{\textit{Variable cost component}}{\textit{of mixed cost}} = \frac{\textit{change in cost}}{\textit{change in activity}}$$

Using our example,

$$\frac{\textit{Variable cost component}}{\textit{of mixed cost}} = \frac{\$40,800 - \$14,800}{18,000 - 5,000}$$

$$= \$26,000/13,000$$

$$= \$2 \textit{ per machine hour}$$

Because the total cost at any volume equals total variable cost at that volume plus total fixed cost, the fixed component of the total cost equals the difference between the total cost and the total variable cost at that volume. In formula notation this becomes, using the high volume,

$$\frac{\textit{Fixed cost component}}{\textit{of mixed cost}} = \frac{\textit{total cost at}}{\textit{high volume}} - \frac{\textit{high}}{\textit{volume}} \times \frac{\textit{variable cost}}{\textit{component}}$$

At 18,000 machine hours,

Total cost at high volume	$ 40,800
Less variable portion (18,000 × $2)	36,000
Fixed component	$ 4,800

We get the same answer using the low volume at 5,000 machine hours.

Total cost at low volume	$ 14,800
Less variable portion (5,000 × $2)	10,000
Fixed component	$ 4,800

The formula that RFC can then use to predict maintenance cost is

Total maintenance cost = $4,800 + ($2 × machine hours)

The rationale for the method is best understood if you recognize that your goal—a cost prediction formula—is simply a formula for a straight line such as that in Exhibit 3-1. The general formula for a straight line is $y = a + bx$, with b being the slope of the line and a the point where the line intercepts the y axis. The formula given above for determining the variable component of a mixed cost computes b, the slope of the line. The formula for the fixed component is solving the general formula for a when you know b (the slope), x (a level of the cost-driving activity, or independent variable, represented on the x axis), and y (the value of the dependent variable, total cost, at that activity level).

    At this point remember that the volume levels used when applying the high-low method must be within the relevant range if the resulting cost prediction formula is to be useful. (Remember from Chapter 2 that the relevant range is that over which per-unit variable cost and total fixed cost should remain constant.) The two-point method has some serious disadvantages, which will become clearer as we discuss the next method.

SCATTER-DIAGRAM METHOD

Like the high-low method, the **scatter-diagram** (or **graphical**) **method** requires cost and volume data from prior periods, and derives an equation (cost prediction formula) based on those data. Again, the goal is a cost prediction formula of the form $y = a + bx$.

The first step is to plot points that represent total cost at various levels of activity within the relevant range. The dots in Exhibit 3-2 show the maintenance cost that RFC incurred at various levels of machine hours. The second step is to draw a line as close to all the points as possible. (Exhibit 3-2 shows such a line.) The placement and slope of the line are matters of judgment; the manager "eyeballs" the data and fits the line visually. Because the fitting is done by hand and eye, as is the determination of the intercept (fixed component) and slope (variable component), different users will get different results. We obtained the following formula to predict maintenance cost for RFC.

Total maintenance cost = $7,200 + ($1.82 × machine hours)

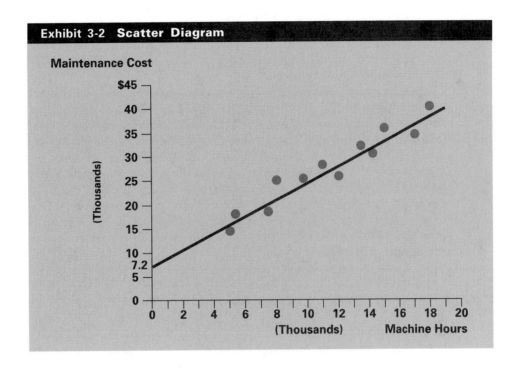

Exhibit 3-2   Scatter Diagram

Maintenance Cost

Like the high-low method, the scatter-diagram method suffers from its reliance on what costs have been, rather than what they are likely to be in the future. But the scatter-diagram method is preferable for two reasons. First, because the high-low method relies on only two observations, it carries the risk that one point or the other (or both) was affected by a random oddity or unusual event. If RFC did a great deal of preventive maintenance in the low-activity month, the resulting prediction formula could be useless. Because the scatter-diagram method uses more observations and permits the manager to see the pattern of costs, the formula is less likely to be influenced by such events and oddities. The second advantage of the scatter-diagram method is that by looking at the plotting of costs at various levels of the activity, a manager will get some idea of how closely the cost follows changes in the cost-driving activity. (This issue is discussed in more detail later.)

Whichever formula it uses, RFC cannot expect to predict maintenance costs exactly. The spread of points on the scatter diagram shows that differences can be expected. Several reasons might explain these differences. One reason is that factors other than machine hours (e.g., the types of materials put through the machinery) might affect maintenance costs. Another is that random elements influence cost, just as they do an automobile's gas mileage.

REGRESSION METHOD

Regression analysis (or just regression) is a more sophisticated method for estimating the fixed and variable components of a mixed cost. Like the high-low and scatter-diagram methods, regression uses cost and volume data from prior periods to yield an equation of the form $y = a + bx$, or Total cost = fixed cost + (variable cost per unit of activity × level of activity). In contrast to the high-low method, regression uses more than two observations. And in contrast to the scatter-diagram method, regression relies on statistical concepts, rather than on the judgment of the manager drawing the line. Regression fits the mathematically best line to the data.

In recent years, accountants have increased their efforts to find techniques for planning administrative costs, partly because such costs have increased more rapidly than many others. A tool that managers are employing with some success in analyzing administrative and other costs is *multiple regression analysis*, which uses two or more independent variables, or cost drivers, to predict the behavior of a cost. Knowledge of some important statistical principles is required before you can understand and apply either simple or multiple regression analysis. But you should be aware that advanced techniques such as these are available for solving cost estimation problems. A discussion of the basic terms and procedures of simple and multiple regression analysis appears in the appendix to this chapter.

PROBLEMS AND PITFALLS IN COST BEHAVIOR ANALYSIS

The methods we have discussed for estimating the behavior of mixed costs are all subject to problems that could decrease the usefulness of cost prediction formulas.

HISTORICAL DATA

The common thread in the high-low, scatter-diagram, and regression methods is that they all use past (historical) information about both the dependent variable (the cost to be predicted) and the independent variable (the measure of activity). Historical information should be used carefully, because formulas based on historical data can give useful predictions only if past conditions also will prevail in the future. For example, observations gathered before a company installed new machinery are suspect because using the new machinery probably will change the cost structure. Similarly, the usefulness of a formula for predicting electricity cost will be reduced if rates have changed since the observations were collected. (The cure in the latter example is to develop the equation using electricity consumption in kilowatt hours, and then apply the expected rates to the predicted use of kilowatt hours.)

The usefulness of a cost-prediction formula can be impaired by nonrepresentative historical data. Remember that the analyst should consider only observations within the relevant range. But even those observations might not be representative of normal circumstances. A company might use temporary, less efficient workers for a few months, making those months nonrepresentative. Formulas developed using nonrepresentative data can lead to major misestimates of costs. Managers should use cost estimation methods only after they review and understand the operating conditions under which cost and activity data were gathered. The scatter-diagram method offers an advantage here because it highlights out-of-line points. Managers often plot data even when they use regression analysis. An out-of-line observation (called an *outlier*) should be ignored.

Finally, cost prediction formulas given by all of the methods are based on observations within a specific range of activity, usually the relevant range. The formulas describe behavior within the range over which the observations fell, so predicting costs at activity levels outside that range (called *extrapolation*) is unwise.

Apart from the problems created by using historical data, analysts must consider the possibility that their predictions will be ineffective because they collected the wrong data. We discuss some of the flaws of data collection in the next section.

CORRELATION AND ASSOCIATION

For an equation to be useful for planning, the relationship between the cost and the activity must be fairly close. The closeness of the relationship is called **correlation** or association. Consider, for example, the costs of preparing invoices to bill customers. The scatter diagram in Exhibit 3-3 relates the total costs of a firm's billing department to sales activity measured by sales dollars. It shows a wide spread of costs around the cost-prediction line, so that using sales dollars to predict the cost is unlikely to be successful. The spread indicates that sales dollars does not drive invoice preparation costs. (Does it take more time or more people to prepare an invoice for $100,000 than one for $10,000?)

Exhibit 3-4 shows billing department costs plotted against another driver, the number of sales orders processed. Because individual sales orders vary in dollar value, it is not surprising that the total cost for invoice preparation varies more closely with the number of sales orders than with the dollars of sales represented by the orders. Finding this better correlated activity measure is important for cost management as well as for cost prediction. Knowing the cost driver, managers can try to reduce the cost by reducing the number of sales orders. Managers might find that salespeople write separate orders for each type of product a customer orders, or for weekly standing orders. They might then devise ways to reduce the number of orders written (and the processing costs) without affecting customer satisfaction.

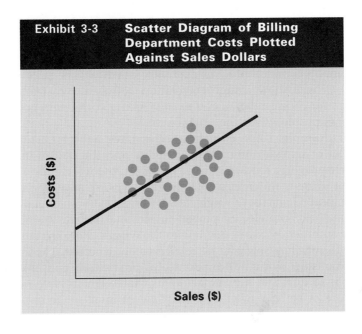

Exhibit 3-3   Scatter Diagram of Billing Department Costs Plotted Against Sales Dollars

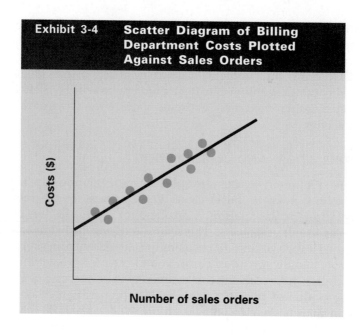

Exhibit 3-4   Scatter Diagram of Billing Department Costs Plotted Against Sales Orders

As stated earlier, the visual aspect of the scatter-diagram method is an important advantage; it allows the manager to see whether the activity chosen as the independent variable is likely to be a good predictor of the dependent variable (cost). Virtually all computer programs for regression analysis, including spreadsheets such as Lotus 1-2-3®, also provide information about correlation. The high-low method, because it includes only two points, does not provide this important information.

SPURIOUS CORRELATION

Determining what activity drives costs is an important objective of cost analysis, enabling managers to monitor and control both the cost and the activity. Computers make it possible to do regression and correlation for hundreds of combinations of activity and cost very quickly. It is quite possible that some analyses will show a high correlation between a cost and an activity even though no causal relationship exists. Such a correlation is called *spurious* and presents problems for the unwary.

For example, some electric utilities have a high correlation between the number of kilowatt hours they generate and the cost of outside maintenance of their property (cutting the grass, etc.). Obviously, producing electric power cannot drive maintenance costs (or vice versa), so why the high correlation? The logical reason for the high correlation is that both depend on another factor: the weather. Both electric power output and outside maintenance are highest in the summer; both are also low in the winter. Because both are related to the same factor, they *appear* to be related to one another. The key, then, in seeking a relationship that will provide useful predictions and enhance cost management is to question high correlations that seem to have no causal basis. The measure of activity used to predict a cost must make sense.

A more subtle example of an unwarranted conclusion about the relationship between a cost and a particular activity occurs when managers *plan* the level of a fixed cost on the basis of the expected level of some activity. For example, many companies budget fixed costs such as advertising, employee training, charitable contributions, and research and development, at some percentage of sales. A scatter diagram or regression analysis will show such costs to be variable with sales, when in reality, managerial action creates that appearance.

STEP-VARIABLE COSTS

Exhibit 3-5 shows a pattern of cost behavior that fits neither the fixed-variable classification scheme nor the pattern of a typical mixed cost. A cost exhibiting such behavior is commonly called a **step-variable cost**. It is fixed over a range of volume, then jumps to a new level and remains fixed at that level until the next jump. The width of the range of volume over which the cost remains fixed depends on the particular cost. Step-variable behavior often occurs because of company policy, such as having one production supervisor for every 20 workers, or one inventory clerk for every 1,000 items of inventory.

Step-variable costs exist because of indivisibility of resources; that is, many resources cannot be acquired in infinitely divisible increments. For instance, an airline can't fly fractions of planes to provide exactly as many seats as passengers demand; it can fly only an entire airplane. Similarly, companies usually cannot rent space one cubic foot at a time. Nor can they hire part-time people for some jobs; it is difficult to hire a sales manager or controller for six or eight months of the year. However, the growing use of temporary employees ("temps") is a way of confronting the indivisibility problem.

Should we plan step-variable costs as if they were mixed, though the fixed component changes within the relevant range? Should we consider them variable, even though they do not vary between steps? Both approaches are used in practice, which means that actual costs will differ from cost predictions under either alternative. Managers are more likely to treat a cost as variable if the steps are relatively short and as a fixed cost if the steps are relatively long (measured horizontally).

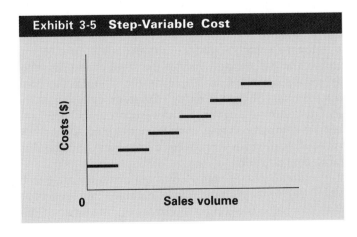

Exhibit 3-5   Step-Variable Cost

Costs ($)

0   Sales volume

Isolating the activity that drives a step-variable cost is often difficult because such costs do not change in direct proportion to short-term changes in activity, but rather respond to changes in activity only over longer periods. Analysts therefore can fail to identify the activity driving the cost, and the real cost-driving activity is less likely to be carefully monitored and controlled. Interviewing can be helpful in analyzing step-variable costs. Many companies have reported success in controlling some types of step-variable costs after interviewing provided clues to the cost-driving activity, enabling managers to concentrate on reducing the level of that activity. For example, companies that have worked closely with suppliers to achieve a high level of quality in purchased materials have reduced inspection and rework costs after recognizing that those costs were driven by the quality, rather than the number, of incoming shipments.

COMMITTED AND DISCRETIONARY FIXED COSTS

 Recall from Chapter 2 that classifying a cost as "fixed" does not imply that the cost cannot be changed, only that it does not vary automatically as volume changes. Some fixed costs can be quickly altered by managerial action and are called **discretionary costs**. Managers frequently decide whether to incur the cost at all and how much to incur. Advertising, employee training, and research and development are examples of discretionary costs. Fixed costs that cannot be changed so quickly are **committed costs**, so called to express the idea that managers have made a commitment that cannot be readily changed. Depreciation is a committed cost. Like other committed fixed costs, depreciation arises from past managerial decisions—some made years ago—and cannot be changed without disposing of the asset to which the depreciation applies.

Deciding whether a cost is committed or discretionary is not always possible just by knowing what the cost is for (rent, salaries, research and development, etc.). For example, rent might or might not be a committed cost depending on the terms of the rental agreement.

Do not misinterpret the discretionary-committed classification as distinguishing between unnecessary and necessary costs, respectively. Advertising is a discretionary fixed cost, but some type of advertising—a sign, a Yellow Pages listing, something—is necessary for many enterprises. Similarly, depreciation is a committed fixed cost; yet most companies could probably operate successfully without one or more of several cash registers, telephone lines, or display racks.

Discretionary costs present unique problems in cost management because managers must determine whether the level of the discretionary activity—the cost driver—is appropriate. For example, should the company hire another research scientist? Should it reduce the number of pages in the annual report? Should it discontinue a particular training program? The larger question is often whether the company should even be performing the activity at all. Should the company pay tuition for employees taking courses? Should the company make charitable contributions?

Unfortunately, discretionary costs are often the first to be attacked in cost-reduction programs, perhaps partly because their effects are not immediately apparent. Consider the long-run effects of cutting such discretionary costs as research and product development, management training programs, and programs to upgrade worker skills.

Research and product development are crucial to the success of companies in such high-technology fields as pharmaceuticals, computers, aircraft, and some consumer products. An executive of **Pfizer** reported that any new drugs that would go on the market from 1994 through 2000 had been discovered well before 1994.[3] Reducing expenditures for personnel development can lead to reduced morale, high turnover, and lessened productivity. Another problem is that cutting discretionary costs does not always reduce the workload and the morale of the remaining employees might suffer. Corporate downsizing, so much in the news today, seems to have had significant effects on morale and loyalty of employees.

AVOIDABLE AND UNAVOIDABLE COSTS

Another useful subdivision of costs hinges on whether the company could avoid the cost by adding, dropping, or curtailing some activity. (Variable costs are nearly always avoidable if we decide to increase or decrease an activity, so for the most part we are concerned with fixed costs.) A particular cost, such as sales salaries, might be partly avoidable, partly not, depending on the decision. A company that stops selling in a geographical region could reduce its salesforce. One that drops a product line might not be able to reduce its salesforce because it still needs all of the salespeople to cover its customers, even though each salesperson would carry fewer lines. Thus, the ideas of avoidability and unavoidability apply only when a decision is at hand. Avoidable if we do, or do not do, what?

At first glance, the avoidable-unavoidable categories might seem to parallel the discretionary-committed categories. This is sometimes so, but significant exceptions may exist, and determining whether or not a cost is avoidable typically requires a case-by-case analysis. Chapters 4 and 5 delve into this topic more deeply.

DIRECT AND INDIRECT (COMMON) COSTS

Another refinement of our basic cost classification scheme is often useful. Costs may be classified as direct or indirect. A **direct cost**, also called a **separable cost** or **traceable cost**, is incurred specifically because of a particular activity of the firm, like a product, product line, or geographical area. (All costs are direct to some activity, if only to the company as a whole.) An **indirect cost**, also called a **common cost** or **joint cost**, does not relate to one specific activity, but rather to several.

Variable costs are direct to a particular product or activity. Some fixed costs are direct to particular products or activities, and some are not. For example, salaries of salespeople who cover particular geographical regions are direct to those regions. But if the salespeople sell several products, their salaries are

---

3 Jerry Flint, *"The Goose that Laid the Golden Pill,"* Forbes, May 9, 1994, 50.

indirect to each of the products. Thus, to classify a cost as direct or indirect, it is necessary first to specify the activity in which the manager is interested.

Direct costs usually are avoidable, although there certainly are exceptions. If a company rents a sales office and the lease has ten years to run, the rent is direct to the office, but is unavoidable. Indirect costs generally are unavoidable; by definition they are incurred to support two or more activities, so they will continue to be incurred if only one of the activities is discontinued. Even here, though, the individual circumstances determine the classification. Consider a large company with six major production departments in a single factory building. Dropping one department could enable the company to reduce such indirect costs as those of operating the payroll and personnel functions, even though no one person in either of those departments works exclusively on the production department being dropped. Thus, some portion of the indirect cost is avoidable.

MANUFACTURING COSTS

A manufacturer incurs costs to make products, so the behavioral classification and management of manufacturing costs concentrates on activities having to do with production.

A typical manufacturer has three types of manufacturing costs: materials and purchased components, direct labor, and manufacturing overhead. The cost of **materials** (sometimes called **raw materials** or **direct materials**) and components that the company buys and transforms into its products (steel, wood, valves, fenders, etc.), normally varies with the volume of production. The cost of **direct labor**, wages paid to employees who work directly on the product, also usually varies with the volume of production. However, in some European countries where it is difficult, or even impossible, to lay off workers in slow times, labor becomes a fixed cost. Some U.S. companies also follow no-layoff policies as well. **Manufacturing overhead**, consisting of all production costs other than materials, purchased components, and direct labor, includes costs that are fixed, variable, and mixed. Many such costs also vary with production, but many others are driven by other activities. Activity-based costing (discussed in the next section) is concerned with analyzing these costs, determining their drivers, and relating the costs to products. Some examples of manufacturing overhead costs appear in Exhibit 3-6.

From the brief listing in Exhibit 3-6, you should see that companies have several pools of manufacturing overhead costs, each driven by a different activity. Some pools of manufacturing overhead will be mixed costs, with variable components based on activities such as labor hours or machine hours. Some pools will be fixed in the short term because they are driven by factors that do not change significantly over short periods. (One example is the costs of some administrative functions that change only as the factory increases the number of products it makes.)

One objective of cost management is to determine the costs of each product so that managers can make decisions about those products. For instance, should we continue to make a particular product or phase it out over the coming year? Should we raise prices on some products? Lower prices on others? A multiproduct company can seldom relate the behavior of most manufacturing overhead costs,

Exhibit 3-6   Examples of Manufacturing Overhead Costs

- Costs of acquiring materials and components, which include finding acceptable vendors and carrying out routine purchasing functions
- Wages of indirect laborers (those who do not work directly on the products), such as maintenance workers, materials handlers, and cleaners
- Costs of data processing related to manufacturing activities
- Salaries of production supervisors
- Costs of changing machinery over from making one product to another (setup costs)
- Accounting and recordkeeping related to manufacturing operations
- Quality control costs, such as salaries of workers responsible for inspecting incoming shipments of materials and components in conventional manufacturers
- Wages of workers responsible for the storage and control of materials
- Heat, light, and power costs for factory
- Depreciation and property taxes on factory buildings and factory machinery
- Salary and office expenses of plant managers and their staffs
- Salaries and expenses of industrial engineers, computer programmers, and other manufacturing support personnel

as well as selling and administrative expenses, to a single, broad measure of output such as the number of units produced or sold, or to the labor content of each product. For example, a company that makes refrigerators, ovens, and toasters could not expect each type of manufacturing overhead cost to vary with the total number of units produced because the units are so different. (Making a toaster does not cause as much overhead as making a refrigerator because a refrigerator requires more labor and machine time, has many more parts, and is a much more complicated product.) Activity-based costing addresses these issues.

ACTIVITY-BASED COSTING

Activity-based costing (ABC) refers to assigning costs to products (or other segments such as customers or geographical areas) by referring to the activities that each product requires. Using ABC requires identifying cost drivers. Because activities cause costs, to understand cost behavior fully requires understanding those activities (cost drivers). Managers who understand activities can determine what costs the activities drive.

As Chapter 2 stated, sales volume drives many costs. However, diversity and complexity of operations also are important cost drivers. Consider how much more complicated your life would be if you took 15 one-hour courses, as opposed to 5 three-hour courses. The constant shifting from one course to another, keeping track of where you are in each course, and allotting time to each course would take up much more time than managing 5 three-hour courses.

Similarly, the more kinds of products a company makes and the wider their variety, the higher its costs. The more kinds of materials, parts, and components a company's products require, the higher its costs. The more processes, machines, and machine setups its products go through, the higher its costs.

Picture two manufacturers of bricks. UniBrick makes 10,000,000 red bricks of a single size, shape, and texture and sells them all to a few customers. *All* of UniBrick's costs relate to its one product and volume is the principal, perhaps the only, cost driver. MultiBrick also makes 10,000,000 total bricks, but in a dozen colors, four textures, and eight sizes/shapes, a total of 384 (12 × 4 × 8) possibilities. MultiBrick mixes and bakes 10-18 batches of bricks per day. Some batches are relatively small, some large, but each batch requires changing and cleaning molds, getting the required materials from storage, and adjusting oven temperatures. MultiBrick sells to over 1,000 customers, whose orders typically include 15-20 different kinds of bricks.

MultiBrick's much more complex and diverse operation generates higher costs than UniBrick. MultiBrick's office deals with many more customers, increasing its costs of order-taking, billing, credit-checking, collection, and customer service. MultiBrick's shipping department incurs higher costs because making up an order requires picking up and taking to the shipping dock various quantities of several kinds of bricks. A forklift truck must search out 15-20 types of bricks and pick up the correct quantities of each. It must make several stops to pick up each order, and probably must make more trips to fill orders than would a truck at UniBrick that goes to a single place and loads up.

Manufacturing operations also will differ. Because it must make varying quantities of many types of bricks, MultiBrick must carefully schedule production to be sure of getting the right quantities of each type of brick its customers require. MultiBrick needs skilled people to determine the best production schedule, communicate that schedule to the factory floor, monitor actual progress, and record results.

MultiBrick must change over from making one type of brick to another 10-18 times a day. These changeovers, or setups, can be very costly. Workers in MultiBrick must clean the old color out of the vats, then put in the correct color. They must change molds if they change the sizes of the bricks. They must change the recipe to accommodate different textures and must get the appropriate ingredients from storage. All of these activities add to costs. UniBrick has no such costs because it cranks out its one model all day long.

Even though both companies have the same sales and production volumes, MultiBrick's total costs will exceed UniBrick's because MultiBrick's costs will be driven by activities other than volume. The number of setups, number of production orders, number of sales orders, and other non-volume activities will drive significant amounts of cost. UniBrick's costs will probably vary only with volume. Of course, despite its higher costs, MultiBrick can still be profitable, perhaps more profitable than UniBrick; MultiBrick can probably command higher prices for its specialty bricks than UniBrick can for its one model.

From a managerial accounting perspective, the significance of diversity and complexity as cost drivers is that managers cannot use a single, volume-based measure to determine overhead costs of individual products. *Of special importance is that using volume-based measures alone overcosts high-volume products and undercosts low-volume products.* Setup costs mount as changeovers increase, and setups increase as the company makes more low-volume products. So, one key to success for MultiBrick is reasonable estimates of the total costs that each of its products generates. Managers will use these costs to make many decisions, including whether to drop some models from the line or emphasize some models over others. **National Semiconductor** eliminated nearly 45 percent of its product line after an ABC analysis showed these products contributing very little to overall profits.

Activity-based costing (ABC) developed as managers understood that low-volume products could not be as profitable as they appeared nor could high-volume products be as unprofitable as they appeared. Under ABC, each product or other segment is apportioned costs based on its consumption of resources as indicated by the cost drivers. MultiBrick needs to develop costs for each of the principal activities that its individual bricks require.

Exhibit 3-7 shows how MultiBrick might determine manufacturing costs using volume as the sole driver and using an ABC approach. Notice that the high-volume brick appears to be less costly under the ABC approach and the low-volume bricks more costly. This is the usual case because a volume-based measure allocates more costs to high-volume products. An ABC system allocates more costs to products that generate activities such as setups, which are not necessarily related to volume.[4]

ABC is not a method of identifying fixed and variable components of costs. Rather, it is concerned with longer-term average costs. Unit costs developed using ABC should not be used to predict total costs at various levels of output in the short run. ABC is excellent for identifying long-term costs. For example, if the average annual cost of dealing with a vendor is $12,324, we cannot say that adding one vendor will increase costs $12,324 per year, but we can say that as we add batches of vendors over time, the average cost increase might be about that. If we then plan new products or manufacturing processes and plan to add 20 vendors, our costs could increase by about $12,300 per vendor. In the long run, companies can change the amount of capacity and personnel they need for such functions as purchasing, machine setups, and customer billing. Thus, costs that are fixed, in the sense of not changing automatically as volume

Exhibit 3-7   MultiBrick Cost Determination Data

Total overhead $8,000,000

Total output   10,000,000 bricks

Data related to two low-volume specialty bricks and a high-volume brick appear below.

	Model A-42	Model A-88	Model C-11
Total production	6,000	4,000	100,000
Material cost per brick	$0.50	$0.40	$0.30
Direct labor cost per brick	$0.60	$0.70	$0.70

(continued)

4 *The works of Professors Robert Kaplan and Robin Cooper are invaluable in studying ABC. For example, see Cooper and Kaplan, "How Cost Accounting Systematically Distorts Product Costs,"* Management Accounting, *April 1988, 20-27.*

Exhibit 3-7 MultiBrick Cost Determination Data (continued)

Panel A: Volume-based allocation of overhead based on units

Overhead rate = total manufacturing overhead costs/total units produced

= $8,000,000/10,000,000

= $0.80 per brick

Cost calculations:

	Model A-42	Model A-88	Model C-11
Material cost per brick	$ 0.50	$ 0.40	$ 0.30
Direct labor cost per brick	0.60	0.70	0.70
Overhead cost at $0.80	0.80	0.80	0.80
Total cost	$ 1.90	$ 1.90	$ 1.80
Times production	× 6,000	×4,000	×100,000
Total cost	$ 11,400	$7,600	$180,000

Panel B: ABC allocations

Cost drivers and activities are summarized below.

Cost Driver	Costs in Pool	divided by	Total Activity of Driver	equals	Rate
Setups	$1,200,000	÷	10,000 setups	=	$120
Baking time	6,000,000	÷	300,000 hours	=	20
Production orders	800,000	÷	5,000 orders	=	160

Activity data, per year

	Model A-42	Model A-88	Model C-11
Number of setups	150	180	30
Baking time	60	50	300
Number of production orders	30	40	20

ABC costs

	Model A-42	Model A-88	Model C-11
Material cost*	$ 3,000	$ 1,600	$ 30,000
Direct labor cost**	3,600	2,800	70,000
Overhead:			
Setup based at $120	18,000	21,600	3,600
Baking time at $20	1,200	1,000	6,000
Production orders based at $160	4,800	6,400	3,200
Total cost	$ 30,600	$ 33,400	$112,800
Divided by annual volume	÷ 6,000	÷ 4,000	÷100,000
Average cost per brick	$5.10	$8.35	$1.128

* $0.50 × 6,000, $0.40 × 4,000, $0.30 × 100,000

** $0.60 × 6,000, $0.70 × 4,000, $0.70 × 100,000

changes in the short term, *will* change as managers adjust to resource requirements. Focusing attention on individual activities helps managers in many
areas.

For instance, a design engineer revising the specifications of a product might
incorporate a component the company does not now use. Unless the company
uses ABC, it will not have a good estimate of the costs associated with introducing a new component and will be much less likely to question the designer's
decision. Introducing that component might require that the purchasing department find vendors who supply it, and then evaluate each potential vendor's
prices, quality control, and ability to meet delivery schedules. The storeroom
will allot space for the component, add the component to its list of stocked
items, and probably generate other paperwork. Until the vendor has satisfied
the company that the quality of the component is acceptable, the company will
inspect incoming shipments. The data processing department must incorporate
the component into whatever computer files are used by various departments.
The accounts payable section will process more invoices and pay more bills.
The company's internal auditors will have to count the component. In short,
a seemingly simple change might send ripples of cost through many areas of
the company, which, though relatively small, can accumulate as more and more
such changes occur.

All of the costs described above must be considered in making such decisions, as well as in other areas. Evaluating the profitability of products or of
geographical areas is one example where ABC is helpful in identifying cost-
driving activities and thereby plays a role in cost reduction and continuous
improvement which JIT operations pursue.

SUMMARY

Cost analysis and management are important to managers. Managers can control costs directly or control the activities that generate them. Costs do not
always fit into fixed or variable classifications, and many costs vary with
activities other than sales. Some manufacturing costs vary with the number of
units manufactured, some selling costs vary with the number of orders placed
by customers, and so on.

Some costs are mixed and contain both fixed and variable elements. Step-
variable costs are fixed over small ranges of activity but at different levels for
different ranges. Scatter diagrams, high-low estimates, and regression analysis
are useful tools for analyzing cost behavior, but must be used with care. Whatever
the method used to analyze cost behavior, actual costs will probably differ from
planned costs.

Identifying value-adding and non-value-adding activities and costs is crucial
for cost management. A company's objectives are to perform value-adding
activities more efficiently and eliminate non-value-adding activities and their
associated costs.

Several other classifications of costs include discretionary or committed,
avoidable or unavoidable, direct or indirect. Discretionary fixed costs can be
changed on relatively short notice. Committed fixed costs normally cannot be

changed quickly. Costs are classified as avoidable or unavoidable only in relation to specific decisions, such as dropping a product. Direct costs relate to a specific activity, while indirect (or common) costs benefit more than one activity.

Manufacturing costs come in three types: materials, direct labor, and overhead. Activity-based costing uses the ideas of cost pools and cost drivers to arrive at costs of products for decision-making purposes. ABC is a long-term approach to associating costs with activities and does not purport to separate costs into fixed and variable components.

KEY TERMS

account analysis   (83)
activity-based costing (ABC)   (95)
committed costs   (92)
correlation   (89)
cost drivers   (80)
cost pool   (80)
direct (separable or traceable) cost   (93)
direct labor   (94)
discretionary costs   (92)
engineering approach   (84)
indirect (common or joint) cost   (93)

manufacturing overhead   (94)
materials (raw or direct)   (94)
mixed (semivariable) cost   (82)
non-value-adding activities   (81)
regression analysis   (87)
scatter-diagram (graphical) method   (86)
step-variable cost   (91)
high-low (two-point) method   (85)
value-adding activities   (81)

KEY FORMULAS

$$\frac{\text{Variable cost component}}{\text{of mixed cost}} = \frac{\text{change in cost}}{\text{change in activity}}$$

$$\frac{\text{Fixed cost component}}{\text{of mixed cost}} = \frac{\text{total cost at}}{\text{high volume}} - \frac{\text{high}}{\text{volume}} \times \frac{\text{variable}}{\text{cost component}}$$

REVIEW PROBLEM

Bartley Company incurs about $860,000 in manufacturing overhead costs each month. The company's former controller had been allocating overhead to individual product lines based on the lines' relative shares of direct labor hours (DLH). The company works about 100,000 DLH per month, so the average overhead cost per DLH is $8.60. The new controller is concerned that using DLH is inappropriate because some costs are driven by other activities. She has developed the following information regarding cost pools and drivers.

Cost Driver	Amount in Pool	Amount of Activity
Direct labor hours	$520,000	100,000
Number of batches	160,000	360
Engineering/design changes	60,000	120
Number of parts	120,000	3,200
Total overhead costs	$860,000	

The controller asks you to analyze two product lines using the existing method of allocating overhead costs based on DLH, and using activity-based rates. She gives you the following data regarding two product lines. Bells are a bread-and-butter line that the company makes in large batches, while whistles are a specialty line that only a few customers buy.

	Bells	Whistles
Direct labor hours	1,600	200
Number of batches	4	12
Engineering/design changes	2	14
Number of parts	22	88

Required

1. Determine the overhead to be allocated to each line using DLH as the only cost driver.
2. Determine the overhead to be allocated to each line using the four drivers identified above.
3. Comment on the differences between your results in items 1 and 2. Why should the differences be so large? What are some implications of the differences for pricing and analyzing the profitability of product lines?

ANSWER TO REVIEW PROBLEM

1.

	Bells	Whistles
Overhead cost, $8.60 × 1,600, $8.60 × 200	$13,760	$1,720

2. Computation of rates

Cost Driver	Amount in Pool	Amount of Activity	Rate
Direct labor hours	$520,000	100,000	$ 5.20
Number of batches	160,000	360	444.44
Engineering/design changes	60,000	120	500.00
Number of parts	120,000	3,200	37.50

	Bells	Whistles
Direct labor hours, $5.20 × 1,600, $5.20 × 200	$ 8,320	$ 1,040
Number of batches, $444 × 4, $444 × 12	1,776	5,328
Engineering/design changes, $500 × 2, $500 × 14	1,000	7,000
Number of parts, $37.50 × 22, $37.50 × 88	825	3,300
Totals	$11,921	$16,668

3. The differences are so large because Whistles consume much more of the non-volume-driven resources, which account for significant amounts of cost. Bells are relatively more labor-intensive and so draw much more overhead cost under the single-driver method. Some implications are:

- The apparent profitability of the two lines, and others, will change considerably under the two methods. Using ABC should give the company a better idea of what product lines are contributing, because it better shows how the lines demand use of resources.
- Prices set under the two methods will differ. The ABC-based prices will better reflect the consumption of resources, especially as between high-volume, bread-and-butter lines and specialty, niche lines.

APPENDIX: REGRESSION ANALYSIS

Regression analysis is a technique for fitting a straight line to a set of data. In contrast to the high-low method, regression analysis can use more than two observations. In contrast to the scatter-diagram method, regression analysis fits a mathematically precise line, rather than one that depends on the judgment of the manager drawing the line to fit the data. The procedures for developing a regression equation are laborious if done by hand, but you can easily set up and solve a regression using a computer spreadsheet. Some hand-held calculators also can solve regressions.

Although regression analysis is used for many purposes, our main interest here is predicting cost behavior—determining the fixed and variable components of a cost or pool of costs associated with a cost driver. Regression provides an equation of the same form as do the high-low and scatter-diagram methods.

Total cost = fixed component + (variable rate × activity)

Regression analysis also provides measures that indicate how well the costs are associated with the measure of activity (cost driver) used. Thus, you can test several drivers to determine which seems to predict costs best. The first step, then, in using regression analysis is deciding which cost driver to use—sales dollars, production in units, number of sales invoices prepared, hours worked by direct laborers, or number of parts and components in a product. Once a possible driver has been selected, the procedures for developing the regression equation are relatively mechanical.

We present two techniques, simple and multiple regression, in this appendix. In simple regression, the equation uses one cost driver (independent variable) to explain costs (dependent variable). In multiple regression, the equation uses more than one independent variable to explain the dependent variable. Assignments in the text do not require the use of multiple regression in this text and discuss it only briefly.

SIMPLE REGRESSION

Developing a regression equation requires the solving of two equations simultaneously. The calculations are quite involved and we shall not illustrate them. Instead, we show the regression results that Lotus 1-2-3® gives using the data in the example in the chapter (page 85).

Regression Output:

Constant	$7,731.78
Std Err of Y Est	$1,763.16
R Squared	0.954921527
No. of Observations	12
Degrees of Freedom	10
X Coefficient(s)	$1.766778
Std Err of Coef.	$0.121390

The constant, 7,731.78 is the value for *a*, the estimate of the fixed component of cost. The variable component, *b* is the 1.766778 shown as the X Coefficient(s). (Lotus 1-2-3 allows you to do multiple regression, where you will have more than one *b* value, hence the (s).) We used 12 observations, shown as No. of Observations. The value for Degrees of Freedom, 10, is not important to us. The other three items relate to the goodness of fit of the regression line. We shall not discuss the standard error of the coefficient, 0.121390, but we take up the other measures below.

CORRELATION AND THE STANDARD ERROR

Managers using the estimates of *a* and *b* want to have some idea about the accuracy of the predictions. Measures of *goodness of fit* tell us how well the regression line fits the data, and therefore suggest to managers how good their predictions are likely to be. The two measures we discuss are the coefficient of determination, often called r^2 (R Squared in the printout) and the standard error of the estimate (Std Err of Y Est in the printout). The coefficient of determination is a measure of how well the regression line accounts for the changes in Y, the dependent variable. The value is the percentage of the variation in Y that is "explained" by the movement of X, so its value can range from zero through 1. A value of 1 means that the regression line is perfect: all points fall on it. A value near zero means that the values of Y are randomly scattered with no relationship to the values of X. The coefficient of determination (r^2) for our example is 0.954921527. The result indicates an excellent fit of the line to the data, so predictions using the regression equation should be good. Again, however, we have only twelve observations to keep down the calculations. Using more observations, say 20 to 30, would make us more confident of the equation.

Exhibit 3-8 shows scatter diagrams for two cases, one with high correlation, one with low correlation. Using machine hours as the independent variable, your predictions of Cost W would be closer to their actual results than those of Cost T. Perhaps you could better predict Cost T using some other measure of activity, or perhaps Cost T is not driven by any activity, but is just random. The coefficient of determination for Cost W will be high, for Cost T it will be low. You might find it helpful to know how the coefficient is calculated.

$$r^2 = 1 - \frac{\Sigma (Y - Y_c)^2}{\Sigma (Y - \overline{Y})^2}$$

The differences, $Y - Y_c$ are the differences between the actual values of Y and those predicted by the regression equation. The differences, $Y - \overline{Y}$ are the

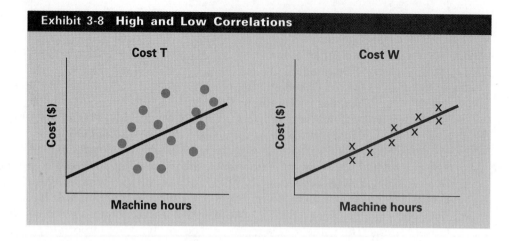

Exhibit 3-8   High and Low Correlations

differences between the actual values of Y and the mean, or average of the values of Y. (The differences are squared for reasons we shall not discuss here.)

A rough interpretation of r^2 follows. If you had no values for X and had to predict Y using only the past values of Y, your best prediction is the average of previous costs. The variation around that mean is the denominator of the last term of the equation and, because that variation is large, your predictions will be well off most of the time. For instance, the average value of Y is $27,858. But the actual values that you would have tried to predict range from $14,800 to $40,800. Your predictions for those months would have been off by about $13,000. In some months you would have been closer, but not as close as you would have been using the regression equation.

The numerator of the last term of the equation is the unexplained variation, the variation that remains after incorporating the independent variable. If r^2 is 1, the unexplained variation is zero, and all of the observations fall on the regression line.

The standard error of the estimate of Y (S_e) is a measure of the variation around the regression line as is shown by its calculation.[5]

$$S_e = \sqrt{\frac{\Sigma (Y - Y_c)^2}{n - 2}}$$

The lower the standard error of the estimate, the better. The standard error is zero if the regression line is perfect and all observations fall on it. (Note that the numerator in the standard error calculation uses the same values as the numerator in the r^2 calculation.). In our example, the standard error is 1,763.16, shown as Std Err of Y Est.

Statistical theory tells us that roughly 68 percent of the actual values of cost lie within one standard error of their predicted values, about 95 percent within

---

5   *The divisor is actually the number of observations minus the number of coefficients estimated in the equation. We estimate* a *and* b *here. In multiple regression, we could have three or more coefficients and the divisor will increase accordingly.*

two standard errors.[6] With the standard error of $1,763, actual cost will be within $1,763 of its predicted value about 68 percent of the time, and within $3,526 (2 × $1,763) about 95 percent of the time. Assuming a cost prediction at the average of about $28,000, 95 percent of the time actual cost should differ by no more than 12.6% ($3,526/28,000). Thus, the standard error of the estimate, like r^2, suggests a good fit of the regression line to the data.

SELECTING A COST-PREDICTION EQUATION

We now have three cost-prediction formulas for maintenance cost. The high-low method result is on page 85, the scatter-diagram result on page 87.

high-low   *maintenance cost = $4,800 + $2   × machine hours*
scatter-diagram   *maintenance cost = $7,200 + $1.82 × machine hours*
regression analysis   *maintenance cost = $7,732 + $1.77 × machine hours*

Which one should the company use? The regression method gives the best results. It is objectively determined, uses all observations, and has good measures of goodness of fit.

PROBLEMS AND PITFALLS

A basic assumption in using regression analysis is that the data that have been collected are representative. That is, it is assumed that the conditions under which the cost-volume observations were assembled were about the same and can be expected to continue. As we suggested in the chapter, if one or more of the observations used in the analysis are not representative of normal conditions, the regression line would not be as useful a prediction tool as desired.

Consider the scatter diagram in Exhibit 3-8 for Cost W. Suppose Cost W is maintenance and repairs plotted against machine hours. Picture an observation of a very high cost at a very low volume, well up the left-hand part of the scatter diagram. Such an observation, called an outlier, has a disproportionate effect on a regression equation. Such an observation is clearly unusual and might best be ignored in developing the equation. That observation might have been from a month in which the plant was shut down for a considerable period for extensive repair work. The high cost of repairs combined with the low volume of machine hours makes the observation nonrepresentative. Great care must be taken in "throwing out" observations, but if a particular observation occurred for unusual reason, it is best to ignore it.

One final caution. Like the predictions from using the high-low and scatter-diagram methods, those resulting from regression analysis depend for their validity on observations over a particular range of activity, that is, the range over which the observations were gathered. Care must be taken in using any of these methods to predict costs for levels of activity not included within the range over which the observations were gathered. For example, if costs of power to operate machines have been analyzed in a range from 500 to 800 hours

---

6 *The following is very rough. We are simply illustrating the principle of the standard error of the estimate. The actual intervals within which predicted costs are likely to fall are wider than the standard error of the estimate.*

of machine time per week; there is no reason to assume that the relationships that held over that range will hold also at 350 hours or 1,100 hours.

MULTIPLE REGRESSION

Multiple regression analysis uses more than one independent variable to generate a cost-prediction equation. In a modern business, many costs depend on more than one activity. The cost of heating a factory depends both on the number of hours it is open and on the outside temperature. Shipping costs depend on both the weight of the goods and the distance over which they must travel.

A multiple regression equation has the following general form.

$$Y = a + b_1X_1 + b_2X_2 + \ldots + b_nX_n$$

where

$$
\begin{aligned}
Y &= \textit{the dependent variable to be predicted} \\
X_1 \ldots X_n &= \textit{the values of the various independent variables influencing the} \\
&\quad\ \textit{value of } Y \\
b_1 \ldots b_n &= \textit{the coefficients of the various independent variables} \\
a &= \textit{the fixed component (as in simple regression)}
\end{aligned}
$$

Suppose the manager of a factory that makes a number of products has requested an analysis of manufacturing overhead costs. The managerial accountant, working in conjunction with a statistician, came up with the following analysis.

Fixed component of manufacturing overhead cost	$32,500 per month (a)
Variable components (independent variables):	
Direct labor hours (X_1)	$2.40 per hour ($b_1$)
Machine hours (X_2)	$1.80 per hour ($b_2$)
Number of setups (X_3)	$80.00 per setup ($b_3$)

The accountant and the statistical consultant have found that variations in three variables (direct labor hours, machine hours, and number of setups) better describe variations in total overhead costs than do variations in any one or combination of two such variables. Such a conclusion is reasonable when one considers that many overhead costs (fringe benefits, for example) are related to labor time and some (like power, supplies, and lubricants) are readily associated with machine time. Still others, such as the wages paid to workers who set up machines and the materials they use, depend on the number of setups or hours spent doing setups.

Suppose, now, that the factory manager expects the following activity in the coming month.

Direct labor hours	20,000
Machine hours	15,000
Setups	200

The manager would predict total manufacturing overhead of $123,500.

$$
\begin{array}{c}
\text{Total} \\
\text{manufacturing} = \\
\text{overhead}
\end{array}
\begin{array}{c}
\text{fixed} \\
\text{cost}
\end{array}
+
\begin{array}{c}
\text{costs} \\
\text{variable with} \\
\text{direct labor} \\
\text{hours}
\end{array}
+
\begin{array}{c}
\text{costs} \\
\text{variable with} \\
\text{machine hours}
\end{array}
+
\begin{array}{c}
\text{costs} \\
\text{variable with} \\
\text{setups}
\end{array}
$$

$$
= \$32,500 + (\$2.40 \times 20,000) + (\$1.80 \times 15,000) + (\$80.00 \times 200)
$$
$$
= \$32,500 + \quad \$48,000 \quad + \quad \$27,000 \quad + \quad \$16,000
$$

The cautions associated with simple regression also apply here, plus one more. Multiple regression analysis requires the assumption that the independent variables are not correlated with each other. In our example, for instance, knowing whether direct labor hours and machine hours (or some other combination of the three independent variables) are closely associated is important. If two (or more) of the independent variables are highly correlated, the results of multiple regression analysis must be used with care and the underlying statistical problems must be understood. Your statistics courses will address these problems.

A multiple regression equation also has a coefficient of determination and a standard error of the estimate, but the calculations are somewhat different than they are for simple regression and we shall omit them.

In summary, when using either simple or multiple regression analysis, you must understand the statistical principles that underlie these approaches. Critical to the production of useful results under either approach is the need for the observations to be representative of conditions expected to prevail during the period for which predictions are being made.

REVIEW PROBLEM—APPENDIX

The controller of Tuscany Products has just received the following results from the company's statistician.

$$
Y = \$326,389 + \$8.625X, \ r^2 = 0.712, \ S_e = \$16,352
$$
$$
Y = \text{monthly factory power cost}, \ X = \text{machine hours}
$$

The statistician collected the data in a range of 20,000 to 30,000 machine hours.

Required
1. Calculate the expected power cost at 22,000 machine hours.
2. Explain the meaning of the equation and of each component of the equation and the measures of goodness of fit. Also indicate the usefulness of each item in cost analysis.

ANSWER TO REVIEW PROBLEM
1. $516,139 ($326,389 + $8.625 × 22,000)
2. The equation itself tells us that factory power cost has a fixed component of $326,389 per month and a variable component of $8.625 per machine hour. We can therefore predict power cost by using the equation, as we did in item 1.

We can find the total variable cost of power for a product or component that we manufacture by multiplying $8.625 by the number of machine hours the manufactured item requires.

The coefficient of determination, r^2 of 0.712, or 71.2%, tells us the percentage of the variation in power cost that is associated with changes in machine hours. The relatively high value for r^2 indicates a good fit.

The standard error of the estimate, S_e, tells us how close our predictions are likely to be to the actual results. In this case, we expect predictions to be within $16,352 about 68% of the time, within $32,704 (2 × $16,352) about 95% of the time.

It is also helpful to understand what the results do not tell you. The equation is not necessarily the best available. Some other factor might predict better. Multiple regression with some other factors might give better results, higher r^2, and a lower standard error.

One last point. The intercept, $326,389, is *not* the estimate of total cost at zero machine hours. The data were collected in the range of 20,000-30,000 hours and it is unsafe to extrapolate outside that range.

ASSIGNMENT MATERIAL

QUESTIONS FOR DISCUSSION

3-1   Cost classification   Indicate whether each of the following items of cost is likely to be discretionary or committed. If in doubt, describe the circumstances under which the cost would fall into one or the other category. If the cost is mixed, consider only the fixed portion.

(a) Straight-line depreciation on building.
(b) Sum-of-years'-digits depreciation on a machine.
(c) Salaries of salespeople.
(d) Salaries of president and vice presidents for production, sales, and finance.
(e) Fees for consultants on long-range planning.
(f) Utilities for factory—heating and lighting.
(g) Management development costs—costs of attending seminars, training programs, etc.

3-2   High-low method   The chief cost analyst of Kraco, Inc. recommended the following approach to estimating the fixed and variable components of manufacturing overhead costs such as supervision, indirect labor, and supplies.

Estimate the total cost the company would incur if it shut down, and treat that amount as fixed cost. Then estimate the total cost working at 100% of capacity, stated in machine hours. Divide the difference in the two cost figures by the machine hours at capacity and treat that as the variable component.

Required
Comment on the suggested procedure. Would the formula derived from it work well for the company if it normally operated between 75% and 90% of capacity?

3-3   Cost analysis   In 1994, **Levi Strauss** announced that it would stop selling to stores that did not order at least $10,000 worth of product annually. (Greenville SC *News*, September 2, 1994, C7)

Required
How do you think Levi Strauss came to this decision? What analyses might have prompted the decision?

3-4   *Methods of cost behavior analysis (related to Appendix)* Discuss the advantages and disadvantages of the high-low, scatter-diagram, and regression methods of cost estimation.

3-5   *Cost classification* Melton Company sells a variety of industrial products. It operates eight regional sales offices. State whether each of the following costs is likely to be (a) avoidable or unavoidable in deciding whether to stop selling in the South-Central region, and (b) direct or indirect to the South-Central office.

(a) Salaries of salespeople in the South-Central region.
(b) Rent on the South-Central office. There are five years left on the lease.
(c) Rent on equipment used in the South-Central regional office. The equipment can be returned with one week's notice.
(d) Salaries of the national vice president for sales and her staff.
(e) National advertising.
(f) Travel expenses of salespeople working in the South-Central region.

3-6   *Cost classification* Talley Industries makes small fiberglass boats. It has two production departments, the Forming Department and the Finishing Department. State whether each of the following costs is likely to be (a) avoidable or unavoidable and (b) direct or indirect to the Forming Department.

(a) Wages of workers in the Forming Department.
(b) Property taxes on the factory building.
(c) Depreciation on machinery used only in the Forming Department.
(d) Salaries of the plant controller and her staff.
(e) Salary of the Forming Department manager.
(f) Wages of maintenance workers who take care of all machinery in the factory.

3-7   *Cost drivers* A recent annual report of **Intuit**, the software company that sells the popular Quicken™ personal finance program, contained the following comments.

"The majority of these costs [customer service and technical support costs, mainly for telephone assistance] consist of fixed costs such as salary expense for permanent, full-time employees, and as such do not fluctuate as a direct function of seasonal variations in the Company's product sales."

Required
What activities do you believe drive these costs?

3-8   *Cost and activities* *Fortune* (September 19, 1994, p. 226, "Companies to Watch") reported that **DIY Home Warehouse** carries fewer models than its competitors, such as 20 types of hammer to 70 for other companies, and that DIY's break-even point is lower because of its lack of variety.

Required
Why do you think DIY's break-even point is lower?

EXERCISES

3-9   *Accuracy of predictions* The following scatter diagrams show two costs plotted against production.

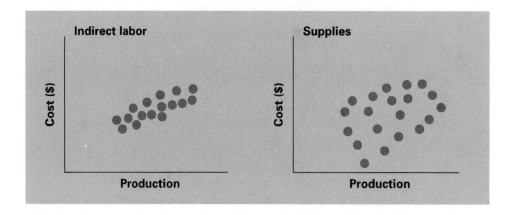

Required

Which cost can you predict and plan for more easily? Explain.

3-10   *Mixed costs*   The president of Gorman Company has asked you to develop a behavioral classification for indirect labor cost. You have the following data from two recent months.

Direct Labor Hours	Indirect Labor Cost
19,000	$47,600
27,000	$60,800

Required

Compute the fixed and variable portions of indirect labor cost based on direct labor hours.

 3-11   *Cost behavior (related to Appendix)*   A study of office supplies used in the regional sales offices of a large manufacturer shows that the cost is mixed. A record of sales and corresponding supply costs in one of the offices is as follows.

Monthly Sales	Cost of Supplies
$430,000	$21,640
480,000	24,860
340,000	21,150
520,000	25,210
370,000	23,150
380,000	24,640
450,000	27,280
560,000	29,840
500,000	26,520

Required

1. Determine the variable cost percentage of sales and the fixed costs using the high-low method.
2. If you have access to a spreadsheet that does regression analysis, use it to determine the fixed and variable components of supplies cost. Comment on the differences between the cost prediction equations given by the two methods.
3. Comment on the measures of goodness of fit the regression analysis generates. Will the equation predict supplies costs well?

3-12   *Revenue and cost analysis—high-low method*   The controller of your firm, a retail store, is attempting to develop CVP relationships to be used for planning and control. He is not sure how this might be done and asks for your assistance. He has prepared two income statements from monthly data.

	October	November
Sales	$ 50,000	$ 60,000
Cost of goods sold	30,000	36,000
Gross profit	$ 20,000	$ 24,000
Operating expenses:		
Selling expenses	$ 7,400	$ 7,700
Administrative expenses	6,200	6,400
Total expenses	$ 13,600	$ 14,100
Income	$ 6,400	$ 9,900

Required
1. Determine the fixed and variable components of cost of goods sold, selling expenses, and administrative expenses.
2. Prepare a contribution margin income statement based on sales of $70,000.

3-13   *Explaining regression analysis (related to Appendix)*   The controller of ARCON, Inc. has received the following regression results from the industrial engineering department.

Y = *monthly manufacturing supplies cost, X = machine hours*
$Y = \$78,331 + \$1.0647X$, $r^2 = .6181$, $S_e = \$10,113$

The data were collected in a range of 40,000 to 50,000 monthly machine hours. The controller wants your assistance in explaining these results to a group of managers.

Required
Write a memorandum that explains the meaning and significance of each of the items in the regression results. Use the guidelines in Appendix A.

3-14   *Interpretation of scatter diagram*   The following graph depicts the costs experienced by Magma Enterprises.

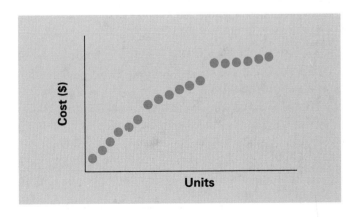

Required

1. Give some possible reasons for the observed behavior of costs.
2. How would you plan for costs that exhibited this type of behavior?

3-15 *High-low method for manufacturing company* The chief accountant of Blackman Industries prepared the following income statements.

	June	July
Sales	$420,000	$450,000
Cost of sales	226,000	235,000
Gross margin	$194,000	$215,000
Selling and administrative expenses	105,000	108,000
Income before taxes	$ 89,000	$107,000

Blackman produces a single product.

Required

1. Determine the fixed and variable components of cost of sales and of selling and administrative expenses.
2. Prepare income statements for June and July using the contribution-margin format. Comment on the differences between the statements above and the ones that you prepared.

3-16 *Relationships* Answer the following questions, considering each situation independently. You may not be able to answer the questions in the order they are asked.

1. A company earns $60,000 selling 80,000 units at $5 per unit. Its fixed costs are $180,000.
   (a) What are variable costs per unit?
   (b) What is total contribution margin?
   (c) What would income be if sales increased by 5,000 units?
2. A company has return of sales of 10%, income of $30,000, a selling price of $10, and a contribution margin of 30%.
   (a) What are fixed costs?
   (b) What are variable costs per unit?
   (c) What are sales in units?
   (d) What are sales in dollars?
3. A company has return of sales of 15% at sales of $300,000. Its fixed costs are $75,000; variable costs are $6 per unit.
   (a) What are sales in units?
   (b) What is contribution margin per unit?
   (c) What is income?

3-17 *Using per-unit data* Nimmer Company expects the following per-unit results at a volume of 80,000 units.

Sales		$4.00
Variable costs	$1.40	
Fixed costs	2.25	3.65
Profit		$0.35

Required

Answer the following questions independently of one another.

1. How many units must the company sell to earn a profit of $90,000?
2. If Nimmer could sell 70,000 units, what selling price will yield a $60,000 profit?
3. Nimmer can undertake an advertising campaign for $6,000. Volume will increase by 3,000 units at the $4 selling price. By how much and in which direction (increase or decrease) will the company's profit change if it takes the action?

3-18 *Percentage income statement* The president of Fillmore Industries has developed the following income statement showing expected percentage results at sales of $800,000.

Sales	100%
Cost of sales	50%
Gross margin	50%
Other expenses	40%
Income	10%

The president tells you that cost of sales is all variable and that the only other variable cost is commissions, which are 20% of sales.

Required

1. Determine the profit that the company expects to earn.
2. Determine fixed costs, the break-even point, and the margin of safety.
3. If sales are $700,000, what will profit be?
4. The president wants a $120,000 profit. Expected unit volume is the same as for the statement above. By what percentage must the company increase its selling price to achieve the goal? Assume the per-unit cost of sales remains constant.

3-19 *Cost behavior graphs (AICPA adapted)* Following are graphs and descriptions of cost elements. For each description, select the letter of the graph that best shows the behavior of the cost. Graphs may be used more than once. The zero point for each graph is the intersection of the horizontal and vertical axes. The vertical axis represents total cost for the described cost and the horizontal axis represents production in units. Be prepared to discuss any assumptions you might have to make in selecting your answers.

1. Depreciation of equipment, using the units-of-production method.
2. Electricity bill, a flat charge plus a variable cost after a certain number of kilowatt-hours are used.
3. City water bill, computed as follows:

First 1,000,000 gallons or less	$1,000 flat fee
Next 10,000 gallons	0.003 per gallon used
Next 10,000 gallons	0.006 per gallon used
Next 10,000 gallons	0.009 per gallon used
etc., etc., etc.	

4. Cost of lubricant for machines, where cost per unit decreases with each pound of lubricant used (for example, if one pound is used, the cost is $10.00; if two pounds are used, the cost is $19.98; if three pounds are used, the cost is $29.94; with a minimum cost per pound of $9.25).

5. Depreciation of equipment, using the straight-line method.

6. Rent for a factory building donated by the city, where the agreement calls for a fixed-fee payment unless 200,000 person-hours are worked, in which case no rent need be paid.

7. Salaries of repairpeople, where one repairperson is needed for every 1,000 hours of machine time or less (i.e., 0 to 1,000 hours requires one repairperson, 1,001 to 2,000 hours requires two repairpeople, etc.).

8. Federal unemployment compensation taxes, where the labor force is constant in number throughout the year and the average annual wage is $16,000. The tax is levied only on the first $8,500 earned by each employee.

9. Rent for production machinery, computed as follows:

First 10,000 hours of use	$20,000 flat fee
Next 2,000 hours of use	$1.90 per hour
Next 2,000 hours of use	$1.80 per hour
Next 2,000 hours of use	$1.70 per hour
etc., etc., etc.	

10. Rent for a factory building donated by the county, where the agreement calls for rent of $100,000 less $1 for each hour laborers worked in excess of 200,000 hours, but a minimum rental payment of $20,000 is required.

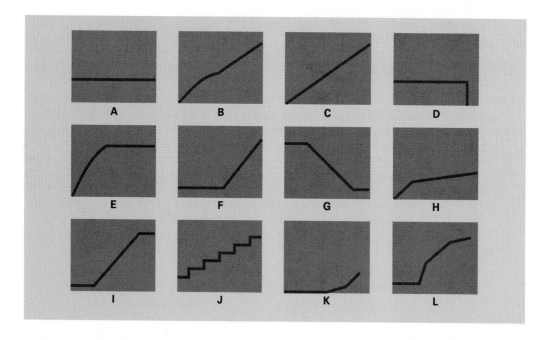

3-20   ABC for shipping department   Boswell Company, a large wholesaler of grocery and household products, has been implementing ABC in several functions. The shipping department, which averages about $626,000 in monthly costs, is now ready for analysis. The controller is interested in attributing shipping costs to two principal types of customers, supermarkets and convenience stores, but wonders whether it is worthwhile to use ABC. Boswell has been using dollar volume of orders to evaluate customers and the controller believes this practice is probably working well.

The controller's assistant worked up the following data using very rough, preliminary estimates, to see whether a more careful study might be likely to produce results significantly different from the current method.

Cost/Pool Driver	Amount in Pool	Amount of Activity	Rate
Dollar volume of orders	$246,000	$6,000,000	$0.04100
Number of customers	180,000	280	642.86
Number of orders	80,000	680	117.65
Number of stocks	120,000	3,200	37.50
Total shipping costs	$626,000		

The number of stocks is a weighted average of the number of items in each order and the number of units of each item. Orders containing many items in small quantities require more time for the forklift operators. The assistant left costs that she could not easily identify with other drivers in the pool driven by dollar volume. Dollar volume also drives some costs, such as credit checking.

The following data relate to the two main classes of customers.

	Supermarkets	Convenience Stores
Dollar volume of orders	$4,500,000	$1,500,000
Number of customers	80	200
Number of orders	220	460
Number of stocks	2,000	1,200

Required
1. Allocate the costs of the shipping department based on the dollar volume of orders.
2. Allocate the costs of the shipping department using ABC rates.
3. Does it appear that the company might benefit from pursuing the use of ABC for the shipping department?

3-21   *Target profits and unit prices* Tina's Handicrafts sells handmade sweaters at $50 apiece. The company acquires the sweaters from Ms. Posey at $30 apiece, but the agreement with her also requires an extra fee of 10% (of selling price) for each sweater sold. Monthly fixed costs are $3,000.

Required
Answer each of the following questions independently.
1. If the company wants to earn a profit of $3,000 a month before taxes, how many sweaters must it sell?
2. The company wants a before-tax profit of $5,000 and expects to sell 500 sweaters. What price must be charged per sweater to obtain the desired level of profit?
3. Suppose the company is selling 500 sweaters per month at $50 and making a before-tax profit of $4,500. Ms. Posey offers to renegotiate the buying agreement so that there would be a charge of $24 per sweater plus a 20% (based on selling price) fee per sweater sold. How many sweaters must the company sell under the new agreement to earn the same $4,500 in before-tax profits?

PROBLEMS

3-22   *Profit improvement alternatives*   Following is the income statement for Meriwether Company for 19X6.

Sales (100,000 × $10)	$1,000,000
Variable costs (100,000 × $6)	600,000
Contribution margin	$ 400,000
Fixed costs	360,000
Profit	$ 40,000

Leslie Meriwether, president of the company, was not happy with the 19X6 results and stated that a profit of $100,000 was a reasonable target for 19X7. She instructed the controller to analyze each component of the statement separately and determine the change in each component that would allow the company to earn the target profit of $100,000. (For example, what change in per-unit selling price would produce the target profit if sales volume, fixed costs, and per-unit variable costs remained constant; or what change in sales volume would be needed, assuming that prices and costs did not change?)

Required
Write a memorandum to Ms. Meriwether that summarizes your findings and indicates what changes might be easier to achieve. Use the guidelines in Appendix A.

3-23   *Interpretation of data*   Your assistant used the following scatter diagram to separate maintenance expenses into the fixed and variable components. She derived the following equation: Monthly total cost = $350 + ($0.80 × machine hours), which is represented by the line drawn on the diagram.

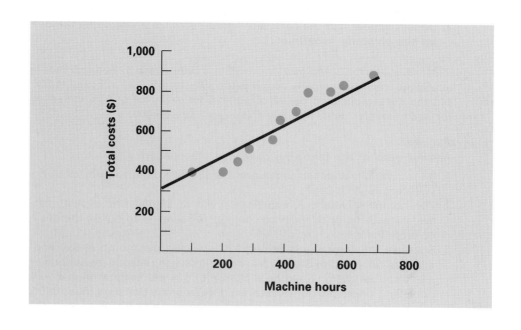

Required

Comment on the way in which your assistant fitted the line to the data and make an alternative recommendation.

3-24 Activity-based cost analysis The controller of the Wellcome Plant of RKD Industries has been analyzing costs of support departments to identify the major cost drivers and is seeking ways to reduce costs. He has just finished analyzing the costs and activity of the production scheduling department. The schedulers determine when particular products will be made, what machinery will be used, and how large the batch will be. Scheduling has come under increasing pressure as the number of products the plant manufactures has increased. The controller has assembled the following information regarding scheduling costs and the number of different products being made. All amounts are in thousands.

Quarter	Number of Products	Costs of Production Scheduling Department
19X6 Q4	5.2	$93.0
19X6 Q3	5.2	84.0
19X6 Q2	4.2	83.8
19X6 Q1	4.1	82.3
19X5 Q4	4.0	75.1
19X5 Q3	3.2	74.0
19X5 Q2	3.2	67.0
19X5 Q1	2.7	66.0

Required

Analyze the scheduling department costs using a scatter diagram or regression analysis. Comment on the usefulness of the results for pursuing cost reduction.

3-25 Cost drivers For each of the following costs, indicate which activity of those listed below might drive it. Some activities might drive more than one cost, some might drive none of the listed costs. You might also suggest activities not listed.

Costs	Activities
Machine maintenance	Direct labor hours
Wages of workers who reset machinery when products change	Number of parts in a product
	Number of employees
Costs of inspecting incoming materials and components	Number of products
	Number of sales orders
Costs of keeping records on workers—how much they produce, what they earn	Number of customers
	Number of components/parts stocked
Costs of inspecting finished products	Number of suppliers
Costs to rework defective units	Number of incoming shipments
Building maintenance	Number of outgoing shipments
Personnel department costs, including payroll processing costs	Number of production runs of individual products
Purchasing department costs, including soliciting bids from vendors and preparing, reviewing, and auditing purchase orders	Production in units
	Sales in dollars
	Machine hours
Customer billing	Space in factory

3-26   Delta Airlines cost structure   A recent annual report of **Delta Airlines** contained the following data, in millions of dollars.

Operating revenues	$8,582.2
Operating expenses	$8,162.7
Operating income	$419.5
Load factor (percentage of available seat-miles occupied)	61.15%
Break-even load factor	57.96%

Required
1. Determine the variable cost as a percentage of revenue for Delta Airlines. (Hint: Find total revenue and total cost at break even, then use the high-low method.)
2. Determine fixed operating costs for Delta Airlines.
3. Determine what operating income Delta Airlines would have earned had it flown its aircraft 62.15% full (one percentage point higher than it actually did).
4. What does your answer to item 3 tell you about how to be successful in the airline industry?

3-27   Multiple regression analysis (related to Appendix)   Your boss at AJK Company has just handed you the following results of a regression analysis.

$$Y = \$49,272 + \$1.78L + \$2.68M$$

where

Y = total monthly manufacturing overhead cost
L = labor hours
M = machine hours

AJK plans to use 12,000 labor hours and 2,000 machine hours next month.

Required
1. Determine the total manufacturing overhead cost that AJK should incur next month.
2. AJK makes a product that has $6 in materials cost. It requires two hours of labor time and 30 minutes of machine time. Laborers earn $10 per hour. What is the product's per-unit variable manufacturing cost?
3. Suppose that AJK could reduce the labor time for the product described in item 2 by 30 minutes, to 1.50 hours. Machine time will remain the same. By how much would the per-unit variable manufacturing cost fall?

3-28   Understanding regression results (related to Appendix)   The controller of the Cromwell Plant of TAYCO Enterprises has the following regression results prepared by the plant's statistician.

$$Y = \$61,424 + \$2.067X, \ r^2 = .7731, \ S_e = \$12,206$$
$$Y = \text{monthly power cost}, \ X = \text{machine hours}$$

The results are based on the past 30 months of operations, during which monthly machine hours ranged from 80,000 to 140,000. The controller wants you to explain the results to some of her staff.

Required

1. If the plant will work 100,000 machine hours next month, what is the predicted power cost?
2. If the plant shuts down next month, should power cost be $61,424?
3. The company is considering a new product that requires 45 machine hours per batch of 100 units. What is the variable cost of power for the product?
4. How close are your predictions of power costs likely to be to the actual results? For example, can you state the range within which actual cost should be some specified percentage of the time?
5. Can you tell whether this equation is the best available to predict power costs?

3-29 Review problem, including income taxes, Chapters 2 and 3 (continued in Chapter 4)   After reviewing its cost structure (variable costs of $7.50 per unit and monthly fixed costs of $60,000) and potential market, Forecast Company established what it considered to be a reasonable selling price. The company expected to sell 50,000 units per month and planned its monthly results as follows.

Sales	$500,000
Variable costs	375,000
Contribution margin	$125,000
Fixed costs	60,000
Income before taxes	$ 65,000
Income taxes (at 40%)	26,000
Net income	$ 39,000

Required

On the basis of the preceding information, answer the following questions independently. Items with an asterisk involve income taxes.

1. What selling price did the company establish?
2. What is the contribution margin per unit?
3. What is the break-even point in units?
4. If the company determined that a particular advertising campaign had a high probability of increasing sales by 3,000 units, how much could it pay for such a campaign without reducing its planned profits?
5. If the company wants a $60,000 before-tax profit, how many units must it sell?
6. If the company wants a 10% before-tax return on sales, what level of sales, in dollars, does it need?
*7. If the company wants a $45,000 after-tax profit, how many units must it sell?
*8. If the company wants an after-tax return on sales of 9%, how many units must it sell?
*9. If the company wants an after-tax profit of $45,000 on its expected sales volume of 50,000 units, what price must it charge?
10. If the company wants a before-tax return on sales of 16% on its expected sales volume of 50,000 units, what price must it charge?
11. The company is considering offering its salespeople a 5% commission on sales. What would the total sales, in dollars, have to be in order to implement the commission plan and still earn the planned before-tax income of $65,000?

3-30   *Cost formula, high-low method* The owner of Bed and Bath Boutique regularly uses part-time help in addition to full-time employees. Some part-time help is needed every day for miscellaneous chores and the owner arranges for additional hours based on estimates of sales for the following week. The following is a record of the wages paid to part-time employees at recent monthly sales volumes.

Sales	Wages Paid to Part-Time Help
$ 8,265	$ 629
1,980	558
6,340	710
17,600	1,360
18,000	1,350
13,800	1,130
15,000	1,466
5,000	675
11,000	1,014

The owner considers these months to be relatively normal; however, in the month with sales of $1,980, the Boutique was closed for over two weeks for repainting and the installation of new carpeting.

Required
Determine the variable cost rate and fixed costs using the high-low method.

3-31   *Fixed costs in decision making* Warren Keith owns a restaurant in a suburb of a large city. The restaurant does not do very much business during August, and Keith is considering closing down and taking a vacation for the month. He develops the following income statement based on planned operations for August.

Sales		$ 22,500
Cost of sales		9,700
Gross margin		$ 12,800
Wages to part-time help	$3,800	
Utilities	1,650	
Rent on building	1,500	
Depreciation on fixtures	750	
Supplies and miscellaneous	4,550	12,250
Income		$ 550

Keith believes it is not worthwhile to stay open unless he can net at least $2,000 for the month. He works hard when the restaurant is open and believes that he deserves at least that much to compensate him for the work he does.

He also tells you that if he closes, he will have to pay a minimum utility bill of $350. Supplies and miscellaneous expenses are fixed, but are avoidable if he closed.

Required
Write a memorandum that advises Mr. Keith about the desirability of staying open for August. Use the guidelines in Appendix A.

3-32   Alternative cost structures—a movie company (continuation of 2-43)   Lois Lane, the president of Blockbusters Incorporated, has reviewed the preliminary analysis of the two contract alternatives and wishes to give further consideration to the arrangements with Kirkwalker. Kirkwalker's agent is also having second thoughts about the alternatives and is wondering what is best for his client.

Required
Answer the following questions.
1. If total paid admissions are expected to be between $9 and $10 million, which compensation scheme is best for (a) Blockbusters and (b) Kirkwalker? (Hint: Refer to your answers in 2-43 regarding break-even points.)
2. If total paid admissions are expected to be about $20 million, which scheme is better for (a) Blockbusters and (b) Kirkwalker?

3-33   Regression analysis (related to Appendix)   Your new assistant has just handed you the following results of a regression analysis.

Factory overhead = $262,203 + ($13.19 × units produced)

You are surprised because your company makes several models of lawn mowers and you had not thought it possible to express factory overhead so simply. Your assistant assures you that the results are correct, giving you the following data.

Month	Units Produced	Factory Overhead
January	1,700	$260,000
February	1,100	280,000
March	2,800	300,000
April	2,300	260,000
May	2,000	360,000
June	1,800	320,000
July	2,400	320,000
August	2,000	200,000
September	2,100	300,000

Required
Comment on your assistant's results. You should do a regression analysis using a spreadsheet or other program.

3-34   Alternative CVP graph   The following data are for three alternatives being considered by the managers of Sanders Company. Each represents a particular strategy for one of its products. The differences result from alternatives such as salaries versus commissions and different levels of product quality, advertising, and promotion.

Alternative	Price	Variable Cost	Fixed Costs
1	$20	$12	$180,000
2	$20	$ 8	$240,000
3	$18	$10	$120,000

When evaluating alternative strategies, the firm's managers prefer the following alternative graphical approach. It represents a graph with Alternative 1 already plotted.

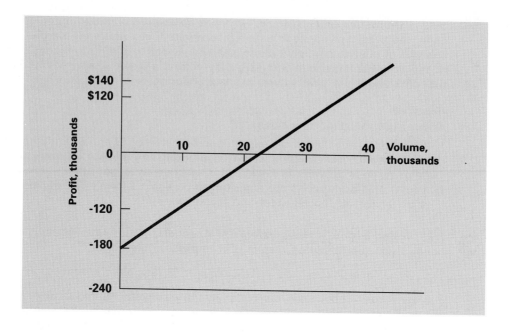

Required

1. Plot the profit lines for alternatives 2 and 3.
2. What general conclusions can you draw from the completed graph? Could you select the best alternative based on the graphical results?

3-35   *Changes in costs* Stoneham Company manufactures a complete line of toiletries. The average selling price per case is $20 and cost data follow.

Variable costs per case:	
Materials	$4.00
Labor	2.00
Other variable costs	2.00
Total variable costs	$8.00
Annual fixed costs:	
Manufacturing	$1,500,000
Selling and administrative	$2,500,000

Art Stoneham, the president, expects to sell 350,000 cases in the coming year. After gathering the above data, Stoneham learned that materials costs will increase by 25% because of shortages.

Required

1. Determine the profit that Stoneham expected before the increase in materials prices.
2. Given the increase in materials costs, determine the price that Stoneham has to charge to earn the profit you calculated in item 1.

3. Suppose that Stoneham decided to raise the price enough to maintain the same contribution margin percentage it had before the cost increase.
   (a) Determine the required price.
   (b) Would Stoneham earn more or less than your answer to item 2 if it charged that price and sold 350,000 cases?

3-36   Cost drivers, activity-based analysis The controller of the Summerton Division of KPL Industries was concerned that costs of some departments normally thought to be fixed had been rising over the past few years. The purchasing department had come in for special review because its costs had been rising rapidly. The purchasing manager argued that the division's increasing number of products and component parts had strained his resources. The division's products are similar, but product designers use parts that differ in size or other characteristics. Purchasing is responsible for finding and evaluating vendors, inspecting incoming shipments, reordering parts when needed, and other tasks associated with managing component parts.

The controller developed the following data related to quarterly costs of the purchasing department and the number of different component parts used in the division's products (not the total number of parts put into products). All amounts are in thousands.

Quarter	Number of Parts	Purchasing Department Costs
19X6 Q4	14.2	$123.1
19X6 Q3	14.1	115.1
19X6 Q2	12.8	111.7
19X6 Q1	11.0	109.0
19X5 Q4	10.9	106.7
19X5 Q3	10.8	106.6
19X5 Q2	10.1	104.6
19X5 Q1	10.1	100.1

Required
Analyze the purchasing department's costs using a scatter diagram or regression analysis. What do your results tell about cost reduction?

3-37   ABC for receiving department Wilson Company is a medium-sized manufacturer of industrial products. The company has implemented ABC for its manufacturing operations and is extending it to other functions. One of the managers involved in the study believes that receiving department costs should be allocated based on total manufacturing costs because it is simple. "I can understand using ABC for manufacturing, but not for some of these minor functions." The controller disagrees, and the two decide to do a brief, preliminary analysis to see if ABC makes sense for the receiving department.

They accumulate the following data.

Cost Driver	Amount of Overhead Cost in Pool	Amount of Activity
Total manufacturing costs	$ 440,000	$8,600,000
Number of shipments received	180,000	1,400
Number of orders requiring inspection	80,000	240
Total overhead cost	$ 700,000	

Orders requiring inspection are from vendors who have not yet passed Wilson's tests. All vendors go through this probationary period and the predominance of such orders is for specialty products that are continually undergoing design and manufacturing changes. The following data relate to Wilson's three major product lines.

	Line A	Line B	Line C
Total manufacturing costs	$4,500,000	$2,200,000	$1,900,000
Number of shipments received	440	320	640
Number of orders requiring inspection	10	25	205

Required

1. Determine the receiving department costs to be apportioned to each line using total manufacturing costs as the only cost driver.
2. Determine the receiving department costs to be apportioned to each line using ABC.
3. Comment on the differences. Should Wilson extend ABC to the receiving department?

3-38   *Cost structures and average costs*   At a dinner meeting of a local association of company accountants, the following conversation took place.

Ruth Hifixed: "My company has enormous fixed costs, and volume is our critical problem. My cost per unit is now $6, at 100,000 units, but if I could get 200,000 units, cost per unit would drop to $4. My selling price is also too low, only $6."

Jim Lofixed: "You are lucky. My cost per unit is $5 at 200,000 units, but we can't produce any more than 200,000. At least we're now better off than we were when sales were 80,000 units. At that volume we lost $0.50 per unit at our $6 price. We kept the same selling price at all volumes."

Required

1. Compute the profit earned by each company at its current level of sales.
2. Determine fixed costs, variable cost per unit, and contribution margin per unit for each firm.
3. Compute the break-even point for each firm.
4. Which company earns more at 150,000 units?
5. Which company earns more at 100,000 units?

3-39   *Cost classification*   Halton's Flower Shop buys and sells floral arrangements. The average selling price is $25, and average purchase cost is $5. Weekly fixed costs are $4,000. Because the arrangements are perishable, the shop cannot sell any units after they have been in inventory for one week. The shop must order a full week's supply at one time.

   Mr. Halton, the owner, would like to earn $1,000 per week from the business. A friend has explained CVP analysis to him and made the following calculation.

$$\text{Unit volume required for \$1,000 profit} = \frac{\$4,000 + \$1,000}{\$25 - \$5}$$
$$= 250 \text{ arrangements}$$

Required

1. Is the above equation correct in the sense that if Mr. Halton orders 250 arrangements per week, he will earn $1,000? Why or why not?

2. Is the purchase cost fixed or variable? Explain.
3. Can you tell Mr. Halton how many arrangements he must sell to earn $1,000 if he purchases 300? If he purchases 400?

3-40 Cost estimation—service business William Jarvis operates his own firm of Certified Public Accountants. For planning purposes, he is interested in developing information about the cost structure of the firm. At times, he hires part-time employees, usually accounting majors from the nearby university.

The best measure of activity for the company is chargeable hours, the number of hours that employees work on client business. The company charges the clients for these hours at hourly rates. Jarvis has the following data regarding wages of part-time employees from recent months.

Total Chargeable Hours	Part-Time Wages
3,000	$3,000
3,500	3,100
2,800	2,990
3,200	3,090
4,800	5,400
5,200	6,180
5,600	6,900

Required

Plot the data on a scatter diagram and comment on the results. Can Mr. Jarvis use your results for planning? What reasons might there be for the pattern that you observe?

3-41 Understanding regression results (related to Appendix) Your assistant in the cost management office has just brought in some regression results sent over by the plant's operations analysis group. The group tried several regressions to analyze power costs. The first equation used direct labor hours as the independent variable.

$$Y = \$182,938 + \$0.5612X, \ r^2 = .2691, \ S_e = \$79,982$$
$$Y = monthly \ power \ costs, \ X = labor \ hours$$

The second equation used machine hours as the independent variable.

$$Y = \$61,122 + \$1.4651X, \ r^2 = .7314, \ S_e = \$8,982$$
$$Y = monthly \ power \ costs, \ X = machine \ hours$$

The number of labor hours per month runs between 15,000 and 25,000. The number of machine hours ranges between 70,000 and 125,000, depending on the mix of products being made.

The controller has requested that your office do a study to help her with planning and you are to discuss the results with her shortly.

Required

Write a memorandum to the controller. Justify your recommendation. Use the guidelines in Appendix A.

3-42 CVP analysis for an airline Icarus Airlines flies a number of routes in the southwestern United States. The company owns six airplanes, each of which can hold 150 passengers. All routes are about the same distance, and all fares are $66 one way. The line is obligated to provide 250 flights per month. Each flight costs $4,000 for gasoline, crew salaries, and so on. Variable costs per passenger are $6, to cover a meal and a head tax imposed for each passenger at every airport to which Icarus flies. Other costs, all fixed, are $130,000 per month.

Required

1. How many passengers must Icarus carry on its 250 flights in order to earn $70,000 profit per month? What percentage of capacity is this number?
2. If the company could cut its flights to 200 per month, how many passengers are required to earn $70,000 per month? What percentage of capacity does this number represent (using 200 flights as capacity)?
3. Is the $4,000 cost per flight fixed or variable?
4. What is the chief problem faced by a company with this type of cost structure?

3-43   Promotional campaign   Ajax Publishers sells magazine subscriptions. Its managers are considering a large promotional campaign in which it will award prizes of $10,000,000. Other costs associated with the campaign follow.

Television time	$ 4,400,000
Fee to Fred Mahon, TV spokesperson	700,000
Mailing	5,300,000
Total	$ 10,400,000

Ajax plans to mail 20,000,000 packages containing entry blanks and forms for subscribing to magazines. Ajax receives 25% of total subscription revenue. Experience indicates that about 15% of those receiving a package subscribe to one or more magazines. The average subscription revenue from a respondent is $35.

Required

1. What profit will Ajax earn if the campaign meets all expectations?
2. What is the break-even point for the campaign expressed as a response rate, assuming that each respondent orders $35 in magazine subscriptions?

3-44   Calculating contribution margin percentage   Bell Company has a 25% margin of safety. Its after-tax return on sales is 6%, and its tax rate is 40%.

Required

1. Determine Bell's contribution margin percentage.
2. Assuming that current sales are $120,000, determine total fixed costs.

3-45   Cost structure and risk   Gladack Company makes a number of products and uses a great deal of machinery. A new product this coming year will require the acquisition of a new machine. The machine can only be leased, not purchased. There are two alternative leasing arrangements: (1) a month-to-month lease that can be canceled on 30-days' notice by either Gladack or the lessor, at a monthly rental of $6,000, and (2) a five-year noncancelable lease at $5,200 per month. The new product is expected to have a life of five years, during which annual revenues will be $250,000 and annual variable costs will be $100,000. There are no new fixed costs other than the lease payments. The president is concerned that the five-year lease removes a great deal of flexibility; if the product does not pan out as expected, the company is stuck with the machine and there are no other uses for it. He does, however, like the idea of saving $800 per month.

Required
Why would the president hesitate between the choices? What could happen to make him regret choosing (a) the five-year lease? (b) the month-to-month lease?

3-46   Loss per unit   A company had a loss of $3 per unit when sales were 40,000 units. When sales were 50,000 units, the company had a loss of $1.60 per unit.

Required
1. Determine contribution margin per unit.
2. Determine fixed costs.
3. Determine the break-even point in units.

3-47   CVP analysis—measures of volume   Acme Foam Rubber Company buys large pieces of foam rubber (called "loaves") and cuts them into small pieces that are used in seat cushions and other products. A loaf contains 5,000 board feet of foam rubber (a "board foot" is one foot square and one inch thick), of which 10% becomes scrap during the process of cutting up the loaf. A loaf costs $700, including freight, and the company is currently processing 100 loaves per month.

The company charges $0.22 per board foot for its good output, $0.07 per board foot for the scrap. Variable costs of cutting the loaf are $100, for labor and power to run the cutting machines. Fixed costs are $18,000 per month.

The president of the company has asked for your assistance in developing CVP relationships.

Required
1. Determine the firm's income when it processes 100 loaves per month.
2. Determine the firm's break-even point expressed as number of loaves processed.
3. The president tells you that your analyses in items 1 and 2 are not what he had in mind. He says that he is accustomed to thinking in terms of board feet of good output sold. He would like to know how many board feet he would have to sell to earn $6,000 per month. Determine the firm's contribution margin per board foot of good output sold and sales required to earn $6,000 per month.

CASES

3-48   *Measures of volume* The controller of Throckton Company has been to a seminar on CVP analysis and wants to use some of the techniques she learned. She gives you the following data and asks that you analyze each cost into its fixed and variable components. She plans to use the information for profit planning. You prepare the following schedules of costs and measures of activity for the previous six months.

Sales	Labor Hours	Production Costs	Selling Expenses	Administrative Expenses
$12,000	500	$ 9,100	$3,250	$3,200
10,000	700	11,000	2,980	3,300
21,000	1,200	14,300	4,130	4,100
30,000	1,300	15,300	4,950	4,500
33,000	900	11,980	5,370	4,300
35,000	800	11,200	5,560	4,800

Required

Analyze the cost behavior patterns in accordance with the request of the controller. Indicate weaknesses and suggest possible improvement.

3-49   *Value-adding and non-value-adding activities and costs* MUL Company manufactures six types of products. The products are relatively standard, not made-to-order. MUL takes orders from customers, then fills the orders from stock or manufactures the required units. The company keeps finished units in a warehouse that it also uses for materials and components. The Quality Control Division inspects all shipments of materials and components, as well as all finished products before they are shipped.

The company holds a two- to three-month supply of parts and components that it uses to make high-volume products. MUL's purchasing manager is responsible for obtaining materials and components at the lowest possible cost and so scours the country looking for the best deals. MUL therefore uses a good many vendors.

Production begins by withdrawing the necessary materials and components from the warehouse, inspecting them for possible deterioration during storage, and transporting them to the first station that works on the product. Each station does one function, such as drilling, planing, welding, or various assembly operations.

Each station has an area to store materials and components for jobs that it has not yet started. The materials wait in the area until the station is ready to begin the job. Setup time in going from one product to another is often substantial at some stations. After the workers at the station have finished with their part of the job, they send the semi-completed units along with the materials and components not yet installed to the next station. There the same process is repeated and so on until all work is completed. In some cases, a job will go to the same station more than once because it requires the same operation at different stages of production.

At the conclusion of production, units go to the Quality Control Division to await testing and inspection. They then go to the warehouse for shipment. The company usually makes 10% more units than needed for an order to allow for defects. Any spare good units are held in the warehouse until another order arrives. Defective units are sometimes reworked, and sometimes sold as scrap. Reworked units are stored in the warehouse. If it is possible to determine which work station caused the defect, its manager is held responsible. (Bonuses for station managers are based largely on total good output.) In cases where it is not possible to determine the source of the defect, no one is held responsible.

The factory manager has said that "it gets pretty hectic at the end of each month when we're trying to finish up jobs and get the stuff out to the warehouse."

The cycle time varies among types of products, but runs from 10 days to 45 days depending on various factors.

Required

What activities described above do not add value to products? What changes in operations can you recommend?

3-50   Determining variable costs of products—activity-based analysis Mel Teague, controller of Rothman Industries, has not been satisfied with the cost analysis that the staff has been doing. Predictions of total costs have been well off the mark and other managers have complained about poor information on which to base their decisions. The staff has used direct labor hours to develop regression equations for all manufacturing overhead costs.

Teague believed that the staff had failed to recognize that drivers other than direct labor hours are at work. She therefore conducted a study of cost pools and drivers and developed the following analysis, showing the fixed and variable components of various cost pools and drivers.

Cost Driver	Variable Amount
Direct labor hours (DLH)	$ 3.00 per DLH
Machine hours (MH)	$18.00 per MH
Number of parts/components	$ 0.05 per part
Total processing time	$ 3.00 per hour

Teague has instructed you to determine the variable cost of two products using the data she has developed. Variable costs for materials and labor and other data for the products follow:

	Product 816	Product 389
Materials cost	$13.00	$11.00
Direct labor cost at $14 per DLH	7.00	14.00
Other data:		
Machine hours	0.50	0.20
Number of parts	120	185
Total processing time	10.0 hours	5.0 hours

Required

1. Determine the total variable cost of each product.
2. Suppose that the staff had estimated variable overhead cost at $40.00 per direct labor hour. Determine the cost of each product using that estimate.
3. Comment on the differences between your answers to items 1 and 2.

Additional Aspects of Cost-Volume-Profit Analysis

4

LEARNING OBJECTIVES

After reading this chapter, you should be able to

1 Calculate contribution margin variances and explain their significance.

2 Understand and use the concepts of weighted-average contribution margin percentages and weighted-average unit contribution margins.

3 Understand why managers treat complementary products and substitute products differently.

4 Understand the importance of fixed costs in a multiproduct company and describe how activity-based costing can help such companies.

5 Understand how pricing strategies can affect volume and profit.

6 Describe the application of CVP analysis in not-for-profit entities.

- **SBC Communications**, formerly **Southwestern Bell**, has adopted a strategy of reducing prices selectively for specific categories of cellular telephone calls. Some of its customers now receive cellular service that is comparable to what they receive at home.

- **Eastman Chemical** reported sales from one segment "...were favorably affected by increases in sales volume, ...partially offset by lower selling prices." About another segment, the company also explained that "The decrease in filter product's selling prices is attributed to excess industry production capacity, ..."

- **Green Mountain Power**, a Vermont electric utility, reported that "... total electricity sales decreased 5.6% due principally to a

> *reduction in wholesale sales. Total operating revenues increased 1.1% in 1992, due primarily to a 5.6% retail rate increase . . . and to increased sales of electricity to retail customers reflecting colder (but normal) temperatures . . . ."*

Budgeted (planned) and actual profits usually differ, and managers analyze these differences, called variances, to evaluate performance and to take corrective action. This chapter illustrates techniques for analyzing contribution margin variances. (Chapter 12 extends the analysis to cost variances.) The chapter also treats some aspects of CVP analysis that we have not yet discussed, with special attention to multiproduct companies and pricing strategy. We discuss activity-based costing in multiproduct companies and CVP analysis in not-for-profit entities.

ANALYZING CONTRIBUTION MARGIN VARIANCES

Profit depends on several factors, including selling prices, sales volumes, and costs. Budgeted and actual incomes rarely coincide because prices, volume, and costs can (and do) vary from expectations. To plan and to evaluate previous decisions, managers need to know the sources of variances.

Our analytical approach concentrates on variances in contribution margin, specifically those that arise because of differences between (1) budgeted and actual sales volume and (2) budgeted and actual selling prices. The same analysis also applies to differences between actual and budgeted gross margins. Additionally, managers often use the same approach to explain differences between the actual results of two periods, such as the current and the prior month, or year. Of course, budgeted and actual contribution margin can differ because of changes in variable costs. Analyzing cost variances requires a full chapter, and we defer that topic until Chapter 12.

As an example, Horton Company expected to sell 20,000 units at $20 with unit variable costs of $12. Horton actually sold 21,000 units at $19. These results and the differences appear in Exhibit 4-1.

We want to explain the $13,000 unfavorable variance, the difference between budgeted and actual contribution margin. Total revenues were $1,000 less than

Exhibit 4-1 Horton Company, Planned and Actual Results

	Actual	Planned	Difference
Units sold	21,000	20,000	1,000
Sales	$399,000	$400,000	$ 1,000
Variable costs	252,000	240,000	12,000
Contribution margin	$147,000	$160,000	$ 13,000

budgeted, while total variable costs were $12,000 more than budgeted. But notice that actual variable cost per unit was $12 ($252,000/21,000), the same as budgeted. So the difference in *total* variable costs is due to the increase in volume, *not* to a difference between budgeted and actual per-unit variable cost.

Two factors caused the difference between total budgeted and total actual contribution margin: a variance in selling price and a variance in sales volume. To isolate the effect of each factor, we hold one factor (price or volume) constant and look at the effect of the other. One simple way to do this is to prepare a statement that shows what would have happened if the company had sold the actual volume, but at the budgeted price, as shown in Exhibit 4-2.

SALES VOLUME VARIANCE

The **sales volume variance** is the difference between (1) the contribution margin the company would have earned selling the budgeted number of units at the budgeted unit contribution margin and (2) the contribution margin it would have earned selling the actual number of units at the budgeted unit contribution margin. The $8,000 favorable difference in Exhibit 4-2 is Horton's sales volume variance. It resulted from Horton's selling 1,000 units more than budgeted at an $8 *budgeted* per-unit contribution margin. Thus, the sales volume variance can also be computed as

$$\begin{array}{ccccc} \text{Sales volume} \\ \text{variance} \end{array} = \begin{array}{c} \text{budgeted} \\ \text{contribution} \\ \text{margin per unit} \end{array} \times \left(\begin{array}{c} \text{actual unit} \\ \text{sales} \end{array} - \begin{array}{c} \text{budgeted unit} \\ \text{sales} \end{array} \right)$$

$$\$8,000 \quad = \quad \$8 \quad \times \quad (21,000 \quad - \quad 20,000)$$

If a company sells more units than budgeted, as Horton did, the variance is favorable. If it sells fewer units than budgeted, the variance is unfavorable.

Exhibit 4-2   Horton Company, Expected Results at Planned Price and Actual Volume

	Actual Results	Actual Volume at Planned Price	Planned Results
Units sold	21,000	21,000	20,000
Sales	$399,000	$420,000	$400,000
Variable costs	252,000	252,000	240,000
Contribution margin	$147,000	$168,000	$160,000
Differences		$21,000	$8,000
		unfavorable	favorable
Total difference		$13,000	
		unfavorable	

Again, please notice that we are holding selling price and per-unit variable cost constant because we want to determine the effect on total contribution margin of selling more (or fewer) units than budgeted. Holding selling price and per-unit variable cost constant holds contribution margin per unit constant.

Even if unit variable cost changed, we still would use budgeted unit variable cost for this analysis, because we want to isolate the effects of sales volume apart from changes in variable costs or selling prices. Remember that we hold all factors but one constant; if we allow both volume and unit variable cost to vary we are confusing the analysis.

SALES PRICE VARIANCE

If unit variable cost does not change, a change in selling price changes unit contribution margin by the same amount and in the same direction. The **sales price variance** is the difference between (1) actual total contribution margin and (2) total contribution margin that would have been earned at the actual volume and budgeted unit contribution margin. Horton sold its product for $19, or $1 less than budgeted. The $21,000 difference between the $168,000 contribution margin that would have been earned selling 21,000 units at the $20 price (Exhibit 4-2) and the actual contribution margin of $147,000 is Horton's sales price variance. The variance is unfavorable because the actual selling price, and therefore actual contribution margin, was less than budgeted.

We can also calculate the sales price variance by multiplying the difference between the actual and budgeted prices by the actual unit volume.

$$Sales\ price\ variance = units\ sold \times (actual\ price - budgeted\ price)$$
$$= 21,000 \times (\$19 - \$20) = -\$21,000$$

The $1 difference between the budgeted and actual selling prices is also the difference between budgeted and actual unit contribution margin, so we could also use contribution margin in the calculation.

$$-\$21,000 = 21,000 \times (\$7 - \$8)$$

A word of caution. An "unfavorable" variance, either sales price or sales volume, is not necessarily bad, nor is a "favorable" variance necessarily good. First, the two variances are often related. Managers often lower prices to increase volume. The wisdom of such a decision depends on the *overall* results, including whether the changes are consistent with the company's strategy, not on either variance considered separately. Pricing policy is discussed in more detail later in the chapter. To interpret variances managers also must know whether conditions were as expected when the original plans were developed. For instance, suppose the budgeted volume was based on forecasts of rapid growth for the industry and that growth failed to materialize. The company probably could not meet its budgeted volume, but the managers are not at fault because they cannot control industry sales. (The managers are responsible for accepting the inaccurate forecast, however.) Managers must also interpret variances in light of the company's strategic objectives, which we also address in this chapter.[1]

---

1 *The works of John Shank and Vijay Govindarajan are especially helpful in this area. See, for example,* Strategic Cost Management, *NY, The Free Press, 1994.*

The accompanying Insight shows samples of narratives about a company's success or failure in meeting objectives or in surpassing the prior year's results, along with one company's analysis of the effects of a competitor's pricing strategy. The very same techniques for explaining differences between budgeted and actual results also apply to explaining differences in results between one period and another.

MULTIPLE PRODUCTS

 Chapter 2 stated that CVP analysis assumes either a single product or a constant sales mix. (Recall that sales mix is the proportion of each product in total sales, expressed in units or in dollars.) If products have widely differing contribution margins, and if the mix changes, the company's contribution margin could change and results could be much different from those predicted. Multiple-

IN SIGHT

From **Golden Poultry Company's** 1994 annual report, "Market prices for broilers weakened in the fall as a result of an increase in the supply of broilers, but returned to more profitable levels as broiler exports increased to the former Soviet Union." And more recently, "The increase [1994 over 1993] in consolidated net sales resulted from a 12% increase in pounds of broiler products sold and a 3% increase in average selling prices .... Market prices for broilers increased as a result of increased exports and the general economic recovery in the United States."

From **RJR Nabisco's** 1993 annual report, "Net sales for RJRT [Tobacco] ... a decline of 20% ... reflecting the impact of industry-wide price reductions and price discounting on higher price brands, a higher proportion of sales from lower price brands and an overall volume decline of approximately 3.6%. The 1993 decrease in overall volume resulted from a decline in the full-price segment that more than offset growth in the lower price segment. The growth in lower price brands was slowed ... by net price reductions on full-price brands."

RJR also commented on a price war in 1993 started when **Philip Morris** reduced the price of its best-selling Marlboro brand, touching off a price war among full-price brands.

"In April, 1993, RJRT's largest competitor announced a shift in strategy designed to gain share of market while sacrificing short-term profits. ... RJRT defended its major full-price brands ... reduced list prices on all its full-price and mid-price brands ... The cost of defensive price promotions and the impact of lower list prices were primarily responsible for the sharp drop in RJRT's 1993 operating company contribution."

product companies can nonetheless use CVP analysis for individual products or for groups of products with approximately equal contribution margins (per-unit or percentage). They also can use CVP analysis when contributions differ greatly, provided that the sales mix remains relatively constant.

Companies have relatively constant sales mixes for several reasons. Some companies sell products that are used together, so that the sales of one affect the sales of the other. Common examples are cameras and film, ice cream and toppings, and tables and chairs. Such products are **complementary products**. Even with no apparent complementary relationship among products, the sales mix still might remain fairly constant. A department store might consistently derive 40 percent of its sales from clothing, 25 percent from furniture and housewares, and 35 percent from its other departments. These percentages might be relatively constant over time despite the absence of obvious causes. Whatever the reasons for the predictability of sales mix, managers of a multiple-product company can apply CVP analysis by using a weighted-average contribution margin. The accompanying Insight gives illustrations of how companies can benefit from recognizing complementary relationships among products.

In applying CVP analysis in a multiproduct company, managers often group similar products together. A natural grouping of products is called a *product line*. An example is a hair-care line, consisting of shampoos, conditioners, colorings, creams, tonics, and restorers. Before proposing a program that could influence sales mix, a manager needs to know price and cost data for each product as well as the current sales mix. These data give the manager some idea of profitability by product and how the sales mix might be enriched. In many cases, managers will treat the entire line as a single "product." Several reasons influence managers to take this simplified approach for analytical purposes.

First, the products might have such similar contribution margins (either per-unit or percentages) that little is gained by examining them individually. After all, planning does involve estimates; moreover, minor differences that may result from grouping products with slightly different contribution margins are not likely to affect decisions. Another reason is that the sheer number of products might make analyzing them individually difficult and time consuming.

A third reason for grouping products relates to the level of the manager for whom an analysis is being prepared. Different managers make different decisions and therefore need different kinds of information. The president of a full-line department store does not look at sales and cost details for every product stocked by the store. However, a lower-level manager—say one in charge of sporting goods—does look at individual products in that line. That manager is concerned about each product and makes decisions about adding and dropping individual products. The store's president is more concerned with the product line as a whole and makes decisions about adding or dropping entire departments.

 An important factor in analyzing either an individual product or a product line is an understanding of the fixed costs associated with that product or line. A later section of the chapter applies principles from Chapter 3 to multiproduct companies.

IN SIGHT

A *Business Week* cover story on the technology paradox highlighted some aggressive uses of the principle of complementary products. **Computer Associates International, Inc.** *gave away* the first million copies of its accounting program, Simply Money. The company expected to recoup more than the cost as users bought upgrades and related, complementary software.

News Corporation operates Star TV, which is beamed down to users from a satellite. In some countries, video pirates intercept the signals, decode them, and sell them to cable users without paying Star TV. Rupert Murdoch, the media giant who owns the Star system, is actually *happy* about these thefts. The more actual viewers of Star TV, whether they pay or not, the higher the advertising rates that Star TV can charge. Thus, sales or thefts of one product, programs, generate higher prices for a related product, advertising revenues. In a more classic type of case, **Nintendo** sells its game consoles at or below cost and derives virtually all of its profits from game software.

A non-technological example is provided by **Victoria's Secret**, the purveyor of women's apparel. The company has played classical music in its stores for some years. Customers began asking to buy tapes or CDs of the music and the company began to sell CDs in 1988. The company has sold 5 million CDs in stores and through its catalogs.

Domino's Pizza, the giant pizza chain, suffered declines in 1992 and 1993 because, according to some observers, it offered only pizza and Coke. **Little Caesars Pizza** offered several other products, as did **Pizza Hut** and other eat-in pizzerias. Domino's fortunes went back up when it added buffalo wings and other complementary products.

Companies follow different strategies with respect to product lines. **Hasbro Toys** used to make school supplies only. In the 1940s it began making toys to use capacity it did not need all year for school supplies. In contrast, **Mattel** gains over half of its revenue from Barbie, Ken, and their clothes.

Sources: Neil Gross and Peter Coy, "The Technology Paradox," Business Week, March 6, 1995, 79-84. Michael O'Neal, "God, Family, and Domino's, That's It," Business Week, January 30, 1995, 57-58.

WEIGHTED-AVERAGE CONTRIBUTION MARGIN PERCENTAGE

As the term suggests, the **weighted-average contribution margin percentage** is the overall contribution margin percentage. It consists of the individual products' percentages weighted by their relative sales. Managers also can use the weighted-average contribution margin percentage just as they use the contribution margin percentage for a single product.

Suppose that TFL (from Chapter 2) has expanded its business. It now sells tote bags and bookbags, as well as backpacks. Increasing the diversity of the business has increased fixed costs to $30,000 per month for additional employees and larger rented quarters. Data for the individual products follow.

	Backpacks	Tote Bags	Bookbags
Selling price	$10	$8	$10
Variable cost	6	2	5
Contribution margin	$ 4	$6	$ 5
Contribution margin percentage	40%	75%	50%
Percentage in sales mix	60% +	10% +	30% = 100%

The percentages shown for sales mix are the proportions of *total sales dollars* coming from each product. (These percentages must total 100 percent.)

TFL has the same questions it had in Chapter 2: What is the break-even point? What sales are required to achieve a particular profit target? When TFL had only one product, it could work equally well with either sales units or sales dollars. With multiple products, it might be more convenient, and simpler, to work with sales dollars, using the weighted-average contribution margin percentage. (As we shall see, some companies could just as easily use sales units.)

We can calculate the weighted-average contribution margin percentage in at least two ways. One way is to prepare a hypothetical partial income statement, such as the one below, down to contribution margin, which assumes total sales of $100,000 and the sales mix that TFL expects.

	Backpacks	Tote Bags	Bookbags	Totals
Sales mix	60%	10%	30%	100%
Sales	$60,000	$10,000	$30,000	$100,000
Variable costs	36,000	2,500	15,000	53,500
Contribution margin	$24,000	$ 7,500	$15,000	$ 46,500

The weighted-average contribution margin percentage is 46.5% ($46,500/ $100,000).

A more direct way to find the weighted-average contribution margin percentage is to multiply the contribution margin percentage for each product by its percentage in the sales mix and add the results. This calculation appears below.

	Backpacks	Tote Bags	Bookbags	Total
Contribution margin percentage	40%	75%	50%	
Multiplied by percentage in sales mix	60%	10%	30%	
Weighted average	24% +	7.5% +	15% =	46.5%

Let's look at the logic of this calculation. With the 60%, 10%, 30% sales mix, the average sales dollar is composed of $0.60 from backpacks, $0.10 from tote bags, and $0.30 from bookbags. The $0.60 sales from backpacks provides $0.24 in contribution margin because the contribution margin percentage on backpacks is 40%. The contribution margin of $0.24 is the 24% in the backpacks column. Similarly, the $0.30 sales of bookbags in the average sales dollar provides $0.15 contribution margin because the rate on bookbags is 50%. The following schedule shows the calculations in dollars.

	Backpacks	Tote Bags	Bookbags	Total
Average sales dollar	$0.60	$ 0.10	$0.30	$ 1.00
Contribution margin percentage	40%	75%	50%	
Contribution margin	$0.24 +	$ 0.075 +	$0.15 =	$ 0.465

Because the average sales dollar yields $0.465 in contribution margin, the weighted-average contribution margin percentage is 46.5%.

Using the 46.5% weighted-average contribution margin percentage, TFL now can do the same analyses it did in Chapter 2. The break-even point is $64,516 ($30,000/46.5%). To earn a $20,000 target profit requires sales of $107,527 [($30,000 + $20,000)/46.5%].

The following income statement shows that the weighted-average contribution margin of 46.5% works.

	Backpacks	Tote Bags	Bookbags	Totals
Sales mix	60%	10%	30%	100%
Sales	$64,516	$10,753	$32,258	$107,527
Variable costs	38,710	2,688	16,129	57,527
Contribution margin	$25,806	$ 8,065	$16,129	$ 50,000
Fixed costs				30,000
Profit				$ 20,000

CHANGES IN SALES MIX

Sales mix is very important when the contribution margin percentages differ greatly among products. (If all products have the same contribution margin percentages, that percentage *is* the weighted-average contribution margin percentage.) Suppose that TFL sees a trend that is likely to change the sales mix to 30% backpacks, 40% tote bags, and 30% bookbags (a shift from backpacks to tote bags). The new weighted-average contribution margin is 57%, an increase of 11.5 percentage points. The increase results from tote bags having a much higher contribution margin percentage than backpacks.

	Backpacks	Tote Bags	Bookbags	Total
Contribution margin percentage	40%	75%	50%	
Percentage in sales mix	30%	40%	30%	
Weighted average	12% +	30% +	15% =	57%

Exhibit 4-3 shows TFL's CVP chart. Note that the horizontal axis shows sales in dollars rather than in units because we are working with contribution margin percentage. The chart shows two total cost lines to represent two sales mixes. The dotted line shows the 53.5% variable cost percentage, which holds when the weighted-average contribution margin percentage is 46.5% (as computed when the sales mix was 60% backpacks, 10% tote bags, and 30% bookbags). The solid total cost line uses a 43% variable cost percentage, which holds when the weighted-average contribution margin is 57% (the second computation, when the sales mix was 30% backpacks, 40% tote bags, and 30% bookbags).

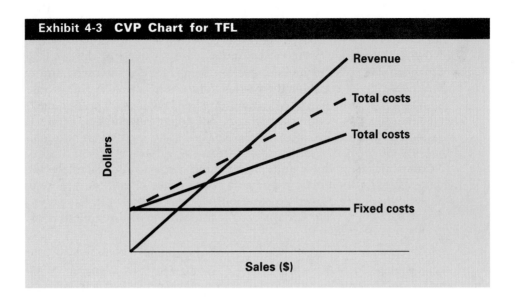

Exhibit 4-3 CVP Chart for TFL

At any level of sales, the break-even point is lower and profits are higher when contribution margin is 57% than when it is 46.5%. Other things being equal, a richer sales mix—one with a higher overall contribution margin percentage—is better, which explains why managers routinely try to enrich sales mix. Under some circumstances, if a company can increase its total sales by some dollar amount, or shift a dollar in sales from one product to another, the product that should be emphasized is the one with the higher contribution margin percentage. Accordingly, managers might shift the emphasis in their advertising towards products with higher contribution margin percentages, while reducing advertising space for products carrying lower percentages. At a simpler level, a salesperson learning that a customer intends to spend $20 for a gift should consider emphasizing suitable $20 items that also have relatively high contribution margin percentages. For a real-life example, **British Airways** richened its sales mix by various tactics aimed at filling more premium-priced seats. The airline recently had 15 percent of its passengers fly first-class and business class, but earned 33 percent of its revenues from these premium seats. The growth that the company experienced in these premium-priced seats in 1994 increased overall passenger revenue per mile by 2.7 percent, a very hefty increase in the airline industry.[2]

Note, however, that some efforts to enrich sales mix might make "other things" unequal. For example, increasing advertising to enrich sales mix also increases fixed costs. Too, if two (or more) products are substitutes, shifting sales from one to the other might not be profitable. That case is best considered in the next section, which deals with contribution margin per unit.

WEIGHTED-AVERAGE CONTRIBUTION MARGIN PER UNIT

Some multiple-product companies use units, rather than dollars, to measure volume and express sales mix. For instance, managers of an automobile

---

2 Jay Palmer, "The British Are Coming," Barron's, *December 12, 1994,* 33.

manufacturer are primarily concerned with the number of cars sold, rather than total dollars of sales. (They are concerned, of course, about dollar sales, but most of the analyses they perform use units—cars—instead of dollars.) Similarly, managers of service businesses, such as firms of CPAs, lawyers, and management consultants, consider their sales volumes in terms of chargeable hours, the hours that their personnel spend on client business. These managers also consider sales mix in unit percentages, not dollar percentages. While TFL says that 40% of dollar sales are from backpacks, a manager of an automaker says that 40% of the cars it sells are sedans.

Companies that think and plan in unit terms could calculate weighted-average contribution margin percentages, but they often find it more useful to calculate a weighted-average contribution margin per unit. Consider the following data for Corbin Company, a manufacturer of three models of desks.

	President	Senior VP	Junior VP
Selling price	$1,000	$800	$500
Unit variable cost	600	500	250
Unit contribution margin	$ 400	$300	$250
Percentage in sales mix, in units	20%	30%	50%

The **weighted-average contribution margin per unit** is calculated in basically the same way as the weighted-average contribution margin percentage. The per-unit contribution margin of each product (in *dollars*, not as a *percentage*) is multiplied by its percentage in the sales mix.

	President	Senior VP	Junior VP	Total
Unit contribution margin	$ 400	$ 300	$ 250	
Multiplied by mix percentage, in units	20%	30%	50%	
Weighted-average unit contribution margin	$ 80 +	$ 90 +	$ 125 =	$295

So long as the sales mix holds, managers can use the weighted-average unit contribution margin of $295 just as they would if the company made a single product. Thus, if Corbin's fixed costs are $500,000, its break-even point is about 1,695 desks (fixed costs of $500,000 divided by the weighted-average per-unit contribution margin of $295). To prove that the per-unit calculation works, suppose that Corbin sells 1,000 desks in the expected mix. Its income statement, through contribution margin, is as follows.

	President	Senior VP	Junior VP	Total
Sales in units*	200	300	500	1,000
Sales	$200,000	$240,000	$250,000	$690,000
Variable costs	120,000	150,000	125,000	395,000
Contribution margin	$ 80,000	$ 90,000	$125,000	$295,000

*1,000 × 20%, 30%, 50%

Total contribution margin is $295,000, which is $295 times 1,000 *total* units. Note also that the weighted-average contribution margin percentage is about 42.8% ($295,000/$690,000). Corbin's managers could use either form of weighted-average contribution margin in their analyses.

Would Corbin's profits increase if its managers tried to shift the sales mix toward the President, the model with the highest per-unit contribution margin? The answer is it depends. Corbin manufactures **substitute products**. That is, customers who buy a desk of one model are unlikely to buy a desk of another model. (A person buying a desk for a home office needs only one. However, Corbin might sell several types of desks to companies with large offices.) Because Corbin earns the contribution margin on only one desk, its managers would certainly prefer to receive the highest contribution margin possible if it will sell only one desk. But managers must recognize that attempting to persuade customers to upgrade to a more profitable model might backfire if customers don't buy *any* desk and go elsewhere. (An unethical, and illegal, effort to persuade customers to buy models carrying higher contribution margins is known as "bait and switch." This scheme involves advertising a very low price on a popular style or model when the company has a very small quantity of that item available to sell.)

Past sales provide clues to sales mix and managers can influence sales mix. But if some products are substitutes or complementary, managers should not adopt strategies to influence the volume of one product unless they have considered the effects on sales of the related products.

FIXED COSTS AND MULTIPLE-PRODUCT COMPANIES

Chapter 3 introduced the concepts of committed/discretionary, direct/indirect, and avoidable/unavoidable fixed costs. These concepts are important in evaluating products, product lines, geographical areas, and other activities, or segments, of a company. The classification of a particular cost depends on the segment being examined. For example, nationwide advertising for a product line is discretionary, avoidable, and direct to the line. But the cost is indirect and unavoidable to any particular geographical region. Similarly, regional advertising promoting several product lines is discretionary, direct, and avoidable to the region, but is indirect and unavoidable to any single line.

The importance of a particular classification, such as direct or avoidable, depends on the purpose of the analysis. If a manager is trying to decide whether to drop a segment (a product, a line, or a region), the important issue is whether a cost is avoidable. If the manager is assessing a segment's profitability, then avoidability is important, but it is also important to know whether a cost is direct or indirect to that segment. Decisions to drop segments are multifaceted and are discussed in detail in Chapter 5. Our focus here is on developing information that will help managers evaluate segments.

Exhibit 4-4 shows a segmented income statement for Davis Department Store, which sells three general types of products. The statement has two important subtotals: short-term margin and long-term margin. **Short-term margin** is contribution margin minus avoidable fixed costs. **Long-term margin**, also called **segment margin**, is short-term margin minus direct fixed costs that are unavoidable in the short term. Generally speaking, a segment with a negative short-term margin is unprofitable and a candidate for immediate

Exhibit 4-4	Davis Department Store Product-Line Income Statement for 19X5 (thousands of dollars)			
	Clothing	Housewares	Furniture	Total
Sales	$2,400	$1,800	$1,300	$5,500
Variable costs:				
Cost of goods sold	$1,050	$ 900	$ 910	$2,860
Commissions	240	180	130	550
Other variable costs	150	120	90	360
Total variable costs	$1,440	$1,200	$1,130	$3,770
Contribution margin	$ 960	$ 600	$ 170	$1,730
Avoidable fixed costs:				
Salaries and expenses of				
department managers	$ 80	$ 65	$ 40	$ 185
Other	30	15	10	55
Total avoidable fixed costs	$ 110	$ 80	$ 50	$ 240
Short-term product margin	$ 850	$ 520	$ 120	$1,490
Direct fixed costs:				
Depreciation on fixtures	$ 80	$ 40	$ 35	$ 155
Other	45	30	20	95
Total direct fixed costs	$ 125	$ 70	$ 55	$ 250
Long-term margin	$ 725	$ 450	$ 65	$1,240
Common fixed costs:				
Rent on store				$ 250
Salaries of administrative staff				365
Utilities				130
Other				300
Total common fixed costs				$1,045
Profit				$ 195

divestiture. A segment with a negative long-term margin is not profitable in the long-term, and a candidate for gradual liquidation.

The exhibit shows that Furniture has a $120,000 short-term margin. This means that Davis's total profit would fall by $120,000 if it dropped Furniture *and* dropping it did not affect the sales of other lines. Because Furniture has a relatively low long-term margin, Davis might begin to explore alternatives.

RELEVANCE OF ACTIVITY-BASED COSTING

 As we discussed in Chapter 3, activity-based costing is especially useful in assigning fixed costs to products based on their use of resources. Tracing as much cost as possible to segments is important because it improves the analysis of product profitability. The smaller the amount of cost directly traceable to products, the more likely that *all* look very profitable. Perhaps if Davis Department Store studied its common fixed costs in more detail it might find some to be driven by activities performed by each segment. **IBM** seeks to identify as much fixed overhead as possible with specific products. One factor that helps to make this tracing possible is that assembly lines in some plants are dedicated to one product, so that relatively little use of common facilities occurs.

Increasing the traceability of costs is an advantage of JIT manufacturing, especially when manufacturing cells each specialize in one product. The more work done on each product in a dedicated area, the more the traceable cost. Moreover, because the people in the cells do the inspection, the materials handling, and much of the required maintenance, less factory-wide cost is incurred for these support activities. If these support activities are performed by centrally managed departments, much of their cost would be common to production departments and products.

ABC AND ETHICS

Because some costs are on the borderline between being direct or indirect to a product or line, managerial accountants must use some judgment in assigning costs to products. Whenever decisions involve judgment, the potential for an ethical conflict exists. For example, managers responsible for products want to keep their costs low and might pressure accountants to treat particular costs as common costs on the income statements for their products. Suppose a product manager, who is also a friend, argues that you should not include a particular cost in the *line's* income statement because the cost cannot be controlled. You then have an ethical conflict: should you treat the cost as common even though you believe it belongs with direct costs? The IMA's Standards of Ethical Conduct, pages 19 and 20, imply that the need for management accountants to maintain professional objectivity outweighs feelings of loyalty to a friend.

PRICING STRATEGY

 Pricing is a very troublesome issue and can give rise to unfortunate effects. Recall from Chapter 2 that target price calculations require estimates of volume and that simply calculating a price does not guarantee that customers will buy the estimated quantity. The "death spiral" occurs when a company sets a high target price, fails to achieve the estimated volume, raises the price, which in turn leads to lower volume, and so on until it goes out of business. Another type of problem arises when a target price is inconsistent with strategy. A company pursuing a differentiation strategy of high quality might not benefit from a low price even if it could earn more in the short run than with a higher price. Long-term considerations such as product image might override short-term profits.

Cutting prices in some market conditions can be a smart strategy, but it is essential that volume increases much more than price decreases or that costs drop. Of course, a company can sell more of a product at a lower price than at a higher price, but consider the following products.

	Product A	Product B
Price	$ 20	$ 5
Variable cost	16	1
Contribution margin	$ 4	$ 4
Unit volume	10,000	10,000
Total contribution margin	$ 40,000	$ 40,000

On which product might a price reduction be wise or unwise? If the company cuts the price of product A by $1, or 5 percent, it reduces contribution margin by 25 percent, from $4 to $3, a huge decrease that requires a 33 percent increase in volume (or $1 cost reduction) to make up. A 5 percent drop in the price of product B only reduces contribution margin by 6.25 percent ($0.25/$4). The schedule below shows results of a 5 percent price drop and a 15 percent unit volume increase for both products.

	Product A	Product B
Price after 5% decrease	$ 19	$ 4.75
Variable cost	16	1.00
Contribution margin	$ 3	$ 3.75
Unit volume up 15%	11,500	11,500
Total contribution margin	$ 34,500	$ 43,125

Total contribution margin for product A drops, while that of product B increases. The general principle is that reducing prices on products with low contribution margin percentages requires very large increases in unit volume to maintain total contribution margin and profit. Perhaps the commonest analytical error in pricing is to calculate the effects of changes on total revenue, rather than on contribution margin. The price that yields the highest total revenue might not be the most profitable. In the example above, reducing the price of product A to $19 and selling 15 percent more units increases total revenue from $200,000 ($20 × 10,000) to $218,500 ($19 × 11,500), but reduces total contribution margin from $40,000 to $34,500.

Despite the difficulties and uncertainties, price reductions can be a sharp strategic, competitive tool. The printer unit of **Hewlett-Packard** (HP) used aggressive pricing as part of a strategy to beat back a challenge by Japanese companies, which held 80 percent of personal computer printer sales in the U.S. in 1985. In addition to cutting prices, HP started getting products to market faster. The increased sales gave HP economies of scale, which lowered average manufacturing costs. HP now sells $8 billion of printers, which is over 30 percent of the U.S. market. The strategy was new at HP, which had rarely cut prices, preferring to compete in high-margin, niche markets. The printer unit was allowed to set prices (and therefore margins) below the company norm to implement its strategy.[3]

Intel Corp., the major maker of computer chips, regularly drops its prices, partly to hurt companies that clone Intel chips. It recently dropped one price

---

3 *Stephen Kreider Yoder, "How HP Used Tactics of the Japanese to Beat Them at Their Game,"* The Wall Street Journal, *September 8, 1994, A1.*

from $495 to $301, another from $479 to $289. One of its chips went from $878 at its introduction in 1993 to $273 at the beginning of 1995. Such drops require aggressive cost-cutting.[4]

CVP ANALYSIS IN NOT-FOR-PROFIT ENTITIES

The term *not-for-profit* describes many kinds of economic entities, including governmental units, universities, churches, charitable organizations such as the Red Cross and American Cancer Society, and clubs and fraternal groups. Though some call such organizations *nonprofit*, we prefer the term *not-for-profit* because it better describes the *intent* of such organizations. (Many businesses turn out to be "nonprofit," but not by choice!)

Income is one measure of how well a business is doing. Although profit is not the only objective of a business company (survival, growth, product quality, and good corporate citizenship are others), earning profits sufficient to attract capital investment is necessary to its survival. How, then, is CVP analysis relevant to entities that do not intend to earn profits?

First, many not-for-profit entities try to earn profits (or at least break even or limit losses) on some activities. College bookstores and food services often operate profitably and help to defray other costs of the college. Municipalities run parking lots, water or electric utilities, and recreational facilities that operate at break even or at a profit. A not-for-profit entity is especially likely to try to break even on a service that benefits only a portion of its constituents. Because not everyone in a city will use a municipal golf course, the city's elected officials might believe that the course should pay its own way.

Second, not-for-profit entities must choose from among alternative ways to accomplish some task. Making choices requires an understanding of cost behavior. For instance, a city can do its own trash collection or contract the task to a private firm. If the outside company charges on the basis of the volume of trash collected, the cost is variable. If the city has its own trucks and personnel, a large portion of the cost is fixed. Recognizing the implications of the different types of behavior, city officials need information about the likely volumes of trash, including estimates about probable growth in volume.

The examples mentioned so far are relatively straightforward applications of cost analysis or CVP analysis. As a rule, however, the major activities of not-for-profit entities are not amenable to such straightforward applications because there is often no objective way to determine the value of the services—there is no revenue. Of course, not-for-profit entities do get revenues—taxes, donations, tuition—but not necessarily from the specific services that they provide. Cities have police forces, but the people do not pay for this service on the basis of use; they pay for it in taxes that also support the other activities of the government.

Despite the difficulties of measuring the results of activities of not-for-profit entities, some evaluations are always being made. Essentially, not-for-profit entities are concerned with analyzing the benefits and costs of activities, not so much with the revenues, costs, and profits. Accordingly, many use benefit-cost analysis.

---

4 The Wall Street Journal, *February 3, 1995, B10.*

BENEFIT-COST ANALYSIS

Managers of not-for-profit entities take many actions based on analyses that incorporate some kind of monetary measurement of both benefits and costs. For instance, governmental studies relating to the construction of a new dam are likely to include both construction costs and estimates of benefits from flood control and new recreational opportunities. Opponents of the dam might offer alternative analyses that measure benefits using different assumptions, attempt to quantify the cost of displacing people who live near the dam site, and state that the proposed dam would do irreparable, unquantifiable harm to various species of wildlife. Interested parties on both sides will dispute each other's figures on quantified points and argue about how to evaluate the unquantified ones.

In other situations, especially those relating to ongoing activities such as public education or police and fire protection, measuring benefits and costs is even more difficult. Most people believe that a better-educated citizen is more beneficial to a community than one less well-educated. But how much more beneficial? Is the difference between the income taxes that the two pay a reasonable measure, or, perhaps, the difference between their incomes?

Benefit-cost analysis often uncovers inefficiencies. The costs of collecting the luxury tax on boats, levied in 1990, exceeded the amounts collected. The General Accounting Office, often called the watchdog of Congress, discovered that costs of filing information returns for state income tax refunds exceeded benefits by $2 million.

As a practical matter, responsible decision makers approach many public service problems in one of two basic ways:

1. Decide on the amount of money to spend on a particular activity and concentrate on getting the most benefit from that level of expenditure.
2. Decide on the level of service to be provided and concentrate on providing that level of service at the most reasonable cost.

As an example of the first approach, a city council might decide to spend $500,000 on police protection. The chief of police then decides how best to spend the allotted money. Should the chief increase the number of patrol cars and cut down on police officers walking beats, or the reverse? Should the department send officers to training programs on advanced crime-fighting techniques, and if so, how many officers and which programs? Unfortunately, establishing the level of expenditure does not avoid the problems of measuring the benefits of public services. The chief must find ways to measure the benefits from alternative plans to provide police protection. Meanwhile, the council must decide whether the city is getting its money's worth, which means finding ways to measure the accomplishments for the approved expenditure. Were the funds well spent if the number of arrests increased? (Not necessarily, because arrests for minor offenses count as much as ones for major crimes.) Are the funds being better used this year if the crime rate has dropped? (Possibly, but many factors besides the quality and quantity of the police force affect the level of crime.)

The second approach—deciding first on the level of service and then trying to achieve that level at reasonable cost—presents many of the same problems as the first. For example, a state legislature might decide that all high school graduates should have the opportunity to attend college whether or not they can afford it. A number of alternatives, with differing costs, are available. Should there be branches of the state university in large population centers? Should the state establish community colleges to prepare students for work at senior colleges? Might it be better to provide money for tuition assistance directly to the students, who could use the funds to attend colleges of their choice? (Should the choices include private colleges? Colleges outside the state?) How does one evaluate whether the stated level of service has been provided at reasonable cost? Choosing among the alternatives involves not only determining the costs but also developing some measures of the benefits of each alternative. Thus, trying to achieve a specified level of service at a reasonable cost does not avoid the problems of measuring the benefits of a public service or evaluating the performance of that service.

In sum, analyzing public service activities is exceedingly difficult because of the lack of objective, unarguable measures of services and performance. Analyzing costs, especially if one is trying to determine whether or not money is spent wisely, is also difficult, but usually less difficult than analyzing activities. The problems are not limited to not-for-profit entities. Businesses spend a great deal of money on employee training, research and development, and other activities where the benefits are not readily measurable in monetary terms. Finding ways to make useful measurements is a constant concern of managers and a goal of much research in universities, business, and government.

SUMMARY

The techniques of CVP analysis are helpful in analyzing the results of operations. Differences between budgeted and achieved contribution margin and income may be attributed to differences in volume, price, and mix. Managers then concentrate on those products or strategies (pricing, promotion, etc.) that are expected to yield the best results. Managers also use contribution margin information to identify profitable products.

Multiproduct companies compute a weighted-average contribution margin to do CVP analysis. This computation requires information about the sales mix, stated either in dollars or units, as well as price and cost data.

Not-for-profit entities use benefit-cost analysis, a counterpart of CVP analysis. Defining and measuring benefits of a particular expenditure in a not-for-profit entity are difficult. Despite these difficulties, more and more managers in such entities are finding that adaptations of the concepts of managerial accounting can be helpful in their organizations.

KEY TERMS

benefit-cost analysis   (146)
complementary products   (135)

long-term (segment) margin   (141)

sales price variance   (133)
sales volume variance   (132)
short-term margin   (141)
substitute products   (141)

weighted-average contribution
    margin percentage   (136)
weighted-average contribution
    margin per unit   (140)

KEY FORMULAS

$$\text{Sales volume variance} = \frac{\text{budgeted contribution margin per unit}}{} \times (\text{actual unit sales - budgeted unit sales})$$

$$\text{Sales price variance} = \text{units sold} \times (\text{actual price - budgeted price})$$

REVIEW PROBLEM

Data on the three types of can openers that are sold by McMichael Company follow. Monthly fixed costs are $90,000.

	Regular	Deluxe	Super
Selling price	$2.00	$3.00	$5.00
Variable costs	1.20	1.50	2.00
Contribution margin	$0.80	$1.50	$3.00
Contribution margin percentage	40%	50%	60%

Required

Consider each part independently.

1. Suppose the sales mix in dollars is Regular, 60%; Deluxe, 30%; and Super, 10%.
    (a) Determine the weighted-average contribution margin percentage and the monthly sales to break even.
    (b) Determine how many units of each model are sold at the break-even point.
    (c) Prepare an income statement by product line for sales of $250,000. Assume that, of the $90,000 fixed costs, avoidable fixed costs for each model are $10,000 and direct unavoidable fixed costs are $5,000, $7,000, and $3,000 for the Regular, Deluxe, and Super models, respectively.
2. Suppose now that the sales mix in units is Regular, 50%; Deluxe, 30%; and Super, 20%.
    (a) Determine the weighted-average contribution margin per unit.
    (b) Determine the total sales dollars required to earn $26,000 profit per month.
3. Suppose that in one month the company expected to sell 40,000 Regular openers at $2 each. It actually sold 39,000 at an average price of $2.20. Compute the sales price variance and sales volume variance.

ANSWER TO REVIEW PROBLEM

1. (a) The weighted-average contribution margin percentage is 45%, computed as follows.

	Regular	Deluxe	Super	Total
Contribution margin percentage	40%	50%	60%	
multiplied by sales mix percentage	60%	30%	10%	
equals contribution margin per sales dollar	24% +	15% +	6% =	45%

Sales required to break even are $200,000 per month (fixed costs of $90,000/ 45%).

(b) Sales are 60,000 units, 20,000 units, and 4,000 units of the Regular, Deluxe, and Super models, respectively. Unit sales for each model are computed by multiplying the sales mix percentage by total sales, to get dollar sales for each model, and then dividing by the selling price per unit.

Regular: ($200,000 × 60% = $120,000)/$2 = 60,000 units
Deluxe: ($200,000 × 30% = $60,000)/$3 = 20,000 units
Super: ($200,000 × 10% = $20,000)/$5 = 4,000 units

(c)

	Regular	Deluxe	Super	Total
Sales[a]	$150,000	$75,000	$ 25,000	$250,000
Variable costs[b]	90,000	37,500	10,000	137,500
Contribution margin	$ 60,000	$37,500	$ 15,000	$112,500
Avoidable fixed costs	10,000	10,000	10,000	30,000
Short-term margin	$ 50,000	$27,500	$ 5,000	$ 82,500
Direct unavoidable fixed costs	5,000	7,000	3,000	15,000
Long-term margin	$ 45,000	$20,500	$ 2,000	$ 67,500
Common fixed costs				45,000
Income				$ 22,500

a Based on the stated sales mix of 60%, 30%, and 10%. $250,000 × 60% = $150,000; $250,000 × 30% = $75,000; $250,000 × 10% = $25,000.
b These figures can be determined by using the variable cost percentages, which are 60%, 50%, and 40% (all are 1 - contribution margin percentages). Or, the number of units of each product can be determined by dividing sales for the product by selling price per unit as given in the problem. Then, the results are multiplied by variable cost per unit as given in the problem. For example, sales of the Regular model are 75,000 units ($150,000/$2). Variable costs are given as $1.20 per unit, so total variable costs are $90,000 for 75,000 units ($1.20 × 75,000).

2. (a) The weighted-average contribution margin per unit is $1.45.

	Regular	Deluxe	Super	Total
Unit contribution margin	$0.80	$1.50	$3.00	
Sales mix, percentage in units	50%	30%	20%	
Weighted-average contribution margin	$0.40 +	$0.45 +	$0.60 =	$1.45

(b) Unit sales required for $26,000 profit, computed using the target profit formula from Chapter 2, are 80,000 units [(fixed costs of $90,000 + target profit of $26,000)/$1.45 weighted-average contribution per unit]. Dollar sales are computed by using the sales mix to determine the number of units sold of each type and then multiplying by the selling price per unit.

Regular: (80,000 × 50% = 40,000 units) × $2 = $ 80,000
Deluxe: (80,000 × 30% = 24,000 units) × $3 =   72,000
Super: (80,000 × 20% = 16,000 units) × $5 =   80,000
Total $232,000

3. Because of the way the information is given, the easiest way to solve the problem is to deal with only the price and volume differences, as follows.

Sales price variance   = quantity sold × (actual price - budgeted price)
      = 39,000 × ($2.20 - $2.00)
      = $7,800 favorable (favorable because actual price was higher than budgeted)

Sales volume variance = budgeted contribution margin × (actual volume - budgeted volume)
      = $0.80 × (39,000 - 40,000)
      = $800 unfavorable (unfavorable because actual volume was less than budgeted)

Alternatively, we could prepare the following schedule.

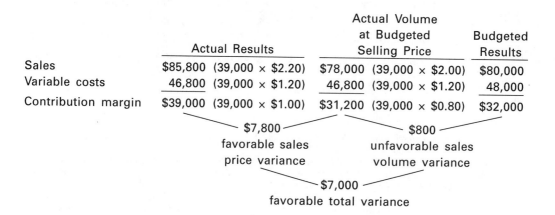

	Actual Results	Actual Volume at Budgeted Selling Price	Budgeted Results
Sales	$85,800 (39,000 × $2.20)	$78,000 (39,000 × $2.00)	$80,000
Variable costs	46,800 (39,000 × $1.20)	46,800 (39,000 × $1.20)	48,000
Contribution margin	$39,000 (39,000 × $1.00)	$31,200 (39,000 × $0.80)	$32,000

$7,800 favorable sales price variance

$800 unfavorable sales volume variance

$7,000 favorable total variance

ASSIGNMENT MATERIAL
QUESTIONS FOR DISCUSSION

4-1   *Price determination—postal service*   What do you think is the major problem in determining prices to be charged for the various classes of mail handled by the postal service? What ethical issues might arise for an accountant studying the question and making recommendations?

4-2   *Sales mix*   **Federal Express** was a well-established express package carrier before it entered the overnight letter business. When it entered the overnight letter business, it set very low, cost-based prices.

Required
Why did Federal Express estimate that its costs for overnight letters would be very low? What other reasons might it have had to set low prices?

4-3 Unit costs and governmental performance The manager of a medium-sized city was quoted as saying that trash collection service in her city was better than that in many neighboring cities because the unit cost was lower. The unit cost was the total cost of collections divided by the number of tons collected. Does having a low unit cost mean that the city is doing a good job?

4-4 Private label sales The newsletter of a national brokerage firm stated that **Cooper Tire & Rubber** was likely to expand its private label sales to **Sears** and **Pep Boys**. Private label products do not carry the manufacturer's brand name, but rather that of the store in which they are sold.

Required
What will increases in private label sales do to Cooper's weighted-average contribution margin per tire?

4-5 Telephone service pricing Long-distance telephone companies (**AT&T, MCI,** Sprint, etc.) will soon be able to offer local service, and local companies (**Bell Atlantic, NYNEX,** and others) will be able to offer long-distance service.

Required
What should happen to the prices customers will pay for both kinds of service? What will happen to the profits of the affected companies?

EXERCISES

4-6 Basic variance analysis Tartan Mills expected to sell 30,000 of its Style 105 knit sweaters at $30 each. It actually sold 29,000 at $29. Variable cost is $14 per sweater.

Required
1. Determine the sales volume variance.
2. Determine the sales price variance.

4-7 Basic sales mix The general manager of Lo-Price Grocery Stores reviewed the following data. Fixed costs are $680,000 per month.

	Produce	Meat/Dairy	Canned Goods
Contribution margin percentage	40%	35%	30%
Sales mix percentage, in dollars	30%	20%	50%

Required
1. Determine the weighted-average contribution margin percentage.

2. Determine the break-even sales volume per month.
3. Determine the sales necessary to earn $90,000 per month.

 4-8   *Improving sales mix* Davis Exterminating Company performs a wide variety of pest control services. George Davis, the owner, has been examining the following forecasts for 19X6.

Type of Service	Expected Dollar Volume for 19X6	Contribution Margin Percentage
Termites	$120,000	60%
Lawn pests	90,000	50%
Interior pests	90,000	70%

Total fixed costs are expected to be $140,000 in 19X6.

Required

1. What is the weighted-average contribution margin percentage?
2. What profit should Davis earn?
3. The actual sales mix turned out to be 20% termites, 30% lawn pests, and 50% interior pests. Total actual sales were $300,000 and total fixed costs were $140,000. Determine (a) the actual weighted-average contribution margin percentage and (b) profit.

4-9   *Relationships* Bruton Syrup sold 12,000 cases of Light Maple. It had a $3,000 favorable sales volume variance and a $2,400 unfavorable sales price variance. It had a budgeted selling price of $10 and variable cost of $7.

Required

1. Determine the number of cases that Bruton had budgeted to sell.
2. Determine the actual price per case that Bruton received.
3. Determine Bruton's budgeted and actual contribution margins.

4-10   *Price and volume variances* Klaxton Company makes large plastic wastebaskets. Budgeted results for March were as follows.

Sales (30,000 units)	$210,000
Variable costs	75,000
Contribution margin	$135,000

Actual results were as follows.

Sales	$212,350
Variable costs	77,500
Contribution margin	$134,850

Variable costs were incurred as expected, per unit.

Required
1. How many wastebaskets did the company sell?
2. What was the actual selling price?
3. What were the volume variance and price variance?

4-11 Product line income statements Campus Laundromat is two years old. Sales have been $4,000 per week, contribution margin is 75% of sales, and weekly fixed costs have been $1,800. Jill Owens, its owner, recently began to sell beer and also installed stereo equipment. She is now selling 800 bottles per week at $1.00. Variable cost is $0.40 per bottle. Additional fixed costs associated with the beer and stereo equipment are $300 per week. The laundry business has also increased to $4,800 per week. Jill's accountant has prepared the following income statement.

	Beer	Laundry	Total
Sales	$800	$4,800	$5,600
Variable costs	320	1,200	1,520
Contribution margin	$480	$3,600	$4,080
Fixed costs	380	1,720	2,100
Income	$100	$1,880	$1,980

The accountant assigned the $300 fixed costs added by the beer business to beer. He also allocated $80 in building rent, light, and heat to beer, based on the relative space occupied by the bar and the laundry equipment.

Required
1. Prepare an income statement for Jill's business before she sold beer.
2. Prepare a new product-line income statement for Jill's business after she started selling beer. Show the $300 fixed costs as direct to beer and the original $1,800 as direct to the laundry business.
3. Does the income statement you prepared for item 2 better show the results of the two lines? Why or why not?

4-12   Basic sales mix Allen Cosmetics makes two facial creams, Allergy-free and Cleansaway. Data are as follows.

	Allergy-free	Cleansaway
Price per jar	$10	$8
Variable cost per jar	$5	$2

Monthly fixed costs are $90,000.

Required
1. If the sales mix in dollars is 60% for Allergy-free and 40% for Cleansaway, what is the weighted-average contribution margin percentage? What dollar sales are needed to earn a profit of $30,000 per month?
2. If the sales mix is 50% for each product in units, what is the weighted-average unit contribution margin? What unit sales are needed to earn $30,000 per month?
3. Suppose that the company is operating at the level of sales that you calculated in item 1, earning a $30,000 monthly profit. The sales manager believes that

it is possible to persuade customers to switch to Cleansaway from Allergy-free by increasing advertising expenses. He thinks that $8,000 additional monthly advertising would change the mix to 40% for Allergy-free and 60% for Cleansaway. Total dollar sales will not change, only the mix. What effect would the campaign have on profit?

4-13 *Weighted-average contribution margin* Blue-Room Products sells three types of simulated brass soap dishes, the Necessary, the Frill, and the Luxury. Detailed selling price and cost data for the products are as follows.

	Necessary	Frill	Luxury
Selling price	$10	$20	$25
Variable cost	$4	$12	50% of selling price

Fixed costs for these products are $286,000.

Required

1. If the company has a choice of selling one more unit of any one of its products, which product should it choose?
2. If the company could sell $1,000 more of any one of its products, which product should it choose?
3. Assume that the sales dollar volume of the company is distributed 40% from Necessary, 20% from Frill, and 40% from Luxury.
   (a) What is the weighted-average contribution margin percentage?
   (b) What is the break-even point for the company in sales dollars?
   (c) At the break-even point, how many units of Luxury are sold?
4. Assume, instead, that the company's sales in units are 40% for Necessary, 20% for Frill, and 40% for Luxury.
   (a) What is the weighted-average unit contribution margin?
   (b) What is the break-even point in units?
   (c) At the break-even point, how many units of Luxury are sold?

4-14 *Variance analysis* The controller of MHA Inc. is examining the following budgeted and actual income statements for its principal product for 19X5. All amounts are in thousands of dollars.

	Budget	Actual
Sales	$4,800.0	$4,967.2
Variable costs	1,680.0	1,780.8
Contribution margin	$3,120.0	$3,186.4

The budgeted unit selling price is $8.00. Actual unit volume is 6% over budget, but the actual selling price is below budget. Per-unit variable costs are incurred as budgeted.

Required

Determine the sales price variance and sales volume variance.

4-15 *Pricing policy—public service* MTA, the city-owned bus service of Middleton, charges $0.90 for all rides. The city has many retired citizens, whose incomes are generally lower than those of working citizens. A member of the city council has proposed that MTA reduce its fares for persons over 65 to $0.40.

At the present time, about 1,200,000 rides per month are made on MTA buses, about 30% of which are by citizens over 65. Buses are rarely crowded. The council member estimates that the decrease in fares to older persons would increase their use of the bus service by 50%. The number of other users would remain the same. Even with the expected increase in riders, buses rarely would be crowded.

Required
1. How much will it cost per month for MTA to reduce fares to riders over 65?
2. Suppose that the bus service is breaking even. By how much would regular fares have to increase to get back to break even if the reduction is granted?

4-16   Product profitability and mix   The sales manager of Worthem Company has been looking at the following extracts from the monthly marketing plan for the coming year. Worthem distributes scented bath oils.

	Paree	Enchante	Whisper
Selling price	$20	$16	$8
Variable cost	6	4	4
Contribution margin	$14	$12	$4
Expected monthly volume, in bottles	5,000	12,000	16,000

Required
1. Determine which product is most profitable (a) per unit sold and (b) per dollar sold.
2. The sales manager would like to achieve a better mix and believes that an advertising campaign could result in buyers of 3,000 bottles of Enchante switching to Paree and buyers of 8,000 bottles of Whisper switching to Paree. The campaign would cost $80,000 per month. Determine whether Worthem should undertake the campaign.

4-17   Price-volume relationships   Watson Brothers manufactures two models of shelving. The standard model sells for $20 and has variable costs of $7. The deluxe model sells for $50 and has variable costs of $35. Unit volume for each model is 8,000 per month. The sales manager believes that a 10% price reduction for either model would increase its unit volume by 25%. Referring to the following schedule, which shows that sales of the deluxe model would increase more than those of the standard model, the sales manager suggests reducing the price for the deluxe model.

	Standard Model	Deluxe Model
Sales after reduction:		
10,000 × $18	$180,000	
10,000 × $45		$450,000
Current sales:		
8,000 × $20	160,000	
8,000 × $50		400,000
Increase in sales	$ 20,000	$ 50,000

Required
1. Determine the total contribution margin that each model currently earns.

2. Determine the total contribution margin that each model would earn after the proposed price reduction.
3. Would you reduce the price of either model?

4-18   Pricing to break even   The Student Senate at Western University sponsors programs for students and faculty. Among the programs is a monthly movie in an auditorium that holds 3,200 people. The movies selected ordinarily would not be shown in the one theater in the small town in which the university is located. Attendance at the university showings is high; a one-evening showing invariably is sold out. When shown on two evenings, attendance at each showing averages 2,375.

Movies are rented at a cost of $2,400 for one showing, $3,200 for two showings. Other fixed costs per showing are $600; variable costs are $0.40 per person for chair rentals, tickets, and miscellaneous items. The Senate wants to break even for the year on the movie program.

Required

1. Determine the prices that must be charged so that the Senate can break even on the movie showings for the year assuming (a) one showing of each movie and (b) two showings of each movie.
2. Write a memorandum that makes a recommendation to the Senate regarding the number of times a movie should be shown. Explain the factors that influenced your decision. Use the guidelines in Appendix A.

4-19   Market share   MBT Company produces and sells consumer products. It recently hired a new vice president for sales who is a great believer in increasing the market share of a product. One of the first proposals was to reduce the price of Kleenbrite, a toothpaste that had a 15% share of the total market of 2,000,000 tubes.

The current price is $1.60 per tube; variable costs are $0.50. The new vice president reduced the price by $0.10, and Kleenbrite increased its share of the market to 16% of the 2,000,000 tube market.

Required

1. Was reducing the price to gain market share a wise move? Show separately the effects of the change in price and the change in volume.
2. What share of the market did Kleenbrite need to achieve in order to justify the $0.10 price reduction?
3. Suppose that the company could increase the market share of Kleenbrite at the $1.60 price by increasing advertising and promotion expenses. What additional expenditures would MBT be able to make to increase market share by one percentage point without reducing its overall profit?

 4-20   Variances from plans (extension of 3-29)   Competitive pressures late in February prompted the managers of Forecast Company to reduce its selling price for March to $9.80. Per-unit variable costs, total fixed costs, and income tax rates continued to behave as budgeted, and total variable costs for March were $420,000.

Required

1. How many units were sold in March?
2. What was the total contribution margin for March?
3. Was the March sales volume variance favorable or unfavorable?
4. What was the sales volume variance?
5. Was the March sales price variance favorable or unfavorable?

6. What was the sales price variance?
7. What income did the company earn in March?

PROBLEMS

4-21 Product profitability Wrynn Company sells three kinds of tobacco jars. The controller has prepared the following analysis of profitability of each of the jars.

	Flavorsaver	Shagholder	Burleykeeper
Selling price	$5.00	$8.00	$11.00
Variable costs	$2.00	$4.00	$ 6.40
Fixed costs	3.00	3.00	3.00
Total costs	$5.00	$7.00	$ 9.40
Profit	—	$1.00	$ 1.60
Profit percentage to selling price	0%	12.5%	14.5%
Annual volume	22,000	15,000	13,000

The company has total fixed costs of $150,000 per year. The controller obtained the fixed cost per unit figure of $3 by dividing $150,000 by 50,000 units (22,000 + 15,000 + 13,000). On the basis of the analysis, the controller suggests that the Flavorsaver model be discontinued if a more profitable substitute can be found. This conclusion upsets the sales manager, who has budgeted a $10,000 promotional campaign for Flavorsaver. He estimates that the $10,000 expenditure on any product would increase its volume by 25%. Sales of the other products would be unaffected, as would existing fixed costs.

Required
Determine which product should be selected for the special promotion.

4-22 Variances in a service business Earl Torgeson, the managing partner of Torgeson, Watts, and Gold, Certified Public Accountants, is comparing budgeted and actual results for 19X1. Because all employees are on salary, there are no variable costs associated with chargeable hours (hours worked on client business).

Employee Category	Budgeted			Actual		
	Hourly Rate	Hours	Total Revenue	Hourly Rate	Hours	Total Revenue
Junior staff	$20	40,000	$800,000	$19	38,000	$722,000
Senior staff	40	12,000	480,000	38	13,000	494,000

Required
For each category, determine the price (rate) and volume variances.

4-23 Segmented income statements—costs of activities Claxton Industries makes three principal product lines: sporting goods, housewares, and hardware.

The company has suffered reduced profitability in the past few quarters, and the top managers have taken a number of actions to try to improve the situation. The most recent quarterly income statement, segmented by product line, follows. Common fixed costs are allocated to the lines based on relative sales or labor content.

Claxton Industries
Income Statement, Second Quarter, 19X9
(in thousands of dollars)

	Total	Sporting Goods	Housewares	Hardware
Sales	$3,337.0	$650.0	$921.0	$1,766.0
Cost of sales	1,928.8	357.3	545.7	1,025.8
Gross margin	$1,408.2	$292.7	$375.3	$ 740.2
Operating expenses:				
Selling expenses	$ 787.6	$157.1	$225.9	$ 404.6
Administrative expenses	514.6	94.2	135.6	284.8
Total operating expenses	$1,302.2	$251.3	$361.5	$ 689.4
Income before taxes	$ 106.0	$ 41.4	$ 13.8	$ 50.8

The managers are still not happy with the 3.2% return on sales, but the $106 thousand pretax profit was a bit higher than the previous quarter's profit. The consensus of the managers is that they should concentrate on sporting goods and hardware because their ROS's are higher than that of housewares. One manager even wants to ignore housewares because its ROS was only 1.5%. "If we only keep a cent and a half from a dollar's sales, why even bother with it?"

   When asked to confirm the judgments about relative profitabilities, the controller points out that some common costs are allocated to the product lines and that some distortions might result from those allocations. Therefore, her assistant has been asked to prepare an alternative income statement without making allocations. The assistant's analysis of Claxton's cost structure reveals the following (in thousands of dollars).

	Sporting Goods	Housewares	Hardware
Variable Costs, Percentage of Sales			
Cost of sales	28.00%	32.00%	35.00%
Selling expenses	2.00%	1.50%	1.80%
Administrative expenses	0.90%	0.70%	2.00%
Direct Fixed Costs			
Cost of sales	$158	$141	$197
Selling expenses	56	87	133
Administrative expenses	13	22	43

The assistant evaluates the costs by examining the activities that generate them. For example, sporting goods require relatively more attention from manufacturing support personnel, such as engineers, than hardware and so is assigned relatively higher direct fixed manufacturing costs. By the same token, hardware consumes considerably more relative administrative time than sporting goods, giving it relatively more direct cost.

Required
1. Prepare a new segmented income statement using the assistant's findings. Show common costs only in the total column, as in Exhibit 4-4.
2. Write a memorandum to the controller that comments on the differences between your statement and the one above. Indicate for example, what decisions are easier, or more difficult, to make with your statement. Use the guidelines in Appendix A.
3. Each line is controlled by a manager. From an ethics standpoint, what can these managers expect from the people who develop the information and prepare the reports? Refer to Exhibit 1-3 on pages 19 and 20.

4-24 Costs and profits per unit Managers of Hylman Company, which manufactures a packaged beverage sweetener, have been trying to decide what price to charge for the product next year. One manager has come up with the following analysis.

Average Price per Case	Likely Results		
	Total Case Volume	Per-Case Cost	Per-Case Gross Margin
$260	60,000	$225.00	$35.00
$250	70,000	$218.00	$32.00
$240	80,000	$212.75	$27.25

"It seems to me," the manager says, "that we should go with the $260 price, since the per-case gross margin is highest at that price."

Required
Determine the price that yields the highest total profit to the firm.

4-25 CVP analysis—product mix Happy Times Brewery produces and sells two grades of beer: regular and premium. Premium sells for $9.50 per case, regular for $7.20. Variable brewing costs per case are $4.80 (premium) and $3.75 (regular). Sales of regular beer, in cases, are double those of premium. Fixed brewing costs are $120,000 monthly and fixed selling and administrative costs are $75,000 monthly. The only variable cost besides variable brewing costs is a 10% sales commission.

Required
1. Compute the break-even point in total cases per month.
2. How many cases of each kind of beer are sold at break even?
3. The brewery is now selling about 90,000 cases per month. The advertising manager believes that sales of premium beer could be increased by 20% if an extensive advertising campaign were undertaken. The campaign would cost $24,000 per month. However, sales of regular beer are expected to fall by about 5% because some customers now buying the regular grade would merely switch to premium. Should the campaign be undertaken?
4. If the campaign were undertaken, what is the weighted-average unit contribution margin?
5. What is the new break-even point in unit sales?

4-26   *Pricing a product*   Watson Camera Company makes cameras and film. The company is introducing a new camera this year, the Super-90. Variable costs are $20 per unit. Associated fixed costs are $2,000,000 per year for production, advertising, and administration. The sales manager of Watson believes that if the camera is priced at $40, about 250,000 units per year will be sold. If the price is $50, about 200,000 units per year would be sold.

Required

1. Determine which price would yield the higher profit.
2. Suppose that for each camera sold, the company usually sells eight packages of film per year. Film sells for $6 per package and the variable cost is $1.20 per package. Would this information affect your analysis in item 1?

4-27   *Pricing decision and average costs*   The sales manager for Markham Pen Company has been trying to decide what price to charge for a pen the company is introducing this year. His staff has prepared a research report that indicates the following price-volume relationships.

Price	Volume (millions)
$3.25	1.6 units
3.10	1.8
2.95	2.0
2.80	2.2
2.65	2.4

The variable cost per pen is $1.50, and total annual fixed costs are estimated at $1.5 million. The sales manager believes that any product should be priced at 150% of total cost. He decides to use 2.2 million units as the volume to determine the average unit cost and computes the cost at $2.182 per pen. He intends to set the price at $3.25.

Required

1. Assuming that the predictions of the staff are correct, determine what profit would be earned if the pen is priced at $3.25.
2. Again assuming the correctness of the staff's predictions, determine which price would yield the highest profit.
3. Suggest what might be wrong with the sales manager's method of setting prices.

   4-28   *Product profitability*   Immediately upon graduation from State University, Jan Wilks took the position of assistant controller with Crow Clothing Company. The controller has given her the following information based on expected operations for the coming year.

	T-Shirts	Sweatshirts	Jeans
Selling price	$6	$ 15	$ 20
Variable costs	3	6	12
Contribution margin	$3	$ 9	$ 8
Sales mix percentage, in dollar sales	40%	40%	20%

Total fixed costs are $840,000.

Required

1. The marketing manager believes that the company could increase sales of any of the three products by one unit for each $4 in additional advertising expenditures. Which product would it be most profitable to advertise?
2. Determine the weighted-average contribution margin percentage.
3. Determine the break-even point.
4. The president wants a profit of $210,000. Determine the sales dollars needed to achieve this goal.
5. After extensive discussions with the sales manager and marketing department, the controller believes that the sales mix will probably change to 20%, 30%, and 50% for T-shirts, sweatshirts, and jeans, respectively.
   (a) Determine the new break-even point.
   (b) Determine the sales needed to earn $210,000.

4-29   Sales promotion   Sales of pizza and beer at Bob's Pizza & Pub have been averaging about $3,000 per week. The weighted-average contribution margin is 60% and weekly fixed costs are $1,200. To attract more business, Bob has hired a local band to play on Saturday nights. The band charges $450 per night. Other costs associated with having the band are $60 per night. Bob charges each person a $1 entry fee when the band is playing. Sales on Saturday nights had been about $600 before the band was hired. Since Bob hired the band, Saturday night attendance has averaged 300 people.

Required

1. Determine the income or loss attributable to having the band. For the moment, ignore the effects that the band might have had on sales of pizza and beer.
2. Determine the increase in sales of pizza and beer that Bob needs to maintain his weekly income at the same level it was before he hired the band.
3. Sales of beer and pizza on Saturday nights actually increased to $1,100, raising total weekly sales to $3,500. Determine the overall effect on Bob's weekly income of hiring the band.
4. Item 3 stated that the entire increase in weekly sales came on Saturday nights. Suppose that weekly sales increased by $500, but that $300 of the increase came on Saturday nights and $200 on other nights. Would your analysis from item 3 still hold? Why or why not?

4-30   Product-line report   Karen Bell is president of Bell & Company, which distributes consumer products to supermarkets. Ms. Bell has been trying to analyze the profitability of her lines. She has available the following information.

Line	Annual Sales	Gross Profit Percentage	Direct Fixed Costs
Paper products	$2,000,000	30%	$110,000
Detergents	1,200,000	40%	150,000

The only variable cost, besides cost of goods sold, is a 10% commission paid on all sales. Bell incurs $350,000 in fixed costs that are common to both lines. All direct fixed costs listed above are discretionary.

Required

Answer each item independently.

1. Prepare an income statement using the format shown in Exhibit 4-4.

2. Ms. Bell believes that she could increase the volume of either line by 10% by increasing promotion of the line by $30,000. Which, if either, line should she select? She cannot select both.

3. Ms. Bell believes that she could increase the volume of either line by 10% if she raised the commission rate on that line to 12%. Which, if either, line should she select? She cannot select both.

4. How does the report format you used for item 1 provide better information than would an income statement showing only combined results for the two lines?

 4-31   Sales interdependencies (AICPA adapted)   Breezway Company operates a resort complex on an offshore island. The complex consists of a 100-room hotel, shops, a restaurant, and recreational facilities. Mr. Blenem, manager of the complex, has asked for your assistance in planning the coming year's operations. He is particularly concerned about the level of profits the firm is likely to earn.

Your conversation with Mr. Blenem reveals that he expects the hotel to be 80% occupied during the 300 days that it is open. All rooms rent for $40 per day for any number of persons. In virtually all cases, two persons occupy a room. Mr. Blenem also tells you that past experience, which he believes is an accurate guide to the future, indicates that each person staying at the hotel spends $10 per day in the shops and $20 per day in the restaurant. There are no charges for use of the recreational facilities. All sales in the shops and restaurant are made to guests of the hotel, which is isolated from the only large town on the island.

After talking with Mr. Blenem, you obtain the following data from the firm's controller.

	Shops	Restaurant
Variable costs, as a percentage of sales dollars:		
Cost of goods sold	40%	30%
Supplies	10	15
Other	5	5

For the hotel, variable costs are $6 per day per occupied room, for cleaning, laundry, and utilities. Fixed costs for the complex are $1,200,000 per year.

Required

1. Prepare an income statement for the coming year based on the information given.

2. Mr. Blenem tells you he believes that the occupancy rate would increase to 90% if the room rate were reduced to $35 per day. Determine the effect on budgeted income if the rate were reduced.

4-32   Variance analysis—brain teaser   Mack Bolend, controller of AMH Industries, received the following budgeted and actual income statements for one of its major products for a recent month. Not having time to analyze them, he requests that you determine why the company did not achieve its budgeted results. All dollar amounts are in thousands.

	Budget	Actual
Sales	$2,350.0	$2,197.8
Variable costs	1,527.5	1,405.3
Contribution margin	$ 822.5	$ 792.5

Per-unit variable costs were incurred as budgeted.

Required
Determine the sales price variance and sales volume variance.

4-33 *Product profitability and pricing* Jackson Confections makes three flavors of jelly: grape, strawberry, and peach. Price and cost data are as follows.

	Grape	Strawberry	Peach
Selling price per case	$10	$12	$14
Variable cost per case	6	9	7

Monthly fixed costs are $250,000.

Required
1. The sales mix, in dollars, is 40%, 40%, and 20% for grape, strawberry, and peach jelly, respectively. Determine the sales dollars that will yield a monthly profit of $50,000.
2. The president would like to earn $50,000 on sales of $800,000. He proposes to do this by increasing the price of strawberry jelly. He expects the mix to remain the same after the price of strawberry jelly increases. What price must Jackson charge for strawberry jelly to achieve the president's goal?

4-34 *Product line reporting, activity analysis* Kelly Company is a retail store specializing in men's clothing. The company has three major product lines: suits, sport clothes, and accessories. The most recent monthly income statement follows.

Kelly Company
Income Statement for April 19X7
(thousands of dollars)

Sales		$800.0
Cost of sales		572.0
Gross profit		$228.0
Operating expenses:		
Commissions	$48.0	
Salaries	71.4	
Rent	21.4	
Shipping and delivery	15.2	
Insurance	14.0	
Miscellaneous	20.8	190.8
Income before taxes		$ 37.2

The president wants a product-line income statement. She gives you the following additional data:

1. The sales mix in April was 30% suits, 50% sport clothes, and 20% accessories, expressed in dollars of total sales.
2. The cost of sales percentages are 80% for suits, 75% for sport clothes, and 50% for accessories.
3. Sales commissions are 6% for all product lines.

4. Each product line is the responsibility of a separate manager, and each manager has a small staff. The salaries that are directly related to each product line are $12,000 for suits, $8,000 for sport clothes, and $5,200 for accessories. These salaries are avoidable. All other salaries are common to the three lines.
5. Rent is for both office and warehouse space, all of which is in a single building.
6. Shipping and delivery costs are for operating expenses and depreciation on the firm's three trucks. Each truck serves a particular geographical area and delivers all three product lines.
7. Insurance includes a $6,000 fixed amount for basic liability coverage. The rest is for coverage of merchandise at the rate of one percent of the selling price of the average inventory on hand during the month. In April, the average inventories at selling prices were equal to sales for each product line.
8. Miscellaneous expenses are committed, but direct. The amounts are $6,000 to suits, $8,800 to sport clothes, and $6,000 to accessories.

Required
Prepare an income statement by product, using the format shown in Exhibit 4-4.

4-35   Product profitability   Messorman Company produces three models of pen and pencil sets, regular, silver, and gold. Price and cost data are as follows.

	Regular	Silver	Gold
Selling price	$10	$20	$30
Variable costs	6	8	15

Monthly fixed costs are $200,000.

Required
1. Which model is most profitable per unit sold?
2. Which model is most profitable per dollar of sales?
3. Suppose the sales mix in dollars is 40% Regular, 20% Silver, and 40% Gold.
   (a) What is the weighted-average contribution margin?
   (b) What is the monthly break-even point?
   (c) What sales volume is necessary to earn a profit of $30,000 per month?
4. Suppose the sales mix in dollars is 30% Regular, 30% Silver, and 40% Gold.
   (a) What is the break-even point?
   (b) What sales volume is necessary to earn $30,000 per month?
5. Suppose that the sales mix in units is 40% Regular, 20% Silver, and 40% Gold.
   (a) What is the weighted-average unit contribution margin?
   (b) What is the break-even point in total units?
   (c) How many total units must Messorman sell to earn $30,000 per month?

4-36   What is profitability?   Kimbell Company sells three products. Data are as follows.

	Product		
	A	B	C
Selling price	$30	$50	$100
Variable cost	20	25	60
Contribution margin	$10	$25	$ 40
Annual unit volume	50,000	10,000	5,000

Required

1. Rank the products in order of profitability as measured by (a) total annual profit, (b) profitability per unit sold, and (c) profitability per dollar of sales.
2. Explain what the rankings mean and how Kimbell's managers might use the information.

4-37   *Product line income statements*   The president of Mifflan Tool Company has just received the firm's income statement for January 19X8. He is puzzled because you had told him last year, when working as a consultant to the firm, that sales of $500,000 should produce a profit of about $46,500 before income taxes.

Mifflan Tool Company
Income Statement for January 19X8

Sales		$500,000
Cost of sales		307,500
Gross profit		$192,500
Operating expenses:		
Rent	$40,000	
Salaries	70,000	
Shipping and delivery	23,000	
Other expenses	30,000	163,000
Income before taxes		$ 29,500

The company sells three lines of power tools, and your analysis assumed the following sales mix in dollars: saws, 30%; drills, 20%; and sanders, 50%. The actual mix in dollars in January was 40%, 30%, 30%. The company does not manufacture its products. Cost of sales and shipping and delivery are variable costs. All others are fixed. Data per unit for each product follow.

	Saws	Drills	Sanders
Selling price	$50	$20	$40
Cost of sales	$30	$15	$20
Shipping and delivery	2	1	2
Total variable costs	$32	$16	$22
Contribution margin	$18	$ 4	$18

None of the fixed costs is directly associated with any particular product line. All costs were incurred as expected, per unit for variable costs, in total for fixed costs. Selling prices were as expected.

Required

1. Prepare a new income statement by product, based on actual results in January. Show both gross profit and contribution margin for each product.
2. Prepare an income statement by product for January, assuming that the expected sales mix had been achieved.
3. Explain the reasons for the differences between the two statements.

4-38   *Revenue variances for an airline*   Big Sky Airline had budgeted for $22 million revenue in March, expecting a 60% load factor (percentage of seat-miles occupied). Actual revenue was $22.8 million. The load factor was 66%. Variable cost per seat-mile is negligible.

Required

Determine the difference between budgeted and actual revenue attributable to (a) price and (b) volume (load factor). Round to the nearest $100,000.

4-39   Decision making for student programs   The Speaker Committee at a large university invites distinguished persons to address students, faculty, and members of the public. Students and faculty are admitted free; members of the public pay $2. Students and faculty must pick up tickets in advance; any tickets left on the day of the speech are sold to the public. The speaker program is expected to break even for the year.

The committee is trying to decide whether to invite Marvin Gardens, a noted environmentalist, or Cayuga Waters, a famous industrialist. One student member of the committee argues that Marvin Gardens is an ideal speaker. His fee is $800. The student states that the auditorium, which holds 2,000 people, will be almost completely filled with students and faculty if Garden speaks. He believes that only about 500 tickets would be available to members of the public and that all available tickets could be sold. Another member, an administrative officer of the university, says that Waters would be a better speaker. She believes that only 500 students and faculty would show up, leaving 1,500 tickets that could easily be sold to the public. Waters charges a fee of $2,000.

Required

1. Assuming that both committee members are correct in their assessments of demand for tickets, which speaker would be more profitable?
2. What other factors should be considered in reaching a decision?
3. What do you recommend?

4-40   Cost analysis in a university   The School of Management at State University currently has 500 students and 25 faculty members. The school's students are juniors and seniors who take all their courses in the school, an average of five courses per semester. The school offers 75 sections per semester, with each faculty member teaching three sections.

Following are the data for the number of sections, average number of students per section, and "student-sections," which is the total number of enrollments in all sections. Since 500 students take five courses each semester, there are 2,500 student-sections.

Number of Sections	×	Average Enrollment	=	Student-Sections
20		20		400
30		35		1,050
25		42		1,050
75				2,500

The university's administration is considering increasing the enrollment in the School of Management to 1,000 students. One university officer objects that the cost would be prohibitive. He states that faculty salaries are now $950,000 per year and would double if enrollment were to double because twice the number of teaching faculty would be required.

Another officer points out that doubling the size of the faculty would not be necessary because the size of the sections could be increased. However, university policy is that no more than 45 students be enrolled in a single section.

You are assigned the task of determining the additional cost of faculty salaries required to support enrollment of 1,000 students. You estimate that demand for the classes now averaging 20 students per section is such that each section would go up to 25 students if enrollment went to 1,000. All other sections would be increased to the 45-student maximum. A faculty member would be hired for each three sections per semester added, at a salary of $30,000 per year.

Required

1. How many sections are needed if enrollment increases to 1,000 students? (Hint: Because 1,000 students will take five courses per semester, you must account for 5,000 individual enrollments.)
2. How much additional cost will be incurred for faculty salaries?
3. After you performed the analyses in items 1 and 2, the chancellor of the university became concerned about the large class sizes. You are asked to redo the analysis of required additional faculty salaries assuming that only 40 sections would hold 45 students, 20 would still hold 25 students, and the rest would have a maximum of 36 students.

4-41   *Multiple products—movie company (continuation of 2-43 and 3-32)* Both the producing company and prospective star have given further thought to the contract terms and concluded that some provision probably should be made for revenues to be earned from contracts authorizing showings of the movie on television. After lengthy negotiations, Kirkwalker's agent proposed the following terms: (a) a payment of $1,000,000, plus (b) 15% of the receipts to the producer from theater admissions, plus (c) 10% of the revenues from sales of television rights. Blockbusters' negotiating team leaves the negotiations to study the potential effect of the new offer.

A study of past productions indicates that the producer can expect revenues from sales of television rights to be approximately one-eighth (12.5%) of producer's revenues from theater admissions. Ms. Lane is pleased with the opportunity to lower the fixed-payment part of the contract but is concerned about the magnitude of the two off-the-top percentages.

Required

1. At what level of receipts to the producer will Blockbusters break even under the new contract proposal?
2. Considering the additional information about the sale of television rights, at what level of receipts to the producer will Blockbusters break even under Kirkwalker's normal contract terms ($1,500,000 plus 5% of the producer's receipts)?
3. Assume that, because of Blockbusters' delay in accepting the contract offer, Kirkwalker's agent decides that his client should also receive a percentage of the revenues Blockbusters will derive from the sale of screening rights in foreign countries, revenues which typically amount to 10% of domestic receipts. If the agent proposes a 5% cut of those revenues for Kirkwalker, what is the break-even point for Blockbusters Incorporated?

4-42   *Interrelationships between products* Rapidcal Company manufactures hand-held calculators. The industry is highly competitive and pricing is critical to sales volume. Warren James, sales manager of Rapidcal, has been trying to set a price for a model that the company will introduce shortly. The new model, the RC-89, is somewhat more sophisticated than the RC-63, which has been successful in recent years. The RC-63 now sells at retail for $20, of which 30% goes to the dealer and 70% to Rapidcal. Variable costs for the RC-63 are $8 per unit. The variable costs for the RC-89, exclusive of dealer share, are $18 per unit.

James is especially concerned about the effects on sales of RC-63 following the introduction of the RC-89. He believes that if the RC-89 is priced at $44 retail, no loss in sales of the RC-63 would occur. However, if the RC-89 were sold at $42, he thinks that some people will buy the RC-89 instead of buying the RC-63. At the $44 price, James expects sales of 150,000 RC-89s per year. For each $2 price cut for RC-89s, sales would increase by about 30,000 units, but about 40% of the increased sales of RC-89 would be at the expense of sales of the RC-63. At any price for the RC-89, Rapidcal receives 70%, the retailer 30%.

Also, James believes that a $38 retail price is rock-bottom for the RC-89. He therefore instructs you to determine the effects on the income of the company of pricing the RC-89 at $44, $42, $40, and $38.

Required

Comply with the sales manager's request and determine the price that should be set for the RC-89.

4-43   Multiple products (extension of 3-29)   The budgeted data for Forecast Company, as shown in 3-29, represent the combined plans for three products: a platter, a cup, and a saucer. The expected sales mix of the three products, in sales dollars, is 40%, 30%, and 30% for the platter, cup, and saucer, respectively.

Required

1. What are the expected sales, in dollars, for each product?
2. If the contribution margin percentage for cups is 10% and that for saucers is 30%, what is the contribution margin percentage for platters?
3. The normal sales mix is one platter for every two cup-and-saucer sets, and the budgeted results reflect that mix. If the expected sales of 50,000 units count each platter, cup, and saucer as a separate unit, what are the budgeted selling prices and per-unit variable costs for each of the three products?
4. Assume that the actual sales for April were $450,000 and that the sales mix, in dollars, was 60% platters and 20% each for cups and saucers.
   (a) What was the actual total contribution margin earned for April?
   (b) What was the actual weighted-average contribution margin percentage for April?
5. B. J. Douglas, sales manager for Forecast Company, considers the April results to be unusual and not likely to be repeated. That is, she believes that sales and cost data reflected in the original plans are appropriate as long as there are no changes in costs or selling prices. But she is convinced that the price of plates (in relation to those charged for the other two products) is too high and not in the firm's best interest. Accordingly, she has developed several plans for improving sales, all involving price reductions for plates. These plans, together with Douglas's best estimates of their effects on sales, are summarized as follows.

Plan A: Reduce the price of a plate to $19. Douglas estimates that unit sales of plates will increase by 10% and that the price reduction will have no effect on the sales of the other two products.

Plan B: Reduce the price of a plate to $16. Douglas estimates that unit sales of plates will increase 20% and that the price reduction will result in more customers buying cups and saucers so that three of each of the other products will be sold for every plate sold.

Plan C: Reduce the price of a plate to $18. Douglas estimates that unit sales of plates will increase 20% and that the present sales mix of two cups and two saucers sold for every plate sold will not change.

Which, if any, of the proposed plans should be adopted?

4-44   Personnel policies and decisions   Patterson Company operates a chain of hardware stores in a metropolitan area. Each store has a manager, several salespeople, and one or two clerks. The vice president has reviewed the performance of each store and is considering closing the Middleton store. The income statement shows the following for 19X8 and future results are expected to be about the same.

Middleton Store
Income Statement for 19X8

Sales		$500,000
Cost of sales	$350,000	
Salaries	85,000	
Commissions, 10% of sales	50,000	
Rent on building	20,000	
Rent on store equipment	4,000	
Miscellaneous expenses	7,000	516,000
Net loss		$(16,000)

If Patterson closes the Middleton store, it will transfer all personnel to other stores. The company is opening several new stores and needs to hire additional people even if the ones from the Middleton store are transferred. The miscellaneous expenses are fixed, but avoidable if the store is closed. If the store closes, none of its former business would go to any of the existing stores.

Required
1. Assume that the leases on building and equipment have 12 years to run. Patterson has no other use for the building and equipment and could not sublease them to another firm. Determine whether the company should close the store.
2. Assume now that the leases are month-to-month and can be canceled at any time. Determine whether the store should be closed.
3. Assume that the leases are unavoidable, as in item 1. However, suppose now that the Middleton store has been losing business because the company has two newer stores relatively close by. The vice president believes that closing the Middleton store will increase total sales in its other stores by $80,000 per year. Cost of sales and commissions, as percentages of sales dollars, are the same in all stores. Fixed costs in the other stores would not be affected by the increases in sales. Determine whether the Middleton store should be closed.

4-45   Line of business reporting (CMA adapted)   Riparian Company produces and sells three products. Each is sold domestically and in foreign countries. The foreign market has been disappointing to management because of poor operating results, as evidenced by the income statement for the first quarter of 19X8.

	Total	Domestic	Foreign
Sales	$1,300,000	$1,000,000	$300,000
Cost of goods sold	1,010,000	775,000	235,000
Gross profit	$ 290,000	$ 225,000	$ 65,000
Selling expenses	$ 105,000	$ 60,000	$ 45,000
Administrative expenses	52,000	40,000	12,000
	$ 157,000	$ 100,000	$ 57,000
Income	$ 133,000	$ 125,000	$ 8,000

Management decided a year ago to enter the foreign market because of excess capacity, but is now unsure whether to continue devoting time and effort to developing it. The following information has been gathered for consideration of the alternatives that management has identified.

	Products		
	A	B	C
Sales:			
Domestic	$400,000	$300,000	$300,000
Foreign	100,000	100,000	100,000
Variable manufacturing costs (percentage of sales)	60%	70%	60%
Variable selling expenses (percentage of sales)	3%	2%	2%

Of the $190,000 total fixed manufacturing costs, $30,000, $40,000, and $70,000 are direct to products A, B, and C, respectively. These amounts are not avoidable in the short term. Additionally, $90,000 in fixed manufacturing costs are direct to the domestic market, $20,000 to the foreign market. These amounts are also unavoidable.

All administrative expenses are fixed and common to the three products and to the two markets. Fixed selling expenses are direct and avoidable by market. Some $40,000 of fixed selling expenses are direct to products, and also avoidable. The percentages of the $40,000 applicable to each product are 30% to A, 30% to B, and 40% to C.

Management believes that if the foreign market was dropped, sales in the domestic market could be increased by $200,000. The increase would be divided 40%, 40%, 20% among products A, B, and C, respectively.

Management also believes that a new product, D, could be introduced by the end of the current year. The product would replace product C and would increase fixed costs by $30,000 per quarter.

Required

1. Prepare an income statement for the quarter by product, using the format of Exhibit 4-4.
2. Prepare an income statement for the quarter by market, using the format of Exhibit 4-4.
3. Determine whether the foreign market should be dropped.
4. Assume that the foreign market will not be dropped. Determine the minimum quarterly contribution margin that product D would have to produce in order to make its introduction desirable.

4-46   *Price and volume variances (AICPA adapted)*   Bay City Gas Company supplies liquefied natural gas to residential customers. Following are the results, both budgeted and actual, for the month of November 19X7. Although he knows that the price of gas per 1,000 cubic feet drops with increases in purchases by a customer, the operations manager is having difficulty interpreting the report.

	Budgeted	Actual	Difference
Number of customers	26,000	28,000	2,000
Sales in thousands of cubic feet	520,000	532,000	12,000
Revenue	$1,300,000	$1,356,600	$56,600
Variable costs	$ 416,000	$ 425,600	$ (9,600)

Required
Compute the sales price variance and sales volume variance.

4-47   *Sales strategies*   Nova Company sells cosmetics through door-to-door salespeople who receive 25% commissions. Nova's national sales manager has been evaluating alternative selling strategies for the coming season. She is trying to decide whether any products should be discounted in price by 30%, receive increased promotional efforts, or be left alone. She is now considering four products, data for which are as follows.

	Mascara	Eyeliner	Lipstick	Cologne
Normal selling price	$2.50	$2.20	$2.00	$12.00
Variable cost	0.90	1.00	0.80	5.00
Contribution margin	$1.60	$1.20	$1.20	$ 7.00
Expected volumes:				
Without discount or special promotion (units)	800,000	750,000	2,000,000	200,000
With 30% discount	1,650,000	1,350,000	3,200,000	380,000
With special promotion	950,000	920,000	2,150,000	240,000

If the special promotion is chosen for a particular product, its price and variable cost will remain the same. Additional fixed costs are $200,000 for each product selected, primarily for advertising and incentive payments to salespeople.

If a product is selected for a 30% price cut, variable costs will remain the same, per unit, because Nova pays sales commissions on the basis of the normal selling price even during such special sales.

Required
1. For each product, determine which of the following should be done: reduce price, do a special promotion, or do nothing.
2. Discuss some additional factors that might influence the sales manager's decisions about each product.

4-48   *CVP for a hospital—patient-days*   The administrator of Brookwood Memorial Hospital has developed the following estimate of costs.

$$\text{Total annual cost} = \$39,000,000 + (\$28 \times P1) + (\$40 \times P2)$$

where

   $P1$ = *patient-days on medical wards*
   $P2$ = *patient-days on surgical wards*

A patient-day is one patient occupying a bed for one day. The administrator expects contribution margins, other than from room charges, to be about $25 per day from each medical patient and $60 per day from each surgical patient. These come from pharmacy, blood bank, operating room charges, and other such sources.

Required

1. Suppose that patient-days on medical wards generally run twice the number of those on surgical wards. The room charges are tentatively set at $75 per day for medical patients and $100 for surgical patients. How many patient-days must the hospital achieve to break even?
2. Suppose now that the administrator forecasts 250,000 medical patient-days and 150,000 surgical patient-days. He wants to set room rates so that the hospital breaks even and also wants each type of patient-day to provide the same dollar contribution margin. What room rates will achieve these objectives? (The $25 and $60 miscellaneous contributions should be included in determining the contribution margins from room charges.)
3. Repeat item 2 assuming that the administrator wants both types of patient-day to provide the same contribution margin percentage.

4-49   Comprehensive review of Chapters 2, 3, and 4   Tacky Company makes three products and sells them in about the same mix each month. Below are income statements for two recent months.

Tacky Company Income Statements
(in thousands of dollars)

	April	May
Sales	$80	$ 60
Costs	60	52
Income	$20	$ 8

Selling price and cost data by product are as follows.

	A	B	C
Selling price	$20	$10	$5
Variable costs	8	3	3
Contribution margin	$12	$ 7	$2
Contribution margin percentage	60%	70%	40%
Percentage of total sales dollars (mix)	40%	40%	20%

Required

1. Using the income statements for April and May, find total fixed cost and variable cost as a percentage of sales dollars.
2. Determine the break-even point in sales dollars.
3. Which product is most profitable per unit sold?
4. Which product is most profitable per dollar of sales?
5. What sales dollars are needed to earn $35,000 per month, and how many units of each product will be sold at that sales level if the usual mix is maintained?
6. The sales manager believes that he could increase sales of C by 10,000 units per month if more attention were devoted to it and less to B. Sales of B would

fall by 2,000 units per month. What change in income would occur if this action were taken?
7. June sales were $100,000 with a mix of 40% A, 30% B, and 30% C. What was income?
8. July sales were $90,000 and income was $22,000.
   (a) What was the contribution margin percentage?
   (b) Which product would you think was sold in a higher proportion than in the usual mix?
9. Suppose the company is currently selling 6,000 units of C. Because this is the least profitable product, management believes it should be dropped from the mix. If C is dropped, it is expected that sales of B would remain the same and those of A would rise. By how much would sales of A have to rise to maintain the same total income?

4-50   *Segmented income statements, activity analysis*   Vic Kemp, executive vice president of Taylor, Inc., is examining the most recent monthly income statements, which are segmented by geographical area. Each area is the responsibility of a regional manager. Taylor, a distributor of products used by paper manufacturers, began operations in the western part of the United States 20 years ago and expanded into the southern and eastern markets only a year ago. Taylor does not manufacture its products, but rather buys them for resale to its customers.

Because Taylor has a good reputation and strong product lines, it has done well in the new markets, or at least Kemp thinks it has. Other than salespeople, Taylor has relatively few people and other assets in the market areas. The bulk of expenses are incurred at the home offices in Corvallis, Oregon.

Kemp is happy with the results in the new territories, but at the same time mistrusts them, not really knowing how the statements are prepared. Kemp is also concerned that the push into the new territories has caused managers to

Taylor, Inc.
Income Statement, October 19X9
(in thousands of dollars)

	Total	Eastern	Southern	Western
Sales	$2,896.0	$589.0	$752.0	$1,555.0
Cost of sales	1,231.9	200.3	300.8	730.8
Gross margin	$1,664.1	$388.7	$451.2	$ 824.2
Selling expenses:				
Salaries and commissions	$ 754.2	$156.2	$192.6	$ 405.4
Shipping and warehousing	187.3	43.2	67.1	77.0
Other selling expenses	84.5	12.1	27.6	44.8
Total selling expenses	$1,026.0	$211.5	$287.3	$ 527.2
Administrative expenses:				
Salaries	$ 147.2	$ 42.6	$ 36.8	$ 67.8
Building occupancy	61.7	22.7	26.5	12.5
Other	56.1	12.3	22.1	21.7
Total administrative expenses	$ 265.0	$ 77.6	$ 85.4	$ 102.0
Total operating expenses	$1,291.0	$289.1	$372.7	$ 629.2
Income before taxes	$ 373.1	$ 99.6	$ 78.5	$ 195.0

neglect the western territory, which seems to be slipping from past levels of profitability. He is quite concerned that the income statements do not give him the kind of information he needs to make judgments and decisions. He has asked the chief accountant for an explanation of the income statements, but to little avail. The chief accountant usually puts him off by saying that it is very complicated and that he does not have the time to explain every number.

Taylor's chief accountant has been allocating costs to the markets using a set of formulas based on relative sales volume in both unit and dollar terms. No one else quite knows how the chief accountant prepares the statements. Kemp finally goes to the controller and asks for a special study to help him get the information he feels is needed. The controller has been concerned with the allocation methods for some time and has collected the following information based on analyses of the activities in each territory.

	Eastern	Southern	Western
Variable Costs, Percentage of Sales			
Cost of sales	34.00%	40.00%	47.00%
Selling expenses	14.00%	13.00%	16.00%
Administrative expenses	0.00%	0.00%	0.00%
Direct Fixed Costs			
Cost of sales	$ 0	$ 0	$ 0
Selling expenses	152	155	207
Administrative expenses	9	12	19

The controller explains that she has developed the information by analyzing the cost driving activities associated with each category. For instance, the eastern territory has relatively heavy direct fixed selling expenses for several reasons. First, there are more established competitors in that region, and new customers are harder to cultivate. Second, shipping costs tend to be higher because orders from the east are smaller than those from the other regions, thus losing economies of large shipments. Other reasons contribute to the differences between the activity-based direct costs and the costs as allocated in the income statement.

Required

1. Prepare a segmented income statement using the contribution margin format. Work with totals only for selling expenses and administrative expenses. Ignore the individual components of those cost categories.

2. Write a memorandum to Mr. Kemp telling him how each territory is doing. Use the guidelines in Appendix A.

3. Write a memorandum indicating the ethical issues that might arise from your analysis, such as what the regional managers have a right to expect from you or another managerial accountant. Refer to Exhibit 1-3 on pages 19 and 20.

4-51   *Comprehensive problem on CVP analysis* You are presented with the following information about Gammon Sales Company, based on plans for the year 19X1.

Sales ($1 per unit)		$100,000
Variable costs:		
Cost of goods sold	$67,000	
Other operating costs	15,000	
Total		82,000
Contribution margin		$ 18,000
Fixed costs		13,140
Budgeted income before taxes		$ 4,860

Required

1. What is Gammon's break-even sales volume?
2. The company's officers have analyzed anticipated cash flows for the year and have determined that it could afford to spend $3,600 on a special advertising campaign. They are not sure, however, that the expenditure would be worthwhile. What is the break-even point if the campaign is undertaken?
3. If, as a result of the advertising campaign, the number of units sold could be expected to increase in an amount equal to the change in the break-even point in units, would the campaign be financially advisable? Explain.
4. Assume that Gammon has decided not to undertake the advertising campaign and is looking for other ways to improve the financial outlook for 19X1. The purchasing agent determines that there is a supplier (other than the one with which the company now deals) that will allow the company to buy at a price 10% below the anticipated purchase price. The sales manager believes that the new supplier does not provide a product of equal quality, and he estimates that sales volume will decrease by about 15% if the new supplier is used. The controller has determined that the switch in suppliers will necessitate minor changes in the administrative procedures, which will increase fixed costs by approximately $1,000. Would the change of suppliers be wise? Explain your answer with supporting computations.
5. Are there some qualitative considerations that might influence the decision on the change in suppliers?
6. After further investigation, you determine that Gammon has not one, but three separate products in its line, each of which has the same selling price. The budgeted activity for 19X1 in more detail is as follows.

	Product			
	1	2	3	Total
Sales ($1 per unit)	$50,000	$ 30,000	$ 20,000	$100,000
Variable costs:				
Cost of goods sold	$30,000	$ 21,000	$ 16,000	$ 67,000
Other operating costs	7,500	4,500	3,000	15,000
Total	$37,500	$ 25,500	$ 19,000	$ 82,000
Contribution margin	$12,500	$ 4,500	$ 1,000	18,000
Fixed costs				$ 13,140
Budgeted income before taxes				$ 4,860

Gammon has decided not to dilute the impact of a special advertising campaign by trying to promote more than one product. Which product should the company probably choose to promote in the $3,600 advertising campaign? Explain.

7. The company has found an alternative supplier for each of its products. Each supplier is willing to sell to the company at a price 10% lower than is currently being paid. In each case, however, the product from the new supplier will probably reduce the total sales of that product by 15%. However, the company can change suppliers for only one of the products at a time. Ignoring any qualitative considerations, decide for which product, if any, Gammon should change suppliers. Support your answer.

8. Assume that Gammon's directors decide to postpone the advertising campaign and continue doing business with current suppliers. At the end of 19X1, despite sales of $110,000, income before taxes was only $360. Analysis of sales by product showed the following.

Sales of Product 1	$ 30,000
Sales of Product 2	20,000
Sales of Product 3	60,000
Total	$110,000

These results surprised the board of directors because operating managers assured the directors that variable and fixed costs had behaved exactly as expected and sales were in excess of the forecast. Explain the reason or reasons for the disappointing results.

4-52   *Explaining revenue differences for a motel*   Great Eastern Inns, a large motel chain, had revenue of $60 million in 19X5, operating at a 70% occupancy rate. In 19X6, Great Eastern raised its room rates by 5%, and its occupancy rate fell to 65%. Variable costs are negligible.

Required

1. Determine Great Eastern's revenue for 19X6.
2. Determine how much of the difference in revenue, from 19X5 to 19X6, is attributable to (a) room rates and (b) room occupancy. You can treat 19X5 in the same way you usually do "budgeted results," and 19X6 as you do "actual results." Round to the nearest $100,000.

CASES

4-53 Product mix, profit planning, taxes Michael Monte, the new assistant controller of Remley Company, has prepared a CVP analysis for the firm based on sales of the firm's three products from 19X7. He will present the analysis to a group of managers later in the week. Data per unit are as follows.

	Products		
	101	102	103
Selling price	$3.50	$4.00	$5.00
Variable costs	1.50	3.00	2.00
Contribution margin	$2.00	$1.00	$3.00

On the basis of the sales mix in 19X7, Michael believed that of every ten units sold, four would be 101s, four 102s, and two 103s. Total fixed costs were predicted to be $90,000. Total sales were expected to be 100,000 units, based on a projection of trends in recent years, and Michael prepared the following budgeted income statement for the year 19X8.

	101	102	103	Total
Sales	$140,000	$160,000	$100,000	$400,000
Variable costs	60,000	120,000	40,000	220,000
Contribution margin	$ 80,000	$ 40,000	$ 60,000	$180,000
Fixed costs				90,000
Income before tax				$ 90,000
Income taxes (40%)				36,000
Net income				$ 54,000

At the meeting, Michael demonstrated that his analysis could be used to predict changes in profits that would be expected to follow changes in sales. As an example, he said that the break-even point for the company is $200,000 in sales, because the contribution margin percentage is 45% and fixed costs are $90,000. He showed the other managers that target profits also can be computed, although the presence of income taxes makes it a bit more complicated than computing the break-even point. He said that if an after-tax profit figure were desired, it was necessary to divide it by 60%, the percentage of net income to income before taxes. The resulting before-tax profit could be added to fixed costs and the sum divided by 45%. Thus, the sales required for profits of $90,000 are about $533,300, since before-tax profits have to be $150,000, and ($90,000 + $150,000)/45% is $533,333.

Some of the managers were becoming restless as Michael explained his analysis. Finally, the production manager said that it was all very interesting, but irrelevant. She told the group that labor costs, which are 50% of variable costs, would increase by 20% under a new union contract.

The controller was somewhat disappointed with Michael's analysis because it had failed to provide for a $40,000 dividend to stockholders that the president of the company had said should be a target. The company has a policy of not allowing dividends to be more than one-third of after-tax profits. The controller had thought that Michael would incorporate the desired dividend into his analysis to show the other managers what had to be done to meet the president's goal.

As the managers began to mumble among themselves about the irrelevance of the analysis, the sales manager announced that the assumed sales mix was no good. "I don't know how this will affect the analysis, but we expect that each product will be sold in equal amounts during this coming year. The demand for 103s is increasing substantially."

The production manager commented that the company was going to rent some additional equipment to increase production of 103s. The rental would be $10,000 per year. She wondered what effect that news would have on Michael's figures.

As he left the meeting, Michael chastised himself for not having obtained more information before going in and looking ill-prepared.

Required

Prepare a new analysis for Remley, incorporating the goals and changed assumptions learned at the meeting. Show the sales necessary to (a) break even and (b) meet the profit required to pay the $40,000 dividend without violating the firm's dividend policy.

4-54   *Explaining territorial differences* Barkman Company sells various types of jams and jellies all across the country. The following income statement shows results for two territories for a recent month, in thousands of dollars.

	Northwest	Southeast
Sales	$2,800	$2,400
Variable costs	840	600
Contribution margin	$1,960	$1,800
Fixed costs	920	920
Territory income	$1,040	$ 880

Variable costs per case are the same in both territories. The territorial managers have wide discretion over setting prices and incurring advertising and promotion expenses.

Required

Compare the pricing strategies of the managers of the territories. Show why the Northwest territory is more profitable than the Southeast.

4-55   *Variance analysis (CMA adapted)* Handler Company distributes two power tools to hardware stores: a heavy-duty hand drill and a table saw. Handler buys the tools from a manufacturer that attaches the Handler label to them.

The 19X4 budgeted and actual results follow. The plan was adopted in late 19X3 based on Handler's estimates of market share for each tool. During the first quarter of 19X4 it seemed likely that the total market for the tools would be 10% less than Handler had estimated. In an attempt to prevent planned unit sales from declining by 10%, Handler's managers instituted a marketing program consisting of price reductions and increased advertising. The table saw was emphasized over the drill in this program.

Handler Company
Income Statement for 19X4
(all data in thousands)

	Drill Plan	Drill Actual	Table Saw Plan	Table Saw Actual	Total Plan	Total Actual
Unit sales	120	86	80	74	200	160
Revenue	$7,200	$5,074	$9,600	$8,510	$16,800	$13,584
Variable costs	6,000	4,300	6,400	5,920	12,400	10,220
Contribution margin	$1,200	$ 774	$3,200	$2,590	$ 4,400	$ 3,364
Unallocated costs:						
Selling					$ 1,000	$ 1,000
Advertising					1,000	1,060
Administration					400	406
Total unallocated costs					$ 2,400	$ 2,466
Income					$ 2,000	$ 898

Required

1. For each product, determine the sales price variance and sales volume variance.
2. Write a memorandum to the president assessing the success, or lack thereof, of the marketing program (price reductions and increased advertising). Use the guidelines in Appendix A.

5

Short-Term Decisions and Accounting Information

As we pointed out very early in this book, an important characteristic of decisions is that they relate to future actions. (You can't decide in August, after the price of a particular company's stock has increased, to buy that stock the previous February.) This characteristic means that managers can never be sure whether their decisions were wise or unwise, because

(1) unexpected events may influence subsequent results and

(2) what would have happened without the decision can never be known.

*When **General Mills'** managers decided, in 1994, to try to end a cereal marketing war, the company dropped the high-cost promotion schemes that symbolized the war and cut prices to levels its managers considered competitively attractive. Just when the lower prices were likely to show up at the supermarkets, an unrelated act by one of the company's vendors resulted in contamination of some of the company's products and caused the scrapping of millions of boxes of cereal. Supply shortages prompted retailers not to pass on the price savings to their customers. In the meantime, other cereal makers took various actions in response to the price cuts.*

*   **General Mills'** volume, market share, and profits declined, but it is impossible to isolate the effects of the pricing decision. Thus, a decision isn't necessarily bad or good just because some unpredictable change in circumstances causes results to differ markedly from expectations. About all managers can do is base their decisions on the best available information and make sure they understand the information that is available.*

"Has General Mills Had It's Wheaties?" Business Week, May 8, 1995, 68-69.

Making decisions means choosing from alternatives. Even continuing to do what we've been doing is a decision, *if* there's some other alternative. Should we raise the price of our product, lower it, or leave it alone? Should we drop a particular product (or product line) or keep it? Should we add a new product or stick with the products we have? Should we make a component of our product in our factory or buy it from another company? Managers are continually considering such sets of alternatives.

This chapter focuses on short-term decisions. Most managers and accountants consider a decision to be short term if it involves a period of one year or less. The cutoff is arbitrary but commonly used, though a better distinction might be that long-term decisions normally require investments in long-lived resources such as buildings and equipment, whereas short-term decisions do not. In any case, short-term decisions are more easily reversible than long-term ones. (You can almost always change prices or the method of compensating salespeople, but you can't so quickly dispose of a factory or a specialized piece of equipment.) The basic principles that apply to short-term decisions also apply to long-term ones, but long-term decisions require some additional considerations because they usually involve a long-term investment to acquire additional resources. Chapters 8 and 9 focus on long-term decisions.

One final matter before we proceed. Virtually every decision has both quantitative and qualitative aspects, and managers must understand both. The analytical approaches we present concentrate on the quantitative, economic aspects of a decision, but we usually mention some of the qualitative issues associated with specific decisions. In practice, qualitative considerations sometimes override quantitative factors; that is, in some cases, managers select an alternative that is not as economically sound as others because of company policy or some belief among its managers about "what's right for the company."

For example, a policy change appears to have prompted **Mitsubishi Electronics America** to stop selling to **Circuit City**, its largest customer at the time of the break in 1993. Later, a Mitsubishi official said "we will not be in a national chain" and asserted that smaller retailers can offer better service.[1] **Taco Inc.**, a company that makes pumps and valves, operates an on-site learning center where employees attend courses—some work-related, many not—both during and after work hours. Asked about the company's commitment to the learning center, Taco's chief executive said "I don't have any idea why the hell it happened except I wanted to do it."[2] **Ben & Jerry's Homemade Inc.** is widely known for implementing policies that reflect its management's interest in social issues (see the accompanying Insight). Such managers cannot be called wrong. But it is critical that they be aware of the costs of the policies they adopt. The techniques described in this chapter help managers to determine such costs.

THE CRITERION FOR SHORT-TERM DECISIONS

The economic criterion for making short-term decisions is simple: *Take the action that you expect will give the highest income (or least loss) to the firm.* Applying this rule is not always simple, and two subrules might be helpful:

1. The only revenues and costs that are *relevant* in making decisions are the expected future revenues and costs that will *differ* among the choices that are available. These are called **differential revenues and costs**. (Because many decisions result in increases in revenues and costs, some use the terms **incremental revenues and costs**.)
2. Revenues and costs that have already been earned or incurred are *irrelevant* in making decisions. Their only use is that they might aid in predicting future revenues and costs.

DIFFERENTIAL (INCREMENTAL) REVENUES AND COSTS

The term *differential* is more inclusive than *incremental*. The latter term suggests increases, and some decisions produce decreases in both revenues and costs. But the terms used are not as important as what they denote. Differential costs are *avoidable* costs, which we discussed in Chapters 3 and 4. If the firm can change a cost by taking one action as opposed to another, the cost is avoidable and therefore differential. Suppose a company could save $50,000 in salaries and other fixed costs if it stopped selling a product in a particular geographical region. The $50,000 is avoidable (differential) because it will be incurred if the company continues to sell in the region and will not be incurred if the firm stops selling in that region. Of course, the company will lose revenue if it discontinues sales in the region. Hence, the lost revenue is also differential in a decision to stop selling in the region.

1 *Marcia Berss, "'We will not be in a national chain',"* Forbes, *March 27, 1995, 50.*
2 *Thomas A. Stewart, "How a Little Company Won Big By Betting on Brainpower,"* Fortune, *September 4, 1995, 121-122.*

SIGHT

Ben & Jerry's Homemade Inc., founded in 1978, is a Vermont-based producer of ice cream. To implement its management concern for environmental issues, its Peace Pops are packed in wrappers and cartons made of recycled materials. The packaging carries messages—in vegetable and water-based ink—that encourage consumers to become involved in social issues. Management's efforts to provide a supportive environment for employees have received national recognition. Examples of the company's support of its employees include an on-site day-care center and a policy of not requiring employees to work after 6 p.m.

Sources: "Ben & Jerry's: a firm with a view," Packaging Digest, *January 1993, 50-55. "Companies respond to changes requiring work/family help," (Cost Containment),* Employee Benefit Plan Review, *October 1992, 49.*

SUNK COSTS AND OPPORTUNITY COSTS

The emphasis on differential revenues and costs gives rise to two other related concepts that you may have encountered in your study of economics: *sunk costs* and *opportunity costs*. A **sunk cost** is one that has already been incurred and therefore will be the same no matter which alternative a manager selects. Sunk costs are never relevant for decision making because they are not differential.

Suppose **Kellogg** spent $500,000 developing a new cereal product and had problems refining the taste and producing the individual pieces of cereal in the right size. The managers must now decide whether or not to market the cereal. The $500,000 is irrelevant to the decision because it is not differential; that is, the cost will be the same whether or not the company markets the product. Similarly, depreciation on a machine is irrelevant in deciding which products to make with that machine. *All historical costs*, whether original cost or book value (cost minus accumulated depreciation), *are sunk costs*.

Even though the historical cost of a resource is sunk, the resource can have a cost for decision-making purposes. If a resource can be used in more than one way, it has an opportunity cost. An **opportunity cost** is the benefit lost by taking one action as opposed to another. The "other" action is the best alternative available other than the one being contemplated.

Suppose **Kmart** owns a warehouse and can use it either to store products or rent it to another company for $80,000 per year. Using the space for storage requires that Kmart forego the opportunity to rent it, which means that there is a difference to Kmart if it chooses to take one action rather than another. When the company considers any action that requires using the space for storage, the relevant cost of the space is its opportunity cost, the $80,000 rent Kmart will not collect. What if Kmart would have to pay $1,000 per year for a license to rent the warehouse? The opportunity cost of using the space for storage falls to $79,000, the net sacrifice Kmart makes by foregoing the rental opportunity.

As another example, suppose PPF Company owns a machine that can be used to produce either of two products, X and Y. The products require the same amount of machine time, but the total contribution margin from X is greater than that from Y. When PPF considers a decision to use the machine to produce X, the cost of using the machine is its opportunity cost, the contribution margin sacrificed by not using it to produce Y. If PPF is considering using the machine to produce Y, the cost is the contribution margin sacrificed by not using it to produce X. As you can see, *opportunity cost depends on what action is being considered.*

The example described in the next section incorporates the concepts of differential revenues and costs, sunk costs, and opportunity costs. As you read, look for examples of these concepts.

BASIC EXAMPLE

Walters Company manufactures clothing. Walters has in stock 5,000 shirts that it cannot sell through normal channels. A chain store has offered to buy the shirts for $12,000. The cost to manufacture these shirts was $17,000. The president says he'd rather throw the shirts away than sell them at a loss of $5,000 ($17,000 manufacturing costs - $12,000 revenue). Is his reasoning sound? If there's no likelihood of getting a better offer, it is not, and the chain's offer should be accepted.

Walters has two alternatives: (1) throw the shirts away or (2) sell them to the chain. Throwing the shirts away yields no revenue and requires no additional costs. Walters should accept the chain's offer, because the *difference* in profit is $12,000. The differential revenues and costs for selling to the chain as opposed to throwing out the shirts are as follows.

Decision: Sell to Chain (*Rather* than Throw Shirts Away)

Differential revenues	$12,000
Differential costs	0
Differential profit	$12,000

The opportunity cost of throwing the shirts away is $12,000, the benefit lost by not taking the best available alternative course of action. What is the opportunity cost of selling the shirts to the chain? Nothing, because Walters obtains no benefit from the alternative, which is to throw the shirts away. This example confirms a principle we stated earlier—that opportunity cost depends on what alternative is being considered.

You understand the concepts of differential and sunk costs if you saw that the $17,000 cost to make the shirts is sunk. It has already been incurred and will not change regardless of which alternative is chosen. True, Walters will have a $5,000 loss if it sells the shirts to the chain ($17,000 - $12,000). But if the shirts are simply thrown out, Walters will have a loss of $17,000. (Note that Walters is better off selling the shirts for $12,000, whether the cost to manufacture them was $2,000, $17,000, or even $50,000, if the only other alternative is to throw them away.)

Let's add another alternative: Another chain store offers to pay $20,000 for the shirts provided that Walters puts on two more pockets and dyes them a different color. The production manager estimates the incremental cost to do the work at $6,000. (The president isn't happy about this alternative either, because the $23,000 total cost [$17,000 + $6,000] is greater than the $20,000 offer.)

Three alternatives are now available, but we already know that the as-is sale is preferable to throwing the shirts away. So, we need only compare the new alternative with the as-is sale. Which of those two alternatives should Walters choose? It should do the work and sell the shirts for $20,000. To understand why, consider the differential revenues and costs to rework and sell the shirts as opposed to selling them to the chain as is.

Decision: Rework and Sell (*Rather* than Sell As Is)	
Differential revenues ($20,000 - $12,000)	$8,000
Differential costs ($6,000 - $0)	6,000
Differential profit	$2,000

Walters would be $2,000 better off by reworking the shirts rather than selling them as is.

What is the *opportunity cost* of an as-is sale of the shirts? The best available alternative is now the rework option, which has a profit of $14,000 ($20,000 revenue - $6,000 cost). Thus, the opportunity cost of the as-is sale is the $14,000 sacrificed by not accepting the rework option. (The opportunity cost of throwing the shirts away is also $14,000.) What is the opportunity cost of accepting the rework offer? The opportunity cost is $12,000, the benefit foregone by rejecting the as-is sale, the best alternative available.

Some decision makers prefer to analyze the alternatives separately but incorporate opportunity costs directly in the analysis. Following are analyses of the alternatives using that approach.

	Throw Out Shirts	Sell Shirts As Is	Rework and Sell
Revenue	$ —	$ 12,000	$ 20,000
Costs:			
Shirts, opportunity cost	(14,000)	(14,000)	(12,000)
Rework			(6,000)
Profit (loss)	$ (14,000)	$ (2,000)	$ 2,000

Once again, the rework alternative is the best choice, and the as-is sale is preferred to throwing the shirts away.

As before, the $17,000 cost of manufacturing the shirts is irrelevant. To emphasize the irrelevance of this sunk cost, consider Walters' income statement for each of the alternatives.

	Throw Out Shirts	Sell Shirts As Is	Rework Shirts
Revenues	$ 0	$ 12,000	$ 20,000
Costs:			
Manufacturing	(17,000)	(17,000)	(17,000)
Rework			(6,000)
Profit (loss)	$ (17,000)	$ (5,000)	$ (3,000)

Reworking the shirts produces the smallest loss, confirming the results of the differential analyses, which showed that alternative to be the best of the three.

The loss incurred by selling the shirts as is is $12,000 less than that from throwing them out, which is equal to the $12,000 differential profit shown in the first analysis. The $3,000 loss reported for reworking the shirts is $2,000 less than the loss from the as-is sale, which is exactly the $2,000 differential profit we found when comparing those choices.

To this point, the opportunity cost of using an available resource — 5,000 shirts — has related to the results of selling it (as is or after rework). To emphasize that opportunity cost is the cost of using some resource in some particular way, let us revise our original example to show that opportunity cost might be the cost of *replacing* the resource. The unchanged fact is that Walters has on hand 5,000 shirts that were manufactured at a cost of $17,000. But now assume that the shirts can be sold at regular prices, so that Walters will have to make similar shirts to meet future sales if it sells the on-hand shirts. The production manager says that the cost of making 5,000 shirts has risen to $20,000. A discount outlet offers Walters $18,000 for the shirts on hand. What should the firm do under these conditions?

The key to the analysis is to understand that, *whatever* Walters decides to do, it must have 5,000 shirts available to meet the expected demand at the regular price. What happens after the shirts must be available — specifically the revenues received from selling them at the regular price — will be the same no matter what Walters decides to do about the shirts now on hand. Hence, the expected revenue from selling 5,000 shirts at regular prices is irrelevant to the decision about accepting the $18,000 offer.

Walters has two alternatives. First, it can hold the shirts to meet expected sales needs at regular prices. Choosing this alternative, Walters receives no revenues it wouldn't otherwise receive and incurs no additional costs, for a net of zero. Second, Walters can sell the on-hand shirts and make others to meet regular sales needs. If this alternative is chosen, Walters receives $18,000 revenue and incurs a cost of $20,000 (to produce the shirts needed for regular sales), for an incremental loss of $2,000. The better choice is to "do nothing" (that is, sell through the regular channel); Walters will be $2,000 better off by choosing that action. The opportunity cost of choosing to sell the shirts now is $20,000, the cost of replacing them later, because selling them now requires replacing them at a $20,000 cost.

From the variations in our basic example, you should discern that decision making requires all of the following.

- Looking for and understanding all the available alternative courses of action.
- Concentrating on differential effects of each alternative.
- Applying the concepts of sunk cost and opportunity cost to the determination of differential revenues and costs.

In the next section we discuss some of the important aspects of developing information needed for decision making.

DEVELOPING RELEVANT INFORMATION

Few short-term decisions relate to all segments of an entity. Most involve a possible change in a segment of the entity — such as a product, product line, factory, or even a single component of one of the entity's products—though an action by one segment might affect some other segments. Finding or developing the information relevant to a decision about a segment isn't a simple task, because the necessary information is seldom available in one place such as an accounting report about the segment of concern.

Suppose a company makes several models of typewriters, copiers, and file cabinets, sells them in several geographical regions to different types of customers (businesses, schools, hospitals, etc.), and operates several factories, some which make only one product or line and others which make several products. Accounting reports might be available regularly by model, product line, factory, sales region, or customer type. But such regular reports might not show information for a specific model of one product by sales region, factory, or customer type. Managers make many decisions that affect a relatively small segment of the company. Often, the segment (individual activity) that managers are reviewing for possible change is not large enough to warrant separate reporting on a regular basis.

An existing accounting report for the segment of concern might include some of the information needed for a decision. (The product-line income statement in Exhibit 4-4 on page 142 is an example of such a report.) But decisions are about what can be expected in the future, so information about past levels of revenues and costs is relevant only if it helps to predict future levels. Estimates of expected future sales of a product or service come from marketing people, and production and design engineers provide information about expected needs for materials, labor, and perhaps other aspects of the manufacturing process.

The increasing use of computers increases the likelihood that internal databases contain details of information that appears only in summary form on reports. For example, from a database that includes many details of inputs for sales transactions, the office equipment producer in our example might be able to develop a special report showing the unit sales of a particular product by sales region and customer type. But, again, information about the past is exactly that, and the concern of decision makers is estimates about the future.

Unfortunately, determining avoidable costs requires more than access to sophisticated computer systems and databases because, as we said in Chapters 3 and 4, avoidability is a function of the decision being contemplated. As an example, consider further the office equipment maker described above. Suppose salespeople are paid salaries, concentrate on specific types of customers, and sell all of the company's products. Neither sales salaries nor travel costs are avoidable costs when analyzing a particular model of copier; if a model is dropped, the salespeople will still call on the same customers. On the other hand, if the segment of concern is a particular type of customer, some sales salaries and related expenses might well be avoidable. Similarly, if salespeople cover specific geographical regions, their salaries and other expenses are avoidable in a segment analysis by region. Thus, costs that are avoidable, and therefore differential, when one segment is under review might be unavoidable when looking at a different segment. Hence, determining avoidability requires close cooperation between managerial accountants and other managers who understand both costs and the decision being considered.

In general, the smaller the segment in question, the less the avoidable cost. Avoidable costs of a typewriter model sold in a particular region are probably limited to the variable costs of producing that model. Those associated with the entire line of typewriters in the same region include variable production costs and perhaps some selling expenses. Some fixed manufacturing costs might also be saved, especially if typewriters sold in that region are made in a factory that does not make other product lines. But even that conclusion depends on the specific circumstances of that plant. As the segment under study expands to an entire product line, more and more costs become avoidable. The most important point about decisions relating to segments is that the analyses will differ with the decisions. There is no magic formula for identifying the costs and revenues relevant to decisions, even when accounting reports exist for the segment in question. As the next section shows, existing accounting reports might even be misleading.

ALLOCATED COSTS

The accounting practice of allocating indirect (common) costs to segments can complicate the task of identifying the costs relevant to a particular decision. **Cost allocation** is the process of assigning indirect costs to individual segments to which the costs are common. For example, manufacturers regularly allocate fixed manufacturing costs to units of product because they are required to do so for financial accounting and tax purposes. Similarly, retailers often allocate the cost of a company-wide purchasing group to individual retail outlets. For reasons discussed in Chapter 10, cost allocations are often incorporated into internal reports that serve as a starting point for decision making.

Earlier in this chapter we emphasized that the basis for decision making was information about the future. In Chapter 2, we showed that per-unit fixed costs—the result of allocations—are not useful in predicting future total costs. Hence, per-unit fixed costs are not relevant for decision making. By definition, common costs are unavoidable to individual segments to which they are common. Allocating such costs to individual segments does not make the allocated amount avoidable in the future. Hence, for making decisions about a segment, common costs allocated to that segment are not relevant; the only relevant costs are those that will change (be differential) if a firm chooses one course of action rather than another.

Although there is a strong presumption that an allocated cost is unavoidable, it is sometimes possible to reduce common costs if a large enough segment is eliminated. For example, suppose that each of the 20 employees of a payroll department works on some part of the payrolls of all six factories that the company operates. The salaries of all of the employees in the payroll department are then common to the six factories. But if one large factory closes, the payroll department might be able to reassign work and people, reducing the staff to 17 or 18 and so reducing some of the common cost. As you saw in Chapters 3 and 4, determining these types of changes in costs is part of analyzing costs in an activity framework, activity-based costing. Again, analyzing costs for decisions requires very careful attention to the specific situation.

The appearance of allocated costs on segment reports raises an important point about internal use of information from existing accounting reports about segments. An information system must provide data for preparing financial statements, completing tax and other government forms, and making decisions. The system is usually designed around the information needs for external reports, because the specific information needed for such reports is well-known and needed regularly. Segment reports produced by the information system often reflect practices required for external reporting. Hence, a manager consulting such reports for information about the costs relevant to a particular decision must understand the basic concepts of both financial and managerial accounting.

ACTIVITY-BASED ALLOCATIONS

Organizations that use activity-based costing (ABC) allocate costs only after making careful studies of cost pools and related cost drivers. Using ABC helps managers focus on what activities change as the result of a decision. Hence, organizations using ABC should be better able to identify costs that will change with a particular decision and should have fewer problems with allocations getting in the way of good decisions.

If, as is the case with companies using ABC, the only costs allocated are those that are clearly driven by activities of the segments, then significant amounts of such allocated costs might be avoidable. Managers who can determine how activities will change as a result of taking particular courses of action should be better able to estimate the effects of the changes on costs. Good estimates are especially likely if the segment will cease certain activities. Even in that case, however, the cost reduction might not be immediate. Moreover, changing the level of an activity might not have a direct, proportional effect on costs; that is, a normal ABC analysis does not automatically determine how much cost is avoidable in any given situation. Activity-based allocations do not substitute for careful analyses of the likely effects of decisions, but they should make those analyses less difficult to develop.

TYPICAL SHORT-TERM DECISIONS

Most of the remainder of this chapter is devoted to typical examples of short-term decisions. Although the situations appear to be quite different, the same principle applies to all: *Find the most profitable alternative by analyzing the differential revenues and costs.* In some cases, it will be relatively easy to determine the differentials and choose among the alternatives. In others, you might find it easier to make your choice by preparing complete income statements for the alternatives. But the two approaches should lead to the same decision.

DROPPING A SEGMENT

You already know there are many ways to segment a firm. Determining the best mix of segments is a continual problem for managers, who sometimes have to decide whether to drop a segment, or perhaps to replace one segment with another. For example, managers of supermarkets regularly consider whether to continue to carry specific nongrocery products or services such as flowers, video rentals, and photo processing. Managers of department stores face similar decisions.

Consider Moorehead Department Store, which uses its available space for three product lines. Following is the income statement for a recent month, and

Moorehead's managers expect these results to continue in the foreseeable future.

	Clothing	Appliances	Housewares	Total
Sales	$ 45,000	$ 40,000	$ 15,000	$100,000
Variable costs	25,000	18,000	11,000	54,000
Contribution margin	$ 20,000	$ 22,000	$ 4,000	$ 46,000
Fixed costs:				
Direct—all avoidable	(4,000)	(3,400)	(1,500)	(8,900)
Indirect (common), allocated based on sales revenues	(9,450)	(8,400)	(3,150)	(21,000)
Income (loss)	$ 6,550	$ 10,200	$ (650)	$ 16,100

Should the store drop the housewares line because it shows a loss? To answer that question we must know what would change if the line were dropped.

Let's begin with a choice between two simple alternatives: keep housewares or drop it and rent the available space to another company for $400 per month. If the housewares line were dropped, Moorehead would lose the $15,000 of sales but could avoid the $11,000 of variable costs of those sales as well as the $1,500 avoidable direct fixed costs shown on the segment report. A careful analysis of the cost drivers for the various common (indirect) fixed costs would show Moorehead's managers how much of those costs could probably be avoided by dropping the line. (Remember the example of the payroll department.) Suppose such an analysis showed that dropping any one segment would reduce common costs by $1,000, so that common costs would drop to $20,000. The changes (differentials) are summarized as follows.

Decision: Rent Out the Space (*Rather* than Sell Housewares)		
Differential revenues:		
Lost sales from housewares		$ 15,000
New rent revenue		400
Net revenue *lost*		$ 14,600
Differential costs:		
Variable costs saved on housewares	$ 11,000	
Direct fixed costs saved	1,500	
Indirect fixed costs saved	1,000	
Total cost saving		13,500
Differential *loss* from dropping housewares		$ 1,100

Assuming only the two alternatives, keeping housewares seems the better choice because dropping it and renting out the space would *reduce* income by $1,100. (You should see that if housewares were simply dropped, the decline in income would be even larger, $1,500 [$1,100 and the $400 rent].) The analysis shows separately the lost revenues and the savings of variable costs, but we could have shown only a $4,000 differential for contribution margin lost. Another way to determine the change in income is to prepare a new income statement that includes only the remaining product lines, the rent revenue, and the lower common costs. (Total income would drop from $16,100 to $15,000, a $1,100 difference.)

Realistic decisions about dropping a segment usually involve other alternatives for using the freed-up resources. For example, Moorehead might be able to use the space to expand one of the other lines, or for an altogether new line. Let's examine a slightly more complicated alternative, and for convenience we'll compare that alternative with simply retaining the housewares line. Suppose Moorehead could substitute a book department in the space now occupied by housewares. Moorehead's managers estimate that a book department would generate contribution margin of $12,000 (revenues of $20,000 and variable costs of $8,000) and would have $2,700 of direct fixed costs. Note, however, that if the book department is substituted for housewares, Moorehead will not reduce common costs because it will still have three departments. Should Moorehead make the substitution?

What will change if the substitution is made? Contribution margin will increase $8,000 ($12,000 from books vs. $4,000 from housewares), but direct fixed costs will increase $1,200 ($2,700 for books vs. $1,500 for housewares). Hence, the substitution would increase income by $6,800 ($8,000 - $1,200). The differential analysis of the substitution option is as follows.

Decision: Substitute Books for Housewares	
Differential contribution margin—increase ($12,000 - $4,000)	$8,000
Differential costs—increase in direct fixed costs ($2,700 - $1,500)	1,200
Differential profit *favoring substitution*	$6,800

If you prepared a complete income statement for the new sales mix, income would be $22,900, $6,800 higher than the current $16,100.

We must emphasize that the decision being considered is whether to substitute books for housewares. The purpose of that decision is to find the best way to use *existing* resources. The analysis would be different if Moorehead was considering adding books to its existing product lines. Adding a line is likely to require some investment in new resources (e.g., display equipment, furniture and fixtures, etc.), a characteristic that distinguishes long-term from short-term decisions.

The alternatives considered thus far serve to remind you that whether a cost is avoidable depends on the decision being considered. If the decision is whether to drop housewares altogether, the $1,000 potential reduction in common costs is relevant because it is avoidable and, therefore, differential. But if the decision is whether to substitute books for housewares, none of the common costs are relevant because they are all unavoidable.

Complementary Effects

The facts of the preceding example didn't include any likelihood that dropping or adding a segment (product line, in this case) might affect the sales of other, continuing segments. But as noted in the discussion of sales mix in Chapter 4, a change in the sales of one product might be accompanied by a change in the sales of another. When such a relationship exists, a decision about the one product is said to have **complementary effects**. Marketing studies of shopping habits can often help quantify the effects of such suspected complementary relationships.

Suppose Moorehead's managers believe that some people coming to shop for books also are likely to buy clothing, and that some people coming to shop for housewares also buy appliances at the same time. After authorizing and reviewing the results of market studies, the managers estimate that appliance sales will drop 10 percent and clothing sales will increase 7 percent if books are substituted for housewares. Considering this new information, should the substitution be made?

You should see that a differential analysis of the substitution decision includes everything in the previous analysis *plus* the impact of the complementary effects. Following is such an analysis.

Decision: Substitute Books for Housewares	
Differential contribution margin:	
Increase due to selling books vs. housewares	$8,000
Increase due to higher clothing sales	
(7% × $20,000 contribution margin on current sales)	1,400
Decrease due to lower sales of appliances	
(10% × $22,000 contribution margin on current sales)	(2,200)
Net increase in contribution margin	$7,200
Differential costs—increase in direct fixed costs	
($2,700 - $1,500)	1,200
Differential profit favoring substitution	$6,000

The advantage of the substitution is less than computed earlier ($6,000 vs. $6,800), but the substitution is still profitable. Again, the outcome of the substitution could have been determined by preparing an income statement to reflect the new sales mix including the complementary effects. (You might want to prepare such a statement to confirm the answer reached using only differentials.) The statement should show total income of $22,100, which is $6,000 greater than the $16,100 income with the current mix.

Loss Leader

A particularly interesting case of complementary effects is the **loss leader**, a product or line that shows a negative profit in the sense that its contribution margin does not cover its avoidable fixed costs. In an extreme case, the product might even have a negative contribution margin! If the complementary effects between the loss leader and the firm's other products are large enough, even such an extreme pricing policy could be beneficial.

Consider the manager of a local pizzeria who is distressed by a lack of business at lunchtime. He attributes this problem to the specials at competing restaurants and is eager to change the situation. (Note that the "segment" in this case is a time period rather than a product or product line.) He has prepared the following income statement, based on a normal week, for the 11 a.m. to 2 p.m. period. The costs shown are all incremental.

	Pizza	Soft Drinks	Total
Sales (200 pizzas @ $1.80)	$360	$100	$460
Variable costs	120	40	160
Contribution margin	$240	$ 60	$300
Wages of part-time employees			80
Income			$220

He is thinking about offering his own luncheon special: with each pizza comes all the free soft drinks a customer can drink. He believes the offer could double lunchtime pizza sales. On the basis of his experience and judgment, he antici-pates that soft drink consumption will increase to two and one-half times the present level. He estimates that the additional part-time help needed to take care of the additional business would increase that cost by $40 per week. Soft drinks will generate no revenue, but the costs will continue, so he will obviously lose money on beverages. Can he gain enough on the sales of pizza to offset the loss?

The following expected income statement for the lunchtime period shows the effects of the special, using the manager's estimates (which are the best information available).

	Pizza	Soft Drinks	Total
Sales	$720	$ 0	$720
Variable costs	240[a]	100[b]	340
Contribution margin	$480	$(100)	$380
Wages of part-time employees ($80 + $40)			120
Income			$260

a *Variable costs computed at the same rate as before, one-third or 33 1/3% of selling price.*
b *Variable costs computed as two and one-half times the previous costs.*

Soft drinks show a negative contribution margin. Yet if expectations about increased sales are realized, total income increases by $40 per week ($260 - $220). In this case, developing a new income statement is probably easier than determining differentials for specific items.

As explained in Chapter 4, the potential for complementary effects is more obvious in some cases than in others. For example, one can readily see the relationship between sales of toothbrushes and toothpaste, or of boiled shrimp and cocktail sauce. The relationship is also fairly clear in **Domino's Pizza** fre-quent offers of a free liter of Coca-Cola with an order for a large pizza. But the loss-leader rationale is also behind many low prices that are expected to en-courage sales of products that are not complementary. Examples include buy-one, get-one-free offers and offers of extremely low prices for some name-brand item—a can of Campbell's tomato soup for 10 cents—to customers spending $10 (or some other specific amount) on other grocery items. In these examples, the complementary products are all other products in the store.

Considering the company as a whole is important in evaluating any decision. A product that is selling at a loss—even at a negative contribution margin—

might be so essential to the sales of other products that it should not be dropped (see the accompanying Insight). Or perhaps a qualitative issue, such as a reputation for offering a complete product line, will be relevant to a decision that could affect that reputation. Of course, a company's managers should want to know the cost of maintaining such a policy.

MAKE-OR-BUY DECISIONS

Most manufactured products consist of several components that are assembled into a finished unit. Many of these components can be bought from an outside supplier or made by the assembling firm. (**Dell Computers**, though known as a computer manufacturer, assembles its final products entirely from components specifically designed for its products.) For each component, a company's managers must decide: make or buy. The Automotive Components Group of **General Motors** makes about 55 percent of the components for GM vehicles. The Group also sells to other vehicle makers who have opted to buy, rather than make, some of the same components.[3]

As with other decisions, the quantitative factors are the differential costs to make and to buy. Suppose XYZ Company makes a component. A manager has prepared the following estimates of costs at the expected volume of 20,000 units.

Materials at $2 per unit	$ 40,000
Direct labor at $5 per unit	100,000
Variable overhead at $3 per unit	60,000
Allocated indirect fixed costs (building depreciation, heat and light, etc.)	120,000
Total costs	$320,000

INSIGHT

Computer information service is an example of an industry that depends on loss leaders. **Prodigy**, a prominent company in the industry, loses money on its monthly charge for basic services. To earn profits, the company counts on advertising and charges for extra services, but the company couldn't provide those extra services without having people signed up for the basic service.

A similar situation exists in the newspaper industry, whose most obvious product, a newspaper, is priced below the cost of production. Sales of advertising space make publishing a newspaper profitable, but both the quantity of advertising a newspaper attracts and the price it can charge for advertising space depend on the newspaper's circulation (quantity of newspapers regularly sold).

Source: "Prodigy Installs a New Program," Business Week, September 14, 1992, 96.

---

3 Steve Kitchen, *"Silk purse maker,"* Forbes, *May 10, 1993, 84–86.*

An outside supplier offers to supply the component at $14 per unit or $280,000 for 20,000 units. Should the offer be accepted?

Because unit sales of the final product will be the same whether the component is made internally or purchased from an outside supplier, revenues are the same either way. Hence, the decision depends on which alternative results in the lower cost. The cost of making the component depends on whether alternative uses can be found for the space and equipment now used to make the component, and whether the total of any of the other allocated fixed costs will change if the company buys the component from an outsider supplier. If no alternative use were available and total allocated fixed costs won't change, the analysis is quite straightforward. The following schedule focuses on the relevant costs for each available course of action.

	Decisions	
	Make	Buy
Materials	$ 40,000	$ 0
Direct labor	100,000	0
Variable overhead	60,000	0
Purchase price	0	280,000
Total	$ 200,000	$ 280,000

The firm saves $80,000 by making the component. (Note that including the fixed overhead of $120,000 under both alternatives would not change the $80,000 advantage of making the component.) Of course, if XYZ could reduce the indirect fixed costs by outside purchase of the component, the avoidable cost should be part of the total cost of making the component internally. The following analysis shows only the differentials of a decision to make the component.

Decision: Make the Component (Rather than Buy)		
New cost—purchase from outside supplier		$280,000
Cost savings —materials	$ 40,000	
—labor	100,000	
—variable overhead	60,000	
Total savings		200,000
Difference *favoring* making the component		$ 80,000

In this case, XYZ is better off making the component unless it can obtain more than $80,000 by using the space and equipment in some other way. Considering only the quantitative data, XYZ should use the available space and equipment to make the component until some other opportunity arises such that the opportunity cost—the benefit to be gained by using the space and equipment for that other purpose—exceeds the $80,000 cost savings available by using those resources to make the component. Such a benefit could come from renting the space and equipment or using them to make a product that would bring more than $80,000 in incremental profit. XYZ might even consider using the resources to make a component it is currently buying from an outsider.

Long-Term Considerations

We remind you that this chapter focuses on short-term decisions, which concern the best way to use existing resources. Thus, our example mentioned possible other *uses* for the equipment devoted to making the component; it did not mention disposing of the equipment. Selling the equipment has long-term consequences, because it eliminates the company's ability to return quickly to in-house production should an outside supplier prove unsuitable. The same is true when managers are considering *making* a component now purchased outside, if in-house production would require an investment in new equipment. (At some point, **General Motors** made decisions to build or buy the 190 factories that comprise its Components Group. In recent years, GM has increased the proportion of components purchased from outside suppliers and reduced its capacity for in-house production.) In Chapter 8 we present techniques managers use to analyze long-term decisions, which usually require a change in existing resources.

Qualitative Issues

Managers consider many qualitative issues when deciding whether to purchase or make a component. Will the quality of purchased components be as good as the company can achieve by producing the part in-house? Will the supplier meet delivery commitments? (For outside buyers from **GM's** Components Group, a relevant question is whether GM would gain inside information about their companies' future products.) A few years ago, a major question was "Will the supplier raise the price later?" That question is still important in some situations, but cost-cutting efforts by large manufacturers have increased pressure on suppliers to *reduce* component prices (see the accompanying Insight). Hence, the relative sizes of the manufacturer and the supplier are also relevant to a make-or-buy decision.

The make-or-buy decision is especially important in an advanced manufacturing environment. A just-in-time manufacturer is extremely concerned with quality and delivery schedules and will not buy a component unless both are guaranteed.

JOINT PRODUCTS

When a single manufacturing process invariably produces two or more separate products, the products are called **joint products**. The process that makes the products is called a **joint process**, and the costs of operating such a process are called **joint costs**. (Note that such costs are a special case of what we have called **common costs**.) Petroleum refiners and meat packers are examples of companies operating joint processes. Refining crude petroleum yields a number of products, such as auto and aircraft fuel, various grades of oil, and kerosene. Processing cattle results in hides, hoofs, various cuts of meat, and other items (fat, bones).

Operators of a joint process can't choose which products will emerge from the process. Some joint products are quite valuable; some have little or no value. Some can be sold just as they emerge from the joint process or can be processed further. For example, a meat packer might sell hides to a tanner. Or, if the meat packer has the expertise and the facilities, it could tan the hides and sell them, or even use the tanned hides to make shoes, gloves, and other products.

SIGHT

The appliance division of **General Electric Co.** announced to its suppliers that it intended to reduce the cost of purchased components by 10 percent annually, beginning in 1993. In the years 1991 to 1993, a major cost-costing effort by **General Motors** saved $4 billion on the cost of purchased components. Other companies announcing major efforts to obtain lower supplier prices since 1992 include **Chrysler, Dow Chemical, DuPont Co., IBM**, and **Mercedes-Benz**.

Many companies approached the task by working with suppliers to find cost savings through improvements in design and processing and encouraging suppliers to make suggestions for cutting costs. (When a suggestion from one of **Chrysler's** suppliers eliminated the need for the part currently being purchased from that supplier, Chrysler rewarded the supplier with new contracts for other parts.) Some companies' tactics to reduce suppliers' prices reflected less interest in cooperation. For example, many of **GM's** suppliers objected to its frequent requests for rebids on existing long-term contracts and its acceptance of low-ball bids from companies having little or no previous experience. Some GM suppliers also complained that its pursuit of the best price included permitting potential suppliers to study engineering drawings that incorporated proprietary information gained from the research efforts of current suppliers.

Sources: Kevin Kelly, Zachary Schiller, and James B. Treece, "Cut Costs or Else: Companies Lay Down the Law to Suppliers," Business Week, March 22, 1993, 128-129.
"Hardball is Still GM's Game," Business Week, August 8, 1994, 26.

Companies that operate a joint process must decide whether to sell each of the joint products at the **split-off point**—the point at which they emerge from the joint process—or to process each further into another saleable product. Such a decision can't be based on the total costs of the individual final products or even on the total variable costs. To produce *any* of the joint products, the firm must undertake the joint process and so incur all the costs to perform that process. For example, a meat packer might pay $300 per animal. This cost does not relate to particular cuts of meat, to hides, or to by-products, because the packer must buy the entire animal to get any of those products. The total cost of purchasing animals varies with the number of animals entering the joint process, but the $300 cost per animal is the same whether any or all of the joint products are sold immediately or processed further. Hence, the costs incurred prior to split-off—the costs of the joint process—are irrelevant to decisions about the joint products. In determining whether to sell a product at the split-off point or process it further, all costs incurred prior to the split-off point are sunk, whether such costs are fixed or variable.

Consider the following example. QBT, a chemical company, operates a joint process that results in two products, Alpha and Omega. Each 1,000 pounds of materials yields 600 pounds of Alpha and 400 pounds of Omega. QBT can sell both Alpha and Omega at the split-off point, but the company has the facilities to process each product further. Selling price and cost data per batch (1,000 pounds of materials) are as follows.

	Alpha	Omega
Selling price at split-off	$1,200 ($2 per pound)	$1,600 ($4 per pound)
Selling price after additional processing	$3,600 ($6 per pound)	$2,000 ($5 per pound)
Costs of additional processing, all variable	$900 ($1.50 per pound)	$500 ($1.25 per pound)

What should QBT do with each product?

We can analyze the results of both alternatives for each product. Alpha is analyzed as follows.

Decision Alternatives for Alpha		
	Sell at Split-Off	Process Further
Sales value	$1,200	$3,600
Incremental cost	0	900
Incremental profit	$1,200	$2,700

Alpha should be processed further because profit will be $1,500 higher ($2,700 - $1,200). The following differential analysis of the decision to process Alpha further suggests the same conclusion.

Decision: Process Alpha Further (*Rather* than Sell at Split-Off)	
Differential revenue ($3,600 - $1,200)	$2,400
Differential costs	900
Differential profit, favoring additional processing	$1,500

A similar analysis of the alternatives for Omega reveals that it should be sold at split-off, not processed further.

Decision: Process Omega Further (*Rather* than Sell at Split-Off)	
Differential revenues ($2,000 - $1,600)	$ 400
Differential costs	500
Differential loss, favoring sale at split-off	$ (100)

QBT would be $100 worse off if it processed Omega further.

The preceding analytical approaches are appropriate in the unlikely case that all incremental costs of additional processing are variable. As a practical matter, doing the additional processing will almost surely require some space, equipment, and people. Also, some of the associated costs might be avoidable. Let's assume that further processing of Alpha requires avoidable fixed costs of $10,000 per month and that QBT usually processes ten batches per month. When the additional processing requires fixed costs, a slightly different approach is necessary. Note that the $10,000 can't be identified with any one batch but rather is common to *all* pounds of Alpha further processed during the month. Hence, to compare costs and revenues, the focus must be on the *monthly* output of 6,000 pounds (10 × 600 pounds per batch). The following analysis indicates a $5,000 advantage ($17,000 - $12,000) to processing Alpha beyond split-off.

Decision Alternatives for Alpha		
	Sell at Split-Off	Process Further
Sales: 10 × $1,200 per batch	$12,000	
10 × $3,600 per batch		$ 36,000
Incremental costs:		
Variable (10 × $900 per batch)	—	(9,000)
Fixed and avoidable	—	(10,000)
Incremental profit	$12,000	$ 17,000

A differential analysis would show the $24,000 additional revenue from selling after further processing ($36,000 - $12,000) and the additional costs of further processing ($19,000), giving the same $5,000 difference in favor of a decision to process Alpha beyond the split-off point. Still another way to look at the decision is to say that the opportunity cost of processing further is the $12,000 given up by not selling at split-off. Incorporating the opportunity cost into the analysis of the decision to process further gives total costs of $31,000 ($9,000 variable costs + $10,000 avoidable fixed costs + the $12,000 opportunity cost to use the output for further processing). Subtracting $31,000 from the $36,000 revenue also gives the $5,000 advantage of processing Alpha further.

The joint products case exemplifies a critical point made earlier: the relevance or irrelevance of a cost depends on the specific decision at hand. The variable costs of the joint process are relevant in deciding whether to operate that process at all, because they are avoidable if the joint process is not operated. But they are irrelevant in deciding whether to sell a given joint product at the split-off point or to process it further. Thus, a managerial accountant cannot respond to the question "What does it cost?" without knowing why the manager wants the answer to that question.

Long-Term Considerations

A condition critical to the legitimacy of analyzing the joint processing decision considered here as short term is that the company already has the facilities and expertise to carry out the additional processing. Such a company has the flexibility to respond quickly to changes in selling prices of a joint product, either at the split-off point or after further processing. If additional capital investment is required, the decision about further processing becomes long term. Similarly, a decision about reducing the firm's short-term flexibility by eliminating the facilities needed for the additional processing of one (or more) of the joint products is a long-term decision.

SPECIAL ORDERS

Companies that make products to be sold under their own brand names often make nearly identical products that are sold at lower prices under the brand names (called *house brands*) of chain stores. For example, at one time **Whirlpool Corp.** sold over 40 percent of the appliances it made to **Sears**, which marketed them under the Kenmore name. Some manufacturers might also sell to chains at lower prices than to smaller dealers selling under the manufacturer's brand name. In addition, manufacturers might accept special one-time orders at lower-than-usual prices when the level of actual sales is lower than that expected when planning production volume. Let's examine the analysis managers need in order to make decisions about special orders.

Griffith Company's income statement for 19X8, is based on planned production and sales of 60,000 units, with sales at $15 per unit. Griffith has the physical capacity to produce 100,000 units, and could hire additional hourly workers to achieve production in excess of 60,000. A chain store has just approached Griffith with an offer to buy 20,000 units at $10. The variable portion of selling and administrative costs is a 2 percent sales commission ($.30 per unit on regular sales), which Griffith would not have to pay on the special order. The president is hesitant to accept the order because the average manufacturing cost of $13 per unit ($780,000/60,000) is greater than the $10 price offered.

	Per Unit	Total	
Sales (60,000 units)	$ 15		$900,000
Manufacturing costs:			
Materials	$ 4	$240,000	
Direct labor	3	180,000	
Overhead (one-third variable)	6	360,000	
Total	$ 13		780,000
Gross margin			$120,000
Selling and administrative expenses			80,000
Operating income			$ 40,000

As always, only the differential elements should be considered in making a decision. Following is a summary of the differentials.

Decision: Accept the Special Order (*Rather* than Reject It)			
	Per Unit	Total	
Differential revenues (20,000 units)	$ 10		$200,000
Differential costs:			
Materials	$ 4	$80,000	
Direct labor	3	60,000	
Variable overhead	2	40,000	
Total	$ 9		180,000
Incremental profit favoring acceptance			$ 20,000

Accepting the order increases income by $20,000; therefore, Griffith should accept it unless its managers believe that unquantifiable factors outweigh that benefit.

In this example, the only differential costs for the order were variable manufacturing costs. In another situation, variable selling and administrative expenses and perhaps some incremental fixed costs might apply to the order. For example, when a special order requires a large increase in production, additional fixed costs might be incurred because the higher production level involves one or more steps in step-variable manufacturing or administrative costs. Those cost increases also should be incorporated in the analysis.

Often, the most important effect of accepting a special order is its potential for affecting sales at regular prices. For instance, an appliance manufacturer deciding whether to supply a discount chain with 100,000 washing machines must consider whether its sales to regular dealers will fall because some customers will buy from the chain instead of from regular dealers. Or perhaps the special order is larger than available capacity, or would cause production delays, so that accepting the order requires foregoing some sales planned at regular prices. (Even a company having the capacity to accommodate both the planned sales and the special order risks lost sales if actual demand is greater than planned.) An excellent example of companies harming their regular sales by offering some product at lower prices is the fleet sales of automakers presented in the accompanying Insight.

We can illustrate the problem of lost sales, and a basic approach for dealing with it, by continuing the example of Griffith Company. Suppose that because of a shortage of labor, Griffith can expect to produce only 75,000 units despite its physical capacity for 100,000 units. If Griffith accepts the special order, Griffith won't be able to fill orders for 5,000 of the 60,000 planned sales at the regular price because filling the order leaves capacity to make only 55,000 units for sale at the regular price (capacity of 75,000 - 20,000 units on the special order). A differential analysis that includes the new information follows. (Remember that there is a commission, a variable selling cost, on regular sales.)

Decision: Accept the Special Order (*Rather* than Reject It)		
Differential revenues:		
New revenues from the order (earlier)	$200,000	
Lost revenues on regular sales (5,000 × $15)	75,000	
Total differential revenues		$125,000
Differential costs:		
Costs for the special order (earlier)	$180,000	
Costs saved by not making regular sales:		
Variable manufacturing cost		
5,000 units × $9 ($4 + $3 + $2)	(45,000)	
Commissions		
5,000 × $0.30	(1,500)	
Total differential costs		133,500
Differential loss, favoring rejecting the order		$ (8,500)

Another approach is to compare the contribution margin obtained from the special order with the contribution margin lost on regular sales.

Decision: Accept the Special Order (*Rather* than Reject It)	
New contribution margin—special order	
20,000 × ($10 - $9 variable manufacturing cost)	$20,000
Lost contribution margin—regular sales	
5,000 × ($15 - $9 - $0.30 = $5.70)	28,500
Loss from accepting order	$(8,500)

SIGHT

The Big-Three U.S. automakers sell many cars to fleets, such as those of **Hertz** and **Avis**. **GM's** fleet sales reached 800,000 cars a year at one time. Accepting fleet sales helped the companies maintain market share and stabilize production at their factories. For many years, the automakers bought back the fleet cars after four to six months and sold them to dealers, who then sold them as used cars. The availability of these cars hurt new car sales and depressed resale values of cars purchased new.

In 1992, U.S. automakers began reducing their reliance on such sales and changed their fleet sales policies to extend the buy-back period. **GM** reduced its fleet sales by 50 percent, which reduction, its CEO admitted, amounted to "two plants' worth of sales." At about the same time Japanese automakers increased their fleet sales in an effort to offset the impact of unfavorable currency exchange rates.

Sources: Neil Templin, "Sales of Rental Cars by Big Three Depress Other Second-Hand Auto Prices,"
The Wall Street Journal, January 6, 1992, B1.
Alex Taylor III, "GM's $11,000,000,000 Turnaround," Fortune, October 17, 1994, 54-56, 58, 62, 66,
70, 74.

Both analyses show the special order to be unprofitable under the revised conditions (total output of 75,000 units).

Consider another example. Suppose Griffith has no capacity constraint but its managers believe that *some* sales at the regular price would be lost because of customers buying from the chain. How many units of sales would Griffith have to lose at the regular price to make the special order unprofitable? At a $5.70 per-unit contribution margin for regular sales (shown before), Griffith could lose sales of up to 3,509 units ($20,000 incremental profit/$5.70 contribution margin) at regular prices without hurting overall profits. The managers must then assess the likelihood that lost sales would approach that critical number.

Long-Term Considerations

Because managers view special-order decisions as short term, they tend to focus on variable costs when quoting a price. Many managers do understand, however, that these decisions can have long-term consequences. For example, a company might accept so much private branding that it must acquire additional manufacturing capacity to meet the continuing growth of its regular sales. Another long-term aspect of accepting special orders at prices based primarily on variable costs is that a company cannot survive indefinitely without covering *all* of its costs. Smaller companies, especially, must be careful not to devote too much capacity to special orders that could turn out to dominate their business. These companies, which are often delighted to acquire large customers such as **Sears, Wal-Mart**, or **JC Penney**, can become captives as their large customers demand more and more of their capacity. Victor Coppola, Director of National Emerging Business Services for **Coopers & Lybrand**, an international public accounting firm, was quoted in *The Wall Street Journal* as saying that there are no success stories of captive suppliers.[4]

Even when managers know that the contribution margin on a particular special order should consider the company's fixed costs, they must still decide what contribution margin is adequate. For a company in which variable costs predominate, the contribution from a special order must be sufficient to allow for errors in computing or forecasting variable costs. For example, the contribution margin on a special order with a $50 selling price changes from positive to negative if the $49 variable cost is underestimated by only 3 percent ($1.47). Where fixed costs predominate, the managers' determination of an adequate contribution margin must consider all special orders, not just a single order, lest the contribution from all orders and regular business still be insufficient to cover fixed costs. Unfortunately, no rules exist for determining an adequate contribution margin for a single special-order opportunity.

FACTORS IN LIMITED SUPPLY

In the special-order example, Griffith's production was limited to 75,000 units because of a shortage of labor. A shortage of some other productive factor, such as space, machine time, or some critical material might also restrict operations. The term *constraint* is often used to describe a shortage of an input factor. A company with two or more products faces the additional problem of deciding how to use the limited quantity of the constraining factor.

Consider Neal Company, which makes a desk tray and a box for computer diskettes. Neal can sell all it can make of either product. Both products require processing on a machine that can operate only 100 hours per week. Data relating to these two products are as follows.

	Desk Tray	Diskette Box
Selling price	$10	$6
Variable cost	6	4
Contribution margin	$ 4	$2
Number of units that can be made per machine hour	60	150

To decide which product to make, Neal's managers cannot look only at contribution margin, because the company can make (and sell) more boxes than trays. If Neal's managers are to make the best possible use of the available machine time, they must consider both the difference in contribution margin and the difference in the production demands on the scarce production factor, machine time.

Two equivalent approaches are available to combine these differences. The first approach compares total contribution margin from the products over some specific time period, such as a week (100 machine hours available).

---

4 *June 10, 1988, 36R.*

Alternative Uses of Machine Time

	Desk Tray	Diskette Box
Maximum weekly production		
(60 × 100)	6,000	
(150 × 100)		15,000
Contribution margin per unit	× $ 4	× $ 2
Total weekly contribution margin	$24,000	$30,000

The analysis shows that producing boxes is the more profitable use of the machine time, and the answer is not affected by the time period chosen. The analysis is useful even if the demand for one or both products is limited. For example, suppose Neal could sell only 9,000 boxes per week, though it could make 15,000. Neal should make as many boxes as it can sell and devote the remaining hours of machine time to making trays. Thus, Neal should spend 60 hours of machine time making boxes (9,000 boxes/150 boxes per hour) and use the remaining 40 hours (100 - 60) to make trays.

The second approach also shows differences in contribution margin but concentrates on a unit of the scarce input. That is, the second approach determines the *contribution margin per unit of the scarce factor.* In Neal's case, the scarce factor is machine time, so the second analysis compares contribution per machine hour.

	Desk Tray	Diskette Box
Number of units that can be made		
per machine hour	60	150
Contribution margin per unit	× $ 4	× $ 2
Contribution margin per hour	$240	$300

The second analysis, like the first, shows that it is more profitable to produce boxes; boxes contribute more than trays, *per hour of machine time used.* Thus, the opportunity cost of using an hour of machine time making trays is the $300 you give up by not using that hour to make boxes.

Neal's managers can use the information derived from the preceding analyses for making decisions about product pricing as well as about the use of available facilities. For example, suppose the managers are considering raising the price of the desk tray. What price must Neal charge for the desk tray to make using machine time for it as profitable as using the time to make boxes? The contribution margins per machine hour have to be equal, which means that the margin for making trays has to be $300 per hour. Since Neal can make 60 trays per hour, the contribution per tray has to be $5 ($300/60). Adding the $5 desired margin to the $6 variable cost per tray gives a required selling price of $11 per tray. At that price, devoting machine time to making trays yields the same contribution margin as spending the time making boxes. The accompanying Insight illustrates how managers applied their understanding of cost and contribution margin data to analyzing the effects of the constraint in a more complex operating situation.

Even operating at full capacity, a plant of the very successful Latex Division of **GenCorp Polymer Products** could not meet the demand for all of its products. The plant's managers faced a difficult problem in analyzing product profitability. The constraining factor was the capacity of reactors, vessels in which the ingredients for each product are cooked. Any product can be made in any reactor. But the reactors differ in size, and the time required to process a product depends on the size of the reactor. Hence, a product's contribution margin per unit of processing time, and any ranking of product profitability based on such a contribution, would apply only to reactors of a particular size. The managers wanted to choose products independent of the reactor size, because they wanted the flexibility of scheduling production in whatever reactors were available at a given time.

To solve their problem, the managers selected a single reactor size and stated the processing time for each product in relative terms, calling the result "product standard processing time." These standardized times were incorporated into a measure called the Product Profit Velocity (PPV), which was used to analyze product profitability. The measure is calculated as follows (materials and freight-out are the only variable costs).

$$PPV = \frac{revenue\ per}{reactor\ run} - \frac{materials\ and}{freight\text{-}out} = \frac{contribution\ margin}{product\ standard\ processing\ time}$$

The products were then ranked, and the lower-ranked products were cut back when capacity was reached. Because of concerns about customer ill will, the plant manager chose to increase prices rather than drop lower-ranking products. The rankings were also used to highlight products to study for ways to reduce costs (for example, by changing the materials mix).

Source: Gary B. Frank, Steve A. Fisher, and Allen R. Wilkie, "Linking Cost to Price and Profit," Management Accounting, *June 1989, 22-26.*

This section suggests analytical approaches for making decisions when a company faces a single constraint. Chapter 16 extends the analysis to situations where there are two or more constraints. Chapter 8 suggests techniques for dealing with decisions to relieve a constraint by making a long-term investment in additional capacity.

DECISION MAKING UNDER ENVIRONMENTAL CONSTRAINTS

When deciding among available courses of actions, managers must, of course, be aware of any laws that might apply. Antitrust laws forbid actions that might substantially reduce competition. Anti-dumping laws address aspects of unfair competition in international trade. Environmental protection laws restrict actions that could harm wildlife or increase pollution. At various times controls on wages and prices have restricted price increases. We shall limit our discussion to the major laws dealing with pricing practices.

The Sherman Act, Clayton Act, Robinson-Patman Act, and the statutes of many states prohibit predatory pricing. Predatory pricing is pricing below cost in the short term to drive competitors out of business and eventually to raise prices. Often, the question in cases under these laws is about what is meant by "cost." For the most part, courts have held that prices below average variable costs are predatory. Occasionally, incremental costs have been used as the standard, particularly in cases involving manufacturers who could show they had excess capacity. In some cases, the determining factor has been an offending company's intention. For example, several pharmacies in Arkansas claimed that **Wal-Mart** engaged in predatory pricing. In refusing to find Wal-Mart guilty, the state supreme court noted that the plaintiffs were still profitable and distinguished between "a sustained effort to destroy competition" and attracting customers by selling items below cost.[5]

The Robinson-Patman Act forbids charging different prices to different customers unless there are intrinsic cost differences in serving the different customers; in other words, this act forbids discriminatory pricing. The Federal Trade Commission (FTC) is the regulatory agency responsible for enforcing the act. Defendants charged with discriminatory pricing under Robinson-Patman can avoid liability by showing that the differences in prices from one customer to another emanate from different methods of manufacturing, different quantities purchased, or attempts to meet competition in good faith. (The last is not a cost issue.)

Justifications based on different methods of manufacture must show that the company sold different products to different customers. Companies that sell private brands usually modify the products to meet this criterion. Companies that custom-make products for different customers also can use this defense. For example, **Pittsburgh Plate Glass** successfully defended itself against a price discrimination suit by showing that it sold to the plaintiff, in smaller quantities than to other customers, a nonstandard size of glass that cost more to make.

One key to a successful defense against price discrimination or predatory pricing is for the company's management accountants to have a thorough understanding of costs. They must be able to amass cost data that support the company's position. Of course, potential ethical problems arise in developing cost studies. Management accountants' objectivity and competence are put at risk if they falsify, or even shade, data to meet the company's needs. The IMA Standards expressly forbid such acts.

In the mid 1990s, after several years with few suits, the FTC renewed efforts to combat a vertical price-fixing arrangement known as resale price maintenance. That practice occurs when, by threatening to cut off deliveries, a manufacturer coerces retailers to agree to maintain the retail prices of its product(s) at a certain level (or within a certain range). The most notable of the recent price-fixing cases involved **Stride Rite** (Ked shoes) and **Reebok International Ltd**, but the FTC also pursued cases involving manufacturers of hockey skates,

---

5 Louise Lee, *"Wal-Mart Wins Ruling on Pricing Policy,"* The Wall Street Journal, *January 10, 1995, B8.*

suntan products, and toys.[6] In 1995, two Japanese companies pleaded guilty to conspiring to fix prices of paper for FAX machines. Costs play no part in price-fixing arrangements, only the ethics of a company's managers and legal advisors.

Many countries, including the U.S., have anti-dumping laws to prevent unfair competitive practices in international trade. These laws, as well as some trade agreements, prohibit a company in one country from selling its products in another country at less than fair value. A company might take such action to establish its position in a new country quickly or to avoid lowering prices during a period of oversupply in its home country. The International Trade Administration, part of the Commerce Department, deals with charges of dumping in the U.S. During the 1990s, U.S. producers have alleged dumping of many products, ranging from steel, color televisions, and components for computers to disposable lighters and fresh roses. Cost data are relevant to a defense against dumping charges, but such cases also involve political considerations.

SUMMARY

Managerial accountants supply information for short-term decision making. The essential quantitative factors influencing such decisions are differential revenues and costs, including opportunity costs. Costs and revenues that will be the same whatever action is taken can be ignored. Historical costs are sunk and are irrelevant for current decisions because they cannot be changed by some current action. Avoidable fixed costs are relevant. Whether a cost is relevant to a particular decision does not always depend on whether the cost is variable or fixed.

Typical examples of short-term decisions are whether to drop a product or product line, whether to produce a component internally or purchase it from an outside supplier, whether to further process joint products, whether to accept a special order, and how best to use the limited supply of some critical input factor. As a general rule, the action that is expected to result in the highest income for the firm should be pursued, subject always to constraints imposed by law. This decision rule considers only the quantifiable factors in a given situation. Most decisions involve some factors that can have monetary effects but for which no reliable estimates can be made. Still other factors, such as a company policy prohibiting certain types of products, may not lend themselves to quantification at all. These qualitative factors should not be ignored.

KEY TERMS

complementary effects (192)
cost allocation (188)
differential revenues and costs (182)

incremental revenues and costs (182)
joint (common) costs (196)
joint process (196)

---

6 *Viveca Novak and Joseph Pereira, "Reebok and FTC Settle Price-Fixing Charges,"* The Wall Street Journal, *May 5, 1995, B1, B8.*

joint products (196)
loss leader (192)
opportunity cost (183)

split-off point (197)
sunk cost (183)

REVIEW PROBLEM

Andrews Company makes three products. Following are the revenue and cost data for a typical month.

| | Product | | | |
	X	Y	Z	Total
Sales	$300	$500	$800	$1,600
Variable costs	100	200	400	700
Contribution margin	$200	$300	$400	$ 900
Fixed costs:				
Avoidable	$ 80	$100	$120	$ 300
Common, allocated on the basis of sales dollar	60	100	160	320
Total fixed costs	$140	$200	$280	$ 620
Profit	$ 60	$100	$120	$ 280

Required

Answer each of the following questions independently.

1. What will total profit be if Andrews simply drops product X?
2. Andrews is considering selling a new product, P, in place of X. P will sell for $7 per unit, have variable costs of $5 per unit, and have avoidable fixed costs of $130. How many units of P would Andrews have to sell to maintain its total income of $280?
3. Andrews charges $10 per unit for product Z. A chain store offers to buy 40 units of Z per month at $8 per unit. The additional sales would not affect total fixed costs or variable costs per unit. Andrews has the capacity to produce 110 units of Z per month. If Andrews accepts the offer, what will its total monthly income be?
4. Closer analysis reveals that X, Y, and Z are joint products of a joint process and all are now being processed beyond the split-off point. The cost of the joint process, including raw material, is the $320 joint allocated fixed cost. All of the other reported costs are incurred to process the individual products beyond the split-off point. If the sales values of X, Y, and Z at split-off are $110, $220, and $230, respectively, could Andrews increase its profits by selling one or more products at split-off? If so, which product(s) should be sold at split-off and what will the increase in total profit be?
5. Unit sales of X and Z are 100 and 200, respectively. Both products are made on a single machine that has a limited capacity. The machine can make five units of X per hour, or eight units of Z.
   (a) If Andrews can sell all that it can make of either product, should it continue to make both products? If not, which product should Andrews make?
   (b) Assume the machine is being operated at its capacity of 45 hours per month. What will happen to monthly profits if Andrews makes only the

more profitable product as determined in part (a)? Give the dollar increase in profits. (Hint: Remember that if only one product is made, the company will save the avoidable fixed costs on the product that it drops.)

ANSWER TO REVIEW PROBLEM

1. $160. Andrews would lose the $200 contribution margin from selling X but would save the $80 avoidable fixed costs. Subtracting the net reduction in profit of $120 ($200 - $80) from the current profit of $280 gives $160. (The $120 drop is the incremental profit on X.)

2. 125 units. To achieve the same total profit, selling P must produce the $120 incremental profit lost by dropping X (per item 1). Hence, selling P must provide contribution margin sufficient to cover both the new avoidable fixed costs and the $120 profit. The new fixed costs are $130, so the contribution margin needed is $250 ($130 fixed costs plus the $120 desired profit). P's contribution margin is $2 per unit ($7 - $5), so Andrews must sell 125 units of P ($250/$2).

3. $350. The important factor is that Andrews will lose some sales at the regular price if it accepts the special order. Capacity is 110 units and planned sales are 80 units ($800/$10 selling price). If Andrews sells 40 units to the *new* customer, it can sell only 70 units at the regular price, 10 units fewer than planned.

   Given that the per-unit variable cost of Z is $5 ($400/80 units), the analysis might proceed as follows.

Gain from contribution margin on special order ($8 - $5) × 40 units	$120
Lost contribution margin because of loss of sales of 10 units at regular price, ($10 - $5) × 10 units	50
Gain on special order	$ 70
Planned profit	280
New monthly income	$350

4. Andrews could increase profits by $20 per month by selling product Y at the split-off point, as shown by the following analysis.

	X	Y	Z
Sales with further processing	$300	$500	$800
Additional processing costs:			
Variable costs	$100	$200	$400
Avoidable fixed costs	80	100	120
Total additional processing costs	$180	$300	$520
Profit if further processed	$120	$200	$280
Split-off values	110	220	230
Advantage (disadvantage) of further processing	$ 10	$ (20)	$ 50

5. (a) Andrews should concentrate on product Z rather than product X. The decision is independent of the number of hours available, because the contribution margin *per hour of machine time* is higher for Z.

	X	Z
Contribution margin per unit	$2 ($200/100)	$2 ($400/200)
Units that can be made in one hour	5	8
Contribution margin per hour	$10	$16

As long as the company can sell all the units it makes of either product, total contribution margin will be greater by making only Z.

(b) Profit will increase by $200. If Andrews uses its capacity of 45 hours to produce only Z, it can make 360 units (45 × 8) for total contribution margin of $720 (360 × $2 per unit). This is an increase of $320 ($720 - $400 contribution margin already anticipated). However, Andrews loses the current $120 *incremental profit* from product X (see item 1). Thus, if Andrews concentrates on product Z it would gain $200 ($320 additional contribution margin from Z - $120 incremental profit lost from not producing X).

ASSIGNMENT MATERIAL

QUESTIONS FOR DISCUSSION

5-1   *"Where do you start?"*   One of your classmates believes he thoroughly understands the principle of incremental cost and so places the following ad in the school paper.

Wanted—Ride to Linville

I will pay all of the extra costs involved in taking me to Linville. Call Bob at 555-6202.

Linville is 1,200 miles from the university. Does your classmate understand the principle of incremental cost as well as he believes he does?

5-2   *Cost analysis*   While standing in line to use a telephone, you hear the following part of a conversation. "I'm going to play golf today, dear." (Pause) "Yes, honey, I know it costs $8 for a caddy and $5 for drinks after the round, but it really does get cheaper the more I play. Look, the club dues are $1,000 per year, so if I play 50 times it costs, ah, let's see, $33 per round. But if I play 100 times it only costs, um, just a second, yeah, about $23 per round." (Pause) "I knew you'd understand. See you at dinner. Bye." How did the golfer figure the cost per round? Comment on her analysis.

5-3   *The generous management*   Several years ago, a leading newspaper ran an advertisement for itself. The advertisement stated that the paper, which cost the customer $0.40, was a bargain because it cost the publisher $1.00 ($0.53 for paper, $0.09 for printers' labor, $0.05 for ink, $0.15 for salaries of editorial employees and $0.18 for other operating expenses such as executives' salaries, rent, depreciation, and taxes). Is the buyer actually paying less than cost? What assumptions did you make to arrive at your answer? How can the publisher be so generous to readers?

5-4   *Pricing policy*   At Washington National Airport you enter the departure area of an airline just before a flight to Los Angeles is to take off. The plane is about 80% full, and the regular fare for the flight is $300. You have neither a ticket nor a reservation for the flight, but you offer to pay $50 to take the flight. Assume there are no variable costs associated with the number of passengers. Do you think the airline would accept your offer? Explain.

5-5 Identifying relevant factors The lay trustees at the Central Westcliff Church are discussing ideas for making more use of church facilities. One trustee suggests that the church sponsor monthly dances for the church's young people in its activity hall, which is almost always unused on Friday evenings. Discuss the costs, revenues, and perhaps unquantifiable factors relevant to a decision about using the activity hall for this purpose.

EXERCISES

5-6 Special order Watt, Inc. manufactures lamps and expects to sell 350,000 units in 19X0 at $21 per unit. Planned per-unit manufacturing costs at that level of production are as follows.

Variable manufacturing costs	$9
Fixed manufacturing costs	$5

Early in 19X0, a new customer approaches Watt offering to buy 15,000 lamps at $11 each. Watt can produce additional units with no change in fixed manufacturing cost or per-unit variable cost. The only additional fixed cost for this order is for packing and shipping, estimated at $3,800.

Required
Determine the effect of accepting the special order on planned profit for the year. Assume that filling the special order will not affect regular sales.

5-7 Joint products Rox Company produces two families of chemicals, orides and octines. The production phase of each chemical group begins with a joint process. Following are production, sales, and cost data for the products that result from each 100-gallon batch of materials going through the joint process that produces orides.

	Boride	Doride	Foride
Gallons produced	40	50	10
Selling price per gallon at the split-off point	$6	$5	$0
Selling price per gallon after further processing	$10	$9	$4
Per-gallon variable cost of further processing	$5	$2	$3

Required
Determine which of the joint products should be sold at the split-off point and which should be processed further.

5-8 Joint products (extension of 5-7) Rox normally processes 120,000 gallons of oride mixture per month. You have determined that, in addition to the variable costs of the additional processing of boride, doride, and foride, there are the following monthly fixed costs associated with such added processing.

	Boride	Doride	Foride
Avoidable fixed costs of additional processing	$ 8,000	$58,000	$ 17,000
Unavoidable fixed costs of additional processing, allocated	25,000	60,000	4,000

Required

1. Does the information about the fixed costs of additional processing of the joint products change your answer from 5-7 as to whether any of those products should be processed after the split-off point?
2. Assume that Rox takes the most profitable course of action with respect to each of the joint oride products. Ignoring the costs of the joint process, what will be the total monthly profit from orides?

5-9 Dropping a segment Colbert Company expects the following results for the coming year.

	Hats	Belts	Jeans	Total
Sales	$ 80,000	$120,000	$250,000	$450,000
Variable costs	$ 30,000	$ 40,000	$100,000	$170,000
Fixed costs	60,000	40,000	120,000	220,000
Total costs	$ 90,000	$ 80,000	$220,000	$390,000
Profit (loss)	$ (10,000)	$ 40,000	$ 30,000	$ 60,000

Required

Answer each of the following questions independently.

1. Suppose that fixed costs, all unavoidable, are allocated based on the floor space each segment occupies. What will total profit be if Colbert drops the hat segment?
2. Suppose that $25,000 of the fixed costs shown for the hat segment are avoidable. What will total profit be if Colbert drops the hat segment?
3. Suppose that Colbert could avoid $25,000 in fixed costs by dropping the hat segment (as in item 2). However, the managers believe that if they do drop hats, sales of each of the other lines will fall by 10%. What will profit be if Colbert drops hats and loses 10% of the sales of each of the other segments?

5-10 Product selection—capacity constraint Winston Company makes three products, all of which require the use of a special machine. Only 200 hours of machine time are available per month. Data for the three products are as follow. Winston can sell as much of any product as it can make.

	Gadgets	Supergadgets	Colossalgadgets
Selling price	$12	$16	$21
Variable cost	7	8	10
Contribution margin	$ 5	$ 8	$11
Machine time required in minutes	6	10	15

Required

1. If all products required the same amount of machine time, which product should Winston make?
2. Given the capacity constraint, determine which product Winston should make and what total monthly contribution margin Winston would earn by making only that product.
3. How much would the selling price of the next most profitable (per machine hour) product have to rise to be as profitable as the product you selected in item 2?

5-11   *Make or buy*   GFA Company is introducing a new product. The managers are trying to decide whether to make one of its components, part #A-3, or to buy it from an outside supplier. Making the part internally requires using some machinery that has no other use and no resale value. The space that could be used to make the part also has no alternative use. The outside supplier will sell the part to GFA for $5 per unit. Following is an estimate of per-unit costs if GFA makes the part.

Cost to Make Part #A-3	
Materials	$1.50
Direct labor	2.00
Variable manufacturing overhead	.50
Fixed manufacturing overhead	2.50
Total cost	$6.50

The estimate reflects expected volume of 10,000 units of the part. The fixed manufacturing overhead consists of depreciation on the machinery and a share of the costs of the factory (heat, light, building depreciation, etc.) based on the floor space that manufacturing the part would occupy.

Required

Determine whether GFA should make or buy part #A-3.

5-12   *Special order*   Devio Company produces high-quality golf balls. A sporting-goods chain offers to buy 25,000 dozen balls at $15 per dozen. The chain would sell the balls for $20, which is $5 less than usually charged by Devio's regular dealers. The chain would obliterate the Devio name so that customers would not be able to tell who had made the balls.

Devio can produce 200,000 dozen balls per year. Following are the planned results for the coming year without considering the special order from the chain.

Sales (150,000 dozen at $18 per dozen)	$2,700,000
Cost of goods sold	1,110,000
Gross profit	$1,590,000
Selling and administrative expenses, all fixed	600,000
Income	$ 990,000

Cost of goods sold contains variable costs of $7 per dozen balls. The rest of the cost is fixed.

Required

1. Determine whether Devio should accept the order.
2. Might your answer to item 1 change if the Devio name were to appear on the balls sold in the chain stores?

 5-13   Short-term decisions Nickolai Company expects the following results in 19X5. Fixed costs, all unavoidable, are allocated based on relative sales dollars.

	Product A	Product B	Total
Sales	$300	$500	$800
Variable costs	150	150	300
Contribution margin	$150	$350	$500
Fixed costs	90	150	240
Profit	$ 60	$200	$260

Required

Answer each of the following questions independently, unless otherwise instructed.

1. The managers are considering increasing advertising for product A by $30. They expect to achieve a 40% increase in volume for product A with no change in selling price, but some of that increase will be at the expense of product B. Sales of B are expected to decline by 5%. What will total profit be if the managers approve the proposed action?
2. What is the maximum percentage decline in volume of product B that would leave the action in item 1 just barely desirable?
3. The managers are considering dropping product A and replacing it with product C. Introducing product C would increase total fixed costs by $30. C's contribution margin percentage is 60%. What dollar sales of product C are needed to maintain the original profit of $260?

5-14   Analyzing data for decisions The expected results for the coming year for Porter Company, which manufactures two lines of products, are as follows, in thousands of dollars.

	Kitchenwares	Officewares	Total
Sales	$3,300	$2,700	$6,000
Variable costs	1,650	810	2,460
Contribution margin	$1,650	$1,890	$3,540
Avoidable fixed costs	650	1,300	1,950
Incremental profit	$1,000	$ 590	$1,590
Common, unavoidable fixed costs			900
Profit			$ 690

Required

Suppose that Porter uses the same production facilities for both products. Demand is such that the firm could sell $500,000 more of either product line but it would have to reduce output and sales of the other line by the same amount. Which line should the company make more of and what is the effect on total profit?

5-15   Changing product lines (extension of 5-14)   Suppose Porter could introduce a new line that is much more profitable than either of the existing ones. To introduce the new line, however, Porter must drop one of the existing lines entirely. The other line—the one not dropped—will continue as originally planned. Which line should Porter drop?

5-16   Joint products   BAT Company produces four joint products at a joint cost of $80,000. The company currently processes all products beyond the split-off point, and the final products are sold as follows.

Products	Sales	Additional Processing Costs
M	$150,000	$110,000
N	180,000	60,000
O	45,000	40,000
P	20,000	15,000

BAT could sell the products at the split-off point for the following amounts: M, $80,000; N, $50,000; O, $15,000; and P, zero.

Required

1. Which products should BAT sell at the split-off point?
2. What would BAT's profit be if it took the most profitable action with respect to each of its products?

5-17   Dropping a product—complementary effects   Kaiser Face Care Company makes three products in the same factory. Following are the revenue and cost data for a typical month, in thousands of dollars.

		Product		
		After-	Shaving	
	Razors	Shave	Cream	Total
Sales	$ 400	$ 600	$ 400	$ 1,400
Variable costs	300	240	120	660
Contribution margin	$ 100	$ 360	$ 280	$ 740
Fixed costs				
Avoidable	$ 120	$ 150	$ 70	$ 340
Unavoidable, allocated on basis of relative sales dollars	80	120	80	280
Total fixed costs	$ 200	$ 270	$ 150	$ 620
Income (loss)	$(100)	$ 90	$ 130	$ 120

Required

1. Determine total income if razors were dropped from the product line.
2. Suppose that if razors were dropped, the sales of after-shave would decline by 20% and those of shaving cream by 10%. Determine income for the company if razors were dropped.

5-18   Inventory values   James Company has 300 pounds of a chemical compound called bysol, bought at $3.20 per pound several months ago. Bysol now costs $3.70 per pound. The company could sell it for $3.40 per pound (shipping costs account for the $0.30 difference between the cost to buy and the selling price).

Required

Answer each of the following questions independently.

1. Suppose James has stopped making the product for which it used bysol and will sell it or use it to make a special order. The special order has a price of $2,000, and incremental costs, excluding the bysol, are $900. What is the relevant cost of using the bysol in the special order? Should the company accept the order?
2. Suppose the company has alternative uses for bysol so that if it accepts the special order it will have to buy more for its regular production. What is the relevant cost of using the bysol in the special order? Should James accept the order?

5-19   Make or buy (AICPA adapted)   MTZ Company manufactures 10,000 units of part Z-101 annually, using the part in one of its products. The controller has collected the following cost data related to the part.

Materials	$ 20,000
Direct labor	55,000
Variable overhead	45,000
Fixed overhead	70,000
Total costs	$190,000

Vortan Company offers to supply the part for $18 per unit. If MTZ accepts the offer, it will be able to rent some of the facilities it devotes to making the part to another company for $15,000 annually and will also be able to reduce its fixed overhead costs by $40,000.

Required

1. Should MTZ accept the offer based on the available information?
2. What is the maximum price that MTZ is willing to pay for the part—the price that would give it the same income it would have if it continued making it?
3. Assuming the $18 price from Vortan, at what annual unit volume will MTZ earn the same income making the part as it would buying it?

5-20   Capacity constraint   Gray Mfg. Inc. can produce either of two products, Product Q and Product Z, with its existing machinery. Making either product requires the use of grinding machines. Gray has 160 grinding machines, each of which can be operated 200 hours per month. Following are the comparative per-unit data for the two products.

	Product	
	Q	Z
Selling price	$10	$15
Variable cost	$6	$9
Required grinding time	2 hrs.	2.5 hrs.

Required

1. If Gray can sell as many units of either product as it can make with its limited supply of grinding machines, which product should Gray make and what will Gray's total contribution margin be per month if it makes that product?
2. Suppose the selling price of Zs has only recently risen to $15. Gray's managers estimate that the maximum sales volume of Z at that price is 80,000 units per year. They believe 180,000 Qs could be sold per year at the $10 price. How should Gray use its grinding machine capacity over the coming year? (That is, how many of each product should Gray produce?)

5-21   Joint products   Grevel Company slaughters cattle and processes the meat, hides, and bones. It tans the hides and sells them to leather manufacturers. The bones are made into buttons and other sundries. In a typical month, it processes about 3,000 cattle. An income statement for such a month follows, in thousands of dollars.

	Totals	Meat	Hides	Bones
Sales	$500	$300	$120	$ 80
Cost of cattle[a]	300	180	72	48
Gross profit	$200	$120	$ 48	$ 32
Additional processing costs, avoidable	(80)	(40)	(20)	(20)
Allocated costs[b]	(60)	(30)	(15)	(15)
Income (loss)	$ 60	$ 50	$ 13	$ (3)

a Allocated on the basis of relative sales value (60% of sales).
b Allocated on the basis of additional processing costs, all unavoidable.

Required

1. Is Grevel losing money by processing the bones into buttons and sundry items?
2. A tanner offers to buy the hides as they are sheared off the cattle for $7 each. He contends that Grevel's income from hides would be $21,000 (3,000 hides × $7) if the hides are sold directly to him. Should Grevel accept the offer?
3. If Grevel could sell the bones without further processing, how much would have to be received per month to keep total profits the same as they are now?

5-22   Opportunity cost pricing   Boyett Company makes three products. Data are as follows.

	Product		
	Wallet	Belt	Hat
Current selling price	$14	$15	$25
Variable cost	4	6	10
Contribution margin	$10	$ 9	$15
Machine time required, in minutes	10	15	30

Boyett has 40,000 minutes of machine time available per week. It can sell all of any of the three products that it can make.

Required

1. Determine which product the firm should make.
2. Determine the selling prices that the firm would have to charge for each of the other two products to make them equally profitable per minute of machine time as the one you selected in item 1.

5-23   Comprehensive review of short-term decisions   The following data relate to the planned operations of Kimble Company before considering the changes described later. All fixed costs are direct, but unavoidable.

	Product		
	Chair	Table	Sofa
Selling price	$120	$ 400	$ 600
Variable costs	$ 40	$ 160	$ 360
Fixed costs	30	120	180
Total costs	$ 70	$ 280	$ 540
Profit per unit	$ 50	$ 120	$ 60
Annual volume	8,000	3,000	4,000

Required

Answer each of the following questions independently, unless otherwise instructed.

1. What is total profit expected to be?
2. What will happen to profit if Kimble drops sofas?
3. What will happen to profit if Kimble drops chairs, but is able to shift the facilities to making more sofas so that volume of sofas increases to 7,000 units? (Total fixed costs remain constant.)
4. Variable cost per sofa includes $60 for parts that the company now buys outside. The company could make the parts at a variable cost of $45. It would also have to increase fixed costs by $35,000 annually. What would happen to profit if the company took the proposed action?
5. Kimble has received a special order for 1,000 tables at $245. Capacity is sufficient to make the units, and sales at the regular price would not be affected. What will happen to profit if Kimble accepts the order?
6. Repeat item 5 assuming now that the order is for 1,500 tables and that capacity is limited to 4,000 tables.

5-24   Using per-unit data   The managers of Ferrara Company expect the following per-unit results at a volume of 200,000 units.

Sales		$10
Variable costs	$6	
Fixed costs	3	
Total costs		9
Profit		$ 1

Required

Answer each of the following questions independently.

1. Ferrara has the opportunity to sell 20,000 units to a chain store for $8 each. The managers expect that sales at the regular price will drop by about 8,000 units as some customers will buy from the chain store instead of from the regular outlets. What will happen to the company's profit if it accepts the order?

2. Of the total unit variable cost of $6, $2.80 is for a part that Ferrara now buys from an outside supplier. Ferrara could make the part for $2.25 variable cost plus $100,000 per year fixed costs for renting additional machinery. What will happen to annual profit if Ferrara makes the part?

3. The company is considering a new model to replace the existing product. The new model has a $6 unit variable cost and the same total fixed costs as the existing product. The new model has expected sales of 100,000 units per year. At what selling price per unit will the new model give the same total profit as the existing one?

PROBLEMS

5-25   Just-in-time, costs of activities   Racine Machinery recently began to change one of its plants to a just-in-time operation. So far, Racine has set up one manufacturing cell to make a product that had formerly been made in large batches. The following analysis of April operations for the cell was disappointing to the controller who had expected dramatic improvements with JIT.

Units produced	20,000
Costs:	
Materials	$ 55,000
Labor	67,000
Overhead	35,000
Total	$157,000
Per-unit cost	$7.85

The overhead cost shown is mostly allocated costs. Roughly $9,000 is incremental, avoidable cost. The per-unit cost to manufacture the product under the old system follows.

Materials	$2.90
Labor	2.80
Overhead	1.80
Total	$7.50

Overhead is based on 22,000 units and is 40% variable, 60% fixed at that level. Under the old system quality control was weak, so the company had to produce about 22,000 units to obtain 20,000 good units. With the JIT cell, workers do their own inspection during production, and only 20,000 total units are produced to obtain 20,000 good units.

Under the old system, manufacturing the product required the following people in addition to direct laborers. The costs given include fringe benefits.

Two inspectors, each earning	$2,000 per month
One production scheduler earning	$2,500 per month
Two maintenance people, each earning	$1,800 per month

When setting up the cell Racine reassigned the people described above and other support personnel who had worked on the product. The other support people earned about $11,000 per month, including fringes.

Required
Determine the incremental cost to produce 20,000 good units in a month under the old method and using the JIT cell. Using the guidelines in Appendix A, prepare a memorandum explaining your results.

5-26   Choosing a product   Hare Company operates a cannery. It buys raw carrots from farmers and can produce three types of canned carrots: sliced, mashed, and pickled. Hare's fixed production costs for a season are $20,000. This season, Hare contracted to purchase 100,000 pounds of raw carrots at $0.25 per pound and will not be able to purchase any more. Following are the price and other data for Hare's three products.

	Sliced	Mashed	Pickled
Selling price per case	$3.50	$3.00	$4.25
Variable processing cost per case	$1.50	$1.75	$2.00
Pounds of raw carrots per case	5 lbs.	2.5 lbs.	5 lbs.

Required
1. Assuming Hare can sell as many cases as it makes of all types of product, which type should it produce?
2. Assuming Hare has no costs other than those already mentioned and that it follows the advice you offered in item 1, what is the maximum profit Hare can make this season?
3. Assume that, despite your advice in item 1, Hare's managers really want to produce and sell pickled carrots and are convinced that they can slightly reduce the volume of carrots in each can of pickled carrots without affecting the selling price. How many pounds of carrots would Hare have to use in each case of pickled carrots to make that product as profitable as the type you selected in item 1?
4. What other factors should Hare's managers consider before deciding to implement the plan proposed in item 3?

5-27   Product pricing—off-peak hours   Marie Angelo, owner of Gino's Pizzeria, is considering a luncheon special to increase business during the slow time from 11 a.m. to 1 p.m. on weekdays. For $2.20 on any weekday, she will give customers all the pizza they can eat. Marie has prepared the following data for weekly business during those hours.

	Pizza	Beverages	Total
Sales (average pizza price, $2.80)	$420	$84	$504
Variable costs	120	24	144
Contribution margin	$300	$60	$360
Avoidable fixed costs—wages of students hired			180
Current incremental profit, lunch period			$180

She estimates that at the special price she will serve about 300 pizzas per week to about 250 customers. (Some customers will eat more than one pizza, given the lower price.) She also anticipates that variable costs per unit will be about 20% higher because people will want more toppings than they now order. Beverage sales will bear the same relationship to the number of customers that they do now when each customer eats one pizza. The increase in the number of customers will entail an increase in personnel during the hours of the special, increasing wage cost by 15%.

Required
Evaluate the monetary effects of the proposed luncheon special.

5-28   Car pool   You and your neighbor carpool to work, driving on alternate days. A colleague at work has injured his hand and will not be able to drive for the next three months. He inquires about riding with you and your neighbor and offers to pay "a fair price." You know that he could ride a bus for $2 per day.

From your house it is a 10-mile round trip to work. If you pick up your injured colleague, the round trip is 14 miles. Last year, your car cost you the following for 15,000 miles. (Your neighbor's car cost the same for the same number of miles.)

Gasoline and oil	$1,350
Maintenance	450
New tires (life of 30,000 miles)	300
Insurance and registration	600
Decline in market value	3,000
Total	$5,700

Required
1. Quote a daily price to your colleague that seems fair to you.
2. What do you think your colleague would say is a fair price?

5-29   Joint products—changes in mix   Brewer Company makes three products in a joint process. The process is set up to yield the following quantities of each product from ten pounds of raw material: Nyron, three pounds; Xylon, three pounds; and Krylon, four pounds. Each product can be further processed; price and cost data are as follows.

	Nyron	Xylon	Krylon
Selling price at split-off, per pound	$2	$4	$ 6
Additional processing costs, per pound	1	3	8
Selling price after additional processing, per pound	8	6	12

Required

1. Which products should the company sell at split-off?
2. Assume that Brewer is now operating in accordance with your answer to item 1. Suppose that by changing the production process Brewer could get eight pounds of Nyron and one pound each of Xylon and Krylon from ten pounds of raw material. The change will increase fixed costs by $60,000 per month. The company generally processes 100,000 pounds of raw material each month. Should Brewer change the process?
3. At what level of output per month, expressed in pounds of raw material processed, would Brewer have the same income under the existing process and under the changed process as described in item 2?

5-30 Hours of operation Bronson Book Store is normally open 12 hours per day, six days per week. Following are typical annual results under current operating hours.

Sales		$361,400
Cost of sales		162,700
Gross margin		$198,700
Operating expenses:		
Salaries	$88,300	
Rent	36,000	
Utilities	11,500	
Insurance	6,500	
Other	17,200	159,500
Profit		$ 39,200

As an experiment, the owner kept the store open for six hours one Sunday. Sales were $750 and additional payroll costs were $110. Doing a few calculations, the owner came up with $511 as the estimated daily cost of operations, exclusive of cost of sales, without Sunday hours. He therefore concluded that about $930 in sales was necessary to make staying open on Sundays worthwhile.

Required

1. Try to determine just what calculations the owner made to get his figures of $511 and $930.
2. With the information available, does it appear profitable to stay open on Sundays?
3. Using the guidelines in Appendix A, prepare a memorandum that describes other information you wish to have before making a final decision.

5-31 Special order—alternative volumes Woolen Products Company makes heavy outdoor shirts. Data relating to the coming year's planned operations are as follows.

Sales (230,000 shirts)	$4,140,000
Cost of goods sold	2,760,000
Gross profit	$1,380,000
Selling and administrative expenses	805,000
Income	$ 575,000

The factory has capacity to make 250,000 shirts per year. Fixed costs included in cost of goods sold are $690,000. The only variable selling, general, and administrative expenses are a 10% sales commission and a $0.50 per shirt licensing fee paid to the designer.

A chain store manager has approached the sales manager of Woolen Products offering to buy 15,000 shirts at $14 per shirt. These shirts would be sold in areas where Woolen's shirts are not now sold. The sales manager believes that accepting the offer would result in a loss because the average total cost of a shirt is $15.50 ([$2,760,000 + $805,000]/230,000). He feels that even though sales commissions would not be paid on the order, a loss would still result.

Required
1. Determine whether the company should accept the offer.
2. Suppose that the order was for 40,000 shirts instead of 15,000. What would the company's income be if it accepted the order?
3. Assuming the same facts as in item 1, what is the lowest price that the company could accept and still earn $575,000?
4. How many units of sales at the regular price could the company lose before it became profitable to accept the order in part 2?

5-32 Make or buy Christensen Appliance Company is bringing out a new washing machine. The machine requires a type of electric motor not used for the current line of products. The purchasing manager has received a bid of $29 per motor from Wright Motor Company for any number that Christensen would need. Delivery is guaranteed within two weeks after order.

Christensen's production manager believes the company could make the motor internally by extensively converting an existing model. Additional space and machinery would be required if Christensen were to make the motors. The company currently leases, for $39,600 per year, space that could be used to make the motors. However, the space is now used to store vital materials, so Christensen would have to lease additional space in an adjacent building to store the materials. That space could be rented for $48,000 per year. It is suitable for storage, but not for converting the motors. The equipment needed to convert the motors could be rented for $45,000 per year.

The treasurer has developed the following unit costs based on the expected demand of 18,000 units per year.

Materials	$11.80
Direct labor	10.60
Rent for space	2.20
Machinery rental	2.50
Other overhead	8.20
Total cost	$35.30

The "other overhead" figure includes $5.40 in fixed overhead that would be allocated to conversion of the motors.

Required
1. Determine whether the motors should be bought or made.
2. Determine the volume of motors at which Christensen would show the same total income whether it bought or made the motors.

3. Suppose that the company had decided to make the motors, however wisely or unwisely according to your analysis in item 1. One-year contracts have been signed for the additional space and for the equipment. These contracts cannot be canceled. Determine the price that Wright Motor would have to offer Christensen to induce it to buy the motors.

5-33   *Dropping a product—opportunity costs* Grothe Company has three product lines. Data for the coming year's operations that reflect the managers' best estimates are as follows.

	Cabinets	Shelves	Bureaus
Sales	$450,000	$320,000	$200,000
Variable costs	200,000	180,000	125,000
Contribution margin	$250,000	$140,000	$ 75,000
Avoidable fixed costs	110,000	60,000	40,000
Product margin	$140,000	$ 80,000	$ 35,000
Investment in receivables and inventories	$350,000	$300,000	$320,000

Unallocated indirect costs total $130,000 and plant and equipment is $560,000.

The managers are not happy with the expected results of the bureau line and are considering dropping it. If they did so, the company could recover the investment in receivables and inventory related to the line and pay off debt of $320,000 that bears 14% interest.

Required
Determine whether Grothe should drop the bureau line.

5-34   *Joint process (extension of 5-7 and 5-8)* Rox's production manager for orides is following the advice you gave in your answer to 5-8. The vice president of manufacturing is satisfied with the results but is now wondering whether Rox should continue competing in the oride market. The controller has provided the following information about the joint process that is the first phase in producing the chemicals in the oride family.

Variable costs per 100-gallon batch	$180
Monthly fixed costs:	
Avoidable	$102,000
Unavoidable	$50,000

Required
Assume that Rox has no alternative uses for the facilities now devoted to operating the joint process that starts the production of orides. Determine whether the company should continue to operate the joint process.

5-35   *Salesperson's time as scarce resource* Lombard Company sells to both wholesalers and retailers. The firm has 30 salespeople and cannot easily increase the size of the sales force. An analysis has shown that a salesperson's call on a wholesale customer yields an average order of $400 and on a retail customer, $180. However, prices to wholesalers are 20% less than those to retailers. Cost of goods sold (all variable) is 60% of prices charged to retailers, 75% of prices charged to wholesalers. A salesperson can call on 7 wholesalers or 12 retailers per day. (The greater number of retailers reduces travel time between calls.)

Required
1. Should salespeople concentrate on wholesalers or retailers? Provide an analysis based on one salesperson for one week showing the difference.
2. Using the guidelines in Appendix A, write a memorandum describing other factors that require consideration.

5-36   Special order—capacity limitation   Weston Tires has been approached by a large chain store that offers to buy 80,000 tires at $17. Delivery must be made within 30 days. Weston can produce 320,000 tires per month and has an inventory of 10,000 tires on hand. Expected sales at regular prices for the coming month are 300,000 tires. Weston's sales manager believes that about 60% of sales lost during the month would be made up in later months. Price and cost data are as follows.

Selling price		$25
Variable costs:		
Production	$12	
Selling	3	15
Contribution margin		$10

Variable selling costs on the special order are only $2 per unit.

Required
1. Determine whether the company should accept the special order.
2. Determine the lowest price Weston could charge on the special order and not reduce its income.
3. Suppose now that the chain offers to buy 60,000 tires per month at $17. The offer is for an entire year. Expected sales are 300,000 tires per month without considering the special order. Also assume that there is *no* beginning inventory and that any sales lost during the year would not be made up in the following year. Determine whether the offer should be accepted and determine the lowest price that Weston could accept.

5-37   Special orders and qualitative factors   Robinson Company has had a reputation for high-quality phonograph products for many years. The company is owned by descendants of its founder, Allan Robinson, and continues the policy of producing and selling only high-quality, high-priced stereo components.

Recently James Giselle, president of a chain of discount stores, proposed that Robinson make and sell him a cheaper line of components than it currently produces. Giselle knows that Robinson has excess capacity and that many other firms produce lower-quality lines for sale in discount stores. Giselle believes that buyers will become aware that Robinson makes the components even though the Robinson name will not appear on them. Giselle tries to convince the management that its only potential for growth lies in the private-brand field, because Robinson now sells only to devoted aficionados who would not settle for less than Robinson components.

Giselle proposes that Robinson sell to the chain at 60% of its current selling price to other outlets. Variable costs are now about 60% of normal selling price but would be reduced by 20% per unit if the cheaper components were made. The first-year order is to be $1,260,000, for which Robinson has enough excess capacity.

Required

1. Evaluate the monetary effects of the proposed deal.
2. Using the guidelines in Appendix A, write a memorandum that evaluates qualitative factors such as the attitudes of the management and the family owners and the reputation of the firm.

5-38   *Cost of being your own boss* Martha and Jim Crain own a leather goods store in a large city. Their most recent year's income statement showed the following results.

Sales		$126,000
Cost of sales		55,000
Gross profit		$ 71,000
Other expenses:		
Rent (monthly lease)	$3,600	
Utilities	2,450	
Advertising	1,000	
Supplies	700	
Insurance	1,150	
Licenses and fees	380	
Miscellaneous	720	10,000
Income		$ 61,000

In discussing the results, Martha and Jim were reminded of their previous jobs. Before they opened the store, he'd been earning $30,000 per year and she'd been earning $35,000. Martha said how nice it was to own one's own business and not have to work for someone else and Jim agreed. "True," she said, we *do* put in more hours at the store than we worked in our other jobs." She went on, "Of course, we have $60,000 invested in the business, which is a lot, but we also don't have to fight the traffic to get there."

Required

Assume that the Crains could sell the business for $60,000, invest the proceeds at 10% interest, and go back to their former jobs. Should they do so?

5-39   *Pricing policy and excess capacity* Electric utilities face several problems in achieving optimal use of their facilities. First, because electricity cannot be stored economically, utilities must be able to generate enough electricity to meet demand at all times. Second, the use of electricity is seasonal, especially in warmer climates where air conditioning produces high-peak requirements in the summer months.

  Executives of Southern Electric Company are evaluating a proposal by the sales manager to offer discounts on electrical service to customers who will use electrical heating equipment. The controller has amassed the following data at the request of the sales manager.

Current generating capacity—monthly	20 million kilowatt-hours (kwh)
Annual sales	120 million kwh
kwh sold—typical winter month	7 million
kwh sold—typical summer month	18 million
Price per 1,000 kwh	$35
Variable cost per 1,000 kwh	$19

The sales manager's proposal is to reduce the price of electricity to $29 per 1,000 kwh if the customer uses electrical heating equipment. He anticipates that about 5 million additional kwh per month could be sold in the winter, a total of about 22 million additional hours per year. Users expected to convert to electrical heating now consume a total of about 30 million kwh per year. Sales to customers currently using electrical heating equipment, who would also qualify for the discount, are about 10 million kwh per year.

Required
Evaluate the monetary effects of the proposed decision.

5-40   Processing decisions   Ayers Sawmill buys pine logs and saws them into boards of two grades, A and B. The grade is determined by factors such as the number of knotholes and quality of the grain. Bark and sawdust also emerge from the sawing operation. Each log usually produces, by volume, about 35% A-grade boards, 55% B-grade boards, and 10% bark and shavings. Charles Ayers, the owner, has just received the income statement for a typical month's operations. Ayers expects much the same results in the foreseeable future.

	Total	Grade A	Grade B	Bark/ Shavings
Sales	$80,000	$36,000	$41,000	$3,000
Costs:				
Logs	$42,000	$14,700	$23,100	$4,200
Sawing	17,000	5,950	9,350	1,700
Trimming	3,200	2,340	860	
Sanding	7,700	4,320	3,380	
Shipping	4,500	1,550	2,430	520
Total costs	$74,400	$28,860	$39,120	$6,420
Income (loss)	$5,600	$7,140	$1,880	$(3,420)

Sawing costs include wages, depreciation, and other nonitemized costs of running the sawmill. The cost of logs and of sawing are allocated based on volume (35%, 55%, 10%). Trimming, sanding, and shipping costs are direct and avoidable. Ayers was disturbed at the results. He told an employee, "The bark and shavings are really hurting me. I might as well throw the stuff out rather than sell it."

Required
1. Tell Ayers whether he should continue selling bark and shavings or throw it out. Explain the reasons for your decision.
2. A chain of lawn and garden stores has offered to buy Ayers's output of bark and shavings if Ayers will grind it into mulch. The grinding would cost about $1,500 per month for wages and equipment rental. The chain will pick up the

mulch at the mill, so Ayers will not incur shipping costs. What monthly revenue does Ayers need to make it profitable to do the grinding?

3. A furniture manufacturer has approached Ayers with an offer to buy all of the sawmill's output of grade B lumber for $30,000 per month as it comes out of the sawing operation. Ayers would not have to trim or sand the lumber. Shipping costs would be $1,200. Determine whether Ayers should accept the offer.

5-41   Evaluating a decision—costs of activities   Six months ago the marketing manager of Arcon Company approved the sale of sizable quantities of the company's principal product to a chain store in a geographical region where the company's products are not currently sold. The sales were made monthly. The sales manager recently asked the controller for an analysis of the business to see whether it should be renewed for another six months as the chain wants to do. The controller prepares the following income statement related to the special order.

Sales	$320,000
Cost of sales	247,000
Gross margin	$ 73,000
Operating expenses	61,000
Profit	$ 12,000

The controller concludes that a $12,000 profit over six months is not enough to justify the added time and effort, as well as the risk of being unable to supply regular customers. Although the company has not operated at capacity during the period, it has come close on occasion.

The sales manager is surprised at the results and asks for more information. The controller provides the following additional data regarding the income statement.

(a) Cost of sales includes the following.

Materials	$ 86,000
Labor	41,000
Overhead, 60% variable	120,000
Total	$247,000

(b) Operating expenses:

Sales salaries	$ 27,000
Clerical	12,000
Other	22,000
Total	$ 61,000

The sales manager is confused about some items and receives the following additional explanation. The sales salaries are for the time of a sales representative who services the account. The representative spends about 80% of her time on the account, and the $27,000 is 80% of her six-month salary. The clerical costs are for a part-time clerk who works exclusively on this account. The bulk of the "other" category is a $16,000 administrative charge. This charge, equal to 5% of sales, is levied on all products to cover administrative expenses of the company. The remaining $6,000 are all incremental costs of various activities as estimated by the controller.

The sales manager seeks your help in understanding the statement and evaluating the order. He is confused and wonders whether to bother discussing renewal of the arrangement.

Required
Prepare a new income statement that will assist the sales manager in evaluating the business.

 5-42   Relevant range The president of Ipswick Company has received an offer to purchase 20,000 of the tables made by his firm. The offer is to be filled any time during the coming year, and the offer price per table is $60. The planned income statement for the year without this order is as follows.

Sales (45,000 tables at $100)		$4,500,000
Cost of goods sold:		
Materials	$ 900,000	
Direct labor	810,000	
Overhead	1,340,000	
Total cost of goods sold		3,050,000
Gross profit		$1,450,000
Selling, general, and administrative expenses		1,220,000
Income		$ 230,000

The president believes that the order should be rejected because the price is below average production cost of $67.78 per table. He asks you to check the matter further because he knows that some costs are fixed and would not be affected by the special order. In your analysis you find that $800,000 in overhead is fixed and that a 10% commission is the only variable selling, general, and administrative expense.

Required
Answer the following questions, considering each situation independently.

1. Assume the relevant range for the firm is between 30,000 and 70,000 tables, that existing sales would not be affected, and that the 10% sales commission would not have to be paid on the special order. What effect would there be on income if the order were accepted? Should it be accepted?
2. The relevant range is the same as in item 1, and existing sales would be unaffected, but the 10% sales commission would have to be paid. Should the order be accepted?
3. The relevant range is now 30,000 to 55,000 tables. If the special order is accepted, sales at regular prices would fall to 35,000 units. The 10% sales commission would not be paid on the special order. Should the order be accepted?

4. The relevant range is the same as in item 3, but production could be increased to meet the special order as well as regular planned sales. For all units produced above 55,000, labor cost per unit and per-unit variable overhead would be 20% higher than planned. Fixed production overhead would increase by $47,000. No sales commission would be paid on the order, and other selling, general, and administrative expenses would remain the same as planned. Should the order be accepted?

5-43   *Value of new products—complementary effects*   Jackman's Grocery is a medium-sized operation in a suburb of a large city. Joe Jackman, the owner, is contemplating the addition of a department to sell either hardware or beer and wine. He has talked to owners of several similar stores and has reached the following conclusions.

1. A hardware department would generate sales of $40,000 per year with a gross profit of 60%. No other variable costs would be added. Fixed costs added would be $12,000. Sales of groceries would increase 5% because of increased traffic through the store.
2. A beer and wine department would generate sales of $60,000 per year with a gross profit of 40%. No other variable costs would be added, and additional fixed costs would be $18,000. Sales of groceries would increase by 8%. The income statement for a typical year for grocery sales alone is as follows.

Sales	$600,000
Cost of goods sold (variable)	240,000
Gross profit	$360,000
Other variable costs	120,000
Contribution margin	$240,000
Fixed costs	140,000
Income	$100,000

Required

1. Ignore the effects on sales of groceries for the moment. Compute the change in income that would result from adding (a) the hardware department and (b) the beer and wine department.
2. Recompute the effects on income of adding each department, considering the effects on sales of groceries. Which department should be added and why?
3. What can be learned from this problem?

5-44   *Special orders—effects on existing sales*   Hunt Company makes high-quality calculators that are sold only by department stores and office equipment dealers. A large discount chain has offered to buy 30,000 calculators this year at an average price of $30. The income statement expected for the coming year shows the following without considering the special order.

Sales (90,000 units at average price of $50)	$4,500,000
Variable production costs (average of $20)	1,800,000
Contribution margin	$2,700,000
Fixed costs (production and selling, general, and administrative)	2,200,000
Income	$ 500,000

The 30,000 units to be bought by the chain are in the same mix as Hunt currently sells. Hunt has the capacity to produce 140,000 units per year.

Required
1. Should the order be accepted if there would be no effect on regular sales?
2. Suppose that accepting the order will result in a 10% decline in sales at regular prices because some current customers would recognize the chain store's product and make their purchases at the lower price. The sales mix would remain unchanged. Should Hunt accept the special order?
3. By how much could sales at regular prices decline before it became unprofitable to accept the order?
4. Assuming the same facts as in item 2, what other factors should Hunt's managers consider before deciding whether to accept the order?

5-45 *Alternative uses of product (CMA adapted)*   So-Clean Corporation manufactures a variety of cleaning compounds and solutions for both industrial and household use. Some of its products share ingredients and some can be refined into others. Grit 337 is a coarse, industrial cleaning powder that sells for $2.00 per pound and has variable costs of $1.60 per pound, all for manufacturing costs. The company currently uses a portion of Grit 337 in making a silver polish that sells for $4.00 per jar. Each jar requires a quarter pound of Grit 337. Other variable production costs for the silver polish are $2.50 per jar and variable selling expenses are $0.30 per jar. Monthly avoidable fixed costs of making the silver polish are $5,600.

Required
1. Assuming that the company cannot sell all of the Grit 337 it can produce, how many jars of silver polish must So-Clean sell monthly to justify continuing to sell it?
2. Suppose now that So-Clean can sell all of the Grit 337 that it can make. How many jars of silver polish must the company sell per month to justify further processing Grit 337 into silver polish?

5-46 *Processing decision*   Most beef bought in stores comes from cattle that have been fattened on feedlots. A feedlot is an area consisting mainly of pens and barns in which cattle are closely packed and fed diets designed to increase their weight rapidly. The cattle are bought from ranchers when they weigh about 500 pounds, at a cost of $260 including freight. After the cattle are fattened, their selling price is $0.50 per pound and the buyer pays the freight to deliver the cattle.

The average animal gains weight in the following pattern.

First month	140 pounds
Second month	130
Third month	120
Fourth month	100
Total potential gain	490 pounds

For each month that an animal is on the feedlot, it eats $52 worth of feed. The lot can hold 5,000 head of cattle at a time.

Required

1. Assume that there is a shortage of animals available for fattening. The lot is only able to buy 600 head per month. Determine the number of months that each animal should be kept on the lot before being sold.
2. Suppose, instead, that the supply of animals is very high so that the lot is operating at full capacity. Determine the number of months each animal should be kept.

5-47   *Special order (CMA adapted)*   Anchor Company manufactures jewelry cases. The firm is currently operating at 80% of its capacity of 7,500 direct labor hours per month. Its sales manager has been looking for special orders to increase the use of capacity. JCL Company has offered to buy 10,000 cases at $7.50 per case provided that delivery is within two months. Per-case cost data for the order are as follows.

Materials	$2.50
Direct labor (1/2 hour at $6)	3.00
Manufacturing overhead	2.00
Total unit cost	$7.50

Variable overhead is $1.50 per direct labor hour and the company allocates fixed manufacturing overhead to units of product based on their direct labor time. Without the order, Anchor has enough business to operate at 6,000 direct labor hours (80% of 7,500) in each of the next two months. The normal selling price of the jewelry case is $10.50. JCL would put its own label on the case.

The production manager is concerned about the labor time that making 10,000 cases would require. She cannot schedule more than 7,500 labor hours per month because Anchor has a policy against overtime. Thus, the company will have to reduce some regular-price sales of the jewelry case if it accepts the order. JCL will not take fewer than 10,000 cases.

Required

1. Determine whether Anchor should accept the order.
2. Determine the price per case for the order that would make Anchor indifferent between accepting and rejecting the order (the price that would give Anchor the same profit under both alternatives).

CASES

5-48   *Services of an athlete—jumping leagues* The Fort Bluff Titans of the Cross Continental Football League (CCFL) have been approached by an agent for Flinger Johnson, the star quarterback of the Snidely Whips, a team in the other major football league—the Nationwide Football League (NFL). Johnson's current contract, at a salary of $300,000 per year, runs out this year and he is free to consider other offers. His goal is a salary of at least $500,000 and he's willing to jump leagues if that's what it takes to meet his goal.

The six teams in the CCFL play each of the other teams twice, for a total of ten games. (Each team plays every opponent once at home and once away.) Tickets sell for $10 per game and variable costs are about $2 per ticket. The home team keeps $7 of the admission price and gives $3 to the visiting team. The home team pays the variable costs, which are about $2 per ticket.

J.J. Box, owner of the Titans, believes that acquiring Johnson would be a boon to attendance. No team in the CCFL, including the Titans, comes close to filling its stadium. Box estimates that having Johnson in the league would be worth 10,000 additional admissions at every game he played, whether at home or on the road, and sellouts are unlikely even with Johnson in the league. Box recognizes that bringing Johnson to his team would affect all owners in the league.

After considering his own financial situation as well as those of his fellow owners, Box decides to meet with the owners of the other CCFL teams before pursuing further negotiations for Johnson's services. At that meeting, Box proposes that, because all owners would benefit from having Johnson in the league, the other owners should be willing to help cover the cost of bringing Johnson to the CCFL. Box says he's willing to do his share, but that he doesn't think he can or should bear the entire cost of bringing in Johnson. Box's legal counsel appeared at the meeting to provide assurance that reasonable financial cooperation among the owners on this matter would not produce legal action by any unit of government.

As might be expected, the press reported whatever it could find out about Johnson's interest in bettering his financial package. After reading about a potential meeting of CCFL owners, Whips' owner, Sal Mindinow, arranged for the owners of NFL teams to meet and discuss the impact of Johnson's possible departure.

The financial facts in the NFL differ somewhat from those in the CCFL. Variable costs are about the same, around $2 per ticket. But tickets to NFL games are $12, NFL teams play 12 games per season, and about 50% of the games of each team are sellouts. (For sold-out games, teams usually have requests for about 3,000 more tickets than seats available.) After much arguing, the owners at the meeting called by Mindinow agreed that if Johnson left the NFL the total number of tickets requested for games in which Johnson's old team plays would drop by about 8,000. Like his counterpart at the meeting of CCFL owners, Mr. Mindinow's legal counsel assured those at the meeting that reasonable financial cooperation among the owners was not likely to prompt government intervention.

Required
Assume that "signing" bonuses are prohibited in both leagues.

1. Develop a proposal that the various owners of teams in the CCFL would consider an economically sound as well as fair way to meet Johnson's salary demands.
2. Develop a proposal that the various owners of teams in the NFL would consider an economically sound as well as fair way to meet Johnson's salary demands.

5-49   Peanuts for peanuts*

The Time: Hopefully never, but then everybody knows the outcome of wishful thinking.

The Scene: A small neighborhood diner in a small New Jersey town about 25 miles from New York City. The operator-owner, Mr. Joseph Madison, is preparing to open for the day. He has just placed a shiny new rack holding brightly colored bags of peanuts on the far end of the counter. As he stands back to admire his new peanut rack, his brother-in-law, Harry, a self-styled efficiency expert, enters from the back door.

Harry. Morning Joe. What're you looking so pleased about?

Joe. I jus' put up my new peanut rack—the one I tole you about the other night.

Harry. Joe, you told me that you were going to put in these peanuts because some people asked for them. But I've been thinking about it and I wonder if you realize what this rack of peanuts is costing you.

Joe. It ain't gonna cost. Gonna be a profit. Sure, I hadda pay $25 for a fancy rack to hol' the bags, but the peanuts cost six cents a bag and I sell 'em for 10 cents. I figger I can sell 50 bags a week to start. It'll take twelve and a ha'f weeks to cover the cost of the rack and after that I make a clear profit of 4 cents a bag. The more I sell, the more I make.

Harry (shaking his finger at Joe). That is an antiquated and completely unrealistic approach. Fortunately, modern accounting procedures permit a more accurate picture which reveals the complexities involved.

Joe. Huh?

Harry. To be precise, those peanuts must be integrated into your entire operation and be allocated their appropriate share of business overhead. They must share a proportionate part of your expenditures for rent, heat, light, equipment depreciation, decorating, salaries for counter help, cook . . .

Joe. The cook? What's he gotta do wit' the peanuts? He don't even know I got 'em yet.

Harry. Look, Joe. The cook is in the kitchen; the kitchen prepares the food; the food is what brings people in; and while they're in, they ask to buy peanuts. That's why you must charge a portion of the cook's wages, as well as a part of your own salary to peanut sales. Since you've talked to me I've worked it all out. This sheet contains a carefully calculated cost analysis which clearly indicates that the peanut operation should pay exactly $1,278 per year toward these general overhead costs.

Joe (unbelieving). The peanuts? $1,278 a year for overhead? That's nuts!

Harry. It's really a little more than that. You also spend money each week to have the windows washed, to have the place swept out in the mornings, to keep soap in the washroom and provide free colas to the police. That raises the actual total to $1,313 per year.

Joe (thoughtfully). But the peanut salesman said I'd make money—put 'em on the end of the counter, he said—and get 4 cents a bag profit.

Harry (with a sniff). He's not an accountant. And remember, he wanted to sell you something. Do you actually know what the portion of the counter occupied by the peanut rack is worth to you?

Joe. Sure. It ain't worth nuttin'. No stool there—just a dead spot at the end.

Harry. The modern cost picture permits no dead spots. Your counter contains 60 square feet and your counter business grosses $15,000 a year. Consequently,

---

* *Used with the permission of Rex H. Anderson, Senior Vice President of INA Reinsurance Company.*

the square foot of space occupied by the peanut rack is worth $250 per year. Since you have taken that area away from general counter use, you must charge the value of the space to the occupant. That's called opportunity cost.

Joe. You mean I gotta add $250 a year more to the peanuts?

Harry. Right. That raises their share of the general operating costs to $1,563 per year. Now then, if you sell 50 bags of peanuts per week, these allocated costs will amount to 60 cents per bag.

Joe (incredulously). What?

Harry. Obviously, to that must be added your purchase price of 6 cents a bag, which brings the total to 66 cents. So you see, by selling peanuts at 10 cents per bag, you are losing 56 cents on every sale.

Joe. Something's crazy!!

Harry. Not at all. Here are the figures. They prove your peanut operation just can't stand on its own feet.

Joe (brightening). Suppose I sell lotsa peanuts—1,000 bags a week mebbe, 'stead of 50?

Harry (tolerantly). No. Joe, you just don't understand the problem. If the volume of peanut sales increased, your operating costs will go up—you'll have to handle more bags, with more time, more general overhead, more everything. The basic principle of accounting is firm on that subject: "The bigger the operation the more general overhead costs must be allocated." No, increasing the volume of sales won't help.

Joe. Okay, you so smart, you tell me what I gotta do.

Harry (condescendingly now). Well—you could first reduce operating expenses.

Joe. Yeah? How?

Harry. You might take smaller space in an older building with cheaper rent. Maybe cut salaries. Wash the windows biweekly. Have the floor swept only on Thursdays. Remove the soap from the washrooms. Cut out the colas for the cops. This will help you decrease the square-foot value of the counter. For example, if you can cut your expenses 50%, that will reduce the amount allocated to peanuts from $1,563 down to $781.50 per year, reducing the cost to 36 cents per bag.

Joe. That's better?

Harry. Much, much better. Of course, even then you'd lose 26 cents per bag if you charged only 10 cents. Therefore, you must also raise your selling price. If you want a net profit of 4 cents per bag, you would have to charge 40 cents.

(Harry is looking very confident, now, but Joe appears flabbergasted.)

Joe. You mean even after I cut operating costs 50%, I still gotta charge 40 cents for a 10-cent bag of peanuts? Nobody's that nuts about nuts! Who'd buy 'em?

Harry. That's a secondary consideration. The point is, at 40 cents, you'd be selling at a price based upon a true and proper evaluation of your then reduced costs.

(Joe does not look convinced; then, he brightens.)

Joe. Look! I gotta better idea. Why don't I jus' throw the nuts out—so I lost $25 on the rack. I'm outa this nutsy business and no more grief.

(Harry is shaking his head vigorously.)

Harry. Joe, it just isn't that simple. You are in the peanut business! The minute you throw those peanuts out, you are adding $1,563 of annual overhead to the rest of your operation. Joe—be realistic—can you afford to do that?

Joe (by now completely crushed). It's unbelievable! Last week I wuz makin' money. Now I'm in trouble—jus' becuz I think peanuts on the counter is gonna bring me some extra profit. Jus' becuz I believe 50 bags of peanuts a week is easy.

Harry (by now smiling and satisfied that his brother-in-law will not be so quick to argue with him in the future). That is the reason for modern cost studies, Joe—to dispel those false illusions.

Curtain falls.

Required

1. Who's nuts?
2. Write a memorandum that evaluates the position(s) that Harry takes.

5-50 *Dropping a segment* Tom Johnson, owner-manager of Johnson's Drugstore, is opposed to smoking and wants to drop the tobacco counter from the store. He has determined from industry statistics and opinions of other drugstore managers that the tobacco counter creates a good deal of other business because many people who come in just for cigarettes, cigars, and pipe tobacco buy other articles. Moreover, some people will go elsewhere for drugs and sundries if they know that tobacco is not being sold.

Johnson estimates that sales of drugs would drop by 5% and sundries by 10% if the tobacco counter were removed. The space now occupied by the tobacco counter would be devoted to greeting cards, which Johnson does not now sell. Estimated annual sales for greeting cards are $8,000, with cost of sales of $3,000.

If the tobacco counter is dropped, one clerk earning $4,000 could be dropped. But a pharmacist would have to handle the greeting card sales, which would result in a further drop in drug sales of 2% (from the current level). Carrying costs of the inventory of greeting cards are expected to be about $300 less per year than those associated with tobacco products.

Johnson has asked you to advise him in this decision. He's provided you with an income statement for the coming year showing his expectations if tobacco products are retained.

Johnson's Drugstore Expected Income Statement for the Coming Year				
	Tobacco	Drugs	Sundries	Total
Sales	$31,000	$128,000	$36,000	$195,000
Cost of goods sold	10,500	54,000	10,500	75,000
Gross profit	$20,500	$ 74,000	$25,500	$120,000
Operating expenses:				
Salaries	$ 9,200	$ 40,000	$10,800	$ 60,000
Occupancy costs (rent, utilities, maintenance, etc.)	3,000	7,000	4,000	14,000
Miscellaneous	1,500	6,700	1,800	10,000
Total operating expenses	$13,700	$ 53,700	$16,600	$ 84,000
Income before taxes	$ 6,800	$ 20,300	$ 8,900	$ 36,000

You learn that occupancy costs are allocated to each product group based on percentages of space occupied for display of those products. These costs will not change in total if greeting cards are substituted for tobacco. The manager's salary, $28,000, is arbitrarily allocated to departments and included in the salaries amount in the income statement. Miscellaneous expenses are allocated based on relative sales volume and would be unaffected by the change except for the cost of carrying inventory.

Required

Comment on the cost to Mr. Johnson of implementing his convictions about smoking.

5-51   *Alternative uses of space*   Several years ago the Star Department Store began leasing space to Clothes Horse, Inc., a chain of boutiques specializing in high-priced women's clothing and accessories. The boutiques are usually separate stores in shopping centers, but the management of Clothes Horse wished to experiment with an operation in a department store and Star was willing, as the space was not then needed for its own operations.

Clothes Horse pays Star a monthly rental of $3,000 plus 5% of its gross sales, and the arrangement has been profitable for both parties. Star pays all electricity, gas, and other costs of occupancy, which are negligible when considered incrementally because the space would have to be lighted and heated anyway. The lease is about to expire, and Clothes Horse is eager to renew it for another year on the same terms. However, some of Star's department heads have indicated a desire to take over the operation of the boutique, and others have requested the use of the space to expand their selling areas.

After reviewing all the requests, Ron Stein and Margot Miller, Star's executive vice president and general manager, respectively, have narrowed the range of choices to the following: (1) renew the lease with Clothes Horse; (2) keep the boutique, but place it under the women's wear department head, Bill Rausch; (3) use the space to expand the shoe department, which is located next to the boutique.

The boutique had total sales of $400,000 in the first ten months of the current year, and the monthly rate is expected to double for the last two months, which come at the height of the Christmas season. Stein and Miller expect a 10% increase in sales in the coming year if Clothes Horse continues to operate the boutique. Mr. Rausch has presented the following expected income statement for the coming year, which he believes he could achieve if he took over the operation of the boutique.

Sales		$380,000
Cost of sales		171,000
Gross profit		$209,000
Operating expenses:		
Salaries	$75,000	
Advertising and promotion	14,000	
Supplies	7,000	
Miscellaneous	8,000	104,000
Profit		$105,000

Mr. Stein commented that Mr. Rausch is generally too optimistic and that his estimate of sales volume was probably about 10% too high. He also noted that Rausch had provided for fewer salespeople than were employed by Clothes Horse and that the somewhat reduced level of service would not help business. Stein felt that expenses other than cost of sales would probably be about as Rausch had estimated, even at the lower volume that Stein thought would be achieved.

The manager of the shoe department believed that if the space were used to expand his department his sales would increase by about $200,000 with a gross profit rate of 45%. He would need to add one salesperson, who would work on a 10% commission, like the other employees in that department. Virtually all other store employees work on salary, not commission.

Miller and Stein both brought up the subject of traffic through the store and both agreed that traffic had increased since Clothes Horse opened the boutique. They were uncertain about the effects of the increased traffic on sales in the store's own departments, so Miller said that she would investigate the matter.

Miller instructed several of her assistants to interview people in the store, particularly in the boutique, regarding their shopping habits. Several days later, the results were in, and she went to Stein's office to discuss them. The following major conclusions were contained in the reports Miller had received.

1. About 40% of sales made in the boutique are to people who come especially to shop there. These people have to walk through parts of the store to get to the boutique and spend about 20% as much in the store as they do in the boutique.

2. The remainder of the boutique's sales are to people who come for other reasons. Many drop in on their way in or out of the store; some plan to shop in the store's other departments as well as in the boutique. These people spend about twice as much in the store's own departments as they do in the boutique.

After a discussion lasting nearly an hour, Stein and Miller decided that the people who came in especially to shop in the boutique would not patronize the store at all if Clothes Horse did not operate it. The executives believed that only the popularity of the Clothes Horse name induced these people to come in.

Of the other group, they believed that about 10% of the patronage would be lost if Clothes Horse did not operate the boutique. This loss of sales would be spread fairly evenly throughout the store. The average gross profit rate in the store is 45%, and other variable costs are an additional 8% of sales.

Required

Determine the best course of action for the store. Using the guidelines in Appendix A, write a memorandum supporting your position.

5-52   *Product processing* Taylor Company makes wall paneling used in homes and offices. The company buys walnut logs and processes them into thin sheets of veneer that are then glued to sheets of plywood to make paneling. Taylor also makes the plywood. The company has enough capacity to make 1,000,000 square feet of veneer per month and 1,200,000 square feet of plywood. Capacity in the gluing operation is 1,300,000 square feet per month. Substantial markets exist for plywood and veneer as well as for paneling, though Taylor's managers think of the company as a paneling manufacturer.

Taylor's senior operating managers meet monthly to discuss recent operating results and their expectations about the coming months. Jim Chen, Taylor's controller, regularly attends these meetings to assist the managers in their deliberations. To facilitate the monthly discussions, Chen developed the following cost data, per 1,000 square feet of product.

	Plywood	Veneer	Paneling
Materials	$18	$16	$ 34
Direct labor	25	20	55
Overhead	32	29	93
Total	$75	$65	$182

When presenting the cost data, Chen pointed out that the figures shown for paneling were cumulative. That is, the amount for each component of paneling cost was the sum of the costs of veneer and plywood plus the additional costs associated with the gluing operation. (Thus, no new materials are added in the gluing operation.) When he first provided the data to operating managers, Chen also pointed out that the variable portion of overhead was approximately 80% of labor cost. After some discussion at that meeting about individual components of fixed overhead, the group agreed that all such costs were probably unavoidable.

At their meeting in March of 19X4, Taylor's managers reviewed operating results for January and February, when the prevailing prices (per 1,000 square feet) of Taylor's products were $178, $74 and $81 for paneling, veneer and plywood, respectively. Mario Franks, Taylor's sales manager, began the meeting with a smile and kind words for everyone present. "I think even Jim Chen will agree we've learned how to use cost data in making our decisions. Our prediction of the selling price for paneling was right on target, and we sold all the paneling we could make in both months."

Sam West, the factory manager, agreed, though with reservations. "Yes, I can see that we did the right thing. But you guys don't have to deal with the flack I'm getting about the layoffs of workers in the plywood shop. And almost every week the manager of the gluing shop—you all know Phyllis—hits me with some new scheme for using the people and equipment in her area to work on jobs that have nothing to do with making paneling."

Anxious that the discussion move on to decisions about what to do in the future, Franks said "All water over the dam. What we need to do now is decide whether we should make any changes in production plans for the near future. Some of my people tell me plywood prices could go up soon, probably to around $86. I hate to say this, because I know that paneling got us where we are; but maybe we should consider other alternatives." To Franks' surprise, Jim Chen chimed in at this point to support consideration of alternatives, though not for the same reason. Said Chen, "I haven't yet seen anything to indicate an increase in plywood prices, Mario, though your field people may be right. But everything I read about new construction projects and the market for remodeling suggests that the price for paneling is in for a drop, perhaps to as low as $164. Even if the field people are wrong and the price of plywood holds at about what it is now, the potential drop in the price for paneling should make us reconsider our position about concentrating on producing paneling."

Gene Draper, the recently hired chief operating officer, entered the discussion with the following comments. "I know I'm the new kid on the block here, but I've tried to do my homework, and it seems to me that whatever the prices for what we produce, a major stumbling block for our company is the unequal capacities of our veneer, plywood, and gluing operations. I know that long-term increases in capacity would involve substantial investments in new assets, and we should discuss such investments at a future meeting. But it seems to me that we should at least be considering ways to equalize capacities in the short run. For example, I'd be willing to authorize spending up to $2,000 a month this year for renting whatever equipment would increase our production capacity of either veneer or plywood by 100,000 square feet, but you'll have to tell me which one to spend the money on."

Required

Evaluate the operating managers' understanding of Taylor's cost structure and the new CEO's offer of short-term support to move toward equalizing capacities.

PART TWO

budgeting

Economic enterprises engage in many activities that require not only planning but also coordination of plans. We explore the relationships among those activities in this part.

The comprehensive budget is a tool to make planning effective and provides a means for monitoring whether activities are going according to plan. In a formal and integrated way, the budget captures and reflects the results of planning decisions, from decisions about prices, product mix and cost structure, to those about dividends and major new investments.

CVP analysis and knowledge of cost behavior are important in budgeting for the relatively near future—the coming year. Those concepts are also important in analyzing the potential of longer-term projects, the expenditures for which might have to be made in the near future. In addition, some of the principles from financial accounting are important in budgeting because a comprehensive budget includes financial statements normally prepared for external reporting.

Budgeting is more than a technical or mechanical exercise. Because it is people who plan and people who act (according to or contrary to plans), the ways that budgets are developed and used can affect people's behavior and vice versa. In this part we introduce some behavioral problems entailed in the budgeting process. A more comprehensive treatment of these problems is given in Part Three.

6 Operational Budgeting

LEARNING OBJECTIVES

After reading this chapter, you should be able to

1. Explain how budgeting relates to the major functions and subfunctions of management.

2. Describe the components and organization of a comprehensive budget.

3. Describe several methods managers use to forecast sales and some of the problems of using each method.

4. Explain the concept of expected value and its application to forecasting.

5. Describe two approaches to setting budget allowances for costs and the types of costs for which each is likely to be used.

6. Describe several behavioral problems associated with the preparation and use of budgets.

7. Prepare a budgeted income statement, a purchases budget, and a simple production budget.

8. Explain why a company's inventory policy is important to budgeting.

The founder of **Grandmother Calendar Company** says his company went bankrupt because it was too successful. Failure to incorporate thoughtful planning into a realistic budget is a more likely reason. Grandmother's only product was personalized calendars. Its marketing strategy, which emphasized the personal nature of the product as a gift, attracted a variety of customers that included several mail-order *catalog companies and several regional retail chains. Grandmother's customers sold calendar kits to their customers; the buyers provided Grandmother with photos and instructions for arranging them and paid Grandmother directly for extra-cost options such as creating collages.*

*Though the initial production capacity for its final product, a finished calendar, was only 150 per day, **Grandmother** contracted to sell kits through thousands of customers. A former company executive told The Wall Street Journal: "Unless you have deep pockets to pay for research and development and equipment for manufacturing, you live and die by sales revenue." By the time orders for finished calendars reached 1,000 per day, Grandmother had managed only to double its capacity. Continued sales of kits and the flood of orders for extra-cost features provided some cash to increase capacity, but not nearly enough. Cash flow was slowed because most people wanting extra-cost features charged their orders to credit cards, and Grandmother could get the money only after the final product was shipped.*

*The backlog of unfilled orders reached five figures, and in early December of 1994 the company told those customers their calendars wouldn't arrive in time for Christmas. By the end of 1994, the company's cash didn't cover paychecks issued to employees. Operations stopped altogether in early January 1995. As **Grandmother's** managers learned, operating a company without a plan that coordinates sales, production, and cash flows is asking for trouble.*

Source: Developed from "A Company Failing From Too Much Success," Louise Lee, The Wall Street Journal, *March 17, 1995, A1, B2.*

The functional areas of a business (marketing, production, personnel, finance, administration) are interdependent and must work in harmony to achieve profit goals. Production must make enough units for marketing to achieve its sales objectives but must not overproduce, because having too much inventory causes excessive costs for storage, insurance, taxes, and interest. For the same reason, a purchasing manager must not overpurchase, yet must ensure that materials and components are available to meet production schedules. Finance must make cash available to pay for materials, labor, and other operating costs, as well as for dividends, acquisitions of assets, and debt repayments. But the timing and amounts of those cash needs depend on the plans of other managers.

The overall plans of the business must be so specified that the manager of each functional area knows what must be done to ensure smooth performance for other areas and for the company as a whole. Companies use comprehensive budgets to coordinate all of these activities.

According to one study, companies that use budgets effectively do four principal things.[1]

1. Generate commitment to budgets.
2. Connect short-term, mid-term, and long-term plans.
3. Adopt detailed, comprehensive procedures to prepare budgets.
4. Analyze budget variances and take corrective action.

---

1 Srinivasan Umapathy, *"How Successful Firms Budget,"* Management Accounting, *February 1987, 25.*

We treat each of these features at various points in this and the following chapter.

COMPREHENSIVE BUDGETS

A **comprehensive budget** is a set of financial statements and other schedules showing the expected, or pro forma, results for a future period. A comprehensive budget normally contains an income statement, a balance sheet, a cash budget (statement of cash receipts and disbursements), and schedules of production, purchases, and fixed-asset acquisitions. The budget package might have other components, depending on the entity's needs.

Comprehensive budgeting requires careful studies of cost behavior patterns. Budgeted income statements are similar to the income statements you developed for CVP analysis and for making short-term decisions. But budgeting involves more than CVP analysis. For instance, budgeting cash collections requires both predicting sales *and* estimating the pattern of cash collections (how much do we collect within 30 days? within 60 days?). Predicted cash collections from sales combine with cash receipts from planned borrowing and other sources to become a cash receipts budget. Exhibit 6-1 offers an overview of the relationships among the components of a typical comprehensive budget. You should refer to this exhibit as we discuss these relationships and the components in detail in this and the next chapter.

Comprehensive budgeting is more complex than CVP analysis because a change in a single assumption affects the whole set of budgets, not just one or

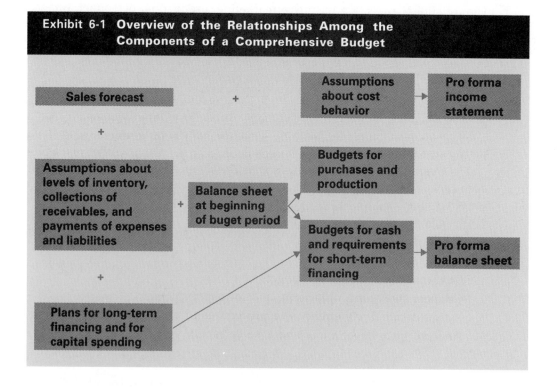

Exhibit 6-1   Overview of the Relationships Among the Components of a Comprehensive Budget

a few items in an income statement. For example, changing budgeted sales for a particular month affects not only variable costs and profit, but also plans for purchasing the items to be sold, the timing and amounts of expected cash receipts, payments for purchases, and perhaps even loans that must be negotiated. The ripple effects of changes in budgets make budgeting ideal for using computer spreadsheets. Spreadsheet users can develop sophisticated budgeting models.

All levels of management are, or should be, involved in putting together some part of the interrelated statements and schedules that make up the comprehensive budget. That is, dealing with budgets is a part of the overall job of managing and helps develop other management skills. (See the accompanying Insight.) Top managers are interested in overall results. Lower-level managers deal only with segments of the total package, and the degree of detail in the schedules they use varies with the breadth of each manager's responsibilities. Thus, a production manager might deal only with schedules of production data. In general, most managers have budgets showing what is expected of *them*—what objectives *they* are to achieve and at what costs.

BUDGETS AND PLANNING

The comprehensive budget is part of a formal strategy and overall plan, in contrast to an intuitive, ad hoc approach to operations. A major benefit of formal planning is that it requires explicit statements not only of objectives (such as sales volume and profit) but also of the means required to achieve those objectives.

Some of the objectives initially considered feasible may prove not so in light of the budget. For example, suppose the budget specifies high sales in the early part of the year. When the production manager tries to plan production on the basis of the initial sales budget, he or she may recognize that productive

IN|SIGHT

Viewing budgets as an integral part of managing is important for managers. For many years, the accounting department at **Elgin Sweeper Company** prepared the company's budgets without participation by the affected managers. Consequently, those managers were not committed to meeting their budgets and didn't view budgets as plans that incorporated or affected their decisions. Top managers made a series of changes in the budgeting process, but it took a long time to get front-line people to prepare budgets. Now Elgin's managers believe that the ". . . key to a successful cost management program was to educate and entrust responsibility to those front-line managers who made the decisions that drive costs."

Source: John P. Callan, Wesley N. Tredup, and Randy S. Wissinger, "Elgin Sweeper Company's Journey Toward Cost Management," Management Accounting, *July 1991, 24.*

capacity is insufficient to meet the budgeted level of sales. Or perhaps the financial manager will see that sufficient production and inventory to meet the budgeted level of sales are possible only if the company obtains a great deal of short-term financing. If securing the necessary financing is undesirable (or even impossible), the budgets must be modified to be consistent with the amount of cash available. The comprehensive budget also incorporates the current effects of plans for long-term financing and for acquisitions of major long-lived assets. The development of those long-term plans, and the related decision making, are discussed in Chapters 7, 8, and 9.

As you know from Chapter 1, decision making is part of the overall planning process. Chapter 5 shows that decision making relies on estimates about future results under alternative courses of action, and one of the alternatives in virtually all decisions is to maintain the status quo (that is, to keep things as they are). Managers use the information in carefully prepared budgets as the status quo, the baseline for determining incremental revenues and costs.

BUDGETS AND CONTROL

Budgets express targets or goals. Actual results express achievements. Comparing budgeted and actual results helps a manager control future operations and provides a useful basis for evaluating performance. Problems showing up in the comparisons prompt managers to take corrective action. The preceding statements are oversimplified but fair statements of the role of budgets in control and performance evaluation. (As reported earlier, analyzing variances from budgets and pursuing corrective action is one of the principal factors important to using budgets effectively.)

Stating the importance of comparing expected and actual results implies nothing about the basis for developing expectations. Such a comparison is meaningful only if expectations are reasonable and consider all available information. For two reasons, past performance is usually inappropriate as the standard for comparison. First, circumstances change. For example, a company might decide to change its marketing strategy to lower selling prices and so spend less on sales-promotion efforts (the strategy adopted by **General Mills** in the mid-1990s). Or perhaps managers believe that, in the second year of producing one of its products, some production costs will be lower than in the first year because workers are more familiar with their tasks. (The cost effects of "learning" are presented in some detail in Chapter 16.) Second, comparisons with past performance tell nothing about whether current performance is as good as it should be. For example, a student who gets 38 percent on one examination and 42 percent on the next has improved but is still not performing adequately. The example confirms the need for a standard of comparison that reflects an acceptable level of performance. Companies adopting the continuous improvement (Kaizen) philosophy, which is discussed more extensively in Chapter 12, set specific cost reduction targets based on past performance.

ORGANIZATION OF BUDGETS

Budgets usually cover specific time periods. Most companies prepare a budget for the upcoming fiscal year, and for short periods within that year—months or even weeks. Many companies also prepare budgets for periods longer than a year, usually for two, three, or four years; these are usually broken down into one-year units.

Because of forecasting difficulties, annual budgets and segments of longer-term budgets are less detailed than are budgets for periods closer at hand. Thus, the budget for one year hence is more detailed than one for periods beyond one year, and budgets for segments of the current year are more detailed than the budget for the full year. Chapter 7 presents the most common approaches to long-term budgeting.

Virtually all companies prepare a separate **capital budget**—a schedule of planned expenditures for long-lived assets. A capital budget often covers several years into the future. Forecasted expenditures from the capital budget become part of the cash budgets for the appropriate periods. Chapters 8 and 9 treat capital budgeting in detail.

The budget for the current year is normally supplemented by budgets for shorter periods, because monitoring progress toward meeting the goals in the annual budget is easier for managers if checkpoints are available along the way. More important, what actually happens is often different from even the most sophisticated plans, so managers might need to make changes in operating plans for the remainder of the period.

Consider the following situation. Suppose actual sales for the first month of the year are higher than budgeted. The sales manager will try to determine whether the additional sales in that month are:

- an indication that the total expectations were too low, or
- likely to be offset by lower sales later.

Suppose the sales manager concludes that sales expectations for the rest of the first quarter, or even for the year, are too low. The sales manager will want production increased to meet the expected demand. An increase in production means acquiring greater quantities of materials and components and perhaps hiring more employees, actions that involve other managers. Changes in plans—such as increased production—go more smoothly and more effectively if managers recognize the need for change well in advance of the point at which a crisis develops. Even with the flexibility provided by a true JIT environment some types of changes are accommodated more smoothly with advance notice.

If the sales manager concludes that sales for the full year will be about the same as budgeted, the higher-than-expected sales in the first month could require changes in plans. For example, inventory at the end of that month will be lower than budgeted because of the higher sales. Managers must decide when to schedule an increase in production to bring inventory to the desired level. Thus, whether sales in excess of expectations are a temporary or a longer-lasting phenomenon, managers must make new plans that have implications for production and cash flows.

Some factors in the business environment also dictate that budgets be developed for periods shorter than a year. Businesses having a heavy concentration of sales in a few months of the typical year (seasonal businesses) must make or buy large quantities of goods in advance of the selling season. Doing so creates a need for cash considerably in advance of cash collections from customers. Cash collections also lag behind cash needs during the busy season of service-providing businesses that are seasonal, such as accounting firms and landscape-maintenance companies. Too, cash requirements vary over the year because some costs are not paid evenly throughout the year. As examples, companies normally pay property taxes in two installments; some insurance premiums are due only annually; interest payments might be required annually, semiannually, or quarterly; and dividends are usually paid quarterly or annually. It makes a big difference whether a $100,000 payment for taxes or dividends must be made in January or July, because the funds must be available when the payment falls due. Cash budgets are an important part of the total budget package, and budgets prepared for the year as a whole conceal these irregular funds requirements and therefore hinder planning.

Companies whose managers want to have plans for at least a year in advance often use continuous budgets. **Continuous budgets** are maintained by adding a budget for a month (or quarter) as one of these periods goes by. Thus, a 12-month budget exists at all times, and managers are aware of the needs for the next 12 months, regardless of the time of the year.

Although comprehensive budgets focus attention on time periods, many managers also find project budgets helpful for controlling operations and evaluating performance. **Project budgets** reflect expectations for various stages of completing specific projects. For example, a company building a new plant will have a time schedule (finish the exterior by June, the interior by November, begin production by March). The periods selected, which may be of unequal length, depend on the project and are of no importance in themselves. The focus in developing a project budget is on completing each stage of the project. Project budgets affect periodic budgeting because cash expenditures for projects must be incorporated in the cash budget. Therefore, project budgets supplement, rather than replace, regular periodic budgets.

DEVELOPING THE COMPREHENSIVE BUDGET

Well in advance of the start of a new budget year, managers begin discussing prospects for the coming year. The earliest discussions normally focus on overall goals relating to profit or growth, such as a 10 percent increase in income, a 2 percent increase in return on sales or assets, a 15 percent increase in sales, or perhaps a 2-point increase in market share. (The overall goals are likely to be derived from longer-term goals and strategies adopted by the firm's top managers.) At least at the outset, most budgets are driven by desired results. But whatever the initial concerns, in every case the budget for the coming period begins with a **sales forecast**, the sales a company expects to achieve. The forecast is critical because expected sales determine the requirements for product, people, other operating costs, cash flows, and financing. The interrelationships among these various elements depend on managerial policies (how much inventory to keep, what credit terms to offer to customers) and operating characteristics (cost structure, cycle time).

Chapters 2 through 5 introduced you to the task of preparing income statements based on expected sales and information about cost behavior. With minor exceptions, preparing a budgeted income statement is an extension of CVP analysis. Other budgets, especially the cash budget and the budgeted balance sheet, present some technical difficulties because of the *leads* and *lags* involved. For example, cash collections usually lag behind the recording of the revenue from credit sales. Similarly, cost of goods sold is recognized when revenue is recorded, but costs to purchase or produce goods for sale are normally incurred before the sale. That is, the costs lead (precede) the sale. Cash payments of incurred costs might be required immediately or might be delayed for varying periods. These leads and lags produce critical technical problems in comprehensive budgeting.

In the remainder of this chapter we present and illustrate sales forecasts, purchases budgets, and expense budgets. These budgets are usually called **operating budgets**. In Chapter 7 we complete the process by considering **financial budgets** (the budgeted balance sheet and the cash budget).

SALES FORECASTING

The sales forecast is the foundation on which a comprehensive budget rests. For a large company, developing the sales forecast is a complex and time-consuming task. For example, when **Xerox's** seven-member forecasting team adopted a sophisticated computer program, developing a forecast took 50 percent less time—but it still took three months. Businesses use many methods to forecast sales. Not all companies use all of the methods we mention, but most use one or more.

INDICATOR METHODS

The sales of many industries are closely associated with one or more factors in the overall economy. Sales of long-lasting consumer goods (cars, washing machines) generally correlate well with widely publicized indicators of general economic activity such as Gross Domestic Product (GDP) and personal income. Sales of baby food are associated with the number of births, and sales of housing units with the formation of new households. Companies in such an industry might first use an indicator of general economic activity (e.g., personal income) to predict total sales for their industry, and then develop a sales budget by estimating the share of the total market they will commit themselves to achieving. Scatter diagrams and regression analysis, which we introduced in Chapter 3, are widely used in forecasting sales, just as they are in predicting costs.

Sales in many industries depend to a great extent on sales of *other* industries. For example, makers of bottles and cans look at forecasts for sales of beer and soft drinks, and steel and tire companies keep abreast of developments affecting the auto industry. In these situations, too, a company might develop a forecast for its industry and then for itself, but the indicator is a forecast for *another* industry.

To be useful for sales forecasting, the value of the indicator must be known, or predictable, in advance of the period for which a budget is being prepared, and the farther in advance the better. For example, an equally strong relationship between their sales and the number of births would be more useful to makers of toddlers' clothes than to makers of baby food, because the known (or predicted) value of the indicator is available farther in advance of the expected change in sales. The availability of predictions of an indicator's value enhances the usefulness of an observed relationship for budgeting purposes, especially if the sales for the industry (baby-food makers, for example) correlate well with actual values of an indicator in the same or *later* periods. In any case, managers must continue to monitor relationships with indicators over time for hints that changes in other factors have made previously observed relationships less useful.

Managers obtain information about indicators from a variety of sources. Various segments of the U.S. government (e.g., the Departments of Commerce and Labor) develop and report data on broad indicators such as GDP, personal income, housing starts, and consumer prices. Some broad indicators originate with the Federal Reserve, private-sector entities such as **Dow Jones & Company** and **Dun & Bradstreet**, and widely distributed business publications such as *Business Week* and *Forbes*. For industry-specific indicators, managers often can refer to data developed by trade publications or associations (e.g., *Ward's Automotive Reports* and the American Iron & Steel Institute.) Exhibit 6-2 shows only a portion of the indicator-like data reported in each issue of *Business Week*.

The scatter-diagram in Exhibit 6-3 on page 256 shows sales of residential carpeting (an industry) plotted against housing starts (a broad indicator). Not surprisingly, the correlation is imperfect, partly because replacement sales do not depend on housing starts. Managers might use either regression analysis or a visual fit of a line to develop a sales forecasting equation. They then would adjust the results for changes they expect to influence the demand in the new and replacement markets.

Sometimes managers can obtain predictions of their industry's sales directly from trade associations, many of which publish forecasts or studies that provide guidance in sales forecasting. For example, an association of appliance dealers might conduct studies to determine the likely sales of various kinds of appliances. Its forecast for the sales of washing machines might take into account the overall economic outlook, forecasts for new housing units, previous sales of washing machines, and the results of a survey of consumers about the age of machines currently in use. The forecast wouldn't indicate how these factors affect the sales of any single dealer, but individual dealers obtain a picture of what is likely to happen to industry sales and can apply it to their own companies.

HISTORICAL ANALYSIS

Companies that operate chains of retail stores (e.g., **Radio Shack**, **Sears**, **The Gap**, **Circuit City**) develop sales data and trends by age of store (i.e., new stores, second-year stores) and begin their forecasts for the coming year by projecting sales from such data and trends. Other companies analyze their total sales of previous years and project the trend to arrive at a forecast. Thus, if sales have been rising at 10 percent per year, the company will start with a forecast based on last year's sales plus 10 percent. However a preliminary forecast is developed, managers then look for factors that suggest the likelihood of higher or lower sales. Were last year's sales abnormally high or low because of a strike or unusual weather conditions? (For example, ice cream, beer, golf balls, and many other products sell better in hot weather.) Are there discernible changes in taste that could affect sales? The past can be used for guidance on what might happen, but differences in conditions can cause the future to differ from the past.

Several sophisticated statistical techniques are available for making predictions from historical data. These techniques are beyond the scope of this book, but you may learn about some of them in other courses.

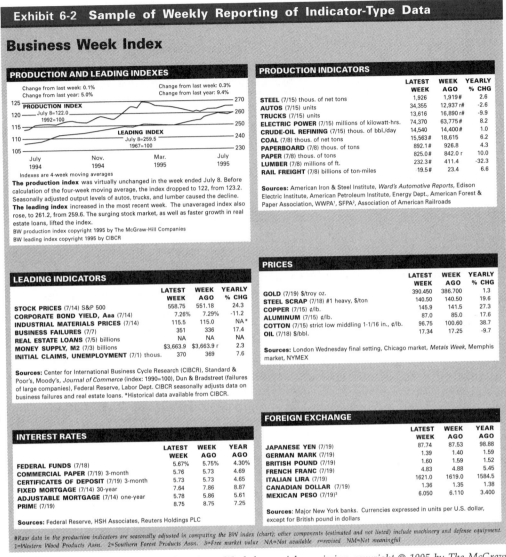

Exhibit 6-2   Sample of Weekly Reporting of Indicator-Type Data

Reprinted from July 15, 1995 issue of Business Week *by special permission, copyright © 1995 by The McGraw-Hill Companies.*

JUDGMENTAL METHODS

Some companies budget sales using judgment based on experience with their customers and products. For example, each regional sales manager, in consultation with the sales staff, might estimate sales in that area, by customer or product line. The chief sales executive would review and discuss the forecasts with the regional managers, then develop a sales budget for each area and for the entire company to submit to top management for approval.

The analysis underlying judgment-based forecasts follows the lines of the other methods described here, but is less formal. Instead of using regression analysis or some other mathematical tool, managers will rely on their own experience and perceptions of changing circumstances to develop a forecast of

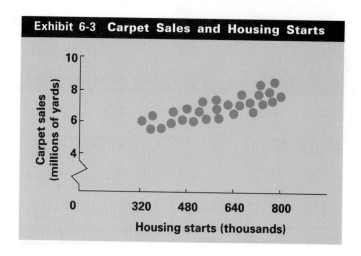

Exhibit 6-3 Carpet Sales and Housing Starts

the prospects for the industry and for the company. For example, a manager may notice an increasing number of newspaper and magazine articles about the decreasing length of the work week and reason that people will have increased leisure time. If the company's products are used for leisure-time activities, the manager is likely to forecast increased sales for the industry and for the company. Perceptive monitoring of world events prompted the top managers of **O'Gara-Hess & Eisenhardt** (a company based in Fairfield, Ohio) to forecast an increase in demand for armor-plated cars. News stories attracting the managers' attention included continuing reports of for-ransom kidnappings and of increasing violence to individuals by advocates of one cause or another.[2]

WHICH METHOD TO USE

Though we identify a limited number of forecasting methods, you should not underestimate the vast differences among companies or the difficulties of applying any one or more of them at any company. The applicability of any of the methods mentioned depends on the characteristics of the company, such as its age, its size, and the industry (or industries) in which it operates. For some companies or industries, no reliable—or predictable—indicators may exist. (Witness the maker of armor-plated cars.) Utilities rely heavily on historical analysis, adjusted for known changes in the population. In contrast, historical analysis is of little use to relatively new companies, companies in relatively new industries, and companies operating in industries heavily influenced by technological developments, such as manufacturers of computers and software.

Relying on any single forecasting method is dangerous. Forecasts using judgment methods alone might reflect unwarranted optimism of the sales manager and sales force. Even where indicators or industry forecasts are available and used, current conditions may differ from those in effect when the relationships among the indicators or forecast and the sales of the company or industry were developed. For example, in 1990 the **Institute of Clean Air Companies** forecast 1993 sales of one type of pollution-control system at $1.2 billion, but actual 1993 sales totaled only $226 million. Apparently, industry experts failed

---

2 *Neil Weinberg, editor (Follow-through), "When bad news is good news," Forbes, January 30, 1995, 14-15.*

to anticipate how hard utilities would look for less expensive ways to meet limits set in 1990 for releasing pollutants into the air.[3]

Most companies use a combination of forecasting methods, and successful forecasting tends to result from combining sound and experienced business judgment with the judicious use of quantitative tools. Whatever methods are used to forecast, the sales budget for the company as a whole is likely to evolve from several forecasts made on a smaller scale. The original forecasts may be by product, product line, geographical area, department, or some combination of these. The scope of the original forecasts and the methods used depend on the entity's organization.

EXPECTED VALUES AND FORECASTING

Some companies generate several forecasts by using different indicators or methods or by consulting several managers. When different methods are used, or different persons are preparing forecasts, the resulting forecasts are likely to differ. Even a single manager might come up with several forecasts based on different assumptions and judgments about conditions for the coming period. With several forecasts at hand, the concept of expected value is sometimes used to reach a single forecast figure to use in budgeting.

An **expected value** is the result of applying a probability assessment to each member of a set of possible future events. For example, to determine an expected value of sales from a collection of forecasts, managers assign a probability to each alternative sales forecast that they believe merits serious consideration. The probabilities reflect the managers' judgments of the likelihood of each forecast actually coming about. Suppose the vice president for sales and the regional managers believe there's a 30 percent probability of sales being $4,500,000 next year, a 50 percent probability that they will be $5,000,000, and a 20 percent probability that they will be $6,000,000. The following schedule shows the expected value of sales to be $5,050,000.

(1) Forecast	(2) Assigned Probability	(1) × (2) Expected Value
$4,500,000	0.30	$1,350,000
5,000,000	0.50	2,500,000
6,000,000	0.20	1,200,000
Expected value	1.00	$5,050,000

The probabilities must, of course, add up to 1, or 100 percent. The vice president would use the $5,050,000 expected value in the budget but would recognize that sales could run from $4,500,000 to $6,000,000. The vice president would monitor actual results and be prepared to revise the budget if conditions warranted. (Although we introduce the expected value concept in connection with forecasting sales, it also applies to budgeting costs.)

Probability assignments are usually based on the manager's judgment and experience, sometimes refined by other statistical techniques. The probabilities are, therefore, said to be *subjective* in that different managers might assign

---

3 Seth Lubove, "The bureaucrat as businessman," Forbes, *August 15, 1994, 64 and 66.*

different probabilities. As with any managerial tool, the quality of the final information or decision rests heavily on the quality of a manager's judgment.

INTERIM PERIOD FORECASTS

The forecasting methods discussed apply to sales forecasts of three distinct types: (1) annual forecasts, (2) longer-term forecasts (three to five years), and (3) quarterly or monthly forecasts. Once a forecast for the year has been approved as a basis for planning, it is necessary to break it down into shorter periods, called *interim periods*.

Often the data used to forecast annual sales (economic indicators, sales for other industries) are also available for quarters. In such cases, managers can base quarterly forecasts on the same indicator used for the annual forecast. Many companies have developed other reliable ways for breaking down annual forecasts. For example, their experience may show that consistent percentages of yearly sales occur in particular quarters or months (15 percent of annual sales are concentrated in March, 40 percent in the first quarter, and so on).

Whatever the methods used to develop the sales forecast, and whatever the length of the forecast period, managers revise budgets when they obtain more information. (Remember the earlier example of revising the budget in the light of heavier-than-expected sales early in the year.) A budget is a plan, not a straitjacket; changing it in the face of changing conditions is sound practice.

EXPENSE BUDGETS

Each manager in an organization is responsible for some specific tasks and the associated costs. Hence, each manager should have a budget allowance, or **expense budget**, stating the acceptable limits for costs the manager may incur in accomplishing assigned tasks.

There are two general ways to develop budget allowances for expenses. One approach sets the budget for a particular cost at a single amount. An allowance set in this way is called a **static budget**, and the approach is used with most fixed costs. Budget allowances for committed costs can generally be set by referring to existing obligations (because costs to be incurred have largely been set by actions already taken). Managerial policies usually determine the budget allowances for discretionary fixed costs, and static budget allowances are often used for such costs.

The second approach sets a variable, or **flexible budget allowance**, based on some measure of activity. Budget allowances are set in this fashion for variable costs and mixed costs, and occasionally for discretionary fixed costs. The character of flexible budget allowances is best exemplified by the budgeting of variable and mixed costs, which we discuss in the next section. Later in the chapter we discuss some special problems relating to the budgeting of discretionary fixed costs.

BUDGETING VARIABLE AND MIXED COSTS

 Chapter 3 introduced the concept that the total amount of a variable or mixed cost varies with the level(s) of the cost-driving activity (activities) identified through cost behavior studies. To develop budget allowances for such costs, managers rely on estimates of the *expected* levels of the relevant activities. For example, the budget allowance for sales commissions is derived from the sales budget. But a budget cannot fulfil its function of revealing deviations from plan unless budget allowances for variable and mixed costs are revised when the *actual* levels of the relevant activities are known. Using the same example, to know whether the cost of sales commissions is under control, managers need a revised budget allowance based on actual sales. Thus, there are two budgeted amounts for costs using a flexible budget allowance: a "before" and an "after."

To illustrate more clearly the need for and use of the flexible budget allowance, consider the budgets of production managers. Some costs are variable, some fixed, and some mixed, and the cost-driving activity will most likely be some measure of production activity. Suppose the manager and supervisor of the Mixing department in a factory agree on the following flexible budget allowances for the listed components of factory overhead in the department. Note that the cost-driving activity for the department's mixed costs is direct labor hours.

Cost	Fixed Amount per Month	Variable Amount per Direct Labor Hour
Indirect labor	$1,200	$0.50
Supplies	200	0.40
Maintenance	2,400	0.10
Depreciation	1,200	0
Miscellaneous	700	0.05
Total	$5,700	$1.05

Suppose further that 1,000 direct labor hours are budgeted for the coming month. The budget allowance for each cost element for the month is computed using the following formula.

$$\begin{array}{c} \textit{Flexible} \\ \textit{budget} \\ \textit{allowance} \end{array} = \begin{array}{c} \textit{fixed cost} \\ \textit{per month} \end{array} + \left(\begin{array}{c} \textit{direct} \\ \textit{labor} \\ \textit{hours} \end{array} \times \begin{array}{c} \textit{variable} \\ \textit{cost per} \\ \textit{hour} \end{array} \right)$$

 The formula for a flexible budget allowance is essentially the same as the cost prediction formula introduced in Chapter 3. The equivalence is logical, because a flexible budget allowance is simply a prediction of the cost to be incurred at a particular level of activity.

The *original* budget allowance for each cost element in the example is computed and reported in the first column of Exhibit 6-4. For example, the original budget amount for indirect labor is $1,700 [$1,200 + (1,000 × $0.50)]. As you can see, Exhibit 6-4 is actually the beginning of a performance report that will be completed later when actual labor hours are known.

Evaluating the manager's performance in controlling costs requires a *revised* budget allowance that is based on the actual level of the cost-driving activity. For example, suppose direct laborers in the department actually work 1,300 hours. The flexible budget allowance for indirect labor would be revised to $1,850 [$1,200 + (1,300 hours × $0.50)], and so on. The revised budget allowances represent goals for the manager's performance.

Exhibit 6-4   Production Performance Report

Month __March__   Department __Mixing__
Manager __E. Jones__

| | Budget Allowances | | | |
	Budgeted Hours	Actual Hours	Actual Costs Incurred	Variance
Direct labor hours	1,000			
Indirect labor	$1,700			
Supplies	600			
Maintenance	2,500			
Depreciation	1,200			
Miscellaneous	750			
Total	$6,750			

In Exhibit 6-5, we complete the performance report by inserting the flexible budget allowances for the achieved level of production. We also insert some *assumed* actual costs, and compute a variance between the revised budget and the actual costs. When actual costs are less than the budget allowance, the variance is favorable; when the reverse is true, the variance is unfavorable. Hence, the variances for supplies, maintenance, and total costs are favorable. In Chapter 12 we introduce methods for analyzing variances.

The activities driving many costs are not related directly to sales, labor hours, or production volume. As we showed in Chapter 3, for example, activities such as the number of vendors from whom the company buys materials and components, the number of employees in a department, or the number of different

Exhibit 6-5   Production Performance Report

Month __March__   Department __Mixing__
Manager __E. Jones__

| | Budget Allowances | | | Variance Favorable (Unfavorable) |
	Budgeted Hours	Actual Hours	Actual Costs Incurred	
Direct labor hours	1,000	1,300		
Indirect labor	$1,700	$1,850	$1,870	$ (20)
Supplies	600	720	705	15
Maintenance	2,500	2,530	2,470	60
Depreciation	1,200	1,200	1,200	—
Miscellaneous	750	765	780	(15)
Total	$6,750	$7,065	$7,025	$ 40

types of products manufactured often generate significant costs. The analytical methods introduced in Chapter 3 help managers identify activities that are useful for budgeting purposes. But the usefulness of the identified relationships for budgeting purposes depends on the availability of estimates or predictions of the level of the cost-driving activities.

BUDGETING DISCRETIONARY COSTS

As stated earlier, discretionary cost allowances are generally set by managerial policies. Static allowances are appropriate for most such costs, but flexible allowances are appropriate when the company's *policy* is to spend an amount equal to some percentage of another factor. Such would be the case if, for example, a company budgets advertising expenditures based on sales or employee training costs based on total wages and salaries.

The real problem with budgeting discretionary costs is determining what level of expenditures is desirable. What *is* optimal spending for employee development? for improving current products? for research on potential products? for in-house legal counsel? Managers must establish budget allowances for such costs without knowing what level of spending is best for their company.

Part of the problem of deciding how much to spend on discretionary items is that expenditures seldom produce immediately measurable output or benefits. Research and development activities might not show results for several years. In some cases, budgets for discretionary items are related to some variable input factor, such as the number of employees being given training or the number of research projects. But, note that the variable factor (e.g., number of employees to be trained or projects to be undertaken) is *also* usually a matter of managerial choice for which there is no right answer.

Occasionally, a manager might be able to specify in some way what benefits could come from a particular level of spending on a discretionary item. For example, the data processing manager might be able to say that leasing a certain software package would speed customer billing by one or two days. (Getting bills out quicker could mean that payments would come in sooner.) Managers might then compare the benefit of faster collections—a reduction of funds tied up in accounts receivable—with the cost of leasing the software package.

Because optimal spending levels for discretionary items can't be determined, static budget allowances for them often are set through negotiations between the affected managers and upper levels of management. Sometimes top managers establish budgets for these areas by specific policy decisions. "We shall increase spending on research and development by 10 percent each year for the next five years" is an example of such a policy decision. Such a statement could be associated with top managers setting a longer-term goal, such as being recognized as the leading innovator in the industry. Whatever the goal accepted by top management, managers of the affected areas have a right to know the reason behind a stated policy so that they authorize actions (and the related expenditures) consistent with the goal.

BUDGETING AND HUMAN BEHAVIOR

Budgeting necessarily involves people, their behavior, their beliefs, even their personalities. Behavioral problems arise when managers' interests conflict, when budgets are imposed from above, when stretch goals are used, and when budgets are viewed as checkup devices or ends in themselves. For both managers and management accountants, budgets and the budgeting process can also raise the most common of behavioral problems, ethical conflicts. Moreover, cultural differences can challenge the effectiveness of budgeting, especially at companies operating in more than one country.

CONFLICTS

We can illustrate the problem of conflicts in budgeting by looking at likely disagreements among managers when a company establishes an inventory policy. An **inventory policy** states the level of inventory the company plans to have on hand at all times. The sales manager of a retailer wants high inventory levels because it's easier to make sales if the goods are available for the customer to see and purchase immediately. The sales manager at a manufacturing company also prefers to have inventory ready for immediate delivery. A financial manager prefers low inventories because of the associated costs (storage, insurance, taxes, interest, and so on). The production manager at a manufacturer isn't interested in inventory per se, but in maintaining steady production—no interruptions for rush orders, no unplanned overtime—and other conditions that minimize production costs. Thus, three managers have different views on the desirable level of inventory. They will be evaluated by reference to how well they do their job, so each has an interest in the company's inventory policy.

In a conventional manufacturing environment, the conflict is resolved with great difficulty, if at all, and the managerial accountant might be called in to help in the negotiating of the final policy. A manufacturing company committed to the JIT philosophy already has established an inventory policy for the level of its materials and finished products: little or none. The company-wide commitment to this common goal not only drops the financial manager's concerns from the conflict, but also encourages the other managers to work together to achieve the maximum sales at the minimum cost.

The conflicting interests of the sales and finance managers persist for retail enterprises. Many retailers have begun to emulate the inventory-reduction efforts of manufacturers by negotiating with their suppliers for quicker and more frequent deliveries. To facilitate speedy replenishment of stock, some retailers maintain computer links with suppliers, providing up-to-date sales data and even sales forecasts. **Wal-Mart** is widely recognized as the pioneer of just-in-time retailing, and many of its suppliers have made major operating changes to accommodate this important customer. For example, the maker of Lee and Wrangler jeans now has a computerized reordering system "so precise that if a Wal-Mart sells a pair of jeans on Tuesday, a replacement pair is back on the shelf by Thursday."[4] But however fast replacements arrive, Wal-Mart's managers must still decide how much inventory to have available on the shelf.

The budgeting of discretionary costs presents opportunities for conflicts between managers if for no other reason than that no one knows the "right" answer. For example, the manager of human resources would favor more training programs for continuing employees than would the managers of the

---

4 *"Just Get It to the Stores on Time,"* Business Week, *March 6, 1995, 66-7.*

employees receiving additional training. The concern of the affected managers is the impact of training time on evaluations of their own performance. If training interferes with timely completion of work assigned to their areas, their ability as managers may be questioned. And if the assigned work is completed despite the training time, higher-level managers might conclude that current staffing levels are higher than necessary.

IMPOSED BUDGETS

Unfortunately, it's not uncommon for senior managers to set performance goals (budgets) without consulting the individuals who will be responsible for meeting those goals. In such cases, the budgets are said to be *imposed*, and serious behavioral problems can arise (or be avoided) depending on the attitudes of the managers imposing the performance goals.

Some managers who impose budgets believe the performance goals they set should be very high (budgeted costs very low)—so high that almost no one could be expected to meet the budget. Such managers sometimes justify their position on the grounds that it "keeps people on their toes" and express the belief that people will be lax in their performance if they can easily meet a budget. Other managers who impose budgets say that budgets should be achievable given a good, but not exceptional, performance.

Sooner or later, imposing unachievable budgets produces problems. Affected managers will become discouraged and feel no commitment to meeting budgeted goals. (Remember that generating commitment to budgets is one of the principal features of companies that use budgets effectively.) Or perhaps the affected managers will take actions that *seem* to help achieve goals (such as scrimping on preventive maintenance to achieve lower costs in the short run) but are really harmful in the longer run (when machinery breaks down and production must be halted altogether).

A major and immediate problem with imposed budgets is that, if unrealistic, they are not useful for planning, when planning is one of a budget's primary purposes. Consider the implications of setting unrealistically high sales goals. The unrealistic sales budget will be the basis for production plans, including perhaps commitments for materials and components and the hiring and training of factory workers. Based on the sales budget, the company also will have planned cash receipts and estimated its needs for short-term financing.[5] What happens if the sales goals are not realized? Unless the company operates under the JIT philosophy, inventory will be higher than expected, and additional storage space may have to be acquired at unfavorable rates. Whatever the company's operating philosophy, cash receipts will not materialize as planned, and additional short-term financing may have to be negotiated on unfavorable terms. If managers decide to adjust subsequent production schedules to bring them into line with lower sales (and to reduce inventory), employee relations may suffer as workers are laid off, and requested delays in delivery of materials may harm relations with suppliers. At their worst, unrealistic budgets can have serious financial effects on the

---

5 *One of the advantages of the cash portion of a comprehensive budget is that it allows managers to identify financing needs before they occur, so the managers have time to seek the best source of financing. More on this in Chapter 7.*

company. At the very least, unrealistic budgets will probably be ignored by those whose actions they were intended to guide.

Even imposed budgets that "imposing" managers believe to reflect achievable, realistic performance goals can produce less-than-optimal performance. There are at least two reasons for adopting a budgeting approach that involves participation by the individuals expected to meet the performance goals in a budget. First, the "imposing" managers can never be as knowledgeable about the costs to perform specific tasks as are the persons actually performing them. Second, a considerable body of empirical evidence suggests that allowing people a say in their expected levels of performance is conducive to better performance than when those individuals are not consulted.

STRETCH GOALS

A recent development in the area of setting performance goals is the use of stretch goals, or more accurately, stretch targets. **Stretch targets** are exceptionally ambitious goals not likely to be achieved without making fundamental changes in the way a job is done. The following are examples of stretch goals set at some well-known companies.[6]

- Produce the new product with half the parts in half the time at half the price (a new VCR introduced by **Toshiba Corporation**).
- Cut the manufacturing cost of a plane 25 percent and its production time more than 50 percent (**Boeing Corporation**).
- Obtain 30 percent of sales revenue from products introduced within the past four years (**3M Company**).
- Raise annual improvement in productivity from 0.3 to 3 percent (**Mead Corporation**).

An executive in charge of executive development programs at **General Electric** said "a stretch target gets your people to perform in ways they never imagined possible. It's a goal that, by definition, you don't know how to reach."[7] Not surprisingly, top managers of companies using stretch goals praise them for spurring innovation in ways not prompted by a commitment to the continuous improvement philosophy mentioned earlier in the chapter. (See the accompanying Insight for examples.)

Target dates for achieving stretch goals are often two or more years away. For example, **Boeing's** top managers set the previously-mentioned goals in 1992, with the production-time goal to be met by 1996 and the cost-cutting goal to be met by 1998. Stretch targets usually supplement, rather than replace, conventional goals such as meeting budgeted earnings and sales for a quarter or year. Nevertheless, the efforts to achieve the longer-term goals necessarily have an impact on periodic reports of budgeted and actual results.

Using stretch goals carries the risk of producing the same problem that can occur with imposed budgets: lack of commitment by lower-level managers to reaching a target they view as unrealistic or even impossible. Convincing lower-

6 Shawn Tully, "Why To Go For Stretch Targets," Fortune, November 14, 1994, 145-6, 148, 150, 154, 158.
7 Strat Sherman, "Stretch Goals: The Dark Side of Asking for Miracles," (Managing: Ideas & Solutions), Fortune, November 14, 1994, 231-2.

SIGHT

Efforts to meet stretch goals set in 1992 by the Chief Executive Officer at **Boeing** changed virtually every phase of production. The company cut parts inventory at assembly locations by $140 million when the unit making parts for doors switched to providing kits containing all the parts needed to assemble each type of door needed. Assemblers previously collected the needed parts from bins in an adjacent warehouse. (The idea to produce kits originated with production workers, who have long been a source of ideas for changing the production practices of manufacturers.) The major change speeding up the design phase of production involved creating a huge computer library of the detailed specifications for parts and plane configurations already developed. The company also began parallel assembly of large sections of each plane, rather than assembling the sections in sequence. By 1994, the time to design and build an order of 747s and 767s had dropped from 18 to 10 months, with the full benefits of several other major changes yet to be realized.

Source: Shawn Tully, "Why To Go For Stretch Targets," Fortune, *November 14, 1994.*

level managers to commit to reaching imposed stretch goals is easiest when those managers know that radical change is necessary to avoid a crisis. But many companies that don't face a perceivable crisis have adopted the stretch philosophy, arguing that only major changes will permit them to continue to prosper in the long run. At such companies, gaining a commitment to stretch goals is more difficult. **Mead's** Chief Executive Officer observed that "a little over half the managers can adjust to stretch goals. For the program to work, the rest have to go." (Mead lost more than a third of its 900 managers in the three years after its productivity goal was announced.)[8] The **General Electric** executive quoted earlier admits the potential for behavior problems in an organization that sets stretch goals. The task of managers who set such goals is difficult at best, because lower-level managers must see a goal as achievable when no one in the company—including the goal setter—yet knows "how to get there."

BUDGETS AS "CHECKUP" DEVICES

Behavioral problems do not arise solely because of the procedure followed to set goals or develop budget allowances. Comparisons of budgeted and actual results and subsequent evaluation of performance also introduce difficulties. Ideally, managers use actual results to evaluate their own performance, to evaluate the performance of others, and to correct elements of operations that seem to be out of control. That is, the budget serves as a *feedback device*, letting managers know the results of their actions. Having seen that something is wrong, they can take steps to correct it.

---

8 *Quoted in Tully, op. cit., p. 146.*

Unfortunately, budgets often are used more for checking up on managers than for providing feedback. Where this is the case, managers are constantly trying to think of ways to explain unfavorable results. The time spent thinking of ways to defend the results could be used more profitably to plan and control operations. Some evaluation of performance is necessary, but the budget ought not to be perceived as a club to be held over the heads of managers. More attention is given to behavioral problems of performance evaluation in Chapters 10, 11, and 12.

10▶
11▶
12▶

UNWISE ADHERENCE TO BUDGETS

Expense budgets set limits on levels of cost to be incurred, allowances managers are not supposed to exceed. If managers view their budget allowances as strict limits on spending, they may spend either too little or too much.

There are times when exceeding the budget could benefit the company. Suppose a sales manager believes that an out-of-town trip to visit several important customers or potential customers will lead to greatly increased sales. The sales manager will be reluctant to authorize the trip if it will result in exceeding the travel budget. At the other extreme, a manager who has kept costs well under budget might be tempted to spend frivolously so that expenditures will reach the budgeted level. The manager may fear a cut in the budget for the following year if costs incurred during the current year are lower than budgeted. The manager might take an undesirable action—authorize an unnecessary trip—so as not to be given a lower budget next year.

Managerial actions influenced by budget concerns in one area are likely to affect the actions taken by managers in other areas. A realistic example involves a manufacturing supervisor who was running a machine at 50 percent of its rated capacity. Asked why, the supervisor said that the machine needed new bearings and would produce only scrap if run faster. A request for maintenance had been ignored for several months because the maintenance supervisor had been controlling costs by not replacing employees who left.

BUDGETING AND ETHICS

For both operating managers and management accountants, budgeting is a fertile field for behavioral problems involving ethical issues. Each of the items we've already discussed offers opportunity for questionable practices.

Managers in some areas might consider preparing—and ask management accountants to help them in doing so—budgets with a great deal of slack so that the managers will be able to meet them with a minimum of effort. Top-level managers who impose budgets on subordinates could ask management accountants to develop budgets so tight that there is little chance of achieving them. Knowing the problems such budgets are likely to create, the management accountants could view responding to the managers' requests to be an ethical problem.

Ethical issues also arise about the reporting of *actual* results for a budget period. When budgets are viewed as checkup devices and budget allowances as strict limits, a manager might be inclined to misclassify some expenditure or to ask the management accountant to delay recording some costs until the next budget period. Actual results also are influenced by revenue-recognition practices, and evidence exists of some managers accelerating recognition of revenues so as to meet sales budgets. The experiences of one company, **Bausch & Lomb** (presented in the accompanying Insight on pages 268-269), include premature revenue recognition and many of the other problems mentioned in this chapter.

Management accountants are particularly uncomfortable if their role appears to be to act as enforcers for upper-level management, because they recognize that necessary requests for explanations are likely to generate distrust (and perhaps misleading information). Some management accountants might believe that continued pursuit of explanations would reduce managers' inclination to seek assistance needed in the future with resultant harm to the firm as a whole.

INTERNATIONAL ASPECTS OF BUDGETING

Companies with foreign operations face several problems that their domestic counterparts do not. One technical problem is translating budgets and actual results from the local currency to the currency of the company's home country. (Chapter 11 addresses this issue.) Both legal and cultural differences among countries affect the effectiveness of budgets and the budgeting process. The differences in laws among countries are too numerous and complex to present here. We will point out, however, that the legal environment of a country affects the flexibility of managers to achieve their goals. For example, the fringe benefits mandated by many countries in western Europe and elsewhere reduce managers' willingness (or ability) to adjust the work force to sales expectations. Of equal, or greater, importance are the beliefs and behavior of the people of different countries.

Both profit and participation in setting goals are still relatively new ideas in the formerly communist countries of eastern Europe and the now independent countries of the former Soviet Union. Managers in such countries had long been accustomed to doing what a central authority said—produce so much of this, so many of that. To many of those managers, thinking in terms of profit is still a formidable task, and many find it difficult to make the transition to responding to the market. For good or ill, some of the individuals adapting well to the changed circumstances were engaged in enterprises illegal under prior regimes. Such individuals bring to their jobs the creativity and independent thinking needed to respond to the market, but their disdain for established guidelines might also carry over to the new environment.

Some cultures foster fatalistic attitudes, and their members see little reason to plan anything. After all, if certain things are going to happen no matter what you do, why bother? In such cultures it is difficult, even impossible, to motivate managers to budget at all. Increased contact with foreigners usually reduces some of the opposition to budgeting, but the change may come about slowly.

The prevailing economic system aside, people in some cultures are inclined to accept authority uncritically. Here, the problem is that anything upper-level managers say is fine with lower-level managers. Lower-level managers will not question their supervisors, nor will they take active roles in developing budgets. Instead, they will wait for clues as to what their managers are looking for and respond only then (and only in line with what they perceive is expected).

Bausch & Lomb (B&L) makes several products (including contact lenses and solution, Ray-Ban sunglasses, and binoculars) and had sales of $1.9 billion in 1993. Consistent with goals publicly announced by its top managers, B&L reported double-digit growth in sales and operating income (excluding non-recurring events) for the 12 years prior to 1994. Maintaining that pace had become increasingly difficult as growth slowed in the markets for the company's products, but the company's budgets continued to reflect the same annual goals.

Several of the company's past and current managers reported tremendous pressure to meet quarterly and annual goals and say they had virtually no part in setting the goals. According to those managers, the Chief Executive Officer's standard advice to managers having trouble meeting budget goals was "Make the numbers, but don't do anything stupid."

Managers adopted a variety of tactics to achieve sales goals. At one or another of **B&L's** segments, all of the following reportedly occurred.

- End-of-quarter promotions so regular that customers learned to delay their normal purchases to take advantage of the lower prices.

- Sales at exceptionably favorable credit terms. (Customers of one **B&L** unit pressing for exceptionally large orders were told they wouldn't have to pay until the ordered products were sold.)

- Threats to stop selling to some regular customers unless they placed unusually large orders.

- Sales of significant quantities of product to customers known to be directing the merchandise elsewhere for sale at discount prices.

- Shipping orders early or shipping unordered merchandise to regular customers.

- Repackaging expensive regular contact lenses as frequent-replacement lenses, which were then sold at lower prices by the unit and its customers.

The last-listed tactic generated a class-action suit by users of the regular product who had paid full price for their lenses. Company officials contend that volume discounts were responsible for the lower prices. (The suit is still unsettled.)

Loading sales into the closing days of a budget period had predictable effects on other aspects of the company.

- Receivables remained uncollected for several months. (**B&L** began selling receivables as collections fell behind budgeted cash receipts.)

- Inventories rose because of higher-than-planned sales returns and production levels budgeted to meet announced sales goals.

- Distribution costs increased because handling the surge of shipments near the end of a budget period required hiring temporary employees and paying overtime to regular employees.

INSIGHT   *(continued)*

- Sales at regular prices suffered as some overstocked distributors sold to discount outlets in the U.S. and elsewhere.

In mid-1994, the company started an internal investigation of revenue-recognition practices at its Hong Kong unit and announced that profits would probably be below forecasts. After the Securities and Exchange Commission announced in late December of 1994 that it would investigate another unit, **B&L's** top managers are reported to have ordered all units to follow conservative revenue-recognition practices. B&L's sales and operating earnings for 1994 were both lower than in 1993. The company's top managers admitted that some wrong-doing occurred at the two units investigated but denied that either corporate policies or the corporate culture encouraged the actions of managers at those units. Specialists in corporate ethics observe that senior managers don't necessarily perceive the message their comments and actions convey to lower-level managers.

Source: Developed from "Blind Ambition: How the pursuit of results got out of hand at Bausch & Lomb,"
Mark Maremont, Business Week, *October 23, 1995, 78-82, 86, 90.*

Home-office managers might also receive the same deferential treatment. As a result, the company loses the benefit of the insights and understanding of its lower-level managers, and those insights might be critical to the company's success.

Whatever the constraints on an individual company, it will benefit from developing a comprehensive budget that reflects its managers' carefully considered plans. The next sections illustrate the development of the initial segments of such a budget for a retailer and present the special problem confronted by a manufacturer. The illustration will be completed in the next chapter.

ILLUSTRATION OF A COMPREHENSIVE
BUDGET FOR A RETAILER (CRANE COMPANY)

We illustrate the preparation of a comprehensive budget by working with Crane Company, a retailer whose managers have prepared the needed sales forecasts and developed a sales budget. (That is, we do not illustrate the sales forecasting process that produced the sales budget.) The illustration will be done in two parts. In this chapter we prepare the tentative budgeted income statement and a purchases budget. In Chapter 7 we prepare the cash budget, which requires some of the data in the budgets developed here. We shall then see how the operating and financial budgets are related, especially how the results in a tentative cash budget could prompt managers to look again at the operating budgets and possibly make changes in them.

The managers at Crane Company are developing a comprehensive budget for the first six months of 19X4. As the first step, they've developed the following sales budget, which extends to August 19X4. (Shortly, you will see why the managers must budget sales beyond the six-month period in order to complete the budget for that period.)

Month	Sales Budget	Month	Sales Budget	Month	Sales Budget	Month	Sales Budget
Jan.	$400	Mar.	$ 800	May	$1,200	July	$700
Feb.	600	Apr.	1,000	June	800	Aug.	800

Sales are obviously seasonal; they increase through May and then drop off, with May sales budgeted at three times those of January.

BUDGETED INCOME STATEMENT

First, we develop a budgeted, or pro forma, income statement. To do so, we must know something about the behavior of the company's costs. We shall assume that Crane's managers have done the necessary cost behavior studies and that they believe the following assertions about cost behavior are a good basis for planning.

- Cost of goods sold will be 60 percent of sales dollars.
- Other variable costs will be 15 percent of sales.
- Total fixed costs will be $240, of which $20 per month is depreciation expense.

With this information we can develop the budgeted income statements for the six months, as shown in Exhibit 6-6.

The next step is to prepare a purchases budget.

Exhibit 6-6 Crane Company Budgeted Income Statements for the Six Months Ending June 30, 19X4

	Jan.	Feb.	Mar.	Apr.	May	June	Six Months
Sales	$400	$600	$800	$1,000	$1,200	$800	$4,800
Cost of goods sold (60% of sales)	240	360	480	600	720	480	2,880
Gross profit	$160	$240	$320	$ 400	$ 480	$320	$1,920
Other variable costs (15% of sales)	60	90	120	150	180	120	720
Contribution margin	$100	$150	$200	$ 250	$ 300	$200	$1,200
Fixed costs (depreciation, rent, etc.)	40	40	40	40	40	40	240
Income	$ 60	$110	$160	$ 210	$ 260	$160	$ 960

PURCHASES BUDGET

A **purchases budget** is a schedule showing how much merchandise must be acquired during the budget period. How much merchandise a company needs to acquire during a period depends on how much it expects to sell, how much is on hand, and how much its managers want to have on hand to start the next period.

Retailers must have *some* merchandise on hand, though the amount considered desirable depends on such things as the products carried and normal delivery times. Hence, to develop Crane's purchases budget we need to know what level of inventory Crane's managers consider desirable. Retailers stock goods in anticipation of sales. (Witness the well-stocked shelves and extra in-aisle displays of department stores early in the Christmas shopping season.) Accordingly, companies usually state their inventory policy as some function of expected sales.

We've already suggested the complexity of a decision about the desired level of inventory, so we'll assume the interested managers at Crane have agreed that inventory should be maintained at a level of two months' sales. That is, Crane's inventory policy is that, at the end of each month, the company should have merchandise on hand to cover the sales expected in the following two months. (Such a policy does *not* mean that everything Crane sells has been on hand for two months. Crane might purchase fast-moving items more than once a month and slow-moving items only three or four times a year.) We chose the specific relationship (two months' sales) so that our illustration would emphasize the importance of expectations in determining purchases.

Moving from budgeting sales to budgeting purchases and inventory, you must also move from using selling prices to using costs. (Remember that merchandise is purchased at cost and carried in inventory at cost until it is sold.) To determine purchasing requirements for any period, we can use the general formula for cost of goods sold (from financial accounting):

$$\text{Cost of goods sold} = \text{beginning inventory} + \text{purchases} - \text{ending inventory}$$

Purchases is the unknown, so we restate the formula to obtain

$$\text{Purchases} = \text{cost of goods sold} + \text{ending inventory} - \text{beginning inventory}$$

A purchases budget follows the revised formula, as you can see in Exhibit 6-7, Crane's purchases budget for the six months. Amounts for cost of sales come from the pro forma income statements in Exhibit 6-6. The sum of the cost of sales for two consecutive months is the amount shown as "ending inventory required" at the beginning of that two-month period. For example, the inventory required at the end of January ($840) is the sum of the cost of sales for February ($360) and March ($480). The circled items show the derivations of the ending inventory for January and April. (Now you see why Crane must forecast sales beyond the six-month period for which it is preparing its budget. Crane could budget purchases only through April if it didn't have sales forecasts beyond June, because the budgeted ending inventories for May and June depend on such forecasts. Whenever a company bases its inventory policy on

**Exhibit 6-7   Crane Company Purchases Budget
for the Six Months Ending June 30, 19X4**

	Jan.	Feb.	Mar.	Apr.	May	June	Six Months
Cost of sales for month (Exhibit 6-6)	$ 240	$ 360 + $ 480		$ 600	$ 720 + $ 480		$2,880
Ending inventory required	840	1,080	1,320	1,200	900ᵃ	900ᵇ	900
Total requirements	$1,080	$1,440	$1,800	$1,800	$1,620	$1,380	$3,780
Beginning inventory	600ᶜ	840	1,080	1,320	1,200	900	600
Purchases required	$ 480	$ 600	$ 720	$ 480	$ 420	$ 480	$3,180

a June and July cost of sales, 60% × ($800 + $700).
b July and August cost of sales, 60% × ($700 + $800).
c Inventory at January 1 is assumed to be consistent with company policy.

expected sales, the company must forecast sales beyond the period being budgeted for.)

The *total* requirement for any one month is the amount needed to cover that month's sales plus what the company has determined must be on hand at the end of that month. The total requirement can be met from two sources: goods already on hand—beginning inventory—and purchases during the month. Of course, the beginning inventory for any month is the ending inventory in the previous month. Thus, required purchases are total requirements less beginning inventory. Work through Exhibit 6-7 to be sure you understand the calculations.

The rows in Exhibit 6-7 for cost of sales and purchases add across to the totals for the six-month period, but the inventory rows and total requirements row do not. The beginning inventory in the six months column is the beginning inventory for the six-month period. The ending inventory is the required inventory at the end of the last month being budgeted. You could arrive at the numbers in the final column if you budgeted only for the six-month period as a whole, but the month-by-month budgets are important for other reasons. As you will see in Chapter 7, the monthly purchases budgets provide information for the monthly cash budgets, and the inventory amount at any month-end will appear on the budgeted balance sheet at that date.

PURCHASES BUDGET—MANUFACTURING FIRM (BRANDON COMPANY)

Retailers purchase merchandise to meet sales goals and adhere to inventory policy. Manufacturers *produce* merchandise in keeping with expected sales and inventory policy. Thus, a manufacturer must prepare a **production budget**. But to meet production requirements, a manufacturer must purchase sufficient materials and components to meet production goals. Hence, both types of companies must plan purchases. The basic idea of such planning is the same, but developing the purchases budget is somewhat more complex for the manufacturer because a manufacturer must develop a budget for production *in units* before developing a purchases budget in dollars. Units must be used first because variable production costs (such as materials) will vary with the number of units produced.

Suppose that Brandon Company, a conventional manufacturer, wishes to keep an inventory of its finished product equal to the budgeted sales for the following one and one-half months (a variation of the policy for Crane Company). Brandon's managers have gathered the following budgeted data for 19X8.

Units of product on hand at December 31, 19X7		200 units
Pounds of material on hand, December 31, 19X7		3,000 pounds

Budgeted sales for the next six months:

January	120 units	March	240 units	May	310 units
February	180 units	April	330 units	June	280 units

Variable manufacturing costs, per unit produced:	
Materials (8 lbs. at $0.50)	$4.00
Direct labor	3.00
Manufacturing overhead:	
Fringe benefits	0.40
Power	0.30
Supplies	0.30
Total	$8.00

Fixed manufacturing costs, per month:	
Rent of machinery	$ 400
Supervisory salaries	600
Insurance	100
Managerial salaries	800
Total	$1,900

Brandon's sales, like Crane's, reflect some seasonality. Also like Crane, Brandon has identified its costs as variable or fixed. But for Brandon, the variable manufacturing costs will vary with the number of units produced, not with the number of units sold. Hence, the production budget must show the number of units that must be produced each period to meet sales and inventory requirements.

Exhibit 6-8 shows Brandon's completed production budget for January, February, March, and April. Note that even though a sales forecast is available for the first six months of 19X8, we can prepare a production budget for only the first four months. This is true because the company's inventory policy for finished units is based on the expected sales for the following two months and we do not know the expected sales beyond June.

Ideal JIT operations allow manufacturers to buy materials and components only as needed. Both conventional manufacturers and JIT manufacturers operating under less than ideal conditions maintain some inventory of materials as a buffer. These manufacturers must have a policy regarding how much material should be on hand. Referring to Brandon's cost data we see that the $4 material cost per unit of product consists of eight pounds of material at $0.50 per pound. Let us assume that Brandon's managers desire to keep materials

Exhibit 6-8	Brandon Company, Production Budget for the First Four Months in 19X4 (in units)					
	Jan.	Feb.	Mar.	Apr.	May	June
Expected sales	120	180	240	330	310	280
Ending inventory required[a]	300	405	485	450	?	?
Total units required	420	585	725	780		
Beginning inventory[b]	210	300	405	485	450	?
Required production	210	285	320	295	?	?

a Sales for the following month + 50% of sales for the second following month. For example, January ending inventory of 300 units is February sales (180 units) + 50% of March sales (50% × 240 = 120).
b Inventory at January 1 is assumed to be consistent with company policy.

inventory equal to 150 percent of the coming month's budgeted production needs. (An inventory policy for materials is based on production, not on sales, because materials are needed when the product is made, not when it is sold.)

Exhibit 6-9 shows completed budgets for materials purchases in January, February, and March. Brandon's inventory policy for materials makes it impossible to budget purchases for April because such purchases depend on an unknown, the budgeted production for May. This example offers further evidence of the problem that lead times can create, and of the need for planning if the company is to operate efficiently.

A retailer needs a purchases budget to develop a cash budget, because the payments for purchased items are not likely to be made at exactly the time of

Exhibit 6-9	Brandon Company, Purchases Budget— Materials, January, February, and March, 19X4			
	Jan.	Feb.	Mar.	Apr.
Budgeted production, in units[a]	210	285	320	295
Needed for current production, budgeted production × 8	1,680	2,280	2,560	2,360
Ending inventory required[b]	3,420	3,840	3,540	?
Total pounds of material needed	5,100	6,120	6,100	?
Beginning inventory[c]	2,520	3,420	3,840	3,540
Required purchases, in pounds	2,580	2,700	2,260	?
Required purchases at $0.50 per lb.	$1,290	$1,350	$1,130	

a From Exhibit 6-8.
b 150% of budgeted production needs for the following month. For example, January ending inventory of 3,420 lbs. is 150% of February's production needs for 2,280 lbs.
c Inventory at January 1 is assumed to be consistent with company policy.

purchase. A manufacturer needs *both* a production budget and a purchases budget in order to budget cash, because payments for purchases of materials and components are not likely to be required at the same time as the payments for other costs associated with production. The development of a cash budget, one of the most critical of the schedules included in a comprehensive budget, is discussed in detail in Chapter 7.

SUMMARY

Comprehensive budgeting is vital to effective planning and control. The comprehensive budget is the major near-term planning document that a company develops and consists of a set of financial statements and other schedules showing the expected results for a future period. Developing a comprehensive budget formalizes management objectives and helps coordinate the many activities performed within a single firm.

Sales forecasting is critical to budgeting because the sales budget drives all other budgets. Several approaches are used for forecasting sales. The approach adopted depends on the reliability of available data, the nature of the product, and the experience and sophistication of the managers. A company must have an inventory policy and information about the behavior of its costs in order to prepare the purchases, production, and expense budgets and a pro forma income statement (called operating budgets).

Flexible budget allowances are appropriate for variable and mixed costs, and occasionally for discretionary fixed costs, because such allowances are useful for identifying problems that require managerial action and for evaluating performance. The production budget for a manufacturer is the equivalent of the purchases budget for a retailer. A manufacturer also needs a purchases budget, but the production budget is the basis for developing the purchases budget of a manufacturer.

Budgeting entails numerous behavioral problems, which can be particularly severe if managers do not participate in the development of the budget for their areas or if budget goals are perceived as unachievable. Budgeting is less effective if the concepts of planning, profit, or participation are inconsistent in some way with the prevailing culture.

KEY TERMS

capital budget (247)	operating budgets (249)
comprehensive budget (244)	production budget (268)
continuous budgets (248)	project budgets (248)
expected value (253)	purchases budget (267)
expense budget (254)	sales forecast (248)
financial budgets (249)	static budget (254)
flexible budget allowance (254)	stretch targets (260)
inventory policy (258)	

KEY FORMULAS

$$\text{Purchases}^a = \frac{\text{cost of}}{\text{goods sold}} + \frac{\text{ending}}{\text{inventory}} - \frac{\text{beginning}}{\text{inventory}}$$

$$\frac{\text{Budgeted}}{\text{production, in units}} = \frac{\text{units needed}}{\text{for current sales}} + \frac{\text{desired ending}}{\text{inventory}} - \frac{\text{beginning}}{\text{inventory}}$$

a For budgeting purchases in a manufacturing firm, "cost of current sales" becomes "cost of units of materials and components needed for current production."

REVIEW PROBLEM

Using the following data for Graham Company, prepare a budgeted income statement and a purchases budget in units and dollars for January 19X4.

Budgeted sales for January	5,000 units at $20	$100,000
Budgeted sales for February	6,000 units at $20	$120,000
Cost data:		
Purchase price of product	$5 per unit	
Commission to salespeople	10% of sales	
Depreciation	$2,000 per month	
Other operating expenses	$40,000 per month plus 5% of sales	

Graham's policy is to maintain inventory at 150% of the coming month's sales requirements. Inventory at December 31, 19X3, is $30,000 (6,000 units at $5), which is less than budgeted.

ANSWER TO REVIEW PROBLEM

Graham Company, Budgeted Income Statement for January 19X4		
Sales		$100,000
Cost of sales (5,000 units at $5)		25,000
Gross profit		$ 75,000
Variable costs:		
Commissions (10% × $100,000)	$10,000	
Variable operating expenses (5% × $100,000)	5,000	15,000
Contribution margin		$ 60,000
Fixed costs:		
Depreciation	$ 2,000	
Other operating expenses	40,000	42,000
Income		$ 18,000

Graham Company, Purchases Budget for January 19X4

	Units	Dollars
Cost of sales	5,000	$25,000
Desired ending inventory (6,000 × 150%)	9,000	45,000
Total requirements	14,000	$70,000
Beginning inventory	6,000	30,000
Purchases required for the month	8,000	$40,000

ASSIGNMENT MATERIAL

QUESTIONS FOR DISCUSSION

6-1   *"I'm too busy to budget"*   Evaluate the following statement: "Budgets are fine for firms that can plan ahead, but I can't. Things are too uncertain for me to make plans. And besides, I have to spend my time looking after day-to-day operations and trying to figure out what is wrong."

6-2   *Expense budgeting*   What are the major factors in setting budgeted amounts for the following?
(a) Commissions to salespeople
(b) Electricity
(c) Taxes on land and buildings
(d) Taxes on personal property (physical assets other than land and buildings)
(e) Charitable contributions
(f) Office salaries

6-3   *Expense allowances*   Indicate whether a company is likely to use a static or a flexible budget allowance for each of the costs listed in 6-2. Explain your answers.

6-4   *Are budgets bad at GE?*   Jack Welch, the CEO of **General Electric**, has long been known for distrust of budgets. GE does not operate under the typical budgeting system. Welch has argued that participation by managers in the budgeting process is unlikely to produce good results and that stretch goals are the best motivators.

Welch has pointed out that budgets can be very deceptive, noting that, on the one hand, GE's plastics business was up over 10% in 1994, but that it should have been up over 30%. The business was caught in a price squeeze and failed to respond in time. He reduced bonuses to the plastics managers. On the other hand, GE's aircraft engine business dropped about 10%, but those managers received significant bonuses. The aircraft business was more successful than its competitors and responded better to the severe drop in military purchases that hurt companies all over the world. Had GE operated under a budget system, the plastics business would have appeared very successful and the aircraft business very unsuccessful, when the opposite was the case.

Required
Should budgeting as described in this chapter produce the results Welch deplores? What is wrong with budgeting that yields the described results?

6-5   *Sales forecasting—effects of external events* Indicate what effect, if any, each of the following events or changes in expected conditions would have on the sales forecast that you have already prepared. Explain your reasoning.

(a) Your company makes building materials. The federal government just announced a cutback in its program to assist low-income families to buy their own homes.

(b) Your company makes toys. The government announces that the economic outlook is better than had been thought. Personal income is likely to increase and unemployment decrease.

(c) You make parts for the automobile industry. A strike against your major customer is announced by the head of the union.

(d) You make heating and air conditioning equipment. The prices of electricity, heating oil, and natural gas are expected to rise rapidly.

(e) You make insulation for houses and other buildings. The prices of electricity, heating oil, and natural gas are expected to rise rapidly.

(f) Your firm publishes college textbooks. Recent statistics show that the numbers of high school seniors and juniors have fallen off from previous years.

(g) You make plumbing pipe from copper. Chile, the major source of copper, has just gone to war with one of its neighbors.

6-6   *Production budgets* From its sales budget, a manufacturing company prepares a production budget in units and then prepares budgets for production costs. Explain why the company must first prepare a production budget in units.

6-7   *Sales forecasting—value of indicators* The following conversation took place between two company presidents.

Grant: "We hired a consultant to help us with our sales forecasting and he has really done a good job. As you know, we make ballpoint pen refills, and he found that our sales are very closely correlated with sales of refillable pens from four months previous. He says that four months seems to be the average life of the cartridges used in most pens. Of course, we don't make pens, but our refills fit the pens that nearly every firm makes."

Harrison: "We did the same thing. Our major product is baby bottles, and our consultant found that the number of bottles we sell is very closely related to the number of births about a month later. People seem to buy bottles about a month before the baby is born."

Required
State which company seems to be in the better position to forecast its sales and explain your answer.

6-8   *What's happening here?* Jack Rolland, the assistant to the controller of Upton Company, was looking at the following report for the marketing department. Upton's fiscal year ends December 31.

Cost Category	Annual Budget	Expenditures Through November	December
Salaries	$240,000	$220,000	$240,000
Travel	36,000	24,000	36,000
Other	96,000	87,000	96,000

Rolland said to you: "I wonder why Cal, the marketing department manager, waited so long to spend his travel money. Maybe a lot of his business is concentrated in December."

Required
Give at least one other explanation for Cal's December spending on travel.

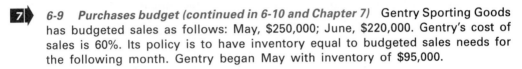

EXERCISES

6-9   Purchases budget (continued in 6-10 and Chapter 7)   Gentry Sporting Goods has budgeted sales as follows: May, $250,000; June, $220,000. Gentry's cost of sales is 60%. Its policy is to have inventory equal to budgeted sales needs for the following month. Gentry began May with inventory of $95,000.

Required
Prepare a purchases budget for May.

6-10   Budgeted income statement (continuation of 6-9, continued in Chapter 7)   Gentry's variable costs other than cost of sales are 10% of sales, and its monthly fixed costs are $22,000, including $3,000 depreciation.

Required
Prepare budgeted income statements for May and June.

6-11   Budgeted income statement and purchases budget (continued in Chapter 7)   Jordan Clothing has the following sales forecast for the first four months of 19X9.

January	$70,000	March	$90,000
February	70,000	April	80,000

Jordan's cost of sales is 60% of sales. Fixed costs are $12,000 per month. Jordan maintains inventory at 150% of the coming month's budgeted sales requirements and has $55,000 inventory at January 1.

Required
1. Prepare a budgeted income statement for the first three months of 19X9.
2. Prepare a purchases budget for the first three months of 19X9, in total and by month.

6-12   Budgeted income statement and purchases budget (continued in Chapter 7)   The following data relate to the operations of Thomas Company, a retail store.

Sales Forecast 19X4	
January	$100,000
February	120,000
March	150,000
April	160,000

(a) Cost of sales is 40% of sales. Other variable costs are 30% of sales.
(b) Inventory is maintained at twice the budgeted sales requirements for the following month. The beginning inventory is $80,000.
(c) Fixed costs are $25,000 per month.

Required

1. Prepare budgeted income statements for the first three months of 19X4 and for the quarter as a whole.
2. Prepare a purchases budget, by month, for the first quarter.

6-13 Expected values You have received the following data from the marketing department regarding the expected monthly unit sales of a new type of coffee maker that your company will introduce in a few months.

Sales	Probability
20,000	0.10
25,000	0.40
30,000	0.40
35,000	0.10

Required

Determine the expected value of sales.

6-14 Budgeting labor costs Kramwer Company's policy is to have a supervisor for every nine workers; whenever the number of supervisors divided into the number of workers is greater than nine, a supervisor is hired. The company is expanding output and has budgeted production in units as follows.

	Jan.	Feb.	Mar.	Apr.	May	Jun.
Production	4,800	5,400	6,100	6,800	7,400	7,200

A production worker can produce 100 units per month. Both workers and supervisors are hired at the beginning of the month in which they are to be added. Workers are paid $1,900 per month, supervisors, $2,800.

Required

Prepare a budget of requirements for workers and for supervisors by month, in units and dollars. What reservations, if any, do you have about the numbers in your budget for June?

6-15 Purchases budget—units and dollars Wells Company expects the following unit sales.

	Feb.	Mar.	Apr.	May	Jun.
Sales	1,900	2,200	2,300	2,100	1,700

The company's policy is to maintain inventory equal to 50% of budgeted sales needs for the following month. The beginning inventory is expected to be 1,000 units. Each unit costs $4.

Required

1. Prepare purchases budgets for as many months as you can in (a) units and (b) dollars.
2. Explain why you had to stop where you did.

6-16   Budgeted income statement for a manufacturer (continued in 6-17, 6-18, and Chapter 7)   HMA Company manufactures a small cabinet for cassette tapes. Its sales budget for the first three months of 19X0 is as follows.

January	$2,000 (50 units)
February	$2,200 (55 units)
March	$1,800 (45 units)

Variable manufacturing costs are $26 per unit, of which $12 is for materials. HMA's fixed manufacturing costs are $150 per month, including $40 of depreciation. Its only variable selling cost is a 15% sales commission. Fixed selling and administrative costs are $70 per month. HMA maintains no inventory of finished cabinets.

Required
Prepare a budgeted income statement for HMA for January.

6-17   Production budget for a manufacturer (continuation of 6-16)   Because HMA carries no inventory of finished cabinets, its production, in units, is the same as its sales. HMA's $12-per-unit materials cost is for four pounds of materials at a price of $3 per pound.

Required
Prepare HMA's production budget for January, in dollars, showing as much detail as the facts permit.

6-18   Purchases budget for a manufacturer (continuation of 6-16 and 6-17)   HMA's policy is to maintain an inventory of material at 20% of what is needed to cover production in the upcoming month. At December 31, 19X9, HMA had 34 pounds of material that cost $102.

Required
Prepare a materials purchases budget for HMA for January, in units and dollars.

6-19   Expense budgets and variances   Burnside Company has found the following formula helpful in predicting the monthly cost of utilities for its factory:

$$Total\ utilities\ cost = \$250,000 + \$5X$$

where X is the number of machine hours worked.

Budgeted production for July was 14,000 units. The machine time needed to produce a unit is three hours, so Burnside budgeted the use of 42,000 machine hours. Actual production in July was 15,000 units, each requiring three machine hours. The actual cost for utilities in July was $410,000.

Required
1. Determine the amount Burnside budgeted for utilities for July.
2. Determine the amount and direction of the July budget variance for utilities based on Burnside's original budget allowance.
3. Determine the amount and direction of the July budget variance for utilities assuming that Burnside uses a flexible budget for utilities.

6-20   Budgeted income statements   Weinstock Building Supply operates a chain of lumberyards in a large metropolitan area. The sales manager has retained an economist to develop sales forecasting methods to enable the firm to plan better. The economist reports that the following equation will forecast sales quite well based on past patterns of behavior.

$$\text{Monthly sales in dollars} = \$136{,}000 + \left(\$0.052 \times \begin{array}{c} \text{dollar value of} \\ \text{building permits issued} \\ \text{in prior month} \end{array}\right)$$

The sales manager shows you the following data regarding building permits. The forecasts were developed by the Association of Builders in the area and have generally been accurate.

March	$3,000,000 (actual)
April	4,750,000 (forecast)
May	6,900,000 (forecast)
June	7,100,000 (forecast)

It is now April 3, and the sales manager would like forecasts of sales and income for as many months as you can prepare. She tells you that cost of goods sold, which is all variable, is 45% of sales, other variable costs are 8% of sales, and fixed costs are $140,000 per month.

Required
Prepare budgeted income statements for as many months as you can, given the data available. Round to the nearest $100.

6-21   Flexible budget and variances   Adams Company makes a single product. Materials for a unit of the product cost $4, direct labor is $3, and manufacturing overhead is $20,000 per month fixed, plus $5 per unit variable (with production). In one month, production was 18,000 units and actual costs were as follows: materials, $71,800; direct labor, $56,100; variable overhead, $89,000; and fixed overhead, $20,000.

Required
1. Prepare a flexible expense budget formula for total production cost.
2. What should costs have been to produce 18,000 units? (Consider each element of cost separately.)
3. What were the variances between actual and budgeted costs for each element of cost?

6-22   Income statement and purchase budget   The managers of Learning Centers, a retail firm, have the following data about the company's main product and its operations.

Selling price per unit	$20
Purchase cost per unit	$8
Sales commission	20% of selling price
Fixed costs per month	$14,000

The managers plan to maintain inventory equal to twice the budgeted sales needs for the following month. Expected unit sales for March, April, and May are 4,000, 4,500, and 3,750, respectively.

Required
1. Prepare budgeted income statements for March and April.
2. Prepare a purchases budget for April, in units.
3. If sales for June are expected to be $100,000, how many units should the company plan to purchase in May?

6-23 *Flexible and static budgets* You just became the supervisor of the grinding department of GHJ Company. The production manager, Carl Mintz, has expressed concern to you about the use of supplies in the grinding department and has, after discussions with you, come up with the following monthly budget formula:

$$Budgeted \; supplies \; expense = \$13,400 + (\$1.85 \times units \; produced)$$

Budgeted production for April was 10,000 units, giving a budget allowance of $31,900. You actually produced 11,500 units and used $33,950 in supplies. Mintz attached a note to your monthly report saying that you needed to get better control of supplies because you exceeded the budget by $2,050.

Required
Using the guidelines in Appendix A, write a memorandum to the production manager showing that you did control the use of supplies in April.

6-24 *Inventory policy—carrying costs* Jack Grant, Frank Milano, and Jill Beary, the Steele Company's managers for production, sales, and finance, respectively, are discussing production and inventory policies. Milano believes that if inventory were increased by 5,000 units, sales would be 2,000 units per month higher, and he would like Steele to stock the additional units. Grant is willing to revise production schedules to do so, but Beary is not in favor of the change. She argues that the cost of storing, insuring, and financing the additional inventory would be prohibitive. She says that it costs Steele $4 per month per unit to cover these costs and that they are variable with the number of units on hand. Contribution margin per unit is $8.

Required
1. What is the value (per month) of the additional sales that would be generated by the increased inventory?
2. What additional monthly costs are associated with carrying the additional 5,000 units in inventory?
3. Using the guidelines in Appendix A, write a memorandum to the three managers giving and supporting your recommendation regarding production and inventory.

PROBLEMS

6-25 *Production budget* Medina Pottery manufactures various products. It has the following sales budget, in sets, for its Mexicali line of dishes: April, 18,000;

May, 24,000; June, 25,000. Medina keeps its inventory at twice the coming month's budgeted sales. At April 1, inventory is expected to be 41,000 sets.

Required
Prepare production budgets for April and May.

6-26 Purchases budget (continuation of 6-25) Making one set of Mexicali dishes requires 12 pounds of materials that cost $2.50 per pound. Medina keeps its inventory of materials at 150% of the coming month's budgeted production. At the beginning of April, Medina expects to have 540,000 pounds of materials on hand.

Required
Prepare a materials purchases budget for April in (a) pounds and (b) dollars.

6-27 JIT manufacturing (continuation of 6-25 and 6-26) Medina's managers are considering adopting just-in-time and flexible manufacturing principles. Some of the managers have studied other companies and believe Medina can implement some aspects of JIT now. They believe the company could very quickly cut finished goods inventory to a constant 800 sets of Mexicali dishes and materials inventory to a two-day supply (1/15th of a month). They believe the company can achieve even greater reductions, with zero inventories as the objective.

Required
1. Prepare production budgets for April and May, and a purchases budget for April. Assume that April's beginning inventories conform to the new policies.
2. Using the guidelines in Appendix A, write a memorandum to Julia Lugo, the factory manager, about the advantages you see in reducing inventory as indicated here.

 6-28 Budgeting production and purchases The production manager of Cram Company wishes to maintain an inventory of materials equal to budgeted production needs for the next two months. Each unit of product takes five pounds of materials. Inventory of finished goods is usually maintained at 150% of the following month's budgeted sales. The sales budget for the first five months of the coming year, given in units, is as follows.

	Jan.	Feb.	Mar.	Apr.	May
Sales	12,000	14,000	10,000	16,000	20,000

Inventories expected at December 31 are 170,000 pounds of materials and 17,000 units of finished product.

Required
Prepare budgets of production and purchases of materials in units and pounds, respectively, for as many months as possible.

6-29 JIT manufacturing (continuation of 6-28) Cram Company's managers have begun to use some principles of just-in-time manufacturing. They have been able to reduce finished goods inventory to a ten-day supply (one-third of the coming month's budgeted sales requirements) and materials inventory to a three-day supply (one-tenth of the coming month's budgeted production). Inventories at August 31 reflect these policies. The sales budget for the coming months, in units, is as follows.

	Sep.	Oct.	Nov.	Dec.
Sales	14,000	15,000	15,500	16,000

Required

Prepare budgets of production and purchases of materials for as many months as you can. (Round all items to the nearest hundred units or pounds.) Comment on the differences between these budgets and those in the preceding assignment and on the advantages of the JIT operation.

 6-30 Preparing flexible budgets As a new assistant to the controller of Elikai Company, you have been assigned the task of preparing a set of flexible budget allowances for overhead costs. You have the following data available.

Cost	Variable Amount per Direct Labor Hour	Fixed Amount
Supplies	$0.70	$17,000
Repairs	0.12	9,200
Power	1.10	15,600
Depreciation		18,800

Supervision, the only other overhead item, is a step-variable cost. It is expected to be $7,000 at 10,000 direct labor hours and to rise by $1,000 for each additional 1,000 direct labor hours.

Required

Prepare a schedule showing the budgeted amount of each cost element, and of total budgeted overhead cost, at 10,000, 12,000, and 14,000 direct labor hours.

6-31 Relationships Following is the pro forma income statement for Habib Company for April. No change in inventories is planned.

Sales (900 units at $50)		$45,000
Variable costs:		
Materials ($5 per unit)	$4,500	
Direct labor ($7 per unit)	6,300	
Overhead—manufacturing ($4 per unit)	3,600	
Selling expenses ($2 per unit)	1,800	16,200
Contribution margin		$28,800
Fixed costs:		
Manufacturing	$9,000	
Selling and administrative	9,100	18,100
Income		$10,700

Required

Fill in the blanks.
1. Budgeted production for April is _____ units.
2. Total variable manufacturing costs for April are $_____.
3. The sale of an additional 10 units would increase income by $_____.
4. Total costs and expenses if 910 units were sold would be $_____.

5. Break-even volume in units is _____.
6. If variable manufacturing costs increased by $2 per unit, income at 900 units sold would be $_____.
7. If fixed costs increased by $4,800, and the firm wanted income of $10,700, sales in units would have to be _____.
8. If ending inventory were to be 30 units higher than beginning inventory, manufacturing costs incurred during the period would be $_____.

6-32   Multiple components—manufacturing firm   Soreto Company expects the following sales by month, in units, for the first five months of the coming fiscal year.

	Jan.	Feb.	Mar.	Apr.	May
Budgeted sales	1,800	1,900	2,500	1,900	2,100

The company's one product, the Tow, is a combination of two components: Tics and Tacs. Each Tow requires three Tics and two Tacs. Soreto follows the policy of having finished goods equal to 50% of budgeted sales for the following two months. Soreto often experiences problems with the quality of components received from suppliers, so inventories of components are maintained at 150% of budgeted production needs for the coming month. Inventories at January 31, 19X8, reflect these policies.

Required

1. Prepare a production budget for Tows for as many months as you can.
2. Prepare purchases budgets for Tics and Tacs for as many months as you can.

6-33   Budgeted income statements—expected values   Burke Company's executives are working on the comprehensive budget for 19X7. After lengthy discussions with regional sales managers, Burke's sales vice president does not wish to pin down a single estimate of sales. He would prefer to give three forecasts, along with his estimates of the probabilities he attaches to them.

Sales	Probability
$ 500,000	0.5
800,000	0.3
1,000,000	0.2

Variable costs are 60% of sales and total fixed costs are budgeted at $250,000.

Required

1. Prepare budgeted income statements based on each of the three forecasts.
2. Prepare a budgeted income statement based on the expected value of sales.

6-34   Smoothing production   Maynard Inc. makes swimsuits, with its sales falling heavily in the April-June period, as shown by the sales budget (in thousands of units).

	Jan.	Feb.	Mar.	Apr.	May	Jun.
Sales	100	100	110	160	200	250

Maynard's normal inventory policy has been to have a two-month supply of finished product. The production manager has criticized the policy because it requires wide swings in production, which add to costs. He estimates that per-unit variable manufacturing cost is $3 higher than normal for each unit produced in excess of 180,000 units per month. Maynard's treasurer is concerned that increasing production in the early months of the year would lead to high costs of carrying inventory. He estimates that it costs the firm $0.80 per unit per month in ending inventory, consisting of insurance, financing, and handling costs. He emphasizes that these costs are incremental.

All of the managers agree that Maynard should have 450,000 units on hand by the end of April. The production manager wants to spread the required production equally over the four months, while the treasurer believes that the firm should stick to its current policy unless it turns out to be costlier.

Required

1. Prepare a budget of production for January through April following Maynard's current policy. Inventory at January 1 is 200,000 units.
2. Prepare a production budget using the production manager's preference.
3. Determine which budget gives lower costs.

6-35   Relationships among sales and production budgets Following are partially completed sales and production budgets for Firmin Company. Firmin maintains an inventory equal to 150% of the budgeted sales for the coming month.

Required

Fill in the blanks.

Sales Budget (in units)

Jan.	Feb.	Mar.	Apr.	May	June	July
3,000	3,400	___	___	___	___	___

Production Budget (in units)

	Jan.	Feb.	Mar.	Apr.	May	June
Ending inventory	___	6,300	___	___	8,700	___
Sales	3,000	___	___	___	___	5,800
Total requirements	___	___	___	13,900	___	___
Beginning inventory	___	5,100	___	6,900	___	___
Production	3,600	___	___	7,000	___	5,200

6-36   Budgeting in a CPA firm Takoski Inoe is a certified public accountant practicing in a large city. He employs two staff accountants and two clerical workers. He pays the four employees a total of $8,800 per month. His other expenses, all fixed, for such items as rent, utilities, subscriptions, stationery, and postage, are $4,700 per month.

Public accounting is, for most firms, highly seasonal, with about four months (January through April) that are extremely busy and eight months that have less activity.

The most relevant measure of volume in a CPA firm is charged hours—the hours worked on client business for which the clients are charged. Mr. Inoe expects his two staff accountants to work an average of 120 charged hours each month during the eight slower months, and 200 hours each per month during the January-April busy season. Clerical personnel work about 600 charged hours each per year, and Mr. Inoe works about 1,400. For both the clerical personnel and Mr. Inoe, approximately 40% of their charged hours fall in the four-month busy season.

Mr. Inoe charges his clients $75 per hour for his time, $35 for the time of a staff accountant, and $15 for the time of clerical personnel.

Required

Prepare a budget of revenues and expenses for a year for Mr. Inoe's firm. Separate the budgets for the periods January-April and May-December.

6-37 Sales forecasting—scatter diagram and regression Ridley Carpet Company has engaged you as a consultant to help in its sales forecasting. After a long discussion with Roberta Ridley, president of the firm, you develop the following data.

Year	Housing Units Built (in thousands)	Sales of Ridley Company (in thousands)
19X1	1,300	$2,440
19X2	1,400	2,610
19X3	1,900	3,380
19X4	1,500	2,760
19X5	2,000	3,520
19X6	1,600	2,875

Required

1. Develop an equation to be used to forecast sales for Ridley Company. Use a scatter diagram and regression analysis.
2. Ms. Ridley has learned that the forecast for housing units to be built in 19X7 is 1.8 million. What is your forecast for Ridley's sales? Are you relatively confident about your forecast? Why or why not?

7▶ **6-38 Comprehensive budget (continued in Chapter 7)** The managers and managerial accountants of Arctic Products Company have been developing information for the comprehensive budget for the coming year. The managers have decided to use the following estimates and policies for planning.

Sales forecast, in units:	
January	20,000
February	24,000
March	30,000
April	25,000
May	22,000
Selling price	$30 per unit
Materials cost	$8 per unit of product
Direct labor and variable overhead	$6 per unit of product
Variable selling costs	$2 per unit sold
Fixed manufacturing costs	$125,000 per month
Fixed selling, general, and administrative costs	$55,000 per month

The managers plan to keep inventory of finished goods equal to budgeted sales for the following two months, and inventory of materials equal to twice budgeted production for the coming month. The planned December 31 inventories are finished goods, 35,000 units and materials, 66,000 units (one unit of material per unit of product).

Required

1. Prepare budgeted income statements for January, February, and the two-month period, using the contribution margin format.
2. Prepare production budgets for January, February, and March.
3. Prepare purchases budgets for materials for January and February.

6-39   *Indicators for sales forecasting* The following economic indicators and other data might be useful in forecasting sales for certain kinds of firms: income per capita, population, car sales, and rate of unemployment.

Required

For each type of business listed below, state which, if any, of the economic indicators you think would be relevant in forecasting sales. Indicate briefly why you think each indicator is relevant or irrelevant.

(a) food company
(b) maker of outboard motors
(c) home construction firm
(d) tire maker
(e) textbook company
(f) jewelry maker
(g) maker of nonprescription drugs

6-40   *Budgeting for a hospital (AICPA adapted)* Dr. Gale, the administrator of Taylor Memorial Hospital, has asked for your help in preparing the 19X7 budget that she must present at the next meeting of the hospital's board of trustees. The hospital obtains its revenues through two types of charges: charges for use of a hospital room and charges for use of the operating room. Use of the basic rooms depends on whether the patient undergoes surgery during the stay in the hospital. Estimated data as to the types of patients and the related room requirements for 19X7 are as follows:

Type of Patient	Total Expected	Average Stay in Days	Percentages Selecting Kinds of Rooms		
			Private	Semiprivate	Ward
Surgical	2,400	10	15%	75%	10%
Medical only	2,100	8	10%	60%	30%

Basic room charges are $100, $80, and $40 for private, semiprivate, and ward, respectively.

Charges for using the operating room depend on the length of the operation and the number of persons involved in the operation. The charge is $0.40 per person-minute. (A person-minute is one person for one minute; if an operation requires three persons for 40 minutes, there would be a charge for 120 person-minutes at $0.40 per person-minute, or $48.) Based on past experience the following is a breakdown of the types of operations to be performed on surgical patients.

Type of Operation	Number of Operations	Average Number of Minutes per Operation	Average Number of Persons Required
Minor	1,200	30	4
Major—abdominal	400	90	6
Major—other	800	120	8
	2,400		

Required

1. Prepare a schedule of budgeted revenues from room charges by type of patient and type of room.
2. Prepare a schedule of budgeted revenues from operating room charges by type of operation.

6-41   *Flexible budget, multiple drivers*   The controller of Ames Industries has analyzed the costs of the Linden Plant. She comes up with the following cost drivers. Data are quarterly.

	Fixed Component	Variable Component	Cost Driver
Inspection	$ 72,500	$120.00	Shipments
Maintenance	61,200	2.40	Machine hours
Data processing	9,700	0.25	Transactions
Purchasing	63,600	180.00	Number of vendors
Other	278,800	2.20	Labor hours

Some of these costs are step-variable, so the variable components do not apply to small changes in activity, but only to relatively large movements. You may assume for this assignment that all changes are large.

Required

Develop flexible budget allowances for each element of cost, and for total cost, for the following two cases.

	Case A	Case B
Shipments	110	75
Machine hours	15,000	22,000
Transactions	220,000	360,000
Number of vendors	120	40
Labor hours	7,000	11,000

6-42   *Manufacturing cost budget*   Horton Company makes a variety of household products, usually in about the same mix. On the average, each unit requires $3 in materials and $2 in variable manufacturing overhead. Direct labor averages $4 per unit at production volumes up to 100,000 units per month. Making more than 100,000 units requires Horton to pay its workers an overtime premium, so that direct labor cost rises to $6 per unit for units over 100,000. The remainder of manufacturing overhead is step-variable, with the following pattern.

Monthly Unit Production	Other Costs
Up to 100,000	$230,000
100,001-120,000	245,000
120,001-140,000	275,000

The pattern of these costs reflects increased supervision, utilities, and other costs associated with operating beyond the normal eight-hour day.

   Budgeted unit production for the next four months is 440,000 units, scheduled as follows.

	Mar.	Apr.	May	Jun.
Production	90,000	115,000	130,000	105,000

Required
1. Prepare budgets for manufacturing costs for each month, and in total.
2. What would total production costs be for the four-month period if the company could equalize production at 110,000 units per month?
3. If Hornton needs to produce only 440,000 units for the entire four-month period, how should it produce by month to obtain the lowest possible total production cost?
4. What reasons might there be for Horton to stick to the original monthly production budget despite its higher costs?

6-43   Budgeting and behavior   Rydell Company sets sales budgets for its salespeople, who are evaluated by reference to whether they achieve budgeted sales. The budget is expressed in total dollars of sales and is $200,000 per person for the first quarter of 19X3. Rydell makes two products, for which price and cost data are as follows.

	Wiffers	Trogs
Selling price	$10	$15
Variable costs	4	10
Contribution margin	$ 6	$ 5

Wiffers are a new product that Rydell's president, Sid Koleski, thinks should become a big seller. At a regular meeting with his sales manager, Koleski said that the sales staff probably would have to seek out customers for Wiffers and convince them of the high quality of the product. Trogs have been popular for some years, and Koleski believes it unlikely that customers who have been buying Trogs for years will buy Wiffers.

The $200,000 budgeted sales per person is a fairly high goal, but is attainable. During the first quarter of 19X3, all salespeople met the $200,000 sales budget.

Required
1. Which product should Rydel's salespeople stress?
2. Under the circumstances described, which product do you think sold most?
3. If your answers to items 1 and 2 conflict, what changes would you suggest for the company's budgeting process?

6-44   Production and purchases budgets—units and dollars   Drummond Company manufactures several products, including a frying pan with a wooden handle. Each frying pan requires a blank sheet of iron that Drummond buys from a single supplier at $2 per sheet and then molds into the appropriate shape. Handles are purchased in ready-to-use condition from another supplier at $0.40 each.

Sales forecasts for the frying pan for the next five months are as follows, in units.

	Apr.	May	Jun.	Jul.	Aug.
Budgeted sales	2,500	3,100	2,800	3,500	2,400

Drummond is able to forecast its total sales for the year fairly well but has experienced less success in breaking down the forecast by month. Finished goods inventory is budgeted at twice the quantity needed for the coming month's sales. Drummond's policy is to maintain the inventory of handles equal to the coming month's production needs. The current supplier of blank iron sheets provides a product of satisfactory quality but is not willing to deliver more frequently or in relatively small quantities. Drummond's purchasing manager has had difficulty finding an alternative supplier that can provide quick delivery of blank iron sheets of the needed quality, so Drummond budgets its inventory of the sheets equal to budgeted production for the coming two months.

Labor costs for shaping the iron and putting on a handle are $1.50 and variable manufacturing overhead costs are $0.80. Fixed manufacturing costs are $4,500 per month.

At the end of March, the company expects to have the following inventories.

Finished pans	5,300
Blank iron sheets	5,600
Handles	4,600

Required

1. Prepare production budgets for April through July, by month, in units and in dollar costs.
2. Prepare purchases budgets in units and dollars for blank iron sheets and handles for April and May.

6-45   *Conflicts in policy*   Timmons Fashions has the following sales budget, in units, for its best-selling line of women's wear.

January	65,000	March	60,000	May	100,000
February	90,000	April	60,000	June	80,000

Timmons manufactures the line in a single factory. Because of union agreements and employment policies, the only feasible amounts of monthly production are 72,000 and 90,000 for a four-day week and five-day week, respectively.

Timmons's policy is to keep inventory of at least 15,000 units at the end of each month to serve as a buffer in case of slow deliveries by suppliers or other problems that could lead to lost sales. Storage space is limited, such that having inventory greater than 40,000 units results in abnormally high costs. The inventory at January 1 is 20,000 units.

Required

Develop a production budget for the six months. If you cannot keep inventory within the limits stated, be prepared to defend the reasoning you used in making your selection.

6-46   *Budgeting administrative expenses*   The controller of Kaufman Company has asked you to prepare a flexible budget for costs in the purchasing department. The normal volume of work in the department is 800 purchase orders per week.

Data entry clerks in the department are paid $5 per hour and work a 35-hour week. The clerks can enter about 100 lines per hour and the average purchase order has 10 lines. When they are not entering orders, the clerks file and perform other work. Order clerks prepare the purchase orders for entry. They are paid $6 per hour for a 35-hour week and generally take 20 minutes to prepare an order. When not preparing orders, the order clerks work at other tasks, such as investigating potential vendors. The purchasing agent is paid $500 per week. Supplies, stationery, etc. average $0.40 per purchase order.

Required
1. Under normal circumstances, how many clerks of each type are required and how much slack time does each type of clerk have available to perform other duties?
2. If salaries for the clerks and costs for supplies and stationery are to be budgeted as variable costs, what is the flexible budget formula for total purchasing costs for each week, and what variance would you expect for a normal week?
3. What is the per-week capacity of the purchasing department given the personnel requirement derived in item 1?
4. What is the flexible budget formula for total weekly purchasing costs if the personnel requirements in item 1 are treated as fixed costs?

6-47   Sales forecasting, budgeted income, and budgeted production (continued in Chapter 7)   Spark Company makes ignition systems for automobile engines. The company has developed the following equation that has been successful in predicting annual sales, in units:

$$Sales = 80,000 + (0.009 \times automobile\ sales)$$

According to two different sources in the automobile industry, this coming year's automobile sales are expected to be 8,000,000 cars.

Each system sells for $80 and contains materials costing $5. Direct labor is $10 per unit and variable manufacturing overhead is $12. Spark's only other variable cost is a sales commission of 10% of dollar sales. Fixed manufacturing costs are $1,200,000 per year; fixed selling and administrative expenses are $1,800,000 per year. Both are incurred evenly over the year.

Sales are seasonal; about 60% of sales are in the first six months of the fiscal year, which begins June 1. The sales forecast for the first six months, in percentages of annual sales, is as follows.

June	5%	August	9%	October	14%
July	8	September	12	November	12

Spark has a policy of keeping inventory of finished product equal to budgeted sales for the next two months. Materials are bought and delivered daily, so no inventory is kept. The inventory of finished product at May 31 is expected to be 19,000 units.

Required
1. Prepare a budgeted income statement for the coming year and for the first six months of the year.
2. Prepare a production budget by month for the first three months, in units.
3. Determine Spark's break-even point (in units) for a year. How might the company's managers interpret that information in light of their successful sales predictions using the given formula?

6-48   Comprehensive budget (adapted from a problem prepared by Professor Maurice L. Hirsch, and continued in Chapter 7)   Banana City is a wholesaler of bananas and nuts. Mr. Bertram A. Nana, the company's president, has asked for your assistance in preparing budgets for fiscal year 19X7, which begins on September 1, 19X6. He has gathered the following information for your use.

(a) Sales are expected to be $880,000 for the year, of which bananas are expected to be 50%, nuts 50%.

(b) Sales are somewhat seasonal. Banana sales are expected to be $77,000 in November, with the rest spread evenly over the remaining eleven months. Sales of nuts are expected to be $40,000 per month except in October and November, when they are expected to be $25,000 per month, and in April and May, when they are expected to be $35,000 per month.

(c) Cost of sales, the only variable cost, is 40% for both products.

(d) Inventory of bananas is generally kept equal to a one-month supply. Inventory of nuts is usually held at a two-month supply.

(e) Income taxes are 40% of income before taxes.

(f) Annual fixed costs, all incurred evenly throughout the year, are expected to be as follows.

Rent	$ 24,000	Depreciation	$ 36,000
Insurance	12,000	Interest	6,000
Wages and salaries	120,000	Other fixed costs	156,000

(g) Inventories expected at August 31, 19X6, are bananas, $14,300 and nuts, $27,500.

(h) The company expects to sell some land that it purchased several years ago for $8,000. The sale is expected to occur in October at a price of $6,000.

Required

1. Prepare a budgeted income statement for the fiscal year ending August 31, 19X7.

2. Prepare a budgeted income statement for each month of the first quarter of the fiscal year and for the quarter as a whole.

3. Prepare a purchases budget by product for each month of the first quarter of the fiscal year and for the quarter as a whole.

CASES

6-49 *Constraints on scheduling production* Robertson Company experiences some seasonality in its sales. Following are its sales forecasts (in units) for the first eight months of 19X5.

January	3,000	March	4,200	May	5,400	July	4,800
February	3,800	April	5,000	June	5,900	August	4,200

The inventory of finished units at January 1 is expected to be 6,800 units and Robertson's policy is to keep inventory equal to a two-month supply.

Robertson's current work force of 100 people is organized into 20 five-member teams. Each team takes responsibility for the product throughout the production process, so that workers can be hired only in groups of five. The 20 teams can produce 4,000 units per month, but overtime can be used to increase output by 10%.

Unlike some firms that face seasonality in sales, Robertson is not constrained by union contracts requiring some guaranteed level of employment for its employees. Nevertheless, Robertson's top managers prefer not to hire and lay off workers when only moderate changes in production are contemplated. As explained to you by Martha Martinez, Robertson's president, this preference is based partly on a perceived responsibility to provide regular employment and partly on a concern about a potential decline in the available work force if skilled workers leave the community due to unstable employment conditions.

Required

Using the guidelines in Appendix A, write a memorandum to Martinez about production and labor needs for the first six months of 19X5. Include in the memorandum a production budget (in units), a budget of worker requirements, any assumptions you made, and any reservations you have about the budgets you propose.

6-50 *Budgeting step-variable costs* Corman Company manufactures several products using a great deal of machinery. Since it is critical to keep the machines running well, Corman pays a good deal of attention to maintenance. Corman's chief engineer has determined that routine maintenance requires a complete shutdown and cleaning every 200 hours a machine has been running. This job costs $250. Excluding the major cleanings, maintenance costs for ten machines have been as follows for the past eight months. Each machine runs about the same amount of time each month as every other machine.

Month	Hours for Ten Machines	Maintenance Costs
1	2,200	$1,400
2	2,100	1,380
3	1,950	1,260
4	2,000	1,290
5	1,700	1,190
6	2,400	1,505
7	2,300	1,455
8	1,800	1,200

Required

1. Using the high-low method, prepare a flexible budget formula for maintenance costs, excluding the major cleaning at 200 hours.
2. Determine the budgeted cost levels for 1,600 hours and at 100-hour intervals up to 2,500 hours. Include maintenance cost using the formula you developed in item 1 and the major cleaning costs.
3. Discuss your reservations about the use of flexible budgets when such costs are present.

6-51   *Reporting budget variances*   Wilkinson Company uses monthly budgets. At the end of each month, the accounting department prepares reports of budgeted and actual results. The reports are circulated to the managers whose operations are being reported on and to their supervisors. Following are excerpts from the reports for the latest two months on the costs in one production department.

	April			May		
	Budget	Actual	Variance	Budget	Actual	Variance
Production in units	8,000	7,000	1,000	10,000	10,500	(500)
Costs:						
Material	$16,000	$14,600	$1,400	$20,000	$20,800	$ (800)
Direct labor	24,000	21,600	2,400	30,000	31,300	(1,300)
Indirect labor	4,000	3,900	100	5,000	5,300	(300)
Power	7,000	6,700	300	8,000	8,400	(400)
Maintenance	5,200	4,700	500	6,000	6,200	(200)
Supplies and other	4,600	4,580	20	5,000	5,050	(50)
Total costs	$60,800	$56,080	$4,720	$74,000	$77,050	$(3,050)

Heated discussions between Wilkinson's production manager, Orel Rhodes, and the heads of production departments are common, and Daniel Dabich, Wilkinson's manufacturing vice president, has often asked Rhodes to explain the heated exchanges. Dabich asks you, his new assistant, to study the budget reports and write a memo for his signature to Retha James, the controller, about the usefulness of the reports his managers receive.

Required

Using the guidelines in Appendix A, comply with Dabich's request. (You will find it helpful to analyze the budgeted amounts of each cost and determine its fixed and variable components.)

7 Financial Budgeting

LEARNING OBJECTIVES

After reading this chapter, you should be able to

1. *Identify the typical leads and lags that complicate the budgeting of cash receipts and disbursements.*

2. *Prepare a cash budget.*

3. *List several decisions managers might consider to resolve cash deficiencies revealed by a cash budget.*

4. *State the sources of the items appearing on a typical budgeted balance sheet and derive the items on a simple budgeted balance sheet from related budgets.*

5. *Explain why managers establish a minimum-cash-balance policy.*

6. *Explain how the cash budget for a manufacturer differs from that for a retailer.*

7. *Describe the basic technique managers use to develop annual and long-term budgets.*

8. *Explain why long-term planning focuses managers' attention on financing decisions.*

9. *Describe some similarities and differences between the budgeting processes in for-profit and not-for-profit entities.*

10. *State how zero-based budgeting and program budgeting differ from the budgeting processes illustrated in Chapters 6 and 7.*

6

You have now been introduced to some of the basic elements of the budgeting process. What follows is a continuation of the story of **Grandmother Calendar Company**, *the subject of the opening vignette in Chapter 6. Before reading further, you should review the company's story, which begins on page 246.*

After the demise of **Grandmother's**, *Harry Harris, the company's founder, told a reporter for the* Daily Oklahoman:

I'm not an attorney; I'm not an accountant. I made mistakes and did not track receivables, payables, and funding. I should have made, well, better decisions.

5

Is Harris correct? Did he make bad decisions because he did not track receivables, payables, and funding? Not really.

As we pointed out in Chapter 5, decision-making involves collecting relevant information and developing expectations about the consequences of a decision. A decision isn't necessarily bad just because results differ from expectations, because unpredictable changes in circumstances influence results. The key word is expectations. *Mr. Harris and other managers at* **Grandmother's** *neglected to develop expectations before taking actions. Hence, they could not readily recognize when results suggested the need for changes in plans.*

Moreover, **Grandmother's** *managers mistakenly viewed the company's many business activities—setting prices and credit policies, selecting production facilities, acquiring financing, signing up customers, producing kits, selling kits, personalizing calendars, paying bills, collecting cash—as unrelated. Prices and credit policies influenced cash flows; the number of sales outlets for kits influenced likely kit-production-needs; sales of kits influenced the inflow of orders for personalized calendars and the facilities and personnel needed to accommodate those orders, and those needs influenced cash flows.*

Budgeting forces managers to develop expectations about their actions. A comprehensive budget brings expectations together to test for conflicts before *the conflicts create a crisis. Identifying problems before they occur is better, especially if those problems are inherent in managers' decisions and would be revealed in the process of developing a budget.*

Source: Developed from "A Company Failing From Too Much Success," Louise Lee, The Wall Street Journal, March 27, 1995, A1, B2.

6 Chapter 6 introduced comprehensive budgeting and some of the major concepts of budgeting, and illustrated the preparation of the operating budgets in the total budget package. Financial budgets are at least as important to the package. This chapter completes the illustration by developing the cash budget and pro forma balance sheet.

We also show how financial statement data are used in the preparation of annual budgets and long-term budgets. Finally, we look at some of the special issues associated with budgeting in not-for-profit entities.

COMPLETION OF ILLUSTRATION—A RETAILER (CRANE COMPANY)

6 In Chapter 6 we prepared the budgeted income statement and purchases budget for Crane Company for the first six months of 19X4. We now proceed to the cash budget for the period and the **pro forma balance sheet** (budgeted balance sheet) at June 30, 19X4.

Exhibit 7-1 shows Crane's balance sheet at December 31, 19X3, the beginning of the six months the managers are planning for. We need the balance sheet at the beginning of the budget period because it shows (1) the resources (assets) already available for use during the budget period and (2) the existing liabilities that must be considered for payment during the budget period. For example, we needed (and used) the inventory figure at December 31 when preparing the purchases budget in Chapter 6.

For ease of reference, we reproduce in Exhibit 7-2 the pro forma income statements and the purchases budgets from Chapter 6 (Exhibits 6-6 and 6-7).

CASH BUDGET

A **cash budget** shows total cash receipts, total cash disbursements, and expected cash balances at various dates, and incorporates loans needed to cover temporary cash deficits. The cash budget is supported by at least one budget schedule for receipts and one budget schedule for disbursements. To identify temporary cash deficits, a company prepares a *tentative* cash budget, and our illustration follows that practice. We begin preparing Crane's cash budget by looking at cash receipts.

Cash Receipts
Crane receives cash when it collects from customers for sales, so preparing a cash receipts budget requires reference to the sales budget. But we need more information, because sales are not necessarily cash flows. Does Crane sell on credit or for cash only? When do credit customers pay their accounts? Assume that experience—adjusted, of course, for any expected changes in conditions—indicates that 20 percent of sales are collected in the month of sale, 48 percent in the month after sale, and the remaining 32 percent in the second month after sale. (Notice that the Accounts Receivable at December 31, 19X3, in Exhibit 7-1 reflects the lag in collecting cash for sales, with $176 and $400 due from November and December sales, respectively.)

Exhibit 7-1 Crane Company Balance Sheet at December 31, 19X3

Assets		Equities	
Cash	$ 60	Accounts payable (merchandise)	$ 360
Accounts receivable:		Accrued expenses	50
Dec. sales	400	Total liabilities	410
Nov. sales	176		
Inventory	600	Common stock	1,000
Plant and equipment, net	600	Retained earnings	426
Total	$1,836	Total	$1,836

Exhibit 7-2 Crane Company, Income Statements and Purchases Budget

Budgeted Income Statements for the Six Months Ending June 30, 19X4

	Jan.	Feb.	Mar.	Apr.	May	June	Six Months
Sales	$400	$600	$800	$1,000	$1,200	$800	$4,800
Cost of goods sold (60% of sales)	240	360	480	600	720	480	2,880
Gross profit	$160	$240	$320	$ 400	$ 480	$320	$1,920
Other variable costs (15% of sales)	60	90	120	150	180	120	720
Contribution margin	$100	$150	$200	$ 250	$ 300	$200	$1,200
Fixed costs (depreciation, rent, etc.)	40	40	40	40	40	40	240
Income	$ 60	$110	$160	$ 210	$ 260	$160	$ 960

Purchases Budget for the Six Months Ending June 30, 19X4

	Jan.	Feb.	Mar.	Apr.	May	June	Six Months
Cost of sales for month	$ 240	$ 360	$ 480	$ 600	$ 720	$ 480	$2,880
Ending inventory required	840	1,080	1,320	1,200	900	900	900
Total requirements	$1,080	$1,440	$1,800	$1,800	$1,620	$1,380	$3,780
Beginning inventory	600	840	1,080	1,320	1,200	900	600
Purchases required	$ 480	$ 600	$ 720	$ 480	$ 420	$ 480	$3,180

We now can determine cash inflows for the six months. Exhibit 7-3 is a good general format for budgeting cash receipts from sales. The first line, expected sales, comes from the pro forma income statements (Exhibit 7-2). The circled items show the pattern of collection of January sales; the total is given below the schedule. Notice that an increase in cash receipts accompanies the increase in sales. But there is a lag (delay). Except for January, the cash receipts for a month do not equal or exceed sales until June, when sales have already declined. By June, collections are being made from the prior months in which sales were considerably higher.

If, as is usually the case, a company pays cash to stock goods in advance of sales, but collects cash well after the point of sale, it can run out of cash while sales are rapidly increasing. That situation, which is commonly experienced by growth companies, will be more obvious when we examine cash disbursements. The uncollected portion of sales from May and June will appear as an *asset* (Accounts Receivable) on Crane's balance sheet as of June 30, 19X4.

Exhibit 7-3 Cash Receipts

	Jan.	Feb.	Mar.	Apr.	May	June	Six Months
Sales for the month	$ 400ᵃ	$ 600	$ 800	$1,000	$1,200	$ 800	$4,800
Collections from Sales							
20% of total sales for the month	$ 80	$ 120	$ 160	$ 200	$ 240	$ 160	$ 960
48% of prior month's sales	240	192	288	384	480	576	2,160
32% of second prior month's sales	176	160	128	192	256	320	1,232
Total cash collections	$ 496	$ 472	$ 576	$ 776	$ 976	$1,056	$4,352

a $400 = total January sales, collected in January, February, and March ($80 + $192 + $128).

Cash Disbursements—Purchases

Crane Company's major cash disbursement is for purchases. To determine cash disbursements for purchases, we need more than the purchases budget reproduced in Exhibit 7-2; we need to know the timing of disbursements for those purchases. In the unlikely event that a company pays for goods on delivery, cash disbursements for purchases equal purchases in each month. Suppose, however, that Crane Company takes advantage of the 30-day credit terms extended by its suppliers so that Crane pays for purchases in the month after purchase. (If Crane used 60-day credit, it would pay in the second month after purchase, and so on.)

To derive cash disbursements for purchases, we need only lag payments a month behind purchases, as in Exhibit 7-4. The January payment is for December purchases, which are Accounts Payable at December 31, 19X3 (from Exhibit 7-1). The other amounts come from the purchases budget reproduced in Exhibit 7-2. Purchases are paid for in the month after purchase. Accordingly, Accounts Payable at the end of any month equal that month's purchases, and cash disbursements (for purchases) in any month equal Accounts Payable at the end of the prior month.

Exhibit 7-4 Cash Disbursements for Purchases

	Jan.	Feb.	Mar.	Apr.	May	June	Six Months
Budgeted purchases	$480	$600	$720	$480	$420	$480	$3,180
Payments	$360	$480	$600	$720	$480	$420	$3,060

Cash Disbursements—Other

We can determine disbursements for other than purchases more easily than those for purchases. You will remember that Crane's expenses include variable costs other than cost of sales and some fixed costs. We need to know the payment practices related to those costs.

Variable costs other than cost of sales are 15 percent of sales. Assume that one-third is paid in the month of incurrence, and two-thirds in the following month. (The portion paid in the month after incurrence could be a 10 percent commission to salespersons, who are paid the commission one month after it is earned.) Thus, in each month, cash disbursements related to variable costs are 5 percent of that month's sales, plus 10 percent of the previous month's sales. A schedule of disbursements, by month, for those variable costs appears in Exhibit 7-5.

The $690 total cash disbursements for variable costs for the six months does not equal the $720 variable costs on the income statement for the six-month period (Exhibit 7-2) because of the timing of the payments. The financial accounting concept of accrued expenses explains that difference. Of the January disbursements, $50 was accrued in December of 19X3 and is not an expense of 19X4. At June 30, 19X4, Crane owes $80 for commissions on June sales of $800. Crane must pay for June commissions in July. The $80 to be paid in July will appear as a *liability* (Accrued Expenses) on Crane's pro forma balance sheet at June 30.

Suppose that the cash component of fixed costs is paid evenly over the six-month period. Of the $240 fixed costs, depreciation, a noncash expense, is $120 ($20 per month × 6), so the cash portion is $120 ($240 - $120), or $20 per month. The *complete* cash disbursements budget shown in Exhibit 7-6 includes the disbursements from Exhibits 7-4 and 7-5.

Tentative Cash Budget

The data developed thus far are combined in the tentative cash budget, shown in Exhibit 7-7. The budget is tentative because we won't know, until after preparing this schedule, whether revisions might be necessary to avoid potential cash shortages.

The last column in Exhibit 7-7 covers the entire six-month period, so the beginning balance is the balance at December 31, 19X3. Although Crane will complete the period with much more cash than it had at the start, the budget

---

Exhibit 7-5   Cash Disbursements—Variable Costs

	Jan.	Feb.	Mar.	Apr.	May	June	Six Months
5% current month's sales	$20	$30	$ 40	$ 50	$ 60	$ 40	$240
10% previous month's sales	50[a]	40	60	80	100	120	450
Total	$70	$70	$100	$130	$160	$160	$690

a December accrued expenses, from December 31, 19X3, balance sheet (Exhibit 7-1).

Exhibit 7-6   Cash Disbursements—All Costs

	Jan.	Feb.	Mar.	Apr.	May	June	Six Months
For purchases (Exhibit 7-4)	$360	$480	$600	$720	$480	$420	$3,060
Variable costs (Exhibit 7-5)	70	70	100	130	160	160	690
Fixed costs	20	20	20	20	20	20	120
Total	$450	$570	$720	$870	$660	$600	$3,870

reveals cash deficits in March and April (and a balance of only $8 at the end of February) if all goes according to plan. Had we prepared a budget only for the entire six-month period, Crane's managers wouldn't have been on notice to make plans for dealing with the temporary cash problem. As we noted in Chapter 6, an important purpose of breaking down cash budgets into relatively short periods is to reveal such temporary problems.

What will Crane's managers do now? They will consider borrowing cash to tide the company over the period during which the deficits appear. They might reconsider the inventory policy, which could mean delaying purchases and consequently delaying the needs for cash payments. They could also consider making policy changes that would accelerate cash collections. But note that both types of policy changes might adversely affect sales. Whatever Crane's managers decide to do to avoid the temporary cash deficits, some portions of previous budgets will require revision. We shall assume Crane's managers decide to offset the expected cash deficiencies with short-term borrowing.

Revised Budgets

When Crane's managers decide to borrow to offset the expected cash deficiencies, the cash budget must be revised to reflect the borrowings and the

Exhibit 7-7   Tentative Cash Budget

	Jan.	Feb.	Mar.	Apr.	May	June	Six Months
Beginning balance	$ 60[a]	$106	$ 8	$(136)	$(230)	$ 86	$ 60
Collections (Exhibit 7-3)	496	472	576	776	976	1,056	4,352
Total available	$556	$578	$ 584	$ 640	$ 746	$1,142	$4,412
Disbursements (Exhibit 7-6)	450	570	720	870	660	600	3,870
Ending balance (deficit)	$106	$ 8	$(136)	$(230)	$ 86	$ 542	$ 542

a From December 31, 19X3, balance sheet (Exhibit 7-1).

repayments (including interest). We shall assume Crane can borrow at 12 percent under the following conditions:

- Borrowings occur at the beginning of the month cash is needed;
- Borrowings and repayments are in $10 increments;
- Repayments occur at the ends of the months that a budgeted surplus of cash is available;
- Interest is paid at the time of repayments, but only for the amounts repaid.

Assume also that Crane has a policy of maintaining a minimum cash balance of $50 at all times. (More about such policies later.) A revised cash budget appears in Exhibit 7-8.

Because of interest expense, we must revise the pro forma income statement for the six-month period. Exhibit 7-9 shows the revised budgeted income statement for that period. The exhibit also includes a separate pro forma income statement for the first three months of the period, so that you can check your understanding and because a company normally prepares pro forma statements more frequently than once every six months.

Exhibit 7-8   Revised Cash Budget

		Jan.	Feb.	Mar.	Apr.	May	June	Six Months
	Beginning balance	$ 60	$106	$ 58	$ 54	$ 50	$ 78	$ 60
	Collections	496	472	576	776	976	1,056	4,352
	Total available	$ 556	$ 578	$ 634	$ 830	$1,026	$1,134	$4,412
	Disbursements	450	570	720	870	660	600	3,870
(1)	Indicated balance	$ 106	$ 8	$ (86)	$ (40)	$ 366	$ 534	$ 542
(2)	Minimum required cash	50	50	50	50	50	50	50
1−2 = (3)	Excess (deficit)	$ 56	$ (42)	$(136)	$ (90)	$ 316	$ 484	$ 492
(4)	Borrowings		50	140	90			280
(5)	Repayments					(280)		(280)
	Interest					(8)[a]		(8)
4 + 1 − 5 = (6)	Ending balance	$ 106	$ 58	$ 54	$ 50	$ 78	$ 534	$ 534
	Cumulative borrowing		$ 50	$ 190	$ 280	$—0—	$—0—	

a 12% × 4/12 (four months) × $50 = $2.00
   12% × 3/12 (three months) × $140 = 4.20
   12% × 2/12 (two months) × $90 = 1.80
                                      $8.00

Exhibit 7-9   Crane Company, Budgeted Income Statements

	Three Months Ending March 31, 19X4	Six Months Ending June 30, 19X4
Sales	$1,800	$4,800
Cost of goods sold (60% of sales)	1,080	2,880
Gross profit	$ 720	$1,920
Other variable costs (15% of sales)	270	720
Contribution margin	$ 450	$1,200
Fixed operating costs	120	240
Operating income	$ 330	$ 960
Interest expense	2.40[a]	8
Income	$ 327.60	$ 952

a At March 31, loans were outstanding for $190. Accrued interest was:

$$\$50 \times 2/12 \times 12\% = \$1.00$$
$$\$140 \times 1/12 \times 12\% = \underline{1.40}$$

Total accrued interest and interest expense $\underline{\$2.40}$

PRO FORMA BALANCE SHEET

A pro forma balance sheet for June 30 is shown in Exhibit 7-10. We also include a pro forma balance sheet at an interim date—March 31—to facilitate your understanding and to recognize normal practice. As we've already explained, the amounts shown for cash in the balance sheets come from the revised cash budgets; balances for Inventory and Accounts Payable come from the purchases budgets. The balances for Accounts Receivable and Accrued Expenses are *derived* from the cash receipts budget and the cash disbursements budgets, respectively. The balances for Plant and Equipment and Retained Earnings are derived from the pro forma income statements and the balance sheet at December 31, 19X3 (Exhibit 7-1). Overall, then, developing and understanding a pro forma balance sheet requires a thorough understanding of the accrual basis of accounting.

One important reason for having pro forma statements (income statement and balance sheet) prior to the end of the six-month period is that the company's managers plan to obtain a short-term loan. A potential lender will want information to help it decide whether Crane can repay the loan and will be interested in whether its managers make good use of budgets. A lender will want to see monthly cash budgets and pro forma statements at least each quarter, if not each month. Later, managers (and lenders) can compare the actual balance sheets at March 31 and June 30 with the pro forma ones to see whether operations are proceeding as planned. For example, suppose the sales forecast proves accurate but Accounts Receivable are higher than budgeted. If customers are paying later than anticipated, Crane still could run into a cash shortage. Increasing receivables might also be a sign that the company is extending credit to less worthy customers in order to meet its sales goals. In that case, bad debts might result, and the need for financing might increase as well.

Exhibit 7-10   Crane Company, Pro Forma Balance Sheets

Assets	As of March 31, 19X4	As of June 30, 19X4
Cash (from cash budget, Exhibit 7-8)	$ 54	$ 534
Accounts receivable (credit sales for month plus 32% of prior month's credit sales)	832	1,024
Inventory (from purchases budget, Exhibit 7-2)	1,320	900
Plant and equipment (beginning balance less depreciation for 3 and 6 months)	540	480
Total assets	$2,746	$2,938
Equities		
Accounts payable (from purchases budget, Exhibit 7-2)	$ 720	$ 480
Accrued expenses (10% of the month's sales)	80	80
Short-term loan (from cash budget, Exhibit 7-8)	190	0
Accrued interest on loan (Exhibit 7-9)	2.40	0
Common stock (beginning balance sheet, Exhibit 7-1)	1,000	1,000
Retained earnings (beginning balance plus income for period)	753.60	1,378
Total equities	$2,746	$2,938

CONCLUDING COMMENTS

 At this point it is useful to return to the overview presented early in Chapter 6 of the relationships among the components of a comprehensive budget. For your convenience, the relevant exhibit from Chapter 6 is reproduced in Exhibit 7-11. As you've now seen, comprehensive budgeting combines basic ideas from both financial and managerial accounting. From financial accounting come the basic financial statements and the accrual concept; from managerial accounting come the emphasis on the future and the need to understand cost behavior. The result is an integrated set of schedules that reflects the expected outcomes of decisions made by managers for planning purposes. We now can point out some other advantages of budgeting and some important items that are missing from our illustration.

The cash budget and pro forma balance sheets are a basis for asset management. Managers can see that an excess amount of cash becomes available at the end of June and begin to look for profitable uses for this cash. At the very least, the company can buy marketable securities such as government bonds and earn safe, though low, returns.

Knowing well in advance when the company will need extra cash, its managers are more likely to be able to find financing to carry the company over the months in which deficits are budgeted. The managers will be able to explain

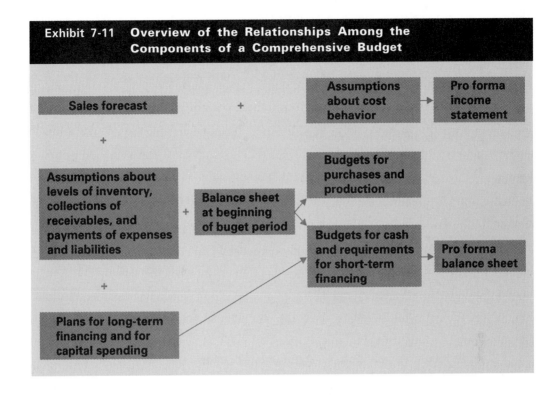

Exhibit 7-11 Overview of the Relationships Among the Components of a Comprehensive Budget

to potential lenders both (1) why the company needs the money and (2) how a loan will be repaid. A company that doesn't seek a loan until its cash balance is precariously low may have to pay a higher interest rate—or may not get a loan on any terms.

Our example is much simpler than is the case in practice. If some portion of Crane's credit sales will never be collected, its receipts budget will reflect only the expected collections. There could be other receipts, such as for interest or dividends on investments. Other cash-disbursement items are also likely, as when a company must make periodic interest payments, repayments of outstanding debt, and perhaps dividend payments. And payment schedules for expenses are likely to be far more complex than those in the example. (For example, fixed costs such as property taxes and insurance are usually paid quarterly or semiannually.)

Perhaps the single most commonly found item missing from our example is disbursements for new long-lived assets. Because such expenditures are usually relatively large, their inclusion is critical if the budget is to fulfill its functions of identifying the timing of financial needs and providing a realistic picture of planned activities. Incorporating the expenditures for major investments into the cash budget is simple once managers have decided what investments are to be made. Making those decisions is not quite so simple, and the next two chapters introduce the analyses that managers use to make them. At this point, you need only recognize that a company's budget is not complete without including budgeted expenditures for new long-lived assets, as well as the means for financing those expenditures.

MINIMUM-CASH-BALANCE POLICIES

For our illustration of budgeting cash for Crane Company we assumed a desire to carry a minimum cash balance of $50. Many companies adopt a policy of maintaining a **minimum cash balance** at all times. The widely publicized efforts of **Tracinda Corporation** to purchase control of **Chrysler Corporation** in the mid-1990s focused attention on the question of how much cash is "enough." (See the accompanying Insight.)

 **IN** *SIGHT*

Tracinda Corporation, which is wholly owned by Mr. Kirk Kerkorian, became **Chrysler's** largest single shareholder in 1990. In a November 1994 letter to Chrysler's Board of Directors, Mr. Kerkorian expressed disappointment with the price performance of the company's stock and with the Board's failure to take actions that would increase the stock's price. He noted that managers "continued to accumulate significant amounts of cash" and recommended that the Board:

- undertake a substantial stock repurchase program;
- effect a 2-for-1 stock split; and
- raise the quarterly dividend on common stock.

Mr. Kerkorian also stated his intention to increase his ownership position and asked the Board to eliminate a corporate policy that made it financially unsound for anyone to attempt to own 10 percent or more of the company's stock. (The specific ownership percentage could vary from one company to another, but such a policy is commonly called a "poison pill.")

Shortly thereafter, **Chrysler's** Board announced the following:

- a 60 percent increase in the annual dividend;
- a 10 percent increase in planned capital expenditures over the $1.2 billion announced for the next five years;
- a $1 billion stock repurchase program; and
- an increase from 10 percent to 15 percent of the ownership level that would trigger the company's poison pill.

At the same time, the Board renewed its commitment to maintaining cash reserves "adequate to fund [**Chrysler's**] business going forward regardless of business cycles, maintaining fully-funded pension plans, and reducing overall financial leverage."

On April 12, 1995, **Tracinda** publicly announced an offer to buy all the remaining outstanding shares of **Chrysler's** common stock. Simultaneously, Chrysler's Board reiterated its belief in the need for adequate cash reserves to finance operations and pursue product development despite downturns in the business cycle. The Board said the proposed buyout plan "contemplated reducing Chrysler's cash reserves by 70%. . . ." The press release after the Board

rejected the buyout offer quoted Chrysler's Chief Executive Officer, Robert Eaton, as follows:

> **Chrysler** does not accumulate cash needlessly. Our accumulated cash reserves were set after careful study of what is necessary to remain globally competitive, especially during the cyclical downturns that affect our business from time to time.
>
> We review our need and our target periodically in light of changing business conditions. Our current cash reserve target is $7.5 billion. To the extent that the Company generates cash in excess of that target, and after taking into account opportunities for investment in our core business and changes in business conditions, **Chrysler** plans to use the excess to create additional shareholder value, through share repurchases or increased dividends.

Mr. Kerkorian claimed that **Chrysler's** after-buyout cash reserves would be $4 billion, which would be adequate, he said, given that Chrysler needed only that much over the three-year downturn ended in 1991. (To meet its cash needs during that period, Chrysler disposed of some assets and issued new stock at a very low price.)

In May of 1995, **Chrysler's** Board announced yet another increase (25%) in its annual dividend. Eaton pointed to weaker-than-expected sales during 1995 and a downward revision in the sales forecast for the year, and emphasized the need for setting a dividend level the company could maintain in good and bad times. In June, **Tracinda** announced its intent to increase its equity interest to just short of 15 percent.

While **Chrysler** was building its cash reserves, both **Ford** and **General Motors** were pursuing a similar cash-retention strategy. Ford's cash-reserve goal was $18 billion, GM's was $15 billion, and both companies were about $5 billion short of their goals in March 1995. One investment advisor supported the auto-makers' needs for huge cash reserves: "They earn $9.50 a share one year and nothing the next. They need the money for the rainy day when it comes." Another noted that the cash-reserve goals of the U.S. auto-makers were far less conservative than those of **Toyota Motor Co.**, whose reserves exceeded $26 billion when Japan's economy was still in a deep recession at the end of 1994.

Whoever's judgment about the needed level of cash reserves was best, **Chrysler's** stockholders (including Mr. Kerkorian) benefitted from the dispute. Per-share cash dividends increased 233 percent in 17 months, and the price of the company's stock rose from the low $40s in March of 1995 to settle in the mid-$50s by the end of the year.

Sources: The primary source for this selective summary of the buyout battle was the June 27, 1995 public document covering Tracinda's offer to buy 14,000,000 shares of Chrysler stock. Other sources include the following: Dave Kansas and Randall Smith, "How Much Cash a Firm Should Keep Is at Issue In Wake of Chrysler Bid," The Wall Street Journal, *April 20, 1995, A1, A7; Robert L. Simison, "A Mountain of Cash is Rising in Detroit as Big Three Build Recession Cushion,"* The Wall Street Journal, *April 28, 1995, A14; Oscar Sures, "Chrysler Plans to Build $1 Billion Plant for Advanced Truck Transmission Line,"* The Wall Street Journal, *August 11, 1995, A2; and David Woodruff and Ronald Grover, "Chrysler: The Inside Story,"* Business Week, *May 15, 1995, 40-2.*

Financial managers devote considerable attention to determining the needed minimum level of cash. As with most decisions, a trade-off between two conflicting factors is involved. On the one hand, a company doesn't want to run out of cash. The lower the minimum required balance, the greater the probability of that happening, if for no other reason than that budgeting involves estimates. (Customers might pay more slowly than expected or cash outflows might be higher.) On the other hand, idle cash earns little or no return. The higher the minimum cash balance, the higher the opportunity cost because the company could invest the cash elsewhere to earn additional income, save interest costs by retiring outstanding debt, or perhaps raise dividends. In deciding on a reasonable compromise, the financial manager must weigh carefully the conflicting objectives.

There are some sophisticated techniques, as well as some generally accepted rules, for approaching the problem of determining an optimal minimum cash balance. Financial management courses discuss the topic of determining minimum cash balances. For now it is enough to say that many firms set a policy of carrying cash equal to, for example, budgeted cash disbursements for the coming two weeks or months. Under such a policy, the minimum required balances change, depending on budgeted receipts and disbursements.

CASH BUDGET FOR A MANUFACTURER (BRANDON COMPANY)

Crane Company, the company in the illustration, is a retailer. Chapter 6 showed that developing a budget for a manufacturer is more complex than for a nonmanufacturer, but that the principles are virtually the same. For example, as we showed in Chapter 6, the production budget for Brandon Company, a manufacturer, is very similar to the purchases budget for a retailer. If we know when the costs of production are paid, we can easily compute cash requirements for production. Let us continue the example started on page 273 with Brandon showing a production budget (Exhibit 6-8) as follows.

Month	Production
January	210
February	285
March	320

Production costs are as follows: materials at $4 per unit, other variable costs at $4 per unit, and fixed costs of $1,900 per month.

Suppose Brandon is a JIT manufacturer (rather than a conventional manufacturer) and so acquires materials as it needs them and keeps no inventory of materials and components. Neither the JIT philosophy, nor having zero inventory, implies anything about the timing of payments for purchases. So, let us assume also that Brandon pays for materials in the month after purchase and pays other cash production costs in the month incurred. Assume further that December production was 300 units. The cash disbursements budget for manufacturing costs appears in Exhibit 7-12. The details of this schedule will become part of the company's overall cash disbursements budget, which will feed into Brandon's cash budget. The remainder of the budget package will be completed accordingly.

Exhibit 7-12 Brandon Company, Cash Disbursements for Manufacturing Costs, January, February, and March, 19X4			
	Jan.	Feb.	Mar.
Production*	210	285	320
Cash disbursements:			
Materials ($4 × prior month's production)	$1,200	$ 840	$1,140
Other variable costs ($4 × current production)	840	1,140	1,280
Fixed costs	1,900	1,900	1,900
Total	$3,940	$3,880	$4,320

* Exhibit 6-8 (page 274)

A quick glance back to the overview of the relationships among the components of a budget (Exhibit 7-11) confirms that there is no difference in principle between the budgets for a retailer and for a manufacturer. In practice, the manufacturer's cash budget is more complicated. Individual production costs are likely to have different payment schedules, and the materials used for production may have to be purchased in advance of production needs. Normally, a separate materials-purchases budget, such as the one in Exhibit 6-9 (page 274), is the basis for determining cash disbursements for materials.

ANNUAL AND LONG-TERM BUDGETS

To facilitate long-term planning, virtually all companies develop forecasts and budgeted financial statements one year in advance, and most companies do so for two, three, or even four years in the future. As we stated in Chapter 6, the usefulness of a company's forecasts for planning purposes is influenced not only by the abilities of its managers but also by characteristics of the company (including the industry or industries in which it operates).

Some of the industry characteristics critical to the company's ability to make useful forecasts are the rate of technological change, applicable legal protections (e.g., patent laws, regulatory requirements), and product development times. For example, the average sales life of a model of personal computer is about six months, which affects the industry's ability to develop useful forecasts. Developers of software face similar problems because only a small proportion of new software packages is successful and competition demands upgrades of successful packages to maintain revenues. Patent laws enhance the reliability of forecasts by makers of prescription drugs, though product development times of up to 15 years complicate forecasts for products that might replace those whose protection is expiring.

Forecasting difficulties notwithstanding, companies do develop budgeted financial statements one or more years in advance. But for obvious reasons, such financial statements (1) are less detailed than those you've seen thus far and (2) do not involve detailed budgets of cash, production, and purchases.

18▶

Rather, companies develop long-term budgets using techniques of financial statement analysis such as are presented in the introductory course in financial accounting. (Chapter 18 discusses such techniques in some detail.) Budgeted financial statements developed in this way are used to help managers plan the asset requirements for meeting long-term corporate goals and assess the company's need for long-term financing.

ASSET REQUIREMENTS

We've shown how operating and financial budgets relate to each other in the short term. Using budgeted sales and expected relationships of certain assets to sales, we developed budgets of purchases and pro forma balance sheets showing budgeted amounts of cash, accounts receivable, and inventory. What was shown on the asset side of those balance sheets was essentially a statement of *asset requirements* – the amounts of various assets required to meet the company's goals of sales and income. We also said that a company might have to reconsider its sales and profit goals if it could not obtain the financing needed to carry its planned levels of assets.

Managers make similar analyses when developing **long-term budgets**. If the company forecasts increasing sales, it must also plan for the assets needed to support those planned levels of sales. Sales can seldom be increased significantly without providing additional production capacity and allowing receivables to increase somewhat. In some situations, significantly higher sales can't be achieved without stocking more inventory. Moreover, the desired minimum cash balance probably will increase with higher sales volume.

In the long term, expected sales levels tend to dictate the necessary levels of assets. Hence, companies normally use *ratios* of various assets to sales to determine the required amounts of those assets. The ratios used will, of course, incorporate the objectives adopted by management, such as faster turnover of inventories. Recognize, however, that the analyses undertaken and numbers used for long-term budgeting are less precise than when budgeting for the shorter term. Moreover, there is more opportunity for circumstances to change. When developing long-term plans, managers try to allow for changes in general economic conditions, selling prices, purchase costs, and production methods. Such changes are extremely hard to predict over relatively long periods, as are the changes likely to result from efforts to meet stretch goals. (See the accompanying Insight.) The predicted asset requirements in long-term budgets are fairly general, with managers trying to see what the company's needs will be in broad terms. As time passes, managers refine their budgets of asset needs and perhaps undertake actions to reduce those needs.

FINANCING REQUIREMENTS

A company requires financing, in the form of liabilities or stockholders' equity, because it needs assets to generate sales. The need for assets creates *financing requirements* – the need for the items listed on the equity side of the balance sheet. (Items on the equity side of the balance sheet – liabilities and owners' equity – are often referred to as the sources of the assets.) As the need for assets increases because of increased sales, so does the need for sources to finance them. A few sources of financing are available almost automatically. For

SIGHT

As explained in Chapter 6, some companies set stretch goals, goals that can be met only through fundamental changes in the way a task is accomplished. The target dates for meeting stretch goals are often two or more years away (e.g., **Boeing's** goal to cut production time 50 percent in four years). Meeting a stretch goal could involve a single major breakthrough or a number of less significant changes. Steps taken to meet a goal are likely to change the company's cost structure and often require investments in new assets.

Being unable to predict likely changes in cost structure is less important to long-term planning than to short-term planning, because long-term plans rely on income goals, not on details of the income statement. The broad approach that managers use to developing long-term plans more easily accommodates the uncertainty about how efforts to meet a stretch target will affect asset requirements.

Source: Shawn Tully, "Why To Go For Stretch Targets," Fortune, *November 14, 1994, 145-6, 148, 150, 154, 158.*

example, most companies buy merchandise on credit. A vendor who extends credit is, in effect, providing a short-term loan—a source of financing. Similarly, when an entity earns income and does not distribute assets to its owners in an amount equal to net income, retained earnings increase. Thus, increases in retained earnings are also sources of financing.

Few businesses can meet all of their financing needs through funds provided by operations and trade creditors. If a company uses short-term loans too liberally, and its current ratio (current assets/current liabilities) gets too low, trade creditors will become increasingly reluctant to extend credit and potential suppliers of new short-term loans may not appear. Thus, growing businesses will need to seek long-term financing.

For long-term financing, companies issue additional stock or take on long-term debt. They can also lease assets. A growing business generally requires higher and higher levels of assets to support its increased sales and so needs more financing than one that is not growing. We've already noted that a company not able to obtain the loan needed to support its short-term requirements might have to scale down its purchases of goods, and that this could, in turn, reduce sales and profits. The same situation occurs in long-term budgeting— a company might not be able to obtain the long-term financing to support the asset levels necessary to reach the projected sales levels.

Managers know that obtaining short- and long-term financing requires advance planning. Potential providers of short-term loans consider the balance of current assets and current liabilities to be important. The focus of interest for potential long-term lenders is the balance between long-term debt and equity capital. Those lenders are likely to expect a borrower to maintain the ratio of long-term debt to equity (long-term liabilities/stockholders' equity) below some particular level, with the maximum level of the ratio being dependent on various characteristics of the borrower. Hence, a company must first study its long-term financing needs *as a whole*, and then pursue specific types and sources of long-term financing with those expectations in mind. The increasing globalization of business has multiplied the available sources of financing, both short term and long term, but has also complicated the decision about which source to use. (See the accompanying Insight.)

ILLUSTRATIONS OF ANNUAL AND LONGER-TERM BUDGETS

Two types of procedures are used in budgeting for long periods: those that are used for a one-year period and those that are more appropriate for three- to five-year periods broken down into annual periods. Differences between the two types are primarily matters of detail; the composition of assets and equities for a one-year budget is more detailed than that for longer periods.

ANNUAL BUDGETS (STRAND COMPANY)

Strand Company, a manufacturer of electrical equipment, had the following income statement for 19X3.

IN SIGHT

As a general rule, businesses benefit from having more potential sources of capital. Choosing a financing source is more complicated when some of the sources are outside the boundaries of a company's "home country," and even companies doing no significant amount of business outside their home country often look at nondomestic sources of funds. When nondomestic sources of funds are available, the financial managers' choice of a source is affected by additional factors such as their expectations about exchange rates and inflation and their willingness to take on risk.

For example, the interest rate for borrowing in a country with a high rate of inflation will incorporate the *lender's* expectations about the inflation rate, which might or might not agree with the *borrower's* expectation. Similarly, borrowers and lenders, if from different countries, might disagree in their expectations about future exchange rates. Moreover, the financial markets have developed some financial instruments (agreements) that could have the effect of balancing the risks associated with engaging in transactions that involve more than one country's currency. Thus, we cannot say, without reservation, that it is better to borrow in the U.S. at a 10 percent interest rate than in Argentina at a 40 percent rate. You will be introduced to the critical factors affecting international capital transactions in your course in financial management.

Source: Gregory J. Millman, "Currency Risk at Monsanto," Management Accounting, *April 1991,* 43.

Strand Company, Income Statement for 19X3

Sales	$800,000
Variable costs at 60%	480,000
Contribution margin	$320,000
Fixed costs	240,000
Income	$ 80,000

Strand's balance sheet at the end of 19X3 follows. We include the percentages of current assets and current liabilities to sales of the same year because we will use them to develop the December 31, 19X4, pro forma balance sheet.

Strand Company, Balance Sheet at December 31, 19X3

Assets			Percentage of Sales
Cash		$ 40,000	5.0
Accounts receivable		120,000	15.0
Inventory		60,000	7.5
Total current assets		$220,000	27.5
Plant and equipment, net		600,000	
Total assets		$820,000	
Equities			
Current liabilities		$ 80,000	10.0
Long-term liabilities		100,000	
Total liabilities		$180,000	
Common stock	$500,000		
Retained earnings	140,000	640,000	
Total equities		$820,000	

Strand's managers forecast a 10 percent increase in sales for 19X4. They expect current assets and current liabilities at the end of 19X4 to bear the same percentage relationships to sales that they did at the end of 19X3. They also expect variable costs to be the same percentage of sales as they were in 19X3 and total fixed costs to increase to $260,000. They budget net plant and equipment at $720,000 at the end of 19X4. (The budgeted level of plant and equipment will have taken into consideration planned acquisitions incorporated in Strand's capital budget. As you will see in Chapters 8 and 9, the acceptability of new investments in long-term assets is evaluated *without regard to the specific means by which those investments will be financed*.) Strand's managers do not expect to declare a dividend in 19X4.

The budgeted income statement for 19X4 is needed for us to determine retained earnings, a significant source of financing, at the end of 19X4.

Strand Company, Budgeted Income Statement for 19X4

Sales ($800,000 × 110%)	$880,000
Variable costs at 60%	528,000
Contribution margin	$352,000
Fixed costs	260,000
Income	$ 92,000

We now determine the asset requirements at the end of 19X4. In Strand's case, the current assets are simply the percentages of sales from the 19X3 balance sheet multiplied by 19X4 budgeted sales. Of course, managers normally would adjust the percentages to reflect their expectations about changes in economic conditions and company practices. For example, a company moving into JIT operations would plan a lower level of inventory. Or perhaps the company will plan to have a larger amount of cash as part of a program to raise its cash reserves. (Remember the plan at **Chrysler** in the Insight on pages 308-309.)

Assets		Percentage of Sales
Cash	$ 44,000	5.0
Accounts receivable	132,000	15.0
Inventory	66,000	7.5
Total current assets	$242,000	27.5
Plant and equipment, net	720,000	
Total asset requirements	$962,000	

The following schedule shows the financing available to support the asset requirements. Current liabilities are at the same percentage of sales as they were in 19X3. Long-term liabilities and common stock are at their 19X3 levels. Retained earnings is the $140,000 beginning balance plus the $92,000 income budgeted for 19X4.

Equities			Percentage of Sales
Current liabilities		$ 88,000	10.0
Long-term liabilities		100,000	
Total liabilities		$188,000	
Common stock	$500,000		
Retained earnings	232,000	732,000	
Total available equities		$920,000	

The $42,000 difference between Strand's asset requirements ($962,000) and its available equities ($920,000) is called a **financing gap**. What can Strand do about the gap?

Strand's managers have several options. With *no* plans to cover the gap, cash at the end of 19X4 will be $2,000 (the budgeted $44,000 - the $42,000 gap), and the company might be unable to pay a bill when due or to meet a payroll. (Remember the month-to-month differences in cash flows illustrated in Chapter 6.) Alternatively, Strand's managers might plan some actions to reduce current asset requirements. For example, they might change credit terms to require speedier payment of receivables, or they might initiate efforts to reduce inventory levels. They might decide to pay current liabilities more slowly or postpone some of the planned capital expenditures. Strand's managers could decide to cover all or part of the financing gap by using additional financing, either debt or equity, or by leasing some assets.

Each of these actions has potential problems. Reducing asset requirements could hamper the company's ability to generate growth in sales and profits. Slower payment of liabilities could harm Strand's credit rating. Obtaining additional financing might be very costly because of unfavorable conditions in the economy, such as a depressed stock market and/or high interest rates. Strand's managers must evaluate all of the options and decide what risks they are willing to accept.

It is possible, of course, that an analysis of expectations and plans for asset requirements and available equities will reveal that available equities exceed asset requirements. In such cases, managers would begin to plan how to use the excess cash. Some possibilities are paying (or increasing) dividends, reducing long-term debt, accelerating planned capital expenditures, and making other investments.

LONGER-TERM PLANNING (KLEP COMPANY)

In the previous section we prepared a pro forma balance sheet to see whether Strand could meet its objectives for the current year. Doing the same for a longer term usually involves preparing a series of schedules containing summary information about asset requirements and financing available from existing sources. Once again, the long-term goals set by top managers will drive the asset requirements. Hence, as we stated earlier, planning for periods beyond the current year is mostly concerned with developing plans for expanding long-term debt and equity capital to meet financing requirements.

The choice between debt and equity can be critical for the company. Most companies adopt some policy about how much debt they will allow. The policy is often stated as a maximum percentage of long-term liabilities to stockholders' equity, or to total long-term financing (long-term liabilities plus stockholders' equity). The advantages and disadvantages of particular kinds of financing are studied in managerial finance. Here, we say only two things: (1) debt can be risky because failing to meet the periodic interest payments can cause bankruptcy; (2) equity financing is less risky but can lead to lower returns for stockholders.

We illustrate long-term planning by using the following data, assumptions, and policies of Klep Company.

Sales forecast in 19X4	$800,000	Current asset requirements are expected at 30% of sales budgeted for the following year.
19X5	$1,000,000	
19X6	$1,300,000	
19X7	$1,700,000	Net fixed assets expected to be required to meet budgeted sales are 75% of sales budgeted for the following year.
19X8	$2,100,000	

Stockholders' equity
  12/31/X3 $412,000

Net income is expected to be 10% of sales over the period of the forecast.

Dividends of 40% of net income will be paid each year.

Desired current ratio of 3 to 1, so that liabilities cannot exceed one-third of current assets.

Desired ratio of long-term debt to equity of 0.5 to 1 (long-term liabilities cannot exceed 50% of stockholders' equity).

These data are the bases of Exhibits 7-13 and 7-14, which determine year-by-year financing requirements. Exhibit 7-13 shows the analysis for 19X4 and 19X5 and how the numbers were derived. See if you can complete the rest of the table.

Exhibit 7-13 Financing Requirements for Klep Company (in thousands of dollars)

		19X4	19X5	19X6	19X7
	(1) Sales	$800	$1,000	$1,300	$1,700
(1) × 10%	(2) Net income	$ 80	$ 100		
(2) × 40%	(3) Dividends	32	40		
(2) – (3)	(4) Add to stockholders' equity	$ 48	$ 60		
(1) for next year × 30%	(5) Current assets required	$300	$ 390		
(5) ÷ 3	(6) Permissible current liabilities	100	130		
(5) – (6)	(7) Working capital to be financed from long-term sources	$200	$ 260		
(1) for next year × 75%	(8) Net fixed assets required	750	975		
(7) + (8)	(9) Total long-term financing required	$950	$1,235		
	(10) Stockholders' equity [prior year plus (4)]	$460	$ 520		
(10) × 50%	(11) Permissible long-term debt	230	260		
(10) + (11)	(12) Total available long-term financing	$690	$ 780		
(9) – (12)	(13) Additional requirements	$260	$ 455		

(Answers appear in Exhibit 7-14.) Such a schedule gives the manager an idea of future financing needs.

Klep's managers can now direct their efforts to devising a plan for obtaining the financing to satisfy line 13 in the Exhibit (Additional requirements). For several reasons, it is generally expensive and undesirable to seek equity financing frequently. Therefore, Klep's managers might plan to obtain enough funds from issuing common stock in 19X4 to avoid taking on additional debt until 19X8. Funds received in excess of current needs might be invested or used to retire existing debt. As needs become more pressing, additional debt could be issued up to the limit prescribed by the 0.5 to 1 debt/equity ratio.

The primary purpose of the example using Klep Company was to illustrate the *approach* used for long-term planning. You should not assume that any of the relationships used for Klep Company reflect desirable, or even normal relationships. (For example, the planned current asset requirements and current ratio for Klep do not reflect the widespread efforts of recent years to operate with low levels of inventory.)

BUDGETING IN NOT-FOR-PROFIT ENTITIES

Not-for-profit (NFP) entities, especially governmental units, make extensive use of budgeting. But the budgeting process differs significantly from the type

Exhibit 7-14 Financing Requirements for Klep Company (in thousands of dollars)

		19X4	19X5	19X6	19X7
	(1) Sales	$800	$1,000	$1,300	$1,700
(1) × 10%	(2) Net income	$ 80	$ 100	$ 130	$ 170
(2) × 40%	(3) Dividends	32	40	52	68
(2) − (3)	(4) Add to stockholders' equity	$ 48	$ 60	$ 78	$ 102
(1) for next year × 30%	(5) Current assets required	$300	$ 390	$ 510	$ 630
(5) ÷ 3	(6) Permissible current liabilities	100	130	170	210
(5) − (6)	(7) Working capital to be financed from long-term sources	$200	$ 260	$ 340	$ 420
(1) for next year × 75%	(8) Net fixed assets required	750	975	1,275	1,575
(7) + (8)	(9) Total long-term financing required	$950	$1,235	$1,615	$1,995
	(10) Stockholders' equity [prior year plus (4)]	$460	$ 520	$ 598	$ 700
(10) × 50%	(11) Permissible long-term debt	230	260	299	350
(10) + (11)	(12) Total available long-term financing	$690	$ 780	$ 897	$1,050
(9) − (12)	(13) Additional requirements	$260	$ 455	$ 718	$ 945

described earlier. First, such entities are likely to budget only for cash flows (receipts and expenditures), not for revenues and expenses. Second, the process is more likely to begin with expenditures rather than receipts. That is, in most cases, NFPs determine what receipts are required only after they've established the desired (budgeted) level of expenditures. We first suggested such an approach in Chapter 4, when we noted that some governmental units provide services they expect to operate on a break-even basis (e.g., municipal golf courses and swimming pools, and perhaps trash collection services, where users' fees are expected to cover costs).

Budgeting cash receipts for NFPs can be relatively simple or quite complex. Property taxes are the chief source of receipts for school districts and many towns and cities. Such taxes are levied on the basis of the assessed valuation of real property (land and buildings) in the area. Once the total assessed valuation is known, the entity can set the tax rate simply by dividing the desired tax revenues by the assessed valuation. If a school district needs $4,580,000 in tax receipts and the assessed valuation of property in the district is $54,000,000, the rate is 0.08482 ($4,580,000/$54,000,000), which is usually reported as $84.82 per $1,000 of assessed value. Because the desired receipts are determined on the basis of the budgeted expenditures, careful planning and monitoring of budgeted expenditures is especially important in NFPs. Some units of government face a legal requirement that limits the tax-rate increase in any year. Such a requirement can trigger the same reconsideration of plans forced on business enterprises whose asset requirements exceed available financing.

For government units that depend heavily on income and sales taxes, as do most states, determining required tax rates is more complex because estimating receipts requires estimates of total incomes subject to the income tax and of transactions subject to the sales tax. Forecasting methods such as those described in Chapter 6 may be used, and states have developed and used very sophisticated forecasting models.

To budget cash receipts, some NFPs use one or more of the methods already discussed to budget revenues. A not-for-profit private school might use forecasts of contributions and enrollments as a basis for setting tuition rates to cover budgeted costs. A not-for-profit hospital might forecast utilization of its various services to set charges that cover the costs of those services. Many NFPs also engage in activities similar to those of for-profit enterprises. For example, the **National Association of Retired Persons** received more than half of its 1994 revenues from sales of insurance, pharmaceuticals, and other goods and services. Some hospitals operate fitness centers for a profit, and museums often operate an on-site restaurant or gift shop.[1] Any of the methods introduced in Chapter 6 might be used by NFPs to forecast revenues from such enterprises. (Note that the profit-making activities of an NFP are taxable if such activities are not related to the entity's purpose. Deciding whether an activity is related to the entity's purpose is often very difficult for the NFP's managers because the managers know that paying income taxes will reduce the funds devoted to fulfilling the entity's purpose.)

Budget allowances for some cost categories at NFPs can be determined by activity analysis. For example, a university might budget faculty positions by applying some formula based on student enrollment. Thus, an academic department might be given one position for each 300 credit hours of expected enrollment. If an academic department is expected to offer 2,700 credit hours during the coming year, it will be authorized nine positions (2,700/300).

Budgets of government units such as towns, states, school districts, and the federal government usually require voter or legislative approval. Once adopted, such a budget must be strictly adhered to. (In some cases, overspending may even be illegal.) In addition, government units tend to practice **line-by-line approval** when authorizing budgets. That is, specific dollar amounts are authorized for specific categories of expenditures, such as salaries, equipment, supplies, travel, and postage. (The detail in such budgets can be overwhelming, with specified amounts for categories such as Grade II Data Entry Clerks and Grade IV Carpenters.) A budgeting process that includes a line-by-line approval procedure tends to have two major disadvantages in practice.

One problem with the line-by-line approval process is that a manager often has no discretion in using the total budgeted funds to achieve the expected objectives. This inflexibility can lead to actions inconsistent with the entity's objectives. For example, suppose that an accounting instructor in a public university is invited to a seminar on a contemporary accounting topic. The dean and faculty are in favor of the trip, but the travel budget is inadequate to cover the cost. Even if funds remain in the budget allowances for supplies, or telephone or secretarial help, the trip can't be authorized. The problem lies

---

1 Paul Magnusson, "It's Open Season on Nonprofits," *Business Week, July 3, 1995, 31.*

in focusing on individual budget items rather than on the objectives to be accomplished by the budget unit.

Another problem associated with line-by-line approval is that it tends to encourage the setting of current budget allowances based on the prior year's (or an average of prior years') budget allowances or actual expenditures for each item. This general approach is called **incremental budgeting**. Under this approach, each budget unit might be given a 5 percent increase (or decrease) in one or more of its line items. In a somewhat broader application of incremental budgeting, each budget unit might be given a 5 percent increase (or decrease) and allowed to spread the total increase (or decrease) over whatever line items are in the budget. Either variation implies that the increased (or decreased) benefits of changes in one segment of the total entity are equal to the increased (or decreased) benefits of any other segment. Further, when the current budget allowance is based on prior expenditures, managers of budget units are inclined to spend the full allowance in order to avoid a reduction in the budget for the next period. With some regularity, the media have reported particularly interesting examples of such responses to incremental budgeting, as when some segment of government makes an end-of-year purchase of a five-year supply of toilet tissue or wastebaskets.

Neither line-item budgeting nor incremental budgeting is unique to NFPs. Many businesses also use these techniques, especially in areas of discretionary spending. What we referred to in Chapter 6 as "unwise adherence to budgets" includes some actions identified in this section. Indeed, all of the behavioral problems discussed in Chapter 6 apply as well to NFPs.

The variety of nongovernmental NFPs rivals that of for-profit entities, with NFPs ranging from a local church or the PTA at a local school, through the local and national units of the **YMCA** and **YWCA**, to the **American Association of Retired Persons** and the national **Muscular Dystrophy Association**. Recent years have seen increasing attention focused on the activities of government and other NFPs. The next section discusses two alternative budgeting approaches, zero-based budgeting and program budgeting, which have been suggested as possible means of alleviating some of the problems.

ZERO-BASED BUDGETING

Strictly interpreted, **zero-based budgeting** means that managers must justify every dollar they request in a budget proposal for a given year. Past budget allowances are considered irrelevant, and managers must start from scratch to convince higher-level managers that the current request is necessary. In a strict but practical application of the zero-based concept, each budget unit develops its budget request as a series of *decision packages*. The most basic of the unit's services constitutes the first package, and incremental packages represent higher levels of service and/or additional services. A critical aspect of the decision packages is that each is associated with a definable level or quantity of services.

For example, the basic package of the parks department for a city might cover a defined level of maintenance and repair service to keep existing parks open for the hours mandated by the city council. A higher-level package could cover on-site security personnel at selected locations, its benefits being described perhaps in terms of reducing repair costs associated with vandalism. At a much higher level, the department might propose a package for providing blooming plants throughout the year at selected parks.

To evaluate and rank the packages from all units, higher-level managers perform cost-benefit analysis and exercise their judgment about the entity's needs. The final budget might include the basic packages from all budget units, plus some incremental packages. This approach helps to circumvent one of the noted flaws of incremental budgeting—the assumption that increased (or decreased) expenditures in all units are equally beneficial (or harmful) to the entire organization. Moreover, forced managerial review of even the most basic functions of each budget unit may reveal budget units that have outlived their usefulness. That is, after reviewing all the decision packages and considering the quantity of potentially available resources, managers might conclude that the most basic service level of some budget units contributes less to achieving desired goals than do higher-than-basic service levels in other units.

Because a full review of each and every budget request every year is incredibly time-consuming, most organizations require such a review of some, or all, budget units only every few years. But the goals of these periodic reviews are the same as under the more strict application of the zero-based concept: to make sure that there is still a need to spend money for a particular service, and that the money being spent is being spent wisely. State-level *sunset laws*, which require that each program or regulatory agency created by the legislature receive a full, regular review and be dropped if it has served its purpose, are a variation of this second approach to the implementation of zero-based budgeting.

PROGRAM BUDGETING

Program budgeting requires that a budget indicate not only how the requested funds are to be spent, but also why the funds are to be spent. A program budget emphasizes the desired results of the unit's efforts and normally provides the unit's manager with considerable discretion in shifting expenditures from one category to another as long as the shift will increase the likelihood of achieving the desired results. For instance, a traditional budget for a school district shows the objects of the expenditures, such as teachers' salaries, textbooks, and supplies. A program budget for the district shows expenditures by such categories as reading, mathematics, remedial work, student activities, and support services. Similarly, a program budget for a police department might show amounts requested for crime prevention, juvenile work, and detection.

One beneficial feature of program budgeting, when implemented properly, is that managers making budget requests are expected to be able to state clearly what would happen if their requests were cut by, say, 10 percent. Thus, the director of parks and recreation for a city should be in a position to say that such a cut would reduce the hours that a swimming pool would be open or require that grass be cut every ten days instead of once a week. In its result, this feature of program budgeting is similar to what can be accomplished with zero-based budgeting, in that different levels of service are associated with each level of requested funding.

The interest in and use of both program and zero-based budgeting probably owes much to the continually increasing public demand for accountability from NFPs. Taxpayers appear to have become dissatisfied with the performance of some government units, and donors to charitable causes have expressed concern about the proportion of contributed funds devoted to fund-raising and other costs not directly related to fulfilling the charitable objectives of the organization. Program budgets that specify goals allow people to see where their money is going and, eventually, to see whether it was spent effectively. (If a school district requests money "to raise the average reading levels of its pupils," board members can later see whether the levels rose.)

Both program and zero-based budgeting are applicable to business entities as well as NFPs. Corporate executives have, for example, adopted variations of these alternative budgeting approaches for all or some portions of their organizations because of an increasing concern with the productivity of research and development, general administration, and other such activities. In the typical business use, however, program budgets are developed in addition to, rather than as a substitute for, more traditional budgets.

SUMMARY

Comprehensive budgeting brings together and coordinates the plans of many managers and many levels of management. A comprehensive budget is the most conspicuous process of communication within a firm, and facilitates the coordination of major functional areas—production, sales, finance, and administration.

Like operating budgets, financial budgets use forecasts and assumptions about the behavior of the various factors incorporated in them. Financial budgeting involves developing detailed budgets of cash receipts and cash disbursements and a pro forma balance sheet. Cash budgets use data from purchases and expense budgets and from the pro forma income statement. Hence, effective financial budgeting depends on good operational budgeting.

Completion of the tentative cash budget might reveal a need for additional financing and/or reconsideration of established policies. Knowing these needs in advance allows managers time to consider alternatives for meeting the needs.

Pro forma financial statements often are prepared one, two, or more years in advance. Such financial statements are less detailed than those prepared for the near term and result from planning relationships among financial statement items rather than from detailed budgets of cash and purchases. Though such budgets are less precise than those prepared for the short term, they can still assist managers in assessing long-term asset and financing requirements.

Budgeting takes place in not-for-profit entities as well as for-profit businesses. Although many of the same principles apply, there are some differences. The most significant difference is that not-for-profit entities normally budget receipts based on budgeted expenditures, while business entities budget expenditures based on budgeted receipts. Two additional budgeting approaches, program and zero-based budgeting, have been introduced for government units to help offset the tendency in not-for-profit budgeting to concentrate on detailed expenditures rather than on objectives. Businesses also use variations of these approaches.

KEY TERMS

cash budget   (295)   minimum cash balance   (304)
financing gap   (312)   pro forma balance sheet   (295)
incremental budgeting   (317)   program budgeting   (318)
line-by-line approval   (316)   zero-based budgeting   (317)
long-term budgets   (308)

REVIEW PROBLEM

 This problem continues the review problem from Chapter 6. Using the following additional data, prepare a cash budget for January 19X4 and a pro forma balance sheet for January 31, 19X4. Prepare supporting budgets for cash receipts and cash disbursements.

Graham Company, Balance Sheet at December 31, 19X3

Assets		Equities	
Cash	$ 20,000	Accounts payable (for	
Accounts receivable	30,000	merchandise)	$ 12,000
Inventory (6,000 units)	30,000	Common stock	200,000
Building and equipment, net	200,000	Retained earnings	68,000
Total	$280,000	Total	$280,000

(a) Sales are collected 40% in month of sale, 60% in the following month.
(b) Purchases are paid 40% in month of purchase, 60% in the following month.
(c) All other expenses requiring cash are paid in the month incurred.
(d) The board of directors plans to declare a $3,000 dividend on January 10, payable on January 25.
(e) The following budgeted income statement and purchases budget from the solution in Chapter 6 are provided for convenience.

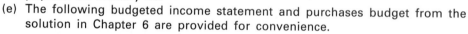

Graham Company, Budgeted Income Statement for January 19X4

Sales		$100,000
Cost of sales		25,000
Gross profit		$ 75,000
Variable costs:		
Commissions	$10,000	
Variable operating expenses	5,000	15,000
Contribution margin		$ 60,000
Fixed costs:		
Depreciation	$ 2,000	
Other operating expenses	40,000	42,000
Budgeted income		$ 18,000

Graham Company, Purchases Budget for January 19X4

	Units	Dollars
Cost of sales	5,000	$25,000
Desired ending inventory	9,000	45,000
Total requirements	14,000	$70,000
Beginning inventory	6,000	30,000
Budgeted purchases	8,000	$40,000

ANSWER TO REVIEW PROBLEM

Graham Company, Cash Budget for January 19X4

Beginning balance	$ 20,000
Receipts (see below)	70,000
Cash available	$ 90,000
Disbursements	86,000
Ending balance	$ 4,000

Graham Company, Cash Receipts Budget for January 19X4

Collection from December sales	$ 30,000
Collection from January sales ($100,000 × 40%)	40,000
Total	$ 70,000

December sales will all be collected by the end of January. Because sales are collected in full by the end of the month following sale, all accounts receivable at the end of a month are expected to be collected in the coming month.

Graham Company, Cash Disbursements Budget for January 19X4

Merchandise [($40,000 × 40%) + $12,000]	$ 28,000
Commissions	10,000
Various operating expenses	45,000
Dividend	3,000
Total	$ 86,000

Graham Company, Pro Forma Balance Sheet as of January 31, 19X4

Assets		Equities	
Cash (cash budget)	$ 4,000	Accounts payable[c]	$ 24,000
Accounts receivable[a]	60,000	Common stock	200,000
Inventory (purchases budget)	45,000	Retained earnings[d]	83,000
Building and equipment[b]	198,000		
Total	$307,000	Total	$307,000

a 60% of January sales of $100,000 (40% was collected in January).
b $200,000 beginning balance less $2,000 depreciation expense.
c 60% of January purchases of $40,000 (40% was paid in January).
d Beginning balance of $68,000 plus budgeted income of $18,000 minus dividend of $3,000.

Notice that cash declined by $16,000 (from $20,000 to $4,000) even though income was $18,000. If Graham's managers believe the budgeted cash balance of $4,000 is too low, they might begin to seek ways to increase that balance (e.g., a short-term bank loan).

ASSIGNMENT MATERIAL

QUESTIONS FOR DISCUSSION

7-1   *Cash budgeting—effects of new information* You are the controller of a large manufacturer and have recently completed the company's cash budget for the coming year. Knowledgeable managers have now given you new information. Considering each item of information independently, indicate (1) whether you expect it to influence your budgets for cash receipts, cash disbursements, or both, and (2) in which direction each budget would be affected. Explain your answers.

(a) The credit manager informs you that customers are not paying their bills as quickly as usual because of high interest rates.

(b) The sales manager informs you that sales should be higher than budgeted because of a strike at the factory of a major competitor.

(c) The purchasing manager informs you that suppliers who have been giving your company 45-day credit are now requiring payment in 30 days.

(d) The vice president of marketing informs you that inventory policy is being changed from the carrying of the next two months' requirements to 80% of the next month's requirements.

7-2   *Publication of budgets* In financial accounting you learned that a company's financial statements are usually distributed to persons outside the company. A comprehensive budgeting program involves the preparation of the same statements using budgeted data, but budgeted financial statements are not normally made available to persons outside the organization. What do you see as the advantages and disadvantages of publishing these budgeted statements as part of a company's annual report?

7-3   *"Something is enough"* The owner of a small chain of shoe stores is dissatisfied with the request from his budget director that he establish a policy regarding a minimum acceptable cash balance. "I see no reason for such a policy," he said. "As long as the monthly budgets show that we can expect to have some cash on hand at the end of the month, why put still another assumption into the budget? There are far too many assumptions in the budget already." Comment on the owner's position.

7-4   *Philanthropy or business sense?* Many public utilities offer "level-payment plans" for their customers. For example, households purchasing natural gas for heating purposes from **CMS Energy Corporation** in Michigan or purchasing electricity from **Texas Utilities** can elect to spread the payments for their purchases over the entire year. The normal plan is for a given month's payment to be 1/12 of the total cost of service provided in the 12 months ending with the current month. Discuss the reasons for a company to offer a level-payment plan.

7-5   *Impact of policy changes on comprehensive budgets* For many years, advertisements for **VanZandt Foods**, a grocery chain, have emphasized the high quality of its produce. The company's top managers have required that local store managers either trash day-old produce or sell it to the highest bidder in the local area. After studying a proposal submitted by the national council of community food banks, VanZandt's top managers decided that directing store managers to donate day-old produce to a local food bank would be in the company's best interests. What aspects of the company's comprehensive budget would be affected by this change in policy?

7-6 Behavior of cash balances and profit Randolph Growing and Harry Declining were talking about the performances of their respective companies in recent months.

Growing: We're making profits hand over fist because of rapid increases in monthly sales. We expected growth and have been keeping our inventories up to meet the increasing demand. But our cash balances have been a problem, and we've borrowed a lot of money lately.

Declining: Things haven't been going as well for us. We have entered our slow season, so sales have been falling. Of course, we knew this would happen and planned accordingly. We aren't making much profit, but do we have cash. Our balance has gone up every month.

Required
Explain why cash is going in the opposite direction from profit for each of these companies.

7-7 "I can't control who pays when." Mark Cable Co. has a franchise to provide cable TV services in a medium-sized city. Mark's owner-president, John Wysocki, tells you he can't budget cash receipts because he can't control when customers pay their bills. Explain how, if at all, the company can influence the timing of cash collections.

EXERCISES

 7-8 Cash receipts budget (continuation of 6-9 and 6-10) Gentry Company collects 40% of its sales in the month of sale and 60% in the following month. Receivables at the end of April were $122,000.

Required
Prepare cash receipts budgets for May and June.

7-9 Cash budget (continuation of 7-8) Gentry Company pays for its purchases in the month after purchase. Accounts payable for merchandise at the end of April were $180,000. Variable costs other than for cost of sales are paid as incurred, as are fixed costs requiring cash disbursement. The cash balance at the beginning of May is $30,000.

Required
1. Prepare cash disbursements budgets for May and June.
2. Prepare cash budgets for May and June.

7-10   Cash receipts budget   Jasica Company expects the following sales for the first six months of 19X7, in thousands of dollars.

	Jan.	Feb.	Mar.	Apr.	May	Jun.
Budgeted sales	$1,600	$2,200	$1,100	$900	$1,600	$2,900

Cash collections expectations are as follows: 2% of sales become bad debts, 40% of sales are collected in the month of sale, 30% in the first month after sale, and 28% in the second month after sale. Sales in November 19X6 were $800,000 and in December, $1,200,000.

Required

Prepare a cash receipts budget for the five-month period ending May 31, 19X7, by month.

7-11   Production and cash disbursements budgets   The following data relate to Corr Company and its single product, a desk lamp.

(a) Sales forecast, January through April, 19X9 (in units): 1,300; 1,600; 2,100; and 2,400.
(b) Inventory policy: inventory is maintained at 10% of budgeted sales needs for the coming month.
(c) Cost data: materials, $6 per unit; direct labor, $10 per unit; and variable manufacturing overhead, $5 per unit. Monthly fixed manufacturing costs are $15,000, including $3,000 depreciation.
(d) Corr uses some JIT principles. It purchases materials daily and pays for them as delivered; all other manufacturing costs requiring cash disbursements are also paid as incurred.
(e) The inventory of finished units at the beginning of January is 130.

Required

1. Prepare a production budget for each of the first three months of 19X9.
2. Prepare a schedule of budgeted cash disbursements for production costs for each of the first three months of 19X9.

7-12   Cash receipts and cash budget (continuation of 7-11)   The lamp sells for $40 per unit. All sales are on account with 30% collected in the month of sale, 70% in the month after sale. Receivables at December 31, 19X8, were $41,000.

   The only variable selling cost is a 10% commission on sales, paid in the month after sale. Unpaid commissions were $4,800 at December 31, 19X8. Fixed selling and administrative costs requiring cash are $7,400 per month, paid as incurred. Depreciation on office and delivery equipment is $1,200 per month.

Required

1. Prepare a cash receipts budget for each of the first three months of 19X9.
2. Prepare a cash budget for each of the first three months of 19X9. Cash at January 1 is $18,000.

  7-13   Cash budget (continuation of 6-11)   Jordan Clothing pays for its purchases 40% in the month of purchase and 60% in the following month. Its accounts payable at December 31, 19X8, were $18,000. It collects 60% of its sales in the month of sale and 40% in the following month. Receivables at December 31, 19X8, to be collected in January, were $30,000. All of its fixed costs require cash disbursements and are paid as incurred. Its cash balance at December 31, 19X8, was $20,000.

Required
1. Prepare a cash receipts budget for each of the first three months of 19X9 and for the quarter as a whole.
2. Prepare a cash disbursements budget for each of the first three months of 19X9 and for the quarter as a whole.
3. Prepare a cash budget for each of the first three months of 19X9 and for the quarter as a whole.

7-14 Pro forma balance sheet (continuation of 7-13) Jordan Clothing had the following balance sheet at December 31, 19X8.

Assets		Equities	
Cash	$ 20,000	Accounts payable	$ 18,000
Receivables	30,000		
Inventory	55,000	Stockholders' equity	87,000
Total	$105,000	Total	$105,000

Jordan rents all of its fixed assets.

Required
Prepare a pro forma balance sheet as of March 31, 19X9.

 7-15 Cash budget (continuation of 6-12) Thomas Company pays for its purchases in the month after purchase. Its accounts payable at December 31, 19X3, were $35,000. It collects 30% of its sales in the month of sale and 70% in the following month. Receivables at December 31, 19X3, to be collected in January, were $63,000. Depreciation is $5,000 per month. All of its other costs require cash disbursements and are paid as incurred. Its cash balance at December 31, 19X3, was $25,000.

Required
1. Prepare a cash receipts budget for each of the first three months of 19X4 and for the quarter as a whole.
2. Prepare a cash disbursements budget for each of the first three months of 19X4 and for the quarter as a whole.
3. Prepare a cash budget for each of the first three months of 19X4 and for the quarter as a whole. If budgeted cash would go below $10,000 assume borrowing and repayments in multiples of $5,000 to maintain at least $10,000. Ignore interest.

7-16 Pro forma balance sheet (continuation of 7-15) Thomas Company had the following balance sheet at December 31, 19X3.

Assets		Equities	
Cash	$ 25,000	Accounts payable	$ 35,000
Receivables	63,000		
Inventory	80,000		
Fixed assets, net	150,000	Stockholders' equity	283,000
Total	$318,000	Total	$318,000

Required
Prepare a pro forma balance sheet as of March 31, 19X4.

7-17   Cash budget and budgeted balance sheet for a manufacturer (continuation of 6-16, 6-17, and 6-18) HMA Company sells only on credit, collecting 70% in the month after sale and 30% the second month after sale. The company pays for its purchases of materials 60% in the month of purchase and 40% in the following month. It pays other cash manufacturing costs as incurred. Monthly fixed selling and administrative costs, all cash, are also paid as incurred, but sales commissions are paid in the month after the sale occurs. In December of 19X9 HMA declared a $220 dividend that it must pay in January of 19X0.

Following is HMA's balance sheet at December 31, 19X9.

HMA Company, Balance Sheet at December 31, 19X9

Assets		Liabilities and Owners' Equity	
Cash	$1,500	Accounts payable for materials	$ 216
Accounts receivable for:		Accrued commissions payable	360
November sales	660	Dividend payable	220
December sales	2,400		
Inventory, materials (34 lbs.)	102	Common stock	5,000
Building, net of depreciation	1,680	Retained earnings	546
Total	$6,342	Total	$6,342

Required
1. Prepare a cash receipts budget for HMA for January, 19X0.
2. Determine HMA's budgeted accounts receivable at January 31, 19X0.
3. Prepare a cash disbursements budget for HMA for January, 19X0.
4. Determine HMA's budgeted accounts payable at January 31, 19X0, for materials purchases.
5. Prepare a cash budget for January, 19X0.
6. Prepare HMA's budgeted balance sheet at January 31, 19X0.

7-18   Cash budget—quarters Walton Company expects the following quarterly results in 19X4, in thousands of dollars.

	1	2	3	4
Sales	$2,400	$3,000	$3,600	$2,100
Cash disbursements:				
Production costs	1,800	2,800	2,200	1,700
Selling and administrative costs	400	600	200	320
Acquisitions of fixed assets	0	300	700	400
Dividends	30	30	30	40

The beginning balance in accounts receivable is $700,000. Cash on hand at the beginning of the year is $120,000, and the desired minimum balance is $100,000. Accounts receivable at the end of a quarter are one-third of sales for the quarter. Any borrowings are made in $10,000 multiples at the beginnings of quarters in which the need will occur, and are repaid at the ends of quarters. Ignore interest.

Required
1. Prepare a cash budget by quarters for the year.
2. What is the outstanding loan at the end of the year?

7-19   *Pro forma balance sheet*   The controller of Lamb Industries is developing an analysis to see what financing requirements will be at the end of the current year. So far the controller has come up with the following data.

Budgeted Income Statement for Year
(in thousands of dollars)

Sales	$1,000
Cost of sales	700
Gross profit	$ 300
Operating expenses	180
Income	$ 120

Outline of Pro Forma Balance Sheet
as of Year End (in thousands of dollars)

Assets		Equities	
Cash	$ 30	Current liabilities	$?
Accounts receivable	?	Long-term debt	100
Inventory	?		
Plant, net	1,400	Stockholders' equity	1,400
Total	$?	Total	$?

Lamb's experience has been that accounts receivable are typically about 25% of sales and inventory about 30% of cost of sales. The company expects to have about the same income statement results for the next few years.

The controller would like to hold current liabilities to about one-half of current assets. The stockholders' equity figure given in the pro forma statement reflects expected profit and dividends for the year.

Required
Determine total asset requirements, total available equities, and the financing gap.

7-20   *Comprehensive budgeting—selected elements*   Following is BLD Company's pro forma balance sheet at December 31, 19X3.

Pro Forma Balance Sheet as of December 31, 19X3

Assets		Equities	
Cash	$ 35,000	Accounts payable	$ 12,000
Receivables	16,000	Expenses payable	5,000
Inventory	63,000	Bank loan payable	20,000
Property, plant		Common stock	160,000
and equipment, net	116,000	Retained earnings	33,000
Total	$230,000	Total	$230,000

The following information is also available about BLD's plans and operations for 19X4.

(a) Expected sales for January through May are shown below.

	Jan.	Feb.	Mar.	Apr.	May
Budgeted Sales	$50,000	$60,000	$70,000	$66,000	$65,000

(b) All sales are on credit and collected 70% in the month of sale and 30% in the month after sale.
(c) Cost of sales is expected to be 55% of sales.
(d) BLD's policy is to maintain inventory equivalent to sales expectations for the following two months.
(e) Variable costs other than cost of sales are 15% of sales, with 40% paid in the month the costs are incurred and the remainder paid in the following month.
(f) Fixed costs are $8,000 per month, including depreciation of $2,000. Cash fixed costs are paid in the month they are incurred.
(g) BLD plans to declare a $1,500 cash dividend in January, to be paid in February.
(h) Purchases are all on credit and paid 80% in the month of purchase and 20% in the month after purchase.
(i) BLD plans to pay $2,200 to its bank on January 31, representing $2,000 of principal on its loan and $200 of interest for January. (Interest is paid monthly, based on the loan outstanding at the beginning of the month.)

Required
1. What are BLD's budgeted cash receipts for January 19X4?
2. What are BLD's budgeted accounts receivable at January 31, 19X4?
3. What is BLD's budgeted inventory for January 31, 19X4?
4. What are BLD's budgeted purchases for January 19X4?
5. What is BLD's budgeted income for January 19X4?
6. What balance would BLD report for retained earnings in its pro forma balance sheet for January 31, 19X4?
7. List the purposes and budgeted amounts of all BLD's expected cash disbursements for January 19X4. (Give supporting computations, if any computations are necessary.)
8. List the names and budgeted amounts of all BLD's budgeted liabilities at January 31, 19X4. (Give supporting computations for your answers, if any computations are necessary.)

PROBLEMS

7-21   Basic cash budget   Before being called out of town on urgent company business, Sandy Banks, the controller of Zonar, Inc., developed the following information for the company's cash budget for the next few months.

	Unit Sales	Unit Production	Materials Purchases
January	1,000	1,400	$130,000
February	1,200	1,600	150,000
March	1,400	1,300	110,000

Zonar's one product, a stereo unit, sells for $600. Customers pay 60% in the month of sale and 40% in the following month. Materials purchases are paid for in the month after purchase. Variable production costs, excluding materials, are $150 per unit of product. Fixed production costs are $150,000 per month, including $30,000 depreciation. Selling and administrative expenses are $50,000 per month, all cash, paid as incurred. Production costs other than those for materials are paid as incurred.

At January 1, the company had $360,000 in accounts receivable from December sales and owed suppliers of materials $500,000. Cash at January 1 was $25,000.

Required
Prepare budgets of cash receipts and disbursements and a cash budget for January and for February. If you show a negative cash balance, assume borrowing to bring it to zero. Ignore interest and repayments.

 7-22   *Comprehensive budget* Borden Hardware Store is preparing its budgets for 19X7.

Forecasted Sales		Balance Sheet Data, December 31, 19X6	
January	$60,000	Cash	$ 8,000
February	80,000	Accounts receivable	24,000
March	70,000	Inventory	54,000
April	90,000	Accounts payable (merchandise)	42,000

Other data are as follows.

(a) Sales are on credit with 40% of sales collected in the month of sale and 60% in the month after sale.
(b) Cost of sales is 60% of sales.
(c) Other variable costs are 10% of sales, paid in the month incurred.
(d) Inventories are to be 150% of next month's budgeted sales requirements.
(e) Purchases are paid for in the month after purchase.
(f) Fixed expenses are $3,000 per month; all require cash.

Required
1. Prepare purchases budgets for each of the first three months of 19X7.
2. Prepare separate cash receipts and disbursements budgets and a cash budget for each of the first three months of 19X7.
3. Prepare a budgeted income statement for the three-month period ending March 31, 19X7.

7-23   *Understanding budgets* Following are Blaisdel Company's balance sheet at December 31, 19X0, and information regarding Blaisdel's policies and past experiences.

Blaisdel Company
Balance Sheet at December 31, 19X0

Assets		Equities	
Cash	$ 41,000	Accounts payable	$ 12,000
Inventory	63,000	Income taxes payable	5,000
Receivables	17,000	Common stock	170,000
Fixed assets, net	89,000	Retained earnings	23,000
Total	$210,000	Total	$210,000

Additional information:

(a) All sales are on credit and are collected 70% in the month of sale and 30% in the month after sale.

(b) Expected sales for the first five months of 19X1 are $50,000, $60,000, $70,000, $66,000, and $65,000, respectively.

(c) Inventory is maintained at a level equivalent to the sales requirements for the following two months.

(d) Purchases are all on credit and are paid 80% in the month of purchase and 20% in the month after purchase.

(e) Other variable costs are 20% of sales and are paid in the month incurred.

(f) Fixed costs are $6,000 per month, including $1,000 of depreciation. Cash fixed costs are paid in the month incurred.

(g) Blaisdel's income tax rate is 25%, with taxes being paid in the month after they are accrued.

(h) Cost of goods sold is expected to be 60% of sales.

Required

1. What are budgeted cash receipts for January 19X1?
2. What is the budgeted inventory at January 31, 19X1?
3. What are budgeted purchases for January 19X1?
4. What is budgeted net income for January 19X1?
5. What is the budgeted cash balance at the end of January 19X1?
6. What are budgeted accounts receivable at February 28, 19X1?
7. What is the budgeted book value of fixed assets at March 31, 19X1?
8. What are budgeted accounts payable at March 31, 19X1?
9. If Blaisdel declared a cash dividend of $1,200 during January, payable in February, what balance would be reported for retained earnings in a pro forma balance sheet as of January 31, 19X1?
10. What amount would show as the liability for income taxes as of March 31, 19X1?

7-24   Cash budget for a student   Bo Phelps is a junior majoring in mathematics at a large university. Bo wants to develop a cash budget for the fall term, which runs from September 1 through November 30. He has collected the following information.

Cash at September 1	$1,250
Tuition, due September 15	2,200
Room rent, due September 15 (for entire term)	800
Cost of meals, per month	300
Clothing expenditures, per month	50
Textbook purchases, due September 15	280

Phelps has been awarded a scholarship of $2,000; the check should arrive by the end of the first week of September. He estimates that expenditures for dates and miscellaneous other items should total about $300 for the term, spread evenly over each month. He also expects that he can get a part-time job that pays $8 per hour. For the most part, Phelps will be able to set the hours he will work each month. His employer, a local business, must withhold 10% of his earnings for income and social security taxes.

Required

Determine how many hours Phelps must work each month to be able to maintain a $100 cash balance for emergencies.

7-25   *Determining required receipts—nursery school*   Westcliff Community Church operates a nursery school on its premises from September through May. Parents can enroll a child for a morning or an afternoon class, but each class is limited to 20 children. The church's Board of Trustees sets the school's monthly fee per child with the intention of breaking even.

The Board has the following report of cash receipts and disbursements for the school for the nine months ended May 31, 19X7.

Receipts		$24,300
Disbursements:		
Teacher's salary	$17,000	
Teacher's assistant ($100 per month)	900	
Payroll-related costs	1,253	
Supplies	3,240	
Food	2,592	
Equipment repair and replacement	552	
Licenses	250	
Miscellaneous	135	
Total		25,922
Deficit		$ 1,622

For the period covered by the report, the monthly fee was $75 per child and average enrollment per month was 36 children.

In a letter accompanying the report, the teacher in charge of the school made the following comments about operations for the coming year.

(a) Costs for food and supplies are likely to increase 5%.
(b) The licensing fees will increase by $50.
(c) The need for a teacher's assistant continues because enrollment reaches 20 in one or both classes in several months.
(d) Payroll-related costs should continue at about the same percentage of payroll costs.
(e) Miscellaneous operating costs are likely to be about the same, but equipment-related costs will probably be about $250.

Based on the multitude of positive comments received about the school's teacher, the Board voted to increase the teacher's salary 15% and to accept the teacher's opinions about costs for the coming year.

Required
1. Prepare a cash disbursements budget for the coming year.
2. Determine what monthly fee per child the Board should set for the coming year to come within $100 of breaking even. Assume an average enrollment of 38 children per month and round the fee to the nearest $5.

7-26   *Pro forma financial statements and cash budget for a retailer*   The following is the expected balance sheet at December 31, 19X1 for Bob's Foods, a specialty retail food store in an affluent suburban area.

Assets		Liabilities and Owners' Equity	
Cash	$ 42,000	Accounts payable	$ 48,000
Accounts receivable	4,500		
Inventory	14,000	Owners' equity	142,000
Equipment, net	95,000		
Other	34,500		
Total	$190,000	Total	$190,000

Robert Granger, owner of Bob's, has regularly permitted about 4% of the customers to place orders on credit and pay for them in the following month. (These customers account for about 10% of dollar sales.) Late in 19X1, Granger decided to increase the number of customers permitted to order on credit. He made no formal analysis of the likely effects of the decision, but he believes that the store would benefit from expanding credit privileges to include a total of 15% of his customers who account for about 40% of the store's sales. Under Granger's new policy, sales would be 60% for cash and 40% on credit, with credit sales being collected in the month after sale.

Granger has developed or collected the following information to help him prepare a budget for the first quarter of 19X2.

(a) Estimated sales:

January	$40,000	March	$60,000
February	45,000	April	50,000

(b) Cost of sales is 70%. Vendors are paid in the month after purchase.
(c) Variable selling costs are 10% of sales.
(d) Administrative costs are fixed at $8,000 per month, including $2,500 depreciation.
(e) Cash operating costs other than for inventory items are paid in the month incurred.

Most suppliers of inventory items deliver at least weekly, but Granger wants to maintain his overall inventory at a 15-day supply (50% of the next month's sales needs). Because the new credit policy will have a fairly immediate impact on the store's cash balance, Granger is concerned that his cash balance may fall below the $20,000 he considers necessary.

Required

1. Prepare a budgeted income statement for the first quarter of 19X2.
2. Prepare a pro forma balance sheet as of March 31, 19X2.
3. Prepare the cash budget for the first quarter of 19X2. If you prepare a cash budget for each month, do not assume any borrowing should the cash balance fall below $20,000.
4. What time frame do you believe Bob's Foods should use to prepare its cash budget? Explain your answer.

 7-27   *Comprehensive budget (adapted from a problem prepared by Professor Robert W. Koehler)* The following data pertain to Elgin's, a specialty store in a large shopping mall.

Sales Forecasts—19X8

January	$ 80,000
February	90,000
March	110,000
April	120,000
May	100,000

Balance Sheet at December 31, 19X7

Assets		Equities	
Cash	$ 15,000	Accounts payable	$ 28,000
Accounts receivable	60,000	Accrued sales commissions	7,000
Inventory	102,000	Common stock	160,000
Net fixed assets	200,000	Retained earnings	182,000
Total	$377,000	Total	$377,000

Other data are as follows.

(a) All sales are on credit with 40% collected in the month of sale and 60% in the month after sale.

(b) Cost of sales is 60% of sales.

(c) The only other variable cost is a 7% commission to salespeople that is paid in the month after it is earned. All sales are subject to the commission.

(d) Inventory is kept equal to sales requirements for the next two months' budgeted sales.

(e) Purchases are paid for in the month after purchase.

(f) Fixed costs are $10,000 per month, including $4,000 depreciation.

Required

1. Prepare a budgeted income statement for the three-month period ending March 31, 19X8.
2. Prepare a cash budget for each of the first three months of 19X8 and all necessary supporting budgets.
3. Prepare a pro forma balance sheet as of March 31, 19X8.

7-28 *Investing idle cash (continuation of 7-27; adapted from a problem prepared by Professor Robert W. Koehler)* The president of Elgin's was pleased with the cash budget you prepared, but felt that the company might be able to invest some of its available cash and thereby earn an additional return. He knows that if the funds are invested in a money market fund the company will be able to earn 0.5% per month interest and can withdraw the money at any time. He believes that a $10,000 cash balance is sufficient and asks you to redo the cash budget to reflect the investing of excess cash at 0.5% per month. (Thus, you can invest $5,000 on January 1, because the $15,000 balance is $5,000 over the required minimum.) Assume that you invest at the ends of months (except for January 1).

Required

Respond to the president's request.

7-29 *Municipal budgeting—revenues* The City of Wentworth is preparing its budget for 19X9. Total required revenues are $44,000,000. The city has two major sources of revenue, sales taxes and property taxes. The sales tax is 3.5% of taxable retail sales, which includes virtually all sales except for food and medicine. The assessed valuation of taxable property is $560,000,000. An economist hired by the city has forecast total taxable retail sales at $860,000,000 for 19X9.

Required

1. Determine the property tax rate needed to meet the city's revenue objective, assuming that the estimate of retail sales is correct.
2. The city council is considering a proposal to reduce property taxes on homes owned by people over 65 years of age. It is proposed that the rate on such homes be set at $20 per $1,000 assessed valuation. The total assessed valuation of homes owned by people over 65 is $45,000,000. Determine the rate that would have to be set on the remaining taxable property in order to meet the revenue objective if the proposal is adopted.

7-30   *Manufacturer's cash budget—three months*   Tompkins Company produces a single product that sells for $15 per unit. Data are as follows.

(a) Variable manufacturing costs, all requiring cash, are $7 per unit.
(b) Variable selling and administrative expenses are $1 per unit.
(c) Fixed manufacturing costs requiring cash are $80,000 per month. Depreciation is $12,000 per month. Fixed selling and administrative expenses are $40,000 per month, all requiring cash.
(d) Tompkins maintains a supply of finished goods equal to 50% of the sales needs for the coming month. The beginning inventory (January 1) is 10,000 units.
(e) Tompkins has partially implemented JIT principles and therefore buys raw materials as needed, maintaining no inventory. The cost of raw materials is included in the variable manufacturing cost of $7.
(f) Tompkins makes all sales on credit, collecting 30% in the month of sale and 70% in the month after sale. The beginning balance in accounts receivable is $140,000.
(g) All cash manufacturing costs are paid for in the month of production.
(h) Tompkins pays 80% of selling and administrative expenses in the month of sale and 20% in the following month. At January 1 Tompkins owed $14,000 from December expenses.
(i) The minimum desired cash balance is $40,000, which is also the amount on hand at the beginning of January. If the company needs to borrow, it does so in multiples of $10,000. It must borrow at the beginning of the month and repay at the end, if sufficient cash is available. The monthly interest rate is 1%, and Tompkins pays interest when it repays loans, whether in full or in part.
(j) The sales budget for the first six months is, in units, January, 20,000; February, 26,000; March, 30,000; April, 32,000; May, 30,000; June, 28,000.

Required

1. Prepare a cash budget and any necessary supporting schedules for the first three months of the year, by month and in total.
2. Given your results in item 1, does the company appear to be profitable? Explain.
3. Suppose that sales stabilize at 25,000 units per month. What will monthly cash collections be? What will monthly cash disbursements for manufacturing costs and for selling and administrative expenses be?

7-31   *One-month cash budget—discounts*   Stony Acres Department Store makes about 20% of its sales for cash. Credit sales are collected 20%, 30%, and 45% in the month of sale, month after, and second month after sale, respectively. The remaining 5% become bad debts. The store tries to purchase enough goods each month to maintain its inventory at 2 1/2 times the following month's budgeted sales needs. All purchases are subject to a 2% discount if paid within ten days and the store takes all discounts. Accounts payable are then equal to one-third of that month's net purchases. Cost of goods sold, without considering the 2% discount, is 60% of selling prices. The store records inventory net of the discount.

The general manager of the store has asked you to prepare a cash budget for August and you have gathered the following data.

Sales:	
May (actual)	$220,000
June (actual)	260,000
July (actual)	300,000
August (budgeted)	340,000
September (budgeted)	300,000
Inventory at July 31, net of discount	455,700
Cash at July 31	73,000
Purchases in July (gross)	210,000
Selling, general, and administrative expenses	
budgeted for August (including $21,000 depreciation)	102,000

The store pays all of its other expenses in the month incurred.

Required
Prepare a cash budget for August.

7-32   Long-range financial budget   Millard Company has retained you to develop a financing plan for the next few years. You collect the following information about the firm's expectations, goals, and policies. All dollar amounts are in thousands.

Sales Forecasts	
19X4	$ 800
19X5	1,000
19X6	1,250
19X7	1,500

Millard expects a return on sales of 12%. The company's directors would like to maintain the policy of distributing dividends in an amount equal to 60% of net income each year. The directors would also like to have a current ratio of at least 2 to 1 and do not want long-term liabilities to exceed 60% of stockholders' equity.

Current asset requirements are 30% of expected sales in the coming year, and net fixed assets are 65% of budgeted sales for the coming year. At the end of 19X3, stockholders' equity is $400.

Required
Prepare a schedule showing financing requirements for 19X4, 19X5, and 19X6.

7-33   Budgeting equations (CMA adapted)   Your firm has just acquired a new computer, and one of the first things the president wants to use it for is preparing the comprehensive budget. He assigns you the task of formulating a set of equations that can be used to write a program to perform the computations required for the budgets. You consult with the chief programmer, and the two of you decide that the following notation should be used, which will make it easy for the programmer to prepare the necessary programs.

S0	= sales in current month (units)
S1	= sales in coming month (units)
S-1	= sales in prior month (units)
S-2	= sales in second prior month (units)
P	= selling price per unit
CGS	= cost of goods sold per unit (purchase price)
OVC	= other variable costs per unit
FC	= total fixed costs per month
FCC	= fixed costs per month requiring cash disbursements
PUR	= purchases in current month (units)
PUR-1	= purchases in prior month (units)

You examine the company's records and decide that the firm's policies or experienced relationships are as follows.

(a) Collections on sales are 30% in the month of sale, 50% in the month after sale, and 20% in the second month after sale.
(b) Inventory is maintained at twice the coming month's budgeted sales volume.
(c) Purchases are paid for 60% in the month after purchase and 40% in the month of purchase.
(d) All other costs are paid as incurred.

Required

Prepare equations that can be used to budget for the following.

1. Income for the current month.
2. Cash receipts in the current month.
3. Purchases in the current month in units.
4. Purchases in the current month in dollars.
5. Cash disbursements in the current month.

7-34   Comprehensive budget (continuation of 6-48; adapted from a problem prepared by Professor Maurice L. Hirsch) The following additional information about Banana City is available.

(a) Sales of bananas are for cash only. Sales of nuts are on credit and are collected two months after sale.
(b) Banana City's suppliers give terms of 30 days for payment of accounts payable. Banana City takes full advantage of the 30-day payments. (Assume all months have 30 days.)
(c) The company must make quarterly payments on its income taxes. The payment for the first quarter of fiscal year 19X7 is due on January 15, 19X7. The liability for taxes payable shown on the balance sheet in item e is to be paid on October 15.
(d) Fixed expenses that require cash disbursement are paid as incurred with the following exceptions: (1) insurance premiums are all paid on November 1 in advance for the next 12 months and (2) interest payments are all made on

January 1. The $156,000 "other fixed expenses" shown in item f of 6-48 all require cash disbursements evenly over the year.

(e) The balance sheet at August 31, 19X6 is as follows.

Assets		Equities	
Cash	$ 15,000	Accounts payable (merchandise)	$ 26,000
Accounts receivable	75,000	Taxes payable	31,000
Inventories	41,800	Accrued interest	4,000
Prepaid insurance	2,000	Long-term debt, 6%	100,000
Land	8,000	Common stock	150,000
Equipment (net)	210,000	Retained earnings	40,800
Total	$351,800	Total	$351,800

(f) Sales expected in the last part of fiscal year 19X6 are as follows.

	June	July	August
Bananas	$31,000	$34,000	$32,500
Nuts	37,000	41,000	34,000

(g) The company plans to pay a dividend of $12,000 in October.

Required
1. Prepare budgets of cash receipts and disbursements for each of the first three months of fiscal year 19X7 and for the quarter as a whole.
2. Prepare a cash budget for the quarter, by month, and in total.
3. Prepare a pro forma balance sheet for November 30, 19X6.

7-35 *Pro forma balance sheet and financing requirements* Jill Eyre, treasurer of Caldwell Company, has collected the following information as part of her planning. She believes the company will have to issue long-term debt during the year, but she is unsure how much.

Budgeted Income Statement for 19X6	
Sales	$300,000
Cost of goods sold	210,000
Gross profit	$ 90,000
Selling, general, and administrative expenses	36,000
Income before taxes	$ 54,000
Income taxes (40% rate)	21,600
Net income	$ 32,400

Balance Sheet Data at December 31, 19X5	
Plant and equipment—net	$150,000
Common stock	200,000
Retained earnings	83,000

Known Asset Requirements, December 31, 19X6	
Cash—minimum desired balance	$25,000
Accounts receivable	30% of sales
Inventory	30% of cost of sales
Plant and equipment—net	$210,000

Jill also knows that accounts payable are normally 50% of inventory and that only half the income tax expense is paid before the end of the year. The company's annual dividend is $22,000 and is normally paid in October.

Required

Prepare a statement of asset requirements and available equities as of the end of 19X6. Determine the amount of long-term debt that Caldwell will need at the end of 19X6.

7-36 Comprehensive budget Following are the balance sheet of your company, Arcon Industries, at December 31, 19X5, and its projected income statement for the first three months of 19X6.

Balance Sheet at December 31, 19X5

Assets		Equities	
Cash	$ 5,000	Accounts payable	$ 16,000
Accounts receivable	10,000	Dividend payable	2,000
Inventory	24,000	Owners' equity	61,000
Plant and equipment, net of accumulated depreciation	40,000		
Total	$ 79,000	Total	$ 79,000

Budgeted Income Statement for the Three Months Ending March 31, 19X6

Sales (10,000 units × $10)		$100,000
Cost of sales (10,000 units × $6)		60,000
Gross profit		$ 40,000
Operating expenses:		
Wages and salaries	$9,000	
Rent	3,000	
Depreciation	3,000	
Other expenses	1,500	
Total operating expenses		16,500
Income		$ 23,500

You are quite happy with the projection, and gloat about it to your banker at lunch. The banker asks if you will need any cash to get through the first quarter. "Of course not" is your reply. Later, back at your office, the chief accountant informs you of the following.

(a) Sales are all on credit and are collected 50% in the month of sale and 50% in the month after sale.

(b) Company policy is to maintain inventory equal to the next two months' sales in units, but inventory at December 31, 19X5, does not conform to policy because of a recent dock strike.

(c) Arcon pays for purchases 50% in the month of purchase and 50% in the following month.

(d) Arcon is committed to paying the recorded cash dividend of $2,000 in March.

(e) All cash expenses are paid in the month incurred, except for purchases.

(f) A breakdown of projected sales by month is as follows:

January	$20,000	March	$50,000	May	$20,000
February	$30,000	April	$20,000		

(g) Maintaining a cash balance of at least $5,000 is necessary to accommodate emergencies and variations from estimates.

Required

Do you regret your reply to your banker? Explain by preparing the appropriate schedules. (If borrowings are necessary, assume that they are in $1,000 multiples at the beginning of the month and that repayments are at the ends of months with 12% annual interest on the amount repaid.)

 7-37 Comprehensive budget (continuation of 6-38) The managers and managerial accountants at Arctic Products have the following additional information.

(a) Sales should be collected 30% in the month of sale and 70% in the following month.

(b) Purchases are paid 40% in the month of purchase and 60% in the following month.

(c) Fixed manufacturing costs include $20,000 per month depreciation.

(d) Manufacturing costs that require cash disbursements are paid as incurred.

(e) Of selling and administrative expenses that require cash disbursements, 80% is paid as incurred; the remaining 20% is paid in the following month.

The balance sheet expected at December 31 appears below.

Arctic Products
Balance Sheet at December 31, 19X5

Assets	
Cash	$ 75,000
Accounts receivable	280,000
Finished goods (35,000 × $14)	490,000
Materials (66,000 × $8)	528,000
Plant and equipment, net	1,200,000
Total assets	$2,573,000

Equities	
Accounts payable	$ 96,000
Accrued expenses	17,000*
Stockholders' equity	2,460,000
Total equities	$2,573,000

* $11,000 of the total relates to fixed costs.

Required

1. Prepare cash budgets for January and February assuming the company desires a minimum cash balance of $60,000 at the end of each month. If projections show that borrowing is necessary to meet the minimum balance and cover a month's cash activity, such borrowings occur at the beginning of the month, in multiples of $10,000. Assume that repayments, in multiples of $10,000, are made at the end of the month, as soon as cash balances permit them. The bank charges interest at 1% per month, but interest payments need to be made only at the time a repayment occurs, and then only for the interest due on the amount being repaid.
2. Prepare a pro forma balance sheet as of the end of February.

 7-38   *Cash budget (continuation of 6-47)* Spark Company collects its sales 30% in the month of sale, 30% in the next month, and 40% in the second month after sale. Fixed production costs not requiring cash are $40,000 per month. All selling, general, and administrative expenses require cash and are paid in the month incurred, except for sales commissions, which are paid in the month after incurrence.

All production costs requiring cash are paid 80% in the month of production and 20% in the month after production. This includes payments for materials, of which no inventory is kept since they are delivered daily.

Selected balance sheet data for Spark Company at May 31 are as follows.

Cash	$120,000 (equals the desired minimum balance)
Accounts receivable:	
From May sales	336,000
From April sales	120,000
Liabilities:	
Sales commissions	48,000
Production costs	66,000

Required

Prepare a cash budget for Spark Company for the first three months of the fiscal year, by month. If the need arises, show borrowings, in multiples of $10,000, required to maintain the desired minimum balance of cash. Repayments are made at the ends of months and interest at 1% per month is paid when a repayment is made.

7-39   *Analysis of budgets of a manufacturing firm* Budgets for Simpson Company appear as follows for the first three months of 19X6.

Budgeted Income Statements
for the Three Months Ending March 31, 19X6

Sales (10,000 units)		$30,000
Variable costs:		
Production	$8,000	
Selling and administrative	7,500	15,500
Contribution margin		$14,500
Fixed costs:		
Production	$1,800	
Selling and administrative	2,400	4,200
Income		$10,300

Production Budget (in units)

	January	February	March
Desired ending inventory	4,500	7,500	6,000
Units sold	2,000	3,000	5,000
Total requirements	6,500	10,500	11,000
Beginning inventory	2,500	4,500	7,500
Production	4,000	6,000	3,500

Cash Receipts Budget

	January	February	March
Collections:			
December sales	$ 750		
January sales	1,500	$4,500	
February sales		2,250	$ 6,750
March sales			3,750
Total collections	$2,250	$6,750	$ 10,500

Cash Disbursements Budget

	January	February	March
Production costs:			
Variable	$3,200	$4,800	$2,800
Fixed	600	600	600
Selling and administrative:			
Variable—current month	600	900	1,500
—prior month	150	900	1,350
Fixed	800	800	800
Totals	$5,350	$8,000	$7,050

Required

Answer the following questions about the assumptions and policies used in formulating the budgets.

1. What are variable manufacturing costs per unit?
2. What are monthly fixed manufacturing costs requiring cash disbursements?
3. What are the company's expectations about cash collections from receivables? (All sales are on account.)
4. What were sales in December 19X5?
5. What are accounts receivable at March 31, 19X6?
6. What proportion of variable selling and administrative expenses is paid in the month incurred, and what proportion is paid the following month? (Hint: Variable selling costs are 25% of sales.)
7. What are accrued expenses payable for selling and administrative expenses at March 31, 19X6?
8. How much cash does Simpson expect to have at March 31, 19X6? (The balance at January 1 is $1,800.)
9. If the company could sell 2,000 additional units in the three-month period, what would income be? (Ignore interest expense.)
10. Look at the production budget. From comparisons of inventories, sales, and so on, determine Simpson's inventory policy.

11. Does the beginning inventory for January reflect Simpson's policy? Show why or why not.
12. What are budgeted sales for April?

7-40   Qualifying for a loan   The president of Stern's Department Store has requested your assistance. He will be seeking a large bank loan in a couple of months for the purpose of opening a new store and has been told by his banker that the March 31, 19X8, balance sheet should look good if the loan is to be granted. The banker said specifically that working capital should be at least $500,000 and that the current ratio should be at least 2.5 to 1.

The end of January is now approaching and the president is becoming anxious. He asks you to prepare a cash budget for February and March and a pro forma balance sheet as of March 31. The balance sheet at the end of January is expected to be as follows, in thousands of dollars.

Assets		Equities	
Cash	$ 110	Accounts payable (merchandise)	$ 410
Accounts receivable	240	Notes payable	40
Inventory	680	Common stock	2,000
Building and equipment (net)	1,830	Retained earnings	410
Total	$2,860	Total	$2,860

The sales forecasts for the months of February, March, April, and May are, respectively, $780,000; $650,000; $600,000; and $820,000. Cost of sales averages 60% of sales. Receivables are collected 60% in the month of sale, 40% in the following month. Inventory is normally maintained at budgeted sales requirements for the following two months. Purchases are paid for in 30 days.

The notes payable shown in the balance sheet are due on March 15. Although the company normally keeps a minimum cash balance of $80,000, the president asks you to disregard this for purposes of the budgets. He also informs you that monthly fixed costs are $265,000, of which $30,000 is depreciation. All fixed costs requiring cash are paid as incurred.

Required

1. Prepare the cash budget and pro forma balance sheet that the president wants. Use thousands of dollars.
2. Determine whether the company will be likely to meet the criteria set by the bank.

7-41   Financing growth   The treasurer of GlenCo Manufacturing has asked you to assist her in long-term budgeting. GlenCo's board of directors has approved a long-term plan that envisions about a 10% return on sales and a 15% annual rate of growth in sales, as reflected in the following sales forecasts, in millions of dollars.

Sales Forecasts		Sales Forecasts	
19X5	$40.0	19X7	$52.9
19X6	46.0	19X8	60.8

At present, current asset requirements generally are about 40% of forecasted sales for the coming year, and net fixed assets are usually about 110% of forecasted sales for the coming year. Stockholders' equity is $32.0 million at the beginning of 19X5.

The directors have imposed some restrictions regarding financing. They wish to continue paying dividends of 40% of net income and want the current ratio to be at least 3 to 1. They also believe that long-term liabilities should not exceed 30% of stockholders' equity.

Required

1. Prepare a schedule to show the treasurer the financing requirements that GlenCo faces from 19X5 through 19X7. Round to the nearest tenth of a million dollars.
2. Reviewing with the treasurer the schedule you prepared in item 1 you realize that, with the exception of the growth in sales, the assumptions and policies in the plan essentially preserve the status quo and ignore trends and conditions you've read about or observed in business. Identify which of the assumptions and policies—if they represent GlenCo's current circumstances—appear to ignore current trends and conditions, and explain your choices.

7-42 *Variable minimum cash balance*   John Lock, chief financial officer of Bland Company, has asked for your help in preparing a cash budget. He plans to maintain a minimum balance based on the budgeted disbursements for the coming month and is unsure how to proceed. He tells you the following about his policy.

> If the coming month's budgeted receipts are greater than budgeted disbursements, I want to hold a balance equal to 10% of budgeted disbursements and invest any excess cash in short-term government notes. If budgeted disbursements are greater than budgeted receipts, I want to have enough cash to make up the budgeted deficit and have 20% of budgeted disbursements on hand to begin the month. We will borrow if the indicated balance is less than required.

The budgets for sales and purchases in the coming months are as follows.

	April	May	June	July	August
Sales	$500,000	$780,000	$900,000	$600,000	$650,000
Purchases	$470,000	$550,000	$560,000	$480,000	$600,000

Sales are collected 30% in the month of sale and 70% in the following month. Purchases are paid for 50% in the month of purchase and 50% in the following month. Sales in March were $450,000 and accounts payable for merchandise at March 31 were $185,000. Cash at March 31 was $140,000. Fixed expenses requiring cash disbursements are $110,000 per month.

Required

1. Prepare a schedule by month for the April-July period indicating the amounts that would have to be borrowed, or would be available for investment, in each month. Borrowings would be repaid as soon as possible and are not included in the determination of disbursements for the purpose of setting the desired balance. Borrowings would be repaid before investments were made and investments would be sold before borrowings are made. Ignore interest.
2. Using the guidelines in Appendix A, write a memorandum to Mr. Lock describing the advantages and disadvantages of his policy in comparison with a policy of having a specific number of dollars as the minimum cash balance.

CASES

7-43   *Financing requirements*   Larsen Company makes fertilizer in a midwestern state. The company has nearly completed a new plant that will produce twice as much as the old plant, which is being scrapped. Swen Larsen, the owner, has consulted you about his financing requirements for the coming year. He knows he will require additional financing because of the doubling of production, and he intends to obtain a loan as soon as possible. He is on good terms with local bankers and anticipates no difficulty in obtaining the loan, but he is anxious that the loan not be too large or too small.

The production process in the new plant is highly automated and can be carried out with a work force of the same size as that used last year in the old plant. The income statement for last year and the year-end balance sheet are as follows:

Income Statement for 19X4

Sales	$1,600,000
Cost of goods sold	1,040,000
Gross profit	$ 560,000
Selling, general, and administrative expenses	390,000
Income	$ 170,000

Balance Sheet at December 31, 19X4

Assets		Equities	
Cash	$ 40,000	Accounts payable	$ 20,000
Accounts receivable	80,000	Common stock	900,000
Inventory of materials	250,000	Retained earnings	150,000
Plant and equipment—old plant	0		
—new plant	700,000		
Total	$1,070,000	Total	$1,070,000

You learn that depreciation expense on the old plant was $80,000 per year, all of which was included in cost of goods sold. The new plant will be depreciated at $120,000 per year. Wages paid last year to production workers were $280,000. Materials purchases were $400,000, which is also the amount of materials cost included in cost of goods sold (the beginning and ending inventories of materials were the same). Factory overhead, other than depreciation, was $280,000 last year and is expected to be $360,000 in the coming year.

Selling, general, and administrative expenses are expected to be $430,000 during the coming year. Sales will be only 120% of last year's sales because it will take some time to reach the full output of the new plant. Larsen expects to spend $250,000 buying new equipment to complete the plant. This expenditure will be made as soon as he obtains the new loan. The factory will be operating at full capacity the last few months of the year, so ending requirements for current assets should be double the beginning amounts. Accounts payable are closely related to the amount of inventory carried. The company ships its products on completion, so all inventory is raw materials.

Required

Prepare a budgeted income statement for 19X5 and a pro forma balance sheet (as far as possible) for December 31, 19X5. State any assumptions you have to make and indicate how much Mr. Larsen must borrow from the bank.

7-44 *Cash budgeting—a lender's viewpoint* You are the chief assistant to Mr. Barnes, the loan officer of Metropolitan National Bank. In December 19X4 Mr. Barnes discussed a loan with Mr. Johnson, manager-owner of a local dry goods store. Mr. Johnson has requested a loan of $250,000 to be repaid at June 30, 19X5. He is expanding the store and needs additional inventory. From the proceeds of the loan, $200,000 will be spent on remodeling and new fixtures. The rest will be spent for additional inventory. At Mr. Barnes' request, Mr. Johnson submitted a budgeted income statement for the six months ending June 30, 19X5.

Sales	$900,000
Cost of goods sold	360,000
Gross profit	$540,000
Selling and general expenses, including $15,000 interest	310,000
Income	$230,000

Mr. Johnson said that, since $50,000 in depreciation was included in selling and administrative expenses, his company would generate more than enough cash to repay the loan with $15,000 in interest (12% annual rate). Mr. Barnes asks you to check out the forecast with Mr. Johnson. From Mr. Johnson you obtain the following information:

(a) Sales are expected to be $100,000 in January, $140,000 in February, and $165,000 in each of the rest of the months of the entire year.

(b) Merchandise is held equal to two months' budgeted sales.

(c) Accounts payable are paid in 30 days.

(d) About half of sales are for cash. The rest are collected in the second month after sale (60 days).

(e) Cost of goods sold is variable, and 15% of sales is the variable portion of selling and general expenses. All selling and general expenses, except depreciation, are paid in the month incurred.

(f) At December 31, 19X4, the following balance sheet is expected.

Pro Forma Balance Sheet as of December 31, 19X4

Assets		Equities	
Cash (desired minimum)	$ 20,000	Accounts payable	$ 30,000
Accounts receivable	40,000	Common stock	200,000
Inventory	60,000	Retained earnings	115,000
Building and equipment	375,000		
Accumulated depreciation	(150,000)		
Total	$ 345,000	Total	$345,000

Required
Using the guidelines in Appendix A, write a memorandum to Mr. Barnes giving and supporting your conclusions regarding the likelihood that Mr. Johnson's company can repay the loan and interest at the end of the first six months of 19X5.

7-45 *Budgeting and industry data* Ralph Robertson is considering opening a menswear store in a new shopping center. He has had a great deal of experience in men's stores and is convinced that he can make a success of his own store.

He plans to invest $10,000 of his own money in the business and has asked you to develop a plan he can take to a bank to obtain a loan to cover the remainder of the needed financing. He knows that a loan officer will be more receptive to an applicant who has made careful plans of his needs.

Ralph gives you the following data obtained from a trade association's study of stores of the kind and size he plans to open (1,200 square feet of selling space).

Average sales per square foot	$70 per year
Average rent	$500 per month plus 5% of sales
Average gross profit	45% of sales
Average annual operating expenses (excluding rent and depreciation):	
At $60,000 sales annually	$19,200
At $90,000 sales annually	$26,700
Inventory requirements	two-month supply
Investment in fixtures and equipment (useful life of five years)	$22,000

Ralph plans to sell for cash only. He will have to pay cash for his first purchase of inventory, but he expects to get 30-day credit from suppliers for further purchases. He will pay his other operating expenses, including rent, in the month incurred.

Ralph expects to have a steady growth in sales for the first four months of operation (January-April 19X8) and to reach the monthly average for the industry in May. His projections for the first four months are as follows: $4,000; $4,500; $5,200; and $6,100.

Required

Using the guidelines in Appendix A, write a memorandum to Mr. Robertson showing his financing requirements through April and a budgeted income statement for 19X8. Include in your memorandum brief comments about the assumptions you used to develop the financial data you are providing.

8 Capital Budgeting—Part I

LEARNING OBJECTIVES

After reading this chapter, you should be able to

1. Explain the concepts of cost of capital and cutoff rates of return.

2. Calculate cash flows from an investment, including the tax effect of depreciation.

3. Use the net present value method to evaluate an investment.

4. Use the internal rate of return method to evaluate an investment.

5. Determine cash flows with income taxes and depreciation.

6. Discuss qualitative reasons for making or not making particular investments.

7. Use the payback method and accounting rate of return method.

8. Understand why discounted cash flow methods are superior.

9. Understand reasons why investing in foreign countries poses special risks.

Capital expenditures are a significant part of the U.S. economy. Investment in the United States by U.S. companies alone is roughly $1.1 trillion per year. In addition, U.S. companies invest overseas, and foreign companies invest in the U.S. Individual organizations, mostly businesses, make huge expenditures for land, buildings, production machinery and equipment, computers and other information technology, office equipment and fixtures, and other physical assets.

• Consider the following capital expenditure amounts made by several companies in a recent fiscal year. We provide sales and net income figures as well to give a perspective on the amounts. All figures are in millions of dollars.

Company	Capital Expenditures	Sales	Net Income
Coca-Cola	$937	$18,018	$2,986
Phillips Petroleum	$1,400	$12,211	$484
Anheuser-Busch	$777	$13,185	$595

• Paper companies spend as much as $400 million for a single machine. From 1988 through 1993, coated-paper manufacturers (which make the paper used in magazines, catalogs, and books) invested $10 billion in 26 machines in North America and Europe. Companies run such machines 24 hours a day and earn high profits when paper prices are high. However, in the 1990s demand for coated paper dropped, prices fell, and companies incurred huge losses.

• **BMW** and some of its suppliers spent nearly $1 billion building a plant in South Carolina. The costs of searching for a suitable site and evaluating such factors as the availability of educated workers, access to transportation, amenities of life for employees, and business climate added to the cost.

• **Manville** spent $800 million on capital investments during a period when it was in bankruptcy from asbestos claims.

If companies make wise capital expenditure decisions, they will reap great rewards, but if they make poor decisions, they could go out of business. How do companies make the decisions that result in such huge outlays? What do they expect to gain from these investments? What techniques do companies use and how does managerial accounting fit into the picture? Is it only profit-seeking companies that make such large expenditures and use managerial accounting techniques?

This and the following chapter require that you understand the principles of the time value of money. Before you begin this chapter, read Appendix B at the back of the book and work through the review problems to be sure that you understand these principles.

     The comprehensive budget, the unifying topic of Chapters 6 and 7, reflects the results expected from a wide variety of planning decisions, such as those about product mix, cost structure, and pricing. Those decisions are intended to produce the best possible results given existing resources. But as you saw in Chapter 7, a comprehensive budget also includes the expected results of planning decisions that involve long-term commitments, called **capital budgeting decisions**. Planned expenditures for new, long-lived assets are often the largest items in the cash disbursements budget.

Capital budgeting decisions, the subject of this and the next chapter, often entail sizable commitments of cash, as indicated by the opening chapter vignette. Such decisions are expected to generate returns (normally, income or cost savings) that will last for more than one year. Capital budgeting decisions are therefore also called *long-term decisions.*

As Chapter 5 pointed out, the usual rule for determining whether a decision is short term or long term is whether its effects will be completed within one year. This rule, while arbitrary, provides a good basis for distinguishing the two types of decisions. Capital budgeting decisions are like short-term decisions in that they use differential revenues and costs. Therefore, these concepts remain relevant to capital budgeting decisions.

Managers use the analytical techniques discussed in this and the following chapter to decide whether to undertake specific long-term projects. The expenditures on those projects selected by management are incorporated into short-term and long-term budgets such as those presented in the preceding chapter. We cover only briefly the issues surrounding decisions about how to finance long-term investments. You will study in more detail the problems of selecting from among financing alternatives in managerial finance.

Considering only quantifiable factors, in short-term decision making an action is desirable if incremental revenues exceed incremental costs. In capital budgeting decisions, the company must include as a relevant cost the **time value of money**, because capital budgeting decisions require investing money now to bring in more money in the future. The time value of money is an opportunity cost; by making a particular investment now, we give up the opportunity to make other investments.

IMPORTANCE OF CAPITAL BUDGETING DECISIONS

Capital budgeting decisions commit companies to courses of action. The success or failure of a particular strategy, or even of the company itself, can hinge on one or a series of such decisions. And, for at least two reasons, capital budgeting decisions are generally riskier than short-term ones. First, the company expects to recoup its investment over a longer period. Much time expires between making the expenditure and receiving the cash. For example, **Intel's** 1994 annual report discussed a $1.3 billion plant the company began in 1994 that would not even start production until 1997. Because capital investments generate returns over several years, a company risks being caught in a business downturn, or recession, that will reduce expected returns. Second, reversing a capital budgeting decision is much more difficult than reversing a short-term decision. For example, suppose a company raises its prices expecting to improve its profits, but sales fall so much that profits fall. Usually the company can simply lower its prices. The company might suffer a decline in profits for a short time, but it can recover fairly quickly once the managers see their error. But a company that buys land and constructs and equips a building to make a particular product is out of luck if the product fails. The plant might have little value in any other use (a low opportunity cost), so if the product is unsuccessful, the company will have made a large, nearly worthless investment. During the 1970s oil crisis, **Reynolds Metals** built a plant to produce aluminum bumpers, which are lighter than steel. It abandoned the plant in 1981, when easing of the crisis prompted automakers to return to steel bumpers.

TYPES OF CAPITAL BUDGETING DECISIONS

Businesses and other economic entities make capital investments for a variety of reasons. The following is a representative list of the types of such decisions. The accompanying Insight describes investment priorities of several companies.

- *Investments mandated by law or policy*   This group includes investments made to comply with environmental, safety, and other laws and regulations. The group also includes investments made because company policy dictates. In these cases, the organization must do something, so the only question is how to do it. For example, a company might have three alternatives that will reduce toxic emissions. The decision is which alternative to select.

- *Investments made to further strategic goals*   This group is composed of investments made for such purposes as securing global distribution of products, increasing quality, and reducing lead time. Companies need not make these investments, but probably will even if they do not meet normal profitability criteria (which we will discuss shortly).

- *Investments to increase capacity or reduce costs*   This group constitutes the bulk of investments that managers evaluate with the techniques in the chapter. Such decisions lend themselves to analytical treatment. These investments aim at increasing profitability.

- *Investments made for non-financial reasons*   A company might build a fitness center or cafeteria without much analysis of the potential benefits, because upper-level managers believe they should do so. Such decisions typically cannot show objective measures of profitability sufficient to justify them, though indirect, intangible benefits might be very high. The decision revolves around how to accomplish the desired result, say, what equipment to purchase for the fitness center.

CAPITAL BUDGETING FUNDAMENTALS

COST OF CAPITAL AND CUTOFF RATES

Appendix B outlines the basic principles of time value of money, including the concept of a discount rate. For capital budgeting decisions, the theoretically correct discount rate is cost of capital. The study of cost of capital is the province of managerial finance. Thus, we include only a brief introduction to the concept. **Cost of capital** is the cost, expressed as a percentage, of obtaining the money needed to operate the company. Capital is obtained from two sources, creditors and owners, corresponding to the divisions of liabilities and owners' equity on the balance sheet. The cost of capital supplied by creditors is the effective interest rate on borrowings. For example, if the company has to make annual interest payments of $80,000 to obtain $1,000,000 from a sale of bonds with that face value, the effective interest rate is 8 percent ($80,000/$1,000,000).[1]

The cost of equity capital is more difficult to determine, for it is based on how much investors expect the company to earn. In a simple situation, this

---

[1] *You might recall the determination of bond prices in financial accounting. If bonds are issued at a premium or discount, the analysis is not so simple, but the refinements are not important to our discussion.*

SIGHT

A great deal of capital spending is aimed at reducing costs, especially in mature industries where competitive advantages are limited and cost leadership is critical. Such investments were once aimed primarily at reducing direct labor, but now also focus on other cost drivers. **H. J. Heinz's Pet Products Co.**, which makes 9-Lives cat food, has faced severe pressures from aggressive competitors. The company has spent to increase efficiency and to integrate vertically by acquiring the capacity to make cans. These cost reduction efforts have enabled the unit to keep prices low enough to compete in a difficult market. **Campbell Soup Company** has invested in programs to reduce costs, particularly in its distribution chain, encompassing such factors as customer order management.

Mattel, the giant toymaker, has many customers that use JIT and, therefore, want quick responses to their orders. Mattel accordingly directs many capital expenditures toward increasing its manufacturing capacity and reducing its cycle time. Most toymakers contract out manufacturing, but Mattel manufactures 75 percent of its core products. The company believes that in-house manufacturing is an important strategic advantage because it reduces costs and response time while increasing quality. Mattel might have a difficult time keeping its existing customer base if it outsourced toy manufacture.

Auto companies have invested in reducing the time required for new car development. **Chrysler** can now bring a car from design to market in 39 months, down from 54 months. The company has also invested in software development that will allow it to reduce factory retooling time from 30 months to 24 months. **Honda** has been able to bring out three new versions of the Accord, while during the same period **Ford** brought out only two versions of the Taurus.

Fieldcrest Cannon, the manufacturer of home furnishings, is one of many companies that have been concentrating on reducing cycle time and inventories through investing in JIT. The Bath Division of Fieldcrest has been building new plants with an eye toward eliminating levels of supervision, empowering employees to solve daily operating problems, and driving up quality.

Colgate-Palmolive Company has invested heavily in new products, so that 26 percent of its 1994 sales were from products less than five years old. The company has also invested in manufacturing facilities in foreign countries, partly to offset the effects of currency fluctuations, a problem we introduced in Chapter 1. Still, the company devotes 60 percent of its capital investment to cost saving projects.

Sources: 1994 annual reports

cost may be approximated by dividing the expected earnings by the market value of the stock. Thus, if a company is expected to earn $3 per share and the market price of the stock is $30 per share, the cost of equity capital is 10 percent ($3/$30).

Cost of capital is also the opportunity cost of investment. A company that invests in any particular project is tying up capital that it could invest elsewhere. The idea of cost of capital as an opportunity cost is illustrated by stock buy-backs that companies undertake from time to time. In a buy-back, the company buys its own shares on the open market, reflecting its view that the best investment available at that time is the company's own stock. Companies bought $99 billion of their own stock in 1995. Among companies that have used this device recently are **Levi Strauss, Bank of America**, and **John Deere**. The 1995 annual report of **Coca-Cola** stated that it bought back 29 million shares for $1.8 billion in 1995. Coca-Cola believes that investing in its own stock offers its shareholders "a significantly higher long-term return than other investment alternatives . . ."

We are interested in cost of capital because it is the minimum acceptable rate of return on investment. But determining cost of capital is usually a complex task. Because of the practical difficulties of the task, managers might simply use their judgment to set a minimum acceptable rate, called a **cutoff rate, hurdle rate**, or **target rate**. Moreover, even if companies do have reasonable estimates of cost of capital, they might use a higher cutoff rate. Companies might set a target rate higher than cost of capital to provide a safety margin against increases in cost of capital. They also might use a higher rate to provide a safety margin against unfavorable changes in cash flows. Remember that cash flows are estimates, some well out into the future, so safety margins are wise. Companies might also use a higher rate because productive investments must not only justify themselves, but must also cover indirect costs and investments that are not productive, such as corporate headquarters costs and investment.

METHODS OF ANALYZING INVESTMENT DECISIONS

When making investment decisions, managers try to determine whether, considering the time value of money, the rate of return associated with the investment is greater or less than the minimum acceptable rate. Two principal techniques are available: (1) find the rate of return associated with the project and compare that rate with the minimum acceptable rate, and (2) use the minimum acceptable rate to find the present value of the future returns and compare that value with the cost of the investment.

The first method is called the **internal rate of return**, or **IRR** method. The second method is called the **net present value (NPV)** method. Using the NPV method, we compare the present value of future returns from an investment with the cost of obtaining those returns—the required investment. (Each proposal to the Federal Base Closure and Realignment Commission included this comparison. That commission was charged with recommending to Congress which specific military bases should be closed.) Both methods use the same basic principles. Later in this chapter, we consider two other commonly used techniques for analyzing long-term investments. These additional techniques are conceptually inferior to either the NPV or the IRR method because neither considers the time value of money.

In three of the four analytical approaches to capital budgeting decisions discussed in this chapter, returns are defined as **cash flows**, not as income. Given the emphasis on income in prior chapters, and probably in your first course in accounting, we will briefly explain why cash flows are so important in capital budgeting.

CASH FLOWS AND BOOK INCOME

Analyses of the short-term decisions covered in Chapter 5 concentrated on whether the decision would increase income. We did not speak of cash flows in Chapter 5 because incremental revenues and incremental costs are the same as incremental cash inflows and incremental cash outflows in the short term. Thus, incremental profit is also incremental cash flow. In the short term, cash flows come in and go out within relatively short periods (during the year), so that the time value of money is not significant.

For long-term investments in depreciable assets, incremental incomes and incremental cash flows will differ in the individual years of the life of the investment because of depreciation. So we cannot use income as a substitute for cash flow. The cash outflow for a depreciable asset occurs in the year of acquisition. Then, for accounting and tax purposes, the cost of that asset is depreciated over its useful life, so the incomes of those years are reduced by depreciation expense. But depreciation expense does not require a cash outlay. Therefore, the income attributable to the investment will be less than the cash flow attributable to the investment because income will be reduced by depreciation expense, which requires no cash flow. For this reason, we must be more specific in our analyses of decisions that involve depreciable assets and future incomes. We cannot use income as a substitute for cash flows (as we did in Chapter 5) because income will not equal cash flow when depreciation expense exists.

Depreciation affects cash flows because it is a legitimate deduction for income and tax purposes, and income taxes are a cash outflow. Hence, to determine incremental cash flow from an investment for a particular year, we must know the depreciation expense for that year. Later in this chapter we show how to deal with depreciation and income taxes.

Bear in mind one final and important point. As with all management decisions that deal with the future, the numbers used (for cash flows, useful lives, etc.) are estimates. They are almost never known with certainty at the time a decision must be made. Chapter 9 illustrates techniques managers use to allow for this uncertainty. The accompanying Insight describes some capital investments that did not pan out or were made obsolete by changes in conditions or strategies.

CAPITAL BUDGETING METHODS

As stated earlier, the principle introduced in Chapter 5 — that the only relevant data for decisions are differential revenues and costs — also governs capital budgeting decisions. The relevant data for capital budgeting decisions are the incremental (or differential) cash flows expected from a decision. The following example illustrates the main points.

A company with a cutoff rate of 12 percent has an opportunity to introduce a new product. The best available estimates from marketing and production people are that the company will be able to sell 3,000 units per year for the next five years at $14 each. Variable costs should be $5 per unit. To make the product, the company will need machinery that costs $60,000, has a five-year life with no salvage value, and requires annual fixed cash operating costs of $5,000 for maintenance, insurance, and property taxes. (Notice that we have not included depreciation as a cost because it does not require a cash payment. We also ignore income taxes for now.)

Anheuser-Busch, brewer of Budweiser and other beers, recently announced that it was selling its snack food division, which had not lived up to its original estimates of profitability. Anheuser-Busch's net investment in the snack operation was about $350 million and it expected to lose $206 million on the sale. Because beer and snack food seem complementary, the original move into snacks seemed very sensible. Many observers believed that Anheuser-Busch could leverage its core competency of consumer marketing, but it did not happen. **Hyundai**, the Korean automaker, abandoned a $300 million plant in Canada because the cars the plant produced did not sell well in North America.

Annual reports sometimes comment on failed investments in ways that stress larger strategic concerns. **Dole Food Companies** stated that it will "reduce our involvement in business segments that require large investments with relatively low returns . . . ." And that Dole is committed to the food business but will "participate in the industry more selectively." Dole sold its juice business for $285 million because its top managers believed the company could not become a major factor in the industry. **Applebee's International**, the restaurant chain, has been sustaining losses in several restaurants in the Dallas area. The company noted that it had closed one, recognizing a loss of $223 thousand, and will "reevaluate its future strategies for these [remaining] restaurants." **CSX** states that it will "evaluate for sale or other disposition" units that fail to earn returns in excess of cost of capital.

Changes in strategy can impair existing investments. In 1994, **Barnes and Noble** closed 49 bookstores it had operated in shopping malls, partly because it had built 268 superstores by the end of the year. The company's superstores are much bigger than mall stores and offer such amenities as cafes serving Starbucks coffee. The company's strategy is to use these superstores to recreate the neighborhood bookstore, even though the superstores harm mall stores. Many companies today stress their "core competencies," the things they do well, and liquidate investments in activities they consider peripheral.

Sources: Annual reports

Following are the annual incremental cash inflows.

	Annual Cash Flows Years 1-5
Revenues ($14 × 3,000)	$42,000
Variable costs ($5 × 3,000)	15,000
Contribution margin ($9 × 3,000)	$27,000
Cash fixed costs	5,000
Expected increase in net cash inflows	$22,000

Using this information, we analyze the proposed investment in two basic ways.

NET PRESENT VALUE (NPV) METHOD

When using the NPV method the question is whether it is wise to invest $60,000 today to receive $22,000 per year for the next five years. The investment is worthwhile if the present value of the $22,000 per year to be received for five years is greater than the $60,000 outlay required today (which, obviously, has a present value of $60,000). The present value of the future cash flows of $22,000 minus the $60,000 required investment is called the NPV or the *excess present value*. If it is positive (present value of the future cash flows exceeds the required investment), the investment is desirable. If it is negative, the investment is undesirable.

To determine the NPV we must first find the present value of $22,000 per year for five years at 12 percent. In the appropriate present value table (Table B in Appendix B), we see that the factor for a series of payments of $1 for five years at 12 percent is 3.605. Multiplying this factor by $22,000, we obtain $79,310 as the present value of the future cash flows. This means that if you desire a 12 percent return and expect annual payments of $22,000 for five years, you would be willing to pay up to $79,310 for this investment. Therefore, you are more than happy to pay only $60,000, and the investment is desirable. The NPV is $19,310 ($79,310 - $60,000). Following is a summary of the analysis.

Present value of future cash flows ($22,000 × 3.605)	$79,310
Investment required	60,000
Net present value	$19,310

INTERNAL RATE OF RETURN (IRR) METHOD

Another approach to analyzing investment opportunities is to find the expected IRR. This method poses the question "What return are we earning if we invest $60,000 now and receive $22,000 annually for five years?" The investment is desirable if the IRR is higher than the cost of capital. The IRR is also called the **time-adjusted rate of return**. **Anheuser-Busch's** annual report states that it evaluates investments using the "discounted cash flow return on investment," which is also the same as the IRR.

Financial calculators calculate NPVs and IRRs, as do most spreadsheets. If net cash flows are equal in each year, the IRR is not difficult to find by hand. The rate equates the present value of the future cash flows with the amount to be invested now. Consider that the computation of the present value of the future flows is as follows:

$$\begin{array}{c} \textit{Present value of} \\ \textit{future flows} \end{array} = \begin{array}{c} \textit{Annual cash} \\ \textit{flows} \end{array} \times \begin{array}{c} \textit{Factor for the discount rate} \\ \textit{and the number of periods} \end{array}$$

To compute the IRR, we set the amount of the investment as the present value and try to determine the discount rate associated with the factor that, when multiplied by the annual flows, equals the cost of the investment. In effect, we are answering the question, "What discount rate gives the investment a net present value of zero?"

The first step is to find the factor related to both the discount rate and number of periods. Rearranging the preceding equation yields

$$\frac{Present\ value\ of\ future\ flows}{Annual\ cash\ flows} = \frac{Factor\ for\ the\ discount}{rate\ and\ the\ number\ of\ periods}$$

In our example,

$$\frac{\$60,000}{\$22,000} = 2.727$$

The second step is to relate this factor, 2.727, to the factor for the discount rate and five periods. We can find the discount rate by looking at the factors listed in the five-period row in Table B. In the five-period row under the 24 percent column, the factor is 2.745; in that row, under the 25 percent column, the factor is 2.689. Hence, the IRR on this project is between 24 and 25 percent. (You should have been able to tell that the IRR on this project was greater than 12 percent because the NPV computed in the previous section is positive.)

Although we could use a financial calculator or spreadsheet to find the rate, we know it falls between 24 and 25 percent and is higher than cost of capital. Hence, the investment is desirable. Because we are dealing with estimates of future cash flows, greater precision is unwarranted.

GENERALITY OF THE ANALYSIS

Our example uses a new product, but the facts and numbers could just as well relate to an opportunity to expand the productive capacity for an existing product, or to an opportunity to reduce costs. Companies responding to changes prompted by the new manufacturing environment are continually evaluating investments that they expect will reduce costs.

Suppose that instead of introducing a new product, the $60,000 investment is for machinery that will cut $9 from the per-unit variable production costs of an existing product through reductions in material waste and quicker processing. (The reduction in variable costs increases the contribution margin on the existing product by $9, which is equal to the contribution margin expected to result from the new product in the original example.) Assume further that the sales volume on the product is 3,000 units per year, and that the additional cash fixed costs for the new machinery are $5,000 (the same as in the original example). The incremental cash flows are then

Savings in variable costs ($9 × 3,000)	$27,000
Less incremental cash fixed costs	5,000
Net increase in annual cash flows (savings)	$22,000

Thus, the pattern of analysis is the same whether the cash flows result from selling new products, expanding output of existing products, or saving on operating expenses. Find the incremental cash flows and then apply one of the methods described. How the cash flows come about is irrelevant.

Not-for-profit entities can also use the basic techniques when they face decisions to acquire long-lived assets. For example, a city might want to decide whether to build a new municipal building or convention center. Because cities are not subject to income taxes, the analysis we have illustrated is adequate. As we noted earlier, however, managers in businesses must also consider the cash outflow for income taxes, which is affected by depreciation. The next section refines the analytical process to recognize the effects of taxes.

TAXES AND DEPRECIATION

Calculating after-tax cash flows is slightly more complex. Continuing with the example of the new product, assume a 40 percent income tax rate and straight-line depreciation for income tax calculations.[2] The initial outlay is still $60,000, but the annual incremental cash flows are different because the income from the project is now subject to income taxes. The net incremental cash inflow for each of the five years is computed as follows:

	Tax Computation	Cash Flow
Net Incremental Cash Flow for Each Year		
Revenues	$42,000	$42,000
Cash expenses (variable and fixed)	20,000	20,000
Cash inflow before taxes	$22,000	$22,000
Depreciation ($60,000/5)	12,000	
Increase in taxable income	$10,000	
Tax at 40% (cash outflow)	$ 4,000	4,000
Net increase in annual cash inflow		$18,000

The tax deduction for depreciation on the asset reduces taxes. Without the deduction, taxes would be $8,800 ($22,000 × 40%). Thus, the $12,000 in depreciation expense saves $4,800 (40% × $12,000). This important saving is called the **tax shield**, or **tax effect of depreciation**.

We do not show net income in the schedule because we want to emphasize that we are concerned with cash flows, not net income. However, you might find it easier, and more understandable, to develop an income statement and then add back depreciation to get net cash flow. (Accountants and financial managers frequently use this calculation.) The income statement converted to a cash basis is as follows:

Revenues (cash inflow)	$42,000
Cash expenses	20,000
Cash inflow before taxes	$22,000
Depreciation	12,000
Income before taxes	$10,000
Tax at 40%	4,000
Increase in net income	$ 6,000
Add back depreciation	12,000
Net increase in annual cash inflow	$18,000
Present value factor for 5 years at 12%	3.605
Present value of future cash inflows	$64,890
Investment required	60,000
Net present value	$ 4,890

---

2 *We introduce income taxes at this stage to emphasize how they affect decisions. Accordingly, we do not yet consider the technical details of U.S. tax law. Chapter 9 introduces the Modified Accelerated Cost Recovery System and other tax issues.*

This approach to computing the increase in net annual cash flow is equivalent to the two-column approach used earlier. Using either approach, you must remember that taxes are determined by tax law, which does not always correspond to financial reporting principles. Chapter 9 discusses some of the differences.

Using either approach, annual incremental cash inflows are now $18,000 per year (rather than $22,000), which, when discounted at 12 percent, have a present value of $64,890. The NPV is $4,890; the investment is still desirable. To compute the IRR, we find the present value factor that, when multiplied by $18,000, equals $60,000. The factor is 3.333 ($60,000/$18,000). The factor closest to this in the five-year row in Table B is 3.274, the factor for 16 percent. The IRR is therefore between 14 and 16 percent, but closer to 16 percent. (You should have expected an IRR greater than 12 percent, since the NPV is positive at a 12 percent cost of capital.)

For the rest of the chapter, any comparisons with this basic example will refer to the analysis *with* taxes.

UNEVEN CASH FLOWS

The basic example has equal annual net cash inflows, but it is not unusual for revenues, or cash expenses, or both, to vary from year to year. For example, revenues from a new product might grow in the early years and decline in later years, or might take several years to reach a particular, expected level. Additionally, companies rarely use straight-line depreciation for income tax purposes. Accordingly, the cash outflow for taxes each year will vary. Or, the investment might have a salvage value that increases cash flow in the last year. Uneven cash flows complicate the arithmetic of the analysis but do not affect the basic principles. We illustrate two situations involving uneven cash flows.

SALVAGE VALUES

Many assets have salvage values at the ends of their useful lives. The simplest way to incorporate this factor into the analysis is to find the after-tax cash flow from the salvage value and discount it separately.

Assume, for example, that the new asset purchased in the basic example has an expected salvage value of $5,000 at the end of its useful life. How would this expectation affect the analysis of the investment? Your knowledge of financial accounting might lead you to expect the salvage value to change the depreciation of this asset. Such is not usually the case. Remember that the cash outflow for taxes depends on what is on the company's tax return. Hence, your interest is in tax-return depreciation, and the tax law specifies that salvage values generally be ignored. For this reason, any proceeds received from selling a depreciable asset at the end of its useful life probably will be taxed.

Using straight-line depreciation and incorporating the expected salvage value into the basic example, we get the following analysis.

Incremental Cash Flows Years 1-5

	Tax Computation	Cash Flow
Revenues	$42,000	$42,000
Cash expenses	20,000	20,000
Cash inflow before taxes	$22,000	$22,000
Depreciation ($60,000/5)	12,000	
Increase in taxable income	$10,000	
Tax at 40%	$ 4,000	4,000
Net cash inflow per year, as before		$18,000

Summary of Present Value of Investment

Operating cash flows ($18,000 × 3.605)		$64,890
Salvage value:		
Total salvage value	$5,000	
Tax on salvage value at 40%	2,000	
After-tax cash inflow from salvage value	$3,000	
Times present value factor for 5 years		
hence at 12%	0.567	
Present value of salvage value		1,701
Total present value		$66,591
Investment required		60,000
Net present value		$ 6,591

NPV was $4,890 when taxes were first considered. The new NPV, $6,591, is higher by the $1,701 present value of the salvage value. We could use a financial calculator or spreadsheet to find the IRR. Note that we cannot simply look up a value in Table B because we no longer have equal cash flows in every year. We could use trial-and-error or interpolate to approximate the IRR. The IRR will be higher than before because the NPV is higher.

VARIATIONS IN ANNUAL FLOWS

We said earlier that cash flows vary if sales vary during the life of a project. The uneven flows change the analysis only in that we need to discount the flows individually, instead of as an annuity.

   To illustrate, let us return to our basic example of a new product. We assume no salvage value, but assume that sales are expected to be 2,000, 3,000, 3,000, 4,000, and 3,000 in years one through five, respectively. (The total is still 15,000 units for the five years.) Without making any calculations, can you tell whether the investment will be more or less desirable than it was when sales were spread evenly over the five years? That is, will NPV be higher or lower than the $4,890 determined earlier? If you decided that the investment will be less desirable (lower NPV) you are correct; sales occur later, so cash will be received later. The present value of a cash receipt declines the longer you must wait to receive it. (Of course, variable costs occur later too, but the inflow from sales exceeds the outflow from variable costs.)

The following schedule shows the calculations using the revised sales fore-cast. For brevity, we use the $9 per-unit contribution margin instead of showing both revenues and variable costs. As expected, NPV is now lower ($3,502 vs. $4,890), but the investment is still desirable because NPV is still positive. Notice that the totals are the same as they were before, which you can verify by multiplying the numbers in the previous schedule by five. Thus, total cash flow before taxes is $110,000 ($22,000 × 5), total income taxes are $20,000 ($4,000 × 5), and so on. The difference arises when the cash flows are converted to present values. The delay in the cash flows reduces the present value of those flows.

Cash Flows and Present Values

			Year			
	1	2	3	4	5	Total
Unit sales	2,000	3,000	3,000	4,000	3,000	15,000
Contribution margin at $9	$18,000	$27,000	$27,000	$36,000	$27,000	$135,000
Less cash fixed costs	5,000	5,000	5,000	5,000	5,000	25,000
Pretax cash inflow	$13,000	$22,000	$22,000	$31,000	$22,000	$110,000
Less depreciation	12,000	12,000	12,000	12,000	12,000	60,000
Income before taxes	$ 1,000	$10,000	$10,000	$19,000	$10,000	$ 50,000
Income taxes at 40%	400	4,000	4,000	7,600	4,000	20,000
Net income	$ 600	$ 6,000	$ 6,000	$11,400	$ 6,000	$ 30,000
Add depreciation	12,000	12,000	12,000	12,000	12,000	60,000
Net cash flow	$12,600	$18,000	$18,000	$23,400	$18,000	$ 90,000
Present value factor (Table A)	0.893	0.797	0.712	0.636	0.567	
Present value	$11,252	$14,346	$12,816	$14,882	$10,206	$ 63,502
Less investment						60,000
Net present value						$ 3,502

Finding the IRR can be difficult when there are uneven cash flows. Trial-and-error and interpolation will give a close approximation of the rate, and financial calculators and spreadsheets can make such calculations. Because the NPV is positive, the IRR must be greater than the 12 percent discount rate used in calculating the present values. (The IRR is about 14.2 percent.)

DECISION RULES

Looking only at the quantitative aspects of an investment opportunity, the decision rules for the two methods of analysis we describe are simple. Under the NPV method, a project having a positive NPV should be accepted; others should be rejected. Under the IRR method, a project having an IRR greater than the company's cost of capital should be accepted. The relationship of the two criteria is as follows:

1.   If IRR is less than the cutoff rate, NPV is negative.
2.   If NPV is positive, IRR is greater than the cutoff rate.

When analyzing any single project for acceptance or rejection, both methods lead to the same decision. The problem of multiple investment opportunities is discussed in Chapter 9.

QUALITATIVE CONSIDERATIONS

Chapter 5 stated that qualitative, or hard-to-quantify, concerns often override quantitative analyses in short-term decisions. The same is true with capital budgeting decisions. As we mentioned at the outset, laws, regulations, and company policy mandate some investments. **CSX's** annual report states that "expenditures to meet safety, environmental, or other regulatory requirements" do not have to provide returns in excess of cost of capital.

The management of **Embassy Suites** found that one of the most frequent complaints was the lack of an iron and ironing board in each suite. Company policy called for each hotel to have a sufficient supply of these amenities. Nonetheless, the company invested $2 million to equip every suite with these conveniences.[3] Employee welfare is an important consideration in many capital budgeting decisions. Morale, safety, and convenience are important factors in decisions regarding such investments as fitness centers, parking lots, and on-site day-care centers. **Toyota Motor Company** has an explicit qualitative goal that investments in plant automation should improve working conditions and make employees more comfortable and put them under less stress. The company expects these better conditions to reduce worker turnover, which in turn will save on training costs. However, the company is committed to such investments even if the tangible, quantifiable benefits are insufficient to justify the investment. Some automated operations now cost more than they would if people were still doing them.[4]

Strategic considerations should also play an important part in major capital investment decisions. Companies usually commit themselves to following particular strategies and must be able to look past purely quantitative analyses to pursue those strategies. **General Motors** new car line, Saturn, required a $5 billion initial investment and has not shown a profit by the spring of 1995. Nonetheless, GM's top management decided that Saturn should be a separate marketing division and carry the company's banner in global competition for clean, fuel-efficient cars. Additional billions will be required to fulfill that role.[5]

Companies following cost leadership strategies will use activity-based costing to look for ways to reduce the levels of various drivers. When **General Electric** modernized its appliance complex in Louisville, Kentucky in the early 1980s, it achieved considerable reductions in costs of scrap, rework, and service calls. But GE had not aimed at cost reduction in undertaking the modernization. Rather, it sought higher product quality because it had adopted the strategy of being the highest quality producer, not the lowest cost producer.[6]

Qualitative concerns are becoming increasingly important as companies adopt advanced manufacturing techniques. Some of the advantages of such techniques

---

3 *"Quality: How to Make It Pay,"* Business Week, *August 8, 1994, 57.*
4 *Alex Taylor III, "How Toyota Copes with Hard Times,"* Fortune, *January 28, 1993, 78-81.*
5 *Gabriella Stern, "Saturn Experiment Is Deemed Successful Enough to Expand,"* The Wall Street Journal, *April 15, 1995, B1-B2.*
6 *Tony Baer, "Cost Justification Is Possible,"* Managing Automation, *August 1986, 57.*

are difficult to quantify and might therefore be overlooked. For instance, while managers agree that increasing the quality of a product is desirable, the monetary effect is not easy to estimate. Similar considerations arise with such benefits as reducing cycle time. An early Insight mentioned that **Chrysler Corporation** cut the technical staff needed to develop a new car from 2,000 to 740 and reduced development time from 54 months to 39 months. These improvements mean that new models get to the market faster and cash inflows come in sooner.[7]

Ford has cut $11 billion from its new product budget for the next five years. It was able to do so because it has been reducing the number of "platforms," or basic cars. (For example, the Ford Taurus and Mercury Sable are built on the same platform.) Ford will use the same platform for more cars and will eliminate some platforms. Ford plans to go from its current 24 platforms to 16 in the year 2000. Ford expects to save $1 billion in 1996 by reducing "complexity, redundancy, and waste in its product-development effort."[8]

These improvements should increase cash flows and bring them in sooner, but managers will have a great deal of difficulty estimating the cash flow effects of such investments. However, while quantitative estimates of benefits of such improvements are difficult, managers cannot assume that doing nothing to improve product quality and reduce cycle time will permit the company to continue as it has. The company could well suffer as a result of not accepting such investments.

Having emphasized the importance of qualitative considerations, we must also point out that ignoring quantitative measures of profitability is also unwise. It is not correct to say that companies should relentlessly pursue objectives that entail many large, unprofitable investments. At some point, reality must intrude and managers must pay attention to profitability or else the company could go under. Where qualitative factors are important, managers should still perform quantitative analyses so they will have a better idea of the cost to the company of accepting a particular qualitative goal as paramount. For example, **AT&T** requires proposals for increasing product quality to show a 10 percent return.[9]

OTHER METHODS OF CAPITAL BUDGETING

Although the NPV and IRR methods are theoretically sound, some managers argue that they are not practical because of the many estimates involved (cost of capital, cash flows, useful lives, etc.). Interestingly, the methods advocated by these managers, payback and book rate of return, require most of the same estimates which NPV and IRR require.

PAYBACK

One of the most commonly used methods of capital budgeting is the **payback** technique. This method poses the question "How long will it take to recover the investment?" If the annual cash inflows are equal,

---

7 William M. Bulkeley, *"The Latest Thing At Many Big Companies Is Speed, Speed, Speed,"* The Wall Street Journal, *December 23, 1994, A5.*
8 Oscar Suris, *"Ford Slashes $11 billion Out of Budget For New Products Over Next Five Years,"* The Wall Street Journal, *February 29, 1996, A4.*
9 *"Quality: How To Make It Pay,"* Business Week, *August 8, 1994, 56.*

$$\frac{Payback}{period} = \frac{Investment\ required}{Annual\ cash\ returns}$$

Payback evaluates the rapidity with which an investment is recovered. In our basic example, the required investment of $60,000 generates annual net cash inflows of $18,000, and so has a payback period of 3.3 years ($60,000/$18,000). As a practical matter, the payback period is automatically computed in the process of calculating IRR on an investment with equal annual cash flows. The investment required was $60,000, and annual cash inflows were $18,000. When computing IRR on this project, we determined that the investment divided by the annual cash inflows was 3.333, which is the payback period for the investment, as well as the present value factor for the discount rate and number of periods covered by the investment.

Decision rules when using the payback technique may be stated in different ways by different companies. Some companies set a limit on the payback period beyond which an investment will not be made. Others use payback to pick one of several investments, selecting the one with the shortest payback period. Some companies impose an implicit payback period by discounting cash flows only up to some specified number of years, and ignoring any potential flows beyond that period. Such a practice compensates for the rapid technological obsolescence that many companies face. **Cyto Technologies** uses a three-year horizon for its investments.[10] **Colgate's** 1994 annual report stated that it directed capital spending to "...rapid-payback, high-return cost savings projects."

ADVANTAGES

The payback period can be particularly important to a company especially concerned about liquidity. Payback also can be used as a rough screening device for investment proposals. A long payback period usually means a low rate of return, and an extremely short payback period very often suggests a good investment. For example, a division of **General Electric** expected a four-month payback period on an investment in a **Pitney-Bowes** Star system that determines the cheapest way to send a parcel.[11] Because the system could readily accommodate rate changes by available vendors, its useful life far exceeds the payback.

Some companies use payback as a measure of risk because, in general, the longer it takes to get your money back, the greater the risk that the money will not be returned. As the time horizon lengthens, more uncertainties arise. Inflation might ease or it might get worse; interest rates could rise or they could fall; new techniques might be developed that would make the investment obsolete. Because of the increased uncertainty, a manager might prefer a project that pays back its investment in two years to one that takes ten years, even if the one with the ten-year payback period has a higher expected NPV and IRR. Payback can therefore be helpful for companies investing in foreign countries, as we shall see in a little while.

---

10 *Suresh Kalagnanam and Suzanne K. Schmidt, "Analyzing Capital Investments in New Products,"* Management Accounting, *January 1996, 31-36.*
11 *Business Week, March 5, 1990, 50.*

FLAWS OF PAYBACK

The payback method has two very serious faults. The first is that it tells nothing about the profitability of the investment. Payback emphasizes the return of the investment but ignores the return on the investment because it ignores the life of the project after the payback period.

Consider the following two investment possibilities.

	A	B
Investment	$10,000	$10,000
Useful life in years	5	10
Annual cash flows over the useful lives	$2,500	$2,000

Investment A has a payback period of four years ($10,000/$2,500), and investment B a payback period of five years ($10,000/$2,000). Using only the payback criterion, investment A is better than investment B because its payback period is shorter. Yet it should be obvious that investment B is superior; the returns from A cease one year after the payback period, while B continues to return cash for five more years.

The second serious fault of the payback method is that it ignores the timing of the expected future cash flows and so ignores the time value of money. This fault, like the method's failure to consider years after the payback period, can lead to poor decisions. Consider the following two investments, X and Y.

	X	Y
Investment	$10,000	$10,000
Cash inflows by year:		
1	$2,000	$6,000
2	2,000	3,000
3	6,000	1,000
4-8	3,000	3,000

Both X and Y have payback periods of three years. They also show equal total returns. But the equal payback periods are misleading because the investment in Y will be recovered much more quickly than that in X. For the same reason, even if the two investments promise equal total returns, the one that generates the returns more quickly is the more desirable. (IRR on investment X is approximately 25 percent, whereas that on investment Y is about 32 percent.)

BOOK RATE OF RETURN

Another commonly used capital budgeting method is the **book rate of return** technique. Under this method, the average annual expected book income is divided by the average book investment in the project. That is,

$$\textit{Average book rate of return} = \frac{\textit{Average annual expected book income}}{\textit{Average book investment}}$$

To illustrate, consider again the $60,000 investment opportunity in our basic example. The book net income for each of the five years of the project's life would be $6,000. The average book investment in this project will be $30,000 ($60,000/2). With an annual net income of $6,000 and an average book investment of $30,000, the average book rate of return is 20 percent ($6,000/$30,000). This return is an average rate of return because we have used the average book investment. The book rate of return for each year will be different because the average book investment in the project will change with each year's depreciation. For example, using the average book investment in year one, the book rate of return is 11.1 percent ($6,000/$54,000); in the last year, the book rate of return is 100 percent ($6,000/$6,000).

Let us compare these results with those obtained using the IRR method. The IRR on this project is something less than 16 percent. If the cutoff rate is 16 percent or higher, both the NPV and the IRR methods of analysis suggest that the investment should be rejected. Use of the book rate of return as the criterion for evaluating investments could mislead managers to accept this investment opportunity.

To emphasize the deficiencies of the book rate of return method, consider another simpler example. As shown in the following analysis, investments A and B require identical investments ($10,000) and produce identical total net incomes, identical average net incomes, and identical book rates of return of 26.7 percent. Investment A is clearly superior to investment B; the flows come in faster for A. (The IRR on investment A is about 23 percent, whereas that on investment B is only about 15 percent.)

	A	B
Pretax cash flows by year:		
1	$10,000	$ 2,000
2	5,000	5,000
3	1,666	9,666
Totals	$16,666	$16,666
Depreciation	10,000	10,000
Income before taxes	$ 6,666	$ 6,666
Income taxes at 40%	2,666	2,666
Total net income	$ 4,000	$ 4,000
Average net income, $4,000/3	$ 1,333	$ 1,333
Average book rate of return, $1,333/$5,000	26.7%	26.7%

The book rate of return method almost always misstates the internal rate of return because it ignores the timing of the cash flows and, therefore, the time value of money. This flaw makes it an unsatisfactory method of capital budgeting.

SUMMARY EVALUATION OF METHODS

Of course, qualitative factors can prevail over the decision rules for all of the methods previously discussed. The critical difference between the NPV and IRR methods and the payback and book rate of return methods is the attention given to the timing of the expected cash flows. The first two methods, called **discounted cash flow (DCF)** techniques, consider the timing of the cash flows; the last two methods do not. Their recognition of the time value of money makes DCF techniques conceptually superior, but payback is often used in conjunction with those techniques.

As stated earlier, some managers argue that DCF techniques are too complex or that they require too many estimates to make them useful in practice. We see little merit in these charges. All four methods require about the same estimates. DCF methods require estimates of future cash flows and the timing of those flows. The book rate of return method requires estimates of future net incomes, which means making essentially the same estimates as those required to estimate cash flows. The payback method requires estimating cash flows but not useful lives. One point in favor of the payback method is that it emphasizes near-term cash flows, which are usually easier to predict than flows in later years. However, as we pointed out, unless consideration is given to useful life, the payback method could lead to very poor decisions.

The NPV, IRR, and book rate of return methods all require an estimate of the cost of capital, or at least a decision as to a minimum acceptable rate of return. The payback method requires a decision regarding the minimum acceptable payback period. Thus, DCF techniques are no less realistic or practical than the other two approaches. The conceptual superiority of DCF techniques argues strongly for their use, though the payback period should probably not be ignored.

INVESTING DECISIONS AND FINANCING DECISIONS

Perhaps you've noticed that none of the examples in this chapter considered how the company will finance the project. That is, we did not say that the company plans to issue debt, common stock, some combination of the two, or finance the investment using cash flows from ongoing operations. The omission was deliberate. The investing decision nearly always should be kept separate from the financing decision.

It might be tempting to argue that if the company plans to finance an investment with 9 percent debt, it should use 9 percent to discount the expected cash flows. Also, it might be tempting to subtract the interest payments as part of the cash flow computation. Resist these temptations!

A company should not accept projects that will return less than the cost of capital, because it must earn a satisfactory return for all investors—both creditors and stockholders. Both types of capital suppliers are concerned about the safety of their investments and therefore monitor company solvency by watching such factors as the ratio of debt to equity. A company that makes too liberal use of debt and earns returns that exceed the interest rate but not the cost of capital will have to pay exorbitant rates to raise capital. (Stockholders will sell their stock, which reduces the price and thus raises the cost of equity capital. Lenders will insist on higher interest rates, thus raising the cost of debt capital.)

Including interest payments as part of the cash flow computation reflects a misunderstanding of the concept of discounting. The discount rate *automatically* provides for not only the recovery of the investment, but also a return on the investment at least equal to the discount rate, which is cost of capital or a cutoff rate. Hence, subtracting interest payments to arrive at the net cash flow provides for the cost of debt twice—once by subtracting the interest payments, and again by using a discount rate that includes the cost of obtaining both the debt and equity capital.

INTERNATIONAL ASPECTS OF CAPITAL BUDGETING

Investing in foreign countries entails special problems and opportunities. On the positive side, many countries eagerly seek foreign investment and will offer tax and other concessions to make them more attractive to foreign companies. **Daewoo and LG Electronics**, a large South Korean company, expanded its manufacturing operations in Europe. European governments gave the company cash grants, low-interest loans, plant sites, exemptions from taxes, and even discounts on electricity.[12] The U.S. is certainly amenable to foreign investment. Several states offered concessions to attract a **BMW** plant a few years ago. The plant went to South Carolina, which, along with some local governments, offered a package of tax abatement and other concessions reported to total $100 million.

In today's global economy, many once-closed nations are opening up for investment, particularly formerly communist nations. Russia and China are the most prominent and have attracted the most attention. Investing in such countries is not for the faint of heart. Investing in any new market is risky because the investor must deal with a new culture, with different customs, practices, and mores. China has offered many concessions in recent years, as have some of the formerly communist countries in Eastern Europe.

Capital budgeting for foreign operations is much more complicated and much less precise. Some factors that can be critical in making investments in foreign countries follow.

- The risk of nationalization (a country seizes the property of foreign companies with limited or no compensation) is very great in some countries.
- Instability in economic, social, and political conditions can cause serious losses. In emerging countries such as formerly communist countries, such risks are magnified.
- Astronomical inflation can wipe out the value of an investment.
- Restrictions on trade and on repatriation of cash can limit the company's ability to return its investment to its home country.
- Exchange rate fluctuations increase risk because overseas investments might be profitable in the local currency, but unprofitable when translated back to the home currency. Building plants and raising capital in foreign countries alleviates this risk.
- Failure to respect local customs and traditions could jeopardize investments.

Problems encountered by companies investing in China, Cuba, and Russia exemplify some of the factors. China has been slow to recognize intellectual property rights and enforceability of contracts. Shortly after **Chrysler** built a plant to make Jeeps, a Chinese factory began making Jeep knockoffs. The government did little to resolve the dispute.[13] Chinese companies have copied or used the trademarks of such products as **Microsoft's** Windows, **Kellogg's** cornflakes, and a vast array of CDs by Western artists. The government's indifference to patent and trademark rights has been a significant factor in decisions by some U.S. companies to avoid the country. One observer stated that companies do not take their most important technology to China.[14]

Creditfinance Securities, a Canadian investment company, rushed to invest in Cuba a few years ago, but has since pulled out because of onerous regulation.[15] **IBM** invested in a plant in Russia, but abandoned it because of changes in the tax and import duty structure. Russia increased the duty on imported parts, on which the plant would rely, but gave some companies exemptions. News reports suggested that some companies gained exemptions through inducements to Russian officials.[16] Of course, foreign companies can run into political problems in the U.S., as well. In 1992, the U.S. Department of Transportation thwarted a bid by **British Airways** to invest in **U.S. Air**. Other U.S. carriers also opposed the investment and it was widely reported that political considerations were paramount in the final decision.

SUMMARY

Decisions to commit resources for periods longer than a year are capital budgeting decisions. Evaluating such decisions requires determining the investment and its resulting cash flows. Future cash flows may occur because of additional revenues and costs, or because of cost savings. Critical to capital budgeting is that most, if not all, of the numbers used in the analyses are estimates. The effects of depreciation on income taxes must also be recognized.

Effective evaluation of capital budgeting decisions requires consideration of the time value of money. The two approaches recommended, called discounted cash flow techniques, are the net present value (NPV) and the internal rate of return (IRR) methods. Two other methods—payback and book rate of return—are often used, but are conceptually inferior because they fail to consider the time value of money. Nevertheless, such methods, particularly payback, may be useful as rough screening devices for investment opportunities.

Discounted cash flow methods are used to decide whether to undertake an investment. An important factor in the successful use of these methods is understanding the company's cost of capital. The expected source for financing a particular investment is not relevant to the analysis of that investment.

---

13 *"Eyeball to Eyeball with China,"* Business Week, *February 20, 1995, 32.*
14 *Louis Kraar, "The Risks Are Rising in China,"* Fortune, *March 6, 1995, 179-80.*
15 *Teo A. Babun, Jr. "Cuba's Investment Boom That Never Was,"* The Wall Street Journal, *March 1, 1996, A15.*
16 *"Market Place," radio program on National Public Radio, March 5, 1996.*

KEY TERMS

book rate of return (364)	net present value (NPV) (352)
capital budgeting decisions (348)	payback (362)
cash flows (352)	target rate (352)
cost of capital (350)	tax effect of depreciation (357)
cutoff rate (352)	tax shield (357)
discounted cash flow (DCF) (365)	time-adjusted rate of return (355)
hurdle rate (352)	time value of money (349)
internal rate of return (IRR) (352)	

KEY FORMULAS

Present value of future flows = Annual cash flows × Present value factor

$$\text{Net present value} = \begin{matrix}\text{Present value}\\\text{of future flows}\end{matrix} - \text{Required investment}$$

$$\text{Payback period} = \frac{\text{Investment required}}{\text{Annual cash returns}}$$

$$\text{Average book rate of return} = \frac{\text{Average annual expected book income}}{\text{Average book investment}}$$

REVIEW PROBLEM

Dwyer Company has the opportunity to market a new product. The sales manager believes the company could sell 10,000 units per year at $15 per unit for five years. The product requires machinery that costs $100,000 and has a five-year life and no salvage value. Variable costs per unit are $8. The machinery has fixed operating costs requiring cash disbursements of $25,000 annually. Straight-line depreciation will be used for both book and tax purposes. The tax rate is 40% and the cutoff rate is 14%.

Required
1. Determine the increase in annual net income and in annual cash inflows expected from the investment.
2. Determine the NPV of the investment.
3. Determine the payback period.
4. Determine the approximate IRR of the investment.
5. Determine the book rate of return on the average investment.
6. Suppose the machinery has salvage value of $5,000 at the end of its useful life, which is not considered in determining depreciation expense. The tax rate on the gain at the end of the asset's life is 40%. How will your answer to item 2 change?

ANSWER TO REVIEW PROBLEM

1.

	Tax Computation	Cash Flow
Sales (10,000 × $15)	$150,000	$150,000
Variable cost (10,000 × $8)	80,000	80,000
Contribution margin (10,000 × $7)	$ 70,000	$ 70,000
Fixed cash operating costs	25,000	25,000
Cash inflow before taxes	$ 45,000	$ 45,000
Depreciation ($100,000/5)	20,000	
Increase in taxable income	$ 25,000	
Income tax at 40% rate	10,000	10,000
Increase in net income	$ 15,000	
Add depreciation	20,000	
Net cash inflow per year	$ 35,000	$ 35,000

2. $20,155, calculated as follows:

Net cash inflow per year	$ 35,000
Present value factor, 5-year annuity at 14% (Table B)	3.433
Present value of future net cash flows	$120,155
Less investment	100,000
Net present value	$ 20,155

3. The payback period is 2.857 years, which is $100,000 divided by $35,000.
4. IRR is just barely over 22%. The factor to seek is 2.857, which is the payback period calculated in item 3. The closest factor in the five-year row of Table B is 2.864, which is the 22% factor. Because 2.857 is less than 2.864, the rate is greater than 22%. (Remember, the higher the rate, the lower the factor.)
5. The book rate of return on the average investment is 30%, which is annual net income of $15,000 divided by the average investment of $50,000 ($100,000/2).
6. The only change required is the determination of the present value of the salvage value less tax on the gain.

Salvage value	$ 5,000
Tax at 40%	2,000
Net cash inflow, end of year 5	$ 3,000
Present value factor for single payment, 5 years at 14% (Table A)	.519
Present value of salvage value	$ 1,557
Net present value from part 2	20,155
Net present value	$ 21,712

Notice that we did not have to recompute annual net cash flows. The company still used $20,000 for depreciation expense. Therefore, at the end of five years, the machinery will have a book value of zero and the gain on disposal will equal the salvage value.

ASSIGNMENT MATERIAL

QUESTIONS FOR DISCUSSION

8-1   Procter & Gamble capital budgeting   P&G, the household and personal products giant, derives over half of its revenues from, and has close to half of its assets in, foreign countries. What factors must P&G consider in its foreign investments, besides those it must consider in U.S. investments?

8-2   Payback and risk   Suppose you are a merchant in medieval Europe and are considering two investments, both of which require $1 million to buy a cargo of merchandise and ship it to a distant country. One voyage will take a year to complete, the other five years. The expected after-tax cash returns at the ends of the periods are $1,160,000 for the one-year voyage and $3,713,000 for the five-year voyage. The expected IRRs on the voyages are 16% and 30%, respectively, and, when a cutoff rate of 10% is used, the NPVs are $54,545 and $1,305,481. Which investment would you take?

8-3   Interest rates and capital investment   The federal government is concerned with regulating the level of economic activity, especially with encouraging production and investment to maintain high employment while not allowing excessive inflation. The Federal Reserve Board attempts to do so partly by changing interest rates. How can the ability to influence interest rates be used to stimulate or discourage investment?

8-4   Boeing's new airplanes   **Boeing** has announced two new versions of the 747 that it expects will require $4 to $5 billion in development costs. One will fly 430 passengers 8,500 miles without refueling (existing 747s are about 400 and 7,500, respectively), the other can carry 500 passengers 7,800 miles. **British Airways** wants to buy the 500-passenger version. **Air Korea** and **Singapore Airlines** are interested in the version that flies 8,500 miles non-stop.

Required
Why are the named airlines especially interested in the specific models? You might reason back from the characteristics of the aircraft to the types of flying the airlines do.

8-5   Capital budgeting—effects of events   You have evaluated a capital expenditure proposal for a new machine. How do each of the following events, not anticipated in the original analysis, affect the evaluation? Consider each event independently.

1. The interest rate on long-term debt increases.
2. Your company signs a new contract with its union. The negotiated wage rate for all categories of workers is higher than the prevailing rate.
3. Your company raises the selling prices of its products.
4. Congress reduces the period over which companies can depreciate assets.

8-6   Exceptions to decision rules

Required

Answer the following questions independently.

1. Using its 14% target rate, GSA Toy Company determined that an investment in a new product, a model tank, had an NPV of $100,000. Give at least four reasons why GSA might reject the project despite its positive NPV.
2. The top managers of J&G Products, Inc., a manufacturer of high-quality electronic equipment, have established a minimum IRR for investment projects of 30%. The analysis of one project shows an IRR of 25%. Suggest at least four reasons why J&G might accept the project despite its failure to meet the 30% minimum IRR.

EXERCISES

8-7   Discounting

Required

1. Find the approximate IRR for each of the following investments.
   (a) An investment of $30,000 with annual cash flows of $6,000 for eight years.
   (b) An investment of $120,000 with a single return of $150,000 at the end of two years.
2. Find the NPVs of the following investments at a 10% discount rate.
   (a) Annual flows of $30,000 for ten years are produced by an investment of $160,000.
   (b) An investment of $30,000 with annual flows of $8,000 for four years and a single return of $4,000 at the end of the fifth year.

8-8   NPV and IRR methods
Jones Secretarial Service is thinking of buying some new word-processing equipment that promises to save $7,000 in cash operating costs per year. The equipment will cost $18,800. Its estimated useful life is four years. It will have no salvage value. (Ignore taxes.)

Required

1. Compute NPV if the minimum desired rate of return is 10%.
2. Determine the approximate IRR.

8-9   Discounting

Required

Solve each of the following problems independently.

1. Larry Paul starts college in one year. His father wishes to set up a fund for Larry to use for the $10,200 he will need each year for four years. Larry will make withdrawals at the beginning of each school year. If Mr. Paul can invest at 8%, how much must he invest today to provide for Larry's college expenses?
2. Henry Jackson is about to retire from his job. His pension benefits have accumulated to the point where he could receive a lump-sum payment of $350,000 or $50,000 per year for ten years, paid at the ends of years. Jackson has no dependents and expects to live for ten years after he retires. If he can invest at 8%, which option should he take?

3. You have just won the $5,000,000 grand prize in a magazine sweepstakes. The prize will be paid in $167,000 installments for 30 years. If your interest rate is 6%, how much would you take now, instead of accepting the annuity?

8-10   *Time value of money relationships*

Required
Answer the following questions.

1. A person received a single payment of $7,880 as a result of investing six years ago at an interest rate of 12%. How much did the person invest?
2. An investment of $3,100 returned a single payment of $6,800 at an interest rate of 14%. How many years elapsed between the investment and the return?
3. A person received seven annual payments of $1,000 from an investment. The interest rate was 12%. What was the amount of the investment?
4. An investment of $1,000 returned $343 annually for some years. The rate of interest was 14%. How many payments were received?
5. A $20,000 investment made today will provide a 14% return. The returns will be paid in equal amounts over 12 years. What is the amount of the annual payment?

8-11   *Basic capital budgeting without taxes*   Crestline Inc. produces custom paper boxes. Its managers have been trying to decide whether to buy a new folding machine for $150,000. It will last five years, have no salvage value, and be depreciated using the straight-line method. The managers anticipate savings in cash operating costs of $50,000 in each of the five years. The cutoff rate is 10%.

Required
1. Calculate the NPV of the investment.
2. Calculate the approximate IRR on the investment.
3. Determine the payback period for the investment.
4. Determine the book rate of return on the average investment.

8-12   *Basic capital budgeting—taxes (continuation of 8-11)*

Required
Redo 8-11 with Crestline Inc. now being subject to a 30% income tax rate.

8-13   *Basic cost savings*   Grove City Pottery currently makes 200,000 large strawberry jars per year at a variable cost of $9.75. Equipment is available for $500,000 that will reduce the variable cost to $7.50, while increasing cash fixed costs by $200,000. The equipment will have no salvage value at the end of its four-year life and will be depreciated using the straight-line method. Norton faces a 40% income tax rate and a 12% hurdle rate.

Required
1. Determine the NPV of the investment.
2. Determine the change in NPV if the equipment has a $25,000 residual value.

8-14   *Basic capital budgeting*   Boston Globes has an opportunity to reduce its annual cash operating costs by $20,000 by acquiring equipment that costs $60,000, has a five-year life, and has no salvage value. Boston uses straight-line depreciation. The cost of capital is 14%. Ignore taxes.

Required
1. Determine the NPV of the investment.
2. Determine the approximate IRR.
3. Determine the payback period.
4. Determine the book rate of return on the average investment.

8-15   Basic capital budgeting with taxes (continuation of 8-14)

Required
Redo 8-14 with a 40% income tax rate.

8-16   Comparison of methods (continued in Chapter 9)   Jason Company has the following three investment opportunities.

	A	B	C
Cost	$ 70,000	$ 70,000	$ 70,000
Cash inflows by year:			
Year 1	$ 35,000	$ 35,000	$ 4,000
Year 2	35,000	10,000	8,000
Year 3	0	45,000	10,000
Year 4	5,000	20,000	98,000
Total	$ 75,000	$110,000	$120,000
Average annual income	$ 1,250	$ 10,000	$ 12,500

Required
1. Rank the investment opportunities in order of desirability using (a) payback period, (b) average book rate of return (use average net book value of the investment as the denominator), and (c) NPV using a 16% discount rate.
2. Comment on the results.

8-17   NPV   Wilson Crocker owns a driving range. He presently pays several high school students $0.80 per bucket to pick up the golf balls that his customers hit. A salesperson has shown him a machine that will pick up balls at an annual cash cost of $6,600 plus $0.05 per bucket. The machine costs $10,000 and has a five-year life. Crocker would use straight-line depreciation. Volume for the driving range is about 21,000 buckets per year. Crocker's combined state and federal tax rate is 30%. He believes that the appropriate discount rate is 16%.

Required
Determine the NPV of the investment and identify one or more nonquantitative factors that might influence the decision.

8-18   Capital budgeting for a hospital   San Lucia Hospital has the opportunity to acquire a used CAT scanner for $250,000. It will last for ten years and have no salvage value. Estimated revenue is $130,000 per year; estimated annual cash costs are $76,000. The hospital uses a 14% discount rate for capital budgeting decisions.

Required
Determine (a) NPV, (b) payback period, and (c) approximate IRR.

8-19   *NPV and IRR* Sargent Company makes high-quality workshoes. Its managers believe that the company can increase productivity by acquiring some new machinery but are unsure whether it would be profitable.

The machinery costs $1,000,000, has a four-year life with no salvage value, and should save about $400,000 in cash operating costs annually. The company uses straight-line depreciation and has a 40% income tax rate and a 12% cost of capital.

Required
1. Calculate the NPV of the investment.
2. Calculate the approximate IRR.

8-20   *Relationships*

Required
Fill in the blanks for each of the following independent cases. In all cases the investment has a useful life of ten years and no salvage value.

	(a) Annual Net Cash Inflow	(b) Investment	(c) Cost of Capital	(d) Internal Rate of Return	(e) Net Present Value
1.	$ 60,000	$251,520	14%	____	$____
2.	$ 80,000	$____	12%	18%	$____
3.	$ ____	$300,000	____	16%	$ 81,440
4.	$ ____	$450,000	12%	____	$115,000

8-21   *Comparison of book return and NPV (continued in Chapter 9)* Welton Company is introducing a product that will sell for $10 per unit. Annual volume for the next four years should be about 200,000 units. The company can use either a hand-fed or a semiautomatic machine to make the product. Data are as follows.

	Hand-fed Machine	Semiautomatic Machine
Per unit variable cost	$4	$2
Annual cash fixed cost	$725,000	$850,000
Cost of machine	$800,000	$1,400,000

Both machines have four-year lives and no anticipated salvage value. Welton uses straight-line depreciation, has a 40% income tax rate, and has a 14% cost of capital.

Required
1. Determine which machine has the higher book rate of return on average investment.
2. Determine which machine has the higher NPV.
3. Determine which alternative has the highest IRR.

PROBLEMS

8-22   *New product decision* Candada Company has the opportunity to introduce a new radio with the following expected results.

| Annual unit sales volume | 300,000 | Selling price per unit | $60 |
| Annual cash fixed costs | $4,200,000 | Variable cost per unit | $35 |

The product requires equipment costing $8,000,000 and having a four-year life with no salvage value. The company has a 12% cost of capital. The income tax rate is 40% and Candada uses straight-line depreciation.

Required

1. Determine the expected increase in future annual after-tax cash flows for this project.
2. Determine the NPV of the investment.
3. Determine the approximate IRR of the investment.
4. Suppose the equipment has a $600,000 salvage value. Candada will still depreciate the full cost of the equipment, so there would be a tax on whatever proceeds are received from its sale. By how much and in what direction will the NPV of the project change because of the expected salvage value?

8-23   *Meaning of IRR*   You want to withdraw $10,000 from a bank account at the end of each of the next three years. The interest rate is 10%.

Required

1. How much must you have in the bank at the beginning of the first year to be able to make the subsequent $10,000 withdrawals?
2. Schedule the activity in the bank account for the three years. Set up columns for Beginning Balance, Interest, Withdrawal, and Ending Balance. Interest is earned at 10% of the beginning balance of each year.

8-24   *Investing in JIT*   Robson Industries operates several plants, one of which is moving toward JIT manufacturing. One of the first investments the plant will make is roughly $4.5 million to rearrange the factory into manufacturing cells. This cost is tax-deductible over five years using the straight-line method. The managers expect to save about $800,000 in annual manufacturing costs for the foreseeable future as a result of using cells. The tax rate is 40% and the cutoff rate is 10%.

Required

Determine the NPV of the investment. Use a 30-year period for the annual cost savings. It will be easier to discount the two types of flows separately.

8-25   *Installing a sprinkler system*   RTP Corp. operates several factories, one of which was built some 50 years ago and is not in good condition. That factory has a fire insurance policy covering machinery, inventory, and the building itself. Premiums on the policy are $26,000 per year.

Recently, a fire inspector from the insurance company recommended that the premium be increased to $73,000 per year because the factory's fire protection has diminished. Its existing sprinkler system no longer works and cannot be repaired at a reasonable cost. The inspector told the plant manager, Jane Strong, that a new system, costing $200,000 and with a 10-year life and no salvage value, would be needed to continue the existing premium of $26,000 per year.

The company uses straight-line depreciation. The tax rate is 40% and the cutoff rate for investments is 14%.

Required

1. Determine the NPV of the investment using only the data provided.
2. Using the guidelines in Appendix A, write a memorandum to Ms. Strong making a recommendation. Include support for your recommendation and suggest relevant factors not mentioned.

8-26   *Employment options* Bob Wiblek is a college senior and an All-American football player. Drafted by the Bay City Beasts of the Tri-Continental League, he has been pondering two alternatives the team has offered. The first is that Bob receives $1,000,000 per year for ten years, the second is that he receives $600,000 per year for 30 years. Either way, Bob and the team both expect his playing career to be over in ten years. Under either alternative, he would get the prescribed amounts whether or not he plays.

Bob will face an income tax rate of 30%. The team has a 40% income tax rate. Bob believes that a 10% discount rate is appropriate. The team has a 14% cutoff rate.

Required

1. Which offer should Bob take?
2. Which offer is better for the owners of the team?
3. If your answers to items 1 and 2 differ, explain why. You need not make any calculations.

8-27   *Importance of depreciation period* Your company has the opportunity to buy machinery for $100,000. It will last for five years, be depreciated using the straight-line method, and save $30,000 in cash operating costs per year. Cost of capital is 10% and the tax rate is 40%.

Required

1. Determine the NPV of the investment.
2. Suppose now that you could depreciate the machinery over two years for tax purposes instead of five years. Determine the NPV of the investment.

8-28   *Bringing out a new product* BDR is considering adding a new product with a selling price of $100 and variable cost of $32. It expects to sell 5,000 units per year. To make the product, BDR must acquire a new machine costing $550,000 and having a useful life of five years. The machine will have no residual value at the end of its life. Managers estimate cash fixed costs to make the product at $150,000 per year. BDR's cutoff rate is 14% and its tax rate is 30%. It uses straight-line depreciation for both financial reporting and tax purposes.

Required

1. What is the expected after-tax annual cash flow from the project?
2. What is the payback period for the project? (Round your answer to three decimal places.)
3. What is the IRR for the project?
4. What is the NPV for this project?
5. Assume BDR has determined that this project could be financed by an 11% loan from a bank. Explain your answer to each of the following.
   (a) Should BDR use 11%, instead of 14%, to compute the project's NPV?
   (b) Should BDR incorporate the annual interest payments on the note into its computation of the project's annual net cash flows?
6. Assume BDR could, for tax purposes only, depreciate the new machine using an accelerated method of depreciation such as double-declining balance. Explain your answers to each of the following.

(a) Would BDR pay less total tax on the income from the project?

(b) Would the project's payback period be different?

8-29　*Manufacturing cells, JIT*　Some of the plant managers of Emsworth Manufacturing Company are trying to switch to JIT manufacturing. The manager of the Seneca Plant has developed the following data on the effects of introducing JIT, mainly from talks with managers whose plants have adopted JIT principles.

	(all amounts in thousands)	
	Current Cost	Estimated JIT Cost
Materials	$1,876.4	$1,692.0
Direct labor	2,845.2	2,312.0
Supervision	434.6	88.3
Maintenance	493.2	23.6*
Inspection, incoming and outgoing	256.3	32.8*
Other	673.9	569.5
Totals	$6,579.6	$4,718.2

Most costs of maintenance and inspection will be carried out by workers in their cells, thus greatly reducing the centrally administered amounts.

Moving to cellular manufacturing requires investments of $7.5 million for rearranging and for new machinery more suited to cellular manufacturing. All of these costs can be deducted for tax purposes over ten years. None of the depreciation and amortization of these costs is included in the figures. The company has a 40% tax rate and a 12% cost of capital. The horizon for discounting the after-tax savings in operating flows is 20 years.

Required

Determine the NPV of the proposed change. You will find it easier to discount the two types of flows separately.

8-30　*Retirement options*　Jerry Waddlum will retire in a few months, on reaching his 65th birthday. His pension plan offers two options: (1) a lump-sum payment of $500,000 on the day of retirement and (2) annual payments of $60,000 per year beginning on the date of retirement and ending at death. Mr. Waddlum is not sure which option he should select and asks for your assistance. He tells you that he has no savings now, that he could earn a 10% return if he invested part of the lump-sum payment, and that he would like to spend $80,000 per year during his retirement. He has no relatives or other heirs and is not concerned about leaving an estate. He tells you that he could live on $60,000 per year but would much prefer to spend $80,000 and be more comfortable.

If he chooses the lump-sum payment, he will take out $80,000 to live on during the first year of retirement and invest the remainder. He will then draw $80,000 at the beginning of every year until the money runs out.

Required

Determine how long Waddlum could afford to keep up an $80,000 per year standard of living if he takes the lump-sum payment.

8-31   *Expanding a product line* Kiernan Company makes office equipment of various sorts, such as tables, desks, chairs, and lamps. The sales manager is trying to decide whether to introduce a new model of desk. The desk will sell for $400 and have variable costs of $220. Volume is expected to be 5,000 units per year for five years. To make the desks, the company will have to buy additional machinery that will cost $1,500,000 and have a five-year life with no salvage value. Straight-line depreciation will be used. Fixed cash operating costs will be $400,000 per year.

Kiernan is in the 40% tax bracket and its cutoff rate is 10%.

Required

1. Use the NPV method to determine whether the new desk should be manufactured.
2. Compute the payback period.
3. Determine the approximate IRR on the investment.

8-32   *Buying air pumps* Mighty Mart is a chain of convenience stores that sells food, beverages, household products, and gasoline. Its product development manager, Carolyn Schmidt, is trying to decide how to acquire coin-operated air pumps that customers can use to fill their tires. One choice is to lease pumps for $850 per year, renewable annually. The other is to buy them for $1,500. Pumps have a three-year life. For each pump, revenue should average $2,400 per year and operating costs, exclusive of lease payments or depreciation, $550 per year.

Mighty Mart is in the 40% tax bracket, has a 10% cutoff rate of return, and uses straight-line depreciation.

Required

Using the guidelines in Appendix A, write a memorandum to Ms. Schmidt giving and supporting your recommendation about which acquisition method to select.

8-33   *Charitable donation* Jan Williamson is a wealthy entrepreneur who wishes to make a substantial donation to her alma mater, Arkwright University. She is considering two alternatives, a $6,000,000 gift now or an equal annual amount in each of the next ten years.

From discussions with the president of Arkwright University, she has learned that the university, which pays no income taxes, earns a 10% return on its endowment fund. The president would be happy with either the $6,000,000 now or with equal annual amounts having a present value of $6,000,000. Mrs. Williamson is able to earn a 9% after-tax return investing in tax-free securities. She faces a combined state and federal tax rate of 35%.

Required

1. Determine the annuity that yields a $6,000,000 present value to the university.
2. Should Mrs. Williamson make the lump-sum donation or pay the annuity that you determined in item 1?

  8-34   *Increasing capacity (continued in Chapter 9)* Pitcairn Manufacturing has regularly been selling out its complete stock of its most popular style of men's socks, Heather. The production and marketing managers have investigated ways to increase capacity and have determined they could produce another 250,000 pairs annually if they bought equipment costing $1,200,000. The equipment has a five-year life with no salvage value. Pitcairn uses straight-line depreciation. The equipment would add $200,000 to annual cash fixed costs. The socks sell for $4 and have a variable cost of $1 per pair. The variable cost would not be affected by using the equipment. The managers are confident of selling 200,000 additional pairs annually. Cost of capital is 14% and the tax rate is 40%.

Required

1. Determine whether Pitcairn should acquire the equipment.
2. Suppose that additional volume is likely to be 250,000 pairs. Determine whether Pitcairn should acquire the equipment.

8-35   *Funding a pension plan* Knowles Company has an agreement with the labor union that represents its workers. The agreement calls for Knowles to pay $25,000 per year for the next ten years into a pension fund. Payments would begin one year from now.

Knowles has excess cash on hand from the sale of some of its assets, so the treasurer approaches the head of the union and asks if it would be all right to make a single, lump-sum payment to discharge the ten-year obligation. Before receiving the union leader's reply, the treasurer decided to determine the maximum amount that Knowles could pay right now. The company is in the 40% tax bracket and has a cutoff rate of 16%. The annual payments are deductible for tax purposes in the years in which they were made and the single payment would be deductible in the current year.

Required

Determine the maximum amount that Knowles could pay in a lump-sum settlement of the obligation.

8-36   *Bond refunding* Expost Company has outstanding a $1,000,000 (par value) issue of bonds bearing a 14% interest rate. The bonds mature in ten years. Interest rates are lower than they were when this issue was sold, and the company can now raise cash on a ten-year bond at 10%. The company's directors are considering retiring the outstanding issue and replacing the old bonds with 10%, ten-year bonds. The company would have to pay a premium of 12% over par value to buy back the currently outstanding issue. It would also have to spend $60,000 in legal fees and other costs to market the new issue. The premium is tax deductible in the year of refunding, but the costs of issuing the new bonds must be amortized evenly over ten years. The tax rate is 40%, and the company's cost of capital is 18%.

Required

Should the old issue be replaced?

8-37   *Capital budgeting by a municipality* The City Council of Alton is considering constructing a convention center in the downtown area. The city has been losing employment to surrounding suburbs, and tax revenues have been falling. The proposed center would cost $22,000,000 to build, and the city would incur annual cash operating costs of $500,000. The city controller estimates that the annual receipts from the center will be approximately $1.8 million. He estimates the center's useful life at 30 years.

The controller's estimate of revenues is based on total annual convention attendance of 200,000 persons. He reports that at 8% interest, the rate the city would have to pay on bonds to build the center, it would be a losing proposition. The present value of $1,300,000 ($1,800,000 - $500,000) annually for 30 years at 8% is $14,635,400, well below the cost of the center. (Assume this computation is correct.)

One member of the council comments that the rentals are not the only source of revenues to the city. To support this position, she offers studies showing that the average person attending a trade show or convention spends $500 in the city in which the event is being held. Because of the various taxes in effect, the city receives, on average, about 1% of all of the money spent in it.

Required

1. Prepare a new analysis, incorporating the additional tax receipts expected if the center is built.
2. Why is 8% used as the discount rate when it is the interest rate, not the cost of capital? (Is the interest rate the same as the cost of capital to a city?)

8-38   *Comparison of NPV and profit*   Graham Auto Products is bringing out a new heavy-duty battery and has two choices with respect to the manufacturing process. No matter which choice it makes, it expects to sell 100,000 units per year for four years at $50 per unit. Data on the two processes are as follows:

	Labor-Intensive Process	Capital-Intensive Process
Per-unit variable cost	$20	$10
Annual fixed cash operating costs	$400,000	$600,000
Investment in equipment	$4,000,000	$6,000,000

Neither set of equipment is expected to have salvage value at the end of four years. The company uses straight-line depreciation. The cutoff rate is 16% and the tax rate is 40%.

Required

1. Which process will give the higher annual profit?
2. Which process will give the higher book rate of return on average investment?
3. Which process will give the higher NPV?
4. Using the guidelines in Appendix A, write a memorandum to Morton Brown, Graham's factory manager, giving and supporting your recommendation regarding which process should be selected.

8-39   *Capital budgeting for a computer service company*   Many companies are in the business of selling computer time to others. Customers include other businesses, universities, hospitals, and so on. One such computer service firm, Compuservice, Inc., currently has a Whizbang 85, a high-speed machine that it rents from the manufacturer for $18,000 per month. The firm is considering the purchase of a Zoom 125, which is the fastest machine of its type available. The Whizbang 85 will be kept even if the Zoom is purchased. Cal Kulate, president of Compuservice, believes that a number of new customers will be attracted if the company acquires the Zoom 125. He estimates additional revenues of $40,000 per month. Additional costs requiring cash would be $4,000 per month for maintenance and salaries for added operators. The Zoom sells for $1,200,000 and has a useful physical life of about fifteen years. However, computer experts have estimated that the Zoom will probably be technologically obsolete in six years.

The company would use straight-line depreciation of $225,000 per year in order to depreciate the computer to its estimated salvage value of $300,000 at the end of four years. The company's tax rate is 40% and its cutoff rate is 16%.

Required

Using the guidelines in Appendix A, write a memorandum to Mr. Kulate giving and supporting your recommendation regarding the proposal.

8-40 *Investing in quality* Pellum Company manufactures a number of products in a relatively old plant. Parts of the manufacturing process are outmoded. One result is that about 10% of output is spoiled in production and must be scrapped. The manufacturing managers have been looking at new machinery and equipment that would reduce the rate of rejects to near zero. Outfitting the plant will cost about $6.5 million. The new machines have five-year lives and no salvage value. The company uses straight-line depreciation. The existing machinery is fully depreciated and has no sales value.

The total manufacturing costs of the plant under current conditions are about $94.6 million, with $58.0 million variable, the rest fixed. Cash fixed operating costs will increase by about $2.2 million annually if the new machinery is acquired. The tax rate is 40% and cost of capital is 12%.

Required

1. Determine the NPV of reducing spoiled output to zero while maintaining the current level of good output.
2. Annual revenue under existing conditions is $117.8 million. Suppose that demand is far above capacity so that the plant could increase sales by 10% if it acquires the new equipment. Determine the NPV of the investment.

8-41 *Reevaluating an investment* Ten years ago Kramer Company, of which you are the controller, bought machinery at a cost of $250,000. The purchase was made at the insistence of the production manager. The machinery is now worthless, and the production manager believes that it should be replaced. He gives you the following analysis, which he says verifies the correctness of the decision to buy the machinery ten years ago. He bases his statement on the 21% return he calculated, which is higher than the 16% cutoff rate of return.

Annual cost savings:	
Labor	$ 41,000
Overhead	28,000
Total	$ 69,000
Less straight-line depreciation ($250,000/10)	25,000
Increase in pretax income	$ 44,000
Income taxes at 40%	17,600
Increase in net income	$ 26,400
Average investment ($250,000/2)	$125,000
Return on investment	21%

Required

Do you agree that the investment was wise? Why or why not?

8-42 *Purchase commitment* Ralston Company buys copper from a number of suppliers, including Boa Copper Company. The president of Boa has offered to sell Ralston up to 1,000,000 pounds of copper per year for five years at $0.80 per pound if Ralston will lend Boa $2,000,000 at 8% interest. The loan would be repaid at the end of five years; the interest would be paid annually.

Ralston uses at least 1,800,000 pounds of copper per year and expects the price to be $1.00 per pound over the next five years. The tax rate is 40% and Ralston's management considers the relevant discount rate to be 12%.

Required
1. Determine whether Ralston Company should accept the offer.
2. Determine the minimum price at which copper would have to sell, per pound, over the next five years to make accepting the offer worthwhile.

CASES

8-43   *New product—complementary effects* Elmendorf Company makes a variety of cleaning products. The company's research and development department has recently come up with a new glass cleaner that is superior to all of the products on the market, including the one that Elmendorf currently makes. The new cleaner would be priced at $22 per case and have variable costs of $12 per case. Elmendorf would have to buy additional machinery costing $10,000,000 to make the new cleaner. The machinery has a ten-year life. Expected volume of the new cleaner is 800,000 cases per year for ten years. Cash fixed costs will increase $1,400,000 per year.

Elmendorf uses straight-line depreciation with no provision for salvage value. The machinery has about $100,000 expected salvage value at the end of ten years. The tax rate is 40% and the cutoff rate is 12%.

One disadvantage of making the investment is that sales of the firm's existing cleaner would be affected. Volume of the existing cleaner is expected to fall by 300,000 cases per year. A case of the existing cleaner sells for $15 and has variable costs of $9.

Required
Determine the NPV of the proposed investment.

8-44   *Uses of space (AICPA adapted)* Lansdown Company manages office buildings in the downtown area of a major city. One of the buildings it manages has a large, unused lobby area. A manager of the firm believes that a newsstand should be placed in the lobby. She has talked to managers of several other office buildings and has projected the following annual operating results if Lansdown establishes a newsstand.

Sales	$49,000
Cost of sales	40,000
Salaries of clerks	7,000
Licenses and payroll taxes	200
Share of heat and light bills on the building	500
Share of building depreciation	1,000
Advertising for the newsstand	100
Share of Lansdown's administrative expense	400

The required investment is $2,000, all for equipment that will be worthless in ten years. Before presenting the plan to her superiors, the manager learned that the space could be leased to an outside firm that would operate the same kind of newsstand. The other firm would pay $750 rent per year for each of the ten years. Because the lobby is heated and lighted anyway, Lansdown would supply heat and light at no additional cost. Lansdown's cutoff rate is 12%. (Ignore taxes.)

Required
1. Determine the best course of action for Lansdown.
2. Determine how much annual rent Lansdown must receive to equalize the attractiveness of the alternatives.

8-45 *Magazine subscriptions* The managers of PC Journal, a magazine for computer users, are working on a campaign to get extended subscriptions. The magazine's base one-year rate is $28 for 12 issues. The managers tentatively set the two-year subscription rate at $50. Both amounts are payable in advance. The variable cost per subscription per year is $10. The cutoff rate is 12%. The company pays no income taxes.

Required

1. Suppose that all one-year subscribers will renew at the end of the year. Therefore, the company will either (a) collect $28 now and $28 in one year or (b) collect $50 now. Determine whether the magazine should offer the $50 rate for a two-year subscription.
2. Again, assuming that all subscribers taking one-year subscriptions would renew at the end of one year, determine the lowest two-year rate that the magazine should offer.
3. Suppose now there is a 40% attrition rate in subscriptions. That is, of every ten one-year subscribers, four will not renew next year. Determine whether the magazine should offer the $50 rate. Assume that the variable costs are paid at the beginning of each year. You might find it convenient to work with a hypothetical batch of ten subscribers.
4. Using the facts from item 3, determine the lowest two-year rate that the magazine should offer.

8-46 *Long-term special order* Nova Company makes indoor television antennae that sell for $12 and have variable costs of $7. The firm has been selling 200,000 units per year and expects to continue at that rate unless it accepts a special order from the Acme Television Company. Acme has offered to buy 40,000 units per year at $9, provided that Nova agrees to make the sales for a five-year period. Acme will not take fewer than 40,000 units.

Nova's current capacity is 230,000 units per year. Capacity could be increased to 260,000 units per year if new equipment costing $100,000 were purchased. The equipment would have a useful life of five years, have no salvage value, and add $20,000 in annual fixed cash operating costs. Variable costs per unit would be unchanged.

Nova would use straight-line depreciation for tax purposes. The tax rate is 40% and the cutoff rate is 14%.

Required

Using the guidelines in Appendix A, write a memorandum to Nova's vice president of manufacturing, Bjorn Hansen, giving and supporting your recommendation about the best course of action.

8-47 *Introduction of new product* Jerry Dollink, controller of Radsiville Industries, Inc., tells you about a meeting of several top managers of the firm. The topic discussed was the introduction of a new product that had been undergoing extensive research and development. Jerry Dollink had thought the product would be brought out in the coming year, but the managers decided to give it further study.

The product is expected to have a market life of ten years. Sales are expected to be 30,000 units annually at $90 per unit. The following unit costs were presented by Jamie Barker, manager of the division that would produce and sell the product.

Materials	$10
Direct labor	17
Overhead (manufacturing)	30
Selling and administrative expenses	12
Total costs	$69

Barker went on to point out that equipment costing $3,000,000 and having an expected salvage value of $100,000 at the end of ten years would have to be purchased. Adding the $900,000 that had already been spent on research and development brought the total outlay related to the new product to $3,900,000.

Depreciation of $300,000 per year would reduce taxes by $120,000 (40% rate). The $21 per-unit profit margin would produce $630,000 before taxes and $378,000 after taxes. The net return would then be $498,000 annually, which is a rate of return of about 4%, far below the 14% cutoff rate. Barker concluded that the product should not be brought out.

Dollink tells you that Barker is a strong believer in "having every product pay its way." The calculation of the manufacturing overhead cost per unit includes existing fixed costs of $600,000 allocated to the new product. Additional cash fixed costs are $200,000 per year. Selling and administrative expenses were also allocated to the product on the basis of relative sales revenue. Commissions of $4 per unit will be the only incremental selling and administrative expenses.

Required
1. Prepare a new analysis.
2. Explain the fallacies in Barker's analysis.

Capital Budgeting—Part II

9

LEARNING OBJECTIVES

After reading this chapter, you should be able to

1 Describe investments in working capital.

2 Analyze replacement decisions using two approaches.

3 Describe and evaluate mutually exclusive investments.

4 Apply preference rules to competing capital investments.

5 Explain and apply sensitivity analysis.

6 Describe the Modified Accelerated Cost Recovery System and use it in evaluating investments.

7 Explain how capital budgeting applies to not-for-profit entities and to social welfare.

Many companies today are replacing assets, or processes. Key-entry data processing equipment is giving way to bar coding. Point-of-sale terminals that provide electronic data interchange are displacing cash registers. New computer software is replacing older versions. **Microsoft** sees much of its business as convincing customers to replace its existing software with new Microsoft products.

When **Mattel** launches a new toy, the required investment in productive equipment is not the whole story. The company will also advertise and promote the product, and must also support the product with finished goods, materials, and work in process inventories because of the seasonal demand for toys. It will also have accounts receivable from the new product's buyers and will probably increase its cash balances to accommodate the increased activity. In fact, Mattel invests nearly three times as much in receivables and inventory as it does in buildings and equipment.

> *Because investments in inventories and other elements of working capital are expensive, many companies devote significant portions of their investments to reducing inventories.* **American Standard***, the diversified manufacturer best known for bathroom fixtures, is one such company. It has cut its inventories in half and implemented JIT principles in its manufacturing plants.* **General Electric** *is another company aggressively reducing inventories. Its Appliances unit reduced the cycle time from receipt of an order to delivery of a finished product from 80 days to under 20 days. In the process, the segment reduced inventory by $200 million and significantly increased profitability through judicious investment.* **Dole Foods** *has been spending money to upgrade its electronic links to its customers and otherwise improve its distribution chain, which should reduce its inventories.*

Sources: *Mattel 1994 annual report; "Prophet of Zero Working Capital,"* Fortune, *June 13, 1994, 113; "Jack Welch's Lessons for Success,"* Fortune, *January 25, 1993, 89; Dole Foods 1994 annual report*

 Chapter 8 treated decisions requiring the purchase of new productive assets. This chapter considers some decisions that differ in several respects from those examined in Chapter 8, but the basic principles of analysis remain the same. The new features require changes in computing net cash flows and investments, but the analyses still concentrate on cash flows and consider the time value of money.

Because of the many estimates in a capital budgeting decision, we introduce an analytical technique managers use to identify the most critical estimates. We also give attention to a few additional aspects of income tax law that affect capital budgeting decisions. Finally, because budgets reflect planning decisions and many of those decisions have social consequences, we conclude the chapter (and Part Two) with a discussion of the social consequences of decision making and a brief look at the special problem of decision making in the public sector.

COMPLEX INVESTMENTS

In many cases, the required investment is not a single cash payment for some new depreciable asset. Some opportunities require a change in the entity's investment in working capital or the replacement of existing assets. These features complicate the determination of the required investment.

CHANGES IN WORKING CAPITAL

Operating virtually any business requires current assets. Businesses selling on credit have accounts receivable, while manufacturers and merchandisers also have inventories. Even companies approaching the JIT ideal have some products in process. And, as Chapter 7 showed, businesses finance some of their current asset requirements with current liabilities. Together, current assets minus current liabilities equal **working capital**. Working capital is a significant investment. For Fortune 500 companies, working capital is about 20 percent of sales.[1]

---

1 Shawn Tully, *"Raiding a Company's Hidden Cash,"* Fortune, *August 22, 1994, 82.*

Tying up cash in working capital is as much an investment as is tying up cash in plant and equipment. Investment decisions requiring increases in working capital must earn satisfactory returns on the entire amount, not just on the plant and equipment portion. Projects aimed at increasing sales usually require an increase in working capital, as you saw in Chapters 6 and 7 when Cross Company increased its sales. Projects can also reduce working capital, and some companies specifically target such investments, as we show in a later Insight. Changes in working capital are not difficult to incorporate in the capital budgeting framework. They have no tax effects, because income taxes are based on accrual accounting. In the introductory analysis we present, such changes affect cash flows in the first and perhaps in the last years of the project. Because of differences in analyzing projects that require increases and decreases in working capital investment, we treat them separately, beginning with increases.

Increases in Working Capital Investment

One difference between investments in working capital and in plant assets is important for our purposes. At the end of its useful life, a tangible asset is almost always worth less than it cost. In contrast, working capital investments are typically recovered *in full*, or nearly so, because the larger receivables and inventory will be turned into cash during the final operating cycle in the life of the project. Remember the time lags, discussed in Chapters 6 and 7, between making a purchase and paying for it and between making a sale and collecting for it. In the final year of a project, the expectation of reduced sales reduces the required inventory, thereby reducing the required purchases, which in turn reduces the amount of cash needed to pay for purchases and *frees such cash for other uses*. Similarly, cash collections in that final year should exceed sales related to the project, because of the delay in collecting for sales made in the previous year.[2]

Consider an investment in a new product that is expected to have a useful life of five years. Revenues from the product are estimated to be $20,000 annually, with additional annual cash costs of $6,000. The investment is $30,000 in equipment and $35,000 in working capital. Straight-line depreciation is used, the equipment has no salvage value, cost of capital is 12%, and the tax rate is 40%. The cash flows and NPV of the project are computed as follows:

	Incremental Cash Flows Years 1-5	
	Tax Computation	Cash Flow
Revenues	$20,000	$20,000
Cash expenses	6,000	6,000
Pretax cash inflow	$14,000	$14,000
Depreciation ($30,000/5)	6,000	
Increase in taxable income	$ 8,000	
Tax at 40%	$ 3,200	3,200
Net cash inflow per year		$10,800

---

2 *As a practical matter, the return of investments in accounts receivable might extend beyond the life of a project because the company will not collect sales made late in the final year until early the next year. Investments in inventory typically will be recovered late in the final year as the company gears down production as sales decline. Such minor timing differences are trivial when we are estimating cash flows years into the future.*

Some companies anticipate recovering less than the full investment in working capital because they expect some over-production in later years. In such cases, the recovery is less than the original investment and a tax effect also occurs.

End of Year 5	
Recovery of working capital investment	$35,000

Summary of Net Present Value of Investment	
Operating cash inflows ($10,800 × 3.605)	$38,934
Recovery of working capital investment ($35,000 × 0.567)[3]	19,845
Total present value	$58,779
Investment required ($30,000 + $35,000)	65,000
Net present value	$ (6,221)

The negative NPV tells us that the investment is undesirable. If only the machinery is considered, the investment appears desirable because it shows a positive NPV of $8,934 ($38,934 - $30,000). The working capital investment was a net $15,155 ($35,000 - $19,845). Failure to consider the working capital requirements would lead to a bad decision.

Decreases in Working Capital Investment

Capital investments that decrease working capital are more and more common. A computerized billing system enables a company to collect its accounts receivable faster. **Wal-Mart** and other retailers have invested in projects that reduce inventories while providing the same levels of service to customers. However, by far the most common type of investment that reduces working capital occurs in companies that are moving toward the JIT ideal of zero inventories.

A company embarking on an inventory-reduction project will draw down existing inventory the first year of the project to meet current sales needs. It will not manufacture or purchase as many units as it sells in the first year. Delaying production or purchases frees up cash for other purposes. Because the company is committed to the JIT philosophy, it does not expect to return to its prior inventory levels at the end of the project's life. The company therefore expects a cash saving in the first year of a project's life but does not expect a cash outflow in the final year. Accordingly, the analysis of an inventory-reducing decision includes only the cash saving from reducing inventory in the first year, with no offsetting outflow in the final year.

The second case of a complex investment to be considered, the replacement decision, is different from investments involving working capital because it involves additional calculations to determine future cash flows.

REPLACEMENT DECISIONS

Businesses frequently face the problem of whether to replace an asset currently in use. Such a question is called a **replacement decision**. Replacement decisions are made when economic or technological factors make it possible to perform tasks at a lower cost. Faster machines that might also reduce waste and labor-saving devices enable the company to earn higher returns. Typically, replacement decisions involve essential operations. The company must perform the function, such as attaching fenders to automobile bodies. The focus is on how to perform the operation.

---

3 *Some analysts prefer to subtract the present value of the recovery from the investment. The effect is the same.*

Determining cash flows for replacement decisions is more complex than for decisions about whether to purchase new assets because (1) depreciation on the replacement is likely to be different from that on the existing assets, and (2) determining the net cost to purchase the replacement requires more steps. We illustrate two methods for evaluating replacement decisions: the incremental approach and the total-project approach.

The **incremental approach** focuses on the differences between the cash flows, given the alternatives of keeping the existing assets or replacing them. The **total-project approach** compares the present values of operating each way. The two approaches give the same results, so selecting one or the other is a matter of computational convenience.

Suppose your company owns a machine for which it paid $100,000 five years ago. Other data relating to the machine are as follows:

Remaining useful life	5 years
Current book value	$50,000
Annual depreciation	$10,000
Expected sales value—now	$20,000
—in 5 yrs.	$10,000
Annual cash operating costs	$30,000

If you continue to use the machine for the next five years, there will be a tax (at an expected rate of 40%) on the expected salvage value because that value was not included in the depreciation calculation. (Annual depreciation of $10,000 for five years equals the $50,000 cost.) If you sell the machine now, the loss for tax purposes will be $30,000 ($50,000 book value - $20,000 sales price).

Suppose a new machine comes on the market that sells for $60,000, has an estimated useful life of five years with no salvage value, and costs only $15,000 per year to operate. The new machine can be depreciated over five years using the straight-line method. Suppose further that the cutoff rate is 16%. Is it wise to replace the old machine now?

As with any capital project, the analysis must consider two things: the initial investment and the future cash flows. In a replacement decision, the computation of each of these is different from the computations we have made previously. First we determine the initial investment.

	Tax Computation	Cash Outlay
Purchase price of new asset		$ 60,000
Book value of old machine	$50,000	
Sale price, which is a cash inflow	20,000	(20,000)
Loss for taxes, which can be offset against regular income	$30,000	
Tax saved (40% × $30,000)	$12,000	(12,000)
Net outlay for new asset		$ 28,000

The book value or cost of an existing asset is sunk and irrelevant to decisions. However, book value *does* affect taxes if the asset is sold and so must be considered in determining those taxes.[4] The sale of the old asset reduces the outlay for the new one by $32,000, because the company will receive $20,000 from the sale and the loss on the sale produces a $12,000 saving in income taxes. Hence, a net outlay of only $28,000 is required to buy the new asset.

Incremental Approach

Following is the computation of future cash flows, using the incremental approach.

Annual Cash Savings Years 1-5

		Tax Computation	Cash Flow
Pretax cash savings:			
Cash cost of using old asset		$30,000	
Cash cost of using new asset		15,000	
Difference in favor of replacement, cash inflow	(1)	$15,000	$15,000
Additional depreciation:			
Depreciation on new asset ($60,000/5)		$12,000	
Depreciation on old asset		10,000	
Additional tax deduction for depreciation with replacement	(2)	$ 2,000	
Increase in taxable income (1) - (2) =	(3)	$13,000	
Additional tax ($13,000 × 40%), cash outflow	(4)	$ 5,200	(5,200)
Additional net cash inflow favoring replacement (1) - (4)			$ 9,800

Salvage Values—End of Year 5

	Tax Computation	Cash Flow
Old asset	$10,000	
New asset	0	
Difference in favor of not replacing	$10,000	$10,000
Tax on difference, cash outflow	$ 4,000	(4,000)
Difference in favor of not replacing (decrease in cash flow)		$ 6,000

We then discount the $9,800 at 16 percent, yielding a present value of $32,085 ($9,800 × 3.274) and also the $6,000 difference in cash flows from salvage values, yielding $2,856 ($6,000 × 0.476). The difference is subtracted from the present value of the $9,800 annual flows because you must give up the salvage value of the old asset in order to obtain the increased annual flows.

---

4 *The* tax basis *of the asset, its original cost less depreciation taken for tax purposes, is the relevant figure. The tax basis and book value will differ if the company uses one method for tax purposes and another for book purposes. Most companies do in fact use different methods for the two purposes.*

Summary of Present Values of Investment—Incremental Approach	
Present value of savings from using new machine	$32,085
Less: Present value of unfavorable difference in salvage values	2,856
Present value of future net savings	$29,229
Required investment	28,000
Net present value of replacing machine	$ 1,229

The present value of future net savings from making a replacement now ($29,229) is greater than the net outlay required ($28,000), so the replacement is desirable. The decision rule, then, using the incremental approach, is to replace when the NPV of the replacement alternative is positive.

TOTAL-PROJECT APPROACH

In the total-project approach we calculate, separately, the present values of the future outflows using the existing asset and using the replacement asset. The decision rule, using the total-project approach, is to accept the alternative with the lower present value of future outflows. This is because the analysis of both alternatives deals with costs (cash outflows), not revenues (cash inflows); the alternative with the lower present value minimizes costs.

For the example just given, the present value of the total outflows if the existing machine is used is calculated as follows.

Decision—Operate Existing Machine	Tax Computation	Cash Flow
Annual operating costs	$30,000	$30,000
Depreciation	10,000	
Total tax-deductible expenses	$40,000	
Tax savings expected (40%)	$16,000	16,000
Net cash outflow expected per year		$14,000
Present value factor for 5 years at 16%		3.274
Present value of future operating outflows		$45,836
Less: Present value of salvage value ($6,000 × 0.476)		2,856
Present value of future cash outflows on existing machine		$42,980

Consider, now, the present value of the total cash flows if the new machine is purchased.

Decision—Sell Existing Machine, Buy New Machine	Tax Computation	Cash Flow
Annual operating costs	$15,000	$15,000
Depreciation	12,000	
Total tax-deductible expenses	$27,000	
Tax savings expected (40%)	$10,800	10,800
Net cash outflow expected per year		$ 4,200
Present value factor for 5 years at 16%		3.274
Present value of future operating outflows		$13,751
Net outlay required for the new machine		28,000
Present value of total cash outflows of buying new machine		$41,751

Comparing the two alternatives, we find

Present value of using existing machine	$42,980
Present value of buying and using new machine	41,751
Difference in favor of replacing machine	$ 1,229

The present value of the total outlays associated with using the existing machine is greater than that of the total outlays associated with acquiring and using the new machine. Note that the $1,229 difference is equal to the NPV we computed using the incremental approach. The two approaches give the same results, and the choice between them is a matter of convenience.

In the replacement decision considered here, it was possible to continue using the currently owned asset. The same two analytical approaches can be used if an essential asset has reached the end of its useful life and alternatives exist as possible replacements. For example, suppose that a company needs a new forklift truck because one of its existing trucks is about to be scrapped. Perhaps two different models are available as replacements, each with a different acquisition cost and associated annual operating costs. Because the firm is committed to replacing the old forklift, the decision becomes how to minimize the future costs, for which either the incremental or the total-project approach could be used. The accompanying Insight describes how one group of consultants approached complex replacement decisions.

MUTUALLY EXCLUSIVE ALTERNATIVES

The decision rules presented in this and the preceding chapter classify investments as wise or unwise. They do not consider whether the company has enough money to make the investments. When resources are limited, all of the company's investment opportunities are *competing* for the available money. In some cases, the competition is even more specific, as when the company has two or more ways of accomplishing the same goal so that selecting one alternative precludes selecting the others. Such competing proposals are **mutually exclusive alternatives**.

Replacement decisions, such as the one just discussed, fit this definition. If the company keeps its present equipment, it doesn't need the newer model, and vice versa. Mutual exclusivity can also arise as a matter of policy. For example, a company might have a policy of introducing no more than one new product in any one year.

Whether exclusivity is inherent in the proposals or is the result of management policy, it is not unusual for competing alternatives to have unequal lives. Some analysts suggest that another evaluation technique, the profitability index, can be particularly useful in ranking and deciding among alternatives. These two special topics are discussed in the next sections.

UNEQUAL LIVES

While both a conveyor belt and a forklift truck might meet the need to move semifinished units from one place to another, the life of the conveyor is likely to exceed that of the truck. To evaluate such investments we must find some

Construction companies, especially road builders, are continually evaluating equipment replacements. Overhauling equipment, rather than replacing it, is usually an option. Companies can also lease equipment for short periods, adding yet another option. To further complicate matters, many companies favor the equipment of a particular manufacturer. The market for used construction equipment is very active, so that companies can buy either new or used equipment.

Companies monitor their equipment carefully to see if operating costs are rising to the point where replacement might be desirable. Repair and maintenance costs, which are sometimes difficult to determine for particular machines, is an important factor. Downtime is an important sign that replacement might be desirable. Downtime is extremely costly because a machine that goes out of service can idle other machines that depend on its work.

The authors consulted XYZ Company on capital replacement decisions for an unidentified company. The consultants used discounted cash flow methods and developed sophisticated indices for repair costs and for productivity to help the company identify candidates for replacement. Their productivity index included downtime, idle time (machine is available, but not being used), travel time from one job to another, and productive time. The repair index encompasses six divisions of equipment, from new through obsolete, each division further subdivided based on the number of hours equipment has run.

Other industries might face less complicated situations, with fewer options and fewer operating factors, but most replacement decisions require careful analysis of many factors.

Source: C. Douglas Poe, Gadis J. Dillon, and Kenneth Day, "Replacing Fixed Assets in the Construction Industry," Management Accounting, *August 1988, 39-43.*

way to make the alternatives comparable. A commonly used method of doing so is to assume a chain of replacements such that the analysis of each alternative covers the same number of years.

To illustrate this method, assume the following facts about two mutually exclusive investment opportunities involving a machine, versions Model G-40 and Model G-70, that is essential to the company's operations.

	Model G-40	Model G-70
Purchase price	$40,000	$70,000
Annual cash operating costs	$8,000	$6,000
Expected useful life	4 years	8 years

Neither machine has any expected salvage value at the end of its useful life. The cutoff rate is 14 percent. So, as to concentrate on the specific problem at hand – the unequal lives of the alternatives – we ignore income taxes and, therefore, need not be concerned with depreciation.

We select eight years as the time period for the evaluation because that is the lowest common denominator for the lives of the two investments. Evaluating first the alternative with the longer life (Model G-70), the present value of the expected cash outflows is $97,834.

Annual operating costs	$ 6,000
Present value factor for 14% and 8 years	4.639
Present value of operating costs	$27,834
Investment required	70,000
Present value of total cash outflows for G-70	$97,834

To provide comparable information about the alternative of using Model G-40, we assume replacement at the end of four years at a cost of $44,000 but no change in annual operating costs. The present value of total cash outflows assuming a choice of Model G-40 is $103,160.

Annual operating costs, years 1-8	$ 8,000
Present value factor for 14% and 8 years	4.639
Present value of operating cash outflows, years 1-8	$ 37,112
Present value of purchase of replacement Model G-40 at the end of year 4 ($44,000 × .592)	26,048
Present value of future cash outlays	$ 63,160
Investment required now	40,000
Present value of total cash outflows for G-40	$103,160

Because we are dealing with cash *outflows* for the two alternatives, we want the one with the *lower* present value, which is Model G-70 ($97,834). However, the company's managers should consider how confident they are in the forecast of the replacement cost of the G-40 as well as the likelihood of a significant change in technology.

RANKING INVESTMENT OPPORTUNITIES

 In Chapter 8 we stated that the two discounted cash flow techniques (NPV and IRR) were conceptually superior to other methods presented in that chapter (payback period and book rate of return). It is possible, however, that if two or more proposals are ranked using each of the two conceptually superior methods, the rankings might not be the same. That is, the proposals ranking first and second using NPV might rank second and first using IRR. If the proposals are mutually exclusive there is now a conflict; the decision rule for NPV argues acceptance of one proposal, while the decision rule for IRR argues acceptance of the other.

To deal with such situations, some accountants and financial specialists prefer a third discounted cash flow technique, the profitability index, which, they argue, is as useful as NPV and IRR in most situations but more useful than those approaches in evaluating mutually exclusive alternatives. The **profitability index (PI)** is the ratio of the present value of the future cash flows to the investment. In general terms,

$$\text{Profitability index} = \frac{\text{Present value of future cash flows}}{\text{Investment}}$$

Thus, a $100,000 investment with present value of future cash flows of $118,000 has a PI of 1.18.

The decision rule using PI is to accept projects with a PI greater than 1.0. In the case of acceptance/rejection decisions, the decision rule for using PI produces the same results as the rules covering NPV and IRR. An investment with a positive NPV and an IRR greater than cost of capital also has a PI greater than 1.0. The advantage of the PI is that it focuses on the present value of future cash flows generated per dollar of investment. The higher the PI, the higher the margin of safety offered by the investment. Consider the following two investments.

	A	B
Present value of future flows	$10,100,000	$500,000
Investment	$10,000,000	$400,000
NPV	$100,000	$100,000
PI	1.01	1.25

Investment A has little margin of safety, considering its size. If the present value of future flows falls only one percent, the NPV is wiped out. Investment B, however, requires a 25 percent drop in the present value of the future cash flows to wipe out the NPV. Most would argue that investment B is therefore safer than investment A.

Nonetheless, if the risk of decreases in future cash flows is not an issue, NPV is generally, theoretically, preferable to either IRR or PI when it comes to ranking competing alternatives. Let us see how the three criteria perform in an example, and explain those special circumstances.

Following are data for two mutually exclusive investment opportunities confronting a company with a 10 percent cost of capital.

	Investment Opportunities	
	X	Y
Investment required	$50,000	$10,000
Life of investment	1 year	1 year
Cash flows, end of year 1	$55,991	$11,403
Present value of cash flows at 10% cost of capital (.909 × cash flow)	$50,896	$10,365
Net present value of project	$896	$365
Internal rate of return:		
Discount rate associated with factor ($50,000/$55,991)	.893 12%	
Discount rate associated with factor ($10,000/$11,403)		.877 14%
Profitability index:		
$50,896/$50,000	1.018	
$10,365/$10,000		1.037

Project Y has both a higher IRR and a higher PI than does project X, which is higher using only the NPV criterion. However, provided that the 10 percent cost of capital is the rate at which other alternative investments can be made, project X should be selected. The simplest way to show this is as follows.

A company considering both opportunities X and Y must have at least $50,000 (the investment required for X) available for investment. If the company accepts project Y (outlay of $10,000), it will have $40,000 available for other projects. Project X returns 12 percent on the entire $50,000, so the question is whether the company can earn more than 12 percent on investment Y and whatever other investments it can make with the $40,000 available.

Now assume that another hypothetical project, Z, is available that requires an investment of $40,000 and shows an expected return of 10.5 percent, slightly above the cost of capital, but lower than the return on X. Z is acceptable using any criterion, but how much cash would the company have at the end of the year if it selected Y and invested the additional funds in Z? The cash position is summarized as follows:

Cash provided by investment in project Y		$11,403
Cash provided by investment in Z:		
Investment returned	$40,000	
Earnings on the investment (10.5%)	4,200	44,200
Total cash available to company at end of year		$55,603

At the end of the year, the company has $55,603 from the two projects. But, had it invested the entire $50,000 in project X, the company would have had $55,991 at the end of the year. Thus, accepting project Y and using the excess funds for another project produces less cash than accepting only project X.

From the illustration we know that managers should exercise care when evaluating mutually exclusive investments that have different rankings under the three criteria (NPV, IRR, PI). If the opportunities competing for available funds include mutually exclusive projects, blind adherence to one criterion or another could lead to poor decisions. The accompanying Insight describes how one company evaluates capital expenditures and how it has changed its criteria since it began having many more projects than available money.

SENSITIVITY ANALYSIS

 Chapter 5 emphasized that decision analysis involves many estimates, errors in one or more of which could lead to an unwise decision. Because of the importance of estimates in decision making, managers analyze the sensitivity of decisions to changes in one or more variables. This testing of the estimates, called **sensitivity analysis**, involves finding out how much the value of a variable can rise or fall before a different decision is indicated. Sensitivity analysis applies to all types of decisions, but is especially beneficial when applied to capital budgeting decisions.

A misestimate of annual cash flow is magnified because it applies to several years and is multiplied by a present value factor. For a project with a ten-year life where the cutoff rate is 20 percent (present value factor of 4.192), a $1 drop

Cyto Technologies, a rapidly growing biotechnology company, manufactures many products and is constantly introducing new ones. Cyto's capital investments begin with an idea that a scientist believes worth developing. Marketing, manufacturing, and R&D managers evaluate such ideas with little regard for financial analysis because estimates of revenues and costs would be too speculative. The next phase, product design, includes determinations of technical and marketing feasibility and preliminary calculations of IRR. Projects that survive that phase enter the product development phase. Here managers do much refining of volume, price, and cost estimates and again calculate IRR. Products that survive this stage go on the market.

Cyto uses nine criteria to evaluate products, only one of which is financial success (IRR). The others relate to advancing corporate strategies and to longer-term profitability such as the potential for spin-off products. These factors are extremely difficult to quantify, but might well be the most critical. Nonetheless, Cyto increasingly relies on IRR for several reasons. Cyto's growth has increased costs that it must cover with profitable investments. Its scientists generate more ideas for projects than the company has money to support. Additionally, increased competition and higher capital costs have made financial success more critical to long-term survival and growth.

Cyto's managers are well aware that changes can provoke behavioral problems. Scientists could become discouraged if the company rejects projects they believe of exceptional scientific merit. Additionally, Cyto considered using higher IRRs for innovative products than for "me-too" products already manufactured by competitors and whose market potentials were better known. While raising the cutoff rate for riskier investments is a long-standing practice, it can have dysfunctional consequences because new products are the lifeblood of companies like Cyto.

Source: Suresh Kalagnanam and Suzanne K. Schmidt, "Analyzing Capital Investments in New Products," Management Accounting, *January 1996, 31-36.*

in annual cash flow produces a drop of $4.192 in the present value of those flows. A capital budgeting decision also works out over an extended time, which is not true of short-term decisions, so a misestimate of useful life could be important.

Suppose an investment of $12,000 is expected to generate cash flows of $3,000 per year for ten years and that the discount rate is 12 percent. The project has a positive NPV. But considering the uncertainties surrounding estimates for years far into the future, a manager might wonder just how long the investment must continue producing an annual flow of $3,000 in order to earn at least the required 12 percent return. Dividing the investment by the annual cash flow gives a present value factor (also the payback period) of 4 ($12,000/$3,000). Knowing the discount rate (12 percent) and the present value factor (4.0) we can consult Table B of Appendix B, look down the 12 percent column, and see that 3.605 is the factor for five years, 4.111 for six years. Hence, the project must yield its annual flows of $3,000 for nearly six years in order to earn the required 12 percent return. In this case then, the estimated useful life of the project has to be in error by 40 percent (from ten to six years), a large error in the original estimate, before the decision changes; so, the decision is not very sensitive to the estimate of useful life.

The outcome of analyzing a capital budgeting decision can also be affected significantly by differences in estimates of sales volumes, selling prices, and per-unit variable costs. (The effect of each such difference is magnified in the analysis, because each unit of volume is multiplied by contribution margin per unit.) Hence, managers might want to determine how sensitive a decision is to estimates of volume, selling price, or variable costs. For example, suppose a company with a cost of capital of 14 percent and a 40 percent tax rate can bring out a new product priced at $22. Variable costs of the product are expected to be $4 per unit, fixed costs requiring cash outlays are estimated at $100,000 annually, and the estimated annual sales volume is 10,000 units. Bringing out the new product requires an investment of $200,000, all for depreciable assets with a five-year life and no salvage value. The company uses straight-line depreciation. The initial analysis for this decision follows.

		Tax	Cash Flow
Expected contribution margin (10,000 × $18)		$180,000	$ 180,000
Fixed costs:			
Cash	$100,000		(100,000)
Depreciation	40,000		
		140,000	
Increase in taxable income		$ 40,000	
Tax at 40% (cash outflow)		$ 16,000	(16,000)
Net cash inflow per year			$ 64,000
Present value factor, 5-year annuity at 14%			3.433
Present value of annual cash inflows			$ 219,712
Investment required			200,000
Net present value			$ 19,712

Based on the available estimates, the project has a positive NPV and should be accepted. But how far can volume fall before the investment becomes only marginally desirable?

Because NPV is now $19,712, we shall find how much a decline in volume will reduce NPV to zero, or equivalently, make the IRR just 14 percent. We can find the decrease in volume that will reduce NPV by $19,712 as follows.

Net present value	$19,712
Divided by 14% present value factor for 5 years	3.433
Equals decrease in annual net cash flows to make investment yield 14%	$ 5,742
Divided by 1 minus the tax rate	.60
Equals decrease in pretax cash flow for 14% IRR	$ 9,570
Divided by contribution margin per unit	18
Decrease in sales to yield 14% IRR	532 units
Volume required for 14% return (10,000 - 532)	9,468

Managers can perform this analysis with other variables, such as selling price, unit variable cost, or total fixed costs. To test the sensitivity of selling price or unit variable cost, simply divide the allowable decrease in total pretax cash flow by unit volume to determine the allowable decrease in unit contribution margin. For our example, $9,570/10,000 = $0.957. A drop in selling price or increase in variable cost of $0.957 will bring the NPV to zero. We analyzed only one variable at a time, holding the others constant. There are ways of allowing several variables to change simultaneously, but these are beyond our scope.

Sensitivity analysis gives managers an idea about how unfavorable occurrences such as lower volumes, shorter useful lives, or higher costs affect the profitability of a project. It is used because of the uncertainty that prevails in almost any real-life situation. Some other ways to deal with uncertainty are introduced in Chapter 16. The accompanying Insight describes how some companies evaluate capital investments after-the-fact.

MORE ON INCOME TAXES

Throughout this book we have treated income taxes rather generally. In particular, we have assumed that a single tax rate applies to all of a company's revenues and expenses, that only revenues and expenses of the current year affect taxes, and that the depreciation rules of financial accounting govern tax deductions for depreciation. None of these assumptions is always true. However, tax law is far too complex to be treated in depth in an introductory text

INSIGHT

An Insight in Chapter 8 described some companies' experience with abandoned investments. How do companies evaluate capital investments, and what lessons can they learn from failures? One way to find out is to conduct a postaudit, or evaluation of a project after it is underway. Postaudits have several major purposes. They serve as control devices by determining whether actual results met expectations. They help managers spot problems with previous decisions and should therefore help managers avoid such problems in the future. Postaudits also alert managers that their decisions will be examined, which should encourage them to do their work more carefully.

A major study showed that about 76 percent of responding companies did postaudits, though some did considerably more analysis than others. Most companies postaudit only major projects involving strategic assets. Few companies postaudit decisions to acquire operating assets such as machinery and equipment. Some companies review projects periodically, such as every three years, while others perform postaudits only once, a year or more after undertaking the project.

Source: Lawrence A. Gordon and Mary D. Myers, "Postauditing Capital Projects," Management Accounting, *January 1991, 39-42.*

in managerial accounting. We therefore point out only a few aspects of the law that bear on capital budgeting decisions (and warn you at the outset that the details are subject to change virtually every time Congress meets).

First, no single tax rate applies to all incomes. Rates are graduated (progressively higher) and depend on whether the business is incorporated. Federal tax rates for corporations begin at 15 percent for income up to $50,000 and increase to 34 percent for income over $75,000. However, above $100,000, the corporation loses the benefit of the lower rates, so that the rate on some incremental income can be as high as 39 percent. The federal rates on incomes of unincorporated businesses depend on, among other things, the incomes of their individual owners from sources other than the business. These rates are 15 percent, 28 percent, and 31 percent, though some can pay as much as 39.6 percent. Most states levy income taxes on individuals and on corporations, which further increases the rates. Because large businesses are likely to be in the top brackets for both federal and state tax purposes, it is reasonable for them to use a single combined federal and state rate for analyzing capital budgeting decisions.

Second, income taxes do not depend solely on revenues and expenses for a given tax year. One feature of tax law, called the operating loss carryback/carryforward, allows businesses to offset losses in one year against profits in another. For example, if a qualifying company lost $200,000 in 19X4, then earns $50,000 in 19X5, it does not have to pay any taxes on the $50,000 because of the loss in 19X4. In fact, with some restrictions, the company does not have to pay income taxes until it earns over $200,000 cumulatively after 19X4.

 The segment of the tax law that introduces the greatest difference between our general approach and the specifics of tax law relates to the treatment of depreciation. As pointed out in Chapter 8, determining the cash outflow for taxes requires considering the tax deduction for depreciation. Because the rules governing depreciation for tax purposes differ considerably from those governing depreciation for financial accounting purposes, we now consider, in some detail, the major factor in producing that difference, the Modified Accelerated Cost Recovery System (MACRS).

MACRS

For many years prior to 1981, business entities were allowed to use a different, and faster, depreciation method for tax purposes than was used for financial accounting purposes. An entity could start using one of the accelerated methods of depreciation and then switch to the straight-line method when that method would produce higher depreciation charges for tax purposes. The life over which an asset could be depreciated for tax purposes was generally its Asset Depreciation Range (ADR) life. (ADR lives were developed by the Internal Revenue Service.) The schedule of ADR lives relieved a business from having to estimate useful lives for its assets for tax purposes.

The Economic Recovery Tax Act (ERTA) of 1981 continued to provide benefits from accelerated depreciation, but narrowed the options by introducing **Accelerated Cost Recovery System (ACRS)**. ACRS specified much shorter depreciation periods than had previously been allowed. The Tax Reform Act of 1986 made some changes in ACRS and introduced **Modified Accelerated Cost Recovery System (MACRS)**. (Both Acts allow businesses to use straight-line depreciation under the ADR lives, but that is usually less advantageous than MACRS.) Under MACRS, the business places individual assets into various classes according to their ADRs. For most industrial and service companies, four classes of property are important:

5-Year Class: This class includes automobiles, light trucks, typewriters, copiers, personal computers, and certain other enumerated items.

7-Year Class: This class includes office furniture and equipment, most types of machinery, and any property not designated by law as being in some other class.

10-Year Class: This class contains property with IRS-specified lives of at least 16 years and less than 20 years, including certain types of transportation equipment.

31.5-Year Class: This class includes nonresidential real property such as factory buildings.

Exhibit 9-1 gives the percentages (rounded to the nearest 1 percent) of cost to be depreciated in each year for the three classes of most relevance to capital budgeting. Depreciation under MACRS for 3-, 5-, 7-, and 10-year classes reflects the 200 percent declining balance method, with a switch to straight-line depreciation when it benefits the business. (The 150 percent declining balance method is used for other classes.) Salvage value is not recognized under MACRS. Also, MACRS uses the half-year convention, which means that assets are assumed to be put in service halfway through the year. Its practical effect is that, as the exhibit shows, assets are depreciated over one year more than their class lives; that is, 5-year assets over six years, 7-year assets over eight years, and so on.

MACRS is usually advantageous because it concentrates depreciation deductions in the earlier years of an asset's life. MACRS class lives are much shorter than ADR lives, so write-offs are considerably faster than they were previously. Tax payments in the early years are less than under the straight-line method. Payments in later years are higher, but remember that the present value of the tax payments is lower the later they are made.

Exhibit 9-1 Percentages of Cost Depreciated Under MACRS			
Year	5-Year Class	7-Year Class	10-Year Class
1	20%	14%	10%
2	32	25	18
3	19	18	14
4	12	12	12
5	12	9	9
6	5	9	7
7		9	7
8		4	7
9			7
10			6
11			3

Calculating depreciation under MACRS can be tedious. Exhibit 9-2 provides a shortcut method for finding the present value of tax savings for 5- and 7-year property at various discount rates. To use the table, multiply the cost of the asset by the factor for the life and discount rate, then multiply by the tax rate.

Let us look at an example to see how the table works. Suppose a company expects pretax cash flows of $3,000 per year from an asset costing $10,000. The asset is in the 5-year class and, to reduce calculations, has a useful life of six years. The tax rate is 40 percent and cost of capital is 12 percent. A year-by-year analysis follows.

	Year					
	1	2	3	4	5	6
Pretax inflow	$ 3,000	$3,000	$3,000	$3,000	$3,000	$3,000
MACRS deduction[a]	2,000	3,200	1,900	1,200	1,200	500
Taxable income	$ 1,000	$ (200)	$1,100	$1,800	$1,800	$2,500
Tax at 40%	400	(80)	440	720	720	1,000
Net cash inflow[b]	$ 2,600	$3,080	$2,560	$2,280	$2,280	$2,000
Present value factors	.893	.797	.712	.636	.567	.507
Present values	$ 2,322	$2,455	$1,823	$1,450	$1,293	$1,014
Total present value	$10,357					

a   From the 5-year column of Exhibit 9-1.
b   Pretax inflows minus tax, year 1, $3,000 - $400 = $2,600.

It is much easier to determine this present value of the operating inflows net of tax, and then to add the present value of the MACRS tax shield.

Exhibit 9-2 Present Value of MACRS Tax Shields[a]		
Discount Rate	5-Year Assets	7-Year Assets
.08	.811	.766
.10	.774	.722
.12	.738	.681
.14	.706	.645
.16	.675	.611
.18	.647	.580
.20	.621	.552
.22	.597	.526
.24	.574	.502

a Factors in this table are the sums of the percentages of depreciation for each period multiplied by the present value factors. For example, the factor for 10% for a 5-year asset is .774 or (20% × .909) + (32% × .826) + (19% × .751) + (12% × .683) + (12% × .621) + (5% × .564). There is some rounding.

Present value of operating flows
$3,000 × (1 - .40) × 4.111 (from Table B) $ 7,400
Present value of MACRS shield
$10,000 × .40 × .738 (from Exhibit 9-2)   2,952
Total present value (rounding difference) $10,352

We needed only two calculations. The operating flow, net of tax, is an annuity of $1,800 [$3,000 × (1 - .40)] for six years, and is discounted using the Table B factor for six years at 12 percent. Exhibit 9-2 gives the factor for a 5-year asset at 12 percent as .738, which, when multiplied by the cost of the asset and by the tax rate, gives the present value of the tax shield.

As noted earlier, the depreciation deductions mandated under MACRS are almost always more advantageous than those available prior to 1981 because of the relatively short lives now acceptable for tax purposes. Note, however, that the shorter lives are unlikely to be used to compute depreciation for financial reporting purposes because they are unlikely to coincide with the useful life of the property. An important result of MACRS is that the tax basis of an asset (cost minus tax depreciation) seldom equals its book value, and it is the tax basis that must be considered in calculating the taxable gain (or deductible loss) when the asset is sold. For capital budgeting decisions involving replacements of existing assets, the analysis of both current cash outlay and cash inflow from salvage value requires a calculation of the tax basis of the asset at the time of disposition.

CRITICISMS OF DCF METHODS

 Chapter 8 gave several examples of companies that explicitly downplayed quantitative analyses because of overriding qualitative, or hard-to-quantify, concerns about particular investments. Companies are much more likely to approve investments that enhance their ability to carry out their strategies than those with no such discernible effect.

Managers today know that they must modernize, automate, and move toward JIT and other advanced manufacturing techniques, but often the costs of investments directed at such results appear prohibitive, with expected *objectively quantifiable* benefits not justifying the investments. For various reasons, high-tech investments often fail discounted cash flow tests. Yet such investments are clearly important. Management accountants are developing new ways of looking at such investments. For example, they are now estimating the effects of failing to adopt new technology, such as losing existing business. Accountants expected typical conventional investments to increase business, or serve existing business at lower cost.[5]

Many companies, especially those using JIT principles, include subjective factors in evaluating capital budgeting decisions. For example, projects that show negative NPVs are more likely to be accepted if they improve one or more

---

5 *Robert E. Bennett and James A. Hendricks, "Justifying the Acquisition of Automated Equipment,"* Management Accounting, *July 1987, 39-46; Robert A. Howell and Steven R. Soucy, "Capital Investment in the New Manufacturing Environment,"* Management Accounting, *November 1987, 26-32.*

of the following factors: cycle time, product quality, competitive position, manufacturing flexibility, and delivery time.

Some criticize the application of DCF methods because of too-high discount rates and the comparison of expected results against the status quo. The issue of discount rates is best left to courses in finance. The question of comparison is whether the company will be able to maintain the status quo. Managers might erroneously believe that if they do nothing to increase quality or reduce cycle time they will continue selling as much as they do now. But in many cases the company that fails to invest in a product will lose sales to competitors who are investing in their products. The comparison should consider realistic sales expectations if the company falls behind its competitors. The accompanying Insight describes three companies' responses to some of the problems we have introduced.

SOCIAL CONSEQUENCES OF DECISION MAKING

Throughout most of this book we have assumed that the consequences of an action were limited to the entity taking that action. Such an assumption is not always warranted. The action of a single entity may have many effects, desirable or detrimental, for other entities.

For example, a company might find that using a machine that saves labor is justified on economic grounds. But the decision to use the machinery might put people out of work. The workers who lose their jobs will suffer if they cannot find other jobs fairly quickly. If they do not find work, they will receive unemployment compensation or some other type of payment that is borne by taxpayers. If they move away from the area to find work, they must incur moving costs, and there may be problems in uprooting their families. The reduced payroll of the plant may adversely affect the community through declines in economic activity such as retail sales. Other jobs may be lost as a result of the layoffs. Some of these implications have been referred to in previous discussions of qualitative considerations of decision making; they were not specifically incorporated into the analyses. Costs that are not borne directly by the entity making a decision and taking an action are called **social costs**, or externalities.

Social benefits (also called externalities) are benefits not accruing directly to the entity making a decision. A company that hires workers who are currently unemployed (as opposed to hiring them away from other companies) provides benefits to the workers in the form of income and increased self-esteem, to the community in the form of increased economic activity and higher taxes, and to the taxpayers in the form of reduced expenditures for unemployment compensation and other social services. The company does not benefit directly from these other benefits, even though its action caused them. Though business managers may not give direct and monetary recognition to externalities, they should at least try to recognize the existence of externalities as individual decisions are studied.

Social benefits and costs are particularly critical in decisions made by government units such as municipalities, states, and the federal government. Decision making in these and other not-for-profit entities is, like that in businesses, based on estimates of discounted benefits and costs. There are several

INSIGHT

Investments in high technology are difficult to evaluate because many of the benefits are not easily quantified. One way to alleviate this difficulty is to "bundle" projects so that the managers evaluate a package, not a single investment. **Caterpillar** bundles projects rather than dealing with each individual component. For instance, its managers will examine an entire process, such as a flexible machining system. One advantage of bundling is that it allows managers to identify costs and benefits more readily than is possible with individual projects. Bundling avoids cost allocation among specific units of a bundle. Bundling also enables managers to evaluate such factors as reduced inventories. They find it easier to estimate inventory reductions that should follow from an entire process than from specific pieces of machinery.

Bundling also focuses managers' attention on the strategic goals of the company, rather than on the performance of a particular machine. Reducing lead time, increasing quality, and other objectives are better achieved, and evaluated, in packages of investment rather than in specific investments.

A plant of **Monsanto's** Fiber Division justified significant investments in high-tech automation on labor savings, reduced waste, lower inventories, and increased quality. The plant spent $37 million on new process controls and related investments because severe marketing conditions made significant improvements mandatory for survival. Management involved the employees in the changes, which included eliminating products and increasing the quality of those that remained. Benefits included better yields of higher-grade fibers and reduced spoilage of inventories through less variation in quality.

High-tech investments are not limited to manufacturers. Service providers such as banks and insurance companies make extensive high-tech investments. **Chemical Bank** has made heavy investments in technology, under the direction of a *technology council* made up of senior managers. The bank has increased productivity in processing routine transactions, but has also developed ways to use information better, even though the benefits are difficult to quantify.

Sources: James A. Hendricks, Robert C. Bastian, and Thomas L. Sexton, "Bundle Monitoring of Strategic Projects," Management Accounting, February 1992, 31-35; Raymond C. Cole, Jr. and H. Lee Hales, "How Monsanto Justified Automation," Management Accounting, January 1992, 39-43; Chemical Bank 1994 annual report.

major differences between the analyses used by businesses and government units. One difference is that government units do not pay income taxes, which makes their decision making somewhat simpler than that of businesses. But other factors in the government decision-making process make decisions much more difficult. These special factors fall into three general categories: (1) measurement problems, (2) problems in determining whether a particular effect is a benefit or a cost, and (3) problems in the distribution of benefits and costs.

Measurement problems arise in decisions of government units because, as mentioned in Chapter 4, not all benefits and costs are monetary. If an unemployed person obtains a job, the government benefits from additional taxes paid by the employed worker. But other benefits such as the worker's increased self-esteem are not readily measurable. Cleaner air is economically beneficial because of fewer deaths from respiratory ailments, less sickness, and reduced cleaning bills for clothing and buildings. But the monetary value of these benefits and of the increased pleasantness that accompanies cleaner air is not readily measurable.

The second factor, determining whether an effect is beneficial or costly, often depends on one's point of view. The government has sanctioned actions to reduce the populations of wolves and coyotes in sheep and cattle-raising states. These programs have been favorably received by ranchers but deplored by conservationists. Programs that result in growth in population of a particular area may also receive mixed reviews. Some states and towns seek industrial development while others discourage it.

The problem of the distribution of benefits and costs has been a difficult social question since the beginning of government. Suppose a city or town is considering the construction of a municipal golf course and analyses show that the fees received will be insufficient to earn the minimum desired rate of return. If the project is accepted, the taxpayers will subsidize those who use the golf course. The town government might still decide to build the golf course because it feels that the people who would use it deserve some inexpensive recreation, even if the general taxpayers must pay some of the costs. Similar reasoning could apply to more widely used municipally owned facilities such as zoos, libraries, and parks.

The criterion that is most generally advocated for decision making by governmental units is the maximizing of "social welfare." Because of the many problems in identifying and quantifying social benefits and costs, this decision rule has generally meant the maximizing of economic benefits—those subject to monetary estimates. To the extent that this can be done, the same general analytical approaches proposed for business decision making can be used in the public sector. And, like the business manager, the decision maker in the public sector must make an effort to at least identify and consider the unquantified but relevant factors before reaching a final decision.

SUMMARY

Proper analyses of investment requirements and future cash flows are critical if a manager is to make good decisions about investing available funds. Required investment should include any required changes in the company's working capital. Where the decision involves a replacement, the analysis may be particularly complex.

Mutually exclusive investment alternatives involve special problems. A third DCF technique, the profitability index, has been suggested to assist in choosing from among such alternatives. This technique can be useful, but the firm's circumstances in terms of available funds and investment opportunities should be considered before selecting a single capital budgeting technique for general use.

Whatever technique is used, managers find it helpful to perform sensitivity analysis. The use of sensitivity analysis is prompted by the number of estimates used in a typical capital budgeting situation.

Computations of cash flows for an investment opportunity require knowing the many special features of income tax laws, particularly the Modified Accelerated Cost Recovery System (MACRS). But other factors, such as differing tax rates for different levels of income in different types and sizes of businesses, can influence both the amounts and the timing of cash flows from a particular investment opportunity.

Qualitative issues are associated with almost every investment opportunity. This is true in both the private and the public sectors. Decision makers in both sectors should make every effort to identify and quantify as many factors as possible and to consider factors that remain unquantified.

KEY TERMS

Accelerated Cost Recovery
   System (ACRS)   (402)
incremental approach   (391)
Modified Accelerated Cost Recovery
   System (MACRS)   (402)
mutually exclusive
   alternatives   (394)

profitability index (PI)   (396)
replacement decision   (390)
sensitivity analysis   (398)
social benefits   (406)
social costs   (406)
total-project approach   (391)
working capital   (388)

KEY FORMULAS

$$\text{Profitability index} = \frac{\text{Present value of future cash flows}}{\text{Investment}}$$

Working capital   =   Current assets - Current liabilities

REVIEW PROBLEM—INVESTMENT IN WORKING CAPITAL

Chapman Products is considering a new product that will sell for $10 and will have variable costs of $6. Expected sales volume is 22,000 units per year. Bringing out the new product requires a $30,000 increase in working capital, as well as the purchase of new equipment costing $150,000 and having a five-year useful life with no salvage value. The new equipment has cash operating costs of $20,000 per year and will be depreciated using the straight-line method, ignoring the half-year convention. Chapman is in the 40% tax bracket and has 12% cost of capital.

Required
Determine the net present value of this investment opportunity.

ANSWER TO REVIEW PROBLEM
The investment appears to be wise, as indicated by the following analysis.

Cash Flow, Years 1-5

	Tax Computation	Cash Flow
Additional contribution margin [22,000 × ($10 - $6)]	$88,000	$ 88,000
Cash operating costs of new machine	20,000	(20,000)
Additional pretax cash flow	$68,000	
Depreciation ($150,000/5)	30,000	
Increase in taxable income	$38,000	
Income taxes, at 40%	$15,200	(15,200)
Net cash flow per year		$ 52,800

Cash Flow, End of Year 5

Recovery of working capital investment ($30,000 × .567)	$17,010

Summary of Net Present Value of Investment

Operating cash flows, years 1-5 ($52,800 × 3.605)	$190,344
Recovery of working capital investment, as above	17,010
Total present value of future cash flows	$207,354
Investment ($150,000 for machine + $30,000 for working capital)	180,000
Net present value of investment	$ 27,354

Note that the analysis shows the $30,000 increase in working capital as part of the investment required for the project, and then includes the recovery of that investment at the end of the project's life as part of the future cash flows. Note also that there is no tax effect of the working capital increase in either part of the analysis.

REVIEW PROBLEM—SENSITIVITY ANALYSIS

Refer to the facts in the first review problem.

Required

1. Determine the annual unit volume required to give Chapman Products a 12% return.
2. With unit volume at 22,000, what selling price will give Chapman a 12% return?

ANSWER TO REVIEW PROBLEM

1. Annual sales must be about 18,838 units. The previous Review Problem shows that the NPV of the investment is $27,354 when annual sales are 22,000 units and the discount rate is 12%. If the project earned exactly 12%, its NPV would be zero. So we can solve the problem by determining the decline in annual

volume that will reduce NPV of $27,354 to zero. That change is 3,162, illustrated as follows:

Change in NPV	$27,354
Divided by the factor for an annuity of five years at 12%	3.605
Equals the equivalent change in annual after-tax cash flow	$ 7,588
Divided by 1 - 40% tax rate	.60
Equals the equivalent change in annual before-tax cash flow, which is also the change in contribution margin	$12,647
Divided by contribution margin per unit ($10 - $6)	4
Equals allowable decline in sales	3,162 units

Hence, the company could sell 3,162 units fewer than its original expectation of 22,000, or 18,838 units, and earn exactly 12% on its investment.
2. We can use the allowable decrease in total contribution margin calculated above.

Allowable decrease in annual total contribution margin	$12,647
Divided by 22,000 unit volume	22,000
Allowable decrease in unit contribution margin	$0.5749

A decrease in selling price or increase in unit variable cost of $0.5749 will bring NPV to zero. Thus a price of $9.4251 or variable cost of $6.5749, or any combination that reduces unit contribution margin by $0.5749, will give a 12% return.

REVIEW PROBLEM—REPLACEMENT DECISION AND REDUCTION IN WORKING CAPITAL

Eamon Company, which has a cutoff rate of 14% and a tax rate of 40%, owns a machine with the following characteristics.

Book value (and tax basis)	$55,000
Current market value	$40,000
Expected salvage value at end of its 5-year remaining useful life	0
Annual depreciation expense, straight-line method	$11,000
Annual cash operating costs	$18,000

Eamon's managers look for opportunities consistent with their desire to create a JIT manufacturing environment. The managers believe that by replacing the old machine and rearranging part of the production area, the company could reduce its investment in inventory by $20,000 as well as save on operating costs. The replacement machine has the following characteristics.

Purchase price	$80,000
Useful life	5 years
Expected salvage value	$5,000
Annual cash operating costs	$3,000
Annual depreciation expense, straight-line, which ignores salvage value	$16,000

Rearrangement costs are expected to be $12,000 and can be expensed immediately for both book and tax purposes. By the end of the life of the new machine, Eamon's managers expect to be further advanced in their implementation of the JIT philosophy and so do not anticipate returning to the prior, higher level of inventory.

Required

Determine whether Eamon should purchase the new machine and undertake the plant rearrangement.

ANSWER TO REVIEW PROBLEM

The project should be accepted. The investment of $21,200 is less than the present value of the future cash flows of $39,320.

Investment Required	Tax	Cash Flow
Purchase price of new machine		$ 80,000
Selling price of existing machine	$40,000	(40,000)
Book value of existing machine	55,000	
Loss for tax purposes	$15,000	
Tax saving at 40%	$ 6,000	(6,000)
Cost of plant rearrangement	$12,000	12,000
Tax savings at 40%	$ 4,800	(4,800)
Reduction of working capital requirements		(20,000)
Net required investment		$ 21,200

Notice that the reduction in working capital is treated as a reduction of the required investment. Because the company does not expect to return to its prior inventory policies at the end of the life of this project, the calculation of cash flows from the project will not include a corresponding outflow in the project's final year. We calculate the annual cash flows and present values for this replacement decision using first the incremental approach and then the total-project approach.

Incremental Approach—Annual Cash Flows

	Tax	Cash Flow
Savings in cash operating costs ($18,000 - $3,000)	$15,000	$ 15,000
Additional depreciation ($16,000 - $11,000)	5,000	
Increase in taxable income	$10,000	
Increased tax at 40%	$ 4,000	(4,000)
Net annual cash inflow		$ 11,000
Present value factor for 5-year annuity at 14%		3.433
Present value of annual cash inflows		$ 37,763
Add present value of after-tax recovery of salvage value ($5,000 × 60% × .519, factor from Table A)		1,557
Present value of future cash inflows		$ 39,320
Required investment		21,200
Net present value		$ 18,120

Because depreciation was computed without regard to salvage value, the new asset will have no book value at the end of its life and the proceeds from its sale will be taxable.

Total-Project Approach—Keep Existing Machine

	Tax	Cash Flow
Cash operating costs	$18,000	$ 18,000
Depreciation	11,000	
Total expenses	$29,000	
Tax savings at 40%	$11,600	(11,600)
Net cash outflow		$ 6,400
Present value factor for 5-year annuity at 14%		3.433
Present value of annual operating flows		$ 21,971

Buy New Machine

	Tax	Cash Flow
Cash operating costs	$ 3,000	$ 3,000
Depreciation	16,000	
Total expense	$19,000	
Tax saving at 40%	$ 7,600	7,600
Net cash inflow		$ 4,600
Present value factor for 5-year annuity at 14%		3.433
Present value of annual inflows		$15,792
Add present value of salvage value (above)		1,557
Net present value of future inflows		$17,349
Net outlay required for machine		21,200
Net present value of future outflows		$ 3,851

The existing machine has a present value of outflows of $21,971, while the new machine has a present value of outflows of $3,851. The NPV in favor of replacing the existing machine is $18,120 ($21,971 - $3,851), as computed under the incremental approach.

Using the new machine will result in new annual cash inflows rather than outflows. This happens because depreciation is so high that the tax saving is greater than the annual cash operating costs. Do not conclude that if a replacement asset yields a positive cash flow, it is automatically a wise investment. In the example used here, if the project had not included the expectation of a reduction in inventory the replacement would not be wise.

REVIEW PROBLEM—MACRS

Strock Company is considering investing in a new machine that costs $100,000 and has an eight-year expected life with no salvage value. The machine is expected to save about $35,000 per year in cash operating costs and falls in the 7-year MACRS class. Cost of capital is 14% and the tax rate is 40%.

Required
Determine the NPV of the investment, discounting the operating flows and the tax shield of depreciation separately. Use Exhibit 9-2 to find the present value of the tax shield.

ANSWER TO REVIEW PROBLEM

Operating flows $35,000 × (1 - 0.40) × 4.639	$ 97,419
Tax shield of depreciation ($100,000 × 0.40 × 0.645)	25,800
Total present value	$123,219
Less investment	100,000
Net present value	$ 23,219

ASSIGNMENT MATERIAL
QUESTIONS FOR DISCUSSION

9-1   *Johnson & Johnson capital budgeting*   Johnson & Johnson, the giant health-care products company, spent $937 million on plant and equipment and $1.2 billion on research and development in fiscal 1995. Can, and should, Johnson & Johnson use capital budgeting techniques to decide what research projects to pursue?

9-2   *Factors in capital budgeting*   Governments frequently take actions that alter the economic climate. For each of the following events, state how it would change companies' capital spending—increase, decrease, or have no effect. Comment on what particular kinds of companies might be affected and how. Consider each independently.

1. Outlawed gasoline engines for automobiles; only electric cars are approved.

2. Discontinued long-standing price supports that have kept the price of cotton artificially high.
3. Levied high tariffs on foreign automobiles.
4. Raised the tax rate on corporate income.
5. Authorized cash grants for attending college to persons with low incomes.
6. Lengthened the period over which companies can depreciate assets.

9-3   Capital budgeting—effects of events   A proposal to acquire a new machine has been analyzed, based on earlier information. How might each of the following events (not anticipated at the time the analysis was done) affect the analysis? Consider each event independently.

1. An increase in taxes on real property (land and buildings) is approved by the voters of the city in which the company has its manufacturing plant.
2. A new tax law provides for a credit against income taxes; the credit is a specified percentage of the investment in new long-lived assets.
3. *The Wall Street Journal* carries a report of a new product that is likely to be a good substitute for the product made by the machine being considered.

9-4   Capital budgeting for a specific company   Suggest some circumstances under which a particular company would evaluate its capital investments projects using straight-line depreciation rather than MACRS.

EXERCISES

 9-5   Comparison of methods (continuation of 8-16)   Determine the profitability index for each opportunity in 8-16 and rank the investments based on these values.

9-6   Basic investment analysis   Cunningham Company can buy a machine that will reduce annual cash operating costs by $60,000. The machine costs $240,000. After its useful life of ten years, it is expected to have no salvage value. The tax rate is 40% and cost of capital is 14%. The company uses straight-line depreciation.

Required
1. What is the NPV for the project?
2. What savings in annual cash operating costs make this project return exactly 14%?
3. Assuming that operating savings are $50,000, what useful life must the machine have to make the investment worthwhile?
4. Suppose the project is not really a new investment but rather a replacement for a machine that has a remaining life of ten years and a current book value of $66,000. The old machine can be sold now for $12,000 and will have no residual value if retained to the end of its useful life. Annual depreciation is $6,600. Should the company replace the old machine with the new one?

 9-7   Basic replacement decision   RTY Company manufactures gear assemblies and has the opportunity to replace one of its existing lathes with a new model. The existing lathe has a book value of $20,000 and a market value of $12,000. It has an estimated remaining useful life of four years, at which time it will have no salvage value. The company uses straight-line depreciation of $5,000 per year on the lathe, and its annual cash operating costs are $63,000.

The new model costs $100,000 and has a four-year estimated life with no salvage value. Its annual cash operating costs are estimated at $22,000. The firm will use straight-line depreciation. The tax rate is 40% and cost of capital is 16%.

Required

1. Determine the investment required to obtain the new lathe.
2. Determine the present value of the net cash flows expected from the investment and the NPV of the investment.
3. Suppose that the new lathe has a salvage value of $5,000. The company will ignore the salvage value in determining annual depreciation and so will have a gain that will be taxed at 40%. Determine the NPV of the investment.

9-8   Relationships   Miller Company invested $250,000 in depreciable assets and earned a 10% internal rate of return. The life of the investment, which had no salvage value, was five years.

Required

1. Determine the net cash flow that Miller earned in each year, assuming that each year's flow was equal.
2. Assume that the tax rate is 40% and that Miller used straight-line depreciation for the investment. Determine the annual pretax cash flow that Miller earned.

9-9   Basic working capital investment   Managers of DeCosmo Enterprises are considering a new high-performance videotape. They expect to sell 60,000 units annually for the next four years at $8 each. Variable costs are expected to be $3 per unit, annual cash fixed costs, $140,000. The product requires machinery costing $300,000 with a four-year life and no salvage value. DeCosmo uses straight-line depreciation. Additionally, accounts receivable will increase about $60,000, inventory about $40,000. These amounts will be returned in full at the end of the five years. The tax rate is 40% and cost of capital is 12%.

Required

Determine the NPV of the investment.

9-10   Replacement decision—working capital   Reynolds Company has the opportunity to replace a large drill press. The replacement press would cost $100,000, have a useful life of two years, and have annual cash operating costs of $30,000. Data on the existing press follows.

Existing Press	
Current book value and tax basis	$40,000
Annual cash operating costs	$90,000
Current market value	$25,000
Annual depreciation	$20,000
Remaining useful life	2 years

The company uses straight-line depreciation. Neither press is expected to have salvage value at the end of its useful life. Using the proposed press will increase inventories by $40,000. The company has a 14% cutoff rate. The tax rate is 40%.

Required

Determine the NPV of the proposed investment.

9-11 Basic MACRS (continued in 9-25) ORM Company has the opportunity to buy a machine for $2,000,000. It is expected to save $600,000 annually in cash operating costs over its ten-year life. For tax purposes, the company will use a 5-year MACRS period. ORM has a 14% cost of capital and a 40% tax rate.

Required

Determine the NPV of the proposed investment.

 9-12 Mutually exclusive alternatives (continuation of 8-21) In 8-21, Welton Company has a choice between a hand-fed machine and a semiautomatic machine to perform a function essential to bringing out a new product.

Required

1. Compute the PI for each alternative.
2. Using the guidelines in Appendix A, write a memorandum to J. Kratz, the production manager. Give and support your recommendation regarding which machine to acquire.

9-13 Investing to reduce inventory, JIT Park Mills manufactures several products in its relatively modern factory. Park maintains large inventories of materials, purchased components, and work in process as buffer stock to offset slow incoming deliveries and production bottlenecks.

Park's managers have been working on ways to reduce the investment in inventory. They have plans that include working with suppliers to have deliveries made right to the production areas instead of to an outside loading dock, revamping the flow of goods through the plant, and coordinating production activities better. Rearranging and outfitting the plant will cost about $8.5 million. The new assets have five-year lives and no salvage value. The company uses straight-line depreciation.

The best estimates are that cash operating costs will increase by about $0.88 million per year if the investment is made, while inventories will be reduced from about $25.7 million to about $1.2 million. The tax rate is 40% and cost of capital is 12%.

Required

Determine the NPV of the proposed investment.

9-14 New product decision—sensitivity analysis Bee Company is considering adding a new product to its Big Bear line of pure honey products. The product will sell for $8 and have per-unit variable costs of $5 and annual cash fixed costs of $60,000. Equipment to make the product costs $210,000 and is expected to last six years with no salvage value. Bee estimates annual sales of the product will be 50,000 units. Bee's income tax rate is 45% and its cost of capital is 14%. Straight-line depreciation would be used.

Required

1. What is the expected annual increase in future after-tax cash flows if the project is accepted?
2. What are (a) NPV, (b) IRR, and (c) PI for this project?
3. How much could annual cash fixed costs on the project be before the project would have an NPV of zero (IRR of 14%)?

4. Approximately how long must the life of the project be to earn an IRR of 16%?
5. How many units of the product must Bee sell each year to have an IRR equal to the 14% cost of capital?
6. How much could variable cost per unit be before the project would have IRR of 14%?

9-15   Working capital   The sales manager of Watlin Tools has received an offer from an overseas company to buy 15,000 power saws for $20 per unit, well below the usual $35 price. Watlin's sales manager believes that no domestic sales would be lost if the offer is accepted. Unit variable cost of the saw is $18. The only drawback the sales manager sees is that, while Watlin must make the units now and incur $270,000 ($18 × 15,000) in cash costs, the customer will pay for the saws one year from now because of restrictions on taking money out of the foreign country. Watlin's cost of capital is 16%. Ignore taxes.

Required
Determine whether Watlin should accept the order.

9-16   Mutually exclusive investments   Miro Manufacturing Company needs additional productive capacity to meet greater demand for its products. Two alternatives are available. The company can choose either one, but not both.

	Hand-fed Machine	Semiautomatic Machine
Required investment in depreciable assets	$1,000,000	$2,000,000
Annual cash operating costs	$1,450,000	$1,230,000
Useful life	10 years	10 years

Under either alternative Miro expects additional revenues of $1,750,000. Additional variable costs are included in the cash costs given. Straight-line depreciation will be used for either investment. Neither is expected to have any salvage value. The tax rate is 40% and cost of capital is 10%.

Required
1. For each alternative, compute: (a) NPV, (b) approximate IRR, (c) PI.
2. Make a recommendation on which alternative should be chosen.

9-17   Sensitivity analysis (continuation of 9-16)   The cost behavior under each alternative in 9-16 is as follows:

	Hand-fed Machine	Semiautomatic Machine
Variable cost as percentage of revenue	70%	40%
Fixed cash operating costs	$225,000	$530,000

Required
Determine the volume, in dollar sales, that will bring each alternative to an IRR of 10%. Does this new information affect the decision you made in 9-16?

9-18   Basic MACRS   Johnstone Manufacturing Company is considering a new machine that is expected to save $150,000 per year in scrap costs because of greater efficiency. The machine costs $600,000 and has a ten-year life with no expected salvage value. Johnstone has a 16% cost of capital and 40% tax rate.

Required

1. Determine the NPV of the investment using straight-line depreciation.
2. Determine the NPV of the investment using 7-year MACRS depreciation. Use Exhibit 9-2 to determine the present value of the MACRS tax shield.

PROBLEMS

 9-19   *Review of chapters 8 and 9* Bullmark Company is considering a new product, the Super Bull, that will sell for $8 per unit and have variable costs of $5 per unit and annual cash fixed costs of $60,000. Equipment required to produce the Super Bull costs $210,000 and is expected to last, and be depreciated on a straight-line basis, for six years, with no expected salvage value. Bullmark estimates that sales of the new product will be 50,000 units per year for six years. Bullmark is subject to an income tax rate of 40% and has cost of capital of 14%.

Required

1. What is the expected increase in future annual after-tax cash flows if the project is accepted?
2. What is the NPV of the project?
3. For this question only, suppose the project also involves an increase in inventories and receivables totaling $40,000. What is the NPV of the project?
4. What is the PI for the project? (Round to two decimal places.)
5. What is the payback period for the project? (Round to two decimal places.)
6. What is the approximate IRR for the project?
7. What is the total annual contribution margin the company must show to earn a return equal to the 14% cost of capital?
8. Approximately how long must the life of the project be to earn a return of exactly 16%?

 9-20   *Relationships* Fill in the blanks for each of the following independent cases. There are no salvage values for the investments.

	(a)	(b)	(c)	(d)	(e)	(f)	(g)
		Annual					
	Years of	After-tax			Internal	Net	
	Project	Cash	Initial	Cutoff Rate	Rate of	Present	Profitability
Case	Life	Flows	Investment	of Return	Return	Value	Index
1	10	$60,000	_____	__%	12%	_____	1.088
2	8	_____	$224,235	16%	18%	_____	_____
3	__	$80,000	$361,600	12%	__%	_____	1.25

 9-21   *Review of chapters 8 and 9* Hand Division of Hand-and-Glove Co. is considering acquiring an asset that has a cost of $141,000, a useful life of four years, and would reduce labor costs by $50,000 per year. Hand is assessed income taxes at a 30% rate, requires a 12% IRR on all investments, and uses straight-line depreciation.

Required

1. What is the IRR of this project?
2. What is the NPV of this project?

3. What is the PI on this project?
4. What must annual savings be for the project to have a 16% IRR?
5. For this part only, assume that Hand could depreciate the asset evenly over three years for tax purposes, though the life of the project and the asset are still four years. What would the NPV of this project be?
6. For this part only, assume that undertaking this project means Hand must increase its working capital by $12,000. What effect would this new information have on the NPV of this project?
7. Assume that the asset in this project is actually a replacement for one now in use that has a remaining life of four years, a book value (and tax basis) of $25,000, and a current market value of $40,000. What is the NPV of the project?

9-22   *Asset acquisition and MACRS* Peyton Company is considering a new asset that costs $1,000,000. Peyton's managers expect to reduce cash operating costs by $260,000 per year over its ten-year estimated life. The asset qualifies for 7-year recovery under MACRS. Cost of capital is 12% and the tax rate is 40%.

Required
Determine the NPV of the investment.

9-23   *Working capital investment (without income taxes)* Alexander Company, a wholesaler of paper products, has been approached by Clark Paper Products. Clark has offered Alexander exclusive rights to distribute its products in the Denver area. The contract runs for three years, after which time either company can terminate the arrangement.

Alexander's managers expect revenue from Clark's products to be about $300,000 per month, with variable costs (all cost of goods sold) about 85% of revenue. Incremental monthly fixed costs should be about $18,000. Additionally, Rawson must carry inventory approximating a two-month supply and accounts receivable of about three months' sales. Alexander will pay cash on delivery of Clark's products. Cost of capital is 20%.

Required
Determine whether Alexander should accept Clark's offer.

9-24   *Replacement decision* Charles Company, a maker of gardening products, is considering replacing a machine. Charles uses straight-line depreciation, has an 18% cost of capital, and has a 40% income tax rate. Neither machine is expected to have salvage value at the end of its useful life. If the company makes the replacement, it will finance the investment with debt bearing 10% interest. The existing machine could be sold now for $35,000.

Existing Machine	
Book value	$60,000
Remaining useful life	3 years
Annual cash operating costs	$130,000
Annual depreciation	$20,000 each of next 3 years

Proposed Machine	
Price	$270,000
Useful life	3 years
Annual cash operating costs	$20,000

Required

Determine the NPV of the proposed investment.

9-25   Sensitivity analysis and MACRS (continuation of 9-11) The managers of ORM Company are not sure of the annual savings in cash operating costs that the machine will generate. One manager has asked how low the savings could be and the company still earn the 14% target rate of return.

Required

Determine the annual cash operating savings that yield a 14% return.

9-26   Comparison of alternatives Stanley Company must choose between two machines that will perform an essential function. Machine A costs $40,000, has a ten-year life with no salvage value, and costs $12,000 per year to operate (cash costs). Machine B costs $80,000, has a ten-year life with no salvage value, and costs $3,000 per year to operate. The tax rate is 40% and cost of capital is 10%. Straight-line depreciation will be used for either machine.

Required

Using the guidelines in Appendix A, write a memorandum to Stanley's vice president of manufacturing, Frank Cousins, giving and explaining your recommendation regarding which machine should be purchased.

9-27   Unit costs Ramor Company manufactures running shoes. Its managers are considering entering the low-priced market and are looking at several alternatives. The model they wish to introduce will, they believe, sell 200,000 pairs annually at $22. Estimates of unit costs for two alternative production methods are as follows:

	Use Existing Facilities	Buy New Machinery
Materials	$ 3.50	$ 3.40
Direct labor	7.50	6.45
Variable overhead	2.50	2.15
Fixed overhead	3.75	4.225
Total unit costs	$17.25	$16.225

Company policy is to charge each product with both fixed and variable overhead. The basic charge for fixed overhead is $0.50 per direct labor dollar. The amount of fixed overhead shown for the new machinery includes $1.00 per unit for depreciation of $200,000 per year ($600,000 cost) on the new machinery, which has a three-year life. Thus, the $4.225 is $1.00 plus the normal overhead charge of $0.50 times $6.45 direct labor cost. One of the managers points out that the $1.025 difference in unit cost works out to $205,000 per year, a significant savings. He also points out that the after-tax savings is $123,000 (the tax rate is 40%), which gives a rate of return of 41% on the average investment of $300,000. Cost of capital is 18%.

Required

1. Determine the NPV of the investment.
2. Determine the approximate IRR on the investment.

9-28   *JIT, Inventory*   The Anderson Plant of Benson Industries is moving toward JIT principles. So far it has been setting up manufacturing cells and smoothing the flow of work. The next phase involves a multitude of changes related to reducing the number of vendors, ensuring the quality of the parts provided by the remaining vendors, opening walls so that trucks can make deliveries straight to the cell where the parts are used, and teaching new skills to workers.

All of these activities are estimated to cost about $4.7 million, of which $2.9 million can be expensed immediately for income tax purposes. The remaining $1.8 million is for changes in the physical plant that must be depreciated over the next ten years, using the straight-line method. The estimated annual cash savings before taxes over the next ten years are $240,000. Based on conversations with other plant managers, the Anderson Plant manager expects inventory to fall to about $120,000 from the current $2.7 million. The tax rate is 40% and cost of capital is 12%.

Required
Determine the NPV of the investment.

9-29   *Pollution control and capital budgeting*   Craft Paper Company operates a plant that produces a great deal of air pollution. The local government has ordered that the polluting be stopped or the plant will be closed. Craft does not wish to close the plant and so has sought to find satisfactory ways to remove pollutants. Craft has found two alternatives, both of which will reduce the outflow of pollutants to levels satisfactory to the government. One, called Entrol, costs $1,000,000, has a ten-year life with no salvage value, and has annual cash operating costs of $180,000. The other, Polltrol, costs $2,000,000, has a ten-year life with no salvage value, and has cash operating costs of $210,000 annually. However, Polltrol compresses the particles it removes into solid blocks of material that can be sold to chemical companies. Annual sales of the material are estimated at $250,000.

Either device will be depreciated on a straight-line basis. Cost of capital is 16% and the tax rate is 40%.

Required
Using the guidelines in Appendix A, write a memorandum to Paula Graves, Craft's vice president of manufacturing, giving and explaining your recommendation about which device to acquire.

9-30   *Replacement decision and sensitivity analysis (without income taxes)*   Hutson Company owns data processing equipment that cost $80,000 five years ago and now has a book value of $40,000 and a market value of $18,000. The equipment costs $45,000 per year to operate and will have no value at the end of five more years.

Hutson can buy equipment that costs $65,000, will last five years with no salvage value, and cost $20,000 per year to operate. It performs the same functions as the existing equipment.

The company has a cutoff rate of 14%.

Required
1. Determine whether the new equipment should be purchased.
2. Determine the approximate IRR on the investment.
3. Suppose the data processing manager knows that the new machine is more efficient than the old, but not how much more. What annual cash savings are necessary for the company to earn 14%?

4. Suppose that the estimate of annual cash flows is reliable, but that the useful life of the new equipment is in question. About how long must the new equipment last in order that the company earn 14%?

9-31 *Alternative production method* Lizmith Co. is considering a change in its manufacturing process, from a labor-intensive to a highly automated method. Information about the current method is as follows:

Book value of existing equipment	$20,000
Remaining useful life of existing equipment	5 years
Annual tax depreciation of existing equipment	$4,000
Current market value of existing equipment	$25,000
Annual cash operating costs, existing method	$64,000

The alternative method requires a machine that costs $100,000 and has a useful life of five years with no salvage value. The new machine can accomplish the same task with annual cash operating costs of $40,000. Straight-line depreciation will be used for tax purposes for the new machine. The tax rate is 40% and cost of capital is 12%.

Required
1. What is the net investment associated with acquiring the new equipment?
2. What is the total present value of the future after-tax cash flows of a switch to the new equipment?
3. What is the NPV of the investment?

9-32 *Sensitivity analysis* The managers of Boston Products Company have been trying to decide whether or not to introduce a new deluxe birdfeeder. They expect it to sell for $30 and to have unit variable costs of $14. Fixed costs requiring cash disbursements should be about $250,000 per year. The feeder also requires machinery costing $600,000 with a four-year life and no salvage value. The company uses straight-line depreciation. Cost of capital is 16%.

The one point of which the managers are unsure is the annual unit volume. Estimates made by individual managers range from 30,000 to 55,000 units.

Required
1. Ignoring income taxes, determine the number of feeders per year the company must sell to make the investment yield just 16%.
2. Redo item 1 assuming a 40% income tax rate.

9-33 *Determining required cost savings* Grunch Company can buy a machine that will reduce variable production costs of a product that sells 10,000 units annually. The machine costs $80,000, has no salvage value, and should last for five years. Annual fixed cash operating costs are $16,000. Cost of capital is 16%.

Required
1. Ignoring taxes, what reduction in unit variable production costs is necessary to make the investment desirable?
2. Answer item 1 assuming a tax rate of 40% and straight-line depreciation.
3. Suppose now that the machine will reduce unit variable production costs by $4, but that annual volume is in doubt. What annual volume is needed to make the investment desirable? Consider income taxes.

9-34   *Benefit-cost analysis* The Department of Health has studied treatments for two diseases, a type of kidney disease and a type of heart disease. The following data have been assembled.

	Kidney Disease	Heart Disease
Cost to save one life	$100,000	$150,000
Average age of victim at death	40 years	50 years
Average annual income of victims	$15,000	$25,000

The heart disease appears to be caused partly by stresses that affect higher-income people, which accounts in part for the difference in incomes between the two types of victims.

The department believes that a discount rate of 10% is appropriate. It also assumes that a person will work until age 70 (30 additional years for persons cured of kidney disease, 20 for those cured of heart disease).

Required
1. Compute the NPV of saving a single life from each disease. The cost to save the life is incurred immediately, and the annual incomes are assumed to be received at the ends of years.
2. Suppose that a lack of trained personnel makes it impossible to pursue treatment for both diseases and that the same amount will be spent regardless of which disease is selected for treatment. Which disease do you prefer to see treated and why?

9-35   *When-to-sell decisions* Smooth Scotch Company has a large quantity of Scotch whiskey that is approaching its sixth anniversary. When it reaches age six it can be sold for $700 per barrel. If it is held until it is ten years old it can be sold for $1,170 per barrel. Cost of capital is 12%.

Required
1. Determine the IRR that would be earned if the Scotch were held until it was ten years old.
2. Suppose that the price of six-year-old Scotch is $700 per barrel, but that the projected price of ten-year-old Scotch in four years is in doubt. What is the minimum price per barrel that the company would have to receive four years hence to justify keeping the Scotch until it is ten years old?
3. Suppose now that the following schedule of prices is expected. Determine the point at which the Scotch should be sold using the criterion of highest IRR. (Assume that the cutoff rate of return is low enough so that all of the rates you compute would be acceptable. That is, the best decision is not to sell now.)

Years of Age	Expected Price
6	$ 700
7	800
8	950
9	1,200
10	1,400

4. Redo item 3 using the NPV criterion to make the decision.

9-36   *Increased sales and working capital* Baker Company now makes several products in a labor-intensive fashion. The products average $4.50 in variable costs, of which labor is $2.25. Fixed costs are $100,000 annually. The company has had difficulty in expanding production to meet increased demand and is considering a large machine that will enable a production increase to 105,000 with the same size work force. Sales are currently 80,000 units at $8 average selling price. The company expects to sell all its production at $7 per unit if the machine is bought.

Variable costs per unit other than labor will remain the same, and fixed costs will increase by the amount of depreciation on the new machine. The machine costs $80,000 and has a useful life of ten years. There will be increased working capital requirements of $80,000. Straight-line depreciation will be used for tax purposes. The tax rate is 40% and cost of capital is 14%.

Required
Determine whether Baker should buy the machine.

 9-37   Sensitivity analysis (extension of 8-34)   The managers of Pitcairn Manufacturing believe that volume will be 250,000 pairs, but are concerned about that estimate. They wish to know how many pairs of socks they must sell to earn an IRR of 14%.

Required
1. Determine the unit volume that will yield an IRR of 14%.
2. How does the calculation for item 1 change your attitude about the investment from your solution to 8-34?

9-38   Backing a play   Kent Clark, a famous playwright, wants your company to back his forthcoming play, I'll Fly Tomorrow. He has prepared the following analysis.

Investment:	
Sets and other depreciable assets (straight-line basis)	$ 300,000
Working capital	100,000
Total investment	$ 400,000
Annual gross receipts, expected to continue for 4 years	$1,000,000
Annual salaries of actors and other personnel	$ 500,000
Rent, $20,000 + 5% of gross receipts	
Royalty to Clark, 10% of gross receipts	
Other cash expenses	$ 140,000

Your company has a target rate of 14% and a tax rate of 40%.

Required
1. Should your company back the play on the basis of the information given?
2. At what level of annual gross receipts does the play yield a 14% IRR?

9-39   Replacement decision   The management of Bettel Metals Inc. is considering a new machine. The new machine is more efficient than the one currently in use and would save the company $6,000 annually because of greater operating speed. To keep the old machine operating at the present level of efficiency requires immediate repairs costing $5,000. The repair cost is tax deductible this year. Annual depreciation on the old machine, which is expected to last ten years, is $1,800. No scrap value is expected at that time.

The new machine costs $37,300, including freight and installation charges. It has an expected useful life of ten years and no expected scrap value. Straight-line depreciation would be used on the new machine. The old machine has a book value of $18,000 and a market value of $12,000. The tax rate is 40%.

Required

1. Compute the net cash outlay if the new machine is purchased.
2. Evaluate the proposal, assuming a minimum required rate of return of 10%.

9-40   Buying an athletic team   A large portion of the purchase price of an athletic team is allocated to the value of the players' contracts. This amount can be amortized for income tax purposes. Some have argued that the principal value of a franchise is the monopoly right to operate and earn revenues from television, ticket sales, and so on. The amount allocated to the monopoly right is not amortizable for tax purposes, much as the cost of land is not depreciable.

Suppose you are in the 28% tax bracket and are considering buying the Midlands Maulers of the Transam Football League. You expect the operations of the team to generate pretax cash inflows of $4,000,000 annually. You also expect the league to fold in ten years, at which time your investment will be worthless. Your discount rate is 14%.

Required

1. Determine the maximum that you are willing to pay for the team assuming that the investment can be amortized evenly over ten years for tax purposes.
2. Determine the maximum that you are willing to pay for the team if you could not amortize the cost. (You then have a lump-sum tax deduction at the end of year 10 equal to your original investment.)

9-41   Investing in quality, JIT   Roush, Inc. manufactures a variety of products in a relatively old plant. Parts of the manufacturing process are very outmoded and the quality of the output is slipping. The company is coming to be viewed as a low-quality producer, which is expected to affect future sales adversely. The manufacturing managers have been looking at new machinery and equipment that would increase quality to the point where the company could enjoy a favorable reputation. They have also been looking at employing JIT principles. Outfitting the plant for the new machinery and to accommodate JIT will cost about $5.5 million. The entire investment can be depreciated over its ten-year useful life. It has no salvage value. The company uses straight-line depreciation. The new machinery will not affect variable costs, but will increase cash fixed costs by $0.7 million per year.

The managers do not expect sales to increase markedly if they fail to make the investment. Rather, they expect sales to fall by about $1.5 million per year if they do not make the investment. The contribution margin ratio is about 60% on the normal product mix. The managers also expect to reduce inventory by $4.8 million if they make the investment. The tax rate is 40% and cost of capital is 12%.

Required

Determine the NPV of the proposed investment.

9-42   Attracting industry   Minerla is a small town with little industry and high unemployment. The mayor and members of the town council have been trying to interest businesses in locating factories in Minerla. Newman Industries has agreed to the following proposal of the town government. The town will build a $4.3 million plant to Newman's specifications and rent it to Newman for its estimated useful life of 20 years at $150,000 per year provided that Newman employs at least 600 currently unemployed citizens of Minerla.

The mayor expects some increases in the cost of town government to result from the additional employees that Newman would transfer to the new factory.

Additional fire and police protection	$ 35,000
Additional school costs	50,000
Additional general governmental costs	20,000
Total additional annual costs	$105,000

An economist from the state university has projected the following annual results if the plant is built.

Increases in retail sales in Minerla	$6,000,000
Increase in property tax base	$4,400,000

The town levies a 1% tax on all retail sales and taxes property at a rate of $80 per $1,000. The state spends about $2,000 per year in direct support for each unemployed person. The economist said that total unemployment is likely to fall by about 1,500 persons because the factory would help to create other jobs.

The council believes that the factory should be built provided that the benefits to the town government do not exceed the costs. The relevant discount rate is 9%.

Required

1. Determine whether the additional receipts to the town, less the additional costs, justify the building of the factory.
2. Assuming that your answer to item 1 is no, list and discuss other factors that might be considered and other actions that might be taken.

9-43   *Modification of equipment*   Pride Company has several machines that have been used to make a product that the company has phased out of its operations. The equipment has a book value of $600,000 and remaining useful life of four years. Depreciation is being taken using the straight-line method at $150,000 per year. No salvage value is expected at the end of the useful life.

Pride can sell the equipment for $320,000 now. Or, at a cost of $400,000, the equipment can be modified to produce another product. The modifications will not affect the useful life or salvage value and will be depreciated using the straight-line method. If the company does not modify the existing equipment, it will have to buy new equipment at a cost of $800,000. The new equipment also has a useful life of four years with no salvage value, and would be depreciated using the straight-line method. The product to be made with the new equipment or modified existing equipment is essential to Pride's product line.

Cash operating costs of new equipment are $50,000 per year less than with the existing equipment. Cost of capital is 16% and the tax rate is 40%.

Required

Using the guidelines in Appendix A, write a memorandum to the company's president, Lee Pride, giving and supporting your recommendation about which alternative should be selected.

9-44   Dropping a product   Stracke Company makes a variety of products in several factories throughout the country. The sales manager is unhappy with the results shown by Quickclean, a spray cleaner for household use. Quickclean is made in only one factory. A typical income statement follows.

Sales	$4,500,000
Variable costs	3,800,000
Contribution margin	$ 700,000
Fixed costs	880,000
Loss	$ (180,000)

The production manager tells the sales manager that about $580,000 of the fixed costs shown require cash disbursements. These are all avoidable. The remaining $300,000 in fixed costs consists of $100,000 in depreciation on equipment used only to make Quickclean and $200,000 in allocated costs. The equipment used to make Quickclean has a useful life of five more years, and no salvage value is expected at the end of five years. The book value is $500,000 and straight-line depreciation is being used.

Stracke has a 14% cutoff rate of return and a 40% tax rate.

Required

1. Assume that the machinery used to make Quickclean has no resale value. If the product is dropped, the machinery will be scrapped. The loss is immediately tax deductible. Determine whether Quickclean should be dropped.
2. Assume that the machinery could be sold for $350,000. Redo item 1.

9-45   New product—complementary effects   Beverly Hill, general manager of the McKeown Division of Standard Enterprises, Inc., is considering a new product. It will sell for $20 per unit and have variable costs of $9. Volume is estimated at 120,000 units per year. Fixed costs requiring cash disbursements will increase by $300,000 annually, mainly in connection with operating machinery that would be purchased for $2,000,000. The machinery has a useful life of ten years with no salvage value, and would be depreciated using the straight-line method.

The new product would be made in a section of the factory that is physically separate from the rest of the factory and is now leased to another firm for $120,000 per year. The lease expires this month, but the other company has expressed an interest in renewing the lease for an additional ten years.

Hill expects inventories to increase by $500,000 if the new product is brought out. She also expects customers to pay for their purchases two months after purchase, but she is uncertain how to consider these factors.

Cost of capital is 20% and the tax rate is 40%.

Required

1. Determine whether the new product should be introduced.
2. Suppose that if the new product were brought out, the sales of an existing product would increase by 30,000 units per year. The existing product sells for

$10 and has variable costs of $6. The increase in sales of this product will lead to increases in inventories and receivables of $60,000. Determine whether the new product should be brought out.

9-46 *Closing a plant—externalities* Fisher Manufacturing Company operates a plant in Vesalia, a small city on the Platte River. The company has been notified that it must install pollution control equipment at the plant at a cost of $4,000,000, or else close the plant. The plant employs 400 people, virtually all of whom will lose their jobs if the plant closes. Fisher will make a lump-sum payment of $80,000 to the people put out of jobs if the plant closes.

A buyer is willing to purchase the plant for $400,000, which equals its book value. Fisher could shift production to the Montclair plant if it closed the Vesalia plant, with no increase in total cash production costs. (The increase in Montclair's cash production costs equals the cash operating costs of the Vasalia plant.) However, shipping costs will increase by $900,000 annually because the Montclair plant is much farther away from customers than the Vesalia plant.

The new equipment has a ten-year useful life with no salvage value. Straight-line depreciation is used for tax purposes. The tax rate is 40% and cost of capital is 14%.

Required

1. Considering only monetary factors, determine whether Fisher should install the pollution control equipment or close the plant.
2. What other factors might be considered by those interested in the decision?

CASES

9-47   *Mutually exclusive investments* Seagle Company requires machinery for an essential task that will be carried out for the next ten years. Two available machines meet the company's needs.

	Rapidgo 350	Rapidgo 600
Purchase cost	$50,000	$90,000
Annual operating expenses, exclusive of depreciation	$12,000	$15,000
Useful life	5 years	10 years

Either machine will be depreciated using the straight-line method. The firm expects to pay $60,000 to replace the Rapidgo 350 at the end of five years, if that machine is selected. The other data applicable to the Rapidgo 350 are applicable to the replacement model as well.

The cutoff rate is 16% and the tax rate is 40%.

Required
Determine the course of action the company should take.

9-48   *Replacement decision, MACRS (CMA adapted)* Lamb Company manufactures several lines of machine products. One valve stem requires special tools that must soon be replaced. The tools are fully depreciated and have no resale value. Management has decided that the only alternative to replacing these tools is to buy the stem from an outside supplier at $20 per unit.

Lamb has been using 80,000 stems over the past few years and this volume is expected to continue, although there could be some decline over the next few years. Cost records show the following at 80,000 units.

Material	$ 3.80
Labor	3.70
Variable overhead	2.20
Fixed overhead	4.50
Total unit cost	$14.20

Replacing the specialized tools will cost $2,500,000. The new tools have a life of eight years and $100,000 salvage value. Lamb will use MACRS. The tools qualify for a five-year recovery period. Cost of capital is 12% and the tax rate is 40%.

Lamb's managers have had discussions with the toolmaker's sales engineers and with another manufacturer that uses similar tools. Indications are that labor and variable overhead will drop, but that material cost will increase because the new tools require higher-quality material than the ones currently used. Their best estimates follow.

Material	$ 4.50
Labor	3.00
Variable overhead	1.80
Fixed overhead	5.00
Total unit cost	$14.30

Cash fixed costs associated with the new tools are $100,000 per year; with the existing tools these costs are $50,000 per year. There will be no such costs if Lamb buys the stem from the outside supplier.

Required

1. Determine whether Lamb should buy the stem or manufacture it using the new tools.
2. Lamb's managers are concerned about making such a large investment when there is a possibility that the volume of the part might drop. Determine the volume of parts that makes Lamb indifferent between making it and buying it.

9-49   *Evaluating an investment proposal* Your new assistant has just brought you the following analysis of an investment you are considering. The investment relates to a new manufacturing process for making one of the company's major products.

Required Investment

New machinery (10-year life, no salvage value)	$350,000
Research and development	60,000
Administrative time	10,000
Total investment	$420,000

Annual Cash Flows (10 Years)

Savings in cost over old process:	
Labor	$ 75,000
Materials	80,000
Variable overhead	40,000
Depreciation	(35,000)
Total operating savings	$160,000
Less: Interest on debt to finance investment	35,000
Net savings before taxes	$125,000
Less: Income taxes at 40% rate	50,000
Net cash flow after taxes	$ 75,000

Your assistant tells you that the new machinery would replace old machinery that has a ten-year remaining useful life with no salvage value. The old machinery will be scrapped if the new machinery is bought, and the salvage value equals the cost of having it removed. The old machinery has a book value of $110,000. The company uses straight-line depreciation for all machinery.

Your assistant also tells you that the listed costs for research and development and for administrative time relate solely to this project and contain no allocations. The costs have already been incurred, so their amounts are certain. The item in the analysis for interest on debt is for $350,000 at 10%, which will be borrowed if the new machinery is acquired.

Based on his analysis and the 16% cost of capital, he recommends that the project be rejected.

Required

Determine whether you should make the investment.

9-50   Alternative uses of assets (AICPA adapted)   Miller Manufacturing Company has been producing toasters and blenders in its Syracuse plant for several years. The rent for the Syracuse factory building is $80,000 per year. Miller's directors have decided to cease operations at that location and scrap the equipment when the lease expires at the end of four years.

Blender production is approximately 50,000 per year and the company expects to continue production at that level. However, because of intense competition and price erosion, the company has decided to stop making toasters.

Two areas of the Syracuse plant, making up about 30% of the total floor space, are devoted to toasters. The equipment used to make toasters has a book value of $140,000 and is depreciated at $35,000 per year. The company has received an offer of $20,000 for all the equipment now used in toaster production, and the buyer is not interested in anything less than all of it. If the equipment were sold, the space now used for toaster production could be subleased for $12,000 per year.

Because the production of blenders is to be continued, the production manager, Hank Schrontz, was asked if he needed the space and/or equipment now devoted to toaster production. He said that though he had no need for additional productive capacity for tasks currently undertaken at the plant, he is interested in using the space and equipment to manufacture a blender part now being purchased from an outside company. The part is a blade assembly that the firm purchases for $5. The contract with the vendor runs for four more years and requires that Miller buy at least 5,000 assemblies per year.

Either of the two areas now used for toaster production could be converted to produce the blade assemblies. Schrontz estimates the variable cost to produce an assembly at $3.60; no additional fixed costs requiring cash would be incurred. However, the equipment now used has to be converted. He estimates the cost at $40,000 to convert enough of the equipment to make 35,000 assemblies per year and $80,000 to convert enough to make 60,000 assemblies. Because the prospective buyer of the equipment wants all or none of it, conversion of any of it means the company must forego the sale.

The company's tax rate is 40% and its cost of capital is 14%. Straight-line depreciation will be used on costs of converting equipment.

Required

Use the guidelines in Appendix A to write a memorandum to Mr. Schrontz explaining your recommendation as to the best course of action.

9-51   Expanding a factory   Fisher Company needs more space and machinery to increase production. The production manager and president have been trying to decide which of two plans to accept.

	Plan A	Plan B
Investment required	$4,000,000	$5,500,000
Additional fixed cash operating costs per year	$600,000	$800,000
Additional capacity in machine-hours per year	200,000	280,000

The company uses straight-line depreciation. No salvage value is expected for either investment at the end of their ten-year useful lives.

The production manager prefers Plan B because the cost per machine-hour and investment per machine-hour are lower than those for Plan A. The president, E. J. Alvarez, is unsure about this and asks the sales manager whether the capacity would be fully utilized. The sales manager provides the following data.

	Product		
	101-X	201-X	305-X
Potential increased sales, in units	30,000	40,000	30,000
Contribution margin per unit	$18	$24	$40
Machine-hours required per unit	2	4	5

Fisher pays income taxes at a 40% rate and has cost of capital of 12%.

Required
Using the guidelines in Appendix A, write a memorandum to E. J. Alvarez giving and supporting your recommendation about expanding capacity and how the expanded capacity should be used.

PART THREE

control and performance evaluation

Part Three concentrates on the management functions of control and performance evaluation. To perform these functions effectively, managers apply the principles and techniques of responsibility accounting. An essential step in the development of a responsibility accounting system is fixing responsibility for each cost. Fixing responsibility for costs is also important to derive the fullest advantage from comprehensive budgeting. In this part, the emphasis shifts from planning to control, and to evaluating actual results in relation to planned or budgeted results.

The major thrust of responsibility accounting is behavioral; the critical factor in its success is the extent to which the system encourages or discourages behavior consistent with the organization's best interests. Human behavior and the ways in which accounting methods encourage particular kinds of behavior are treated extensively in the three chapters in this part, including recent theories that cast doubt on traditional approaches.

10

Responsibility Accounting

LEARNING OBJECTIVES

After reading this chapter, you should be able to

1. Define goal congruence and explain its relationship to control and performance evaluation.

2. Identify the types of responsibility centers and explain the differences among them.

3. Determine the positive and negative aspects of specific criteria used for evaluating the performance of responsibility centers.

4. Explain the differences between the two basic types of organizational structure and how each affects the responsibility accounting system.

5. Describe the pros and cons of including cost allocations in performance reports.

6. Describe some approaches to allocating costs to responsibility centers.

7. Explain how cost allocations can create ethical problems.

Chapter 5 described some difficulties that **General Motors** experienced since centralizing its purchasing functions a few years ago. GM has made other changes too. It used to allow its product line managers to develop cars for any segment of the market. Its lines overlapped and its costs were high because of the proliferation of models. The top design executive reported directly to the company's vice-chairman, and had no responsibility to either manufacturing (who had to make the cars) or marketing (who had to sell them).

> *In 1995 **GM** began restructuring its North American Operations. GM created a new level executive, called a vehicle-line executive, to whom design, engineering, brand-development, and manufacturing would be responsible.*
>
> *Until early 1996, **Coca-Cola** divided its soft drink business into two units, North America and International. In 1996 it set up five soft drink units, Africa, Middle and Far East, Latin America, Greater Europe, and North America. Within each region are divisions such as Brazil and North Latin America. According to Chief Executive Officer Roberto Goizueta, "This move flattens our management structure." Coca-Cola has only one other top-level segment, Coca-Cola Foods, which accounts for about 10 percent of total revenue. Its manager has worldwide responsibilities.*
>
> *Why do companies organize in particular ways? How do managers respond to different sets of responsibilities? Did **GM's** product line managers work in the company's best interests? How can companies motivate managers to work in the best interests of the company?*

Sources: Jolie Solomon, Myron Stokes, Theresa Waldrop, and Frank Washington, "He Loves GM, He Loves It Not," Newsweek, March 29, 1993, 42; Keith Naughton and Kathleen Kerwin, "At GM, Two Heads Might Be Worse Than One," Business Week, August 14, 1995, 46; Alex Taylor III, "GM's $11,000,000 Turnaround," Fortune, October 17, 1994, 54-74; "GM: Some Gain, Much Pain," Fortune, May 29, 1995, 78-80; and 1995 annual report of The Coca-Cola Company.

Thus far we have concentrated on applying the concepts of managerial accounting to the management functions of planning and decision making. We now look more closely at managerial control, particularly performance evaluation. Managers exercise control through a management control system, a set of policies and procedures used to determine whether operations are going as planned and, if not, to suggest corrective action. Responsibility accounting is the gathering and reporting of information that is used to control operations and evaluate performance. The **responsibility accounting system** is the formal, financial communication system within the overall management control system. These systems use both financial and nonfinancial information.

Nonquantifiable factors are even more important for effective control and evaluation than they are for planning and decision making. The potential for accounting reports to influence the actions of managers is of particular concern. The problem of cost allocation introduced in Chapter 5 is also relevant here. There are good reasons for allocating costs—to encourage particular kinds of behavior and to assist in evaluating performance. But there are also good reasons not to allocate costs, so that the issue is less clear than it was in decision making, where allocation was virtually always undesirable.

GOAL CONGRUENCE AND MOTIVATION

Employees, including managers, work to achieve their own goals, which can include salary increases, promotion, and recognition. (When a company is downsizing, just keeping a job might be an important goal.) Much as students try to perform well on tasks that affect their grades, employees pursuing their goals try to perform well on the measures by which they are evaluated.

People do not need incentives to pursue their own goals. They might face ethical problems if such actions conflict with other personal values. For example, some companies, including CPA firms, evaluate people partly on how long they take to perform assigned tasks. Employees then have incentives to under-report time. Other companies evaluate people partly on how much billable time they generate, so such employees have an incentive to over-report time.

Whether or not they seek profits, economic entities have goals. For any entity, the important question is whether employees are working toward achieving the *entity's* goals. A major objective of management control is to encourage **goal congruence**, which means that as people work to achieve their own goals, they also work to achieve the goals of the company. People must have incentives to work toward the company's goals. To accomplish that objective, managers must assign responsibilities and develop performance evaluation criteria that motivate employees to work toward the company's goals.

A responsibility accounting system generates reports to employees, including managers, about the performance of their assigned responsibilities. Because the reports influence behavior, they must be carefully designed and thoroughly understood both by the evaluators and those being evaluated. Most of the major problems in developing an effective responsibility accounting system are behavioral. Persons must trust the system; they must also believe that the system is fair. They must know the criteria used for evaluation and they must have a reasonable amount of control over their performance. Consider your response to learning, on the last day of class, that your clothing will be a factor in your grade. Or, learning on the first day of class that your grade will be based partly on how well a randomly selected student performs on examinations. Evaluatees must also believe that the system reasonably depicts their performance with regard to the evaluation criteria, again, making controllability an important issue.

A management control system is most effective when it establishes evaluation criteria that encourage goal-congruent behavior and is implemented through a responsibility accounting system that employees trust to report their performance. The first step in implementing responsibility accounting is to establish responsibility centers.

RESPONSIBILITY CENTERS

To be held accountable for performance, managers must have clearly defined areas of responsibility—activities they control. A **responsibility center** is an activity, such as a department, that a manager controls. You might think it is relatively easy to identify activities with specific managers. You might expect a plant manager to be responsible for producing budgeted quantities of specific products within budgeted cost limits, or a sales manager to be responsible for getting orders from customers. In the real world, a company's size, operating characteristics, and the philosophies of its upper-level managers influence the assignment of responsibility. Generalizing about the responsibilities of specific managers is unwise.

A factor that complicates the evaluation of performance in even the simplest of organizations is that the performance of one manager can affect the performance of others. For example, the best salespeople in the world will have difficulty selling poorly made products. By the same token, no production manager can minimize costs if production schedules change daily to accommodate rush orders. Such interdependencies cannot be eliminated entirely, but their effects can be minimized by careful selection of responsibility centers, appropriate use of rewards and penalties, and proper use of performance reports by managers who understand the information that they receive. For example, holding the production manager responsible for the quality of output as well as for production costs can reduce the potential for conflict between sales and production. Each situation where conflict might arise must be considered by itself and appropriate procedures and responsibilities assigned to the managers potentially in conflict; few general rules exist to which one can turn for guidance.

While most managers' responsibilities include meeting nonfinancial goals, responsibility centers are typically defined by financial responsibility. The four types of responsibility centers are cost centers, revenue centers, profit centers, and investment centers. The type of responsibility center depends on the breadth of control of the manager.

COST CENTERS

A **cost center** is a segment whose manager is responsible for costs but not for revenues. A cost center can be relatively small, such as a manufacturing cell, the office of the chief executive, or the legal department. A cost center could also be quite large, such as a factory or the entire administrative area for a large firm. Large cost centers might be composed of smaller cost centers. For example, a factory might be segmented into many work stations, each of which is a cost center with several stations combined into departments that are also cost centers.

Identifying a responsibility center as a cost center doesn't mean that its manager is responsible only for controlling costs. A purchasing department manager is responsible for evaluating and selecting vendors, and is therefore responsible for the quality of materials and components the vendors supply.

REVENUE CENTERS

Revenue centers are responsibility centers whose managers are held responsible for earning revenues, but not for the costs of generating revenues. Hospitals are the principal users of revenue centers, largely because of cost allocation issues and third-party reimbursers (such as Blue Cross, Medicare, and Medicaid). Some companies evaluate marketing managers by revenue, and ignore costs. But any center generates costs, if only the salary of its manager, so revenue centers exist because the organization chooses not to make the manager responsible for costs.

Again, managers of revenue centers might be held responsible for nonfinancial goals. Companies whose strategies include remaining only in markets where their products meet criteria such as specified market shares or rank will hold marketing managers responsible for such goals. **General Mills'** annual report lists the ranks of many of their products in their respective markets and **General Electric's** strategy is to compete only where it is number one or two in sales.

PROFIT CENTERS AND INVESTMENT CENTERS

A **profit center** is a segment whose manager is responsible for revenues as well as costs. For such a center, profit, defined in various ways, is used to measure performance. In some cases, the profit calculation includes only direct costs; in others the calculation includes some (or all) indirect costs.

An **investment center** is a segment whose manager is responsible not only for revenues and costs, but also for the investment required to generate profits. For such centers, companies calculate return on investment. Return on investment relates profit to the resources (plant and equipment, inventory, receivables) required to earn it. In both kinds of centers, the profit figure rarely reflects the generally accepted accounting principles (GAAP) that govern external reporting. The focus of internal responsibility accounting is the effectiveness and efficiency of the unit and its manager. The principle of controllability we discussed earlier argues against including such items as the annual audit fee in reports for profit and investment centers.

 In practice, the term *profit center* often refers to both types of segments. Later in this chapter, and in parts of Chapter 11, we discuss various questions about how profit and investment might be measured. Of course, managers of profit and investment centers are also responsible for meeting nonfinancial performance goals such as market share, customer satisfaction, and employee development.

A major reason for using profit and investment centers is that profit and return on investment are more comprehensive measures of success than is cost alone. To survive, a company can't just control its costs; it must earn profits and profitability is not necessarily a goal of managers whose responsibilities include only revenues or costs. **JKL Advertising** provides an example of a company that increased profitability and control by redefining its managers' responsibilities. The agency had grown rapidly, then began to show losses because it failed to evaluate the profitability of accounts. Because managers were responsible either for revenues or costs, but not both, none were in charge of ensuring that each account was profitable. The agency made managers responsible for budgeting the profitability of every new account, so they consider themselves responsible for profitability.[1] **Fieldcrest Cannon**, the giant home-products manufacturer, reorganized into four major business units partly because the new setup allowed better measurement of results. Part of the reason the company could measure results better was that cost allocation problems, which we consider later in this chapter, were less significant under the new structure.[2]

The idea that profit is a more comprehensive measure of performance than is cost has led some companies to create **artificial profit centers**, segments that deal with outsiders very little, if at all, but rather "sell" most of their goods or services to other segments within the company. The price that one center charges another center within the company is called a **transfer price**. (We discuss transfer prices in detail later in this chapter and in Chapter 11.) For example, a data processing department might charge the other departments that use its services. The department could then have an income statement, instead of just a statement of costs. The department's failure to show a profit—

1 William B. Mills, "Drawing Up a Budgeting System for an Ad Agency," Management Accounting, December 1983, 46-51.
2 Fieldcrest Cannon, 1994 annual report.

or to earn a satisfactory return on its investment—*might* indicate that it is inefficient. A loss might even indicate that the company would be better off to contract for the services from an outside company. With many companies now outsourcing ancillary functions to concentrate on their core businesses, efficiency measures of such functions are more important than ever. However, we say "might" because factors outside the control of the data processing manager could affect the results and cause the department to appear inefficient. A common example of such a confounding factor occurs when a growing company acquires more equipment and personnel than it currently needs because it expects higher use in the future. (Costs are now higher than necessary. But the decision to acquire higher capacity might be wise.)

Pacific-Telesis Group recently turned its in-house legal department into a subsidiary that must compete against outside law firms for PacTel business. **Metropolitan Life Insurance** and **BankAmerica** have similar operations, but have maintained their legal departments as cost centers.[3]

 Chapter 8 emphasized the need for investments to earn returns greater than the cost of the required capital. Companies that use investment centers recognize this principle by relating profits to the investment required to earn them. Managers responsible for both profit and investment have incentives to increase revenues, reduce costs, and reduce investment, all of which, taken by themselves, increase return on investment. Investment centers that fail to earn satisfactory returns might be candidates for elimination. Again, other factors might argue for keeping a center that appears to be performing poorly.

PERFORMANCE EVALUATION CRITERIA

Selecting criteria to measure and evaluate performance is important because the criteria influence managers' actions. (How might a student's day-to-day actions be influenced by knowing that part of a course grade depended on appearance and punctuality?) The most common deficiencies in performance measurement are (1) using a single measure that emphasizes only one objective of the organization and (2) using measures that either misrepresent or fail to reflect the organization's objectives or the employee's responsibilities.

Managers want to use a single measure of performance. Such a measure would be objective because everyone would be measured the same way. It would be simpler to apply because there would be no question about how to weight several measures (such as examination scores, class contribution, and grades on projects). Unfortunately, such a measure is seldom found, and attempts to use a single measure often lead to unwanted results. Consider an example reported from the former Soviet Union. The government was unhappy with the output of nails and decided to evaluate managers of nail factories by the weight of the nails produced. The managers could produce much greater weight by making only large spikes, and they did. Once the government saw that its performance measure was not working, it changed the basis of evaluation to the number of nails produced—and the factories began to pour out carpet tacks and small brads. A single measure could be equally unsuccessful in other settings. For example, evaluating salespeople on total dollar sales fails

---

3 Amy Stevens, "*Lawyers and Clients*," The Wall Street Journal, *July 24, 1995, B8.*

to consider the profitability of the products sold. If, as seems probable, lower margin product are easier to sell than higher margin products, salespeople will concentrate on low margin products to the detriment of the company.

Failing to link performance measures to the entity's goals can also encourage dysfunctional actions. *The Wall Street Journal* reported the case of a school district that was offered the use of an interactive video system that could reduce by 30 percent the time required for sub-literate adults to complete an educational program. Because his budget was based on average daily attendance, and getting students through the program faster would reduce average attendance, the director of the program turned down the offer. The director's action illustrates not only a poor choice of evaluation criteria, but also ethical blindness, since the people in the program would be served better by finishing faster.[4]

Linking performance measures to the goals and objectives at a given time is important. For example, a young company in a rapidly growing industry does not need to be overly concerned with cost control because its early success depends on gaining customer acceptance and building a high market share. Prices and profit margins are usually high during the growth phase, so costs are not critical. But as the company and its industry mature, cost control becomes much more important. Many companies in the computer industry have begun to pay more attention to costs. Companies such as **Apple**, **Sun Microsystems**, and **Compaq** that used to achieve 70 percent gross margins now work hard to achieve 30 percent margins because of falling prices and cutthroat competition. The accompanying Insight illustrates how changes in strategy might prompt changes in evaluation criteria and how evaluation criteria affect the achievement of strategic objectives.

Whether dealing with a cost, profit, or investment center, performance can only be evaluated by comparing actual results *with* something. The most common comparison is actual and budgeted results. Managers of production departments could be evaluated on producing budgeted quantities of product at budgeted costs. (Product quality expectations would, of course, be considered in establishing budgeted output and costs.) Managers of nonmanufacturing departments, such as a computer center or market research group, could be evaluated on whether they performed their assigned tasks and met budgeted costs. Managers of profit centers are evaluated by comparisons of actual and budgeted profit, and managers of investment centers might be evaluated on the basis of return on investment. (The special problems of evaluating investment centers are discussed in Chapter 11, but most of the comments on profit centers also apply to investment centers.)

The legitimacy of evaluating a manager's performance by comparing budgeted and actual results depends on (1) how the budgeted amounts were determined and (2) the extent to which the comparisons consider the control- lability of differences. As discussed in Chapters 6 and 7, managers are likely to try to achieve budgeted results that reflect currently attainable performance, or if they are convinced that stretch goals are necessary. We also noted that managers tend to react more favorably to an evaluation based on a budget they helped to set. But even with budgets that are agreed upon in advance, an uncontrollable change in conditions can influence results, and managers do not

---

Emerson Electric Co. has annual sales of $8 billion in industrial products such as pressure gauges and appliance motors. The industry is mature and competition from domestic and foreign companies is fierce. In such cases, companies cannot raise prices, nor can they count on growth in unit volume to enhance profitability. Cost reduction is often the most important strategic objective in mature industries. In the mid-1980s Emerson's top managers adopted its "best-cost producer" strategy, which meant a relentless pursuit of cost reduction. Cost reduction became a principal corporate objective and managers' compensation was tied closely to it. The company's efforts were successful over an entire decade. However, top managers concluded that the company had overlooked other avenues such as new products and new markets. They attributed these oversights to the emphasis on reducing costs, which discouraged efforts to develop new products and enter new markets.

In the early 1990s, **Emerson** changed its compensation scheme. Managers were no longer rewarded so much on cost reduction to the exclusion of other objectives. Their compensation was tied also to meeting sales objectives, introducing new products, and expanding internationally. The company introduced four times as many new products in 1994 as it had in 1990.

Source: Seth Lubove, "It ain't broke, but fix it anyway," Forbes, August 1994, 56-60.

react favorably to a reporting and evaluation system that fails to allow for variations due to circumstances beyond their control.

Besides comparing budgeted and actual results, some companies evaluate managers on the basis of improvement over some prior period, or by comparison with other segments of the same company. Whatever the type of responsibility center, and whatever bases used to compare with actual results, evaluating a segment is different from evaluating its manager. A manager might be doing an excellent job even though the segment is performing poorly. For example, the manager of a segment doing business in a declining industry might be doing an excellent job if segment profits are steady or decline more slowly than those of the industry as a whole. Similarly, a segment operating in a growing market might look healthy even if its manager is not doing as good a job as another manager could. The question in both cases is the standard for comparison: what should the segment be able to accomplish? The performance of each segment is important to those corporate managers who are concerned with allocating resources to their best uses.

ORGANIZATIONAL STRUCTURE

The way a company is organized, which depends on such things as the culture of its home country and the philosophy of its top managers, influences its reporting system. Different organizational structures result in different groupings of responsibilities. That is, the way a company is structured affects the areas controlled by individual managers. For instance, in one company a factory manager might also have responsibility over the sales force that sells the products from that factory and so is in charge of a profit center or investment center. A company similar to the first in product lines, factories, and other physical aspects might assign the responsibility for the sales force to a corporate vice president of sales. Factory managers in such a company manage cost centers. The reporting requirements for the two companies are quite different.

In general terms, an organization is characterized as centralized or decentralized depending on the extent of the responsibilities granted to its managers. If employees, both managers and non-managers, have a good deal of responsibility and authority and can make many types of decisions without the approval of higher levels of management, **decentralization** exists. Where managers can act less freely, and decisions are made at the top, **centralization** exists. Chapter 11 takes up the question of decentralization more fully. Profit and investment centers are more commonly associated with decentralization than are cost centers because managers of profit and investment centers have broader responsibility than do managers of cost centers. In visual terms, a centralized organizational structure tends to be hierarchical, or pyramid-like. Centralized organizations are usually organized by function, production, marketing, administration, etc. A decentralized organizational structure appears flatter, and is organized by product line, geographical area, or other non-functional basis.

The abbreviated organizational structure depicted in Exhibit 10-1 follows functional lines. Because responsibilities for sales, production, and administration are separated throughout the company, it is likely to have many cost centers and few, if any, investment centers.

Exhibit 10-2 shows an alternative organizational structure in which managers of each region are responsible for both production and sales. Such an organization is likely to have many profit/investment centers.

Note that the finance function is centralized in both structures. Responsibility for financing the entity is limited to the highest level of management. One reason for centralizing financing decisions is a legal consideration: the issuance of bonds and/or stock commits the entire entity and so must be approved by top managers. Another reason is that capital requirements can be met at less cost if the needs of its segments are aggregated and filled as a unit. Companies will centralize other units for various reasons. **Procter & Gamble** centralizes Research and Development and Administration, while decentralizing all operating units. **Maytag Corp.** once operated its Jenn-Air and Magic Chef lines as separate businesses. In 1996 it announced that it would consolidate their sales and marketing functions, and partially consolidate their manufacturing.[5]

RESPONSIBILITY REPORTING FOR COST CENTERS

Exhibit 10-3 on page 446 shows the interrelationships among reports for cost centers. Reports for a real company show more detail, more itemizations of individual costs. We restricted the number of items for simplicity.

---

5 *Susan Carey, "Maytag To Close A Plant, Take A Big Charge,"* The Wall Street Journal, *February 9, 1996,* A6.

Exhibit 10-1 Sample of Organizational Structure

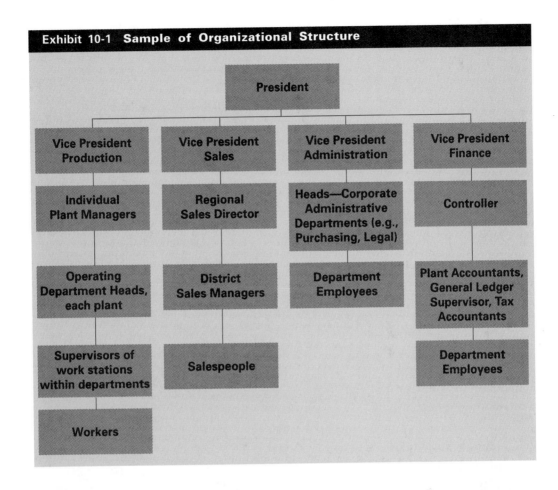

Exhibit 10-2 Sample of Organizational Structure

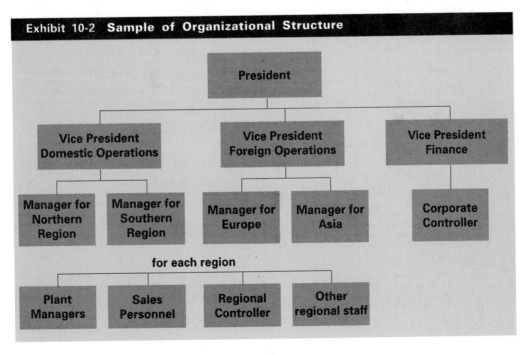

Exhibit 10-3　Responsibility Reports for Cost Centers

	Current Month		Year to Date	
	Budget	Over (Under)	Budget	Over (Under)
Report to Supervisor of Work Station 106—Drill Press				
Materials	$　3,200	$　(80)	$　12,760	$　110
Direct labor	14,200	170	87,300	880
Supervision	1,100	(50)	4,140	(78)
Power, supplies, miscellaneous	910	24	3,420	92
Totals	$ 19,410	$　64	$ 107,620	$ 1,004
Report to Supervisor of Fabrication Department				
Station 106—Drill Press	$ 19,410	$　64	$ 107,620	$ 1,004
Station 107—Grinding	17,832	122	98,430	(213)
Station 108—Cutting	23,456	876	112,456	1,227
Total work stations	$ 60,698	$ 1,062	$ 318,506	$ 2,018
Departmental costs (common to work stations):				
General supervision	12,634	0	71,234	0
Cleaning	6,125	324	32,415	762
Other	1,890	(67)	10,029	(108)
Totals	$ 81,347	$ 1,319	$ 432,184	$ 2,672
Report to Manager of Factory				
Fabrication department	$ 81,347	$ 1,319	$ 432,184	$ 2,672
Milling department	91,234	(2,034)	405,190	(4,231)
Assembly department	107,478	854	441,240	1,346
Casting department	78,245	(433)	367,110	689
Total departments	$358,304	$　(294)	$1,645,724	$　476
General factory costs (common to departments):				
Engineering	14,235	261	81,340	842
Heat and light	8,435	178	46,221	890
Building depreciation	3,400	0	20,400	0
General administration (includes accounting, travel, plant manager's office, etc.)	23,110	340	126,289	776
Total factory costs	$407,484	$　485	$1,919,974	$ 2,984

The company whose reports are exhibited operates a factory that has three levels of supervision: (1) work stations, which are relatively small units under the control of supervisors; (2) departments, which are collections of work stations under the control of departmental supervisors; and (3) the factory as a whole, which is under the control of the factory manager. In addition, though not reflected in the reports, the factory manager is under the direction of the vice president of manufacturing. Two features of this set of sample reports are noteworthy and apply to all responsibility centers.

1. The amount of detail in a report declines as the level of the manager receiving it rises.
2. The reports are not necessarily *additive*.

The first feature is easy to understand. Managers are usually concerned most with the performance of those directly under their control. Routine reports to department managers do not detail all of the costs of each work station. Managers who want such detailed information can get it if they are particularly concerned.

The second feature, lack of additivity, requires further explanation. The total cost on the report to a manager is *not* the sum of the costs on the reports to the managers under her or his supervision. For example, Exhibit 10-3 shows that the total cost reported to the fabrication department supervisor is greater than the sum of the costs reported to the supervisors of the work stations. As we stated earlier, an important characteristic of good responsibility reporting is that reports separate controllable and uncontrollable costs (or omit uncontrollable costs entirely).

The company in Exhibit 10-3 omits uncontrollable costs. But all costs are controllable by *someone*. In the example company, the plant manager is responsible for some costs that the departmental supervisors are not: engineering, heat and light, building depreciation, and general administration. These costs are common to all of the departments and are therefore not controllable by any one departmental supervisor. Similarly, the department supervisors are responsible for some costs that the supervisors of work stations are not, and so on.

Lack of additivity also results from decisions not to hold particular managers responsible for costs they could control. In the preceding example, building depreciation is clearly not controllable by an individual department supervisor. However, the department managers can control the amount of electricity used to light their space by turning lights on and off as needed. The company simply does not consider it worthwhile to install separate meters in every department, so it does not try to hold the individual department managers responsible for the cost. Whether it is worthwhile to adopt procedures to assign responsibility for a particular cost to lower levels of management depends not only on the significance of the cost but also on the benefits to be gained by doing so. Benefits might include savings from lower-level managers using less of particular items (electricity, supplies, repair services, whatever). But the benefits must be weighed against the cost of obtaining the additional information (meters, time required to fill out more detailed requisition forms and to produce more detailed reports, etc.). In any case, the facts in a particular case determine whether a cost is controllable at a given level of management, and the responsibility reporting system should follow, as closely as possible, the principle of including only controllable items.

RESPONSIBILITY REPORTING FOR PROFIT CENTERS

The principle of controllability also applies to responsibility reporting for profit centers (and for investment centers, which we consider in more detail in Chapter 11). Exhibit 10-4 provides sample reports for a company that organizes profit centers around product lines and geographical regions. Managers at the lowest level of profit centers are responsible for product lines. They are responsible

Exhibit 10-4   Responsibility Reports for Profit Centers (thousands of dollars)

	Current Month		Year to Date	
	Budget	Over (Under)	Budget	Over (Under)
Report to Product Manager— Appliances, European Region				
Sales	$122.0	$ 1.5	$ 387.0	$ 3.2
Variable costs:				
Production	$ 47.5	$ 2.8	$ 150.7	$ 5.9
Selling and administrative	12.2	1.8	38.7	1.9
Total variable costs	$ 59.7	$ 4.6	$ 189.4	$ 7.8
Contribution margin	$ 62.3	$(3.1)	$ 197.6	$ (4.6)
Direct fixed costs	36.0	(1.2)	98.5	(3.1)
Product margin	$ 26.3	$(1.9)	$ 99.1	$ (1.5)
Report to Manager— European Region				
Product margins:				
Appliances	$ 26.3	$(1.9)	$ 99.1	$ (1.5)
Industrial equipment	37.4	3.2	134.5	7.3
Tools	18.3	1.1	59.1	(2.0)
Total product margins	$ 82.0	$ 2.4	$ 292.7	$ 3.8
Regional expenses (common to all product lines)	18.5	0.8	61.2	(1.3)
Regional margin	$ 63.5	$ 1.6	$ 231.5	$ 5.1
Report to Executive Vice President				
Regional margins:				
European	$ 63.5	$ 1.6	$ 231.5	$ 5.1
Asian	78.1	(4.3)	289.4	(8.2)
North American	211.8	(3.2)	612.4	(9.6)
Total regional margins	$353.4	$(5.9)	$1,133.3	$(12.7)
Corporate expenses (common to all regions)	87.1	1.4	268.5	3.1
Corporate profit	$266.3	$(7.3)	$ 864.8	$(15.8)

to the managers of the geographical regions, who are in turn responsible to the executive vice president.

Here again, the reports show decreasing detail to higher-level managers and are not additive. Unallocated costs—regional expenses common to product lines, or corporate expenses common to regions—include many items. For instance, regional expenses include the salaries of people at regional headquarters, including those in accounting, personnel, finance, and other functions administered from regional headquarters. These costs are not direct to product lines, and product managers cannot control them. In addition, image-building advertising not aimed at particular product lines could also be under the control of a regional manager. At the total-firm level there are similar kinds of common costs.

For simplicity, the sample report for the regional manager shows only product margins for each product group. In some companies, such managers receive more detail, such as sales, costs, contribution margin, and perhaps some expenses of special concern, such as advertising and promotion. Exhibit 10-5 shows an approach that provides more detail on individual components of the appliance segment in the European region and draws attention to costs that are common to the different categories of appliances. (To focus attention on the format, we have omitted budgeted figures.) The critical point in responsibility reporting is conveying the best information; the selection of the elements to include and the format are secondary. Notice that the amount of detail is greater in the alternative format and that some costs shown as direct to product lines in Exhibit 10-4 are shown as common to the individual products in the line in Exhibit 10-5.

In both Exhibit 10-4 and Exhibit 10-5, the sample reports to the manager of appliance sales for the European region include production costs. This report

Exhibit 10-5   Alternative Responsibility Reporting Format Report to Product Manager—Appliances, European Region (thousands of dollars)

	Small Home Appliances	Large Home Appliances	Commercial Appliances	Total
Sales	$39.0	$34.2	$48.8	$122.0
Variable costs:				
Production	$12.1	$ 9.4	$26.0	$ 47.5
Selling and administrative	3.9	3.4	4.9	12.2
Total variable costs	$16.0	$12.8	$30.9	$ 59.7
Contribution margin	$23.0	$21.4	$17.9	$ 62.3
Direct fixed costs	4.2	15.2	8.1	27.5
Margin	$18.8	$ 6.2	$ 9.8	$ 34.8
Costs common to products in the appliance line				8.5
Product margin				$ 26.3

implies that the manager for the region can control, and is responsible for, production costs, but control of production is not necessary to justify this type of reporting. From earlier chapters you know that decisions about individual products or product lines are based on profitability. For decision-making purposes, then, regional sales managers must know the costs of manufacturing the products they sell. Accordingly, reports to managers who are responsible only for sales and regional selling costs often include a charge for the products, even though such reporting does not follow strictly the principle of controllability. (We discuss ways to bring such reporting more in line with the controllability principle later in the chapter.)

CHOOSING AN ORGANIZATIONAL STRUCTURE

Should a company organize into profit and investment centers or into cost centers? Should it centralize or decentralize decision making? The most important factor is the attitudes and philosophies of top managers. Company presidents who are uncomfortable delegating critical decisions tend to centralize decision making. Those who are comfortable delegating such decisions tend to decentralize. **Wal-Mart** wants its managers, and other employees, to act as entrepreneurs and have a "bias for action." Wal-Mart's managers receive considerable information and support to allow them such freedom. Managers use income statements, inventory turnover data, and other information to increase profitability. But some very successful companies feature centralized decision making. At **Southwest Airlines**, the CEO approves every expenditure over $1,000, not because he doesn't trust his people, but to make them ever more careful.

For an international company, communication time and types of operations carried on in each country (sales offices, manufacturing) are also influential factors, as is the ability of on-site managers. Local managers empowered to make decisions should make better decisions than those at central headquarters. **Johnson & Johnson** has a policy of decentralized management, and also a policy of hiring citizens of the countries in which it operates to manage its operations. **Procter & Gamble** markets different versions of its products in different geographical regions, all tailored to local tastes. One example is a Head and Shoulders® hair conditioner specially formulated for hot, humid areas of China.[6] It is unlikely that a manager in Ohio, where P&G is based, would think of such a version of a popular product. The accompanying Insight describes how top management attitudes and strategies affect organizational choices and the degree of decentralization.

Even after a company decides to use profit centers, it must decide how to divide up operations. Should the company segment along product lines, geographical areas, types of customers (industrial, government), or markets (leisure, household products, mining)? The choice should be influenced by whether the segmentation facilitates evaluation, and that depends to some extent on the amount of common costs associated with each alternative structure. If each factory serves a particular region and makes many products, segmenting by region is more reasonable than segmenting by product line. If each factory produces a single product (or line) and serves all regions, to segment by product or line is more reasonable. (Even if there is a sales manager in each region, the

---

6 Johnson & Johnson 1995 annual report and Procter & Gamble 1995 annual report.

SIGHT

Sysco Corp. is a Houston-based wholesaler with annual sales exceeding $10 billion. It has about sixty operating companies in the United States and Canada. Each company has its own chief executive with broad responsibility over its operations. Innovation is common, but the desire for decentralized decision making is so strong that top corporate managers do not require operating units to adopt innovations proven successful in other, similar units.

Sysco's CEO has traced his commitment to decentralizing to experiences early in his career at a large manufacturer. After being promoted to a supervisory position that he believed would give him the opportunity to influence management policies, he was shocked to discover that eighteen levels remained between him and the company's president.

United Technologies is a $21 billion conglomerate with operating units all over the world. Its CEO describes himself as "a rampant believer" in decentralization. UT gives operating managers considerable responsibility and uses local managers to run its foreign units.

NationsBank has developed an initiative called the Freedom To Act. The program was promulgated by the president of the bank in seventeen half-day rallies with the company's banking center managers. It gives people who deal with customers the power and authority to act immediately to satisfy customers, without going through channels. NationsBank is also among the companies in the U.S. that uses the term "associates," rather than "employees" to describe the people who work there.

Sources: Toni Mack, "V-Ps of planning need not apply," Forbes, October 25, 1993, 84-86; Tim Smart, "Global Mission," Business Week, May 1, 1995, 132-3; NationsBank 1994 annual report.

profit centers could be product lines. Costs incurred by regional managers would be common to product lines.)

Setting up an organizational structure is difficult. Rarely does only one structure make sense for a given firm. Moreover, a structure found useful at one time, by one set of managers, will not remain useful forever. Managers, including top managers, change; products and product lines are added, dropped, or regrouped; manufacturing activities are transferred among plants or otherwise changed, perhaps because of technological innovations. Hence, the structure of the organization, for both responsibility reporting and for operating purposes, requires regular review and reconsideration. For example, after the breakup of **AT&T**, the regulatory environment prompted the newly independent, regional operating companies to segment along state lines. Prospects for increased competition because of continuing deregulation encouraged managers of regional units to concentrate more on specific types of customers and services. **Ameritech**, one of the regional units, restructured itself into segments related to the type of customer served.[7]

---

7 Gary Samuels, "A Meeting at the Breakers," Forbes, June 20, 1994, 51 ff.

COST ALLOCATIONS ON RESPONSIBILITY REPORTS

A real-world fact that complicates responsibility accounting is that responsibility centers include both operating and service departments. **Operating departments** in a manufacturing company work directly on products. Operating departments in a retail company serve customers directly. Virtually all operating departments use services provided by other centers. **Service departments** or **service centers** provide such services to operating departments and to one another. Examples of service departments are human resources, accounting, building security, maintenance, and data processing.

A common reason to establish a service department is that having such a department can be cheaper than contracting for the service with an outside vendor or having each responsibility center perform or acquire the service on its own. For example, if there is no personnel department, each department must screen and hire its employees, maintain their records, and do all the other tasks that a personnel department performs—or contract with an outside company to handle these tasks. A company sometimes establishes a service department because its managers believe that a qualitative issue, such as a need for confidentiality, makes it wise to perform a particular service inside rather than have outsiders do it. For example, an auto company might prefer to have its own employees provide custodial services at research and development facilities.

Managers of centers using services cannot directly control the costs of those services. Managerial accountants often refer to such costs as *indirect*, and the emphasis in responsibility accounting on controllability suggests that such costs not be included in responsibility accounting reports. Yet because the departments receiving services benefit from those services, it seems natural that they should "pay" for those services. Moreover, users often can control the *amount* of the service they use, if not its cost. For example, the manager of a factory department can often use as much preventive maintenance service as she deems desirable. The manager of a product line can order as much market research as he thinks wise. Companies use two basic approaches to such payments, cost allocations and transfer prices.

You have encountered allocations before. In Chapter 2 you saw that a total cost per unit gives misleading information because it requires allocating fixed costs to units of product. In Chapter 5 you saw that the only costs relevant for decision making are incremental costs and that allocated costs are not incremental and therefore not relevant. But accountants and other managers disagree about whether to allocate indirect costs for control and performance evaluation. (And the allocation issue has become increasingly important because indirect costs of operating modern factories are growing rapidly as direct laborers are replaced by robots, creating a need for computer operators and maintenance workers.) Thus, while users unquestionably benefit from the activities of service departments, there are serious questions about whether to charge users for the services and, if so, how.

REASONS FOR ALLOCATING COSTS

As we show in later chapters, the full-cost idea is important in product costing—determining the unit cost of products to determine inventory and cost of goods sold for financial reporting and income tax purposes. Because companies *must* allocate costs for financial reporting, some managers might be inclined to use them as well for internal reporting, arguing that failing to allocate understates the full cost of operating the service-using centers. But most proponents of allocating offer behavioral reasons.[8]

A behavioral reason for allocating is to remind managers of the existence of indirect costs and the need to cover them. If the company as a whole is to make a profit, its revenues must cover not only the direct costs of its profit centers, but also its indirect costs. As an example of such a reminder, the Financial Services Department of **Weyerhauser**, a large integrated paper company, charges each department a fee for transactions related to each salaried employee (payroll checks, issuing tax forms, etc.). Managers of using departments who are considering adding salaried personnel therefore know what the costs will be.[9]

Such allocations have some basis in cost behavior, for, as we discussed in several earlier chapters, fixed costs are not fixed forever at the same amounts. Step-variable costs (from Chapter 3) move up or down as activity changes by large amounts. Chapter 5 mentioned the need to consider incremental fixed costs. Moreover, arguing that allocations direct managers' attention to long-term survival is consistent with the view reflected in Chapter 3, that operating managers are apt to accept the soundness of allocations that are based on their use of activities that drive costs. A benefit of adopting JIT principles is that managerial accountants and other managers who find non-value-adding activities in the course of analyzing service departments will try to eliminate the activities and costs. Operating managers can then be more confident that they are not being charged with inefficiencies or with costs driven by activities irrelevant to their operations.

Proponents of allocations also argue that if indirect costs are not allocated, managers might overuse services because they view the services as "free." For example, if a company does not allocate its computer costs, managers might use more computer time than is economically justified, thus straining capacity and perhaps leading to an unwise purchase of additional capacity. Allocating computer costs could discourage overuse and help prevent incurring unnecessary costs. For a different example of using cost allocation to control costs, consider a sales manager who controls credit terms offered to customers and the level of inventory maintained. Sales managers normally want to carry a high inventory and offer liberal credit terms, with the company incurring costs to carry the investment in inventory and receivables. Sales managers are less likely to allow those assets to increase excessively if they are charged a financing fee based on the investments in those assets. (Note, however, that if the major objective of a relatively new company is to establish a strong demand for its products by getting as much market penetration as possible, allocating financing costs to the sales manager works against achieving the firm's objective.)

Some proponents of using cost allocations on performance reports offer a conflicting argument, also behavioral. They suggest that allocations are helpful

8 *A major study found that the most common reasons for allocating corporate indirect costs to profit centers were (1) to remind managers of the existence of the costs, (2) to make the sum of profit center profits equal company-wide profit, (3) to reflect fairly each center's use of services, (4) to encourage managers to pressure service providers to control costs, and (5) to encourage use of services. See James M. Fremgen and Shu S. Liao, The Allocation of Corporate Indirect Costs, (NY; National Association of Accountants, 1981).*
9 *H. Thomas Johnson and Dennis A. Loewe, "How Weyerhauser Manages Corporate Overhead Costs,"* Management Accounting, *August 1987, 20-26.*

when a service is underused. The reasoning behind this argument is that managers will use the service more because they are already paying for it through the cost allocation.

Another behavior-oriented reason for allocating indirect costs is that the managers to whom costs are allocated will encourage the managers of service departments to keep the cost of the service under control. For example, suppose the manager of computer services wants to buy newer, faster equipment. The manager must convince the users that it is economically sound for them. In the absence of allocations, users have no reason to object to decisions that increase computer costs.

Whatever the reasons for allocating, remember that virtually all allocations are arbitrary. By arbitrary we mean that there is no way to prove that one allocation method is better than another. Nevertheless, some allocation methods are more reasonable than others. Also, as stated earlier, different allocation methods might influence managers differently. We shall, therefore, discuss further how allocations are made and the potential behavioral effects of various allocation methods. The accompanying Insight describes a real case of behavior-influencing aspects of cost allocations.

REASONS FOR NOT ALLOCATING COSTS

Accountants and other managers agree that allocating *variable* costs of a service center to service-using departments is reasonable because the managers of those departments can cause an increase in such costs. For example, a manager who orders 1,000 copies of a document from the Central Copying Center should pay for at least the variable cost of the copies. Note, however, that users cannot control the *per unit* variable cost, so that allocating variable costs violates the principle of controllability. We shall see shortly how companies get around this difficulty.

Where managerial accountants disagree is on the matter of allocating indirect fixed costs. There are two principal arguments against allocating indirect fixed costs, both of which stress the potential for adverse behavioral consequences.

1. Because indirect fixed costs are not controllable by the users, allocating them violates the principle of controllability. Managers charged with costs they cannot control might come to distrust the whole system of control and evaluation. Worse, they might attempt to "beat the system" and so take actions inconsistent with the company's objectives. An example appears later in this chapter.

 2. Including allocated costs on performance reports could lead to poor decisions because managers will treat the costs as differential. As shown in Chapter 5, making sound decisions requires using differential revenues and costs.

Companies can avoid these undesirable consequences by carefully selecting allocation methods and bases.

ALLOCATION METHODS AND EFFECTS

Once managers have decided to allocate indirect costs, they have two decisions. One is to select the costs to be allocated, called **cost pools**. A cost pool often

The Portables Group of **Tektronix Company** had been allocating overhead based on direct labor, but its design and process engineers had driven direct labor costs down to less than 7 percent of total manufacturing cost (just over 3 percent on some of its newer products). Because overhead costs were high and rising, the overhead allocation rate per direct labor hour was extremely high. Thus, though direct labor cost was fairly low, the high overhead cost allocated on the basis of direct labor made the total cost that seemed to be labor-related very high. Many managers interpreted the situation as encouraging efforts to further reduce direct labor, but labor-reducing efforts that also increased overhead simply raised the overhead allocation rate. Finally, the Group undertook an internal study that showed that costs related to materials and components—purchasing, receiving, inspecting, storage, and record keeping—constituted roughly half of overhead costs. Follow-up of this study showed that design and process engineers often recommended using more parts when their use reduced direct labor because, there being no overhead charge on parts, there was no incentive either to reduce the number of components or to standardize those in use.

After its study of overhead costs, the Portables Group began to allocate its material-related overhead based on the number of component parts needed and their annual use. A sample calculation of the two-step allocation process is as follows:

Total material-related overhead	$5,000,000
Total number of parts needed, all types	6,250
Annual cost to carry a part	$800
Cost per part (example):	
Part A, annual use, 20,000 units	$800/20,000 = $0.04
Part B, annual use, 500 units	$800/500 = $1.60

The first step in the allocation process is to determine a cost per part, regardless of the annual volume of use of that part. The next step uses the annual volume of the part to determine a cost per unit, which is then allocated to the product based on the quantity of each part used in the product. Adopting the new cost allocation plan influenced behavior in three important ways. First, it encouraged engineers to reduce the number of parts in existing products. Second, it encouraged standardization of parts for use in several products. Third, it encouraged use of fewer, and more standardized, parts in new products.

Source: John W. Jonez and Michael A. Wright, "Material Burdening," Management Accounting, *August 1987, 27-31.*

 consists of the costs of a particular service department, but, as Chapter 3 described in relation to ABC, cost pools can cut across departmental lines. The other decision is to select a basis, or bases, for making the allocations. The basis is usually some measure of activity or use of the service. For instance, some companies use the number of employees in each department as the basis for allocating the costs of its personnel department. Similarly, costs related to a building (such as depreciation, property taxes, and insurance) are probably allocated on the basis of the space occupied by the departments.

The best allocation basis is the cost driver—the activity that reflects the causal relationship of use to cost. That is, if the users' actions cause the cost to increase, then the costs should be charged accordingly. The next best basis is one that reflects the benefits that the user receives. For instance, it is reasonable to allocate heating expense based on the space that each department occupies—a measure of the benefits received. Even if the managers of using departments cannot control heating expense, they must have heated space to operate.

When neither a use nor a benefit basis is available, allocations are often made on the basis of a department's "ability to bear" indirect costs. For example, there is no reasonable measure of how much each segment benefits from costs such as the salary of the president or the annual audit fee. Therefore such costs are often allocated based on sales or assets, with the idea that these measures reflect the segment's ability to bear them. (Or they might not be allocated at all.) Finally, sales is often used as the allocation basis when no measure of benefits received is available.

Assuming a decision to allocate on the basis of use, there are still several approaches to allocating indirect costs (both fixed and variable) and it is not easy to select a method that will work, in the sense of accomplishing goal congruence. Using the following information, we shall illustrate some common methods.

Raleigh Company has one service department, Maintenance, and two operating departments, Fabrication and Assembly. Data for the departments follow.

Operating Department	Hours of Maintenance Service Used	
	Budgeted	Actual
Fabrication	20,000	20,000
Assembly	20,000	10,000
Total	40,000	30,000

	Maintenance Department Costs for Year		
	Budgeted Original	Flexible	Actual
Variable:			
$5 per hour	$200,000	$150,000	
$5.10 per hour			$153,000
Fixed	75,000	75,000	79,500
Totals	$275,000	$225,000	$232,500

ALLOCATING ACTUAL COSTS BASED ON ACTUAL USE

The simplest—and worst—allocation method is to allocate the actual total cost of the Maintenance Department based on the operating departments' relative use of the service. Using the actual per-hour cost of providing the service of $7.75

($232,500 actual cost divided by 30,000 hours), the allocations are as follows:

Fabrication (20,000 × $7.75)	$155,000
Assembly (10,000 × $7.75)	77,500
Total maintenance cost allocated	$232,500

This method is flawed in two respects. First, it allocates actual costs rather than budgeted costs. The maintenance manager is responsible for controlling maintenance costs. Operating managers might be responsible for the use of the service, but cannot control the cost. Allocating actual costs passes the inefficiencies (or efficiencies) of the Maintenance Department on to the operating departments.

The second flaw of the method is that it allocates fixed costs based on use. This aspect too, allows the performance report of one manager to be affected by the actions of other managers. To see this, consider that each of Raleigh's operating departments budgeted 20,000 hours of maintenance for the year. The budgeted rate is $6.875, computed as follows:

Variable rate	$5.000
Fixed rate ($75,000/40,000)	1.875
Total rate (per hour)	$6.875

Budgeted total maintenance costs were $275,000 and each operating manager budgeted $137,500 in maintenance cost. Allocating on the basis of *actual* use, the manager of the Assembly Department looks good because $60,000 less than budget is charged ($137,500 budget minus the actual allocation of $77,500, as computed earlier). But the manager of Fabrication looks bad. The Fabrication Department is charged $155,000 (as previously computed), $17,500 over budget, even though used exactly the budgeted amount for this service. The additional charge arose partly because the Maintenance Department was over *its* budget, but more importantly because *another* user—the Assembly Department—used less of the service than it had budgeted.

If an allocation is to be used in evaluation, the allocation to a given department should not be affected by the actions of other departments. In general, allocating fixed costs based on actual use encourages managers to underuse the service because the allocation depends not only on how much service a particular manager uses, but also on how much the other managers use.

ALLOCATING BUDGETED COSTS USING DUAL RATES

A better allocation method is to allocate only *budgeted* costs. Using **dual rates**, a company allocates fixed costs and variable costs differently. The method allocates budgeted variable costs based on actual use of the service, and budgeted fixed costs based on expected long-term use.

Using dual rates overcomes the problems of allocating fixed costs based solely on actual use because each department's allocated fixed cost is a lump sum determined before the year begins. The idea supporting this approach is that service departments incur fixed costs to provide the capacity to serve, and the decisions that determined the capacity of the Maintenance Department were based on estimates made earlier by the managers of the operating departments.

The argument is that if the manager of the Assembly Department has requested some amount of capacity, he or she should pay for it.

Suppose, for example, that the estimated long-term use is 60 percent for the Fabrication Department and 40 percent for the Assembly Department. We then have the following allocations, which assign variable costs at the budgeted rate of $5 per hour of use and fixed costs at the budgeted total of $75,000.

	Fixed	Variable	Total
Fabrication (60% × $75,000)	$45,000	$100,000	$145,000
Assembly (40% × $75,000)	30,000	50,000	80,000
Total	$75,000	$150,000	$225,000

The dual rate method has several advantages. One is that operating managers do not absorb the inefficiencies of the Maintenance Department because only budgeted costs ($225,000) are allocated. The allocation to each department is not affected by the use of another department. Another advantage is that operating managers probably will not overuse the service because there is a charge for use. Moreover, because they know in advance that they will be charged the lump-sum as well as the charge based on use, managers probably will not underuse the service. Finally, operating managers are less likely to consider the allocated fixed costs in making decisions because the amount of allocated fixed cost is independent of the actual use of the service.

ALLOCATING THROUGH TRANSFER PRICES

Early in the chapter we mentioned that some companies create artificial profit centers by having cost centers charge other centers a transfer price for their service. Transfer prices are not cost allocations in the strict sense of the term because the charge is not necessarily related to the costs of the service department. But using a transfer price accomplishes many of the goals sought through cost allocations, such as reminding managers of the need to cover indirect costs and encouraging goal-congruent behavior. Transfer prices can encourage less or more use of a service, whichever result upper-level management desires. It is probably easier to encourage or discourage use through transfer prices than through cost allocations.

Often, the transfer price approximates the market price for the services, which is the price that operating departments would have to pay to obtain the services from an outside company. Because the transfer price is set in advance, the using manager knows exactly how much will be charged to employ another ten hours of maintenance time. In this respect, the transfer price shares the advantage of the dual-rate method of allocation.

Suppose that in our example the transfer price for maintenance services was set at $8 per hour—a price management considered to be the best estimate of the cost to acquire maintenance services from another company. The amounts charged to each department are as follows:

Fabrication (20,000 × $8)	$160,000
Assembly (10,000 × $8)	80,000
Total maintenance cost charged	$240,000

Using a transfer price does not change the actual cost incurred anymore than does using a cost allocation. Actual total cost was $232,500. The report to the Maintenance Department will show revenues of $240,000, actual costs of $232,500, and a profit of $7,500. Reports to the operating departments will show maintenance costs of $240,000. The Maintenance Department's $7,500 profit, netted against the $240,000 of cost, is $232,500, the actual cost Raleigh incurred.

Using transfer prices to create artificial profit centers is not a simple task, as evidenced by the experience of **Weyerhauser Company**. Weyerhauser requires all of its corporate-level service departments to charge for their services. The Financial Services Department provides general accounting and payroll services, and its charges are based on a variety of factors. For example, charges to account for receivables are based on invoice volume and number of customers and are adjusted for situations that require hand-processing. In developing its charges for general accounting work, the Department used separate rates for employees of three types: analytical, clerical, and systems. A critical factor in Weyerhauser's system is that users are free to acquire services from outside the company. Consistent with comments made earlier, one result of the transfer-pricing system (called "charge-backs" at Weyerhauser) was that service department managers became profit-conscious, seeking to provide better services to the company and seeking outside customers for their services.[10]

Not all transfer-pricing systems include the freedom to purchase services from, or sell services to, outsiders. For example, upper-level managers might believe that a need for confidentiality overrides the benefits of permitting its segments to purchase secretarial services from an outside dealings. Permitting an artificial profit center to make outside sales can also create problems. Should the service department give preference to the needs of internal customers when time constraints exist? Might the "hard money" available from external customers prompt the manager to assign a lower priority to either anticipated or unanticipated needs of internal customers?

Determining a transfer price that approximates the outside cost for a service is often very difficult. But if reliable outside prices are available, there is a significant advantage to using that price as a transfer price and treating a service department as a profit center. A center consistently showing losses under such a pricing system alerts upper-level managers to the possibility that the company could benefit from shutting down the department and buying outside. Such a decision must consider the structure of fixed costs (avoidable and unavoidable) and would be analyzed along the lines described in Chapter 5 in connection with make-or-buy decisions.

The widespread efforts at cost-cutting in recent years have often resulted in companies going outside to purchase goods and services once produced internally. Responding to the same need to reduce costs, many companies have consolidated services once performed at individual units. And, as noted earlier, some companies have turned service centers into profit-seeking businesses that solicit outside and inside business. Some examples follow. **Geon Co.**, a $1 billion manufacturer of polyvinyl chloride, has stopped running its own trucks. It no longer writes its own checks, nor does it operate warehouses. **Xerox** has farmed out its computer needs to **Electronic Data Systems**. **IBM** changed its employee

---

10 *Ibid.*

benefits operation into a separate business that seeks outside, as well as inside, business. **General Electric** replaced the accounting centers at its operating units with five regional accounting centers, then consolidated the regional centers into one. **Johnson & Johnson** encourages its operating companies to share services such as finance, purchasing, and human resources administration. **Ryder** manages flows of parts and automobiles for **Saturn**.

WHAT TO DO ABOUT ALLOCATIONS IN PERFORMANCE REPORTING

Virtually everyone agrees that managers should be charged with at least the incremental costs of carrying out their functions. If allocations are to be made, amounts allocated should be budgeted, rather than actual, costs. Charges should be for the quantity of the service at budgeted variable costs of providing the services. If fixed costs are allocated, the allocation should be budgeted fixed costs and should be based on the long-run percentages of the service capacity expected by each operating department. In any case, the allocation to a particular department should not be affected by the actions of other departments.

Compromises are possible. Performance reports can show controllable and allocated costs separately. If reports draw the attention of the higher-level managers who use the reports to the distinction, there is less likelihood of misunderstanding and complaining from the lower-level managers.

What all managers must understand is that allocations and their close relative, transfer prices, are *managerial accounting devices*, not economic activities. By themselves, neither allocations nor transfer prices can change a company's total income. Changes in income can occur only if a change in an allocation or transfer price induces managers to act differently.

ETHICS AND ALLOCATIONS

When discussing why allocations might appear on performance reports we pointed out that allocations are needed for product costing. Some organizations must make allocations for other purposes. For example, public utilities must allocate some costs between classes of users (residential, commercial, industrial). Hospitals must allocate costs to determine their reimbursements under Medicare, Medicaid, and Blue Cross. Some federal grants to cities, counties, states, and universities require allocations to determine allowable costs.

The Cost Accounting Standards Board (CASB) operated from 1970 to 1980, and again after 1990. CASB was a powerful force in support of allocations. CASB had jurisdiction over accounting practices of companies that did certain kinds of business with the federal government. The Board's pronouncements remained in effect after it was terminated in 1980, and in 1988 Congress broadened their applicability. The Board issued standards and interpretations regarding many aspects of allocation, including bases to use, and costs to include or exclude from the pool of costs to be allocated. Since it began anew in 1990, the Board has recodified earlier pronouncements and addressed issues arising after 1980.

Even though a grant, contract, GAAP, or a regulatory agency demands allocations, this does not make them correct. Indirect costs cannot be allocated "correctly," in the sense that one allocation is clearly right and all others clearly wrong. Nor do allocations change an entity's total costs. Yet allocations do have real-world consequences. We have seen that one reason for using allocations is to influence behavior, and changed behavior can change costs and revenues. Allocations can also influence profits by affecting revenues and taxes. In such circumstances, ethical problems can loom large.

Some governmental units, especially the Department of Defense, contract with businesses to do work on a cost-plus basis. Such contracts permit the company to be reimbursed for its costs, including an allocation of indirect costs, plus a specified profit. The temptation for a business involved in such contracts is to allocate as much cost as possible to government work. One way to do so is to include questionable costs in the pool of costs to be allocated. Government auditors probe allocation methods of some companies, but they do not audit every contract. Less than careful attention in determining the costs to be included in a pool had serious consequences for **Stanford University**, which does a great deal of research for agencies of the U.S. government. In an address to alumni, Stanford's then-president conceded that the cost pool allocated to government research had mistakenly included, among other things, the cost of flowers, furniture, and repairs for the president's house and the cost of a yacht.

State regulation of rates charged by public utilities presents another opportunity for allocations to affect revenues, because regulators are expected to approve rates that cover a utility's costs. Public utilities charge different rates for different classes of customers and must allocate costs to each class of customer to justify the rates. A major charge leading to the breakup of **AT&T** was that long-distance service was allocated so much cost that it heavily subsidized local service. That is, local rates were lower and long distance rates higher than they should have been. Moreover, utilities that operate nonregulated businesses are tempted to allocate large amounts of indirect costs to regulated services. They will receive increased revenues to pay for these costs.

Companies operating in more than one state and/or country often must allocate indirect costs among the jurisdictions where they operate. If income tax rates differ among those jurisdictions, the temptation is to assign higher costs to the jurisdictions with higher tax rates. Auditors of taxing authorities are aware of the temptation and give special attention to allocation methods. (Chapter 11 discusses this point further in connection with multinationals.)

In recent years, some charitable organizations have come under fire for questionable allocations. Donors naturally prefer charities that devote the bulk of their resources to charitable purposes and spend a relatively small portion of their money on fund-raising and administrative activities. A number of organizations have been accused of painting a false picture of their activities. In several cases, the false picture has been attributed to questionable cost allocations. For example, some charities spend money, quite legitimately, on public education. But some charities have allocated significant amounts of the cost of fund-raising literature (including administrative costs) to their reported spending on public education programs on the basis of including a few pieces of educational material with those communications. Organizations that carry on both for-profit and not-for-profit activities (e.g., the **American Association of Retired Persons**) have come under scrutiny for similar reasons.

APPENDIX: OTHER ALLOCATION METHODS

As indicated in the chapter, common costs must be allocated for some purposes and allocations can be useful for influencing behavior. Allocation schemes are, therefore, of considerable interest. The chapter illustrated the direct method. The **direct method** ignores the services that service departments provide to other service departments. This appendix describes two techniques that many managerial accountants believe to be superior to the direct method: the step-down method and the reciprocal method.

STEP-DOWN METHOD

Many companies and other organizations, particularly those that work with cost-reimbursement contracts, use a multistep allocation called the **step-down allocation**, the **step method**, or simply, step-down. It is seen in legislated or regulated methods for determining how much to reimburse hospitals for services performed for patients. State and local governments often receive reimbursements for indirect costs of programs that use the step method.

The principle of the step-down method is to recognize that service departments provide services for other service departments as well as for operating departments. We accomplish, partially, the objective of recognizing this service by allocating the costs of service departments one at a time. As a result, the costs of all service departments, except the first to be allocated, will reflect their shares of the costs of some of the other service departments. An example should make this idea clear.

Consider GNL Manufacturing Company, which has two operating departments and two service departments. The operating departments, Forging and Machining, receive services from Personnel and Administration. Personnel keeps all employee records and handles payrolls; Administration handles all other administrative tasks. Each service department provides services to the other service department as well as to the two operating departments. Data for the most recent month follow.

Department	Direct Costs	Number of Employees
Personnel	$ 200,000	10
Administration	500,000	30
Forging	1,800,000	100
Machining	3,000,000	300
Totals	$5,500,000	440

As with any allocation, we must select the bases for making the allocations. Suppose that GNL's managers decide to allocate Administration costs based on the direct costs of the departments and Personnel costs based on the number of employees.

Because the step-down method allocates the costs of one service department at a time, we must decide which service department's costs to allocate first. Several guidelines are available. One is to start with the department that serves the most other service departments. Another is to order the departments based on the percentage of their services that go to other service departments. Suppose GNL's managers decide to allocate Administration costs first.

The following schedule shows the allocation of the $500,000 of Administration costs, using direct costs as the basis.

	Personnel	Forging	Machining	Total
Direct costs	$200,000	$1,800,000	$3,000,000	$5,000,000
Percentage of total	4%	36%	60%	100%
Allocation	$ 20,000	$ 180,000	$ 300,000	$ 500,000
Previous totals	200,000	1,800,000	3,000,000	5,000,000
New total cost	$220,000	$1,980,000	$3,300,000	$5,500,000

Total costs are still $5,500,000, the total direct costs before allocation. But the total is spread differently, with the $500,000 from Administration now in the other three departments.

We are now ready to allocate the costs for Personnel on the basis of the number of employees. Notice that we allocate $220,000, the new total of costs in Personnel. Under the step-down method, a service department's costs build up through successive allocations to it. Note also that no Personnel costs are allocated to Administration. Once you allocate costs from a department, you do not allocate any back to the department. Following is the allocation of the Personnel costs and the final totals allocated to the operating departments.

	Forging	Machining	Total
Number of employees	100	300	400
Percentage of total	25%	75%	100%
Allocation of personnel costs	$ 55,000	$ 165,000	$ 220,000
Previous totals	1,980,000	3,300,000	5,280,000
New total cost	$2,035,000	$3,465,000	$5,500,000

By their nature, allocations are arbitrary no matter how sophisticated the method used to calculate them. The results are always influenced by the allocation basis chosen. Had we selected different bases for allocating the costs of either of the service departments, the final results would be different. Also, the results are influenced by the order in which allocations were made. That is, had we chosen to allocate Personnel first, the final total costs for each operating department would have been different. In summary, the allocation process succeeds in assigning the costs of service departments to the operating departments, but does not change the fact that the costs of service departments are common to the departments serviced. All of the reservations stated in the chapter about allocations and decision making apply regardless of the allocation scheme used. The 1995 annual report of **Procter & Gamble** noted the allocation problem: "The Company's operations are characterized by interrelated raw materials and manufacturing facilities and centralized research and staff functions. Accordingly, separate profit determination by segment is dependent upon assumptions regarding allocations."

The following schedule summarizes the procedures and explicitly shows the step-down feature as each department's costs are allocated.

	Administration	Personnel	Forging	Machining	Total
Direct costs	$ 500,000	$ 200,000	$1,800,000	$3,000,000	$5,500,000
Administration	(500,000)	20,000	180,000	300,000	
Personnel		(220,000)	55,000	165,000	
Total	$ 0	$ 0	$2,035,000	$3,465,000	$5,500,000

The total costs of the two operating departments ($5,500,000) are, of course, the same as the total costs of all departments before the allocation procedure began. As stated many times, allocations do not, by themselves, change total costs.

RECIPROCAL METHOD

The **reciprocal**, or **simultaneous**, **method** of allocation fully recognizes the services that each service department renders to other service departments. This means, in terms of the example, that not only are Administration costs allocated to Personnel, but Personnel costs are also allocated to Administration. To accomplish this reciprocal allocation we first find the percentages that each service department receives from the other. The original data from the example are presented as follows, in somewhat modified form, to facilitate the calculations.

Services Provided By	Services Provided To				
	Personnel	Administration	Forging	Machining	Total
Administration:					
Direct costs	$200,000		$1,800,000	$3,000,000	$5,000,000
Percentages	4%		36%	60%	100%
Personnel:					
No. of employees		30	100	300	430
Percentages		6.98%	23.25%	69.77%	100%

The next step in the reciprocal method is to calculate what are called the adjusted costs of the service departments, to recognize that the departments provide services to each other. We set up simultaneous equations, letting P = the adjusted costs for Personnel and A = the adjusted costs for Administration.

The equations are

$$P = \$200,000 + 0.04A$$
$$A = \$500,000 + 0.0698P$$

One way to solve these equations is to substitute the equation for A in that for P, as follows. (You could use other ways, of course.)

$$P = \$200,000 + 0.04 (\$500,000 + 0.0698P)$$

Simplifying and rearranging this equation yields

$$P = \$220,616$$

and substituting for P in the equation for A yields

$$A = \$515,399$$

The final step is to allocate these adjusted costs to the two operating departments using the percentages computed. (That is, we do not adjust the percentages as was done using the step-down method.)

Service Departments	Operating Departments		Total Costs
	Forging	Machining	
Allocations			
Personnel			
$220,616 × 23.25%	$ 51,293		
$220,616 × 69.77%		$ 153,924	
Administration			
$515,399 × 36%	185,544		
$515,399 × 60%		309,239	
Total allocated	$ 236,837	$ 463,163	$ 700,000
Direct costs	1,800,000	3,000,000	4,800,000
Total cost	$2,036,837	$3,463,163	$5,500,000

Notice that the total costs allocated equal the direct costs of the two service departments ($500,000 for Administration and $200,000 for Personnel). The final total cost is still $5,500,000, the sum of the direct costs of the four departments, showing once again that the method of allocating costs does not, by itself, change the total cost incurred.

Those who favor the reciprocal method claim it is more accurate than other methods (including step-down) because it recognizes all reciprocal services. But the results still depend on the choice of an allocation basis for each department. Moreover, the method is subject to the same objection as is any other allocation method. It is arbitrary and so cannot be said to yield a "true" or "correct" cost for an operating department (especially if the costs of one or more of the service departments are largely fixed).

In this case, the choice between the step-down and reciprocal methods does not produce a significant difference in the total costs finally assigned to individual operating departments. (The difference is $1,837, which is less than 1 percent of the final total cost for each department.) In other cases, the difference could be much larger, and the need for managers to understand the potential impact of alternative allocation methods is much greater.

SUMMARY

Managers use accounting information to control operations and evaluate their subordinates' performance. Those evaluated must be evaluated on bases that are consistent with the goals of the firm. Responsibility accounting should assist in achieving goal congruence and in motivating managers. No single responsibility accounting system is appropriate for all companies, or for the same company over its lifetime. The responsibility accounting system must parallel the structure of the organization. The structure of the organization depends on the nature of its operations and on the attitudes and management styles of top managers.

The reporting segments of a responsibility accounting system might be cost centers, revenue centers, natural or artificial profit centers, or investment centers. Most companies use cost, profit, and investment centers. Whatever the plan for segmenting the company for reporting purposes, individual managers can be held responsible for only that which they can control.

Cost allocations can be troublesome in responsibility accounting, as they have been shown to be in decision making. The principle of including on performance reports only items that a manager can control conflicts with management's desire to charge for benefits received and to use allocations to encourage goal-congruent behavior. Transfer prices can alleviate some of the problems of cost allocations. However, the pervasiveness of behavioral considerations in all aspects of responsibility accounting makes it difficult to draw general conclusions about the best or most useful approaches to follow.

KEY TERMS

artificial profit centers   (440)
centralization   (444)
cost center   (439)
cost pools   (454)
decentralization   (444)
direct method   (462)
dual rates   (457)
goal congruence   (438)
investment center   (440)
operating departments   (452)
profit center   (440)

reciprocal (simultaneous)
    method   (464)
responsibility accounting
    system   (437)
responsibility center   (438)
revenue centers   (439)
service centers   (452)
service departments   (452)
step-down allocation   (462)
step method   (462)
transfer price   (440)

REVIEW PROBLEM

Wolfert Company makes and sells air conditioners and operates in three regions: the Northeast, Southeast, and Southwest. Data for 19X5 are as follows in thousands of dollars.

	Northeast	Southeast	Southwest
Sales	$2,400	$5,600	$3,800
Variable cost of sales	1,220	2,200	1,700
Variable selling costs	170	330	240
Direct fixed costs:			
Production	310	810	440
Selling	240	400	280
Administrative	320	440	380

Common fixed costs were $450,000 for administration and $110,000 for selling.

Required

Prepare a performance report by region, showing contribution margin and regional profit. Show common costs as lump-sum deductions in the total column.

ANSWER TO REVIEW PROBLEM

Performance Report for 19X5
(in thousands of dollars)

	Northeast	Southeast	Southwest	Total
Sales	$2,400	$5,600	$3,800	$11,800
Variable costs:				
Production	$1,220	$2,200	$1,700	$ 5,120
Selling	170	330	240	740
Total variable costs	$1,390	$2,530	$1,940	$ 5,860
Contribution margin	$1,010	$3,070	$1,860	$ 5,940
Direct fixed costs:				
Production	$ 310	$ 810	$ 440	$ 1,560
Selling	240	400	280	920
Administration	320	440	380	1,140
Total direct fixed costs	$ 870	$1,650	$1,100	$ 3,620
Regional profit	$ 140	$1,420	$ 760	$ 2,320
Common fixed costs:				
Selling				$ 110
Administration				450
Total common costs				$ 560
Income				$ 1,760

ASSIGNMENT MATERIAL

QUESTIONS FOR DISCUSSION

10-1 Responsibility versus control The manager of a store of a large chain of supermarkets said the following to the controller of that chain.

"My son is taking a managerial accounting course at CU, and he's been telling me about something called responsibility accounting and how it can help to motivate employees. How come we don't have responsibility accounting in our stores? I've got a meat manager who pretty much keeps that department in my store going. My son says the meat department would be a good candidate for what he calls a profit center."

Required

What do you think?

10-2 Procter & Gamble's allocations The Appendix to this chapter quoted from Procter & Gamble's 1995 annual report: "The Company's operations are characterized by interrelated raw materials and manufacturing facilities and centralized research and staff functions. Accordingly, separate profit determination by segment is dependent upon assumptions regarding allocations."

Required
Explain the quotation.

10-3   *Responsibility centers—universities* What problems do you see in establishing and evaluating responsibility centers in the following: (a) universities, (b) colleges or schools within universities, and (c) departments within colleges?

10-4   *Responsibility reporting* The annual report of a major manufacturer carried the following paragraph (paraphrased).

"Specialization also continues within each marketing force as we increase the number of personnel. We are experiencing a steady rise in the number of customers as well as in the variety and complexity of products and equipment. As a result, an increasing proportion of our salespeople concentrate on just one or a few industries—or on certain product categories."

Required
Suppose that in the past, the salespeople sold all products to all kinds of customers in different industries. What effects will the new method of directing the efforts of the individual salespeople have on the responsibility reporting system?

10-5   *Archer Daniels Midland operations* The **Archer Daniels Midland** 1994 annual report stated that a few years ago ADM had been a "conglomeration of free-standing processing plants and free-standing elevators . . . some still operating as independent companies. . . ." Things have changed. "Our multi-purpose refineries now refine eight different kinds of vegetable oil. . . . Ships often carry five or more grains, oilseeds, and finished products . . . The 150,000 tons processed each day are purchased mostly by the same purchasing organization, and many of the products manufactured in these plants are sold by one sales organization. . . . Our overhead is thus spread over this entire combination of activities." The report went on to say that management perceives ADM to be a one-purpose company and that it had become nearly impossible to determine how much ADM earned on any particular product.

Required
How would the changes in ADM's operations likely have influenced its organizational structure and its responsibility reporting?

10-6   *Change in organizational structure* In recent years, popular business periodicals have carried many stories about the decentralization of major companies that were viewed previously as centralized, and vice versa. Suggest some of the factors likely to affect the ease or difficulty of implementing change in each direction.

10-7   *Evaluating a performance measure* The top-level administrators of Mid-State University announced that, henceforth, the major factor in evaluating the performance of a faculty member will be the number of students who enroll in classes taught by that faculty member.

Required
Discuss how the proposed performance evaluation measure does or does not (a) reflect application of the principle of controllability and (b) contribute to goal congruence.

10-8   *Pricing, timing, allocations, and public relations*   For many years telephone companies did not charge for directory assistance (calling an operator to get a number). When they did begin to charge (usually 20 cents per request after three free requests per month), a commentator said, "This is ridiculous. They have operators on duty anyway, so there is no additional cost for their giving out a number. Ma Bell has just found another way to get into our pockets."

Required
Comment on the quotation.

10-9   *Artificial profit centers*   A national trade association held a seminar for chief executives where one of the topics discussed was responsibility accounting and the profit center concept as a means of evaluating departments. Two executives who attended the conference made the following statements to their respective chief accounting officers.

Executive A: I want you to set up as many profit centers as possible, beginning with the legal department. From now on, departments using legal services will be charged at $40 per hour. That's about twice the average lawyer's salary and ought to cover the nonsalary costs of the legal department. We haven't even allocated the costs of the legal department up to now, and we might as well do something to let our managers know that when they ask for legal advice they can expect to pay for it.

Executive B: Well, you accountants have done it again. Like all the other high-priced professionals, you insist on coming up with special names for something that everyone already understands. For years now we've been allocating the costs of the legal department, like all other corporate departments, to the operating units in our company. Now I'm told that what we need to do is set up a 'transfer price.' That's just a fancy name for allocating the costs.

Do you foresee any problems with the first executive's intentions? Do you agree with the position taken by the second executive?

EXERCISES

10-10   *Alternative allocation bases*   The following data refer to the three departments of ABC Company.

	A	B	C
Sales	$500,000	$800,000	$700,000
Square feet of space occupied	6,000	10,000	4,000

Total common costs are $200,000.

Required
Allocate the common costs to the departments on the bases of (a) sales dollars and (b) square feet of space occupied.

10-11   *Basic allocation methods*   Pro Mart Stores has three profit centers and one service center, a central purchasing department. Data are as follows:

	Profit Centers		
	Groceries	Meat	Canned Goods
Percentage of central purchasing services used in current year	50%	20%	30%
Expected long-term use of central purchasing services	40%	40%	20%

Budgeted central purchasing costs were $600,000 fixed and $300,000 variable. Actual fixed costs were $620,000, and actual variable costs were $290,000.

Required

1. Allocate the actual central purchasing costs to the profit centers based on actual use of the services.
2. Allocate the budgeted variable central purchasing costs to the profit centers based on actual use of the services and the budgeted fixed costs based on expected long-term use.
3. Which of the two methods do you prefer? Why?

10-12   *Performance report* York Tool Company operates six departments in its main plant. Each department manager is responsible for materials, direct and indirect labor, supplies, small tools, and equipment maintenance. The factory manager is responsible for buying equipment and for all other costs. Last month, the manager of the Stamping Department received the following performance report. The costs of building occupancy have been allocated to the department.

	Budget	Actual	Over (Under)
Materials	$ 32,900	$ 33,800	$ 900
Direct labor	34,200	34,500	300
Indirect labor	15,250	14,220	(1,030)
Supplies	5,600	5,450	(150)
Small tools	4,200	4,340	140
Equipment:			
Depreciation	12,800	12,800	0
Maintenance	5,700	4,950	(750)
Building:			
Depreciation	2,200	2,200	0
Maintenance	980	950	(30)
Property taxes	760	770	10
Total	$114,590	$113,980	$ (610)

Required

Prepare a new performance report that shows only the costs for which the manager of the Stamping Department is responsible.

10-13   *Step-down allocation method (related to Appendix)* Mott Company has two service departments, Personnel and Administration, and two operating departments, Foundry and Assembly. The following schedule shows the costs in each service department and the percentages of activity that each service department provides each of the other departments, both service and operating.

Department Providing Service	Costs of Department	Department Receiving Service			
		Personnel	Administration	Foundry	Assembly
Personnel	$200,000	0%	60%	30%	10%
Administration	$300,000	20%	0%	20%	60%

A member of the controller's staff made the following allocations.

	Foundry	Assembly
Personnel:		
$200,000 × (.30/.40)	$150,000	
$200,000 × (.10/.40)		$ 50,000
Administration:		
$300,000 × (.20/.80)	75,000	
$300,000 × (.60/.80)		225,000
Totals	$225,000	$275,000

The controller is wondering whether it would make any difference to use the step-down method, instead of the direct method shown.

Required

1. Allocate the service department costs using the step-down method, beginning with Personnel costs.
2. Explain why the controller would begin the step-down with Personnel costs.

10-14 Reciprocal allocation (continuation of 10-13) Perform the allocation in 10-13 using the reciprocal method.

10-15 Allocations—actual versus budgeted costs Merion Turf Products produces lawn fertilizers and grass seed. The company's Research Department, which works to improve both types of products, had budgeted costs of $450,000, virtually all fixed. These costs were to be allocated to the two product lines based on the relative amounts of time spent on each. All of the scientists keep time sheets showing which projects they work on each month.

At year-end the Research Department had actually spent $496,000 as a result of unanticipated cost increases and some inefficiencies in the department. The manager of the Fertilizer Department had budgeted $225,000 for allocated research costs but found that he was actually charged with $276,760. The final allocation was based on actual costs and actual relative time spent on work for his department. He was not happy with the situation, especially when he learned that the manager of the Grass Seed Department had canceled a major project, resulting in lower-than-budgeted research on grass seed.

Required

Suggest a way to allocate research costs that will not unduly penalize the managers of the Fertilizer and Grass Seed Departments.

10-16 Assignment of responsibility Klee Company is organized by function: sales, production, finance, and administration. The production manager is upset about the following performance report. She contends that costs of $8,000 were incurred solely because the sales manager ordered changes in production for rush orders from customers.

Performance Report—Production Department

Controllable costs:	Budget	Actual	Variance (Favorable)
Materials	$ 80,000	$ 79,000	$ (1,000)
Direct labor	160,000	162,000	2,000
Other labor	46,000	53,000	7,000
Idle time*	1,000	4,000	3,000
Other production costs	21,000	20,000	(1,000)
Totals	$308,000	$318,000	$ 10,000

* Wages paid to workers while they are idle, as when machines are being reset because of a change from one product to another.

The production manager argues that the $3,000 shown on the performance report as idle time was caused by changing the production process to meet special orders. In addition, she claims that about $5,000 in other labor was for costs incurred to make the necessary changes and for the overtime premium paid to workers to get the work finished in time to meet the deadlines given for rush orders.

Required

What is wrong and what do you recommend?

10-17 *Transfer prices and goal congruence* The controller of MicroDot has set transfer prices for service departments, all of which had been cost centers. One is for stenographic services. The charge is $18 per hour, based on total budgeted hours of available service and total budgeted costs for the stenographic pool. The manager of one operating department, a profit center, has obtained a price of $15 per hour for stenographers' time from an outside agency for a task that will take about 50 hours. The manager informs the controller and the manager of the stenographic pool of the outside price and is told to take it if she wishes; the transfer price will not be lowered.

Required

Comment on the position taken by the controller and the manager of the stenographic pool. (Budgeted costs for the pool are about 90% fixed.) Make a recommendation.

10-18 *Set of performance reports* Arcon, Inc., manufactures office equipment. The Raleigh Plant produces several models of copiers. The following schedule shows year-to-date controllable costs for the Assembly Department and for all others as a whole, in thousands of dollars.

	Assembly		All Others	
	Budget	Over (Under)	Budget	Over (Under)
Materials	$12.8	$ 1.1	$ 64.2	$ 3.2
Direct labor	28.9	(2.2)	256.8	4.3
Other controllable costs	15.3	1.8	102.2	(1.5)

There were $74,000 in budgeted costs controllable by the plant manager, but not by any of the department managers. Actual costs were $1,200 over budget. The

Raleigh Plant is part of the Southeast region. Regions, like plants, and departments are cost centers. Budgeted costs of the other plants in the region totaled $3,265,200, actual costs were $12,300 over budget. Budgeted costs of $120,600 (actual were $1,300 over budget) were controllable by the regional manager, but not by the plant managers.

Required
Prepare a set of responsibility reports for the Assembly Department, the Raleigh Plant, and the Southeast region using the format shown in Exhibit 10-3.

10-19   Development of performance report   Stratton Company is organized by functional areas: sales, production, finance, and administration. The Sales Department has product managers who are responsible for a particular product and who are evaluated based on the following typical performance report.

Activity Report—Product Zee
May 19X4—Manager, J. Harrison

Sales		$475,000
Cost of goods sold		281,000
Gross profit		$194,000
Other expenses:		
Advertising	$26,000	
Travel	14,000	
Depreciation	5,000	
Office expenses	21,000	
Administrative expense	25,000	91,000
Product profit		$103,000

The following additional information about the report is available.

(a) Because of problems in the production process, cost of goods sold is $11,000 higher than budgeted.
(b) Harrison authorized spending $16,000 on product advertising. The remainder of the advertising cost reported is an allocated share of general advertising costs incurred by the firm.
(c) Depreciation charges consist of the following: 20% on furniture and fixtures in Harrison's office and 80% for the product's share of depreciation on the building that houses all the firm's activities.
(d) Office expenses include $4,000 allocated from the expenses of the vice president for sales.
(e) Administrative expenses are allocated based on relative sales.

Required
Revise the performance report for product Zee to reflect the principle of controllability.

PROBLEMS

10-20   Cost allocation—direct method   The following schedule shows the costs of the service departments of HabsCon Inc. and the percentages of service that the service departments provide to each other and to Winston's operating departments.

Department Providing Service	Costs of Department	Department Receiving Service			
		Purchasing	Administration	Trimming	Cutting
Purchasing	$300,000		20%	60%	20%
Administration	$500,000	30%		20%	50%

Required

Use the direct method to allocate the service department costs to the operating departments. Exercise 10-13 shows how to calculate the percentages.

10-21   Cost allocation—step-down method (continuation of 10-20, related to Appendix)   Use the information from 10-20 to do a step-down allocation, beginning with the Administration Department.

10-22   Cost allocation—reciprocal method (continuation of 10-20, related to Appendix)   Use the information from 10-20 to do a reciprocal allocation.

10-23   Performance reporting and allocations   Newton Company, a furniture outlet, allocates indirect costs to its two product lines based on sales. The income statement for 19X5 is as follows:

	Indoor Furniture	Outdoor Furniture	Total
Sales	$400,000	$400,000	$800,000
Direct costs	150,000	150,000	300,000
Controllable profit	$250,000	$250,000	$500,000
Indirect costs	225,000	225,000	450,000
Income	$ 25,000	$ 25,000	$ 50,000

In 19X6, price increases on indoor furniture increased sales of that line to $500,000, while unit sales remained contant. Prices of outdoor furniture were not changed, and sales remained at $400,000. Direct costs of each line were again $150,000, and total indirect costs were again $450,000.

Required

1. Prepare a product-line income statement for 19X6, allocating indirect costs based on sales.
2. Comment on the results. (Are they logical? Did the manager of outdoor furniture do a better job in 19X6 than in 19X5?)

10-24   Responsibility for rush orders   Howard Company's sales manager, Ken Perrier, often requests rush orders from the production department. Howard's production process requires a great deal of setup time whenever changes in the production mix are made. The production manager, Brad Givens, has complained about these rush orders, arguing that costs are much lower when the process runs smoothly. Perrier argues that the paramount consideration is to keep the customer's goodwill and that, therefore, all sales orders should be made up as quickly as possible.

Required
1. Identify the issues creating the conflict.
2. Using the guidelines in Appendix A, write a memorandum to the two managers suggesting what steps might be taken to effect a satisfying solution.

10-25 Performance measurement Eleanor Klein, the sales manager of Warner Company, is evaluated on the basis of total sales. Exceeding the sales budget is considered good performance. The sales budget and cost data for 19X3 follow.

	Alpha	Beta	Gamma	Total
		Product		
Sales budget	$150,000	$300,000	$550,000	$1,000,000
Variable costs	75,000	135,000	165,000	375,000
Contribution margin	$ 75,000	$165,000	$385,000	$ 625,000

Actual sales for the year were as follows:

Alpha	Beta	Gamma	Total
$500,000	$400,000	$200,000	$1,100,000

Actual prices were equal to budgeted prices, and variable costs were incurred as budgeted (per unit).

Required
1. Did Klein perform well? Support your answer with calculations.
2. Using the guidelines in Appendix A, write a memorandum to Warner's controller, George Karpinski, explaining what the changes in the firm's performance evaluation might contribute to goal congruence.

10-26 Behavioral problem Watson Company recently bought a copier with a capacity of 10,000 copies per day. Annual fixed costs of the copier are $24,000; the variable cost is $0.01 per copy. Previously, Watson had leased a similar copier with annual fixed costs of $14,000 and variable costs of $0.06 per copy. Watson allocates the fixed costs of the copier based on expected long-term use of the copier and the variable costs based on actual use.

Total copying had run about 8,000 per day with the old machine. The new copier is nearly always running at capacity, and people have complained that they cannot get copies within a reasonable time. Some managers have been forced to send material to outside copying services, which charge about $0.08 per copy.

Required
What seems to be happening, and what do you recommend, if anything?

10-27 Hospital allocations and decisions Blake Memorial Hospital is a full-service hospital with several departments. Departments that perform services directly for patients are called revenue centers and include the Medical, Surgical, and Emergency Departments. Other departments, such as Admissions, Patient Records, Laundry, and Housekeeping, are called service centers. Costs of service centers are allocated to revenue centers. Following is a schedule showing the percentages of costs allocated from two service centers to two revenue centers, together with the direct costs of each of the service centers.

| | | Revenue Center | |
Service Center	Costs	Medical	Surgical
Admissions	$300,000	70%	30%
Records	$400,000	20%	80%

The hospital receives reimbursements from Blue Cross, Medicaid, and other third parties for services performed for some patients. The reimbursement contracts typically allow recovery of both direct and indirect costs. Such reimbursements amount to about 30% of total Medical Department costs and about 90% of total Surgical Department costs. Thus, at the present time, the hospital is reimbursed for $144,000 of its Admissions costs, calculated as follows:

Through medical reimbursements ($300,000 × 70% × 30%)	$ 63,000
Through surgical reimbursements ($300,000 × 30% × 90%)	81,000
Total	$144,000

The hospital administrator is considering some different procedures that will increase the cost of Records by $10,000, while reducing Admissions costs by $6,000. Obviously, the change would increase total cost, but the administrator is well aware of the differing reimbursement rates.

Required

1. Calculate the total reimbursement that the hospital now receives for the indirect costs of Admissions and Records.
2. Calculate the total reimbursement that the hospital will receive if the new procedures are adopted.
3. Comment on the effects of the procedural changes beyond Blake Memorial.

10-28 Allocations, expense reimbursement, and ethics You need to take a business trip from your office in Atlanta to a branch in Los Angeles sometime in the next few weeks. You have also planned to play in a golf tournament near San Francisco. You manage to combine the trips so that you fly to Los Angeles, finish your business, then go to the tournament. Some airfares are as follows:

Atlanta-Los Angeles each way	$380
Los Angeles-San Francisco each way	$105
Atlanta-San Francisco each way	$420

Because you will be staying over a weekend, you get a special excursion ticket that allows you to make the entire trip for $740. You spend three days working, two days playing golf. Your company reimburses your business expenses.

Required

1. How much airfare will you show on your expense account?
2. Suppose that you were your boss. How much airfare would you allow the company to reimburse?

10-29 Step-down allocation (related to Appendix) Walker Company has two operating departments—Machining and Assembly—and three service departments—Personnel, Data Processing, and General Administration. The controller wishes to allocate service department costs using the step-down method, beginning with Data Processing, then Personnel, and lastly, General Administration. She wants to use the following bases: Data Processing, number of transactions; Personnel, number of employees; General Administration, total direct costs (before any allocation of service department costs).

The controller has assembled the following data.

Department	Total Direct Costs	Number of Employees	Number of Data Processing Transactions
Data processing	$ 300,000	20	0
Personnel	200,000	30	20,000
General administration	400,000	100	30,000
Machining	2,000,000	300	40,000
Assembly	3,000,000	600	10,000

Required

Prepare a step-down allocation.

10-30   *Performance report for a cost center*   Dominic Porter, the manager of the Casting Department of Western Foundries, was disturbed by the report that he received last month.

Monthly Cost Report—Casting Department
July, 19X6

Materials	$ 32,800
Direct labor	66,800
Indirect labor	2,380
Power	18,900
Maintenance	5,700
Other	9,350
Total	$135,930

The factory manager had commented unfavorably to Porter about power and maintenance costs, both of which were higher than in previous months. Both costs are mixed. The variable portions are relatively controllable by the department managers, but the fixed portions are not controllable at the departmental level. The amounts shown are allocations based on the department's use of the services each month. The Casting Department used 9,500 kilowatt-hours of power and 800 hours of maintenance service in July. The budgeted monthly costs of the two services are as follows:

Power cost = $130,000 + $0.05 per kilowatt-hour
Maintenance cost = $24,000 + $0.80 per maintenance-hour

The Casting Department's long-term shares of the services are estimated at 10% for power and 15% for maintenance. All other costs on the report are controllable by the department manager.

Required

Prepare a new performance report for the Casting Department that shows controllable costs and noncontrollable costs separately and allocates fixed power and maintenance costs based on the department's long-term use of those services.

10-31   *Ethics and allocations*   Tempest Foundry, a maker of heavy-duty machinery parts, now serves only commercial customers, but soon will begin doing work for the U.S. government. Cost-plus contracts are necessary because so much of the work is special-order parts, ones the company has not made before. Therefore, the company has no idea of what they will likely cost to manufacture.

The government's cost-plus contracts provide for the government to pay the cost of the work plus a profit based on a percentage of the cost of the work. The cost of work includes materials and labor, plus a "fair share" of overhead. The company will keep track of the materials and labor used on each government project.

Tempest's managers have been trying to decide how to allocate overhead costs between government and commercial business. They agree that they should, each month, allocate actual overhead costs to commercial and government business, but they are not sure what basis to use. One manager argues that they should base the allocations on labor time because government work is likely to be more labor-intensive than commercial work and will therefore be allocated more overhead. Another says that they should analyze overhead costs to see what activities drive them and use the drivers as the bases for allocation. A third argues that it really makes little difference and spending time on the issue is fruitless.

Required

Using the guidelines in Appendix A, prepare a memorandum to Tamara Vasilatos, the controller, discussing the issues and suggesting a solution.

10-32   *Performance report in a service company*   Louis Wardlaw heads the Tax Department at Bryan & Cummings, a large firm of Certified Public Accountants. The firm also has an Audit Department and a Management Services Department. Wardlaw recently received the following performance report for his department.

	February	March
Revenues	$140,600	$148,400
Costs:		
Staff salaries	$ 76,800	$ 77,400
Travel and supplies	7,800	8,100
Occupancy and utilities	9,800	10,900
General office expense	15,400	21,800
Total costs	$109,800	$118,200
Income	$ 30,800	$ 30,200

Wardlaw thought that his department had done much better in March than in February and was surprised by the report. He talked to the firm's internal accountant, who had prepared the report, to gather additional information. Staff salaries, travel, and supplies are all direct to the department. Occupancy and utilities are allocated based on space occupied. In March, the lease on the firm's office expired and was renewed at a higher rent. General office expense is allocated to departments based on revenue. The Audit and Management Services Departments both experienced drops in revenue in March, resulting in a higher share going to the Tax Department.

Required

1. Revise the preceding report to show revenue, direct costs, controllable profit, allocated indirect costs, and income.

2. Did the Tax Department perform better in February than in March? Why or why not?

10-33 *Compensation plan (CMA adapted)* Parsons Company compensates its salespeople with commissions and a year-end bonus. The commission is 20% of a "net profit," which is computed as the normal selling price less manufacturing costs. (Such costs contain some allocated fixed overhead.) The profit is also reduced by any bad debts on sales written by individual salespeople. The granting of credit is the responsibility of the firm's credit department, and credit approval is required before sales are made.

Salespeople can give price reductions, which must be approved by the sales vice president. Commissions are not affected by such price concessions. The year-end bonus is 15% of commissions earned during the year provided that the individual salesperson has achieved the target sales volume. If the target is not reached, there is no bonus. The annual target volume is generally set at 105% of the previous year's sales.

Required
Using the guidelines in Appendix A, write a memorandum to Ralph Samson, vice president of sales, identifying the features of the compensation plan that are the least and most likely to be effective in motivating salespeople to work in the firm's interests.

10-34 *Selecting an allocation base* Amelia Strelcyzyk, controller of Carter Brothers Discount Mart, is considering allocating indirect costs to its departments. She proposes to allocate annual building rent of $2,000,000 based on the floor space that each department occupies. Jennifer Bynum, manager of the Children's Department, objects to this basis. She contends that the basis should be the relative value of the space. Her department is on the second floor. Comparable second floor space rents for about $10 per square foot, while first floor space rents for about $15 per square foot.

The Children's Department occupies 20,000 square feet of the total 100,000 square feet on the second floor. The first floor also has 100,000 square feet.

Required
1. Determine the amount of cost that the Children's Department would be allocated using the controller's method.
2. Determine the amount of cost that the Children's Department would be allocated using the department manager's method.
3. Using the guidelines in Appendix A, write a memorandum to Ms. Strelczyk, giving and supporting your recommendation about which allocation method to use.

10-35 *Allocations and decisions* Cramer Company has several product lines, each controlled by a different manager. Each manager is evaluated partly on profit. The expenses charged to each line are the direct costs of the line plus 15% of sales. (The 15% covers costs not directly associated with the lines, such as salaries of the corporate staff, interest on corporate debt, and service functions such as personnel, building security, and cafeteria. These costs are virtually all fixed.) The president of the company estimated that 15% would cover these expenses at budgeted sales of $6,000,000 for the coming year. Each year the percentage is adjusted based on budgeted costs and budgeted sales for the entire company.

The manager of the small appliances line has the opportunity to sell 20,000 units to a chain store at $30 each. Per-unit variable costs are $27, ignoring the 15% charge. There would be no incremental fixed costs associated with the order, and there is sufficient capacity to make the additional units.

Required

1. Given the existing plan for evaluating performance, will the manager of small appliances accept the order? Why or why not?
2. Is it in the company's best interests for the manager to accept the order? Why or why not?

10-36   Performance measures   Following are five job titles and the measure by which performance in that job is judged. Comment on the usefulness of each in achieving goal congruence.

Job or Job Title	Performance Measure
(a) Director of mental health program	Number of patients released from treatment
(b) Director of a program to reduce unemployment	Number of jobs found for unemployed people, as a percentage of total unemployed persons
(c) Director of a regional program to rehabilitate substandard housing	Number of homes now meeting local building codes that had previously been classified substandard
(d) Machine operator	Number of hours the machine runs
(e) Salesperson	Dollars of sales orders divided by number of customers visited

10-37   Evaluation of compensation plans (AICPA adapted)   Gibson Company was established some years ago to bring several new products to the market. Its founder, Gilbert Wilson, believed that once customers tried their products, they would become well accepted. For the first several years, Gibson grew at a rate Wilson considered to be satisfactory. In recent years, some problems have developed both in the firm's profitability and in the morale of and harmonious relationships among the firm's salespeople. Since the company began, salespeople have been paid a base salary plus an 8% commission. The following data are available for two salespeople for the most recent year.

	Ronald McTavish	James Christy
Gross sales orders written	$270,000	$200,000
Commissions	21,600	16,000
Sales returns	18,500	8,000
Cost of goods sold—all variable	139,500	68,400
Discretionary expenses of salespersons (travel, entertainment, etc.)	19,200	21,500

Required

1. Determine which salesperson contributed more to the company's profit by preparing a performance report for each.

2. Using the guidelines in Appendix A, write a memorandum to Mr. Wilson recommending (and supporting) changes in Wilson's method of compensating its salespeople.

10-38 *Allocations and ethics* A slightly edited excerpt from an appeal for contributions from a charity is as follows:

The Fund's expenses were $26,893,345. Of that amount, 21% was spent in support of research programs and 43% of expenses went in support of the Fund's public education programs in connection with fund-raising appeals. Combined research and public education programs accounted for 64% of total expenses. Fund-raising expenses were 22% of total expenses and administrative expenses were 14% of total expenses.

The mailing included five health tips (such as cut down on fats, do not smoke, and exercise regularly) that occupied about 15% of the mailing.

Required

1. To which of the given categories do you think the charity allocated the costs of mailing? What sorts of costs might the charity have included as part of mailing costs?
2. With the information available, are you inclined to support the charity? Why or why not?

10-39 *Allocation and behavior* Brenner Company allocates common production costs such as depreciation, property taxes, payroll office, and factory accounting on the basis of the cost of materials used on jobs in each production department. Budgeted material costs for the coming year are $300,000, common production costs are $750,000.

The manager of the Fabricating Department has developed a new process that requires 10% more materials than the old process, but 20% less labor time. Without the new process, she expects to incur materials costs of $60,000 and labor costs of $50,000 during the coming year.

Required

Determine the desirability of introducing the new process from the viewpoints of both the firm and the manager of the Fabricating Department. If your answers conflict, suggest a solution.

10-40 *Performance reporting—alternative organizational structure (CMA adapted)* Cranwell Company sells three products in a foreign market and a domestic market. An income statement for the first month of 19X2 shows the following.

Sales		$1,300,000
Cost of goods sold		1,010,000
Gross profit		$ 290,000
Selling expenses	$105,000	
Administrative expenses	72,000	177,000
Income		$ 113,000

Data regarding the two markets and three products are as follows:

| | Products | | |
	A	B	C
Sales:			
Domestic	$400,000	$300,000	$300,000
Foreign	100,000	100,000	100,000
Total sales	$500,000	$400,000	$400,000
Variable production costs (percentage of sales)	60%	70%	60%
Variable selling costs (percentage of sales)	3%	2%	2%

Product A is made in a single factory that incurs fixed costs (included in cost of goods sold) of $48,000 per month. Products B and C are made in a single factory and require the same machinery. Monthly fixed production costs at that factory are $142,000.

Fixed selling expenses are joint to the three products, but $36,000 is direct to the domestic market and $38,000 to the foreign market. All administrative expenses are fixed. About $25,000 is traceable to the foreign market, $35,000 to the domestic market.

Required

1. Assume that Cranwell has separate managers responsible for each market. Prepare performance reports for the domestic and foreign markets.
2. Assume that Cranwell has separate managers responsible for each product. Prepare performance reports for the three products.

10-41   Cost allocations, transfer prices, and behavior Several top executives of Millard Company are discussing problems they perceive in the company's methods of cost allocation. For each of the following costs, indicate what changes will help accomplish the stated objectives.

(a) Computer cost, which is 95% fixed, is allocated using a transfer price of $100 per hour of use. The executives believe that lower-level managers do not use the computer enough.

(b) Maintenance costs, which are budgeted at $10 per hour variable and $200,000 per year fixed, are allocated by dividing total incurred cost by total maintenance hours worked and distributing the resulting per-hour cost to operating departments according to the number of hours of maintenance work done. The executives believe that operating managers request maintenance work only when machinery is about to break down. Production has halted while repairs were made on critical machines. Operating managers have complained that the per-hour cost is too high.

(c) Millard has a consulting department that advises operating managers on various aspects of production and marketing. The costs of the department are fixed but discretionary and have been rising in recent years because of heavy demand for its services. The costs are not allocated because it was felt that managers should be encouraged to use the service. One executive commented that operating managers call the department to find out where to go for lunch.

10-42   Allocations and behavior R. A. Shore is a large mail-order company dealing in men's and women's clothing and accessories. Shore operates its six regional distribution centers as profit centers. Until now, each distribution center handled its own trucking requirements. Shore has just acquired a fleet of trucks that are under the control of the traffic manager, who is based at central headquarters.

The traffic manager anticipates having to hire outside truckers because Shore's fleet is insufficient to meet peak demands. He wants the managers of the distribution centers to provide monthly estimates of their trucking needs, from which he will decide how much, if any, outside trucking to hire. For the following two reasons, costs will be higher than necessary if the estimates he receives are either too high or too low.

First, the typical agreement with an outside trucker provides for a payment of $1.20 per mile, but with a guarantee of 2,000 miles for a month. Thus, a trucker who drives 1,000 miles will be paid $2,400. The guarantees can add up to a substantial amount if the estimates are too high. Second, if the estimates are too low, the traffic manager must scramble to find additional truckers in the middle of the month, also adding to costs. Therefore, accurate estimates of trucking needs are desirable. The controller wants a cost allocation scheme that will encourage accuracy.

Required

1. Suppose the controller decides not to allocate trucking costs. Do you expect managers of the distribution centers to pay much attention to their monthly estimates of needs?
2. Answer the question in item 1 assuming that the controller decides to allocate all trucking costs, both for the owned fleet and for outsiders, based on mileage used by each center.
3. What would you do to encourage the managers of the distribution centers to act in Shore's best interests?

10-43 *Allocations and managers' bonuses* Katherine Grove, the owner of GroveMart, wants to pay her department managers bonuses totaling $7,500. Grove wants the $7,500 allocated based on the profit each department earns. In the following income statement, all indirect costs are allocated based on sales.

	Dry Goods	Housewares	Total
Sales	$250,000	$500,000	$750,000
Total direct costs	166,000	437,000	603,000
Controllable profit	$ 84,000	$ 63,000	$147,000
Indirect costs (all fixed):			
Sales salaries	$ 16,000	$ 32,000	$ 48,000
Other	8,000	16,000	24,000
Total indirect costs	$ 24,000	$ 48,000	$ 72,000
Profit	$ 60,000	$ 15,000	$ 75,000

Some salespeople work in one department or the other, while some cover both departments. The manager of Housewares argues that the allocation of indirect sales salaries is inappropriate. He believes that the allocation should be based on the relative direct sales salaries of $60,000 for Dry Goods and $20,000 for Housewares. (These amounts are included in direct costs.) He says that the work of the salespeople is related to the total sales effort.

Required
1. Compute each manager's bonus given the existing allocations.
2. Prepare a new income statement allocating indirect sales salaries as suggested by the manager of Housewares. Compute each manager's bonus.
3. Comment on the results. Which method of allocation gives the better result?
4. How might Grove distribute the $7,500 to the managers in a reasonable way without getting into arguments over allocations?

 10-44   *Performance report* Caldwell Department Store has three major lines— housewares, clothing, and sporting goods. The controller is developing performance analyses for the managers of the lines and has prepared the following income statement, in thousands of dollars.

	Housewares	Clothing	Sporting Goods	Total
Sales	$900	$1,200	$400	$2,500
Cost of goods sold	500	680	180	1,360
Gross profit	$400	$ 520	$220	$1,140
Other expenses:				
Selling	$ 60	$ 90	$ 40	$ 190
Advertising	45	60	20	125
Rent	40	40	20	100
Depreciation	20	16	12	48
General and administrative	90	120	40	250
Miscellaneous	60	85	32	177
Total expenses	$315	$ 411	$164	$ 890
Profit	$ 85	$ 109	$ 56	$ 250

You learn the following about the data in the income statement.
(a) Cost of goods sold is direct.
(b) Salaries expense includes allocated salaries of $75,000 for employees whose work takes them into different departments. The controller used relative sales to make the allocations.
(c) Advertising is partly allocated. Each department is charged at standard market rates for newspaper space, radio time, and television time that its manager requests. The $50,000 cost of general advertising ordered by the sales vice president was allocated based on sales dollars.
(d) The rent allocation is based on floor space occupied. The three departments occupy 100,000 square feet. Sporting Goods is in the basement, the others on the first floor. Similar property in the city rents for $1.05 per square foot for first floor space, $0.80 for basement space. Rent on space occupied by the administrative offices is included in general and administrative expenses.
(e) Depreciation is all for furniture and fixtures within the departments.
(f) General and administrative expenses are allocated based on sales dollars.
(g) Miscellaneous expenses are partly separable, partly allocated. The allocated amounts by department are as follows: Housewares, $28,000; Clothing, $36,000; and Sporting Goods, $16,000.

Required
Prepare a new performance report using the principle of controllability. Include a column for unallocated costs, as well as one for each department.

10-45   *Transfer prices and behavior* All operating departments of Jacson Company are profit or investment centers, and some service departments are artificial profit centers. The Maintenance Department is an artificial profit center that charges $10 per hour for work it does for operating departments. The variable cost per hour is $4, and fixed costs are $40,000 per month.

The manager of Department A, an operating department, has just determined that some changes in the production process can be made. If the changes are made, maintenance requirements will drop from 2,100 hours per month to 1,600. However, the variable cost to produce a unit of product will increase from $6 to $7. Department A produces 4,000 units of product per month.

Required

1. Determine the change in monthly profit for Department A if the production process is changed.
2. Determine the change in profit of the Maintenance Department if Department A changes its production process.
3. Determine the effect of the change in Department A's production process on Jacson's monthly profit.
4. Suppose that the manager of Department A is prompted to study possible changes in the production process because the transfer price for maintenance work is to be raised to $12 per hour. The Maintenance Department expects a $1 increase in variable cost per hour and approval of other expenditures that will raise fixed costs by $8,000 per month. For the last several months, the Maintenance Department has shown a profit of $8,000, and the proposed new transfer price was designed to maintain that profit level.
   (a) How many hours of maintenance work per month are currently done by the Maintenance Department?
   (b) If the manager of Department A makes the change in the production process, what profit will Maintenance show for a month?

10-46   *Cost allocation* Galco Industries allocates indirect costs to departments and product lines using direct labor hours as the basis. The 19X5 allocations are based on 400,000 direct labor hours and $1,910,000 indirect costs. Data related to one product line, cleaners, and to all others as a group, for 19X5 follow.

	Totals	Cleaners	All Others
Direct labor hours	400,000	50,000	350,000

Galco's managers have become convinced that they need several bases to reflect the activities that drive their indirect costs. After careful study, the controller developed the following information regarding cost pools and activities that drive the pools.

Cost Driver	Amount of Activity	Amount of Related Indirect Costs
Labor hours	400,000 hours	$1,580,000
Record keeping	150,000 entries	180,000
Number of parts	4,000 parts	150,000
Total indirect costs		$1,910,000

Data related to one product line, cleaners, and to all others as a group for 19X5 follow.

	Totals	Cleaners	All Others
Direct labor hours	400,000	50,000	350,000
Record keeping entries	150,000	6,000	144,000
Number of parts	4,000	100	3,900

Required

1. Allocate the indirect costs to cleaners and to the other products based on direct labor hours.
2. Allocate each group of costs separately to cleaners and to the group of others using the separate bases.
3. Galco sells 30,000 cases of cleaners annually. Its direct costs are $16.50 per unit. Separately calculate the total per-case costs using your results from items 1 and 2. Comment on the difference.

10-47   *Performance report*   Budgeted and actual results for the carpet line of Glenn Products follow, along with selected other data. Glenn makes a wide variety of products, with each line under a single manager.

Carpet Line, January 19X6 (in thousands of dollars)

	Budget	Actual	Over (Under)
Sales	$434.0	$446.4	$12.4
Cost of sales	262.0	279.1	17.1
Gross margin	$172.0	$167.3	$ (4.7)
Operating expenses	97.0	100.0	3.0
Profit	$ 75.0	$ 67.3	$ (7.7)

Other data:

(a) The carpet line is manufactured in several plants, all of which make other products using fabric and other materials that go into carpets. The fixed costs of all of these factories, totaling about $8 million per month, are allocated to product lines based on relative variable manufacturing costs. Budgeted variable manufacturing costs for the carpet line were about 38% of sales, while actual costs were about 39% of sales because of some price reductions.
(b) The carpet line had budgeted and actual fixed operating expenses traceable to its operations of $32,600. Variable operating expenses, both budgeted and actual, were 6% of sales. The remaining costs shown in the statement were allocated expenses common to the entire business of the firm. These costs are allocated based on relative sales.

Required

Prepare a report on the carpet line that identifies the responsibility of the manager in charge. Use the format shown in Exhibit 10-4 but include a column for actual results as well as for budgeted results and amounts over or under.

CASES

10-48   Cost allocations in a university   Ed Cranston, the new dean of the School of Business at Midstate University, is concerned. It is only early February, and he has just received a report from the university's printing and duplicating service showing that the school has exceeded its budget for duplicating for the academic year. The report appears as follows:

Printing and Duplicating Department Statement of Budget and
Charges for the School of Business, September–January

Annual Budget	Actual Charges	Over (Under)
$4,200	$4,350	$150

An enclosed note states that Ed must either stop using the service or obtain approval of a supplemental budget request from the university's chief fiscal officer. Ed pulls out his latest statement, from December, and finds that actual charges at that time were $1,830. Since the school was on vacation during a good part of January, he wonders how $2,520 could have been incurred in January.

He finds out that costs for the Printing and Duplicating Department in January were $6,300, of which $700 was for paper, $2,000 for salaries, $2,000 for machine rentals, and $1,600 for general overhead (allocated share of all university utilities, depreciation, etc.). A total of 35,000 copies was made in January, a relatively low number because of the vacation. However, several faculty members in the School of Business had a substantial amount of printing done for scholarly papers that they were circulating to other professors throughout the country. The School of Business was responsible for 14,000 of the 35,000 copies. The $2,520 charge was computed by dividing total department costs for the month by the number of copies ($6,300/35,000) to arrive at a charge of $0.18 per copy. Ed also learned that during a typical month about $8,600 in cost is incurred and 150,000 copies are processed. Paper is the only variable cost.

Required
Evaluate the cost allocation system used and recommend changes if you think any are necessary.

10-49   Allocation of costs—distribution channels   Weisner Company sells its products through wholesalers and retailers. Erica Stern is in charge of wholesale sales, and Ralph Pike manages retail sales. Frieda Weisner, president of the firm, has ordered an analysis of the relative profitability of the two channels of distribution to determine where emphasis should be placed. The data on the next page show the operations for the last six months.

The same products are sold to both wholesalers and retailers, but prices to wholesalers are about 20% less than those to retailers.

Required
1. Comment on the reasonableness of the allocation methods used.
2. Recast the statement based on the principle of controllability.
3. What further information would help in assigning costs to the responsible managers?

10-50   Allocations and behavior   Clifford Electronics operates a single plant. Clifford allocates indirect costs to departments and then to product lines based

	Wholesalers	Retailers
Sales	$2,000,000	$3,000,000
Cost of sales—all variable	$1,600,000	$2,000,000
Sales commissions (3% of sales)	60,000	90,000
Managers' salaries	18,000	18,000
Advertising (allocated as a percentage of sales dollars)	12,000	18,000
Selling expenses—salespeople's expenses, delivery, order processing, credit checking (allocated on the basis of number of orders from each group)	80,000	160,000
General expenses (allocated as a percentage of sales dollars)	40,000	60,000
Total expenses	$1,810,000	$2,346,000
Income	$ 190,000	$ 654,000

on their direct labor content. Each department concentrates on one product line. The cost of an average unit of one of its major lines, made in Department Z, follows. The data relate to a recent month when the company made 50,000 units of the product line.

Materials and components	$ 90
Direct labor at $12 per hour	24
Indirect costs at 500% of direct labor	120
Total cost	$234

The indirect cost rate of 500% of direct labor cost is based on actual total indirect costs divided by the $4,000,000 total company-wide labor cost for the most recent month. Because of the high combined labor and indirect costs, the department manager urged the Design Engineering Department to work on reducing the labor time in the product. The engineers did a great deal of redesigning that resulted in a 25% reduction in labor time over a six-month period, largely by using costlier parts and components that required less time to assemble. The department manager was then surprised to see the following analysis for the sixth month of the program, when production was 50,000 units.

Materials and components	$ 95
Direct labor at $12	18
Indirect at 650% of direct labor	117
Total cost	$230

The manager was aghast at the results and could not understand why such a concentrated effort had shown so little payoff. The manager of engineering was also distressed at the results. The most disappointing aspect was the sharp increase in the indirect cost rate, and the manager decided to determine its cause. He learned that total labor hours for the company decreased about 10% over the six-month period because other departments were also trying to reduce labor costs.

Required

1. Determine total indirect costs allocated to the product line in each month.
2. What reasons might there be for the disappointing results?

10-51 *Allocations and behavior (continuation of 10-50)* Sarah Torg, controller of Clifford Electronics, was well aware of the problems created by the company's use of direct labor to allocate all indirect costs. She did considerable analysis and developed the following plant-wide pools of average monthly indirect costs, as they related to particular cost drivers.

Activity	Amount of Activity	Amount of Related Indirect Costs
Labor cost	$3,480,000	$ 9,880,000
Record keeping	2,400,000 entries	840,000
Materials	$48,000,000 cost of materials	11,350,000
Engineering hours	4,000 hours	770,000
Total indirect costs		$22,840,000

Torg noted that using direct labor cost to allocate the indirect costs gave a rate of about 650%, as Department Z experienced in a previous month. That is, $22,840,000/$3,480,000 = 656%. She wanted to see how the allocations would change using these four bases, instead of just direct labor. She collected the following data for the line described in the preceding assignment.

Labor cost	$900,000
Record keeping	400,000 entries
Cost of materials used	$4,750,000
Engineering hours	300 hours

Required

1. Calculate the rate per unit of activity for each group of indirect costs.
2. Use the rates calculated in part 1 to allocate indirect costs to Department Z, and determine the unit cost of the average product in Z's line using the new allocation.
3. Using the guidelines in Appendix A, write a memorandum to Ms. Torg commenting on the differences between the alternative allocation schemes.

10-52 *Performance measurement in an automobile dealership* In automobile dealerships the sales managers of new and used cars are commonly evaluated according to the profits on sales of new and used cars, respectively. Complicating such evaluations is the interrelationship that often exists between the actions taken by the two segments.

A new-car sales agreement may include some allowance for a traded-in used car. The trade-in allowance is often based on what the used-car manager is willing to pay the new-car manager for the car. For example, suppose that a customer wants to buy a new car that has a list price of $12,000 and trade in a used car. If there were no trade-in, the price of the car would be $11,200. If the used-car manager will give $3,500 for the used car to be traded in, the new-car salesperson could allow up to $4,300 to the customer, because the net price would still be satisfactory. The $7,700 cash paid ($12,000 list price - $4,300 allowed on the old car) is the same as the difference between the $11,200 desired price and the $3,500 that the used-car manager will pay for the car.

Sometimes the used-car manager will offer lower prices than at other times, say, if the used-car lot is full and sales are slow. If the used-car manager will pay only $2,800 for the car, the salesperson could give only a $3,600 trade-in allowance to obtain $11,200.

Required

1. Assuming that each manager is evaluated on profits in his respective area, what is the disadvantage of the system to the new-car manager? Is there a disadvantage to the used-car manager?
2. Suppose the dealership's policy provides that the new-car manager can try to sell the car to another used-car dealer if he is unhappy with the price offered by the used-car manager. In the second example, suppose the new-car manager believed that the trade-in automobile could be sold to another used-car dealer for $3,500. The $11,200 deemed acceptable for the new car would be obtained ($7,700 from the customer plus $3,500 from selling the trade-in), so this deal for the new car would be accepted despite the lower bid from the used-car manager. Does the system encourage the managers to act in the best interests of the total firm?

10-53   *Home office allocations and decisions*   Worcester Manufacturing Company has fourteen sales offices throughout the United States and Canada. Each sales office is a profit center, with the local manager able to set prices and offer special discounts to obtain customers. Many functions such as checking creditworthiness of customers, billing, and others are centralized in the home office. A few years ago, Marquarite Campau, the president, decided to charge the sales offices for these functions. After some thought, she set the charge at 8% of revenue. Home office costs are almost all fixed.

The firm's factories bill the sales offices for goods at prices established annually. The charge includes both variable manufacturing costs and a margin to cover fixed costs. Variable manufacturing costs average about 40% of revenue at current prices.

Lee Mott, manager of the Miami office, has come to you for advice. She is considering a price reduction that she expects to add considerably to unit volume but is unsure of the effects on profit. She begins by showing you an income statement that reflects her expectations for the coming year without the price reduction.

Miami Office Budgeted Income Statement for 19X2		
Sales		$2,400,000
Cost of sales		1,200,000
Gross margin		$1,200,000
Salaries and commissions	$490,000	
Rent, utilities, insurance	86,000	
Home office charge	192,000	768,000
Profit		$ 432,000

Mott believes that it is possible to obtain the following increases in unit volume given the associated decreases in selling prices.

Decrease in Price	Increase in Unit Volume
5%	20%
10%	35%

Mott tells you that the only variable costs of running the office are the 15% commissions that salespeople earn. Of course, her "cost of sales" is variable because it depends on unit volume, as is the home office charge because it depends on total revenue. Mott is evaluated on the profit that her office generates.

Required
1. Determine whether or not Mott should reduce prices, and if so, by how much.
2. Using the guidelines in Appendix A, write a memorandum to Ms. Mott giving and supporting your recommendation about which action (hold prices, reduce prices by 5%, reduce prices by 10%) is in Worcester's best interests.

10-54 Incurred costs and performance   Weldon Oil Company operates a refinery in the northeastern United States. During the winter about 200 workers are employed as drivers of fuel-oil trucks to deliver oil for heating purposes. Drivers are paid $10 per hour. During the summer there is no need for their services as fuel-oil truck drivers, and they are given jobs in the refinery. These refinery jobs pay only $7 per hour. However, company policy is to pay the drivers their usual $10 rate.

The refinery manager is charged with the $10 wage paid to the drivers while they work in the refinery. The manager of fuel-oil distribution bears no charge except when the workers are delivering fuel oil. The refinery manager does not object to employing the drivers during the summer. Even with this addition to his regular work force he must hire students and other temporary employees in the summer. He does, however, object to the $10 charge in the summer, because he can obtain equally qualified (for those jobs) workers at $7 per hour and he must use the drivers as a matter of company policy.

Required
Using the guidelines in Appendix A, write a memorandum to Ms. Cohen, Weldon's controller, pointing out the problems by the firm's present cost-assignment policies and recommending an alternative approach for assigning the charges for drivers' wages during the summer.

11

Divisional Performance Measurement

LEARNING OBJECTIVES

After reading this chapter, you should be able to

1 Explain some of the advantages and disadvantages of decentralization.

2 Describe the commonly used measures of evaluating the performance of investment centers and their managers.

3 Describe how performance evaluation methods can encourage managers to act against the best interests of the company.

4 Describe variations in measuring income and investment.

5 Explain how evaluating a division is different from evaluating the manager of the division.

6 Explain the problems in developing transfer pricing policies.

7 Describe performance evaluation problems specific to multinational companies.

In the 1994 annual report, Alex Trotman, CEO of **Ford Motor Corp.**, told stockholders that the company was reorganizing from its former geographical basis to a product-line basis. The reorganization was prompted by the company's strategy to use a single platform for each car world-wide. Previously, a car made in the United States would be quite different from one made in Europe, increasing costs and making the company's operations needlessly complex and duplicative. The reorganization was also to reduce bureaucracy and increase decision making at lower levels, " . . . pushing authority and accountability down into the organization as far as they will go, to keep us fast and innovative and in touch with our customers." Ford now wants decisions made "at the level closest to the action."

General Electric dropped three layers of management, cleared a thicket of bureaucracy, and gave its businesses more freedom. One objective was to create what CEO Jack Welch called "a small business culture." As part of the reorganization, GE has increased from about 400 to over 22,000 the number of managers who have stock options, reflecting a spreading of responsibility throughout the company.

Hershey Corp. reorganized to streamline its decision making. It established a new division to market its products to grocery stores, saying that the "ability to dedicate sales and marketing resources to specific categories provides a distinct competitive advantage."

For *IBM*, decentralization came in response to serious erosions of profitability in the late 1980s and into the 1990s. IBM was too ponderous and slow to respond to its more nimble competitors, particularly in the personal computer market. The company's 1991 annual report announced that top management was "... redefining IBM from a single, centralized company into a network of more competitive businesses." Businesses will be more free-standing, but with access to "IBM's technological and financial resources."

Companies throughout the world are reorganizing, spreading responsibility, and loosening lines of authority. Such changes are often responses to the rapid pace of change that characterizes global competition. But how do companies control and evaluate managers and segments in these conditions?

Sources: Ford Motor Corp. 1994 annual report, 3-5; General Electric 1995 annual report, 2-4; Hershey Corp. 1994 annual report, 4-6; IBM 1991 annual report, 2-5.

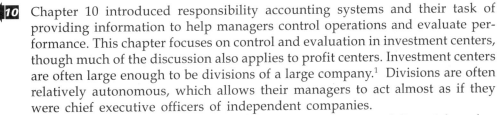 Chapter 10 introduced responsibility accounting systems and their task of providing information to help managers control operations and evaluate performance. This chapter focuses on control and evaluation in investment centers, though much of the discussion also applies to profit centers. Investment centers are often large enough to be divisions of a large company.[1] Divisions are often relatively autonomous, which allows their managers to act almost as if they were chief executive officers of independent companies.

Investment centers control all the major components of financial performance: revenues, costs, and investments. They therefore can be evaluated by more comprehensive measures of performance than can cost centers or profit centers, which do not control all these elements. The more comprehensive the performance measure the better. The measures described in this chapter are more comprehensive than cost or profit measures.

DECENTRALIZATION

 From Chapter 10 you know that the term **decentralized** refers to companies that give managers broad authority. Companies that use investment centers are usually highly decentralized. In highly decentralized companies, operating units (usually called *divisions* or **business units**) are almost autonomous;

---

1 *The term* division *can refer to any large operating unit, but in this chapter we use it to refer to investment centers.*

division managers are responsible for both production and marketing, as well as for functions such as personnel and accounting. Division managers also prepare and submit capital budgets to central headquarters for approval.

BENEFITS OF DECENTRALIZATION

Proponents of decentralizing argue that it promotes better decision making. They believe that the managers closest to an operation make better decisions because they are better able to gather and evaluate information than are centrally located corporate managers. Managers at the scene can also act more quickly because they need not report to headquarters and wait for approval of their proposed actions. **General Electric** uses a program called Work Out, which is based on the belief that people closest to the situation know best. Groups including shop floor workers, supervisors, and managers meet to solve problems.[2]

Considerable evidence suggests that the broader responsibility accompanying decentralization increases motivation. Studies have shown that employees (including managers) tend to perform better as their responsibilities increase. In general, the least-motivated people are those who perform a single task again and again throughout the day. One effect of establishing manufacturing cells in companies using JIT is to broaden the responsibilities of workers that make up the cell. The term *job enlargement* describes giving increased responsibility. People who do much of the work on a product, as opposed to doing only one small operation, and managers who control most of the factors that affect profitability become more committed to their jobs and are more likely to view their jobs as sources of satisfaction, not just as sources of income. In recent years, work teams that manage themselves have become an important tool. Many companies use such teams.

Rubbermaid Corp. has been at the top of *Fortune's* list of most admired corporations for several years. The company uses teams extensively and its CEO credits its decentralized approach with making the company more nimble and entrepreneurial.[3]

Decentralization is particularly advantageous to companies that operate in different industries. As companies widen their range of products, the need to give broad responsibility to division managers increases. A company's president or other chief operating officer can't be thoroughly familiar with a great many product lines, such as textiles, furniture, appliances, automobile supplies, movies, and sporting goods. Similarly, increasing international operations has increased the need for knowledgeable on-site managers with decision-making authority. Managers of nearly autonomous divisions are also well prepared for higher positions. They appreciate all aspects of a company's operations. With such increased responsibility comes higher rewards, but greater risk. The accompanying Insight describes how some companies compensate managers of decentralized units such as investment centers and how one company sees decentralization as important in developing top executives.

As a practical matter, it is impossible to operate a modern business of any complexity without delegating some authority to lower-level managers. The

---

2 *General Electric 1995 annual report,* 4.
3 *Rahul Jacob, "Corporate Reputations,"* Fortune, *March 6, 1995, 56.*

Fluor Corporation, a world-wide engineering and construction firm, has the following to say. "Fluor's management team, which has the ultimate responsibility for creating value, . . . is even more closely aligned with the creation of shareholder value. Fluor's management compensation philosophy recognizes this responsibility. . . . A significant portion of management compensation is directly linked to financial and stock performance, and increases at successively higher levels of responsibility. More than 78 percent of the compensation of the five highest paid Executive Officers is at risk and dependent upon achievement of aggressive performance and stock price objectives."

Campbell Soup Company uses "pay for performance," which ties compensation to the achievement of corporate objectives. Up to 75 percent of executives' compensation is linked to meeting goals. Additionally, Campbell requires some 70 executives to own stock in amounts from one-half to three times their base salaries to increase their commitment.

The chief executive of **Container Corporation of America**, in an annual report, commented on the value of decentralization in preparing top managers: "The corporate organization consists of over 21,000 men and women, working in plants and offices, laboratories, forests and paperboard mills in the U.S. and six other countries. Its 140 plants and mills operate as relatively independent businesses, under a management system that delegates authority and responsibility to local managers. This decentralized organization, which provides for successful development of local markets, also constitutes an environment which encourages individual self-development. One measure of its success, over the years, is that virtually all of the company's present senior management team is a product of this system."

Sources: Fluor Corporation, 1994 annual report, 4; Phyllis Berman and Alexandra Alger, "Reclaiming the Patrimony," Forbes, March 14, 1994, 50-51; Container Corporation of America annual report, 1972.

interdependence of functional areas and factors in the corporate culture make conflicts between managers inevitable. When the chief executive is the only manager whose span of responsibility includes the managers in conflict, arbitration and settlement of disputes must necessarily take place at the top. In most situations, decentralization allows conflicts among managers to be resolved at a lower level.

PROBLEMS OF DECENTRALIZATION

Decentralization has its problems, the major one being that managers operating in nearly autonomous fashion might make decisions that harm the company. Indeed, perhaps the most formidable problem of decentralization is achieving goal congruence while at the same time promoting and maintaining divisional autonomy. **Magna International**, a leading auto-parts supplier, decentralized to extremes in the early 1980s. The company rewarded plant managers almost solely on profits and gave them near-complete freedom. Unlike most companies, Magna permitted plant managers to borrow money, build new factories, and sign long-term contracts. The plant managers added huge amounts of debt until the burden almost sank Magna in 1990, as the recession hit the company's sales.[4]

Decentralization can create other problems. In the early 1980s, **Levi Strauss** decentralized into divisions that each handled a product line. It reconsolidated because retailers were unhappy having to buy from several divisions instead of only one. Pressures from large customers who buy across product lines have prompted organizational changes at many other companies, whether the changes redefined segments, established segments to deal with such customers, or centralized ordering, distribution, billing, and other functions. For example, **Fieldcrest Cannon**, the home furnishings manufacturer, organized one of its units by type of customer: department and specialty stores, mass merchants, institutions, and international. This organization made the unit more responsive to the differing requirements of the customers.

Two managerial accounting issues are especially related to decentralization. First is the need to develop methods of evaluating performance that work to benefit the company as a whole. Second is a need to develop transfer prices that produce decisions in the best interests of the company. We turn first to the problem of selecting performance measures for divisions.

MEASURES OF PERFORMANCE

Companies use three principal measures to evaluate divisions: income, return on investment, and residual income.

INCOME

Net income for financial reporting purposes, computed under GAAP, is the most widely examined (and least understood) financial datum. For several reasons income is unsatisfactory for measuring the performance of divisions.

- In calculating net income, companies subtract interest and taxes, neither of which is normally under the control of divisional managers and so are not typically shown in internal reports.
- A division's expenses usually include some charges (allocations) for services provided by central headquarters. For example, much of the payroll work for divisions of **Ford Motor Company** is done by an artificial profit center that bills divisions for its services.
- Factors that influence GAAP-based income do not necessarily apply to internal reports. For example, companies must expense research and development expenditures because of the importance of verifiability and objectivity in financial reporting. Because these qualities are less important in internal reporting, companies can capitalize and amortize R&D expenditures to reflect their long-term benefits.
- Income is not a comprehensive measure of success. A division that earns $10 million on a $200 million investment is far less successful

---

4 Brian O'Reilly, "The Perils of Too Much Freedom," *Fortune, January 11, 1993, 79.*

than one earning $3 million on a $10 million investment. This objection applies not only to GAAP-based income, but to any other calculation such as we have made in earlier chapters, particularly Chapters 4 and 5.

Although income is not the most useful performance measure, neither is it irrelevant. Indeed, two of the three other widely used performance measures discussed in this chapter include income. But the importance of income is as a part of other measures rather than as a measure in itself.

RETURN ON INVESTMENT

Return on investment (ROI) is the general term used to describe a ratio of *some measure of income to some measure of investment.* In financial accounting you might have seen the ratio net income divided by stockholders' equity, usually called *return on equity (ROE).* ROE is one type of ROI. Another is *return on assets (ROA),* usually measured as income before interest and taxes divided by total assets. Some companies use the term *return on capital employed,* or just return on capital, to designate the same ratio. For internal performance evaluation, managers generally use an ROI measure of the following form.

$$ROI = \frac{divisional\ income}{divisional\ investment}$$

Companies define and measure **divisional income** (also called *segment income* or *operating profit*) and **divisional investment** (also called *invested capital* or *identifiable assets*) in various ways. We examine some of these ways shortly.

ROI is the most frequently used criterion for divisional performance measurement, though the use of other measures is growing. ROI has a distinct advantage over income as a performance measure, because companies usually have divisions of different sizes. A division earning $300,000 on an investment of $1,000,000 is more efficient than one earning the same profit on an investment of $5,000,000. ROI makes it possible to compare the efficiency of different-size divisions by relating output (income) to input (investment).

Some managers find it helpful to restate the ROI formula when they are looking for ways to improve operating performance. The restatement expands the basic formula (income ÷ investment) into two ratios.

$$ROI = \frac{income}{sales} \times \frac{sales}{investment}$$

The expanded version gives the same final answer because "sales" appears in the numerator of one factor and the denominator of the other and thus cancels out. But the expanded form helps to focus the manager's attention on the two components of ROI.

The first ratio, income ÷ sales, is the familiar **return on sales (ROS)** ratio introduced in Chapter 2, also called *profit margin* or just *margin.* The second, sales ÷ investment, is **investment turnover**, or just *turnover.* This expanded version clearly shows that an increase in sales, by itself, will not increase ROI because sales cancels out. But a decrease in investment, with other factors remaining the same, will increase ROI (as will an increase in income with other factors held constant).

With the expanded formula, a manager can readily determine the effect on ROI of a decision expected to change two factors. Suppose that ROS is now 15 percent and investment turnover is 2 times; ROI is 30 percent (15% × 2). A manager considering changing the product mix to items with lower margins and faster turnover, which will increase turnover to 2½ times while reducing ROS to 10 percent, can see that ROI will fall to 25 percent (10% × 2½).

The values of the two components of ROI often give clues to the strategies used by companies or divisions. For example, a single company might operate divisions that follow a differentiation strategy, and should therefore have high margins, as well as divisions that follow a cost leadership strategy, and should have high turnovers. The values can also offer clues as to why one division is outperforming another. The following data are for the 1993 U.S. operations of toy companies **Hasbro** and **Mattel**. Amounts are in millions of dollars.

	Hasbro	Mattel
Sales	$1,670	$1,873
Operating profit	242	188
Identifiable assets	1,541	719
Return on sales	14.5%	10.0%
Investment turnover	1.08	2.61
ROI	15.7%	26.1%

Hasbro's profit margin is much higher than **Mattel's**, but Mattel turns its investment over twice as fast as does Hasbro, giving Mattel a wide lead in ROI. We cannot be sure why Mattel has better results, but we can surmise that it manages its assets better. We should point out that these numbers come from annual reports that do not describe in detail how the numbers are calculated. The two companies might well calculate things differently, making comparisons less clear. Of course, a company doing these calculations for several of its divisions can be sure it defines numbers consistently.

While the advantages of ROI in considering relative sizes and alternative strategies are obvious, absolute size still matters in assessing a segment's contribution to the entity as a whole. Depending on the circumstances, a 12 percent ROI for a very large division might be making a greater contribution than a 40 percent ROI in another division. Recall from Chapter 8 that a company is wise to accept all proposed investments with expected returns greater than cost of capital. Residual income recognizes the same general principle in evaluating divisions.

RESIDUAL INCOME

Residual income (RI) is the income a division produces in excess of the **minimum required (desired, target) rate of return**. Top management establishes the minimum rate of return, which should be greater than cost of capital, as described in Chapter 8. For one reason, the target ROI usually does not recognize income taxes because companies do not include income taxes in computing divisional income. Some companies set different minimum rates of return for different divisions to reflect differences in the risks associated with their businesses. A division in a risky industry such as fashion merchandise should earn higher returns than one in a more stable industry such as paper.

Residual income is computed as follows.

$$RI = income - (investment \times target\ ROI)$$

The parenthetical term is the profit that must be earned to satisfy the minimum requirement. It is the minimum required *dollar* return. Anything over that amount benefits the company. (Of course, *any* income benefits the company, but the minimum required ROI is needed simply to keep it going.) If the company earns less than investors demand, they will invest their capital elsewhere and the company will decline and perhaps go out of business. The most basic argument for using RI, in preference to ROI, for evaluating divisional performance is that RI explicitly recognizes the critical point that the capital invested in any division comes with a cost, as you know from Chapter 8. When the minimum ROI approximates cost of capital or the cutoff rate (pretax) for the company as a whole, RI measures the profit that the division provides to the company over and above the minimum profit required for the amount invested.

Proponents of RI argue that it reflects the contribution a division makes to the company better than does ROI. Suppose that Division A produces a $200,000 income on an investment of $1,000,000, an ROI of 20 percent, while Division B earns $1,500,000 on an investment of $10,000,000, an ROI of 15 percent. Depending on the required ROI for the company, the contributions of the divisions to the company as a whole will appear quite different. Consider two possibilities: (1) required ROI is 10 percent and (2) required ROI is 18 percent. The RIs for each division are as follows:

| | 1 | | 2 | |
| | Required ROI is 10% | | Required ROI is 18% | |
	Division A	Division B	Division A	Division B
Investment	$1,000,000	$10,000,000	$1,000,000	$10,000,000
Divisional income	$ 200,000	$ 1,500,000	$ 200,000	$ 1,500,000
Required minimum return (investment × minimum ROI)	100,000	1,000,000	180,000	1,800,000
Residual income	$ 100,000	$ 500,000	$ 20,000	$ (300,000)

If the minimum required ROI is 10 percent, Division B contributes more to the company than does Division A, despite Division B's lower ROI. In this situation we could say that Division B was more valuable to the company. On the other hand, if the company has an 18 percent minimum ROI, Division A contributes more and is more valuable under the RI criterion. The accompanying Insight describes a concept akin to RI that is becoming popular for evaluating both divisions and entire companies.

Because numbers for divisional income and divisional investment are needed to compute both RI and ROI, the same questions arise as to how those numbers should be computed. These questions are discussed later in the chapter.

BEHAVIORAL PROBLEMS

We pointed out in Chapter 10 that goal congruence is an important objective of a management control system. From Chapter 8 you know that, in the absence

SIGHT

In recent years, well-known companies as diverse as **AT&T**, **Briggs & Stratton**, **Coca-Cola**, and **Quaker Oats** have adopted a performance measure called **EVA**, for **economic value added**. They use this measure not only for divisions, but for the company as a whole. *Fortune* publishes lists of companies ranked by EVA and many espouse it as an excellent performance measure for a company as a whole. The concepts of EVA and RI are very similar. EVA uses after-tax operating profit, which is RI's divisional profit less income taxes. EVA also uses cost of capital as the target ROI, while RI uses a pretax target return that is also higher than cost of capital. Those using RI often begin with a pretax cost of capital, then adjust the target return upward to allow for risk, indirect costs and investment, and other factors. We discussed this type of adjustment in Chapter 8. Suppose that the company in the example has a cost of capital of 11 percent and a 30 percent income tax rate. EVA for Division A is

Divisional profit	$200,000
Less income taxes	60,000
After-tax profit	$140,000
Less required minimum, $1,000,000 × 11%	110,000
EVA	$ 30,000

The CEO of **Quaker Oats** credits EVA with instilling an excellent attitude in managers, making them act as if they were owners. Quaker Oats calls EVA *controllable profit*. **Coca-Cola** increased EVA simply by moving some vending machines to higher-traffic locations. Coke has published a brochure detailing how it uses EVA, and distributes it to anyone who asks. **CSX Corporation's** 1994 annual report stated that "Using EVA to measure financial performance, CSX has reduced costs, utilized assets more effectively, conserved capital, increased productivity, and improved service." The report also stated that the EVA concept recognizes that "companies create wealth only when they generate returns above their cost of capital."

Because EVA recognizes that a division must cover cost of capital to thrive, it shares RI's advantage over ROI as a performance measure. The interest in EVA generated by the attention that *Fortune* and other publications have given it has encouraged companies to identify the investments of business units and to make more extensive use of investment centers. For example, before adopting EVA, **Quaker Oats** evaluated its divisions—and rewarded its managers—on income. **Briggs & Stratton** did not identify investment with any segments within its engine business. It has since organized those segments into five investment centers. Similarly, **AT&T** had only a few, very large investment centers before 1993. It reorganized one of those units into 40 investment centers.

Directing managers to thinking about both income *and* investment encourages them to think about ways to use capital more efficiently—to get more income from their existing capital or to reduce capital and hold income constant. Many of the profitable actions claimed as results of using EVA stem from directing managers' attention to *both* income and investment.

Sources: Shawn Tully, "The Real Key to Creating Wealth," Fortune, September 20, 1993, 38-50; Coca-Cola brochure and annual reports; CSX annual report, 1994.

of some overriding qualitative issue, a company should accept an investment that will yield a positive net present value, or equivalently, that has an internal rate of return greater than cost of capital or the cutoff rate. Investment centers make significant capital investments, most of which must be approved by corporate headquarters. Divisional management must decide whether or not to seek approval for the investment opportunities it sees or to fund those for which it need not obtain corporate approval. A performance measure is dysfunctional if it encourages managers to make poor investment decisions. We can examine the performance measures so far discussed in relation to goal congruence.

ROI VERSUS RI

Using ROI to evaluate divisions can encourage the divisions to reject good investments and accept poor investments.

Rejecting Valuable Investments—Division Q

Consider the manager of Division Q, who expects $300,000 income on a $1,000,000 investment for a 30 percent expected ROI. The manager has an opportunity offering a $75,000 incremental profit on an incremental investment of $300,000 (ROI of 25 percent on the additional investment). Suppose further that the company's minimum rate of return is 20 percent. From the company's viewpoint, the proposed investment should be undertaken because its 25 percent expected ROI exceeds the 20 percent required minimum. But if the performance of the division (and its manager) is evaluated on the basis of ROI, the manager will be inclined to reject the new investment because ROI (now 30 percent) will fall, as can be seen in the following computations.

Divisional profit:	
Current	$ 300,000
From new project	75,000
Total divisional profit	$ 375,000
Investment before new project	$1,000,000
Additional investment for the project	300,000
Total investment	$1,300,000
Divisional ROI after new investment ($375,000/$1,300,000)	28.8%

Using RI to evaluate performance encourages goal congruent behavior.

	Without New Project	With New Project
Divisional investment	$1,000,000	$1,300,000
Minimum required ROI	20%	20%
Divisional profit	$ 300,000	$ 375,000
Less minimum required	200,000	260,000
Residual income	$ 100,000	$ 115,000

A division manager evaluated on the basis of RI will undertake this project because performance improves. This should not be surprising because the 25 percent ROI exceeds the required 20 percent. The ROI criterion encourages maximizing the ratio of profit to investment. The RI criterion encourages maximizing total dollars of profit in excess of the minimum required dollar return. In fact, we could have said in advance that the project was desirable, and that it would increase RI by $15,000, which is the increase in income less the additional dollar return required [$75,000 - ($300,000 × 20%)].

Accepting Value-Losing Opportunities—Division Z

Suppose that the manager of Division Z of the same company expects income of $200,000 on an investment of $2,000,000, for a 10 percent ROI. How would the manager respond to an opportunity to increase income $15,000 by investing $100,000? The investment is unwise for the company because it earns less than the 20 percent minimum. But the manager will accept the investment because divisional ROI increases to 10.2 percent.

$$New\ ROI\ =\ \frac{\$200,000\ +\ \$15,000}{\$2,000,000\ +\ \$100,000}\ =\ \frac{\$215,000}{\$2,100,000}\ =\ 10.2\%$$

Yet the proposed action actually generates negative residual income of $5,000 because a $100,000 investment requires income of $20,000 to meet the 20 percent minimum required rate of return. A manager evaluated on RI will reject the investment because the already negative RI of $200,000 [$200,000 - ($2,000,000 × 20%)] grows to $205,000 if the investment proposal is accepted.

In most companies, Division Z would not be able to make the undesirable investment because capital budgeting proposals must go to the corporation for approval. But that manager still might invest in receivables and inventory to increase income, investments which do not require headquarter approval.

ROI AND RI

Because ROI and RI use book values, they can both encourage divisional managers to act against the company's best interests. Consider the following example. A manager is considering a project that requires a $100,000 investment and provides pretax cash flows of $40,000 per year for five years. The company requires a minimum pretax ROI of 25 percent. The present value of the $40,000 stream of payments discounted at 25 percent is $107,560 ($40,000 × 2.689). Under the decision rules developed in Chapter 8, the investment is desirable because it has a positive NPV of $7,560 ($107,560 - $100,000). The book rates of return and RIs for the first two years of the investment are as follows, using straight-line depreciation.

Year	Additional Cash Flow	Additional Depreciation	Increase in Book Income	Average Additional Investment[a]	ROI on Additional Investment	RI[b]
1	$40,000	$20,000	$20,000	$90,000	22.2%	$(2,500)
2	$40,000	$20,000	$20,000	$70,000	28.6%	$ 2,500

a Book value of investment at beginning of year plus book value at end of year, divided by two.
b Book income of $20,000 minus 25 percent required return on average additional investment.

In the first year, ROI is below the 25 percent required minimum and RI is negative. The division manager, seeing that undertaking the project will penalize performance in the first year, is not encouraged to accept the project.

Because investment declines through depreciation, both ROI and RI rise over time unless income from the investment declines sharply. The pattern is more extreme if the company uses an accelerated method of depreciation. Even if cash flows, and therefore book income, decline, the pattern of increasing ROI is likely to occur.

The rise in ROI based on book values is even more pronounced in more realistic situations where returns do not begin immediately or do not reach their peaks in the early years. Ordinarily some lead time is required—to build a plant, install machinery, test the operation, remove bugs, and generally get the operation going. Heavy startup costs are common in the opening of a new plant or even the remodeling of an existing one. The returns are likely to increase over the first few years as the plant gains efficiency. If a new product is involved, its sales will usually begin low and rise over time, and so too will profits.

Thus, two factors work against the manager—lower income in early years and the natural tendency of ROI to rise as the book value of the investment falls because of depreciation charges. What can be done to encourage the manager to pursue worthwhile investments?

One way to avoid the first-year drop in ROI and thereby encourage managers to accept desirable investments is to leave the new investment out of the base for calculating ROI until the project is on-stream and running well. Of course, many major projects will take a relatively long time before they are running well. **Quaker Oats** allows units extra time to reach positive EVAs if they start out with especially large investments.

Another approach is to amortize the costs of starting up over several years instead of expensing them all in the first year of an investment's life. A third possibility, seldom observed in practice, is to base depreciation charges on budgeted income to be earned over several years; this results in lower depreciation in early years and higher charges in later years.

Essentially, the problem just described is a conflict between the long and the short terms. As stated several times in this book, many actions that can help meet short-term goals are harmful in the long run. Such actions could reduce profits, ROI, and RI in the long term, but by then the manager might have been promoted to another job. Conversely, a manager who takes actions that benefit the division and company in the long run, while hurting short-term performance, could be fired, not promoted, or otherwise penalized. The manager who takes over could well reap the benefits of the predecessor's good decisions. Something we said in Chapter 10 bears repeating here: evaluating managerial performance with a single quantitative measure is unwise. Managers should use other quantitative measures, as well as qualitative measures, to evaluate their subordinates. **AT&T** spends a good deal of money collecting and analyzing data from which it derives measures of customer satisfaction. The company uses this measure, as well as measures of employee satisfaction, in addition to EVA.[5]

---

5 Rhona L. Ferling, *"Quality in 3D: EVA, CVA, and Employees,"* Financial Executive, July/August 1993, 51.

PROBLEMS IN MEASUREMENT

Whether using ROI or RI as the evaluation criterion, a company must determine what revenues, costs, and investments are to be included in the calculations. The determinations should be made along the lines of responsibility, with controllability as the principal criterion for including costs and investments. A division manager who is held responsible for earning returns (income) on investment should control the elements of both income and investment.

INCOME

To compute the income for which division managers are responsible, we must identify variable costs and direct fixed costs. As discussed in Chapter 10, some companies also allocate common indirect fixed costs for several reasons. If common fixed costs are allocated to divisions, they should be separated from direct fixed costs and clearly labeled as allocated. Companies using RI or EVA should exclude interest on corporate debt from the income calculation because cost of capital includes interest on debt. An upcoming Insight describes how several companies compute income by business unit for their annual reports.

INVESTMENT

Opinions differ as to what to include in and how to measure divisional investment. Everyone includes assets that are used exclusively by a particular division. Most assets can be readily identified with specific divisions. For financial reporting purposes, companies presenting segmented information often refer to *identifiable assets*, as the upcoming Insight shows. For example, virtually all plant and equipment (or fixed assets) falls under the control of specific divisions. Inventory and receivables, which are also investments, are under divisional control if the divisional manager controls production and credit terms. Divisional managers control some cash, but in many cases central headquarters receives payments directly from customers and pays bills submitted by the divisions. Centralizing the cash management function usually reduces costs for the company as a whole. Some assets are controlled only at the highest level of management. Central headquarters controls the headquarters building and equipment, cash and marketable securities (often called cash equivalents), long-term investments, and such intangible assets as goodwill and organization costs. An upcoming Insight describes how some companies report segment information to external parties.

Suppose we have analyzed the revenues, costs, and assets of Multiproducts, Inc., and have identified these by divisions as shown in Exhibit 11-1. The company has three operating divisions, A, B, and C, and a central corporate office. The minimum required ROI is 10 percent.

From the data in Exhibit 11-1 we can compute ROI and RI for each division and for the company as a whole, as in Exhibit 11-2. The latter computation should be based on an investment defined as the total assets of the company. Note that no performance measurement is given for unallocated assets.

When a company does not allocate all costs and all investment to divisions, the company cannot earn the target ROI unless the divisions earn *more than* the target ROI. Although the company's ROI is 11.1 percent, only one division earns so low a rate. Note also that the combined RI of the divisions is partly consumed

Exhibit 11-1 Multiproducts, Inc. (in millions of dollars)

	Division A	Division B	Division C	Unallocated	Total
Investment					
Cash	$ 20	$ 30	$ 60	$ 30	$ 140
Accounts receivable, net	60	80	90		230
Inventory	100	180	240		520
Prepaid expenses	10	10	20	20	60
Plant and equipment— net of depreciation	200	320	440	60	1,020
Investments	10	—	—	100	110
Total assets	$400	$620	$850	$210	$2,080
Income					
Sales	$100	$400	$700		$1,200
Variable costs	30	220	400		650
Contribution margin	$ 70	$180	$300		$ 550
Direct fixed costs	30	90	140		260
Divisional profit	$ 40	$ 90	$160		$ 290
Common fixed costs					60
Income					$ 230

by the unallocated costs and assets, so that, although the divisions earn residual income of $103 million ($0 + $28 + $75), the company earns only $22 million in excess of a 10 percent return on total assets. Therefore, companies that do

Exhibit 11-2 Multiproducts, Inc. (in millions of dollars)

	A	B	C	Company as a Whole
Computation of ROI				
Profit of segment	$ 40	$ 90	$ 160	$ 230
Investment in segment	400	620	850	2,080
ROI (profit/investment)	10%	14.5%	18.8%	11.1%
Computation of RI:				
Profit of segment	$ 40	$ 90	$ 160	$ 230
Required return (investment x minimum return of 10%)	40	62	85	208
RI (profit - required return)	$ 0	$ 28	$ 75	$ 22

not allocate all costs and investment to divisions must set the target ROI for divisions higher than cost of capital to the *company as a whole*. If the company allocates all costs and investments to divisions, the target ROI for the divisions can be the cost of capital to the company.

Managers favoring complete allocation argue that divisional managers should be made aware of the substantial costs and investment involved in running the company as a whole, which each of the divisions must work to offset. This argument was explored in Chapter 10. Another and perhaps more persuasive justification for complete allocation is that corporate managers are interested in whether a division is earning returns comparable to those of independent companies in the same industry. If the division is to be treated more or less as an independent, autonomous entity, corporate managers argue that it should bear the costs and assets that a competing independent company must. An independent company must incur many costs, and maintain many assets, that a division often does not. For example, an independent company performs research and development, while a division can often rely on a centrally administered R&D organization. Similarly, an independent company must maintain more cash than a division that relies on a centralized cash management function. To make reasonable comparisons between the division and an outside company, then, corporate management might allocate central costs and assets to divisions (also reminding divisional managers of the needs met by the central administration).

Companies that allocate corporate costs among divisions do so in many ways. In some companies, central headquarters charges each division a management fee for services provided. For instance, divisions need financing, just as if they were separate companies; so the charge reflects that service. The fee might be a percentage of revenue, total investment in the division, or some other base. The desire to avoid having unallocated costs and investment has motivated top managers to study more closely the divisional activities that drive some of those costs and investments.

Efforts to make division managers realize that they must consider the performance of the entire company might be worthwhile, but allocating central costs and assets to divisions must be understood for what it is—allocation. Whatever the allocation methods used, managers at both the divisional and corporate levels must be aware that allocations in no way change the nature of the costs or assets as indirect to the divisions and not controllable by the divisional managers.

LIABILITIES

Assigning liabilities to divisions increases their ROIs and RIs because it decreases investment. Some current liabilities (payables, accrued expenses) are readily associated with particular divisions. But assigning all liabilities to divisions is seldom possible without arbitrary allocations. As a rule, divisions cannot issue long-term debt, and their managers are not responsible for it. Long-term debt results from financing decisions made at the highest level of management on the basis of the organization's overall needs and goals. Companies do not usually allocate long-term liabilities to divisions. For performance measurement purposes, many companies include only those liabilities that are

INSIGHT

Companies' annual reports do not necessarily list all investment centers. Companies refer to "segments" that might include several investment centers, so their annual reports might not reflect their internal reporting.

Procter & Gamble reports income after taxes when reporting for geographic segments, but uses income before taxes when reporting for product-line segments. The company reports "Identifiable Assets" for each segment with no reduction for liabilities. P&G does not allocate all corporate costs and investment to its segments. **Sonoco**, a world-wide maker of paper, packaging, and related products, excludes interest, income taxes, and unallocated corporate expenses from its calculations of segment income. The company also reports identifiable assets as those used by each segment in its operations. **Anheuser-Busch** allocates all corporate costs except interest and income taxes to its three major segments, but it identifies some assets only with the company as a whole.

IBM discloses revenues by product-line segment, but not profits and assets. The 1994 annual report states that the "company operates in the single industry segment that creates value by offering services, software, systems, products, and technologies." The report also has extensive footnotes regarding the ambiguities of treating specific products as part of one product line or another.

Sources: Annual reports.

definitely (not arbitrarily) related to divisions, and define divisional investment as controlled assets minus divisional liabilities.

Exhibit 11-3 uses assumed values for liabilities to illustrate the computations of ROI and RI when a company uses liabilities in calculating investment.

As expected, both RI and ROI are higher for all divisions and for the company as a whole when liabilities are included in the computations.

From a behavioral standpoint, the question of whether to include liabilities is undecided. In favor of their inclusion is that most current liabilities are related to the operating level of the division and provide financing to it and to the company. On the negative side, divisional managers could be encouraged to allow liabilities to rise too high in order to reduce investment and increase ROI. If divisional managers delay payments to suppliers, the credit rating of the company as a whole might suffer. A reasonable compromise might be a corporate policy that allows managers to carry, say, trade payables up to the length of time specified by suppliers. Then, if a division had 40 days' purchases in accounts payable and suppliers offered 30-day credit, the division could not deduct the extra 10 days' worth of liabilities to determine divisional investment. Under this policy, the manager has no incentive to allow payables to extend beyond the suppliers' credit terms. (Note that divisional managers have no opportunity for delaying payments if cash disbursements are handled at the central headquarters.)

Exhibit 11-3 Multiproducts, Inc. (in millions of dollars)

	A	B	C	Company as a Whole
Computation of ROI				
Profit of the segment	$ 40	$ 90	$ 160	$ 230
Total assets	$ 400	$ 620	$ 850	$2,080
Divisional liabilities (assumed)	60	170	310	540
Divisional investment	$ 340	$ 450	$ 540	$1,540
Unallocated liabilities (assumed)				730
Total investment	$ 340	$ 450	$ 540	$ 810
ROI	11.8%	20.0%	29.6%	28.4%
Computation of RI:				
Profit of the segment	$ 40	$ 90	$ 160	$ 230
Required return (investment × minimum return of 10%)	34	45	54	81
RI	$ 6	$ 45	$ 106	$ 149

FIXED ASSETS

For all computations to this point, you have been given the amount of the investment in assets. In Exhibit 11-1, for example, the investments in cash, inventory, and fixed assets were given, but there was no mention of how these amounts were determined. There are many views about what values to use for fixed assets. Some of the valuation bases used are original (gross) cost, original cost less accumulated depreciation (often called net cost, or net book value), and current replacement cost. The basis used can have a significant effect on ROI and RI, and each basis has advantages and disadvantages.

The most popular basis by far is net book value. Its principal advantages are that it conforms to financial accounting practice and that it recognizes the decline in productivity that usually accompanies increasing age. Many believe it to be the most reasonable basis, given that the computation of divisional income includes a deduction for depreciation expense. The major disadvantage of net book value is that it gives, as shown earlier, rising ROI and RI over time. Using gross (original) cost for valuing fixed assets overcomes the objection about rising ROI and RI. **DuPont** believes that its managers should maintain facilities in excellent condition throughout the facilities' lives. The company also considers it inappropriate to hold operating managers responsible for earning a return on only net book values. Finally, the company pointed out that using net book values would relate returns to "an ever-decreasing investment."[6]

---

6 *Frank R. Rayburn and Michael M. Brown, "Measuring and Using Return on Investment Information," in James Don Edwards and Homer A. Black, eds,.* The Managerial and Cost Accountant's Handbook *(Homewood, IL: Dow-Jones-Irwin, 1979), 331.*

Yet virtually all assets do lose productivity as they age, and continued use of gross cost ignores that decline. Moreover, the company's investment in a fixed asset *does* decline over time, as the company recovers its investment through the cash flows that the asset produces.

Both gross and net book values suffer from the defect that they reflect costs the company has already incurred, perhaps many years ago. Managers who have older assets generally have lower investment bases (either gross or net) than managers using similar assets that are newer and, in all likelihood, costlier. For this reason, many accountants and managers advocate valuing investments at replacement cost.

There are at least three ways to define replacement cost.

1. The current cost of new assets just like those now in use.
2. The current cost of acquiring assets of the same age and condition as those being used.
3. The current cost of obtaining similar productive capacity or service.

The third interpretation considers how the company would choose to accomplish a particular task today. For example, suppose a company has a fleet of fork-lift trucks to move materials within its factory, but would install a conveyor system if it were starting over today. Under the third interpretation, the replacement cost of the fleet is the cost of the conveyor system. Because managers should continuously evaluate the alternatives available for accomplishing tasks, we prefer the third interpretation (equivalent productive capacity) for evaluating divisional performance. However, much disagreement on this point exists.

Whatever definition of replacement cost is adopted, its use eliminates the problems of different depreciation methods *and* changes in prices of fixed assets. Thus, managers are not penalized or rewarded simply because of the depreciation methods used or the ages of their assets. The normal accounting system does not automatically provide information about current replacement costs, and the practical difficulties and costs of determining replacement costs continue to discourage their use. Despite the disadvantages, original cost less accumulated depreciation remains the most popular approach for valuing fixed assets.

THE SUBJECT OF EVALUATION—DIVISION OR MANAGER

As we stated in Chapter 10, it is important to distinguish between evaluating a division and evaluating its manager. Evaluations of divisions are strategic. Should the company invest more in a particular division? Should it "milk" a division and use its cash flow to finance investments in other divisions? Should it allow the division to wither away, or should it try to sell it now? ROI and RI give clues to where the company might be wise to increase, maintain, or reduce investment; other things being equal, higher ROI and RI are desirable. However, for evaluating managers of divisions, both ROI and RI have drawbacks, depending on how the results for a division are interpreted. The critical issue is the standard used for comparison. With what should we compare a division's results? Several bases for comparison are available, including comparisons among divisions within the company, with historical results in the same division, with industry averages, and with budgets.

INTERNAL RANKING

Ranking divisions within the company in terms of ROI and RI provides insight into the relative contributions of the divisions. But such a ranking should not be used to rank the managers of the respective divisions, because different kinds of divisions *should* have different ROIs. For example, ROI is generally higher for businesses (divisions or companies) operating in consumer markets than for those selling mostly to other industrial companies. Both ROI and RI should be higher for divisions taking on high risks. (For example, a division in plant genetics, a very risky field, should have a higher ROI than one making clothing.) The performance of a particular division manager must not be obscured by intracompany comparisons that ignore the nature of the division. A mediocre manager might be able to earn a respectable ROI in a division operating in a growing industry. On the other hand, an excellent manager might be doing a great job to maintain an ROI of 5 percent in a division operating in a declining industry. The responsibility of top managers is to decide which divisions the company should continue to operate and which it should fold or seek to sell. The business press and even the general interest press carries stories daily about companies disposing of divisions.

HISTORICAL COMPARISONS

Comparing current results with historical results in the same division overcomes differences in results stemming from divisions being in different industries. If there is a change in managers, the relative performance of two managers can also be compared. Historical comparisons also indicate relative improvement or decay. However, historical comparisons should be interpreted carefully. Historical experience can be good or bad and relative improvement might not be enough. A division now earning an 8 percent ROI is not doing well even if it has doubled ROI in the past few years. Conditions in the industry might change. If industry conditions improve, then a division should improve at more than its historical rate.

INDUSTRY AVERAGES

Comparing divisional results with industry averages can be useful because differences among divisions resulting from differences in industry do not influence the comparison. A division (and its manager) can be seen as better or worse than the companies with which it competes. Such comparisons present their own problems, however, because, as noted earlier, a division should be expected to earn a higher ROI than an entire company operating in the same industry. A division benefits from being part of a larger organization. As the trend to diversification continues, it becomes increasingly difficult to find companies to which the performance of a single division can be compared.[7]

---

7 *Comparisons are difficult even if independent companies operate in the same industry. Such companies might also operate in other industries, or in different parts of the value chain, or follow different strategies. Chapter 18 points out how different accounting methods, such as LIFO-FIFO, affect comparisons.*

BUDGETS

Budgets developed with participation by divisional managers are valuable tools for assessing the performance of division managers. When managers participate and commit themselves to meeting budgeted goals, comparisons of actual and budgeted results are excellent comparisons for evaluation purposes. Exhibit 11-4 shows budgeted and actual statements of income and financial position for a division. Allocated costs are shown separately. The only assets shown are those controlled by the division's manager. The exhibit also shows why budgeted and actual ROI were not the same. The division earned more profit than budgeted, but its receivables and inventories climbed much higher than budgeted, resulting in a reduced ROI. This type of report gives more information than simple comparisons of ROI, RI, or both.

TRANSFER PRICES

A great deal of intracompany buying and selling occurs in many companies, which necessitates setting transfer prices. A segment of **Anheuser-Busch** is the third largest U.S. maker of aluminum cans, which it sells both internally and externally. **Sonoco**, a world-wide supplier of paper and packaging products, has a paper division that sells 80 percent of its output internally for conversion into packaging materials. Sonoco also manages 80,000 acres of timberland to supply its paper-making operation and to sell wood for furniture. The company uses market-related transfer prices.[8]

Exhibit 11-4   Divisional Performance Report (in millions of dollars)

	Budget	Actual	Variance
Sales	$ 573.0	$ 591.0	$ 18.0
Variable costs (perhaps detailed)	246.0	251.2	5.2
Contribution margin	$ 327.0	$ 339.8	$ 12.8
Direct fixed costs	140.0	141.4	1.4
Divisional profit	$ 187.0	$ 198.4	$ 11.4
Allocated costs	12.0	15.0	3.0
Profit	$ 175.0	$ 183.4	$ 8.4
Assets employed:			
Cash	$ 15.5	$ 17.0	$ 1.5
Receivables	110.0	141.0	31.0
Inventory	90.0	122.5	32.5
Fixed assets, net	450.0	453.4	3.4
Total assets employed	$ 665.5	$ 733.9	$ 68.4
ROI	26.3%	25.0%	12.3%

---

8 *Sonoco annual report, 1994, 14-15, 37.*

PRICING POLICIES

Transfer prices are important because they are revenues to the selling division and costs to the buying division and therefore affect divisional performance. We know from Chapter 10 that changes in transfer prices do not, in themselves, affect total company profit. Total profit is affected only if individual managers change their operations because of a change in transfer prices. But because of their *potential* for encouraging actions that might not be in the interest of the total company, transfer prices are important factors in divisional performance measurement. The following examples explore some implications of several transfer-pricing policies.

1. *Actual cost with or without a markup for the selling division.* We know from Chapter 10 that basing transfer prices on actual costs is unwise. The selling manager has no incentive to keep costs down. Worse, a price that is actual costs plus a percentage markup gives the selling manager more profit the higher costs go. The buying manager would naturally object that costs (and hence reported performance) are adversely affected.

2. *Budgeted cost, with or without a markup.* This method does not reward the selling manager if costs go up and actually encourages the selling manager to keep costs down. If there is a markup, the selling division can earn a profit. The buying manager appreciates not having cost inefficiencies passed on from the selling division but prefers no markup at all. Thus, discussions center on budgeted cost and markup percentages.

3. *Market-based prices.* This method is generally considered the best. It puts both the buying and selling managers on an independent basis, provided that they are free to buy or sell on the outside as well as within the company. One difficulty in using this policy is that outside market prices might not exist, or the prices that are available might not be representative. For example, available market prices might reflect relatively small transactions, whereas the divisions deal in very large quantities. Under such circumstances, buying managers might contend that they should pay less because of the quantities bought.

    In many cases, the transfer price is less than the market price to reflect cost savings from dealing internally. For instance, suppose a division pays a 15 percent commission on outside sales, none on inside sales. The transfer price should be 85 percent of the market price to reflect that saving. Selling divisions will often accept less than market price when they are operating below capacity, just as Chapter 5 showed a company might accept a less-than-normal price on a special order.

4. *Incremental cost.* Such prices are theoretically best *from the company's viewpoint when the selling division is operating below capacity.* The manager of the selling division will object to this price because it yields no profit to that division. Incremental cost can be as low as the variable cost of the goods or services, but might also include fixed costs that increase as a result of the transfer.

5. *Negotiated prices.* This method allows managers to bargain with each other and alleviates some problems that arise with other methods. A

manager who is dissatisfied with the offered price can buy or sell in the outside market, if it exists. Some see as a disadvantage that managers with better negotiating skills will tend to prevail. Others contend that negotiating skills are part of effective management.

Despite our suggestion that market-based transfer prices are generally best, we hasten to point out that the autonomous division manager who is setting a transfer price must use judgment and *understand the information available.* Like the managers making decisions discussed in earlier chapters, division managers must understand the concepts of contribution margin and incremental cost, and the implications of those concepts in light of the available alternatives. For example, Chapter 5 presented the analysis underlying a decision whether to accept a special order at less than the normal selling price. Critical to that analysis was whether the company had an alternative use for the facilities and whether the additional contribution margin covered incremental fixed costs. The same principles apply when a division manager has to propose a selling price for an order from another division. When the selling division has excess capacity, its results (and the manager's reported performance) will be improved if the price is greater than variable costs and incremental fixed costs. When the division's capacity can be fully used without taking the order, the selling manager should demand the market price less any costs saved by dealing internally, such as commissions.

In summary, if treated as heads of autonomous units, division managers should be free to offer transfer prices that reflect the cost structures of their divisions and the available alternatives. When the division is operating at full capacity, with sales to customers outside the company, a market-based transfer price is nearly always best. When the selling division is operating below capacity, a transfer price that falls between incremental cost and market price is usually best. Hence, division managers must understand the cost structures of their divisions and use that knowledge in setting transfer prices. If they have the freedom to negotiate prices, the resulting actions are likely to be in the company's best interests. To see why this is true, let us consider an example.

ILLUSTRATIONS

Division A buys 6,000 units of a component for its major product from an outside supplier for $13 per unit. The component is very much like a product made by Division B, another division of the same company, and the manager of A has asked B to supply the item at $13. Division B now sells its output to outside customers at $15. The budgeted income statement for the coming year for Division B is as follows:

Budgeted Income Statement, Division B	
Sales, 10,000 × $15	$150,000
Variable costs, 10,000 × $7	70,000
Contribution margin	$ 80,000
Fixed costs	30,000
Income	$ 50,000

Let us assume, for simplicity, that Division B could make the component needed by A with no change in fixed costs and with the same variable cost per unit that it has now. How should the manager of B respond to the requested transfer price? What price serves the best interests of the divisions and of the company?

Suppose that Division B has capacity of 11,000 units, and cannot increase its outside sales above 10,000 units. If it accepts Division A's business, it loses 5,000 units of outside sales. (Capacity of 11,000 less 6,000 to Division A leaves 5,000 units available for sales to outsiders, a reduction of 5,000 from present sales of 10,000 units.) Following is a budgeted income statement for the division if a transfer takes place at $13, the price that A now pays to an outside supplier.

Budgeted Income Statement, Division B (Component Sold Internally for $13)	
Sales to outsiders, 5,000 × $15	$ 75,000
Sales to A, 6,000 × $13	78,000
Total sales	$153,000
Variable costs, 11,000 × $7	77,000
Contribution margin	$ 76,000
Fixed costs	30,000
Income	$ 46,000

Because Division A is already paying $13 to an outside supplier, purchasing the component internally for that price will not change Division A's income and its manager is indifferent to the source of supply. The manager of Division B will not accept the $13 price, because profit will decline by $4,000 (from $50,000 to $46,000). Is the manager's decision not to make the sale also in the best interest of the company as a whole?

From the standpoint of the company, the decision is a make-or-buy decision such as you studied in Chapter 5. That is, if Division B makes the component and sells it to Division A, the component is made by the company; alternatively, the component could be bought from an outside supplier. We can, therefore, look at the decision from the point of view of the company as we did in Chapter 5.

Lost contribution margin from outside sales by Division B [5,000 × ($15 - $7)]	$40,000
Savings of variable costs paid to outside supplier [6,000 × ($13 - $7)]	36,000
Loss to company	$(4,000)

The change in the company's income (a $4,000 decline) equals the combined changes in the incomes of its divisions (no change for A, a $4,000 decline for B).

Now suppose that Division B can produce 20,000 (rather than 11,000) units, and it can still sell only 10,000 units to outsiders. If fixed costs will not be affected by producing additional units for sale to Division A, Division B's results will improve by selling to A at any price greater than B's variable cost of $7 per unit. For example, a budgeted income statement for Division B if the transfer takes place at as little as $8 per unit follows.

Budgeted Income Statement, Division B
(Component Sold Internally for $8)

Sales to outsiders, 10,000 × $15	$150,000
Sales to A, 6,000 × $8	48,000
Total sales	$198,000
Variable costs, 16,000 × $7	112,000
Contribution margin	$ 86,000
Fixed costs	30,000
Income	$ 56,000

The manager of Division A will be happy to accept an $8 price, for that division's income will increase by $30,000 [6,000 units × ($13 - $8)]. Division B's manager should accept the $8 price because that division's income will improve by $6,000, the $1 contribution margin ($8 - $7) on the 6,000 additional units. If you understood the previous example, you should see that the company's top managers also want the transfer to take place. The company's total income will increase by $36,000, the combined changes in the incomes of its divisions ($30,000 + $6,000). Analyzing the situation as a make-or-buy decision, the company saves $36,000 in variable costs [6,000 × ($13 - $7)] by making the unit rather than buying it outside.

It would be unfortunate if the manager of Division B didn't understand the division's cost structure and considered the $8 price to be unacceptable. For example, suppose the manager had reviewed the original budgeted income statement and concluded that the cost was $10 per unit (variable costs of $70,000 plus fixed costs of $30,000, divided by the 10,000 units of planned production). The decision not to sell at $8 would have been, as indicated earlier, detrimental to Division A, to the company, and to Division B.

As long as Division B has excess capacity, any price less than the market price of $13 and greater than B's variable costs of $7 is advantageous to both divisions and to the company as a whole. Division A acquires the component at a lower price than it would have to pay to an outside supplier. Division B gains some contribution margin. And the company benefits from having a lower total cost of the product (the $7 variable cost from Division B rather than the $13 outside price). Indeed, even a transfer price of $7 should be acceptable. Division B loses nothing and could gain by being able to retain good workers who might otherwise have left the area for other jobs, or by keeping good relations with suppliers who might be concerned about the low levels of B's orders for materials.

So long as the company gains from an internal exchange, the managers of the divisions should be able to agree on a price because they can both benefit from the exchange. The total gain to the company is also the total gain to the two divisions; the transfer price simply allocates the gain between the two divisions.

In summary, the major issue from the standpoint of the company as a whole is not the choice of a transfer price but whether the transfer should take place at all.

- The company faces a make-or-buy decision.
- For the buying division, the question is simply which supplier (sister division or outside company) offers the lower price (assuming equal quality, delivery schedules, etc.).

• The selling division faces a special-order decision, as in Chapter 5; the concern is whether the contribution margin from selling inside offsets the loss, if any, of contribution margin from lost outside sales.

If the transfer is profitable from the standpoint of the company as a whole, the best transfer-pricing system is one that prompts the managers to make a decision in the best interests of the company as a whole. Thus, setting transfer prices requires judgment and a full understanding of the circumstances and of the accounting information available.

MULTINATIONAL COMPANIES—SPECIAL PROBLEMS

Companies that operate in several countries are called *multinationals.* Some multinationals operate divisions in foreign countries, others set up separate, legal corporations. Whether a division or a subsidiary corporation, a segment that operates in a particular country does business in the currency of that country, pays taxes in that currency, and reports its financial results in that currency. Many U.S. companies are multinationals, as are many foreign companies such as **British Petroleum, Toyota,** and **Unilever**. Multinationals face special problems related both to evaluating performance and to transfer pricing.

Multinational companies have more complicated reporting needs than domestic companies. Besides the currency translation problems discussed in earlier chapters, significant cultural and language barriers and little or no on-site supervision of operations by home-office managers present serious problems in evaluating performance. These factors contribute to a heavy reporting load. **Eastman Kodak** states that its managers receive 200 financial reports containing a total of 1,300 documents per year. Continuing advances in communications technology such as satellites and the Internet make reporting easier, but do not reduce its volume.

With respect to evaluation, multinationals must cope with changes in exchange rates, which are the relationships of foreign currencies to U.S. dollars. One problem for performance evaluation is that the local manager in the foreign country does business in the foreign currency, but the multinational cares about the results in its home currency (dollars for U.S. multinationals). The trouble is that the local manager and the division can look good or bad in U.S. dollars simply because of changes in exchange rates, over which the local manager has no control.

Consider the following division's monthly income statement in Xs, the currency of country X.

	Division X
Sales	X3,000
Expenses	2,000
Income in local currency	X1,000

If an X was worth $10 during the month, the division would also show $10,000 income for the month. Suppose that next month the division does exactly the same business and has the same income statement, but that the value of an X drops to $8. The division then shows $8,000 income, a 20 percent drop from last month even though it did the same business. Evaluating the manager's (or the division's) performance on the basis of reports using the currency of the home country penalizes the division and the manager for a decline in the exchange rate (and gives undue credit when the rate rises). Of course, one factor that influences exchange rates is the relative inflation in the two countries and managers should consider inflation when making decisions. So the results do have some validity. A drop in the exchange rate for Xs from $10 to $8 suggests that X experienced, or anticipates, higher inflation than does the United States. If Division X could only maintain its position (sales of X3,000, profit of X1,000) during inflation, it is actually falling behind. The question of translating foreign currency also vexes financial accounting.

Evaluating the performance of foreign units (and their managers) can also be complicated by legal, cultural, and philosophical differences that direct attention to special areas or restrict a local manager's actions. For example, some Latin American countries limit staffing by foreigners, and Japanese companies are not inclined to employ foreign nationals in management positions. Some European countries virtually outlaw layoffs.[9]

Transfer-pricing problems for multinationals are equally troublesome. In a 1995 study, **Ernst & Young**, a major international accounting and consulting firm, showed transfer-pricing issues to be the leading concern of multinationals. Because different countries have different income tax rates, multinationals want to show higher profits in low-tax countries and lower profits in high-tax countries. Doing so is sometimes termed *income shifting* and transfer prices are an ideal vehicle. For example, suppose that Division A buys a product from Division B. The divisions are in different countries, but both use the same currency, denoted as T. Data are as follows:

Selling price of Division A's product	T100
Variable cost, excluding transfer price	T20
Tax rate in Division A's country	20%
Variable cost of Division B's product	T30
Tax rate in Division B's country	60%

The following income statements show the effects, including income taxes, of transferring 1,000 units of Division B's product at T30 and at T60.

	Division A	Division B
Sales (1,000 × T100)	T100,000	
(1,000 × T30)		T 30,000
Variable cost [1,000 × (T20 + T30)]	50,000	
(1,000 × T30)		30,000
Contribution margin	T 50,000	T 0
Income tax at 20% and 60%	T 10,000	T 0

	Division A	Division B
Sales (1,000 × T100)	T100,000	
(1,000 × T60)		T 60,000
Variable cost [1,000 × (T20 + T60)]	80,000	
(1,000 × T30)		30,000
Contribution margin	T 20,000	T 30,000
Income tax at 20% and 60%	T 4,000	T 18,000

Total income taxes are only T10,000 at the lower price, T22,000 at the higher price. (The corporation minimizes its total taxes if Division B gives the product to Division A, but the authorities in Division B's country would certainly not permit that.) If the company forces Division B to sell at a low price, it saves considerable taxes, but penalizes the performance of Division B and its manager and enhances the reported performance of Division A and its manager. Dictating transfer prices also reduces the sense of independence and autonomy that managers value.

The income-shifting potential of transfer prices is not limited to sales of product. As you know from Chapter 10, companies use transfer prices for services, and multinationals often charge foreign (and domestic) units a management fee or allocate some corporate costs to those units. A multinational could therefore shift income from a foreign country to the home country through such charges. Obviously, the temptation is to charge higher fees to units in high-tax countries, lower fees to those in low-tax countries. Here again, the performance of local managers is affected by a corporate decision.

Similar problems arise with import duties, or tariffs, which are typically based on values reported for incoming goods. If one division is transferring goods to another division located in a high-tariff country, a low transfer price reduces the tariff.

Besides the problems associated with portraying performance, some of the practices described are, if arbitrarily imposed, unethical and in some countries illegal. Various government authorities such as those responsible for collecting income taxes in the various countries will try to ensure that artificially high or low transfer prices are disallowed and that corporate charges actually reflect the services provided at the corporate level. Transfer prices and corporate fees are also of interest to the authorities in countries having significant currency restrictions. For example, for many years Brazil had severe restrictions on foreign companies taking out of the country profits made by local operating units (called *repatriation of profits*). Its extreme currency restriction policy, which permitted currency to leave the country only in payment for goods, might have been influenced by the ethically debatable efforts of some multinationals to repatriate profits through management fees or allocations of corporate costs.

Transfer pricing entered the public arena in the 1992 presidential campaign when President Clinton claimed that foreign-based multinationals were avoiding over $11 billion in annual taxes by manipulating transfer prices. Early in 1993 the IRS issued new regulations that required companies to use pricing methods that accurately reflected business conditions, such as assets employed, functions performed, and risks taken by the subsidiaries or divisions. These regulations allowed more flexibility than older proposals that required that profits on intracompany business approximate profits on transactions with outsiders. Most authorities accept transfer prices that clearly represent arms-length transactions, those that would be the same if the buyer and seller were unrelated companies.

SUMMARY

Evaluating investment centers requires determining which revenues, costs, and investments the manager can control. Commonly used performance measures are return on investment (ROI) and residual income (RI), along with its variant, economic value added (EVA). ROI is the most popular measure, but RI is advantageous from a behavioral point of view. Use of either criterion requires answering difficult questions about which items to include in divisional income and investment and opinions differ about how some items should be measured.

Intracompany sales and purchases require transfer prices. Such prices can encourage managers to take actions that harm the company as a whole. However, managers who are free to negotiate transfer prices are likely to make decisions that benefit both the divisions and the company. Companies with divisions in countries using a different currency have special problems in evaluating the performance of those divisions. Such companies also have problems in setting transfer prices that take into consideration the different tax structures and currency restrictions of the countries in which their divisions operate.

KEY TERMS

business units (493)
decentralized (493)
divisional income (497)
divisional investment (497)
economic value added (EVA) (500)
investment turnover (497)

minimum required (desired, target) rate of return (498)
residual income (RI) (498)
return on investment (ROI) (497)
return on sales (ROS) (497)

KEY FORMULAS

$$\text{Return on investment (ROI)} = \frac{\text{divisional income}}{\text{divisional investment}}$$

$$\text{Return on investment (ROI)} = \frac{\text{income}}{\text{sales}} \times \frac{\text{sales}}{\text{investment}}$$

$$\text{Return on sales (ROS)} = \frac{\text{income}}{\text{sales}}$$

$$\text{Investment turnover} = \frac{\text{sales}}{\text{investment}}$$

$$\text{Residual income (RI)} = \text{income} - (\text{investment} \times \text{target ROI})$$

REVIEW PROBLEM

The manager of the Bartram Division of United Products Company has given you the following information related to budgeted operations for the coming year, 19X5.

Sales (100,000 units at $5)	$500,000
Variable costs at $2 per unit	200,000
Contribution margin at $3 per unit	$300,000
Fixed costs	120,000
Divisional profit	$180,000
Divisional investment	$800,000

The minimum required ROI is 20%.

Required
Consider each part independently.

1. Determine the division's expected ROI using the expanded second formula.
2. Determine the division's expected RI.
3. The manager has the opportunity to sell an additional 10,000 units at $4.50. Variable cost per unit would be the same as budgeted, but fixed costs would increase by $10,000. Additional investment of $50,000 would also be required. If the manager accepts the special order, by how much and in what direction will RI change?
4. Bartram's budgeted volume includes 20,000 units that Bartram expects to sell to the Jeffers Division of United Products. However, the manager of Jeffers Division has received an offer from an outside company to supply the 20,000 units at $4.20. If Bartram Division does not meet the $4.20 price, Jeffers will buy from the outside company. Bartram could save $25,000 in fixed costs if it dropped its volume from 100,000 to 80,000 units.
    (a) Determine Bartram's profit assuming that it meets the $4.20 price.
    (b) Determine Bartram's profit if it fails to meet the price and loses the sales.
    (c) Determine the effect on the company's total profit if Bartram meets the $4.20 price.
    (d) Determine the effect on the company's total profit if Bartram does not meet the price.

ANSWER TO REVIEW PROBLEM
1. 22.5%

$$\frac{income}{sales} \times \frac{sales}{investment} = \frac{\$180,000}{\$500,000} \times \frac{\$500,000}{\$800,000} = 0.36 \times 0.625 = 0.225 = 22.5\%$$

2. $20,000

Profit budgeted	$180,000
Minimum required return ($800,000 × 20%)	160,000
Residual income budgeted	$ 20,000

3. RI would increase by $5,000. This can be determined either by considering the changes in the variables or by preparing new data for total operations. Considering only the changes:

Increase in sales (10,000 × $4.50)	$45,000
Increase in variable costs (10,000 × $2)	20,000
Increase in contribution margin	$25,000
Increase in fixed costs	10,000
Increase in profit	$15,000
Increase in minimum required return ($50,000 × 20%)	10,000
Increase in RI	$ 5,000

A new income statement and calculation of new total RI shows the following.

Sales ($500,000 + $45,000)	$545,000
Variable costs (110,000 × $2)	220,000
Contribution margin	$325,000
Fixed costs ($120,000 + $10,000)	130,000
Divisional profit	$195,000
Minimum required return ($850,000 × 20%)	170,000
Residual income	$ 25,000

The new $25,000 RI is $5,000 more than RI based on budgeted operations without the special order.

4. (a) $164,000. If Bartram accepts the lower price, revenue (and hence contribution margin) will be reduced by $0.80 per unit for 20,000 units. With no change in fixed costs, the $16,000 drop in contribution margin means a similar drop in profit. An income statement under the new assumption would show the following.

Sales [($5 × 80,000) + ($4.20 × 20,000)]	$484,000
Variable costs ($2 × 100,000)	200,000
Contribution margin	$284,000
Fixed costs	120,000
Divisional profit	$164,000

(b) $145,000. If Bartram does not accept the lower price, the full contribution margin from sales to Jeffers will be lost. The avoidable fixed costs will be saved. The contribution margin lost would be $60,000 (20,000 units at $3), and the fixed costs saved would be $25,000. Hence, divisional profit would drop $35,000 ($60,000 - $25,000) to $145,000 ($180,000 budgeted profit - $35,000).

    The answer could also be arrived at by reference to the income statement prepared in item a. The contribution margin lost would be $44,000

(20,000 x the lower contribution margin of $2.20), with fixed costs savings of $25,000. The net decline in profits would be $19,000 ($44,000 - $25,000), which, when subtracted from the $164,000 total profit shown in the income statement in item a, equals $145,000.

A third, somewhat longer, approach to the problem would be to prepare an income statement assuming the sales to Jeffers are not made. This approach, too, shows a new divisional profit of $145,000.

Sales ($5 × 80,000)	$400,000
Variable costs ($2 × 80,000)	160,000
Contribution margin	$240,000
Fixed costs ($120,000 - $25,000)	95,000
Divisional profit	$145,000

(c) If you concluded that the company's total profit would change as a result of the change in the transfer price, you have forgotten a very important point made in Chapter 10. Changes in transfer prices do not, in themselves, change total profit. Only if changes in transfer prices cause managers to change their operations and actions can total profit change. In this situation, the manager of Bartram Division had planned to sell to Jeffers Division and the income statement was budgeted accordingly. If he accepts the lower price, he will still be selling to Jeffers. Similarly, the manager of Jeffers Division had planned to buy from Bartram Division. He will still buy from Bartram Division, but at a lower price. The only thing that has changed is the transfer price. The reduction in the profit of Bartram Division (because of the lower contribution margin) will be exactly offset by the increased profit of Jeffers Division (because of that division's lower costs). Hence, the company's total profit will not change.

(d) The company will lose $19,000 if Jeffers buys from an outside supplier. From the point of view of the company as a whole, the decision is a make-or-buy decision such as was discussed in Chapter 5. Consider, therefore, the two possible decisions, from the company's point of view.

	Decision	
	Buy from Outside Supplier	Make Product Inside (Bartram)
Purchase price (20,000 × $4.20)	$84,000	
Variable cost to produce (20,000 × $2)		$40,000
Avoidable fixed costs		25,000
Costs of each decision	$84,000	$65,000

As this analysis indicates, the decision to produce internally carries a $19,000 advantage.

Another approach to this problem is to consider the profits of the individual divisions and how those profits would differ from originally budgeted profits if a purchase were made from an outside supplier. If Jeffers can buy at $4.20 from either source, its profits will increase $16,000 (20,000 units × $0.80 saved) over what has been budgeted with an original transfer price of $5.00. For this reason, the manager of Jeffers would be eager to obtain the lower price. Now consider the position of the manager of Bartram Division, who has budgeted profits of $180,000. The profit of his division will decline $35,000 (budgeted profits of $180,000 - $145,000 profits, computed in item b) if he does not get the order from Jeffers. For this reason, Bartram's manager should not want to lose the order from Jeffers. Putting these two changes in divisional profits together, we see that there will be a $19,000 loss (a $16,000 gain by Jeffers and a $35,000 loss by Bartram).

The important factor in this second approach is that if each division's manager evaluates his own situation properly, each will make a decision consistent with the good of the company as a whole. The manager of Jeffers Division will wisely seek the lower price because it will increase his profits. The manager of Bartram Division will wisely consider the lower price because failing to do so will decrease his profit.

ASSIGNMENT MATERIAL

QUESTIONS FOR DISCUSSION

11-1   *Value menu*   McDonalds, Pizza Hut, and various other restaurant chains have announced some variant of the "value menu" idea, whereby consumers get more food value for their money. How will these programs likely affect the margins and turnovers of the restaurants? Can you tell how the programs will affect ROI?

**11-2   *Alternative accounting methods*   **Explain how various inventory cost flow assumptions (last-in first-out, first-in first-out, weighted average) can affect the measurement of return on investment for a division.

**11-3   *Product-line reporting*   **Financial analysts often express the desire that companies publish annual reports broken down by division or principal lines of activity. They have said they would like to see financial statements broken down by products, or perhaps separated into wholesale and retail business, or maybe separated into government and commercial business. What problems might arise from attempting to fulfill this desire for additional information? What recommendations might you make?

**11-4   *Types of responsibility centers*   **Assume that the following multiple-choice question appeared on an examination covering this chapter and that the instructions were to select the single best answer.

Which of the following is true?

(a) All investment centers qualify as profit centers, but not all profit centers qualify as investment centers.
(b) All profit centers qualify as investment centers, but not all investment centers qualify as profit centers.
(c) All cost centers qualify as profit centers, but not all profit centers qualify as cost centers.
(d) All cost centers qualify as investment centers, but not all investment centers qualify as cost centers.

Forced to make a choice, most students would correctly select answer (a). If, however, only the first alternative were presented and the instructions were to indicate whether the statement was true or false, some of those same students might decide that the statement was false. What line of reasoning would those students present to justify their answer and how would you respond to their position?

11-5   *Whirlpool's operating results*   Whirlpool's 1994 annual report reveals that it sells 19% of its output to **Sears** under private label, the rest under the Whirlpool name. What effects might the Sears sales have on margin, turnover, and ROI?

EXERCISES

**11-6   *RI, ROI, and CVP analysis*   The following data refer to the PID division of MMC Corporation.

Average selling price	$25
Average variable cost	$15
Total fixed costs	$400,000
Investment	$800,000

Required
Answer each of the following questions independently.
1. If the manager of DCB desires a 20% ROI, how many units must she sell?
2. If the division sells 60,000 units, what will ROI be?
3. The minimum desired ROI is 15%. If the division sells 60,000 units, what is RI?
4. The manager desires a 25% ROI and wishes to sell 50,000 units. What price must she charge?
5. The minimum desired ROI is 20% and RI is $30,000. What are sales, in units?

**11-7   *Comparison of ROI and RI, investment decisions*   The manager of Technic Division of Microprod, Inc. has developed the following schedule of investment opportunities. The schedule shows the amount to be invested and the expected annual profit. Currently, investment is $8,000,000 and profits are $2,000,000.

Investment Opportunity	Amount of Investment	Annual Profit
A	$ 600,000	$ 90,000
B	700,000	200,000
C	1,000,000	230,000
D	1,100,000	290,000
E	1,200,000	170,000

Required
1. The division manager wishes to maximize ROI. (a) Which projects will he select? (b) What ROI will he earn?
2. The manager wishes to maximize RI. Determine which projects he will select and the RI he will earn if the minimum desired ROI is (a) 15% and (b) 25%.
3. Assuming that the ROI on each project approximates the IRR discussed in this chapter and in Chapter 8, which policy (maximizing ROI or maximizing RI) is

better for the company? Assume that the minimum desired ROI equals cost of capital.

11-8   *Basic transfer pricing* Wharton Division of Turner Industries manufactures furniture. Data on a sofa the division makes follows.

Selling price		$700
Variable costs:		
Fabric	$150	
Other variable costs	250	
Total variable costs		400
Contribution margin		$300
Expected volume		4,000 units

Wharton buys the fabric from an outside supplier. The manager of Wharton learns that Seagrave Division of Turner makes a fabric that meets her requirements. Seagrave sells the fabric to outside customers for $180. Variable cost to Seagrave is $100. Wharton's manager offers to buy the fabric at $120.

Required
1. Seagrave has plenty of capacity to serve its outside customers and meet Wharton's needs. If Wharton buys 4,000 units from Seagrave at $120:
   (a) What will happen to Seagrave's income?
   (b) What will happen to Wharton's income?
   (c) What will happen to Turner Industries' income?
2. Redo item 1 assuming that Seagrave has no excess capacity and will lose outside sales if it supplies Wharton.

11-9   *Product line evaluation* "My division as a whole is evaluated on ROI and RI, so why shouldn't I use those measures to evaluate my product lines?" The speaker was Lynn Cathcart, manager of the Household Products Division of General Enterprises, Inc. Cathcart provided the following data regarding the three major lines that the division handles.

	Cleaners	Disinfectants	Insect Sprays
Margin	15%	18%	20%
Turnover	3 times	2 times	2.5 times
Annual sales, millions	$60	$30	$40

Required
1. For each product line, determine ROI, total investment, and annual profit.
2. The minimum required ROI is 30%. Determine RI for each product line.

11-10   *Basic transfer pricing* The Games Division of Toys-and-Stuff Inc. uses 500,000 batteries per year for its products. Currently, Games buys the batteries from an outside supplier for $1.40 each. Power Division of Toys-and-Stuff makes batteries of the type used by Games Division and sells them at $1.50 each. Power's variable cost to produce each battery is $0.90. Power Division has ample manufacturing capacity to serve its regular customers and also meet the needs of Games Division.

Required

Answer each of the following questions independently.

1. If Power agrees to supply the batteries at $1.20, what will be the effect on the incomes of each of the divisions and on Toys-and-Stuff as a whole?
2. Why might Power's manager accept an offer as low as $0.90 per battery from Games?
3. Repeat item 1 assuming that Power has no excess capacity and so would lose outside sales if it supplies the batteries to Games, and then find the lowest per-battery price that Power's manager would accept for the 500,000 batteries.
4. Repeat item 1 assuming that Power has only 200,000 units of excess capacity and so would lose outside sales of 300,000 units if it supplied the 500,000 batteries needed by Games.
5. Power again has 200,000 units of excess capacity. What is the lowest price that Power can accept for 500,000 units without reducing its income?

11-11   *Procter & Gamble's ROI components*   The following information comes from **Procter & Gamble's** 1994 annual report.

	Laundry and Cleaning	Food and Beverages	Health Care
Sales	$10,224	$6,507	$3,025
Operating profit	1,695	736	360
Identifiable assets	5,375	5,511	3,321

Required

1. Compute ROI for each segment, using the ratios of ROS and investment turn-over.
2. Assume each segment could increase its ROS by one percentage point with the same sales as are currently shown. Recompute ROI and comment on the differences between the results here and those in item 1.

 11-12   *ROI, RI, and CVP analysis*   The following data refer to the operations of Ross Division of Hunter Enterprises.

Selling price per unit	$40
Variable cost per unit	$15
Annual fixed costs	$800,000
Investment	$1,500,000

Required

1. Determine the number of units that must be sold to achieve a 25% ROI.
2. The manager has been approached by a company that wishes to buy 10,000 units per year at a reduced price. Current volume is 50,000 units. Accepting the special order will increase fixed costs by $30,000 and investment by $80,000.
   (a) Determine ROI without the special order.
   (b) Determine the lowest price at which the manager can sell the additional 10,000 units without reducing ROI.
3. Suppose that the minimum required ROI is 20%.
   (a) Determine the change in RI that will occur if the special order goes at the price you computed in item 2 (b).
   (b) Determine the lowest price that will not reduce RI.

11-13 ROI, RI, and EVA for Warner-Lambert The Chewing Gum and Mint Division of **Warner-Lambert** had the following results, in millions of dollars, in 1994.

Profit	$264
Investment	$872

Required
1. Determine ROI and RI if the minimum required return is 20%.
2. Warner-Lambert faced a 35% income tax rate. Cost of capital is 13%. Determine EVA.

11-14 Basic RI relationships Hughes Division had RI of $3 million, investment of $25 million, and asset turnover of two times. The minimum required ROI was 20%.

Required
1. Determine Hughes's sales, profit, and ROS.
2. Determine the ROS that Hughes needs to raise its RI to $4 million, holding sales and investment constant.
3. With the ROS calculated in item 1, determine the sales required to earn $4 million RI, holding investment constant.

11-15 Transfer pricing—increased costs and sacrificed sales Division A of ABC Inc. has a capacity of 100,000 units and expects the following results for 19X8.

Sales (80,000 units at $7)	$ 560,000
Variable costs (at $3)	(240,000)
Fixed costs	(260,000)
Income	$ 60,000

Division B, another division of ABC, currently purchases 25,000 units of a part for one of its products from an outside supplier at $7 per unit. B's manager believes she could use a minor variation of A's product instead, and offers to buy the units from A at $6. The variation desired by B would cost A an additional $1 per unit and would increase A's annual fixed costs by $12,000. A's manager agrees to the deal offered by B's manager.

Required
Determine the amount and direction of the effect of the deal on the 19X8 income for Division A, for Division B, and for ABC as a whole.

11-16 Transfer prices and decisions Green Inc. consists of two divisions, Armonk and Braser. Armonk makes only one product, a chemical compound, at a variable manufacturing cost of $2.50 per gallon. The division sells both to outsiders (at $5 per gallon) and to Braser (at $4 per gallon). Braser spends $2 per gallon converting what it buys from Armonk into a product that it sells to outsiders at $9 per gallon. The budgeted income statements for Green and its divisions follow.

	Armonk	Braser	Green
Sales to outsiders:			
Armonk (200,000 × $5)	$1,000,000		$1,000,000
Braser (60,000 × $9)		$540,000	540,000
Sales to Braser			
60,000 × $4	240,000		240,000
Total	$1,240,000	$540,000	$1,780,000
Variable costs:			
$2.50 per gallon × 260,000	$ 650,000		$ 650,000
$4 paid to Armonk × 60,000		$240,000	240,000
$2 per gallon × 60,000		120,000	120,000
Total variable costs	$ 650,000	$360,000	$1,010,000
Contribution margin	$ 590,000	$180,000	$ 770,000
Direct fixed costs	300,000	120,000	420,000
Division profit	$ 290,000	$ 60,000	$ 350,000
Common costs			130,000
Income			$ 220,000

An outside supplier has offered to sell Braser 60,000 gallons of the needed chemical compound at $3.50 per gallon. Neither the outsider supplier nor Armonk is willing to supply anything less than Braser's total needs of 60,000 gallons.

Required
Answer each of the following questions independently.

1. If Armonk reduces the transfer price to $3.50 and Braser continues to buy from Armonk, what will happen to the incomes of each of the divisions and of Green Inc. as a whole?
2. If Armonk refuses to reduce the transfer price and Braser buys outside, what will happen to the incomes of each of the divisions and of Green Inc. as a whole? (Assume Armonk cannot increase its sales to outside customers.)
3. Assume that Armonk's capacity is 260,000 gallons and that, if Braser doesn't buy from Armonk, Armonk can increase its outside sales by 45,000 gallons. Should Armonk reduce its price to meet that offered by the outside supplier? (Consider the question from both Armonk's and Green's points of view.)

11-17   *Range of transfer price*   Microtec Division of CR Industries makes a microchip that it presently sells only to outside companies. The Consumer Products Division of CR is bringing out a new oven that requires a sophisticated chip and has approached Microtec for a quotation. Microtec sells the chip for $47 and incurs variable costs of $12. It has excess capacity. The Consumer Products Division can acquire a suitable chip from outside the company for $41.

Required
1. Determine the advantage to CR Industries as a whole for the Consumer Products Division to buy the chip from Microtec, as opposed to buying it outside.
2. Determine the minimum price that Microtec would accept for the chip.
3. Determine the maximum price that Consumer Products would pay Microtec for the chip.
4. How would your answers to each of the preceding items change if Microtec was working at capacity?

11-18   Basic ROI relationships   Gandolf Division of Nationwide Motors had sales of $30 million, ROI of 30%, and asset turnover of 3 times.

Required

1. Determine Gandolf's (a) investment, (b) profit, and (c) ROS.
2. Suppose that by reducing its investment, Gandolf could increase its asset turnover to four without affecting sales or income. What will its ROI be?

11-19   ROI and RI relationships   Fill in the blanks in the following schedule. Each case is independent of the others. In all cases, the minimum desired ROI is 20%.

	Case			
	A	B	C	D
Sales	$____	$ 400	$ 700	$ 400
Income	$____	$____	$____	$____
Investment	$ 300	$ 200	$____	$____
Margin	8 %	____ %	6 %	15 %
Turnover	3 times	____ times	____ times	____ times
ROI	____ %	____ %	____ %	30 %
RI	$____	$ 15	$ 22	$____

11-20   Relationships   Fill in the blanks for each of the following independent situations. In all cases the minimum required ROI is 20%.

	(a) Income	(b) Investment	(c) ROI	(d) RI
1.	____	$20,000	30%	____
2.	____	$25,000	____	$1,000
3.	$4,000	____	____	$ 500
4.	$5,400	____	30%	____
5.	____	____	30%	$3,000

11-21   Transfer prices—pushing capacity   For several years, ABC Division of Slavic Corp. has been selling some (currently 8,000 units) of its product to XYZ Division of the same company at a price slightly below that charged to outside customers. Budgeted income statements for the two divisions follow.

	ABC Division	XYZ Division
Sales of ABC:		
To outsiders (80,000 at $6)	$480,000	
To XYZ (8,000 at $5)	40,000	
Sales of XYZ:		
To outsiders (8,000 at $70)		$560,000
Total sales	$520,000	$560,000
Variable costs:		
ABC (88,000 at $2)	$176,000	
XYZ (8,000 at $5)		$ 40,000
XYZ (8,000 at $35)		280,000
Total variable costs	$176,000	$320,000
Contribution margin	$344,000	$240,000
Direct fixed costs	250,000	95,000
Divisional profit	$ 94,000	$145,000

XYZ Division has received an offer from an outside supplier to sell 8,000 units such as those currently being purchased from ABC for $4.50.

Required

1. Assume that ABC's manager refuses to meet the outside supplier's price and cannot increase outside sales.
   (a) How will ABC's profit be affected if XYZ purchases the units from the outside supplier?
   (b) How will total profit of Slavic Corp. be affected if XYZ buys the units from the outside supplier?
2. Assume that ABC's manager doesn't want to meet the price offered by the outside supplier because she believes that she's already giving XYZ a bargain. She says that meeting XYZ's needs is stretching her factory's capacity and that, while she couldn't make outside sales beyond the current level (80,000), her per-unit variable cost would drop to $1.85 for all units and her fixed costs would drop by $18,000 if she didn't sell to XYZ. How will total profit of Slavic Corp. be affected if XYZ accepts the offer from the outside supplier to provide 8,000 units at $4.50?

11-22   Transfer prices for service work   The service department of an automobile dealership does two general kinds of work: (1) work on cars brought in by customers and (2) work on used cars purchased by the dealership for resale. The service manager is often evaluated on the basis of gross profit or some other dollar measure. Because of the evaluation measure, the prices to be charged to the used-car manager for reconditioning and repair work on cars bought for resale are particularly important. The used-car manager is also likely to be evaluated by his profits. Thus, he wants service work done as cheaply as possible. The service manager naturally wants the prices to be the same as those he charges outside customers.

Required

1. What possible transfer prices could be used, and what are their advantages and disadvantages?
2. What do you recommend?

 11-23   Review of Chapters 10 and 11   Selected information about the only two divisions of Major Corp. follows.

	Noble	Seneca
Sales	$3,200,000	$4,800,000
Income	480,000	320,000
Investment	2,000,000	1,600,000

Unallocated costs common to the two divisions are $200,000 per year. Assets (net of liabilities) that are not associated with either division are $600,000.

Required

Answer the following questions. Note: The answers to most questions do not depend on the answers to previous questions.

1. What is ROS for Noble Division?
2. What is investment turnover for Noble Division?
3. What is ROI for Noble Division?
4. What is ROI for the company as a whole?

5. What is RI for Seneca Division if Major's minimum required ROI is 12%?
6. Suppose Major's top managers decide to allocate common costs to its divisions on the basis of divisional sales.
   (a) Determine Seneca Division's ROI.
   (b) Determine the ROI for the company as a whole.
7. If Major's top managers decide to allocate common costs on the basis of divisional investment, what will ROI be for the company as a whole?

PROBLEMS

11-24   *Performance evaluation criteria*   Hawthorne Company has two divisions, Hi and Lo. The company evaluates divisional managers based on ROI. Budgeted data for the coming year are as follows:

	Hi	Lo	Total
Sales	$ 600,000	$ 300,000	$ 900,000
Expenses	300,000	200,000	500,000
Divisional profit	$ 300,000	$ 100,000	$ 400,000
Investment	$1,200,000	$1,000,000	$2,200,000

An investment opportunity is available to both divisions. It is expected to return $40,000 annually and requires an investment of $200,000.

Required
1. Given that the divisional managers are evaluated based on ROI, which, if either, of the managers will accept the project? Explain.
2. Assume that the managers are evaluated on residual income. If the minimum required ROI is 18%, which, if either, of the managers will accept the project? Explain.
3. If the minimum required ROI is 18%, is it in the company's best interest for a division to accept the project? Explain.

11-25   *Components of ROI*   The managers of two divisions of Diversified Company were recently discussing their operations. Fran Margin commented, "I get a good return on sales, about 25%, but my investment is a drag. Turnover last year was only 0.60 times." Florence Turns said, "My problem is margins; turnover is about 3 times, but return on sales is only 5%."

Required
1. Compute ROI for each division.
2. (a) Assume that Margin's division will maintain the same ROS. Determine the investment turnover required to achieve a 20% ROI.
   (b) Assume that Turns' division will maintain its turnover. Determine the ROS required to achieve a 20% ROI.

11-26   *Appropriate transfer price*   Rohn Division of kSystems expects the following results in 19X6 from selling only to outside customers.

Sales (100,000 units at $9)	$900,000
Variable costs at $5	500,000
Contribution margin	$400,000
Fixed costs	180,000
Profit	$220,000

Early in 19X6, the manager of Wood Division of kSystems asked the manager of Rohn to supply 30,000 units to Wood. Wood would modify the units at a variable cost of $4 and sell the resulting product for $11. Rohn Division has capacity of 120,000 units and will therefore lose 10,000 units in outside sales if it supplies the 30,000 to Wood. Rohn's fixed costs remain constant up to capacity.

Required

1. If Rohn does transfer 30,000 units to Wood, which modifies and sells them as described, what will happen to the profit of kSystems as a whole?
2. What is the minimum transfer price that Rohn will accept from Wood for the 30,000 units?
3. What is the maximum transfer price that Wood will pay?
4. Redo item 1 assuming that Rohn's capacity is 150,000 units and that outside sales cannot increase over 100,000 units.

11-27   ROI and RI on a special order   The Appliance Division of TVM Industries has the opportunity to sell 250,000 units of one of its principal lines to a large chain store at $24 per unit. Selected data follow.

Annual unit volume	1,700,000
Normal selling price	$40
Unit variable cost	$18
Annual fixed costs	$30,000,000
Divisional investment	$25,000,000

The manager of the Appliance Division expects a 50,000 unit decline in sales at the normal price if she supplies the chain. She also expects fixed costs to increase by $100,000 and investment to increase by $1,200,000 if she accepts the order.

Required

1. Determine whether the manager of the Appliance Division should accept the order, assuming that she is evaluated based on ROI.
2. Determine whether the manager of the Appliance Division should accept the order, assuming that she is evaluated based on RI and that the minimum required ROI is 20%.

11-28   Comprehensive review   The following information relates to the Glove Division of Hand-and-Glove Company.

Selling price	$12
Variable cost, per unit	$8
Annual direct fixed costs, all unavoidable	$160,000
Total divisional investment	$500,000

Required

Answer each of the following questions independently.

1. Assume Glove's current sales are 80,000 units.
   (a) What is its ROI?
   (b) What is its RI if the required ROI is 20%?
2. Suppose Hand-and-Glove expects a minimum ROI of 18%. How many units must Glove sell to earn an RI of $50,000?
3. If Glove's return on sales is 20% and ROI is 48%, what are its sales, in dollars?
4. Assume that Glove expects to produce and sell 80,000 units but has the capacity to produce 100,000 units. The manager of Hand Division, which is currently buying 25,000 units of a similar product from an outside supplier for $11, offers to buy the units from Glove only if Glove will supply the full 25,000 units needed.
   (a) What is the maximum price that Hand's manager is likely to offer for the units?
   (b) What is the minimum price that Glove's manager is likely to accept on a sale of 25,000 units to Hand Division?
   (c) If Hand's manager offers $9 per unit and Glove's manager accepts the offer, what will be the amount and direction of the effect on the total income of Hand-and-Glove?

11-29 *Transfer prices and required profit margins* Johnna Roberts is the used-car manager of the Snappy Wheels automobile dealership. She is expected to earn a gross profit of 25% of sales in the used-car operation, and she is distressed by the company's transfer-pricing policy. Roberts is charged with the trade-in price she sets for a used car plus any reconditioning work. The charge for reconditioning is based on actual costs by the service department plus a one-third markup over cost (25% on sales). Roberts believes she is being unduly penalized by the one-third markup.

Ellen Black, the service manager, is held responsible for earning a 25% gross profit on sales. She argues that it would not be fair to force her to do reconditioning work any cheaper than the work she does on customers' cars.

Roberts has recently been approached by Joe Sharp, the owner of Sharp's Garage, an independent repair shop. Sharp offers to do reconditioning work for Roberts at 20% over cost, the work to be done during Sharp's slack periods. The work will generally take about four days longer than work done by the service department, which has no excess capacity.

Required

Should Roberts take her reconditioning business to Sharp?

11-30 *Make-or-buy and transfer pricing* Viscount Enterprises, Inc. has three divisions, A, B, and C. One of the company's products uses components made by A and B, with the final assembly done by C. One unit from A and one from B are required.

Data for the product are as follows:

Selling price (C division)	$110
Variable costs:	
A division	$ 36
B division	20
C division	16
Total variable costs	$ 72
Volume	10,000 units

Divisions A and B charge Division C $44 and $28, respectively, for each unit. Division C has been approached by an outside supplier who will sell the component now made by Division A at $40 per unit.

Required

1. Prepare partial income statements, down to contribution margin, for A, B, and C based on current operations.
2. Determine whether the offer from the outside supplier should be accepted. If A meets the outside price, C will continue to buy from A.
3. Suppose that A can sell its entire output of 10,000 units per year at $48 if it performs additional work on the component. The additional work will add $5 to variable cost per unit; fixed costs will be unchanged. Capacity of Division A is 10,000 units. Should A meet the outside supplier's price or allow C to buy from the outside supplier? Support with calculations. Is A's decision good for the company?

11-31   *Goal congruence and motivation*   Roth Company manufactures furniture and related products. Tammie Bills, manager of the Redfern Division, has been seeking bids on a particular type of chair to be used in a new living room suite she wants to market. No division within the company can supply the chair.

The lowest outside bid is $140 from Thomas Chair Company. Wisner Chair Company has bid $150 and would buy some of the materials from the Ronson Upholstery Division of Roth Company. The Ronson Division has excess capacity, would incur variable costs of $35 for the amount of material needed for one chair, and would be paid $56 by Wisner. Bills knows that Wisner would buy the materials from Ronson and that Thomas would not. Each division manager is evaluated on the basis of ROI.

Required

1. As manager of the Redfern Division, which bid would you accept, Thomas's or Wisner's?
2. As Roth's president, which bid do you want to see accepted? Explain.
3. Using the guidelines in Appendix A, write a memorandum to Jan Blane, Roth's president, giving and explaining your recommendation about how to handle this situation.

11-32   *Performance of international division*   CWK Industries is a division of Martek, Inc. CWK operates in Hungary, where the currency is the forint (F). The information CWK used to develop its operating budgets for the first quarter of 19X7 follow. The exchange rate is four forints per dollar.

Unit sales	100,000
Unit price	F300
Cost of sales percentage	40%
Operating expenses	F13,000,000 per month

Required

1. Prepare a budgeted income statement for the first quarter of 19X7, in forints.
2. Translate the budgeted income statement to dollars.

11-33   *Performance of international division (continuation of 11-32)*   CWK's actual results for the first quarter of 19X7 follow. After the budgets were prepared, the exchange rate quickly went to five forints per dollar and remained there over the quarter, during which sales were 104,400 units. Prices and costs were incurred as expected.

CWK Division
Income Statement
First Quarter, 19X7 (000's)

Sales, 104,400 × F300	F31,320
Cost of sales	12,528
Gross profit	F18,792
Operating expenses	13,000
Income	F 5,792

Required

1. Translate the actual income statement to dollars.
2. Comment on the results. Did the managers of CWK perform well, badly, about as expected?

11-34   *Divisional performance—interactions*   Acme Camera Company has two divisions, Film and Camera. The manager of the Film Division, John Kretzmar, has just received a report from his laboratory indicating a breakthrough in a new type of film that produces much clearer pictures. The film can only be used in the X-40, a low-priced camera made by the Camera Division. The film currently sold for the X-40 has a variable cost per roll of $0.90 and sells for $3.00 per roll. The film currently sells 2 million rolls per year.

Kretzmar is confident that if he devoted his efforts and facilities to the production and sale of the new film he could sell 2.5 million rolls at $2.80 each. Additionally, he believes, on the basis of several market research studies, that if the Camera Division sold 200,000 more X-40s per year, sales of the new film could reach 4.8 million rolls. The variable cost of the new film is $0.80 per roll, additional fixed costs to produce it are $250,000 per year, and additional required investment totals $600,000.

Samantha Brewer, manager of the Camera Division, is not happy with the proposal that she increase production of X-40s. She argues that the camera has a contribution margin of only $6 and that she would have to increase her investment by $4,000,000 and her fixed costs by $500,000 in order to increase production by 200,000 units. She is virtually certain, as is Kretzmar, that the extra units could be sold, but she is also well aware that the Acme's minimum required ROI is 20%.

Required

1. Compute the change in RI for the Camera Division if production and sales of X-40s are increased by 200,000 units to show why Brewer is not eager to expand its production.
2. If the manager of the Camera Division will not increase production, what is the best action for the Film Division?
3. What is the best action for the company as a whole?

11-35   *RI, ROI, CVP analysis, and effects of decisions*   The following data refer to the Pratt Division of Standard National Company.

Selling price	$40
Variable costs	$24
Total fixed costs	$200,000
Investment	$800,000
Budgeted sales in 19X9	30,000 units

Required

Answer each of the following questions independently.

1. What is planned ROI for 19X9?
2. The minimum required ROI is 20% and the division manager wishes to maximize RI. A new customer wants to buy 10,000 units at $32 each. If the order is accepted, the division will incur additional fixed costs of $40,000 and will have to invest an additional $160,000 in various assets. Should the order be accepted?
3. The minimum desired ROI is 20% and the manager wishes to maximize RI. The division makes components for its product at a variable cost of $4. An outside supplier has offered to supply the 30,000 units needed at a cost of $5 per unit. The units that the supplier would provide are equivalent to the ones now being made and the supplier is reliable. If the component is purchased, fixed costs will decline by $20,000 and investment will drop by $40,000. Should the component be bought or made?
4. Again, minimum required ROI is 20% and the goal is maximizing RI. The manager is considering a new product. It will sell for $20, variable costs are $12, fixed costs will increase by $80,000, and sales are expected to be 15,000 units. What is the most additional investment that can be made without reducing RI?
5. Assume the same facts as in item 4 except that investment in the new product is $400,000 and introducing the product will increase sales of the existing product by 2,000 units. What increase in unit sales of the existing product is needed to justify introducing the new product?

11-36   *Corporate charges and behavior*   MST Company charges its operating divisions a percentage of sales to cover corporate expenses, which are virtually all fixed. The percentage is based on budgeted sales and budgeted corporate expenses and is predetermined for each year. In 19X6 the charge is 3%. The charge is included in calculating the profit of each division and its ROI, which is the basis for evaluating the performance of divisional managers.

Calco Division makes electronic equipment and has some excess capacity. Its manager has found a customer who will pay $10 million for a batch of product that has variable costs of $8.8 million. No incremental fixed costs are associated with the order. Accepting the order will require increased investment in receivables and inventories of about $5.1 million. The 3% charge is not included in the $8.8 million.

The divisional manager expects to earn $15.5 million on an investment of $70.5 million without the order.

Required

1. Should the divisional manager accept the order, acting in her own best interests?
2. Assuming that the minimum required ROI is 20%, is it to the company's advantage to accept the order?

11-37 *Performance measurement—athletic programs* Haltom University is a medium-sized private university with a religious affiliation. Perhaps prompted by the prospect of declining college enrollment, a number of faculty members at Haltom have become increasingly concerned about the costs of the school's athletic program. The football program has been subjected to particular scrutiny. One professor assembled the following data and argues, based on these data, that football is clearly a drain on funds needed elsewhere in the university.

19X4 Football Program

Revenue from ticket sales		$300,000
Revenue from concessions		25,000
Total revenue		$325,000
Associated costs:		
Tuition for players on scholarship	$120,000	
Room rent in dormitories for players	22,000	
Board and incidentals for players	110,000	
Coaches' salaries	90,000	
Portion of salaries of athletic director, ticket office personnel, attendants, etc.	17,000	
Uniforms, equipment, etc.	10,000	
Total costs		369,000
Net loss on football program		$ (44,000)

Required
1. Comment on each item. Should it be included? If you are uncertain, state the conditions under which it should be included or excluded.
2. What other information do you want before reaching a decision on the desirability of the football program?

11-38 *Transfer prices* Following is a budgeted income statement for Superdivision of Weaver, Inc. The division sells both to outsiders and to a sister division.

	Intercompany Sales to Subdivision	Sales to Outsiders
Sales:		
100,000 units at $10	$1,000,000	
50,000 units at $8		$400,000
Variable costs ($4 per unit)	400,000	200,000
Contribution margin	$ 600,000	$200,000
Fixed costs ($300,000, allocated at $2 per unit)	200,000	100,000
Profit	$ 400,000	$100,000

Required
1. Subdivision can buy all of its requirements from an outside supplier at $7 per unit and will do so unless Superdivision meets the $7 price. Superdivision's manager knows that if he loses the Subdivision business he will not be able to increase sales to outsiders and fixed costs will not change. Should he meet the $7 price from the standpoint of (a) the company and (b) Superdivision?

2. Superdivision meets the $7 price. Superdivision then is offered the opportunity to sell 60,000 units to a chain store at $7 each. The price of the 100,000 units now sold to outsiders will not be affected. However, Superdivision has capacity of 190,000 units. If Superdivision cannot fill all of the requirements of Subdivision, then Subdivision will have to buy all the units outside at $7. Should Superdivision accept the order, considering (a) the company and (b) Superdivision?

3. Suppose now that Subdivision has received the offer from the outside supplier, who will provide as many units as Subdivision wants to buy at $7. Superdivision no longer has the opportunity to sell the 60,000 units to the chain store. The manager of Superdivision believes that reducing prices to outsiders could increase those sales greatly. Best estimates are that reducing the price to $9.20 would yield sales of 120,000 units; to $8.40, 150,000 units; and to $7.80, 170,000 units. Capacity is 190,000 units. Superdivision can sell any amount up to 50,000 units to Subdivision. Subdivision will buy units from the outside supplier as necessary. What should be done? How many units should Superdivision sell to outsiders, and how many units should it sell to Subdivision at $7?

11-39   ROI, RI, and investment decisions   The manager of Brandon Division of Greene Industries has been analyzing her investment opportunities. The division currently has profits of $1,250,000 and investment of $5,000,000.

Investment Opportunity	Annual Profit	Amount of Investment
A	$300,000	$ 900,000
B	300,000	1,600,000
C	240,000	1,200,000
D	280,000	800,000
E	260,000	1,000,000

Required

1. Assume that the manager wishes to earn the highest ROI possible. Determine which projects will be selected and the ROI that will be earned.
2. Assume that the manager wishes to maximize RI. Determine which projects will be selected and the total RI that will be earned if the minimum required return is (a) 20% and (b) 28%.
3. Assume that the ROI on each project approximates the IRR discussed in Chapter 8 and that the minimum desired ROI approximates cost of capital. Determine which policy is better for the company: maximizing ROI or maximizing RI.

11-40   Transfer pricing   MST Division of 3K Company expects the following results in 19X6.

Sales (100,000 at $3)		$300,000
Variable costs	$120,000	
Fixed costs	150,000	270,000
Profit		$ 30,000

Sparkman Division of 3K Company wants to buy 30,000 units of MST's product. Sparkman will incur an additional $0.80 per unit and sell the resultant new product for $4.50. MST has capacity for 120,000 units.

Required

1. What will happen to 3K's profit if the transaction takes place at a transfer price of $1.50?
2. What will happen to the profit of each division if the transaction takes place at the $1.50 transfer price?
3. What is the minimum transfer price MST will accept for the 30,000 units?

11-41 Transfer prices and goal congruence (CMA adapted) A. R. Oma Company manufactures a line of men's perfumes and aftershave lotions. The manufacturing process is a series of mixing operations with the adding of aromatic and coloring ingredients. The finished product is bottled and packed in cases of six bottles each.

The bottles are made by one division, which was bought several years ago. Management believes that the appeal of the product is partly due to the attractiveness of the bottles and so has spent a great deal of time and effort developing new types of bottles and new processes for making them.

The bottle division has been selling all of its output to the manufacturing division at market-based transfer prices. The price has been determined by asking other bottle manufacturers for bids on bottles of the appropriate size and in the required quantities. At present, the company has the following bids.

Quantity, Cases of Six Bottles	Price per Case	Total Price
2,000,000	$2.00	$ 4,000,000
4,000,000	1.75	7,000,000
6,000,000	1.6666	10,000,000

The bottle division has fixed costs of $1,200,000 per year and variable costs of $1 per case. Both divisions are investment centers, and their managers receive significant bonuses based on profitability, so the transfer price is of great interest to both of them.

The perfume manufacturing division has variable costs, excluding the cost of bottles, of $8 per case and fixed costs of $4,000,000 annually. The market research group has determined that the following price-volume relationships are likely to prevail during the coming year.

Sales Volume in Cases	Selling Price per Case	Total Revenue
2,000,000	$12.50	$25,000,000
4,000,000	11.40	45,600,000
6,000,000	10.65	63,900,000

The president, Miguel Enez, believes that the market-based transfer price should be used in pricing transfers. The bottle division has no outside sales potential because the company does not wish to supply its highly appealing bottles to competitors.

Required

1. Of the three levels of volume given, determine which will provide the highest profit to the (a) bottle division, (b) perfume division, and (c) company as a whole.
2. Do the results in item 1 contradict your understanding of the effectiveness of market-based transfer prices? Explain why or why not.
3. Using the guidelines in Appendix A, write a memorandum to Mr. Enez giving and supporting your recommendation about the course of action that should be selected.

11-42   *Transfer pricing (CMA adapted)*   The manager of the Arjay Division of National Industries, Inc. has the opportunity to supply a brake assembly to an aircraft manufacturer for $50. The manager is willing to accept the order if he can break even on it because he has excess capacity and will be able to keep skilled workers busy who would otherwise have to be laid off. Additionally, he believes there is a good chance of getting more business from the same company at better prices.

Bradley Division of National Industries makes a part that is used in the brake assembly. Bradley is operating at capacity and producing the part at a variable cost of $4.25. Its selling price is $7.50 to outsiders. None of its output is currently being sold internally.

The manager of Arjay decides to offer Bradley a price that will result in breaking even on the order. He determines that the other costs involved in filling the order are as follows, per unit.

Parts purchased outside	$23
Other variable costs	14
Fixed overhead and administration	8
Total, before fitting	$45

He decides to offer the manager of Bradley $5 per fitting, which brings the total cost per unit to $50, the selling price of the assembly. The company is decentralized and the managers are evaluated based on ROI.

Required

1. Determine whether the manager of Bradley is likely to accept the $5 offer.
2. Determine whether it is to the company's advantage for Bradley to supply the part at $5.
3. As the controller of National Industries, what do you advise be done?

11-43   *Budgeted and actual results*   Managers of divisions of Wycliff Company receive bonuses based on ROI. The bonuses constitute about 30% of total compensation of the average manager. Part of the bonus depends on whether the manager meets budgeted ROI.

F. C. Smith took over as general manager of the Poursh Division in late 19X1. Budgeted and actual results for 19X6 follow, in thousands of dollars.

	Budget	Actual
Sales	$ 2,500	$ 2,480
Cost of sales	(1,250)	(1,310)
Operating expenses	(750)	(610)
Profit	$ 500	$ 560
Investment		
Current assets (50% of sales)	$ 1,250	$ 1,240
Current liabilities (40% of current assets)	(500)	(496)
Plant and equipment, net	1,800	1,770
Total investment	$ 2,550	$ 2,514
ROI	19.6%	22.3%

Smith received a sizable bonus. Smith commented on the results by saying that once he saw sales would not meet budget, he began to cut costs, especially in discretionary areas such as maintenance, employee training, and engineering. (Engineers were responsible for improving the quality of products and methods of manufacturing.) He also held off payments to suppliers, letting them finance more of the division's asset requirements.

Required
Discuss Smith's performance. Include in your discussion the long-term implications of the specific actions mentioned and the ethical aspects of his actions.

11-44 Divisional performance, cost allocations, and dropping a product line
Sonya Rathman is the manager in charge of two product lines for Kingston Company. She has just received the following income statement for the three months ended March 31, 19X7. The statement shows Rathman's two product lines and the total results for the company. The company has ten product lines.

	A	B	Total Company
Sales	$100,000	$200,000	$2,000,000
Cost of sales	$ 60,000	$100,000	$1,050,000
Selling and general	29,000	50,000	450,000
Total separable expenses	$ 89,000	$150,000	$1,500,000
Common costs (allocated on basis of sales dollars)	15,000	30,000	300,000
Total expenses	$104,000	$180,000	$1,800,000
Income (loss)	$ (4,000)	$ 20,000	$ 200,000

Rathman is disturbed by the showing of product line A. She believes that the line is contributing to the common costs of the company and should be kept, but she is worried about the effect on her performance.

Required
1. Prepare an income statement assuming that product line A is dropped. Show the effects on both Rathman's and the company's performance. All separable costs are avoidable. Be sure to reallocate common costs to product line B based on its relative percentage of the new sales for the company. Round to the nearest $500.
2. Comment on the results. Does Rathman's performance look better if product line A is dropped? Is it better? Is the decision good for the company?

11-45 Developing divisional performance data Dixon Company has three divisions, X, Y, and Z. The following data regarding operations and selected balance sheet elements have been prepared by the company's accountant (in thousands of dollars).

	X	Y	Z
Sales	$2,000	$3,000	$5,000
Cost of goods sold	1,000	1,400	3,300
Gross profit	$1,000	$1,600	$1,700
Selling and administrative expense	400	900	800
Income	$ 600	$ 700	$ 900
Current assets	$400	$700	$600
Current liabilities	$300	$200	$100
Fixed assets (net)	$2,250	$3,000	$3,750

After determining costs and assets directly traceable to the divisions, the accountant allocated the remainder in the following way.

(a) Common cost of goods sold of $1,800 was allocated based on sales dollars.
(b) Common selling and administrative costs of $1,000 were allocated on the basis of relative sales dollars.
(c) Common fixed assets of $3,000 were allocated on the basis of relative shares of directly assignable fixed assets of $1,500, $2,000, and $2,500, for X, Y, and Z, respectively.
(d) All current assets except cash (which is held and managed by corporate headquarters) are directly assignable. Cash of $200 is allocated based on sales.

Required

1. On the basis of the data developed by the company, rank the divisions according to ROI on net assets and RI, with a 15% minimum required ROI.
2. Recast the statements, computing divisional profit and assets employed without allocations. Rank the divisions on the same bases as in item 1. Comment on the differences between your rankings.

CASES

11-46 Transfer pricing Westfall Division of Bailey Enterprises makes stereo-phonic speakers and sells them to other companies for use in complete systems. The division can make 45,000 speakers per year and cannot increase production because of shortages of specialized skilled labor. Data for the division's product follow.

Selling price		$80
Variable manufacturing costs	$48	
Variable selling costs	8	56
Contribution margin		$24

Westfall has just lost a customer and volume is projected at 40,000 speakers per year for the next several years. Another division of Bailey, Leakes Division, is interested in buying speakers from Westfall and putting them in sets to be sold through retail outlets. Leakes now buys speakers of somewhat higher quality than those made by Westfall at $84 each. The speakers are of better quality than the rest of the components of the set, so the manager of Leakes intends to reduce prices and predicts higher volume if she changes to the lower-quality speakers. Volume of the set in which the speakers are to be used is currently 3,500 per year. If the price were reduced from $680 to $600, volume is expected to be 4,500 units per year. Variable costs are currently $460 per set, including the $168 for two speakers now purchased outside. Leakes Division wants 9,000 speakers per year from Westfall and has offered $62 per speaker. Westfall will not incur variable selling expenses on speakers sold to Leakes.

Required

1. Determine whether it is in the company's best interests if Westfall sold speakers to Leakes.
2. At the suggested transfer price, is it in the interests of each of the managers to have Westfall sell to Leakes?
3. Determine the limits on the transfer price—that is, the highest price that Leakes would be willing to pay and the lowest price that Westfall will accept.

11-47 Problems of market-based transfer prices Planton Division of Borgan Industries has developed an electronic measuring system that requires a sophisti-cated microprocessor. CLI Division makes such a microprocessor and currently sells it for $200 on the outside market. CLI incurs variable costs of $50 per unit. CLI has a lot of excess capacity. It now sells 30,000 units of the microprocessor per year and could make close to 40,000 units. However, increasing outside sales to 36,000 units would require reducing the selling price on all units to $160. Accordingly, CLI has been restricting output.

The manager of Planton received a bid of $200, the current market price, from CLI for the microprocessor and then analyzed data regarding expected volume at different selling prices. He intended to set the price of the measuring system at either $600 or $550 based on the following.

	Selling Price	
	$600	$550
Expected variable costs, per unit:		
Materials	$ 90	$ 90
Microprocessor from CLI	200	200
Labor and variable overhead	110	110
Total variable costs	$400	$400
Contribution margin	$200	$150
Expected volume	5,000 units	6,000 units

Required

1. At the $200 transfer price, what price will the manager of Planton Division set for the measuring system?
2. From the standpoint of the company, which price is better, $600 or $550?
3. The manager of CLI Division knows that Planton will buy 5,000 microprocessors at the $200 price. What is the minimum price he will accept for 6,000 units— the price that gives him the same total contribution margin he could earn selling 5,000 at $200?
4. Will the transfer price you calculated in item 3 induce the manager of the Planton Division to try to sell 6,000 units of the measuring system at $550? Assume that the two managers have to agree on both the transfer price and the quantity to be taken. That is, the alternatives that the Platon manager faces are to (1) buy 5,000 microprocessors at $200 and (2) buy 6,000 at $175.

11-48   Divisional performance and accounting methods A division manager for McKy Company has been criticized for allowing ROI to fall in the past two years. She has explained that the division made some large investments on which a 30% before-tax ROI is expected. She argues that the use of straight-line depreciation is hurting ROI, on which her performance is evaluated. Following are comparative income statements and other data for the past three years.

	19X1	19X2	19X3
Sales	$2,200	$2,900	$3,800
Variable costs	1,200	1,500	1,800
Contribution margin	$1,000	$1,400	$2,000
Total fixed costs	600	950	1,400
Divisional profit	$ 400	$ 450	$ 600
Invested capital			
(principally plant and equipment)	$1,000	$1,600	$2,400
ROI	40%	28%	25%
Capital expenditures	$200	$900	$1,500
Depreciation included in fixed costs	$300	$450	$600

Required

1. Explain why the falling ROI might not indicate poor performance.
2. What possible solutions are there?

11-49   Capital budgeting and performance evaluation Arnold Donald, manager of the Western Division of Global Enterprises, Inc., is considering an investment. He can save $10,000 in cash operating costs per year using a machine that costs

$40,000 and has a ten-year life with no salvage value. Donald calculates the ROI in the first year as 15% [($10,000 - $4,000 depreciation)/$40,000]. He decides that the machine is not a wise investment because his current ROI is 20% and he is evaluated based on ROI. (Current income is $40,000 and investment is $200,000.)

The seller of the machine offers to lease it at $8,500 per year if Donald will accept a noncancellable lease for ten years. He asks your advice and specifically requests that you consider the effect of the lease on ROI. The company's minimum desired ROI before taxes is 12%, which approximates cost of capital.

Required

Using the guidelines in Appendix A, write a memorandum to Mr. Donald explaining his choices and the effects of each alternative from his standpoint and that of the company.

11-50   National Automobile Company—introduction of a new model   National Auto Company consists of four relatively autonomous divisions. In the past each division has concentrated on a relatively limited range of models designed to appeal to a particular segment of the automobile market. The Kalicak Division has been producing mid-sized cars for many years. They range in price (to dealers) from $14,000 to $25,300.

One day last August, Noel Mack, general manager of the Kalicak Division, was studying some reports prepared by the company's market research department at central headquarters. Mack had been considering for some time the possibility of bringing out a stripped-down version of the division's most popular model, the Panther. He had been hesitant to do so because he feared that sales of the higher-priced Panthers would suffer. The market research indicated, however, that lost sales of higher-priced versions would be negligible if a new Panther were introduced and priced to sell to the customer for about $20,800. The lowest price at retail now charged for a Panther is $24,700.

Mack was pleased at the results of the study and instructed his production manager to determine the costs of producing 80,000 units of the new model per year—the number of units that the study indicated could be sold. Mack also asked for information about additional investment in equipment, inventories, and receivables necessitated by the higher volume.

A few days later Mack had the additional information. The production manager estimated the cost per unit to be $17,800, composed of the following basic categories.

Variable costs	$13,800
Fixed costs	4,000
Total	$17,800

The fixed cost per unit included $100 million in existing fixed costs that would be reallocated to the new model under a complicated formula used by the division's cost accounting department. The additional investment in equipment was $300 million and in receivables and inventories about $200 million.

Mack was reasonably certain that the information he had gathered was as accurate as estimates are likely to be. He consulted with several large dealers and concluded that the model could be priced at $18,100 to dealers. Any higher price would encourage the dealers to charge more than $20,800, with a consequent decline in volume below the 80,000 per year target.

Like the other divisional managers, Mack is evaluated based on the residual income earned by his division. The minimum required return is 18%. Income taxes are ignored in determining residual income for the divisions.

Required

Determine whether the new Panther should be brought out.

11-51   National Automobile Company—interaction effects of decisions (continuation of 11-50)   While mulling over his decision whether to introduce the new Panther model, Noel Mack was eating lunch with Deborah Warren, general manager of the Hatfield Division, which specializes in compact and subcompact cars. Mack told Warren about the study he had ordered and gave a general picture of the results, including the projection of 80,000 units of volume of the new model.

After lunch, Warren called Hanna Joost, the chief of market research for the firm, and requested more information about the study. Joost said that the study indicated a potential decline in volume of 30,000 units of one of the Hatfield Division's best-selling higher-priced models if Kalicak brought out the new lower-priced model. Warren asked why that information had not been included in the report given to Mack and was told that Mack had only asked for estimates in declines in volume of Kalicak Division cars. Warren then immediately telephoned her production manager and sales manager. She informed them of the situation and demanded that they quickly collect information.

Several days later, the production manager informed Warren that the model in question, which sold to retail dealers for $16,700, had unit costs of $16,400 at the division's current volume of 160,000 units per year. Fixed costs of $3,500 were included in the $16,400 figure. Warren asked what savings in fixed costs might be expected if volume were to fall by 30,000 units and was told that the fixed cost per unit would rise to about $4,000, even though some fixed costs could be eliminated. Conversations with other managers revealed that the division's investment could be reduced by about $100 million if volume fell as stated.

Warren was visibly distressed by what she had heard. She was concerned with her division's interests, but realized that Mack had the right to operate in accordance with his best interests. She pondered the possibility of going to the company's executive vice president for advice.

Required

1. Determine the effect on Hatfield of the introduction of the new Panther.
2. Determine the effect on the company of the introduction of the new Panther.

11-52   ROI at Burlington Industries, Inc.   Burlington Industries, Inc. is a very large and widely diversified manufacturer of textiles and associated products. The organization consists of several largely autonomous divisions, the performances of which have been evaluated using, among other measures, ROI and dollar profit. Profit measures are before tax but after a special deduction called the Use of Capital Charge (UOCC). The minimum required ROI for a division is the weighted average of the minimum required ROIs for three different types or classes of assets.

The classes are (1) accounts receivable less accounts payable, (2) inventories, and (3) fixed assets.

The central managers at Burlington have stated that the use of different required ROIs recognizes the different risks of the different types of investment. They feel that fixed assets, which are committed for relatively long periods and lack liquidity, should earn a higher ROI than assets committed for a shorter time. Receivables, which are turned into cash more quickly than are inventories, require a lower ROI. The minimum required ROIs for the three classes are 7% for receivables-less-payables, 14% for inventories, and 22% for fixed assets. These minimums are based on estimates of cost of capital and of relative investment in each class of assets for the company as a whole.

The following data relate to a hypothetical division of Burlington, stated in thousands of dollars.

Sales	$23,450
Cost of sales	16,418
Selling and administrative expense	1,678
Other expenses, not including UOCC	1,025
Accounts receivable less accounts payable	2,540
Inventories	3,136
Net fixed assets	3,560

Required
1. Prepare an income statement for the hypothetical division. Use the same basis as is used by Burlington.
2. Compute ROI for the division and the weighted-average minimum required ROI.
3. Comment on the method used by Burlington. Does it seem to encourage desirable behavior on the part of managers? Is the use of different minimum ROIs a good idea?

Control and Evaluation
of Cost Centers

LEARNING OBJECTIVES

After reading this chapter, you should be able to

1 *Develop standard variable costs for a product.*

2 *Calculate direct labor, variable overhead, and materials variances.*

3 *Discuss the advantages and disadvantages of approaches to setting standards.*

4 *Describe new approaches to cost control and management, as described by proponents of JIT and other continuous improvement approaches.*

Trane Company, *a leading manufacturer of air conditioning systems and fixtures for home and commercial use, uses a standard costing system that focuses on getting costs of its various products "close enough," that is, not precisely right. The company's cost system is designed to support its operating philosophy of on-time delivery of quality products. Simplicity and lowest total cost are part of the company's philosophy. The company applies the principle of simplicity to its accounting as well as to its operations, paying little attention to immaterial elements of cost. Because labor cost is less than 5 percent of total cost, Trane does no detailed reporting of labor productivity. The company expenses low-cost parts such as screws and nuts.*

In contrast, **Sally Industries,** *a manufacturer of entertainment robots for theme parks, pays considerable attention to labor cost and productivity because labor constitutes a high percentage of total cost. Moreover, Sally must pay careful attention to which workers perform which tasks because the rates of pay vary considerably among tasks.*

> *Sally's system makes workers much more conscious of how they use their time and reduces non-value-adding work.*

Sources: Ronald B. Clements and Charlene W. Spoede, "Trane's SOUP Accounting," Management Accounting, *June 1992, 46-52.*
Thomas L. Barton and Frederick M. Cole, "Accounting for Magic," Management Accounting, *January 1991, 27-31.*

This chapter applies the concepts of responsibility accounting to cost centers, principally in manufacturing companies. We explain how managers set performance standards and what behavorial problems they encounter in setting and using standards. We examine the role of standard costs in planning and control, with major emphases on developing standards for variable costs and interpreting variances from those standards. We also look at the use of standards in JIT operations. Finally, proponents of continuous improvement, such as those using JIT, and some advocates of emerging schools of managerial thought dispute the benefits of standard costs, and we consider their arguments and proposals.

COST CONTROL

All companies need to control costs and increase productivity because competition is now global. Chapter 3 described cost management, including the management of the activities that drive costs. Chapter 6 described how companies use budgets to control costs while other chapters, especially Chapters 8 and 9, discussed increasing productivity. Eliminating non-value-adding activities is one way to increase productivity; another is to use better manufacturing technology.

Cost control is critically important for companies in mature industries where total demand for the product is not growing. Such companies cannot significantly increase profits unless they can produce at lower costs than their competitors. Recognition of this principle is evidenced in a recent annual report of **Kellogg's**, the giant cereal company, which stated that the company used its leadership in manufacturing technology to control costs and increase productivity. In addition, the report stated that cost leadership allowed Kellogg to maintain the highest quality for its products. A company that does not make high-quality products will not long prosper no matter how good its cost control.

STANDARDS AND STANDARD COSTS

A **standard cost** is the per-unit cost a company should incur to make a unit of product. Companies develop and use standard costs for materials, direct labor, and overhead. This chapter concentrates on standards for variable costs, materials, direct labor, and variable overhead. A standard cost has two components: a standard price, or rate, and a standard quantity. Both standards relate to the input factor (materials, direct labor, variable overhead). The standard price, or rate, is the amount that should be paid for one unit of the input factor: $2 per pound of materials, $8 per hour of direct labor, and $4 variable overhead per machine hour. The standard quantity is the amount of the input factor that should be used to make a unit of product: three pounds of materials and 0.25 direct labor hours (DLH). Thus, if a unit of product should require 0.25 direct labor hours and the standard labor rate is $8 per hour, the standard direct labor cost per unit is $2 (0.25 hours × $8).

STANDARD COSTS AND BUDGETS

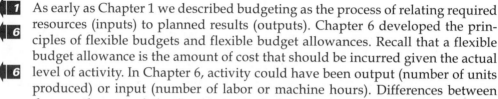

As early as Chapter 1 we described budgeting as the process of relating required resources (inputs) to planned results (outputs). Chapter 6 developed the principles of flexible budgets and flexible budget allowances. Recall that a flexible budget allowance is the amount of cost that should be incurred given the actual level of activity. In Chapter 6, activity could have been output (number of units produced) or input (number of labor or machine hours). Differences between the actual cost and the flexible budget allowance are variances.

The relationship of standard costs to flexible budgets is simple and direct: a standard cost is a per-unit expression of a flexible budget allowance *based on actual output*. Thus, with the standard quantity of labor of 0.25 hours per unit of product and the standard labor rate of $8 per hour, the standard cost for labor is $2 per unit of product. The flexible budget allowance for one unit is also $2. If the company makes 20,000 units, the flexible budget allowance for labor is $40,000 ($2 × 20,000). [Notice also that the total standard time to make 20,000 units is 5,000 hours (0.25 hours per unit × 20,000 units). Multiplying 5,000 total standard hours by the $8 standard rate gives the same $40,000 flexible budget allowance.] If actual direct labor cost was $42,200, a variance of $2,200 ($42,200 minus the flexible budget allowance of $40,000) exists. In the pages that follow we show how to analyze that variance.

We also can establish a flexible budget allowance based on *inputs* rather than outputs, and we use such an allowance in analyzing variances. Remember that for any of the required input factors (for example, labor), two factors determine total cost: the quantity of the input used (the number of hours worked by laborers) and the cost of a unit of such input (the hourly wage paid to laborers). In the situation previously described, if 5,100 hours of labor were used, the flexible budget allowance based on *input* is $40,800 ($8 per hour × 5,100 hours worked).

STANDARD VARIABLE COSTS AND VARIANCES

Coulter, Inc., a manufacturer of wooden packing crates, uses standard variable costs to aid in planning and control. Careful study has determined that if workers are producing at normal efficiency, the direct labor time per crate is one-half hour. Also, 20 feet of lumber should be used per crate at normal efficiency. The company expects to pay direct laborers $10 per hour. Lumber costs $0.80 per foot. Coulter estimates the variable overhead rate as $2 per direct labor hour. Using these data, we compute the standard variable cost of a crate as shown in Exhibit 12-1. Actual results for a recent month are also shown. While this example is simplified, it illustrates all of the principles of standard variable costs.

In practice, making almost any product requires several materials, perhaps several kinds of direct labor paid at different rates, and variable overhead

Exhibit 12-1   Standard Variable Costs

Cost Factor	Standard Quantity	×	Standard Price	=	Standard Cost
Materials	20 feet		$0.80		$16.00
Direct labor	1/2 hour		$10.00		5.00
Variable overhead	1/2 hour		$2.00		1.00
Total standard variable cost per crate					$22.00

Actual results:

Crates produced	1,000
Materials purchased (23,000 feet at $0.82/foot)	$18,860
Direct labor (480 hours at $10.10)	$4,848
Variable overhead incurred	$980

driven by several factors. We use a single type of each factor to focus on the general concepts. The same reason prompts our use of a single measure of activity, hours of direct labor, for variable overhead. We could use more than one measure of activity for variable overhead. Selecting measures for overhead requires identifying the cost drivers for each overhead pool using the techniques described in Chapter 3. In many plants, some variable overhead is related to machine hours or processing time, and some to the number and complexity of parts and components in each product. The pool of costs driven by a particular activity also includes the variable portions of such mixed costs as utilities, supplies, and payroll fringe benefits. Many companies use several activity-based rates.

Managers compare actual costs with standard costs to evaluate performance. The per-unit standard cost for each input factor consists of a price component and a quantity component. Hence, for any given factor, the actual total cost will differ from the total standard cost when either or both the actual price or quantity differs from the standard price or quantity. The total variance, therefore, is separated into price and quantity variances. Many terms are used to describe such variances. Price variances are sometimes called *rate*, *budget*, or *spending* variances. Quantity variances are sometimes called *use* or *efficiency* variances. The particular term you use is not important as long as you know which kind of variance is being referred to. We begin the illustration of variance analysis with direct labor costs. With a single exception, the analysis is the same for the other cost factors.

LABOR VARIANCES

Given that the company made 1,000 crates, what should direct labor cost be? The total standard direct labor cost, or flexible budget allowance, for 1,000 crates is $5,000, computed as follows from the data in Exhibit 12-1.

Actual production (units)	×	*Standard direct labor cost per unit*	=	*Total standard direct labor cost*
1,000	×	$5.00	=	$5,000

We could also compute the flexible budget allowance for 1,000 crates by multiplying the 1,000 crates by the 0.50 standard hours, giving 500 standard hours allowed, and then multiplying by the $10.00 standard rate. The calculation to be used is largely a matter of convenience. *Standard hours allowed* is the term for the number of direct labor hours that should have been used to produce 1,000 units.

Exhibit 12-1 shows that direct laborers actually worked 480 hours during the month and earned $10.10 per hour, for $4,848 total actual cost. Actual costs were $152 less than standard (standard cost of $5,000 - $4,848 actual cost). But why? And who is responsible for the difference?

10 In the performance reports we presented earlier (as in Chapter 10, for example), we made no distinction between variances in prices paid and quantities used. However, it is likely that some managers control either prices or quantities, but not both. The supervisor of a manufacturing cost center normally is responsible only for the quantities of labor and materials used, not for wage rates or materials prices. Therefore, we want to isolate each type of variance so that we can identify the manager responsible for it. Here, we want to separate the $152 total variance into two components: (1) the difference due to price, or labor rate, and (2) the difference due to the quantity of labor used.

We shall illustrate two common approaches to separating a total variance into its components. The first deals with *total* costs. We hold one of the factors constant (either price or quantity) and see what portion of the total variance is due to the effect of the other factor. We can represent actual total labor cost as follows:

Actual input quantity	×	*Actual rate for input factor*	=	*Actual cost of input factor*
480 hours	×	$10.10	=	$4,848

To separate the variances, we need a flexible budget allowance based on the actual quantity of our *input* factor, labor. That budget allowance is $4,800—the number of hours actually worked times the standard wage rate.

Actual input quantity	×	*Standard rate for input factor*	=	*Budget allowance for actual quantity of input factor*
480 hours	×	$10	=	$4,800

The only difference between the two calculations is the rate used for the input factor. The input factor (circled in the calculations) is the same for both, 480 hours. Hence, the difference between the actual cost incurred ($4,848) and the flexible budget allowance ($5,000) is due to the difference between the standard wage rate and the actual wage rate. That $48 difference ($4,848 - $4,800) is the

labor rate variance, and it is unfavorable because the actual cost is greater than the flexible budget allowance for that quantity of input (480 hours).

The variance due to quantity is calculated in much the same way. We previously calculated the flexible budget allowance *based on the actual output of 1,000 units* as $5,000. A slightly different, but equivalent, calculation follows.

Standard input quantity		*Standard rate for input factor*		*Budget allowance for actual quantity of output*
1,000 units × *½ hour per unit* *= 500 hours*	×	*$10*	=	*$5,000*

Compare this formula with the one immediately preceding it, where a budget allowance was computed for the actual quantity of the input factor, labor hours. Note that both calculations use the $10 standard rate for the input factor (boxed in the calculations). The only difference between the two calculations is the quantity of input, labor hours. Hence, the $200 difference between the two budget allowances ($5,000 - $4,800) is due to the difference in the quantity of labor used. This difference is the **labor efficiency variance** or *direct labor efficiency variance* and is favorable because laborers worked fewer than the 500 standard hours allowed for 1,000 units of output. Our analysis shows that the $152 total variance can be explained as follows:

Labor rate variance	$ 48 unfavorable
Labor efficiency variance	200 favorable
Total labor variance	$152 favorable

Exhibit 12-2 diagrams these relationships. The left-hand figure is actual cost, the middle figure is a flexible budget allowance based on input, and the right-hand figure is the budget allowance based on output. The chart can be used to determine the variance for any adjacent numbers: if the number to the right is larger than the one to the left, the variance is favorable; the variance is unfavorable if the opposite is true.

Labor Efficiency and Idle Time

The labor efficiency variance should indicate how efficient direct laborers are *when they make a product*. Hence, the labor hours used to compute that variance should not include **idle time**, the time when laborers do not have productive work to do. Idle time occurs for a variety of reasons having nothing to do with worker efficiency. For example, lack of orders for the finished product, unavailability of materials, or bottlenecks in earlier stages of production could idle workers.

Including idle time in the computation could mask problems in production scheduling or some other function, or could mislabel as labor inefficiency the cost of a manager's (or top management's) conscious decision or company policy not to lay off laborers when there is not enough work to keep them busy. Moreover, including idle time in the computation discourages goal congruence, because supervisors whose performance is evaluated in part by the efficiency

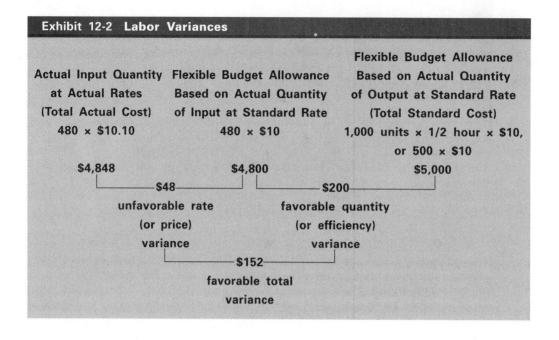

Exhibit 12-2 Labor Variances

Actual Input Quantity at Actual Rates (Total Actual Cost) 480 × $10.10	Flexible Budget Allowance Based on Actual Quantity of Input at Standard Rate 480 × $10	Flexible Budget Allowance Based on Actual Quantity of Output at Standard Rate (Total Standard Cost) 1,000 units × 1/2 hour × $10, or 500 × $10
$4,848	$4,800	$5,000

———$48———
unfavorable rate
(or price)
variance

———$200———
favorable quantity
(or efficiency)
variance

———$152———
favorable total
variance

variance might take actions that are not in the company's best interest. For example, the supervisor of laborers who would otherwise be idle might assign them to making units and components not required by production schedules, so that the company will incur unnecessary costs for storage, financing, insurance, taxes, etc. until the units are needed. Such actions are obviously contrary to the efforts of many manufacturing companies who are, as we have noted throughout this book, adopting JIT and other modern techniques that do not tolerate such production.

Alternative Computation

We also can calculate variances by using the differences between the standard and actual figures for rate and quantity. We could compute the labor rate variance as follows:

$$\frac{Actual}{hours} \times \left(\frac{Standard}{rate} - \frac{Actual}{rate}\right) = \frac{Labor\ rate}{variance}$$

$$480 \times (\$10 - \$10.10) = -\$48$$

Direct laborers were paid $0.10 per hour more than standard (an unfavorable occurrence) and earned this amount over 480 hours.

Using the same approach to calculate the labor efficiency variance results in the following:

$$\frac{Standard}{rate} \times \left(\frac{Standard}{hours} - \frac{Actual}{hours}\right) = \frac{Labor}{efficiency}\ variance$$

$$\$10 \times (500\ hours - 480\ hours) = \$200$$

Employees worked 20 fewer hours than the standard for producing 1,000 units (a favorable occurrence).

When the number inside the parentheses (using these alternative formulations) is negative, as in the rate variance, the variance is unfavorable. When the number inside the parentheses is positive, as in the efficiency variance, the variance is favorable. Do not memorize these relationships. Rather, think of favorable variances as those giving lower total cost and vice versa.

You may use either or both methods. A minor difficulty with the alternative method is that the actual rate might require rounding. For example, if workers were paid $4,910 for 480 hours of work, the actual rate is $10.229166. . . . You then would have a small difference between the rate variance computed in this way and that computed using the method described earlier.

VARIABLE OVERHEAD VARIANCES

We used labor variances to illustrate the computations, but we could have used variable overhead. The computations are essentially the same.

As shown in Exhibit 12-1, variable overhead costs for the month are $980. What are the variable overhead variances? Total standard variable overhead cost for 1,000 units of output is $1,000 ($1 standard cost per crate × 1,000 crates, or 500 standard direct labor hours at $2 standard rate per hour). So, the total variance is $20 favorable (actual cost of $980 compared with a standard of $1,000).

Exhibit 12-3 shows the diagrammatic approach to determining variable overhead variances. Note that actual direct labor hours are used to determine the middle term (the flexible budget based on the actual quantity of input), and that standard labor hours are used to determine the right-hand term. (The right-hand term is also given by $1 standard variable overhead per unit × 1,000 units.) Both variable overhead variances, the **variable overhead budget variance** (or **spending variance**) and the **variable overhead efficiency variance**, are calculated in the same fashion as are the labor variances. Exhibit 12-3 shows the calculations. If we based variable overhead on another activity, say machine hours, we would substitute actual and standard machine hours for actual and standard direct labor hours. We also could use more than one cost driver to assign variable overhead to a unit of product. An example appears later in the chapter.

Although the variable overhead budget variance is calculated in much the same way as the labor rate variance, it is not a rate variance in the sense of being the result of the prices paid for the input factor (overhead). For example, using more factory supplies than standard will show up in the variable overhead budget variance, not in the variable overhead efficiency variance.

Alternative Computation

The $20 budget variance can be computed using the alternative calculation method described earlier. However, because we were given only total overhead incurred, we must divide the total cost of $980 by the actual hours of 480 to determine the actual rate at which the variable overhead was incurred. That rate is about $2.0417 ($980/480). The format of the calculation is the same as for the computation of the direct labor variance.

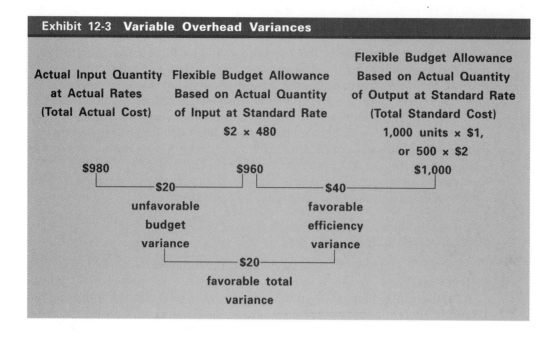

Exhibit 12-3   Variable Overhead Variances

$$\text{Variable Overhead Budget Variance} = 480 \times (\$2.00 - \$2.0417)$$

$$= -\$19.97 \text{ (difference due to rounding)}$$

We can also calculate the $40 variable overhead efficiency variance using the standard rate per direct labor hour of $2 and the difference between the actual and standard hours.

$$\text{Variable Overhead Efficiency Variance} = \$2 \times (500 - 480) = \$40$$

Interpreting Variable Overhead Variances

No matter what drives variable overhead cost pools, variable overhead efficiency variances indicate efficient (or inefficient) use of the *drivers*, *not* of the factors making up variable overhead. Thus, for a pool of variable overhead that is related to machine time, the variable overhead efficiency variance will reflect the efficient or inefficient use of *machine hours*, not the use of power, lubricants, maintenance, and other elements of variable overhead driven by machine hours.

Of course, some elements of variable overhead might be related directly to the number of units produced, rather than to an input factor such as labor hours. For example, costs such as packaging materials (boxes, padding, lining) are directly related to units produced. Workers who pack the products should use standard quantities of these materials for each packaged product even if they work more or less efficiently than standard (take more or less time to package the product). If variable overhead contains significant amounts of such cost elements, the conventional calculations of variable overhead efficiency and budget variances are not appropriate for analysis and may be difficult for a manager to interpret.

It is important to identify the cost drivers to achieve the best possible estimates of cost. If a considerable amount of overhead cost is driven by the number of components in a product, but the company uses direct labor hours as the driver, the company will have large, unexplainable budget variances because it is using the wrong driver. The reason is that, as we said earlier, use of overhead elements themselves is reflected in budget variances, while use of the driver is reflected in efficiency variances. If a company uses the wrong driver, it will compute the budget allowance based on input using the wrong driver. Such budget allowances will be well off the mark.

The choice of cost drivers for overhead is also important for behavioral reasons. Product designers, engineers, and other technical personnel whose responsibilities include cost reduction naturally will concentrate on high-cost factors. Thus, in a company using direct labor to assign variable overhead, these technical personnel will bend their efforts toward reducing labor time. Their efforts will be misplaced if direct labor does not drive significant amounts of overhead. The Tektronix example in Chapter 10 illustrates this point.

MATERIALS VARIANCES

When we speak of materials, we also mean parts, components, and subassemblies that a company buys. The **material use variance** is calculated in the same way as the labor and overhead efficiency variances. The **material price variance** differs from its counterparts in labor and variable overhead because materials, unlike labor, can be stored. What is purchased in one period is not necessarily used in that period, but the economic effect of paying more or less than standard price for materials occurs at the time of purchase, so the material price variance is based on the quantity of materials purchased, not the quantity used. Another reason for this is that the earlier that managers are aware of variances, the sooner they can take corrective action. Consequently, it makes sense to isolate the material price variance at the time of purchase rather than at the time the material is used. Coulter Inc. (see Exhibit 12-1) bought 23,000 feet of lumber for $18,860, an average price of $0.82 ($18,860/23,000). The standard price per foot of lumber is $0.80 (also from Exhibit 12-1). In calculating the material price variance, the flexible budget allowance is based on what you expect to pay for the quantity purchased: $18,400 (23,000 feet × $0.80 per foot). The material price variance is diagrammed in Exhibit 12-4.

We can also use the alternative formula.

$$\begin{array}{ccccc} \text{Material} \\ \text{price} & = & \begin{array}{c}\text{Actual} \\ \text{quantity} \\ \text{purchased}\end{array} & \times & \left(\begin{array}{c}\text{Standard} \\ \text{price}\end{array} - \begin{array}{c}\text{Actual} \\ \text{price}\end{array}\right) \\ \text{variance} \\ -\$460 & = & 23{,}000 & \times & (\$0.80 - \$0.82) \end{array}$$

The material use variance is calculated the same as the direct labor and variable overhead efficiency variances. Coulter used 19,500 feet of lumber to make 1,000 crates. The standard quantity of lumber per crate is 20 feet (see Exhibit 12-1), so the total standard quantity for 1,000 crates is 20,000 feet. The standard cost of lumber for 1,000 crates is $16,000 (20,000 feet at $0.80 per foot, or 1,000 crates multiplied by the standard materials cost per crate of $16, as shown in Exhibit 12-1). The material use variance is diagrammed in Exhibit 12-5.

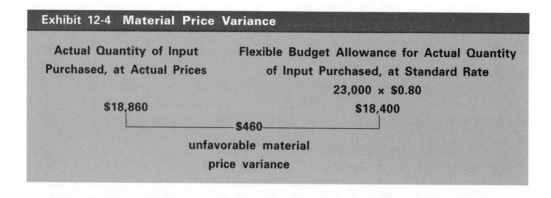

Exhibit 12-4   Material Price Variance

Actual Quantity of Input
Purchased, at Actual Prices

$18,860

Flexible Budget Allowance for Actual Quantity
of Input Purchased, at Standard Rate
23,000 × $0.80
$18,400

└──────────── $460 ────────────┘
unfavorable material
price variance

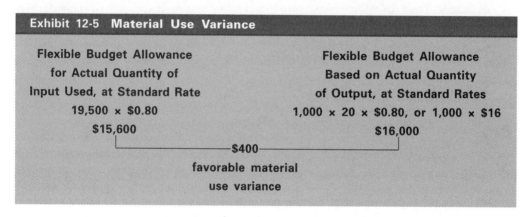

Exhibit 12-5   Material Use Variance

Flexible Budget Allowance
for Actual Quantity of
Input Used, at Standard Rate
19,500 × $0.80
$15,600

Flexible Budget Allowance
Based on Actual Quantity
of Output, at Standard Rates
1,000 × 20 × $0.80, or 1,000 × $16
$16,000

└──────────── $400 ────────────┘
favorable material
use variance

Again, we can calculate the material use variance using the differences.

$$\begin{array}{c} \text{Material use} \\ \text{variance} \end{array} = \text{Standard price} \times \left(\begin{array}{c} \text{Standard quantity} \\ \text{for actual output} \end{array} - \text{Actual quantity} \right)$$

$$\$400 \qquad = \qquad \$0.80 \quad \times \qquad (20,000 - 19,500)$$

We were able to determine labor and variable overhead variances in one schedule for each (see Exhibits 12-2 and 12-3, respectively). We cannot do that with materials variances because we have two actual quantities, one for units purchased, the other for units used. This is the only difference between materials variances and the other types of variances.

STANDARDS IN MULTIPRODUCT COMPANIES

So far we have dealt with a company making a single product, but multiproduct companies also use standard costs. (As Chapters 14 and 15 show, many multiproduct companies have no other choice than to use standard costs.) No conceptual problems are introduced simply because a company makes more than one product. But practical questions arise about the extent to which detailed information should be produced and the cost of obtaining the additional information.

Seldom does a multiproduct company encounter problems in developing standard costs. But isolating variances for each product is a different matter if products use the same facilities and the same workers, and the company cannot determine the actual use of materials, labor, and variable overhead drivers (such as machine time, setups, or production orders) for each product. The costs of materials, labor, and overhead are traceable to *production as a whole*. But under such circumstances it might be very costly (even impossible) to keep track of materials, direct labor time, and overhead drivers used to make each product.

Despite the difficulties of obtaining information about the actual costs of individual products, managers are interested in knowing such costs for planning and decision making. As a practical matter, a company might *periodically* keep track of materials and labor by product as a check on standards. In addition, managers who suspect inappropriate standards might investigate if efficiency variances fluctuate significantly as product mix changes. The overriding issue is whether the costs of keeping track of materials, direct labor, and overhead drivers by product is less than the benefits of having that information.

STANDARD COSTS AND ACTIVITY-BASED COSTING

TGH Company has two principal variable overhead cost pools. One pool is driven by machine time and includes such costs as power, supplies, abrasive materials, and maintenance. The other pool is driven by the number of machine setups. These costs include wages of setup workers, supplies used in changeovers, and materials destroyed in testing machine settings and calibrations. The variable component of overhead related to machine hours is $6.00 per hour, and the variable component related to setups is $140 per setup. Data and calculations for a 1,000 unit batch of one of TGH's products are as follows:

Standard machine hours	1,500	
Variable overhead rate per hour	$6	
Standard variable overhead related to machine hours		$ 9,000
Number of setups per batch	20	
Variable overhead rate per setup	$140	2,800
Total standard variable overhead per batch		$11,800

Suppose that TGH made 10,000 units (10 batches) of this product using 14,000 machine hours. Actual machine-hour driven variable overhead was $85,000; setup-driven variable overhead was $27,500. Because of scheduling problems, TGH required 210 setups to achieve the output. A diagrammatic presentation showing the calculations of variances is as follows:

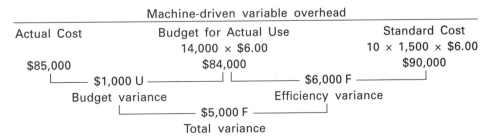

Machine-driven variable overhead

Actual Cost	Budget for Actual Use 14,000 × $6.00	Standard Cost 10 × 1,500 × $6.00
$85,000	$84,000	$90,000

$1,000 U — Budget variance

$6,000 F — Efficiency variance

$5,000 F — Total variance

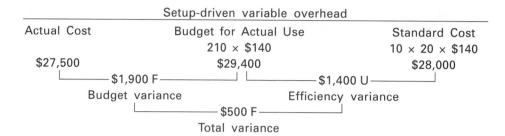

Of course, the company would also have materials and labor variances that it would calculate in the usual way.

VARIANCES AND PERFORMANCE EVALUATION

Isolating price and quantity variances is the first step toward providing information for performance evaluation. Quantifying price and use variances is not the same thing as identifying the causes of, and the responsibility for, those variances. Knowing that laborers were paid more or less than the standard rate, or worked more or fewer than the standard hours, does not explain why these variances occurred. As we pointed out in Chapter 10, the relevant factors in evaluating the performance of an individual manager are those that the manager is responsible for and can control.

Two issues complicate the interpretation of variances. First, variances signal nonstandard performance only if they are based on up-to-date standards that reflect current production methods and current prices of input factors. A company that increases labor time to increase product quality, but does not adjust its standards, will have unfavorable labor efficiency variances. These variances are not the fault of the managers responsible for using labor; the fault lies with the standard. Most companies continually seek to improve production methods. Developing new standards every time a change occurs is costly, and frequent revisions of standards might cause the standards to lose their meaning. Accordingly, the decision to revise standards must compare the cost of making the revision with the expected benefits in the form of better control and performance evaluation, and managers must interpret variances in the light of changes in manufacturing conditions not incorporated in standards.

Second, many variances are interdependent. One variance might be directly related to others, either in the same or a different department. (We confronted a similar situation in Chapter 10, where the use of a particular cost-allocation scheme could cause one manager's actions to affect the reported performance of another.) For example, a purchasing manager could buy lower-quality materials at a favorable price. If the materials are hard to work with, labor time increases. Unfavorable labor and perhaps variable overhead efficiency variances (for the variable overhead that is driven by direct labor) in processing departments have the same cause as the favorable material price variance — the purchase of lower-quality materials. Thus, knowing that there was a variance for some element of cost (materials, labor, or overhead) is not the same as knowing why the variance occurred or which manager was responsible for it.

INVESTIGATING VARIANCES

Once they have calculated variances, managers must decide whether to investigate them. As a general rule, managers should investigate a variance if they expect to be able to take corrective action that will reduce costs by an amount greater than the cost of the investigation. Because of the difficulty of estimating the relevant costs, many companies use rules of thumb, or rules derived from statistical analyses, to decide whether to investigate.

Because they want to investigate only significant variances, managers use two general criteria: absolute size of the variance and its percentage of standard cost. A variance of $5 is almost certainly not worth investigating, whereas a variance of $100 might be. If actual cost is $500 and standard cost is $400, the $100 variance is 25 percent of standard. This large variance percentage might well be worth investigating, whereas a $100 variance from a standard cost of $85,000 is almost certainly not. Thus, absolute size of a variance is probably less important than its percentage of standard cost.

The cost of investigating variances is difficult to determine. Managers with a fixed amount of time to spend on various tasks are wise to concentrate on variances that are likely to be correctable and whose correction may be expected to yield large savings. (There is a significant opportunity cost of managerial time.)

Many companies use **control charts** to decide when a particular variance should be investigated. These charts show past cost behavior patterns so that efforts will not be wasted investigating costs that normally show wide fluctuations. A control chart is shown in Exhibit 12-6.

The dots on the chart represent actual costs related to actual outputs. The *dotted* lines represent the limits within which managers have decided not to investigate variances. Managers could set the lines closer to or farther away from total standard cost. The closer the limits, the more variances will be investigated, and vice versa. The wide scattering of costs in a chart suggests high variances. A manager who believes that the production process is under adequate control and that the variances are unavoidable will set wide limits. A manager who thinks that most variances are caused by correctable factors will set narrow limits. Statistics courses cover many sophisticated ways of developing control charts.

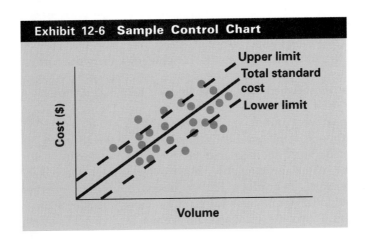

Exhibit 12-6 Sample Control Chart

What should *not* be important in deciding whether to investigate a variance is whether the variance is favorable or unfavorable. As we pointed out in the previous section, variances are not necessarily independent; a favorable variance in one area of responsibility might have unfavorable effects on another area. Moreover, favorable variances can be caused by actions that could harm the company in the long run. For example, favorable variances in material prices or labor efficiency could stem from lessened concern for the quality of the finished products. When customers see reduced quality, the reputation and subsequent sales of the company will be hurt. Short-run profits might increase because of lower costs (favorable variances), but long-run profits may suffer.

Because, as we suggested early in the chapter, standards can be useful for planning, one of the most important reasons for investigating variances is to detect bad standards. Variances can occur because of out-of-date standards. Variances also can result if standards are set at levels that are either too tight or too loose. If standards are used for planning and decision making, they must reflect current information about attainable performance.

SETTING STANDARDS—BEHAVIORAL PROBLEMS

Companies use a variety of approaches to setting standards, and the approach used can influence how people respond to them.

Engineering Methods

Some companies develop standard quantities for materials and labor by carefully examining production methods and determining how much of an input factor is necessary to obtain a finished unit. Time-and-motion study, a method developed in the early 20th century, is often used to set labor standards. Industrial engineers analyze the various movements necessary to perform each task. For example, a worker might have to reach into a bin, pick up a part, place it on the workbench, drill two holes in specified places, then place the part into another bin. Each movement is timed. The total time required to perform the entire task becomes the standard time allowed. Similarly, industrial engineers study the characteristics of the product and its materials to determine how much material is required per unit. Such studies also determine the materials wasted through cutting and trimming. One caution in applying engineering methods is that workers under observation might work much slower than usual, leading the company to set standards too low (standard costs too high).

Engineering methods also are used to set standards for some overhead items, such as maintenance. Industrial engineers specify the components of a desirable maintenance program and estimate the costs of each component. A standard is then established that allows for specified maintenance expense per machine-hour used, with allowance for other maintenance that occurs because parts break or wear out.

Although some overhead items can be analyzed using engineering methods, it is usually difficult to analyze overhead by starting with a unit of product. Unlike materials and labor, most overhead costs are not directly related to single units of product. Rather, large amounts of overhead are likely to be related to large quantities of product, labor hours, machine hours or other cost drivers. Therefore, standards for elements of variable overhead are more often developed using the methods illustrated in Chapter 3: high-low, scatter diagram, and regression analysis.

Managerial Estimates

Some companies rely on the judgment of managers closest to a task to determine quantities of input needed to produce a unit of product. Such managers understand current production conditions and specifications. This approach to setting standards is advantageous because, as we noted in Chapter 6, managers who participate in setting standards and budgets are more likely to commit to meeting them. There is, however, some reluctance to allow managers to set standards without guidance, because some higher-level managers believe—rightly or wrongly—that standards set in this way will include unnecessary slack (that is, standards will be too loose). Hence, standards initially determined by managerial estimates usually are carefully reviewed at higher levels of management.

Even companies that can carefully engineer standards rely on comments from managers because manufacturing managers understand that some factors are difficult to capture in engineering analyses. More important, as early as Chapter 6 we noted that managers who participate in setting goals (such as standards) are much more likely to commit themselves to achieving them.

The evidence is persuasive, but not conclusive, that performance also improves when *workers* participate in setting standards. The general idea of increasing employee involvement in managerial decisions extends to setting standards.

Product designers and managers developing standards should understand that cost reduction is not the only objective. Designing products that will be of high quality and relatively easy to manufacture are important as well. These facets of manufacturing have become even more important for U.S. companies that want to do business in the European Community. Companies that want to sell in the European Community must demonstrate that their products meet the standards established by the International Standards Organization (ISO) of Geneva. For example, ISO 9000 requires companies to document each step their workers perform that affects the quality of the product. Companies applying for ISO certification must meet stringent requirements in 20 functional areas, ranging from design to employee training. ISO dispatches independent auditors to verify that companies follow required procedures.[1]

What Standard—Ideal, Attainable, or Historical?

Perhaps the most critical issue of behavioral responses to standards is the level of performance of the standard. Should the standard be based on what can be done under the best possible conditions? Should it include allowances for waste, fatigue, and bottlenecks—that is, currently attainable performance? Should it be based on past performance, an historical measure?

An **ideal standard** can be attained only under perfect conditions. It assumes that laborers continuously work at the peak of their abilities, that materials always arrive at work stations on time, that machines never break down, that maintenance on machinery never stops production, and that no one makes mistakes. In short, an ideal standard is not likely to be achieved under anything

---

1 *"You Want EC Business? You Have Two Choices,"* Business Week, *October 19, 1992, 58.*

like normal working conditions. Using an ideal standard is sure to result in unfavorable variances.

Some argue that ideal standards are best because the resulting unfavorable variances alert managers to deviations from the ideal and motivate workers to do the best possible job. Whether ideal standards really do assist managers in these ways is questionable. Some evidence from the behavioral sciences suggests that motivation is *reduced* rather than increased by the use of ideal standards. Being unattainable goals, ideal standards can foster discouragement, lack of commitment to the goal, and distrust of higher levels of management. Frustrated managers and workers might even ignore standards they know to be unattainable. However, we shall explain later in this chapter why some companies that focus on continuous improvement use ideal standards.

Setting a **currently attainable standard** recognizes expectations about efficiency under normal working conditions. Such a standard allows for unavoidable losses of efficiency due to recurring problems that can never be eliminated. But currently attainable standards are not lax. Performance requirements are high, but they are attainable if everything goes reasonably well.

Research in the behavioral sciences indicates that managers and workers respond well to standards as goals when they have participated in setting the standards and when the standards are attainable. Such standards also can be useful for planning, whereas ideal standards cannot. (Managers who use ideal standards must make adjustments to plan accurately for expenses, pro forma financial statements, and cash flows.) Additionally, currently attainable standard costs are of more value than ideal standard costs for decision-making purposes. Acceptance of special orders, price reductions or increases, promotional campaigns, and other special decisions must be based on expected variable costs, not those that could be obtained only under ideal conditions.

An **historical standard** is based on experience. Using historical performance as a standard has serious drawbacks. Such standards perpetuate inefficiencies and ignore changes in product design and work methods that affect labor and materials requirements. Historical achievements have no particular significance except as they may aid in predicting the future. (Compare this reservation with those expressed earlier—particularly in Chapters 5, 6, 7, and 11—about the usefulness of historical information for predicting the future.)

STANDARD COSTS, PRODUCT LIFE CYCLE, AND STRATEGY

It is important to use any managerial tool to its best advantage. Some work well in certain circumstances, poorly in others. Two factors affecting how well standard costs are likely to work are the life-cycle stage of the product and the strategy the company is following for the product. As to life cycle, most products begin their lives with rapid sales growth, then mature and have stable sales, and finally decline. As to strategy, some companies strive to be cost leaders, others try to differentiate their products through style, function, quality, customer service, or other factors.

Standard costs and variance analysis work best for mature, stable products (such as automobiles) and for undifferentiated commodities (such as paper and most building products) where companies follow a cost leadership strategy. In the mature stage of product life, when price competition is important, cost control is one of the principal competitive weapons. Low costs allow a company to maintain its margin and to weather poor periods.

Products in growth stages often are highly differentiated and use rapidly changing technology. They compete on style or function, but not on price. The critical success factors are increasing volume and achieving high market share. Margins tend to be high, so that being a low-cost producer contributes less to overall profitability than does volume.

Standard costs do have a place with growing products, or differentiated products, but they should not be emphasized at the expense of gaining volume and a secure share of the market. Even **Merck**, the giant maker of prescription drugs that are patented and therefore highly differentiated, stresses cost control through productivity gains and eliminating non-value-adding activities and costs.

REPORTING VARIANCES

Managers of cost centers typically receive reports like the one in Exhibit 12-7. The exhibit shows that the number of units produced is less than the number budgeted, which *might* indicate that the manager was ineffective because he or she failed to meet the production goal. But a problem in a department that had previously worked on the product could also have caused the failure to meet the production goal, in which case this manager cannot be held responsible for the shortfall in production. If the production shortfall is the manager's fault, then shortfalls are likely to appear in any departments that subsequently work on the product. In any case, the cause of the production shortfall must be determined before this manager's performance can be evaluated.

The "actual" costs reported to the manager on the sample report have been adjusted to eliminate price variances. That is, the amounts in the Actual column for materials, labor, and supplies are actual quantities multiplied by standard prices. This approach is used when the manager controls only the quantities of each factor used.

Because calculating a variance does not explain its cause, performance reports usually contain a section for comments and explanations of variances. The department manager can then concentrate on those variances that need explanation and, if the cause of the variance is in that department, comment on the prospects for improvement.

The sample performance report clearly labels some costs as noncontrollable and shows them separately. Chapter 10 pointed out reasons for doing this. In general, variable costs are controllable over short periods, whereas many fixed costs are not. Thus, depreciation on equipment in the machining department is direct to the department, but not controllable in the short run. Allocated costs are not controllable by the department to which they are allocated.

CONTROL OF FIXED COSTS

From earlier discussions we know that the total cost per unit of product changes with a change in production because there is a fixed component in the total cost. As we will discuss in Chapters 13 and 14, companies use per-unit fixed costs, including standard fixed costs, for product costing purposes. But for *control*

Exhibit 12-7   Departmental Performance Report

Month May 19X7

Department Machining   Manager R. Jones

Date Delivered 6/4   Date Returned 6/6

	Budgeted	Actual	Variance
Production, in units (original budget 11,000 units)	11,000	9,000	2,000
Controllable costs, for actual production of 9,000 units:			
Materials, standard of $2 *	$18,000	$18,800	$800 U[1]
Labor, standard of $3 *	27,000	28,800	1,800 U[1]
Supplies, standard of $0.10 *	900	880	20 F
Repairs	1,100	1,200	100 U
Indirect labor	900	900	0
Total controllable costs	$47,900	$50,580	$2,680 U
Noncontrollable costs:			
Depreciation Machinery used in department	$1,500	$1,500	0
Heat and light (allocated)	200	220	$20 U
Other allocated costs	800	860	60 U
Total noncontrollable costs	$2,500	$2,580	$80 U
Total costs	$50,400	$53,160	$2,760 U

*Actual costs are at standard prices.

Comments and Explanations
[1] Faulty materials required more time and created more waste.

purposes, the notion of a standard fixed cost *per unit* has little meaning. The total cost incurred for each element of fixed overhead is, however, relevant for planning and control.

Fixed overhead includes many components, such as depreciation, property taxes, supervisory and managerial salaries, and the fixed components of mixed costs, such as maintenance and power. Each item is budgeted separately for the department that controls it. There are two fixed cost variances. For cost control, only the budget variance is relevant. The other variance is described in Chapter 14.

BUDGET VARIANCE

The **fixed overhead budget variance** is simply the difference between actual and budgeted fixed cost and is computed for each element of cost for a particular department. Budget variances occur for many reasons. Since the company prepared the budget, there may have been changes in the prices for resources (a raise in salaries, an increase in property taxes); some discretionary costs, such as employee training or travel, might have been increased or decreased by managerial action; and quantities of resources used might have been greater or less than budgeted, as when more or fewer industrial engineers were hired than were budgeted.

The major considerations in analyzing fixed cost budget variances are behavioral. Managers who are worried about exceeding their budget might postpone discretionary costs (such as employee training). On the other hand, as we saw in Chapter 6, managers might incur unnecessary costs if they fear that being below budget this period will lead to a budget cut for the next period.

Managers can manipulate some discretionary costs to achieve low total budget variances (total fixed costs incurred less total fixed costs budgeted), so focusing only on totals can obscure critical problems. Managers who scrimp on employee training or maintenance are improving short-run performance to the detriment of long-run performance. This type of undesirable action might escape notice if only the totals were considered.

As you know from Chapter 6, managers hold different philosophies about budgeting fixed costs. Some advocate tight budgets, some loose budgets, and some prefer budgets based on currently attainable performance levels. Our preference is for the use of currently attainable budgets, with the persons whose budgets are being set participating in the determination of what is currently attainable. Likewise, the methods used in setting standard variable costs— historical analysis, engineering methods, and managerial judgment—can also be applied to the budgeting of fixed costs.

FIXED COSTS ON PERFORMANCE REPORTS

Notice that the cost center performance report shown in Exhibit 12-7 distinguishes between controllable variable costs and controllable fixed costs. Whereas materials and direct labor are usually variable, the other controllable items could be variable, fixed, or mixed.

For planning, the manager wants to know whether a variance is likely to recur. It might be easier to plan for future variances if the fixed and variable controllable costs are separated. If a fixed cost is running $1,000 per month more or less than budgeted, and this variance is expected to continue, the manager can count on the variance being $1,000 per month. A direct labor efficiency variance of 10 percent of standard cost will be a different dollar amount in each month, depending on production. Thus, planning for future operations requires different analyses for the two kinds of costs—fixed and variable.

A PROBLEM AREA—SEPARATING FIXED AND VARIABLE COSTS

Some companies cannot determine separate budget variances for variable overhead and fixed overhead because they cannot determine how much of the *actual* cost incurred is fixed and how much is variable. For example, a cost such as electricity usually has both a fixed and a variable component. But it might not be possible to determine how much of the actual cost relates to the fixed component and how much to the variable component.

Suppose that electricity is budgeted using the following formula: Total cost = $2,450 + ($0.80 × machine hours). The fixed portion is for lighting; the variable portion is for machinery that runs only during production. Assume that the standard and actual price per kilowatt-hour is $0.03. Any difference between actual electricity cost and the flexible budget amount must be caused by the quantity of electricity used.

Suppose that a product requires two standard machine hours, production was 4,000 units, 8,100 machine hours were used (100 hours over standard), and actual electricity cost was $9,210. The total standard hours allowed for production of 4,000 units are 8,000 (4,000 × 2). The total budgeted cost for electricity is $8,850 [$2,450 + ($0.80 × 8,000 standard machine hours)]. Because we cannot, in the absence of separate meters, analyze the actual cost into its fixed and variable components, we cannot calculate separately the budget variances for the fixed and variable elements. In such cases, companies calculate a single budget variance for the mixed cost as a whole. Using the data in our example, the budget variance is as follows:

$$
\begin{aligned}
\textit{Total budget variance} &= \textit{Actual cost - Flexible budget based on input} \\
&= \$9,210 - [\$2,450 + (\$0.80 \times 8,100)] \\
&= \$9,210 - \$8,930 \\
&= \$280 \textit{ unfavorable total budget variance}
\end{aligned}
$$

The variance is unfavorable because actual cost exceeds the budget allowance. We also know that actual machine hours were 100 over standard, so we know there is an $80 unfavorable variable overhead efficiency variance (100 × $0.80).

Why might a company not isolate the fixed and variable components of the actual cost? Why, for example, would the company in the preceding example not install meters on its machines to determine how much electricity is related to machines and how much to lighting the factory? As stated earlier, especially in Chapter 10, the answer is usually that the cost to obtain the additional information exceeds the probable benefits. In this instance, the cost to install and maintain meters might exceed the savings that could be achieved through better control. Recall that a fundamental principle of managerial accounting is that obtaining additional information is desirable only if the benefits exceed the costs.

STANDARD COSTS, VARIANCES, AND CONTINUOUS IMPROVEMENT

Historically, conventional manufacturers paid considerable attention to labor variances because direct labor was a significant proportion of total manufacturing cost and also drove much overhead cost. Direct labor is much less important in many of today's manufacturers, being about 10 to 20 percent of total manufacturing cost; direct labor can be as little as 3 to 5 percent of total cost in some operations. Nor does direct labor drive as much overhead cost as it once did. Accordingly, direct labor should receive correspondingly less attention.

As we noted earlier, including idle time in labor efficiency variance calculations can be dysfunctional. The possibility that supervisors will violate goal congruence by overproduction is especially harmful in JIT companies. Moreover, many managers believe that reporting labor efficiency variances, even excluding idle time, detracts from the main objective of rapid, smooth throughput of high-quality products. Managers committed to continuous improvement believe that the very idea of standards and standard costs conflicts with their philosophy. They argue that standards stifle improvement because people will strive to *meet* standards, which violates the principle of continuous improvement. They also argue that variances relate to cost centers, which typically are small units, when managers and workers should be concerned with the performance of the entire manufacturing operation.

Advanced manufacturers emphasize developing worker skills and teamwork. Because many foreign countries have lower wage rates than the United States, U.S. companies will have to take measures to compete world-wide. **Levi Strauss**, maker of Levi's, now uses teams to produce an entire garment, replacing an assembly line where each worker did only a small part of the work. The company cut cycle time from six days to seven hours, so it can switch products quickly and respond better to customer needs. Defects also dropped when the workers took over production of the entire garment.[2]

Despite these reservations, some JIT companies and others seeking continuous improvement use standards (and analyze variances) much as do companies using conventional operations. Others use standards, but continually tighten them (lower standard costs) to encourage improvement. JIT companies that do *not* use standards compare current period actual costs with prior period actual costs (or an average of actual costs for the past few periods) to gauge their improvement. Such comparisons are similar to variance calculations, with the prior period costs acting as the "standard."

KAIZEN COSTING AND TARGET COSTS

Japanese manufacturers have used a technique called **kaizen**, or **kaizen costing**, for many years. Kaizen stresses continuous improvement, rather than simply meeting standards. Under kaizen, performance standards are continually raised (standard costs lowered), so the objective is to meet targeted *reductions*, not standard costs.

Previous chapters have discussed the importance of the product design stage of developing a product, where managers make decisions that commit perhaps

---

2 *"The Global Economy: Who Gets Hurt?"* Business Week, *August 10, 1992, 48.*

80 percent of total costs to make the product over its life. Kaizen comes in when products are being made and sold. It aims at achieving systematic, steady reductions through continuous improvement. Kaizen companies establish annual and monthly target cost-reduction rates, which they then translate into amounts for individual cost elements and products. For instance, suppose a company has established a 5 percent target reduction rate beginning from a standard labor cost of $25 per unit. The first target is $23.75, 5 percent less than $25, or a reduction of $1.25. Companies adjust target rates and amounts for changes in manufacturing conditions such as design changes and changes in input factor costs (e.g., increase in labor rates).

We introduced target costs in Chapter 2 as costs determined by working from the market price of a product to the cost that will allow the company to earn a target profit. **Chrysler**, among other companies, uses Kaizen and target costing principles in dealing with its suppliers. Chrysler takes the target price for an automobile and works backwards to determine what it can pay for each part. Chrysler then works with its suppliers to meet or beat those prices.

Drifting costs are costs achievable with current methods and technology. Managers view them as interim steps toward achieving target costs. Companies try to identify ways to move the drifting cost toward the ultimate target by focusing on areas where reduction can be most effectively pursued.[3]

NONFINANCIAL MEASURES

Managers of JIT operations use many nonfinancial measures to evaluate performance. Measures used instead of, or along with, standard costs include the following:

1. *Supplies of inventories*   You already know that companies try to keep inventories low because they are costly to carry. Such measures as turnover and days' supply of inventory help managers judge how efficiently they are operating. Inventory supply is often expressed as turnover, which is the days' supply divided into 360 (or 365). Thus, a 10-day supply is the same as a turnover of 36 times. A company that can manufacture its products with only a 4-day supply of materials and components is doing better than one that requires a 12-day supply to keep its production lines running.

2. *Cycle time*   This is the total time a company takes from receiving a customer's order through making the product and shipping it to the customer. Time spent making the product is value-adding time, while the rest of the cycle time is non-value-adding. The closer cycle time is to manufacturing time, the greater is the value-adding time. Additionally, the shorter the cycle time, the higher customer satisfaction.

3. *Setup time*   This is the time it takes to change over from making one product to making another. It is a non-value-adding activity.

4. *Percentage of deliveries to customers made on time*   This indicates how well the company is meeting its commitments to customers.

3 Malcolm J. Morgan, *"A Case Study in Target Costing, Accounting for Strategy,"* Management Accounting (England), May 1993, 20-22.

5. *Quality measures* There are many ways to assess and measure quality. Some common ways are the percentage of defective units, number of warranty claims or customer complaints, and number of units reworked.

6. *Throughput measures* These indicate how much work a cell, a department, or an entire factory is doing. Measures of throughput include number of units finished, number of units finished divided by processing time available, and value-adding time divided by total time. These measures, as well as others, are consistent with the objectives of JIT manufacturing. They also can be used by conventional manufacturers. The accompanying Insight describes one company's use of such measures as well as data regarding the extent of use of some measures.

Materials and Purchasing

World-class manufacturers do not evaluate their purchasing functions solely on the basis of the prices they pay for materials and components. **McKinsey & Co.**, a large consulting firm, reported a number of measures of performance for the purchasing function, some of which are as follows:

	Typical Company	World-class Company
Agents per $100 million purchases	5.4	2.2
Purchasing costs as percent of purchases	3.3%	0.8%
Time spent placing order, weeks	6	0.001
Percentage deliveries late	33%	2%
Percentage deliveries rejected	1.5%	0.0001%
Materials shortages, per year	400	4

Some of these measures relate to the cost of the purchasing function, while others relate to the quality of suppliers. It is important that companies reduce lead time of their suppliers because that fosters the JIT objective of reducing cycle time and inventory. Of course, quality measures are especially important for JIT companies.[4]

A major study concluded that evaluating purchasing managers by material price variances is especially unwise for manufacturers that have embarked on supply chain management. Companies such as **AlliedSignal** are developing long-term, strategic relationships with only a very few suppliers. Buyers give such suppliers large orders on long-term contracts in exchange for annual price decreases. Purchasing managers are also trying to reduce administrative costs of the purchasing function, which are non-value-adding and can run to millions of dollars annually. AlliedSignal reduced its payments for maintenance, repair, and operating supplies (MRO) by $50 million in 1994 through using fewer suppliers, placing orders through electronic data interchange (no paperwork), and other such economies.

The same study also found that competitive bidding is not always a good idea, either. Suppliers of Japanese automakers established factories close to auto plants, have face-to-face contact with customers (suppliers stationed engineers

---

4 *"Quality,"* Business Week, *November 30, 1992, 72.*

INSIGHT

AT&T's New River Valley Works utilizes the JIT philosophy with several product lines. A partial list of performance measures used on its Communications Transformer Line appears as follows:

Measure	Goal
Number of defectives	0
Percentage of orders shipped on time	100%
Manufacturing interval (cycle time)	5 hours
Supply of inventories	0.5 days
Cost of scrap	$1,500
Scrap as a percentage of output	1%
Number of line disruptions	0
Percentage of people cross-trained to do more than one job	100%

The plant is further along toward achieving some goals than others. We said earlier that people given ideal standards might not be motivated to work to achieve them. In a JIT environment, goals are not used as standards for monthly achievement, but rather as pinnacles of success.

Another study of measures of operating performance found the following measures, and percentages of companies using each.

Measure	Percentage Using Measure
Inventory supply	75%
Labor efficiency	73%
Physical scrap counts	72%
Cost of rework	72%
Materials use	61%
Customer delivery performance	55%
Machine utilization percentage	54%
Machine downtime	48%
Throughput rates	46%
Warranty costs	38%

The author found it interesting that so many companies tracked labor efficiency because, on average, labor costs for these companies were only 13 percent of total manufacturing cost.

Sources: F. B. Green, Felix Amenkhienan, and George Johnson, "Performance Measures and JIT," Management Accounting, *February 1991, 34.*
James A. Hendricks, "Applying Cost Accounting to Factory Automation," Management Accounting, *December 1988, 24.*

in customers' plants), and dedicated a considerable portion (about 22%) of assets to those customers, thus focused more on those customers, which increased product quality. U.S. suppliers are farther away, dedicating only 15 percent of assets. The study concludes that a tightly integrated production network with dedicated suppliers will outperform a loosely coupled one.[5]

The behavioral aspects of standards and variances extend to many areas of management. The accompanying Insight illustrates one.

STANDARD COSTS FOR NONMANUFACTURING ACTIVITIES

Some companies have developed standard costs for nonmanufacturing activities. Such activities have certain traits that render the development of standard costs difficult. Most basically, measuring output in nonmanufacturing activities is difficult. Rarely do homogeneous physical units flow out of the work done by the product design, legal, accounting, marketing, and general administration departments. There is seldom a definable measure of output because there is no standard product.

Costs associated with administrative work also tend to be more fixed than those of manufacturing. Consequently, it might be impossible to develop standard variable costs per unit of output even if an appropriate unit of output

IN SIGHT

Charles Machine Works manufactures the Ditch Witch®, the well-known trenching equipment used to lay underground utility lines. In moving toward JIT and total quality management (TQM), the company used a tool called Socio-Technical Systems Analysis (STSA), which is especially useful for identifying variances that cause problems further down the production line. The company had found that some variances or quality problems were caused early in the process, but were not discovered until later. The worker who discovered the problem often scrapped the defective piece because to repair it would make his performance suffer.

For instance, at an early step, a worker could cause burrs in the barrel of a cylinder. These burrs would not show up until assembly, when the barrel would leak. The assembly worker who discovered the burrs simply tossed the defective barrels aside where they piled up until an engineer was notified. Additionally, the worker responsible for the burrs was not motivated to inspect and correct them because it would slow him down. "Someone else" would find them later. The task is to alleviate such problems through better teamwork and more coordination. The company used activity-based costing and standard costs to help TQM efforts by "focusing on activities that give 'the best return for the dollar.'"

Sources: Michael F. Thomas and James T. Mackey, "Activity-Based Cost Variances for Just-in-Time," Management Accounting, April 1994, 49-54.

5 *Jeffrey Dyer, "Dedicated Assets: Japan's Manufacturing Edge,"* Harvard Business Review, *November 1994.*

could be found. Therefore, administrative activities usually are controlled by static budgets rather than by standard variable costs. Thus, the earlier discussion on control of fixed costs is applicable to nonmanufacturing activities, but the discussion on standard variable costs usually is not.

Benchmarking is a relatively recent development that companies use to determine whether their operations and costs compare favorably to those of world-class companies. The concept is not limited to costs of manufactured products. **L.L. Bean**, the mail-order retailer, has such an excellent order-filling system that companies from all over have gone to its headquarters to study its operations. Companies can also use published databases to make such comparisons. One example is KnowledgeView®, published by **Price-Waterhouse**, the international CPA firm. The Texas Society of CPAs conducts annual studies of various operating and financial characteristics of CPA firms in the Southwest and publishes the results.

Companies evaluating their operations can find all kinds of comparisons. For instance, one company investigating its accounting function found that it cost a world-class company $4.60 to prepare an invoice and $7.30 to process a payroll check.[6] In reengineering its accounts payable function, **ITT Automotive** used the **Hackett Group** database to evaluate the efficiency of various functions such as the number of invoices processed per person per year.[7]

SUMMARY

Standard costs are a tool for planning, control, and evaluation of cost centers. Managers of cost centers, along with their managers, receive information showing the efficiency of the operation.

The standard for each major element of product cost (materials, labor, and overhead) is a combination of two separate standards: one for the quantity of the factor used in the product, the other for the price of a unit of that factor. The total variance between budgeted and actual cost can be analyzed into one variance related to a difference in price and another variance related to a difference in the quantity of the factor used. Since a single manager usually is not responsible for both the prices and quantity of resources used, separating total variances into price and use components assists in assigning responsibility. The separation also is helpful in planning future operations.

Because managerial functions and activities of cost centers are interdependent, variances shown on the performance report for a manager cannot automatically be attributed to the good or bad performance of that manager. The causes of variances are not always easy to determine and include poor management in the department showing the variance or poor management in an entirely different department. The cause also could be a bad standard. Some JIT advocates argue against the use of standards. Most JIT manufacturers use other measures to evaluate operations, whether or not they use standards.

---

6 *Steve Coburn, Hugh Grove, and Cynthia Fukami, "Benchmarking with ABCM,"* Management Accounting, *January 1995, 58.*
7 *Richard J. Palmer, "Reengineering Payables at ITT Automotive,"* Management Accounting, *July 1994, 39.*

KEY TERMS

benchmarking (574)
control chart (561)
currently attainable standard (564)
fixed overhead budget
  variance (567)
historical standard (564)
ideal standard (563)
idle time (553)
kaizen costing (569)

labor efficiency variance (553)
labor rate variance (553)
material price variance (557)
material use variance (557)
standard cost (549)
variable overhead budget
  (spending) variance (555)
variable overhead
  efficiency variance (555)

KEY FORMULAS

$$\begin{matrix} \text{Total standard} \\ \text{cost for} \\ \text{input factor} \end{matrix} = \begin{matrix} \text{Actual} \\ \text{production} \end{matrix} \times \begin{matrix} \text{Standard quantity} \\ \text{of input factor} \\ \text{per unit of} \\ \text{product} \end{matrix} \times \begin{matrix} \text{Standard price} \\ \text{(rate) for unit} \\ \text{of input factor} \end{matrix}$$

$$\begin{matrix} \text{Price} \\ \text{variance} \end{matrix} = \begin{matrix} \text{Actual quantity} \\ \text{of input acquired} \end{matrix} \times \left(\begin{matrix} \text{Standard price} \\ \text{per unit of input} \end{matrix} - \begin{matrix} \text{Actual price} \\ \text{per unit of input} \end{matrix} \right)$$

$$\begin{matrix} \text{Quantity} \\ \text{variance} \end{matrix} = \begin{matrix} \text{Standard price} \\ \text{per unit of input} \end{matrix} \times \left(\begin{matrix} \text{Total standard quantity} \\ \text{of input required} \end{matrix} - \begin{matrix} \text{Actual quantity} \\ \text{of input used} \end{matrix} \right)$$

REVIEW PROBLEM

Baldwin Company makes cabinets. One model, the Deluxe, has the following requirements.

Materials	40 feet of wood at $1.20 per foot
Direct labor	4 hours at $7 per hour
Variable overhead	$5 per direct labor hour

During June 19X4, the company made 1,200 Deluxe cabinets. Operating results were as follows:

Materials purchases (58,000 feet at $1.15)	$66,700
Materials used	51,200 feet
Direct labor (4,750 hours at $7.10)	$33,725
Variable overhead	$23,900

Required
Compute the standard variable cost per Deluxe cabinet and the variances for June 19X4.

ANSWER TO REVIEW PROBLEM

Standard Variable Cost	
Materials (40 feet of wood at $1.20)	$48.00
Direct labor (4 hours at $7 per hour)	28.00
Variable overhead at $5 per direct labor hour	20.00
Total standard variable cost	$96.00

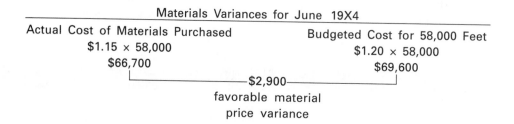

Materials Variances for June 19X4

Actual Cost of Materials Purchased
$1.15 × 58,000
$66,700

Budgeted Cost for 58,000 Feet
$1.20 × 58,000
$69,600

$2,900
favorable material
price variance

Alternatively, 58,000 × ($1.20 - $1.15) = $2,900 favorable

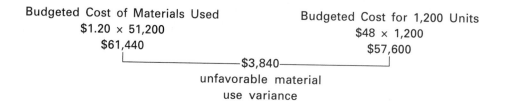

Budgeted Cost of Materials Used
$1.20 × 51,200
$61,440

Budgeted Cost for 1,200 Units
$48 × 1,200
$57,600

$3,840
unfavorable material
use variance

Alternatively, $1.20 × [(1,200 × 40) - 51,200] = $3,840 unfavorable.

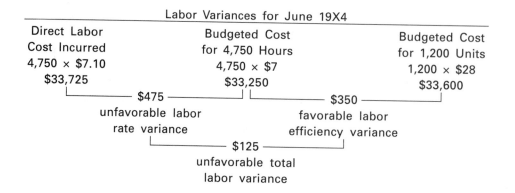

Labor Variances for June 19X4

Direct Labor
Cost Incurred
4,750 × $7.10
$33,725

Budgeted Cost
for 4,750 Hours
4,750 × $7
$33,250

Budgeted Cost
for 1,200 Units
1,200 × $28
$33,600

$475
unfavorable labor
rate variance

$350
favorable labor
efficiency variance

$125
unfavorable total
labor variance

Alternatively, the labor rate variance is:

$$4{,}750 \times (\$7 - \$7.10) = -\$475 \ unfavorable$$

The labor efficiency variance is:

$$\$7 \times [(1{,}200 \times 4) - 4{,}750] = \$7 \times (4{,}800 - 4{,}750) = \$350 \ favorable$$

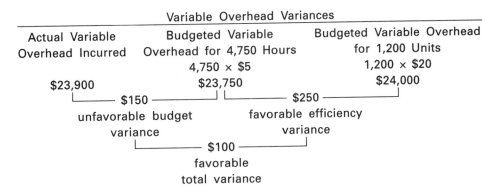

Variable Overhead Variances

Actual Variable Overhead Incurred	Budgeted Variable Overhead for 4,750 Hours 4,750 × $5	Budgeted Variable Overhead for 1,200 Units 1,200 × $20
$23,900	$23,750	$24,000

└─── $150 ───┘ └─── $250 ───┘
unfavorable budget   favorable efficiency
variance   variance
└─────── $100 ───────┘
favorable
total variance

Alternatively, we can compute the budget variance by calculating the actual rate of about $5.032, subtracting it from the standard rate of $5, then multiplying by 4,750 hours.

$$4,750 \times (\$5 - \$5.032) = -\$152 \text{ unfavorable (difference due to rounding)}$$

The efficiency variance is also given by $5 × (4,800 - 4,750) = $250 favorable. Note that because the variable overhead standard is based on direct labor hours, the only difference between the computation of the labor efficiency variance and the variable overhead efficiency variance is the rate used.

ASSIGNMENT MATERIAL

QUESTIONS FOR DISCUSSION

12-1 Budgeting and standards Budgeting aids managers in planning and control. Standard costs are useful for assisting in budgeting and for planning and control in general. What does the use of standard costs accomplish that budgeting does not?

12-2 Interpreting variances For each of the following situations, (a) indicate whether a variance is likely to occur, (b) state which variance(s) might be affected and in what direction, and (c) state whether an investigation should be undertaken and whether corrective action could be taken.
1. Wage rates have risen because a new union contract has been signed.
2. To increase safety, the plant manager has reduced the speeds at which forklifts carrying materials and semifinished products can be driven.
3. The firm sells its waste materials, chiefly metals, to a scrap dealer. Lately, revenue from waste sales has increased, while production has been steady.
4. Exceptionally heavy rainfall necessitates the drying out of materials that are stored outside.
5. The electric utility that supplies the company has been having difficulty with its generators. There are frequent blackouts and brownouts.
6. Many part-time workers are hired because of increases in production.

12-3 Changes in automakers' operations Various publications have reported on how the major auto companies have changed their operations in recent years. (One of the best is Alex Taylor III, "The Auto Industry Meets the New Economy," *Fortune*, September 5, 1994, 52-60.) For each of the following items, indicate how costs, including standard costs, might be affected.

1. Companies have begun buying many components that they once made. The only parts that **BMW** will make for its new roadster to be produced in South Carolina are the engine, transmission, and suspension. American companies will supply all other parts.
2. Companies are reducing the number of suppliers, and requiring suppliers to do more design and development work. In the past, companies gave suppliers detailed specifications and awarded contracts to the low bidder. For instance, the 1994 Ford Tempo required over 700 suppliers, the 1995 Ford Contour only 227.
3. **Ford** and **General Motors** have centralized purchasing for their U.S. and European operations.
4. **Chrysler** involves its suppliers in product design, soliciting their ideas for parts and components.

12-4   *Long-term contracts*   A recent annual report of **Borden** stated that the company had long-term contracts to buy chemicals from various suppliers at fixed prices. Many other companies use such arrangements, which sometimes obligate the company to buy a specified minimum quantity of the commodity or product.

Required
What are the advantages and disadvantages of such arrangements to the buyers?

12-5   *Effects of changed conditions*   Each of the following describes a change that occurred after standards had been set for the period and then lists three of the variances that were discussed in the chapter. For each item, select the variance most likely to be affected by the change and explain your choice.

1. To meet a shortage of workers in the face of a steady demand for the product, the firm decided to hire less experienced workers than it hired in the past.
   Variances: Material price variance, labor rate variance, labor efficiency variance.

2. Faced with the prospect of a shortage of the firm's normal materials, the firm decides to use a new, more expensive material that produces less waste and is easier to handle.
   Variances: Labor rate variance, variable overhead budget variance, variable overhead efficiency variance.

3. Based on a suggestion from a worker, the process for assembling certain parts of the final product has been changed so that a single employee assembles six components. Before the change, two employees of the same department worked independently to assemble three components each and a third employee in that department put together the subassemblies produced by those two employees.
   Variances: Material use variance, labor efficiency variance, variable overhead spending variance.

12-6   *Responsibility for variances (CMA adapted)*   Phillips Company uses a standard cost system. Variances for each department are calculated and reported to the department manager. Reporting has two major purposes: evaluating performance and improving operations.

Jack Smith recently was appointed manager of the Assembly Department. He has complained that the system does not work properly and discriminates against his department because of the current practice of calculating a variance for rejected units. The procedures for making this calculation are as follows: (1) all units are inspected at the end of the assembly operation, (2) rejected units are examined to see if the cause of rejection can be assigned to a particular department, (3) units that are rejected but cannot be identified with a particular department are totaled, (4) the unidentifiable rejects are apportioned to each department on the basis of the identifiable rejects. Thus, if a department had 20% of the identified rejects, it will be charged with 20% of the unidentified rejects. The variance, then, is the sum of the identifiable rejects and the apportioned share of unidentified rejects.

Required
Write a memorandum to Henry Berger, Smith's supervisor, evaluating the validity of Smith's claim and making a recommendation for resolving the problem.

12-7 Significance of variances Ann Jackson, controller of Stone Company, was recently told by several production managers that "as long as total costs do not exceed budgeted costs, based on standard prices and quantities, there is no reason to do any investigating or analysis."

Required
Comment critically on the statement. Cite at least two reasons why the policy is unwise.

EXERCISES

12-8 Standard cost computations Blivet Company makes a plastic deck chair. It has established the standard prices and quantities for a finished unit as follows:

Materials	4 pounds at $3 per pound
Direct labor	3 hours at $10 per hour
Variable overhead	$6 per direct labor hour (DLH)

Blivet also has fixed overhead of $100,000 per year.

Required
Fill in the blanks in the following items.

1. The standard cost per unit of finished product is
   (a) _____ for materials.
   (b) _____ for direct labor.
   (c) _____ for variable overhead.
2. At 70,000 direct labor hours, total variable overhead cost should be _____.
3. At 90,000 direct labor hours, production should be _____ units.
4. If 100,000 pounds of materials are used, production should be _____ units.
5. At 60,000 direct labor hours, total materials used should be _____ pounds.
6. If 66,000 pounds of materials are used, total variable overhead cost should be _____ and total labor cost should be _____.

12-9 Fundamentals of standard costs and variances Bryant Company manufactures decorative statues. Each statue requires 20 pounds of special clay and

30 minutes of direct labor. The standard price of clay is $3 per pound. The standard direct labor rate is $10 per hour and the standard variable overhead rate is $12 per direct labor hour.

During November, Bryant manufactured 1,000 statues. It bought 25,000 pounds of clay for $71,800 and used 22,000 pounds. Bryant paid direct laborers $4,770 for 480 hours and incurred $5,400 in variable overhead.

Required

1. Determine the standard variable cost of a statue.
2. Determine all variable cost variances.

12-10   Basic material and labor variances   Fergon Company makes a lamp shade and had the following budgeted and actual results in December.

	Budget	Actual
Unit production	10,000	11,000
Direct labor hours	20,000	21,600
Materials used, yards	40,000	44,700

The standard labor rate is $12 per hour; standard materials price is $4 per yard.

Required

Calculate the direct labor efficiency variance and the material use variance.

12-11   Basic variance relationships, materials   Fill in the following blanks. You can work them in order, but you do not have to.

Standard materials cost per unit of product	$30
Material use variance	$1,800F
Standard material use for quantity produced, in pounds	25,000
Number of pounds of materials purchased	30,000
Material price variance	$2,000U
Standard price per pound of materials	$6
Standard pounds of materials per unit of product	_____
Units produced	_____
Number of pounds of materials used	_____
Amount paid for materials purchased	_____

12-12   Ethics and overhead assignment   Ben Grayson, manager of a product line at FGH industries, was complaining about the calculation of standard costs. "My line has only three products. They are very simple and require no machine setups, no special quality control, and little machine time. Only direct labor and three or four kinds of materials are required. But some of the other lines we carry have products that require all manner of setup time, extra record keeping, and more vendor analysis because they have many more materials and components. Most of them are also machine-intensive. It's just not fair for them to bear overhead based only on direct labor. I've talked to the controller, but she just tells me to do my job and she'll do hers."

Required

Comment on Grayson's complaints. Is the controller abiding by the IMA Standards reproduced in Exhibit 1-3? If not, why not?

12-13 *Variance computations* Following are the standard variable costs for one of Halsey Knitting's sweaters, the Highlander.

Materials, 2 pounds of yarn at $6 per pound	$12
Labor, 2 hours of labor at $8 per hour	16
Variable overhead, $3 per labor hour	6
	$34

Actual results in March follow.

Production	1,000 sweaters
Materials purchased	2,100 pounds for $12,100
Materials used	2,200 pounds
Hours of labor worked	1,900 hours
Cost of labor	$16,100
Variable overhead incurred	$6,500

Required
Compute all variable cost variances.

12-14 *Comprehensive variance analysis* 4N Company makes industrial cleaners. Standard costs for Scumaway are as follows, along with actual results for March.

Materials, 5 pounds at $6 per pound	$30
Direct labor at $10 per hour	20
Variable overhead at $6 per DLH	12
Total standard variable cost	$62

Actual results for March:

(a) Production was 1,200 units.
(b) Material purchases were 3,200 pounds at $5.90 per pound.
(c) The company used 6,200 pounds of materials in production.
(d) Direct laborers worked 2,250 hours at $10.10, earning $22,725.
(e) Variable overhead was $13,800.

Required
Compute all variable cost variances.

12-15 *Evaluation in JIT manufacturing* Baskin Products recently implemented JIT principles and its controller is having difficulty in analyzing performance. She has collected the following statistics and asks you to tell her how each could help evaluate performance in the two months.

	July	September
Average processing time, hours	42	36
Average cycle time, days	33	22
Production, units	7,400	7,180
Maximum capacity, units	7,800	7,800
Defective units	96	72
Inventory of materials, days' supply	9	6
Inventory of work in process goods, days' supply	13	9
Inventory of finished goods, days' supply	3	4

Required

Use the data to describe where Baskin is improving and where it is not. You might wish to calculate some ratios using these raw numbers.

12-16   *Revision of standard costs* Clarkson Company manufactures toys. One group of toys consists of small cars, each of which requires the same quantities of materials and direct labor. The cars are packaged and sold in batches of 50. The standard variable cost of a batch is as follows:

Materials	$20.00
Direct labor (0.50 hours)	8.00
Variable overhead	4.00
Total standard variable cost	$32.00

The production supervisor is uncertain how to prepare the budget for the coming year. He tells you the following.

(a) Materials costs will average 20% higher because of price increases.
(b) Laborers will get a 5% raise at the beginning of the year.
(c) Increased efficiency will reduce direct labor hours by 10% and material use by 5%.
(d) The variable overhead rate will increase to $9 per direct labor hour.

Required

Prepare revised standard variable costs.

12-17   *Relationships—labor variances* Each of the following independent situations relates to direct labor. Fill in the blanks.

	a	b	c	d
Units produced	4,000	_____	3,000	_____
Actual hours worked	1,900	4,200	_____	_____
Standard hours for production achieved	2,000	_____	_____	6,000
Standard hours per unit	_____	0.5	2	3
Standard rate per hour	$12	$10	$4	_____
Actual labor cost	_____	$41,800	_____	$24,500
Rate variance	$310U	_____	$300U	$300F
Efficiency variance	_____	$1,000U	$600F	$800U

12-18   *Variance analysis* Kuhn Car Products makes automobile antifreeze. Kuhn has developed the following formula for budgeting monthly factory overhead costs: Total overhead cost = $140,000 + ($10 × direct labor hours). Other data relating to the cost of a case of the product are as follows:

Materials	4 gallons at $1.50 per gallon
Direct labor	20 minutes at $10 per hour

Last month Kuhn produced 12,000 cases and had the following costs.

Materials purchased (49,000 gallons)	$73,000
Materials used	51,200 gallons
Direct labor (3,920 hours)	$38,750
Overhead	$188,500

Required
Compute the price and quantity variances for materials and direct labor and the total variance for overhead.

12-19   *Performance reporting* Bryan Sklar, the president of your company, has asked you to investigate some unfavorable variances that occurred in one of the departments last month. You were given the following summary of the department's performance report.

	Budget	Actual	Variance
Production (in units)	3,000	3,200	200F
Costs (based on budgeted production):			
Direct labor	$ 9,000	$ 9,700	$ 700U
Supplies	600	650	50U
Repairs	1,500	1,500	
Power	1,200	1,400	200U
Total costs (all variable)	$12,300	$13,250	$ 950U

Required
1. Was performance poor?
2. Write a memorandum to Mr. Sklar recommending changes in the company's reporting. Use the guidelines in Appendix A.

12-20   *Variances—relationships among costs* Read the following in its entirety and then fill in the blanks.

1. Standard variable costs per unit:
   (a) Materials   4 pounds @ $_____ $ _____
   (b) Direct labor _____ hours @ $12.00 $24.00
   (c) Variable overhead $3 per DLH $ _____
2. Production   8,000 units
3. Materials purchases   33,000 pounds $62,000
4. Materials used, at standard prices   31,200 pounds $ _____
5. Direct labor, actual _____ hours $191,200
6. Material price variance $4,000 F

7. Material use variance	$ _____
8. Direct labor rate variance	$3,200 F
9. Direct labor efficiency variance	$ _____
10. Variable overhead spending variance	$1,500 F
11. Variable overhead efficiency variance	$ _____
12. Actual variable overhead cost	$ _____

12-21   Standards—machine-hour basis   Wilkens Company is highly automated and uses machine-hours to set standard variable costs. A unit requires two pounds of material costing $6 per pound and 12 minutes of machine time. The standard variable overhead rate is $10 per machine-hour. There is no direct labor; all workers are classified as indirect labor, and their wages are considered part of variable overhead.

During June, 23,000 units were produced using 5,200 machine-hours. Variable overhead costs were $50,300. Purchases of materials were 54,000 pounds for $318,000 and 45,000 pounds were used.

Required

1. Compute the standard variable cost of a unit of product.
2. Compute the variances for June.

PROBLEMS

12-22   Standards in a service function   Graham Labs performs blood tests for local physicians. Dr. Graham, head of the company, has instituted a standard cost system to help control costs and measure employee efficiency. After extensive consultations with his employees, he developed the following standards for some high-volume tests.

Test	Standard Time (in minutes)
Blood sugar	12
Cell count	10
Others	6

The company's 12 lab technicians earn an average of $11 per hour, with a range of $10.25 to $11.50. During July, the first month the system was in effect, the lab had the following results.

Test	Number Performed
Blood sugar	4,600
Cell count	2,400
Others	5,400

Lab technicians earned $21,500 for 1,880 hours.

Required

Determine the labor rate variance and labor efficiency variance.

12-23   Investigation of variances   The production manager of ComPlast Company tells you that she exercises management by exception. She examines a performance report and calls for further analysis and investigation if a variance is greater than 10% of total standard cost or is more than $1,000. She is not responsible for any rate or price variances and is therefore concerned only with efficiency variances. During April, the following occurred.

(a) Materials used, 4,650 gallons
(b) Direct labor hours, 7,920
(c) Production, 2,000 units

The standard cost of a unit is as follows:

Materials (2 gallons at $4)	$ 8
Direct labor (4 hours at $8)	32
Variable overhead ($6 per DLH)	24
Total standard variable cost	$64

Required
1. Compute the variances for which the production manager should be held responsible.
2. Determine which variances should be investigated according to her criteria.

12-24   *Determining a base for cost standards*   The production manager of Rolland Company recently performed a study to see how many units of product could be made by a worker who had no interruptions, always had materials available as needed, made no errors, and worked at peak speed. He found that a worker could make 20 units in an hour under these ideal conditions. In the past, about 15 units per hour was the actual average output. However, new materials handling equipment had recently been purchased and the manager is confident that an average of 18 units per hour can be achieved by nearly all workers.

All workers earn $15 per hour. A month after the study was made, workers were paid $1,200,000 for 80,000 hours. Production was 1,410,000 units.

Required
1. Compute the standard labor cost per unit to the nearest $0.001 based on
   (a) historical performance
   (b) ideal performance
   (c) currently attainable performance
2. Compute the labor efficiency variance under each of the standards in item 1 and comment on the results.
3. Using the guidelines in Appendix A, write a short memo to Bonnie Gardella, the production manager, stating which method of setting the standard you prefer for planning purposes and for control purposes.

12-25   *Investigation of variances*   The supervisor of the Boiling Department is pleased with her performance this past month, which showed a favorable material use variance of $2,000. The following data relate to the operation.

Units produced	4,000
Standard costs for materials:	
Libidinum, 3 pounds at $3	$ 9
Larezium, 2 pounds at $4	8
Total standard materials cost	$17

The operation used 10,000 pounds of libidinum and 9,000 pounds of larezium.

Required
1. Verify the amount of the material use variance.
2. Did the supervisor do a good job this month? What questions must be answered before coming to a conclusion about the manager's performance?

12-26 *Determining standard costs* Vernon Company makes its single product, Shine, by mixing the materials Dull and Buff in 500-pound batches in a 3:2 ratio (three pounds of Dull for each two pounds of Buff). The mixing is done by two laborers and takes three hours. The resulting mixture is boiled for four hours, which requires four workers. The mixture that comes out of the boiler yields four pounds of finished product for each five pounds of raw material, so that the 500 pounds of material mixed become 400 pounds of final product. (Evaporation during boiling reduces the volume.)

All laborers earn $12 per hour. Variable overhead is $4 per direct labor hour. Dull costs $2.80 per pound; Buff costs $2 per pound.

Required
Determine the standard variable cost per pound of Shine.

12-27 *Activity-based variances* In the past, KC Valves, Inc. has used standard costs with all variable overhead being associated with direct labor. Some managers are unhappy with the results because direct labor is not the only cost driver. The managers have amassed the following data for a standard batch of 1,000 units of model GY-44.

Materials, various	$1,900
Direct labor, 40 hours at $15	600
Labor-driven variable overhead at $8	320
Machine setups, 80 hours at $20	1,600
Laboratory tests, 5 at $20	100
Total standard variable cost	$4,520

Actual results in March follow.

Production	10 batches
Direct labor hours	390
Labor-driven variable overhead	$3,300
Setups	880 hours, $17,500
Laboratory tests	47 tests, $960

The managers are unsure what variances to calculate, and how, aside from those related to direct labor.

Required
Determine all overhead variances that you can for March and explain your calculations.

12-28   *Standards and variances, two products* Bascomb Company makes two coffee tables. Both go through essentially the same process, and the company does not keep records regarding the amounts of materials and labor used in making each model, only for the two models as a whole. Standard cost data are as follows:

	Harcombe	Exeter
Materials:		
3 pounds at $4 per pound	$12	
4 pounds at $4 per pound		$16
Direct labor	16	24
Variable overhead	12	18
Total standard costs	$40	$58

All direct laborers earn $8 per hour, and the variable overhead rate is $6 per direct labor hour. The same materials are used in both models.

During March, the company had the following results.

Production	2,000 Harcombe, 1,500 Exeter
Materials purchased	9,000 pounds at $4.15 per pound
Materials used	11,900 pounds
Direct labor	8,750 hours at $7.95 per hour
Variable overhead	$55,500

Required

1. Compute all variable cost variances for production as a whole.
2. Can you compute variances for each model? If not, why not? Explain why you might want to isolate variances to the individual models.

12-29   *Overhead rates, ABC, and pricing* Darlene Bhada, controller of TGF Industries, was discussing the company's most recent operating results with Jim Simmons, the sales manager. Both were disappointed because a downward trend in profit was accelerating, even though sales were remaining about the same. Simmons said "Our major line is selling poorly because our competitors are undercutting our prices. I don't see how they do it! We have cut prices down to the bone. Fortunately, some of our minor lines are doing very well." Bhada replied that "The problem could be with our costs. Look at the standards for these representative products from the major line and one of the minor lines."

	Major Product	Minor Product
Materials	$35	$ 65
Direct labor at $12/hour	24	24
Variable overhead at $18/DLH	36	36
Total standard variable cost	$95	$125
Annual volume	80,000	4,000
Selling price	$100	$165

Bhada continued, "We have been revising our overhead rate by looking at the requirements of each product. I have divided our variable overhead costs into three pools and developed variable rates for each. My chief accountant has collected data for each product." The data Bhada referred to follow.

Driver for Cost Pool	Variable Rate	Major Product	Minor Product
Direct labor	$3.00/DLH	2 DLH	2 DLH
Machine setups	$8.00/setup	1 setups	7 setups
Number of parts	$0.50/part	8 parts	18 parts

"Perhaps," Bhada went on, "we can get a better idea of our costs by incorporating this new information."

Required

1. Develop standard variable costs using the new information.
2. Write a memorandum to Ms. Bhada explaining the differences between your standard costs and the original standards as previously given. State why the company seems to be experiencing the results given previously. Follow the guidelines in Appendix A.
3. In general, do you expect that high-volume or low-volume products are more likely to show higher overhead costs under ABC than under labor-based assignment? Why?

12-30   Input standards versus output standards   Foelber Company manufactures a commercial solvent. Foelber budgets manufacturing costs based on direct labor hours. The production manager is unable to interpret the report he has just received and asks for your assistance. The report contains the following data.

	Actual Cost at 10,000 Direct Labor Hours	Budgeted Cost for 10,000 Hours
Materials used at standard prices	$ 26,700	$ 24,000
Direct labor	69,200	68,000
Indirect labor	28,100	26,500
Other variable overhead	26,100	27,300
Total variable costs	$150,100	$145,800

Foelber budgeted 50,000 gallons of production. Actual production was 51,000 gallons, which requires 10,200 direct labor hours at standard performance.

Required

For each component of cost, determine the variance due to efficiency (or inefficiency) and that due to spending or price.

12-31   Bases for standard costs and decisions   Sewell Company uses very tight standards for determining standard costs. The production manager believes that the use of standards achievable only under ideal conditions helps to motivate employees by showing them how much improvement is possible and therefore giving them goals to achieve.

The sales manager has criticized the use of such high standards for performance and correspondingly low standard costs because it increases his difficulty in determining whether business at lower than normal prices should be accepted. In one specific instance, the sales manager was offered the opportunity to sell 4,000 units at $8.50, which is $4 below the normal selling price. He rejected the offer. The standard variable cost per unit of product is as follows:

Materials (3 pounds at $0.50)	$1.50
Direct labor (½ hour at $6 per hour)	3.00
Variable overhead ($4 per direct labor hour)	2.00
Total standard variable cost	$6.50

The sales manager was uncertain whether the order should have been accepted. He knew that the standards were never met. What bothered him was the extent to which they were not met. He asked his assistant to try to determine whether the order would have been profitable. The assistant developed the following information: material price and labor rate variances are negligible. However, during a normal month when 10,000 units are produced, the material use variance, direct labor efficiency variance, and total variable overhead variance are about $2,000, $6,000, and $5,200, respectively, all unfavorable.

Required
1. Assuming that the experience of the month presented would have applied when the special order was being made up, should the order have been accepted?
2. Develop new standard variable costs based on currently attainable performance, assuming that the month described reflected currently attainable performance. Be sure to include both prices and quantities for each input factor.

12-32   Multiple products Cross Company manufactures three models of small plastic chairs. The standard material cost is $0.80 per pound, standard labor rate is $8.00 per hour, and standard variable overhead rate is $3.00 per direct labor hour. The standard quantities of each cost factor for each model are as follows:

	Model 1	Model 2	Model 3
Materials, pounds	24	24	42
Direct labor hours	5	5	2

Actual results for March were as follows:

Production:	
Model 1	12,000
Model 2	16,000
Model 3	14,000
Materials purchased	1,400,000 pounds at $0.78
Materials used	1,275,000 pounds
Direct labor	173,000 hours for $1,365,200
Variable overhead	$497,000

Required
Determine the variable cost variances.

12-33   Standards and idle time Prescott Textiles manufactures a single kind of cloth in its Petzel Mill. The standard labor cost per 100 yards of cloth is $14.00, which is two standard labor hours at $7 per hour. In August, orders were slow and the mill turned out only 1,200,000 yards, well below the usual volume. Workers were paid for 29,000 hours. The company guarantees a 40-hour work-week to employees with five years of service. About 5,500 of the 29,000 hours were idle time, when eligible employees were paid, but had no work to do.

Required

1. Calculate the labor efficiency variance using the 29,000 hours actually worked.
2. Can you conclude from your answer to item 1 that the work force was inefficient in August? Why or why not? What do you recommend?

12-34   *Evaluation in JIT manufacturing* Crystal Enterprises has been using JIT principles for a short time and has been developing a variety of performance measures. Jill Fennell, the controller, recently received the following statistics and asks you to tell her how each could help evaluate performance.

Production in units	8,150
Number of defectives	240
Percentage of orders shipped on time	88%
Manufacturing interval (cycle time)	36 hours
Supply of inventories	5 days
Cost of scrap	$4,600
Scrap as a percentage of output	3%
Number of line disruptions	5
Percentage of people cross-trained on more than one job	65%

Required

Write a memorandum to Ms. Fennell telling her how each measure can help her evaluate operations. Use the guidelines in Appendix A.

12-35   *Analyzing results—sales and cost variances* Managers of Reed Blanket Company were disappointed at the shortfall in profit for 19X7, as shown in the following income statements. Amounts shown are in millions.

	Budgeted	Actual
Unit sales	10.0	10.8
Sales	$120.0	$122.1
Variable manufacturing costs:		
Materials	$ 20.0	$ 21.8
Direct labor	15.0	17.0
Variable overhead	5.0	5.2
Total variable costs	$ 40.0	$ 44.0
Contribution margin	$ 80.0	$ 78.1
Fixed costs:		
Manufacturing	$ 50.0	$ 50.8
Selling and administrative	20.0	19.9
Total fixed costs	$ 70.0	$ 70.7
Profit before taxes	$ 10.0	$ 7.4

Required

The president wants an analysis showing why profit fell short of budget. He wants you to determine the effects of the difference between budgeted and actual unit volume, budgeted and actual selling prices, and budgeted and actual costs for the volume achieved. Production equalled sales. Prepare such an analysis and be sure that it fully accounts for the difference between budgeted and actual profit.

12-36   Flexible and static budgets   Grace Manufacturing Company is managed by a family, none of whose members understand accounting. Ralph Grace, one of the managers, was elated at the following performance report.

	Budget	Actual	Variance
Production	30,000	26,000	
Materials	$ 75,000	$ 72,000	$ 3,000F
Direct labor	45,000	40,000	5,000F
Variable overhead	90,000	86,000	4,000F
Fixed overhead	60,000	60,000	
Total	$270,000	$258,000	$12,000F

Grace showed the report to Denise Cohen, the newly hired assistant controller, saying that one did not need to understand accounting to see that coming in under budget was a good thing.

Required

As Cohen, what would you say to Grace?

12-37   Actual to actual comparisons—JIT   Trivet Company operates a factory utilizing JIT operations. Results for two recent months follow.

	June	May
Direct labor hours worked	21,500	20,200
Number of units produced	11,000	10,300
Rate paid to direct laborers	$7.20 per hour	$7.00 per hour
Price paid for materials	$0.96 per gallon	$0.98 per gallon
Materials purchased and used in production	45,000 gallons	41,000 gallons
Variable overhead incurred	$85,800	$83,400
Unit cost	$25.80	$25.73

Required

The production manager wants to know if performance improved in June. Write a memorandum detailing the differences between May and June. Determine the differences in May and June costs resulting from changing input factory prices and changing efficiency.

12-38   Variance analysis—changed conditions   Grimes, Inc. makes a warm-up outfit with the following standard costs.

Materials (3 pounds at $4)	$12
Direct labor (2 hours at $8)	16
Variable overhead ($4 per DLH)	8
Total standard variable cost	$36

The standards have proved to be currently attainable and are generally met within small variances each month. In August, the manufacturing vice president brought in a glowing report from the purchasing department. The company bought materials for $3.50 per pound. The new materials were different from the old but were of equal quality for the finished product. The materials bought during August were used in September with the following results.

Production scheduled	4,000 units
Actual production	3,700 units
Direct labor (8,350 hours)	$66,100
Variable overhead	$34,200
Materials used	12,300 pounds

Required

1. Compute all variances that you can.
2. Why might the variances have occurred?
3. Assuming that the experience of September will continue, should the company continue buying the new materials?

12-39   Economic cost of labor inefficiency   Columbia Windows makes high-quality bay windows for houses. It sells to wholesalers who in turn sell to building contractors or homeowners. Some months of the year the company has trouble keeping up with demand and loses sales because customers generally are unwilling to wait and buy from a competitor. Direct labor time is constrained by the production process, so that the company can obtain a maximum of 280,000 direct labor hours per month. The typical product mix results in an average standard labor time of 14 hours per unit. The standard labor rate is $10 per hour, and the standard variable overhead rate is $8 per direct labor hour. Average materials cost is $82 per unit; average selling price is $620 per unit. Results for two recent months follow. January is typically a slow month, June a busy one, with orders for over 22,000 units.

	January	June
Units produced	12,500	19,200
Actual labor hours	179,400	280,000

Materials costs were at standard. The actual labor rate equalled the standard rate, and variable overhead was incurred as budgeted for actual direct labor hours.

Required

1. Compute the labor efficiency variance and variable overhead efficiency variance for each month.

2. Do the variances for both months reflect the true cost to the firm of labor inefficiency? Why or why not?

12-40   Unit costs and total costs   Wilton Matthews, the production manager of KRL Industries, was disturbed at the following results for November. Budgeted production was 90,000 units, and actual production was 100,000 units.

	Budget for 90,000 Units	Actual for 100,000 Units
Materials	$ 288,000	$ 341,800
Direct labor	679,500	773,800
Variable overhead	339,750	391,300
Fixed overhead	850,000	860,700
Total costs	$2,157,250	$2,367,600
Cost per unit	$23.969	$23.676

Purchases of materials were about equal to use and were at 5% over standard prices. Labor rates were 2% over standard.

Matthews tells you that the 5% material price variance and 2% labor rate variance were the source of the unfavorable results, offering the following calculations to support his case.

Adjust budgeted costs to 100,000 units ($2,157,250 × 100/90)	$2,396,944
Material price variance ($288,000 × 100/90 × .05)	16,000
Labor rate variance ($679,500 × 100/90 × .02)	15,100
Total allowable costs	$2,428,044

"Look, these guys who prepare the reports can't hold me to a budget for 90,000 units when I put out 100,000. Besides, they charged me with variances that I am not responsible for, so I actually came in way under budget. Even with the stupid way they made up the report, you can see that my unit cost was below budget, but I should look even better."

Required

Matthews is responsible for materials and labor use and for all overhead costs. Determine whether his claim of good cost control is correct by calculating the total variances for which he is responsible. Calculate as many individual variances as you can.

12-41   Design change variances   Grogan Company manufactures machine tools and often changes the design of a tool during the year to make it more suitable for customers. Grogan does not change the standards when it changes the design, which has caused some grumbling by production managers. The controller wants to be able to reconcile the year's actual results with the original budget and argues that changing standards during the year makes it virtually impossible to do so.

As a compromise, a production manager has suggested dividing the efficiency variances into two parts, one that captures the effects of design changes, the other to reflect efficiency in meeting the standard created by the revised design. The total efficiency variance will still be the difference between actual inputs at standard prices and the original standard inputs at standard prices.

The following data are representative of design changes.

	Original	Redesigned
Materials:		
6 feet at $3 per foot	$18.00	
7 feet at $3 per foot		$21.00
Direct labor:		
.60 hours at $10 per hour	6.00	
.55 hours at $10 per hour		5.50
Variable overhead at $7 per DLH	4.20	3.85
Totals	$28.20	$30.35

Production of the tool was 2,000 units, requiring 13,700 feet of materials and 1,180 direct labor hours.

Required

1. Determine the material, direct labor, and variable overhead efficiency variables, ignoring the redesign.
2. For each variance, determine how much resulted from the design change and how much from efficient or inefficient use of input factors.

12-42   *Use of unit costs*   The supervisor of the machining department of Glenmills Company has just received the following performance report, which was prepared by the new cost accountant.

	Costs per Unit		
	Budget	Actual	Variance
Materials	$ 3.00	$ 2.96	$(0.04)
Direct labor (1.5 standard hours)	9.00	9.204	0.204
Variable overhead:			
Indirect labor	2.40	2.48	0.08
Power	0.90	0.93	0.03
Fixed overhead	4.00	4.95[a]	0.95
Totals	$19.30	$20.524	$ 1.224

a Actual cost incurred divided by actual production in units.

Budgeted production was 12,000 units; actual production was 10,000 units. Budgeted fixed overhead per unit is based on budgeted production. You learn that actual materials cost in the report is based on standard prices and that all other actual cost figures are based on actual prices and quantities.

The supervisor is not responsible for direct labor rates, which were $5.90. He is also not responsible for variable overhead spending variances, but he is responsible for fixed overhead budget variances.

Required

Prepare a new report including only those items for which the supervisor is responsible. (You might wish to use a different type of presentation from that shown.)

12-43   *Analysis of income statement*   The controller of Taylors Company has given you the following income statement.

Sales (20,000 × $20)		$400,000
Standard variable cost of sales		240,000
Standard variable manufacturing margin		$160,000
Variances:		
Materials	$ 6,000F	
Direct labor	4,000U	
Variable overhead	3,000U	1,000U
Actual variable manufacturing margin		$159,000
Fixed costs:		
Budgeted manufacturing costs	$75,000	
Fixed cost budget variance	2,000U	
Selling and administrative expenses	40,000	117,000
Income before taxes		$ 42,000

The controller gives you additional data. Production was 22,000 units. Materials purchased were all made at standard price. Direct laborers averaged 0.85 hours per unit, which was 0.05 hours above the standard time. Actual direct labor cost was $144,800. The standard variable overhead rate is $2 per direct labor hour.

Required
Answer the following questions.

1. What was the direct labor efficiency variance?
2. What was the direct labor rate variance?
3. What was the standard materials cost per unit?
4. What was actual total variable overhead?
5. What was the variable overhead efficiency variance?
6. What was the variable overhead budget variance?
7. What was actual total fixed manufacturing cost?
8. If the standard materials price is $2 per pound, how many pounds are needed at standard to make a unit of product?
9. How many pounds of materials did the firm use?

12-44 Forecasting income Robyn Company had the following income statement in 19X7.

Sales (110,000 × $20)		$2,200,000
Standard variable cost of sales		880,000
Standard variable manufacturing margin		$1,320,000
Variances:		
Materials	$ 2,400U	
Direct labor	1,800F	
Variable overhead	1,600F	1,000F
Actual variable manufacturing margin		$1,321,000
Fixed costs:		
Manufacturing	$560,000	
Selling and administrative	470,000	1,030,000
Income		$ 291,000

The details of standard cost were as follows:

Materials (0.50 pounds at $4 per pound)	$2.00
Direct labor (0.40 hours at $10 per hour)	4.00
Variable overhead at $5 per direct labor hour	2.00
Total standard variable cost	$8.00

The company's industrial engineers have redesigned the product so that (1) materials requirement should be 0.45 pounds and (2) direct labor hours should be 0.35. The company expects to produce 120,000 units in 19X8 and to sell 115,000. Materials costs will increase to $4.20 per pound. Each element of fixed cost should increase by 5%.

The managers and engineers expect to see materials use about 2% over the 0.45 pounds standard because it will take some time for workers to learn the new production methods. They also expect direct labor for the year to be about 6% above standard for the same reason. They do want to use the 0.45 pounds and 0.35 hours as the standards, however, because they expect workers to operate at standard by midyear. The standard variable overhead rate will increase by $0.20 per hour because of rising prices for input factors such as supplies and power. All elements not mentioned should be about the same as they were in 19X7.

Required

1. Determine the standard cost for the product for 19X8.
2. Prepare an income statement for 19X8 reflecting the manager's expectations, using the same format as the one for 19X7.

12-45 *Relationships among data* Dempsey Company uses standard variable costs. Variable overhead rate is based on direct labor hours. The following data are available for operations during April 19X4.

Total production	_____
Actual labor cost	$ 61,600
Actual materials used	5,900 pounds
Actual variable overhead	$ 37,150
Standard labor cost per unit	$_____
Standard materials cost per unit	$4.50
Standard variable overhead cost per unit	$_____
Materials purchased (8,200 pounds)	$ 12,800
Material price variance	$500 U
Labor rate variance	$2,500 U
Variable overhead spending variance	$_____ F or U
Material use variance	$_____ F or U
Labor efficiency variance	$900 F
Variable overhead efficiency variance	$_____ F or U
Direct labor hours worked	9,850 hours
Standard labor rate	$_____
Standard direct labor hours per unit	5 hours
Variable overhead rate per DLH	$4

Required

Fill in the blanks. (Hint: You cannot do the parts in the order given.)

12-46   Standard costs—alternative raw materials   Visodane, Inc. manufactures a household cleaner called Kleenall that is sold in 32-ounce (1/4 gallon) plastic bottles. The cleaner can be made using either of two basic raw materials— anaxohyde or ferodoxin. Their respective costs are $10 and $8 per pound. Whichever material is used is mixed with water and other chemical agents and is then cooked. The product is then bottled, and the bottles are packed into cartons of 20 bottles each.

Each batch is made with 1,200 gallons of water, costing $0.30 per 100 gallons. Chemical agents other than raw materials cost $120 per batch. If anaxohyde is used, 100 pounds are mixed with the water and chemical agents. If ferodoxin is used, 110 pounds are needed. Mixing takes three hours and requires three laborers.

The mixture is then cooked, for 80 minutes if anaxohyde is used and for 90 minutes if ferodoxin is used. One worker is needed for the cooking process. With either raw material, the output of the cooking process is 1,000 gallons because of evaporation. Bottling and packing requires one laborer working two hours.

All laborers are paid $6 per hour. Variable overhead is based on the time required in each process because the high degree of mechanization makes direct labor a poor measure of activity for variable overhead. Overhead per hour is $30 for the mixing process, $120 for the cooking process, and $60 for the bottling and packing process. Bottles cost $0.04 each and the cartons cost $0.20 each.

Required

1. Compute the standard cost of a carton of 20 bottles of Kleenall, assuming (a) anaxohyde is used and (b) ferodoxin is used.
2. Suppose that each carton sells for $20 and that cooking time available each month is 1,000 hours. Which material should be used?

CASES

12-47   *Selecting a vendor* Brenda Olesky, controller of the Industrial Products division of NVT, Inc., was trying to decide between two vendors for a valve for a product. Olesky gathered the following data regarding the two finalists. The data came from other divisions that do business with both companies. The division expects to use 100,000 valves per year.

	Boston Metals	Barnett, Inc.
Unit price	$45	$51
Discount for payment within 10 days	2%	2%
Normal lead time, purchase order to delivery	22 days	6 days
Percentage times missed delivery date	20%	5%
Reject rate	3%	1%
Technical support	good	excellent

Required

State which vendor you would choose and why.

12-48   *Developing standard costs (CMA adapted)* The controller of Berman Detergents has asked for your help in preparing standard variable costs for its major product, Sudsaway. Berman has never used standard costs, and the controller believes that better control will be achieved if standards are used. She wants the standards to be based on currently attainable performance.

The following data are available for operations in 19X6.

Materials used (1,350,000 gallons at $0.80 per gallon)		$1,080,000
Direct labor (160,000 hours at $5.50 per hour)		880,000
Variable overhead:		
Indirect labor	$240,000	
Maintenance and repairs	80,000	
Packaging materials	370,000	
Other variable overhead	480,000	1,170,000
Total variable production costs		$3,130,000

During 19X6, 740,000 cases of Sudsaway were produced. Each case contains 12 bottles of 16 ounces each, a total of 1.5 gallons per case. During 19X6 the firm used an inferior raw material. During 19X7 the firm expects to pay $0.90 per gallon for a better material. Even with the better material, some shrinkage will occur during production. The controller expects that output of Sudsaway in gallons will be 90% of the raw material put into process.

The firm employed a number of inexperienced workers in 19X6. They worked about 48,000 of the total direct labor hours, which is about 12,000 more than standard hours. During 19X7 the controller expects all workers to be normally productive and to earn an average wage of $5.80.

According to the controller, variable overhead costs were under control during 19X6, given the excessive labor hours worked. Packaging materials were not affected by the excessive labor hours, being related to cases actually produced. Indirect laborers will receive a 10% wage increase early in 19X7.

Required

Prepare standard variable costs, by category of cost, for a case of Sudsaway.

12-49   Standard costs, variances, and evaluation (CMA adapted)   Bergen Company manufactures a single product. Standard variable cost of a unit is as follows:

Materials (1 pound plastic at $2)	$ 2.00
Direct labor (1.6 hours at $4)	6.40
Variable overhead	3.00
Total standard variable cost	$11.40

The variable overhead cost is not related to direct labor hours, but rather to units of product because production is thought to be the causal factor in the incurrence of the variable overhead elements. The elements of variable overhead, based on a yearly volume of 60,000 units of production, are as follows:

Indirect labor (30,000 hours at $4)	$120,000
Supplies, oil (60,000 gallons at $0.50)	30,000
Maintenance costs, variable portion (6,000 hours at $5 per hour)	30,000
Total budgeted variable overhead	$180,000

Fixed overhead is budgeted as follows, based on 60,000 units of product.

Supervision	$ 27,000
Depreciation	45,000
Other fixed overhead (includes fixed maintenance costs of $12,000)	45,000
Total budgeted fixed overhead	$117,000

During November, 5,000 units were produced and actual costs were as follows:

Materials (5,300 pounds used at $2)	$10,600
Direct labor (8,200 hours at $4.10)	33,620
Indirect labor (2,400 hours at $4.10)	9,840
Supplies (6,000 gallons of oil at $0.55)	3,300
Variable maintenance costs (490 hours at $5.30)	2,597
Supervision	2,475
Depreciation	3,750
Other fixed overhead (includes maintenance of $1,100)	3,600
Total	$69,782

Purchases of materials were 5,200 pounds at $2.10 per pound. The firm has divided responsibilities so that the purchasing manager is responsible for price variances for materials and oil and the production manager is responsible for all quantities of materials, labor (direct and indirect), supplies, and maintenance. The personnel manager is responsible for wage rate variances and the manager of the maintenance department is responsible for spending variances.

Required

1. Calculate the following variances.
   (a) material price
   (b) material use
   (c) direct labor rate
   (d) direct labor efficiency
   (e) total variable overhead
   (f) total fixed overhead

2. Prepare a report that details the overhead variances of each element by responsibility. (A convenient method is to list the managers across the top, and under each show the variances for which they are responsible.) You should account for all variable and fixed overhead variances. That is, the total of your answers to item 1 should be distributed to individual managers.

12-50 *Analyzing results (CMA adapted)* Aunt Molly's Old Fashioned Cookies bakes cookies for retail stores. The company's best-selling cookie is Chocolate Nut Supreme which is marketed as a gourmet cookie and regularly sells for $8.00 per pound. The standard cost per pound of Chocolate Nut Supreme, based on Aunt Molly's normal monthly production of 400,000 pounds, is as follows:

Cost Item	Quantity	Standard Unit Cost	Total Cost
Direct materials			
Cookie mix	10 oz.	$0.02/oz.	$0.20
Milk chocolate	5 oz.	$0.15/oz.	0.75
Almonds	1 oz.	$0.50/oz.	0.50
			$1.45
Direct labor*			
Mixing	1 min.	$14.40/hr.	$0.24
Baking	2 min.	$18.00/hr.	0.60
			$0.84
Variable overhead**	3 min.	$32.40/hr.	$1.62
Total standard cost per pound			$3.91

* *Direct labor rates include employee benefits.*
** *Applied on the basis of direct labor hours.*

Aunt Molly's management accountant, Karen Blair, prepares monthly budget reports based on these standard costs. Following is April's contribution report that compares budgeted and actual performance.

Contribution Report
April 1995

	Budget	Actual	Variance
Units (in pounds)	400,000	450,000	50,000F
Revenue	$3,200,000	$3,555,000	$355,000F
Direct material	$ 580,000	$ 865,000	$285,000U
Direct labor	336,000	348,000	12,000U
Variable overhead	648,000	750,000	102,000U
Total variable costs	$1,564,000	$1,963,000	$399,000U
Contribution margin	$1,636,000	$1,592,000	$ 44,000U

Justine Molly, president of the company, is disappointed with the results. Despite a sizable increase in the number of cookies sold, the product's expected contribution to the overall profitability of the firm decreased. Molly has asked Blair to identify the reasons why the contribution margin decreased. Blair has gathered the following information to help in her analysis of the decrease.

Use Report
April 1995

Cost Item	Quantity	Actual Cost
Direct materials		
Cookie mix	4,650,000 oz.	$ 93,000
Milk chocolate	2,660,000 oz.	532,000
Almonds	480,000 oz.	240,000
Direct labor		
Mixing	450,000 min.	108,000
Baking	800,000 min.	240,000
Variable overhead		750,000
Total variable costs		$1,963,000

Required
1. Prepare an explanation of the $44,000 unfavorable variance between budgeted and actual contribution margin for the Chocolate Nut Supreme cookie product line during April 1995 by calculating the following variances.
   (a) sales price variance
   (b) sales volume variance
   (c) material price variance (assume purchases of material equal use)
   (d) material quantity variance
   (e) labor efficiency variance
   (f) variable overhead efficiency variance
   (g) variable overhead spending variance
2. Explain the problems that might arise in using direct labor hours as the basis for allocating overhead.
3. How might activity-based costing solve the problems described in item 2?

PART FOUR

product costing

Part Four deals with product costing—determining unit costs of products. The emphasis is on manufactured products, but the material applies to services as well. Knowledge of product costing is important to nonaccounting managers because they use reports that use the methods considered in Part Four. An understanding of cost behavior and of the significance of unit costs is particularly important in interpreting reports of manufacturers. Identifying cost drivers and developing activity-based costs is important because product costs are used for many managerial purposes such as pricing and evaluating the profitability of products and lines. Cost allocation is further considered together with some of its effects. The discussion of product costing methods also covers some behavioral problems. Thus, product costing has implications for control and performance evaluation.

Introduction to Product Costing

13

LEARNING OBJECTIVES

After reading this chapter, you should be able to

1. Trace the flow of costs for a manufacturer.

2. Identify the three types of inventory that a manufacturer carries.

3. Identify and describe three types of manufacturing processes and their related costing requirements.

4. Describe and illustrate job-order costing, including overhead application.

5. Determine product costs under actual and normal costing systems.

6. Analyze misapplied overhead into budget and volume variances.

7. Prepare income statements using actual and normal costing.

8. Develop ABC overhead rates and apply them to job-order companies.

9. Discuss the role that overhead application can play in pursuing corporate strategies.

Sally Industries of Jacksonville, Florida, makes robotic characters and props for entertainment parks. Most of the robots are unique and made to order for the customer, though Sally does make some standard models. The prices of robots are set in advance because Sally bids on its jobs. The company bases its bids on careful estimates of cost and must be very careful to keep its costs in line with estimates. Sally must also meet delivery dates to keep its customers, *even if doing so increases costs. Keeping costs under control is critical to the company's survival.*

*To develop its costs, **Sally** uses what is called a job-order cost system, which means simply that the company keeps track of the costs of each and every order of robots it makes. Sally uses its expertise and experience to bid on jobs, relying partly on its cost system to generate accurate cost estimates. Because of the high direct labor content of robots, the company is especially careful to track how much time each worker spends on various tasks.*

Sally uses some aspects of standard costs, as when it can modify a standard product. In such cases, the company can use standard times for making various standard components and estimate the additional time that customization will require. The company uses a personal computer spreadsheet to gather historical and budgeted information to use in developing bids.

Source: Thomas J. Barton and Frederick M. Cole, "Accounting for Magic," Management Accounting, January 1991, 27-31.

Chapters 13 through 15 introduce the basic approaches and cost accumulation methods of product costing. Product costing encompasses several areas, though its central focus is on determining the costs of manufactured products for reporting inventory and cost of goods sold in external financial statements. Because amounts reported for inventory are important for published financial statements, product costing is an important topic for financial reporting. While manufacturers must adhere to GAAP for their published financial statements, they are not required to do so for internal reporting and have more flexibility in preparing financial statements to meet their needs for planning and control.

Product costing topics obviously relate to manufacturers, but much of the material is relevant to other kinds of companies and to not-for-profit organizations. While service and merchandising companies do not face the same GAAP requirements as manufacturers, they nonetheless have similar concerns regarding costs of products. Insurance companies market different types of insurance policies, banks provide services such as various checking account options and different types of loans. Such companies need to understand the costs of their products.

Product costing presents many subtle and complex issues that only a competent cost accountant needs to understand. We discuss only basic product costing principles because managers in manufacturing companies receive and interpret reports that use those principles and must understand them. You are already familiar with the basic techniques used in product costing, one of which is assigning overhead cost to products through drivers such as labor time, number of setups, or number of component parts for a product. While discussing ABC in prior chapters we included selling and administrative expenses in determining the costs associated with products because we were, and are, concerned with the overall long-term profitability of products, not just the margin of selling price over manufacturing cost. In this chapter, however, we are concerned only with manufacturing costs. *Selling and administrative expenses are not part of the cost of manufactured goods for determining inventories and cost of goods sold for financial reporting and income tax accounting.*

COST FLOWS

 As early as Chapter 3, we saw that manufacturers incur costs for materials and components, for the labor required to turn materials into finished product, for the facilities needed for the manufacturing process, and for selling and administrative efforts. Under GAAP, which governs product costing, selling and administrative costs are expensed in the period incurred and are called **period costs**. In general, manufacturing costs are expensed (as cost of goods sold) when the product is sold and are called **product costs**. The accounting path followed by a product cost, from the time it is incurred to the time it becomes an expense, is called the *flow of costs*. From your study of financial accounting you are familiar with the flow of product costs for a merchandising company. The cost of purchased products (including the purchase cost and freight-in) flows into inventory and then into cost of goods sold. For a manufacturing company, the flow is basically the same—costs flow into inventory and then to cost of goods

 sold. But two factors noted in Chapters 3 and 6 complicate the situation: (1) manufacturers typically have three types of inventory and (2) the cost associated with manufacturers' inventories includes more than the purchase price of materials needed in the manufacturing process. Taking up the first factor, a typical manufacturer has three types of inventory.

1. **Finished goods inventory**, consisting of units that are ready for sale. This inventory is equivalent to what is called inventory by a merchandising concern.

2. **Work in process inventory**, consisting of semifinished units (such as automobiles without windshields, doors, or engines). Reaching this semifinished state requires not only materials and purchased parts but also labor and machinery. This inventory has no equivalent in a merchandising concern.

3. **Materials and purchased parts/components inventory**, consisting of the various materials (steel, glass, wood) and components (items such as switches, valves, and handles purchased from other manufacturers) that go into a finished product but which have not been put into production. Here again there is no equivalent in a merchandising concern. For brevity, we shall use the term *materials* to refer to both materials and purchased parts/components.

Manufactured inventories have three types of cost: materials, direct labor, and manufacturing overhead. Direct labor and overhead costs are necessary to transform or convert materials into finished products, a principle that we covered

 in Chapter 3. These costs all flow through inventory and eventually to cost of goods sold.

The flow of costs for a manufacturer is shown in Exhibit 13-1. The costs of materials are first collected in the Materials account.[1] As materials are requisitioned for use in production, their costs flow to Work in Process Inventory.[2]

---

1 *Terminology differs in practice. For example, some companies use the term "stores" for inventory of materials and purchased parts.*
2 *To facilitate the discussion, we capitalize the names of accounts and use lowercase to denote the things themselves. Thus, "Work in Process Inventory" refers to the account and "work in process inventory" refers to the physical, semifinished products.*

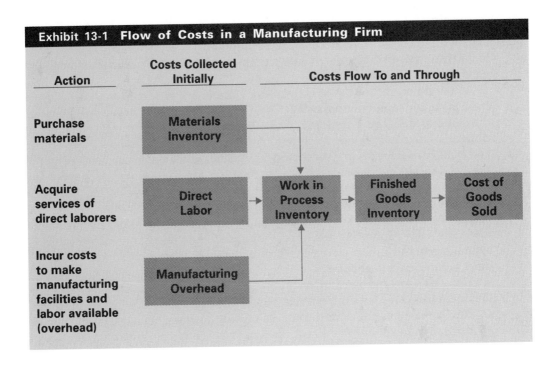

The cost of labor is first collected in Direct Labor and then flows to Work in Process to show that work was done to transform materials to a semifinished state. Manufacturing overhead costs are collected in a temporary account called Manufacturing Overhead, and then flow to Work in Process to reflect the role of such items as supervision, power, and depreciation in transforming materials into finished product. Thus, Work in Process collects the costs of materials, labor, and manufacturing overhead. As goods are completed, their costs are transferred from Work in Process to Finished Goods. Finally, as goods are sold their costs are transferred from Finished Goods to Cost of Goods Sold. The approach to *accumulating* cost and production information differs depending on whether the company makes a single product or a variety of dissimilar products.

MANUFACTURING PROCESSES

Some factories make a single, homogeneous product in a more or less continuous process. Every pound of sugar or flour, gallon of tomato juice, or ton of newsprint is virtually the same as any other made in the same plant. In such cases, it makes perfect sense to calculate a unit cost by dividing total production costs by the number of units (pounds, gallons, etc.) produced. Thus, cost per unit is calculated as

$$\frac{Cost\ per}{unit\ of\ product} = \frac{Total\ production\ costs}{Total\ units\ processed}$$

Such factories use *process costing*, which we discuss in Chapter 15. Note that because such factories make only one product, they have no need for activity-based costing for products because *all* costs relate to that one product. As Chapter 4 discussed, such companies might still use ABC to develop costs to analyze the profitability of other segments such as types of customers or geographical regions.

At the other end of the spectrum are companies or factories that rarely, if ever, make the same product twice. Construction companies never build exactly the same bridge, office building, or house twice. A printer might work on 50 different books in a month, each with a different number of pages, type of ink, and quality of paper. For either company, calculating an average cost using the previous equation is senseless, because the units are so different. Moreover, the managers of such companies are keenly interested in the cost of each unit or batch. For, while they might not make the same product (house, bridge, 300 page book) again, they will make similar ones—requiring similar amounts of materials, labor, and other resources—and will use the costs of current jobs to estimate costs of future jobs. Such companies use *job-order costing*, which we discuss later in this chapter.

Along the spectrum are many hybrids: many modern companies and factories are *mass producers* or *repetitive manufacturers*. They make many products, so they cannot use the simple process costing formula. However, all of their products are relatively standard, so that each batch or unit of a particular product is much like every other. An automobile manufacturer is a good example. Such companies typically use *standard costing*, which we introduced in

Chapter 12 and continue in Chapter 14. In addition to the three product costing methods just mentioned, companies must make two choices regarding their cost accounting. First is a choice that applies only to internal reporting.

ABSORPTION COSTING AND VARIABLE COSTING

For financial reporting and income tax purposes manufacturers must use **absorption costing**, sometimes called **full costing**. Under absorption costing, inventory cost includes fixed manufacturing costs. From previous chapters, you know that expressing fixed costs as per-unit amounts can give misleading results, especially for short-term decisions. You also know that ABC assigns fixed costs to products, partly for use in long-term evaluations of products (or other segments). Absorption costing can create problems in interpreting results,

which we consider in Chapter 14.

Accounting systems must produce absorption costing information to satisfy these external requirements. Companies often use data required for external purposes for internal purposes. Managers who receive absorption costing reports must understand how the information was developed and, more importantly, how to interpret that information. Because ABC apportions virtually all costs to products, managers whose companies use ABC must also understand the principles. Managers need to know the average total cost, including the fixed costs, of manufacturing a product or providing a service, such as is provided by ABC. For the most part, our objections to using unit fixed costs relate to short-term results, particularly short-term decision making, as well as to the danger in projecting unit costs to different levels of activity. In the longer term, the distinction between fixed and variable costs becomes less critical because the company periodically renews the commitments that give rise to fixed costs. The accompanying Insight describes a situation where just finding manufacturing costs is a difficult matter.

GAAP does not govern internal reporting, so companies do not have to use absorption costing for internal, managerial purposes. Variable costing or direct costing is a technique that does not include fixed costs in calculating per-unit inventory cost. We consider absorption costing for the most part in this chapter and take up variable costing in Chapter 14.

JOB-ORDER COSTING

We begin with **job-order costing**, which requires keeping track of the cost of materials and labor used on each job and then *applying, absorbing,* or *assigning* some amount of manufacturing overhead to each job. Tracing material and labor cost to specific jobs is usually straightforward; workers simply keep track of time and materials they use on each job and report them on forms designed for that purpose. Such recording adds no value to the product, so companies continually strive to reduce or eliminate such activities and their related costs. Technological developments such as bar coding have made gathering and recording data much less tedious and less costly than they once were. In fact, some factories have achieved paperless operations. No one fills out forms!

The idea that managers should have a good idea of the costs of manufactured products might seem obvious, but in former communist countries there was little need for cost information. "How do you determine the cost of a manufactured product?" was one question put to an American accountant who led a delegation of accountants to Minsk in the former Soviet republic of Belarus. Soviet accounting aimed at providing information that was suitable for central planning and the controlling of the economy. Factories did not need to earn profits, but to supply goods as specified by central planners.

Mielec, a Polish company, has made golf carts for over 20 years, solely for export. (Poland has no golf courses.) U.S. cart manufacturers sued Mielec on grounds that it was selling its carts in the U.S. for below cost. But because Poland's government administered all prices and wages, it was impossible to determine the cost, in U.S. dollars, to produce a golf cart. The solution was to develop cost data by using factor prices (materials, labor, power, supplies, and other overhead items) from comparable market economies, such as Spain. The analysts applied Spanish prices to Mielec's physical quantities of resources to estimate the final costs of a golf cart. Nonetheless, the case is still dragging on.

Sources: Newton D. Becker, "Russia Faces a New Accounting World," The New Accountant, *December 1992, 12.*

Manufacturing overhead costs—such as heat, light, power, and machinery depreciation—cannot be traced directly to specific jobs. Rather, overhead costs are applied (assigned) to jobs indirectly, by determining overhead rates per unit of input activities (drivers) with which overhead cost pools vary most closely. Such activities are often called *allocation bases*. Common bases are direct labor hours, direct labor cost, machine hours, number of machine setups, number of material moves, and cycle time. Managers use the techniques described in Chapter 3 to determine the activities with which overhead cost pools are most closely associated. Historically, direct labor has been used more than any other base. More recently, companies with significant automation switched to machine hours. With the rise of activity-based costing, companies now use multiple bases. Of course, to apply overhead, the company must track how much of these other resources each job requires.

In Chapter 3, we introduced the concept of assigning overhead costs to one activity (a job) based on some other activity (such as labor hours). We applied the concept in other chapters, most recently in Chapter 12, where we noted that variable overhead is usually related to input factors such as labor time or machine time. We do the same in product costing. Our basic example uses a single rate for simplicity. We cover multiple rates later in this chapter. Exhibit 13-2 contains the basic information for our example. (For now, ignore the lower part of the exhibit, which deals with budget information.) Farr Company manufactures electronic sensing devices to customer order. Farr worked on three jobs (J-1, J-2, and J-3) in July. Farr uses machine hours to apply overhead.

Materials costs, direct labor costs, and machine hours in Exhibit 13-2 were determined from forms employees prepared that show how much materials, labor time, and machine time were used. There are two commonly used methods of applying overhead to jobs: actual costing and normal costing. We shall illustrate both methods, and then discuss the effects of those procedures on the financial statements, particularly on the income statement.

Exhibit 13-2   Farr Company Data for July

| Total overhead costs | | | | $140,000 |
| Total machine hours | | | | 7,000 |

Job Data	J-1	J-2	J-3	Total
Machine hours	2,000	1,000	4,000	7,000
Materials used	$20,000	$62,000	$30,000	$112,000
Direct labor cost	$20,000	$10,000	$40,000	$70,000

Budgeted data for year:				
Machine hours				100,000
Overhead costs, $1,200,000 + $5 per machine hour (MH)				$1,700,000

a Job J-1 was finished and sold in July. Job J-2 was finished, but not yet sold, and job J-3 was incomplete at the end of July.

ACTUAL COSTING

Under **actual costing**, the overhead incurred during a period is applied to all jobs that were in process during the period. To assign all of the overhead costs to jobs, we calculate the overhead rate by dividing total actual overhead by the total amount of the relevant input factor—machine hours here. In general form we have

$$Overhead\ rate\ =\ \frac{Total\ manufacturing\ overhead}{Total\ manufacturing\ activity}$$

In this specific situation,

$$Overhead\ rate\ =\ \frac{\$140,000}{7,000}$$
$$=\ \$20\ per\ machine\ hour$$

We can now determine the total costs on the three jobs.

	Job Number		
	J-1	J-2	J-3
Overhead ($140,000):			
2,000 hrs. at $20	$40,000		
1,000 hrs. at $20		$20,000	
4,000 hrs. at $20			$ 80,000
Materials	20,000	62,000	30,000
Direct labor	20,000	10,000	40,000
Total cost of job	$80,000	$92,000	$150,000

Notice that all $140,000 of overhead cost is assigned to the three jobs ($40,000 + $20,000 + $80,000 = $140,000). Under actual costing, total overhead incurred is assigned to individual jobs.

Let us move to the financial statements. Exhibit 13-2 states that job J-1 was sold in July, J-2 was finished, but not sold, and J-3 was not finished at the end of July. The cost of job J-1 appears in the July income statement as Cost of Goods Sold (as we shall show later). The cost of job J-2 appears in the July 31 balance sheet as Finished Goods Inventory and that of job J-3 appears on the balance sheet as Work in Process Inventory.

Actual job-order costing is simple, but is not commonly used because it can produce misleading results. The reason is that overhead rates can fluctuate significantly from month to month. The differences in monthly rates are related to fixed overhead costs and there are two causes. First, activity (machine hours in our example) often differs from month to month because of seasonality or changes in the economy. Second, fixed overhead costs can fluctuate—heating is an obvious example. Although heating costs are higher in winter, to say that products made in the winter "cost more" is not logical. Customers are unlikely to pay more for products made in January just because the manufacturer had to heat its factory. Let us illustrate this point using Farr Company data. Exhibit 13-2 shows that Farr's variable overhead cost is $5 per machine hour and that its fixed overhead averages $100,000 per month. Suppose that in May its fixed overhead is $100,000, but in December, because of seasonal cost factors, it is $110,000. Machine hours are 10,000 in May and 5,000 in December, again because of seasonal factors. Under actual job-order costing, the overhead rates for the two months are as follows:

	May	December
Total overhead costs:		
$100,000 + (10,000 × $5)	$150,000	
$110,000 + (5,000 × $5)		$135,000
Machine hours	10,000	5,000
Overhead rate per machine hour	$15	$27

Suppose that Farr does two similar jobs in May and December, each requiring 100 machine hours at $10 per hour and $800 in materials. Actual costing shows the following total costs of each job.

	Job Done In	
	May	December
Materials	$ 800	$ 800
Labor (100 × $10)	1,000	1,000
Overhead, 100 hours at $15 and $27	1,500	2,700
Total	$ 3,300	$ 4,500

Does the job done in December really cost $1,200 more than the one done in May? Will customers pay more for jobs just because they were made in a slow month? Actually, customers often pay lower, not higher, prices in slow months, because companies need the business to keep their workers busy. Yet the profitability of the two jobs will appear different if they were sold at the same price, and this appearance might mislead a manager trying to develop a price quotation on a similar job. Most companies avoid this problem by using normal costing, but companies that have relatively little overhead to allocate might be well-served by actual costing. The accompanying Insight describes a company that relies on its job-order system for pricing and has little overhead.

NORMAL COSTING

Normal costing uses the same overhead rate all year, smoothing the fluctuations of actual costing. The vehicle that accomplishes this smoothing is a **predetermined overhead rate**. A predetermined overhead rate is one calculated in advance. The rate is based on budgeted results, not actual costs and activity. The calculation follows.

$$\frac{Predetermined}{overhead\ rate} = \frac{Budgeted\ manufacturing\ overhead\ for\ year}{Budgeted\ production\ activity\ for\ year}$$

Again, budgeted production activity can be expressed as direct labor hours, machine hours, or whatever other measure managers think appropriate. The activity measures used in normal costing are the same as those used in actual costing; the difference is in the use of budgeted rather than actual figures. Let

SIGHT

Atlantic Dry Dock does various ship repairs and conversions, each of which is typically a large, expensive job. Atlantic uses job-order costing. When a shipowner requests a bid, the company prepares a cost estimate that it uses in setting its bid. Good bidding, neither so high that the company does not get enough jobs, nor so low that it cannot cover its costs, is crucial to the company's success, even its survival, because competition is very tough. If Atlantic gets a job, it uses its original estimate as the budget for the job. The company's estimators are excellent. Their estimates come within 10 percent of actual cost of material and labor for the job the vast majority of the time.

Atlantic maintains a large database that is invaluable in estimating costs. The estimator can find the most recent purchase price of any required material and can examine previous jobs to see their requirements of materials and direct labor. In such a complicated business, the company must rely on experience with previous jobs in bidding on new jobs.

Atlantic's estimators use spreadsheets to perform sensitivity analysis on important factors such as labor rates and times for various categories, such as blasters and painters. Estimators also analyze costs and gross profits for various bid prices. Low-balling, bidding low to get business, is anathema to the company's founder, who is quoted as saying that "I have never seen an empty shipyard go bankrupt. I have seen a lot of them that bid too low to get the job go broke." Accordingly, the company's management carefully reviews bids, again analyzing the estimates of material and labor requirements.

Overhead cost is relatively low in relation to materials and direct labor costs. Even so, **Atlantic** is unusual in that it does not apply overhead to jobs; however, it traces many items of variable overhead directly to jobs. Such items as small tools, consumable supplies, or even rental or purchase of small equipment for a specific job are charged directly to jobs as materials. Not applying overhead to jobs simplifies the accounting system, and makes it less expensive to operate. At year-end, Atlantic allocates overhead to jobs in inventory to accommodate financial reporting and income tax requirements.

Source: Thomas L. Barton and Frederick M. Cole, "Atlantic Dry Dock's Unique Cost Estimation System," Management Accounting, October 1994, 32-39.

us illustrate normal job-order costing with Farr Company, using the budgeted data at the bottom of Exhibit 13-2. The budget formula for overhead costs has the same form we saw in earlier chapters.

$$\text{Budget allowance} = \text{Fixed costs} + \left(\text{Variable cost per unit of activity} \times \text{Amount of activity} \right)$$

Total budgeted overhead is $1,700,000, budgeted fixed costs of $1,200,000 plus $500,000 of variable cost ($5 variable overhead per machine hour × 100,000 budgeted machine hours). The predetermined overhead rate is $17 per machine hour ($1,700,000/100,000). This rate, multiplied by the number of hours worked on each job, gives the overhead costs of the jobs. Overhead assigned to jobs is called **applied** (or **absorbed**) **overhead**.

	Job Number		
	J-1	J-2	J-3
Overhead:			
2,000 hrs. × $17	$34,000		
1,000 hrs. × $17		$17,000	
4,000 hrs. × $17			$ 68,000
Materials, as before	20,000	62,000	30,000
Direct labor, as before	20,000	10,000	40,000
Total cost of job	$74,000	$89,000	$138,000

This schedule has several important points. First, materials costs and direct labor costs are the same as they were under actual costing. Only the overhead cost allocations are different. Differences in allocated overhead give the differences between the two costing methods. The following analysis should help you understand the different treatments of overhead under actual costing and normal costing. Under actual costing, the overhead cost assigned to a particular job is

$$\frac{\textit{Overhead assigned}}{\textit{to job}} = \frac{\textit{Actual hours}}{\textit{worked on job}} \times \frac{\textit{Total actual overhead}}{\textit{Total actual hours}}$$

Under normal costing, the overhead assigned to a job is

$$\frac{\textit{Overhead assigned}}{\textit{to job}} = \frac{\textit{Actual hours}}{\textit{worked on job}} \times \frac{\textit{Total budgeted overhead}}{\textit{Total budgeted hours}}$$

Thus, under actual costing, total actual overhead is spread over all jobs. But under normal costing, the total amount of overhead assigned to jobs will equal total actual overhead only if (1) total actual overhead equals total budgeted overhead and (2) total actual hours equal total budgeted hours. (Offsetting differences could make the assignment come out even, but that is very unlikely.)

   Which set of costs, actual or normal, is "correct"? There is no answer to this question, much as there is no answer to the question of whether first-in first-out or last-in first-out is the "correct" inventory cost flow assumption. Normal costing has the advantage of minimizing the effects of fluctuations in the overhead rate, and is therefore more popular than actual costing. Normal costing nearly always shows a difference between actual overhead and applied overhead. The difference between actual overhead and applied overhead under normal costing is called misapplied overhead.

MISAPPLIED OVERHEAD

Let us look at the total overhead costs assigned under the two methods to jobs worked on in July.

	Overhead Applied to Jobs Using	
	Actual Costing	Normal Costing
Job J-1	$ 40,000	$ 34,000
Job J-2	20,000	17,000
Job J-3	80,000	68,000
Total	$140,000	$119,000

Note that you can also calculate total applied overhead by multiplying the predetermined overhead rate of $17 by the 7,000 total machine hours: $17 × 7,000 = $119,000. Please note also that applied overhead is *not* the amount you expect to incur; overhead application is a product costing device. Farr budgets overhead as $100,000 per month plus $5 times machine hours, *not* as $17 per machine hour. *The $17 rate is for product costing, not for budgeting.* Misapplied overhead is $21,000 ($140,000 - $119,000). When actual overhead is greater than applied overhead, as above, the difference is called **underapplied** (or **underabsorbed**) **overhead**. When applied overhead is greater than actual overhead, we call the difference **overapplied** (or **overabsorbed**) **overhead**. Farr has $21,000 of underapplied overhead.

 At first glance, misapplied overhead looks much like the variances we studied in Chapter 12. That is, if one views applied overhead as akin to a standard cost, overapplication and underapplication appear to be analogous to favorable and unfavorable cost variances. But the analogy should not be carried too far. Although overapplied or underapplied overhead can result from actual costs being lower (a favorable variance) or higher (an unfavorable variance) than budgeted, misapplication *also* can result from differences between actual activity and the activity level used to calculate the predetermined overhead rate.

OVERHEAD VARIANCES

To illustrate these two points, let us look more closely at Farr's July results, when machine time totaled 7,000 hours. The budget formula for annual overhead cost is $1,200,000 fixed costs plus $5 per machine hour variable cost. With monthly fixed overhead budgeted at the average of $100,000 (one twelfth of the annual amount), we can compare July's actual costs with the flexible budget allowance based on 7,000 hours.

Actual costs, fixed and variable	$140,000
Budgeted costs [$100,000 + ($5 × 7,000 hours)]	135,000
Budget variance, unfavorable	$ 5,000

Farr incurred $5,000 more overhead cost than budgeted, an unfavorable budget variance. Calculating a **budget variance** is not new with this chapter. In this case, we cannot determine how much of this variance relates to fixed cost and how much to variable cost because we do not know the actual amounts of fixed and variable costs. (This point was discussed in Chapter 12.) But we do know now that $5,000 of the $21,000 underapplied overhead is an unfavorable budget variance because actual costs were higher than budgeted costs.

The other factor affecting the predetermined rate and, therefore, the amount of overhead applied, is activity. We know (again from Exhibit 13-2) that Farr planned 100,000 machine hours for the year, for a monthly average of 8,333 $^1/_3$ hours. But only 7,000 hours of machine time were used in July. The variance caused by a difference between actual machine hours and the budgeted hours used in the calculation of the predetermined rate is called the **volume variance**, or the **idle capacity variance**, and is the difference between budgeted overhead and applied overhead.

Budgeted overhead, as computed before	$135,000
Applied overhead ($17 × 7,000 actual hours)	119,000
Volume variance, unfavorable	$ 16,000

When applied overhead exceeds budgeted overhead, the volume variance is said to be favorable; when the opposite is true, the variance is said to be unfavorable. Hence, we have now identified two unfavorable variances that add up to the $21,000 difference between actual and applied overhead for the month. The meaning of a budget variance is clear; Farr incurred $5,000 more overhead cost than budgeted. But what does the volume variance mean? Only that actual activity was different from budgeted activity—the level of activity used to set the predetermined overhead rate. What is the economic significance of the volume variance? Very little, if any. Whether it is favorable or unfavorable is not good or bad *per se*, because it relates solely to the smoothing of fixed overhead and arises only because actual hours do not equal the monthly average of budgeted hours. To demonstrate this point more clearly, let us look further at the $17 predetermined overhead rate.

The budgeted overhead cost used in the calculation of the $17 predetermined overhead rate has both a fixed and a variable component. The variable portion of the rate is $5 per hour, so the fixed portion is $12. (Alternatively, budgeted fixed overhead is $1,200,000 and budgeted hours are 100,000, also giving a $12 fixed portion.) Now, look at the difference between actual hours (7,000) and the 8,333 $^1/_3$ monthly share of the hours budgeted for the year. The $16,000 volume variance is exactly that 1,333 $^1/_3$ hour difference multiplied by the $12 rate for fixed overhead. Perhaps this point is more easily seen if you recast the calculation of the volume variance and separate budgeted and applied costs into their variable and fixed components, as follows:

	Variable Portion	Fixed Portion
Budgeted cost (7,000 hours × $5)	$35,000	$100,000
Applied cost:		
7,000 hours × $5	35,000	
7,000 hours × $12		84,000
Volume variance (1,333 $^1/_3$ hours × $12)	—	$ 16,000

The flexible budget allowance for variable costs depends on the actual level of activity. But because fixed costs do not change with the level of activity, the budgeted amount is not affected when more (or fewer) hours are worked than were budgeted. Thus, what produces the volume variance is the difference between budgeted and actual production activity, the 1,333 $^1/_3$ hours. We now have three different, but equivalent, formulas for calculating the volume variance.

$$\frac{Volume}{variance} = \frac{Total\ budgeted}{manufacturing\ overhead} - \frac{Total\ applied}{manufacturing\ overhead}$$

$$= \frac{Total\ budgeted\ fixed}{manufacturing\ overhead} - \frac{Total\ applied\ fixed}{manufacturing\ overhead}$$

$$= \frac{Predetermined\ overhead}{rate\ for\ fixed\ costs} \times \left(\begin{array}{ccc} Budgeted & & Actual \\ production & - & production \\ activity & & activity \end{array}\right)$$

You should use whichever formula is most convenient in a given situation; they all give the same answer. We can also use the graphical format shown in Chapter 12 to compute the overhead budget variance and volume variance.

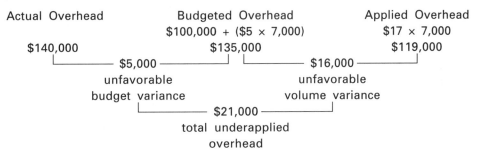

Before leaving this topic we want to remind you again that *applying overhead is an accounting device.* Managers do not expect to incur overhead at the rate used to apply it. Rather, they expect to incur overhead according to the budget formula.

INCOME STATEMENTS, ACTUAL AND NORMAL COSTING

We have illustrated two methods for assigning overhead costs to product. We now look at how the two methods affect the income statement. Exhibit 13-3 shows the July income statement for Farr Company under the two methods. We also assume that Farr had $50,000 of selling and administrative expenses and that, as stated earlier, job J-1 was completed and sold for $150,000. Costs accumulated on jobs J-2 and J-3 remain in inventory at the end of the month. In internal reports, many companies show additional detail about underapplied overhead, showing separately the budget and volume variances as computed earlier. The most obvious difference between the statements is the amount of income ($20,000 under actual costing and $5,000 under normal costing). What caused the $15,000 difference?

The difference between incomes under actual costing and normal costing lies in the treatment of overhead, not in the amount of overhead incurred, which is the same $140,000 regardless of the method used. The actual costing income statement shows the actual overhead in a single amount; the normal costing income statement shows the actual overhead in two amounts, $119,000 assigned to jobs and $21,000 as a separate deduction.

Exhibit 13-3   Farr Company, Income Statements for July

		Normal Costing	Actual Costing
Sales		$150,000	$150,000
Normal cost of sales	$74,000 [a]		
Plus underapplied overhead	21,000		
Cost of sales		95,000	80,000 [b]
Gross profit		$ 55,000	$ 70,000
Selling and administrative expenses		50,000	50,000
Income		$ 5,000	$ 20,000
Details of cost of sales			
Cost of sales:			
Beginning inventories		$ 0	$ 0
Materials		112,000	112,000
Labor		70,000	70,000
Overhead		119,000	140,000
Total costs		$301,000	$322,000
Less ending inventory		227,000 [c]	242,000 [d]
Normal cost of sales		$ 74,000	
Underapplied overhead		21,000	
Cost of sales		$ 95,000	$ 80,000

a Cost of job J-1 from page 614.
b Cost of job J-1 from page 611.
c Job J-2 ($99,000) + job J-3 ($128,000) = $227,000.
d Job J-2 ($102,000) + job J-3 ($140,000) = $242,000.

If you look closely at the statements you will see that the source of the $15,000 difference in income is the $15,000 difference in the ending inventories. The cost of job J-2 is $3,000 greater and that of J-3 is $12,000 greater under actual costing than under normal costing. That difference occurs because more overhead is assigned to those jobs under actual costing. Remember that overhead was assigned at the actual rate under actual costing, but at a predetermined rate for normal costing, so that for a single period within the year such differences are very common. The difference in incomes, then, relates to the differences in overhead assigned to inventory. We have shown underapplied overhead as an addition to normal cost of sales. Another possibility is to show an amount called normal gross margin (sales minus normal cost of sales) and then subtract underapplied overhead from normal gross margin. Either approach can be used and income will be the same. The choice is a matter of preference. The income statement in Exhibit 13-4 shows the alternative format and also separates underapplied overhead into the budget variance and volume variance.

Exhibit 13-4 Farr Company, Normal Costing Income Statement for July		
Sales		$150,000
Normal cost of goods sold		74,000
Normal gross margin		$ 76,000
Variances:		
Budget variance	$ 5,000U	
Volume variance	16,000U	21,000
Gross margin		$ 55,000
Selling and administrative expenses		50,000
Income		$ 5,000

ACTIVITY-BASED OVERHEAD RATES

Our example used a single overhead rate, which implies that virtually all overhead is driven by machine hours—an unreasonable assumption for most manufacturers. As you know from previous chapters, companies using activity-based costing (ABC) identify cost drivers for each pool of costs. You also know that ABC assigns selling and administrative expenses to products or other segments. ABC is also relevant to product costing, but for product costing ABC does not assign selling and administrative expenses to jobs or units of product.

Cost pools might be departments, or pools related to such activities as materials use, labor time, machine time, or number of setups or engineering changes. Some companies allocate such costs as purchasing, receiving, inspecting, and storing—costs associated with materials—to jobs based on the materials cost of each job. They also might recognize multiple cost drivers by using different rates for labor time and for machine time, even in a single department.

As you know, using multiple ABC rates often provides better information than does a single plant-wide rate. But it is more costly to operate a system where overhead is applied differently from department to department, or on multiple bases. For instance, it is necessary not only to identify the cost drivers and pools, but to keep track of the amount of activity associated with each job, product, or other object of allocation. Keeping such records can be quite costly. Accordingly, using ABC rates is wise only when the expected benefits, in the form of better control and decision making, exceed the additional costs. It is no easy task to determine whether benefits exceed costs, for the benefits are not usually experienced in dollar terms. Nonetheless, managers must make judgments about benefits.

Multiple rates are better than a single plant-wide rate in two general cases. One is when overhead is related to more than one input factor. In our example, Farr applied overhead using machine hours, which reflects an automated, machine-intensive operation. However, a department with a low investment in machinery and many laborers could use labor hours to apply overhead. Another example of the same case is if some overhead is clearly related to materials and other overhead to labor or machine time; here again, ABC rates make sense. The other case is when the same input factor applies to all departments, but the overhead rates in the departments differ greatly from one to another. We now show how ABC overhead rates can improve pricing decisions. The following data relate to Reinhart Company, which makes electrical equipment.

| | Data for Cost Driver | | |
	Direct Labor	Machine Setups	Total
Budgeted overhead costs	$800,000	$400,000	$1,200,000
Budgeted direct labor hours	100,000		
Budgeted number of setups		2,000	
Rates $800,000/100,000; $400,000/2,000	$8/hour	$200/setup	

If Reinhart uses only direct labor to apply overhead, it will calculate a rate of $12 per direct labor hour, which is total overhead of $1,200,000 divided by 100,000 direct labor hours. The $12 rate does not capture the differences between the two types of overhead, and using it could lead to poor decisions. Suppose that Reinhart works on the following two jobs and sets prices at 150 percent of manufacturing costs, including overhead applied at the $12 rate.

	Job A	Job B
Direct labor hours	800	200
Materials cost	$10,000	$10,000
Direct labor cost at $10/hour	8,000	2,000
Overhead applied at $12/DLH	9,600	2,400
Total cost	$27,600	$14,400
Price at 150% of cost	$41,400	$21,600

If job A requires two machine setups and job B requires 25 setups, the cost of each job using the activity-based rates is as follows:

	Job A	Job B
Materials cost	$10,000	$10,000
Direct labor cost at $10/hour	8,000	2,000
Overhead:		
Labor-related at $8/DLH	6,400	1,600
Setup-related at $200/setup	400	5,000
Total cost	$24,800	$18,600
Price at 150% of cost	$37,200	$27,900

Using the single, labor-based rate, Reinhart will charge lower prices for jobs requiring lots of setups (compare the prices on job B). If Reinhart has a competitor that has a similar cost structure and uses activity-based rates, Reinhart will bid higher than the competitor on labor-intensive jobs (like job A) and will lose much of that business to the competitor. Reinhart will obtain a great deal of setup-intensive business because it will underbid the competitor. The problem is that Reinhart will suffer losses in profitability if it bids so low on setup-intensive jobs. (Remember that Reinhart's prices must cover selling and administrative expenses as well as manufacturing costs.)

Determining cost drivers for JIT manufacturers is in some respects easier than it is for conventional manufacturers. Costs that are indirect in a conventional manufacturing environment are often direct in a JIT environment. Activities such as materials handling, maintenance, and other support services are carried out by centrally administered units in conventional manufacturing but are done by the workers in each manufacturing cell of a JIT operation. The costs of these activities, which are direct to the output of a particular manufacturing cell, make product costing much simpler. We examine product costing in JIT environments in Chapter 15.

Service organizations have become increasingly interested in cost analysis and especially in ABC. **Fireman's Fund**, the large property/casualty insurer, uses a technique it calls *cost sampling* to determine how much effort its people are directing toward specific types of activities such as screening policy applications, soliciting business, gathering information, negotiating price and coverage, and doing routine paperwork. The company uses various ways to sample people's efforts. One was for the people gathering the information to interrupt employees briefly and determine what type of work they were doing and on what product. The company also analyzed work by reference to type of policy and size of policy, which resulted in setting up a "fast-track" for routine smaller policies to reduce processing costs.[3]

ETHICS IN PRODUCT COSTING

Ethical and legal questions can arise in product costing, especially when a company works on a "cost-plus" basis (where the price is a multiple of cost, or cost plus a specified dollar amount). Such work is quite common in regulated companies, such as electric utilities, and in work done for governmental agencies, especially the Department of Defense. The legal and ethical issues center on how much overhead is allocated to specific jobs or customers. Selecting drivers, classifying costs in pools, and setting bases for calculating rates can all create potential problems. Chapter 10 described the difficulties that Stanford University encountered because of costs it included in particular pools. Some of the widely publicized cost overruns on defense contracts could be traced at least partly to allocations.

Companies that operate both regulated and non-regulated businesses, such as many telephone companies, have incentives to load costs onto regulated businesses, where regulators typically allow cost recovery plus a reasonable profit. The non-regulated operations of such companies will therefore absorb less cost and be more profitable than they would be if they absorbed more costs. Managers of not-for-profit entities also face difficult decisions about cost allocations because such entities often conduct both taxable and nontaxable activities. Paying taxes reduces the money available to the entity, so managers have incentives to allocate as much cost as possible to taxable activities, perhaps exceeding reasonable amounts. Management accountants are enjoined to perform allocations of overhead in objective ways by the Standards for Ethical Conduct, but gray areas will always require judgment.

---

3 *Michael Crane and John Meyer, "Focusing on True Costs in a Service Organization,"* Management Accounting, *February 1993, 41-45.*

PRODUCT COSTS AND VALUE-CHAIN ANALYSIS

A company that wants to analyze its position in the value-chain, perhaps to enter or leave a particular stage in the chain, must have good estimates of the costs of its products. As you now know, product costing, whether job-order or other, treats selling and administrative expenses as non-inventoriable, thus making product costs unsuitable for such analyses. In many companies selling and administrative expenses exceed manufacturing costs by wide margins, so value-chain analysis (or any other analysis focusing on product profitability) must supplement product costing information with information about selling and administrative expenses. ABC and other techniques can assign some selling and administrative expenses to products for strategic analyses.

Companies are not only concerned with their own costs, but also with their competitors. Many strategic analyses require determining whether you or your competitors have cost advantages. The accompanying Insight describes how **Caterpillar** uses product costing techniques to analyze its competitors' costs.

OVERHEAD APPLICATION, BEHAVIOR, AND STRATEGY

 Allocating overhead to products, like other topics we have discussed, is fraught with behavioral problems, one of which is whether a particular approach will advance the company's pursuit of specific strategic goals. Chapter 10 introduced this question.

INSIGHT

Caterpillar has been following a strategy of being the lowest-cost, highest-value manufacturer in the equipment industry. In the normal course of analysis, management accountants and other professionals analyze competitors' products, financial statements, and other sources to estimate competitors' product costs. The analysts use various methods to arrive at cost estimates, such as working backwards from their prices. If all approaches lead to about the same cost estimates, the analysts can be more confident that their estimates are sound. Of particular importance is if a competitor develops a cost advantage that cannot be overcome by standard cost reduction methods, but requires a radical approach.

Caterpillar credits competitor cost analysis with stimulating significant reductions in its own costs through product simplification, consolidation of manufacturing operations, and other steps. An additional step is to streamline merchandising and support so that manufacturing cost advantages are not dissipated by those functions. Finally, the process also stimulates searches for ways to add value to products while reducing costs.

Source: Lou Jones, "Competitor Cost Analysis at Caterpillar," Management Accounting, *October 1988, 32-38.*

Perhaps the major source of problems is the choice of allocation bases, or drivers. As we said earlier, labor has been the principal basis for overhead application for many years. But as we noted several times, labor costs are a smaller percentage of total costs, especially those adopting new manufacturing techniques such as just-in-time, flexible manufacturing, and computer-integrated manufacturing. At the same time, however, overhead costs have been rising, both in absolute dollars *and* as a percentage of total manufacturing cost. The rise in overhead is a natural consequence of changing the manufacturing environment to one that requires more brainwork. Support personnel such as industrial engineers, mechanical engineers, electrical engineers, computer experts, and highly skilled maintenance workers are more in demand.

A company whose cost structure is moving toward less labor and more overhead (which also means more fixed cost and less variable cost) can make serious errors if it allocates overhead using direct labor hours or direct labor cost. When overhead is rising while direct labor hours and cost are falling, an overhead rate calculated using direct labor hours will become astronomically high (perhaps to hundreds of dollars per direct labor hour). Careful studies of cost drivers led many companies to use activity-based rates to direct attention to areas where cost control was most needed. The accompanying Insight describes three cases of companies using overhead application bases to influence behavior, especially to lower costs.

SUMMARY

Product costing is determining costs of inventory and of cost of goods sold for manufacturers. For financial reporting and income tax purposes, manufacturers must use absorption costing, which requires that all manufacturing costs, variable and fixed, be included in unit cost.

Manufacturing costs flow through inventory accounts to cost of goods sold. Cost data are accumulated in various ways, depending on the type of manufacturing process. Factories that produce essentially identical products accumulate costs using process costing. Factories that seldom produce the same product accumulate costs using job-order costing.

Some companies compute product costs based on actual costs incurred. Others use a normal costing system, under which the company applies overhead to products using a predetermined overhead rate based on budgeted manufacturing overhead and budgeted production activity. The rate is usually stated as a cost per unit of some input measure such as direct labor hours or machine hours. Predetermined overhead rates can be calculated for each department or for a factory as a whole.

Factories that use normal costing will almost always see a difference between actual overhead and overhead applied. The difference, called underapplied or overapplied overhead, can be reported in an income statement as an adjustment to either normal cost of sales or normal gross margin. Underapplied or overapplied overhead can be analyzed into a budget variance and a volume variance. The latter variance has little economic significance. Activity-based overhead rates are useful for many companies because they can provide better

The Portables Group of **Tektronix**, which we discussed briefly in Chapter 10, had based its overhead allocations on direct labor, but direct labor had declined to less than 7 percent of total manufacturing cost, as low as 3 percent on newer products. Simultaneously, overhead costs were rising because the Group was introducing new manufacturing methods and operations had become increasingly technological. These two factors combined to make labor-based overhead rates extremely high. A serious consequence was that manufacturing people believed that reducing labor time was the best way to reduce total costs. While labor cost *per se* was low, when an hour of direct labor was loaded with a huge overhead charge, the total labor-related cost loomed very large. Design engineers drove labor time down by using special parts and other devices, but that did not have the desired effect. Overhead costs continued to rise.

As Chapter 10 reported, the Group studied overhead costs and concluded that costs of activities such as purchasing, receiving, inspecting, storage, and record keeping were significant drivers. The Group changed its allocation procedures, using both materials and conversion activities (labor and machine time). The new allocation methods contributed to better understanding and to greater potential for cost reduction.

Hitachi, the giant electronics company, took a different view in one of its factories that manufactured VCRs. Upper-level management decided that lowering labor time was an essential component of a successful strategy. Accordingly, the factory applied overhead based on labor precisely to encourage designers and engineers to drive labor as low as possible.

Peterson Ranch, a world-class grower of nuts and fruits in the Sacramento Valley, uses overhead application to encourage desired behavior. Managers are responsible for individual fields and are charged for labor and overhead they use. Peterson rates tractors and other equipment based on horsepower so that managers use smaller, less expensive equipment. The equipment fleet is actually dropping both in number of pieces and in size, cost, and complexity.

Sources: John W. Jonez and Michael A. Wright, *"Material Burdening,"* Management Accounting, August 1987, 27-31.
T. Hiromoto, *"Another Hidden Edge — Japanese Management Accounting,"* Harvard Business Review, July-August 1988, 22-24.
Donald E. Keller and Paul Krause, *"'World Class' Down on the Farm,"* Management Accounting, May 1990, 39-45.

information than a single plant-wide rate or departmental rates based on labor or machine time. Companies using such rates have found that they improved decision making. An ABC system costs more to operate than a conventional system, so managers must weigh the benefits of an ABC system against the additional costs. The product-costing system can affect behavior and should encourage people to act in goal-congruent ways. In some organizations, choices related to cost allocation raise ethical and legal questions.

KEY TERMS

absorption (or full) costing   (608)
actual costing   (611)
applied (or absorbed) overhead   (614)
budget variance   (615)
cost pools   (619)
finished goods inventory   (606)
idle capacity variance   (616)
job-order costing   (609)
materials and purchased
   parts/components inventory   (606)

normal costing   (612)
overapplied (or overabsorbed)
   overhead   (615)
period costs   (606)
predetermined overhead rate   (612)
product costs   (606)
underapplied (or underabsorbed)
   overhead   (615)
volume variance   (616)
work in process inventory   (606)

KEY FORMULAS

$$\text{Predetermined overhead rate} = \frac{\text{Budgeted manufacturing overhead for year}}{\text{Budgeted production activity for year}}$$

$$\begin{matrix}\text{Variable overhead} \\ \text{budget variance}\end{matrix} = \begin{matrix}\text{Actual} \\ \text{variable} \\ \text{overhead}\end{matrix} - \begin{matrix}\text{Flexible budget} \\ \text{allowance for actual} \\ \text{production activity}\end{matrix}$$

$$\begin{matrix}\text{Underabsorbed} \\ \text{(overabsorbed)} \\ \text{overhead}\end{matrix} = \begin{matrix}\text{Actual} \\ \text{manufacturing} \\ \text{overhead}\end{matrix} - \begin{matrix}\text{Applied} \\ \text{manufacturing} \\ \text{overhead}\end{matrix}$$

$$\begin{matrix}\text{Fixed overhead} \\ \text{budget} \\ \text{variance}\end{matrix} = \begin{matrix}\text{Actual} \\ \text{fixed} \\ \text{overhead}\end{matrix} - \begin{matrix}\text{Budgeted} \\ \text{fixed} \\ \text{overhead}\end{matrix}$$

$$\text{Volume variance} = \begin{matrix}\text{Budgeted (fixed)} \\ \text{manufacturing} \\ \text{overhead}\end{matrix} - \begin{matrix}\text{Applied (fixed)} \\ \text{manufacturing} \\ \text{overhead}\end{matrix}$$

$$\text{Volume variance} = \begin{matrix}\text{Predetermined} \\ \text{overhead rate for} \\ \text{fixed overhead}\end{matrix} \times \left(\begin{matrix}\text{Budgeted} \\ \text{volume}\end{matrix} - \begin{matrix}\text{Actual} \\ \text{volume}\end{matrix}\right)$$

$$\text{Total overhead budget variance} = \begin{matrix}\text{Actual} \\ \text{total overhead}\end{matrix} - \begin{matrix}\text{Budgeted} \\ \text{total overhead}\end{matrix}$$

REVIEW PROBLEM

Boulder Company makes drill presses to customer order and uses job-order costing. The company began the month of March with no inventories. During March, it worked on two jobs, for which data is as follows:

	Job #15	Job #16
Materials used	$69,000	$45,000
Direct labor at $10 per hour	$35,000	$60,000

Boulder incurred factory overhead costs of $209,000. Budgeted monthly factory overhead is $150,000 + ($5 × direct labor hours). The company uses a predetermined overhead rate based on 10,000 direct labor hours per month. Activity does not usually fluctuate much from one month to another.

Required
1. Calculate the predetermined overhead rate per direct labor hour.
2. Determine the amounts of overhead to apply to each job.
3. Determine the overhead budget variance and volume variance.
4. Suppose that job #15 was sold for $240,000 and job #16 remained in inventory. Selling and administrative expenses for March were $24,000. Prepare an income statement for March. Treat variances as adjustments to normal cost of sales.
5. Suppose now that the company used actual costing, allocating overhead to jobs based on the actual overhead rate per direct labor hour. Determine the amounts of overhead applied to each job and prepare an income statement assuming the relevant data from item 4.

ANSWER TO REVIEW PROBLEM
1. $20.00 per direct labor hour, calculated as follows.

$$Predetermined\ rate = \frac{Total\ budgeted\ overhead}{Total\ budgeted\ activity}$$

$$= \frac{\$150,000 + (\$5 \times 10,000)}{10,000}$$

$$= \$20$$

The rate consists of $15 fixed and $5 variable. Because there is no significant fluctuation in activity during the year, it is reasonable to use the monthly rather than the annual figures to calculate the rate. In fact, with annual fixed overhead of $1,800,000 ($150,000 × 12) and 120,000 direct labor hours (10,000 × 12), we would have exactly the same result.

2.

	Job #15	Job #16	Total
Direct labor hours:			
$35,000/$10	3,500		
$60,000/$10		6,000	9,500

Overhead at $20 per hour: $70,000 + $120,000 = $190,000

3.

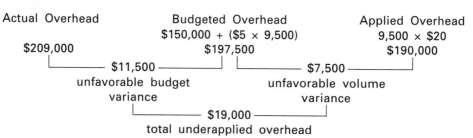

4.

Sales		$240,000
Cost of sales:		
Normal cost of sales[a]	$174,000	
Variances:		
Budget variance	11,500U	
Volume variance	7,500U	
Cost of sales		193,000
Gross profit		$ 47,000
Selling and administrative expenses		24,000
Income		$ 23,000

a Job #15, materials + direct labor + applied overhead = $69,000 + $35,000 + $70,000 = $174,000.

5. The problem here is simply to determine the actual overhead rate.

$$Actual\ rate = \frac{Actual\ overhead}{Actual\ activity}$$

$$= \frac{\$209,000}{9,500\ hours}$$

$$= \$22.00\ per\ hour$$

The applied amounts are as follows:

	Job #15	Job #16	Total
Direct labor hours	3,500	6,000	9,500
Overhead applied at $22 per hour	$77,000	$132,000	$209,000

All overhead goes to individual jobs, so there are no variances. The income statement shows the following, with job #15 costing $181,000 ($69,000 + $35,000 + $77,000).

Sales	$240,000
Cost of sales	181,000
Gross margin	$ 59,000
Selling and administrative expense	24,000
Income	$ 35,000

The difference in incomes ($23,000 versus $35,000) arises from the differences in inventory. Under normal costing, as in item 2, overhead of $120,000 is applied to job #16, which is still in inventory. Under actual costing, as shown here, overhead of $132,000 is applied to job #16. The $12,000 difference in income under the two methods is explained by the $12,000 difference in the overhead assigned to the job remaining in inventory (job #16).

ASSIGNMENT MATERIAL

QUESTIONS FOR DISCUSSION

13-1   *FedEx's handling costs*   A recent annual report of **FedEx** stated

"In fiscal 1994, our average daily U.S. domestic package volume rose 12%, or more than 196,000 packages per day. Our average cost for handling that volume declined, however to an amount 1.5% lower than our fiscal 1993 per-package cost. Internationally, the high fixed costs of our world-wide network are steadily being offset by greater volume."

Required

1. Do you think FedEx's *total costs* for handling domestic packages rose or fell from 1993 to 1994? You might wish to work out an example using the figures given and an arbitrary per-package cost for 1993 of $10.
2. Explain the meaning of the last sentence in the quotation.

13-2   *Trane Company's overhead absorption*   Trane Co., whose operations were described in Chapter 12, sets its overhead rates to allow it to absorb overhead costs at 85% of capacity. What does that statement mean?

13-3   *Overhead application*   "Underapplied overhead is a bad sign because the more overhead you apply, the lower your fixed cost per unit." Discuss this statement critically.

13-4   *Costing methods and inventories*   World-class manufacturers keep very little inventory. Suppose such a company begins and ends a year with no inventories. Will there be any difference between its income computed using actual costing and using normal costing? Why or why not?

13-5   *"What's normal about it?"*   A student sitting near you in class just asked this question. The student does not see how you can apply overhead using a predetermined rate, and went on to say: "If overhead cost per hour is $15 in one month and $6 the next, that's the way it goes. All this 'applying' business is a bookkeeping trick, but it doesn't make any sense in the real world."

Required

Comment on the statements.

13-6   *Are cost accountants the villains?*   Mr. Robert Fox, executive vice president of **Creative Output**, a management consulting firm in Connecticut, was quoted as arguing that allowing cost accounting "to dictate the way a factory floor is organized and run" is harmful. Fox was further quoted as saying that, "The cost accounting system assigns part of overall costs of running the factory to each step in the manufacturing process. Each hour a machine is running, for instance, may be costed at a given amount. A foreman will then try to get as much material as he can through that machine . . . to keep the costs assigned to his particular work stations as low as possible."

Required

Discuss the quotation. What does Mr. Fox mean and how must a company be applying overhead for the quotation to be correct?

EXERCISES

13-7 Basic actual job-order costing StorTech Furniture uses actual job-order costing, applying overhead to jobs based on direct labor hours. StorTech worked on two orders in March.

	MK-11	JO-8
Direct labor hours	11,000	9,000
Material cost	$150,000	$60,000
Direct labor cost	$95,000	$75,000

StorTech incurred $180,000 overhead cost in March.

Required
1. Determine the actual overhead rate for March.
2. Determine the amount of overhead to be applied to each job.
3. Determine the total cost of each job.

13-8 Basic normal job-order costing (continuation of 13-7) Suppose now that StorTech uses normal costing, with a predetermined overhead rate of $10 per direct labor hour.

Required
1. Determine the amount of overhead to be applied to each job.
2. Determine the total cost of each job.
3. Determine the amount of overapplied or underapplied overhead for March.
4. Suppose that StorTech budgeted annual overhead using the formula $1,500,000 + ($4 × direct labor hours). The predetermined overhead rate was based on 250,000 budgeted direct labor hours. Assuming that budgeted monthly fixed overhead is $125,000, what were the budget and volume variances?

13-9 Job-order costing income statements (continuation of 13-7 and 13-8) StorTech Furniture's job JO-8 was incomplete at the end of March, while job MK-11 was sold for $600,000. Selling and administrative expenses were $150,000.

Required
1. Prepare an income statement for March using the results from 13-7.
2. Prepare an income statement for March using the results from 13-8. Show any misapplied overhead as an adjustment to normal cost of sales.

13-10 Job-order costing—income statement MQL Company uses normal job-order costing. Its predetermined overhead rate is based on the following data.

Variable overhead per machine hour	$2
Total budgeted fixed overhead	$600,000
Total budgeted machine hours	200,000

The company began 19X5 with no inventories. A summary of materials, direct labor cost, and machine hours for 19X5 is as follows:

	Total	Jobs Sold	Jobs in Ending Inventories
Materials costs	$700,000	$600,000	$100,000
Direct labor cost	$1,900,000	$1,700,000	$200,000
Machine hours	180,000	160,000	20,000

Total sales were $5,500,000, selling and administrative expenses were $1,900,000, and total actual manufacturing overhead was $840,000.

Required
1. Compute the predetermined overhead rate for 19X5.
2. Prepare an income statement for 19X5 with overapplied or underapplied overhead shown as an adjustment to cost of sales.

13-11   Predetermined overhead rates   For each of the following situations, fill in the missing data. The predetermined overhead rates are based on budgeted fixed costs and budgeted machine hours for the year. There is no variable overhead.

	(a) Fixed Overhead Rate	(b) Budgeted Fixed Overhead	(c) Budgeted Hours	(d) Actual Hours	(e) Fixed Overhead Applied
1.	_____	$240,000	30,000	32,000	_____
2.	$5	_____	20,000	22,000	_____
3.	_____	$70,000	_____	11,000	$77,000
4.	$4	$160,000	_____	_____	$172,000

13-12   Ethics and overhead application   Milton Machine does considerable work for the U.S. government on cost-plus contracts. The typical cost-plus contract provides that the government will pay for materials, direct labor, and overhead. The government requires that overhead assigned to jobs be reasonable and in conformity with the company's usual methods. An allowance for profit is then added to the total cost to determine the price.

Milton has been using machine hours to apply overhead but its controller believes that the company should shift to labor hours. He explains, "Our government business could be a lot more profitable if we used labor time to apply overhead. Government business is much more labor-intensive than commercial business and would therefore shoulder more overhead."

Required
Comment on the controller's proposal.

13-13   Overhead relationships—variances   Each of the following cases is independent. Fill in the blanks, being sure to indicate whether a variance is favorable or unfavorable. The amounts for "total budgeted overhead" are the flexible budget allowances for the actual level of activity for the period. In each case, the company uses a single rate to apply both fixed and variable overhead.

Case	(a) Total Budgeted Overhead	(b) Total Actual Overhead	(c) Total Applied Overhead	(d) Budget Variance	(e) Volume Variance
1	$400,000	$397,000	$402,000	————	————
2	$600,000	————	$585,000	$4,000U	————
3	$400,000	————	————	$6,000 F	$10,000U
4	————	$310,000	————	$6,000U	$18,000F

13-14 *Job-order costing—assigning overhead* Marquette Boatworks uses normal costing and its predetermined overhead rate is based on the following information. Monthly budgeted overhead = $600,000 + ($0.80 × direct labor cost). Monthly budgeted direct labor cost is $1,000,000. At the end of March, the following information was available.

	Total	Jobs Sold	Jobs in Ending Inventory of Work in Process	Finished Goods
Materials cost	$650,000	$510,000	$80,000	$60,000
Direct labor cost	$1,010,000	$820,000	$100,000	$90,000

Actual overhead for the month was $1,407,000.

Required
1. Compute the predetermined overhead rate based on direct labor cost.
2. Determine cost of goods sold for the month.
3. Determine ending inventory of work in process.
4. Determine ending inventory of finished goods.
5. Determine overapplied or underapplied overhead.
6. Determine the volume variance.
7. Determine the budget variance.

13-15 *Predetermined overhead rates—job-order costing* Walton Company uses predetermined rates for fixed overhead, based on machine hours. The following data are available relating to 19X5.

Budgeted fixed factory overhead cost	$240,000
Budgeted machine hours	40,000
Actual fixed factory overhead cost incurred	$242,000
Actual machine hours used	39,000

Actual machine hours by job	
Job No.	Machine Hours Used on Job
12	8,000
13	14,000
14	7,000
15	10,000

Required
1. Compute the predetermined overhead rate.
2. Determine the overhead to be applied to each job.
3. Determine the budget variance and the volume variance.

13-16   Job order costing—activity-based overhead rates   MFG Industries applies overhead to jobs using two rates—one based on the number of parts used on each job, the other based on machine hours for each job. Because of the high amounts of overhead associated with purchasing, receiving, storing, and issuing materials, the managers believe that simply using machine hours to allocate this overhead is inappropriate. Summary data for 19X5 follow.

	Budget	Actual
Part-related overhead	$240,000	$234,000
Machine-related overhead	$700,000	$697,000
Cost of materials used on jobs	$1,600,000	$1,582,000
Direct labor cost	$900,000	$869,000
Machine hours	100,000	98,000
Number of parts	1,000,000	1,040,000

Data related to jobs worked on in 19X5 follow.

			Jobs in Ending Inventory of	
	Total	Jobs Sold	Work in Process	Finished Goods
Materials cost	$1,582,000	$1,321,000	$82,000	$179,000
Direct labor cost	$869,000	$788,000	$33,000	$48,000
Machine hours	98,000	77,000	7,000	14,000
Number of parts	1,040,000	980,000	25,000	35,000

Sales were $3,890,000 and administrative expenses were $356,000.

Required
1. Compute the predetermined overhead rates for parts and for machine hours.
2. Determine the cost of jobs sold and the cost of each type of ending inventory.
3. Prepare an income statement showing misapplied overhead as an adjustment to normal cost of sales.

13-17   Basic job order costing   Tucker Machinery, Inc. manufactures large custom drills. It uses a predetermined overhead rate of $4.20 per machine hour. During August, Tucker worked on three jobs. Data are as follows:

	Z-101	K-221	K-341
Machine hours	2,180	1,130	2,810
Direct labor cost	$23,400	$14,200	$36,320
Materials cost	$24,570	$9,220	$26,245

Job Z-101 was completed and sold. The other jobs were unfinished. Actual overhead for August was $25,210.

Required
1. Determine the overhead to be applied to each job.
2. Determine normal cost of sales and ending inventory.
3. Determine overapplied or underapplied overhead.

13-18   Comparison of actual and normal costing   Riopelle Company uses actual job-order costing, assigning overhead to jobs based on direct labor cost. During March, Riopelle had the following activity.

	Jobs Worked on in March		
	M-1	M-2	M-3
Materials cost	$22,000	$51,000	$38,000
Direct labor cost	$24,000	$18,000	$28,000

Total actual overhead was $196,000; selling and administrative expenses were $28,000. Job M-1 was sold for $160,000. Jobs M-2 and M-3 were incomplete at the end of March.

Required
1. Determine the actual overhead rate per direct labor dollar.
2. Determine the overhead assigned to each job and the total cost of each job.
3. Prepare an income statement for March.
4. Suppose now that Riopelle uses normal costing. Its predetermined overhead rate is based on $2,100,000 budgeted overhead and $700,000 budgeted direct labor cost for the year. Calculate the predetermined overhead rate and redo items 2 and 3 using normal costing. Show any misapplied overhead as an adjustment to normal gross margin.

13-19   *Graphical analysis of overhead* The following graph shows the budgeted manufacturing overhead for Minich Company.

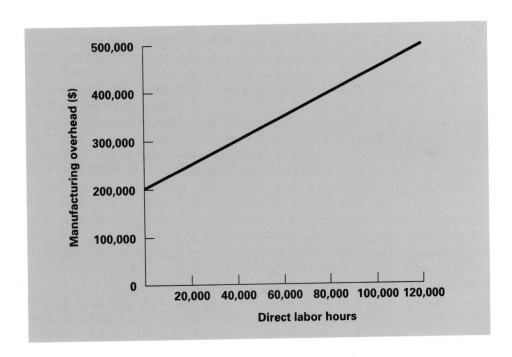

Required
1. Draw the line that represents applied overhead for each of the following two cases.
   (a) The predetermined overhead rate is $5 per direct labor hour.
   (b) The predetermined overhead rate is based on 100,000 direct labor hours.
2. Suppose that actual overhead equals budgeted overhead and that volume is 90,000 direct labor hours. What are the volume variances under each of the two cases from item 1?

13-20   *Job-order costing for a service business*   D. J. Grimm Co. is an engineering consulting firm that specializes in mining work. The company uses a job-order cost system to accumulate costs for each job. Data on operations for August follow.

	Grand Bay Gold	Big Butte Copper	Flake River
Engineers' time, hours	300	250	150
Engineers' cost	$6,400	$7,800	$3,600
Other expenses	$2,100	$1,700	$1,200

Other expenses include travel, lodging, auto rentals, meals and other items that are charged to clients. Grimm applies overhead to jobs using a predetermined overhead rate. The rate is based on $6,400,000 budgeted overhead cost and 200,000 budgeted engineering hours.

Required
1. Calculate the predetermined overhead rate.
2. Determine the cost of each job worked on in August.

13-21   *Basic job-order costing*   Kelton Company makes a wide variety of gear assemblies for industrial applications. The company uses normal costing, with a predetermined overhead rate of $4.40 per machine hour. During March 19X6, Kelton worked on the following jobs.

	Job Number		
	311	312	313
Materials used on job	$12,260	$24,340	$7,890
Direct labor cost	$17,250	$13,550	$10,100
Machine hours	1,480	1,230	860

Required
1. Compute the amounts of overhead to be applied to each job and the total cost of each job.
2. Actual overhead for March was $16,980. What was overapplied or underapplied overhead?

13-22   *Overhead application*   The controller of Williams Company received the following budgeted data for manufacturing overhead costs of 19X7.

	Fixed Amount	Variable Cost per Direct Labor Hour
Indirect labor	$ 42,800	$0.50
Supplies	19,300	0.15
Lubricants	7,700	0.12
Utilities	36,400	0.51
Repairs	22,400	0.17
Property taxes	7,000	0
Depreciation	31,000	0
Total	$166,600	$1.45

The controller estimates that 70,000 direct labor hours will be worked in 19X7.

Required
1. Compute the predetermined fixed overhead rate per direct labor hour.
2. Assume that 67,000 direct labor hours are worked on jobs in 19X7.
   (a) How much fixed overhead will be applied?
   (b) How much variable overhead should be incurred? How much applied?
   (c) If actual overhead costs are $274,800, what are the budget and volume variances?

PROBLEMS

13-23 Overhead application VanMeter Company runs a highly automated operation that measures its activity by machine hours. Its managers have budgeted 400,000 machine hours for 19X2. They budget annual manufacturing overhead as total budgeted overhead = $800,000 + ($4 × machine hours). The company had no beginning inventories.

Required
1. Compute the predetermined overhead rate for 19X2.
2. At the end of 19X2, the controller collected the following information.

Total manufacturing overhead incurred	$2,285,000
Machine hours on jobs sold	350,000
Machine hours on jobs in ending inventories	40,000

Determine the amounts of applied overhead in cost of goods sold and in ending inventories. Determine the amount of overapplied or underapplied overhead and break it down into the budget variance and volume variance.

13-24 Job order costing—activity-based overhead rates Hughes Machines uses two rates to apply overhead to jobs. One rate is based on materials cost, the other on machine time. Hughes has relatively high overhead that is related to buying, receiving, storing, and issuing materials; hence the managers believe that applying this overhead through the relative materials cost of jobs is appropriate. The following data relate to 19X4.

	Budget
Materials-related overhead	$880,000
Machine-related overhead	$1,100,000
Cost of materials used on jobs	$1,760,000
Machine hours	200,000

Data related to three jobs worked on in March follow.

	Job XT-56	Job XR-23	Job XY-67
Materials cost	$21,000	$82,000	$39,000
Direct labor cost	$16,000	$13,000	$18,000
Machine hours	8,500	4,500	2,900

Actual material-related overhead was $74,200 and actual machine-related overhead was $92,800.

Required

1. Compute the predetermined overhead rates for materials and for machine hours.
2. Determine the amount of overhead to be applied to each job and the total cost of each job.
3. Determine overapplied or underapplied overhead for each type of overhead.

13-25   Job-order costing—two departments   WestCo makes industrial robots to customer order in two departments, Machining and Assembly. Machining is highly mechanized, and Assembly is labor intensive. Accordingly, the company applies overhead using machine hours in the Machining Department and direct labor hours in the Assembly Department. Budgeted data for 19X6 are as follows:

	Machining Department	Assembly Department
Total budgeted overhead	$840,000	$180,000
Machine hours	120,000	
Direct labor hours		60,000

During March WestCo worked on two jobs.

	Job #1029	Job #1030
Materials used	$23,000	$35,000
Direct labor, Assembly Department, at $6 per hour	$12,000	$19,200
Machine hours in Machining Department	4,000	5,000

Required

1. Calculate the predetermined overhead rate for each department.
2. Calculate the overhead applied to each job and the total cost of each job.
3. Actual overhead in the Machining Department was $65,500, in the Assembly Department, $14,200. Calculate overapplied or underapplied overhead for each department.

13-26   Basic job-order costing   Walker Company manufactures precision optical instruments to customer order. Walker uses normal costing and sets its predetermined overhead rate based on machine hours. For 19X4, the rate is $11.40 per hour, based on $3,420,000 budgeted overhead and 300,000 budgeted hours. During January, the company worked on three jobs.

	Job Number		
	M-101	R-12	Z-610
Materials used	$35,800	$73,200	$40,600
Direct labor cost	$123,200	$120,200	$78,300
Machine hours	8,800	8,200	7,200

Job M-101 was completed and sold while the other two remained in inventory at the end of January. Actual overhead incurred in January was $271,300.

Required

1. Determine the amount of overhead that should be applied to each job.

2. Determine normal cost of goods sold for January and ending inventory.
3. Determine overapplied or underapplied overhead for January.

13-27   *Job costing in a service firm* Barnes and DiLello form a partnership of architectural engineers operating in a single office in a medium-sized city. The firm charges clients for the time that each person on the staff spends on the client's business, using a rate of 2 ½ times the person's salary, based on an 1,800-hour working year. Thus, an architectural draftsperson earning a salary of $25,000 is charged out to clients at $35 per hour [($25,000/1,800) × 2.5 = $34.73, rounded to $35]. The rate is intended to cover all costs and to yield a profit.

	Budget for 19X9
Salaries of professional staff	$ 750,000
Salaries of support personnel (clerks, typists, etc.)	78,000
Other costs	680,000
Total expected costs	$1,508,000

The listed costs do not include salaries for Barnes and DiLello. Each partner expects to work about 1,200 chargeable hours at a rate of $60 per hour. About 80% of the professional staff's time is chargeable to clients, as well as about 40% of the support personnel's time. Nonchargeable time is for general firm business, professional activities (attending seminars and continuing-education programs), and business development.

Required

1. What total income will the partners earn if their estimates prove correct?
2. Suppose that two professional employees work on a design for a particular client. One earns $18,000 per year, the other $21,000, and each works 12 hours on this particular project. How much will the firm charge the client for the project assuming that neither the partners nor the support staff is involved in this project? (Round hourly rates to the nearest dollar.)

13-28   *Overhead costs and pricing policy* HortonWorks is a medium-sized machine shop that does custom work for industrial customers. Business is seasonal, with about four busy months, three slack months, and the rest about average. HortonWorks uses an actual job-order costing system, assigning overhead to jobs at the end of each month based on the labor cost of each job. Rae Horton, the owner, sets prices using the following format, with typical data.

Estimated material cost	$32.50
Estimated labor cost	16.80
Subtotal	$49.30
Allowance for overhead at 60%	29.58
Subtotal	$78.88
Allowance for profit at 10%	7.89
Price	$86.77

Horton developed the formula based on experience and on the financial results of the past few years. Overhead has averaged about 60% of the sum of materials and labor costs, and a 10% profit is reasonable in the industry. Horton has found that similar jobs seem to be more or less profitable depending on the month in which they are done. This bothers her, and she has begun to wonder whether her pricing policy is sensible.

Required

1. In which months, busy or slack, will jobs appear more profitable? Why?
2. Should Horton modify the pricing policy? What should Horton do?

 13-29   *Job-order costing* The following data pertain to the March operations of Covera Machine Tool Company. The company uses JIT principles and ships jobs as it completes them, keeping no inventory of finished goods.

Jobs in beginning work in process:	
Materials	$237,670
Direct labor	$322,200
Factory overhead	$467,190
Materials put into process in March:	
To jobs in ending inventory	$228,310
To jobs finished and sold in March	$881,480
Direct labor for March:	
To jobs in ending work in process	$452,400
To jobs finished and sold in March	$892,880

The company uses normal costing and applies overhead at $1.50 per direct labor dollar. The materials and labor costs for jobs finished and sold include the cost to finish the beginning inventory of work in process. The company had March sales of $4,680,000 and selling and administrative expenses of $453,650.

Required

1. Determine the overhead cost in ending inventory of work in process and in cost of goods sold.
2. Overhead was overapplied by $18,430 in March. What was actual overhead?
3. Prepare an income statement for March, treating overapplied overhead as an adjustment to normal cost of sales.

13-30   *Job order costing—comparison of overhead rates* Rubenstein Foundry uses a single overhead rate based on machine hours. One of its managers believes that the company could benefit from using two rates, one based on materials cost, the other on machine time. The manager believes that because Rubenstein has relatively high overhead related to buying, receiving, storing, and issuing materials, applying this overhead through the relative materials cost of jobs is appropriate. The following data relate to 19X4.

	Budget
Materials-related overhead	$ 540,000
Machine-related overhead	1,462,500
Total overhead	$2,002,500
Cost of materials used on jobs	$1,700,000
Machine hours	225,000

Data related to three jobs worked on in March follow.

	Job XT-56	Job XR-23	Job XY-67
Materials cost	$21,000	$82,000	$39,000
Direct labor cost	$16,000	$13,000	$18,000
Machine hours used	8,500	4,500	2,900

Actual materials-related overhead was $41,800 and actual machine-related overhead was $111,300.

Required
1. Compute the predetermined overhead rate per machine hour assuming that Rubenstein uses only machine hours to apply overhead, as it has been doing.
2. Determine the amount of overhead to be applied to each job and the total cost of each job.
3. Redo parts 1 and 2 using the two rates as suggested by the manager. Comment on the differences in job costs here and in part 2.

13-31   *Job-order costing for a service business* D. J. Westlake Co. is a partnership of Certified Public Accountants specializing in tax work. The firm uses a job-order cost system to accumulate costs for each job it does for a particular client. Data on operations for June follow.

	Walton Estate Planning	GHK, Inc Federal Return	All Other Jobs
Senior accountant time, hours	80	40	3,000
Junior accountant time, hours	20	150	12,000

Westlake pays senior accountants an average of $60,000 per year for an expected 2,000-hour year. It pays juniors an average of $30,000 per year for the same expected hours. Westlake uses the average hourly pay to determine the cost of accountants' time on jobs. Westlake also charges an hourly amount to cover overhead costs and provide a profit. The client is charged for the time and the combined overhead/profit rate. This year, the rate is based on the following data.

Budgeted overhead cost	$9,200,000
Budgeted profit	$800,000
Budgeted hours	200,000

Required
1. Calculate the salary rates Westlake will use for senior accountants' and junior accountants' time.
2. Calculate the predetermined rate that Westlake must use to cover its overhead costs and meet its profit objective.
3. Determine the "cost" of each job worked on in June and the cost of "all other jobs."
4. How is Westlake's accounting different from that of a manufacturer? Does its method make sense?

13-32   *Job-order costing, beginning inventory* Wisconsin Machinery Company makes large industrial machines. It uses a job-order costing system applying overhead at $15 per direct labor hour. Direct laborers earn $8 per hour. The following data relate to jobs worked on in March 19X4.

	4-22	4-23	4-24	4-25
Costs in beginning inventory:				
Materials	$ 34,000	$ 10,000	0	0
Direct labor	48,000	8,000	0	0
Overhead	90,000	15,000	0	0
Total	$172,000	$ 33,000	0	0
Costs incurred in March:				
Materials	$11,000	$ 46,000	$60,000	$9,000
Direct labor	$16,000	$ 32,000	$52,000	$12,000

Jobs 4-22, 4-23, and 4-24 were completed and sold. Job 4-25 was not finished at the end of March. Total overhead incurred during March was $212,000.

Required
1. Compute the amounts of overhead to be applied to each job.
2. Compute the amount of overapplied or underapplied overhead for March.
3. Compute cost of goods sold for March and the inventory at March 31.
4. Revenue from the three jobs sold was $860,000. Selling and administrative expenses for March were $180,000. Prepare an income statement for March.

13-33   CVP analysis for a job-order company   Brill Optics manufactures special lenses to customer order. Kim Brill, the owner, is trying to develop a profit plan and has collected the following budgeted data for 19X7.

Materials cost	$200,000
Labor cost (40,000 hours at $9 per hour)	360,000
Variable overhead	160,000
Fixed overhead	240,000
Selling and administrative expenses, all fixed	120,000

Brill has set a predetermined overhead rate of $10 per direct labor hour. The company sets prices at 120% of total manufacturing cost, including applied overhead.

Required
1. What profit will Brill earn if operations meet expectations?
2. Suppose that Brill is able to generate only 35,000 direct labor hours worth of work, a 12.5% decline. Materials and variable overhead also decline by 12.5%. Brill treats misapplied overhead as an adjustment to normal cost of sales. What will profit be, assuming prices were set using applied overhead?
3. What pricing policy, stated as a percentage of total manufacturing cost, will give a $100,000 profit at 40,000 direct labor hours?

13-34   Costing and pricing in a hospital   The controller of Prairie Memorial Hospital has recently decided to set prices for laboratory tests using a formula based on costs. She has analyzed each type of test as follows.

Class of Test	Time Required (minutes)	Number Performed in Average Year
I	12	38,000
II	15	17,000
III	30	9,000

Variable costs are negligible. The controller believes that because all lab technicians are salaried, it is best to treat their salaries as overhead costs. Total annual overhead costs are $960,000.

Required

1. Calculate a predetermined overhead rate per minute. Round to the nearest $0.001.
2. Determine the price for each class of test that will make the laboratory break even. Round prices to the nearest cent.
3. Suppose that the laboratory performs 37,000 Class I, 17,000 Class II, and 10,000 Class III tests. Total costs are $965,000. Determine profit or loss.

13-35   *Overhead application and pricing decisions* Westminster Furniture, a high-quality manufacturer, has just received an offer from a large wholesaler for a single batch of goods. The offered price is $43,000, which is about $12,000 less than normal for similar work. Westminster has never done business with the wholesaler and the sales manager wants to get a foot in the door. She is sure that existing sales would be unaffected by the special order and wants to accept the order if any profit can be made. The production manager provided the following estimates of cost for the order.

Materials	$ 12,000
Direct labor (3,000 hours)	18,000
Overhead	15,000
Total	$ 45,000

The production manager informed you that the overhead cost is based on the overhead application rate of $5 per direct labor hour. The rate includes both fixed and variable overhead and was based on 60,000 expected direct labor hours and $300,000 budgeted total overhead costs. The rate last year was $5.50, based on 50,000 direct labor hours and $275,000 total overhead costs. The production manager told you that the difference in rates is due to the difference in budgeted direct labor hours—the cost structure is the same this year as last year.

Required

1. Determine the incremental cost of the order. Should it be accepted?
2. What other factors should be considered in deciding whether to accept this special order?

13-36   *Overhead rates and cost analysis* Walton Machinery Company has been operating well below capacity, and Frank Williams, the sales manager, has been trying to increase orders. He recently received an offer to bid on a large industrial press and submitted the specifications to Walton's cost estimators. Their estimate follows.

Materials	$29,600
Direct labor at $9 per hour	19,800
Overhead at $12 per direct labor hour	26,400
Total manufacturing cost	$75,800
Standard allowance for selling and administrative expenses, 10% of manufacturing cost	7,580
Total cost	$83,380
Standard allowance for profit at 15% of total cost	12,507
Suggested price	$95,887

Williams told the executive vice president that the suggested price is not low enough to get the job. He said that the customer expected a price in the neighborhood of $75,000, which another company had already bid. The vice president called in the controller, who said that the overhead rate was about 60% variable, 40% fixed, and that variable selling and administrative expenses were negligible. The vice president was reluctant to meet the $75,000 price but agreed to think it over and get back to Williams.

Required
Write a memorandum to Mr. Williams indicating whether Walton should meet the $75,000 price.

13-37   Pricing policy and profits   Sumter Milling is a job-order company. It uses material supplied by its customers, so that virtually all of its manufacturing costs are direct labor and overhead. Jackie Wiggins, the controller, prepared the following data for use in establishing the company's pricing policy for the coming year.

| Total budgeted direct labor hours | 240,000 |
| Total budgeted manufacturing costs | $4,800,000 |

Total budgeted manufacturing costs were developed using the following formula:

Total manufacturing costs = $1,200,000 + ($15 × direct labor hours)

Total selling and administrative expenses are budgeted as $800,000 + ($0.10 × revenue). The management of the company seeks an $880,000 profit.

Required
1. Determine the revenue Sumter must earn to achieve its profit objective.
2. Determine the price per direct labor hour Sumter must charge to achieve the objective.
3. Suppose that the company uses the pricing policy you developed and actually works 230,000 direct labor hours. What will its profit be?
4. Suppose that the company uses your pricing policy and works 250,000 hours. What will its profit be?

13-38   Overhead rates, ABC, and pricing   Jarod Kane, controller, and Renee Poston, sales manager of Hicks Furniture, were discussing the company's dismal operating results. Poston said "Some of the products in our high-volume lines just are not selling. Our competitors' prices are less than ours, but we are leaving almost no margin to cover selling and administrative expenses and provide a reasonable profit. However, some of our low-volume products are doing quite well, especially some of those we make in small jobs."

Kane had begun a study of the company's costs and thought that part of the problem might lie with the way it applied overhead to jobs. "Look," he said, "an order of our high-volume chairs might be 200-300 units, while for some of the others, say an expensive sofa, a typical job size is more like 20. There have to be significant costs of making up many such small batches instead of a few large ones. After all, we have to do a cost estimate and start some paperwork for each job, workers have to log in their time, we have to track the job through the plant, and so on. Plus, some of our costs are related to such activities as setting up machinery, moving materials and semifinished product, and packing up a shipment; they typically are made in large batches. My new assistant is completing the study I started and I expect to hear about the findings this afternoon."

You, the new assistant, have accumulated the following information that you believe is accurate enough for preliminary analysis.

Costs and activities under current procedures

	Model 807 Chair	Model 5052 Table
Number in typical order	200	30
Average cost per job:		
Materials	$24,000	$20,400
Direct labor at $10/hour	6,000	1,500
Overhead at $25/DLH	15,000	3,750
Total unit cost	$45,000	$25,650
Price at 120% of manufacturing cost	$54,000	$30,780

Activity-based data

Driver for Cost Pool	Total Cost in Pool	Annual Activity of Driver
Direct labor	$4,800,000	300,000
Machine setups	1,200,000	5,000
Number of parts/components	900,000	450,000
Number of record keeping transactions	400,000	400,000

Amounts of Cost Driver per Job

Model 807	Model 5052
600 DLH	150 DLH
1 setup	12 setups
400 parts	800 parts
200 transactions	500 transactions

Required

1. Calculate overhead rates for each cost driver and determine the cost and price of each model.
2. Write a memorandum to Mr. Kane explaining the differences between your costs and the original costs. State why the company seems to be experiencing the operating results described by Poston. Use the guidelines in Appendix A.
3. In general, would you expect high-volume or low-volume products to show higher overhead costs under ABC than under labor-based assignment? Why?

13-39   Changing overhead rates   Benson Electronics has been on a cost-cutting program designed to help it meet foreign competition. The cost of a typical unit of Benson's major product is as follows:

Materials and components	$180
Direct labor	44
Overhead at 400% of direct labor	176
Total cost	$400

The overhead cost reflects actual overhead divided by actual labor hours at 50,000 units, the expected production level of the product. Benson's engineers did considerable redesigning of the product line to reduce labor cost. They introduced some custom-made components, which, though more costly than the existing components, were easier to assemble into the units. They also changed some job descriptions and rerouted product flow. The head of engineering understood that the changes would raise material/component costs by about $16, but would reduce labor cost by roughly $16 and therefore reduce overhead by about $64 at the 400% rate. The results in the first six months were not encouraging as the following unit cost calculation, which as before is based on actual overhead costs and direct labor for 50,000 units, shows.

Materials and components	$190
Direct labor	29
Overhead at 600% of direct labor	174
Total cost	$393

The heads of production and engineering, as well as the controller, were not happy with the results. A great deal of work had resulted in little net decrease in unit cost. The most disappointing aspect was the sharp increase in the overhead rate occasioned by the drop in direct labor.

Required
1. Determine total overhead before and after the cost-cutting program.
2. Suppose that the entire difference you found in part 1 is attributable to the component of overhead that varies with direct labor. Determine the variable component of overhead, with respect to direct labor. Can you now explain why costs did not fall as much as one might have thought?
3. What do you recommend?

13-40   Normal costing   Boardman Company manufactures equipment used to cap bottles. The following data summarize 19X3 activities.

Beginning inventories of work in process and finished goods	$ 360,000
Materials put into process	2,240,000
Direct labor	1,780,000
Manufacturing overhead incurred	2,520,000
Selling and administrative expenses	880,000
Sales	7,960,000

The company uses an overhead application rate of $1.40 per direct labor dollar, based on budgeted direct labor cost of $1,800,000 and the following formula for budgeting manufacturing overhead: Manufacturing overhead = $1,440,000 + ($0.60 × direct labor cost). At the end of the year, the controller prepared the following analysis of costs.

	Total	Jobs Sold	Incomplete Jobs	Finished Jobs
Materials	$2,240,000	$1,890,000	$120,000	$230,000
Direct labor	$1,780,000	$1,480,000	$100,000	$200,000

Required

Prepare an income statement for the year, using normal costing and showing the budget variance and volume variance as separate adjustments to gross margin.

13-41 *Overhead rate behavior* Ned Clinton, controller of Walcott Industries, has been puzzled by the behavior of overhead rates. The company has been engaged in a program to reduce costs and the focus has been on direct labor and associated overhead costs. Because the average cost per direct labor hour (DLH) was in the $10.20-$10.40 range and the average overhead rate around $39 per DLH, Clinton expected savings in the area of $50 for reductions in DLH. Clinton has been collecting data (see below) for the past few quarters to track the progress of the program. Output was about the same in each quarter, so the decreased labor hours represent improved performance.

Quarter	Actual Direct Labor Hours	Direct Labor Cost	Overhead Cost	Overhead per DLH
3rd 19X1	62,000	$634,500	$2,432,000	$39.23
4th 19X1	61,100	629,450	2,431,900	39.80
1st 19X2	61,200	630,180	2,431,200	39.74
2nd 19X2	58,300	601,100	2,428,800	41.66
3rd 19X2	55,400	569,900	2,427,200	43.81

Clinton was puzzled at the behavior of the overhead rate. He knew that overhead was not totally variable with direct labor, but thought that there surely should have been a considerable drop in overhead as direct labor hours declined.

Required

1. Using the high-low method, determine the component of overhead costs that varies with direct labor hours.
2. State why you think Clinton might have been incorrect in his estimates of the effects of reducing labor time and what he might do now.

13-42 *Job-order costing and decisions* Last month, Marchmont Furniture Company began work on custom-made chairs ordered by a retail store. When the work was nearly complete, the retailer went bankrupt and was not able to pay for the chairs. The sales manager of Marchmont immediately called other stores in an effort to sell the chairs. The original price was $280,000, but the best price the sales manager could get if the chairs were finished according to the original specifications was $182,000. This offer was from the Z-Store chain. Randle Company, which also operates a chain of stores, offered $202,000 for the chairs provided that different upholstery and trim were used. The sales manager talked to the production manager about the order and got the following information.

	Costs Accumulated to Date
Materials	$ 31,500
Direct labor (7,000 hours at $11)	77,000
Factory overhead at $10 per hour	70,000
Total accumulated costs	$178,500

The factory overhead rate includes $4 variable overhead and $6 fixed overhead. The additional work required to complete the chairs was estimated as follows by the production manager.

	Original Specifications	Randle's Specifications
Materials	$4,000	$6,000
Direct labor hours	800 hours	1,800 hours

Required

1. Using the company's costing method, determine the total costs to be charged to the job assuming (a) the work is completed based on the original specifications and (b) the chairs are modified as required by Randle Company.
2. Determine which offer Marchmont should accept.

13-43   *Job-order costing—service business*   Sofdat Inc. develops computer programs for businesses, hospitals, local governments, and other organizations. The company has been having difficulty analyzing the profitability of jobs and estimating costs for use in bidding.

The company has hired you to develop a job-order costing system. So far, you have decided that production costs should include the following costs.

Programmers' salaries	$480,000
Supervisors' salaries	120,000
Other costs of programming	240,000

You decide that the company should use normal costing, treating programmers' salaries as direct labor with each programmer having an hourly rate equaling his or her salary divided by the normal 2,000-hour working year. You also decide to treat the other two elements of cost as manufacturing overhead. You intend to use programming hours to set the predetermined overhead rate because programmers earn different salaries. Finally, you intend to treat the cost of idle programming time (actual salaries paid less salaries charged to jobs) and "excess cost" (amounts charged to jobs in excess of actual salaries paid) as part of overhead.

The president expects selling and administrative expenses to be $180,000. She also expects programmers to work about 24,000 hours, and you decide to use this figure to compute the predetermined overhead rate.

The president is interested in seeing how the system will operate and gives you the following information for a typical month. There was no beginning inventory and sales were $170,000. All costs incurred were one-twelfth of the estimated annual amounts given. Jobs sold had a total of 1,350 programming hours and jobs in process at the end of the month had 450 programming hours, so that actual charged hours for the month were 1,800 (1,350 + 450). Information on programmers' salaries follows.

Salaries on jobs sold	$27,000
Salaries in ending inventory	$9,200

Idle time was $3,800 ($40,000 incurred - $27,000 - $9,200).

Required
1. Calculate the predetermined overhead rate per hour of programmers' time.
2. Determine the cost of ending inventory of jobs in process.
3. Determine overapplied or underapplied overhead cost for the month, including idle time.
4. Prepare an income statement for the month showing overapplied or underapplied overhead as a separate expense or negative expense.

13-44   Comparing actual and normal costing—seasonal business   Barnett Company has used actual job-order costing for several years. At the end of each month, a clerk divides total manufacturing overhead cost incurred during the month by total direct labor cost for the month to get an overhead rate per labor dollar. He then applies overhead at this rate to each job worked on during the month. Because the company uses actual costing, there is no underapplied or overapplied overhead.

The president has been unhappy with this method because it results in widely differing overhead costs in different months. The work is highly seasonal, with the summer months very heavy and the winter months light. The president has asked you to show how normal costing differs from actual costing and has given you the following data regarding two similar jobs done in the past year.

	Job J-12	Job A-16
Materials cost	$10,410	$10,310
Direct labor	16,900	16,400
Overhead	40,560	29,520
Total	$67,870	$56,230

Job J-12 was done in January, when total overhead was $528,000 and total labor cost was $220,000. Job A-16 was done in August, when total overhead was $1,179,000 and total labor cost was $655,000. The company budgets annual overhead using the formula Total annual overhead = $3,200,000 + ($1.20 × direct labor cost). Total budgeted labor cost for the current year is $4,000,000.

Required
1. Develop the predetermined overhead rate based on total budgeted overhead and labor cost.
2. Determine the costs of the two jobs using the rate calculated in item 1.
3. Comment on the advantages of using predetermined overhead rates.

13-45   Activity-based overhead rates   Percan Industries has been using a single overhead rate, but its managers have become convinced that they need several rates to reflect the activities with which overhead costs are associated. After careful study, the controller developed the following budgeted information regarding cost pools and activities that drive the pools.

Activity	Amount of Activity	Overhead Costs in Pool
Labor hours	400,000 hours	$1,600,000
Machine setups	2,000 set ups	$600,000
Record keeping	150,000 entries	$150,000

Data related to jobs worked on in 19X5 follow.

	Totals	Jobs Sold	Jobs in Ending Inventories
Materials cost	$2,582,000	$2,321,000	$261,000
Direct labor cost	$4,169,000	$3,788,000	$381,000
Direct labor hours	410,000	371,000	39,000
Machine setups	1,950	1,870	80
Entries	152,000	136,000	16,000

Actual overhead costs were, by pool: labor hour-based, $1,620,000; machine setup-based, $592,000; and record keeping, $148,000.

Required

1. Compute the predetermined overhead rate for each activity.
2. Determine the amount of each type of overhead to apply to jobs sold and jobs still in inventory.
3. Determine the total cost of jobs sold and the cost of ending inventory.
4. Determine the amount of misapplied overhead for each cost pool.

**13-46   *Effects of separate overhead rates (continuation of 13-45)*   One of the managers of Percan Industries says that the new system with its three overhead cost pools is more elaborate and costly than the company needs. He proposes to go back to the old basis, where all overhead was applied using labor hours. In trying to convince him of the wisdom of the separate rates, you pull out the following information about two products that the company manufactures regularly. The data are for typical-sized batches of each product. The company makes several models of each product, but they are all roughly the same. The company prices its products at 150% of total manufacturing cost.

	Product XT-12	Product JY-09
Materials costs	$260	$780
Labor cost	$280	$2,880
Direct labor hours	20	200
Machine setups	12	0
Record keeping entries	400	80

Required

1. Determine the cost and price of each product using the overhead rates you developed in the previous assignment.
2. Determine the cost and price of each product using a single overhead rate based on labor hours. Use the budgeted data from the previous assignment

and remember to include all of the overhead cost, not just the labor-driven cost.

3. Comment on the results.

13-47   *Analyzing overhead*   The president of your company has asked you some questions about overhead. You recently changed the accounting system from actual to normal costing, with some opposition from other managers who could not see the advantages. Although the president was not happy with the actual costing system, he is not convinced that normal costing is a significant improvement.

The specific questions he wants you to answer relate to determining whether or not costs are under control and what information he can get from the figures for underapplied and overapplied overhead. He gives you the following results from the most recent three months.

	March	April	May
Direct labor hours worked on jobs	14,000	8,000	5,000
Total overhead incurred	$ 71,000	$ 52,000	$ 51,000
Total overhead applied at $6 per direct labor hour	84,000	48,000	30,000
Underapplied (overapplied) overhead	$ (13,000)	$ 4,000	$ 21,000

The predetermined rate of $6 per hour was calculated using budgeted direct labor hours for the year of 120,000 and budgeted overhead of $480,000 fixed and $2.00 variable per direct labor hour. Budgeted fixed overhead is $40,000 for each of the three months.

Required

Making any calculations you consider relevant, tell the president what he can learn using the given data.

13-48   *Departmental versus plant-wide overhead rates*   Caldwell Company operates two departments, Grinding and Assembly, in a plant that makes optical devices such as binoculars and telescopes. Because nearly all of its products are made to customer order, Caldwell uses job-order costing. In the past, it has used a single overhead application rate based on total budgeted direct labor hours and total budgeted overhead. The rate for 19X8 was computed using the following data.

	Grinding Department	Assembly Department	Total
Total budgeted overhead	$1,200,000	$800,000	$2,000,000
Budgeted direct labor hours	200,000	50,000	250,000
Rate ($2,000,000/250,000)			$8

Budgeted overhead was based on the following formulas.

Grinding Department $800,000 + ($2 × direct labor hours)
Assembly Department $500,000 + ($6 × direct labor hours)

The company bases its bid prices on total estimated cost including direct labor, materials, and overhead at $8 per direct labor hour. The controller has been thinking about changing to departmental rates and has collected the following data regarding two jobs recently completed. All direct laborers earn $10 per hour.

	Job 391	Job 547
Direct labor hours:		
Grinding	330	80
Assembly	30	180
Materials cost	$3,000	$2,500
Direct labor cost	$3,600	$2,600

The policy is to bid a price of 150% of total estimated manufacturing cost.

Required

1. Determine the overhead that the company will apply to each job using the $8 plant-wide rate. Determine the total cost of each job. Assuming that the actual results for each job were also the estimated results that the company used to set the bid prices, determine the price that the company bid for each job.
2. Compute the predetermined overhead rate for each department.
3. Determine the amounts of overhead applied to each job, the total cost of each job, and the bid price for each job using the predetermined departmental overhead rates that you computed in item 2.
4. Comment on the differences in your results for the two jobs using the plant-wide rate and departmental rates. Do you recommend that the company switch to departmental rates?

13-49   CVP analysis in a job-order company   Carthage Machine Works manufactures industrial machinery, principally small cutting equipment. Virtually all machines are custom made and Carthage uses job-order costing. The president has developed the following estimates for the coming year, 19X8.

Materials cost	$280,000
Direct labor hours	20,000
Direct labor wage rate	$9 per hour
Variable manufacturing overhead	80% of direct labor cost
Fixed manufacturing overhead	$200,000
Selling and administrative expenses	$70,000

The president tells you that her pricing policy is to charge the customer 125% of material cost plus a per-hour amount for direct labor. She wants to earn a profit of $60,000 before taxes in 19X8.

Required

1. Determine the price per direct labor hour the company must charge to meet the target profit.
2. Suppose that the company adopts the per-hour charge you computed in item 1 and has the following results: material costs, $300,000; direct labor hours, 18,000. All overhead costs are incurred as expected (variable per unit of activity and fixed in total). Determine the profit that the company will earn.

13-50   Overhead application and cost control   Guinn Print Shop had the following results in three recent months.

	April	May	June
Actual overhead costs	$25,000	$28,000	$34,000
Applied overhead costs	18,000	27,000	36,000

Arief Guinn, the owner, said that cost control was poor in April, better in May, and excellent in June. "We really need to overapply overhead because that reflects good cost control," he said.

Guinn budgets overhead as $2 variable per direct labor hour and $240,000 fixed per year. Monthly fixed overhead is budgeted at $20,000. Guinn uses 60,000 direct labor hours per year to set its predetermined overhead rate.

Required

1. Determine Guinn's predetermined overhead rate.
2. Determine the number of direct labor hours worked in each month.
3. Determine the budget variance for each month.
4. Explain to Mr. Guinn why his conclusions about cost control were, or were not, correct.

CASES

13-51   *Cost justification* The following material is taken from a column by Rowland Evans and Robert Novak that appeared in the July 8, 1976, *Knickerbocker News* (Albany, New York). At that time, the federal election laws required that candidates for the presidency limit spending before their parties' conventions to $13 million.

When Treasury Secretary William Simon traveled to Raleigh, N.C., last Jan. 20 to address the state Chamber of Commerce and then a President Ford Committee (PFC) reception, the taxpayers' bill was $2,310. The reimbursement to Uncle Sam for the PFC for political expenses: $17.44 .... The method used for Simon's Jan. 20 journey to North Carolina, an important primary state, is the model. The Air Force charged $2,310 for a Jetstar carrying Simon and seven others (including aides and Secret Service agents) to North Carolina. Since Simon occupied only one of eight seats, his share of the cost is $288.75. The 30 minutes spent at the PFC reception amounted to only 5 percent of the portal-to-portal time from Washington. So, 5 percent of $288.75 is $14.44. Add $3 for the share of meals, and the cost to the PFC is $17.44.

Required

1. Suppose that you had been engaged as a consultant to former President Ronald Reagan, who was President Ford's opponent in that campaign for the Republican nomination. What would you say about the method used to determine the cost billed to the PFC? What other information would you seek?
2. Suppose that you were engaged as a consultant to the PFC. How would you defend the $17.44 charge?

13-52   *What is cost?—consumer action* Easy Ed Johnson's Belchfire Auto Agency advertises that it will sell cars at $100 over cost and that anyone who can prove that Johnson is making more than $100 on a sale will get a $5,000 prize. Phyllis Henley decides to disprove Johnson's claim. She obtains the following information from a consumer magazine.

Cost Data from Consumer Scoop—
Belchfire 8 with Standard Equipment

Invoice cost to dealer	$13,400
Commission to salesperson	100
Variable cost of make-ready services (lubrication, washing, etc.)	40
Total cost to dealer	$13,540

Since Henley knows that Johnson has been selling this particular model for $14,190, she marches into the showroom and demands a $5,000 prize because she can "prove" that Johnson is selling this model at $650 over his cost. Johnson, with considerable aplomb, summons his accountant, who presents the following information to Henley.

Invoice cost to dealer	$13,400
Commission to salesperson	100
Cost of make-ready services	160
General overhead	430
Total cost	$14,090

The accountant points out that Henley failed to consider the "real" costs of running a large automobile dealership. He states that the make-ready and general overhead costs are based on the total service department cost and total overhead costs divided by the number of cars sold last year (500). General overhead costs are virtually all fixed. Johnson pleasantly and politely offers his condolences to Henley for having failed to win the $5,000 and invites her back any time she wants to buy a car at $100 over cost. Henley is not at all happy with her reception at Johnson's or the data provided by his accountant, and she decides to sue for the $5,000.

Required

Assume that Henley loses the case at the local level and appeals the decision to a higher court. The trial judge (original decision) agreed with the explanation of Easy Ed's accountant. Nevertheless, Henley argues that Easy Ed is defrauding the populace and owes her $5,000. Her lawyer has asked you to serve as an expert witness. What will your testimony be?

13-53   Determining product costs   Renata Tomato Company processes and cans tomato paste. The company has the capability to can whole tomatoes as well, but has not done so for about a year because of lack of profitability. The company has the capacity to process 5,000,000 pounds of tomatoes per month, whether for canning whole or making into paste.

The production manager and controller were recently discussing the production budget for the next several months. They agreed, on the basis of the information in the following schedule, that the company should continue to process only tomato paste.

	Whole Tomatoes	Tomato Paste
Selling price per case	$ 6.00	$5.80
Variable costs:		
Tomatoes[a]	$ 3.10	$2.00
Direct labor	0.90	1.00
Variable overhead	1.80	2.00
Packaging	0.52	0.60
Total variable costs	$ 6.32	$5.60
Contribution margin	$(0.32)	$0.20

a Whole tomatoes must be grade A tomatoes, which cost $0.155 per pound.

Paste is made from grade B tomatoes, which cost $0.08 per pound. There are 20 pounds of tomatoes in a case of whole tomatoes, 25 pounds in a case of paste.

A few days after the decision had been made to process only paste, the president received a call from a large tomato grower who offered to sell Renata as many pounds of tomatoes as it could use for the next six months. The price was to be $0.095 per pound, and the batches would be mixed A and B grades. The grower guaranteed that at least 40% of the tomatoes would be grade A.

The president told the production manager about the offer. The latter replied that it should cost $0.005 per pound to sort the tomatoes into the two grades, but that there would be no other additional costs if the offer were accepted. The company's capacity to process 5,000,000 pounds per month would not be affected. The company can sell all it can produce of either product.

The production and sales managers decided to investigate the probable effects of taking the offer. They agreed that it was profitable to can whole tomatoes if the price were much less than the current $0.155 per pound, but they were uncertain of the effects on the contribution margin of paste. They agreed to ask the controller to prepare a new analysis of relative profitability of the two products. The controller's analysis showed that paste was now a losing proposition, while whole tomatoes were extremely profitable. For the cost of tomatoes, the controller used $0.10 per pound, the purchase price plus additional sorting costs.

	Whole Tomatoes	Tomato Paste
Selling price per case	$6.00	$ 5.80
Variable costs:		
Tomatoes	$2.00	$ 2.50
Other variable costs	3.22	3.60
Total variable costs	$5.22	$ 6.10
Contribution margin	$0.78	$(0.30)

The production manager and sales manager wondered about the wisdom of using the $0.10 per pound cost of tomatoes for both products. "After all," said the sales manager, "aren't we paying more for the grade A tomatoes and less for the grade B? It seems unreasonable to say that they cost the same." The controller said that other methods were possible, suggesting that the costs could also be assigned based on the ratios of costs of buying tomatoes already sorted. "If we did it that way," he said, "buying 2,000,000 pounds of grade A tomatoes at $0.155 would cost $310,000. The 3,000,000 grade B tomatoes would cost $240,000 at $0.08. The total cost is $550,000. The cost of grade B is thus about 43.6% of the total. So we could assign $218,000 ($500,000 × 43.6%) to the grade B tomatoes in the package deal. That gives a cost per pound of $0.07267. Doing the same with the grade A produce gives $0.141 per pound."

At this point the president entered the room and commented that it seemed to her that the company was buying $240,000 worth of grade B tomatoes at $0.08 per pound and the rest of the purchase and sorting costs should be assigned to the grade A tomatoes. "That gives $260,000 to the grade A ($500,000 - $240,000), which is $0.13 per pound. Isn't that best?"

Required

1. Determine whether the company should buy the unsorted tomatoes.
2. Discuss the appropriateness of the methods of determining the cost of tomatoes suggested by each of the managers and make a recommendation.

14

Standard Costing and Variable Costing

LEARNING OBJECTIVES

After reading this chapter, you should be able to

1 Describe standard costing and explain why it is the predominant costing method.

2 Develop standard fixed costs and apply fixed overhead to products.

3 Prepare standard absorption costing income statements.

4 Compare, contrast, and distinguish actual, normal, and standard costing.

5 Explain how variable costing differs from absorption costing.

6 Explain why variable costing offers advantages over absorption costing for internal reporting purposes.

7 Prepare variable costing income statements.

The Hamilton, Ohio mill of **Champion International**, the giant paper company, generates over $250 million revenues per year. Demand for paper is very cyclical and prices fluctuate considerably, creating a feast-or-famine environment. The industry suffers from chronic over-capacity as companies add capacity in good times, only to see paper go unsold in poor times. Historically, paper mills have stressed high levels of production, even if prices were too low to enable the mills to make profits. Mills emphasized production partly because of extremely high fixed costs and huge capital investment. A single paper-making machine can cost $400 million and managers did not like to see such expensive machines lying idle. The problem was that mills produced too much paper, with too much waste, and at too-great cost. One

> reason for this situation is that product costing, especially absorption costing, can actually encourage overproduction. We develop this topic in the chapter.
>
> The Hamilton mill took a new approach, focusing on customer satisfaction, reduction of inventory, and reduction of waste. To bring its performance evaluation into congruence with its new strategy, the mill scrapped its existing cost system and installed throughput accounting. We introduce this technique later in this chapter. Throughput accounting penalizes increasing inventory and rewards reducing it, which focuses the attention of mill managers. Variable costing, also developed in the chapter, does not reward overproduction, but does not penalize it either.

Source: Kim Constantinides and John K. Shank, "Matching Accounting to Strategy: One Mill's Experience," Management Accounting, September 1994, 32-36.

Chapter 12 showed how standards can be used to help manage costs. Chapter 13 introduced absorption costing—the product costing method required for external reporting under GAAP. This chapter shows how standard costs can be used in product costing and presents an alternative to absorption costing, called variable costing, or direct costing. Variable costing excludes fixed production costs from inventory and cost of goods sold calculations and uses the familiar contribution margin format of the income statement. Variable costing is acceptable, and widely used, for internal reporting purposes and for decision making. It can be used by job-order and process cost companies, and with actual, normal, or standard costing.

STANDARD ABSORPTION COSTING

Under **standard costing** inventories appear at standard cost, not actual or normal cost. The accounting system for a factory using standard costing automatically calculates and records manufacturing cost variances in separate accounts. Standard costing is much more widespread among manufacturing companies than actual or normal costing, the methods described in Chapter 13. One important reason is that because standard costing integrates standard costs and variances into the company's records, variances are calculated as a normal part of record keeping with little or no additional cost. Capturing as much information as possible directly in the accounts is wise, because such information is very easy to retrieve and is more likely to be accurate. Another reason is that standard costing is often simpler to implement than actual or normal costing.

Chapter 12 showed how to determine standards for variable production costs. Under standard absorption costing, manufacturers also determine a standard fixed overhead cost per unit for each product. The resulting total standard cost per unit is used to calculate the cost of inventory and the cost of goods sold. Unfavorable variances are treated as expenses; favorable variances are treated as negative expenses. They are reported separately in the income statement. The development of a standard for fixed overhead follows from Chapter 13, which showed how to calculate and use a predetermined overhead rate. We begin with a simple, one-product company. Such a company can determine a standard fixed cost per unit simply by dividing total budgeted fixed manufacturing overhead by some number of units of its product. Because all resources are devoted to that one product, there is no need to use an input factor such as direct labor hours or machine hours, nor to develop activity-based measures.

Exhibit 14-1 presents data for SMP Company, which produces an automobile part. The company has standards for labor, materials, and variable overhead. To simplify the situation, we group all standard variable costs into a single per-unit variable cost. Because you already have learned to analyze variable cost variances, we will not give data to identify each variable cost variance, but will calculate only total variable cost variances. Notice that variable selling and administrative expenses are incurred based on units sold, not on units produced.

CALCULATING A STANDARD FIXED COST

The **standard fixed cost per unit** depends, as did the predetermined overhead rate, on two things: (1) the choice of *a measure of activity* (e.g., number of units, direct labor hours, or machine hours) and (2) *a level of activity* (e.g., budgeted units or hours). Since we are dealing with a single-product company, the obvious measure of activity is units of product, but we must choose the level of activity.

◀**13** In Chapter 13, under normal costing, we used budgeted activity to set the predetermined overhead rate. We can use that same level of activity, but we also could use other levels: normal activity (or normal capacity), practical capacity, and theoretical capacity. **Normal activity** is the average activity expected or budgeted over the coming two to five years. The objective in using this activity level is to develop a standard fixed cost that reflects the company's expected long-term per-unit costs, not the cost for a single year (as budgeted activity reflects).

Exhibit 14-1 SMP Company, Operating Data for 19X5	
Production in units	110,000
Sales in units, at $80 each	90,000
Ending inventory in units	20,000
Actual production costs:	
Variable	$2,255,000
Fixed	$3,200,000
Selling and administrative expenses:	
Variable at $5 per unit	$450,000
Fixed	$1,400,000
Standards and budgets:	
Budgeted fixed production costs	$3,000,000
Standard variable production costs	$20 per unit

Practical capacity is the maximum activity the company can achieve given the usual kinds of interruptions. (Events such as strikes or severe shortages of materials are not considered usual.) As with budgeted and normal activity, the measure of activity might be units of product, direct labor hours, or a set of activity-based measures. Standard costs based on practical capacity reflect the lowest reasonable long-term average fixed cost. **Theoretical capacity** is the absolute maximum that a plant can produce, with no interruptions or problems at all. Using practical capacity and theoretical capacity yields very low unit costs, costs that most companies can use as goals, but rarely reach. JIT factories that use standard costs often use practical capacity, or even theoretical capacity, *because* these levels give goals that the company can strive to reach.

Suppose that SMP's managers decide to set the standard per-unit fixed cost using normal capacity of 100,000 units. The standard is then $30 per unit, computed as follows:

$$\textit{Standard fixed cost per unit} \; = \; \frac{\textit{Budgeted fixed production costs}}{\textit{Level of activity}}$$

$$= \; \frac{\$3{,}000{,}000}{100{,}000}$$

$$= \; \$30 \; \textit{per unit}$$

The total standard cost per unit is $50, consisting of the $20 standard variable cost per unit and the $30 standard fixed cost per unit. We shall use this standard fixed cost per unit to determine variances and, if variances are not significant, the standard will also be used in external financial statements for the period.

VARIANCES

We first calculate variable manufacturing cost variances. From Exhibit 14-1 we know that actual production was 110,000 units, so total variable cost variances are $55,000 unfavorable, calculated as follows:

Total actual variable production costs (Exhibit 14-1)	$2,255,000
Standard variable costs (110,000 × $20)	2,200,000
Unfavorable variable cost variances	$ 55,000

13 Fixed overhead variances follow the general pattern of Chapter 13. There is a budget variance and a volume variance.

The total fixed overhead variance (misapplied fixed overhead) is $100,000, computed as follows:

Total actual fixed overhead	$3,200,000
Fixed overhead applied (110,000 × $30)	3,300,000
Overapplied overhead	$ 100,000

The volume variance under standard costing is budgeted fixed overhead minus applied fixed overhead. (The volume variance under normal costing is calculated the same way, but applied overhead is based on inputs, not output.) The budget variance under standard costing is, just as under normal costing, actual fixed overhead ($3,200,000) minus budgeted fixed overhead ($3,000,000).

Following is an analysis of fixed overhead variances using the diagram format introduced in Chapter 12. The budget variance is $200,000 unfavorable, and the volume variance is $300,000 favorable.

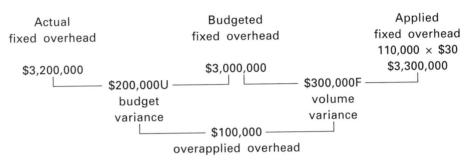

The unfavorable budget variance, as in the previous chapter, means that SMP incurred more fixed manufacturing overhead than it budgeted. The favorable volume variance, similar to the meaning in the previous chapter, means only that SMP worked more standard hours than it used to set the standard fixed cost.

Exhibit 14-2 provides a graphical analysis of SMP's results.

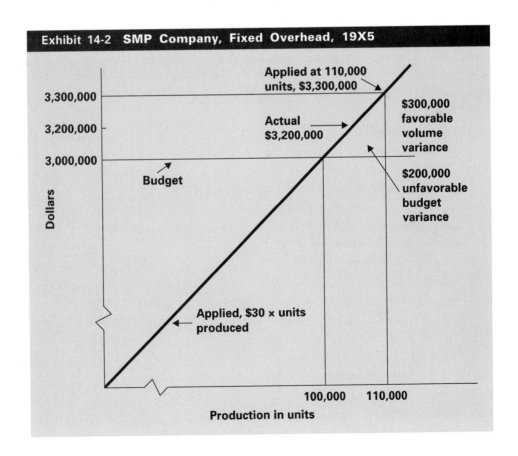

Exhibit 14-2 SMP Company, Fixed Overhead, 19X5

INCOME STATEMENTS

Using the standard cost per unit and the operating data from Exhibit 14-1, we can prepare an income statement for SMP Company for 19X5. Exhibit 14-3 shows the statement. As you can see, the format is similar to those used for actual and normal absorption costing in Chapter 13, which in turn were based on the typical income statement presentation used in financial accounting. That is, cost of sales is computed by adding the standard production costs for the year to the beginning inventory and then subtracting the ending inventory.

Notice that the variable production costs and fixed production costs added to the beginning inventory are at standard cost per unit multiplied by unit production. Under standard costing, all amounts in the calculation of standard cost of goods are standard cost per unit multiplied by the number of units. This is true for the beginning inventory, applied production costs, cost of goods available for sale, and standard cost of goods sold. Therefore, *if* the standard cost of units in the beginning inventory is the same as the standard cost for the current year, standard cost of sales is simply the per-unit standard cost multiplied by the number of units sold. In such cases, we have no need to show the details of the section for the standard cost of sales, because it equals the number of units sold times the standard cost per unit. Thus, we can also prepare an income statement such as the one in Exhibit 14-4, which omits the details of the cost of goods sold section.

Exhibit 14-4 also shows variances as adjustments to standard cost of goods sold instead of as adjustments to standard gross margin. You should see that

Exhibit 14-3   SMP Company, Income Statement for 19X5

Sales		$7,200,000
Standard cost of sales:		
Beginning inventory	$ 0	
Standard variable production costs		
(110,000 × $20)	2,200,000	
Applied fixed production costs (110,000 × $30)	3,300,000	
Cost of goods available for sale (110,000 × $50)	$5,500,000	
Ending inventory (20,000 × $50)	1,000,000	
Standard cost of sales (90,000 × $50)		4,500,000
Standard gross margin		$2,700,000
Variances:		
Fixed manufacturing cost budget variance	$ 200,000U	
Fixed manufacturing cost volume variance	300,000F	
Variable manufacturing cost variances	55,000U	45,000F
Actual gross margin		$2,745,000
Selling and administrative expenses*		1,850,000
Profit		$ 895,000

* *Fixed costs of $1,400,000 plus variable costs of $450,000, 90,000 × $5*

Exhibit 14-4   SMP Company, Income Statement for 19X5 (Alternative format)

Sales		$7,200,000
Cost of sales:		
Standard cost of sales (90,000 × $50)	$4,500,000	
Variances:		
Fixed manufacturing cost budget variance	200,000U	
Fixed manufacturing cost volume variance	300,000F	
Variable manufacturing cost variances	55,000U	
Cost of sales		4,455,000
Gross margin		$2,745,000
Selling and administrative expenses*		1,850,000
Profit		$ 895,000

* Fixed costs of $1,400,000 plus variable costs of $450,000, 90,000 × $5

the final results for actual gross margin and income will be the same regardless of where the variances appear in the statement.

Finally, please remember that we do not expect to *incur* fixed overhead at the standard fixed cost per unit—we expect to incur total *budgeted* fixed overhead. The application of fixed overhead to units of product is an accounting device used to avoid the fluctuating per-unit fixed costs that could result from using actual absorption costing. Standard fixed costs are an extension of the predetermined overhead rates of Chapter 13. Before we show how standards are used in a multiproduct company, complete the following review problem to make sure you understand the basics of standard costing.

REVIEW PROBLEM

SMP continued to use the same standard costs for 19X6. Its operating data for 19X6 were as follows:

Production, in units	95,000
Sales, in units, at $80 each	100,000
Ending inventory, in units	15,000
Actual production costs:	
Variable	$1,881,000
Fixed	$2,950,000
Selling and administrative expenses:	
Variable at $5 per unit	$500,000
Fixed	$1,400,000
Standard variable production cost	$20 per unit
Budgeted fixed production costs	$3,000,000

Prepare an income statement for 19X6. The solution that appears in Exhibit 14-5 uses a slightly different format from that in Exhibit 14-3. Here we show

Exhibit 14-5   SMP Company, Income Statement for 19X6

Sales (100,000 × $80)		$8,000,000
Standard cost of sales:		
Beginning inventory (Exhibit 14-3)	$1,000,000	
Standard variable production costs (95,000 × $20)	1,900,000	
Applied fixed production costs (95,000 × $30)	2,850,000	
Cost of goods available for sale (115,000 × $50)	$5,750,000	
Ending inventory (15,000 × $50)	750,000	
Standard cost of sales (100,000 × $50)	$5,000,000	
Variances:		
Fixed manufacturing cost budget variance	50,000F	
Fixed manufacturing cost volume variance	150,000U	
Variable manufacturing cost variances	19,000F	
Cost of sales		5,081,000
Gross margin		$2,919,000
Selling and administrative expenses*		1,900,000
Profit		$1,019,000

Variances:

Variable cost, $1,881,000 - ($20 × 95,000) = $19,000F

Fixed cost

Actual fixed overhead	Budgeted fixed overhead	Applied fixed overhead (95,000 × $30)
$2,950,000	$3,000,000	$2,850,000

$50,000F — budget variance

$150,000U — volume variance

$100,000 — total fixed overhead variances

* Fixed costs of $1,400,000 plus variable costs of $500,000, 100,000 × $5

variances as an adjustment to standard cost of goods sold instead of as an adjustment to standard gross margin. Exhibits 14-3, 14-4, and 14-5 offer three possibilities for placement of variances, but all three eventually arrive at an actual gross margin figure.

MULTIPLE PRODUCTS AND ACTIVITY-BASED COSTING

As we said earlier, standard costing is the overwhelming choice of repetitive manufacturers, companies that make many standard products. It also can be used by companies that make several products of different design. So long as the products are relatively standard, even a job-order company can use standard costing. Any company that can develop standards can use a standard costing system.

As early as Chapter 3 we began discussing the idea of activity-based costing (ABC), under which companies (and other organizations) associate overhead cost pools with their respective drivers and assign the costs in each overhead pool based on the relative use of drivers. Most recently, Chapters 12 and 13 used those concepts in applying overhead. ABC also applies to standard costing, especially for multiproduct companies. The idea behind activity-based costing—to associate as much cost as possible with activities, and subsequently with products, to determine how much resource use is traceable to the product—is certainly applicable to standard costing. The objective is to get better information about the costs and profitability of individual products.

Suppose that ARG Company has two major types of fixed overhead. Overhead related to materials and component parts, such as purchasing, inspection, warehousing, and handling is budgeted at $500,000. Overhead related to direct labor is $3,000,000 and the rate per direct labor hour is $4.00, based on 750,000 hours at normal activity. (You learned how to make that calculation in Chapter 13.) Material-related overhead is allocated based on the total number of component parts budgeted for use during a year. ARG makes two types of instruments. Data and calculations are as follows:

	Portable Model	Table Model
Standard direct labor hours	8	12
Number of component parts	100	200
Budgeted production	6,000	2,000
Total budgeted use of components	600,000	400,000
Standard fixed overhead rate		
per component $500,000/(600,000 + 400,000) = $0.50		

We can calculate the standard overhead costs per unit as follows:

	Portable Model	Table Model
Material-related:		
Portable Model (100 × $0.50)	$50	
Table Model (200 × $0.50)		$100
Direct labor-related:		
Portable Model (8 hours × $4)	32	
Table Model (12 hours × $4)		48
Total standard fixed overhead cost per unit	$82	$148

The $50 and $100 for material-related overhead are treated just like any other overhead. The company will apply both types of overhead, just as we did in Chapter 13. It also will calculate misapplied overhead, budget variances, and volume variances separately for each pool of overhead. Let us illustrate for the material-related overhead. Assume the following results for the year.

Actual material-related overhead	$510,000
Actual production:	
Portable Model	7,000
Table Model	2,000
Standard use of components	1,100,000
Fixed overhead applied	$550,000

The standard use of components is based on total production of each model, 7,000 × 100 plus 2,000 × 200 = 1,100,000 components, which, when multiplied by the $0.50 standard rate, gives $550,000 applied overhead. Variances are as follows:

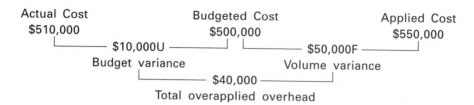

The calculations are the same no matter how many cost pools the plant uses.

COMPARISON OF STANDARD AND NORMAL COSTING

Although the normal costing concept of a predetermined overhead rate is related to the idea of a standard fixed cost per unit, the results reported under the two types of costing systems are not the same. Remember that, under normal costing, overhead is applied based on the actual level of the activity. Under standard costing, overhead is applied based on the number of units produced, or standard quantity of inputs used.

The two systems will always give the same budget variance, because the budget variance is simply actual cost minus budgeted cost. But unless standard hours equal actual hours, the volume variances will differ because different amounts of fixed overhead are *applied* under the two methods. The difference in volume variances serves to remind you of what we said when introducing the concept of a volume variance in Chapter 13: the variance has little or no economic significance and reflects only the effect of using some activity level other than the actual level to determine the overhead application rate.

We have presented several costing methods in this and previous chapters. The following table summarizes the similarities and differences among the three methods—actual costing, normal costing, and standard costing—by showing the basis for determining the inventoriable cost of a unit of product.

Cost Element	Actual Costing	Normal Costing	Standard Costing
Materials	actual cost	actual cost	standard cost
Direct labor	actual cost	actual cost	standard cost
Overhead	actual cost	applied cost	standard cost
	(actual input ×	(actual input ×	(actual output ×
	actual rate)	predetermined rate)	standard cost)

The table shows that actual costing and normal costing differ only in the treatment of overhead, as explained in Chapter 13. Standard costing differs from both of the other methods by using standard costs for all input factors. The only difference between standard costing and normal costing with respect to overhead is that standard costing applies overhead based on *standard* quantities of the input factor (or, what amounts to the same thing, on actual unit production), while normal costing applies overhead based on *actual* quantities of input factors.

   While standard costs for product costing are invaluable for many companies, their use in control and performance evaluation can create problems, some of which we introduced in Chapter 12. The accompanying Insight describes two such experiences.

IN SIGHT

Case 1

Teijin Seiki Co., Ltd. manufactures machines and components for a variety of industries as diverse as textiles, aerospace, and printing. Managers at a division that made reduction gears for earthmoving equipment were dissatisfied with the standard costing system. The division applied direct labor and overhead to products based on standard machine times. The managers therefore expected that when they reduced standard machine times, costs should also drop, but results were disappointing. The problem was that the standard machine time, which is value-adding time, was much less than the lead time, or total time a component was in process. Lead time includes waiting time, which is, of course, not value-adding, but which generates significant amounts of overhead.

   The division changed its allocation base from standard manufacturing time to lead time, so that managers were motivated to reduce lead time, which in turn reduced inventories and costs. The overhead rate was then calculated as

$$Overhead\ rate\ =\ \frac{Total\ budgeted\ overhead}{Total\ lead\ times}$$

The denominator, total lead times, was the sum of the lead times for all of the parts the division made. Reducing machine time still saves costs under the new method, but the new method directs managerial attention to the entire flow of parts through the factory.

Case 2

Companies have always strived to reduce conventionally calculated product costs, and have based many performance evaluations on such reductions. The rigors of modern global competition necessitate other measures of success, including product-related measures. The **J. I. Case Agricultural Equipment Group** focuses on quality, delivery, cycle time/process time, and cost. To evaluate progress, the unit monitors, among other things, scrap and rework costs. Because such costs result from failures in production, they are non-value-adding and should be eliminated. The Group has been measuring other non-value-adding costs such as after-the-fact-inspection, setup, material movements, and downtime.

Some flexibility measures and objectives the Group pays attention to include:

1. reducing setup time, so that the company can respond quickly to changes in demand or other changes that affect production schedules.
2. reducing downtime, so that the company can operate more efficiently, meet production schedules, and eliminate unscheduled maintenance, a non-value-adding activity. Preventive maintenance is a value-adding activity.
3. reducing material handling by using manufacturing cells.
4. increasing the commonality of parts and processes, which reduces inventory requirements and makes operations more efficient.

Sources: Makoto Kawada and Daniel F. Johnson, "Strategic Management Accounting – Why and How," Management Accounting, *August 1993, 32-38.*
Michael R. Sellenheim, "Performance Measurement," Management Accounting, *September 1991, 50-53.*

VARIABLE COSTING

Thus far, we have discussed only absorption costing systems. Such systems are required for financial reporting and for income tax purposes and are often used, as we mentioned earlier, for internal purposes. However, throughout this book we have recommended internal reports using the contribution margin format, which treats all fixed costs as period costs. When this approach is applied to product costing the result is called variable costing (direct costing).

Variable costing excludes fixed production costs from the unit costs of inventories, and treats all fixed costs as expenses in the period incurred. It is possible — and we think preferable — to use variable costing for internal reports. The flow of manufacturing costs using variable costing can easily be shown by a slight variation of the cost flow figure presented in Chapter 13. Exhibit 14-6 depicts the difference in cost flows under variable and absorption costing systems.

Exhibit 14-7 presents variable costing income statements using actual costing for SMP (the subject of our earlier example) for 19X5 and Exhibit 14-8, page 668, shows an actual variable costing income statement for 19X6. Except when a company uses job-order costing, actual costing requires a cost flow assumption. We use FIFO.

Variable costing can also be used with standard costs, as shown in Exhibits 14-9 and 14-10, pages 668 and 669, respectively, for SMP for 19X5 and 19X6. We use the $20 per unit standard variable cost here. Note that there is no need to select a level of activity to calculate a predetermined fixed overhead rate because variable costing does not include fixed costs in the calculation of inventory cost per unit. The variable cost variances are the same as they are under standard absorption costing, as is the fixed overhead budget variance. The

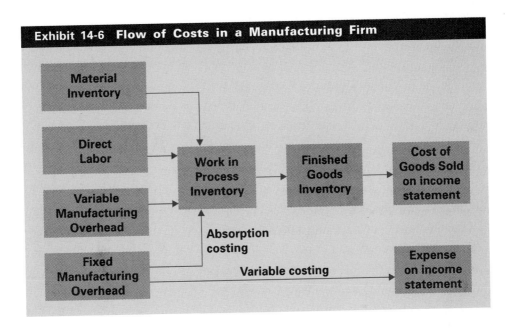

Exhibit 14-6 Flow of Costs in a Manufacturing Firm

volume variance does not appear under variable costing because no fixed over-head is applied to products. Note that we show total budgeted fixed manufac-turing costs and the fixed overhead budget variance separately. Recall from Chapter 12 that companies calculate fixed overhead budget variances because they are economically significant. (A variable costing company *recognizes* fixed costs—it just does not *inventory* them. It expenses them as they are incurred.)

**Exhibit 14-7 SMP Company, Income Statement for 19X5—
Actual Variable Costing**

Sales		$7,200,000
Variable cost of sales:		
Beginning inventory	$ 0	
Actual variable production costs	2,255,000	
Cost of goods available for sale	$2,255,000	
Ending inventory*	410,000	
Variable cost of sales		1,845,000
Variable manufacturing margin		$5,355,000
Variable selling and administrative expenses		450,000
Contribution margin		$4,905,000
Actual fixed costs:		
Manufacturing	$3,200,000	
Selling and administrative	1,400,000	4,600,000
Profit		$ 305,000

* $2,255,000/110,000 = $20.50 *unit cost,* 20,000 *units times* $20.50 = $410,000.

**Exhibit 14-8   SMP Company, Income Statement for 19X6—
Actual Variable Costing**

Sales		$8,000,000
Variable cost of sales:		
Beginning inventory	$ 410,000	
Actual variable production costs	1,881,000	
Cost of goods available for sale	$2,291,000	
Ending inventory*	297,000	
Variable cost of sales		1,994,000
Variable manufacturing margin		$6,006,000
Variable selling and administrative expenses		500,000
Contribution margin		$5,506,000
Actual fixed costs:		
Manufacturing	$2,950,000	
Selling and administrative	1,400,000	4,350,000
Profit		$1,156,000

* $1,881,000/95,000 = $19.80 unit cost, 15,000 units times $19.80 = $297,000.

**Exhibit 14-9   SMP Company, Income Statement for 19X5—
Standard Variable Costing**

Sales		$7,200,000
Standard cost of sales:		
Beginning inventory	$ 0	
Standard variable production costs (110,000 × $20)	2,200,000	
Cost of goods available for sale (110,000 × $20)	$2,200,000	
Ending inventory (20,000 × $20)	400,000	
Standard variable cost of sales (90,000 × $20)		1,800,000
Standard variable manufacturing margin		$5,400,000
Variable manufacturing cost variances		55,000U
Variable manufacturing margin		$5,345,000
Variable selling and administrative expenses		
(90,000 × $5)		450,000
Contribution margin		$4,895,000
Fixed costs:		
Budgeted fixed manufacturing costs	$3,000,000	
Fixed manufacturing cost budget variance	200,000U	
Selling and administrative expenses	1,400,000	
Total fixed costs		4,600,000
Profit		$ 295,000

Exhibit 14-10   SMP Company, Income Statement for 19X6—Standard Variable Costing

Sales		$8,000,000
Standard cost of sales:		
Beginning inventory (20,000 × $20)	$ 400,000	
Standard variable production costs (95,000 × $20)	1,900,000	
Cost of goods available for sale (115,000 × $20)	$2,300,000	
Ending inventory (15,000 × $20)	300,000	
Standard variable cost of sales (100,000 × $20)		2,000,000
Standard variable manufacturing margin		$6,000,000
Variable manufacturing cost variances		19,000F
Variable manufacturing margin		$6,019,000
Variable selling and administrative expenses		
(100,000 × $5)		500,000
Contribution margin		$5,519,000
Fixed costs:		
Budgeted fixed manufacturing costs	$3,000,000	
Fixed manufacturing cost budget variance	50,000F	
Selling and administrative expenses	1,400,000	
Total fixed costs		4,350,000
Profit		$1,169,000

 Though it might seem otherwise, variable costing does not introduce new concepts. Suppose that at the end of Chapter 3 you were asked to prepare an income statement based on the following data.

Sales	90,000 units at $80 per unit
Variable costs per unit:	
Manufacturing	$20.50
Selling and administrative	$5.00
Total fixed costs:	
Manufacturing	$3,200,000
Selling and administrative	$1,400,000

Your income statement would probably have looked like the one in Exhibit 14-11.

The income statements in Exhibits 14-7 and 14-8 *appear* to be different from and more complex than statements you have seen in earlier chapters, but the only *real* difference is in the amount of detail on cost of sales. Whether you use the shortened format of Exhibit 14-11 or the expanded format of Exhibit 14-7, the incomes for the year are the same and reflect an expensing of fixed costs in the year incurred. Without knowing it, you have been preparing actual variable costing income statements since Chapter 3.

Exhibit 14-11 SMP Company, Income Statement for 19X5—Actual Variable Costing (Alternative Format)

Sales (90,000 x $80)		$7,200,000
Variable costs:		
Manufacturing (90,000 x $20.50)	$1,845,000	
Selling and administrative (90,000 x $5)	450,000	2,295,000
Contribution margin		$4,905,000
Fixed costs:		
Manufacturing	$3,200,000	
Selling and administrative	1,400,000	4,600,000
Income		$ 305,000

COMPARING VARIABLE AND ABSORPTION COSTING RESULTS

Compare the 19X5 and 19X6 results under variable costing (Exhibit 14-9 and 14-10) with the results under absorption costing for the same economic activity (see Exhibits 14-3 and 14-5). *Absorption costing income is higher than variable costing income for 19X5 and lower for 19X6.* Absorption costing income in 19X5 is higher because absorption costing transfers some of the fixed costs of 19X5 into 19X6 as part of the cost of the ending inventory of 20,000 units. Absorption costing income in 19X6 is lower because a similar shift of 19X6 costs (to 19X7) was smaller (fixed costs in an ending inventory of only 15,000 units) than the amount of fixed costs transferred in from 19X5.

In more general terms, the differences are traceable to the relationship between production and sales. Subject to a few technicalities, *when production exceeds sales* (so that ending inventory is greater than beginning inventory) *absorption costing gives a higher income than variable costing.* When sales exceed production, absorption costing gives a lower income than variable costing. The difference in incomes is due entirely to the fixed costs carried forward in inventory under absorption costing. Such costs are shown on the balance sheet as part of inventory and are expensed only when the goods are sold. Exhibit 14-12 shows the amounts of fixed production costs expensed in each year under the two approaches, along with a reconciliation of the incomes under standard costing.

If the standard fixed cost per unit does not change from year to year, the difference between absorption costing income and income under variable costing can be computed directly by multiplying the standard fixed cost per unit by the change in units in inventory. Thus, we could have made the reconciliation shown in Exhibit 14-12 simply by using the formula

$$\begin{array}{c}\text{Difference}\\\text{in}\\\text{incomes}\end{array} = \left(\begin{array}{c}\text{Units in}\\\text{beginning}\\\text{inventory}\end{array} - \begin{array}{c}\text{Units in}\\\text{ending}\\\text{inventory}\end{array}\right) \times \begin{array}{c}\text{Standard}\\\text{fixed cost}\\\text{per unit}\end{array}$$

$$\begin{array}{c}\text{Difference}\\\text{19X5}\end{array} = \quad (0 \quad - \quad 20,000) \quad \times \quad \$30 = \$(600,000)$$

Exhibit 14-12 Reconciliation of Incomes—Variable and Absorption Costing

	19X5	19X6
Comparison of reported income:		
Variable costing (Exhibits 14-9 and 14-10)	$ 295,000	$1,169,000
Absorption costing (Exhibits 14-3 and 14-5)	895,000	1,019,000
Difference to be explained	$ (600,000)	$ 150,000
Explanation of income difference:		
Fixed production costs in beginning inventory		
(transferred from prior year):		
0 units × $30	$ 0	
20,000 units × $30		$ 600,000
Fixed production costs incurred during		
the year	3,200,000	2,950,000
	$3,200,000	$3,550,000
Less fixed production costs in ending inventory		
(being transferred to a future year):		
20,000 units × $30	600,000	
15,000 units × $30		450,000
Total fixed costs expensed under absorption		
costing for the year	$2,600,000	$3,100,000
Total fixed costs expensed under variable		
costing—equal to total fixed costs incurred	3,200,000	2,950,000
Difference between fixed costs incurred and		
expensed for the year	$ (600,000)	$ 150,000

$$\frac{Difference}{19X6} = (20,000 - 15,000) \times \$30 = \$150,000$$

ABSORPTION COSTING, PRODUCTION, AND INCOME

Of more importance than reconciling incomes under the two methods is that *absorption costing income increases as production increases*. Absorption costing therefore encourages high production, because managers evaluated on income will show higher incomes the more they produce, regardless of whether they sell the output. Of course, production in excess of sales violates the principles of JIT and other advanced manufacturing techniques. Similarly, a manager following JIT principles who *reduces* inventory will suffer because reported income under absorption costing will be lower than it would be if she produced more. None of this holds for variable costing. Production does not affect variable costing income, which is a major reason many managers prefer it for internal purposes.

EVALUATION OF METHODS

We have already stated that we believe variable costing to be generally superior to absorption costing for internal reporting purposes. Not all managers, in accounting or elsewhere, agree with our position.

EXTERNAL REPORTING

Although arguments about the suitability of either method for external reporting are not relevant to internal reporting, we mention some here to alert you to the principal justifications offered for absorption costing.[1]

The matching concept, which you studied in financial accounting, holds that costs must be matched against related revenues or against the revenues of the periods that have benefited from the costs. As an example, the cost of a fixed asset is assigned, through depreciation, to the years of its life.

Fixed production costs "benefit" the company in the sense that, without them, few companies could produce anything at all. Thus, having a factory building and equipment entails depreciation, property taxes, some level of maintenance, and other fixed costs. Moreover, many supervisory personnel in a factory are salaried. Because these fixed costs are essential to the production of goods, one could argue that they should be expensed when the goods are sold, not when the goods are still in inventory. This argument is made by those favoring absorption costing.

Advocates of variable costing for financial reporting purposes counter by arguing that fixed production costs benefit production, but production as a whole, rather than any single unit of product. In other words, fixed costs provide the capacity to produce. Thus, once the company is in business and producing goods, fixed production costs have done their job; they are not needed for this or that unit, only for production as a whole. Accordingly, the argument continues, considering fixed costs on a per-unit basis is inappropriate because fixed costs cannot be identified with individual units; fixed costs are joint to all the units produced. Controversy about the most appropriate method for external reporting purposes has raged for many years, and we do not expect it to stop in the foreseeable future.

INTERNAL REPORTING AND COST STRATEGY

Variable costing has important advantages for internal reporting. It presents information in the form that is most useful for managers—the form needed for CVP analysis—and its results do not depend on production.

Separating fixed and variable costs and reporting contribution margin enable managers to perform the CVP analysis that cannot be done working directly with absorption costing statements. Managers cannot predict income for future periods using an absorption costing income statement for two reasons: (1) they must predict not only sales for that future period, but also production, and (2) they must break down the cost figures into their fixed and variable

---

1 *For income tax reporting, tax law, which can be extraordinarily complex, governs determination of inventory and cost of sales. In a growing economy, inventories will rise, so that companies will pay higher taxes under absorption costing than under variable costing.*

components (i.e., managers must develop the information that is already provided by variable costing).

As we stated earlier, production has no effect on income under variable costing. Managers can concentrate on the effects of changes in sales without having to allow for production. If sales fall from one period to another, variable costing income also will fall. Using absorption costing, income might well rise when sales fall if production is higher than sales. Most managers think of sales, not production, as the income-generating activity. Therefore, variable costing is more in tune with a manager's basic understanding of income than is absorption costing.

Behavioral problems regarding costing methods extend to people's natural resistance to change. Overcoming top management's objections to changing accounting systems is critical, and often difficult. The controller of **Martin Industries**, a manufacturer of heating products, successfully introduced variable costing in part by securing the support of top management. The company benefited from the use of variable costing as well as from other changes, but might have continued with its old system had the controller not been careful to seek support.[2]

Variable costing offers a significant strategic advantage because its income figure is not affected by production. Over the long run, production and sales for a given product will be about the same, so both absorption costing and variable costing will give the same total income. Variable costing income represents an equilibrium income in the sense that it shows what the company would earn over the long run if sales continued at the same level. Absorption costing income can be misleadingly high when production exceeds sales because the income cannot be maintained at the same level of sales. (A company cannot indefinitely produce in excess of current sales unless sales are rising.) Managers developing strategies for products are better served by incomes that represent equilibrium amounts, rather than by incomes influenced by inventory changes. The accompanying Insight describes **throughput accounting**, which has some of the characteristics of variable costing. Throughput accounting follows principles of the Theory of Constraints, which we introduce in Chapter 16. Throughput accounting is a radical departure from other methods in that it treats all costs except unused materials as expenses.

Absorption costing requires allocating fixed costs to units of product. We have consistently argued that allocations are unwise for managerial purposes because they obscure CVP relationships, can lead to poor decisions, and are not helpful in control and performance evaluation. Absorption costing can therefore be criticized because it requires allocations.

A multiple-product company using absorption costing allocates fixed production costs to its products and to the individual units of each product. The many costs that are common to several products (depreciation on factory building, salary of plant manager, etc.) will thus be allocated first to products and then to units of each product. Hence, statements prepared by product or by product line will contain two sets of allocations, making it extremely difficult to analyze the relative profitability of a product or a product line.

---

2 *Russell F. Briner, Michael D. Akers, James W. Truitt, and James D. Wilson, "Coping with Change at Martin Industries,"* Management Accounting, *July 1989, 45-49.*

In summary, the information that managers need is provided much more directly by variable costing statements. Where absorption costing is used, a manager must recast statements to perform many of the analyses needed to plan, make decisions, control, and evaluate performance.

Advocates of absorption costing argue that variable costing may prompt managers to take a short-run approach to problems when a long-run approach

IN SIGHT

Companies using throughput accounting inventory materials, just as do other companies. But throughput companies do not record work in process or finished goods inventories. Throughput accounting treats all direct labor and manufacturing overhead costs as period costs, expensing them as they are incurred. Cost of goods sold is the cost of materials *put into process*. A sample income statement appears at the end of this Insight, along with absorption and variable costing income statements that reflect the same facts. This technique is being successfully used by a paper mill of **Champion International**, which we introduced in the chapter opening, and by a British auto parts maker, among others.

The British company, **Garrett Automotive** (now **AlliedSignal Limited, Turbochargers**) faced a serious challenge in 1989, when its European operations changed. The company had to manufacture more product lines and make units in smaller batches. The company also had to make 3.5 percent reductions in cost under a contract with a major customer. Managers credit throughput accounting with helping the company by focusing managers' attention on turning materials into sales, not just into products. The right products to make are those that are sold; any products unsold are the wrong ones to have been made. Garrett's managers, like those of the mill described earlier, wanted to penalize overproduction and reward inventory reduction, which throughput costing does very well. The company considered ABC, but found it unhelpful because overhead costs were relatively low and increasing record keeping costs to obtain more accurate identification of overhead costs probably would not yield commensurate benefits.

Example of Throughput Costing

Units produced	10,000	
Units sold at $20	9,000	$180,000
Cost of materials *used*, $5 per unit	$50,000	
Other variable manufacturing costs, $2 per unit	$20,000	
Fixed manufacturing costs	$30,000	
Selling and administrative expenses	$15,000	

Standard fixed manufacturing cost (absorption costing), $3 based on 10,000 units at normal capacity; no beginning inventories; unit costs, variable costing, $7 per unit, $5 + $2; unit costs, absorption costing, $10 per unit, $5 + $2 + $3

(IN)SIGHT   *(continued)*

	Absorption Costing	Variable Costing	Throughput Costing
Sales	$180,000	$180,000	$180,000
Cost of sales*	90,000	63,000	50,000
Gross margin	$ 90,000	$117,000	$130,000
Other expenses:			
Other manufacturing costs**		$ 30,000	$ 50,000
Selling and administrative	15,000	15,000	15,000
Total other expenses	$ 15,000	$ 45,000	$ 65,000
Income	$ 75,000	$ 72,000	$ 65,000

* 9,000 × $10 = $90,000, 9,000 × $7 = $63,000, cost of materials used, $50,000
** Fixed manufacturing costs = $30,000, other variable manufacturing costs plus fixed manufacturing costs = $50,000

The $7,000 difference between throughput income and variable costing income is the $7 variable manufacturing cost times 1,000 units in inventory. Notice that throughput costing results in even lower income than does variable costing when production exceeds sales. Throughput costing will also show higher in comes than does variable costing when sales exceed production. So while variable costing neither rewards nor penalizes production that is higher or lower than sales, throughput costing does penalize high production and reward low production. Throughput costing is therefore very much in tune with JIT and other philosophies that seek lower inventories.

Sources: John Darlington, John Innes, Falconer Mitchell, and John Woodward, "Throughput Accounting: The Garrett Automotive Experience," Management Accounting (England), April 1992, 32-39.

is more desirable. Although they acknowledge the usefulness of variable costing information for specific short-run decisions (like the acceptance of special orders), they argue that concentrating on variable costs can be harmful in the long run. Their major objection is that if fixed costs are not treated as costs of product, managers might set prices too low to cover fixed costs and earn profits. They argue that managers who become accustomed to reports prepared using variable costing could come to ignore the fixed costs that might be the great bulk of production costs. In short, advocates of absorption costing argue that it is useful because it alerts managers to the need to cover both fixed and variable costs.

Advocates of variable costing offer two counterarguments. One is that even absorption costing does not include all costs as product costs. Selling and administrative costs are excluded from inventory under both costing methods. In many cases, these costs exceed production costs. In the same vein, when a standard fixed cost per unit is used, the amount of fixed cost included in product cost (and therefore in inventory) is decided in advance. Since fixed costs will probably be overapplied or underapplied, some of them will not be included in inventory.

The other counterargument is that it is unnecessary to allocate fixed costs to units in setting prices when the company faces competition and cannot charge any price it chooses. For example, suppose a company could analyze the expected volume-price relationships as suggested in Chapter 4 and select the best combination of price and expected volume. If a company has discretion over prices and can expect to sell about the same volume no matter what price is charged, there is no harm in using a total cost per unit to set prices. However, companies in these circumstances are much less common than companies that face competition and therefore cannot charge any price they wish.

A major study of pricing practices showed that 70 percent of manufacturers surveyed used full costs to set prices, 12 percent used variable costs, and 18 percent did not use costs, but rather prices based on their competitors' prices. The authors describe a similar study done in 1983 that found 82 percent using full costs, 17 percent using variable costs, and 1 percent "other." They concluded that full-cost pricing continues to be the norm, but with less dominance than before.

About half of those using full costs used full manufacturing costs, while the other half used manufacturing costs plus some selling and administrative expenses. About half of those using variable costs used only manufacturing costs, with the other half using some other variable costs as well.

The authors attribute some of the strength of full-cost pricing to the use of ABC, which better rationalizes individual product costs and eliminates much of the arbitrariness characteristic of older costing systems.[3]

If absorption costing is to be used, it seems better to use a standard fixed cost per unit than an actual fixed cost per unit. When a standard fixed cost is used, the effect of production's being different from production used to set the standard is isolated in the volume variance. (The volume variance tells us what the effect is, but is not helpful for control purposes.) Using standard fixed costs might alleviate the problem of a manager's changing prices at frequent intervals, if only because total cost per unit will not change as production changes.

SUMMARY

Standard costing is a method of product costing that uses standard costs instead of actual or normal costs. One major benefit of standard costing is that it ties the accounting records to the calculations of the variances used for control purposes. Another very important benefit is that it simplifies record keeping for a company that makes several products.

Standard absorption costing requires calculating a standard fixed cost per unit. Like normal costing, standard absorption costing yields a volume variance

3 *Eunsup Shim and Ephraim F. Sudit, "How Manufacturers Price Products,"* Management Accounting, *February 1995, 37-39.*

as well as a fixed overhead budget variance. But the volume variance is of little, if any, economic significance. Setting a standard fixed cost per unit requires selecting a level of activity, the most common of which is normal activity or practical capacity. The magnitude and direction of the volume variance depend on the activity level chosen for the standard.

The required use of some type of absorption costing for external reporting has contributed to the internal distribution of, and the need for managers to understand, reports reflecting this approach to product costing. For internal managerial purposes, some companies use standard variable costing or even actual variable costing, which consider only variable production costs as product costs and treat fixed manufacturing costs as expenses in the period in which they are incurred. Variable costing is compatible with both CVP analysis and the contribution margin format of the income statement.

KEY TERMS

normal activity
  (normal capacity) (657)
practical capacity (658)
standard costing (656)

standard fixed cost per unit (657)
theoretical capacity (658)
throughput accounting (673)
variable (direct) costing (666)

KEY FORMULA

$$\text{Volume variance—standard costing} = \left(\begin{array}{c}\text{Actual} \\ \text{units} \\ \text{produced}\end{array} - \begin{array}{c}\text{Units at} \\ \text{selected} \\ \text{activity}\end{array}\right) \times \begin{array}{c}\text{Standard} \\ \text{fixed cost} \\ \text{per unit}\end{array}$$

REVIEW PROBLEM

In 19X7, SMP Company again used a $20 standard variable cost and $30 standard fixed cost based on $3,000,000 and 100,000 units. SMP produced 112,000 units and sold 102,000. It incurred all manufacturing costs as expected. Selling and administrative expenses were again $5 variable per unit and $1,400,000 fixed.

Required
1. Prepare an income statement using absorption costing.
2. Prepare an income statement using variable costing.
3. Suppose that $8 of the $20 standard variable cost is for materials. Prepare an income statement using throughput costing.

ANSWER TO REVIEW PROBLEM
1.

SMP Company, 19X7 Income Statement—Absorption Costing		
Sales (102,000 × $80)		$8,160,000
Standard cost of sales:		
Beginning inventory (15,000 × $50)	$ 750,000	
Variable production costs (112,000 × $20)	2,240,000	
Fixed production costs (112,000 × $30)	3,360,000	
Cost of goods available (127,000 × $50)	$6,350,000	
Ending inventory (25,000 × $50)	1,250,000	
Standard cost of goods sold (102,000 × $50)		5,100,000
Standard gross margin		$3,060,000
Fixed cost volume variance, favorable		360,000
Actual gross margin		$3,420,000
Selling and administrative expenses		1,910,000
Profit		$1,510,000

The volume variance can be computed in either of two ways. It is the difference between budgeted fixed production costs of $3,000,000 and applied fixed production costs of $3,360,000. Because applied costs exceeded budgeted costs, the variance is favorable. Volume variance is also the difference between the 112,000 units produced and the 100,000 units used to set the standard fixed cost, multiplied by the standard fixed cost (12,000 units × $30 = $360,000).

2.

SMP Company, 19X7 Income Statement—Variable Costing		
Sales (102,000 × $80)		$8,160,000
Standard variable cost of sales:		
Beginning inventory (15,000 × $20)	$ 300,000	
Variable production costs (112,000 × $20)	2,240,000	
Cost of goods available (127,000 × $20)	$2,540,000	
Ending inventory (25,000 × $20)	500,000	
Standard variable cost of sales (102,000 × $20)		2,040,000
Standard variable manufacturing margin		$6,120,000
Variable selling and administrative expenses		510,000
Contribution margin		$5,610,000
Fixed costs:		
Production	$3,000,000	
Selling and administrative expenses	1,400,000	4,400,000
Profit		$1,210,000

As explained in the chapter, the $300,000 difference in income under the two methods results because of the fixed overhead costs in the beginning and ending inventories under absorption costing. The beginning inventory of 15,000 units included fixed overhead costs of $450,000 (15,000 × $30 standard fixed cost per unit) carried forward from 19X6. The ending inventory of 25,000 units includes fixed overhead costs of $750,000 (25,000 × $30) being carried forward to 19X8. The $300,000 difference in income occurs because the fixed costs being carried forward from 19X7 ($750,000) are greater than those carried forward to 19X7 ($400,000). That is, the income difference results from the increase in inventory or, described another way, because 19X7 production (112,000 units) was greater than 19X7 sales (102,000 units).

3.

SMP Company, 19X7 Income Statement—Throughput Costing	
Sales (102,000 × $80)	$8,160,000
Standard throughput cost of sales, 112,000 × $8*	896,000
Throughput	$7,264,000
Other manufacturing costs**	4,344,000
Manufacturing margin	$2,920,000
Selling and administrative expenses	1,910,000
Profit	$1,010,000

* *$8 material cost per unit times units produced.*
** *$12 non-material variable manufacturing costs times 112,000 units, plus $3,000,000 fixed manufacturing costs.*

The $200,000 difference between variable costing income ($1,210,000) and throughput income ($1,010,000) is the $20 total variable manufacturing cost multiplied by the 10,000 units produced, but not sold.

ASSIGNMENT MATERIAL

QUESTIONS FOR DISCUSSION

14-1   Variable and absorption costing   "The trouble with variable costing is that I have to put all of the fixed costs on the income statement right away. With absorption costing I can put some of them into inventory where they belong and take care of them later when the products are sold." Discuss these statements critically.

14-2   Period costs—product costs   The distinction between product costs and period costs is a major point of contention between the advocates of variable costing and those of absorption costing. Is the distinction important for decision making?

14-3   Comparison of costing methods   Absorption costing rewards high production with increased income. Variable costing does not reward higher production with higher income, but throughput costing actually penalizes higher production. Explain these statements.

EXERCISES

14-4   Basic standard costing—absorption and variable   Rath Company makes Zuds, a household cleaning product. Zuds sells for $5 per case and has a standard variable manufacturing cost of $1 per case. Fixed production costs are $300,000 per month; fixed selling and administrative expenses are $50,000 per month. The firm began March 19X1 with no inventories and had the following activity in March and April.

	March	April
Production in cases	120,000	90,000
Sales in cases	100,000	100,000

The president wants two sets of monthly income statements: one showing monthly income using variable costing, the other showing monthly income using absorption costing. Use practical capacity of 150,000 cases per month to set the standard fixed cost.

Required

Prepare income statements by month as the president requested. Use the format that shows the details of beginning and ending inventories and of production costs in the cost of goods sold section.

14-5   Standard costing income statements   The following data pertain to the operations of Lindsey Corporation for 19X8.

Normal capacity	200 units
Practical capacity	300 units
Budgeted production	240 units
Actual production	250 units
Actual sales ($25 per unit)	240 units
Standard variable production cost per unit	$10
Fixed production costs—budgeted and actual	$2,400

During 19X8 there were no variable cost variances and actual fixed costs incurred equalled the budgeted amount. There were no beginning inventories and no selling or administrative expenses.

Required

1. Determine the standard cost per unit assuming that standard fixed cost is based on (a) normal capacity, (b) practical capacity, and (c) budgeted production.
2. Prepare income statements for each of the three bases computed in item 1.

14-6   Basic absorption costing   Perry Industries manufactures disk drives for microcomputers. Data related to its best-selling model, which is the only one made in its Bristol plant, follow.

Production:	
April	11,000 units
May	9,000 units
Sales:	
April	8,000 units
May	11,000 units
Standard variable manufacturing cost	$125
Standard fixed manufacturing cost	75
Total standard manufacturing cost	$200

Perry has set its standard fixed manufacturing cost based on normal activity of 10,000 drives per month and budgeted fixed manufacturing costs of $750,000 per month. There was no inventory at the beginning of April. The drive sells for $300. Selling and administrative expenses are $350,000 per month. All manufacturing costs were incurred as expected (variable per unit and total fixed) in both months.

Required
Prepare standard absorption costing income statements for April and May.

14-7   Basic variable costing (continuation of 14-6)   Using the data in the previous assignment, prepare standard variable costing income statements for Perry Industries for April and May.

14-8   Throughput costing (continuation of 14-6)   Of the $125 standard variable manufacturing cost, $90 is for materials.

Required
Prepare throughput costing income statements for April and May.

14-9   Effect of measure of activity (continuation of 14-6)   The president of Perry Industries has heard that some companies use practical capacity as the basis for determining standard fixed manufacturing costs. He asks you to show him how using Perry's practical capacity of 15,000 drives per month would affect the income statements you prepared for 14-6.

Required
Prepare the income statements that the president wants. Comment on the differences between these statements and the ones you prepared for 14-6.

   14-10   Absorption costing   L-Gate, Inc. makes network connectors that sell for $500. Standard variable manufacturing cost is $200, and the standard fixed manufacturing cost is $100, based on budgeted fixed costs of $10,000,000 and budgeted production of 100,000 units. During 19X6, the company produced 96,000 units and sold 90,000. Actual fixed manufacturing costs were $9,870,000; actual variable manufacturing costs were $19,300,000. Selling and administrative expenses were $11,350,000, all fixed. There were no beginning inventories.

Required
Prepare a standard absorption costing income statement.

14-11   Variable costing (continuation of 14-10)   Prepare an income statement for L-Gate using standard variable costing.

14-12   Standard fixed cost and volume variance   The following data refer to the operations of Hinson Company for 19X8.

Normal capacity	240,000 units
Practical capacity	300,000 units
Actual production	250,000 units
Fixed costs—budgeted and actual	$600,000

Required

1. Compute the standard fixed cost per unit based on (a) normal capacity and (b) practical capacity.
2. Compute the volume variances for each of the methods given in item 1.

 14-13   *Relationships* For each of the following independent situations, fill in the missing data. In all cases, the standard fixed cost per unit is based on normal capacity of 10,000 units.

	(a) Standard Fixed Cost per Unit	(b) Total Budgeted Fixed Costs	(c) Actual Production	(d) Volume Variance (Favorable)
1.	$_____	$_____	8,000	$ 8,000
2.	$ 3	$_____	_____	$ 6,000
3.	$_____	$ 40,000	8,000	$_____
4.	$_____	$ 30,000	_____	$ (7,500)

14-14   *Effects of changes in production—standard variable costing* The following data relate to Elliot Pencil Company's best-selling model.

Sales (30,000 cases at $10)	$300,000
Production costs:	
Variable costs, standard and actual	$4 per case
Fixed, budgeted and actual	$150,000

The company has no beginning inventories and no selling and administrative expenses.

Required

Prepare income statements using standard variable costing assuming the company produced (a) 30,000 cases and (b) 31,000 cases. Show the details of the cost of sales section of the income statements.

14-15   *Effects of change in production—standard absorption costing (continuation of 14-14)* Assume that Elliot Pencil Company uses standard absorption costing with a standard fixed cost per case of $5 based on normal activity of 30,000 cases.

Required

Prepare income statements assuming that production is (a) 30,000 cases and (b) 31,000 cases. Show details of cost of sales.

14-16   *"Now wait a minute here."* The title of this problem is the statement your boss made when you showed him the results of completing item 1 of this assignment.

Hownet makes panes for greenhouse windows, selling them for $10 each. Standard variable manufacturing cost is $2 and total fixed manufacturing costs are $60,000. Normal volume is 10,000 units, so that the standard fixed cost per unit is $6. Your boss had asked you to determine the firm's gross profit (after any production variances) from selling 10,000 units. The company treats all variances as adjustments to standard gross margin. Being conscientious, you decided to check your results by preparing income statements down to actual gross margin under each of the following cases. There are no beginning inventories.

(a) Sales are 10,000 units, production is 10,000 units.
(b) Sales are 10,000 units, production is 10,001 units.
(c) Sales are 10,001 units, production is 10,001 units.
(d) Sales are 9,999 units, production is 10,001 units.

Required

1. Prepare the income statements.
2. Explain why your boss gave the response he did.
3. Tell your boss why the results came out as they did.

14-17   All fixed cost company Fixed Company was organized on January 1, 19X5, and began operations immediately. The balance sheet immediately after organization showed plant and equipment of $2,400,000 and common stock of $2,400,000. The plant is completely automated and makes its one product from air. Its only cost is $240,000 depreciation, based on a ten-year life and the straight-line method. During the first two years of operation the company had the following results.

	19X5	19X6
Units produced	140,000	100,000
Units sold	120,000	120,000

All sales were at $5 per unit and were for cash. The company uses a standard fixed cost of $2 per unit based on normal volume of 120,000 units. There were no cash disbursements in either year so that cash at the end of each year was $5 multiplied by cumulative sales.

Required

1. Prepare income statements for each year.
2. Prepare a balance sheet as of the end of each year.
3. Repeat items 1 and 2 using variable costing.

14-18   Interpreting results The president of Stockley Jellies, Inc. has been reviewing the income statements of the two most recent months. She is puzzled because sales rose and profits fell in March, and she asks you, the controller, to explain.

	February	March
Sales ($30 per case)	$ 540,000	$ 660,000
Standard cost of sales	270,000	330,000
Standard gross profit	$ 270,000	$ 330,000
Volume variance	40,000	(50,000)
Selling and administrative expenses	(150,000)	(150,000)
Income	$ 160,000	$ 130,000

The standard fixed cost per case is $10, based on normal capacity of 20,000 cases per month.

Required

1. Determine production in each month.

2. Explain the results to the president.
3. Prepare income statements using variable costing.

14-19   Income determination—absorption costing   The following data apply to Malkovich Company's 19X4 operation.

Sales (80,000 units)	$1,600,000
Production	90,000 units
Variable costs of production, standard and actual	$900,000
Fixed production costs, budgeted and actual	$360,000
Selling and administrative costs	$250,000

Required
Prepare income statements for 19X4 using standard absorption costing with (1) 90,000 units and (2) 100,000 units used to set the standard fixed cost.

14-20   Income determination—variable costing (continuation of 14-19)   Prepare an income statement for Malkovich for 19X4, using standard variable costing.

14-21   Relationships   Fill in the blanks for each of the following independent situations. In all situations, selling price is $10, standard and actual variable manufacturing cost is $6, fixed production costs—budgeted and actual—are $100,000, and the volume used to set the standard fixed cost per unit is 50,000 units. There are no selling and administrative expenses.

	(a)	(b)	(c)	(d)
			Income—	Income—
	Unit	Unit	Variable	Absorption
Case	Sales	Production	Costing	Costing
1	80,000	_____	$_____	$210,000
2	_____	_____	$ 80,000	$120,000
3	50,000	55,000	$_____	$ _____

14-22   All fixed company   Earthcare, Inc., manufactures a single product from garbage. It sells for $5 per unit. The production process is automated and there are no variable costs. Earthcare's production costs are $20,000 per month. Normal activity is 10,000 units per month, and the standard fixed cost per unit is $2. Earthcare has no selling and administrative expenses. Earthcare began May with no inventory. Its activity for May, June, and July is summarized as follows, in units.

	May	June	July
Production	11,000	10,000	9,000
Sales	9,000	10,000	11,000

Required
1. Prepare income statements for each of the three months using standard absorption costing. Show the details of the cost of sales calculations.
2. Prepare income statements for each of the three months using standard variable costing.

PROBLEMS

14-23 *Standard costing—absorption and variable* EauPlume Company makes shaving lotion and uses standard absorption costing. Standard labor and materials per case are as follows:

Materials (3 gallons at $5 per gallon)	$15
Direct labor (0.50 hour at $12 per hour)	6

Total annual manufacturing overhead is budgeted according to the formula $500,000 + ($2 × direct labor hours). The company uses normal capacity of 25,000 direct labor hours (50,000 cases) to set the standard fixed cost.

EauPlume began 19X7 with no inventories. It produced 45,000 cases and sold 40,000 at $40 each. Selling and administrative expenses were $200,000. There were no variable cost variances, and fixed production costs were incurred as budgeted ($500,000).

Required

1. Determine the total standard cost per case.
2. Prepare an income statement for 19X7.
3. Prepare an income statement for 19X7 using variable costing.

14-24 *Absorption costing and variable costing* Gordon Soups, Inc. makes a variety of soups. Data related to its chicken gumbo follow.

Selling price per case	$90
Variable manufacturing costs per case	$25
Fixed manufacturing costs per month	$600,000
Selling and administrative expenses, all fixed, per month	$160,000

Gordon uses standard absorption costing, basing its unit fixed cost on normal activity of 15,000 cases per month. In July, Gordon produced 16,000 cases and sold 14,000. There were 3,000 cases in beginning inventory at standard cost. All costs were incurred as expected.

Required

1. Determine the standard fixed cost per unit.
2. Prepare an income statement for July. Use the short form of the income statement but calculate cost of goods sold separately.
3. Prepare an income statement for July assuming that Gordon uses variable costing. Remember that inventory at the beginning of July will be at standard variable cost.

14-25 *Absorption costing and variable costing—variances* VCX Company uses standard absorption costing, basing its standard fixed cost on 300,000 units of product per year, and $900,000 annual budgeted fixed manufacturing overhead. Standard variable manufacturing cost is $6 per unit. Results for 19X6 follow. There were no beginning inventories.

Unit production	290,000
Unit sales (at $20 per unit)	270,000
Actual variable manufacturing costs	$1,715,000
Actual fixed manufacturing costs	$910,000
Actual selling and administrative expenses, all fixed	$800,000

Required
1. Determine the standard fixed cost per unit and the total standard cost per unit.
2. Compute all variances.
3. Prepare an income statement for 19X6. Show any variances as adjustments to standard cost of sales.
4. Prepare an income statement using variable costing.

 14-26   Budgeted income statements   Morrison WinterSports manufactures several lines of skiing equipment. Its Riverdale Plant makes a single model, the M-80 ski. Budgeted data for 19X7 follow.

Sales (37,000 pairs at $70)	$2,590,000
Production	39,000 pairs
Standard variable cost	$15
Standard fixed cost	25
Total standard cost	$40
Selling and administrative expenses:	
Fixed	$600,000
Variable	$8 per pair

Morrison uses normal activity of 40,000 pairs per year and budgeted fixed manufacturing costs of $1,000,000 to set its standard fixed cost. There were no beginning inventories.

Required
1. Prepare a budgeted income statement using standard absorption costing.
2. Prepare a budgeted income statement using standard variable costing.

14-27   Analysis of results (extension of 14-26)   The Riverdale Plant of Morrison WinterSports actually produced 41,000 pairs and sold 40,000. All costs were incurred as expected—fixed in total and variable per unit.

Required
1. Prepare an income statement using standard absorption costing.
2. Prepare an income statement using standard variable costing.
3. Which set of statements (standard absorption costing or variable absorption costing) from this and the previous assignment gives better information for analyzing results?

14-28   Analysis of income statement—standard costs   The income statement for Bourque Manufacturing Company for 19X6 follows. The company has established the following standards for a unit of finished product.

Materials (16 pounds at $0.50)	$ 8
Direct labor (2 hours at $12)	24
Variable overhead ($1 per direct labor hour)	2
Fixed overhead	2
Total	$36

The fixed overhead standard is based on normal capacity of 20,000 units. During 19X6, 49,000 direct labor hours were worked and 370,000 pounds of materials were used.

Bourque Manufacturing Company
Income Statement for 19X6

Sales (20,000 units at $50)		$1,000,000
Cost of goods sold—at standard		720,000
Standard gross profit		$ 280,000
Variances:		
Materials	$3,000U	
Labor	3,000U	
Variable overhead	3,000U	
Fixed overhead:		
Spending variance	5,000F	
Volume variance	8,000F	4,000F
Gross profit		$ 284,000
Selling and administrative expenses		230,000
Income		$ 54,000

Required
1. Based on the information provided, determine the following:
   (a) number of units produced
   (b) material use variance
   (c) material price variance
   (d) direct labor efficiency variance
   (e) direct labor rate variance
   (f) variable overhead efficiency variance
   (g) variable overhead spending variance
   (h) fixed overhead incurred
2. Prepare an income statement using standard variable costing.

14-29   Conversion of absorption costing income statement from normal to practical capacity (continuation of 14-28)   The standard costs and the income statement for Bourque Manufacturing Company use a standard fixed cost per unit based on normal capacity of 20,000 units. Assume, instead, that Bourque bases its standard fixed cost per unit on its practical capacity of 25,000 units.

Required
1. Determine the standard fixed cost per unit.
2. Prepare an income statement for 19X6.

14-30   *Reconciling incomes—absorption costing*   TriCom Co. had the following budgeted income statement for March 19X5 in thousands of dollars.

Sales	$4,230.0
Standard cost of sales	1,903.5
Standard gross margin	$2,326.5
Selling and administrative	
expenses (all fixed)	1,800.0
Income	$ 526.5

Budgeted volume was 211.5 thousand units at a selling price of $20. Standard cost of sales was $9, of which $5 was fixed. The assistant who prepared the statement had no information about budgeted production, so assumed that it would be equal to normal activity of 220 thousand units per month, eliminating the volume variance.

Tri-Com actually sold 214 thousand units and produced 210 thousand. Actual fixed production costs were $1,100 thousand, actual variable production costs were $840 thousand. Selling and administrative expenses were as budgeted.

Required

1. Prepare an income statement reflecting the actual results.
2. Does it make sense that actual income is less than budgeted income when actual sales were higher than budgeted sales? Write a memorandum to Lynn Maffett, Tri-Com's president, explaining why the actual results were different from budget. Use the guidelines in Appendix A.

14-31   *Reconciling incomes—variable costing*

Required

1. Use the information from the previous assignment to prepare budgeted and actual income statements for TriCom using variable costing.
2. Explain the difference between budgeted and actual income.

14-32   *Analysis of income statements*   As chief financial analyst of Markem Enterprises, Inc., you have been asked by the president to explain the difference between the two income statements prepared for her consideration. One was prepared by the controller, the other by the sales manager. Both used the same data from last year's operations. Markem had no beginning inventories.

	Statement A	Statement B
Sales (10,000 units)	$2,000,000	$2,000,000
Cost of goods sold:		
Production costs	1,200,000	1,800,000
Ending inventory	(400,000)	(600,000)
Cost of goods sold	$ 800,000	$1,200,000
Gross profit	$1,200,000	$ 800,000
Other costs	900,000	300,000
Income	$ 300,000	$ 500,000

Variable costs of production, the only variable costs, are $80 per unit.

Required

1. Determine which statement was prepared using variable costing, which using absorption costing.
2. Determine (a) fixed production costs, (b) selling and administrative expenses, (c) production in units, and (d) cost per unit of inventory for both statements.
3. Which statement do you think was prepared by which manager and why do you think so?

14-33 *Conversion of income statement* The manager of the Morgan Division of Rorshoot Industries has been on the job only a short time. The following income statement, for the third quarter of 19X7, is the first report she has received. She is having some difficulty understanding it because she is familiar only with variable costing, and she has asked you to convert the statement to a variable costing basis.

Sales		$1,324,000
Cost of sales		893,700
Gross profit		$ 430,300
Operating expenses:		
Selling and administrative	$276,300	
Unabsorbed fixed overhead	21,600	297,900
Income		$ 132,400

From reviewing internal records you have determined the following:

(a) Selling and administrative costs are all fixed.
(b) The division sells its one product at $40 per unit.
(c) Fixed manufacturing overhead is applied at $12 per unit.
(d) There was no fixed overhead budget variance.
(e) Production during the quarter was 38,200 units.

Required

Prepare an income statement using standard variable costing.

14-34 *Effects of costing methods on balance sheet* McPherson Company has a loan with a large bank. Among the provisions of the loan agreement are (a) the current ratio must be at least 3 to 1 and (b) the ratio of debt to stockholders' equity must be no higher than 75%. The balance sheet at December 31, 19X4 follows.

Assets		Equities	
Cash and receivables	$ 460,000	Current liabilities	$ 200,000
Inventory (40,000 units at			
variable cost)	200,000	Long-term bank loan	300,000
Total current assets	$ 660,000	Stockholders' equity	760,000
Fixed assets (net)	600,000		
Total assets	$1,260,000	Total equities	$1,260,000

Current ratio: $660,000/$200,000 = 3.3/1
Debt/stockholders' equity: $500,000/$760,000 = 66%

The budgeted income statement for 19X5 follows.

Sales (100,000 units)		$1,000,000
Variable cost of sales		500,000
Variable manufacturing margin		$ 500,000
Other variable costs (variable with sales)		50,000
Contribution margin		$ 450,000
Fixed costs:		
Manufacturing	$300,000	
Other	50,000	350,000
Income		$ 100,000

Budgeted production is 100,000 units. The company's president foresees substantial expenditures for fixed assets and intends to obtain a loan to finance these expenditures. He projects the following pro forma balance sheet for December 31, 19X5.

Assets		Equities	
Cash and receivables	$ 400,000	Current liabilities	$ 240,000
Inventory (40,000 units at			
variable cost)	200,000	Long-term bank loan	460,000
Total current assets	$ 600,000	Stockholders' equity	860,000
Fixed assets (net)	960,000		
Total assets	$1,560,000	Total equities	$1,560,000

He sees that the company will be in default on both provisions of the loan agreement. (Compute the current ratio and debt/stockholders' equity ratio to verify his finding.) Trying to resolve the problem, he lists the following points.

(a) Practical capacity is 150,000 units.
(b) The company might benefit by using absorption costing.

Required

1. Prepare the income statement and balance sheet using standard absorption costing, with production of 150,000 units used to set the standard fixed cost. Also assume production of 150,000 units. Assume that all increased production costs are paid in cash.
2. Is the company safely within the limits of the loan agreement?
3. Is the company better off using absorption costing?

14-35 CVP analysis and absorption costing The Baltic Division of Samar Industries manufactures large drill bits. The division had the following plans for the first quarter of 19X5.

Unit sales	80,000
Selling price	$40
Variable cost	$24
Fixed costs	$800,000

The divisional manager expected profit of $480,000 from these results. The actual income statement for the quarter follows. The divisional manager was surprised to see that the targets for volume, price, and costs were met or exceeded, but that profit was less than anticipated.

Sales (82,000 units at $40)	$3,280,000
Standard cost of sales at $30	2,460,000
Standard gross margin	$ 820,000
Production variances	(180,000)
Actual gross margin	$ 640,000
Selling and administrative expenses	200,000
Profit	$ 440,000

The divisional manager was informed that all variable costs and 75% of fixed costs were for manufacturing. The division uses standard costing, with practical capacity of 100,000 units per quarter used to set the standard. Actual production was only 70,000 units in the first quarter of 19X5 because of a large supply of inventory left over from the previous period.

Required

1. Prepare an income statement using variable costing.
2. Tell the divisional manager how your income statement would be of more help to her than the one shown above.

14-36 Standard costing—activity-based overhead rates Cannon Industries applies overhead to products using two rates—one based on machine hours, the other on the number of component parts. The latter rate is used because of the high amounts of overhead associated with purchasing, receiving, storing, and issuing parts. The company does not classify any employees as direct labor because production is highly automated. Summary data for 19X5 follow.

	Budget
Parts-related overhead	$1,200,000
Machine-related overhead	$6,480,000
Machine hours	100,000
Total number of parts to be used	8,000,000

The overhead costs are largely fixed with respect to output. Data for product GT-1029 follow.

Component parts, 11 parts at average $2.50 price	$27.50
Machine time	0.15 hours

During March 19X6, the company made 60,000 units of product GT-1029, and no other products. Parts-related overhead was $105,300; machine-related overhead was $542,230. The managers expect both of these categories of cost to be incurred evenly throughout the year. Use of parts was at standard.

Required

1. Calculate the predetermined overhead rates for parts and for machine hours.
2. Determine the standard cost of product GT-1029.
3. Determine whatever variances you can.

14-37   *Preparing income statements*   Bob Cransk, president of BC Company, has been receiving monthly reports like the one which follows since he founded the company ten years ago. As BC's newly hired controller, you have been discussing the reports with Cransk, trying to decide whether to make any changes. (All numbers are in thousands of dollars.)

	March	February
Sales	$1,256.8	$1,452.4
Standard cost of sales	$ 769.3	$ 879.7
Production variances	7.3U	29.8U
Cost of sales	$ 776.6	$ 909.5
Gross margin	$ 480.2	$ 542.9
Selling and administrative expenses	406.4	412.6
Profit before taxes	$ 73.8	$ 130.3
Summary of variances:		
Materials	$ 8.4U	$ 7.1U
Direct labor	7.8U	6.9U
Overhead	8.9F	15.8U
Total	$ 7.3U	$ 29.8U

Cransk has told you that he is generally satisfied with the reports, but he is sometimes surprised because they seem to contradict what he believes from his knowledge of operations. He attributes some of his surprise to his lack of understanding of accounting principles.

"For example," he said, "February is a good month. March starts our slow season. I expected February to be a little better than it was, but it seemed okay. March showed better than I had thought it would. I know that our production affects income, so I sort of make mental adjustments for it, but I'd rather not have to."

A review of the records reveals that standard variable cost of sales was $580.5 in February and $510.3 in March. Total fixed manufacturing overhead was $305.2 in February and $299.8 in March. Budgeted fixed manufacturing overhead was $304.5 in both months. Variable overhead variances were $3.2 unfavorable in February, $2.3 unfavorable in March. Although there is some variation in selling and administrative expenses, they can be considered fixed.

Required

1. Prepare income statements for February and March using standard variable costing.
2. Tell Cransk how much of the variances in the income statements are attributable to the use of absorption costing.

14-38   *Incorporating variances into budgets*   Viner Company is developing its budgets for the coming year. The company uses the following standard costs for its final product.

Materials (3 gallons at $3)	$ 9
Labor (4 hours at $5)	20
Variable overhead ($6 per DLH)	24
Total standard variable cost	$53

Budgeted fixed manufacturing costs are $300,000. Selling and administrative expenses, all fixed, are budgeted at $400,000. Generally, there is about a 10% variance over standard quantity for materials, but the materials usually cost 5% less than the standard price. Direct laborers will receive a 6% wage increase at the beginning of the year, and labor efficiency is expected to be 4% better than standard. An unfavorable variable overhead spending variance of 5% is expected. Sales for the year are budgeted at 20,000 units at $100; production schedules indicate planned production of 24,000 units. There are no beginning inventories. Purchases of materials are budgeted to be equal to expected materials use.

Required

1. Determine the expected variable cost variances for the year.
2. Prepare a budgeted income statement for the coming year using standard variable costing.

14-39 Costs and decisions "You're fired!!" was the way your boss, the controller of Saran Bathing Suit Company, greeted you this morning. His ire was based on the following two income statements. A few months ago you recommended accepting an offer from a national chain for 10,000 suits at $12 each. At that time, inventories were rising because of slow sales. Things have not improved noticeably since then. Your recommendation was based on the variable production costs of $10 per unit, which are the only variable costs. The total standard cost of $16 per suit includes $6 in fixed costs, based on normal production of 130,000 units.

Income Statements for 19X4

	If Special Order Had Not Been Accepted	Actual, with Special Order
Sales: 100,000 × $25	$2,500,000	$2,500,000
10,000 × $12		120,000
Total sales	$2,500,000	$2,620,000
Cost of sales at $16 standard cost	1,600,000	1,760,000
Standard gross profit	$ 900,000	$ 860,000
Volume variance (20,000 × $6)	120,000U	120,000U
Actual gross profit	$ 780,000	$ 740,000
Selling and administrative expenses	710,000	710,000
Income	$ 70,000	$ 30,000

"Your recommendation cost us $40,000! Now clean out your desk and leave."

Required

Write a memorandum to your boss, Mr. Beatty, that will get your job back. Use the guidelines in Appendix A.

14-40   *Actual versus standard costs—multiple products* Brennan Company makes luggage. For some time, its managers have been dissatisfied with the firm's cost information. Unit costs have fluctuated greatly and have not been useful for planning and control purposes.

Under the present system, unit costs are computed at the end of each month. The costs are determined by allocating all actual production costs for the month to the various models produced, with the allocation based on the relative materials costs of the various models.

The controller has decided to develop standard costs for product costing purposes. She has analyzed the materials and labor requirements for each model, based on what she believes to be currently attainable performance. The results of her analysis follow. (For simplicity, the problem is limited to three models.)

	Briefcase #108	Cosmetic Case #380	Two-Suiter #460
Materials costs	$12.00	$14.00	$18.00
Labor hours required	0.5	0.8	1.5

Workers all earn $8 per hour, and the company usually works about 6,000 labor hours per month. The controller intends to use 6,000 hours to set the standard fixed cost per unit. Her analysis of monthly manufacturing overhead yielded the formula $90,000 + ($7 × direct labor hours).

During April the company had the following results. There were no inventories at April 1.

	Briefcase #108	Cosmetic Case #380	Two-Suiter #460
Production in units	3,000	2,500	1,200
Sales in units	2,400	1,800	1,000
Sales in dollars	$84,000	$90,000	$85,000

There were no variable cost variances and fixed production costs were $92,000.

Required

1. Compute the standard cost for each model.
2. Compute the ending inventory of finished goods.
3. Prepare an income statement for April. Selling and administrative expenses were $28,000.

14-41   *Interim results, costing methods, and evaluation of performance* Kleffman Company sells a product with a highly seasonal demand. The budgeted income statement for 19X7 is as follows:

Sales (240,000 units)		$2,400,000
Cost of goods sold—at standard:		
Materials	$420,000	
Direct labor	540,000	
Manufacturing overhead	600,000	1,560,000
Gross profit—at standard		$ 840,000
Selling and administrative expenses		420,000
Income before taxes		$ 420,000

Budgeted production is 240,000 units, the number used to set the standard fixed cost per unit. The controller has determined that materials, labor, 40% of manufacturing overhead ($240,000), and $120,000 of the selling and administrative expenses are variable. All fixed costs are incurred evenly throughout the year.

January and February are relatively slow months, each with only about 5% of annual sales. March is the first month of a busy period, and production in February is generally high in order to stock up for the anticipated increase in demand. The actual income statements for January and February 19X7 are as follows:

	January	February
Sales (12,000 units)	$120,000	$120,000
Cost of goods sold—at standard	78,000	78,000
Gross profit—at standard	$ 42,000	$ 42,000
Manufacturing variances:		
Variable costs	3,000F	4,000U
Fixed cost—budget	2,000F	3,000U
Fixed cost—volume	9,000U	7,500F
Gross profit—actual	$ 38,000	$ 42,500
Selling and administrative expenses	31,000	31,000
Income	$ 7,000	$ 11,500

Although the president is pleased that performance improved in February, she has asked the controller why the two months showed different profits, since sales were the same. She also wonders why profits were not about 5% of the $420,000 budget, as each month's sales were 5% of the annual budget.

Required
1. Explain to the president why profits in January and February would be less than 5% of the budgeted annual profit, even though each month's sales were 5% of the budgeted annual amount.
2. Explain to the president why profits differed in the two months. Comment on the president's being pleased that "performance improved in February."

14-42 Income statements and balance sheets Arens Company makes a single product, a microwave oven that sells for $300. Standard variable cost of production is $180 per unit, and the only other variable cost is a 10% sales commission. Fixed production costs are $3,600,000 per year, incurred evenly throughout the year. Of that amount, $800,000 is depreciation and the remainder all require cash disbursements. Fixed selling and administrative expenses of $200,000 per month all require cash disbursements.

For inventory costing Arens uses a standard fixed cost of $45 per unit, based on expected annual production of 80,000 units. However, during 19X6 the company experienced the following results, by six-month periods.

	January-June	July-December
Sales in units	30,000	40,000
Production in units	32,000	42,000

The company sells for cash only and pays all of its obligations as they are incurred. Its balance sheet at December 31, 19X5, in thousands of dollars was as follows:

Assets			Equities	
Cash	$ 400			
Inventory (1,000 units)	225		Common stock	$3,000
Plant and equipment (net)	3,000		Retained earnings	625
Total assets	$3,625		Total equities	$3,625

During 19X6, all costs were incurred as expected (variable costs per unit and fixed costs in total).

Required

1. Prepare income statements (in thousands of dollars) for each of the two six-month periods and the year as a whole.
2. Prepare balance sheets as of June 30 and December 31, 19X6, in thousands of dollars.

14-43   *Pricing dispute* Calligeris Company manufactures brake linings for automobiles. Late in 19X2 the company received an offer for 10,000 linings from Phelan Company. Phelan was unwilling to pay the usual price of $5 per lining but offered to buy at a price that would give Calligeris a $0.50 gross profit per lining.

Without consideration of the order, Calligeris expected the following income statement for the year.

Sales (100,000 linings at $5)		$500,000
Cost of goods sold at standard:		
Beginning inventory (20,000 at $4)	$ 80,000	
Variable production costs (100,000 units at $2.50)	250,000	
Fixed production costs at $1.50 per unit	150,000	
Cost of goods available for sale	$480,000	
Ending inventory (20,000 at $4)	80,000	
Cost of goods sold at standard		400,000
Standard gross profit		$100,000
Volume variance (20,000 at $1.50)	$ 30,000F	
Selling and administrative expenses	50,000	20,000
Income		$ 80,000

The production manager decided that the order could be filled from inventory, so no additional production was planned. The company shipped 10,000 linings to Phelan Company, billing that company for 10,000 units at $4.50 per lining. No additional costs were incurred in connection with this order.

Required

1. Prepare an income statement for 19X2 assuming that the actual results for the year were as planned except that the additional sale was made to Phelan company. Do the results show that the company earned the agreed gross profit?
2. Suppose that you were the controller of Phelan Company. Would you dispute the $4.50 price? If so, why? What price would you propose and why?

14-44   *Predetermined overhead rates—multiple products* The controller of Salmon Company has been developing a new costing system. He believes that the use of standard costs would reduce the cost of record keeping and simplify the firm's internal reporting to managers. He has asked your assistance and you have collected the following information relating to the firm's three products.

	Model 84	Model 204	Model 340
Variable production costs	$4.00	$7.00	$11.00
Direct labor hours required	0.50	0.80	1.50

The company works 50,000 direct labor hours per year at its normal operating level, and the controller uses that figure to set the predetermined overhead rate. Budgeted fixed production costs are $300,000. Operating results for 19X4 follow. There were no beginning inventories.

	Production in Units	Sales in Units	Sales in Dollars
Model 84	30,000	25,000	$250,000
Model 204	24,000	20,000	$280,000
Model 340	20,000	18,000	$450,000

All production costs were incurred as expected, including variable costs per unit and total fixed costs. Selling and administrative expenses were $140,000.

Required
1. Compute standard fixed costs per unit for each model.
2. Compute the ending inventory in dollars for each model.
3. Prepare an income statement for 19X4.

14-45   *Comprehensive review, budgeting, overhead application* Ruland Company makes and sells a single product. The product sells for $20 and Ruland expects sales of 880,000 units in 19X5. The distribution of sales by quarters is expected to be 20%, 25%, 25%, and 30%. The company expects the following costs in 19X6.

Manufacturing Costs		
	Fixed	Variable per Unit
Materials (4 pounds at $0.80)	—	$3.20
Direct labor (0.5 hour at $5)	—	2.50
Maintenance	$ 46,000	0.20
Indirect labor	422,000	0.40
Supplies	316,000	0.05
Power	186,000	0.10
Depreciation	1,900,000	—
Supervision	310,000	—
Miscellaneous	320,000	0.05
Totals	$3,500,000	$6.50

Selling, General, and Administrative Expenses

	Fixed	Variable per Unit
Sales commissions	—	$2.00
Salaries and wages	$1,200,000	—
Other expenses, including interest	4,350,000	
Total	$5,550,000	$2.00

Budgeted production and purchases are as follows:

Quarter	Production (units)	Material Purchases (pounds)
1	210,000	733,000
2	220,000	950,000
3	260,000	904,000
4	210,000	795,000
Total	900,000	3,382,000

Other information relating to Ruland's operation follows.

(a) The company uses a standard fixed cost of $3.50 per unit.
(b) Sales are collected 60 days after sale.
(c) Purchases of raw materials are paid for in the month after purchase.
(d) Direct labor costs unpaid at the end of a quarter are about 10% of the cost incurred in that quarter. All other manufacturing costs requiring cash disbursements (all but depreciation) are paid as incurred, except for raw material purchases.
(e) All selling and administrative expenses require cash disbursements and are paid as incurred except for salesperson's commissions. These are paid in the month after incurrence.
(f) The company has a 40% income tax rate. At year end, the amount of unpaid taxes is about 25% of the total expense for the year.
(g) A dividend of $300,000 will be paid in 19X5.
(h) Purchases of plant assets, all for cash, will total $2,100,000 in 19X5.
(i) Assume that sales, production, and purchases of raw materials are spread evenly over the months of each quarter (one-third of the quarter in each month of the quarter).

The balance sheet at the end of 19X4 appears as follows, in thousands of dollars.

Assets		Equities	
Cash	$ 840	Accounts payable (materials)	$ 240
Accounts receivable	2,800	Accrued commissions	120
Inventory—finished goods		Accrued payroll (direct labor)	64
(146,000 units)	1,460	Income taxes payable	80
Inventory—materials			
(530,000 pounds)	424	Long-term debt	4,000
Plant and equipment	16,200	Common stock	7,000
Accumulated depreciation	(8,400)	Retained earnings	1,820
Total	$13,324	Total	$13,324

Required

1. Prepare a budgeted income statement for 19X5.
2. Prepare a cash budget for 19X5 for the year as a whole, not by quarter.
3. Prepare a pro forma balance sheet for the end of 19X5.
4. Without preparing new statements, describe the differences that would occur in your prepared statements if the company were using variable costing.

CASES

14-46   *Standard costs and pricing*   The controller of Carolina Mills has been discussing costs and prices with the treasurer. The controller wants to use 2,400,000 machine hours to set standard fixed costs, while the treasurer prefers to use 3,000,000 hours. The controller feels that the lower base will make it easier for the company to absorb its fixed overhead, but the treasurer is concerned that the company might set its prices too high to be competitive with other companies.

"Look," the treasurer said, "suppose we use our formula for budgeting total manufacturing costs, materials, labor, and overhead."

$$\text{Total manufacturing cost} = \$7,680,000 + \$4.25 \text{ per machine hour}$$

"Now," she went on, "if we use your basis of 2,400,000 hours and our usual pricing formula, setting prices at 150% of total manufacturing cost, we will have higher prices than competition will permit, with consequent loss of volume."

The controller replied, "I can't agree with you. Your basis of 3,000,000 hours is very close to practical capacity, and we'd be taking the risk of having a significant amount of underabsorbed overhead that would really hurt our profits."

Required

1. Suppose that selling and administrative expenses are $6,200,000, all fixed. What profit will the company earn if it uses 2,400,000 hours to set standard fixed costs, sets prices using the given formula, and sells output requiring 2,400,000 machine hours? (Assume no inventories.)
2. Repeat item 1 substituting 3,000,000 machine hours for 2,400,000 hours.
3. Is the real issue here the selection of the base for applying fixed overhead? Why or why not? If not, what is the real concern?

14-47   *Product costing methods and CVP analysis*   Tollgate Company expects to produce 190,000 units in 19X6. The company uses a predetermined overhead rate for fixed overhead based on 210,000 units, which is normal capacity. Overabsorbed or underabsorbed overhead is shown separately in the income statement. The selling price is $16 per unit. At the expected level of production Tollgate expects the following costs.

Variable production costs	$1,330,000
Fixed production costs	630,000
Fixed selling and administrative costs	434,000

In addition, there are variable selling costs of $2 per unit. The company had no inventory at the end of 19X5.

Required

1. Determine the break-even point assuming that variable costing is used.
2. Determine the number of units that must be sold to break even given that production will be 190,000 units. Assume absorption costing.
3. If your answers to the first two items differ, explain the difference, showing calculations.
4. Would your answer to item 2 be different if the company had a beginning inventory of 10,000 units costed at the same per-unit amount that the company will use in 19X6? Explain why or why not, with calculations.

14-48 Costing methods and evaluation of performance Donita Boroff is the manager of the Wallace Division of Fizer Industries, Inc. She is one of several managers being considered for the presidency of the firm, as the current president is retiring in a year.

All divisions use standard absorption costing; normal capacity is the basis for application of fixed overhead. Normal capacity in the Wallace Division is 40,000 units per quarter, and quarterly fixed overhead is $500,000. Variable production cost is $50 per unit. Boroff has been looking at the report for the first three months of the year and is not happy with the results.

Wallace Division Income Statement for First Quarter		
Sales (25,000 units)		$2,500,000
Cost of goods sold:		
Beginning inventory (10,000 units)	$ 625,000	
Production costs applied	1,562,500	
Total	$2,187,500	
Less ending inventory	625,000	1,562,500
Gross profit		$ 937,500
Volume variance		(187,500)
Selling and general expenses		(500,000)
Income		$ 250,000

The sales forecast for the second quarter is 25,000 units. Boroff had budgeted second-quarter production at 25,000 units but changes it to 50,000 units, which is practical capacity for a quarter. The sales forecasts for each of the last two quarters of the year are also 25,000 units. Costs incurred in the second quarter are the same as budgeted, based on 50,000 units of production.

Required

1. Prepare an income statement for the second quarter.
2. Does the statement for the second quarter reflect Boroff's performance better than that for the first quarter? Can you make any suggestions for reporting in the future? Do you think Boroff should be seriously considered for the presidency of the firm? Why or why not?

14-49 Costing methods and performance evaluation Warren Progman, the new manager of the Oliver Division of General Products Company, was greatly displeased at the income statements that his controller, Hal Gannon, had been giving him. Progman recently had been placed in charge of the division because it had not been showing satisfactory results. Progman was upset because, although sales had risen in each of the last two months, profits had not kept pace. Income statements for the last three months are as follows:

	March	April	May
Sales	$360,000	$440,000	$560,000
Cost of sales	198,000	264,000	381,000
Gross profit	$162,000	$176,000	$179,000
Other expenses	142,000	150,000	162,000
Profit before taxes	$ 20,000	$ 26,000	$ 17,000

Progman asked Gannon why profits had declined when sales had increased and why a substantial increase in sales from March to April had produced only a small increase in profits. Gannon's reply was simply that operations had gone according to plans that Progman had set, and that the problems that Progman wanted to know about were due to the method of accounting for product costs and the relationships of sales to production.

Progman was unimpressed with this explanation and rather testily pointed out that he had been put in charge of the division to "turn it around." He was not about to let accounting conventions give corporate management second thoughts about placing him in charge. Gannon, who was fully aware of the claims Progman had made when being considered for the manager's job, had not liked Progman from the start. To the suggestion that accounting conventions were standing in the way of Progman's performance, Gannon replied only that the reports for all divisions were prepared from the same uniform accounting system and in the form required for corporate reporting. He told Progman that the reports were prepared using GAAP, which was necessary because the corporation was publicly held and had to issue reports to shareholders. He did not tell Progman that he believed the methods used by the company for external reporting were inappropriate for internal purposes.

Later, at lunch with Theodora Holloway, the division's sales manager, Gannon related the conversation that he had had with Progman. Holloway, who had also wondered about the firm's accounting methods, asked Gannon why he didn't just explain the statements to Progman. "Not on your life," said Gannon. "I see no reason to help that braggart. Let him explain to the top brass why things aren't going the way he said they would if he were put in charge instead of me."

"Actually," Gannon continued, "what he's worried about just isn't a difficult problem. Cost of sales included both standard cost and the adjustment needed when production for the month did not equal the 25,000-unit volume that was used to set the standard fixed cost of $9 per unit. In fact, things have gone very well. We had no variances at all except for volume. Selling prices held very well at $20 per unit, and the division is doing much better now. But would I like to be there when the brass asks Progman why things are not going so well! Why, even production in April was right on target at 25,000 units budgeted."

Required

1. Explain the results in the three-month period. You may wish to compute standard fixed costs per unit and production in each month.
2. Prepare income statements for the three months using variable costing.

14-50   *Costing methods and product profitability* At a recent meeting, several of the managers of Cornwall Valve Company were discussing the firm's costing and pricing methods. Although there was general agreement that the methods should be helpful to managers in determining which products to emphasize, there was considerably less agreement on which methods would accomplish this.

The sales manager, Nado Oho, expressed his preference for product costs based on variable costs only. "I see no reason to charge a product with fixed costs. Contribution margin is, after all, the critical question in selecting the products to push."

"I just can't agree with you," said Perrie Emerson, the production manager. "If you'd just take a walk through the plant you'd be reminded that people and materials aren't the only things needed to produce one of our valves. There are tons of machinery that cost money too. Ignoring those costs can only get you into trouble, and it sure isn't very realistic anyway. You've got to consider the machine time required for each product, and that can only be accomplished by allocating the fixed production costs to products. Machine time is critical, and production costs should be allocated on a machine-hour basis."

To make this point, Emerson put an example on the conference room blackboard. "Look, let me show you. Let's take just three of our basic products that all require time in the grinding department. That department has a capacity of 1,000 machine hours a month, and the monthly fixed costs of the department are $10,000." Following is the schedule Emerson put on the board.

	101-27	101-34	101-56
Selling price	$9.00	$12.00	$17.40
Variable costs	5.00	6.00	8.40
Contribution margin	$4.00	$ 6.00	$ 9.00
Fixed costs	1.00	1.25	2.50
Profit per unit	$3.00	$ 4.75	$ 6.50
Number of valves processed per hour	10	8	4

Emerson continued, "Now what I've done is compute a fixed cost per unit by dividing the $10 per hour fixed cost by the number of valves of each type that we can process in one hour. You can see that what I use the grinding machinery for does make a difference. It seems to me that this approach is much better at showing which products to emphasize. This shows that the 56 is the best bet and the 27 is the worst."

"But Perrie," said Oho, "we don't disagree. The 56 is a winner because it has the highest contribution margin, and we wouldn't push the 27 because it contributes the least. What are we arguing about?"

Emerson was not too happy about having her own example used to counter her argument. She admitted that, in the case she used, the relative rankings of the products were the same as they would be using the contribution margin approach. But she still felt that her method would be more valuable to the sales manager than a simple contribution margin approach, and she looked around the room for support.

"Well, now, it's nice to hear that you two are so interested in the information my staff has to offer," commented Joe Anderson, the controller. "But if you want to be realistic, let's consider something else. We're committed to making some of each of these valves, though not nearly enough to keep the grinding department operating at capacity. So the big decision isn't really which valve to produce and sell. What we really need to know is which one to produce after we've met the commitments we made. And the kicker is that we could probably sell all of whatever we produce. The way I see it, we have about 600 hours of grinding time available for discretionary production. So what do we do?"

Emerson continued to argue for her approach, and she specifically attacked the question of pricing. "The way we price our products just isn't rational; I know we could do better if we considered the fixed costs the way I said. We should be selling the 27s for $12.50 if we want to make them as profitable as the 56s, and we'd have to jack the price of 34s by $1.75 to equal the profit on the 56s. Okay, okay, I can see you're getting upset about the idea of such increases, Nado. I know the customers would be unhappy. But if we cater to their needs by producing these models, we ought to get a fair return for doing it."

Required

Determine which valve should be produced once the committed demand is satisfied. Criticize the analyses of the sales manager and the production manager, including their comments about pricing.

14-51 Budgeting, cash flow, product costing, motivation After almost two decades of profitable operations, Pennywise Company experienced its first loss in 19X6, and all internal reports during the first 11 months of 19X7 indicated a second losing year. At the meeting of the board of directors at the end of December 19X7, the members were given the first draft of the basic operating data for 19X7. (Exhibit 1 shows the basic data available to the directors at the meeting.) Public announcement of the data is made shortly after the directors' meeting.

Exhibit 1 Pennywise Company—Operating Data for 19X7
Part A: Condensed Statement of Income

Sales (1,200,000 units at $12 per unit)	$ 14,400,000
Cost of goods sold	11,760,000
Gross margin on sales	$ 2,640,000
Selling and administrative expenses	3,630,000
Net operating loss for the year 19X7	$ (990,000)

Part B: Miscellaneous Operating Data

Normal operating capacity, in units	1,875,000
Fixed costs:	
Manufacturing	$6,000,000
Selling and administrative	$750,000
Variable costs, per unit:	
Manufacturing	$4.80
Selling and administrative	$2.40

The directors had maintained the dividend so as not to antagonize the stockholders or give the impression that the recent losses were any more than a temporary setback. Most of the directors had come to realize, by the end of 19X7, that future dividends were advisable only if the company returned to profitable operations. Consequently, the board members were willing to consider any plans that might help minimize inefficiencies, reduce costs, and build a profitable operation once again.

The chair of the board (and principal stockholder), Mr. Ira Hayes, had recently attended a conference sponsored by the National Association of Manufacturers on motivating personnel to better performance. Mr. Hayes was not particularly impressed with most of the discussions. He told the personnel manager, Ms. Gray: "Those speakers all seemed to concentrate on qualitative and nonquantifiable issues like working conditions and improving the general atmosphere to promote creativity and individuality. There was the usual noise about implementing methods of 'participatory management,' and the like, and coordinating the efforts of the management team. But really, there wasn't much in the way of concrete suggestions."

Having been closely associated with the company since its founding by Mr. Hayes sixteen years before, Ms. Gray was well acquainted with Mr. Hayes' feelings on the matter of motivation. As Mr. Hayes had said on many occasions, he was convinced that the surest (and easiest) way to motivate people was to provide monetary incentives of some kind and then let them know exactly what measures would be used to assess their performance. In keeping with this philosophy, Mr. Hayes proposed, at the first board meeting in 19X8, that the company adopt a profit-sharing plan in which all employees could participate. The other members of the board were receptive to the idea and a committee was appointed to draw up a plan.

According to the plan devised by the committee, the company would set aside cash equal to a certain percentage of before-tax profits. The cash would be distributed to all employees on the basis of a preestablished formula. Or, more correctly, a set of such formulas was needed because the performances of employees in different areas of the company had to be measured in different ways. Mr. Ira Hayes Jr., the president, wanted to provide his own incentives to encourage better performance by sales and production personnel. He gave the sales and production manager, individually, several long and enthusiastic pep talks on expanding their respective areas to higher levels. He further authorized an expenditure for $450,000 on a national advertising program.

Production in the plant reached the normal capacity of 1,875,000 units for the year 19X8. At the board meeting in early 19X9, the president remarked: "Back in the black again. The field people did a great job pushing sales up by almost 17%." (Exhibit 2 shows the data presented to the board at that meeting.)

Exhibit 2 Pennywise Company—Operating Data for 19X8

Sales (1,406,250 units at $12)		$16,875,000
Cost of goods sold:		
Fixed costs	$ 6,000,000	
Variable costs (1,875,000 @ $4.80)	9,000,000	
	$15,000,000	
Less: Ending inventory (468,750 units @ $8.00)	3,750,000	11,250,000
Gross margin on sales		$ 5,625,000
Selling and administrative expenses:		
Fixed costs	$ 1,200,000	
Variable costs (1,406,250 @ $2.40)	3,375,000	4,575,000
Operating profit before taxes and allowance for profit-sharing pool		$ 1,050,000
Provision for profit-sharing pool		210,000
Operating profit before taxes		$ 840,000
Provision for federal income taxes		420,000
Net income for the year 19X8		$ 420,000
Dividends to common stockholders ($0.20 per share)		$ 200,000

The board was pleased with the results of their new plan and with its apparent immediate effectiveness. There was, in fact, much optimistic talk at the meeting about the effect that the new plan would have on 19X9 operations, especially because the special sales campaign would probably not be repeated regularly. The board voted to continue the plan for at least one more year. After the vote, Mr. Hayes, Jr. suggested that it probably would be good for employee relations if the board would announce soon when the pool for profit sharing would be distributed in cash to the employees because the dividend announcement had already been widely publicized. In an outer room, the sales manager, the production manager, and the controller were discussing the advantages and disadvantages of nepotism and of nonoperating management on the board of directors.

Required

The questions following this paragraph are not designed to limit your discussion or specifically direct your analysis. Nor is there any particular significance to the order in which they are listed. You will find it worthwhile to answer the first one first because it may provide some clue as to how you might proceed. It is probably inefficient to answer each of the questions directly and in order because some are interrelated, but you may want to incorporate some comments about each of them in your answer.

1. What is the company's break-even point?
2. What is the company's system for implementing the management functions of planning and control?
3. Are profits likely to continue?
4. Has the profit-sharing plan contributed to efficiency? to cost reduction? to a return to profitable operations?
5. Should the board announce a cash distribution to employees relatively soon?

15

Process Costing and the Cost Accounting Cycle

The drive to eliminate non-value-adding activities has been part of management accounting for years and management accountants have long believed that developing information was wise only if the value of the information exceeded its cost. One benefit of JIT and other advanced manufacturing techniques is simpler and less costly accounting. But not all managers are amenable to drastic changes in cost accounting systems and companies have used needlessly complicated practices for years.

For example, until recently, **Boeing** had a cumbersome process that manually tracked every part that went into every aircraft. The company spent enormous amounts of time doing such unnecessary work as writing each aircraft's identification number on the drawings of every part in the aircraft. Because each aircraft has several million parts, such non-value-adding costs are considerable.

Trane Company, whose pursuit of simplicity in its product costing system we introduced in Chapter 12, redesigned its system in many ways. One important change was the adoption of a simplified method of accounting for costs, called backflushing, which we describe in the chapter. Backflushing requires far less record keeping than conventional methods and frees management accountants to do more analytical work. Another example is that the company stopped keeping detailed bills of materials (BOM) that showed the relationship of

> *every part to the subassemblies in which it was used. Several depart-*
> *ments, including manufacturing, engineering, and finance, had used*
> *this detailed information, but the company found that simplifying the*
> *BOM did no harm. Costs declined because fewer records, engineering*
> *drawings, and part numbers were needed.*

Sources: Alex Taylor III, "Boeing, Sleepy in Seattle," Fortune, August 7, 1995, 92-98.
Ronald B. Clements and Charlene W. Spoede, "Trane's SOUP Accounting," Management Accounting,
June 1992, 46-52.

Chapter 13 introduced product costing—determining the cost of a unit of manufactured product. Chapter 13 emphasized job-order costing. However, the concepts (such as cost flows and application of overhead) apply to all types of manufacturing. While job-order costing is used by companies producing non-standard products, companies that make a single, homogeneous product can use a cost accumulation method called process costing. The first part of this chapter discusses process costing and includes an example describing how a bank uses process costing concepts.

We complete our study of product costing by illustrating the cost accounting cycle. The illustrations cover the journal entries and accounts employed in the three principal types of cost accumulation systems: job-order costing, process costing, and standard costing. Because they keep low inventories, ideally none, advanced manufacturers have fewer problems with product costing. We illustrate one way that they account for product costs.

PROCESS COSTING

Some examples of companies that can use process costing are makers of sugar, bricks, cement, and bulk chemicals. The essence of **process costing** is the accumulation of costs by process, or department, for a period of time. The company calculates per-unit costs for goods passing through a process by dividing costs for the process by production for the period.

For internal reporting, a process costing factory, like a job-order factory, can use either variable or absorption costing, as described in Chapter 14. We concentrate on absorption costing in this chapter. A process coster can also use actual costing, normal costing, or standard costing.

Because process costers manufacture a single, homogeneous product, they can use the basic formula we described earlier:

$$Unit\ cost\ =\ \frac{Production\ costs}{Production}$$

The unit cost is then applied to inventories and cost of goods sold. The key to process costing is determining production, which depends on the treatment of units of work in process. Look at the data for our illustration in Exhibit 15-1. The company finished 100,000 units in August, and also did 60 percent of the work on 5,000 units. What is production for the period? The 100,000 units finished? No, because the $206,000 cost was incurred not only to finish those 100,000 units, but also to work on the 5,000 units. Because some work is done

Exhibit 15-1 Data for Ronn Company

	August	September
Production costs	$206,000	$191,400
Unit data:		
In process at beginning of month	0	5,000
Completed during month	100,000	90,000
In process at end of month	5,000	10,000
Percentage of completion for end-of-period		
work in process	60%	40%

on units in process at the end of a period, we cannot simply use the number of units finished as the denominator. Instead, we use equivalent unit production (or equivalent production) in the denominator, as we discuss shortly. To do so, we must select a cost flow assumption, typically either first-in first-out or weighted average. We shall use the weighted-average method in this chapter. (We describe the FIFO method in the Appendix at the end of this chapter.)

Recall from financial accounting that the **weighted-average inventory method** applied to a merchandiser combines the cost of the beginning inventory with the costs incurred during the period and also combines the units in the beginning inventory with those purchased during the period. The principle is the same for manufactured products.

EQUIVALENT UNIT PRODUCTION AND UNIT COST

Under the weighted-average method, **equivalent unit production** is the sum of (1) the units finished during the period and (2) the equivalent units in the ending inventory of work in process.

The formula for weighted-average equivalent production is as follows:

$$\begin{matrix} \text{Equivalent} \\ \text{production} \end{matrix} = \begin{matrix} \text{Units} \\ \text{completed} \end{matrix} + \left(\begin{matrix} \text{Units in} \\ \text{ending inventory} \end{matrix} \times \begin{matrix} \text{Percentage} \\ \text{complete} \end{matrix} \right)$$

In our example, the 5,000 units in process at the end of August are equivalent to 3,000 complete units (5,000 × 60%). Thus, at the end of August there were 3,000 equivalent units and at the end of September there were 4,000 equivalent units (10,000 × 40%).

In our example, equivalent unit production for August is as follows:

Units completed	100,000
Equivalent units in ending inventory, 5,000 × 60%	3,000
Weighted-average equivalent unit production	103,000

The weighted-average unit cost formula is as follows:

$$\text{Unit cost} = \frac{\text{Cost of beginning inventory} + \text{Current period cost}}{\text{Weighted-average equivalent unit production}}$$

Because there is no beginning inventory for August, the numerator is simply production cost for August. The unit cost for August is therefore $2.00: $206,000/ 103,000 = $2.00.

ENDING INVENTORY AND TRANSFERS

We use the $2 unit cost for both the units completed and those in the ending inventory of work in process. Thus, $200,000 is transferred to Finished Goods Inventory (100,000 × $2) and $6,000 is left in Work in Process Inventory (5,000 × 60% × $2). Notice especially that Work in Process Inventory reflects equivalent whole units. That is, we do not multiply the 5,000 physical units in process by the $2 unit cost because those 5,000 units are only 60 percent complete.

We account for the total production costs of $206,000 in the following schedule. Such a schedule helps you to be sure of your work. The costs accounted for in the schedule should equal the beginning inventory of work in process plus the current period production costs. In August, there is no beginning work in process, so we account only for the $206,000 August production costs.

Cost of finished units transferred to finished goods (100,000 × $2 per unit)	$200,000
Cost of ending inventory (5,000 units × 60% × $2 unit cost)	6,000
Total production costs accounted for	$206,000

BEGINNING INVENTORY

Ronn began September with 3,000 equivalent units of work in process with a cost of $6,000, as we just calculated. As the formula showed, these units do not affect the denominator of the unit cost calculation for September, but the $6,000 cost does. September equivalent production is as follows:

Units completed	90,000
Equivalent units in ending inventory, 10,000 × 40%	4,000
Weighted-average equivalent unit production	94,000

Unit cost is calculated as follows:

$$\frac{\$6,000 + \$191,400}{94,000} = \frac{\$197,400}{94,000} = \$2.10$$

The $2.10 is the weighted-average cost, which includes both the September results and the inventory carried over from August. The disposition of the costs follows.

Ending inventory of work in process 10,000 × 40% × $2.10	$ 8,400
To finished goods inventory, 90,000 × $2.10	189,000
Total	$197,400

The sum of the cost of the beginning inventory and September production costs is $197,400. Therefore, the $197,400 cost in ending inventory and transferred to finished goods inventory accounts for those costs. The total costs from August and September were accounted for by the costs transferred out of the process plus the costs remaining in process. This calculation offers a check on your work. If the total costs accounted for as either transferred out or still in process do not equal the beginning inventory plus current period cost (with due regard for rounding errors), you have made an error.

Although no other conceptual problems arise under process costing, one common situation increases the number of calculations and another common situation requires special care. The first is when units in work in process are not equally complete with respect to all components of manufacturing cost (materials, labor or machine time, and overhead). The second situation is when — as in most manufacturing companies — units pass through more than one department or process. The next two sections discuss these refinements.

MATERIALS AND CONVERSION COSTS

The Ronn Company example assumed that the same percentage-of-completion figure applied to all productive factors — materials, labor or machine time, and overhead. Such equality is unlikely because materials are usually put into process at an early stage. (Obviously, *some* materials must go into process immediately because you cannot work on nothing.) Labor and overhead are added more or less continuously. Thus, work in process inventories usually include all (or nearly all) of the necessary materials, but *always* less than the total required labor and overhead (else the units would be finished). Consider a company that refines sugar from sugar beets. At any given time, all of the beets in process are 100 percent complete with regard to materials: the beets must be in process before any work is done. But grinding beets into sugar takes time, so that in-process beets are not complete with regard to labor and overhead.

Converting raw materials into finished product requires labor and overhead — power, supplies, maintenance, and so on. Labor and overhead together are called **conversion costs** and are generally assumed to have the same completion percentage. In a machine-driven department where labor is insignificant, there might be only materials and overhead — no direct labor cost at all.

Differing degrees of completion for materials and conversion costs do not change the general formula for computing unit costs; they only require calculating costs separately for materials and conversion costs. We shall illustrate the computations using the data and computations of unit cost for Borne Company in Exhibit 15-2.

As before, we use these unit costs to determine the cost of the ending inventory of work in process and the cost of the units transferred to finished goods inventory.

Ending inventory:	
Materials cost (5,000 units × 100% × $0.80)	$ 4,000
Conversion cost (5,000 units × 60% × $1.20)	3,600
Total cost of ending work in process inventory	$ 7,600
Transferred to finished goods:	
Materials cost (45,000 units × $0.80)	$36,000
Conversion cost (45,000 units × $1.20)	54,000
Total cost transferred to finished goods	$90,000

Exhibit 15-2 Production Data for Borne Company for May

		Materials	Conversion Costs
Costs of beginning inventory		$4,000	$5,600
Production costs incurred in May		$36,000	$52,000
Unit data:			
Units completed	45,000		
Units in process at May 31	5,000		
Percentage of work complete		100%	60%
Equivalent production:			
Units completed		45,000	45,000
Equivalent units in ending inventory:			
5,000 × 100%		5,000	
5,000 × 60%			3,000
Equivalent unit production		50,000	48,000
Unit costs:			

$$= \frac{\$4,000 + \$36,000}{50,000} \quad = \frac{\$5,600 + \$52,000}{48,000}$$

$$= \$0.80 \qquad = \$1.20$$

Taking advantage of the checkpoint presented in earlier sections, we can see that the total costs are fully accounted for through the transfer of completed units and the costs assigned to the ending inventory.

Total costs to be accounted for:	
Costs in beginning inventory ($4,000 + $5,600)	$ 9,600
Costs for current month ($36,000 + $52,000)	88,000
Total	$ 97,600
Total costs accounted for as:	
Cost of finished units transferred to finished goods	$ 90,000
Cost of ending inventory	7,600
Total	$ 97,600

Thus, the different percentages of completion for materials and conversion costs require only that we compute different amounts of equivalent production and separate total costs by type. No new concepts are involved.

MULTIPLE PROCESSES

When a product passes through several processes, its total cost obviously must include the costs of all the processes. Suppose that Borne Company's manufacturing process includes a cutting operation (cutting large blocks of raw material into smaller blocks) and a sanding operation (refining the shapes to common specifications). The data in Exhibit 15-2 relate to the cutting operation and the 45,000 units that department finished were transferred to the Sanding Department. The cost of a unit transferred from sanding to finished goods includes the cost of both the forming and the sanding processes. The cost of a unit in process in the Sanding Department includes not only the cost of that operation but also the cost of the Forming Department.

Let us extend the example of Borne Company, whose basic production data for May appear in Exhibit 15-2. The 45,000 units completed in May were actually transferred to the Sanding Department. The Sanding Department adds no materials, so all costs it incurs are for conversion. Its overhead is closely associated with labor hours worked. Operating data for May for the sanding process follow.

Unit Data:
Units on hand at beginning of June	0
Transferred in from prior department (cutting)	45,000
Completed and transferred to finished goods	40,000
On hand at end of period (70% complete)	5,000

Cost Data:
Beginning inventory	$0
Transferred in from prior department	$90,000
Sanding Department's conversion costs for June	$156,600

The first step, of course, is to calculate the equivalent production for the sanding process.

Units completed	40,000
Equivalent units in ending inventory, 5,000 × 70%	3,500
Weighted-average equivalent unit production	43,500

So unit cost *for the Sanding Department* is calculated as follows:

$$\frac{\$0 + \$156,600}{43,500} = \$3.60$$

The cost of a unit transferred from sanding to finished goods is the $2.00 from the Cutting Department plus $3.60 from the Sanding Department, a total of $5.60. Finding the cost of Sanding Department ending work in process inventory requires two steps because the units have had all of the work done by the prior department, but only 70 percent of the work of the Sanding Department.

Ending work in process:
Cost from prior department, 5,000 × 100% × $2.00	$10,000
Conversion costs, 5,000 × 70% × $3.60	12,600
Ending work in process	$22,600

The total cost to be accounted for by the Sanding Department consists of the costs transferred in ($90,000), the costs in the beginning inventory (none), and the month's production costs ($156,600), or $246,600. That total is accounted for as follows:

Transferred to finished goods, 40,000 × $5.60	$224,000
Ending inventory of work in process	22,600
Total	$246,600

THE COST ACCOUNTING CYCLE

◀13 Chapter 13 presented an overview of the flow of manufacturing costs (Exhibit 13-1), noting that costs are first accumulated by object (materials, labor, and overhead) and are then passed on to Work in Process to Finished Goods and, **◀14** ultimately, to Cost of Goods Sold.[1] Chapter 14 noted that the choice between absorption and variable costing determines whether fixed manufacturing costs are inventoried or assigned directly to expense. Using journal entries and accounts, we show how these costs flow through the accounting records.

◀13 The transition from a set of ideas to an accounting flow is not difficult. Exhibit 15-3, which is but a minor variation of similar figures in Chapters 13 **◀14** and 14, translates cost flows to changes in specific accounts. Exhibit 15-3 also points out the difference between absorption and variable costing: the latter

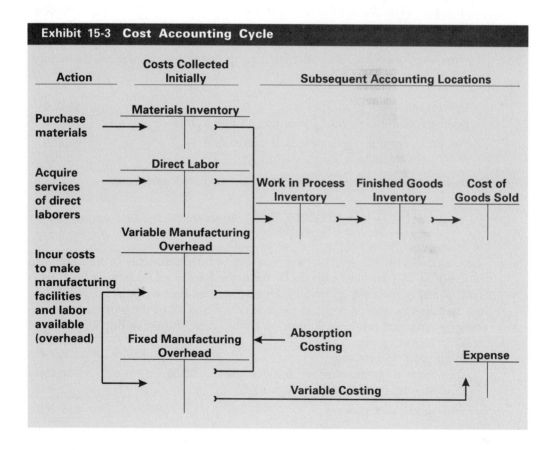

Exhibit 15-3   Cost Accounting Cycle

---

1 *Following the pattern in Chapter 13, we capitalize the names of accounts and use lowercase to designate the objects themselves. Thus "work in process" refers to physical, semifinished products, while "Work in Process" refers to the account.*

assigns fixed manufacturing overhead to expense in the period in which those costs are incurred. Absorption costing assigns fixed manufacturing costs to Work in Process; hence, they flow through Finished Goods and, ultimately, to Cost of Goods Sold. We shall concentrate our discussion of accounting entries on those relevant to absorption costing, but the application to variable costing, or throughput accounting for that matter, should follow naturally.

The two principal cost accumulation systems are process and job-order costing. Actual or normal costing can be used under either system, and standard costs can always be used by process costers and sometimes by job-order manufacturers. Despite the differences among the various combinations available, the journal entries to record the flow of costs differ little from one system to another because, as Exhibit 15-3 shows, there is a limited number of places for costs to be collected or transferred. The first illustration is actual process costing, the second is a job-order company using normal costing. We also illustrate standard costing in a simple setting to concentrate on the accounting issues specific to standard costing.

ILLUSTRATION OF ACTUAL PROCESS COSTING

Mason Company produces a special type of plywood. The manufacturing process requires sequential applications of layers of wood until the plywood reaches the required thickness. Mason had no beginning inventories of work in process. (The implications of beginning work in process inventories for the calculation of equivalent production were discussed on pages 710-711.) Mason had the following transactions in 19X5. (We omit explanations of the journal entries because the descriptions of the transactions serve the same purpose.)

Purchase of materials: Mason bought 1,400,000 feet of wood at $0.095 per foot.

1. Materials Inventory (1,400,000 × $0.095)	$133,000	
Cash or Accounts Payable		$133,000

Materials put into process: Mason used 1,300,000 feet of wood.

2. Work in Process (1,300,000 × $0.095)	$123,500	
Materials Inventory		$123,500

Direct labor: Direct laborers earned $344,400 for 41,000 hours of work at $8.40 per hour.

3a. Direct Labor	$344,400	
Cash or Accrued Payroll		$344,400
3b. Work in Process Inventory	$344,400	
Direct Labor		$344,400

Overhead costs incurred: Mason incurred the following overhead costs. For brevity we list only a few individual items, lumping the bulk of overhead costs into the "Other" category. Overhead costs are first recorded by type of cost.

4. Indirect Labor	$ 84,000	
Supplies	12,000	
Other Variable Overhead	155,300	
Supervision	74,000	
Depreciation	96,000	
Other Fixed Overhead	291,000	
Accumulated Depreciation		$ 96,000
Various, Cash, Accrued Expenses		616,300

Overhead costs usually are not put directly into Work in Process Inventory. Instead, they are gathered into either an account called Manufacturing Overhead or into two such accounts: one for variable overhead and one for fixed overhead.

5a. Variable Manufacturing Overhead	$251,300	
Indirect Labor		$ 84,000
Supplies		12,000
Other Variable Overhead		155,300
5b. Fixed Manufacturing Overhead	$461,000	
Supervision		$ 74,000
Depreciation		96,000
Other Fixed Overhead		291,000

The manufacturing overhead accounts are for convenience and are especially helpful when standard costing is used, as we shall show shortly. The amounts put into the manufacturing overhead accounts are now transferred to Work in Process Inventory.

5c. Work in Process Inventory	$251,300	
Variable Manufacturing Overhead		$251,300
Work in Process Inventory	$461,000	
Fixed Manufacturing Overhead		$461,000

Production: Mason finished 40,000 square yards of plywood. Another 3,000 square yards were still in process at the end of 19X5. These 3,000 square yards were two-thirds finished for both materials and conversion costs.

To transfer the cost of finished units to Finished Goods Inventory, we need the per-unit cost of production. Therefore, we need equivalent production, which is calculated as follows:

$$\text{Equivalent production} = 40,000 + (3,000 \times 2/3) = 42,000 \text{ square yards}$$

The 42,000 equivalent production is used to determine the cost per unit. At this point we have $1,180,200 in Work in Process Inventory, composed of the following costs. The numbers in parentheses refer to journal entries.

Materials (2)	$ 123,500
Direct labor (3b)	344,400
Variable overhead (5c)	251,300
Fixed overhead (5c)	461,000
Total	$1,180,200
Divided by equivalent production	42,000
Equals cost per unit	$ 28.10

The $28.10 cost per unit is used to transfer to Finished Goods Inventory.

6. Finished Goods Inventory		
(40,000 × $28.10)	$1,124,000	
Work in Process Inventory		$1,124,000

Sales: Mason sold 35,000 square yards at $40 each.

7a. Cash or Accounts Receivable
   (35,000 × $40) $1,400,000
      Sales $1,400,000
7b. Cost of Goods Sold (35,000 × $28.10) $983,500
      Finished Goods Inventory $983,500

Selling and administrative expenses: The company incurred $340,000 in selling and administrative expenses.

8. Selling and Administrative Expenses $340,000
      Cash, Accrued Expenses $340,000

At this point the accounts for direct labor, variable overhead, and fixed overhead all have zero balances. The other key accounts show the following:

Work in Process Inventory

(2)	$ 123,500		
(3b)	344,400		
(5c)	251,300	$1,124,000	(6)
(5c)	461,000		
	1,180,200	1,124,000	
Bal.	$ 56,200		

Finished Goods Inventory

(6)	$1,124,000	$983,500	(7b)
Bal.	$ 140,500		

Materials Inventory

(1)	$133,000	$123,500	(2)
Bal.	$ 9,500		

Cost of Goods Sold

(7b)	$983,500	

An income statement for Mason Company appears in Exhibit 15-4.

We said earlier that non-manufacturing organizations use product costing. The accompanying Insight describes a bank's use of process costing concepts.

ILLUSTRATION OF JOB-ORDER COSTING

Portland Mill Works makes industrial products that require work in two departments, stamping and assembly. The Stamping Department uses costly machinery and relatively little direct labor. Accordingly, the managers believe that machine hours (MH) is the appropriate measure of activity for applying overhead in that department. The Assembly Department is relatively labor

Exhibit 15-4   Income Statement for Mason Company—Actual Process Costing

Sales (7a)[a]	$1,400,000
Cost of goods sold (7b)	983,500
Gross profit	$ 416,500
Selling and administrative expenses (8)	340,000
Income	$ 76,500

a Figures in parentheses indicate journal entry numbers from the earlier illustrations.

Banks operate telephone service centers that answer inquiries about a variety of topics. Some banks have a center for each large department, such as the mortgage department. Because mortgage departments offer both fixed and adjustable rate mortgages, it is essential that managers determine the costs of servicing each type for pricing and for analyzing profitability. The traditional way that banks developed such costs was a simple process costing calculation:

$$Unit\ cost\ of\ call = Total\ cost\ of\ center/Total\ number\ of\ calls$$

Banks then allocated costs to each type of mortgage based on the number of calls related to each type.

Managers of a regional bank were concerned that the simple approach failed to recognize that some types of calls required considerably more time than others. The three basic types of calls are inquiries about rates and terms, inquiries about the status of mortgage applications, and problem solving/other. Inquiries about the status of applications took about the same time whether the application was for a fixed or adjustable rate mortgage. But problem-solving calls regarding adjustable rate mortgages took over twice the time as those regarding fixed rate mortgages. The bank incorporated the average time per call into the cost calculation, to develop a cost per minute.

The bank actually developed three cost-per-minute figures. One is based on historical costs. One is based on practical capacity, which gives the lowest possible cost and serves as a target. One is based on expected activity over five years and is used to estimate costs over the planning period.

Source: Gilbert Y. Yang and Roger C. Wu, "Strategic Costing and ABC," Management Accounting, May 1993, 33-37.

intensive, with machinery limited to small devices. The managers use direct labor hours (DLH) as the measure of activity for applying overhead in that department.

The company has established the following predetermined overhead rates.

	Stamping Department	Assembly Department
Total budgeted overhead	$600,000	$250,000
Divided by budgeted levels of activity	200,000 MH	100,000 DLH
Equals predetermined overhead rates	$3.00 per MH	$2.50 per DLH

Exhibit 15-5 presents the actual results for the year, including the overhead applied for each department.

Exhibit 15-5   Portland Mill Works, Results for 19X6

Activity Data	Totals	Jobs Sold	Jobs in Ending Work in Process Inventory	Jobs in Ending Finished Goods Inventory
Machine hours in Stamping Department	210,000	190,000	7,000	13,000
Direct labor hours in Assembly Department	95,000	80,000	5,000	10,000
Cost Data				
Materials used	$ 650,000	$ 580,000	$30,000	$ 40,000
Direct labor	800,000	720,000	20,000	60,000
Applied overhead:				
Stamping Department at $3.00[a]	630,000	570,000	21,000	39,000
Assembly Department at $2.50[b]	237,500	200,000	12,500	25,000
Total costs	$2,317,500	$2,070,000	$83,500	$164,000
Actual Overhead				
Stamping	$ 608,000			
Assembly	244,000			
Total	$ 852,000			

a Total, 210,000 × $3.00 = $630,000; jobs sold, 190,000 × $3.00 = $570,000, etc.
b Total, 95,000 × $2.50 = $237,500; jobs sold, 80,000 × $2.50 = $200,000, etc.

We can calculate misapplied overhead as follows:

Total actual overhead ($608,000 + $244,000)	$852,000
Total applied overhead ($630,000 + $237,500)	867,500
Total overapplied overhead	$ 15,500

The journal entries and accounts of a job-order company are similar in form to those of a process costing company (or one that uses standard costs). Job-order costing is a specific identification method, so that transfers from Work in Process Inventory to Finished Goods Inventory and to Cost of Goods Sold are based on the particular jobs finished and sold and do not require a cost flow assumption. For Portland Mill Works, the following entries summarize our knowledge of the flows. All of the information comes from Exhibit 15-5.

Materials used

1. Work in Process Inventory	$650,000	
Materials Inventory		$650,000

Direct labor

2a. Direct Labor	$800,000	
Cash or Accrued Payroll		$800,000
2b. Work in Process Inventory	$800,000	
Direct Labor		$800,000

Overhead incurrence and application (For brevity, we omit recording the specific items of overhead.)

3a. Factory Overhead—Stamping Department	$608,000	
Factory Overhead—Assembly Department	244,000	
Various Credits, Cash, Accrued Expenses, Accumulated Depreciation		$852,000
3b. Work in Process Inventory	$867,500	
Factory Overhead—Stamping Department		$630,000
Factory Overhead—Assembly Department		237,500

Completion of jobs

| 4. Finished Goods Inventory | $2,234,000 | |
| Work in Process Inventory | | $2,234,000 |

This entry is the total cost of all jobs completed during the year, which consists of the $2,070,000 cost of jobs sold plus the $164,000 cost of jobs still in Finished Goods Inventory at year end.

Cost of sales

| 5. Cost of Goods Sold | $2,070,000 | |
| Finished Goods Inventory | | $2,070,000 |

At this point, the various manufacturing overhead and inventory accounts appear as follows:

Factory Overhead—Stamping			
(3a)	$608,000	$630,000	(3b)
		$ 22,000	Bal.

Factory Overhead—Assembly			
(3a)	$244,000	$237,500	(3b)
Bal.	$ 6,500		

Work in Process Inventory			
(1)	$ 650,000		
(2b)	800,000		
(3b)	867,500	$2,234,000	(4)
	2,317,500	2,234,000	
Bal.	$ 83,500		

Finished Goods Inventory			
(4)	$2,234,000	$2,070,000	(5)
Bal.	$ 164,000		

Cost of Goods Sold	
(5)	$2,070,000

The amounts shown as ending balances in Cost of Goods Sold and the two inventory accounts agree with the amounts shown in Exhibit 15-5. The balances of the factory overhead accounts represent the overapplied or underapplied overhead for the departments. The net overapplied overhead of $15,500 ($22,000 overapplied in stamping minus $6,500 underapplied in assembly) agrees with the misapplied overhead computed on page 719.

◀13   What happens to the balances representing misapplication (actual different from applied) of overhead? As Chapter 13 stated, the $15,500 can be shown in the income statement, as an adjustment either to cost of goods sold or to gross margin. For financial reporting purposes, if misapplied overhead is material, the company must convert to an actual costing basis. Doing so requires allocating misapplied overhead to cost of sales and ending inventories based on the amounts of applied overhead in each account.

ILLUSTRATION OF STANDARD COSTING

Our final illustration of the cost accounting cycle is of a standard costing system. Virtually all such systems require that transfers of costs from Work in Process Inventory to Finished Goods Inventory be made at the total standard cost of units completed. But costs can be put into Work in Process Inventory in two ways: (1) put in actual quantities of inputs at standard prices or (2) put in standard quantities of inputs at standard prices. We shall illustrate the latter technique. We also note that standard product costing can be used without

◀12   using standard costs and variances to evaluate performance. As Chapter 12 stated, some companies do not use standards because they believe standards limit performance and stifle continuous improvement. Such companies can still benefit from using standard product costing because it is likely to be cheaper and simpler. They can do so without using standards and variances to evaluate performance.

Data for one of DMV Company's products appear in Exhibit 15-6. For simplicity, we assume that the company has no inventories of work in process — that it finishes the units it starts each day. With the information given, we can calculate variances as we make the entries.

One objective of a standard costing system is to isolate variances in the accounts as quickly as possible, instead of making separate calculations outside of the accounting system. Timely determination of variances helps in control because the sooner that managers know about variances, the sooner they can decide whether or not to investigate and possibly act.

The journal entries describing the events of March isolate price variances when the cost is incurred, which is when the variance first becomes known. They isolate quantity variances when costs go into process. Thus, the entries putting costs into process are made at the end of the period, when production is known, because you must know production to determine the efficiency variances and fixed overhead volume variance. As we have said, there are other possible patterns, but they all share the essential characteristic of standard costing: all inventories appear at standard cost at the ends of periods.

Materials purchases

1. Materials Inventory (30,000 pounds × $3)	$90,000	
Material Price Variance	2,000	
Cash or Accounts Payable		$92,000

Exhibit 15-6 DMV Company: Data for Illustration

Standard Costs

Materials (3 pounds at $3 per pound)	$ 9
Direct labor (2 hours at $8 per hour)	16
Variable overhead at $6 per DLH	12
Fixed overhead[a]	20
Total standard cost	$ 57

Results for March 19X6

Beginning inventory of finished units at standard cost (500 units × $57)	$28,500
Units produced in March	9,000
Units sold in March	9,200
Ending inventory of finished units	300

Costs in March

Materials purchased (no beginning inventory)	$92,000
Materials used, 26,000 pounds	
Direct labor (19,000 hours × $8.20)	$155,800
Variable overhead	$112,000
Fixed overhead	$198,000

a Budgeted fixed overhead $200,000 per month/normal capacity of 10,000 units.

Materials use

```
2. Work in Process Inventory
     (27,000 pounds × $3)              $81,000
         Material Use Variance                     $ 3,000
         Materials Inventory
         (26,000 pounds × $3)                       78,000
```

Direct labor

```
3a. Direct Labor (19,000 × $8)        $152,000
        Direct Labor Rate Variance       3,800
            Cash or Accrued Payroll                $155,800
3b. Work in Process Inventory (18,000 × $8)  $144,000
        Direct Labor Efficiency Variance     8,000
            Direct Labor                           $152,000
```

Variable overhead

```
4a. Variable Manufacturing Overhead
        (19,000 × $6)                   $114,000
            Variable Overhead Spending
            Variance                               $  2,000
            Various Credits, Cash, Accrued
            Expenses                                112,000
```

4b. Work in Process Inventory (18,000 × $6) $108,000
    Variable Overhead Efficiency Variance   6,000
      Variable Manufacturing Overhead $114,000

Fixed overhead

5a. Fixed Manufacturing Overhead $200,000
    Fixed Overhead Budget Variance $ 2,000
    Various Credits, Cash, Accumulated
    Depreciation   198,000
5b. Work in Process Inventory (9,000 × $20) $180,000
    Fixed Overhead Volume Variance   20,000
      Fixed Manufacturing Overhead $200,000

Completion of goods

6. Finished Goods Inventory (9,000 × $57) $513,000
    Work in Process Inventory $513,000

Cost of sales

7. Cost of Goods Sold (9,200 × $57) $524,400
    Finished Goods Inventory $524,400

The T-accounts for each type of inventory and for Cost of Goods Sold follow. The beginning balance in Finished Goods Inventory is the standard cost of the 500 units on hand at the beginning of March (from Exhibit 15-6). The ending balance reflects the standard cost of the remaining 300 units (300 × $57 = $17,100). Materials Inventory shows the standard price of the 4,000 pounds in the ending inventory, which is the 30,000 pounds bought less the 26,000 used.

Work in Process Inventory				Finished Goods Inventory	
(2)	$ 81,000		3-1 Bal.	$ 28,500	
(3b)	144,000		(6)	513,000	$524,400 (7)
(4b)	108,000			$541,500	$524,400
(5b)	180,000	$513,000 (6)	3-31 Bal.	$ 17,100	
	$513,000	$513,000			

Materials Inventory				Cost of Goods Sold	
(1)	$90,000	$78,000 (2)	(7)	$524,400	
3-31 Bal.	$12,000				

What is the disposition of the variance account balances? As with misapplied overhead, there usually are two alternatives: variances can be carried to the income statement as adjustments to either cost of goods sold or to gross margin, or they can be prorated among those accounts still containing the cost elements that gave rise to the variances. Thus, variances other than the material price variance could be prorated among Cost of Goods Sold, Finished Goods Inventory, and Work in Process Inventory. The proration of a material price variance also includes Materials Inventory if materials were still on hand. As stated earlier, the need for proration depends on the magnitude of the variances and the ending inventories, since GAAP accepts standard costs for financial reporting purposes as long as the income statement results of using such costs do not differ materially from the results under actual costing. However, what constitutes a "material" difference is a matter of continuing debate.

Virtually all accounting systems must serve several purposes. In the U.S., systems must handle externally imposed requirements of financial reporting and income tax compliance, as well as provide information managers can use to improve operations. Product costing is important in many legal settings, for example, in complying with provisions of international trade agreements. The accompanying Insight describes one set of requirements that a system must meet if a company hopes to benefit from the North American Free Trade Agreement (NAFTA).

PRODUCT COSTING IN AN ADVANCED MANUFACTURING ENVIRONMENT

Advanced manufacturers, such as JIT operations, usually have no significant work in process inventory and so have relatively few problems in accounting

INSIGHT

NAFTA gives preferences to products "made" in member countries. However, most modern products contain parts and components made in various countries. For instance, some automobiles consist largely of components made in Japan and the U.S. that are then assembled in Mexico or Canada. Determining a product's nationality is complex and fraught with elaborate allocations. NAFTA provides two ways of determining whether a product qualifies for preferential treatment, both of which require calculations involving transaction value or net cost. *Transaction value* is the price of the product, *net cost* is total cost less some enumerated costs including sales promotion, packing, shipping, and royalties.

Companies seeking preferential treatment for their products must be prepared to document their costs. Most companies will have some products for which they will not seek preferential treatment, so they must make extensive allocations of costs common to the two types.

Companies can calculate net cost in three ways, which differ only in the point at which they allocate manufacturing and nonmanufacturing costs to specific products. One method is to subtract the unallowable costs from total cost to determine net cost for all of the products the company makes, then allocate that amount to each product. The company can also allocate all costs to products, then subtract the unallowable costs. The third method is to allocate individual costs to each product, excluding the unallowable costs. After all this is done the company must calculate the percentage of cost incurred in the NAFTA member countries. The percentages vary by product, with 62.5 percent of the cost for cars and 60 percent for buses required to be incurred within the region.

Thorny problems can still arise. Can a Mexican manufacturer include depreciation on equipment bought in Austria (a nonmember country) as incurred within the region?

Source: Abdel Agami, "Accounting for NAFTA," Management Accounting, *May 1994, 30-33.*

for that type of inventory. Some operations might, however, have significant finished goods inventories, in which case product costing is still a concern. One technique used by such companies is backflushing, or backflush costing.

Backflushing concentrates on completed units, rather than on the units making their way through work in process. Backflushing therefore requires relatively few entries. Backflushers do not try to maintain Materials Inventory, Work in Process Inventory, or Finished Goods Inventory at their "correct" balances. Rather, companies using this technique maintain two inventory accounts, one for finished goods and the other for both materials and work in process.

Terminology and procedures vary, but the fundamentals are straightforward. The following example shows one way to record events using a backflush system. Data for the example follow.

Beginning inventories	None
Materials and components purchased and put into process	$250,000
Labor and overhead costs incurred	$180,000
Units completed	40,000
Units sold	35,000

Because materials are put into process almost immediately after being received, backflushing factories do not need two separate accounts for materials and for work in process. They might record material purchases in the following manner.

Materials and Work In Process Inventory	$250,000	
Cash or Accounts Payable		$250,000

Conversion costs are collected in a single account as follows:

Conversion Costs	$180,000	
Cash, Accounts Payable, Accumulated Depreciation, etc.		$180,000

The two entries are made throughout the period as events require.

Average cost of production for the period is $10.75 [($250,000 + $180,000)/ 40,000]. At the end of the period, the company records the cost of the ending inventory of finished units and the cost of units sold.

Cost of Sales (35,000 × $10.75)	$376,250	
Finished Goods Inventory (5,000 × $10.75)	53,750	
Materials and Work In Process Inventory		$250,000
Conversion Costs		180,000

The entry could also be made using standard costs, though JIT operations typically use actual rather than standard costs.

The pattern of entries shown is not the only possibility. Some companies charge all costs to Finished Goods Inventory on the basis of reports of the number of units completed, and make a transfer of Cost of Sales only at month-end. Because backflush costing has the potential for reducing the information provided to managers during an accounting period, it is best suited to a company with relatively stable levels of production activity and few work in process units.

Trane Co. uses a backflushing system along with standard costs. The company accounts for materials and conversion costs only when it finishes units. Using standard costs makes record keeping simpler.[2]

Backflushing is an instance of accountants reducing non-value-adding costs by reducing record keeping. Much of the analysis and work that management accountants have performed in record keeping has to do with reducing the volume of transactions by eliminating recording that is non-value-adding, while preserving information needed for managing operations. The accompanying Insight describes several ways that companies have tried to meet these objectives.

IN SIGHT

In an earlier chapter we said that a **Hewlett-Packard** operation eliminated 100,000 entries *per month* when it adopted JIT techniques. Other companies have had similar successes, often in eliminating detailed reporting on direct labor. The journal entries illustrated in this chapter are summaries of many entries made weekly or even more often, depending on circumstances. Eliminating such low-level recording not only reduces costs, but also frees up valuable resources, such as the time of management accountants, for more productive use. Instead of spending time explaining details of labor variances, management accountants can be performing more valuable analyses. The rest of this Insight describes two innovative approaches to product costing and record keeping.

Before **Borg-Warner's** Automotive Chain Systems Operation changed its production methods, it literally had piles of work in process inventory that necessitated very involved and detailed accounting. Work in process contained many defective units that remained undiscovered for long periods. The division now does not start a new batch until the previous batch has cleared a production process. The division uses cells and teams of workers, rather than assembly lines, and strives for continuous, level production.

Performance measures used to include the number of units produced, regardless of quality, which encouraged supervisors to produce as much as they could, increasing inventories and their associated costs. Now, departments are credited only with good units completed. Many workers were on piecework, paid for the number of units they made, which was clearly dysfunctional. All workers are now paid a daily rate.

Accounting is greatly simplified, with entries to record labor and overhead made only when units are finished, not periodically as costs are incurred. The system is much like the backflushing system described in this chapter.

Of greater importance than reduced and simplified record keeping is the better management information generated by the new system. Management no

longer pores over detailed reports of individual "piles" of work in process built up at each production station. Managers now look only at physical units and costs that pass through the entire process.

A technique called *engineered costs* greatly simplifies record keeping, as does standard costing, but differs from standard costing in several respects. Engineered costs are actual costs, not standard costs. Engineered costs have been validated by experience with factory operations and do not represent targets or goals as standard costs often do. **Best Baking Company** found that its production costs were barely fluctuating from month to month, so it simply used those costs to value inventory and cost of sales. The company was able to eliminate materials requisitions and time cards for its workers. Best updates its costs when material prices or wage rates change, or when recipes change. Using engineered costs greatly reduced record keeping at Best, freed up computer resources, and eliminated vast quantities of clerical time.

Validating engineered costs could take considerable time and some companies might never achieve the objective. Companies with rapidly changing products probably could not use engineered costs.

Sources: *Al Phillips and Don E. Collins, "How Borg-Warner Made the Transition from Pile Accounting to JIT,"* Management Accounting, *October 1990, 32-35.*
Richard P. Mager, "Valuing Production Using Engineered Costs," Management Accounting, *March 1993, 50-53.*

FINAL COMPARATIVE COMMENTS

We have illustrated the cost accounting cycle in four situations. We showed a processing company using actual costing, a job-order company using normal costing, an operation using standard costs, and finally, a JIT operation. At this point we pause to review briefly the many topics covered as part of our three-chapter discussion of product costing.

Any cost accounting system uses either variable costing or absorption costing, the difference being that only the latter assigns fixed manufacturing overhead to units of product. Any system must use either actual, normal, or standard costs. The nature of the manufacturing operation separates cost accumulation systems into job-order and process. Both types of manufacturers can use either absorption or variable costing, and actual, normal, or standard costs. (Job-order cost systems are least likely to use standard costs because of the uniqueness of the products made on the various jobs.)

Yet, with all these possibilities, the only real differences among the various methods and systems lie in the valuation of inventories. That is, total fixed and variable manufacturing costs incurred in a particular period are facts that do not depend on the costing system, so the choice of a cost system does not change *actual* costs. The different techniques are simply different ways of *assigning those costs to cost of goods sold and to inventories. If a company has no inventories, every one of the various approaches will give the same income on the income statement.*

Thus, managers who must use accounting reports to help them in decision making must know the basis used for those reports and must understand the effects that any given method has on those reports.

SUMMARY

The type of manufacturing operation determines whether a company uses job-order or process costing. Calculating unit costs under process costing is complicated by incomplete units of inventory at the beginning or end of a period. The concept of equivalent production is used to resolve this complication, but the existence of beginning inventories requires further refinement of the concept to adopt a cost flow assumption (weighted-average or first-in first-out).

The flow of costs through a manufacturing company can be accounted for in several ways regardless of whether a company uses job-order or process costing. Specifically, a company can use either actual or normal costing in the assignment of manufacturing overhead, or it can use standard costs. (In addition, of course, a company could use either variable or absorption costing, but the latter is required for external reporting.)

The journal entries to record cost flows are quite similar for all costing systems. They are more complex when standard costs are used, because entries under standard costing must isolate variances into separate accounts.

JIT operations, or others where work in process inventories are negligible or constant, can use simpler methods such as backflushing, which records far fewer transactions than conventional systems and therefore costs much less to operate.

KEY TERMS

backflushing (or backflush costing) (725)
conversion costs (711)
cost accounting cycle (714)

equivalent unit product (equivalent production) (709)
process costing (708)
weighted-average inventory method (709)

KEY FORMULAS

$$\text{Equivalent production—weighted average} = \text{Units completed} + \left(\text{Units in ending inventory} \times \text{Percentage complete}\right)$$

$$\text{Equivalent production—first-in first-out} = \text{Units completed} + \left(\text{Units in ending inventory} \times \text{Percentage complete}\right) - \left(\text{Units in beginning inventory} \times \text{Percentage complete in prior period}\right)$$

$$\text{Cost per unit—weighted average} = \frac{\text{Cost of beginning inventory} + \text{Costs incurred during the period}}{\text{Equivalent production—weighted average}}$$

REVIEW PROBLEM—PROCESS COSTING

Stambol Manufacturing Company makes a chemical solvent and uses weighted-average process costing. Data for April 19X8 are as follows:

Beginning inventory of work in process	$6,000
Materials used	$485,000
Direct labor	$648,000
Overhead	$604,000
Gallons completed and sent to finished goods	800,000
Gallons in ending inventory (75% complete)	40,000

Required
1. Determine equivalent production and cost per unit.
2. Determine the cost of the ending inventory of work in process.
3. Prepare a T-account for Work in Process Inventory. Check the ending balance with your answer to item 2.
4. There was no inventory of finished product at the beginning of April. During April, 730,000 gallons were sold and 70,000 gallons remained in ending finished goods inventory. Determine cost of goods sold and the cost of the ending inventory of finished product.

ANSWER TO REVIEW PROBLEM
1. Equivalent production and cost per unit.

Equivalent Production

Gallons completed	800,000
Equivalent production in ending inventory (40,000 × 75%)	30,000
Equivalent production for April	830,000

Cost per Unit—Weighted Average

Beginning inventory of work in process	$ 6,000
Costs incurred:	
Materials	485,000
Direct labor	648,000
Overhead	604,000
Total	$1,743,000
Divided by equivalent production	830,000
Equals cost per unit	$ 2.10

2. Ending inventory of work in process is $63,000 (30,000 equivalent units × $2.10).

3.

Work in Process Inventory			
Beginning balance	$ 6,000		
Materials	485,000		
Direct labor	648,000		
Overhead	604,000	$1,680,000 transferred out (800,000 × $2.10)	
	1,743,000	1,680,000	
Ending balance	$ 63,000		

The $63,000 balance equals the answer to item 2.

4. Cost of goods sold is $1,533,000, 730,000 gallons multiplied by $2.10. Ending inventory of finished goods is $147,000, which is 70,000 gallons (800,000 - 730,000) multiplied by $2.10.

REVIEW PROBLEM—STANDARD COSTING

Mason Company, whose actual operations were accounted for in the chapter, has changed to standard costing. It developed the following standards per square yard of plywood.

Materials (30 feet of wood at $0.10 per foot)	$ 3
Direct labor (1 hour at $8 per hour)	8
Variable overhead ($6 per direct labor hour)	6
Fixed overhead*	9
Total standard cost	$26

* Based on budgeted fixed overhead of $450,000 and normal capacity of 50,000 square yards ($450,000/50,000 = $9 per square yard).

Required

1. Using the actual results detailed in the chapter, calculate the variances from standard cost.
2. Prepare journal entries to record the events.
3. Prepare T-accounts for Work in Process Inventory, Finished Goods Inventory, Materials Inventory, and Cost of Goods Sold at standard.
4. Prepare an income statement for the year and contrast it with the one shown in Exhibit 15-4 that uses actual costing.

ANSWER TO REVIEW PROBLEM

1.

Materials Variances	
Price variance [1,400,000 feet × ($0.10 - $0.095)]	$7,000 favorable
Use variance {[1,300,000 - (42,000 × 30 feet)] × $0.10}	4,000 unfavorable

Direct Labor Variances

Rate variance [41,000 hours × ($8.40 - $8)]	$16,400 unfavorable
Efficiency variance {[41,000 hours - (42,000 × 1)] × $8}	8,000 favorable

Variable Overhead Variances

Spending variance [$251,300 - (41,000 × $6)]	$5,300 unfavorable
Efficiency variance {[41,000 hours - (42,000 × 1)] × $6}	6,000 favorable

Fixed Overhead Variances

Budget variance ($461,000 - $450,000)	$11,000 unfavorable
Volume variance [(50,000 - 42,000) × $9]	72,000 unfavorable

2.

1. Materials Inventory (1,400,000 × $0.10) $140,000
      Material Price Variance $ 7,000
      Cash or Accounts Payable   133,000

2. Work in Process (1,260,000 × $0.10) $126,000
      Material Use Variance   4,000
      Materials Inventory $130,000

3a. Direct Labor (41,000 × $8) $328,000
      Direct Labor Rate Variance   16,400
      Cash $344,400

3b. Work in Process Inventory
   (42,000 × 1 × $8) $336,000
      Direct Labor Efficiency Variance $ 8,000
      Direct Labor   328,000

4a. Variable Manufacturing Overhead
   (41,000 hours × $6) $246,000
      Variable Overhead Spending Variance   5,300
      Cash, Accrued Expenses $251,300

4b. Fixed Manufacturing Overhead $450,000
      Fixed Overhead Budget Variance   11,000
      Accumulated Depreciation $ 96,000
      Cash, Accrued Expenses   365,000

5a. Work in Process Inventory (42,000 × $6) $252,000
      Variable Overhead Efficiency
      Variance $ 6,000
      Variable Manufacturing Overhead   246,000

5b. Work in Process Inventory (42,000 × $9) $378,000
      Fixed Overhead Volume Variance
      (8,000 × $9)   72,000
      Fixed Manufacturing Overhead $450,000

6. Finished Goods Inventory (40,000 × $26) $1,040,000
      Work in Process Inventory $1,040,000

7a. Cash or Accounts Receivable
   (35,000 × $40) $1,400,000
      Sales $1,400,000

7b. Cost of Goods Sold (35,000 × $26) $910,000
      Finished Goods Inventory $910,000

8. Selling and Administrative Expenses $340,000
      Cash, Accrued Expenses $340,000

3.

Work in Process Inventory		
(2)	$ 126,000	
(3b)	336,000	
(5a)	252,000	
(5b)	378,000	$1,040,000 (6)
	1,092,000	1,040,000
Bal.	$ 52,000	

Finished Goods Inventory		
(6)	$1,040,000	$910,000 (7b)
Bal.	$ 130,000	

Materials Inventory		
(1)	$140,000	$130,000 (2)
Bal.	$ 10,000	

Cost of Goods Sold	
(7b)	$910,000

4.

Income Statements for Mason Company—Absorption Costing

	Actual Costing	Standard Costing
Sales (7a)	$1,400,000	$1,400,000
Cost of goods sold (7b)	983,500	910,000
Gross profit	$ 416,500	$ 490,000
Manufacturing variances:		
Material price (1)		$ 7,000F
Material use (2)		4,000U
Direct labor rate (3a)		16,400U
Direct labor efficiency (3b)		8,000F
Variable overhead spending (4a)		5,300U
Variable overhead efficiency (5a)		6,000F
Fixed overhead budget (4b)		11,000U
Fixed overhead volume (5b)		72,000U
Total variances		$ 87,700U
Gross profit		$ 402,300
Selling and administrative expenses (8)	340,000	340,000
Income	$ 76,500	$ 62,300

APPENDIX: PROCESS COSTING—THE FIFO METHOD

We stated in this chapter that we must choose a cost flow assumption (weighted average or first-in first-out) when work in process inventory exists at the beginning and end of a period.

The illustration in the chapter used the weighted-average method. It is just as reasonable — and intuitively more appealing — to argue that the costs incurred in the current period apply only to that portion of the work done in the current period. This alternative leads to the use of the first-in first-out (FIFO) method. Adopting this method changes the calculation of the unit cost for the current period because it affects both the numerator and the denominator of the calculation of current period unit cost. The numerator includes only the production costs of the current period, and the denominator includes only the work done during the current period.

ILLUSTRATION OF FIFO

To illustrate FIFO, let us return to the data used in this chapter to illustrate the weighted-average method. For your convenience, the data in Exhibit 15-1 are reproduced in Exhibit 15-7.

The company starts the month of August with no units in process. Hence, there is no need to know the cost flow assumption. FIFO gives the same result as does the weighted-average method.

The situation in September is different. In September, 90,000 units were completed and 10,000 were on hand, 40 percent complete. But of the 90,000 units completed, 5,000 units were 60 percent complete at the beginning of the period, so that the production costs for September apply to those beginning inventory units only to the extent of the 40 percent of the work done in September. Therefore, we calculate the cost of processing a unit of product in September by using only September's costs and an equivalent production figure that reflects only September's work. We already know that production costs in September were $191,400, so the task is to calculate equivalent production related only to the September work. The easiest approach is to calculate weighted-average EUP, then subtract the work done in August. Thus, the calculation of equivalent production for September using the FIFO method follows.

Units completed in September (90,000 × 100%)	90,000
Work done on units partially complete at the end of September (10,000 × 40%)	4,000
Weighted-average equivalent production	94,000
Less work done in August on units completed in September EUP in beginning inventory, (5,000 units × 60%)	3,000
Equivalent production, FIFO	91,000

We can generalize this calculation in this way.

$$
\begin{array}{l}
\text{Equivalent} \\
\text{production} \\
\text{—first-in} \\
\text{first-out}
\end{array}
=
\begin{array}{l}
\text{Units} \\
\text{completed}
\end{array}
+
\left(
\begin{array}{l}
\text{Units in} \\
\text{ending} \\
\text{inventory}
\end{array}
\times
\begin{array}{l}
\text{Percent} \\
\text{complete}
\end{array}
\right)
-
\left(
\begin{array}{l}
\text{Units in} \\
\text{beginning} \\
\text{inventory}
\end{array}
\times
\begin{array}{l}
\text{Percent} \\
\text{complete} \\
\text{in prior} \\
\text{period}
\end{array}
\right)
$$

Exhibit 15-7   Data for Ronn Company

	August	September
Production costs	$206,000	$191,400
Unit data:		
In process at beginning of month	0	5,000
Completed during month	100,000	90,000
In process at end of month	5,000	10,000
Percentage of completion for end-of-period work in process	60%	40%

Under FIFO, equivalent production reflects only work done during the current period. Thus, the calculation of FIFO unit cost uses only the production costs for the period. The formula under FIFO is as follows:

$$Unit\ cost-FIFO = \frac{Current\ period\ production\ costs}{Equivalent\ production-FIFO}$$

In our example, $191,400/91,000 = $2.1033.

The reconciliation follows.

Costs of beginning inventory (5,000 units × 60% × $2)	$ 6,000
Production costs for September	191,400
Total cost to be accounted for	$197,400

These costs either have been transferred to finished goods (for the completed units) or are associated with the units still in process. Under FIFO, the cost of the units in process at the end of the period is the unit cost for work done in September, or $2.1033 per equivalent unit. The cost assigned to the ending inventory of 10,000 units that are 40 percent complete is $8,413 (10,000 × 40% × $2.1033).

The costs transferred to finished goods can be determined by analyzing the units transferred.

Transfer of units that were in process at the beginning of the month:	
Cost from prior period, beginning inventory (5,000 × 60% × $2)	$ 6,000
Completion costs (5,000 × 40% × $2.1033)	4,207
Total	$ 10,207
Transfer of units started and completed in September	
[(90,000 - 5,000) × $2.1033]	178,780
Total	$188,987

Thus, the total cost of $197,400 can be accounted for as follows:

Costs transferred to finished goods	$188,987
Costs in ending inventory	8,413
Total cost accounted for	$197,400

If you compare the FIFO results with the weighted-average results shown in the chapter, you will see that the unit cost for September under FIFO ($2.1033) is slightly higher than that under weighted average ($2.10). Hence, the total cost of the ending work in process under FIFO ($8,413) is slightly higher than that under weighted average ($8,400). The magnitude of the difference is a function of the illustrative data; you should not assume that the difference will always be so small.

WHY CHOOSE FIFO?

At the start of this appendix, we suggested that FIFO is intuitively appealing. This is so because the costs incurred in a given period are applicable only to the work done during that period. The method is also appealing because it supports a manager's interest in controlling costs. The per-unit cost given by the weighted-average method is not suitable for control purposes because it mixes performance of the current period with performance in prior periods.

Because the unit cost calculation under FIFO uses (1) an equivalent production that includes only current work and (2) only the current period production costs, managers obtain performance data for different periods. From Chapter 12 we know that some companies establish standard costs for certain aspects of the manufacturing process, and that comparisons of actual costs with standards give managers useful information for control and performance evaluation. For a company that uses standard costs and process costing, FIFO is particularly useful because it does not intermingle actual costs from two periods.

ASSIGNMENT MATERIAL

QUESTIONS FOR DISCUSSION

15-1 Borden's costing methods A recent annual report of **Borden** stated that it operates a plant that produces *Cracker Jack*, bouillon, and dehydrated soup. The products share some productive facilities. Do you think the plant uses job-order, process, or standard costing?

15-2 Kinds of standards If you were president of a manufacturing firm, which of the following income statements would you prefer to receive and why?
(a) One showing actual costs only.
(b) One showing standard costs and variances, with standard costs based on ideal standards.
(c) One showing standard costs and variances, with standard costs based on currently attainable standards.

EXERCISES

15-3 Basic process costing Waste Specialities, Inc. uses weighted-average process costing. It makes its product from garbage and so has no material costs. The following data relate to July.

Beginning inventory, 6,000 units, 70% complete	$6,400
Units completed in July	30,000 units
Units in ending work in process, 60% complete	5,000 units
July conversion costs	$39,800

Required
1. Determine equivalent production for July.
2. Determine the unit cost.

736   *Part Four   Product Costing*

3. Determine the cost of the ending inventory of work in process.
4. Determine the cost of goods transferred to finished goods.
5. Prepare journal entries for the month. Use the account, Conversion Costs, to record the costs incurred.

15-4   Job-order costing—journal entries   Briscoe Machine Shop had the following activity in March. Briscoe uses actual job-order costing.

(a) The company used $5,120 in materials on jobs.
(b) Direct labor was $8,760.
(c) Factory overhead was $9,610.
(d) The cost of jobs finished was $13,660.
(e) The cost of jobs sold was $11,480.

Required
Prepare journal entries to record these events.

15-5   Basic process costing—weighted average   The following data relate to the operations of Sweeney Milling, Inc. for March. The company puts materials, labor, and overhead into process evenly throughout.

Beginning inventory, (8,000 units, 80% complete)	$8,880
Units completed in March	65,000 units
Ending inventory, 60% complete	15,000 units

Production costs incurred in March were $250,120. The company uses the weighted-average method.

Required
1. Compute equivalent production.
2. Compute unit cost.
3. Compute the cost of the ending inventory.
4. Compute the cost of units finished and transferred to finished goods inventory.

15-6   Basic process costing—FIFO *(continuation of 15-5, related to Appendix)*
Redo the previous assignment using the first-in first-out method.

15-7   Journal entries *(continuation of 15-5)*   Additional information about Sweeney's March operations follows.

Materials purchases, on account	$81,000
Materials use	$68,000
Conversion costs:	
Direct labor	$52,040
Overhead	$130,080

Required
Prepare journal entries to account for Sweeney's March operations using the weighted-average method and show a T-account for Work in Process Inventory.

15-8   Journal entries (continuation of 15-6 and 15-7, related to Appendix)   Refer to 15-6 and to the additional information in 15-7.

Required
Prepare journal entries to account for Sweeney's March operations using FIFO and show a T-account for Work in Process Inventory.

15-9   Relationships—income, production, and volume variance   Perkins Company sells a single product at $30 per unit. There are no variable manufacturing costs, and fixed manufacturing costs are budgeted at $400,000. In 19X5 the company had a standard gross profit of $280,000 and income of $174,000 on sales of 20,000 units. Selling and administrative expenses were $90,000, and fixed manufacturing costs were incurred as budgeted.

Required
1. Compute the standard fixed cost per unit.
2. Compute the volume variance for 19X5.
3. Determine how many units were produced in 19X5.
4. Determine what income Perkins would have earned using variable costing.

15-10   Relationships—income, sales, and volume variance   In 19X3, Bishop Company sold 102,000 units of product. Variable cost per unit was $6, both standard and actual. Standard fixed manufacturing cost per unit is $8 and selling and administrative expenses were $200,000. Fixed manufacturing costs were incurred as budgeted. Income for 19X3 was $224,000 after considering a favorable volume variance of $16,000. Beginning and ending inventories were the same.

Required
1. Determine the selling price of a unit of product.
2. Determine the level of volume used to set the standard fixed cost per unit.
3. Determine budgeted fixed manufacturing costs.

15-11   Process costing—T-account   Valley Manufacturing Company uses a process costing system. The following data apply to July 19X9. Percentages of completion are the same for materials and for conversion costs.

Units:	
Beginning inventory, 20% complete	3,000
Finished during July	35,000
Ending inventory, 60% complete	5,000
Production costs:	
Cost in beginning inventory	$23,700
Incurred during July	$766,700

Required
1. Compute the cost per unit of the units finished during the period, using the weighted-average method.
2. Compute the amount of ending work in process inventory and transfers to finished goods.
3. Prepare a T-account for Work in Process Inventory.

15-12   Process costing (continuation of 15-11, related to Appendix) Redo 15-11, using the first-in first-out method.

15-13   Backflush costing Timmins Company has completed the transition to just-in-time manufacturing and is attempting to simplify its record keeping. The controller has given you the following data for January and asked what is the simplest, most direct way to record the events.

Beginning inventories	none
Units finished	100,000
Units sold	90,000
Materials purchased and used	$455,000
Direct labor and manufacturing overhead	$640,000

There was no ending inventory of materials or of work in process.

Required

Determine ending inventory and cost of goods sold.

15-14   Backflush costing, journal entries (continuation of 15-13) Prepare journal entries for Timmins Company's January activity.

15-15   Backflush costing with standards (continuation of 15-13) Suppose that Timmons uses the following standard costs.

Materials	$ 4.50
Direct labor and overhead	6.50
Total standard cost	$11.00

Required

Repeat 15-13 using standard costs to value inventory. Show variances as adjustments to standard cost of sales.

15-16   Process costing—two departments The Westminister Plant of Byron Chemicals makes an industrial cleaner called Argot. The product requires two processes, mixing and distilling. The following data apply to May 19X7. There were no beginning inventories. Percentages of completion are the same for materials and for conversion costs.

	Mixing	Distilling
Barrels completed during May	70,000	70,000
Barrels on hand at May 31, 60% complete	9,000	0
Production costs incurred	$30,160	$49,000

Required

1. Compute the cost per barrel for each process.
2. Compute the amount of ending work in process inventory in the Mixing Department.

3. The company had no finished product on hand at the beginning of May. Of the 70,000 gallons finished during May, 60,000 were sold. Compute cost of goods sold and ending inventory of finished goods.

15-17 *Process costing* Hittite Company makes a water-soluble paint. All materials are put into process and are then mixed for several hours. Data for July follow.

Unit Data

Gallons completed in July	180,000
Gallons in ending inventory	30,000
Percentage complete:	
Materials	100%
Conversion costs	80%

Cost Data

	Materials	Conversion Costs
Beginning inventory	$3,240	$9,620
Incurred during July	$42,960	$127,060

Required

1. Using the weighted-average method, compute equivalent production for (a) materials and (b) conversion costs for the month of July.
2. Compute unit costs for each cost factor using the weighted-average method.
3. Prepare the journal entry to transfer the cost of finished gallons to Finished Goods Inventory.
4. Prepare a T-account for Work in Process Inventory.
5. Prove that your ending balance in Work in Process, from item 4, is correct.

PROBLEMS

15-18 *Equivalent production and unit costs* VanDoerr Company manufactures fertilizer in a single process. Data for April are as follows:

Beginning inventory of work in process	10,000 pounds
Completed in April	200,000 pounds
Ending inventory of work in process	40,000 pounds
Cost of materials used in production	$712,150
Conversion costs incurred	$321,080
Costs in beginning inventory:	
Materials	$84,650
Conversion costs	$19,400

The inventories were 100% complete for materials. The beginning inventory was 75% complete for conversion costs, and the ending inventory was 60% complete. VanDoerr uses the weighted-average method.

Required

1. Determine equivalent production for materials and for conversion costs.
2. Determine unit costs for materials and for conversion costs.
3. Determine the cost of the ending inventory of work in process and the cost transferred to finished goods inventory.

15-19   Equivalent units and standard costs (related to Appendix)   The production manager of Knox Company has just received his performance report for June 19X1. Among the data included are the following:

	Costs		
	Budget	Actual	Variance
Materials	$ 10,000	$ 11,400	$ 1,400 U
Direct labor	20,000	21,500	1,500 U
Variable overhead	15,000	15,400	400 U
Fixed overhead	18,000	18,800	800 U
Total	$ 63,000	$ 67,100	$ 4,100 U

The budgeted amounts are based on 2,000 units, the number actually completed during June. The production manager is upset because 600 units 75% complete are still in process at the end of June and are not counted as part of production for the month. However, at the beginning of June, 300 units were one-half complete.

Required

1. Compute equivalent unit production on a first-in first-out basis.
2. Prepare a new performance report.

15-20   Costing methods and pricing   The sales manager and the controller of Emerson Company were discussing the price to be set for a new product. They had accumulated the following data.

Variable costs	$8 per unit
Fixed costs	$160,000 per year

The sales manager had set a target volume of 20,000 units per year. He determined average fixed cost to be $8 per unit, bringing average total cost per unit to $16. The company follows a policy of setting prices at 200% of cost, so the sales manager stated that the price should be $32 per unit.

The controller said that $32 seemed high, especially as competitors were charging only $30 for essentially the same product. The sales manager agreed, stating that perhaps only 18,000 units per year could be sold at $32. However, he was convinced that the price should be set at 200% of cost. He added that it was unfortunate that fixed costs were so high, because he thought that 20,000 units could definitely be sold if the price were $30, and probably 24,000 at $28. However, it would not be possible to achieve the desired markup at those prices.

Required

1. Point out the fallacies in the reasoning of the sales manager. (You might wish to show what would happen at the $32 price. Would the company achieve the desired markup?)

2. Determine which price ($32, $30, $28) will give the highest profit.

15-21   *Overhead rates, standard cost income statement* The following data
pertain to the operations of Dickson Company for 19X5.

Budgeted production	100,000 units
Actual production	90,000 units
Budgeted costs for 100,000 units:	
Materials	$ 400,000
Direct labor	300,000
Variable overhead	200,000
Fixed overhead	300,000
Actual costs:	
Materials	350,000
Direct labor	280,000
Variable overhead	190,000
Fixed overhead	320,000
Administrative	400,000
Actual sales (80,000 units)	1,600,000

There were no beginning inventories. Dickson uses a standard fixed cost based
on budgeted production.

Required
Prepare a standard cost income statement. Show variances separately for each
category of manufacturing cost.

15-22   *Standard cost system—journal entries* Watson Company makes a single
product. Its standard cost is as follows:

Materials (2 pounds at $4)	$ 8
Direct labor (3 hours at $10)	30
Variable overhead ($6 per direct labor hour)	18
Fixed overhead (based on normal capacity of 50,000 units)	10
Total standard cost	$66

At the beginning of 19X9 there were no inventories. During 19X9 the following
events occurred.
(a) Materials purchases were 120,000 pounds for $455,000.
(b) Direct laborers were paid $1,490,000 for 151,000 hours of work.
(c) Variable overhead of $895,000 was incurred.
(d) Fixed overhead incurred was $490,000.
(e) Materials used were 95,000 pounds.
(f) Production was 48,000 units. All units started were finished.
(g) Sales were 45,000 units at $100 each.

Required
Prepare journal entries to record these events. Isolate variances as early as
possible.

15-23 Process costing—journal entries Swanson Company makes a single type of pump on an assembly line. The company uses process costing and applies manufacturing overhead at the rate of $12 per direct labor hour. Inventories at the beginning of 19X6 were as follows:

Raw materials	$ 34,000
Work in process	67,000
Finished goods	125,000

During 19X6 the following transactions took place.
(a) Materials purchases were $286,000.
(b) Wages earned by direct laborers for 35,000 hours were $289,000.
(c) Raw materials costing $271,000 were put into process.
(d) Other manufacturing costs incurred were

    (1) Indirect labor, $46,000
    (2) Supervision and other salaries, $182,000
    (3) Utilities and insurance, $23,500
    (4) Depreciation, $72,000
    (5) Other miscellaneous costs, $112,000

(e) Transfers from Work in Process to Finished Goods were $863,000.
(f) Sales were $1,314,000.
(g) Cost of goods sold was $818,000.
(h) Selling and administrative expenses were $387,000.

Required
1. Prepare journal entries to record these events.
2. Determine the ending balance in each inventory account.
3. Prepare an income statement for 19X6.

15-24 Product costing and CVP analysis The president of Landry Company asked for your assistance in analyzing the firm's revenue and cost behavior. You gathered the following data relating to the firm's only product.

Selling price		$ 10
Variable costs:		
Production	$4	
Selling	2	6
Contribution margin		$ 4
Fixed production costs		$120,000 per month
Fixed selling and administrative expenses		$30,000 per month

You calculated the monthly break-even point as 37,500 units and the monthly sales required to earn the president's $8,000 target profit as 39,500 units.

    Three months after you provided the analysis, the president called you. On your arrival at her office she gave you the following income statements.

	April	May	June
Sales	$380,000	$395,000	$420,000
Cost of goods sold	243,200	269,300	316,125
Gross profit	$136,800	$125,700	$103,875
Selling and administrative costs	106,000	109,000	114,000
Profit (loss) before taxes	$ 30,800	$ 16,700	$ (10,125)

The president is extremely upset. She asks why your analysis did not work, particularly because the production manager assured her that variable costs per unit and fixed costs in total were incurred as budgeted during the three months. The sales manager has also assured the president that selling prices were as expected.

After a few minutes you talk to the controller, who tells you the company uses actual absorption costing and produced the following quantities of product during the three months: April, 50,000 units; May, 40,000 units; June, 32,000 units. There were no inventories on hand at the beginning of April.

Required
Explain the results to the president. Show calculations of the determination of cost of goods sold for each month.

15-25 *Process costing* Stockton Company makes a chemical spray that goes through two processes. Data for February are as follows:

	Mixing Department	Boiling Department
Gallons transferred to Boiling Department	75,000	
Gallons transferred to finished goods		68,000
Gallons on hand at end of month	9,000	15,000
Percent complete:		
Prior department costs	—	100%
Materials	100%	— [a]
Labor and overhead	60%	40%
Costs incurred during February:		
Materials	$18,480	—
Labor and overhead	$32,160	$25,900
Beginning inventories:		
Gallons	8,000	8,000
Costs:		
Materials	$1,680	—
Prior department costs	—	$6,350
Labor and overhead	$4,020	$2,220

a No material is added in this department.

Required
1. Determine the weighted-average equivalent production by cost category for each department.
2. Determine the per-unit cost by cost category for the Mixing Department.

3. Prepare the journal entry to record the transfer from the Mixing Department to the Boiling Department.
4. Determine the per-unit cost by cost category for the Boiling Department.
5. Prepare the journal entry to record the transfer of product from the Boiling Department to Finished Goods.
6. Prepare the T-accounts for Work in Process for each department. Verify the ending inventory balances.

15-26   Process costing (continuation of 15-25, related to Appendix)   Assume that Stockton Company uses FIFO and that the beginning inventory in the Mixing Department was 60% complete as to materials and 70% complete as to conversion costs.

Required

1. Determine the FIFO equivalent production by cost category for the Mixing Department and the unit cost for each category.
2. Determine the total cost to be transferred to the Boiling Department.
3. Prepare a T-account for Work in Process in the Mixing Department and verify the ending inventory balance.

15-27   Standard costs—performance evaluation   Topham Company is opening a new division to make and sell a single product. The product is to be made in a factory with practical capacity of 150,000 units. Production is expected to average 120,000 units after the first two years of operation. During the first two years, sales are expected to be 80,000 and 100,000, respectively, with production being 100,000 and 110,000 in those years.

The product is to sell for $20, with standard variable manufacturing costs of $8. Fixed production costs are expected to be $360,000 annually for the first several years. Selling and administrative costs, all fixed, are budgeted at $300,000 annually.

Dee Yost, controller of Topham Company, has suggested that the normal capacity of 120,000 units be used to set the standard fixed cost per unit. The other managers agree that Yost's idea is sound, and Bill Van Der Meer, the controller of the new division, is given the task of developing budgeted income statements based on the data given.

The operations of the first year are summarized as follows:

Sales (77,000 units)	$1,540,000
Production	118,000 units
Costs incurred:	
Variable production costs	$ 954,000
Fixed production costs	370,000
Selling and administrative expenses	300,000

Required

1. Prepare a budgeted income statement based on the expected results in the first year of operations.
2. Prepare an income statement based on actual results.
3. Comment on the results. Was performance better than expected or worse? Explain.

15-28   Standard cost income statement—relationships and variances   The income statement for Rider Company for 19X6 follows.

Sales (200,000 units)		$2,000,000
Cost of sales:		
Materials	$300,000	
Direct labor	400,000	
Overhead	600,000	1,300,000
Standard gross profit		$ 700,000
Manufacturing variances:		
Materials	$ 12,000U	
Direct labor	18,000F	
Variable overhead spending	4,000U	
Variable overhead efficiency	8,000F	
Fixed overhead budget	7,000F	
Other underabsorbed overhead	20,000U	3,000U
Actual gross profit		$ 697,000
Selling and administrative expenses		600,000
Income		$ 97,000

Other data are as follows:
(a) There were no beginning inventories.
(b) Fixed overhead absorbed per unit is $2, based on budgeted production of 200,000 units, and budgeted fixed costs of $500,000.
(c) The standard direct labor rate is $4 per hour.
(d) Variable overhead standard cost is based on a rate of $2 per direct labor hour.
(e) Direct laborers worked 116,000 hours.
(f) The standard price for materials is $0.50 per pound.
(g) Materials purchases were 800,000 pounds at $3,000 over standard price.

Required
Determine the following:
1. Standard cost per unit, including standard prices and quantities for each element of cost.
2. Standard variable cost per unit.
3. Production for the year.
4. Ending inventory at standard cost.
5. Fixed overhead costs incurred.
6. Cost of materials purchased.
7. Material use variance.
8. Pounds of materials used in production.
9. Direct labor efficiency variance.
10. Direct labor rate variance.
11. Direct labor costs incurred.
12. Variable overhead costs incurred.
13. Amount by which income would have increased if one more unit had been sold, no more produced.
14. Amount by which income would have increased had one more unit been produced and sold.

15-29   Interpretation of standard cost statement   The following income statement represents the operations of c-Trin Company for June. Variable manufacturing costs at standard are 50% of total standard manufacturing cost. Standard fixed cost per unit is based on normal activity of 30,000 units per month.

c-Trin Company
Income Statement for June, 19X4

Sales (20,000 units)		$200,000
Standard cost of sales		120,000
Standard gross profit		$ 80,000
Manufacturing variances:		
Materials	$2,000U	
Direct labor	1,000F	
Overhead budget	1,000U	2,000U
		$ 78,000
Volume variance		24,000U
Gross profit, actual		$ 54,000
Selling and administrative costs		48,000
Income		$ 6,000

Required

Answer the following questions.

1. What are fixed and variable standard costs per unit?
2. What are monthly fixed manufacturing costs?
3. How many units were produced in June?
4. If beginning inventory of finished goods was $60,000 at standard cost, how much is ending inventory at standard cost? (Hint: Prepare an expanded cost of goods sold section.)

15-30   Income statement for standard costing, practical capacity (continuation of 15-29)   Assume the same facts as in 15-29, except for the following.

(a) Production is 22,000 units.
(b) Total fixed production costs are $90,000.
(c) c-Trin bases its standard fixed cost per unit on its practical capacity of 40,000 units per month.
(d) There were no beginning inventories.

Required

Prepare a new income statement. (Hint: The standard fixed cost per unit will not be the same as in 15-29.)

15-31   Standard costs, budgets, variances, journal entries   The following data relate to the operations of Warner Company for 19X2.

Budgeted sales (100,000 units)	$1,000,000
Budgeted production	140,000 units
Budgeted costs:	
Materials (2 pounds per unit)	$210,000
Direct labor (1 hour per unit)	420,000
Variable overhead ($1 per direct labor hour)	140,000
Fixed overhead—manufacturing	300,000
Selling and administrative (all fixed)	180,000

The company uses a standard cost system; the preceding production costs are based on standard cost per unit. Standard fixed cost per unit is based on 150,000 units of production at practical capacity. The inventory of finished goods at December 31, 19X1, is 13,000 units. There were no other inventories at December 31, 19X1.

Actual results for 19X2 follow:

Sales (95,000 units)	$950,000
Production	130,000 units
Materials purchased (250,000 pounds)	$192,500
Materials used	236,000 pounds
Direct labor (133,000 hours)	$402,000
Variable overhead	$128,000
Fixed overhead	$285,000
Selling and administrative expenses	$175,000

Required

1. Prepare a budgeted income statement for 19X2.
2. Prepare all necessary journal entries to record events in 19X2. The production manager is responsible for all variances except material price and labor rate.
3. Prepare an income statement for 19X2.

15-32 Actual process costing, journal entries, and income statement Wilberforce Company uses actual process costing. The following data relate to its operations in July 19X7. There were no beginning inventories.

(a) Materials purchases were $39,600 for 12,000 pounds ($3.30 per pound).
(b) Payments to direct laborers were $28,850 for 7,300 hours of work.
(c) Variable overhead costs incurred were $58,510.
(d) Fixed overhead costs incurred were $86,500.
(e) Materials use was 11,000 pounds.
(f) Units completed totaled 7,200. At the end of July 19X7, units in process totaled 500 and were 40% complete.
(g) Sales were 6,500 units at $50 per unit.
(h) Selling and administrative expenses were $106,000.

Required

1. Prepare journal entries for July.
2. Prepare an income statement for July.

15-33 Standard process costing, journal entries, and income statement (continuation of 15-32) The president of Wilberforce Company needs your assistance. She wants to know whether her company could use standard costing and how it works. She believes that the following standards are appropriate.

Materials (1.5 pounds at $3.20)	$ 4.80
Direct labor (1 hour at $4)	4.00
Variable overhead at $8 per direct labor hour	8.00
Fixed overhead at $12 per direct labor hour	12.00
	$28.80

The president tells you that the $12 fixed overhead rate is based on normal capacity of 7,000 direct labor hours per month.

Required

1. Prepare journal entries for July using standard process costing.
2. Prepare an income statement for July using standard process costing.

15-34   Special order   Western Corn Oil Company has found that its sales fore-cast for 19X6 was too high by about 40,000 cases of oil. Because the production budget was not revised, inventory is expected to be about 40,000 cases above normal at year end. In early December the sales manager was offered the op-portunity to sell 25,000 cases at $4.80, well below the normal price of $8. Regular sales would not be affected by the order. He asked the controller for an analysis of the order and was given the following partial income statement. The controller said that because general and administrative expenses would not be affected, it was only necessary to determine the effect on gross profit.

Expected Income Statements

	Without Order	With Order
Sales	$2,400,000	$2,520,000
Standard costs of sales, $6 per case	1,800,000	1,950,000
Standard gross profit	$ 600,000	$ 570,000
Volume variance	(120,000)	(120,000)
Actual gross profit	$ 480,000	$ 450,000

The sales manager was puzzled and asked the controller about the volume vari-ance. The controller replied that the volume variance related to production, not sales, and that production would not be increased because inventory was already too high. She said that the volume variance resulted because the company used 400,000 cases on which to base the standard fixed cost, and actual production was expected to be only 340,000 cases.

Required

1. Determine whether the order should be accepted.
2. Prepare new partial income statements, using variable costing.
3. Prepare a new partial income statement assuming that production would be increased by 25,000 cases if the order were accepted.

15-35   Job-order costing—standards and variances   Carlson Company makes a variety of furniture. The company has established the following standard variable costs for some of its high-volume models.

	Chair Model 803	Sofa Model 407
Materials:		
Wood	$ 24	$ 58
Fabric	46	92
Other	13	21
Total materials	$ 83	$171
Direct labor at $5 standard rate per hour	65	90
Variable overhead at $8 per direct labor hour	104	144
Total standard variable cost	$252	$405

During June the company worked on two jobs. Order 82 was for 80 units of Model 803, and order 83 was for 50 units of Model 407. Both jobs were finished and sold for a total of $97,000.

Cost data are as follows:

Materials used, at standard prices:	
Wood	$ 4,855
Fabric	8,360
Other	2,090
Direct labor (2,050 hours × $5 per hour)	10,250
Variable overhead incurred	16,850

Fixed production costs were incurred as budgeted, $24,600. Selling and administrative expenses were $18,700. There were no material price variances.

Required
1. Determine the standard cost of each job order, by individual cost category.
2. Determine the following variances: material use, by type of material; direct labor efficiency; variable overhead spending; variable overhead efficiency.
3. Prepare an income statement for June using standard variable costing. Show the variances calculated in item 2 as a lump sum.

15-36   Comprehensive problem on costing methods   The following data relate to Gagner Company operations for 19X5.

	Budgeted	Actual
Production (units)	200,000	180,000
Sales (units)	190,000	160,000
Direct materials	$400,000	$375,000
Direct labor	$600,000	$580,000
Variable overhead	$400,000	$395,000
Fixed overhead	$200,000	$208,000
Selling and administrative expenses	$700,000	$700,000

There were no beginning inventories; sales prices averaged $15 per unit; practical capacity is 250,000 units.

Required
1. Prepare income statements based on the following costing methods:
   (a) actual absorption costing.
   (b) standard absorption costing—fixed overhead based on budgeted production (show the total variance for each element of cost).
   (c) standard absorption costing using practical capacity as the fixed overhead allocation base.
   (d) standard variable costing.
   (e) actual variable costing.
2. Compare and contrast the results obtained in item 1.

15-37   Comprehensive problem on costing methods (continuation of 15-36)
Gagner Company now has data regarding operations for 19X6, during which selling prices again averaged $15 per unit. The following data relate to 19X6 activity.

	Budgeted	Actual
Production (units)	150,000	190,000
Sales (units)	140,000	200,000
Direct materials	$300,000	$400,000
Direct labor	$450,000	$590,000
Variable manufacturing overhead	$300,000	$410,000
Fixed manufacturing overhead	$200,000	$215,000
Selling and administrative expenses	$700,000	$720,000

Required

Prepare income statements for 19X6, using each of the methods listed in the previous assignment.

15-38   Standard costs and product profitability   Tucumcary Office Products Company makes three sizes of file folders. The company has practical capacity of 50,000 machine hours per year and uses that figure to set standard fixed costs for each size of folder. At the beginning of 19X6 the controller had prepared the following data regarding the three sizes of folders (all data per carton of 50 folders).

	Two-Inch	Three-Inch	Four-Inch
Selling price	$17.00	$24.00	$31.00
Standard variable costs	$ 8.00	$11.00	$16.00
Standard fixed costs	4.80	6.40	9.60
Total standard costs	$12.80	$17.40	$25.60
Standard gross profit	$ 4.20	$ 6.60	$ 5.40
Expected sales in cartons	44,000	25,000	30,000
Machine hours required per carton	0.3	0.4	0.6

The sales manager has informed the controller that he has been approached by a large office supplies chain. The chain wants to buy 24,000 cartons of a six-inch folder and is willing to pay $40 per carton. The sales manager discussed the offer with the production manager, who stated that the folders could be made using the existing equipment. Variable costs per carton should be $19, and 0.8 machine hours should be required per carton.

Because the chain will take not fewer than 24,000 cartons, the sales manager was fairly sure that the company did not have the capacity to fill the special order and still manufacture its other products in the volumes required by the expected sales. He therefore asked the controller to develop data on the proposed order and to decide which of the existing products should be partially curtailed. The controller then prepared the following analysis, which is incomplete because he was called away before finishing it. The sales manager was not sure how to proceed from this point and asked you to help him make the decision.

	Six-Inch Folder
Selling price	$40.00
Standard variable cost	$19.00
Standard fixed cost	12.80
Total standard cost	$31.80
Standard gross profit	$ 8.20

The controller also prepared the following analysis of budgeted profit for the year.

	Two-Inch	Three-Inch	Four-Inch	Total
Standard gross profit per carton	$ 4.20	$ 6.60	$ 5.40	
Expected volume	44,000	25,000	30,000	
Expected gross profit—standard	$184,800	$165,000	$162,000	$511,800
Expected volume variance				140,800
Expected actual gross profit				$371,000
Budgeted selling and administrative expenses, all fixed				327,000
Budgeted profit before taxes				$ 44,000

The company generally manufactures about as many cartons of each size of folder as it sells. Because it rarely experiences differences between standard and actual machine hours for given levels of production, it computes its volume variance based on the difference between 50,000 hours and actual hours worked.

Required
Prepare an analysis for the sales manager showing him whether the special order should be accepted and for which products, if any, production and sales should be reduced.

15-39   Review problem   Sally Ann Frocks is a manufacturer of dresses. Its relevant range is 1,500 to 5,000 dresses per month. For the month of May 19X5, it has prepared the following forecast.

Sales, 2,500 dresses @ $30 each
Variable manufacturing costs per dress:
  Materials, 3 yards @ $2 per yard
  Direct labor, 2 hours @ $0.50 per hour
  Variable overhead, $1 per DLH
Fixed manufacturing overhead, $3,000
Variable selling expenses, commissions at 10% of sales
Fixed selling and administrative costs, $6,000
Inventories:
  May 1, 19X5 none
  May 31, 19X5 materials, 500 yards; finished dresses, 500

Normal capacity is 3,000 dresses per month, which is the basis for overhead application.

Required
Answer the following questions.
1. What is practical capacity?
2. What is budgeted production for May?
3. How many yards of materials should be purchased during May?
4. How many hours does it take to produce a dress?
5. What are total variable manufacturing costs per dress?
6. What are total manufacturing costs per dress?

7. What is contribution margin per dress?
8. What is the cost per dress if variable costing is used?
9. What is the cost per dress if actual absorption costing is used?
10. What is the cost to produce one additional dress?
11. What is the cost to produce and sell an additional dress?
12. What is the predetermined fixed overhead rate per direct labor hour?
13. What are total budgeted manufacturing costs for May?
14. Give a formula for total manufacturing costs in the range of 1,500 to 5,000 dresses per month.
15. What would the predetermined fixed overhead rate be per direct labor hour if practical capacity were used as the base?
16. What is budgeted income for May?
17. What is the break-even point, in dresses?
18. By how much could budgeted sales fall before a loss was incurred?
19. By how much would income increase for each unit sold above budgeted volume?

15-40 Process costing, second department (continuation of 15-25 and 15-26, related to Appendix) The beginning inventory in the Boiling Department of Stockton Company was 50% complete as to conversion costs.

Required

Using the data from 15-25 and 15-26 and the above information, do the following.

1. Determine the FIFO equivalent production for conversion costs in the Boiling Department and the per-unit conversion cost.
2. Determine the total cost to be transferred from the Boiling Department to Finished Goods.
3. Prepare a T-account for Work in Process in the Boiling Department and verify the ending inventory balance.

15-41 Review of Chapters 12, 13, 14, and 15 ARC Industries makes fiberglass insulation, selling it for $20 per roll. The standard variable cost per roll is as follows:

Materials (25 pounds at $0.20 per pound)	$5
Direct labor (0.20 hour at $10 per hour)	2
Variable overhead at $5 per direct labor hour	1
Total standard variable cost per roll	$8

Budgeted fixed production costs are $1,500,000 per year.
ARC began 19X3 with no inventories. Actual results for 19X3 follow.

Sales (230,000 rolls)	$4,600,000
Production	260,000 rolls
Production costs:	
Materials purchased (7,000,000 pounds)	$1,425,000
Materials used	6,450,000 pounds
Direct labor (53,000 hours)	$520,000
Variable manufacturing overhead	$270,000
Fixed production overhead	$1,480,000
Selling and administrative costs, all fixed	$800,000

The company uses actual absorption costing for most purposes, though it has established standard variable production costs. The treasurer wants to see how standard costing works for income determination and asks you to prepare income statements using the two approaches. One statement is to be a standard variable costing statement, the other a standard absorption costing statement, with 250,000 rolls used to set the standard fixed cost.

Required
1. Determine all variances from standard costs, including the fixed overhead budget and volume variances.
2. Prepare the income statements that the treasurer requested. On each, show the variances as a lump sum subtracted from the standard gross margin or contribution margin.

15-42 Review of Chapters 12, 13, 14, and 15 (continuation of 15-41) During 19X4, ARC Industries produced 240,000 rolls and sold 250,000. The same standards and budgets in effect in 19X3 applied to 19X4, and the selling price remained at $20 per roll. Actual costs follow.

Materials purchased (6,200,000 pounds)	$1,210,000
Materials used	5,900,000 pounds
Direct labor (47,000 hours)	$475,000
Variable overhead	$240,000
Fixed production overhead	$1,510,000
Selling and administrative costs	$810,000

Required
Prepare income statements using the same bases as for 15-41. Again, calculate all variances and show the appropriate total as a lump sum on each statement.

15-43 Unit costs (CMA adapted) Wood Glow Manufacturing Co. produces a single product, a wood refinishing kit that sells for $17.95. The final processing of the kits occurs in the Packaging Department. An internal quilted wrap is applied at the beginning of the packaging process. A compartmented outside box printed with instructions and the company's name and logo is added when units are 60% through the process. Conversion costs, consisting of direct labor and applied overhead, occur evenly throughout the packaging process. Conversion activities after the addition of the box involve package sealing, testing for leakage, and final inspection. The following data pertain to the activities of the Packaging Department during the month of October.

Beginning work in process inventory	10,000 units, 40% complete
Units started and completed in October	30,000 units
Ending work in process	10,000 units, 80% complete

The Packaging Department's October costs were as follows:

Quilted wrap	$80,000
Outside boxes	50,000
Direct labor	22,000
Applied overhead	66,000 ($3.00/per direct labor dollar)

Costs transferred in from prior processing were $3.00 per unit. Cost of goods sold for the month was $240,000, and the ending finished goods inventory was $84,000. Wood Glow uses the first-in first-out method of inventory valuation. Wood Glow's controller, Mark Brandon, has been asked to analyze the activities of the Packaging Department for the month of October. Brandon knows that in order to properly determine the department's unit cost of production, he must first calculate the equivalent units of production.

Required

1. Determine equivalent units of production for the October activity in the Packaging Department. Be sure to account for the beginning work in process inventory, the units started and completed during the month, and the ending work in process inventory.
2. Determine the cost per equivalent unit of the October production.
3. Actual overhead incurred during October was $5,000 more than the overhead applied. Describe two ways the company could account for this amount.

CASE

15-44   *Cost of rejected units*   Pacific Compressors manufactures a variety of industrial equipment, but its Redwood Plant specializes in a single type of valve. The company uses the following standard variable costs.

Materials	$22
Conversion costs at $18 per machine hour	36
Total standard cost	$58

During March the plant produced 20,000 units, of which 19,000 passed inspection. The remaining 1,000 were scrapped. The variance report showed the following. The figures shown for "actual cost" are actual quantities at standard rates, so all variances are efficiency variances.

	Actual Cost	Standard Cost	Variance
Materials	$ 451,000	$ 418,000	$33,000U
Conversion costs	712,000	684,000	28,000U
Totals	$1,163,000	$1,102,000	$61,000U

The production manager and controller had never been satisfied with the variance report because a manager could not tell from the report whether variances related to efficiency or to rejected units.

Required

1. How many units were used in calculating the total standard costs for March?
2. Devise a variance analysis that shows separately the cost of rejected units and the efficiency or inefficiency with which the plant operated. How does your analysis improve matters?

PART FIVE

special topics

The last part of this book covers three topics that are often treated in managerial accounting courses, but that are also frequently included as parts of other courses. Chapter 16 introduces several quantitative decision-making techniques that are commonly employed in approaching real-world problems. Chapter 17 covers the cash flow statement. Chapter 18 introduces financial statement analysis and is geared primarily to the uses of financial statements by managers, creditors, and stockholders.

16
Quality and Quantitative Methods in Managerial Accounting

LEARNING OBJECTIVES

After reading this chapter, you should be able to

1 Describe and illustrate four categories of quality costs.

2 Understand the difficulties in determining quality costs.

3 Describe and apply statistical decision theory to several situations.

4 Prepare payoff tables.

5 Describe and apply linear programming.

6 Describe and illustrate sensitivity analysis and shadow prices.

7 Describe the theory of constraints, including the focusing steps.

8 Describe and illustrate learning curves.

"Find your main bottleneck and attack it relentlessly." said Fred Wenninger, CEO of **Iomega**, a high-tech manufacturer. Wenninger believes that reducing cycle time is the best way for a small company to increase quality. Low cycle times mean that inventories cannot pile up and therefore defects appear immediately. Workers can then isolate the cause of the defects and correct it before they run off a large number of defective units. Wenninger pointed out that "When your cycle is 28 days and you spot a defect at the end of the line, you can imagine how hard it is to isolate the problem."

Procter & Gamble follows a "value strategy," meaning that it strives to give customers high-quality products at reasonable prices, partly through continuously improving products and operations. **First Union** and other banks use sophisticated statistical models to determine their exposure to risks of changes in interest rates and decide how to respond.

> *What is the role of managerial accountants in product quality?*
> *What sorts of tools are available for analyzing risk and uncertainty?*

Sources: "Quality," Business Week, *November 30, 1992, 67-70; Procter & Gamble 1995 annual report, 3-7; First Union 1995 annual report, 28-30.*

Earlier chapters have stressed the importance of quality and continuous improvement. This chapter discusses the costs of quality, including two competing views of the behavior of those costs. This chapter also covers a selected group of quantitative methods of analyzing decisions. We have stressed throughout this book that making decisions requires considering both quantitative and qualitative factors. Increases in the mathematical sophistication of managers and the availability of computers have refined the uses of quantifiable data in decision making.

Any manager, and most certainly a managerial accountant, should be familiar with these techniques, their uses, and their limitations. First, managers must be able to describe the problems and to specify the relevant information to the specialist who sets up and solves them. Second, managers must be able to comprehend what the specialist is saying and grasp the basics of the proposed solution. Third, managers must understand the limitations of a given technique, so that they can evaluate the applicability of a proposed technique to the problem at hand and suggest changes if the proposed solution appears to be ineffective.

COST OF QUALITY

 The emphasis on quality we began discussing in Chapter 1 has caused accountants and other managers to rethink many ideas about the cost of increasing quality. At various places throughout this book we have described companies' efforts at increasing quality. Experts have estimated the **cost of quality**, defined as the cost of not doing it right the first time, to American businesses in the range of 10 to 30 percent of sales. A simple definition was adopted by the president of **Kodak**, who, in the 1994 annual report, said of the cost of quality, "It's basically the sum of all costs that would disappear if we did everything right the first time. Corporations like Kodak spend lots of time looking over people's shoulders to assure quality. That costs money. We want to get rid of that cost and still produce the quality."

We can analyze and categorize quality costs in several ways. One set of categories is costs of conformance to quality standards versus costs of nonconformance. Further subdivisions of costs of conformance are prevention costs and appraisal costs. Subdivisions of costs of nonconformance are internal failure costs and external failure costs. (We can also classify quality costs as voluntary and involuntary, with prevention and appraisal costs being voluntary and internal and external failure costs being involuntary.[1] The advantage of this classification is that it focuses on what the organization can do and the consequences of its inability to eliminate failure.) These four categories are

---

1 *Lawrence P. Carr and Thomas Tyson, "Planning Quality Cost Expenditures,"* Management Accounting, *October 1992, 52-56.*

generally acknowledged as capturing the relevant elements. Exhibit 16-1 lists a variety of examples of each type of cost.

MEASURING QUALITY COSTS

Measuring and reporting the total cost of quality is extremely difficult. A glance at external failure costs reveals that some are opportunity costs and cannot be known, only estimated. How can a company determine the cost of losing future sales to dissatisfied customers, let alone the cost of those customers telling other people of their bad experiences? One analysis suggests that opportunity costs are three to four times cash costs of failure.[2] Some observers in the automobile

Exhibit 16-1   Quality Costs

Prevention costs, incurred to increase the likelihood that products will meet quality standards

- design costs
- costs of improving production processes and methods
- costs of upgrading worker skills and instilling in them the importance of quality
- higher wages paid to workers who produce higher quality work
- preventative maintenance

Appraisal costs, incurred to determine whether particular units of product meet quality standards

- inspection costs for materials, semifinished units, and finished units
- costs of automated monitoring of processes and products, such as lasers that scan products for defects
- cost of maintaining a laboratory to test for conformance to specifications

Internal failure costs, incurred when company determines that specific units do not meet quality standards

- lost contribution margin on lost output
- cost to repair or rework defective units
- cost of defective units that must be scrapped
- cost of downtime on machinery while rework is done
- cost to readjust malfunctioning machinery

External failure costs, incurred when a unit of product fails to perform to customers' expectations

- cost to repair or replace returned units
- cost of processing customer complaints
- cost to send servicepeople to customer's premises
- ill-will of customers who might not buy from you again, and might inform others of problems with your products

---

2 Francis X. Brown and Roger W. Kane, "Quality Cost and Profit Performance," in Quality Costs: Ideas and Applications, *American Society for Quality Control, Milwaukee, WI, 1984, 203-9.*

industry believe that satisfied customers tell 8 people about their cars, while dissatisfied customers tell 22 people about their problems.[3] They hesitate to suggest how many of the 22 are deterred from buying a particular company's cars, so they are still a step away from estimating the cost of having a dissatisfied customer.

Serious difficulties work against determining whether some costs relate to quality at all, and if so, whether they might belong to one category or another. Do all training costs advance quality? How about worker safety programs? Such costs have some relationship to quality, but serious allocation problems arise with many costs that are common to several purposes.

For many years managers believed that total quality costs plotted against the number or percentage of defective units (or of good units) was a saucer-shaped curve, such as that depicted in Panel A of Exhibit 16-2. Prevention and appraisal costs increase as the company produces a higher percentage of good units, while failure costs, both internal and external, fall. Thus, as the percentage of good

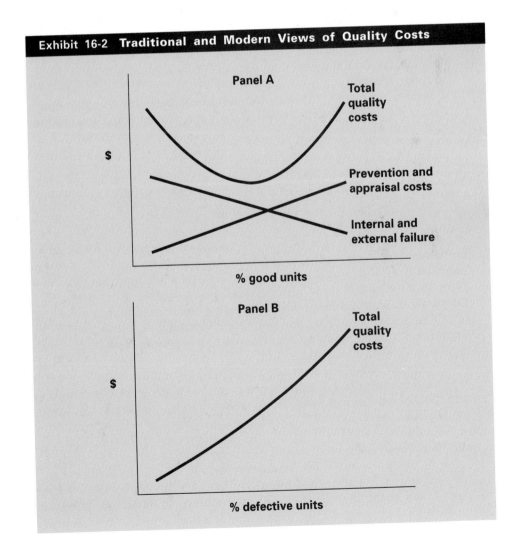

Exhibit 16-2 Traditional and Modern Views of Quality Costs

3 *Carr and Tyson, op. cit.,* 53.

units rises (or of defective units goes down) *total quality costs* decline, but then begin to rise because the costs of preventing defectives exceed the costs of producing defectives. Using this model, the idea was to find the optimal percentage of defectives, where total costs were lowest. This view accepts some percentage of defectives as normal and regards the pursuit of zero defects as not cost-effective.

The saucer-shaped curve and approach to finding the optimal percentage of defects is now in disrepute. Many managers now believe that total quality costs continually decline as defects decline. One major reason for the new way of thinking is the more comprehensive view of costs that now prevails. Many managers now believe that the costs of defectives rise so fast that the total cost curve never goes up regardless of expenditures on prevention and appraisal. Such a curve is depicted in Panel B of Exhibit 16-2.

The traditional view of quality included the ideas that workers were responsible for defects, that periodic inspection was the way to catch defects, and that an "acceptable level" of quality existed that the company should try to achieve, but not exceed. The modern view is that increasing quality decreases total costs, expressed by one expert as "quality is free." The accompanying Insight describes **Xerox's** experience with evaluating quality costs as well as an initiative **Ford Motor Company** uses as part of its view that quality is an important strategic weapon.

Increasing quality involves techniques discussed in the following section. Part of evaluating quality includes analyzing statistics and interpreting trends in defectives.

INSIGHT

Some companies have found that concentrating on quality actually reduces costs, which accords with the view of many experts in the field. **Xerox Corporation** is a good example, having saved considerable amounts of money by increasing the quality of its business processes, as well as its products. The **US Customer Operations** group (USCO), a service business, applied cost of quality (COQ) principles and saved the company $200 million in four years. USCO set up various projects using multifunctional teams to find areas of the business process that were not working well.

One project involved reducing the $22 million annual cost (7.3 percent of revenues) of excess and obsolete spare parts. The team of experts from several areas of the business met weekly until the solution was implemented. They first established a benchmark of 2.1 percent of sales, then studied the problems. One of their findings was that no end-of-life strategy existed. No one told anyone else that the need for a part would cease, leading to unexpectedly high inventories at phase-out time. The team recommended a communication network between product planners and parts planners. Another finding was that spare parts failed at too high a rate based on engineering standards. They recommended making engineering responsible for the failure rate so that it had incentives to design in quality.

USCO ran into apathy as projects were completed and improvements made. One response was to report on quality costs quarterly to maintain the focus of managers.

Ford Motor Company has long accepted quality as a strategic imperative. Its advertising stresses that it considers quality Job 1. Ford also operates, as do other auto manufacturers, a Customer Assistance Center, where from 120 to 140 people answer customers' questions and register their complaints. Service representatives are college graduates destined for the marketing department, or temporaries hired from an agency. All get four and a half weeks of training, including two days spent learning how to handle irate customers.

A large screen in the Center continuously flashes the number of callers waiting for a live representative. An average call takes two minutes. Calls range from customers who want refunds on alleged lemons to those wanting to know how to set the clock, a popular topic when time changes go into effect.

Representatives will not recommend specific dealers because **Ford's** franchising agreements with its dealers precludes it, but the representative will divulge the names of dealers cited as Chairman's Award winners. Ford recognizes these dealers for outstanding customer service.

How would you classify the cost of maintaining the Center? Is it appraisal cost, or perhaps external failure cost? Not a quality cost at all? The cost is common to several functions, including marketing, as well as quality. Many of the calls do not relate to quality, the ones about setting the clock, for example. Some might argue, however, that people make such calls because it is too difficult to read the owners's manual, which most would consider a quality defect.

Source: Lawrence P. Carr, "How Xerox Sustains the Cost of Quality," Management Accounting, August 1995, 26-37.

STATISTICAL DECISION THEORY

We applied the expected value concept to sales forecasting in Chapter 6 when managers believed that several outcomes were possible and assigned probabilities to each of these outcomes. The concept is applicable to many other situations, including variance investigation, which we introduced in Chapter 12.

Chapter 12 stated that a variance should be investigated when the expected savings from investigation exceed the cost of the investigation. Suppose a $300 variance has occurred and is expected to continue for six months if not corrected. Investigating to find the cause will cost nothing. But the chances are about 80 percent that even after identifying the cause, the variance cannot be corrected. The expected values of the costs of investigating and of not investigating are summarized below.

Choice 1—Do Not Investigate	
Expected cost of $300 for six months	$1,800

Choice 2—Investigate

Event	Probability of Event	×	Conditional Value	=	Expected Value
Cause is correctable	.20		0		0
Cause is not correctable	.80		$1,800		$1,440
Total	1.00				$1,440

It is worthwhile to investigate the variance; it costs nothing to investigate, and there are potential savings of $1,800. The $360 ($1,800 - $1,440) difference between expected values has special significance. It is the maximum amount you would be willing to spend to investigate whether the variance can be corrected. This amount is called the value of perfect information, which is the difference between (1) the expected value of the best alternative, given the existing information, and (2) the expected value of alternatives when you know in advance what event will occur. One point to note is that the probabilities sum to one, or 100 percent. *Something* must be true, the cause is, or is not, correctable. Be sure that your probabilities add up to one.

To confirm that $360 is the maximum you would pay to investigate the variance, suppose that it will cost $360 to investigate. What are the expected values (costs) of the two choices?

Choice 1—Do Not Investigate

Cost of $300 for six months	$1,800

Choice 2—Investigate

Event	Probability of Event	×	Conditional Value	=	Expected Value
Cause is correctable	.20		$ 360[a]		$ 72
Cause is not correctable	.80		2,160[b]		1,728
Total	1.00				$1,800

a *The cost to investigate will be incurred.*
b *The cost to investigate plus the cost of the continued variance will be incurred.*

Thus, the expected cost of both choices is the same.

Let us modify the circumstances. The cost to investigate the variance is $200 and there is a 30 percent probability that the variance was caused by a random disturbance and will not continue beyond the first period. The usual expected value approach can be used under these circumstances also. The analysis follows.

Choice 1—Do Not Investigate

Event	Probability of Event	×	Conditional Value	=	Expected Value
Variance is random, will stop without action	.30		0		0
Variance will continue	.70		$1,800		$1,260
Total	1.00				$1,260

Choice 2—Investigate

Event	Probability of Event	×	Conditional Value	=	Expected Value
Variance is random, will stop without action	.30		$ 200		$ 60
A problem exists that can be corrected	.14[a]		200		28
A problem exists that cannot be corrected	.56[b]		2,000		1,120
Total	1.00				$1,208

a The 20% chance of being able to take corrective action now applies to only 70% of the cases. The probability thus becomes 70% × 20%, or 14%. (Remember the total probabilities must be 1.0.)
b Same reasoning as in Note a except that the probability of there being an uncorrectable problem is 70% × 80%, or 56%.

Under the new conditions, the expected cost of investigating ($1,208) is still less than the expected cost of not investigating ($1,260). But the difference between the two choices is less ($52 as opposed to $360). This makes sense because not only is there a cost to investigate, but now there is a 30 percent chance that you do not have to do anything and the variance will stop.

Another approach to solving the problem is the **decision tree**, a commonly used device that provides a graphical representation of the problem. The tree for this decision, shown in Exhibit 16-3, works essentially the same as the

Exhibit 16-3   Decision Tree

		Cost ($)	Probability	Expected values ($)
Do not investigate	No problem, variance stops—30%	0	.30	0
	Problem, variance continues—70%	1,800	.70 / 1.00	1,260 / 1,260
Do investigate	No problem, variance stops—30%	200	.30	60
	Problem exists—70% / Can be corrected— 70% × 20%	200	.14	28
	Cannot be corrected— 70% × 80%	2,000	.56 / 1.00	1,120 / 1,208

tabular format but has the advantage of allowing a step-by-step determination of probabilities when there are several possible events within other events (such as the 80 to 20 percent probabilities within the 70 percent probability). Both approaches show that the expected cost of investigating is less than the expected cost of not investigating.

A CAVEAT

Relying solely on expected values is not always wise. Consider a simpler example. Suppose you were given the following choices: (1) take $10,000 now or (2) flip a coin, heads you win $40,000, tails you lose $10,000. Compute the expected values (assuming an honest coin, of course).

Choice 1—A certain gain of $10,000.

Choice 2—An expected value of $10,000, as indicated below.

Event	Probability	×	Conditional Value	=	Expected Value
Heads	.50		$40,000		$20,000
Tails	.50		-10,000		- 5,000
	1.00				$15,000

Choice 2 has a higher expected value, but unless you have a great deal of money, you probably would not select choice 2. The difficulty with relying solely on the expected value is that the concept is based on probabilities, and probability theory is based on mathematical laws that govern large numbers of occurrences. If you had 1,000 chances to play the game, you could expect the odds to work in your favor and you should win a substantial sum. But with only one try, you do not have the laws of large numbers on your side. You therefore have a 50 percent probability of losing $10,000, an event most people would shy away from.

Operations researchers incorporate such considerations into the simple expected value model by attaching utilities to the various outcomes. Utility represents the degree of "better-offness" or "worse-offness" associated with the events. By using utilities, operations researchers recognize that generally it detracts more from your well-offness to lose $10,000 than is added by winning $40,000. But assigning utilities to outcomes is a matter of judgment, and assigned values differ markedly depending on who is doing the choosing. Different managers make different decisions, even if they all use the same data. Some are more willing than others to accept risks. We consider this point in more detail in the following section.

PAYOFF TABLES

Managers use the expected value concept most often when they must make the same decision several times and have several available strategies with probabilities attached to the possible outcomes of each. A typical application is deciding how many units of a product to buy (or make) when there are given probabilities for sales and the unsold units are discarded or sold at substantial losses.

Suppose a florist must decide how many corsages to buy each week. All units must be bought in advance and no additional purchases are possible once the week has begun. Unsold corsages are discarded. The florist has estimated the following demand. (For computational simplicity we assume only three possible outcomes. Computers make it possible to analyze more realistic situations quickly.)

Demand in Units	Probability of Demand
4,000	20%
8,000	50%
12,000	30%

The variable cost per corsage is $6 and the selling price is $10. Because the florist purchases the corsages in advance and discards unsold ones, it loses $6 on each unsold corsage. This is the problem with a perishable good: buying (or making) more than can be sold brings a penalty of the variable cost of the unsold units (less any salvage value, or plus any disposal cost). Perishability is an economic concept, not a physical one. Corsages deteriorate rapidly; newspapers do not. But day-old newspapers do not sell any better than wilted flowers. High-fashion goods are another example of a perishable good in the economic sense.

The approach to analyzing the purchasing decision for perishable goods is to prepare **payoff tables**. For each purchasing strategy, prepare a table of **conditional values**, profits earned given the strategy and demand, without regard to the probabilities of each event. Then prepare a second table that shows the **expected values** (that is, considering the probabilities) of each strategy. (We could combine the tables, but that makes it much harder to follow the logic.) Exhibit 16-4 shows the conditional values.

Each entry in the table is the contribution margin, or loss, from that particular combination of demand and purchases. Thus, if the company bought 4,000 units, it would sell 4,000 units no matter what the demand because it could not buy any more even if it learned that buyers would demand 8,000 or 12,000 units. Hence, if purchases are 4,000 units, the company will earn $16,000 contribution margin by selling 4,000 units ($4 per unit × 4,000 units) and will lose nothing by having to discard units bought but not sold.

If the company buys 8,000 units and can sell only 4,000 units, costs will be $48,000 (8,000 × $6) and revenues only $40,000 (4,000 × $10), for a loss of $8,000. Put another way, the company earns $16,000 contribution margin on the 4,000

Exhibit 16-4 Conditional Values of Strategies

	Strategy: Purchases of		
Event: Demand	4,000	8,000	12,000
4,000	$16,000	$ (8,000)	$(32,000)
8,000	16,000	32,000	8,000
12,000	16,000	32,000	48,000

units sold but loses $6 per unit for the 4,000 unsold units discarded. If the company did sell 8,000 units, it would earn revenues of $80,000, have costs of $48,000, and a contribution margin of $32,000 ($4 × 8,000). The same contribution margin would be earned if the company could have sold 12,000 units but only sold 8,000, because only 8,000 were purchased.

The next step is to compute the expected value of each possible outcome, using the probabilities of demand. Exhibit 16-5 summarizes the expected values.

Notice that the expected value of the strategy of purchasing 4,000 units ($16,000) is equal to the conditional value of each outcome: demand of 4,000, 8,000, and 12,000. This should not be surprising, because the company can sell only 4,000 units if it buys only that many. The problem with that strategy is that the company foregoes contribution margin if it could have sold more than 4,000 units.

Notice also that the outcomes, both conditional and expected values, of buying 12,000 units are more widely dispersed than the others. We would expect this because the more you buy and sell, the higher the profit, but the more you buy and do not sell, the lower the profit or higher the loss. Buying 12,000 is the riskiest strategy.

Using the expected value criterion, the florist would buy 8,000 units, the strategy with the highest expected value ($24,000). But remember that we are dealing with expectations; the actual values might be different from the ones expected. Most managers recognize how important the estimated probabilities are to the results and will perform "what-if" analysis (the sensitivity analysis discussed in earlier chapters). For example, the manager might compute what happens if the probability of selling 12,000 units increases to 40 percent with an offsetting decrease in the probability of selling 8,000 units, or might try several plausible combinations of probabilities. Using a microcomputer and one of the many available software packages, the manager could obtain information about many such combinations in just a few minutes.

Again, we stress the point that no quantitative method, from CVP analysis through expected value calculations, tells you what to do. It tells you only what will happen if—and "if" is a big word—all your predictions are correct. Accordingly, companies that continually make decisions about producing or purchasing perishable goods do this type of analysis often.

Exhibit 16-5   Expected Values of Strategies

| | | Strategy: Purchases of | | | | | |
| | | 4,000 | | 8,000 | | 12,000 | |
Demand	Probability	CV[a]	EV[b]	CV[a]	EV[b]	CV[a]	EV[b]
4,000	.20	$16,000	$ 3,200	$ (8,000)	$ (1,600)	$(32,000)	$ (6,400)
8,000	.50	16,000	8,000	32,000	16,000	8,000	4,000
12,000	.30	16,000	4,800	32,000	9,600	48,000	14,400
Expected values			$ 16,000		$24,000		$12,000

a Conditional values from Exhibit 16-4.
b Conditional value multiplied by probability.

The **value of perfect information** can also be computed from payoff tables. In this application, it equals the difference between the contribution margin that would be earned if the company knew how many units would be demanded and therefore purchased exactly that many, and the expected value of the strategy it would follow using only probabilities.

If the company knew in advance how many corsages would be demanded, it would buy exactly that many and would have the following expected value of contribution margin, selling 4,000 units in 20 percent of the weeks, 8,000 units in 50 percent of the weeks, and 12,000 units in 30 percent of the weeks.

Sales	Contribution Margin, Conditional Value (Exhibit 16-4)	×	Probability	=	Expected Value
4,000	$16,000		.20		$ 3,200
8,000	32,000		.50		16,000
12,000	48,000		.30		14,400
Expected value			1.00		$ 33,600

In this case, then, the value of perfect information is $9,600 ($33,600 - $24,000, the expected value of the strategy of buying 8,000 units each week). We can confirm the $9,600 value of knowing the level of demand by showing the expected sales for a ten-week period, following the strategy of buying 8,000 units each week and following the optimal strategy when the florist knows in advance what the week's demand will be.

During the ten-week period, the company should sell 4,000 corsages twice (20 percent × 10 weeks); 8,000 corsages five times; and 12,000 corsages three times. Following the strategy of buying 8,000 each week, it would have losses of $8,000 twice and gains of $32,000 eight times. (As shown in Exhibit 16-4, the company loses $8,000 when demand is 4,000 units and gains $32,000 when demand is 8,000.) Total contribution margin for the ten-week period is $240,000 [($32,000 × 8) - ($8,000 × 2)]. With perfect information, the florist buys and sells 4,000 corsages twice, 8,000 corsages five times, and 12,000 corsages three times. The contribution margin for the period is as follows:

Sales (in units)	Number of Weeks	×	Contribution Margin per Week	=	Total
4,000	2		$16,000		$ 32,000
8,000	5		32,000		160,000
12,000	3		48,000		144,000
Total					$336,000

The difference between the expected contribution margin with perfect information ($336,000) and using the optimal strategy without such information ($240,000) is $96,000, which is ten times—for ten weeks—the $9,600 calculated earlier as the value of perfect information.

In the real world it is impossible to obtain perfect information, but the concept is still valuable. Some additional information is almost always obtainable at a cost; test-marketing new products is an example of an effort to obtain more information. The questions are whether the information gained would result in a change in strategy, whether decisions would be better if the information were available, and whether the cost of obtaining the information is less than the benefits.

DEVELOPING PROBABILITIES

The probabilities used to compute expected values can be intuitive and judgmental, or they can be developed using more objective, sophisticated statistical techniques.

At one extreme, probabilities might be "best estimates" of experienced managers. There might be some historical basis for the estimates, as when managers develop rules through experience and believe that the current situation is similar to previous situations. For example, if a machine is not operating at peak efficiency, the manager might rely on several years of experience with similar machines to estimate a probability of about 60 percent that an internal part is wearing out, and 40 percent that some random factor is at work that will not continue.

In some cases, managers' estimates of probabilities are based on the presence or absence of external factors. Businesses that depend greatly on the weather provide good examples. A company that sells hot dogs and soft drinks at baseball parks might develop its sales probabilities based on weather forecasts. The hotter the day is expected to be, the more soft drinks the company can expect to sell. Of course, the validity of the manager's estimates depends on the accuracy of the weather forecasts.

Managers often try to narrow the range of estimates by getting additional information and using statistical techniques to evaluate the information. Market research is one commonly used way to obtain additional information. A firm might be considering a new product that will require a nationwide advertising and promotional campaign. Because such campaigns are very costly, the company might test-market the product using a regional campaign. After the small-scale campaign is underway, the managers can analyze the results and gain a better perspective on probable nationwide sales. You might study some of these techniques in your courses in marketing and statistics.

Because probabilities are estimates, some managers react negatively to quantitative techniques that use them. Such managers argue that "sound business judgment" is better than quantitative analysis because the former does not require a lot of assumptions. But when a manager makes a decision, with or without the help of quantitative analysis, the decision implies some beliefs about the future. Consider a decision to set a production level without first estimating demand for the product. Such a decision implies some expectation about demand. Any manager who selects a particular course of action—say, ordering 4,000 corsages—is making assumptions about the future, whether or not those assumptions are specifically stated.

LINEAR PROGRAMMING

 Chapter 5 showed that profits are maximized when the company makes the combination of products that maximizes the contribution margin per unit of a fixed resource. The example in that chapter involved only one fixed resource, but it is more likely that several resources will be fixed.

A multiproduct company facing several constraints can use **linear programming** to determine the combination of products that maximizes profits. Linear programming can also be used to find the combination of input factors that minimizes the cost of an activity. A cattle feeder can determine the least-cost mix of various feeds to provide a specific level of nourishment. Or, a company with several factories and warehouses can determine the least-cost way to move the required quantities of finished product from factories to warehouses.

The mathematics involved in linear programming is complex and is not detailed in this book. However, you should be able to recognize the kinds of problems that can be solved with linear programming, understand the formulation of the problem, and see what is being done when the problem is solved. Essentially, linear programming is the solving of a system of simultaneous linear equations. The system includes an objective function specifying what is to be maximized (usually contribution margin) or minimized (usually cost). The rest of the system's equations state the constraints.

A company makes two products, X and Y. Both products require time in the Assembly Department and the Finishing Department. Data on the two products follow.

	X	Y
Hours required in Assembly Department	2	4
Hours required in Finishing Department	3	2
Selling price	$65	$100
Variable cost	40	60
Contribution margin	$25	$ 40

Each week, 100 hours are available in the Assembly Department and 90 hours are available in the Finishing Department. Using these data we can formulate the linear program in the following four steps.

Step 1.
Formulate the objective function, which in this case is to maximize total contribution margin per week.

$$Maximize: contribution\ margin = \$25X + \$40Y$$

where X and Y stand for the numbers of units of each product that will be produced.

Step 2.
Formulate the constraints as inequalities.

$$2X + 4Y \leq 100$$
$$3X + 2Y \leq 90$$

Each inequality describes the constraint of available time in a department. The first states that the hours spent assembling X (2 hours per unit) plus those spent assembling Y (4 hours per unit) cannot exceed (must be equal to or less than) 100, the available capacity of the Assembly Department. Similarly, the second inequality states that the hours used in finishing X (3 hours per unit) plus those spent in finishing Y (2 hours per unit) cannot exceed the 90 hours available in the Finishing Department.[4]

Following is the entire set of equations and inequalities.

Maximize: contribution margin = $25X + $40Y

Subject to the constraints:

$$2X + 4Y \leq 100$$
$$3X + 2Y \leq 90$$

Step 3.

Graph the lines representing constraints. The capacity constraints of the two departments are shown in Exhibit 16-6. The nonnegativity constraints are implicit because we show only the upper right-hand quadrant of the graph, where production of both products is zero or positive.

The lines representing the capacity constraints can be drawn by determining the two extreme points. For example, the assembly constraint is $2X + 4Y \leq 100$.

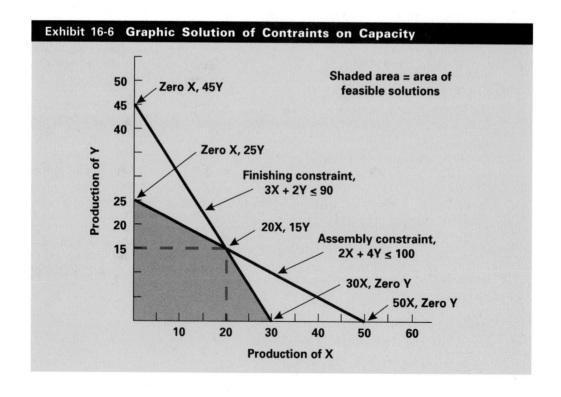

Exhibit 16-6   Graphic Solution of Contraints on Capacity

If only product X is made, maximum production is 50 units, which is 100/2. If only Y is made, maximum production is 25 units (100/4). Hence, the points on the axes are determined and the line is drawn to connect them. Each point on the line represents a possible combination of production. For example, assembling 30 units of X requires 60 hours of assembly time. There would be 40 hours left (100 - 60) to assemble units of Y. In that time, 10 units of Y could be assembled.

The shaded area in the graph is the area of feasible solutions. All points within the shaded area are achievable combinations of production; all points outside the area are unachievable because they require more time than is available in one or the other department.

Step 4.

Determine the contribution margin at each of the corners in the area of feasible solutions. In linear programming an optimal solution always occurs at a corner, an intersection of two lines. (The axes are considered to be lines.)

Corner		Contribution Margin		Total Contribution Margin
X	Y	X	Y	
0	0	$ 0	$ 0	$ 0
30	0	750	0	750
20	15	500	600	1,100
0	25	0	1,000	1,000

The corner 20X, 15Y produces the best solution.

It is often possible to solve for the intersections of constraints using simultaneous equations. This enables you to find the intersection of two constraints without having to draw an accurate graph. Using our illustration, we turn the inequalities into equations.

$$(1)\ \ 2X + 4Y = 100$$
$$(2)\ \ 3X + 2Y = 90$$

Multiplying equation (2) by 2 and subtracting equation (1) we obtain

$$4X = 80$$
$$X = 20$$

Substituting 20 for X in equation (1) gives

$$40 + 4Y = 100$$
$$4Y = 60$$
$$Y = 15$$

Many other types of constraints are possible. Exhibit 16-7 shows the graph when market conditions limit the sales of product X to 16 units per week. The formerly optimal solution of 20X, 15Y is no longer feasible. Two new corners have been created: 16X, zero Y and 16X, 17Y. Clearly, 16X and 17Y must be more desirable than 16X and zero Y. The question is now whether 16X, 17Y is better than zero X, 25Y, which was the second best solution in the original problem. At 16X,

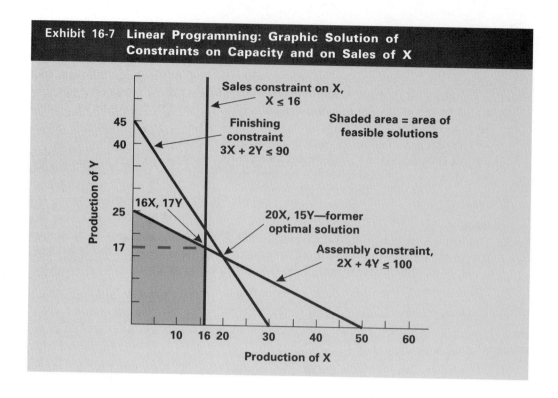

Exhibit 16-7   Linear Programming: Graphic Solution of Constraints on Capacity and on Sales of X

17Y, total contribution margin per week is $1,080 [($25 × 16) + ($40 × 17)]. This is better than the $1,000 earned producing only 25 units of Y.

The constraint of the Finishing Department is no longer critical. It now lies completely outside the area of feasible solutions which means that the time in the Finishing Department will not be fully used. The Finishing Department will have eight hours of unused capacity because 16 units of X and 17 of Y can be finished in 82 hours.

$$3X + 2Y \leq 90$$
$$3 \times 16 = 48$$
$$2 \times 17 = 34$$
$$Total \quad \underline{82}$$

Managers would consider reducing the available capacity of the Finishing Department if they expected the constraint on sales of X to continue. They might also pursue opportunities to do finishing work for another company to use the capacity.

SENSITIVITY ANALYSIS

Sensitivity analysis, the testing of a solution to see how much it changes if one or more variables were to change, is, as we have seen throughout this book, important in decision making. Let us consider the original situation when there was no constraint on the sales of product X. The sales manager might expect the price of X to fall, which would lower its contribution margin. Total contribution margin would also fall so long as the company stayed with its original plan to produce 20 units of X and 15 units of Y. At some point the drop in contribution margin would make it more profitable for the company to produce 25 units of Y, none of X, than to continue with the original plan. That point is an indifference point, as described in Chapter 2.

The manager is interested in knowing how far the contribution margin of X has to fall before the company should stop producing it. The manager can determine that by finding what contribution margin from X in the 20X, 15Y combination equals the total contribution margin from zero X, 25Y. Using C to denote the contribution margin from a unit of X, the manager can frame the following equation.

$$
\begin{array}{ll}
\textit{Produce 25Y} & \textit{Produce 20X, 15Y} \\
\$40 \times 25 = & (C \times 20) + (\$40 \times 15) \\
\$1{,}000 = & 20C + \$600 \\
C = & \$20
\end{array}
$$

Consequently, if the contribution margin per unit of X falls below $20 (from $25), the company would stop producing X and devote its facilities solely to making Y.

Similarly, a rise in the price and contribution margin per unit of Y would make the company more likely to stop producing X and begin producing more of Y. The following equation states that when the contribution margin of 25 units of Y equals that of 15 units of Y plus 20 units of X, the company will earn the same with either production mix. Here, C represents contribution margin per unit of Y.

$$
\begin{array}{rcl}
C \times 25 & = & (C \times 15) + (\$25 \times 20) \\
C \times 25 & = & (C \times 15) + \$500 \\
C \times 10 & = & \$500 \\
C & = & \$50
\end{array}
$$

If the contribution margin of Y rises above $50 per unit (from $40), the company will earn more total contribution margin producing 25Y, zero X, than 15Y, 20X.

SHADOW PRICES

Managers confronted with capacity constraints often wish to know whether it would be beneficial to add capacity in a particular department. They are interested in the value of adding, say, an hour per week of assembly time. The value of adding an hour of capacity is the additional contribution margin that could be earned. This amount is the shadow price of the resource. A **shadow price** is an opportunity cost—the cost of not having an additional unit of capacity.

We shall calculate the shadow price of the assembly constraint using our original illustration in which there was no constraint on the sales of product X. To make it easier to show graphically, we shall add eight hours of capacity to the Assembly Department, rather than one hour. Exhibit 16-8 shows the new assembly constraint. It also shows the former optimal solution, where the

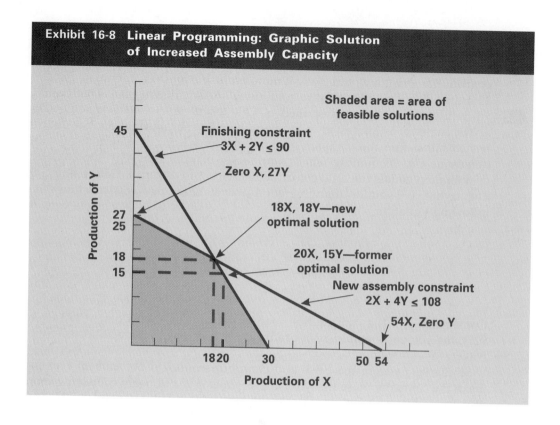

Exhibit 16-8   Linear Programming: Graphic Solution of Increased Assembly Capacity

assembly constraint and finishing constraint lines intersected when capacity in the Assembly Department was 100 hours per week. Notice that the new corner, 18X, 18Y, shows the company making fewer units of X than before, but more units of Y.

Checking the new corners for the optimal solution, we have

Corner		Contribution Margin		Total Contribution
X	Y	X	Y	Margin
18	18	$450	$ 720	$1,170
0	27	0	1,080	1,080

The new optimal solution of 18X, 18Y has a total contribution margin of $1,170 per week. That is $70 higher than the $1,100 earned under the optimal solution of 20X, 15Y when the Assembly Department had 100 available hours. Therefore the firm would be willing to pay up to $70 per week to get an additional eight hours of assembly capacity. The shadow price is $8.75, which is $70/8 hours. (Had we structured the example to add one hour instead of eight, we would have had contribution margin of $1,108.75 and a noninteger solution requiring production of fractional units of both products.) In linear programming, capacity is fixed for the planning period (a week, day, month, or year). In the long run the company can add to capacity or reduce it. Shadow prices give an idea of the value of adding capacity and are important information for long-run planning.

THEORY OF CONSTRAINTS

Theory of constraints (TOC) is a set of techniques developed by Eli Goldratt and his associates.[5] TOC encompasses many aspects, but its most common application lies in increasing production in the face of some constraint. In TOC, a **constraint** limits a system from achieving higher performance relative to its goal. Constraints can be external, such as market demand or vendor quality, or internal, such as labor or machine capacity, behavior of managers or workers, logistics, or policy. TOC holds that, at any one point in time, *only one* constraint prevents a system from achieving its goal. Some constraint always exists, else a company could sell an infinite number of units. Managers must seek solutions that address the constraint, not another (nonconstraining) element within the system. Overcoming the constraint and thus improving the system's performance results only from solving the *right* problem. The TOC approach is iterative and continuous—a process of ongoing improvement.

TOC might appear to be a simpler concept than linear programming, where we solved problems involving several constraints. It is not. In TOC, constraints arise because of randomness and interdependence. Linear programming does not provide for either. LP assumes that units are always ready to be processed by a potentially constraining resource, that is, it ignores sequencing of operations. LP is also deterministic, ignoring random fluctuations. TOC advocates argue that linear programming is also too simple to deal with real-world factories. Consider an assembly line where every worker processes from three to seven units per hour, averaging five units per hour. Each worker sends output to the next worker until the product is complete. Will the system as a whole average five units per hour? No! Work will pile up in front of a worker who has a few slow hours (or whose predecessors have fast periods), while those downstream from the slow worker will run out of work. Even though each worker can average five units per hour, the system as a whole cannot achieve that average. If workers, or machines, do not average the same output, the situation becomes even more complicated.

The basic steps in TOC, called *focusing steps*, are:

1. Identify the constraint. Determine what limits the system's performance.
2. Decide how to exploit the constraint. Develop a logical plan for overcoming the limitation.
3. Subordinate everything else to the plan in step 2. Make effective management of the existing constraint the top priority. Measure performance by reference to meeting the plan, not by reference to meeting local objectives.
4. Elevate the constraint. Inject improvement into the system to break the constraint.
5. If, in the previous steps, you break the constraint, go back to step 1, but do not allow inertia to become the new constraint. Go back and find the new weakest link that limits system performance.

The TOC steps can be applied to any kind of constraint, a bad company policy for example. (Management inertia often lies behind the failure of many laudable programs such as those directed at improving quality or morale.) Market demand

---

5 *See, for example, E. M. Goldratt,* It's Not Luck, *Croton-on-Hudson, NY, North River Press, 1994.*

might be too low, an external constraint. For the most part, however, the use of TOC relates to internal bottlenecks. And proponents of TOC are quick to blame accounting methods and techniques for many of the difficulties that managers face. The accompanying Insight describes how one company applied TOC.

TOC is a method of continuous improvement, much like JIT and TQM. Some observers believe that TOC can help to identify areas where organizations can best apply TQM principles. Others believe that TOC's concentration on constraints is an integral part of TQM, especially because TOC, like JIT, aims at reducing inventories and cycle time.

IN SIGHT

The Stanleytown factory of **Stanley Furniture Company** was quoting lead times of 45 days, even though 95 percent of its sales were standard, made-to-stock items. Of the 45 days, 25 were for manufacturing and 20 were for administrative/distribution activities including order processing, credit approval, and shipping. The company suffered from the "hockey stick" production pattern, where output was relatively low until month-end, when it shot upward to meet monthly sales targets. The rush of production increased overtime and generated expediting costs. Management wanted to reduce the lead time to provide better service. It first made several improvements to the manufacturing process, then turned its attention to administrative/distribution activities.

Order processing went as follows. Sales representatives sent orders to headquarters, where clerks entered them into a sales order system. Other employees approved credit for the customer. Only after credit approval was the order placed on the production schedule. The traffic department then consolidated orders into groups and scheduled deliveries.

The team applying the focusing steps found, in step 1, that credit approval was the bottleneck. Work piled up in this operation because its employees reviewed each customer's credit history and had different procedures for different-size orders. In step 2, the company reduced the steps required to approve orders from customers with good credit. The result was a drop in the backlog at each station and a reduction in the administrative lead time.

In step 3, the team subordinated all other activities to credit approval, and management de-emphasized other departments goals and objectives.

In step 4, the company eliminated the constraint by changing the flow. Instead of waiting for credit approval before allocating inventory for an order, the company allowed the warehouse to allocate inventory before final credit approval. The company was able to do this without disrupting its production schedules, fear of which was one reason it had not taken the step earlier.

In step 5, the team determined that the constraint had been broken and turned its attention to the shipping function, starting again with step 1.

Source: Michael S. Spencer and Samuel Wathen, "Applying the Theory of Constraints Process Management Technique," National Productivity Review, Summer 1994, 381-383.

LEARNING CURVES

Even before they faced serious competition from overseas companies, U.S. companies paid a great deal of attention to improving employee productivity and recognized that people generally need less time to do a task as they become more familiar with the task. For instance, airplane manufacturers long ago determined that the labor time required for each airplane of a given model declines as the workers learn.

The **learning curve** is a measure of increases in efficiency. The rate of performance improvement, expressed as a percentage, is called the learning rate. The most common form of the learning curve is expressed as follows: as output doubles, the average time to make a unit or batch of units drops to the learning rate percentage multiplied by the average time at the previous point. An example will clarify this relationship.

Northern Manufacturing is about to begin making a new product. The expected labor time for the first batch is 10 hours, and the expected learning rate is 80 percent. Exhibit 16-9 illustrates the learning curve for Northern. The exhibit shows, for selected numbers of batches, both the average time per batch and the total time.

Notice that the exhibit shows results only at doubling points (2 is double 1, 4 is double 2, 8 is double 4). To determine the average time for some other number of batches, we can use the following formula.

$$Y = aX^b$$

where

> Y = *average time for X number of batches;*
> a = *the time required for the first batch (or unit);*
> X = *total output (number of batches);*
> b = *the learning exponent.*

The value of b is the logarithm of the learning rate (expressed as a decimal) divided by the logarithm of 2. (Because many calculators include both logarithm and exponentiation functions, using the formula is not difficult.) With the

---

Exhibit 16-9   Examples of Expected Average and Total Times— 80% Learning Curve

Total Ouput in Batches	Expected Average Time per Batch (hours)	Expected Total Time (hours)[a]
1	10 (given)	10
2	8 (10 × 80%)	16 (2 × 8)
4	6.4 (8 × 80%)	25.6 (4 × 6.4)
8	5.12 (6.4 × 80%)	40.96 (8 × 5.12)

a Number of batches × average time per batch.

formula you can find the average time for any output level. For instance, in the example, the value of b is about -.322. Thus, the per-batch average time for seven batches is

$$Y = 10 \times 7^{-.322}$$
$$= 10 \times .5344$$
$$= 5.344$$

We stress that the learning curve is expressed in terms of the per-batch average time for some total number of batches, not the incremental time to produce some number of additional batches. Thus, if we refer to Exhibit 16-9, the second batch does not require eight hours; rather eight hours is the per-batch average time to produce both of the first two batches. To find the incremental time for a batch, you must first find the total times for that number of batches and for one batch fewer. For Northern, we know from Exhibit 16-9 that eight batches require 40.96 hours. Seven batches require 37.408 hours (7 × 5.344, the average time computed above using the formula). Hence, the eighth batch requires 3.552 hours (40.96 - 37.408).

You can also apply the learning curve directly to cost, rather than to time. For example, we could have said that labor and labor-related variable overhead costs were $10 for the first batch. In that case, the answers derived in the exhibit or from the formula would be expressed in dollars.

The learning curve is useful in planning and controlling. Managers can estimate labor time, and therefore labor and labor-related variable overhead costs, for specific quantities of output. They can then determine, by comparing actual time or cost with the estimated values, whether learning is as expected.

Suppose that CompuCom is considering a customer's offer to buy eight batches of a specialized microprocessor. (A batch could be 500, 1,000, or any other number of units, so long as all batches are the same size.) The customer has offered to pay $80,000 for the entire order. No incremental fixed costs are associated with the order. Materials and purchased components will cost $3,500 for each batch. (This portion of the cost is not subject to learning.) CompuCom estimates the cost of direct labor and labor-related variable overhead for the first batch at $3,000 and has usually experienced an 80 percent learning rate.

Suppose CompuCom's managers have decided not to accept the order unless they expect more than the $35,000 in contribution margin which the company could earn doing other business if the order is rejected. If the managers ignore the potential for lower costs because of learning, they would reject the order on the basis of the following analysis.

Revenues		$80,000
Variable costs:		
Materials and components (8 × $3,500)	$28,000	
Labor and labor-related overhead (8 × $3,000)	24,000	52,000
Expected contribution margin		$28,000

But, the order does have the desired profit potential if the learning factor is considered. The following schedule shows the expected costs of labor and labor-related variable overhead, based on the 80 percent learning rate and expected costs of the first batch.

Total Output in Batches	Expected Average Cost per Batch	Expected Total Cost[a]
1	$3,000 (given)	$ 3,000
2	2,400 ($3,000 × 80%)	4,800 (2 × $2,400)
4	1,920 ($2,400 × 80%)	7,680 (4 × $1,920)
8	1,536 ($1,920 × 80%)	12,288 (8 × $1,536)

a *Number of batches × average cost per batch.*

With this cost information, the order shows higher profit.

		$80,000
Revenues		
Variable costs:		
Materials and components (8 × $3,500)	$28,000	
Labor and labor-related overhead, previously given	12,288	40,288
Expected contribution margin		$39,712

Total expected contribution margin from the order is nearly $12,000 more than that shown by the analysis that ignores the cost reduction expected to result from learning and the order is more profitable than the available alternative (contribution margin of $35,000). The lesson here is that managers must study their companies' experiences for evidence of potential cost reductions as a result of learning and, where it exists, incorporate that potential into decision making.

SUMMARY

Quality costs are an important component of operations. Companies striving to improve quality can use the four categories of quality cost to assist in their analyses. Theory of constraints provides a scheme for achieving continuous improvement that concentrates on one problem at a time.

Managers use a variety of quantitative techniques to help them make decisions. Statistical decision theory enables managers to incorporate the effects of uncertainty. Linear programming helps managers decide how best to use existing resources. Shadow prices help managers to understand the significance of existing constraints and the potential gains from expanding capacity. Learning curves are useful in planning and controlling labor and labor-related costs.

Much of the information needed for using these techniques is supplied by managerial accountants. Managers and accountants must be aware of the objectives and information requirements of such techniques. The managerial accountant will sometimes have to assist in formulating the problem and must therefore understand the capabilities and limitations of the techniques available.

KEY TERMS

conditional values   (767)
constraint   (777)
cost of quality   (759)
decision tree   (765)
expected values   (767)
learning curve   (779)

linear programming   (771)
payoff tables   (767)
shadow price   (775)
theory of constraints   (777)
value of perfect information   (769)

REVIEW PROBLEM

In March, Grauger Company experienced an unfavorable cost variance of $2,000. Based on experience and judgment, the production manager believes there is a 40% probability that the variance was due to random causes and will not continue. A 60% probability exists that there is some difficulty in the production process and that the variance will continue at $2,000 per month for the next two months. Investigating the variance would cost $800. If the variance is investigated and something is wrong with the process, there is a 70% probability that corrective action could be taken and a 30% probability that nothing can be done.

Required

Determine the expected costs of investigating and of not investigating the variance.

ANSWER TO REVIEW PROBLEM

Expected Cost of Investigating

Event	Cost	Probability	Expected Value
Variance is random and will not continue	$ 800	.40	$ 320
Variance is caused by problem in process that can be corrected	800	.42[a]	336
Variance is caused by problem that cannot be corrected	4,800[b]	.18[c]	864
Expected cost of investigating		1.00	$1,520

a 60% × 70%.
b $800 + (2 × $2,000).
c 60% × 30%.

Expected Cost of Not Investigating

Event	Cost	Probability	Expected Value
Variance is random	0	.40	0
Variance is caused by problem in process and will continue	$4,000	.60	$2,400
Expected cost of not investigating		1.00	$2,400

The variance should be investigated because the expected cost to investigate is less than that of not investigating.

ASSIGNMENT MATERIAL

QUESTIONS FOR DISCUSSION

16-1   Quality costs   Of the four categories of quality costs, which is the hardest to estimate? Why?

16-2   Learning curves   Which of the following operations of companies do you think experience significant learning effects?
1. **General Motors'** automobile assembly plants
2. **Pillsbury's** flour mills
3. **Colgate-Palmolive's** toothpaste plants
4. **Boeing's** aircraft plants.

16-3   Classifying quality costs   Classify each of the following costs as prevention, appraisal, internal failure, external failure, or as not a cost of quality. State any assumptions you make.
1. Training new workers.
2. Upgrading skills of existing workers.
3. Inspecting purchased components.
4. Reworking defective units.
5. Routine maintenance on machinery.
6. Salaries of field engineers who assist customers with problems and service products in the field.
7. Sales returns.

16-4   Expected values and risk   You have $100,000 to invest and only two opportunities. Would you invest in a bond yielding 7% and maturing in one year, or buy shares in a start-up biotech company that has a 50% probability of bringing you $400,000 (including your original investment) at year end, and a 50% probability of losing your investment? Why?

16-5   Theory of constraints   Suppose you work with a team of people assembling small engines. All of you have about equal ability except for Bob, who is considerably slower than everyone else. What would you do to maximize the output of the group?

EXERCISES

16-6   Variance investigation   Tuck Company's controller has determined that it costs $800 to investigate a variance and that corrective action is possible in one out of five cases investigated. An unfavorable variance of $1,500 has occurred. The production process will be changed after next month, so that any savings will be for only one month if corrective action can be taken. Should the variance be investigated?

16-7   *Basic learning curve* Industrial engineers at Krum Inc., a manufacturer of industrial presses, expect the first unit of a new model, the TN-22, to require 5,000 direct labor hours. They also expect an 80% learning curve.

Required

1. Determine the average direct labor time and the total direct labor time to make four units of the TN-22.
2. Determine the average direct labor time and the total direct labor time to make eight units of the TN-22.

16-8   *New products—expected values and risk* The sales manager of Happy Toy Company is considering two new toys, a doll and a game. On the basis of market research and experience, she has formulated the following table.

Event	Doll		Game	
	Cash Flow	Probability	Cash Flow	Probability
Big success	$80,000	.2	$110,000	.3
Fair success	50,000	.5	70,000	.4
Flop	20,000	.3	(20,000)	.3

Required

1. Determine the expected value of cash flows associated with each new toy.
2. Which one would you select, and why?

16-9   *Formulating a linear programming problem* Greer Carson Company makes three products, A, B, and C. Their respective contribution margins are $80, $70, and $60. Each product goes through three processes: cutting, shaping, and painting. The numbers of hours required by each process for each product are as follows:

Product	Hours Required in Each Process		
	Cutting	Shaping	Painting
A	3	2	4
B	5	1	3
C	2	3	2

The following numbers of hours are available per month in each process: cutting, 8,000; shaping, 9,000; and painting, 5,000.

Required

Formulate the objective function and constraints to determine the optimal production policy.

 16-10   *Linear programming* LM Company makes two products.

	L	M
Selling price	$60	$20
Variable costs	$35	$10
Machine minutes required per unit:		
Grinding Department	3	1
Assembly Department	2	2

LM has 900 minutes of machine time available in the Grinding Department and 800 available in the Assembly Department.

Required
Determine the optimal product mix.

16-11   Learning curve JayCo Industries is bidding on a contract to make eight batches of landing gear assemblies for an aircraft company. JayCo's engineers expect direct labor and variable overhead for the first batch to be $60,000. Variable overhead is related to direct labor. JayCo usually achieves an 85% learning rate.

Required
1. Determine the expected average cost for direct labor and variable overhead for the eight batches.
2. Determine the expected total cost for direct labor and variable overhead for the eight batches.

16-12   Learning curve (continuation of 16-11) JayCo's managers expect the cost of materials and purchased components to be $25,000 per batch (not subject to learning). They also want an average contribution margin of $15,000 per batch.

Required
1. Determine the price that JayCo must bid to earn $15,000 average contribution margin per batch for eight batches.
2. Suppose now that the contract is for 16 batches. Redo item 1.
3. Suppose that the contract is still for eight batches, but that JayCo's managers believe that the learning rate will actually be 80%. Redo item 1.

16-13   Cost structure and probabilities The production manager of Omega Company is considering modifying one of her machines. The modification will add $10,000 per month to the cost of running the machine but will reduce variable operating costs by $0.20 per unit produced. The modification itself costs nothing, and the machine can be returned to its current operating method at any time.
   The product made on the machine has an uncertain demand; the best estimates available are as follows:

Monthly Demand	Probability
35,000	.20
50,000	.40
60,000	.20
70,000	.20

Required
1. Determine the number of units that must be produced to justify the modification.
2. Determine the expected value of making the modification. Should it be made?

16-14   Payoff table Campus Program sells programs at football games. The owner has collected the following data regarding the pattern of sales.

Quantity Sold (cases)	Probability
400	.20
600	.50
700	.30

The owner is uncertain of the number of cases of programs to order. He must order one of the given quantities. A case of programs sells for $300 and the purchase price is $100. Unsold programs are thrown away.

Required

Construct a payoff table to determine the number of cases of programs the firm should order.

PROBLEMS

16-15   *Linear programming, formulation of problem*   Carter Company makes two models of its basic product. Data are as follows:

	X	Y
Selling price	$80	$100
Materials requirements, pounds	2	1
Labor time, hours	2	3

Materials cost $8 per pound and the combined labor and variable overhead rate is $12 per labor hour. The company has 400 pounds of materials and 500 hours of labor available. It can sell all of either model that it can make. Fixed costs are $2,000, of which $700 is depreciation. All fixed costs are unavoidable.

Required

Formulate the objective function and constraints.

16-16   *Linear programming (continuation of 16-15)*

Required

1. Determine the optimal mix.
2. Determine the shadow price of the labor constraint. Assume the addition of 20 hours of labor.

16-17   *Sensitivity analysis*   The florist for whom you prepared the payoff table (Exhibit 16-5) is not impressed. He has decided to order 4,000 corsages per week because he does not want to be stuck with unsold goods. Because you own a share of the business, you would like him to order 8,000 per week. In an effort to show him that he is being unduly conservative, you decide to show him how low the risk is by using more pessimistic probabilities. Because you would not order 12,000 corsages, you can lump together the probabilities of selling 8,000 and 12,000. (The contribution margin from ordering 8,000 corsages is the same whether demand is 8,000 or 12,000.)

Required

Determine the expected values of ordering 8,000 corsages with the following probabilities:

Case	Demand in Units	Probability of Demand
1	4,000	.30
	8,000	.70
2	4,000	.40
	8,000	.60
3	4,000	.50
	8,000	.50

16-18   Quality costs   RST Company has the following costs, among others.

Inspection of outgoing shipments	$ 70,000
Employee training	50,000
Salaries of laboratory personnel who test samples of product	150,000
Rework of defective units	40,000
Salaries of customer service personnel, who spend 40% of their time fixing products, 60% taking orders	200,000
Product design	250,000
Vendor certification, principally determining whether vendors' quality controls are adequate	80,000
Inspection of incoming shipments	40,000

Required

1. Determine the total amounts the company is spending on each of the four quality cost categories.
2. Do these costs capture all of the costs of quality the company incurs? Assume that all costs are recorded correctly.

16-19   Expected values—a law firm   The firm of Smith, Perez, and Jamison has been approached by Hirt, who suffered a whiplash injury in an automobile accident. He wants the firm to represent him in a court suit, with the firm's fee being one-third of the total judgment given by the court.

Jamison estimates that 2,000 hours are needed to prepare and try the case, with the opportunity cost being $80 per hour. Based on experience with similar cases, she believes that the following judgments and associated probabilities are reasonable estimates on which to decide whether to accept the case.

Judgment for Hirt	Probability of Judgment
0	.40
$150,000	.20
$400,000	.30
$600,000	.10

Required

Determine whether the firm should accept the case.

16-20   Learning curve in administrative work   The Dean of Admissions at Mid-State University needs student help to process 6,400 application forms. She has found that a new student helper can process 40 forms the first day. The helpers usually achieve an 85% learning rate. The Dean plans to hire ten helpers, so each will process 640 forms. You may consider 40 forms to be a batch.

Required

Determine how many days it will take ten new helpers to process the 6,400 forms.

16-21   *Variance investigation* DePardeu Company has just experienced a $4,000 unfavorable variance. The production supervisor believes that there is a 40% chance that the variance was a one-time thing and will not continue. She believes that if an investigation is made, the chance of correcting the variance is 60% and of not correcting it is 40%. It costs $800 to investigate a variance. The most that will be lost if the variance continues is $4,000.

Required

Determine whether to investigate the variance.

16-22   *Linear programming* Fast Class Company makes two products, the Fast and the Class. Fasts sell for $18 and have variable costs of $5. Classes sell for $14 and have variable costs of $6. Both products go through two processes—cutting and forming. Each Fast requires two minutes of cutting and four minutes of forming. Each Class requires three minutes of cutting and two of forming. The company has available 3,000 minutes of cutting time and 2,400 minutes of forming time per month. Fixed costs in cutting are $400 and in forming are $300, all unavoidable.

Required

Determine the number of Fasts and Classes that should be produced each month.

16-23   *Shadow prices and sensitivity analysis (continuation of 16-22)*

Required

Consider each item independently.

1. Determine the shadow price of the forming constraint.
2. Determine the price of Fasts that would make the company indifferent between the current optimal mix (from 16-22) and making all Fasts.
3. Determine the price of Classes that would make the company indifferent between the current optimal mix (from 16-22) and making all Classes.

16-24   *Product selection* Henson Electronics is trying to decide which of three products to introduce. The managers think that only one should be brought out in order to concentrate promotional effort. Information about the products follows.

	Radio	Toaster	Coffee Maker
Selling price	$22	$37	$45
Variable cost	13	20	25
Contribution margin	$ 9	$17	$20
Sales forecasts, in units, with probabilities in parentheses	25,000 (20%)	12,000 (10%)	15,000 (60%)
	40,000 (40%)	19,000 (25%)	20,000 (20%)
	50,000 (30%)	25,000 (50%)	25,000 (20%)
	75,000 (10%)	38,000 (15%)	

Required
1. Compute the expected values of contribution margins for the three products.
2. Which product would you select, and why?

16-25   *Expected value of hole-in-one* The sponsors of the Eastern Open, a major golf tournament, have decided to give a new automobile to any player who gets a hole-in-one during the tournament. The car they have selected costs $28,000. One of the sponsors owns an insurance agency and offers to insure the tournament against a hole-in-one for $1,400. If the sponsors buy the policy and someone does get a hole-in-one, the insurance company will buy the car. Statistics show that a hole-in-one occurs about once in every 30 tournaments.

Required
Determine the expected value of *not* buying the insurance. Would you buy the insurance if you were a sponsor?

16-26   *Learning curve in make-or-buy decision* Barfield Company currently buys a component for one of its products at $22 per unit. Barfield needs 32,000 units of the component in the coming year. The product will be redesigned, so that the component will not be needed beyond the coming year. The production manager believes that Barfield could make the component with the following costs for the first batch of 1,000 units.

Materials	$13,000
Direct labor and variable overhead	15,000
Total variable cost	$28,000

There are no incremental fixed costs because Barfield could use existing equipment. The production manager expects an 85% learning rate on direct labor and variable overhead. Consider a batch to be 1,000 units.

Required
Determine whether Barfield should make or buy the component.

 16-27   *Make or buy* Walters Company manufactures ceramic figurines. Sometimes the company subcontracts production of its designs to other companies, paying a set amount per piece. The chief designer has come up with a new item that most of the managers expect to be a best seller. Some of the managers are less sure and want to be as cautious as possible.

If Walters manufactures the item, it must lease additional space and machinery at a cost of $80,000 for the coming year. The lease could not be canceled for one year. Unit variable cost is $14 and the selling price is $36. Alternatively, the company could subcontract production. A local outlet has agreed to produce the item and sell it to Walters Company at $23.

Based on her experience with other, similar items, the company's sales manager has developed the following estimates of demand and probabilities for the new figurine.

Demand	Probability
7,000	.20
9,000	.30
12,000	.30
14,000	.20

Required

Determine the expected value of the profit on the figurine if Walters (a) makes it internally and (b) subcontracts it.

16-28   Special order decision—probabilities The sales manager of Schieren Company has been approached by a chain store that would like to buy 10,000 units of the firm's product. The sales manager believes that the order should be accepted because the price offered is $6 and variable costs of production are $5.

In a conversation with the production manager, the sales manager extracted the following information: (1) sufficient capacity exists to meet the special order and (2) prices for materials and wage rates are expected to increase by the time the order would be manufactured, but the amounts of the increases are not certain. The best estimates follow.

New Variable Cost	Probability
$5.20	.30
5.70	.40
6.60	.30

Required

1. Determine the expected contribution margin on the special order.
2. What other factors should be considered in reaching a decision?

16-29   Cost of investigating a variance Gilgenbach Company's production manager has been trying to decide whether a particular variable overhead variance should be investigated. The variance was $300 unfavorable this past month, and is expected to continue at the rate of $300 for five more months if nothing is done. The estimated cost to investigate the variance is $600, and the chances are four out of five that nothing can be done to correct the variance even if its cause can be isolated. If the variance is found to be correctable, the total savings, not considering the cost of the investigation, will be $1,500 (the total cost of the variance over the next five months).

Required

Determine whether the variance should be investigated.

16-30   Expected values and utilities The sales manager of Wonderland Toy Company has been studying a report prepared by a consultant. The company had asked the consultant to study the advisability of bringing out a new doll that would be quite different from anything on the market. The report indicated that there was considerable variation in sales expectations. The consultant concluded that there was about a 60% chance of selling 50,000 dolls and a 40% chance of selling only 10,000.

The doll's price is to be $24, with variable costs of $20. Incremental fixed costs, primarily for advertising, are $120,000.

The sales manager decided, on the basis of the expected value of profit, that the doll should be introduced, but the president of the firm was leery. The president felt that the doll was apt to lose money and that the company had had too many duds in recent years. After some discussion, the president decided that losing a dollar was twice as bad as earning a dollar was good. He instructed the sales manager to prepare a new analysis incorporating his utility, although he did not call it that.

Required
1. Prepare a schedule showing the expected value of profit without consideration of the president's views.
2. Prepare a new schedule in which the president's views are incorporated. Determine whether the doll should be brought out.

16-31   *Variance investigation*   Mayan Company experienced an unfavorable variance of $2,000 in May. The production manager found, from past data, that 30% of the time a variance of this size is experienced, nothing is wrong with the process and the variance stops. When there is a problem, 60% of the time the variance continues for two additional months, at $2,000 per month, and 40% of the time it continues for three additional months, also at $2,000 per month.

Investigating the variance costs $800. If there is a problem with the production process, it can be corrected 40% of the time. The other 60% of the time nothing can be done. The 40% and 60% probabilities apply both to variances that would continue for two additional months and to those that would continue for three additional months. If the investigation has been done and the cause of the variance found to be correctable, correcting it costs an additional $600.

Required
1. Determine the expected cost of not investigating the variance.
2. Determine the expected cost of investigating the variance.

16-32   *Variance investigation (CMA adapted)*   Cilla Company manufactures a line of women's handbags. A summary of Cilla's cutting department operations for May 19X5 showed a $16,000 unfavorable materials use variance.

Veronique Antek, the supervisor of the department, gathered the following information to assist her in deciding whether to investigate the variance.

Estimated cost to investigate the variance	$4,000
Estimated cost to make changes if the department is operating incorrectly	$8,000
Estimated savings if changes are made	$40,000
Estimated probability that the department is operating incorrectly	10%

Required
Determine whether Antek should investigate the variance.

16-33   *Capital budgeting probabilities*   The following estimates have been prepared by the production manager of Hector Company. They relate to a proposed $60,000 investment in a machine that will reduce the cost of materials used by the firm. Cost of capital is 16%. Ignore taxes.

Annual Cash Savings		Useful Life	
Event	Probability	Event	Probability
$20,000	.30	9 years	.40
14,000	.30	8 years	.40
12,000	.40	6 years	.20

Required

1. Compute the expected values of annual cash savings and useful life. Determine whether the machine should be purchased.
2. The production manager wishes to see whether the machine would be a good investment if each of his most pessimistic estimates came true, but not both at the same time. Determine whether the investment would be desirable if (a) the useful life is the expected value computed in item 1 and annual cash flows are only $12,000, and (b) the annual cash flows are equal to the expected value computed in item 1 and the useful life is only six years.

16-34   *Expected values* The managers of Hawkins Company are trying to decide how to operate in the coming year. The company rents a machine that performs essential operations on the product; the rental period is one year. The product sells for $10 per unit and has variable costs of $1.

Three machines are available; operating and other data are as follows:

Machine	Productive Capacity	Annual Rent
Standard	11,000 units	$50,000
DeLuxe	12,000 units	54,000
Super	13,000 units	55,500

The sales forecast for the coming year has been based on the 10,000 units sold the prior year; demand for the product is expected to increase, but the size of the increase is uncertain. The best estimates follow.

Sales in Units	Probability
11,000	.30
12,000	.50
13,000	.20

Required

Determine the best course of action for the company.

16-35   *Payoff table* *The Evening News* is a large metropolitan newspaper. The paper is sold through dealers who are charged $0.20 per copy that they sell. Unsold copies are returned to *The Evening News* and full credit is given. The unsold copies are sold as wastepaper for $0.02 each. The variable cost of producing a paper is $0.10.

The Evening News currently prints 500,000 papers each day. Management is considering a change and has asked for your help. A recent study showed the following results.

Papers Returned	Percentage of Time
100,000	20%
50,000	20%
0	60%

The study also indicated that when 500,000 copies were all sold, there were often more papers demanded. The best estimates are that 25% of the time 500,000 copies are demanded, 25% of the time 550,000 are demanded, and 10% of the time 600,000 papers could be sold if they were available.

Required
1. Determine the best strategy for *The Evening News.*
2. Determine the value of perfect information.

16-36 Linear programming, graphical solution Salinas Furniture Company makes two types of sofas, traditional and modern. Because of their different types of construction, they require different amounts of machine time and skilled labor time. The company has available, per week, 1,000 hours of skilled labor and 1,200 hours of machine time. The variable costs associated with skilled labor, including both wages and variable overhead, are $7 per hour; for machine time, the variable costs are $6 per hour. The firm can sell all of the modern sofas it can make, but only 200 traditional sofas per week.

Additional data on the two sofas are as follows:

	Traditional	Modern
Selling price	$240	$180
Materials costs (the only other variable cost)	$80	$60
Labor hours required, per unit	4	2
Machine hours required, per unit	3	4

The following figure plots the constraints.

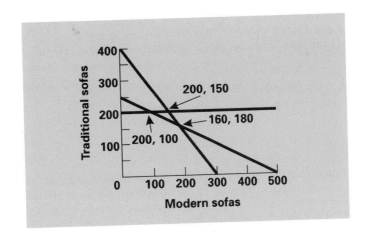

Required
1. Determine the number of each sofa that should be produced each week.
2. Assuming that the price of modern sofas remains constant, at what price for traditional sofas should the firm increase its production of traditional sofas and reduce that of modern sofas?

16-37 Expected values—capital budgeting Fleming Company plans to build a factory to manufacture a new product. The product and the factory are expected to have useful lives of ten years. No salvage value is expected for any of the components of the factory. The firm's marketing research staff has studied the potential demand for the product and has provided the following information.

Expected Annual Demand	Probability of Demand
200,000 units	60%
250,000 units	40%

The firm can build a factory with capacity of either 200,000 or 250,000 units. Data on the two possible factories follow:

Capacity	Total Cost, All Depreciable Assets	Annual Fixed Costs Requiring Cash
200,000	$1,500,000	$300,000
250,000	1,800,000	380,000

The product will sell for $5 and have variable costs of $1. The tax rate is 40% and cost of capital is 16%. Straight-line depreciation is used for tax purposes.
    Management has decided to base its decision on NPV. Whichever factory shows the greater favorable difference between the present value of the expected value of future cash flows and the required investment will be built.

Required
Prepare analyses of the expected values of future cash flows under the two investment possibilities. Determine which factory should be built.

16-38   Expected values (AICPA adapted)   Wing Manufacturing Company makes a chemical compound, product X, that deteriorates rapidly. Any left unsold at the end of the month in which the firm makes it becomes worthless. The variable cost of manufacturing the product is $50 per pound and the selling price $80 per pound. The demand for the product, with associated probabilities, is as follows:

Monthly Demand	Probability
8,000	.25
9,000	.60
10,000	.15

The management of Wing believes that it is necessary to supply all customers who order product X. Failing to do so would result, in the managers' judgment, in losing not only sales of product X, but also sales of other products. Wing has found a company that will sell product X to it at $80, plus $10 freight per pound. The managers want to develop a policy regarding production. Some argue that the high cost of obtaining additional amounts from the outside supplier makes it desirable to produce 10,000 pounds per month. Others argue that it is safer to produce less and to buy from the supplier as needed.

Required
Determine what production strategy maximizes the expected value of profit.

Statement of Cash Flows

17

LEARNING OBJECTIVES

After reading this chapter, you should be able to

1. Explain why people outside a company are interested in a statement of the company's cash flows.

2. State the three types of activities reported in a cash flow statement and classify cash flows according to the type of activity they represent.

3. Name the two approaches to presenting operating cash flows and describe their differences.

4. Describe the supplementary information disclosed in a cash flow statement.

5. Recognize financial statement items that are likely to be part of a reconciliation of income and operating cash flow.

6. Develop cash flow statements.

The 1995 annual report of **The Coca-Cola Company** posed the question,

What do we produce with our secret formula? and gave as the answer, Superior cash flow.

Coca-Cola characterized its "financial fundamentals" as "superior and reliable," describing how it generated superior cash flow and what it did with the cash it generated. To the query of why the company did not pay higher dividends, Coca-Cola responded that its returns on capital justified reinvesting in the business rather than paying dividends. The company also uses cash to buy back its own stock to further increase returns to shareholders.

> *Your previous work in accounting has included studying the concept of income, which has been important throughout this book, as well. The financial press constantly reports that income data and stock prices rise and fall based on income. So, given all of the attention paid to net income and earnings per share, both based on accrual accounting, why does* **Coca-Cola** *(and many other companies) express its success so much in terms of cash flow? Of what interest to investors is cash flow?*

Source: *1995 annual report of The Coca-Cola Company, 18-21.*

As Chapters 13 through 15 discussed, accounting information systems serve both financial and managerial accounting. Much of the information prepared for distribution outside the company is also used by internal managers. For example, data from income statements and balance sheets are used for budgeting (Chapters 6 and 7) and performance measurement (Chapters 10 and 11).

A third statement required for financial reporting is the statement of cash flows. A cash flow statement is similar to the internally used cash budget introduced in Chapter 7. But because the cash flow statement is part of the financial statement package contained in annual reports, its form and content are subject to GAAP.[1] This chapter discusses the form and content of the statement.

The chapter also illustrates the preparation of cash flow statements because readers of the statement often misunderstand its contents and how they relate to the other financial statements.

INTEREST IN CASH FLOWS

Profitability is but one of the factors important for the survival and growth of a business. Also important are current and future inflows and outflows of cash. From Chapter 7 we know that managers develop cash budgets to anticipate shortages of cash. Their concern is that cash be available for such matters as operations, capital expenditures, repaying debt, and dividends.

Managers are responsible for planning how and when cash will be obtained and used. When budgeted cash outflows are more than budgeted inflows, managers must decide what to do. Sometimes they obtain financing (through borrowing or issuing stock) or dispose of some existing investment (by selling an asset or perhaps an entire segment of the business). Sometimes they curtail budgeted activities by revising plans for operations (e.g., dropping a special advertising campaign), new investments (e.g., delaying acquisition of new machinery), or payments to financing sources (e.g., delay debt repayment or reduce dividends). Whatever they do, the managers' goal is to balance the cash available and the needs for cash.

Lenders, stockholders, suppliers, and other outsiders are also aware of the importance of planning and of decisions for balancing available cash and cash

---

1 The official pronouncement governing cash flow statements is *Statement of Financial Accounting Standards Board, No. 95* (Stamford, Conn., Financial Accounting Standards Board, 1987). That publication is the source of statements in the chapter about GAAP requirements.

needs. They know that cash flows into the company from operations, financing sources, and sales of fixed assets and other investments. They know that cash is used for operations, dividends, repayment of debt, and expansion. They are interested in cash flows and changes in cash because these reflect the company's decisions for implementing its short-term and long-term plans for operations, investment, and financing. Stated more generally, outsiders are interested in information about the company's **operating**, **investing**, and **financing activities** and the cash flows generated by those activities. The cash flow statement provides information to assess managerial decisions and performance and prospects for future profit, payments to financing sources, and growth.

CASH FLOW STATEMENT

As you might have guessed from the preceding discussion, the **cash flow statement** has three basic parts, which classify cash inflows and outflows as related to operating, investing, or financing activities. The following lists provide examples.

Operating flows: Inflows include cash received from customers and from interest and dividends on investments. Outflows include cash paid for inventory, salaries and wages, interest, taxes, and other expenses. The net amount of these flows is **cash flow from operations**, or cash provided by operations, or other similar title.

Investing flows: Inflows include receipts from sales of long-lived assets, such as property, plant, equipment, and patents and from sales of investments. Cash outlays to acquire these same types of assets, or to lend to others, are examples of investing outflows.

Financing flows: Inflows include cash received from long-term or short-term borrowing, from issuing common or preferred stock, and from selling treasury stock. Dividends, purchases of treasury stock, retirements of bonds, and repayments of other long-term loans are examples of financing outflows.

Note that interest payments are operating items while dividends are financing items even though both are payments to suppliers of financing. The FASB apparently classified interest as an operating item because it is included on the income statement, while dividends are not. The FASB also requires disclosure of total interest payments so that a reader can reclassify such payments.[2]

Beyond the basic classification scheme, a few other considerations affect the content and format of a cash flow statement. Before we present an example of a typical statement and illustrate its development, we discuss the three most important considerations.

DEFINING CASH

Cash is an essential asset. Financial managers often invest cash in excess of immediate needs in highly liquid, income-producing securities such as govern-

---

2 *The same reasoning appears to apply to interest and dividend revenues, which are cash inflows from investing activities. However, the FASB required separate disclosure of such revenues only if a company presents its operating cash flows using the "direct method," which is discussed later in the chapter.*

ment notes. The company's immediately available funds include not only its cash but also those highly liquid securities (called **cash equivalents**).

GAAP requires that the cash flow statement report the changes in the sum of cash and cash equivalents. That is, the amount reported as the net change in cash equals the change in the sum of cash and cash equivalents. The practical implications of using the sum are that the cash relating to the purchases and sales of cash equivalents will not be reported among the investing activities, and that the gain or loss from sales of the securities will be included among the operating cash flows. In this chapter, we use the term *cash* to refer to both cash and cash equivalents.

REPORTING OPERATING CASH FLOWS

Reread the examples of operating cash flows provided earlier. Does the income statement report these inflows and outflows? Does net income equal net cash flow from operating activities? The answer to both questions is "no." From your study of financial accounting you know that the income statement uses the accrual basis of accounting and does not necessarily reflect cash transactions relating to operations. For this reason, information about operating cash flows is not directly available from an income statement. Exhibit 17-1 shows the net income and net cash flow from operations reported for three companies. The net cash provided (or used) by operations can be smaller or larger than net income, and of course the change in cash over the year differs from both of those amounts.

The FASB permits two reporting methods for operating cash flows. The first, called the **direct method**, separately reports operating cash inflows and out-flows such as collections from customers and payments to employees, suppliers of goods, and other vendors such as utilities. A reporting of operating cash flows under this method resembles a cash budget showing receipts and disbursements for operations.

The second approach, called the **indirect method**, reports the same net cash flow from operations as does the direct method, but does so by starting with net income and then adjusting that amount for the effects of noncash items that affected net income. The indirect approach *reconciles*, describes the differences between, reported net income and the net cash flow from operations. This calculation is called a **reconciliation of net income and cash flow from**

Exhibit 17-1   Net Income versus Changes in Cash, Selected Companies, 1994 (in thousands of dollars)

	Net Income (Loss)	Net Cash Provided (Used) by Operations	Net Increase (Decrease) in Cash
Ben Franklin Retail Stores, Inc.	$ 1,558	$ (5,998)	$ (5,455)
Biogen, Inc.	(4,897)	34,886	(19,864)
Wendy's International	97,156	165,711	47,941

operations. Users are so interested in the explanation of why income differs from net operating cash flow that a reconciliation must be provided if a company uses the direct method of presenting operating cash flows.

Because the indirect method does not show cash flows for specific purposes, companies that use it must supplement their statements with disclosures of two specific cash flows. The first, which we explained earlier, is cash paid for interest. The second is total cash flow for income taxes. Some observers suggest that widespread public misunderstanding of the accounting for deferred taxes motivated the tax reporting requirement.

We use the indirect method in the sample format and illustration because (1) it is the method most often used in practice and (2) you will have to understand the reconciliation approach whether or not the cash flow statement uses that method of presentation.

NONCASH TRANSACTIONS

Some important operating, investing, and financing activities do not affect cash. For example, during the year ended January 18, 1995, **Pep Boys**, the auto parts company, acquired some property in part by assuming an obligation to pay off an existing mortgage on the property. Acquiring the property is an investing activity and taking on a mortgage is a financing activity, but no current cash flow reflects these activities. As another example, two years earlier, some holders of Pep Boys convertible bonds converted their bonds into common stock. Both cancelling debt and issuing stock are financing activities, but no cash changed hands.

Significant activities not involving cash must also be reported, either in a supplementary schedule or in narrative form. Whichever alternative is adopted, noncash transactions must be reported in a way that clearly distinguishes them from the cash flows for each of the three major types of activities. For simplicity, we use the supplementary schedule approach in the sample format and basic illustration.

CASH FLOW STATEMENT FORMAT

Exhibit 17-2 shows the cash flow statement of **Procter & Gamble**. The statement uses the indirect method of presenting operating cash flows and reports important noncash transactions and other required disclosures in a supplementary schedule. Notice that P&G reports both additions to, and reductions of, long-term debt. From the beginning-of-year and end-of-year balance sheets we could determine the net change in long-term debt, but not the separate amounts of new debt and repayments of existing debt. Another noteworthy point in the statement is that, as required by GAAP, it combines the net change in cash with the cash balance at the beginning of the year to produce the end-of-year cash balance. This calculation ties the cash flow statement to the balance sheet, just as starting the operating activities section with net income ties the statement to the income statement. Some companies show the beginning cash balance at the end of the schedule, after the change in cash.

Also notice the description of the net cash flow in each of the three major sections. Depending on the transactions during the year, the net flow in any

Exhibit 17-2   Procter & Gamble Company Statement of Cash Flows for 1995 (millions of dollars)

Cash and Cash Equivalents, Beginning of Year	$ 2,373
Operating Activities	
Net earnings	$ 2,645
Depreciation and amortization	1,253
Deferred income taxes	181
Change in accounts receivable	(225)
Change in inventories	(401)
Increase in payables and accrued liabilities	435
Change in other liabilities	(157)
Other	(163)
Total Operating Activities	$ 3,568
Investing Activities	
Capital expenditures	$ (2,146)
Proceeds from asset sales	310
Acquisitions	(623)
Change in investment securities	96
Total Investing Activities	$ (2,363)
Financing Activities	
Dividends to shareholders	$ (1,062)
Reduction of short-term debt	(429)
Additions to long-term debt	449
Reduction of long-term debt	(510)
Proceeds from stock options	66
Purchase of treasury shares	(114)
Total Financing Activities	$ (1,600)
Effect of Exchange Rate Changes on Cash and Cash Equivalents	$ 50
Change in Cash and Cash Equivalents	(395)
Cash and Cash Equivalents, End of Year	$ 2,028
Supplemental Disclosure	
Cash payments for:	
Interest, net of amount capitalized	$ 444
Income taxes	1,047
Noncash transactions:	
Reductions in employee stock ownership plan debt guaranteed by the Company	53
Liabilities assumed in acquisitions	575
Conversion of preferred to common shares	29

section could be an inflow or an outflow and the description would be worded accordingly. A few companies simply give a total for each classification, but most use descriptive titles. Note also that **P&G's** statement provides the required supplementary disclosures for interest and income taxes.

With the outline and the **P&G** example in mind as our final product, we shall illustrate how to develop a cash flow statement.

ILLUSTRATION

The subject of our illustration is USL Corporation, a retailer whose other financial statements are provided in Exhibits 17-3 and 17-4. Exhibit 17-4 also includes information about some USL activities in 19X5. For convenience, Exhibit 17-4 also shows the increase or decrease in each balance sheet item.

The comparative balance sheets show that USL's cash decreased $174,500 and that there are no short-term investments that might qualify as cash equivalents. Our objective, then, is to develop a statement that shows how USL's operating, investing, and financing activities combined to produce that decrease. If the net result of all such activities during the current year was to decrease cash by $174,500, the changes in the other items in the balance sheet must offset the change in cash. We will refer to these other changes as we develop the cash flow statement. When we have explained all of those changes, the cash flow statement will be complete except for some required supplementary disclosures. Let us begin by determining cash flow from operations.

Exhibit 17-3   USL Corporation Combined Statement of Income and Retained Earnings for 19X5

Sales		$1,000,000
Cost of goods sold		
Beginning inventory	$100,000	
Purchases	540,000	
Cost of goods available for sale	$640,000	
Less ending inventory	190,000	
Cost of goods sold		450,000
Gross profit		$ 550,000
Expenses:		
Depreciation	$ 56,000	
Interest	12,000	
Income taxes	123,700	
Other	128,800	
Total expenses		320,500
Net income		$ 229,500
Retained earnings at the beginning of the year		190,000
		$ 419,500
Dividends declared and paid during the year		30,000
Retained earnings at the end of the year		$ 389,500

Exhibit 17-4   USL Corporation Balance Sheets as of December 31

	19X5	19X4	Increase (Decrease)
Assets			
Current assets:			
Cash	$ 185,500	$ 360,000	$ (174,500)
Accounts receivable	272,000	130,000	142,000
Inventory	190,000	100,000	90,000
Prepaid expenses	8,000	20,000	(12,000)
Total current assets	$ 655,500	$ 610,000	
Noncurrent assets:			
Plant and equipment, at cost	$ 928,000	$ 600,000	328,000
Less accumulated depreciation	215,000	160,000	55,000
Total noncurrent assets	$ 713,000	$ 440,000	
Total assets	$1,368,500	$1,050,000	
Equities			
Current liabilities:			
Short-term bank loans	$ 34,000	$ 50,000	(16,000)
Accounts payable	135,000	105,000	30,000
Accrued expenses—taxes	38,000	2,000	36,000
—wages	12,000	3,000	9,000
Total current liabilities	$ 219,000	$ 160,000	
Bonds payable, due 20X5	100,000	100,000	
Total liabilities	$ 319,000	$ 260,000	
Owners' equity:			
Common stock	$ 660,000	$ 600,000	60,000
Retained earnings	389,500	190,000	199,500
Total owners' equity	$1,049,500	$ 790,000	
Total equities	$1,368,500	$1,050,000	

Additional information:

(a) USL issued common stock for $22,000 cash and additional stock of $38,000 for new equipment.

(b) USL obtained a new short-term bank loan for $80,000 and paid off a total of $96,000 on that and previous loans.

(c) USL bought new plant and equipment for $300,000 cash (in addition to that acquired by issuing stock).

(d) USL received $9,000 cash on the sale of equipment that had cost $10,000 and had accumulated depreciation of $1,000.

CASH FROM OPERATIONS

Using the indirect method, we begin with net income, which was $229,500. (Note that in analyzing net income we are actually dealing with one of the two factors that explain the net change in Retained Earnings. Dividends is the other factor.) Deriving net operating cash flow from net income is not difficult if you keep in mind the makeup of the income statement and the balance sheet. Look at Exhibit 17-3 and ask yourself the following questions.

- Why might revenues on the income statement differ from cash collected from customers?
- Why might cost of goods sold differ from the cash paid to purchase merchandise for sale?
- Why might the amounts reported as expenses not equal the cash paid for those items?

The answers to these questions give the content of the "Adjustments" section of the cash flow statement and come from your understanding of accrual accounting.

Revenues Versus Cash Inflows

Differences between sales and cash receipts occur for two reasons. First, early in the year a company receives cash from customers for sales made last year and included in last year's income statement. (This amount was the balance of accounts receivable at the start of the year.) Second, for some sales made late in the year, cash will not be collected until next year. (Amounts still due at year-end are accounts receivable at the end of the year.) Thus, net income reflects sales made this year regardless of the period in which cash was collected, while cash receipts reflect cash collected this year regardless of the period in which the sales were made.

To move from the amount of net income to the cash flow for the year, we must (1) add the accounts receivable at the beginning of the year and (2) subtract the accounts receivable at the end of the year. In USL's case, we add $130,000 and subtract $272,000, or we can simply subtract the $142,000 increase in Accounts Receivable. This is the second of the items in the Adjustments section of the cash flow statement's section on operating activities. (You might want to look briefly now at the completed statement shown in Exhibit 17-5.)

Cost of Sales Versus Cash Outflows

Consider next why there is a difference between cost of goods sold ($450,000) on the income statement and the amount of cash actually paid for merchandise. Two factors create a difference.

First, the beginning and ending inventories affect cost of goods sold for the year regardless of the year in which the company pays for inventory. The beginning inventory increased cost of goods sold and so decreased net income; the ending inventory decreased cost of goods sold and so increased net income. Thus, net income includes the effects of inventories, while cash payments for merchandise do not. To remove from net income the effect of inventories, we must (1) add the beginning inventory and (2) subtract the ending inventory. In USL's case, we add $100,000 and subtract $190,000, or we can simply subtract the $90,000 increase. This is the third adjustment in the statement in Exhibit 17-5.

The second reason for a difference between cost of goods sold and cash outflows for merchandise is that cost of goods sold shows the merchandise

Exhibit 17-5   USL Corporation, Statement of Cash Flows for 19X5

Cash flow from operating activities:		
Net income		$ 229,500
Adjustments for noncash expenses, revenues,		
losses, and gains included in income:		
Depreciation	$ 56,000	
Increase in accounts receivable	(142,000)	
Increase in inventory	(90,000)	
Increase in accounts payable	30,000	
Increase in accrued taxes	36,000	
Increase in accrued wages	9,000	
Decrease in prepaid expenses	12,000	
Total adjustments		89,000
Net cash flow from (for) operating activities		$ 140,500
Cash flows from investing activities:		
Purchase of plant and equipment	$(300,000)	
Sale of equipment	9,000	
Net cash (used) by investing activities		(291,000)
Cash flows from financing activities:		
New short-term borrowing	$ 80,000	
Repayment of short-term debt	(96,000)	
Proceeds from issuing common stock	22,000	
Dividends paid on common stock	(30,000)	
Net cash (used) by financing activities		(24,000)
Net change (decrease) in cash		$(174,500)
Cash balance, beginning of year		360,000
Cash balance, end of year		$ 185,500
Supplementary Disclosures:		
Interest paid		$12,000
Income taxes paid		$87,700
Issuance of common stock to acquire new equipment		$38,000

purchases made this year regardless of when the purchased merchandise was paid for. From your knowledge of financial accounting you know two things. First, early in the year the company pays cash for some of the purchases made in the prior year. (This amount was the beginning balance in accounts payable.) Second, some purchases made late in the year will not be paid for until the next year. (Unpaid amounts at the year's end are the ending balance in accounts payable.) Thus, the amount shown as cost of goods sold in this year's income statement can be higher or lower than cash payments for merchandise, depending on the relationship between the beginning and ending balance in Accounts Payable. To move from net income to the cash flow for the year, we must (1) subtract the accounts payable at the beginning of the year and (2) add the accounts payable at the end of the year. In the case of USL, we subtract $105,000 and add $135,000, or we can simply add the $30,000 increase in Accounts Payable. This is the fourth adjustment in Exhibit 17-5.

Operating Expenses and Cash Outflows

Finally, let us consider why other expenses shown on the income statement might not equal cash disbursements. One reason for a difference is well known to you. The first expense listed, depreciation, requires no current disbursement of cash. Depreciation expense reduced net income without having any effect on cash flows this period. Hence, to remove from net income the effect of depreciation expense, we must add depreciation (in USL's case, $56,000) to net income. This is the first adjustment in Exhibit 17-5 and is typically shown first on published statements.

There are two other reasons for the difference between the amounts shown in the income statement for various expenses and the cash payments for such expenses: accruals and prepayments. Let us consider accruals first.

Early in the year cash is paid to liquidate liabilities for expenses of the prior year (accrued expenses at the beginning of the year); in the latter part of the year expenses are incurred for which cash will not be paid until the next year (the ending balance of accrued expenses). Thus, the current year's income is reduced by this year's expenses regardless of the year in which the payments were made. To move from net income to cash flow for the year, we must (1) subtract accrued expenses at the beginning of the year and (2) add accrued expenses at the end of the year. In the case of USL, we subtract $2,000 and $3,000, the beginning balances in the two accrued expense accounts (for taxes and wages); then we add $38,000 and $12,000, the ending balances of the same two accruals. For simplicity, we will add $36,000 and $9,000, the increases in the two accounts. These are the fifth and sixth adjustments in the completed cash flow statement.

Prepayments of expenses are similar to expense accruals in that the year in which cash is paid is not the year in which the expense affects net income. For prepayments, however, the cash flow occurs before the item appears in the income statement. Thus, the current year's income was reduced by some expenses paid for in the previous year (the beginning balance of prepaid expenses), but cash was paid this year for expenses that will not reduce income until next year (the ending balance of prepaid expenses). To move from net income to the cash flow for the year, we must (1) add the beginning-of-year prepayments and (2) subtract the end-of-year prepayments. USL will add $20,000 and subtract $8,000, or simply add the $12,000 decrease in Prepaid Expenses. This is the seventh and final adjustment in the cash flow statement and completes the reconciliation of the difference between USL's net income and its cash flow from operations.

INVESTING AND FINANCING ACTIVITIES

Look again at the comparative balance sheets in Exhibit 17-4. Every item on the balance sheet, except Bonds Payable, shows a change over the year. We know already that the changes in Accounts Receivable, Inventory, Prepaid Expenses, Accounts Payable, the two expense accruals, and part of the changes in Accumulated Depreciation and Retained Earnings relate to operating activities. What brought about the other changes? Unless our investigation of these changes reveals some way in which they affected net income, they must be related to financing and investing activities.

From the combined statement of income and retained earnings (Exhibit 17-3) we know that USL paid $30,000 in dividends, which is a financing activity, and the change in Retained Earnings is now fully explained. The additional information in Exhibit 17-4 explains the other changes in the balance sheet. The stock issued for cash (item a) is a financing activity; the stock issued for new equipment is a significant noncash activity to be shown in the schedule of supplementary disclosures. Taking on a new bank loan and repaying old loans (item b) are also financing activities. Items c and d describe the acquisition and sale of property, two types of investing activities.[3]

The cash flow statement is now complete except for the required disclosures of payments for interest and for income taxes. Because the balance sheet shows no accrued interest at either the beginning or the end of the year, the $12,000 interest expense on the income statement is also the cash paid. Deriving the cash paid for income taxes involves using the same type of reasoning needed to derive the adjustments to net income. The $123,700 tax expense is not the cash paid because (1) early in the year USL paid $2,000 for taxes of the prior year (the beginning balance of accrued taxes) and (2) $38,000 of the tax for the current year will not be paid until next year (the ending balance of accrued taxes). To find the cash paid this year, we must add the $2,000 and subtract the $38,000 from the reported expense of $123,700. The result, $87,700, is the needed supplementary disclosure.

To summarize briefly, we started with comparative balance sheets for USL and noted that cash had decreased by $174,500. To explain that change, we analyzed the changes in all the other items on the balance sheet. The results of that analysis appear in the cash flow statement shown in Exhibit 17-5, which is further discussed in the next section.

CASH FLOW STATEMENT

The cash flow statement in Exhibit 17-5 provides a basis for further discussion. Consider first the adjustments to net income. If you reflect for a moment about the adjustments, you will recognize that the first, for depreciation, is quite different from the others.

The depreciation adjustment, required because depreciation expense appears on the income statement, has no relation to the operating cash inflows or outflows for the current period. The other six adjustments are needed because of short-term timing differences between cash flows and appearance on the income statement. Once you understand the reasoning for the treatment of these other adjustments, you may find the following rules helpful.

---

3 *Completing the cash flow statement without some of the additional information in Exhibit 17-4 would be difficult. It is sometimes possible to study the information available within the financial statements, deduce what transactions might have occurred, and then ask questions about such transactions. For example, because accumulated depreciation increased by $55,000 when depreciation expense was $56,000, we could infer a sale of some asset(s) with accumulated depreciation of $1,000 and know that the $328,000 increase in plant and equipment was a combination of the sale and some acquisitions. Similarly, the $60,000 increase in common stock would prompt a question about what the company received when the new stock was issued. The availability of the cash flow statement to interested parties outside a company eliminates the need for the parties to make and pursue such inferences, though that approach might be necessary when a statement is not available for some reason.*

1. Add to net income a decrease in an asset (or an increase in a liability) resulting from operating activities.
2. Subtract from net income an increase in an asset (or a decrease in a liability) resulting from operating activities.

Note that the net change in cash, a decrease of $174,500, agrees with the decrease shown in the comparative balance sheets in Exhibit 17-4. The two statements are thus linked, with the cash flow statement describing the cash inflows and outflows that contributed to the decline in cash, a balance sheet item. The link with the income statement is provided by using the indirect method to present cash flow from operations.

As we have shown, the information for a cash flow statement can be developed by analyzing the other financial statements and gathering some other information. Because the company's managers have access to information about its actual cash flows, the task is relatively easy. Without access to information about actual flows, the task is more difficult but not impossible. But for anyone—manager, stockholder, or creditor—presented with a cash flow statement, what is important is to understand its contents and implications; and that understanding begins with an understanding of how the statement is developed. The accompanying Insight describes how some companies discuss their cash flows in annual reports.

OPERATING FLOWS—SPECIAL CONSIDERATIONS

In developing USL's cash flow statement, we used the indirect method of presenting operating cash flows. We also used fairly common transactions. In this section we discuss and illustrate two important variations of these basic circumstances.

THE DIRECT METHOD, INFLOWS AND OUTFLOWS

Although the indirect method of reporting the cash flow from operating activities is acceptable, the FASB and many financial statement users prefer the direct method. Supporters of the direct method stress their interest in its separate disclosure of inflows and outflows. Of course, the *net* operating cash flow is the same regardless of the method used to present information about it. Hence, the same items that reconcile net income with net operating cash flow under the indirect method also explain the differences between cash inflows and outflows for specific items included in the income statement.

Consider the three income statement categories that affected net income for USL Corporation: sales, cost of goods sold, and other expenses. What is the difference between sales reported in the year's income statement and cash received during the year from customers? You answered that question already: the beginning and ending balances in Accounts Receivable. What is the difference between reported cost of goods sold and cash payments to acquire merchandise? You already answered that question, too: the beginning and ending balances in Inventory and Accounts Payable. Finally, why are the expenses shown on the income statement different from the year's cash payments for operating expenses? The answer you already know is that accruals, prepayments, and the noncash expense of depreciation explain the difference.

**SIGHT**

The importance of cash flow is illustrated by comments from companies' annual reports. **Procter & Gamble**, whose cash flow statement appears in Exhibit 17-2, pointed out that its $3,568 million cash flow from operations in 1995 was enough to finance its capital expenditures of $2,146 million, as well as pay $1,062 million in dividends to shareholders. P&G stated that it uses its cash to repay debt and buy back its own stock ($114 million addition to treasury stock). Exhibit 17-2 shows that P&G was able to repay $429 million in short-term debt and $510 million long-term debt while borrowing only $449.

Colgate-Palmolive commented that its cash flow from operations as a percentage of sales rose to 11 percent after being 10 percent in the previous year, reflecting "improved profitability and continued management emphasis on working capital." Colgate used its cash to finance acquisitions, repurchase shares of stock, and pay increased dividends.

In contrast, look at the totals of categories for **Brookstone**, the specialty retailer, for fiscal 1995.

Cash provided by operating activities	$ 1,884
Cash flows from investing activities, all	
expenditures for plant and equipment	(13,894)
Cash flows from financing activities, mainly	
proceeds from stock issuances	1,426
Change in cash during fiscal 1995	$ (10,584)

Brookstone cannot continue to make such plant and equipment expenditures without generating more cash from operations, which eventually must pay for everything a company does.

Sources: Procter & Gamble annual report, 1995, 20-21, 26; Colgate-Palmolive Company annual report, 1994, 20-2; Brookstone annual report, 1995, 21.

Thus, the same type of analysis that produced the information needed to reconcile net income with net operating cash flow provides the information needed to present net operating cash flow under the direct method. The only difference is that, to develop the information about inflows and outflows separately, we must adjust individual items in the income statement rather than the net result of those items (net income). Let us determine the separate operating cash flows for USL using the information developed earlier. In each case we begin with the amount shown on the income statement (see Exhibit 17-3) and compute the cash flow for that item.

Cash Receipts from Customers

Reported sales were $1,000,000, but Accounts Receivable increased by $142,000. We can compute the cash received from customers as follows:

Sales		$1,000,000
Add Accounts Receivable, beginning of year		
(additional current cash collections)	$ 130,000	
Deduct Accounts Receivable, end of year		
(uncollected sales)	(272,000)	
Increase in Accounts Receivable		(142,000)
Cash receipts from customers		$ 858,000

Cash Payments to Merchandise Suppliers

Cost of goods sold reported for the year was $450,000, but we know that this amount differed from cash payments to suppliers because of changes in Inventory and in Accounts Payable. To convert Cost of Goods Sold to cash payments to suppliers, we adjust for changes in these two balance sheet items, as follows.

Cost of goods sold		$450,000
Add Inventory, end of year	$ 190,000	
Deduct Inventory, beginning of year	(100,000)	
Increase in inventory		90,000
Add Accounts Payable, beginning of year	$ 55,000	
Deduct Accounts Payable, end of year	(85,000)	
Increase in Accounts Payable		(30,000)
Cash payments to merchandise suppliers		$510,000

If you have trouble seeing why an increase in Inventory should be added to cost of goods sold to arrive at cash payments while an increase in Accounts Payable is subtracted, consider again how these items affect cost of goods sold and review our earlier explanation.

Cash Payments for Expenses

From the earlier analysis we know that depreciation and the changes in Prepaid Expenses and the two accrued expense accounts explain the difference between reported expenses and the cash flows for expenses. As stated earlier, the FASB requires separate disclosure of the cash paid for two expense items, interest and income taxes, regardless of which method is used to present operating cash flows. Hence, although the same calculations apply to all the expenses, we separated these two items from other expenses. Accordingly, we can calculate the cash payments for expenses as shown on the top of the next page.

As you can see, the $87,700 calculated as payments for income taxes agrees with the amount computed and disclosed earlier.

Formal Presentation

Exhibit 17-6 shows the cash flow statement for USL Corporation using the direct method of presenting cash flow from operations. As you can see, the net cash flow from operations is the same as that shown in Exhibit 17-5 when the indirect method was used. Note that, with the use of the direct method, the details of the computations (i.e., the descriptions of the adjustments) are not part of the presentation. Remember, however, that a reconciliation of net income and net cash flow from operations must also be provided.

		Total	Interest	Income Taxes	Other
Expenses for the year		$320,500	$12,000	$123,700	$184,800
Eliminate effect of depreciation		(56,000)			(56,000)
Eliminate effect of change in prepaid expenses:					
Deduct beginning prepaid expenses	$ 20,000				(20,000)
Add ending prepaid expenses	8,000				8,000
Decrease in prepaid expenses		(12,000)			
Eliminate effect of change in accrued expenses:					
Add beginning accrued expenses	$ 5,000			2,000	3,000
Deduct ending accrued expenses	(50,000)			(38,000)	(12,000)
Increase in accrued expense		(45,000)			
Cash payments for expenses		$207,500	$12,000	$ 87,700	$107,800

Exhibit 17-6 USL Corporation, Statement of Cash Flows for 19X5

Cash flow from operating activities:		
Cash receipts from customers	$ 858,000	
Cash payments to merchandise suppliers	(510,000)	
Interest paid	(12,000)	
Income taxes paid	(87,700)	
Cash paid for other operating costs	(107,800)	
Net cash flow from operating activities		$ 140,500
Cash flows from investing activities:		
Purchase of plant and equipment	$ (300,000)	
Sale of equipment	9,000	
Net cash (used) by investing activities		(291,000)
Cash flows from financing activities:		
New short-term borrowing	$ 80,000	
Repayment of short-term debt	(96,000)	
Proceeds from issuing common stock	22,000	
Dividends paid on common stock	(30,000)	
Net cash (used) by financing activities		(24,000)
Net change (decrease) in cash		$ (174,500)
Cash balance, beginning of year		360,000
Cash balance, end of year		$ 185,500
Supplementary Disclosure:		
Issuance of common stock to acquire new equipment		$38,000

Companies using the direct method differ in the number and types of items reported separately as operating flows. For example, some highlight amounts paid for wages and fringe benefits, rent, or some other major expense. In the next section we discuss a common circumstance that affects both the computation and reporting of operating cash flows regardless of which reporting approach is followed.

NONOPERATING GAINS AND LOSSES

One transaction included in the example is unrealistic: the sale of plant and equipment at book value. Because there was no gain or loss on the sale to appear in the income statement, USL had only to report the proceeds as an inflow from investing activities. It is highly unlikely that a company selling a noncurrent asset will receive an amount exactly equal to the book value of that asset. Thus, when a sale occurs, the difference between the cash received and the book value of the asset sold will appear in the income statement as a gain or loss. Reporting a gain or loss on the sale of an asset in no way changes the fact that the *sale* is an investing activity. The proceeds from the sale are still an inflow to be reported under investing activities. The complication presented by such sales is that the resulting gains or losses do not reflect a cash flow from operating activities.

For example, suppose a long-term investment that cost $30,000 is sold for $45,000. The sale provides $45,000 cash, and the cash inflow should appear on the cash flow statement with the investing activities. But the income statement for the year includes the $15,000 gain on the sale. Hence, net income was increased by $15,000 as a result of a nonoperating activity. Under either the direct or the indirect method of presenting operating cash flows, the $15,000 income effect of the sale has to be eliminated. (If the book value of the investment had been $60,000, so that a $15,000 loss, rather than a $15,000 gain, occurred on the sale, the cash inflow would still be $45,000, and the $15,000 loss on the sale would also have to be eliminated to arrive at the cash flow from operating activities.)

Thus, gains and losses from investing activities are adjustments in deriving operating cash flows from amounts reported in an income statement. In a cash flow statement that uses the indirect method of reporting flow from operating activities, losses appear as additions to net income and gains as subtractions.

Let's look at the logic of why gains and losses on sales of noncurrent assets do not directly affect cash. Suppose a company sells a plant asset that cost $50,000 and has accumulated depreciation of $30,000 (book value of $20,000). First, suppose the sale is for $24,000, giving a $4,000 gain; then suppose the sale is for $15,000, giving a $5,000 loss. In journal entry form, the sales would show as follows:

Sale for $24,000:		
Cash	$24,000	
Accumulated Depreciation	30,000	
Plant and Equipment		$50,000
Gain on Sale of Equipment		4,000

Sale for $15,000:		
Cash	$15,000	
Accumulated Depreciation	30,000	
Loss on Sale of Equipment	5,000	
Plant and Equipment		$50,000

In both cases, the cash flow is the amount of cash received. The gain or loss is reported on the income statement. Because the gain or loss is not a cash flow and the sale of a noncurrent asset is not an operating activity, the gain or loss must be removed to determine cash provided by operations using the indirect method. Using the direct method, the gain or loss is simply not reported and no adjustment is needed.

CONCLUDING COMMENTS

Over the years, a common misconception has arisen that depreciation and similar expenses are inflows of cash. This misconception is understandable if we recognize that (1) the indirect method of computing operating cash flows has predominated in practice and that (2) under that method depreciation is added to net income to arrive at cash flow from operations. As you know, depreciation neither increases nor decreases cash. Depreciation requires no current outlay of cash; rather, a cash outflow occurs at the time the asset is acquired, and that outflow is reported as an investing activity.

In one sense, however, depreciation influences cash flows. Because depreciation is deductible for tax purposes, a company's income tax payment— which *is* an operating cash flow—is lower than it would have been had there been no depreciation to deduct. Hence, net cash inflow from operations is higher than would be the case had there been no depreciation.

We should also point out that the cash flow statement provides information beyond a classified listing of the company's cash flows. As we note in the next chapter, an understanding and evaluation of a company's activities requires study of more than one year's financial statements. At this point we comment only briefly on insights that might be provided by review of the cash flow statements.

Consider USL, the company whose cash flow statements we developed. Exhibit 17-5 (and Exhibit 17-6) shows that USL's net cash expenditure for long-term investments ($291,000) was more than the cash made available from normal operations ($140,500) and traditional sources of long-term financing sources ($22,000 from new common stock). Is this a good or bad sign? As you might expect, the answer is that it depends. A substantial net new investment in plant and equipment suggests expansion and the potential for growth in earnings. True, normal operating activities and financing sources didn't provide enough cash for USL's new investment. But USL's cash balance at the beginning of 19X5 was relatively large (about 34 percent of total assets), which might indicate that significant new financing was obtained in the preceding year. (Remember that managers plan in advance to meet cash needs for planned capital expenditures.) Thus, a reader should review USL's prior year's financial statements, particularly the cash flow statement, before drawing any conclusions. To return to the ideas presented at the beginning of this chapter, perhaps the primary value of a cash flow statement is that it shows managers' current responses to planned short-term and long-term needs for cash.

SUMMARY

Information about flows of cash is important to both managers and external parties. Generally accepted accounting principles require a cash flow statement as part of the financial statement package. Some short-term investments qualify as cash equivalents.

A company's activities are generally classified as operating, investing, or financing activities. A cash flow statement reports a company's cash flows under these three headings. Significant activities having no effect on current cash flows are also reported, either in narrative form or in a separate schedule of the cash flow statement.

Two approaches are acceptable for presenting information about cash flows relating to operating activities. One approach, the indirect method, reconciles net income with the net cash flow from operations. The indirect method does not report operating inflows and outflows separately. The preferred approach, the direct method, reports inflows and outflows separately but does not offer a direct link between the cash flow statement and reported net income. To provide that link, companies using the direct method must also provide a reconciliation of net income to net cash flow from operations. Cash flow statements prepared using either the direct or the indirect method will report the same net cash flow from operations, the same cash flows relating to investing and financing activities, and the same net change for cash, and will disclose the cash paid for interest and for income taxes.

KEY TERMS

cash equivalents   (798)
cash flow from operations   (797)
cash flow statement   (797)
direct method   (798)
financing activities   (797)

indirect method   (798)
investing activities   (797)
operating activities   (797)
reconciliation of net income and
    cash flow from operations   (798)

REVIEW PROBLEM

Comparative balance sheets and a combined statement of income and retained earnings for Harold Company are given in Exhibits 17-7 and 17-8 on pages 814 and 815, respectively.

The following additional information is also available.

(a) Common stock was issued for $200 cash.
(b) Investments costing $40 were sold at a gain of $30.

Exhibit 17-7   Harold Company, Balance Sheets at December 31

	19X7	19X8	Change Increase (Decrease)
Assets			
Current assets:			
Cash	$ 205	$ 190	$ 15
Accounts receivable, net	420	430	(10)
Inventory	350	310	40
Total current assets	$ 975	$ 930	
Investments	120	160	(40)
Plant and equipment	2,500	2,250	250
Accumulated depreciation	(800)	(720)	80
Total assets	$2,795	$2,620	
Equities			
Current liabilities:			
Accounts payable	$ 210	$ 220	(10)
Accrued expenses—taxes	28	22	6
—interest	6	16	(10)
—other	31	32	(1)
Total current liabilities	$ 275	$ 290	
Long-term debt	100	250	(150)
Total liabilities	$ 375	$ 540	
Owner's equity:			
Common stock, no par value	$1,800	$1,600	200
Retained earnings	620	480	140
Total owner's equity	$2,420	$2,080	
Total equities	$2,795	$2,620	

(c) Equipment costing $30 and with accumulated depreciation of $20 was sold for $10.

Required
1. Determine cash flow from operations using the indirect method.
2. Prepare a cash flow statement for 19X7.
3. Show the cash flow from operations using the direct method. Show separately the cash inflow from sales and the cash outflows for merchandise purchases, operating expenses, interest, and income taxes.

ANSWER TO REVIEW PROBLEM
1. To compute cash flow from operations we must determine the adjustments to net income. Review of the company's income statement reveals the need for three adjustments:
(a) Depreciation, a noncash expense, has reduced income.

**Exhibit 17-8   Harold Company, Combined Statement of
Income and Retained Earnings for 19X7**

Sales		$2,350
Cost of goods sold:		
Beginning inventory	$ 310	
Purchases	890	
Cost of goods available for sale	$1,200	
Less ending inventory	350	
Cost of goods sold		850
Gross profit on sales		$1,500
Operating expenses:		
Depreciation	$ 100	
Other operating expenses	359	
Total operating expenses		459
Operating income		$1,041
Other income and expense:		
Gain on sale of investment	$ 30	
Interest expense	21	
Net other income		9
Income before taxes		$1,050
Income tax expense		320
Net income		$ 730
Retained earnings as of December 31, 19X6		480
		$1,210
Dividends declared and paid		590
Retained earnings at December 31, 19X7		$ 620

(b) The sale of a long-term investment, a nonoperating transaction, has increased income.

(c) The change in Inventory, which is not directly related to cash flows, has increased net income.

The change in Inventory (an increase) produced higher net income because the ending inventory (which reduced cost of goods sold and hence increased income) was greater than the beginning inventory (which increased cost of goods sold and hence decreased income).

We can then turn to the comparative balance sheets for any other facts that might cause the reported components of net income (revenues, cost of goods sold, and operating expenses and other income and expense) to differ from cash flows relating to operations. Review of the comparative balance sheets reveals the need for three additional adjustments:

(d) The change in Accounts Receivable means there is a difference between cash inflows from operations and reported revenues.

(e) The change in Accounts Payable means there is a difference between cash outflows for operations and the reported cost of goods sold because there is a difference between cash outflows for purchases and reported purchases.

(f) The change in various accrued expenses means that there is a difference between operating cash outflows for expenses and reported operating expenses, interest, and taxes.

Changes in the other balance sheet items, though they may have affected cash, would not have given rise to operating cash flows. If such changes affected net income, their effects should be eliminated from net income as we compute the cash flow from operating activities. Let us look at the other balance sheet changes.

A change in noncurrent investments is normally from an investing activity, a sale or purchase. A cash flow from such a change does not result from operations. We have already recognized that net income must be adjusted to remove the effect of the sale of investments on net income (from adjustment (b)). A change in plant and equipment is also an investing activity, a sale or purchase. The income statement shows no evidence that either type of investing activity affected net income. The only operations-related change in Accumulated Depreciation is the depreciation for the year, which has no effect on cash flow from operations. We have already identified an adjustment (a) to remove the effect of the depreciation expense from net income.

The changes in long-term debt and common stock, whatever their causes, give rise to financing flows. Again, there is no evidence (such as a gain from retirement of debt) in the income statement that financing activities affected net income. The change in Retained Earnings is explained by net income, which we have already considered, and the payment of dividends, which is a financing activity.

Thus, we can compute the cash flow from operations by starting with net income and making the six adjustments (a) through (f).

Reconciliation of Net Income and Cash from Operations	
Net income	$730
Adjustments for noncash expense, revenues and gains:	
(a) Depreciation for the year	100
(b) Gain on sale of long-term investment	(30)
(c) Increase in inventory	(40)
(d) Decrease in various accounts receivable	10
(e) Decrease in accounts payable	(10)
(f) Decrease in various accrued expenses	(5)
Cash flow from operations	$755

2. In item 1, the information needed for one section of the statement, cash flow from operations, was developed. Our objective now is to find any nonoperating inflows or outflows of cash. For this information we refer again to the balance sheet changes that did not affect cash flow from operations. The changes, already discussed briefly, are summarized as follows:

Item	Change Increase (Decrease)	Change Already Explained Increase (Decrease)
Investments	$ (40)	$ (30)
Plant and equipment	250	80
Accumulated depreciation	80	
Long-term debt	(150)	
Common stock	200	
Retained earnings	140	730

Let us examine each of these changes carefully.

- The $40 decrease in Investments was the result of a sale that produced a gain of $30. Since the investments that were sold cost $40 (the amount of the balance sheet decrease in Investments), the proceeds from the sale must have been $70. Hence, we have an investing cash inflow of $70 to be reported on the statement.
- The normal reason for an increase in Plant and Equipment is a purchase of new equipment. But, we already know that during the year the company sold equipment that originally cost $30, thus reducing Plant and Equipment by $30. Thus, the purchases of new plant and equipment must have been enough to offset this decrease and produce a net increase in Plant and Equipment of $250, or $280 ($250 + $30). So we have two transactions: sale of equipment and purchase of equipment, both of which involve investing cash flows. The old equipment was sold for $10, and this amount should be reported as an investing cash inflow. The new equipment must have cost $280 and should be reported as an investing use of cash.
- As we know, depreciation neither produces nor uses cash. Hence, the change in Accumulated Depreciation is not a cash inflow or outflow. We have already explained the $80 increase for the year. Accumulated Depreciation increased by $100 because of the current year's depreciation expense, as shown on the income statement. Accumulated Depreciation decreased by $20 because an asset on which depreciation of $20 had accumulated was sold. The net change is an increase of $80 (an increase of $100 offset by a decrease of $20). In our analysis of Plant and Equipment, we determined that an investing cash inflow of $10 should be reported in connection with the sale of equipment.
- The normal reason for a decline in long-term debt is that some of the debt was repaid. Such a repayment is a financing outflow. Since we have no evidence to indicate some other reason for the decrease, we shall report the decline as a financing outflow in the amount of $150.
- Common Stock increased by $200; the usual explanation for such an increase is that additional shares of stock were issued. This conclusion is confirmed by the information obtained at the beginning of the problem, and so we include among the financing inflows of cash the issuance of additional stock for $200.
- The lower portion of Exhibit 17-8 reports that the net change in Retained Earnings resulted from an increase because of net income and a decrease because of dividends. Net income is an operating source of cash, and we have already dealt with cash from operations. The payment of dividends should be reported on our statement as a $590 financing outflow of cash.

Having analyzed and explained all the changes in balance sheet accounts during the year, we now incorporate our conclusions into the cash flow statement, as shown in Exhibit 17-9.

3. Calculating cash flow from operations under the direct method requires you to look at the individual sections of the income statement and apply the adjustments determined in item 1 to specific sections. Following Exhibit 17-9 are the calculations of specific operating cash inflows or outflows. We already know that the only other item to affect net income, the gain on sale of investments, resulted from an investing, rather than an operating, activity. Hence, neither the gains nor the proceeds from the sale would be reported as a part of the cash flow from operations. If Harold Company used the direct method of reporting its cash flow from operations, that segment of its cash flow statement would appear as on page 819.

Exhibit 17-9 Harold Company, Cash Flow Statement for 19X7

Net cash flow from operating activities:		
Net income	$ 730	
Adjustments for noncash expenses, revenues, and gains:		
Decrease in accounts receivable	10	
Increase in inventory	(40)	
Decrease in accounts payable	(10)	
Depreciation for the year	100	
Decrease in various accrued expenses	(5)	
Gain on sale of long-term investment	(30)	
Net cash provided by operating activities		$ 755
Cash flows from investing activities:		
Acquisition of plant and equipment	$(280)	
Sale of equipment	10	
Sale of investments	70	
Net cash used by investing activities		(200)
Cash flows from financing activities:		
Retirement of long-term debt	$(150)	
Proceeds from issuance of common stock	200	
Dividends on common stock	(590)	
Net cash used by financing activities		(540)
Net increase in cash		$ 15
Cash balance, beginning of year		190
Cash balance, end of year		$ 205

Computation of Cash Receipts from Customers

Sales		$2,350
Add Accounts Receivable, beginning of year (additional current cash collections)	$ 430	
Deduct Accounts Receivable, end of year (uncollected sales)	(420)	
Decrease in Accounts Receivable		10
Cash receipts from customers		$2,360

Cash Payments to Merchandise Suppliers

Cost of goods sold		$ 850
Eliminate effect of change in Inventory:		
Add Inventory, end of year	$ 350	
Deduct Inventory, beginning of year	(310)	
Increase in Inventory		40
Eliminate effect of change in Accounts Payable:		
Add Accounts Payable, beginning of year	$ 220	
Deduct Accounts Payable, end of year	(210)	
Decrease in Accounts Payable		10
Cash payments to merchandise suppliers		$ 900

Exhibit 17-9   Harold Company, Cash Flow Statement for 19X7 *(continued)*

Cash Payments for Operating Expenses

	Operating	Interest	Taxes
Expenses for the year	$ 459	$21	$320
Eliminate effect of depreciation (noncash expense)	(100)		
Eliminate effect of change in accrued expenses:			
Add accrued expenses, beginning of year	32	16	22
Deduct accrued expenses, end of year	(31)	(6)	(28)
Cash payments for expenses	$ 360	$31	$314

Net cash flow from operating activities:	
Cash receipts from customers	$ 2,360
Cash payments to merchandise suppliers	(900)
Cash paid for interest	(31)
Cash paid for income taxes	(314)
Cash payments for operating expenses	(360)
Net cash provided by operating activities	$ 755

Note that the $755 thousand cash provided by operating activities agrees with the amount shown in Exhibit 17-9, where the indirect method was used.

ASSIGNMENT MATERIAL

QUESTIONS FOR DISCUSSION

17-1   Depreciation and cash It is often said that cash generated by operations consists of net income plus depreciation. Explain why this statement is or is not true.

17-2   Net income and cash flow Walter Bryant started Bryant Machine Shop five years ago. The shop has been profitable and Mr. Bryant has been withdrawing cash in an amount equal to net income each year. He has taken out an amount equal to nearly half of his original investment of $80,000, most of which was used originally to purchase machinery. Mr. Bryant's customers pay cash on completion of work. He keeps very little inventory and pays his bills promptly, and he is puzzled because the cash balance keeps growing despite his withdrawals. Can you explain the increase in cash?

17-3   Net income and cash Suppose that a large retail chain and a railroad earned the same income. Which company would you expect to show the higher cash provided by operations? Explain your answer.

17-4   Explanation of a cash flow statement   You have provided the president of Ralston Company with a full set of financial statements, including a statement of cash flows. He understands everything except some of the adjustments in the operations section of the statement. He has three specific questions.

1. "Why do you subtract the increase in accounts receivable? We don't pay out cash for our accounts receivable, we collect it."
2. "You show the decrease in inventory as an addition. We sure didn't get any cash because our inventory decreased. In fact, the decrease means that we have less to sell next year and will have to spend more cash to replenish our supply. So why add it back to net income?"
3. "Our accrued expenses increased, and you showed this as an addition? Look, we had especially heavy payroll costs at the end of the year, and we paid them the third day of the new year. So it seems to me that we had to use more cash because of the increase, not less."

Required

Explain each of the items to the president.

17-5   Cash flow and growth   ABC Company has two divisions, one growing rapidly, one stable and mature. Both are profitable. Which division will generate positive cash flows and which will generate negative cash flows? Explain your answer referring to sections of the cash flow statement.

EXERCISES

17-6   Cash receipts from customers   Fill in the blanks in the following schedule.

	Case A	Case B	Case C	Case D
Sales in 19X8 income statement	$700,000	$900,000	$_____	$910,000
Net accounts receivable:				
At beginning of 19X8	32,000	47,000	18,000	31,000
At end of 19X8	25,000	55,000	25,000	
Cash collected from customers in 19X8	$_____	$_____	$853,000	$925,000

17-7   Cash payments to merchandise suppliers   For each of the following three cases, compute the cash paid in 19X7 to merchandise suppliers.

	Case A	Case B	Case C
Cost of goods sold in 19X7 income statement	$631,000	$795,000	$3,316,000
Merchandise inventory:			
Beginning of 19X7	205,000	152,000	846,000
End of 19X7	183,000	101,000	872,000
Accounts payable:			
Beginning of 19X7	21,000	22,000	78,000
End of 19X7	32,000	18,000	64,000
Cash paid to merchandise suppliers in 19X7	$_____	$_____	$_____

17-8 Relationships Fill in the blanks in the following schedule.

	Case A	Case B	Case C
Cost of goods sold in 19X3 income statement	$609,000	$521,000	$ _____
Merchandise inventory:			
Beginning of 19X3	81,000	47,000	262,000
End of 19X3	74,000	61,000	245,000
Accounts payable:			
Beginning of 19X3	32,000	68,000	93,000
End of 19X3	41,000	_____	85,000
Cash paid to merchandise suppliers in 19X3	$ _____	$523,000	$2,824,000

17-9 Components of cash flow from operating activities Which of the following items appears in the operations section of the cash flow statement for Washburn Company? Washburn uses the indirect method of presenting operating cash flows.

1. Depreciation expense.
2. Increase in Dividends Payable.
3. Decrease in Income Taxes Payable.
4. Loss from sale of long-term investments.
5. Decrease in Prepaid Insurance.
6. Increase in Inventory.
7. Proceeds from sale of long-term investments.
8. Increase in Accounts Receivable.
9. Amortization of patents covering Washburn's major product.
10. Payment for machinery to be used to produce Washburn's major product.

17-10 Classifying activities Classify each of the following transactions as an operating, investing, or financing activity.

1. Sale of merchandise (an inventory item) for cash.
2. Sale of merchandise (an inventory item) on account.
3. Sale of a fully depreciated machine for cash.
4. Declaration of a cash dividend on common stock.
5. Payment of a previously declared cash dividend on common stock.
6. Purchase of merchandise (for resale) on credit.
7. Payment of cash for purchase made in item 6.
8. Payment of the premium on a three-year policy for theft insurance on the company's inventory.
9. Acquisition of land by issuing a long-term note payable.
10. Payment of wages.
11. Purchase of 10,000 shares of the company's common stock from some of its stockholders. The price paid is less than that at which the shares were originally issued.
12. Sale of 5,000 shares of treasury stock at a price in excess of that paid to acquire that stock.
13. Accrual of interest due on a 20-year mortgage note payable.
14. Payment of previously accrued wages and salaries for employees.

17-11 Reconciliation of net income and cash from operations Prepare a reconciliation of net income and cash from operations using the relevant items from the following list.

Increase in land	$ 48,000
Increase in accounts receivable	42,000
Increase in accrued expenses payable	6,800
Decrease in inventory	26,500
Decrease in accounts payable	112,000
Decrease in prepaid insurance	1,500
Increase in common stock	85,000
Loss on sale of long-term investment	53,000
Net income	254,000
Depreciation expense	61,000
Decrease in cash	14,000
Cash received from sale of long-term investment	156,300
Cash provided by operations	248,800

17-12   Cash payments for operating expenses   For each of the following three cases, compute the cash paid in 19X7 for operating expenses.

	Case A	Case B	Case C
Operating expenses in 19X7 income statement	$576,900	$21,425	$4,150,000
Prepaid expenses:			
Beginning of 19X7	22,000	863	97,100
End of 19X7	19,300	541	105,400
Accrued expenses payable:			
Beginning of 19X7	21,200	2,260	57,800
End of 19X7	25,100	1,045	53,400
Cash paid in 19X7 for operating expenses	$ _____	$ _____	$ _____

17-13   Relationships   Fill in the blanks in the following schedule.

	Case A	Case B	Case C
Operating expenses in 19X7 income statement	$627,400	$123,800	$ _____
Prepaid expenses:			
Beginning of 19X7	35,400	25,500	103,000
End of 19X7	29,300		81,000
Accrued expenses payable:			
Beginning of 19X7	48,800	21,400	193,000
End of 19X7	51,100	24,300	242,000
Cash paid in 19X7 for operating expenses	$ _____	$118,400	$4,250,000

 17-14   Cash from operations—indirect method   In 19X9, Drew Company reported net income of $48,000. You also have the following information about 19X9.

1. Depreciation expense for the year was $110,000.
2. Accounts Receivable increased by $17,000.
3. Inventory declined by $9,000.
4. Accounts Payable decreased by $14,000.
5. Accrued Expenses increased by $6,000.

Required
Compute cash flow from operations.

17-15   Effects of transactions   Determine the effect, if any, of each of the following transactions on (a) net income and (b) cash. Show the amount of the change and its direction (+ or -).

1. Common stock worth $400,000 was issued in exchange for equipment.
2. A cash dividend of $100,000 was declared, but not paid.
3. The dividend in item 2 was paid.
4. An account receivable of $20,000 was written off against the Allowance for Doubtful Accounts.
5. A customer who owed the company $22,000 on account gave the company equipment with a fair market value of $22,000 in settlement of the receivable.
6. Interest payable was accrued in the amount of $14,000.
7. The interest payable in item 6 was paid.
8. The company bought 100 shares of its own stock for the treasury. The cost was $4,600, paid in cash.
9. Inventory with a cost of $18,000 was written off as obsolete.
10. Plant assets that had cost $45,000 and were one-third depreciated were sold for $12,000 cash.

17-16   Classifying activities   Indicate whether each of the following transactions is an operating, investing, or financing activity.

1. Cash collected on previously recorded credit sale of merchandise.
2. Sale of factory machinery for an amount of cash that exceeds the machine's book value.
3. Sale of factory machinery for an amount of cash that is less than the machine's book value.
4. Payment of cash for a previously recorded credit purchase.
5. Payment of the premium on a three-year policy for theft insurance on the company's inventory.
6. Acquisition of land by issuing common stock having a market value in excess of par.
7. Payment of wages.
8. Purchase of 10,000 shares of the company's common stock from some of its stockholders. The price paid is in excess of the price at which the shares were originally issued.
9. Sale of 5,000 shares of treasury stock at a price in excess of that paid to acquire the stock.
10. Payment of previously accrued interest on a 5-year note payable.
11. Receipt of insurance proceeds as a result of destruction of the company's factory buildings and machinery because of an earthquake. (The proceeds exceeded the book value of buildings and machinery destroyed.)

17-17   Analysis of noncurrent accounts   The following data were taken from the records of Miller Mining Company.

	End of Year	
	19X6	19X5
Plant and equipment	$4,240,000	$3,980,000
Accumulated depreciation	(980,000)	(740,000)
Mineral properties, net of depletion	7,750,000	6,950,000

You have also determined that plant and equipment costing $240,000 and with accumulated depreciation of $90,000 was sold for $80,000 and that depletion expense related to mineral properties was $440,000. The only other transactions affecting the accounts shown were depreciation expense, purchases of plant and equipment, and purchases of mineral properties.

Required

1. Determine the amount of cash provided by sales of plant and equipment.
2. Determine the gain or loss to be added or subtracted in the reconciliation of net income to cash flow from operations.
3. Determine the amount of depreciation expense to be added to net income in the reconciliation of net income to cash flow from operations.
4. Determine the amount of cash paid to buy plant and equipment.
5. Determine the amount of cash paid to buy mineral properties.

17-18   Cash flow from operations—special situations (continuation of 17-14)
After more careful study of Drew Company's income statement for 19X9, you determine that the following items also affected net income.

1. Amortization of intangible assets, $22,000.
2. Loss of sale of plant assets, $3,000.
3. On one sale, for $24,000, the customer gave Drew Company a 5-year note bearing interest at 9%.

Required

Recompute cash provided by operations.

PROBLEMS

 17-19   Statement preparation Following is a list of items for the cash flow statement for Collins Company for the year 19X8.

Net income for the year	$450,000
Dividends paid during the year	140,000
Proceeds from sale of a 10-year bond issue	350,000
Amortization of patents	57,000
Depreciation expense	143,000
Cash received from sale of land	106,000
Decrease in inventory	17,000
Increase in accounts receivable	74,000
Gain on sale of land	20,000
Decrease in accrued expenses	12,000
Cash purchase of new equipment	510,000
Cash purchase of a long-term investment	265,000
Increase in income taxes payable	6,000
Decrease in accounts payable	48,000
Purchase of land and buildings by giving a 10-year note	350,000

Required

Prepare a cash flow statement for 19X8 using all the items given. (Hint: The change in cash was an increase of $60,000.)

17-20   *Converting cash flow to income*   Boyd Company uses the direct method of reporting cash flow from operations. Following is the operations section of its cash flow statement for 19X7.

Cash receipts from customers		$857,000
Cash payments for:		
Merchandise for resale	$520,000	
Wages and salaries	160,000	
Income taxes	25,000	
Other operating expenses	120,000	
Total cash payments for operating activities		825,000
Cash provided by operations		$ 32,000

Other data taken from Boyd's records for 19X7 show the following.

(a) Accounts receivable increased by $20,000.
(b) Accounts payable decreased by $8,000.
(c) Inventory remained constant at $50,000.
(d) Accrued wages and salaries (the only accrued expense) increased by $3,000.
(e) Depreciation expense was $55,000.

Required

Determine Boyd Company's net income for 19X7.

17-21   *Reconciliation of net income and cash flow from operations (continuation of 17-20)*   Using the data provided in 17-20 prepare a reconciliation of net income and cash flow from operations.

17-22   *Cash flow statement from comparative balance sheets*   Following are balance sheets for Lorelei Company at December 31, 19X5 and 19X6.

	December 31	
	19X5	19X6
Cash	$14,000	$23,000
Accounts receivable, net	15,000	19,000
Inventory	12,000	10,000
Property, plant, and equipment, net	30,000	47,000
Total assets	$71,000	$99,000
Accounts payable	$ 3,000	$ 5,000
Notes payable, due in 1 year	4,000	3,000
Long-term notes payable	10,000	18,000
Common stock	48,000	48,000
Retained earnings	6,000	25,000
Total equities	$71,000	$99,000

The following information is also available about the company's transactions in 19X6.

(a) Net income was $27,000.
(b) Depreciation on plant and equipment was $3,000.
(c) Property, plant, and equipment costing $12,000 was purchased for cash.
(d) Dividends of $8,000 were declared and paid.
(e) Equipment was purchased by giving an $8,000 long-term note.

Required
Prepare a cash flow statement for 19X6. Use the indirect method to present operating cash flows.

17-23 *Determining cash flow from operations* Use the information provided to determine cash flow from operations.

From the income statement:	
Sales	$1,850,000
Cost of goods sold	925,000
Operating expenses, total	683,000
Depreciation (included in expense total)	73,000
From the balance sheet:	
Increase in Accounts Receivable	25,000
Decrease in Prepaid Expenses	12,000
Decrease in Inventory	37,000
Decrease in Accounts Payable	68,000
Increase in Accrued Expenses	17,000

17-24 *Cash from operations—direct method (continuation of 17-23)* Use your results from 17-23 to prepare the operations section of the cash flow statement using the direct method of presenting operating cash flows.

17-25 *Distinguishing operating cash flows* In 19X5, Bard Company reported net income of $168,600. The following facts are also known about the year's activities.

Increase in Inventory	$ 5,000
Decrease in Prepaid Expenses	400
Depreciation expense—company cars	31,000
Increase in Accounts Receivable	12,000
New short-term bank borrowings	45,000
Decrease in Dividends Payable	32,000
Amortization expense—patents	9,000
Decrease in Accounts Payable	4,000

Required
1. Compute the cash flow from operations for 19X5.
2. Explain how your answer to item 1 would change if you also knew that during 19X5 Bard sold some machinery for $2,800 cash, incurring a loss of $1,300.

17-26 *Selecting relevant information* Use the following information as necessary to compute cash flow from operations for the year.

Net income	$ 80
Increase in Accounts Receivable	12
Increase in Inventory	40
Decrease in Accrued Interest Receivable	3
Increase in Long-term Investments	135
Depreciation and amortization expense	161
Gain on sale of machinery and equipment	27
Proceeds from sale of machinery and equipment	198
Increase in Accounts Payable	74

17-27 *Cash flow statement from transaction information* Fisher Company began 19X4 with $18,000 cash. The following information is available for 19X4 activities.
(a) Net income was $115,000.
(b) Depreciation expense was $70,000.
(c) Fisher retired bonds payable that were due in 19X9. The cash paid to retire the bonds was equal to their $60,000 book value.
(d) Fisher paid $90,000 cash for new plant and equipment.
(e) Fisher declared dividends of $18,000 to be paid in January of 19X5. Dividends payable at the end of 19X3 were $3,000.
(f) One of Fisher's long-term investments in stock was written off as a loss in 19X4 because the company in which Fisher had invested went bankrupt. The book value of the investment was $30,000.
(g) Accounts Receivable increased by $15,000 during the year.
(h) Inventory increased by $26,000 during the year.
(i) Prepaid Expenses decreased by $8,000 during the year.
(j) During 19X4 Fisher sold, for $54,000 cash, a patent with a $38,000 book value.

Required
Prepare a cash flow statement for Fisher Company for 19X4.

17-28 *Cash flows from transactions* Transactions of Martin Company for 19X6 and other selected data are as follows:
(a) Sales, all on account, were $800,000.
(b) Cost of goods sold was $360,000.
(c) Depreciation expense was $60,000.
(d) Other operating expenses, all paid in cash, were $210,000.
(e) Equipment was purchased for $220,000 cash.
(f) Long-term investments were sold at an $8,000 gain. They had cost $57,000.
(g) Common stock was issued for cash of $150,000.
(h) A building that had cost $80,000 and had accumulated depreciation of $72,000 was destroyed by fire. There was no insurance coverage.
(i) Over the year, the following changes occurred in the current accounts.

Cash	+$ 17,000
Accounts receivable, net	+ 128,000
Prepaid expenses	+ 12,000
Inventory	+ 82,000
Accounts payable	+ 14,000

Required
1. Determine net income for 19X6.
2. Prepare a cash flow statement for 19X6.

17-29   *Effects of transactions*   Explain how each of the following affects the 19X9 cash flow statement of Gray Company.

1. A long-term investment in the common stock of Black Company was sold for $183,000, which was $42,000 less than its book value at the date of sale.
2. At the beginning of 19X9, Gray had a patent with a book value of $180,000. On November 15, 19X9, Gray sold the patent for $98,000. Amortization expense (for 19X9) to the date of sale was $45,000.
3. On October 31, 19X9, Gray sold some of its equipment for $18,000. The book value of the equipment at the beginning of 19X9 was $13,000, and 19X9 depreciation on the equipment to the date of sale was $2,200.
4. On July 3, 19X9, when the market value of its common stock was $28 per share, Gray declared a 10% stock dividend on its 100,000 shares of outstanding $20 par-value stock. The dividend was distributed on October 1, 19X9.
5. On April 1, 19X9, Gray retired an outstanding issue of bonds, paying $103,500 in cash. The bonds had a book value at the date of retirement of $98,300. Amortization of discount on these bonds between January 1 and April 1 of 19X9 was $200.
6. On March 19, 19X9, Gray acquired new machinery valued at $460,000. Gray paid $85,000 in cash for this machinery and gave a 5-year, 10% note for the difference.

17-30   *Cash flow*   As you were walking down the hall to your office at Complan Company, you met the president of the company. She was disturbed at the latest financial statements and wanted your help. She explained that the company was faced with a serious shortage of cash even though profits were high and working capital increased. She showed you the following condensed financial statements. (All data are in thousands of dollars.)

Complan Company, Income Statement for 19X7

Sales	$6,720
Cost of sales	3,850
Gross profit	$2,870
Operating expenses	2,140
Net income	$ 730

Complan Company, Balance Sheets as of December 31

	19X7	19X6	Change
Assets			
Cash	$ 25	$ 380	$(355)
Accounts receivable, net	990	860	130
Inventory	1,445	1,200	245
Plant and equipment, net	3,850	3,370	480
Totals	$6,310	$5,810	
Equities			
Accounts payable	$ 190	$ 280	(90)
Accrued expenses	110	200	(90)
Long-term debt	2,250	2,200	50
Common stock	2,080	2,080	—
Retained earnings	1,680	1,050	630
Totals	$6,310	$5,810	

The president told you that it had been touch-and-go whether the company would have enough cash to pay a $100,000 dividend that had been declared when the directors realized that the company was having an excellent year. To pay the dividend, the company had to increase its long-term borrowings by $50,000. "We made $730,000 and had depreciation expense of $150,000. We did buy $630,000 worth of plant assets, but I figured that our cash would stay about the same as it was last year. Look at this stuff and tell me what happened."

Required
Explain the results to the president.

17-31   Cash flow statement from comparative trial balances   Following are the beginning and ending balances of the balance sheet accounts for Truitt Company for 19X3.

	Beginning of Year Dr.	Beginning of Year Cr.	End of Year Dr.	End of Year Cr.
Cash	$ 36,000		$ 26,000	
Accounts receivable	50,000		60,000	
Allowance for bad debts		$ 10,000		$ 12,000
Inventory	70,000		85,000	
Buildings and equipment	190,000		240,000	
Patents	26,000		20,000	
Accounts payable		30,000		40,000
Accrued wages payable		4,000		5,000
Accumulated depreciation on buildings and equipment		96,000		100,000
10-year bonds payable		80,000		104,000
Premium on bonds payable		—		1,000
Treasury stock		—	4,000	
Common stock		100,000		135,000
Retained earnings		52,000		38,000
Totals	$372,000	$372,000	$435,000	$435,000

The following information is also available about the company's activities in 19X3.

(a) Net income was $14,000.
(b) Dividends of $8,000 were declared and paid.
(c) A stock dividend was declared and distributed, and for this reason $20,000 was charged to Retained Earnings, which represented the par and market value of the stock issued in connection with the dividend.
(d) Depreciation in the amount of $8,000 was recorded as an expense this year.
(e) Machinery costing $6,000 and having a book value of $2,000 was sold for $3,000 cash in 19X3.

Required
Prepare a cash flow statement for Truitt Company for 19X3. You may assume that any changes other than those described are attributable to reasonable transactions with which you should be familiar.

17-32   Treatment of transactions   Explain how each of the following transactions is reflected on a cash flow statement. Be specific.

1. Depreciation expense was $340,000.
2. A $110,000 dividend was declared late in the year and will be paid early next year.
3. Fixed assets costing $380,000 with accumulated depreciation of $170,000 were sold for $80,000 cash.
4. Long-term investments were written off because the companies issuing the securities were bankrupt. The write-off was $220,000.
5. The company issued long-term debt in exchange for land. The value of the land was $640,000, which equaled the value of the debt.
6. Near the end of the year the company sold a parcel of land for $300,000, which was $60,000 more than its cost. The buyer gave the company a 5-year, 8% note for $300,000.
7. The company paid $50,000 in settlement of a dispute relating to its income tax return of three years ago. The company debited Retained Earnings for $50,000.

17-33   *Statements from limited data*   The following changes in the balance sheet accounts for Rohmer Company occurred during 19X8.

	Change	
	Debit	Credit
Cash	$120	
Accounts receivable, net		$180
Inventory	120	
Plant and equipment	350	
Accumulated depreciation		90
Accounts payable	80	
Accrued expenses		30
Long-term debt	15	
Common stock		200
Retained earnings		185
Totals	$685	$685

The company had net income of $225 and paid dividends of $40. No plant assets were sold or retired.

Required

Prepare a cash flow statement. In the absence of available information, make the most reasonable assumption about the cause of a change.

17-34   *Classification of items in cash flow statements*   A list of items follows, most of which appear on a cash flow statement for Brillan Company for 19X8. During the current year, cash increased by $101,000.

(a) Dividends declared during the year were $125,000, but dividends actually paid in cash were $103,000.
(b) An issue of 10-year bonds payable was sold for $275,000 cash.
(c) Amortization of the company's franchise cost was $6,000.
(d) Depreciation on the company's tangible fixed assets was $159,000.
(e) Land was sold at a loss of $14,000; cash received for the sale was $74,000.
(f) Decrease in Inventory was $6,000.
(g) Increase in Accounts Receivable was $81,000.
(h) Increase in Accrued Expenses Payable was $11,000.

(i) Decrease in Income Taxes Payable was $24,000.
(j) Increase in Accounts Payable was $51,000.
(k) Decrease in Prepaid Expenses was $1,000.
(l) Increase in Allowance to Reduce Short-term Investments to Lower-of-Cost-or-Market was $3,000.
(m) Decrease in short-term bank borrowings (debt) was $13,000.
(n) Cash paid for new equipment was $500,000.
(o) Cash paid for a long-term investment was $158,000.
(p) A 10-year note payable for $200,000 was given to acquire land and buildings.
(q) Amortization of discount on the 10-year bond issue mentioned in item (b) was $2,000.
(r) Cash received as dividends on stock held as a long-term investment and accounted for on the equity basis was $25,000.
(s) Amortization of discount on a long-term investment in bonds was $3,000.
(t) Cash received from sale of treasury stock was $6,000; the stock cost the company $4,000.
(u) Increase in the credit balance of Deferred Taxes was $4,000.
(v) Brillan's portion of net income of the company whose stock is mentioned in item (r) was $56,000.
(w) Net income for the year was $402,000.

Required
Prepare Brillon's cash flow statement for 19X8.

17-35 Comprehensive problem Comparative balance sheets and an income statement for RJM Company follow. All data are in millions of dollars.

RJM Company, Balance Sheets as of June 30

	19X7	19X6
Assets		
Cash	$ 9.5	$ 28.7
Accounts receivable, net	125.8	88.6
Inventories	311.4	307.0
Prepayments	12.6	11.4
Total current assets	$ 459.3	$ 435.7
Investments	68.3	71.8
Plant and equipment	1,313.9	1,240.6
Accumulated depreciation	(753.1)	(687.4)
Intangible assets	42.5	46.2
Total assets	$ 1,130.9	$ 1,106.9
Equities		
Accounts payable	$ 62.6	$ 59.8
Taxes payable	32.4	29.6
Accrued expenses	38.9	52.6
Total current liabilities	$ 133.9	$ 142.0
Long-term debt	505.3	496.2
Common stock, no par value	384.2	377.4
Retained earnings	107.5	91.3
Total equities	$ 1,130.9	$ 1,106.9

RJM Company, Income Statement for 19X7		
Sales and other revenues		$896.3
Expenses:		
Cost of goods sold	$493.2	
Depreciation	69.3	
Amortization	3.7	
Income taxes	85.0	
Other expenses	203.5	
Total expenses		854.7
Net income		$ 41.6

Sales and other revenue includes a gain of $0.8 million on sale of investments. Amortization expense is related to intangible assets. Other expenses include losses of $1.3 million on sales and other disposals of equipment. These assets had cost $9.6 million and had accumulated depreciation of $3.6 million. Long-term debt and common stock were issued for cash.

Required

Prepare a cash flow statement for the year ended June 30, 19X7.

17-36   Cash flow statement from comparative trial balances—comprehensive problem   Following are the trial balances for Mesmer Company at the beginning and the end of 19X5.

	Beginning of Year		End of Year	
	Dr.	Cr.	Dr.	Cr.
Cash	$ 50,000		$ 60,000	
Accounts receivable	150,000		200,000	
Inventory	250,000		270,000	
Prepaid expenses	50,000		70,000	
Land	250,000		307,000	
Buildings and equipment	700,000		838,000	
Bond discount—5% bonds	—		8,000	
Allowance for bad debts		$ 25,000		$ 35,000
Accumulated depreciation		300,000		421,000
Accounts payable		170,000		220,000
Accrued expenses		105,000		115,000
Bonds payable:				
5% bonds		—		200,000
6% bonds		175,000		—
Bonds premium—6% bonds		4,000		—
Long-term notes payable		—		80,000
Capital stock—par value		450,000		475,000
Paid-in capital in excess of par		81,000		83,500
Retained earnings		140,000		123,500
Totals	$1,450,000	$1,450,000	$1,753,000	$1,753,000

The following data are available regarding Mesmer Company's 19X5 activities.

(a) Net income was $70,000, including gains and losses on transactions relating to fixed assets and bond retirements.

(b) Land costing $100,000 was purchased, paying 20% in cash and giving long-term notes payable for the remainder of the purchase price. The only other transaction related to land was a sale that produced a gain of $12,000.

(c) Equipment that had originally cost $82,000 and had a book value of $23,000 was sold for $8,000 cash. Additional equipment was purchased for cash.

(d) At the beginning of the year, bonds payable carrying an interest rate of 5% and a maturity value of $200,000 were sold for $190,000 cash. Very shortly thereafter, the 6% bonds were purchased on the open market for $159,000 and retired.

(e) During the year, a stock dividend was declared and issued and was accounted for by a charge against Retained Earnings for $27,500, the market value of the stock distributed in connection with the dividend. The market value was 10% higher than the par value for the shares issued. Cash dividends were declared and paid as usual.

Required

Prepare a cash flow statement for 19X5.

CASE

17-37   Brookstone's cash flow statements Cash flow statements for **Brookstone**, the specialty retailer, follow, in thousands.

	Year Ended		
	January 28 1995	January 29 1994	January 30 1993
Cash flows from operating activities:			
Net income	$ 5,143	$ 9,972	$ 6,320
Adjustments to reconcile net income to net cash provided by operating activities:			
Depreciation and amortization	4,276	3,099	3,565
Loss on sale of Peterborough facility	—	590	—
Deferred taxes	1,202	306	(2,659)
Extraordinary gain	—	(3,074)	—
Increase (decrease) in long-term liabilities	398	(1,401)	3,244
Cumulative effect of adoption of FAS 106 and FAS 109	—	—	(2,844)
Changes in working capital:			
Accounts receivable, net	(1,063)	(980)	(121)
Merchandise inventories	(7,443)	(6,373)	676
Other current assets	(435)	83	(1,140)
Other assets	(199)	(93)	—
Accounts payable	2,300	573	3,385
Other current liabilities	(2,295)	1,921	2,529
Net cash provided by operating activities	$ 1,884	$ 4,623	$12,955
Cash flows from investing activities:			
Proceeds from sale of Peterborough facility	—	$ 2,400	—
Expenditures for plant and equipment	$ (13,894)	(7,699)	$ (2,555)
Net cash used for investing activities	$ (13,894)	$ (5,299)	$ (2,555)
Cash flows from financing activities:			
Repayment of term loans	—	$ (18,930)	—
Payments for capital lease	$ (63)	(26)	$ (1,300)
Proceeds from exercise of stock options and related tax benefit	1,875	—	—
Payments for issuance costs	(521)	—	—
Issuance of common stock	135	19,648	—
Net cash provided by (used for) financing activities	$ 1,426	$ 692	$ (1,300)
Net increase (decrease) in cash and cash equivalents	$ (10,584)	$ 16	$ 9,100
Cash and cash equivalents at beginning of period	14,742	14,726	5,626
Cash and cash equivalents at end of period	$ 4,158	$ 14,742	$14,726

Supplemental disclosures of cash flow
  information:
Cash payments for:

Cash paid for interest	$177	$258	$1,413
Cash paid for income taxes	$4,136	$3,012	$941

Required

Answer the following questions.

1. Was Brookstone profitable during the three-year period?
2. Did Brookstone add to or reduce its cash over the three-year period?
3. Did accounts receivable increase or decrease in 1995?
4. Did accounts payable increase or decrease in 1995?
5. Why is the loss on sale of Peterborough facility, a distribution center, a positive adjustment in the operations section in 1994?
6. How much cash did the company receive for the Peterborough facility?
7. What was the book value of the Peterborough facility?
8. Cash paid for interest and for income taxes is highlighted at the bottom of the statement. Why aren't these items added back to net income in the operations section?
9. What is the biggest reason for Brookstone's 1995 cash flow from operations being so much less than its net income?
10. Is Brookstone using its suppliers to finance its inventories? Has it done so over the three-year period?
11. Where did the company get the money to repay the term loan in 1994?
12. Did the company pay dividends in any of the latest three years?
13. Was the extraordinary gain in 1994 included in calculating net income?
14. Did the cumulative effect of adopting FAS 106 and FAS 109 require cash payments?

18 Analyzing Financial Statements

LEARNING OBJECTIVES

After reading this chapter, you should be able to

1 Explain why financial analysts use ratios to evaluate companies.

2 Explain liquidity and show how ratios can measure a company's liquidity.

3 Explain profitability and show how ratios can measure a company's profitability.

4 Explain solvency and show how ratios can measure a company's solvency.

5 Describe leverage and show how it changes returns to stockholders.

6 Explain some limitations of ratio analysis.

The price of a company's stock is of major interest to its employees and stockholders, among others. A company's stock price depends principally on investors' expectations about profitability and financial strength. Changes in these expectations can have significant effects.

For example, on April 17, 1996, **IBM** reported excellent profits for the first quarter of 1996 and announced an increase in its dividend. But its stock price suffered a huge 9 percent drop because investors were concerned about comments from top management that suggested some slowing down over the next few quarters. On the same day, **Ford Motor Company** reported a 58 percent drop in profits but its stock price jumped $1.25 because investors believed that the company had turned the corner on profitability, and that the worst was over. How do investors reach such conclusions? What sorts of analyses do investors perform to make judgments about profitability and financial strength? How do they use these analyses?

Sources: Various issues of The Wall Street Journal, *various news reports on television.*

Throughout this book we have stressed the importance of expectations and the ways that accounting and other information help managers form reasonable expectations. We have also used ratios among financial statement elements. Chapter 2 showed that managers often express target profits as a ratio of income to sales (return on sales). In Chapter 11 you saw that managers commonly use the ratio of income to total assets (or some other measure of return on investment) to measure divisional performance. Chapter 7 illustrated the cash squeeze that can accompany buildups of inventories and receivables, as well as how managers use ratios when developing long-term plans. This chapter addresses the analysis of financial statements, including the calculation, interpretation, and evaluation of financial ratios.

Many people and organizations outside a company, such as suppliers and investors in debt or equity securities, are interested in the company's activities. Banks that provide short-term loans, insurance companies that buy long-term bonds, brokerage firms that give (or sell) investment advice to their customers, mutual funds that buy stocks or bonds—all of these, and many other institutions, employ financial analysts to help make decisions about individual companies. Individual investors also perform financial analyses. Our approach to analyzing financial statements is that of a financial analyst, who makes recommendations to investors after studying financial statements and other sources of information about a business. Because an analyst's recommendations can affect a company's ability to obtain credit, sell stock, and secure new contracts, internal managers must also be aware of what concerns financial analysts.

EXPECTATIONS AND PERFORMANCE

Like a company's managers, financial analysts base their decisions on expectations about the future. Just as managers focus on forecasts, financial analysts concentrate on what the future holds. Analysts want to know what to expect from a company—whether it will be able to pay its employees and suppliers, repay its loans, pay dividends on its stock, and expand into new areas. As with company managers, financial analysts also are concerned with the past only insofar as they can use the past as a reliable guide to the future. For example, an impressive history of growth in net income, sales, financial stability, and capable management is overshadowed if the company's major product is determined to be harmful in some way (e.g., tobacco, leaded gasoline), or becomes illegal (e.g., asbestos, the insecticide DDT) or obsolete (e.g., early types of computers and calculators). Nevertheless, analysts assume that what has held true in the past is likely to continue unless they have information that indicates otherwise, much as managers use a cost prediction formula developed on the basis of past experience. Hence, both analysts and a company's managers must be continually alert for signs that the future will differ from the past. In addition to focusing on the future, managers and financial analysts use many of the same analytical approaches.

METHODS OF ANALYSIS

Financial analysis consists of a number of interrelated activities. Among the most important are considerations of ratios and trends and the comparison of ratios and trends against some norms. (A *norm* is a standard for comparison, which could be an average value for a particular industry or for all companies in the economy.) Trends are of interest as clues to the future.

AREAS OF ANALYSIS

Different types of investors are interested in different aspects of a company. Short-term creditors, such as suppliers and banks considering loans of relatively short duration (90 days or six months), are concerned primarily with a company's short-term prospects. They want to know whether a company will be able to pay its obligations in the near future. Banks, insurance companies, pension funds, and other investors considering relatively long-term commitments (e.g., ten-year loans) cannot ignore short-term prospects, but are more concerned with the long-term outlook. Even if such investors are satisfied that a company has no short-term problems, they want to be reasonably sure that it has good prospects for long-term financial stability and can be expected to repay its longer-term loans with interest.

Stockholders, current and potential, are also interested in both the short-term and long-term prospects of the company. But their interest goes beyond the company's ability to repay loans and make interest payments. Their concern is with profitability—the ability to earn satisfactory profits and pay dividends—and the likelihood that the market price of the stock will increase.

We have divided the discussion of these aspects of a company's prospects into three major areas: liquidity, solvency, and profitability. For the most part we work with ratios. Apart from expressing relationships between two factors, ratios are useful because they facilitate comparisons among companies of different sizes.

ILLUSTRATION

We shall use the comparative financial statements and the additional financial information about Graham Company shown in Exhibit 18-1.

The analysis has actually begun in the exhibit because it shows the percentages of sales for each item on the income statement and the percentage of total assets or total equities for each balance sheet item. These percentage statements, or **common size statements**, can help an analyst to spot trends.

Two of the more important percentages on the income statement are the gross profit ratio, which is gross profit divided by sales, and return on sales (ROS), which is net income divided by sales. These ratios for Graham in 19X6 are 38.5 and 7.9 percent, respectively. The gross profit ratio improved in 19X6 over 19X5, but ROS declined.

Both financial analysts and internal managers are interested in ROS and the gross profit ratio because these ratios indicate how valuable a dollar of sales is to the company. (These ratios are not the same as the contribution margin ratio, but they do give a rough idea of the profit/sales relationship.) A relatively low ROS, combined with a gross profit ratio that is normal for the industry, could indicate that operating expenses are higher than those of other companies. Similarly, a decline in ROS or the gross profit ratio could also suggest weakening prices, which could be very serious. In late 1995, the stocks of many manufacturers of computer chips fell sharply because of concerns over

Exhibit 18-1 Graham Company, Balance Sheets as of December 31

	19X6		19X5	
	Dollars	Percent	Dollars	Percent
Current assets:				
Cash	$ 80,000	5.2%	$ 50,000	3.6%
Accounts receivable, net	180,000	11.6	120,000	8.7
Inventory	190,000	12.2	230,000	16.7
Total current assets	$ 450,000	29.0	$ 400,000	29.0
Plant and equipment—cost	$1,350,000	87.1	$1,150,000	83.3
Accumulated depreciation	(340,000)	(21.9)	(250,000)	(18.1)
Net plant and equipment	$1,010,000	65.2	$ 900,000	65.2
Other assets	$ 90,000	5.8	$ 80,000	5.8
Total assets	$1,550,000	100.0%	$1,380,000	100.0%
Current liabilities:				
Accounts payable	$ 110,000	7.1%	$ 105,000	7.6%
Accrued expenses	40,000	2.6	15,000	1.1
Total current liabilities	$ 150,000	9.7	$ 120,000	8.7
Long-term debt	600,000	38.7	490,000	35.5
Total liabilities	$ 750,000	48.4	$ 610,000	44.2
Common stock, 22,000				
shares	$ 220,000	14.2	$ 220,000	15.9
Paid-in capital	350,000	22.6	350,000	25.4
Retained earnings	230,000	14.8	200,000	14.5
Total stockholders' equity	$ 800,000	51.6	$ 770,000	55.8
Total equities	$1,550,000	100.0%	$1,380,000	100.0%

Graham Company, Income Statements for the Years Ended December 31

	19X6		19X5	
	Dollars	Percent	Dollars	Percent
Sales	$1,300,000	100.0%	$1,080,000	100.0%
Cost of goods sold	800,000	61.5	670,000	62.0
Gross profit	$ 500,000	38.5	$ 410,000	38.0
Operating expenses	280,000	21.6	210,000	19.4
Income before interest				
and taxes	$ 220,000	16.9	$ 200,000	18.6
Interest expense	48,000	3.7	42,000	3.9
Income before taxes	$ 172,000	13.2	$ 158,000	14.7
Income taxes at 40% rate	68,800	5.3	63,200	5.9
Net income	$ 103,200	7.9%	$ 94,800	8.8%

a Including depreciation of $90,000 in 19X6 and $75,000 in 19X5

softening prices, reflected in falling margins. **Intel**, the giant computer chip maker, stated that its gross profit ratio declined in 1994 because of such factors as price decreases and inventory writedowns. As we mention several times in this chapter, ratios provide clues or indicators, but they do not tell you that a company's managers are acting wisely or unwisely.

Balance sheet ratios show whether the proportions of particular assets or liabilities are increasing or decreasing, and whether they are within reasonable bounds. We explore balance sheet ratios in more detail later in the chapter.

LIQUIDITY

Liquidity is a company's ability to meet obligations due in the near future. The more liquid the company, the more likely it is to be able to pay its employees, suppliers, and holders of its short-term notes payable. A company with excellent long-term prospects could fail to realize them because it was forced into bankruptcy when it could not pay its debts in the near term. Hence, while liquidity is most important to short-term creditors, it also interests long-term creditors and stockholders.

WORKING CAPITAL AND THE CURRENT RATIO

Working capital, the difference between current assets and current liabilities, is a very rough measure of liquidity. Graham had the following amounts of working capital at the end of 19X5 and 19X6.

	19X6	19X5
Current assets	$450,000	$400,000
Current liabilities	150,000	120,000
Working capital	$300,000	$280,000

Working capital is positive and increased. But this does not necessarily mean that Graham has adequate liquidity or became more liquid. Most analysts consider changes in working capital as only a very rough indication of changes in liquidity and supplement their analysis with several other calculations. Working capital is stated in absolute dollar terms and hence is greatly influenced by the size of the company.

The current ratio is a measure of relative liquidity that takes into account differences in absolute size. It is used to compare companies with different total current assets and liabilities as well as to compare the same company's liquidity from year to year.

$$Current\ ratio\ =\ \frac{current\ assets}{current\ liabilities}$$

Graham has current ratios of 3.33 to 1 in 19X5 ($400,000/$120,000) and 3 to 1 in 19X6 ($450,000/$150,000). On the basis of the current ratio, we would say that the company seemed to be less liquid at the end of 19X6. With good reason we said "seemed to be less liquid." One major problem that arises with any ratio, but especially the current ratio, is that of composition. The **composition problem** arises when one uses a total, such as total current assets (or current liabilities), that might mask information about the individual components. How soon will the current assets be converted into cash so that they can be used to pay current liabilities? How soon are the current liabilities due for payment? You already know that current assets normally are listed in order of liquidity from cash, the most liquid, to prepaid expenses. The analyst obtains a general idea of the magnitude of the composition problem by reviewing the common-size balance sheet to see how much of current assets consists of relatively liquid items.

QUICK RATIO (ACID-TEST RATIO)

The quick ratio, or acid-test ratio, is cash plus marketable securities plus accounts receivable divided by current liabilities. It is similar to the current ratio, but includes only those assets that are cash or "near cash" (called **quick assets**). Hence, the ratio gives a stricter indication of short-term debt-paying ability than does the current ratio.

$$Quick\ ratio\ =\ \frac{cash\ +\ marketable\ securities\ +\ accounts\ receivable}{current\ liabilities}$$

Graham had no marketable securities at the end of either year, so its quick ratios are as follows:

$$19X5 \quad \frac{\$50,000\ +\ \$120,000}{\$120,000}\ =\ 1.42$$

$$19X6 \quad \frac{\$80,000\ +\ \$180,000}{\$150,000}\ =\ 1.73$$

Graham seems to have increased its liquidity because its quick ratio increased. We could say that the company was better able to meet current liabilities at the end of 19X6; but we would still like to know how soon its current liabilities have to be paid and how rapidly it can expect to turn its receivables and inventory into cash. The next section presents ratios that measure the liquidity of current assets.

WORKING CAPITAL ACTIVITY RATIOS

Two commonly used ratios provide information about the time within which a company should realize cash from its receivables and inventories. And, although we cannot tell the time within which the company must pay its various current liabilities simply by examining the financial statements, one commonly used ratio offers some insight into the company's bill-paying practices.

Accounts Receivable Turnover

Accounts receivable turnover measures how rapidly a company collects its receivables; in general, the higher the turnover the better.

$$Accounts\ receivable\ turnover\ =\ \frac{credit\ sales}{average\ receivables}$$

Average receivables are usually defined as the beginning balance plus the ending balance, divided by 2. This simple averaging procedure is satisfactory so long as there are no extremely high or low points during the year (including the end of the year). If a company's receivables fluctuate widely, using a monthly average for receivables is better. For illustrative purposes we assume that all of Graham's sales are on credit. Because we do not have the beginning balance for 19X5, we can only calculate the turnover of *average* receivables for 19X6 for Graham Company. (Some analysts do compute turnovers using end-of-year values.)

$$\frac{\$1,300,000}{(\$120,000\ +\ \$180,000)/2}\ =\ \frac{\$1,300,000}{\$150,000}\ =\ 8.67\ times$$

Some analysts make a related calculation called number of days' sales in accounts receivable. This figure indicates the average age of ending accounts receivable.

$$Days'\ sales\ in\ accounts\ receivable\ =\ \frac{ending\ accounts\ receivable}{average\ daily\ credit\ sales}$$

Average daily sales is simply credit sales for the year divided by 365. For Graham Company, we have average daily credit sales of about \$2,959(\$1,080,000/365) for 19X5 and about \$3,562 (\$1,300,000/365) for 19X6. Hence, days' sales in accounts receivable are

$$19X5\quad \frac{\$120,000}{\$2,959}\ =\ 41\ days$$

$$19X6\quad \frac{\$180,000}{\$3,563}\ =\ 51\ days$$

On average, then, Graham's accounts receivable were 41 days old at the end of 19X5 and 51 days old at the end of 19X6. The collection period has lengthened considerably in one year, but the period must be interpreted in light of the credit terms offered to customers. The faster customers pay, the better, but there are always trade-offs. If a company loses sales because of tight credit policies, the advantage of faster collection might be more than offset by the loss of profits from lower total sales. The increase in the average collection period might well be the result of a management decision to offer more liberal terms to stimulate sales.

We used Graham's total sales to compute the two receivables-related ratios because we assumed that all sales were on credit. An outside analyst seldom knows what portion of sales is on credit and uses total sales for lack of better information. The ratios so computed are not misleading as long as the proportions of cash and credit sales did not change significantly (another instance of "the composition problem"). An internal manager, of course, has access to information about the composition of total sales and could make a more precise calculation of the receivables ratios. Moreover, the internal manager is extremely interested in the precise patterns of customer payments, for cash budgeting and control purposes. Nevertheless, as a first step in the analysis, the internal manager is likely to use the same ratios as the external analyst.

Inventory Turnover

The type of analysis discussed in connection with receivables also applies to the company's inventory. Inventory turnover is calculated as follows:

$$\textit{Inventory turnover} \ = \ \frac{\textit{cost of goods sold}}{\textit{average inventory}}$$

Again, average inventory is the sum of the beginning and ending balances divided by 2 unless the company has much higher and lower inventories for significant portions of the year because of seasonal business. It is then better to use monthly figures to determine the average.

Graham's inventory turnover for 19X6 is about 3.8 times, calculated as follows:

$$\frac{\$800,000}{(\$230,000 \ + \ \$190,000)/2} \ = \ \frac{\$800,000}{\$210,000} \ = \ 3.8 \ \textit{times}$$

Using only the year-end inventory for 19X5, turnover is 2.9 times (\$670,000/ \$230,000).

Inventory turnover indicates the efficiency with which a company uses its inventory. High inventory turnover is critical for many businesses, especially those that sell at relatively low markup (ratio of gross profit to cost) and depend on high sales volumes to earn satisfactory profits. For example, discount stores and food stores rely on quick turnover for profitability. Companies with very high markups, such as jewelry stores, do not need such rapid turnovers to be profitable.

As discussed in Chapters 1, 6, and 9, maintaining inventory can be very expensive. Some costs—insurance, personal property taxes, interest on the funds tied up in inventory, and obsolescence—can be very high. Therefore, managers prefer to keep inventory as low as possible. The problem is that if inventory is too low, particularly in retail stores, sales might be lost because customers cannot find what they want.

Analysts will also sometimes calculate the number of days' sales in inventory, which is a measure of the supply that the company maintains.

$$\textit{Days' sales in inventory} \ = \ \frac{\textit{ending inventory}}{\textit{average daily cost of goods sold}}$$

Average daily cost of goods sold is simply cost of goods sold for the year divided by 365. For Graham, this is \$1,836 (\$670,000/365) for 19X5 and \$2,192 (\$800,000/365) for 19X6. Days' sales in inventory are as follows:

$$19X5 \quad \frac{\$230,000}{\$1,836} \ = \ 125 \ \textit{days}$$

$$19X6 \quad \frac{\$190,000}{\$2,192} \ = \ 87 \ \textit{days}$$

The decline in days' sales in Graham's inventory could indicate a deliberate change in inventory policy, or perhaps just a temporary reduction of inventory because of heavier than expected sales near the end of the year.

As you may remember from your study of financial accounting, generally accepted accounting principles (GAAP) allow several formats for the income statement. Some formats do not show cost of goods sold, so that an outside analyst cannot compute inventory turnover using the approach just presented. In such cases, the analyst will use sales as a substitute for cost of goods sold, even though sales and inventory are not measured in the same way. (Sales is measured in selling prices, while inventory is measured in cost prices.) The inventory turnover so derived is *overstated*—a unit costing $1 and sold for $2 will reflect two inventory turnovers when only one unit has been sold. If analysts recognize the overstatement in the calculation, they will not be misled by the results.

PROFITABILITY

Profitability can be measured in absolute dollar terms, such as net income, or by ratios. The most commonly used measures of profitability fall under the general heading of return on investment (ROI). As described in Chapter 11, ROI is actually a family of ratios having the general form

$$\textit{Return on investment} = \frac{\textit{income}}{\textit{investment}}$$

External investors, especially stockholders and potential stockholders, are interested in the return that they can expect from their investments. A company's managers want to earn satisfactory returns on the investments that they control. As a practical matter, then, different analysts and managers will define both income and investment differently when trying to measure the same basic relationships. In this section, we present some of the most often used alternative ways of looking at this basic relationship of accomplishment (return, income) to effort (investment).

RETURN ON ASSETS (ROA)

ROA measures operating efficiency, how well managers have used the assets under their control to generate income. The following ratio is one way to make the calculation.

$$\textit{Return on assets} = \frac{\textit{net income} + \textit{interest} + \textit{income taxes}}{\textit{average total assets}}$$

For Graham, ROA was about 15 percent for 19X6, calculated as follows:

$$\frac{\$103,200 + \$48,000 + \$68,800}{(\$1,380,000 + \$1,550,000)/2} = \frac{\$220,000}{\$1,465,000} = 15.0\%$$

Adding interest and income taxes back to net income is equivalent to using income before interest and income taxes. Remember that we are concerned with operations: Interest and, to some extent, income taxes depend on how the company finances its assets—how much debt it uses. Moreover, income taxes are affected by many matters not related to operations, which is another reason for adding them back. (Some of these nonoperating factors are the company's investments in securities and its use of tax benefits such as percentage depletion.) Some analysts add back only interest; others add back only the after-tax effect of interest. There are arguments to support several measures of the numerator in the ROA calculation. Choosing one alternative over another is a matter of both personal preference and of the particular objective.

Average total assets is normally the sum of the beginning and ending balance sheet amounts divided by 2, although if significant fluctuations occur from month to month, it is better to use monthly data to determine the average. Some analysts use end-of-year assets in the denominator, some use beginning-of-year amounts, and still others use total assets minus current liabilities. (Analysts in the latter group argue that current liabilities are operating sources, rather than financing sources.) In this chapter, we use average total assets, or total year-end assets, with no consideration of current liabilities, but we caution you that this is a matter of choice and preference.

Both internal and external analysts can obtain the information for this ratio directly from publicly available financial statements, and can make direct comparisons with companies in the same industry.

RETURN ON COMMON EQUITY (ROE)

ROA is a measure of operating efficiency. Common stockholders are also concerned with the return on their investment, which is affected not only by operations but also by the amount of debt and preferred stock in the company's capital structure.

ROE is computed as follows.

$$\textit{Return on common equity} \ = \ \frac{\textit{net income - dividends on preferred stock}}{\textit{average common stockholders' equity}}$$

In the absence of preferred stock, average common stockholders' equity is simply the sum of the beginning and ending amounts of stockholders' equity divided by 2. If there is preferred stock, preferred dividends must be subtracted from net income in the numerator, and the amount of total stockholders' equity attributable to preferred stock is subtracted in the denominator to obtain common stockholders' equity.

Graham Company has no preferred stock, but it does have debt. ROE for Graham in 19X6 is a bit over 13 percent.

$$\frac{\$103,200}{(\$770,000 \ + \ \$800,000)/2} \ = \ \frac{\$103,200}{\$785,000} \ = \ 13.1\%$$

Notice that Graham's ROE is less than its ROA. If a company finances its assets solely with common stock, such a relationship will hold between ROE and ROA because ROE is computed using after-tax income. But debt holders do not participate in the earnings of the company; they receive a stipulated, constant amount of interest. Hence, the company can increase its ROE if it uses debt, provided that ROA is greater than the interest rate it must pay to debt holders. This method of using debt (or preferred stock) to increase ROE is called

leverage or **trading on the equity** (sometimes *financial leverage*). Leverage increases both risk and the potential for greater return.

THE EFFECTS OF LEVERAGE

Suppose that a company with a 40 percent tax rate requires total assets of $1,000,000 to earn $180,000 per year before interest and income taxes, for an ROA of 18 percent. Three possible financing alternatives are (1) all common stock, (2) $400,000 common stock and $600,000 in 7% bonds (interest expense of $42,000), and (3) $400,000 in common stock and $600,000 in 8% preferred stock (dividends of $48,000). The following schedule shows the differing effects of the three alternatives on ROE.

	(1) All Common Stock	(2) Debt and Common Stock	(3) Preferred Stock and Common Stock
Income before interest and taxes	$ 180,000	$180,000	$180,000
Interest expense at 7%	0	42,000	0
Income before taxes	$ 180,000	$138,000	$180,000
Income taxes at 40%	72,000	55,200	72,000
Net income	$ 108,000	$ 82,800	$108,000
Less preferred stock dividends	0	0	48,000
Earnings available for common stock	$ 108,000	$ 82,800	$ 60,000
Divided by common equity invested	1,000,000	400,000	400,000
Equals return on common equity	10.8%	20.7%	15.0%

Note that dividends on preferred stock must be subtracted from net income to reach earnings *available for common stockholders* (because the preferred shareholders have a prior claim on the company's earnings). Note also that, although the plans that include debt or preferred stock both result in lower earnings available for common equity, both produce a higher ROE than would be achieved if all common equity were used. That is, these two plans provide the benefits of leverage.

However, leverage works both ways. It is good for the common stockholder when earnings are high and bad when they are low. If in one year the company earns only $60,000 before interest and taxes, it has the following results.

	(1) All Common	(2) $600,000 Debt	(3) $600,000 Preferred
Income before interest and taxes	$ 60,000	$ 60,000	$ 60,000
Interest expense at 7%	0	42,000	0
Income before taxes	$ 60,000	$ 18,000	$ 60,000
Income taxes at 40%	24,000	7,200	24,000
Net income	$ 36,000	$ 10,800	$ 36,000
Less preferred stock dividends	0	0	42,000
Earnings available for common stock	$ 36,000	$ 10,800	$ (6,000)
Divided by common equity invested	1,000,000	400,000	400,000
Equals return on common equity	3.6%	2.7%	negative

As you can see, ROE is highest if all common equity is used, but the return is very low. Companies having relatively stable revenues and expenses, such as public utilities, can use considerable leverage. Leverage is very risky for companies in cyclical industries such as automobile and aircraft manufacturing, and construction, where income fluctuates greatly from year to year. A couple of bad years in a row could bring a heavily leveraged company into bankruptcy. During the 1980s, leverage was so important in the acquisition of entire companies that the term *leveraged buyout* (LBO) became a standard part of financial discussions. Often such acquisitions were financed with high-yield bonds, called junk bonds because of their high risk.

EARNINGS PER SHARE (EPS)

Investors in common stock are less concerned with a company's total income than with their share of that income as expressed by the company's earnings per share (EPS). EPS is the most widely cited statistic in the financial press, the business section of newspapers, and recommendations by brokerage firms and other investment advisers. In simple cases, EPS is calculated as follows:

$$\textit{Earnings per share (EPS)} = \frac{\textit{net income - dividends on preferred stock}}{\textit{weighted-average common shares outstanding}}$$

The weighted average of common shares outstanding is the best measure of the shares outstanding throughout the period when the income is earned. If Graham had 22,000 shares outstanding all through 19X5 and 19X6, as well as at the ends of those years, its EPS figures are

$$19X5 \quad \frac{\$94,800 - \$0}{22,000} = \frac{\$94,800}{22,000} = \$4.31$$

$$19X6 \quad \frac{\$103,200 - \$0}{22,000} = \frac{\$103,200}{22,000} = \$4.69$$

EPS in 19X6 was $0.38 higher than in 19X5. This is an 8.8 percent growth rate, which we calculate as follows:

$$\textit{Growth rate of EPS} = \frac{\textit{EPS current year - EPS prior year}}{\textit{EPS prior year}}$$

The greater the growth that investors expect, the more they are willing to pay for the common stock. Of course, an increase in EPS from one year to the next does not always mean that the company is growing; it might simply reflect a rebound from a particularly poor year. EPS could also increase (or decrease) because of an unusual event that is unlikely to recur frequently. (Financial accounting refers to such events as extraordinary items.) Many analysts compare EPS numbers without the effects of extraordinary items and other one-time events such as the discontinuance of a major segment of the business or a change in accounting principle used to prepare financial statements, such as a change from FIFO to LIFO. GAAP accommodates that practice by requiring the reporting of an EPS number before extraordinary items, gains or losses on discontinuances, and changes in accounting principle. In any case, growth rates should be calculated over a number of years, rather than for a single year as we have done here. The upcoming Insight explores the importance of growth rates in stock prices.

Some companies issue **convertible securities**, bonds and preferred stock that can be converted into common stock at the option of the owner. Conversion poses the problem of potential **dilution** (decreases) in EPS, because earnings have to be spread over a greater number of shares.[1] Calculating EPS when dilution is possible can be extremely complex. We shall show a single, relatively simple, illustration. Assume that a company has net income of $200,000, 80,000 common shares outstanding, and an issue of convertible preferred stock. The preferred stock pays dividends of $20,000 and is convertible into 30,000 common shares. Using the basic formula, EPS is $2.25.

$$\frac{\$200,000 - \$20,000}{80,000} = \frac{\$180,000}{80,000} = \$2.25$$

IN SIGHT

Many investors, called growth investors, seek out stocks with rapidly increasing profits, and such stocks can be very volatile. If a slow-growing stock typically maintains a PE ratio of 10, a slight change in its growth rate will have little effect on its price because its PE ratio will probably stay around 10. But the price of a high-growth stock with a PE ratio of 30 will change considerably if its growth rate changes. Changes in growth rates affect PE ratios. For example, on April 16, 1996, the stock of **Informix** increased 24 percent on heavy volume after the company announced an EPS of 10 cents, only a single cent above Wall Street concensus estimates, but apparently enough to indicate faster growth than previously expected. On the same day, shares of **DSP Group** fell nearly 10 percent after it reported an EPS slightly below analysts' expectations, suggesting the possibility of slowing growth.

Following are the growth rates and PE ratios of four companies, as published by a national brokerage firm.

Company	Growth Rate	PE Ratio
Altera	30%	24.8
Promus Hotel	25%	25.1
Bell Atlantic	10%	14.0
GTE	10%	14.9

---

1 *The computation of EPS is governed by Accounting Principles Board Opinion No. 15 (New York: American Institute of Certified Public Accountants, 1969) and Unofficial Accounting Interpretations of APB Opinion No. 15 (New York: American Institute of Certified Public Accountants, 1970). Together, these two documents contain about 100 pages.*

In some cases the $2.25 is presented on the income statement and called *primary earnings per share*. Then, the income statement will report another EPS number, called *fully diluted earnings per share*. Fully diluted EPS is calculated assuming that the convertible securities had been converted into common stock at the beginning of the year. Had this occurred, there would have been no preferred dividends, but an additional 30,000 common shares would have been outstanding for the entire year. We calculate fully diluted EPS by adding back the preferred dividends on the convertible stock to the $180,000 earnings available for common stock and adding 30,000 shares to the denominator.

$$\frac{\$180,000 + \$20,000}{80,000 + 30,000} = \frac{\$200,000}{110,000} = \$1.82 \text{ } \textit{fully diluted EPS}$$

PRICE-EARNINGS RATIO (PE)

The PE ratio is the ratio of the market price of a share of common stock to its EPS. The ratio indicates the amount investors are paying to buy a dollar of earnings. PE ratios of high-growth companies are often very high; those of low-growth or declining companies tend to be low. Assume that Graham's common stock sold at $60 per share at the end of 19X5 and $70 at the end of 19X6. The PE ratios are

$$\textit{Price-earnings ratio} = \frac{\textit{market price per share}}{\textit{earnings per share}}$$

$$19X5 = \frac{\$60.00}{\$4.31} = 13.9$$

$$19X6 = \frac{\$70.00}{\$4.69} = 14.9$$

The increase in the PE ratio from 19X5 to 19X6 could have happened because EPS had been growing rather slowly until 19X6 and investors believed the growth rate would increase in the future. Such a situation justifies a higher PE ratio. Or perhaps PE ratios throughout the economy increased because of good economic news and expectations of good business conditions.

DIVIDEND YIELD AND PAYOUT RATIO

We have been viewing earnings available for common stockholders as the major return accruing to owners of common stock. But, investors do not "get" EPS. They receive dividends and, they hope, increases in the market value of their shares. The dividend yield is a measure of the current cash income that an investor can obtain per dollar of investment.

$$\textit{Dividend yield} = \frac{\textit{dividend per share}}{\textit{market price per share}}$$

Graham declared and paid dividends of $63,000 in 19X5 and $73,200 in 19X6 on 22,000 shares, giving dividends per share of $2.86 and $3.33 for 19X5 and

19X6, respectively. Given per-share market prices of $60 and $70 at the ends of 19X5 and 19X6, dividend yields are

$$19X5 \quad \frac{\$2.86}{\$60.00} \;=\; 4.77\%$$

$$19X6 \quad \frac{\$3.33}{\$70.00} \;=\; 4.76\%$$

The payout ratio is the ratio of dividends per share to EPS. For Graham, the payout ratio in 19X6 is 71 percent ($3.33/$4.69) and in 19X5 was 66 percent ($2.86/$4.31). In general, companies with high growth rates have relatively low dividend yields and payout ratios. Such companies are investing the cash they could use for dividends. Investors who favor high-growth companies are not looking for dividends so much as for increases in the market price of the common stock. Because such hoped-for increases might or might not occur, investing in high-growth companies is generally riskier than investing in companies that pay relatively high, stable dividends.

ECONOMIC VALUE ADDED (EVA)

◀ 11 Chapter 11 referred to EVA in the context of divisional performance evaluation and compared it with residual income. The proponents of EVA argue that it is the best measure of the success of a company as a whole. EVA is computed as

EVA = After-tax operating income - (cost of capital × investment)

After-tax operating profit is income before interest and taxes multiplied by one minus the tax rate. EVA proponents define investment differently from GAAP. Some explanations of EVA give investment as total assets less current liabilities, plus expenditures made for long-term purposes. Expenditures for research and development and for employee training are common examples. They advocate amortizing such investments over five years. Suppose Graham's cost of capital is 9 percent and that it has no investments we need to add back. Its EVA for 19X6 is

$$
\begin{aligned}
EVA \;&=\; \$220,000 \times (1 - 40\%) - [9\% \times (\$1,550,000 - \$150,000)] \\
&=\; \$132,000 - 9\% \times \$1,400,000 \\
&=\; \$6,000
\end{aligned}
$$

The $6,000 EVA says that Graham is covering its cost of capital and providing additional economic value to its shareholders.

SOLVENCY

Solvency refers to long-term safety, the likelihood that the company will be able to pay its long-term liabilities. Solvency is similar to liquidity but has a much longer time horizon. Both long-term creditors and stockholders are interested in solvency—long-term creditors because of a concern about receiving interest payments and a return of principal, stockholders because they cannot receive dividends and benefit from increased market prices unless the company survives.

DEBT RATIO

One common measure of solvency is the debt ratio, which is calculated as follows:

$$Debt\ ratio\ =\ \frac{total\ liabilities}{total\ assets}$$

This ratio measures the proportion of debt in a company's capital structure. It is also called the debt-to-assets ratio. As with other ratios, variations provide much the same information. For example, some analysts calculate a debt-to-equity ratio, dividing total liabilities by stockholders' equity; others calculate a ratio of long-term liabilities to total assets or of long-term liabilities to long-lived assets, such as property, plant, and equipment. All of these variations have the same basic objective: to determine the company's degree of debt. The higher the proportion of debt in the capital structure, the riskier the company. Companies in different industries can handle different percentages of debt. For example, public utilities typically have very high percentages of debt because they have stable cash flows, manufacturers somewhat lower.

The debt ratios for Graham Company for 19X5 and 19X6 are

$$19X5\ =\ \frac{\$610,000}{\$1,380,000}\ =\ 44.2\%$$

$$19X6\ =\ \frac{\$750,000}{\$1,550,000}\ =\ 48.4\%$$

Notice that if we subtract the debt ratio from 100 percent, we get the proportion of stockholders' equity in the capital structure. This is usually called the *equity ratio*. Like the debt ratio, it is a way of measuring solvency, but from a different standpoint.

Graham's debt ratio increased from 19X5 to 19X6, but we cannot tell whether it is near a dangerous level without knowing a good deal more. We can obtain some additional information by calculating the burden that interest expense places on the company.

TIMES INTEREST EARNED

Times interest earned, or interest coverage, measures the extent to which operations cover interest expense. The higher the ratio, the more likely the company will be able to continue meeting the interest payments.

$$Times\ interest\ earned\ =\ \frac{income\ before\ interest\ and\ taxes}{interest\ expense}$$

Graham had interest coverage of 4.8 times in 19X5, but slipped to 4.6 times in 19X6.

$$19X5 \quad \frac{\$200,000}{\$42,000} = 4.8 \; times$$

$$19X6 \quad \frac{\$220,000}{\$48,000} = 4.6 \; times$$

We use income before interest and taxes because interest is a tax-deductible expense. Some analysts also add depreciation in the numerator. Reasoning that depreciation does not require cash payments, these analysts believe that the numerator in their ratio approximates the total amount of cash available to pay interest.

CASH FLOW TO TOTAL DEBT

A major study of ratios computed for actual companies showed that the single best ratio for predicting a company's failure was the ratio of **cash flow to total debt**.[2] In that study, cash flow was defined as net income plus depreciation, amortization, and depletion, and total debt was defined as total liabilities plus preferred stock.

$$\frac{Cash \; flow}{to \; total \; debt} = \frac{net \; income + depreciation + amortization + depletion}{total \; liabilities + preferred \; stock}$$

Graham has no amortization or depletion and no preferred stock. Therefore, the values of the ratio are

$$19X5 \quad \frac{\$94,800 + \$75,000}{\$610,000} = \frac{\$169,800}{\$610,000} = 27.8\%$$

$$19X6 \quad \frac{\$103,200 + \$90,000}{\$750,000} = \frac{\$193,200}{\$750,000} = 25.8\%$$

The research study drawing attention to this ratio was conducted before companies were required to provide a cash flow statement as part of the financial statement package. Using the operating cash flow taken *directly* from Graham's cash flow statement, the ratios are

$$19X5 \quad \frac{\$177,600}{\$610,000} = 29.1\%$$

$$19X6 \quad \frac{\$203,200}{\$750,000} = 27.1\%$$

Though both versions of this solvency ratio show a decline, the decline does not seem serious. Nevertheless, comparison of the ratio with the industry average might indicate a potential problem.

Other uses of cash flow ratios have become popular, especially now that GAAP requires virtually every publicly traded company to publish its cash flow

---

2 See William H. Beaver, *"Financial Ratios as Predictors of Failure," Empirical Research in Accounting, Selected Studies, 1966,* Journal of Accounting Research, *1967, 71-111.*

statement. Brandt et al. propose a number of such ratios.[3] Analysts use ratios to assess the adequacy of a company's cash flow for financing operations and its growth. The accompanying Insight describes how one company views the relationships among its financial strategies and ratios.

RATIOS AND EVALUATION

Calculating ratios for the current year is only the starting point in analyzing a company's operations and prospects. Comparisons are critical and many factors besides the magnitudes of the ratios must be considered.

Analysts should compare ratios with those from prior years, evaluate trends, and explore related ratios. (Is the company becoming more or less liquid? More or less profitable? Were changes in sales and ROA consistent with changes in turnovers of receivables and inventory?) Whenever possible, analysts also compare a company's ratios with those of similar companies and with those for the industry as a whole. (Are the company's ratios consistent with, and moving in the same direction as, those for the industry? Are out-of-line ratios or trends explainable?)

SIGHT

Hon Industries is a major manufacturer of office furniture. The company is very profitable and has grown rapidly over the past 25 years. In its 1994 annual report, the Chair and CEO described Hon's strategies. Among the salient points were that they required a 25 percent ROA of their operating units, based on beginning-of-year assets employed. The company seeks productivity improvements and also pursues international growth. The company has an objective of a 15 percent annual growth rate in profits, which requires a careful financial strategy. Hon requires considerable financial resources to meet its growth objectives.

Hon stresses increasing ROA through various means, one of which is increasing inventory turnover. The company increased turnovers from 11.7 in 1991 to 14 in 1994, which reduced assets by $8.2 million and thereby increased ROA.

Hon strives to keep a strong balance sheet, but with judicious use of leverage. Hon's top management targets a debt ratio of 20 to 40 percent as providing leverage without sacrificing financial safety. The company maintains a payout ratio of about 25 to 35 percent, reinvesting the rest in the business. Hon has also repurchased over 14 million shares of its stock over ten years, which increases earnings per share. With its use of debt and payout, it has been able to finance all of its growth without issuing common stock since 1971.

Source: Hon Industries 1994 annual report, 2-5, 18-23.

---

3 *For an excellent discussion of cash flow ratios, see Lloyd Brandt Jr., Joseph R. Danos, and J. Herman Brasseaux, "Financial Statements Analysis: Benefits and Pitfalls,"* The Financial Accountant, *June 1989, 69-78.*

Several factors make both inter-company and industry comparisons difficult. Comparisons become more difficult as more and more companies diversify their operations. Highly diversified companies might operate in fifteen or more different industries. A welcome trend in financial reporting is increased disclosure of data about the major segments of diversified companies. Such additional disclosure allows analysts to make comparisons that were not possible when only overall results were available.

Even comparisons with fairly similar companies must be made with care, because ratios can differ considerably when companies use different accounting methods. For example, differences in the accounting methods used to value inventory (e.g., FIFO and LIFO) can influence many ratios. If purchase prices have generally been rising, a company using LIFO will show a lower inventory, current ratio, ROS, and EPS, and a higher inventory turnover than a company using FIFO. The longer the price trend has continued and the longer the company has used LIFO, the more marked the effects of the difference in inventory method. Consider too the effects of different depreciation methods on ratios. A business using the sum-of-the-years'-digits method will show lower book values for its plant assets than one using the straight-line method; the differences will affect all ratios involving total assets, net income, or both.

Before 1977, profitability measures were significantly influenced by whether a company acquired the use of property, plant, and equipment by issuing long-term debt or stock or by arranging long-term leases. The effects of this particular difference in financing arrangements were eliminated to a great extent by the issuance of *Financial Accounting Standard No. 13*, but some differences still remain.[4]

Even comparisons among similar companies using similar accounting methods can be misleading in the sense that one business could show up better than another in several measures of liquidity, profitability, or solvency and still not be better managed, more successful, or stronger than the other. For example, a company might be *too* liquid. Too much cash is not as bad as too little cash, but having excessive cash is unwise, because cash does not earn profits unless it is used for something. Faster turnover of inventory could be the result of unnecessarily low selling prices. A shorter collection period on receivables could result from highly restrictive credit policies. Hence, turnovers must be studied in relation to ROS and gross profit ratios, and to trends in the industry. In short, no single ratio, or group of ratios, should be considered in a vacuum.

Another factor to consider in evaluating a company is the extent to which one or more ratios can be affected by a single transaction. For example, consider the effects of a large cash payment for a current liability. Such a payment reduces both cash and current liabilities, and has no effect on total working capital. Yet it can improve the current ratio. To illustrate, look at the ratios for Graham Company for 19X6 and assume that it paid current liabilities of $30,000 just before the end of that year. Its current assets before the payment would have been $480,000 ($450,000 + $30,000), and its current liabilities would have been $180,000 ($150,000 + $30,000), giving a current ratio of 2.67 to 1. This ratio is lower than the 3 to 1 we calculated earlier. Before the payment the acid-test ratio would have been 1.6 to 1 [($80,000 + $180,000 + $30,000)/($150,000 +

4 Financial Accounting Standards Board, Statement of Financial Accounting Standards No. 13, Accounting for Leases (Stamford, Connecticut: Financial Accounting Standards Board, 1976).

$30,000)]. This is also lower than the ratio calculated earlier (1.73 to 1). Taking actions to improve ratios is called **window dressing**. This type of window dressing is possible if the current ratio and acid-test ratio are greater than 1 to 1. If those ratios are less than 1 to 1, paying a current liability will reduce them, but window dressing is then possible by delaying payments of current liabilities.

Any evaluation based on ratios and comparisons of them must recognize the relative importance of the ratio to the particular industry. The nature of the product and of the production process, the degree of competition in the industry, and many other industry-related factors are relevant in interpreting a particular company's liquidity, profitability, and solvency ratios. For example, consider the utility industry. Because a utility is a monopoly, the government unit granting the monopoly right also regulates many of the utility's actions. In most cases, the regulating authority both ensures and limits the utility's profitability. Utilities seldom have liquidity problems, because their cash flows are relatively stable, because selling a service means they need not maintain inventories, and because their ability to shut off the service minimizes problems in collecting their receivables. For the same reasons, the investing public tolerates more leverage and a lower, but more stable, level of profitability in a utility.

All of the preceding considerations point out the need for understanding (1) the company being analyzed and (2) the industry in which the company operates. That a company's ratios differ from those in the past, or are in-line or out-of-line with those of other companies in the industry, is not good or bad in itself. (In the 1980s, **Chrysler Corporation** improved its liquidity, profitability, and prospects for solvency, in relation to both its prior performance and to the average for the industry. Nevertheless, the entire industry performed poorly during that period.) Finally, as the accompanying Insight describes, financial statements do not tell analysts all they want to know.

SUMMARY

Ratio analysis is used in making investment decisions. Analysts are concerned with trends in ratios and with whether a company's ratios are in line with those of other companies in the same industry. Ratios can be classified into three major types: liquidity, profitability, and solvency.

Which ratios to use and which to emphasize depend on the type of decision to be made. Short-term creditors look primarily at liquidity. Long-term creditors are concerned more with solvency than with liquidity and profitability, but the latter aspects are still important. Current and potential holders of common stock are most interested in profitability, but liquidity and solvency are still significant.

Ratio analysis must be used with care. Ratios provide information only in the context of a comparison. Comparisons must be made with other companies and with norms for the industry. Different accounting methods, such as LIFO and FIFO, sum-of-the-years'-digits depreciation and straight-line depreciation, can cause similar companies to show quite different ratios.

SIGHT

Accountants and financial analysts acknowledge that financial statements do not reveal all of the important factors of a company's success or failure. The stock of **Fibreboard**, a forest-products company, ran up in 1995 at least partly because investors became aware of the value of its timber acreage. The company owns 80,000 acres of timberland worth about $240 million, but carried on the books at $35 million, the acquisition cost. Investors have been aware of the value of the **Coca-Cola** trademark for many years. The company carries the trademark at $1, but the annual report states that it is probably worth more like $39 billion.

Information reported in one section of financial statements might be contradicted by information reported elsewhere. **Duracraft**, a large manufacturer of home heaters, reported excellent quarterly earnings in April 1995, but the stock price fell. One analyst suggested that the quality of the company's earnings was suspect. He pointed to an increase in inventories that might hide costs or be a sign of some developing problem that would affect earnings adversely in a later period. The analyst also mentioned a large decrease in the allowance for doubtful accounts. The allowance, he thought, might not be enough to cover the eventual bad debts.

For some other examples, consider a *Forbes* survey of analysts in early 1996. One recommended avoiding **Chesapeake Energy** because of its high debt ratio. Another suggested that **Organogenesis** was a bad buy because it relied so heavily on one product. The debt ratio is available from the balance sheet, but reliance on a single product is revealed only in supplementary disclosures in annual reports.

Sources: Gene G. Marcial, "Moving Past an Asbestos Cloud," and "Curious Math at Duracraft?", Business Week, May 22, 1995, 122; Coca-Cola annual report, 1995, 17; Shlomo Z. Reifman and John H. Christy, "Riding the Bull," Forbes, January 1, 1996, 248-50.

KEY TERMS

cash flow to total debt (852)	liquidity (840)
common size statements (838)	quick assets (841)
composition problem (841)	solvency (850)
convertible securities (848)	window dressing (855)
dilution (of earnings per share) (848)	working capital (840)
leverage (trading on the equity) (846)	

KEY FORMULAS

Liquidity Ratios

Accounts receivable turnover $= \dfrac{\text{credit sales}}{\text{average receivables}}$

(840)   Current ratio $= \dfrac{\text{current assets}}{\text{current liabilities}}$

(842)   Days' sales in accounts receivable $= \dfrac{\text{ending accounts receivable}}{\text{average daily credit sales}}$

(843)   Days' sales in inventory $= \dfrac{\text{ending inventory}}{\text{average daily cost of goods sold}}$

Inventory turnover $= \dfrac{\text{cost of goods sold}}{\text{average inventory}}$

(841)   Quick ratio $= \dfrac{\text{cash + marketable securities + accounts receivable}}{\text{current liabilities}}$

Profitability Ratios

(849)   Dividend yield $= \dfrac{\text{dividend per share}}{\text{market price per share}}$

Earnings per share (EPS) $= \dfrac{\text{net income - dividends on preferred stock}}{\text{weighted-average common shares outstanding}}$

EVA = After-tax operating profit - (cost of capital × investment)

(838)   Gross profit ratio $= \dfrac{\text{gross profit}}{\text{net sales}}$

(850)   Payout ratio $= \dfrac{\text{dividend per share}}{\text{earnings per share}}$

Price-earnings ratio (PE) $= \dfrac{\text{market price per share}}{\text{earnings per share}}$

Return on assets (ROA) $= \dfrac{\text{net income + interest + income taxes}}{\text{average total assets}}$

Return on common equity (ROE) $= \dfrac{\text{net income - dividends on preferred stock}}{\text{average common stockholders' equity}}$

(838)   Return on sales (ROS) $= \dfrac{\text{net income}}{\text{sales}}$

Solvency Ratios

(851)   Debt ratio $= \dfrac{\text{total liabilities}}{\text{total assets}}$

(851)   Times interest earnings $= \dfrac{\text{income before interest and taxes}}{\text{interest expense}}$

Cash flow to total debt $= \dfrac{\text{net income + depreciation + amortization + depletion}}{\text{total liabilities + preferred stock}}$

REVIEW PROBLEM

Financial statements for Quinn Company follow.

Quinn Company, Balance Sheets at December 31

	19X7	19X6
Assets		
Cash	$ 180,000	$ 200,000
Accounts receivable, net	850,000	830,000
Inventory	620,000	560,000
Total current assets	$ 1,650,000	$ 1,590,000
Plant and equipment	7,540,000	6,650,000
Accumulated depreciation	(1,920,000)	(1,500,000)
Total assets	$ 7,270,000	$ 6,740,000
Equities		
Accounts payable	$ 220,000	$ 190,000
Accrued expenses	450,000	440,000
Total current liabilities	$ 670,000	$ 630,000
Long-term debt	1,000,000	950,000
Total liabilities	$ 1,670,000	$ 1,580,000
Common stock, no par value	4,000,000	4,000,000
Retained earnings	1,600,000	1,160,000
Total equities	$ 7,270,000	$ 6,740,000

Quinn Company, Income Statement for 19X7

Sales		$8,650,000
Cost of goods sold		4,825,000
Gross profit		$3,825,000
Operating expenses:		
Depreciation	$ 420,000	
Other	2,135,000	
Total		2,555,000
Income before interest and taxes		$1,270,000
Interest expense		70,000
Income before taxes		$1,200,000
Income taxes at 30%		360,000
Net income		$ 840,000

Quinn Company, Cash Flow Statement for 19X7		
Net cash flow from operating activities:		
Collections from customers		$ 8,630,000
Payments to suppliers		(4,855,000)
Payments for operating expenses		(2,163,000)
Interest paid		(72,000)
Taxes paid		(320,000)
Net cash provided by operations		$ 1,220,000
Cash flows for investing activities—purchase		
of plant and equipment		(890,000)
Cash flows for financing activities:		
Payment of dividends	$(400,000)	
Proceeds from new long-term debt issue	50,000	
Net cash for financing activities		(350,000)
Change in cash (decrease)		$ (20,000)
Cash balance, beginning of year		200,000
Cash balance, end of year		$ 180,000

Quinn had 200,000 shares of common stock outstanding throughout the year. The market price of the stock at year end was $65 per share. All sales are on credit.

Required

Compute the following ratios as of the end of 19X7 or for the year ended December 31, 19X7, whichever is appropriate.

1. Current ratio.
2. Quick ratio.
3. Accounts receivable turnover.
4. Days' sales in accounts receivable.
5. Inventory turnover.
6. Days' sales in inventory.
7. Gross profit ratio.
8. Return on sales (ROS).
9. Return on assets (ROA).
10. Return on equity (ROE).
11. Earnings per share (EPS).
12. Price-earnings ratio (PE).
13. Dividend yield.
14. Payout ratio.
15. EVA, assuming cost of capital is 12%.
16. Debt ratio.
17. Times interest earned.
18. Cash flow to total debt.

ANSWERS TO REVIEW PROBLEM

1. Current ratio

$$\frac{\$1,650,000}{\$670,000} = 2.46 \text{ to } 1$$

2. Quick ratio

$$\frac{\$180,000 + \$850,000}{\$670,000} = 1.54 \text{ to } 1$$

3. Accounts receivable turnover

$$\frac{\$8,650,000}{(\$850,000 + \$830,000)/2} = 10.3 \text{ times}$$

4. Days' sales in accounts receivable

$$\frac{\$850,000}{\$8,650,000/365} = 36 \text{ days}$$

5. Inventory turnover

$$\frac{\$4,825,000}{(\$620,000 + \$560,000)/2} = 8.2 \text{ times}$$

6. Days' sales in inventory

$$\frac{\$620,000}{\$4,825,000/365} = 47 \text{ days}$$

7. Gross profit ratio

$$\frac{\$3,825,000}{\$8,650,000} = 44.2\%$$

8. ROS

$$\frac{\$840,000}{\$8,650,000} = 9.7\%$$

9. ROA

$$\frac{\$840,000 + \$70,000 + \$360,000}{(\$7,270,000 + \$6,740,000)/2} = 18.1\%$$

10. ROE

$$\frac{\$840,000}{(\$5,600,000 + \$5,160,000)/2} = 15.6\%$$

11. EPS

$$\frac{\$840,000}{200,000} = \$4.20$$

12. PE ratio

$$\frac{\$65.00}{\$4.20} = 15.5 \text{ times}$$

13. Dividend yield

$$\frac{\$2}{\$65} = 3.1\%$$

14. Payout ratio

$$\frac{\$2.00}{\$4.20} = 47.6\%$$

15. EVA

$$\$1,270,000 \times (1 - 30\%) - [12\% \times (\$7,270,000 - \$670,000)] = \$97,000$$

16. Debt ratio

$$\frac{\$1,670,000}{\$7,270,000} = 23.0\%$$

17. Times interest earned

$$\frac{\$1,270,000}{\$70,000} = 18 \ times$$

18. Cash flow to total debt

$$\frac{\$840,000 + \$420,000}{\$1,670,000} = 75.4\%$$

ASSIGNMENT MATERIAL

QUESTIONS FOR DISCUSSION

18-1   Dividend yield   Your friend bought stock in NMC Corporation five years ago for $20 per share. NMC is now paying a $5 dividend per share and the stock sells for $100. He says that the 25% dividend yield is an excellent return. How did he calculate the dividend yield?   Is he correct?

18-2   Ratios and accounting methods   LIFO Company uses the last-in first-out method of inventory determination; FIFO Company uses first-in first-out. They have virtually identical operations, physical quantities of inventory, sales, and fixed assets. What differences would you expect to find in the ratios of the companies?

18-3   Ratios and operating decisions   Bronson Company and Corman Company are in the same industry and have virtually identical operations. The only difference between them is that Bronson rents 60% of its plant and equipment on short-term leases, while Corman owns all of its fixed assets. Corman has long-term debt of 60% of the book value of its fixed assets, Bronson has none. The two companies show the same net income because Bronson's rent and depreciation are the same as Corman's depreciation and interest. What differences would you expect to find in the ratios of the two companies?

18-4   Foreign exchange risk   Coca-Cola gains about 82% of its operating profit outside the U.S. It makes most of the product it sells overseas in the host countries. If the dollar strengthens against foreign currencies (dollar buys more units of foreign currency), will that help or hurt the company? Why?

18-5   Liquidity   You are the chief loan officer of a medium-size bank. Two companies have applied for short-term loans, but you can only grant one because of limited funds. Both companies have the same working capital and the same current ratio. They are in the same industry and their current ratios are well above the industry average. What additional information about their current positions would you seek?

18-6   Seasonality and ratios
1. At December 31, 1994, Mattel, Inc., the toy company, had $762 million accounts receivable. Sales for 1994 were $3,205 million. What are days' sales in accounts receivable? Why might Mattel's days' sales in receivables seem high at December 31?

2. Mattel's inventories at December 31, 1994 were $339 million and its cost of sales for 1994 was $1,604 million. What was its inventory turnover? Do you think the figure reflects what Mattel experiences throughout the year?

18-7   Price-earnings ratio   Your friend says that his investment strategy is simple. He buys stocks with very low PE ratios. He reasons that he is getting the most for his money that way. Do you agree that this is a good strategy?

18-8   Relevance of ratios to industry   The 1995 annual report of **Entergy Corporation**, a major electric utility, contained the usual set of financial statements. A condensed balance sheet follows, in millions of dollars.

	December 31	
	1995	1994
Assets		
Utility plant	$15,821	$15,917
Current assets	2,315	2,234
Deferred debits and other assets	4,130	4,471
Total assets	$22,266	$22,622
Capitalization and Liabilities		
Stockholders' equity	$ 6,472	$ 6,351
Preferred stock	954	1,000
Long-term debt	6,777	7,094
Other long-term liabilities	622	585
Current liabilities	2,100	2,040
Deferred credits	5,341	5,552
Total capitalization and liabilities	$22,266	$22,622

Required
Discuss the relevance of the three ratio groups to the analysis of a company such as Entergy.

18-9   Ratio variations   The Financial Highlights section of an annual report of **Motorola Inc.** included the values of the following ratios.

1. Return on average invested capital (stockholders' equity) plus long-term and short-term debt, net of marketable securities.
2. Percent of total debt less marketable securities to total debt less marketable securities plus equity. To which of the three general categories of ratios does each of these ratios belong? How would you explain why the components of these ratios differ from those given in the chapter?

EXERCISES

18-10   Effects of transactions   Indicate the effects of each of the following transactions on the company's (a) current ratio and (b) acid-test ratio. There are three possible answers: (+) increase, (-) decrease, and (0) no effect. Before each transaction takes place, both ratios are greater than 1 to 1.

	Effects on	
	(a)	(b)
	Current	Acid-Test
Transaction	Ratio	Ratio
Example: Purchase inventory for cash.	0	-
1. Purchase inventory on account.	_____	_____
2. Pay a current account payable.	_____	_____
3. Borrow cash on a short-term loan.	_____	_____
4. Purchase plant assets for cash.	_____	_____
5. Borrow cash on a long-term loan.	_____	_____
6. Collect an account receivable.	_____	_____
7. Record accrued expenses payable.	_____	_____
8. Sell a plant asset for cash at a profit.	_____	_____
9. Sell a plant asset for cash at a loss.	_____	_____
10. Buy marketable securities, for cash, as a short-term investment.	_____	_____

18-11 *Relationships* Answer the questions for each of the following independent situations.

1. The current ratio is 1.5 to 1. Current liabilities are $120,000. What are current assets?
2. ROA is 18%; ROE is 25%. There is no preferred stock. Net income is $2 million and average total assets are $16 million. What is average total stockholders' equity?
3. The current ratio is 4 to 1; the acid-test ratio is 2.2 to 1; cash and receivables are $440,000. The only current assets are cash, receivables, and inventory. (a) What are current liabilities? (b) What is inventory?
4. Accounts receivable turnover is 6 times; inventory turnover is 5 times. Both accounts receivable and inventory have remained constant for several years. All sales are on credit. On January 1, 19X8, the company bought inventory. (a) On the average, how long will it be before the new inventory is sold? (b) On the average, how long after the inventory is sold will cash be collected?
5. A company had current assets of $400,000. It then paid a current liability of $80,000. After the payment, the current ratio was 2 to 1. What were current liabilities before the payment was made?
6. Accounts receivable equal 35 days' credit sales. The coming year should see credit sales of $730,000 spread evenly over the year. What should accounts receivable be at the end of the year?

18-12 *Leverage* Balance Company is considering the retirement of $800,000 in 10% bonds. These bonds are the company's only interest-bearing debt. The retirement plan calls for the company to issue 20,000 shares of common stock at a total price of $800,000 and use the proceeds to buy back the bonds. Stockholders' equity is now $1,000,000, with 25,000 shares of common stock outstanding (no preferred stock). The company expects to earn $300,000 before interest and taxes in the coming year. The tax rate is 40%.

Required

1. Determine net income, EPS, and ROE for the coming year, assuming that the bonds are retired before the beginning of the coming year. Assume no change in stockholders' equity except for the new stock issue.

2. Determine net income, EPS, and ROE for the coming year, assuming that the bonds are not retired. Again, assume that year-end stockholders' equity will be the same as at the beginning of the year.
3. Is the proposed retirement wise?   Why or why not?

18-13   *Return on assets and return on equity* Z-Way Corporation had ROS of 6% and sales of $22 million. Interest expense is $0.8 million; total assets are $36 million; the debt ratio is 60%. There is no preferred stock. Ignore taxes.

Required
1. Determine income, ROA, and ROE.
2. Suppose the company could increase its ROS to 9% and keep the same level of sales. What would net income, ROA, and ROE be?
3. Suppose that the company reduced its debt ratio to 40% by retiring debt. New common stock was issued to finance the retirement, keeping total assets at $16 million. Net income is $1.72 million because of lower interest expense that now totals $0.40 million. What are ROA and ROE?

18-14   *Financing alternatives* The founders of Marmex Company are trying to decide how to finance the company. They have three choices:

(a) Issue $4,000,000 in common stock.
(b) Issue $2,400,000 in common stock and $1,600,000 in 10% bonds.
(c) Issue $2,400,000 in common stock and $1,600,000 in 12% preferred stock. Income before interest and taxes is expected to be $1,000,000. The tax rate is 40%.

Required
1. Compute net income, earnings available for common stock, and ROE for each financing choice.
2. Suppose that the tax rate increases to 60%. Redo item 1. Can you draw any conclusions about the effects of tax rates on the relative desirability of the three choices?

18-15   *Effects of transactions* Indicate the effects of each of the following transactions on the company's (a) receivables turnover, (b) inventory turnover, (c) gross profit ratio. The possible answers are (+) increase, (-) decrease, and (0) no effect. Before each transaction, the ratios are (a) receivable turnover of 8 times, (b) inventory turnover of 6 times, and (c) gross profit ratio of 25%.

	Effects on		
	(a)	(b)	(c)
	Receivables	Inventory	Gross
Transaction	Turnover	Turnover	Profit Ratio
1. Buy merchandise on account.	___	___	___
2. Sell merchandise for cash at normal price.	___	___	___
3. Sell merchandise on account at below-normal price.	___	___	___
4. Sell plant asset at a profit for cash and short-term note.	___	___	___

18-16   *Return on assets and equity* Randolph Company has average total assets of $4,000,000 and a debt ratio of 30%. Interest expense is $120,000, and return on average total assets is 12%. The company has no preferred stock. Ignore taxes.

Required
1. Determine income, average stockholders' equity, and ROE.
2. Suppose that sales have been $3,600,000 annually and are expected to continue at this level. If the company could increase its ROS by one percentage point, what would be its income, ROA, and ROE?
3. Refer to the original data and your answers to item 1. Suppose that Randolph retires $600,000 in debt and therefore saves interest expense of $60,000 annually. The company would issue additional common stock in the amount of $600,000 to finance the retirement. Total assets would remain at $4,000,000. What would be the income, ROA, and ROE?

18-17   Effects of transactions—returns ratios   Indicate the effects of each of the following transactions on the company's (a) ROS, (b) ROA, and (c) EPS. There are three possible answers: (+) increase, (-) decrease, and (0) no effect. Before each transaction takes place, the ratios are as follows: (a) ROS, 10%; (b) ROA, 5%; (c) EPS, $0.25.

	Effects on		
	(a) ROS	(b) ROA	(c) EPS
1. Sell a plant asset for cash, at twice the asset's book value.	———	———	———
2. Declare and issue a stock dividend.	———	———	———
3. Purchase inventory on account.	———	———	———
4. Purchase treasury stock for cash.	———	———	———
5. Acquire land by issuing common stock.	———	———	———

18-18   Ratios   The financial statements for Massin Company, a merchandising company, follow (in thousands of dollars). Massin has 200,000 common shares outstanding. The price of the stock is $21. Dividends of $0.80 per share were declared. The balance sheet at the end of 19X5 showed approximately the same amounts as that at the end of 19X6.

Massin Company, Income Statement for 19X6		
Sales		$3,200
Cost of goods sold		1,400
Gross profit		$1,800
Operating expenses:		
Depreciation	$ 240	
Other	1,060	
Total		1,300
Income before interest and taxes		$ 500
Interest expense		60
Income before taxes		$ 440
Taxes at 40%		176
Net income		$ 264

Massin Company, Balance Sheet at December 31, 19X6

Assets		Equities	
Cash	$ 200	Accounts payable	$ 210
Accounts receivable	400	Accrued expenses	280
Inventory	350	Total current liabilities	$ 490
Total current assets	$ 950	Long-term debt	680
Plant and equipment	3,200	Common stock	920
Accumulated depreciation	(1,200)	Retained earnings	860
Total assets	$ 2,950	Total equities	$ 2,950

Required

Calculate the following ratios.

1. Current ratio.
2. Acid-test ratio.
3. Accounts receivable turnover.
4. Inventory turnover.
5. Gross profit ratio.
6. ROS.
7. ROA.
8. ROE.
9. EPS.
10. PE ratio.
11. Dividend yield.
12. Payout ratio.
13. EVA, assuming a 10% cost of capital.
14. Debt ratio.
15. Times interest earned.
16. Cash flow to total debt.

PROBLEMS

 18-19   Analyzing ROE (adapted from a paper by Professor William E. Ferrara)
Chapter 11 introduced the idea of separating the components of ROI as follows:

$$ROI = \frac{net\ income}{sales} \times \frac{sales}{investment}$$

Applying this separation to the calculation of return on stockholders' equity, we could express ROE as

$$ROE = \frac{net\ income}{sales} \times \frac{sales}{stockholders'\ equity}$$

This separation is less enlightening than it might be, however, because net income combines the effects of financing choices (leverage) with the operating results. Letting total assets/stockholders' equity stand as a measure of financial leverage, we can also express return on stockholders' equity as follows:

$$ROE = \frac{net\ income}{sales} \times \frac{sales}{total\ assets} \times \frac{total\ assets}{stockholders'\ equity}$$

Sales and total assets cancel out, leaving the ratio net income/stockholders' equity. The three-factor expression allows the analyst to look at operations (margin × turnover, the first two terms) separately from financing (the last term).

The separation is not perfect because interest (financing expense) is included in calculating net income, but the expansion is adequate for many purposes. Thus, the product of the first two terms is a measure of operating efficiency, while the third is a measure of leverage and therefore of financial risk.

The following data summarize results for three companies.

Company Results (in thousands of dollars)

	Co. A	Co. B	Co. C
Sales	$4,500	$6,000	$5,000
Net income	$450	$400	$480
Total assets	$4,500	$4,500	$4,400
Stockholders' equity	$3,000	$2,000	$4,000
ROE	15%	20%	12%

Required

Calculate ROE for each company using the three-factor expression and comment on the results. You should be able to draw tentative conclusions about the relative operating and financing results of the companies.

18-20 **Current asset activity** The treasurer of Billingsgate Company has asked for your assistance in analyzing the company's liquidity. She provides the following data.

	19X6	19X5	19X4
Total sales (all on credit)	$480,000	$440,000	$395,000
Cost of goods sold	320,000	290,000	245,000
Accounts receivable at year end	64,000	48,000	31,000
Inventory at year end	50,000	44,000	38,000
Accounts payable at year end	37,000	29,000	28,000

Required
1. Compute accounts receivable turnover for 19X5 and 19X6.
2. Compute days' sales in accounts receivable at the end of 19X5 and 19X6.
3. Compute inventory turnover for 19X5 and 19X6.
4. Compute days' sales in inventory at the end of 19X5 and 19X6.
5. Comment on the trends in the ratios. Do the trends seem to be favorable or unfavorable?

18-21 **Constructing financial statements from ratios** The following information is available concerning Warnock Company's expected results in 19X7 (in thousands of dollars). Turnovers are based on year-end values.

Required
Fill in the blanks.

Return on sales	8%
Gross profit percentage	30%
Inventory turnover	4 times
Receivables turnover	5 times
Current ratio	3 to 1
Ratio of total debt to total assets	40%

Condensed Income Statement

Sales	$ 800
Cost of sales	_____
Gross profit	_____
Operating expenses	_____
Net income	$_____

Condensed Balance Sheet

Cash	$ 30	Current liabilities	$_____
Receivables	_____	Long-term debt	_____
Inventory	_____	Stockholders' equity	_____
Plant and equipment	670		
Total	$_____	Total	$_____

18-22 Effects of transactions on ratios Indicate the effects of each of the following transactions on the company's current ratio, acid-test ratio, and debt ratio. There are three possible answers: increase (+), decrease (-), and no effect (0). Before each transaction takes place, the current ratio is greater than 1 to 1 and the acid-test ratio is less than 1 to 1.

	Effects		
	Current Ratio	Acid-Test Ratio	Debt Ratio
Example: An account payable is paid.	+	-	-
1. Bought inventory for cash.	_____	_____	_____
2. A sale is made on account; cost of sales is less than selling price.	_____	_____	_____
3. Issued long-term bonds for cash.	_____	_____	_____
4. Sold land for cash at its book value.	_____	_____	_____
5. Marketable securities held as temporary investments are sold at a gain.	_____	_____	_____
6. Issued common stock in exchange for plant assets.	_____	_____	_____
7. Collected an account receivable.	_____	_____	_____
8. Issued long-term debt for plant assets.	_____	_____	_____
9. Declared, but did not pay, a cash dividend.	_____	_____	_____
10. Paid the dividend in item 9.	_____	_____	_____
11. Paid a short-term bank loan.	_____	_____	_____
12. Recorded depreciation expense.	_____	_____	_____
13. Wrote off some obsolete inventory, debiting a loss account.	_____	_____	_____

18-23   Comparisons of companies Condensed financial statements for Amex Company and Corex Company follow (in thousands of dollars). Both companies are in the same industry and use the same accounting methods. Balance sheet data for both companies were the same at the end of 19X4 as at the end of 19X5.

Balance Sheets, End of 19X5

	Amex Company	Corex Company
Assets		
Cash	$ 185	$ 90
Accounts receivable	215	170
Inventory	340	220
Plant and equipment (net)	850	810
Total assets	$1,590	$1,290
Equities		
Accounts payable	$ 150	$ 140
Other current liabilities	80	90
Long-term debt	300	500
Common stock	700	300
Retained earnings	360	260
Total equities	$1,590	$1,290

Income Statements for 19X5

	Amex Company	Corex Company
Sales	$3,050	$2,800
Cost of goods sold	1,400	1,350
Gross profit	$1,650	$1,450
Operations expenses:		
Depreciation	$ 280	$240
Other	1,040	900
Total	1,320	1,140
Income before interest and taxes	$ 330	$ 310
Interest expense	30	55
Income before taxes	$ 300	$ 255
Income taxes at 40%	120	102
Net income	$ 180	$ 153
Earnings per share	$0.90	$0.77
Dividends per share	$0.40	$0.20
Market price of common stock	$12.00	$11.50

Required

On the basis of the data given, answer the following questions. Support your answers with whatever calculations you believe appropriate.

1. Which company seems to be more liquid?
2. Which company seems to be more profitable? Suppose cost of capital is 12% for both companies.
3. Which company seems to be more solvent?
4. Which stock seems to be a better buy?

18-24 *Effects of transactions—selected ratios* In the following exhibit, several transactions or events are listed in the left-hand column and the names of various ratios and the value of that ratio before the associated transaction are listed in the right-hand column. Indicate the effect of the transaction on the specified ratio. There are three possible answers: (+) increase, (-) decrease, and (0) no effect.

Transaction	Effect on Ratio	
1. Write off an uncollectible account receivable.	_____	Current ratio of 3 to 1
2. Sell merchandise on account, at less than normal price.	_____	42 days' sales in accounts receivable
3. Borrow cash on a short-term loan.	_____	Acid-test ratio of 0.9 to 1
4. Write off an uncollectible account receivable.	_____	Return on sales of 18%
5. Sell treasury stock at a price greater than its cost.	_____	Return on equity of 20%
6. Acquire plant asset by issuing long-term note.	_____	Debt ratio of 40%
7. Record accrued salaries payable.	_____	Times interest earned of 3.2
8. Record depreciation on plant assets.	_____	Cash flow to debt ratio of 60%
9. Return inventory items to supplier for credit.	_____	Inventory turnover of 8 times
10. Acquire plant assets by issuing common stock.	_____	Debt ratio of 60%

18-25 *Construction of financial statements using ratios* The following data are available for Wasserman Pharmaceutical Company as of December 31, 19X4 and for the year ended.

Current ratio	3 to 1
Days' sales in accounts receivable	60 days
Inventory turnover	3 times
Debt ratio	40%
Current liabilities	$300,000
Stockholders' equity	$1,200,000
Return on sales	8%
Return on common equity	15%
Gross profit ratio	40%

Wasserman has no preferred stock, no marketable securities, and no prepaid expenses. Beginning-of-year balance sheet figures are the same as end-of-year figures. All sales are on credit and the only noncurrent assets are plant and equipment.

Required

Prepare a balance sheet as of December 31, 19X4 and an income statement for 19X4 in as much detail as you can with the available information.

18-26 *Dilution of EPS* Boston Tarrier Company has been very successful in recent years, as shown by the following data.

	19X6	19X7
Net income	$3,400,000	$2,600,000
Preferred stock dividends	800,000	800,000
Earnings available for common stock	$2,600,000	$1,800,000

The treasurer of the company is concerned because he expects holders of the company's convertible preferred stock to exchange their shares for common shares early in the coming year. All of the company's preferred stock is convertible, and the number of common shares issuable on conversion is 300,000. Throughout 19X6 and 19X7 the company had 500,000 shares of common stock outstanding.

Required

1. Compute primary EPS for 19X6 and 19X7.
2. Compute fully diluted EPS for 19X6 and 19X7.

18-27   *Inventory turnover and return on equity*   Timmons Company is presently earning net income of $300,000 per year, which gives a 10% ROE. The president believes that inventory can be reduced with tighter controls on buying. Any reduction of inventory frees cash, which would be used to pay a dividend to stockholders. Thus, stockholders' equity would drop by the same amount as inventory.

Inventory turnover is 3 times per year. Cost of goods sold is running at $2,700,000 annually. The president hopes that turnover can be increased to 5 times. He also believes that sales, cost of goods sold, and net income will remain at their current levels.

Required

1. Determine the average inventory that the company currently holds.
2. Determine the average inventory that would be held if turnover could be increased to 5 times per year.
3. Determine ROE if Timmons can increase turnover and reduce stockholders' equity by the amount of the reduction in investment in inventory.

18-28   *Ratios—industry averages*   The president of Brewster Company has been concerned about its operating performance and financial strength. She has obtained, from a trade association, the averages of certain ratios for the industry. She gives you these ratios and the company's most recent financial statements (in thousands of dollars). The balance sheet amounts were about the same at the beginning of the year as they are now.

Brewster Company, Balance Sheet as of December 31, 19X6

Assets		Equities	
Cash	$ 860	Accounts payable	$ 975
Accounts receivable	3,210	Accrued expenses	120
Inventory	2,840	Taxes payable	468
Total current assets	$ 6,910	Total current liabilities	$ 1,563
Plant and equipment, net	7,090	Bonds payable, due 19X9	6,300
		Common stock, no par	4,287
		Retained earnings	1,850
Total assets	$ 14,000	Total equities	$ 14,000

Brewster Company, Income Statement for 19X6	
Sales	$11,800
Cost of goods sold	7,350
Gross profit	$ 4,450
Operating expenses, including $650 depreciation	2,110
Operating profit	$ 2,340
Interest expense	485
Income before taxes	$ 1,855
Income taxes at 40%	742
Net income	$ 1,113

Brewster has 95,000 shares of common stock outstanding, which gives earnings per share of $11.72 ($1,113,000/95,000). Dividends are $5 per share and the market price of the stock is $120. Average ratios for the industry are as follows:

Current ratio	3.8 to 1	Return on equity	17.5%
Quick ratio	1.9 to 1	Price-earnings ratio	12.3
Accounts receivable turnover	4.8 times	Dividend yield	3.9%
Inventory turnover	3.6 times	Payout ratio	38.0%
Return on sales	7.6%	Debt ratio	50.0%
Return on assets	17.6%	Times interest earned	6 times
Cash flow to total debt	25.0%		

Required
1. Compute the ratios shown above for Brewster Company.
2. Prepare comments to the president indicating areas of apparent strength and weakness for Brewster Company in relation to the industry.

18-29   *Generation of cash flows* Humbert Company must make a $600,000 payment on a bank loan at the end of March 19X9. At December 31, 19X8, Humbert had cash of $95,000 and accounts receivable of $355,000. Estimated cash payments required during the first three months of 19X9, exclusive of the payment to the bank, are $315,000. Humbert expects sales to be $810,000 in the three-month period, all on credit. Accounts receivable are normally equal to 40 days' credit sales.

Required
1. Determine the expected balance in accounts receivable at the end of March 19X9. Assume that the three-month period has 90 days.
2. Determine whether the company will have enough cash to pay the bank loan on March 31, 19X9.

CASES

18-30   Evaluation of trends and comparison with industry   Comparative balance sheets and income statements for Marcus Manufacturing Company follow (in thousands of dollars). Your boss, the chief financial analyst for Hanmattan Bank, has asked you to analyze trends in the company's operations and financing and to make some comparisons with the averages for the same industry. The bank is considering the purchase of some shares of Marcus for one of its trust funds.

Marcus Manufacturing Company, Balance Sheets as of December 31

	19X7	19X6
Assets		
Cash	$ 170	$ 180
Accounts receivable	850	580
Inventory (all finished goods)	900	760
Total current assets	$1,920	$1,520
Plant and equipment, net	2,050	1,800
Total assets	$3,970	$3,320
Equities		
Current liabilities	$ 812	$ 620
Long-term debt	1,640	1,300
Common stock	1,000	1,000
Retained earnings	518	400
Total equities	$3,970	$3,320

Marcus Manufacturing Company, Income Statements

	19X7	19X6
Sales, all on credit	$4,700	$4,350
Cost of goods sold	2,670	2,460
Gross profit	$2,030	$1,890
Operating expenses	1,470	1,440
Income before interest and taxes	$ 560	$ 450
Interest expense	130	100
Income before taxes	$ 430	$ 350
Income taxes at 40%	172	140
Net income	$ 258	$ 210
Earnings per share	$2.58	$2.10
Market price of stock at year end	$32.00	$28.00
Dividends per share	$0.96	$0.80

Selected data from the 19X5 balance sheet (in thousands of dollars) include the following:

Accounts receivable	$ 510
Inventory (all finished goods)	620
Total assets	2,940
Stockholders' equity	1,320

The following are averages for Marcus's industry.

Current ratio	2.7 to 1	Receivables turnover	8.5 times
Quick ratio	1.4 to 1	Inventory turnover	4.2 times
Debt ratio	52%	Return on assets	15.0%
Price-earnings ratio	11.5	Return on equity	13.5%
Dividend yield	4.5%	Return on sales	5.0%
Payout ratio	48.0%		

Required
Compute the above ratios for Marcus for 19X6 and 19X7 and comment on the trends in the ratios and on relationships to industry averages.

18-31   Trends in ratios   As the chief investment officer of a large pension fund, you must make many investing decisions. One of your assistants has prepared the following ratios for MBI Corporation, a large multinational manufacturer.

	Industry Average All Years	19X7	19X6	19X5
Current ratio	2.4	2.6	2.4	2.5
Quick ratio	1.6	1.55	1.6	1.65
Receivable turnover	8.1	7.5	7.9	8.3
Inventory turnover	4.0	4.3	4.2	4.0
Debt ratio	43.0%	38.0%	41.3%	44.6%
Return on assets	17.8%	19.1%	19.4%	19.5%
Return on equity	15.3%	15.1%	15.6%	15.9%
Price-earnings ratio	14.3	13.5	13.3	13.4
Times interest earned	8.3	9.7	9.5	8.9
Earnings per share growth rate	8.4%	7.1%	6.9%	7.0%

Required
What is your decision in the following cases?   Give your reasons.
1. Granting a short-term loan to MBI.
2. Buying long-term bonds of MBI on the open market. The bonds yield 7%, which is slightly less than the average for bonds in the industry.
3. Buying MBI common stock.

18-32   Financial planning with ratios   The treasurer of MaxiMart, Inc., a large chain of stores, has been trying to develop a financial plan. In conjunction with other managers, she has developed the following estimates, in millions of dollars.

	19X3	19X4	19X5	19X6
Sales	$100	$120	$150	$210
Plant assets, net	80	95	110	125

In addition, for planning purposes she is willing to make the following estimates and assumptions about other results.

Cost of goods sold as a percentage of sales	60%
Return on sales	10%
Dividend payout ratio	30%
Turnovers based on year-end values:	
Cash and accounts receivable	4 times
Inventory	3 times
Required current ratio	3 to 1
Required ratio of long-term debt to stockholders' equity	50%

At the beginning of 19X3 the treasurer expects stockholders' equity to be $60 million and long-term debt to be $30 million.

Required

Prepare pro forma balance sheets and any supporting schedules you need for the end of each of the next four years. Determine how much additional common stock, if any, the company will have to issue each year if the treasurer's estimates and assumptions are correct.

18-33   Leverage Mr. Harmon, treasurer of Stokes Company, has been considering two plans for raising $2,000,000 for plant expansion and modernization. One choice is to issue 9% bonds. The other is to issue 25,000 shares of common stock at $80 per share. The modernization and expansion is expected to increase operating profit, before interest and taxes, by $320,000 annually. Depreciation of $200,000 is included in the $320,000. Condensed financial statements for 19X4 appear below and on the top of the next page (in thousands of dollars).

Stokes Company, Balance Sheet as of December 31, 19X4			
Assets		**Equities**	
Current assets	$ 3,200	Current liabilities	$ 1,200
Plant and equipment, net	7,420	Long-term debt, 7%	3,000
Other assets	870	Stockholders' equity	7,290
Total assets	$ 11,490	Total equities	$ 11,490

Mr. Harmon is concerned about the effects of issuing debt. The average debt ratio for companies in the industry is 42%. He believes that if this ratio is exceeded, the PE ratio of the stock will fall to 11 because of the potentially greater risk. If Stokes increases its common equity substantially by issuing new shares, he expects the PE ratio to increase to 12.5. He also wonders what will happen to the dividend yield under each plan. The company follows the practice of paying dividends equal to 50% of net income.

Stokes Company, Income Statement for 19X4

Sales		$8,310
Cost of sales	$5,800	
Operating expenses	1,200	
Total		7,000
Operating profit		$1,310
Interest expense		210
Income before taxes		$1,100
Income taxes at 40%		440
Net income		$ 660
Earnings per share*		$6.60
Dividends per share		$3.30

Based on 100,000 outstanding shares

Required

1. For each financing plan, calculate the debt ratio that the company would have after the securities (bonds or stocks) are issued.
2. For each financing plan, determine the expected net income in 19X5, expected EPS, and the expected market price of the common stock.
3. Calculate, for each financing plan, the dividend per share that Stokes would pay following its usual practice and the yield that would be obtained at the market prices from your answer to item 2.
4. Suppose that you now own 100 shares of Stokes Company. Which alternative would you prefer the company to use? Why?

APPENDIX A

guidelines for preparing memoranda

Some assignments require you to write a memorandum about a specific problem. In most cases, such memoranda are short and focused on a few points. The general guidelines in this appendix regarding names, headings, supporting schedules, jargon, and environmental constraints apply to memoranda. In addition, other things to consider include:

1. Use proper memorandum format, including a heading, to whom the memorandum is addressed, who wrote the memorandum, the date, and the subject, as the following illustrates.
2. Be direct and to the point. Do not use fancy words and avoid jargon as much as possible. Define your audience and make sure that you provide information in an understandable way. Take the viewpoint of the reader. What would you like to see if you were the reader?

Illustration of Memorandum Format

MEMORANDUM

To: John Jones, Controller
From: Mary Smith, Smith & Co. Certified Public Accountants
Date: January 19, 19X4
Subject: Analysis of Plant Location

At your request, we evaluated alternative plant locations. We have concluded that the Middleton location best suits your needs. Only the question of transportation charges remains. We used the net present value of the cost savings from each alternative location to develop our analysis (exhibit attached).

3. Make your purpose clear. Executives are busy. If you do not grab their attention and hold it, they will scan your report with little interest or not read it at all. Make clear what response you would like from the reader.

4. Use the opening of your memorandum to establish a link between what you have been asked to do and your recommendations/conclusions. See the previous illustration. At the end of the memorandum tie things together. Also, end in such a way that the reader understands what you have done and is comfortable with your analysis.

GENERAL GUIDELINES

What follows are some guidelines for writing any report or memorandum. Some might not apply to a particular assignment, but they are generally useful.

AUDIENCE ANALYSIS

No writing assignment can be successful without your defining and analyzing your audience. Ask yourself these questions: Who will be reading this? What is my relationship with the reader? What do my readers know about the subject? Do my readers have strong feelings about this subject? Answering these questions will help you develop an audience profile to shape what you say and how you say it.

ANALYSIS VERSUS RESTATEMENT

Many students confuse analysis with restatement. Restatement is a summary of the facts in a situation. An analysis involves critical thinking and requires that you go beyond the facts to answer the following questions: What are the implications of this information? How does this information affect the present or future situation? What effect does this information have on my audience? By answering these questions, you are performing an analysis. All memoranda and cases require analysis; restatement is insufficient.

NAMES AND ABBREVIATIONS

The first time names of individuals and companies are used, they should be fully stated. Do not substitute "Co." for "Company," "Inc." for "Incorporated," or make any change in the name of a company. Define your abbreviations. For example, you could state, "In 1989, the situation at Federal Paper, Incorporated (Federal) involved— . . . ." From that point, you could refer to the company as Federal. Once you have defined an abbreviation, use it consistently. If you want to abbreviate an individual's name, use the last name (e.g., Smith for Robin Smith) or use a courtesy title with the last name (Ms. Smith). Your perspective will dictate how formal or informal to be with names.

SUPPORTING SCHEDULES

All supporting schedules, exhibits, graphs, and tables must be labeled and referred to in your analysis. Supporting materials can be called exhibits or tables and should be numbered in the order that they are referred to in the memorandum. All exhibits must have headings that describe their content.

We encourage you to generate material for exhibits and/or figures using programs such as Lotus 1-2-3. You will use such programs in your working career. However, be selective in what you include in exhibits. Consider your audience, role, and task; carefully format your exhibits; make sure they are properly titled; and provide appropriate references to sources. Finally, define all abbreviations.

USE OF JARGON

Avoid using jargon (topic or industry-specific terminology). You should be able to present your analyses without jargon, buzzwords, and clichés.

ENVIRONMENTAL CONSTRAINTS

Most assignments include constraints imposed by the internal or external environment. You should clearly state these constraints. They might affect your analysis.

ASSIGNMENTS

The assignments are glimpses of situations, some real, some not. Your knowledge is limited. The issues might or might not be clear. Ambiguity and uncertainty are characteristic of the real world. Nevertheless, you can see what problems are emerging and the kinds of decisions needed to solve them. Lack of information is not an excuse to avoid dealing with the issues.

READING THE ASSIGNMENT

Carefully read and reread the assignment. Get an overall understanding of the situation and supporting facts. When you reread the assignment, take notes about key facts, assumptions, and issues. Outline appropriate analytical techniques to help you gain additional information (e.g., CVP analysis, NPV analysis, transfer pricing). Examine the quantitative information for clues. Look at the assignment's questions for hints on how to approach your analysis.

First, avoid rushing to conclusions. You might overlook important information or distort it to fit a preconceived idea. Second, be sure that you fully understand the assignment before you try numerical analysis. Third, differentiate between facts, estimates, and assumptions or suppositions. As you read, ask yourself a broad range of questions: What are the problems and opportunities here? What information given will aid in solving these problems? What information is lacking? What is going on here? Why are these problems still unsolved? What is happening among the people in this organization? When you use an appropriate analytical technique, what will you learn? How sensitive is your analysis to changes? How probable are these changes? What assumptions and/or estimates do you have to make?

You should be very careful not to confuse the basic problem with its symptoms. For example, a decline in sales is probably a symptom of a problem, not the problem per se. Make sure you understand what background information is needed. Depending on the assignment, you might have to discuss factors inside the organization (management team, marketing issues, finances, etc.) and outside the organization (industry makeup, foreign competition, economic conditions, government regulations, etc.). The more a problem relates to strategic planning issues, the more important it is to identify the strengths and weaknesses of the company in relation to its internal and external environment.

In analyzing and planning how to respond to an assignment, do not be limited by the specific questions asked. Do not feel bound to address specific questions in lockstep. Remember that an assignment should be used as a springboard for any relevant issues that can usefully be brought into the analysis. Also, remember that you will write this response after having done all the supporting analysis. Thus, you should integrate your presentation. For example, if there are four sequential parts to an assignment, your answers to part 1 should not be presented as if you had not read and analyzed parts 2, 3, and 4.

Because an assignment extends the text in many instances, do not expect to always find specific text references or techniques for your analysis or solution. You might have to draw on ideas and/or techniques from several sources.

PERSPECTIVE OF WRITER AND READER

Take the detached role of a person observing the information and problem(s) who is analyzing and commenting on appropriate issues. Your audience is another person who is detached from the situation. Instructions should be clear about how much information your audience requires (how much background information is known and how much you should explain and/or summarize). If you are writing from the perspective of an outside consultant hired by a company or a member of management of a company, you are working with management to deal with appropriate issues. The assignment instructions or specific instructions from your instructor will let you know what perspective to take and for what audience. Knowing your audience should help you decide how much background information or explanation is appropriate.

HEADINGS

Headings provide transitions between sections and help the reader know where you are going. In addition, they provide a framework for your analysis and can help you write a more organized memorandum. They are valuable and you should use them whenever you change from one principal topic to another.

GENERAL WRITING GUIDELINES

The following guidelines for memoranda should be amended depending on your instructor and your assigned perspective (neutral, consultant, member of management).

Beginning/Introduction

The introduction to your analysis should include a statement of the problem(s) you have identified. You should state how you approached the analysis and solution to the problems and what courses of action you have identified. List the decisions you need to make. If you have made assumptions and/or estimates, state them clearly and justify them. If there is additional information that you could use to make a more informed decision, state what it is. Finally, include a brief summary of your conclusions (including actions recommended). Make sure that you use the specific evidence in the assignment to support your position.

   The introduction sets the tone. Make sure that you build a sufficient foundation regarding the problems or issues, the facts, your approaches, etc. Make sure it is clear to the reader what you are doing and why.

Middle/Analysis

This is the heart of the memorandum, where you present your analyses and bases for your conclusions. What criteria are you using to select a course of action?   What are the results of your analysis? Make sure to support your analysis. Do not make assertions without evidence or argument to support them. Here is where you need to spend the greatest amount of time and space. Your conclusions and recommendations should be clear and should logically follow your analysis. Finally, there must be a way to measure the consequences of your recommendations. Therefore, this section should:

1. Identify and explain courses of action open to the organization. Not all such courses of action are necessarily delineated in the assignment.

2. Clearly explain the criteria used to select the final course of action (increase profits, reduce risk, report only controllable costs). If criteria are mentioned in the assignment, you should evaluate them and justify their use. If no criteria are presented, you should develop realistic and applicable criteria through your analysis of the assignment's information and your knowledge from the course and from other courses.

3. Select a course of action. If appropriate, indicate how to implement your proposal.

4. Discuss means to measure the consequences of your recommendation(s). Establish standards by which the success or failure of your proposed course of action should be judged.

You should build a logical, integrated presentation, developing the ideas and issues within this section. Organization and the use of headings is very important. Everything should flow in a logical order; it should be clear how you have come to your conclusions and why you have made particular choices.

End/Conclusion

Your ending section should summarize your solutions. If there are unanswered questions, state them and indicate what you would do to resolve them. Give whatever recommendations you have. This final section should bring everything together in a natural end to the paper. There should be no surprises or new material; everything should continue logically from the previous sections and must be fully supported by discussion and facts presented earlier.

APPENDIX B

time value of money

Suppose you had the choice between receiving $10,000 now or one year from now. Suppose you are absolutely sure to receive $10,000 at either time. Virtually everyone would choose the first alternative. A dollar now is worth more than a dollar to be received in one year, or at any later date. This statement sums up an important principle: *money has a time value*. The reason that a dollar now is worth more than the certainty of a dollar to be received in the future is that you could invest the dollar now and have more than a dollar at the later date. It does not matter whether you expect inflation or deflation to change the purchasing power of money; you always prefer money now to the promise of *the same amount* of money later.

Many economic decisions involve investing money now in the hope of receiving *more* money later on. Any analysis of such decisions must consider the **time value of money**. Suppose you can invest $10,000 today with a promise that you will receive $10,800 at the end of one year. Should you make the investment? You know that to justify waiting for the money, the amount to be received should be larger than the amount available to you now. But how much larger? It depends on what else you could do with the cash you have to invest—the opportunities that are available.

Suppose your best alternative investment would earn 10 percent interest per year. If you invest $10,000 at 10 percent per year, you will have $11,000 at the end of one year [$10,000 + ($10,000 × 10%)]. Comparing the two alternatives, you could have $11,000 at the end of the year as a result of a $10,000 investment now, or you could have $10,800 at the end of the year for a $10,000 investment now. You should choose the first alternative.

What happens when the time horizon is extended beyond one period? Suppose you can invest $10,000 today and receive $12,500 at the end of two years. Should you make the investment if the interest rate on another alternative is 10 percent? First determine how much you would have at the end of two years if you invested at a rate of 10 percent, as follows.

Now	You have $10,000
At the end of year 1	You have $11,000 [$10,000 + ($10,000 × 10%)]
At the end of year 2	You have $12,100 [$11,000 + ($11,000 × 10%)]

The interest earned in the second year is 10 percent of the total amount you have at the end of the first year, *not* 10 percent of the $10,000 you originally invested. This is **compound interest**: you earn the quoted interest rate both on the original amount invested and on the interest that you subsequently earn. The $12,100 you have at the end of two years is the **future value** of the $10,000 at a 10 percent interest rate. The $10,000 is the **present value** of $12,100 at a 10 percent interest rate.

By comparing the values of each available alternative at the end of the two years, you can see that you are better off to invest $10,000 now to receive $12,500 at the end of the two years. You could have only $12,100 by investing elsewhere. We show this by comparing the two values at the *end* of the investment term. The practice of comparing present values is more common.

PRESENT VALUE OF A SINGLE AMOUNT

To evaluate an opportunity to receive a single payment at some date in the future at some interest rate, we determine the present value of that choice. Instead of determining how much we would have at some future date if we invested $1 now, we want to know how much we would have to invest now to receive $1 at some future date. The preceding example showed that, at a 10 percent interest rate, an investment of $10,000 will accumulate to $12,100 at the end of two years. The present value of $12,100 two years from now at 10 percent is thus $10,000. The procedure to determine present values is called **discounting**, and the interest rate used is called the **discount rate**. The amount of money to be received later is always a combination of the original investment (sometimes called *principal*) and the interest on that investment.

Formulas are available for determining the present value of a sum of money to be received in the future. Computer spreadsheets and many calculators have functions to find present and future values. You can also use tables to determine present values without the formulas. Suppose we want to find the present value of $1.21 to be received two years from now when we know that the interest rate is 10 percent. (We know already that the present value is $1, and this is the answer the table should give us.) Table A on page 895 shows the present value of $1 to be received at various times in the future and at various interest rates. Referring to the 10% column and the row for two periods, we find the factor .826. This means that the present value of $1 to be received two years from now is $0.826 when the interest rate is 10 percent. Because we expect to get $1.21 we multiply the factor by $1.21. This multiplication produces a present value of $0.99946, which is not significantly different from $1. (The slight difference is due to rounding in preparing the table.) The factors in Table A are generated by the following formula.

$$(1 + i)^{-n}$$

where

$$i = the\ interest\ rate$$
$$n = the\ number\ of\ periods$$

Two characteristics of Table A are significant and should be understood. First, as you move down any column in Table A, the factors become smaller. You should expect this because the longer you must wait for a payment, the less it is worth now. If a dollar now is worth more than a dollar to be received in one year, then surely a dollar to be received one year later is worth more than one to come two years later. Second, the factors become smaller as you move across the table in any row. As the interest rate increases, the present value of the amount to be received in the future decreases. This should also be expected. The higher interest rate you can expect to earn on the sum invested now, the less you need to invest now to accumulate a given amount at the end of some number of years. In summary, the longer you have to wait for your money and the higher the interest rate you can earn, the less it is worth to you now to receive some specified amount at a future date.

PRESENT VALUE OF A STREAM OF EQUAL RECEIPTS

Sometimes it is necessary to compute the present value of a *series* of equal amounts to be received at the ends of a series of years. Such a stream is an **annuity** and describes, for example, bond interest received annually for a number of years. You can find the present value of an annuity by finding the present values of each component of the stream and adding them. For example, what is the present value of an annuity of $1 per year for four years at 10 percent?

Received at End of Year	Amount to Be Received	Present Value Factor (from Table A)	Present Value of Future Receipt
1	$1	.909	$0.909
2	$1	.826	0.826
3	$1	.751	0.751
4	$1	.683	0.683
Present value of annuity			$3.169

This procedure is cumbersome, especially if the annuity lasts for many years. You are multiplying the same number ($1) by several different numbers (the present value factors). From your study of mathematics, you know that the sum of these multiplications is equal to the product of the constant number ($1) and the sum of the different numbers. If you add up the present value factors (3.169) and multiply that sum by $1, you will get the same answer. (This can be verified at a glance because we are using an annuity of $1.)

Many practical situations deal with a series of equal receipts over several periods. These could be analyzed by using Table A and the lengthy procedure described above. But the task is made simpler by using a table like Table B on page 895, which adds the present value factors for you. Look at Table B in the column for 10% and the row for four periods. The factor is 3.170. This is the present value of a series of four $1 receipts when the interest rate is 10 percent. (The factor, 3.170, is rounded up from the sum of the factors given in Table A.)

The values shown in Table B are the cumulative sums of the factors from Table A (with an occasional rounding difference). The factor for an annuity for one period in Table B is the same as the factor for a single receipt in Table A, at the same interest rate. Try adding down Table A and checking each successive sum with the factor in Table B. The factors are generated by the following formula.

$$\frac{1 - (1 + i)^{-n}}{i}$$

where

i = *the interest rate*
n = *the number of periods*

All the factors in both tables relate to future receipts (or payments) of $1. When dealing with amounts other than $1, you multiply the factor by the number of dollars involved to compute the present value. But remember, you can use Table B only when all payments in the stream are equal.

STREAMS OF UNEQUAL AMOUNTS

What if the payments to be received in the future are not equal? You could use the factors from Table A, but that can be cumbersome. If most of the payments are equal, you can find the present value of the equal portions of each payment using Table B, then discount the remainder separately. We shall illustrate this method by modifying the previous example. Instead of receiving $1 per year for four years, you will receive $1 at the end of each of the first three years and $2 at the end of the fourth year.

From Table B we know that $1 per year for four years has a present value of $3.170 at 10 percent. That is the present value of the stream *except* for the extra $1 to be received at the end of year 4. Looking in Table A (for the present value of $1 to be received at the end of four years) we find that the extra $1 has a present value of $0.683. Adding the $0.683 to the $3.170, we obtain $3.853. We can check this by discounting each receipt separately.

Received at End of Year	Amount to Be Received	Present Value Factor (from Table A)	Present Value of Future Receipt
1	$1	.909	$0.909
2	$1	.826	0.826
3	$1	.751	0.751
4	$2	.683	1.366
Present value of this series of payments			$3.852*

The difference ($0.001) is due to rounding.

Suppose that only $0.60 is to be received at the end of the fourth year. We now have a stream of equal payments of $1 for three years, then a $0.60 payment at the end of the fourth year. Use Table B to find the present value of a stream of $1 payments for three years, then add to it the present value of $0.60 to be received at the end of four years (from Table A). The solution is as follows.

Present value of $1 per year for 3 years at 10% ($1 × 2.487)	$2.4870
Present value of $0.60 at end of year 4 at 10% ($0.60 × .683)	0.4098
Present value of this series of payments	$2.8968

COMPUTATIONS FOR PERIODS OTHER THAN YEARS

It is common practice to quote an annual interest rate. Nevertheless, many investments make payments more than once a year. For example, a savings bank might credit interest quarterly or even daily, and interest on most bonds is paid semiannually.

If interest is *compounded* more often than annually, the rate of interest actually earned is higher than the quoted interest rate. Suppose a savings bank pays 6 percent annual interest compounded semiannually. How much will you have at the end of a year if you deposit $1,000 today? You earn $30 for the first six months ($1,000 × 0.06 × ½). For the second six months, you earn interest on $1,030 ($1,000 + $30) and the interest earned is $30.90 ($1,030 × 0.06 × ½). Hence, at the end of the year you have $1,060.90. In effect, you earned at the rate of 6.09 percent per year, because the interest of $60.90 for one year is 6.09 percent of the $1,000 investment. The 6.09 percent is called the **effective interest rate** and must be distinguished from the quoted, or **nominal interest rate**, of 6 percent. We could say that the investment is earning 3 percent *per period* (6 percent divided by the two compoundings per year). You are earning 3 percent on the investment at the beginning of each period. For any given nominal interest rate, the effective interest rate rises as the number of compoundings per year increases.

Compound interest tables such as Tables A and B are constructed on the basis of an interest rate *per period*. Therefore, you must be careful to determine the interest rate you should use in any given situation. If you want the present value of an amount to be received ten years from now using an *effective* rate of 10 percent, you look in Table A in the 10% column and the row for ten periods. (Remember that an effective rate is a rate per year.) If, on the other hand, you want the present value of an amount to be received ten years from now using a nominal interest rate of 10 percent compounded semiannually, you look in Table A in the *5% column* (10 percent divided by the number of compoundings per year) and the row for *20 periods* (10 years times the number of compoundings per year).

In most situations you know the nominal interest rate. Therefore, to complete the desired computation you convert the nominal rate to a rate per compounding period and revise the number of periods to take into account the compoundings. *When consulting the tables, the number of periods is the number of years times the number of compoundings per year, and the interest rate is the nominal annual rate divided by the number of compoundings per year.* Doing this you are stating the interest rate per compounding period.

One practical example involves applying almost every technique in this appendix. Suppose you can buy a bond that will mature in ten years. The bond carries a nominal interest rate of 6 percent and interest is paid semiannually. You *want* to earn 10 percent compounded semiannually. How much would you be willing to pay for a bond with a face (maturity) value of $10,000?

First, you must recognize that your investment has two components. If you buy the bond you contract to receive (1) $10,000 ten years from now and

(2) payments of $300 ($10,000 × 0.06 × ½) every six months for ten years. What is each of these components worth to you now? The price you would be willing to pay for the bond is the sum of the present values of the components.

To compute the price you would pay for the bond, you need the following:

1. The present value of $10,000 to be received ten years from now. You want to earn 10 percent compounded semiannually, so you refer to Table A for the present value factor for 20 periods (10 years × 2 compoundings) at 5% (10 percent divided by 2 compoundings). The factor is .377, so the present value you are looking for is $3,770 ($10,000 × .377).

2. The present value of an annuity of $300 to be received each six months for ten years. You want to earn 10 percent compounded semiannually, so you refer to Table B for the present value factor for 20 periods (10 years × 2 compoundings) at 5% (10 percent divided by 2 compoundings). The factor is 12.462, so the present value you are looking for is $3,739 ($300 × 12.462).

Thus, the price you would pay for this $10,000, 6 percent bond is $7,509 ($3,770 + $3,739). Note that the interest rate per period (5%) and the number of periods (20) are the same for both calculations. The bond is a single investment and earns a single rate of interest even though it provides both a single payment and an annuity.

USES AND SIGNIFICANCE OF PRESENT VALUES

Should you invest a sum of money now in order to receive a larger amount later (whether the amount comes in a single payment, a stream of payments or both)? Your decision should be based on the amounts of the cash to be invested and received later, the length of time over which the inflows are received, and the interest rate.

When the dollars to be received in the future are known, you can refer to the tables for an appropriate factor, multiply by the number of dollars to be received in the future, and compare that amount with the money that must be invested now to receive the amount or amounts in the future. If the result of the multiplication is greater than the amount to be invested now, the present value of the future returns is greater than the investment and the investment is desirable. Such an investment has a positive **net present value (NPV)**. If the result of the multiplication is smaller than the required investment, the opportunity is not desirable. (It has a negative NPV.)

The most common use of present value is to find values of future payments. In some situations, however, you want to find the interest rate earned by investing so many dollars now and receiving so many in the future. The procedures are discussed in the next section.

DETERMINING INTEREST RATES

When you wish to know the interest rate on an investment with known future receipts, you also use present value tables. The interest rate is also called the discount rate, the **time-adjusted rate of return**, or the **internal rate of return (IRR)**. The last term is the most common.

To find the present value of a stream of equal future receipts (annuity), you multiplied the annuity by a factor that incorporated both the length of the series of receipts and the interest rate being earned. This can be shown mathematically.

$$\begin{array}{c} \textit{Present value of} \\ \textit{future receipt(s)} \end{array} = \begin{array}{c} \textit{amount of each} \\ \textit{future receipt} \end{array} \times \begin{array}{c} \textit{factor for discount} \\ \textit{rate and waiting period} \\ \textit{(present value factor)} \end{array}$$

In previous examples, you were looking for the value to the left of the equal sign. In trying to find the interest rate on a given investment when you know the future receipts, you look for the interest rate that *equates* the present value of the future receipts with the investment required to produce those receipts. Using the preceding equation, you state that the value to the left of the equal sign is the investment required now. You know the amount of the future receipts, and you know one element in determining the factor required—the waiting period. You want the missing element in our equation—the interest rate, or IRR.

Suppose you can invest $3,791 today and receive $1,000 per year for five years beginning one year from now, and you want to know the interest rate you would be earning. Substituting in the preceding equation yields

$3,791 = $1,000 \times$ *(the factor for the interest rate for five periods)*

The factor is 3.791, which is obtained by rearranging the equation to show

Present value factor for five periods = $3,791/$1,000 = 3.791

The $1,000 payments are an annuity, so you can look in Table B for the factor in the five-period *row* that is closest to 3.791. That exact factor is found in the 10% column, so the investment yields a rate of return of 10 percent. (We can check this by multiplying $1,000 by 3.791, giving $3,791 as the present value.) In general terms, this basic equation can also be shown as

$$\textit{Present value factor} = \frac{\textit{present value of receipts (required investment)}}{\textit{periodic receipts}}$$

The basic formula can also be used with a single payment. Suppose you could receive $1,450 at the end of four years if you invested $1,000 today. The factor to look for in *Table A* is 0.690 (rounded), which is $1,000/$1,450. Looking across the four-period row in Table A, we come to .683 in the 10% column. The rate of return is therefore a bit less than 10 percent.

You can also use this modification of the basic equation if you know the receipts, the amount of investment (which is the present value), and the interest rate, but you want to know the length of time. Suppose you could invest $1,000 now and receive $300 per year, but the number of years is uncertain. If you want a 14 percent rate of return, you can compute the number of years over which you would have to receive the $300 payments.

$$\textit{Present value factor} \; = \; \frac{\$1,000}{\$300} \; = \; 3.333$$

This factor is for 14 percent and an unknown number of years. Therefore you look down the 14% column in Table B and find that 3.433 is the factor for five years. If you received five $300 annual payments you would earn slightly more than the desired 14 percent.

DETERMINING REQUIRED RECEIPTS

For some decisions you want to know the receipts, either single payment or annuity, needed to earn a particular interest rate (or IRR), given the necessary investment and the life of the receipts. The basic formula can be rearranged as follows.

$$\textit{Periodic receipt} \; = \; \frac{\textit{present value of receipts (required investment)}}{\textit{present value factor}}$$

Suppose you can invest $10,000 now expecting to receive $3,000 per year for six years. You would like to earn a 12 percent return. If you *do* receive $3,000 per year, your rate of return will be about 20 percent ($10,000/$3,000 = 3.33, which is close to the factor for 20% and six years). However, you are uncertain whether you *will* actually receive $3,000 and want to know the minimum annual receipt for six years that will give a 12 percent return.

$$\textit{Periodic receipt} \; = \; \frac{\$10,000}{\textit{4.111 (the factor for six years and 12\%)}} \; = \; \$2,432$$

Thus, if you receive at least $2,432 each year for the next six years you will earn at least a 12 percent return.

This method can also be applied to single payments; the only difference is the table to be used. Suppose you can invest $1,000 and receive a single payment at the end of five years. If you wish to earn a 14 percent return, you would have to receive $1,927 (rounded), which is $1,000/.519, the factor for a single payment at 14 percent at the end of five periods.

SUMMARY

Many decisions involve cash inflows and outflows at different times. Such situations require recognizing the time value of money. To evaluate a situation that involves cash flows occurring at different times, it is necessary to use the values of those flows at the same point in time.

Almost all managerial accounting decisions involving cash flows at different times use the present value of those flows as the point of analysis. The present value of a single cash flow at some time in the future can be computed manually or determined with the help of tables such as Table A. When several future cash flows are involved, it is usually easier to compute their present value by using tables such as Table B. Although tables such as Table B apply only when the individual amounts in the series of cash flows are equal, it is possible to deal with uneven cash flows by using Tables A and B.

The present value of a future cash flow (or a series of future cash flows) depends on the amount of the flow(s), the interest (discount) rate, and the length of the waiting period. Sometimes, the present value is known, but one of the other elements is not. The tables can also be used to determine the value of the unknown element.

Applications of the concept of present values include the computation of bond prices and the evaluation of other long-term investment opportunities. Chapters 8 and 9 of this book include managerial decisions that must be analyzed using present values. The use of present values is not limited to accounting. You may apply your knowledge of present values in the study of economics, finance, and statistics.

KEY TERMS

annuity (884)
compound interest (883)
discounting (883)
discount rate (883)
effective interest rate (886)
future value (883)

internal rate of return (IRR) (888)
net present value (NPV) (887)
nominal interest rate (886)
present value (883)
time-adjusted rate of return (888)
time value of money (882)

KEY FORMULAS

Present value of future receipt(s)	=	amount of each future receipt	×	factor for discount rate and waiting period (present value factor)

$$\text{Present value factor} = \frac{\text{present value of receipts (required investment)}}{\text{periodic receipts}}$$

$$\text{Periodic receipt} = \frac{\text{present value of receipts (required investment)}}{\text{present value factor}}$$

REVIEW PROBLEMS

1. Find the present value of the following sets of payments if the discount rate is (a) 10% and (b) 16%.

Received at End of Year	i	ii	iii	iv
1	$1,000	$2,000	$1,500	$ 0
2	1,000	2,000	2,000	3,000
3	1,000	2,000	2,000	3,000
4	1,000	2,000	2,000	3,000
5		5,000		4,000

2. Find the discount rates for the following situations.

Case	Investment Required Now	Periodic Receipts	Number of Years for Receipts
i	$3,605	$1,000	5
ii	$12,300	$2,000	10
iii	$9,380	$3,000	5

3. Fill in the blanks for each of the following situations. All involve a single payment to be received at the end of the number of years given.

Case	Investment	Year in Which Payment to Be Received	Payment to Be Received	Interest Rate
i	_____	4	$4,000	14%
ii	$1,000	5	$1,464	___
iii	$3,000	—	$5,290	10%
iv	$5,000	7	_____	14%

4. Fill in the blanks for each of the following situations. All involve streams of equal annual payments. Round dollar calculations to the nearest $1.

Case	Investment	Annual Cash Payments	Number of Years Payments to be Received	Interest Rate
i	_____	$1,000	10	14%
ii	$10,000	_____	8	10%
iii	$20,000	$5,000	—	8%
iv	$10,000	$2,000	8	___

ANSWERS TO REVIEW PROBLEMS

1. i.   Stream of equal payments of $1,000 per year for four years.
   (a) At 10%—3.170 × $1,000 = $3,170
   (b) At 16%—2.798 × $1,000 = $2,798

   ii.   Stream of four equal payments and larger amount at end of fifth year. We will discount the four equal payments and add the present value of the fifth one.

   (a) At 10%—3.170 × $2,000 $6,340
       (Table A, five years, 10%) .621 × $5,000   3,105
                                      $9,445

(b) At 16%—2.798 × $2,000 $5,596
    (Table A, five years, 16%) .476 × $5,000   2,380
                                     $7,976

iii. Stream of unequal payments for four years. The easiest method is to find the present value of a $2,000 stream of payments for four years and subtract the present value of $500 at the end of one year.

    (a) 10%—3.170 × $2,000 $6,340.00
        (Table A, one year, 10%) .909 × $500   (454.50)
                                 $5,885.50

    (b) At 16%—2.798 × $2,000 $5,596.00
        (Table A, one year, 16%) .862 × $500   (431.00)
                                 $5,165.00

iv. Stream of unequal payments beginning at the end of year two. Although there are shortcuts, it is probably simplest to discount separately.

    (a) At 10%

Received at End of Year	Amount to Be Received	Present Value Factor (from Table A)	Present Value of Future Receipt
1	0		
2	$3,000	.826	$2,478
3	$3,000	.751	2,253
4	$3,000	.683	2,049
5	$4,000	.621	2,484
Present value of this series			$9,264

    (b) At 16% the present value is $7,712. Computations are similar to those for (a), except that the factors for 16% are used.

2. All of these problems require the use of Table B.

$$\frac{Investment\ required}{periodic\ receipt} = the\ factor$$

i.

$$\frac{\$3,605}{\$1,000} = 3.605\ for\ five\ years = 12\%$$

ii.

$$\frac{\$12,300}{\$2,000} = 6.15\ for\ ten\ years;\ 6.145\ for\ 10\%\ is\ the\ closest\ factor$$

iii.

$$\frac{\$9,380}{\$3,000} = 3.127\ for\ five\ years;\ the\ factor\ for\ 18\%$$

3. All of these problems require the use of Table A.
  i. $2,368. $4,000 × .592 (the factor for 14% for four years)
 ii. About 8%. $1,000/$1,464 = .683, which is very close to .681, the factor for a single payment in five years at 8%.

iii. About six years. $3,000/$5,290 = .567, which is very close to the 6-year factor at 10% (.564). In this case, you know the interest rate, so you are looking for the column with a factor that is closest to .567.

iv. $12,500. $5,000/.400 (the factor for seven years at 14%)

4. All of these problems are solved by using Table B and the equation

Present value = annual payment × present value factor

The present value, in each case, is the amount of the investment.

i. $5,216. $1,000 × 5.216 (the factor for ten periods at 14%)

ii. $1,874. $10,000/5.335 (the factor for eight periods at 10%)

iii. About five years. $20,000/$5,000 = 4.0, which is the factor for 8% and an unknown number of years. Moving down the 8% column in Table B, we find 3.993, which is the closest factor to 4.0 under 8%.

iv. About 12%. $10,000/$2,000 = 5.0, which is the factor for eight years and an unknown interest rate. The closest factor in the 8-period row is 4.968, which is the factor for 12%. The true rate is slightly less than 12%.

ASSIGNMENT MATERIAL

EXERCISES

B-1 Computations—present values Find the present value of the following sets of payments if the discount rate is as noted for each set.

Received at End of Year	Set A at 8%	Set B at 10%	Set C at 20%
1		$2,000	$(3,000)
2		2,000	4,000
3		2,000	4,000
4		2,000	4,000
5		2,000	4,000
8	$10,000		

B-2 Missing factors Fill in the blanks for each of the following independent investment opportunities.

Case	Investment Required Now	Periodic Receipt	Number of Years of Receipt	Interest (Discount) Rate
A	$16,950	$3,000	10	____
B	$16,775	_____	10	8%
C	_____	$5,000	13	18%
D	$10,000	$2,500	__	24%

B-3 Computation of bond prices You are considering investing in some corporate bonds. Each bond is different, and because the companies are different, you believe you should earn a different rate of interest (effective interest rate) on each investment. The relevant data for each bond are as follows.

	Bond of Company		
	A	B	C
Face value	$10,000	$5,000	$20,000
Nominal (stated) interest rate	10%	8%	6%
Years to maturity	7	8	7
Interest paid	Annually	Annually	Semiannually
Desired interest rate	12%	10%	10%

Required

Compute the price you would pay for each bond.

B-4   *Present values and rates of return*   The following information is available about two investments.

	A	B
Required investment now	$10,000	$20,000
Cash flows, annually for 7 years	$2,500	$4,700

Required

1. Compute the approximate IRR for each investment.
2. Compute the present value of each investment if the desired rate of return is 10%.
3. Determine the annual cash flows that would have to be received for each year in the 7-year period to make each investment provide a 16% return.
4. For each investment, determine the number of years that the stated annual cash flows would have to be received to make the investment provide a 20% return.

B-5   *Present values—unusual timing*   Many situations involve cash flows occurring at or near the end of a period. Still others involve flows at or near the beginning of a period. Tables A and B can be used to deal with both types of situations. For each of the following situations, compute the present value of the cash flows described.

(a) A receipt of $5,000 four years from today; the interest rate is 9%.
(b) A receipt of $1,000 per year at the beginning of each of five years beginning today; the interest rate is 8%.
(c) A receipt of $10,000 per year for seven years, the first receipt to arrive exactly six years from today; the interest rate is 12%.

B-6   *Relationships*   Fill in the blanks for each of the following investments.

Item	Case			
	1	2	3	4
a. Investment required now	_____	$416,250	$32,280	_____
b. Present value at desired rate of return	_____	_____	$31,080	$358,000
c. Annual cash receipt	$9,000	$125,000	_____	50,000
d. No. of years cash to be received	16	8	4	_____
e. Desired rate of return	16%	14%	_____	9%
f. Rate of return yielded	20%	_____	18%	14%

Table A
Present Value of $1

Number of Periods	Interest Rates												
	5%	6%	8%	9%	10%	12%	14%	16%	18%	20%	22%	24%	25%
1	.952	.943	.926	.917	.909	.893	.877	.862	.847	.833	.820	.806	.800
2	.907	.890	.857	.842	.826	.797	.769	.743	.718	.694	.672	.650	.640
3	.864	.840	.794	.772	.751	.712	.675	.641	.609	.579	.551	.524	.512
4	.823	.792	.735	.708	.683	.636	.592	.552	.516	.482	.451	.423	.410
5	.784	.747	.681	.650	.621	.567	.519	.476	.437	.402	.370	.341	.328
6	.746	.705	.630	.596	.564	.507	.456	.410	.370	.335	.303	.275	.262
7	.711	.665	.583	.547	.513	.452	.400	.354	.314	.279	.249	.222	.210
8	.677	.628	.541	.502	.467	.404	.351	.305	.266	.233	.204	.179	.168
9	.645	.592	.500	.460	.424	.361	.308	.263	.225	.194	.167	.144	.134
10	.614	.558	.463	.422	.386	.322	.270	.227	.191	.162	.137	.116	.107
11	.585	.527	.429	.387	.350	.287	.237	.195	.162	.135	.112	.094	.086
12	.557	.497	.397	.355	.319	.257	.208	.168	.137	.112	.092	.076	.069
13	.530	.469	.368	.326	.290	.229	.183	.145	.116	.093	.075	.061	.055
14	.505	.442	.340	.299	.263	.205	.160	.125	.099	.078	.062	.049	.044
15	.481	.417	.315	.274	.239	.183	.140	.108	.084	.065	.051	.040	.035
16	.458	.394	.292	.251	.218	.163	.123	.093	.071	.054	.042	.032	.028
20	.377	.312	.215	.178	.149	.104	.073	.051	.037	.026	.019	.014	.012
30	.231	.174	.099	.075	.057	.033	.020	.012	.007	.004	.003	.002	.001

Table B
Present Value of $1 Annuity

Number of Periods	Interest Rates												
	5%	6%	8%	9%	10%	12%	14%	16%	18%	20%	22%	24%	25%
1	.952	.943	.926	.917	.909	.893	.877	.862	.847	.833	.820	.806	.800
2	1.859	1.833	1.783	1.759	1.736	1.690	1.647	1.605	1.566	1.528	1.492	1.457	1.440
3	2.723	2.673	2.577	2.531	2.487	2.402	2.322	2.246	2.174	2.106	2.042	1.981	1.952
4	3.546	3.465	3.312	3.240	3.170	3.037	2.914	2.798	2.690	2.589	2.494	2.404	2.362
5	4.329	4.212	3.993	3.890	3.791	3.605	3.433	3.274	3.127	2.991	2.864	2.745	2.689
6	5.076	4.917	4.623	4.486	4.355	4.111	3.889	3.685	3.498	3.326	3.167	3.020	2.951
7	5.786	5.582	5.206	5.033	4.868	4.564	4.288	4.039	3.812	3.605	3.416	3.242	3.161
8	6.463	6.210	5.747	5.535	5.335	4.968	4.639	4.344	4.077	3.837	3.619	3.421	3.329
9	7.108	6.802	6.247	5.996	5.759	5.328	4.946	4.607	4.303	4.031	3.786	3.566	3.463
10	7.722	7.360	6.710	6.418	6.145	5.650	5.216	4.833	4.494	4.192	3.923	3.682	3.571
11	8.306	7.887	7.139	6.805	6.495	5.988	5.453	5.029	4.656	4.327	4.035	3.776	3.656
12	8.863	8.384	7.536	7.160	6.814	6.194	5.660	5.197	4.793	4.439	4.127	3.851	3.725
13	9.394	8.853	7.904	7.487	7.103	6.424	5.842	5.342	4.910	4.533	4.203	3.912	3.780
14	9.899	9.295	8.244	7.786	7.367	6.628	6.002	5.468	5.008	4.611	4.265	3.962	3.824
15	10.380	9.712	8.559	8.061	7.606	6.811	6.142	5.575	5.092	4.675	4.315	4.001	3.859
16	10.838	10.106	8.851	8.313	7.824	6.974	6.265	5.669	5.162	4.730	4.357	4.033	3.887
20	12.462	11.470	9.818	9.129	8.514	7.469	6.623	5.929	5.353	4.870	4.460	4.110	3.954
30	15.372	13.765	11.258	10.274	9.427	8.055	7.003	6.177	5.517	4.979	4.534	4.160	3.995

company index

A

Adolph Coors Company, 17
Air Korea, 371
Allen-Bradley, 12
AlliedSignal Limited, Turbochargers, 571, 674
Altera, 848
American Airlines, 37
American Association of Retired Persons, 317, 461
American Standard, 388
Ameritech, 451
Anheuser-Busch, 348, 354-355, 507, 511
Apple, 442
Applebee's International, 354
AT&T, 151, 362, 451, 461, 500, 503, 572
Atlantic Dry Dock, 613
Avis, 202

B

BankAmerica, 441
Bank of America, 352
Barnes and Noble, 354
Bausch & Lomb, 263-265
Bell Atlantic, 151, 848
Ben & Jerry's Homemade Inc., 182
Best Baking Company, 727

BMW, 348, 367, 578
Boeing Corporation, 260-261, 309, 707, 783
Borden, 578, 735
Borg-Warner, 726
Briggs & Stratton, 500
British Airways, 139, 368, 371
British Petroleum, 516
Brookstone, 808, 834

C

Calvin Klein, 79
Campbell Soup Company, 351, 495
Caterpillar, 407, 622
Champion International, 655, 674
Charles Machine Works, 573
Chase Manhatten Bank, 10
Chemical Bank, 407
Chesapeake Energy, 856
Chrysler Corporation, 197, 304-305, 312, 351, 362, 368, 570, 578, 855
Circuit City, 182, 250
CMS Energy Corporation, 322
Coca-Cola Company, 21, 30-31, 37, 348, 437, 500, 795-796, 856, 861
Colgate-Palmolive Company, 351, 363, 783, 808
Compaq Computer, 4, 12, 442

Computer Associates International, Inc., 136
Container Corporation of America, 495
Coopers & Lybrand, 203
Cooper Tire & Rubber, 55, 151
Creative Output, 628
Creditfinance Securities, 368
CSX Corporation, 354, 361, 500
Culp, Inc., 15
Cyto Technologies, 363, 399

D

Daewoo and LG Electronics, 367
Dell Computers, 194
Delta Airlines, 37, 49, 118
DIY Home Warehouse, 109
Dole Food Companies, 354, 388
Domino's Pizza, 136, 193
Dow Chemical, 197
Dow Jones & Company, 250
DSP Group, 848
Duke Power, 1
Dun & Bradstreet, 250
DuPont Co., 197, 508
Duracraft, 856

E

Eastman Chemical, 130
Eastman Kodak, 15, 516, 759
Electronic Data Systems, 459
Elgin Sweeper Company, 245
Embassy Suites, 361
Emerson Electric Co., 443
Entergy Corporation, 862
Ernst & Young, 78, 517

F

Federal Express, 150, 628
Fibreboard, 856
Fieldcrest Cannon, 351, 440, 496
Fireman's Fund, 621
First Union, 758
Fluor Corporation, 495
Ford Motor Company, 14, 305, 351, 362, 492, 496, 578, 762-763, 836

G

Gap, 250
Garrett Automotive, 674
GenCorp Polymer Products, 205
General Electric Co., 197, 260-261, 273, 361, 363, 388, 439, 460, 493-494
General Mills, 8-10, 14-15, 79, 181, 246, 439

General Motors, 194, 196-197, 202, 305, 361, 436-437, 578, 783
Geon Co., 459
Golden Poultry Company, 134
Grandmother Calendar Company, 242-243, 294
Green Mountain Power, 130
GTE, 848

H

Hackett Group, 574
Harley-Davidson, 13
Hasbro Toys, 136, 498
Hershey Corp., 493
Hertz, 202
Hewlett-Packard, 81, 144, 726
Hitachi, 624
H. J. Heinz Pet Products, 46, 351
Honda, 351
Hon Industries, 853
Hyundai, 354

I

IBM, 12, 143, 197, 368, 459, 493, 507, 836
Informix, 848
Institute of Clean Air Companies, 252
Intel Corp., 15, 144, 349, 840
Intuit, 109
Iomega, 758
ITT Automotive, 574

J

JC Penney, 202
J. I. Case Agricultural Equipment Group, 665
JKL Advertising, 440
John Deere, 352
Johnson & Johnson, 414, 450, 460

K

Kellogg's, 183, 368, 549
Kmart, 183

L

Levi Strauss, 77, 108, 352, 496, 569
Little Caesars Pizza, 136
L.L. Bean, 574

M

Magna International, 495
Manville, 348

Martin Industries, 673
Mattel, Inc., 136, 351, 387, 498, 861
Maytag Corp., 444
McDonalds, 523
MCI, 151
McKinsey & Co., 571
Mead Corporation, 260-261
Mercedes-Benz, 79, 197
Merck, 12, 565
Metropolitan Life Insurance, 441
Microsoft, 368, 387
Mielec, 609
Minnesota Mining and Manufacturing
    Company (3M), 17, 260
Mitsubishi Electronics America, 182
Monsanto, 407
Motorola Inc., 30-31, 862
Muscular Dystrophy Association, 317

N

National Association of Retired Persons,
    316
National Semiconductor, 97
NationsBank, 451
New Balance, 14
News Corporation, 136
Nintendo, 136
Nokia, 15
NYNEX, 151

O

O'Gara-Hess & Eisenhardt, 252
Organogenesis, 856

P

Pacific Gas & Electric, 21
Pacific-Telesis Group, 441
Panhandle Eastern, 1
Pep Boys, 151, 799
Peterson Ranch, 624
Pfizer, 93
Philip Morris, 134
Phillips Petroleum, 348
Pillsbury, 783
Pitney-Bowes, 363
Pittsburgh Plate Glass, 206
Pizza Hut, 136, 523
Price-Waterhouse, 574
Procter & Gamble, 371, 444, 450, 463, 467,
    507, 758, 799-801, 808
Promus Hotel, 848

Q

Quaker Oats, 500, 503

R

Radio Shack, 250
Red Lobster Restaurants, 15
Reebok International Ltd., 206
Reynolds Metals, 349
RJR Nabisco, 134
Rubbermaid Corp., 494
Ryder System, 12, 460

S

Sally Industries, 548, 604-605
Saturn, 12, 460
SBC Communications, 130
Sears, Roebuck and Co., 56, 151, 199, 202,
    250
Shawmut National Corporation, 78-79
Singapore Airlines, 371
Sonoco, 507, 511
Southwest Airlines, 22, 30-31, 79, 82-83, 450
Southwestern Bell, 130
Sprint, 151
Stanford University, 461
Stanley Furniture Company, 778
Stride Rite, 206
Sun Microsystems, 442
Sysco Corp., 451

T

Taco Inc., 182
Teijin Seiki Co., Ltd., 665
Tektronix Company, 455, 624
Texas Utilities, 322
Toronto Blue Jays, 21
Toshiba Corporation, 260
Toyota Motor Company, 1, 12, 305, 361, 516
Tracinda Corporation, 304-305
Trane Company, 548, 628, 707, 726

U

Unilever, 516
United Airlines, 77-78
United Technologies, 451
U.S. Air, 368
US Customer Operations, 762, 763

V

VanZandt Foods, 322
Victoria's Sectret, 136

W

Wal-Mart, 30-31, 49, 79, 202, 206, 258, 390, 450
Weyerhauser Company, 453, 459
Whirlpool Corp., 199

X

Xerox Corporation, 249, 459, 762

Y

YMCA, 317
YWCA, 317

index

A

Absorbed overhead, *def.,* 614
Absorption costing, *def.,* 608
    comparing results of variable and, 670
    production and income, 671
Accelerated Cost Recovery System (ACRS),
   def., 402
Account analysis, *def.,* 83
Accountants, activities of managerial, 15
Accounting
    financial, *def.,* 2
    management and, *illus.,* 8
    management functions and, 3
    managerial, *def.,* 2
Accounts receivable turnover, 841
Acid-test ratio, 841
Activities
    financing, *def.,* 813
    investing, *def.,* 797
    non-value-adding, *def.,* 81
    operating, *def.,* 797
    value-adding, *def.,* 81
Activity-based costing (ABC), *def.,* 95; *illus.,*
  97
    ethics and, 143
    multiple products and, 662
    relevance of, 142
    standard costs and, 559

Activity-based overhead rates, 619
Actual costing, *def.,* 611
Actual process costing, illustration of, 715
Advanced manufacturing, *def.,* 10
Allocated costs. *See* Cost allocations
Annual budgets, 310
    long-term and, 307
    illustrations of, 310
Annuity, *def.,* 884
Applied overhead, *def.,* 614
Artificial profit centers, *def.,* 440
Asset requirements, 308
Avoidable costs, 93

B

Backflushing, *def.,* 725
Balance sheet, *illus.,* 296, 839
    pro forma, 301; *def.,* 295; *illus.,* 302
Beginning inventory, 710
Benchmarking, *def.,* 574
Benefit-cost analysis, *def.,* 146
Book income and cash flows, 353
Book rate of return, *def.,* 364
Break-even point, *def.,* 38
    target dollar profits and, 39
Budgeted income statements, *illus.,* 266, 301
Budgeting, *def.,* 3

asset requirements, 308
capital. *See* Capital budgeting
conflicts, 258
discretionary costs, 257
ethics and, 262
financing requirements, 308
human behavior and, 257
incremental, *def.,* 317
international aspects of, 263
in not-for-profit entities, 314
program, *def.,* 318
variable and mixed costs, 254
zero-based, *def.,* 317
Budgets
annual, 310
annual and long-term, 307
illustrations of, 310
capital, *def.,* 247
cash, *def.,* 295
for a manufacturer, 306
revised, *illus.,* 300
tentative, 298; *illus.,* 299
as checkup devices, 261
comprehensive, *def.,* 244
developing, 248
overview of relationships in, *illus.,*
244, 303
continuous, *def.,* 248
control and, 246
divisional performance, 511
expense, *def.,* 254
financial, *def.,* 249
flexible allowance, *def.,* 254
imposed, 259
long-term, *def.,* 308
operating, *def.,* 249
organization of, 246
planning and, 245
production, *def.,* 268
project, *def.,* 248
purchases, *def.,* 267; *illus.,* 268, 270, 296
for manufacturing firm, 268
revised, 299
standard costs and, 550
static, *def.,* 254
unwise adherence to, 262
Budget variance, 567; *def.,* 615
separating fixed and variable costs, 568
Business units, *def.,* 493

C

Capacity constraints, *illus.,* 772, 774, 776
Capital
cost of, *def.,* 350

working, *def.,* 388
Capital budget, *def.,* 247
Capital budgeting
cash flows and book income, 353
decisions. *See* Capital budgeting
decisions
decision rules, 360
effects of taxes and depreciation, 357
fundamentals, 350
income taxes and, 401
international aspects of, 367
investing and financing decisions, 366
methods. *See* Capital budgeting
methods
mutually exclusive alternatives, 394
other methods, 362
qualitative considerations, 361
ranking investment opportunities, 396
salvage values in, 358
sensitivity analysis, 398
unequal lives, 394
uneven cash flows in, 358
Capital budgeting decisions, *def.,* 348
importance of, 349
methods of analyzing investment, 352
types of, 350
Capital budgeting methods
book rate of return, 364
discounted cash flow (DCF), 365
internal rate of return, 352, 355
net present value, 352, 355
other, 362
payback period, 362
advantages of, 363
flaws of, 364
summary evaluation of, 365
Cash
defining, 797
from operations, 802
Cash budget, *def.,* 295
for a manufacturer, 306
revised, *illus.,* 300
tentative, 298; *illus.,* 299
Cash disbursements
all costs, *illus.,* 299
for manufacturing costs, *illus.,* 307
other than purchases, 298
for purchases, 297; *illus.,* 297
variable costs, *illus.,* 298
Cash equivalents, *def.,* 798
Cash flow from operations, *def.,* 797
Cash flows, 352
and book income, 353
cost of sales versus cash outflows, 803
financing, 797

incremental approach, 391, 392
interest in, 796
investing, 797
operating, 797
    reporting, 798
    special considerations, 807
operating expenses and cash outflows, 805
reporting operating, 798
    direct method, *def.*, 798
    indirect method, *def.*, 798
revenues versus cash inflows, 803
salvage values in uneven, 358
total-project approach, 391, 393
uneven, 358
variation in annual, 359
Cash flow statement, 806; *def.*, 797; *illus.*, 804, 810
    format, 799; *illus.*, 800
    illustration, 801
Cash flow to total debt ratio, *def.*, 852
Cash receipts, 295; *illus.*, 297
Centralization, *def.*, 444
Committed costs, *def.*, 92
Common costs, *def.*, 93, 196
Common size statements, *def.*, 838
Complementary effects, 191; *def.*, 192
    and loss leaders, 192
Complementary products, *def.*, 135
Complex investments, 388
Composition problem, *def.*, 841
Compound interest, *def.*, 883
Comprehensive budget, *def.*, 244
    developing, 248
    illustration of for retailer, 265
    overview of relationships in, *illus.*, 244, 303
Computer-integrated manufacturing (CIM), *def.*, 14
Conditional values, *def.* and *illus.*, 767
Conflicts in budgeting, 258
Constraint, *def.*, 777
    capacity, *illus.*, 772, 774, 776
Continuous budgets, *def.*, 248
Continuous improvement, standard costs, variances, and, 569
Contribution margin, *def.*, 32
Contribution margin income statement, 33
    comparison of financial accounting and, *illus.*, 35
Contribution margin percentage, 41; *def.*, 32
    weighted-average, 136
Contribution margin per unit, weighted-average, 139; *def.*, 140

Contribution margin variances, analyzing, 131
Control, *def.*, 5
    budgets and, 246
Control chart, *def.* and *illus.*, 561
Control reports, *def.*, 5
Conventional manufacturing, 11
    compared to JIT manufacturing, *illus.*, 16
    material and product flows in, *illus.*, 13
Conversion costs, *def.*, 711
    materials and, 711
Convertible securities, *def.*, 848
Correlation, *def.*, 89
    and association, 89
    spurious, 90
Cost accounting cycle, *illus.*, 714
Cost allocation methods
    actual costs based on actual use, 456
    budgeted costs using dual rates, 457
    direct, 462
    reciprocal, 464
    simultaneous, 464
    step-down, 462
    transfer pricing, 458
Cost allocations, *def.*, 188
    activity-based, 189
    and ethics, 460
    methods and effects, 454
    reasons for, 452
    reasons for not using, 454
    on responsibility reports, 452
Cost behavior, 31
    account analysis, 83
    analysis, problems and pitfalls in, 88
    engineering approach, 84
    estimating, 82
    mixed, *illus.*, 82
Cost centers, *def.*, 439
    responsibility reporting for, 444
    responsibility reports for, *illus.*, 446
Cost control, 549
Cost drivers, *def.*, 80
Cost flows, 606
    in a manufacturing firm, *illus.*, 607, 667
Costing
    ethics in product, 621
    target, *def.*, 44
Cost management, 78
Cost of capital, *def.*, 350
Cost of quality, *def.*, 759
Cost pools, *def.*, 80, 454, 619
Costs
    activity-based costing and standard, 559

avoidable, 93
budgeting discretionary, 257
budgeting variable and mixed, 254
budgets and standard, 550
common, *def.*, 93, 196
differential, *def.*, 182
direct, *def.*, 93
drifting, 570
fixed, *def.*, 32. *See also* Fixed costs
flow of, in a manufacturing firm, *illus.*, 607, 667
incremental, *def.*, 182
indirect, *def.*, 93
joint, *def.*, 93
manufacturing, 94
manufacturing overhead, *illus.*, 95
mixed, *def.*, 82. *See also* Mixed costs
nonvariable, *def.*, 34
objectives of analyzing, 78
opportunity, *def.*, 183
period, *def.*, 606
product, *def.*, 606
quality, 760
    traditional and modern views of, *illus.*, 761
semivariable, *def.*, 82
separable, *def.*, 93
standard, for nonmanufacturing activities, 573
step-variable, *def. and illus.*, 91
sunk, *def.*, 183
traceable, *def.*, 93
unavoidable, 93
unit, 35
variances and standard variable, 550
Cost structure and managerial attitudes, 45
Cost-volume-profit (CVP) analysis, *def.*, 31
    assumptions and limitations of, 48
    in not-for-profit entities, 145
Cost-volume-profit chart, *illus.*, 139
Cost-volume-profit graph, 37; *illus.*, 38
Currently attainable standard, *def.*, 563
Current ratio, 840
Cutoff rate, *def.*, 352
Cycle time, *def.*, 11

D

Days' sales in accounts receivable, 842
Days' sales in inventory, 843
Debt ratio, 851
Decentralization, 493; *def.*, 444
    benefits of, 494
    problems of, 495

Decentralized, *def.*, 493
Decision making, *def.*, 4
    and behavior, 5
    developing relevant information for, 186
    long-term considerations, 196
    make-or-buy, 194
    qualitative issues, 196
    short term, 189
    social consequences of, 406
    under environmental constraints, 205
Decision tree, *def. and illus.*, 765
Departmental performance report, *illus.*, 566
Deregulation, 21
Desired rate of return, *def.*, 498
Differential revenues and costs, *def.*, 182
Dilution (of earnings per share), *def.*, 848
Direct cost, *def.*, 93
Direct labor, *def.*, 94
Direct materials, *def.*, 94
Direct method, *def.*, 462
Direct method of reporting operating cash flows, 798
Discounted cash flow (DCF) techniques, 365
    criticisms of, 405
Discounting, *def.*, 883
Discount rate, *def.*, 883
Discretionary costs, *def.*, 92
    budgeting, 257
Dividend yield, 849
Divisional income, *def.*, 497
Divisional investment, *def.*, 497
Divisional performance
    assets, 508
    behavioral problems, 499
    budgets, 511
    historical comparisons, 510
    income, 504
    industry averages, 510
    internal ranking, 510
    investment, 504
    liabilities, 506
    measures of, 496
        income, 496
        residual income, 498
        return on investment, 497
    pricing policies, 512
    problems in measurement, 504
    report, *illus.*, 511
    subject of evaluation, 509
    transfer prices, 511
Drifting costs, 570

Dropping a segment, 189
Dual rates, *def.,* 457

E

Earnings per share (EPS), 847
Economic value added (EVA), 850; *def.,* 519
Effective interest rate, *def.,* 886
Ending inventory and transfers, 710
Engineering approach, *def.,* 84
Environmental constraints, decision making under, 205
Equivalent unit production, *def.,* 709
    and unit cost, 709
Ethics, 18
    budgeting and, 262
    in product costing, 621
Expected value, *def.,* 253, 767; *illus.,* 768
    and forecasting, 253
Expense budget, *def.,* 254

F

Financial accounting, *def.,* 2
    income statement, comparison of contribution margin and, *illus.,* 35
    managerial accounting and, 6
Financial budgets, *def.,* 249
Financial statements
    areas of analysis, 838
    common size statements, *def.,* 838
    methods of analysis, 837
Financing activities, *def.,* 813
    and investing activities, 805
Financing cash flows, 797
Financing decisions and investing decisions, 366
Financing gap, *def.,* 312
Financing requirements, 308; *illus.,* 314-315
Finished goods inventory, *def.,* 606
Fixed costs, *def.,* 32
    calculating standard, 657
    committed, 92
    control of, 565
    discretionary, 92
    multiple-product companies and, 141
    on performance reports, 567
Fixed overhead budget variance, *def.,* 567
Flexible budget allowance, *def.,* 254
Flexible manufacturing, 14
Flexible manufacturing system, *def.,* 14
Forecast, sales, *def.,* 248. *See also* Sales forecasting
Full costing, *def.,* 608
Future value, *def.,* 883

G

Gains and losses, nonoperating, 811
Goal congruence, *def.,* 438
    and motivation, 437
Graphical method, *def.,* 86

H

High-low method, *def.,* 85
Historical analysis, 250
Historical data, 88
Historical standard, *def.,* 564
Human behavior, budgeting and, 257
Hurdle rate, *def.,* 352

I

Ideal standard, *def.,* 563
Idle capacity variance, *def.,* 616
Idle time, *def.,* 553
    and labor efficiency, 553
Imposed budgets, 259
Income, divisional, *def.,* 497
Income statements, 660; *illus.,* 296, 660-662
    actual and normal costing, 617; *illus.,* 618
    actual process costing, *illus.,* 717
    actual variable costing, *illus.,* 667-668, 670
    budgeted, *illus.,* 266, 301
    comparison of contribution margin and financial accounting, *illus.,* 35
    contribution margin, 33
    formats, 35
    normal costing, *illus.,* 619
    product line, *illus.,* 142
    standard variable costing, *illus.,* 668-669
Incremental approach, 392; *def.,* 391
Incremental budgeting, *def.,* 317
Incremental revenues and costs, *def.,* 182
Indicator methods of sales forecasting, 249
Indifference point, *def.,* 47
Indirect cost, *def.,* 93
Indirect method of reporting operating cash flows, 798
Interim period forecasts, 254
Internal rate of return (IRR), *def.,* 352, 888
    method, 355
Interviews, 84
Inventory
    finished goods, *def.,* 606
    and lead time, 12
    materials, *def.,* 606
    policy, *def.,* 258

turnover, 843
work in process, *def.,* 606
Investing activities, *def.,* 797
and financing activities, 805
Investing cash flows, 797
Investing decisions and financing decisions, 366
Investment center, *def.,* 440
Investment decisions, methods of analyzing, 352
Investment turnover, *def.,* 497
Investments
complex, 388
divisional, *def.,* 497

J

Job-order costing, *def.,* 609
illustration of, 717
Joint costs, *def.,* 93, 196
Joint process, *def.,* 196
Joint processing, long-term considerations of, 199
Joint products, *def.,* 196
Judgmental methods of sales forecasting, 250
Just-in-time (JIT) manufacturing, *def.,* 11
compared to conventional manufacturing, *illus.,* 16
inventory and lead time, 12
material and product flows in, *illus.,* 13

K

Kaizen costing, *def.,* 569
and target costs, 569

L

Labor efficiency and idle time, 553
Labor efficiency variance, *def.,* 553
Labor rate variance, *def.,* 553
Labor variances, 551; *illus.,* 554
Lead time, 12; *def.,* 11
Learning curve, *def.,* 779
examples of, *illus.,* 779
Leverage, *def.,* 846
effects of, 846
Linear programming, 770; *def.,* 771; *illus.,* 774
sensitivity analysis, 774
shadow prices, 775; *illus.,* 776
Line-by-line approval, *def.,* 316
Liquidity, *def.,* 840
Long-term budgets, *def.,* 308

annual and, 307
Long-term decisions, 349
Long-term margin, *def.,* 141
Long-term planning, 313
Loss leader, *def.,* 192

M

Make-or-buy decisions, 194
Management and accounting, *illus.,* 8
Management functions and accounting, 3
Managerial accountants, activities of, 15
Managerial accounting, *def.,* 2
financial accounting and, 6
international aspects of, 20
Managerial attitudes and cost structure, 45
Manufacturing
advanced, *def.,* 10
cell, *def.,* 13
computer-integrated, *def.,* 14
conventional, 11
costs, 94
firm, flow of costs in, *illus.,* 607, 667
flexible, 14
overhead, *def.,* 94
overhead costs, *illus.,* 95
processes, 607
Margin of safety (MOS), *def.,* 46
Material and product flow, *illus.,* 13
Material price variance, *def.,* 557; *illus.,* 558
Materials, *def.,* 94
and conversion costs, 711
and purchased parts/components inventory, *def.,* 606
Material use variance, *def.,* 557; *illus.,* 558
Material variances, 557
Minimum cash balance, *def.,* 304
Minimum-cash-balance policies, 304
Minimum required rate of return, *def.,* 498
Mixed costs, *def.,* 82
behavior, *illus.,* 82
budgeting variable and, 254
estimation methods
high-low, 85
regression analysis, 87
scatter-diagram, 86
Modified Cost Recovery System (MACRS), *def.,* 402
percentage of cost depreciated under, *illus.,* 403
present value of tax shields, *illus.,* 404
Multinational companies, 560
Multiple processes, 712
Multiple-product companies, fixed costs and, 141

Multiple products, 134
    and activity-based costing, 662
Multiple regression analysis, 88
Multiproduct companies, standards in, 558
Multiskilled workers, 13
Mutually exclusive alternatives, *def.*, 394

N

Net present value (NPV), *def.*, 352, 887
    method, 355
Nominal interest rate, *def.*, 886
Noncash transactions, 799
Nonmanufacturing activities, standard costs for, 573
Nonoperating gains and losses, 811
Non-value-adding activities, *def.*, 81
Nonvariable costs, *def.*, 34
Normal activity, *def.*, 657
Normal costing, *def.*, 612
    comparison of standard and, 664
Not-for-profit entities
    budgeting, 314
    cost-volume-profit analysis in, 145

O

Operating activities, *def.*, 797
Operating budgets, *def.*, 249
Operating cash flows, 797
    direct method of reporting, 798
    indirect method of reporting, 798
    reporting, 798
    special considerations, 807
Operating departments, *def.*, 452
Operating expenses, cash outflows and, 805
Opportunity cost, *def.*, 183
Organizational structure, 443; *illus.*, 445
    choosing, 450
Overabsorbed overhead, *def.*, 615
Overapplied overhead, *def.*, 615
Overhead
    absorbed, 614
    applied, 614
    misapplied, 614
    overabsorbed, 615
    overapplied, 615
    underabsorbed, 615
    underapplied, 615
Overhead application, behavior, and strategy, 622
Overhead rates, activity-based, 619
Overhead variances, 615

P

Payback, *def.*, 362
Payback period, 362
    advantages of, 363
    flaws of, 364
Payoff tables, 766; *def.*, 767
Payout ratio, 849
Performance evaluation, *def.*, 5
    criteria, 441
    nonfinancial measures, 570
    variances and, 560
Performance report
    departmental, *illus.*, 566
    fixed costs on, 567
Period costs, *def.*, 606
Planning, *def.*, 3
    budgets and, 245
    longer-term, 313
Practical capacity, *def.*, 658
Predetermined overhead rate, *def.*, 612
Preparing memoranda, guidelines for, 877
Present value, *def.*, 883
    of a single amount, 884
    of a stream of equal receipts, 885
    of streams of unequal amounts, 886
Price-earnings ratio, 849
Pricing policies, 512
Pricing strategy, 143
Probabilities, developing, 770
Process costing, *def.*, 708
    illustration of actual, 715
Product costing
    ethics in, 621
    in advanced manufacturing environment, 724
Product costs, *def.*, 606
    and value-chain analysis, 622
Product life cycle, standard costs, and strategy, 564
Product-line income statement, *illus.*, 142
Production budget, *def.*, 268; *illus.*, 270
Production performance report, *illus.*, 256
Profitability, 844
Profitability index (PI), *def.*, 396
Profit center, *def.*, 440
    artificial, *def.*, 440
Pro forma balance sheet, 301; *def.*, 295; *illus.*, 302
Pro forma statements, *def.*, 3
Program budgeting, *def.*, 318
Project budgets, *def.*, 248
Purchases, cash disbursements for, *illus.*, 297
Purchases budget, *def.*, 267; *illus.*, 268, 296
    for manufacturing firm, 268

Q

Qualitative issues, 196
Quality, cost of, *def.*, 759
Quality costs, *illus.*, 760
    measuring, 760
    traditional and modern views of, *illus.*,
      761
Quick assets, *def.*, 841
Quick ratio, 841

R

Ratios
    accounts receivable turnover, 841
    acid-test, 841
    cash flow to total debt, 852
    current, 840
    days' sales in accounts receivable, 842
    days' sales in inventory, 843
    debt, 851
    dividend yield, 849
    earnings per share, 847
    and evaluation, 853
    inventory turnover, 843
    payout, 849
    price-earning, 849
    return on assets, 844
    return on common equity, 845
    times interest earned, 851
    working capital activity, 841
Raw materials, *def.*, 94
Reciprocal method, *def.*, 464
Reconciliation of net income and cash flow
  from operations, *def.*, 798
Regression analysis, *def.*, 87
    multiple, 88
Relevant range, 36; *def.*, 37
Replacement decisions, *def.*, 390
    incremental approach, 391-392
    total-project approach, 391, 393
Residual income (RI), *def.*, 498
    and return on investment, 502
    versus return on investment, 501
Responsibility accounting system, *def.*, 437
Responsibility center, *def.*, 438
Responsibility reporting
    alternative format, *illus.*, 449
    cost allocations, 452
    for cost centers, 444; *illus.*, 446
    for profit centers, *illus.*, 448
Return on assets (ROA), 844
Return on common equity (ROE), 845
Return on investment (ROI), *def.*, 497
    and residual income, 502
    versus residual income, 501

Return on sales (ROS), *def.*, 36, 497
    target, 42
Revenue center, *def.*, 439
Revenues
    differential, *def.*, 182
    incremental, *def.*, 182
    versus cash inflows, 803
Revised budgets, 299
Revised cash budget, *illus.*, 300

S

Sales, cost of, versus cash outflows, 803
Sales forecast, *def.*, 248
Sales forecasting, 249
    expected values and, 253
    historical analysis, 250
    indicator methods, 249
    interim period forecasts, 254
    judgmental methods, 250
    which method to use, 252
Sales mix, *def.*, 48
    changes in, 138
Sales price variance, *def.*, 133
Sales volume variance, *def.*, 132
Salvage values, 358
Scatter diagram, *illus.*, 87, 89, 90
Scatter-diagram method, *def.*, 86
Segment margin, *def.*, 141
Selling prices, target, 43
Semivariable cost, *def.*, 82
Sensitivity analysis, 774; *def.*, 398
Separable cost, *def.*, 93
Service centers, *def.*, 452
Service departments, *def.*, 452
Shadow price, *def.*, 775
Short-term decisions
    complementary effects, 191
    criterion for, 182
    developing relevant information for,
      186
    dropping a segment, 189
    long-term considerations, 196
    loss leader, 192
    make-or-buy, 194
    qualitative issues, 196
    typical, 189
Short-term margin, *def.*, 141
Simultaneous method, *def.*, 464
Social benefits, *def.*, 406
Social costs, *def.*, 406
Solvency, *def.*, 850
Special orders, 199
    factors in limited supply, 203
    long-term considerations, 202

Spending variance, *def.*, 555
Split-off point, *def.*, 197
Spurious correlation, 90
Standard absorption costing, 656
Standard costing, *def.*, 656
    comparison of normal and, 664
    illustration of, 721
Standard costs, *def.*, 549
    and activity-based costing, 559
    and budgets, 550
    for nonmanufacturing activities, 573
    product life cycle, and strategy, 564
    and standards, 549
    variances, and continuous improvement, 569
Standard fixed cost per unit, *def.*, 657
Standards
    ideal, attainable, or historical, 563
    in multiproduct companies, 558
    setting, 562
        engineering methods, 562
        managerial estimates, 563
    and standard costs, 549
Standards of Ethical Conduct, *illus.*, 19
Standard variable costs and variances, 550
Statement of cash flows, 806; *def.*, 797;
    illus., 804, 810
Static budget, *def.*, 254
Statistical decision theory, 763
Step-down allocation, *def.*, 462
Step method, *def.*, 462
Step-variable cost, *def. and illus.*, 91
Strategy, standard costs, product life cycle,
    and, 564
Stretch goals, 260
Stretch targets, *def.*, 260
Substitute products, *def.*, 141
Sunk cost, *def.*, 183

T
Target costing, *def.*, 44
Target costs and kaizen costing, 569
Target dollar profits and break-even point,
    39
Target profit, *def.*, 39
    achieving, 39
Target rate, *def.*, 352
Target rate of return, *def.*, 498
Target return on sales, 42
Target selling prices, 43
Tax effect of depreciation, *def.*, 357
Taxes and depreciation, 357
Tax shield, *def.*, 357
Theoretical capacity, *def.*, 658

Theory of constraints, *def.*, 777
Throughput accounting, *def.*, 673
Time-adjusted rate of return, *def.*, 355, 888
Times interest earned ratio, 851
Time value of money, *def.*, 349, 882
Total-project approach, 393; *def.*, 391
Total quality control, 14
Traceable cost, *def.*, 93
Trading on the equity, *def.*, 846
Transactions, noncash, 799
Transfer price, 511, *def.*, 440
Two-point method, *def.*, 85

U
Unavoidable costs, 93
Underabsorbed overhead, *def.*, 615
Underapplied overhead, *def.*, 615
Unequal lives, 394
Uneven cash flows, 358
    salvage values in, 358
Unit costs, 35

V
Value-adding activities, *def.*, 81
Value chain, *def.*, 4
Value-chain analysis and product costs, 622
Value of perfect information, *def.*, 769
Variable costing, *def.*, 666
    comparing results of absorption and,
        670
Variable cost percentage, *def.*, 32
Variable costs, *def.*, 32
    budgeting mixed and, 254
    variances and standard, 550
Variable overhead budget variance, *def.*, 555
Variable overhead efficiency variance, *def.*,
    555
Variable overhead variances, 555; *illus.*, 556
    interpreting, 556
Variances, 658
    analyzing contribution margin, 131
    budget, 567; *def.*, 615
    fixed overhead budget, *def.*, 567
    idle capacity, *def.*, 616
    investigating, 561
    labor, 551; *illus.*, 554
    labor efficiency, *def.*, 553
    labor rate, *def.*, 553
    material price, *def.*, 557; *illus.*, 558
    materials, 557
    material use, *def.*, 557; *illus.*, 558
    overhead, 615
    and performance evaluation, 560

reporting, 565
sales price, *def.*, 133
sales volume, *def.*, 132
spending, *def.*, 555
standard costs, continuous improvement, and, 569
and standard variable costs, 550
variable overhead, 555; *illus.*, 556
variable overhead budget, *def.*, 555
variable overhead efficiency, *def.*, 555
volume, *def.*, 616
Volume variance, *def.*, 616

W

Weighted-average contribution margin percentage, *def.*, 136

Weighted-average contribution margin per unit, 139: *def.*, 140
Weighted-average inventory method, *def.*, 709
Window dressing, *def.*, 855
Working capital, *def.*, 388, 840
activity ratios, 841
changes in, 388
decreases in, 390
increases in, 389
Work in process inventory, *def.*, 606

Z

Zero-based budgeting, *def.*, 317
Zero defects, 14

check figures

Chapter 1

1-5 $25,800 net income, $456,000 total assets
1-6 $76,000 cash provided by operations
1-7 $25,000 income before taxes, $488,000 total equities
1-8 $22,000 net increase in cash

Chapter 2

2-4   (2a) 40,000 units, (3) 100,000 units
2-5   (2) $625,000, (3) $975,000
2-6   (1) $28,000 income, (2b) $640,000
2-7   (1) $42,000 income, (2) $975,000
2-8   (1b) $1,000,000, (3a) 44,444, (4) $35.33
2-9   (1b) $6,250,000, (2) $31.89, (3) $32.10
2-10   (1c) 4,875, (2e) $90,000, (3d) $75,000
2-18   (2a) 10,750, (3) $20.40
2-20   (2) 50,000, (3) $15.20
2-21   (1) $94,800, (3) $145.66
2-22   (2) 6,000
2-23   (2) 4,571
2-24   (2a) $21, (3b) $200,000
2-25   (1b) 833,333, (3) $21.20
2-26   (2) $370,000, (4) $270,000, (5) $18.50
2-27   (2) $20
2-28   (2) 45
2-29   (1) a, (2) a, (3) 60,000
2-31   (2) $28,000 increase
2-32   (2b) 324
2-33   (2) $16
2-34   (2) $39
2-35   (1) $200,000, (2) 56,667
2-36 $38,000 April contribution margin
2-37   (1) $70,000 model 440
2-38   (1) $460, (2) 1,324

2-39   (1) $1,608.2 fixed costs
2-40 $8,500
2-41   (2) $29.60 businesses
2-42   (2) 12,838
2-43   (1) $4,210,526 for normal, (2) $1,605,000 for special
2-44 $85,000 total fixed costs
2-45   (1b) 60%
2-46   (2a) 10,800
2-47 $700,000 indifference point
2-48 $1,146,520 income
2-49   (1) 14.9%, (2) $203,000
2-50   (1) $2,960

Chapter 3
3-10 $1.65 variable cost
3-11 $7,720 fixed component
3-12   (1) 3% variable selling cost, (2) $13,400 income
3-15   (1) $100,000 fixed cost of sales
3-16   (1b) $240,000, (2d) $300,000, (3a) 30,000
3-17   (2) $4.83
3-18   (3) $50,000, (4) 6.25%
3-20   (1) $469,350 supermarkets, (2) $336,900 supermarkets
3-21   (2) $51.11
3-26   (1) 6.3% variable, (3) $551.1 million
3-27   (2) $30.90
3-29   (3) 24,000, (5) 48,000, (9) $10.20, (11) $625,000
3-30 $415 fixed
3-32   Blockbusters prefers S in (1) and N in (2), Kirkwalker prefers N in (1) and S in (2)
3-35   (2) $21, (3a) $22.50
3-37   (1) $366,300 line A, (2) $289,593 line A
3-38   (1) $0 Hifixed, (3) 100,000 for both
3-42   (1) 20,000, (2) 55.56%
3-43   (2) 11.66%
3-45 $78,000 annual profit with monthly lease
3-46   (3) 70,000
3-47   (1) $4,500, (2) 80, (3) $0.05
3-48 $5,225 + $7.75 (high-low)
3-50   (1) $66.50 for 816, (2) $65 for 389

Chapter 4
4-6 $29,000 U price variance
4-7   (2) $2,000,000
4-8   (1) 60%, (2) $40,000
4-9   (1) 11,000, (2) $9.80
4-10   (3) $4,500 F volume variance
4-11   (2) $180 income from beer
4-12   (1) 60%, (2) $5.50
4-13   (3a) 52%, (3b) $550,000
4-14 $187.2 F volume variance

4-16   (2) $6,000 income increase
4-17   (2) $210,000 total contribution margin
4-19 $32,000 U price variance
4-20   (2) $128,800, (6) $11,200, (7) $41,280
4-22 $78,000 U total variance for junior staff
4-23 $222.1 margin for sporting goods, $356.1 for housewares
4-25   (1) 63,518, (2) 21,173 premium
4-26 $3,000,000 income at $40 price
4-27   (1) $1.3 million
4-28   (2) 52%, (3) $1,615,385
4-29   (1) $210 loss
4-30   (1) $290,000 margin for paper products, (3) $9,600 increase for detergents
4-31   (2) $54,000 increase
4-32 $65.8 U volume variance
4-33   (1) $833,333
4-34 $13.2 margin for suits
4-35   (3a) 48%
4-36   (1b) C, B, A
4-37 $72,000 contribution margin for saws
4-41   (2) $4,210,500
4-42 $1,920,000 contribution margin at $44 price
4-43   (2) 32.5%, (4a) $123,750
4-45 $143,000 margin for product A, $220,000 for domestic
4-46 $26,000 F price variance
4-48   (1) 443,182
4-49   (6) $6,000, (7) $29,000, (9) 1,000 units
4-50   Eastern $145.2 margin
4-51   (2) $93,000
4-55 $340 U volume variance for drill

Chapter 5
5-6 $26,200
5-7 $2 profit on Doride
5-8 $561,000
5-9   (2) $35,000
5-10   (2) Colossalgadgets $8,800
5-11 $4 variable cost to make
5-13   (1) $12.50 increase
5-16   (2) $140
5-17   (2) $40,000
5-18   (1) $80 incremental profit
5-19 $5,000 difference
5-20   (1) $76,800 contribution margin
5-22   (2) $21 for belts
5-23   (2) $960,000 decrease, (4) $25,000 increase, (6) $7,500 increase
5-24   (2) $10,000 increase
5-25 $31,340 difference
5-26   (3) 4.5 pounds
5-27 $25 decrease

5-29 $1 loss on Xylon further processing
5-30   (2) $302 gain
5-31   (1) $67,500 gain
5-32   (1) $546,600 cost to make
5-35   (1) $4,320 gross margin from retailers
5-36   (2) $16.50
5-37   (1) $252,000
5-39 $20,000 loss
5-40   (2) $3,980
5-41 $76,000 profit
5-42   (2) $80,000
5-43   (2) $125,200 with beer and wine
5-44   (2) $30,000 gain
5-45   (1) 7,000, (2) 8,000
5-47   (1) $4,500 loss
5-50 $18,930
5-51 $66,800 from leased department

Chapter 6
6-9 $187,000
6-10 $44,000 June income
6-11   (2) $60,000 February purchases
6-12   (2) $68,000 March purchases
6-13   27,500
6-14   72 workers, 8 supervisors in June
6-15   (1a) 2,200 April purchases
6-16 $180 income
6-18 $630
6-19   (2) $50,000 F
6-20 $40 May income
6-21 $900 U variance
6-22   (2) 3,000 units
6-23 $725 F variance
6-24   (2) $20,000
6-25   26,000 May production
6-26 $570,000
6-27 $552,000
6-28   8,000 units for February
6-29   71,900 purchases in September
6-30 $92,640 at 12,000
6-31   (2) $14,400, (4) $34,480
6-32   1,900 March production, 3,550 purchases of Tacs in February
6-33   (2) $26,000 income
6-34   200 March production
6-35   5,100 January EI, 4,200 March sales, 6,300 March BI, 5,600 May production
6-36 $51,200 January—April income
6-38   (1) $156 February income, (2) 22,000 March production, (3) 19,000 February purchases
6-40 $3,072,000 total revenue

6-42   (1) $1,505 May
6-44   (1) $10,610 July, (2) $520 April handles
6-47 $2,604,000 six months income, (2) 21,280 August production
6-48   (1) $103,200 income, (3) $29,200 November purchases

Chapter 7
7-8 $222,000 May
7-9   (1) $228,000 June disbursements, (2) $38,000 ending balance
7-10 $1,696 February
7-11   (1) 2,130 March, (2) $46,650 February
7-12   (1) $55,600 February, (2) $18,290 March ending balance
7-13   (1) $70,000 February, (2) $66,000 February and March
7-14 $170,000 total assets
7-15   (1) $93,000 January, (2) $112,000 February, (3) $27,000 February ending balance
7-16 $387,000 total assets
7-17   (2) $2,720, (4) $252, (6) $6,278 total assets
7-18   Borrow $840 quarter 2
7-19 $1,745 available equities
7-20   (1) $51,000, (3) $71,500, (5) $6,800 income
7-21 $880,000 January disbursements, $132,000 February ending cash
7-22   (1) $39,000 February, (2) $65,000 February disbursements, (3) $54,000 income
7-23   (2) $78,000, (4) $3,000, (6) $18,000, (8) $7,800, (9) $24,800
7-24   about 81 hours in September
7-25   (1) $28,691, (2) about $85
7-26   (1) $5,000 income, (2) $185,500 total assets
7-27   (1) $62,400 income, (2) $60,000 March purchases, $98,000 March receipts, (3) $472,100 total assets
7-29   (2) $25.2427
7-30   (1) $327,000 February receipts, 31,000 March production, $43,800 ending cash
7-31 $87,920 ending cash
7-32 $98.6 financing gap in 19X4
7-34 $117,000 November receipts, $83,800 November disbursements, $55,600 November cash
7-35 $52,300 gap
7-36 $25,000 February receipts, $18,500 March disbursements, $5,910 ending cash
7-37 $636,000 February receipts, $527,600 February disbursements
7-38 $1,386,240 October receipts, $425,904 June disbursements for production costs, $181,176 June cash
7-39   (2) $600, (5) $11,250, (7) $2,250, (8) $900
7-40   (1) $1,410 total receipts, $492 March purchases, $62 ending cash, $2,944 total assets
7-41 $23.9 gap in 19X6
7-42 $63,000 June cash
7-43 $1,570,000 required assets
7-44 $692,000 required assets

Chapter 8

8-7   (1a) 9%, (2a) $24,350
8-8   (1) $3,390
8-9   (3) $2,298,755
8-10 (3) $4,564, (5) $3,534
8-11 (1) $39,550
8-12 (2) about 14%
8-13 (2) $9,540 increase
8-14 (1) $8,660
8-15 (1) $(2,326)
8-16 (1) B, $7,485 NPV
8-17 $12,934
8-18 (b) 4.63
8-19 (1) $32,580
8-20 (1e) $61,440, (2e) $92,480
8-21 (1) 41.75% for hand-fed machine, (2) $319,260 NPV for semiautomatic
8-22 (2) $443,000
8-24 $1,390,000 NPV
8-25 (1) $(11,181)
8-26 (1) $4,301,500 for 10 years
8-27 (1) $(1,434)
8-28 (1) $166,000
8-29 $2,536.4
8-31 (1) $92,220
8-32 $266 NPV
8-33 (1) $976,404
8-34 (2) $262,458 NPV
8-36 $13,358 against retirement
8-37 (1) $3,893,400
8-38 (3) $1,484,080 for labor-intensive
8-39 $(57,339)
8-40 (2) $16.1 million
8-41 $(1,584)
8-42 (2) $1.04037
8-43 $8,551,320
8-44 $7,605 NPV of operating
8-45 (2) $53
8-47 $1,616,712

Chapter 9

9-6   (1) $(2,150)
9-7   (1) $84,800
9-8   (1) $65,946
9-9 $46,262
9-10 $816 NPV
9-11 $442,560
9-12 (1) 1.330 hand-fed
9-13 $16.55 million
9-14 (2a) $43,757, (5) $43,181
9-15 $(11,440)

9-16   (1) $408,840 for semiautomatic
9-17 $1,431,857 for hand-fed
9-18   (1) $(49,038)
9-19   (1) $68,000, (2) $54,452, (7) $126,663
9-20   (1c) $339,000, (3a) 10 years
9-21   (2) $(2,589), (4) $56,883, (7) $27,217
9-22 $153,800
9-23 $88,734
9-24 $(20,644)
9-27 $(34,760)
9-28 $260.4
9-29 $(1,328,644) for Entrol
9-30   (1) $38,825
9-31   (3) $(2,016)
9-32   (1) 29,027
9-33   (2) about $4.61
9-34   (1) $41,405 NPV kidney
9-35   (2) $1,100
9-36 $(437)
9-37   205,527
9-38   (2) $947,100
9-39   (1) $19,900
9-40   (2) $16,250,627
9-41 $1,221 thousand
9-43 $59,980 in favor of replacing
9-44   (2) $13,504 favoring drop
9-45   (1) $(155,160)
9-46 $268,800 favoring closing
9-47 $116,098 for Rapidgo 350
9-48   (1) $4,769,280 PV of buying
9-49 $303,791 NPV
9-51 $354,300 PV plan B

Chapter 10
10-11   (1) $455,000 groceries, (2) $300,000 meat
10-12 $97,850 budget
10-13 $165,000 foundry
10-14 $184,091 foundry
10-18 $554.2 Raleigh plant
10-19 $157,000 profit
10-20 $367,857 trimming
10-21 $437,500 trimming
10-22 $393,617 cutting
10-23 $100,000 indoor income
10-27   (1) $456,000 reimbursement
10-29 $2,404,400 machining
10-30 $112,445 controllable costs
10-32 $30,800 February income
10-34   (2) $160,000
10-35 $60,000 profit increase

10-40   (1) $285,000 domestic margin, (2) $152,000 product C profit
10-44 $136,000 sporting goods margin
10-45   (2) $3,000 decrease, (4b) $4,500
10-46   (2) $208,450 to cleaners
10-49 $892,000 retailers' income
10-51   (2) $191 total cost
10-53   (1) $409,320 for 10% reduction, (2) $957,600 for 5% reduction

Chapter 11
11-6   (1) 56,000, (2) 25%
11-7   (1) select B and D
11-8   (1b) $120,000 increase, (2c) $120,000 decrease
11-9   (2) $0.9 million for disinfectants
11-10   (3) games gains $100,000
11-11   (1) laundry 31.5%
11-12   (1) 47,000, (2b) $20.40
11-13   (2) $58.2
11-14   (1) $50 million sales, (2) 18%
11-15   company gains $43,000
11-16   (2) $90,000 drop for Armonk, $30,000 increase for Braser
11-17   (1) $29, (3) $41
11-18   (1b) $3 million, (2) 40%
11-19   (A) RI $12, (C) investment $100
11-20   (1d) $2,000, (3b) $17,500, (5a) $9,000
11-21   (2) $10,000 increase
11-23   (2) 1.6 times, (5) $128,000
11-25   (1) 15% for both, (2a) 0.80
11-26   (2) $6.33, (3) $7
11-27   (2) $60,000 increase
11-28   (1b) $60,000, (2) 75,000, (4a) $11
11-32   (2) $1,250
11-33   (1) $1,158.4
11-34   (1) $100,000 reduction
11-35   (2) $8,000 increase
11-36   (1) 21.6% overall ROI
11-38   (1) $150,000 difference to division
11-40   (1) $57,000 increase, (3) $54,000
11-41   (1a) $1,800,000 profit at 4,000,000 cases
11-44   (1) $18,500 income to division
11-46   (1) $88,000 increase to company

Chapter 12
12-8   (1b) $30, (4) 25,000, (6) $297,000
12-9   (1) $71, (2) material price variance $3,200 F, direct labor efficiency variance $200 F, variable overhead budget variance $360 F
12-10   material use variance $2,800 U
12-11   24,700 pounds used
12-13   direct labor efficiency variance $800 F, variable overhead efficiency variance $300 F

12-14   direct labor rate variance $225 U, variable overhead budget variance $300 U

12-16 $34.41

12-17   (a) $23,110 actual cost, (c) 6,000 standard hours, (d) 6,200 actual hours

12-18   material use variance $4,800 U, overhead $8,500 U

12-20   (1a) $2 per pound, (4) $62,400, (7) $1,600 F, (12) $47,100

12-21   variable overhead budget variance $1,700 F, variable overhead efficiency variance $6,000 U

12-22   direct labor efficiency variance $220 U

12-23   material use variance $2,600 U, variable overhead efficiency variance $480 F

12-24   (2) $142,500 U for ideal

12-25 $4,000 U for larezium

12-26 $1,592 standard cost per batch

12-27 $80 F efficiency variance for labor-related overhead, $1,600 U efficiency variance for set-up related overhead

12-28   material price variance $1,350 U, variable overhead budget variance $3,000 U

12-29   (1) $77 for standard product

12-30   material use variance $2,220 U, direct labor rate variance $1,200 U

12-31   (2) $7.82

12-32   material use variance $12,000 U, direct labor efficiency variance $40,000 U

12-35 $6.4 F sales volume variance, $0.80 U variable cost variances

12-36 $16,000 U total variance

12-37 $1,189 U material use, $3,268 F variable overhead

12-38   direct labor efficiency variance $7,600 U, variable overhead budget variance $800 U

12-39   (2) June loss is $430,400

12-40   direct labor efficiency variance $3,700 U, fixed overhead budget variance $10,700 U

12-41   (1) material use variance $5,100 U, direct labor efficiency variance $200 F, (2) material use variance $900 F, direct labor efficiency variance $800 U

12-43   (1) $8,800 U, (3) $4, (5) $2,200 U, (9) 41,000

12-44   (2) $346,510 profit, material use variance $4,536 U, direct labor efficiency variance $25,200 U

12-45 $30 standard labor cost, $20 standard overhead cost, material use variance $150 F, variable overhead efficiency variance $600 F

12-46   (1) $8.838 for Anaxohyde

12-48 $4.19

12-49   (1a) $520 F, (1d) $800 U, (1e) $737 U

12-50   (1) $204,500 F sales volume variance, (1c) $133,000 U, (1e) $30,000 F

Chapter 13

13-7   (1) $9, (2) $81,000 to JO-8, (3) $344,000 for MK-11

13-8   (1) $90,000 to MK-11, (2) $225,000 JO-8, (4) $25,000 F, $5,000 U

13-9   (1) $106,000 (2) $115,000

13-10   (2) $3,040,000 cost of sales, including overapplied overhead

13-11   (1e) $256,000, (3a) $7, (4c) 40,000

13-13   (2b) $604,000, (3c) $390,000, (4a) $304,000
13-14   (2) $2,478,000, (4) $276,000, (6) $6,000 F
13-15   (3) $2,000 U, $6,000 U
13-16   (2) $2,883,200 cost of sales, (3) $655,400
13-17   (1) $4,746 applied to K-221, (2) $102,533 EI
13-18   (2) $113,200 M-1, (3) $18,800
13-20 $18,800 Grand Bay Gold
13-21 $21,774 for 313
13-22   (2b) $97,150
13-23   (2) $55,000 overapplied
13-24   (2) $160,750 for XR-23
13-25 $98,800 for 1030
13-26   (2) $259,320 cost of sales
13-27   (1) $214,000, (2) $648
13-29   (1) $1,806,510 in cost of sales, (3) $104,040 profit
13-30   (1) $8.90, (2) $135,050 XR-23, (3) $87,550 for XY-67
13-31   (3) $12,950 for GHK
13-32   (1) $97,500 for 4-24, (3) $43,500 for 4-25
13-33   (1) $72,000, (2) $18,000, (3) 22.9% over cost
13-34   (3) $13,180 profit
13-37   (1) $7,200,000, (3) $760,000
13-38   (1) $245.04 for 807
13-40 $1,250 income
13-42   (1) $222,300 Randle specs, (2) $3,000 advantage to Randle
13-43   (2) $15,950, $100,950 income
13-44   (2) $59,510 for A-16
13-45   (2) $2,181,000 in cost of sales, (3) $8,290,000 cost of sales, (4) $17,000 overapplied
13-46   (1) $6,810 for JY-09, (2) $987 for XT-12
13-47   (1) $10,770 for job 547, (3) $13,590 for job 391
13-49   (1) $29.20, (2) $39,000
13-50   (2) 3,000, 4,500, and 6,000
13-53   (1) $42,000 contribution margin from buying unsorted tomatoes

Chapter 14
14-4 $50,000 March income variable costing, $90,000 absorption costing
14-5   (1) $22, $18, $20, (2) $1,280 practical capacity income
14-6 $525,000 income April, $675,000 May
14-7 $300,000, $825,000 incomes April and May
14-8 $(75,000), $1,075,000 incomes April and May
14-9 $450,000, $725,000
14-10 $370,000 U total variances, $6,280,000 income
14-11   (1) $5,680,000
14-12 $25,000 F, $100,000 U
14-13   (1b) $40,000, (2c) 8,000, (3a) $4 per unit, (4c) 12,500
14-14 $30,000 income
14-15 $30,000, $35,000 incomes
14-16 $20,000, $20,006, $20,008, $20,004
14-17   (1) $400,000, $320,000 (3) $360,000, $360,000
14-18   (1) 24,000, 15,000 (3) $100,000, $200,000

14-19 $230,000, $226,000 incomes
14-20 $190,000 income
14-21   (1c) $220,000, (2b) 65,000, (3d) $110,000
14-22   (1) $29,000, $30,000, $31,000, (2) $25,000, $30,000, $35,000
14-23   (1) $32, (2) $70,000
14-24   (1) $40, (2) $230,000
14-25   (2) $10,000 U, $30,000 U budget and volume variances, (4) $2,095,000
14-26   (1) $189,000, (2) $139,000
14-27   (1) $305,000, (2) $280,000
14-28   (1b) $7,000 F, (1d) $12,000 U, (1f) $1,000 U, (1h) $35,000
14-29   (1) $1.60
14-30   (1) $504.0
14-31   (1) $484 budgeted income, $524 actual
14-32   (2a) $600,000, (2d) 5,000
14-33   33,100 units sold, $480,000 fixed costs
14-34   (1) $280,000 income, (2) $1,740,000 total equities
14-35 $512,000 income
14-36   (1) $64.80 per MH, (2) $38.87
14-37   (1) $21.8, $136.9 incomes, (2) $6.5 F, $11.9 U
14-38 $11,800 F material price variance, $27,648 U labor rate variance, (2) $217,224 income
14-39   The company is $20,000 better off for the sale.
14-40   (1) $27, $38, $63, (2) $55,400, (3) $22,300 income
14-42   (1) $(210), $690 for six-month periods, (2) $140, $780 cash balances
14-43   (1) $85,000
14-44   (1) $3, $4.80, $9, (2) $771,000 standard cost of sales, $85,200 volume variance
14-45   (1) $684,000, (2) $16,880,000 receipts, $17,391,100 disbursements, $328,900 ending cash, $1,660,000 FGI, $249,600 materials
14-46   (1) $2,740,000, (2) $4,015,000
14-47   (1) 152,000, (2) 123,500
14-48   (1) $125,000 F volume variance, $562,500 income
14-49   (2) $(61,000), $(1,000), $89,000 incomes
14-51   New BE = 1,500,000

Chapter 15
15-3   (1) 33,000, (2) $1.40, (3) $4,200, (4) $42,000
15-5   (1) 74,000, (2) $3.50, (3) $31,500, (4) $227,500
15-6   (1) 67,600, (2) $3.70, (3) $33,300, (4) $225,700
15-9   (1) $16, (3) 24,000, (4) $110,000
15-10   (1) 18,000, (3) $800,000
15-11   (1) $20.80, (2) $728,000 to FG
15-12   (1) $20.50, (2) $728,900 to FG
15-13 $985,500 cost of sales
15-15 $5,000 U, $10,000 F materials and conversion variances
15-16   (1) $0.40, $0.70, (3) $66,000 cost of sales
15-17   (2) $0.22, $0.67, (3) $160,200
15-18   (1) 240,000, 224,000, (3) $169,280 EI
15-19   (1) 2,300, (2) $69,750 budget
15-20   (2) $28

15-21 $60,000 U total variances, $180,000 income
15-24   Variable costing incomes, $2,000, $8,000, $18,000
15-25   (1) 84,000, 80,400 EUP Mixing, (2) $0.24, $0.45, (3) $51,750, (4) $1.08 total, (5) $73,440
15-26   (2) $51,922
15-27   (1) $360,000 income, (2) $367,000 income
15-28   (1) $6.50, (2) $4.50, (5) $4.93, (9) $16,000 F, (12) $236,000
15-29   (2) $90,000, (4) $72,000
15-30 $4,500 income
15-31   (1) $50,000 income, (3) $40,500 income
15-32   (3) $184,600 cost of sales
15-33   (2) $34,660 income
15-35   (1) $20,250 for job 83, (3) $11,295 income
15-36 $315,112, $302,000, $298,000, $282,000, $292,000 incomes
15-37 $576,888, $588,333, $587,000, $595,000, $588,684 incomes
15-39   (1) 5,000, (3) 9,500, (5) $9, (7) $18, (11) $12, (15) $0.30 per hour, $0.60 per dress, (17) 500
15-40   (1) $0.37, (2) $73,788
15-41 $25,000 U material price variance, $10,000 U labor use variance, $60,000 F volume variance, (2) $455,000, $635,000 incomes
15-42 $30,000 F material price variance, $5,000 U labor rate variance, $5,000 F variable overhead efficiency variance, $735,000, $675,000 incomes
15-43   (1) 50,000, 44,000, 44,000, (2) $8
15-44   (1) 19,000, (2) $58,000 quality cost

Chapter 16
16-6 $2,000 cost to investigate
16-7   2,560 for 8 batches
16-8 $47,000, $35,000 EVs
16-10   250 L, 150 M
16-11 $36,848 for 8 batches
16-12   (1) $76,850
16-13   (2) $600 EV
16-14 $108,000 EV for 600 units
16-15 $40, $56 CMs
16-16   175 X, 50 Y
16-17   (2) $16,000, (3) $12,000
16-18 $380,000 prevention, $260,000 appraisal
16-19 $210,000 EV
16-20   Less than 9 days
16-21 $1,760 cost of investigating
16-22   900 C, 150 F
16-23   (1) $2.88
16-24 $410,550 for toaster
16-25 $933
16-26 $75,000 advantage to making
16-27 $151,000 EV to make
16-29 $1,800 EV of investigating
16-30   (1) $16,000 EV
16-31   (2) $2,984 EV

16-32 $4,800 cost of not investigating
16-33   (1) $5,160 NPV
16-34 $51,600 EV for super
16-35 $43,750 EV for 550,000
16-36   160, 180
16-37 $239,880 for 200,000 unit plant
16-38 $212,000 for 10,000

Chapter 17
17-6   A $707,000, C $860,000
17-7   A $598,000, C $3,356,000
17-8   A $593,000, C $2,833,000
17-11 $248,800
17-12   A $570,300, B $22,318
17-13   A $619,000, C $4,321,000
17-14 $142,000
17-17   (2) $70,000 loss, (4) $500,000
17-18 $143,000
17-19 $(669,000) for investing, $210,000 from financing activities
17-20 $2,000
17-22 $9,000 increase
17-23 $242,000 net income
17-24 $1,825,000 cash receipts, $956,000 payments to merchandise suppliers
17-25   (1) $188,000 cash from operations
17-26 $239 cash from operations
17-27 $67,000 increase in cash
17-28   (1) $170,000, (2) $22,000 cash from operations
17-30 $355,000 decrease in cash
17-31 $10,000 decrease in cash
17-33 $120 increase in cash, $325 cash from operations
17-34 $520,000 cash from operations, $101,000 increase in cash
17-35 $64.2 cash from operations, $19.2 decrease in cash
17-36 $215,000 cash from operations, $10,000 increase in cash

Chapter 18
18-11   (1) $180,000, (2a) $200,000, (5) $240,000
18-12   (1) 10% ROE, (2) $5.28 EPS
18-13   (1) 13.3% ROA, (2) 22.3% ROE, (3) 17.9% ROE
18-14   (1) 15%, 21%, 17% ROE
18-16   (2) $396,000, (3) $420,000
18-18   1.22:1 acid test ratio, 4 inventory turnovers, 3.8% dividend yield
18-19   15%, 20%, 12% ROE
18-20   (2) 49, 40 days, (3) 6.8, 7.1 turnovers
18-21 $560 cost of sales, $64 income, $160 receivables
18-23   (1) 1.7:1, 1.1:1 acid test ratios, 89, 59 days sales in inventory, (2) 5.9%, 5.5% ROS, 17%, 27.3% ROE, (3) 11, 5.64 times interest earned
18-25 $180,000 net income, $2,250,000 sales, $450,000 inventory, $500,000 long-term debt
18-26   (1) $5.20, $3.60
18-27   (2) $540,000, (3) 11.4%

18-29 $585,000 available to repay loan
18-30   19X7 ratios, 2.4:1 current, 62% debt, 12.4 PE, 3.2 inventory turnover, 15.4% ROA
18-32 $149 for 19X4 total assets, $177.5 for 19X5
18-33   (2) $744,000, $852,000, (3) 4.55%, 4%